June 1988

To my mom —
With all my love —

Well, I've just accomplished to make Best New Poets for two years in a row. With your love and encouragement, who knows where or what will happen next?

Thank you, mom, for believing in me!

All my love,
Ruth

Best New Poets of 1987

Edited, with introduction, index
and biographical sketches

By

JOHN FROST

And the staff of the American Poetry Association

THE AMERICAN POETRY ASSOCIATION
Santa Cruz, California

INTRODUCTION

I once had occasion to embark on an extended journey. Alone, I drove straight to the end of my street and out on across this expanse of land we call America. During my long adventure I opened not a single volume of poetry, nor did I relax into the gentle comfort of a favorite novel. For six months I learned to see the world without retreating into the safety of my love of poetry.

What I found between the crossing of each state line was a humanity full of a new and vigorous spirit. I learned to watch for the mundane and the painful. I flung my heart into the experiences of the people I met: their love of God, their fear of aging, their family outings, their children, and their laughter. I stopped along the roadside to simply sit within great and sun-baked fields of cotton, wheat, corn, strawberries, and even lettuce. I walked along relentless city streets, feeling strong and curious, but always searching with my senses for that unmistakable pulse of human spirit.

That was many years and many miles ago. Although I now make a practice of seeing the world rather than reading on all my travels, I am imminently grateful to return to my patient library and to the many poems sent literally from all over the world immortalizing what others, like myself, have paused long enough to *see*.

Best New Poets of 1987 is hereby presented as a testimony to the uniquely human impulse to transform into verse what is seen with open eyes and experienced with the singular and insatiable mind. Most of these fine poets have been published before, yet, in general, they have not received wide reputations. With this collection we wish to promote the sharing of poetic vision throughout our growing worldwide community of poets. Thirty grants were awarded in conjunction with this book, and we believe that their recepients, as well as all the poets chosen for this volume, will continue to grow and refine their work.

Therefore, I urge the reader to relax, sit down, and wander with these poets across their landscape of experience: the best of their poetic vision.

John Frost

John Frost
Chief Editor
Santa Cruz, California
February 24, 1988

THE SEEKER

I sought the marketplace in Midas town
    Where Mammon laid a crafty snare,
But though the clink of coins played merry tunes
    I could not buy my freedom there.

I lingered in the temple's pious halls,
    Dreaming its god had summoned me.
What tangled webs the tongues of men could spin
    To trap my reason's liberty!

The firebrand lured me by his easy pledge
    To win a world with bread and peace.
I ate my crust behind a barricade
    And sought in vain my mind's release.

I battled on the earth's far bloody rim
    To set my shackled brother free.
A liberation bomb gouged out my grave.
    O Death, thou crowning tyranny!

Dorice McDaniels

WOMAN, ARISE!

Find your own movement of the feminine within,
You bring awareness to the wisdom of Mother Earth inside you,
Bring awareness to your earth knowing
You begin to thaw of petrified layers of conditioned freeze,
Begin the thaw of your energetic streams of the life force
You water and nourish the seeds of Truth in your belly,
Embody and embrace the truth of your deepest self
You nourish the budding seedlings of your own power,
Encourage the buds of your heart to bloom,
Your Essence begins to flower into recognition
The *artist* begins to sing through and move you
transforming your living into growing and evolving,
being and becoming fully filled *You*
The ripening fruits of Essence
bursting into rainbow
Rainbow blooms of the heart
Waves of soul-mind body dancing
Lyrics of your own heart-song.

Avonelle Gadsby

THE FORGOTTEN SEA

I once walked the shore of the sea
Breaking the powerful gusts of wind
That blew from the side.
The world was many and I was one
Still I persisted strongly
To break ahead . . .
Until I narrowed in the opposing sun.
I then drifted with the wind;
It seemed to be much simpler
Than to be strong, but one.

I hear stories that the persisting sea
Shall win the battle with the shore that restrains it.
I think I once knew how this story was begotten,
But being blinded in the sun . . . I seem to have forgotten.

Oleg Melamed

MOONLIGHT HOEDOWN
PART I

Cy Storm and his fiddle were a well-known pair;
no dance in Badger, unless Cy was there.
When the hay was new; when the moon was bright
and lanterns low, he would fiddle all night.

It has been nigh on fifty years since old Cy died.
The township mourned, and the family cried;
but Nevada said, "He'll be back to play
when the moonlight shines on new-mown hay.
There is magic in the night, when the moon is high,
like a great orange globe, hanging in the sky."

The pot-holed roads have reversed all time;
broken posts, like ghosts, white, encrusted with lime.
Spare stalks of wheat stand for scythe
that will not return in the autumn burn.
Late September day, jack rabbits run and play.
Weatherbeaten barn, siding all aslant,
forsaken by all man, and the baking dusty land.

Cobwebs on the beams, sunlight lanterns stream;
initials on the walls, on the stanchions, and the stalls.
Hayloft looks to the sky, remnants of a rope swing high.
Musty telltale sign of long-gone horses, plows, and kine.
Shadows lengthen trees, from the west an evening breeze;
riding full moon in sight, all the magic of the night.
        moonlight magic.

Dorothy R. Wellman

MOONLIGHT HOEDOWN
PART II

Autumn Glow

Scent of new-mown hay, tuning guitars start to play.
Picking strings on rafters high, resin, bow, a bottle of rye.
Happy click of heel and toe, swing your partner, 'do-si-do.'
Petticoats swing, ready now, sashay, turn and bow.
Ladies to the right, gents to the left,
listen to the caller; no partner bereft.

Cy Storm face beaming pats the floor,
banjos twang, dancers plead for more,
Nevada lifts his lady high, whirls her around as if to fly.
Arms brush foreheads, beaded and wet;
flushed cheeks, eyes sparkle, the best is yet.

Cy lifts his hand, raises his bow —
'Three O'Clock Waltz,' serene, soft and low.
Lady's head on partner's shoulder, gent's hand on her waist,
she raises her lips for good-night embrace.
Music is quiet, lights fade away,
cobwebs are hanging, no moonlight hay.

Wise moon in orbit, soon out of sight,
winks as he waits for the next moonlight night —
        moonlight magic.

Dorothy R. Wellman

I TROTH MY SPIRIT TO HUMAN RESCUE

Beyond Homestead Valley, while Midnight
Sun plants a radiant kiss upon
Forget-Me-Not Hill, I pledge: ''I do''
to reclaim this lost generation —
most endangered human species.

I send it reverberating across
Gold lake, Mad River, Sex Mountains
that all who are lost, troubled, misled
might hear, come and find their own missions.

I venture out free as elephant
brownies, harvesting tundra berries —
ready as the miles of caribou
answering their Northern Call — sure as
lake-browsing moose and mountain-terraced
sheep, I move forth into my life mission

Tooled with native gifts: faith, hope and love.
Excited as Falls Creek, racing to
the sea, anxious as time reaching for
eternity, I go recycling —
give first aid, befriend and fulfill needs —
leave jungle trails blazed with miracles.
What a world I have to inherit!

Lola Beall Graham

A FIRE IN MY SOUL

Because of you there is a fire in my soul,
And to keep it burning, forever, is my goal.
It surely has made my life completely whole,
Without asking of thee or me, a toll!

Bernice Prill Grebner

BLUEBERRY WINE

Sapphire Lace, and
Blueberry Wine:
Bushell of sea shells
That grow from a vine . . .
If you have a minute,
Then I have the time;
To tell you the tales,
Of my Blueberry Wine.

Chocolate Champagne, and
Raspberry Rocks;
Lemony seconds, ticking away,
Composing the hours
On Strawberry Clocks . . .
Crimson are the hands,
Magenta is the face.
So carefully bathed
In Sapphire Lace, and

Blueberry Wine;
Bushels of sea shells
The grow from a vine . . .
If you have a nickel,
Or even a dime,
I'll tell you the secrets
Of Blueberry Wine.

Maria Silvagnia-Macatangay

A LIFE JUST BEGUN

You depart
    from my threshold
Caressing me
    as you leave
You meet those who
    have gone before
In the flow
    of the moment
    I go with you
For otherwise
    I could not bear
    the pain
The chains of duty
    pull me back
But your life
    has just begun.

Wilson Reid Ogg

ALL I NEED TO KNOW

The cloth is yours
I am your understudy
You train me
    in the art of needlework
Your patterns
    guide my hands
And my flowers reflect
    the sun's vitality
I recognize you
    as the filament
    of thought
And that's all
    I need to know.

Wilson Reid Ogg

LIKE A SILLY CLOWN

Like a silly clown,
I stand in the rain and watch,
    as the clouds cry
and come near to the ground.
I stand at attention,
    at the rolling thunder.
Startled by an arrow of lightning,
    I bow and frown.
I stand there and listen
    to the wind,
at the howling, fading sound.
Standing there thinking of life;
    As I nearly drowned.
Just like a silly clown . . .
    Suddenly the rain stopped,
    the clouds drifted away,
    as I looked around . . .
    The sum came out,
    as it drifted down.
    Yet I stood there,
    like a silly clown.

Robert O. Pugh

TREE REMOVAL

Shortsightedness exists
For those
Who think
That by cutting
Down a tree
They are gaining
Beauty.
In actuality,
Aren't they really
Losing a friend
In good standing?

Paul J. Volkmann

DAYS GONE BY

yellow roses ramblin'
across a wooden trellis,
blue jays bathing
in a stone fountain,
brown needles spread
upon rocky earth,
white railing encompassing
the redwood deck,
it was a home,
comfortable and quiet
nestled among tall pines
now, just a memory
of days gone by

Pamela McKean

LONELY FACE

As I walked into this building,
I knew it was not a happy place,
Oh, it was full of people,
But there were no smiles upon a face,
They are the old, the weak, the lonely,
Their burdens they can no longer bear,
They are placed inside this building,
And they think, No one seems to care,
Forgotten by their loved ones,
Forsaken, yea, are some,
Just knowing that day by day,
Death is soon to come,
People all about them,
Busy though they may be,
Why can they not just take the time,
And show more sympathy.
The old, the weak, the lonely,
We will all soon be that way,
If you make it until then,
Who will help you, come, that day?

Helen Matthews

THROUGHOUT ETERNITY

You will never be free of me.
We are joined by a tinseled strand of love.
Feel me playing it now
as my fingers tug?

eLizabeth King

AUCTION ON THE OLD HOMESTEAD

It was listed in the local paper . . . the place, the time
  and the day.
All the property would be sold, though some had been given away.
The neighbors were gathered to buy things
  they thought they would need.
It might be a plow, a chair or a dish, maybe some left-over seed.
''A dollar, now two, who'll give me a five?'' he called out
  loud and clear.
As he stood on top the old wagon bed. It was the chant
  of the auctioneer.

Old shovels and rakes, pails and pipes, some hand tools, chain or two.
An old meat grinder, minus the handle would bring
  antique prices he knew.
The auctioneer kept on with his chant . . .
  ''A quarter, a half, a dollar or two.''
He was selling treasures from the old homestead.
  A nod of the head was the cue.

Old crock jars once filled with pickles, were empty,
  but up for sale now.
You could picture Grandma filling those jars, in the heat,
  with sweat on her brow.
Old pots and pans, rusty and black. Even a gilded bird cage.
Old picture frames with glass broken out . . . but antiques
  are the current rage.

The auctioneer rapped his cane on the wagon, as his bookkeeper
  stood with the pen.
The chant continued 'til each item was sold.
  ''Give me a dollar, a five or a ten.''
Now up for sale, the old horse-drawn plow . . . many years it had
  turned this land.
Then an old corn planter that's swung o'er Grandpa's arm
When the corn was planted by hand.

The sale went on . . . with each nod of a head . . .
  another item was eventually sold.
Those old antiques held memories of love, work and hard times untold.
One item left . . . the last to be sold . . .
  a battered reed rocking chair.
A tired mother and a sleepy child had often found peace and rest there.

The auction was over . . . all items were sold . . .
  they were now being carried away.
But the memories of all those old treasures
  in the heart would forever stay.

Jane Luciene Nowak

THE OLD COW-BELL

Gathering cobwebs, corroded thick with rust,
The old cow-bell is silent, covered with dirt and dust.
Hanging from a leather strap near an old cow stall.
Muffled . . . deathlike . . . no answer to the ''come boss'' call.

Remembering . . .
I see the herd come home, following the lead cow, Nell.
One after the other . . . single file. I hear the ring of the bell.
It's keeping time with a clear tone to the tired, marching feet.
While tails switch in unison in the dusty summer heat.

The barn door is open . . . the cows are now inside.
Each one in a special stall . . . standing . . . side by side.
Contented, chewing their cuds . . . fresh milk filling the pail.
The cow-bell rings softly
With movement of head or tail.

My memories . . .
Are like an enchanting spell.
I must not disturb that old cow-bell.
It remains . . . silent, corroded with rust.
Hanging on the wall, covered with dirt and dust.

Jane Luciene Nowak

WHAT ECSTASIES! WHAT WINGINGS! WHAT EXUBERANCES!

Beyond imagination South Africa's apartheid laws:
Its betrayal of all human dignity and sensibility of love!
Its limiting despair! Its impoverishment of spirit!
Its neverending, devastating, destructive environment!
Its persecutions and bloodletting of young and old!

Renews ancient chrysalis and moonbeam aspirations.
Blacks locked — tear — pearl dreams wing into life.
Gloriously tasting the strange wine of self-ferment,
Freedom's implausible truths sprout happenings.
Implementations of lightnings and thunderings
Shock the eyeballs and eardrums of the globe.

These awed, combustible awakenings are unstoppable;
Spurring kindred-hearted demonstrations worldwide.
Thrusting deep! Lifting high! The black's ''roots
Of hope'' have enkindled a wild, uncontrolled, fiery
Response, the first budding songs of liberty.
It usurps . . . escalates . . . maximizes . . . reality.

Destiny's magic, invisible triumphs sunder chains by the
Glorious chemistry of incarnated peace blossoms, like ''The
Prickly Poppys'' beauteous white petals and golden heart,
Pre-viewing a fresh, fruited freedom-filled genesis.
A star-blest heart-rending *release* from the *chrysalis;*
What Ecstasy! What Wingings! What Exuberances!

Don Blondeau

EMBRACING OUR HERITAGE

Tune: O Store Gud, Irregular
#17 Methodist Hymnal

O Lord, our God, we search in awesome wonder,
  Thy saintly souls who served thee faithfully:
Grant us their heights of Holy aspiration;
  That we, like they, project Thy future day.

Recharge our faith;
  Thou source of boundless strength;
That we may serve
  At Thy desire.
Recharge our fears, that in conflicting strife;
  We testify
Redemptive life.

LeRoy H. Klaus

STRUGGLE

Torn asunder by conflicting desires
Our game of life plays out

How the cards are arranged — that's a clue
For selection of your card accepts the role
That the card plays out for you

Our choices are innumerable in the flower of youth
Adulthood reduces the array
Creating the inner struggle that one must choose
Selecting the right card to play

Placing one in the game for better or worse
To survive for another day

Stanley S. Reyburn

TURNING TO LIES

It never ceases to amaze me.
I never get over the surprise.
When feelings I thought were so strong,
Turn out to be all lies.
So how am I to feel,
How am I to judge.
I used to think my feelings would lead the way,
To follow what I deeply felt,
That more than once has been proven wrong.
Now I have no base to believe in.
No judge of honesty to trust.

Marcia M. Korbar

SUMMER

Finally.

It's here.

After nine long months
I wish I could cheer.

But with all the frustration
of facts, theories and multiplication

I
feel
too
tired
and
unclear.

I guess I'll just say
in a very quiet way,

summer is here.

Andy Macera

THE SEASON OF LOVE

The fall is fast in coming.
I can feel it in the cool night air,
as the chill of aloneness creeps through me.
The brilliant blue of a midnight sky
is darkened by the slow-moving clouds,
as my life has now darkened without you.
The light of the bright full moon,
is greyed by the menacing clouds,
as my heart is shadowed in pain.
A lone, lifeless and browned leaf
silently flutters to the ground,
like my tears sliding down my cheeks.
The colorful flowers are quickly fading,
their petals withering in their last days,
as my love for you can no longer bloom.
The long sunny days will soon be gone,
shortening, as fall is drawing near,
like my days with you, now are no longer.
And as the season of summer fades
into the rapidly approaching fall,
so I have lost the season of your love.

Debi Buettner

MEMBERS ONLY

If I want to join the club
I have to knock on Mr. Carver's door,
And say to him, "How's your stub?"
For he lost one leg in a war.

Kyle says all his teeth are fake
And sometimes slip out onto his chin,
The sight almost more than you can take
To watch him stuff them back in.

While Quinn says he only comes out at night
Along with Snag his big pet rat,
To find a meal or just a bite
Of sleeping bum or stray cat.

And Jim says Snag's so big
He even answered when Jim called,
With part of an old lady's wig
Dangling from his jaw.

But Bonnie whispered to me aside
Not to worry about my dare:
"Whatever they tell you it's a lie,
Ain't nothing but ghosts in there."

I suppose it's now or never.
The others are urging me on.
The sidewalk feels like forever
And every step twice as long.

Andy Macera

KNOWING HER

She's hard to know
But the learning's worth the cost
She teases with her loving
When she melts the morning frost

She touches me
As no one has before
And I am drawn concentrically
To beg her love once more

As slowly she reveals
Her hidden self to me
I revel in the knowledge gained
That she could really be

She's sultry, happy, moody, sad
A rainbowed soul in hue
A bit like flint but soft as silk
In pink and aqua blue

M. Dwight Hurst

SENSES

For a moment I thought
I smelled . . .
No, heard . . .
There. There it is again.
That wind born of home;
so warm and moist with
just a touch of summer crickets . . .
It takes me back again.

eLizabeth King

REPETITION

If I've ever lived before,
As certain sectors claim,
I have to wonder of the point
That calls us back again.

To learn home hidden mystery,
Encompassed in this life . . .
Or love beyond our primal ways,
And triumph over strife?

Well, pal, it's all okay with me,
Yet in the dead of night
Can't help but wish the first time out
I could have done it right.

Bonnie L. Nott

NEED

It's love they need
  Boys of thirteen
Mother's tender
  All-enfolding
Love. Warm content
  With one adored —
A well of deep
  Affection at
Which to quench heart's
  Bewildering.
Oh, yes, for boys
  Of every age
'Tis love they need.

Helen deLong Woodward

GOD GAVE US MOTHERS

God gave us mothers
To help us grow tall and strong,
To help us know right from wrong,
To wipe away our tears
To alleviate our fears.
God gave us mothers
Who always understand,
When things go wrong
She lends a helping hand.
Those gentle, loving hands
Guide us wisely and caress,
Laughter echoed through her house,
Little incidents that bless.
Mothers are God's sentinels
Guiding with her smile,
Guarding us all the while.

Patricia J. Kelly

THE MOOD

The mood is translucent light,
Like stars on a clear summer night;
But I sense a subtle passion,
Weaving in and out in opaque fashion!

Bernice Prill Grebner

WHERE ARE THE WORDS

Where are the words when a loved one is gone
To fill the void that enters one's life

Where are the words of consolation
To soothe the emptiness filling a widow's bosom

Where are the words of cheer and support
To rally the home team when they're down

Language is a God-given gift by which we converse
Yet it becomes entrapped in times of stress

Sometimes the words can be reduced to three
In the universal language of "*I love you*"

Stanley S. Reyburn

SPARKLES

Bright shiny spangles bedazzle the eyes
As the dancer clicks her flashing castanets

Feet beat a steady staccato on the hardwood floor
Showcasing flamenco as a feverish display of Latin art

From the glittering array of clinging costumes
To the electric glances of dancer's feverish eyes

From the strains of Malagueña caressing viewer's ears
To the lightning moves across the ballroom floor

The room sparkles with sweat beading in the effort
That arouses as well as entertains those who watch

The sensual dancers whirl in a kaleidoscopic brightness
Softened by the tune of a mellower refrain

Catch the madness of this dancing frenzy
Be hypnotized by the mystery of its spell

Stanley S. Reyburn

THE CHEAT OR THE CHEATED?

The chance meeting; the knowing greeting.
The secret sighs; the blatant lies.
The promises remiss; the adder's hiss.
The rendezvous; the tainted two.

The fleeting trysts; the forbidden mists.
The meager joys; the devil's toys.
The fire consuming; the ending looming.
The discovery starting; the final parting.

The love that's lost; the weighty cost.
The heart a-rending; the pain ascending.
The soul ignored; the loneliness restored.
The gigolo's haste; the utter waste!

The unremitting quest; the psyche ne'er at rest.
The unfulfilling plight; the neverending flight.
The peace that's never found; the hauntings that abound.
The play fore'er repeated; the cheat — or more the cheated?

Dr. John A. Short

THE PROCESS OF TOGETHERNESS

There we were — clinging together; expanding our dreams.
There we were — growing together; exploring our extremes.

There we were — moving together; mate holding mate.
There we were — expanding together; ignoring our fate.

There we were, diverging — but together, entertaining
different goals.
There we were, independent — but together, playing
different roles.

There we were, individual — but together, seldom
talking at all.
There we were, soulless — but together, each hearing
another call.

There we were, little in common — but together; just hope,
little more.
There we were, a dialogue beginning together, communicating
as never before.

There we were, bonds broken — but together, just beginning
to feel.
There we were, despondent — but together, wounds beginning
to heal.

There we were — recovering together; rebonding anew.
There we were — as one again together; no longer two.

There we were — threatened together; nearly asunder;
nearly apart.
Here we are now — realigned together, creating a new life;
a new start!

While the fire that was in the beginning dimmed to but embers
in the ash,
Our Phoenix rose to tower above it — together ever;
nevermore to clash!

Dr. John A. Short

THE VALLEY OF NO RETURN

More and more, we are surrounded by those who
have moved down into the Valley of Discontent.
The Valley is populated by the legions of fellow
mourners whose lives have been twisted, their dreams bent.

One upon one, their emotional mirrors reflect
rather faithfully each other's dissatisfactions.
The tattered fabrics of their relationships hang torn.
They are duplicated everywhere — in their actions.

From their embattled emotional fortresses their
ragged replicas hang, like so many charred and torn
banners. For most, the once proud colors are forever
frayed and faded, their causes now they forever mourn!

They do gain consolation — but meager still — from the
multitudes that share their discontent and their sorrow.
Now they play at life — their true dreams dashed and shattered.
They play the fool, betting the never-coming morrow.

It could have been different; it could have followed the plan.
The banners could have stayed ever bright and a-flowing.
Had they worked together within their dreams, their cause would
not — as now — be shallow. No, theirs could still be growing!

All it would have taken was some effort. A common cause
would have kept the dream alive. Communion of spirits would
have preserved it, and made it real. But now all that's left
is a nightmare — with playing at living understood!

Dr. John A. Short

STARPOINT ETUDE

Within my fragile craft
  I traverse the Milky Way.

Perceiving that
  in every direction
  from those distant lights,
  and for my ears alone,
  the music plays.

It is an adagio of prophetic
  promise at last fulfilled:

Terran out among the stars.

eLizabeth King

WINE, ROSES AND MEMORIES

He pushed us together
Then pulled us apart,
Your memory has burned
Its place in my heart.

You promised the pain
Would soon go away,
Why couldn't you find
A way to stay.

Wine, roses and memories
So dear to our souls,
I try to deny it
But still it grows.

The look on your face,
The strength in your form,
They touched me so gently
And still make me warm.

I'll worship our love
'Til eternity's end,
Wine, roses and memories,
You're my best friend . . .

Mary Anne Burton Majure

Remember —

Murders and obscenities everywhere
After the night of broken glass
No more children ever to bear
So much pain to many a lass.

Jews, Protestants, and Catholics —
All endured Nazism's pain.
Together all can fix
That neverending stain

By all remembering
Thus, never to happen again.
You cannot be forgetting
Or it will happen again.

Charlotte Moriggia-Fantry

I'VE CHANGED

My world is now changing
So different I am
My work is now ranging
And I am to blame.

To have seen so much
To know there is more
To know how to touch
To make pain no more.

I know it is a gift
That surely came from God
It gave me a lift
Life — no longer hard.

Charlotte Moriggia-Fantry

GOODBYE VERNON

You left this world
I wished you stayed.
Gloria loved you so.
Her heart now cries.
Tears from her eyes.
So many whys
So many tears
Such inner fears.
You will be missed
No more kissed.
Peace she so needs
Sadness now feeds.
Help from God
Things are hard
For her I ask
In her new task.
Goodbye Vernon for now;
No more pain to allow
As your soul is free
In eternity.
We will meet you there
For you we so care.
Our love we send
Your soul to mend.

Charlotte Moriggia-Fantry

MY CHILDREN

You support me in what I do,
And give me encouragement too.
You make me feel royal,
Because you are so loyal.

When I feel so much despair,
You are like a breath of spring air.
You give heed when I am sad,
You manage to make me glad.

You know how to inspire,
You have ways to admire.
I am proud to boast,
Because you are the most.

Ruth Robertson

ATOMIC POWER

Man has unleashed
Theobroma,
The food of the Gods,
The power of the universe.

Without divine hearts
And minds to guide
Our faltering hands.
We have eaten of the

Forbidden fruit of
The Garden of Eden.
We have touched
The beauty of the heavens

With dirty hands
And unclean hearts,
Without the heart
Of kindness and love

Of our Divine Creator.
With war and hatred
And destruction
On our mind. Without God.

We have said to God:
''You have no hands.''

Ruth Johnsson Hegyeli, M.D.

A SINGLE VOICE

A single voice, a solo
Above the chatter.

The solo flute.
The green of spring,

The heat of summer,
The harvest of fall,

The green, the heat,
The harvest.

The beginning,
The middle,
The end.

The freshness of spring,
The vigor of summer,
The glory of fall

All coming to
A chilling end.

The dramatic
Tingling of winter,

The death of nature,
The single voice

Of all mankind.
The solo of death.

Ruth Johnsson Hegyeli, M.D.

TRUE FRIENDS

True friends are precious, let's drink a toast
The loving creator to Him let us boast

His blessings are many to all us below
True knowledge and wisdom the best ones I know

How thoughtful of Him to cause friendships to grow
Its value is worth much more than mere dough

Without true friends life is oh so blah
The bitterness of it can stick in your craw

How good to share happiness with those that we meet
The joy of it all is so fine and so sweet

Yes, you must move to touch on the lives
Of others about you, men and their wives

Little children and grown ones to be treated with care
Getting to know them their life you can share

Yes, sharing with them the good and the bad
Can bring true friends, no need to be sad

Lois Lumsden

ACROSS THE CHASM OF TIME

The world has eagerly become a lair for deception
Allowing humanity to decay and fester
Forcing civilization to resurrect sodality
The oncoming calamity encircles mankind
Embracing with certain fatality

Across the chasm of time
The child of freedom reaches out a hand of salvation
Beckoning unto mankind to grasp a hold
The child reaches further
And is greeted only by the wind.

Richard K. Evans

THROUGH THE YEARS

In memory of Robert L. Williams

In early days, a while ago
We looked up to a face full of smiles & angel glow
    Through the years
He dried a many tears
    Robert, we love you still even though your face is
    no longer near
You are still the calm for all our fears
    No finer Big Brother ever could exist
Always know Dear Brother you are truly missed
    No finer son there could be anywhere
Mama says, "Thanks" for all your love & tender care
    Though your face is no longer here & your hands can dry
    no more tears
We feel you grow closer through the years
    You are in our hearts to stay
This kind of love & closeness, no death can steal away
Oh, how we long for sweet yesterday
    Please know that if you look to us and see tears
It's because the love will still grow, through the years.

Karen Denise Bynum Jones

MARY, HIS MOTHER

'Tis almost Christmastime again,
    A time that warms the hearts of men —
As they think of a Babe so far away
    Lying near His mother in a manger of hay,
A mother whose heart was strangely stirred
    When the wise men brought gifts —
Gold, frankincense and myrhh,
    A mother in whose care this babe was sent
As from the manger to Calvary He went.

What were her thoughts as she watched Him grow,
    She must have loved this sweet One so,
What were her thoughts at the set of each sun
    When there was time to ponder
After the work was done?
    Time to reflect about His birth,
To reflect about His time on earth —
    To reflect about the crowds who gathered near
The words of this, her Son, to hear?
    When news of His healing ones came, did she
Wonder how long until Calvary?

From the time that the angel told her that she would be
    His mother, until the day that He hung on the tree,
What did she ponder in her mother heart,
    This woman, Mary, who in Christ's life had such a part?
What did she think when He arose? I'm sure only God in
                    heaven knows.

Mary Quinn

ARE WE TOO SECURITY CONSCIOUS?

A small bird was blown from the nest during a furious rainstorm
    one night.
It was too weak and cold to even try to go in flight.
Being so helpless just lying there on the wet ground,
But luckily for this helpless bird, the next morning it was found.
Kind hands took it to give it love and much tender care,
Because of the necessities of life, nothing did they spare.
It was placed in a cage near an open window and it could see
Other birds hopping and singing as they gathered high in the tree.
As those who had cared for the bird felt it was time to set it free,
They opened the window and cage while the bird flew to the tall tree.
It sat there waving in the breeze as if trying to decide
As to whether to stay out here or to go back and stay inside.
Then, as a streak out of the blue, it to the open window flew,
And hopped into the cage feeling secure as would me or you.

C. D. McKay

WINO'S ELEGY

Of late I dream of Sarah,
        of late I dream of southeast,
Town Hall, an' all the liquor
            stores I been, ya know,
    and smashed glass, and crushed dreams, and piss on the wall.
        Then too the genius of the dance,
            of putting your soul into your feet . . .

but I could never dance.

Fred Denney, Jr.

TRANSFORMATION — BY VAN GOGH

Transformation,
The artist's vision
Illuminating the
Ordinary object

With light from within
To set aglow
The souls of men,
Generations into the
Future.

An ordinary object,
A pair of old,
Worn shoes,
Left unlaced
On a dirty floor.

An ordinary object, transformed
By the artists' vision
To tell the story of its owner,
About a hard and tired life
Of struggle and defeat.

A transformation by Van Gogh,
Projecting the hurting feet,
Relieved of the old shoes
By the end of the day,
Happy at rest.

Ruth Johnsson Hegyeli, M.D.

RUTH INGEBORG ELISABETH JOHNSSON HEGYELI. Pen Name: Andrews; Born: Stockholm, Sweden, 8-14-31; Married: Dr. Andrew F. Hegyeli (deceased), 7-2-66; Education: University of Toronto, B.A., Sciences, 1958; M.D., 1962; Occupations: Government executive, Physician, Scientist; Expert in international relations; Memberships: Academy of Medicine, Toronto, Canada; New York Academy of Sciences; AAAS; American Society Artificial of Internal Organs; Poetry: 'The Statue of Liberty,' *Best New Poets of 1986*, 1987; 'The Power of Love Created by Children,' *Hearts on Fire: A Treasury of Poems on Love, Vol. III*, 1986; 'Bitter Tears,' *Poems of the Century*, 1986; 'The People of the Planet,' 1986; 'Openings to Eternity,' *American Poetry Showcase*, 1985; Themes: *Love, life, death, philosophy, international relations, spiritual dimensions, the future of mankind, art, music, history.*

THE DILEMMA

Please, don't leave.
 I need you by me always
 Away from other lustful,
 Greedy eyes, my selfish pleasure.

Please, let me go.
 My life is away from here,
 Among new faces and
 People desiring less selfish pleasure.

Don't leave me alone
 With only a few words
 And stolen hours to
 Remember my selfish pleasure!

Let me go my way
 To hear old promises and half-
 Truths from new hearts whose
 Desire is less selfish pleasure.

Don't leave!
Farewell.

Patricia Cody

LET THERE BE PEACE

Let our words of peace
 reach far and wide
  across the sea . . .
  across the countryside . . .
Let love be our aim
 because death on a battlefield
  brings sorrow and pain . . .
Let war be a thing of the past
Let peace reign in each nation
 at last . . .
Let it — be yours
Let it be — mine
Let there be peace
 for all — in our lifetime.

Phyllis Joan Smith

FEEL SUCH LOVE

One day when I had a problem,
A friend sat at the table with me,
And as I shared how I felt,
In her face the Lord I could see.
She listened ever so quietly,
About the things I really feel,
The response I saw in her,
Was a love I knew was so real.
There were times with her,
When I would almost cry,
That I saw such compassion,
As I'd see a tear in her eye.
As she left my house that day,
I prayed to the Lord above,
And thanked for sending one,
Who could make me feel such love.

Patricia Lawrence

BROKEN DREAMS

When it rains I miss him most.
My room is dark with gloomy ghosts.
My heart and mind are filled, it seems,
With wisps and coils of broken dreams.

There was a time when he was here,
And chased away my every fear.
He brightened every starless night,
And sunless days were ever bright.

His cheery smile, a golden sphere,
Warmed my heart when he held me near.
His gentle touch and kiss so right,
Made darkest nights blaze glory bright.

But now, across the sea he's gone.
He never writes, he never phones.
And all my nights I spend at home,
Amid the mists of my tears, alone.

My heart is sad and dulled with pain.
My days and nights are drenched in rain,
Which sweeps away in rushing streams,
All my hopes and fondest dreams.

When it rains I miss him most.
My soul is filled with shadowy ghosts.
Each day and night are fraught, it seems,
With wisps and coils of broken dreams.

Carol K. Pancoast

BEING NEAR

My eyes were wet with tears,
Because I was so happy you were near,
Now my heart sings with cheer
As you, darling Jeff, are so very dear!

Bernice Prill Grebner

SOMEWHERE ALONG THE FEMORAL TRAIL

In a dream-like state
You can find me somewhere
Along the arching pectoral slope.
A night-veiled courier
Bringing warmth to coolness,
Turgidity to flaccidity,
And activity to dormancy.

In a dream-like trance
You can find me somewhere
Along the mesial femoral slope.
A nocturnal emissary
Bringing light to thought,
Life to stillness,
And motion to quietude.

On my somnambulistic steed
You can find me somewhere
Along the gentle femoral trail.
A visitor into darkness
Bringing light to understanding,
Coming from aloneness,
Leaving separateness behind,
Momentarily.

William J. Russell

A BLOSSOM FROM THE GARDEN OF OUR HERITAGE

Walked past the garden and saw buds already in bloom
Their bright colors splashed life and lifted my gloom
With blossoms of orange, red, yellow, and pink
Gives a man reason to pause and think

The life of the garden is like the life of the land
With action growing from roots deep in the sand
Growth from a root of thought might spring life into a stalk
Just like heartfelt feelings about our faith, we could talk

Roots deep in the earth start from a tiny seed
So think about what you think this mighty nation might need
Believe in yourself and share your heart with a friend
Ask the Almighty for guidance to blend

We have a mighty heritage in the U.S. of A.
One for future generations really does need to stay
So seek if you will in the heart of the Founding Father
And thank the good Lord that they took time to bother

And go back to the garden and look at the bees
Envision a thousand wings beating faith into the breeze
And join us in thanksgiving for a Pope who sees us as brother
Who encourages us to speak in terms of Faith to each other

David E. Dowd

COPPER BEECHES

Standing beneath our tall copper beech
we pause and gaze down at the network of roots.
Knotty and spread, they lie middling, above
and below the cool soft surface of the soil.

Eighty feet high our copper beech stands
with purple leaves branching a royal plume.
This beech has bested one hundred years
and will probably more than double that.

In the smooth gray bark of the beech's trunk
we ring our middle years, resilience less
but strength enduring to double too our span,
as the beech, through sun, wind, rain, chance.

Should our middle years add double their score,
age continuing and surviving in the young
bodies we carried, nourished, guided, protected,
we will then plant more copper beech trees.

To see growth beneath the surface of things
to plumb the mysteries of roots, reality, truth
to unravel those tangles, ties, perplexities
that lie buried or half-perceived, nature's wisdom.

Not a bad job, planting copper beeches,
young trees growing tall and strong, new life
taking root, rising as the wind rises, meeting
our middling beech in coppery coated salute.

Addie Lee

SING ME HOME

Deep in the park by a campfire's glow, an old man huddled in the snow
Reached out with trembling hands, bent low.
Picked up his violin, his bow
    Knelt on the sacks that made his bed
    A threadbare blanket 'round him spread
    Tears turned to ice. He raised his head
    Please, sing me one last song, he said

Sing me a song, old violin. Sing me the laurel in the wind
Sing me the way the willows bend above the brook. My soul suspend
    Across the arc of time and space
    To meadows, where the dogwood trace
    White lines of purity and grace
    Against the mountain's ancient face

Sing me a song of home, old friend.
I'll close my eyes and I'll pretend
There still might be a way to mend life's broken pieces. To transcend
    All of the failures. All the pain
    The pathways lost. The sad refrain
    Of empty bottles in the rain
    And start the long way back again

Deep in the park by a campfire's glow.
Quiet and cold and covered with snow
As an old man dies, a whisper low begins to rise and ring, as though
    A thousand homeless voices blend
    Throb like the strings of a violin
    And far across the dark night send
    The sound of the laurel in the wind

Jeanne Heath Heritage

TEARS

I don't cry very often.
Not as often as I should.
They say that tears are a cleansing
thing.
Tears can make you feel good.

I'm the person who can't cry easily.
I have held tears back for so long.
I cry because I'm angry . . .
    hurt . . .
    frightened . . .
But rarely in front of anyone.

But once I cried because I was happy.
I couldn't find the words to tell you
how much I love you.
How happy you have made me.

Because I could not tell you how I feel,
I cried.
Because you made me so happy,
I cried.
Because I love you so very much,
you saw the tears.

Nancy Stewart-Tornai

I LOSE YOU

The other day I lost a word,
One not often heard.
And though I search, it's all in vain,
As there is nothing that can explain,
Why the other day I lost a word.
The other night I dreamed my plight.
A dream that led to an awesome fright.
How I lost a word the other day;
One I may never again write or say,
A word with healing power and might.
Something is missing since the word was lost,
A price I pay at an unknown cost.
But perhaps, my dear, I worry too much,
So I'll sign this note with a losing touch,
My dear wife, I lose you much,
More than just any old word as such.

William J. Russell

WILLIAM JOHN RUSSELL. Born: Chicago,
Illinois, 1933; Education: St. Martin's College,
Lacey, Washington, B.A., Psychology; Occupa-
tions: LVN, LPT, QA/UR Coordinator for Men-
docino County Mental Health; Memberships:
Certified Human Service Worker; American As-
sociation of Orthopedic Technologists; Awards:
Golden Poet Award, 1987; Poetry: *Poems to
Splice Time By,* self-published collection, 8-8-87;
Comments: *Using the tool of language, one may
be able to study behavior in a way that helps to
unveil hidden psychological thorns, and perhaps,
even help remove them. My poetry seems to help
others, especially when read aloud. A constant
theme that runs throughout has to do with time
and self-healing.*

TOMORROW

How long is forever
  And what is the depth of endless?
I don't know
Can't see that far
I don't even know it exists
Does it matter?
I only know today will determine tomorrow
For it was yesterday that caused today
If we help each other
We will help ourselves
Tomorrow can be a better day.

Roger S. Harkness

REMEMBER ME

Remember me in the morning's light,
when birds fly by and the day is bright.
Remember me, as the hours go by,
and sunshine floods the noontime sky.
Remember me, when the sun sinks low,
and the western sky is a golden glow.
Remember me, when the land is dark,
and the sky with stars is bright apart.
I loved it all, remember me?

Doris Kent McAllister

THE RIGHT CHOICE

Be kind to all
Help those in need
But choose your friends
With care indeed!

Be careful with
Your heart's desire
Choose your partner
Don't play with "fire" —

Be wise with time
Work hard at all
You choose to do —
Learn from each fall —

With all the choices
To make each day
Be sure that God
Will lead your way!

Edna M. Parker

METAMORPHOSIS

A lonely worm fed close to earth
Where he had wiggled since his birth.
Other worms came near to feed,
But none discerned his crying need.

In search of his identity,
He stated most emphatically:
"It's me; it's me I want to be."
That was his constant, earnest plea!

But then he made a sudden turn,
And he no longer was a worm.
He changed from worm without a sigh
To reign as monarch of the sky.

In his new role, he now could be
The creature he was meant to be:
In flight, a joy to all who knew
And loved the worm before he flew!

Neva Dawkins

LOVE THOSE TEENAGERS!

When doubts arise
Then pushed by peers
Gray clouded skies
Eyes filled with tears

Keep your own goals
Try your talents
Never give up
Keep your balance!

Remember now
When times are rough
And all seems lost
Love proves enough!

Edna M. Parker

FREEDOM

Children have so much to learn
In this "topsy-turvy" world:
First, a baby learns to walk
Falls and spills around him hurled —

School then throws him "for a loop"
All those years filled with learning
Chores to do at home and school —
For *freedom* he is yearning!

His responsibility
When curbed with goals set for life
Will prove the greatest *freedom*
In both mind and heart, from strife!

Edna M. Parker

COLORS

We stood upon a hill
Staring at the moon
The clouds turned silver
The evening sky maroon

One hour later
We were strolling by a lake
The fish were dying
And the flowers all looked fake

Morning arrived
And we gazed upon the mountain range
The grass was blue
And the birds flew strange

Somewhere, somehow
We lose the innocence of youth
A thousand lies
Become the undisputed truth

We misrepresent everything we hear
We distort everything we see
Until we reach the point
When you're not you and I'm not me

And life's a myriad of colors.

Nicholas Sarro

ONE HUNDRED ROUNDS

One hundred rounds, is all that stands between myself and a
Visit to the Netherworld.
One hundred rounds, stacked away neatly in five magazines,
Twenty rounds each, within easy reach.
One hundred rounds to be introduced to an enemy that's hardly seen.

One hundred rounds . . .
I lie in this tall grass, two holes in my leg, sweat rolls
Down my face; the sun beating down on my back, with its rays
Spread out like a Golden Eagle's wings.
One hundred rounds to keep me company, and help me listen for
Anything that my sun-red eyes can't see, ears straining, fingers
Stroking the rounds, praying that they are enough to keep this
Out-of-the-way spot from becoming my death bed.

Who are these hundred rounds, that know no kind of discrimination?
One hundred rounds, carriers of sorrow or joy, blessings or plagues,
One hundred seeds to be planted, seeds that can take life, or give
Life; Seeds that can maim, cripple, or, to diminish in strength,
And quantity; man-made objects created to change the course of
Human events. So small, yet, so hypocritical in their being.

One hundred rounds, I have to stake my life on our brief association.

Col. J. Nicholas Jones

TRADE OFF

Sitting in a hotel in the heart of L.A.
Pope's coming to visit the very next day.
Secret Service agents pushing the homeless away.
Three million dollars to host the pope.
Street vendors selling pope on a rope.
While the pontiff is here, we have to be discreet.
Can't have the homeless on the street.
The pontiff's visit was uplifting and grand.
But 3 million dollars would house and feed the homeless —
and I'm sure he would understand!

Chris Drury

DECADE OF ACHIEVEMENT

''Congratulations!'' seem to be in order,
    While I celebrate the anniversary of my tenth year;
''No, it did not come to me that easy, you see
    the job I worked at was adequate
    'til I decided to build a career!''

Certain projects that need special attention,
    I decided to work on at home;
No, I would not get paid, but would be fulfilled
    with the satisfaction of getting it done!

My husband questioned my actions asking,
    ''Why did you go back to school?''
I replied, ''You can never stop learning, and
    I won't be anyone's fool!''

He respected my decision, and
    commended me as his wife;
I'll never cease to amaze him, thus exclaiming,
    ''You only go 'round once in life!''

Yes, quite a lot has changed
    over the course of ten years, and
    I'm mighty proud to say,
''My work is my life, I'm happy I've succeeded,
    look what I have accomplished, and did it my way!''

Veronica Rychter-Danczyk

THE BEST TIMES THAT I'VE EVER HAD

You've shown me different faces of life.
You are always willing to listen and lend a sympathetic ear,
to share thoughts, moods, feelings, give a smile, a warm hug,
a joke, and a cheerful hello.
Helping to put some adventure and creativity into life,
curing loneliness, sadness and boredom are what you achieve
by giving words of comfort, reassurance,
encouragement, peace, and kind words of wisdom.
You are caring, trustworthy, loving, understanding,
    honest, and patient.
We can talk and share memories that are special,
which only we have in common.
The companionship I have in you
has given me a strong inner spirit.
You've seen and known me at my best and worst.
We've worked, partied, learned, laughed, and
grown wiser from and with each other.
I hold my unconditional guarantee in our special friendship
true in my heart constantly.
We have a common bond, which can never
be broken by
anything at all.
I'm rich in having such a wonderful, genuine, true friend —
You!
You've made the times which I've spent with you
the best times that I've ever had.

Janice M. Chang

MY LIFE WILL NEVER END

I'll never go into an empty world
of death.
That word only means a temporary short state
of peaceful rest in sleep.
My life here will never end.
The people that I've known
and those who've known me
will always keep me alive
through their thoughts and lives.
Life is neverending,
where I'm going.
It is the most beautiful place,
which I can't begin to describe in only words.
You'll have to see this
wonderful place for yourself.
Come see it with me.
This place where I'm going to
knows no pain, suffering, or death.
The only things that exist are
happiness, the feelings of joy, and most of all, love.
These are all found in eternal life
in a place like no other — *Heaven.*
Meet me there, along with our friends and family.
See you again, soon!

Janice M. Chang

SATIETY

Hawks silent for their supper
twist ice cold blood land
red, wet, blind.
Cows choking, full of cud,
cannot graze grass blades
cutting stone.
Magnolia incense
burns, churns, turns
my head toward
the western sky.
I carry paper,
printed words,
heavy beneath my crippled arm.
Sweet misery,
overtaxing eyes,
I yearn for lean,
thin, painless life.

Lori Lata

Polygons erect monuments
to the stars;
wheels turn an
endless cargo
crumbling to dust.
I see a crayfish wrestling
with the shark;
it wins,
and so a statue stands erect
to the stars.
Bloodbaths pool
the tales of victory,
remembrance of a lore.
Passages cut deep into caves
lend themselves to replication.
Pictures on the wall
capture enemies at bay;
they dare not thrust together
for the avalanche of stars.

Lori Lata

CONTRARINESS

I am never leaving earth.
I will stay here
till I die
till my body lies still
beneath the soil
till my flesh putrifies
till my bones decay
till there is nothing left
of me to see
but everything left
to read, hear, speak
aloud.
I am never leaving earth.

Lori Lata

TRY

If with speed,
goals in life
we don't succeed.

Take to note,
keep in mind
this old quote.

Never in vain,
that we try,
again and again.

Lonnie Louis

ME FIRST

Inspiration: Luke 9:61,62

I heard Him calling in the night,
"Come . . . walk with Me a mile."
My creature comforts tugged at me,
"Can't I linger for awhile?"

I heard Him calling through the dawn
When the grass was dewy wet.
But the hours of my days were planned,
"Oh . . . I'm just not ready yet."

He called again at eventide
As the sun crept from the sky.
"Won't You follow me?" He asked.
"Oh yes, Lord . . . by and by."

I heard Him call from near and far
Then a year became a score.
I've sadly learned what time has bought —
For I hear His call no more.

E. J. Brock

ODE TO PAIN

Let me know pain
'Til I have found the source of power
Of its eccentric orbit.

Then, turning thought
To trace its tortuous path,
Mayhap I'll tame that troubled wave
And in its ascent build a form
To manifest new life . . .
Or in its descent, speed its path
To shores where pain finds surcease
At journey's end.

Neva Dawkins

FATEFUL FASCINATION

Your glance grips my heart
And holds it for your etching.

If my heart must bleed,
Let it not be from the
  Pain of parting,
But from the imprint of love
  To depths uncharted.

Neva Dawkins

THE POOR MAN

A poor man works hard
Nearly all his life
To take care of his kids and wife
He has lots of worries
And very little fun
And he has nothing
When his working days are done.
They retire him when he gets old
A tired, weary soul
They give him a pension
Too small to mention.
When the good Lord calls him in
He leaves this world
Without a thing.
The only thing he leaves behind
Are his footprints
On the sands of time.

Wilson Molero

DO I DARE?

Do I dare
reap into the past
and sow the rejection I knew then?
Would the hurt feel just the same
as the day it happened?
Do I dare
disturb the conscious inside of me?
To make it remember
what should be erased from memory?
Do I dare
create another avalanche of anger;
thrusting it against family and friends?
Do I dare
do all this in the name of revenge?
Do I dare?

Albertha C. Dawson

SHE COMES

A woman comes from the rib of a man,
  as Eve did come from Adam.

We have forgotten,
  and strive yet not to remember.

Lisa L. Woititz

THE PERFECT PICTURE — MADE WITH LOVE

The beauty of the sea is spectacular.
Where the waves lie on the ocean line
is the point which soft white sand
unites with the mighty hands of the sea.
There, the grandest sights of
blooming flowers surrounded by green grass
and tall mountains topped with shimmering snow
can be enjoyed to the fullest.
Off in a distance, there is a peaceful island,
surrounded by water and little creatures contained within.
Palm trees sway back and forth,
waving to the one who sees them.
Just above, are cream-white clouds amidst the deep blue sky.
The sun shines through, to give this wonderful sight
a warm and special glow.
Back on shore, is a tall white lighthouse
which guards the lives of many on ships and boats.
Footprints of sea gulls flow gracefully
like a cool breeze around the gifts of the sea.
Polished rocks, delicate sand dollars, precious sea shells,
and little creatures carefully crafted with love
by the Master Designer are among these gifts.
But the greatest gift is that of love, which our Creator has shown
by giving us a breathtaking view, that is indeed the perfect picture.

Janice M. Chang

JANICE MAY CHANG. Born: Loma Linda, California, 5-24-70; Education: Loma Linda Academy, 6-14-87; California State University, San Bernardino; Occupation: Student; Membership: Loma Linda Chapter, National Honor Society; Poetry: 'Special Gifts — Friends,' 'The Happiness Bug!' 'An Invitation To Stop Hunting and To Start Living,' *American Poetry Anthology*, 1987; Themes: *Love, friendship, and the beauty of nature, which God has given to us, are aspects in everyday life. My poems portray these aspects which everyone can relate to. It is my desire that my expressions of thoughts and feelings will affect the lives of people by bringing out happiness and by helping them to realize that what they have is special.*

A REQUEIM FOR WHERE GOD IS FORBIDDEN

Amid strains of martial music
And the stained, curling posters of
Heroic workers,
The sad old horns of the Soviet press
Are blowing a requeim, now,
For those who are dead and dying
In the land along the edge of the trees,
The Polessa.*

> *'The Polessa' is what the people who lived
> near Chernobyl called their homeland —
> 'The land along the edge of the trees.'*

Fred Denney, Jr.

ONE MORE SONG TO SING

Stopping . . . I watched the woods fill up with evening shadows
And things creeping, and winged things
That found with one last twitter, flutter and rustle
What they were seeking . . . their nightly perches and secret dens
And . . . far . . . far into the dark cover of night I sought out
One song more . . .
Walking . . . I could have walked out to the stars . . .
They were so close
At fingertip . . . up . . . up through the blackened treetops
And away to celestial endlessness . . .
Watching . . . I sought out the moon . . . as far as eye could search
And found it reflected into silvery watery images from lake beyond
And finally . . . shouting back *boldly* at me
As it sprang 'round . . .
Full, yellow, and brilliant over ancient oak and . . .
Turning up the wick of night in a grand finale of shining lights
Pushing on . . . and leaving behind . . .
And singing ahead . . . I traveled on
For . . . I still had one more song to go . . .

Dian Belohovek

THOSE THINGS

I was once somebody's hero, someone's special pride and
joy;
Someone's friend; another's lover; someone else's
bright-eyed boy!
I was even once a fighter; and, a leader I have been . . .
Gee! I wonder if I'll ever get to do those things again?

I have lived life as a student, looking wise and acting
''cool'';
Often, selfish and complacent, played the ever-pompous
fool;
There were nights I dreamed of glory, honors, favors I
might win . . .
Now I wonder, will I ever get to do those things again?

As a somewhat bold romantic with an empathy for pain,
Sometimes, looking for the rainbow, staying too long in the
rain;
I have been a timid gallant, certain love would never
end . . .
And I wonder, will I ever get to do those things again?

Steve Boone

SUMMER PORCH

The porch's being
lies in abnegation,
unaware of or perhaps not acknowledging a deluge of years
which has coated its concrete with moss
and robbed mortar of its bricks.
Sitting porch,
where dusty leaves and shadows drift with breeze and time
amid dirty pillars under a slate canopy in a leaf-hued summer twilight.

Sadly summer porch creeks
with old men nodding in the dark to old men walking in the park
red match flares framing sweating faces lighting cigarettes
dangling from mouths that have forgotten more than they know.

Fred Denney, Jr.

ODE TO A BIG MAN

You have always cheated and lied to me
not caring what I'd feel
You have made me buckle under
crushing my stamina — crimping my will

You have sniggered in my face — made jokes —
for my attempts at art
You've tied a string around my thoughts
threading it through my heart

You've called me cutting hateful names
that wounded so very deep
You've left me feeling worthless
while crying myself to sleep

You've caused my very soul to bleed
through my efforts to make things right
I've grown weary of this marriage
and *your* internal fight

I don't want to hear the apologies
come raining down on me
How very cheap my life has been
for loss of dignity

Go crawl upon your manly throne — sir —
call me the stupid fool
Smile as you see the emptiness
of the kingdom you now rule

Jean Lockamy Kaplan

MARRIAGE

Do you ever pause a moment
   In the journey of the day
Just to rest your faithful team-mate
   From their toil along the way?
Do you work a little harder
   Than you would really need to
Just to make the workload lighter
   For the one who's helping you?

When they find a duty irksome,
   Do you come to their relief?
Do you speak a word of comfort
   When their heart is deep in grief?
Do you often say, "I love you"?
   Do you try to cheer their life?
Do you give them any joy-rides
   From the happy side of life?

Do you set aside your business
   For a moment or a day
And refresh their drooping spirits
   With a joke or carefree play?
Are you making good those pledges
   So your teammate can't forget?
Are you certain that your futures
   Will be free from all regret?

Nadine R. Mickelson

A MIRROR

A mirror hanging on the wall
For one and all to see
And if you stand and look within
What will you see but thee.

Yes, thee is all that you see there
An image graven well,
Thus molded by the hand of God
And in it you do dwell.

Your actions speak so well of you
So do the best you can
To help yourself and others to
Respect the Image Man.

Mirror mirror on the wall
Who is the fairest of them all?
Answer is so plain to see
The image God did give to me.

Deloris Ballinger

SHYLAH FOR THE SUMMER

Sunny Sundays chasing dreams
best of lovers
best of friends
adoring you for contrasts.

Fragile lady bound in nylon
sleeping nude
or hanging sideways off a Harley.

You were sounds
and smells
and silent tears
love
and lust
and cool propriety.

Always moving
lonely searching
restless bird in endless flight.

A summer gift.

Ben Pierce

PATRICK I MISS YOU

I got so excited,
I almost forgot to say, I love you.
I told you about your eyes
and what they do to me.
I told you how I'd never lie,
you mean too much you see. But
I almost forgot to say, I love you.

I told you of the long, long nights,
how I'm alone and so, so blue.
And of the many different sights
I wished I'd seen with you, but
I almost forgot to say, I love you.

In the end you remembered first,
to my wonder and surprise.
Hearing your words took me to the
night, I saw that love in your eyes.
   I love you.

Mary E. Correll

WEDDING DAY

This is the end of a perfect day
The happiest day of our lives
A day we have been planning for
For now we are husband and wife;

We are young and have had many dreams
Have built many castles in the air
Now we must try to make the dreams come true
We must help each other, our burdens to bear.

Our house will be a home of love
Friends will always be welcome there
We must face the world with all its moods
With lots of faith and much prayer.

Our love for each other must never fail
As we travel along life's rugged ways.
With pitfalls and much sinking sand
We will need his presence each day.

Life has many deep and unseen pits
And stormy gales will often blow.
But our love will always overcome such
As onward through this life we will go.

Never forget to look at the road map
The book that is so old and so true.
If you follow the signs that are written there
Your love and faith will carry you through.

Bryan Roesch

Parents are hard to understand
remember we are just woman and man
we were born just like you
in a land messed up, and sometimes cruel

Money problems, are a common fright
but yet we try to do what's right
we raise our children best we can
and yes we love you all we can

When you are sick, so are we
when you get hurt, we're there to see
we doctor you, we listen too
to all the foolish things that you do

Sure parents are a burden too
because we don't understand all you do
our times were rough yet we survived
today we try to keep you alive

Say *I love you* all you can
try not to live your life in sin
tell your parents, you love them too
someday they'll die and they'll leave you.

Albert C. Moreau

Lovers' Walk.

PLEASE ANSWER ME

I walked the wilderness of despair,
  I walked and walked, I knew not where.
I had no thought for man or beast,
  And for myself, the very least.
I wasted hours alone, to brood,
  In lonely, dreary, solitude;
No one near, to clasp my hand,
  No one who could understand.
Then passion found me, confused, alone —
  Wooed me, won me, for its own,
Set pulsing heart and loin afire,
  With age-old lust and desire.
Could this be love, this my fate —
  Will I awaken, much too late?
Will there be no one left to care,
  Will I be left without a prayer?
Without hopes a dreamworld, could fulfill,
  With silver stars and moonlit hill,
God's wisdom to guide my heart and soul,
  A plan to reach, some hidden goal.
Am I to live, to love, then die —
  Is this to be my lonely cry?
Am I now lost, for all eternity,
  Oh! My Lord, please answer me.

Mildred M. Brookins

THE DESERTED HOUSE

The house across the way could tell,
A story of its own —
The windows once were sparkling,
The grass was newly mown —
But now it sits alone — forlorn,
The weeds grow 'round the door,
The laughter that rang through its rooms,
Has been silenced, evermore.

The old mailbox is empty — cobwebs
Are everywhere,
The realtor's sign says it's for sale,
But no one is ever there.
Old newspapers line the driveway,
Which adds to its sad neglect,
The neighbors are praying a buyer
Will give this old house respect.

I remember the day they moved away,
I could almost feel their pain —
Though they never said why, I knew that I
Would never see them again.
So that's the story of the house
That's deserted — so alone,
And the shipwreck of a marriage,
In a house that was once a home.

Toni Figueroa

GRANDPA

I have lost someone very dear
I have shed many a tear
I have always loved him a lot
But, I know he has reached that certain spot
He made a promise I wish he could have kept
But, he took each day step by step
Then the day came when he could walk
  no more
And silently he fell to the floor
My love grows stronger and stronger
It will go on with the days as they grow
  longer and longer.

Christy Bybee

DADDY IS FOREVER

''Here I come, Daddy.''

See the child run along the sea,
the water is up to her knee.

''Catch me, Daddy.''

See the sun, see the sea,
watch the child run to me.

''I want to go higher, Daddy, higher.''

Did you really love me that much?
I should have been able to tell by your touch.

''Can I really have the world?''

He would have given it to me,
all I had to do was ask for the key.

''Sing me a song, Daddy.''

Even though he's gone,
I still hear his song.

Christy Bybee

WHERE IS YESTERDAY

Where is yesterday — where did it go?
It was here, and then so suddenly
It seems so long ago.

I see myself a-running
Through clouds of smoky gray,
Looking for an opening
To go back to yesterday.

But yesterday is gone — yesterday is gone,
No searching will ever give it back to me,
Yesterday is gone.

Like ashes 'round a fire
Are first warm and then grow cold,
The ashes of my yesterday
Are scattered to and fro.

Yes, yesterday is gone — yesterday is gone,
It's locked away inside my mind,
No key will fit the door.

Janette Lestina

A JOYFUL WISH

If love was mine,
I would hold it tight.
And wrap it about me,
Like a deep, dark, star-filled lonely night.

I would wear its fragrances of harmony,
Sweetly upon my soul.
And dance in the misty mornings,
Upon a grassy knoll.

I would gather all the love I could find,
And keep it as a friend of mine.
It would be with me all of the time,
To make me feel, oh, so fine!

Lisa Kristin Braaten

SUNFLOWERS

They bloom in the most desolate places,
a vacant field,
a railroad track,
a barren lot.

They are there to brighten
a lonely spot,
a lonely heart.

They are there to change
the dross to gold.

These flowers of the wild
are sent to tell there's
hope wherever we dwell,
whatever we know!

Helene A. Donohoe

MAILMAN

Mailman! Make my dreams come true,
a note from my love,
a wager won,
a bill marked 'paid.'

Mailman! Do you know what you bring?
Hope!
Joy!
Love!
Anger!
Despair!

Mailman! Most of all you bring a presence,
a suspense.

What will it be today?
Something!
Nothing!
Care?

Helene A. Donohoe

IF I WERE A SUNDAY

If I were a Sunday . . .
I'd sit upon my cushioned windowseat
And contemplate some new venturous feat
Or . . . watch the winter rain tic-tic down my window pane
And . . . in anticipation wait, for stormy clouds to dissipate
And there in concentration try to find the rainbows in the sky
I'd trace their some mysterious end . . . up and over and around again
If I were a Sunday . . .
I'd sail the fabled seven seas in winter's gale and driving rain
And stand watch upon the bridge at midnight
To hear the echoing twelve bells refrain
And when the blackened clouds would part
I'd gaze at stars so luminously bright . . . as they appear one by one
twinkling into the night
If I were a Sunday . . .
I'd take a trip by camel to some far-off Eastern place
And in the sands I'd let my footprints trace
Some memory of my being there . . .
And leave something on this earth to share
In joy with others who, like me . . . only dream dreams, you see
Of . . . cabbages and kings . . . and other exciting
    and adventurous things

Dian Belohovek

DIAN ELLIANA BELOHOVEK. Pen Name: Deborah James; Born: Ontario, California, December; Married: Richard; Education: Cal State Long Beach, B.S., Health Care Adm., Chapman College, HMRD M.S., in process; Occupation: State Department of Health Supervisor; Memberships: California State Health Care Supervisors' Association; California Lutheran College Guild; Licensed Psychiatric Technician; Awards: 'The Merry Cycle,' 1986; Other Writings: "To A Franklin Stove," "Another," "On My Way," "Inconspicuous Things," "Sounds From A Bush Orchestra," all prose, 1973; Themes: *Capturing quiet and heartfelt moments in time spiced with some humor or comic wit; contemplation and adventurousness are what I attempt to convey in my themes and ideas in my poetic writings. Hopefully, adding some positive qualities that are uplifting and just plain thought-provoking.*

MOST ARE NO LONGER HERE

I overlooked so many things that matter to me now.
The friends I took for granted are no longer friends
            somehow.
Life was bright and easy but the price extremely dear;
For, of all the things I cared about, most are no longer
            here.

It seems to me I used to laugh more often than I do;
For, though I often try, I fear my smiles are far too few.
The songs I used to sing have lost the magic I found dear.
Yes, of all the things I cared about, most are no longer
            here.

I used to find myself in love! I'd throw all cares aside
And open up my hidden heart to show the fears inside.
I'd often hoped my love and I might love for many a year;
But, of all the things I cared about, most are no longer
            here.

Steve Boone

AND NOW SHE'S MARRIED

I read that the love of my life has been wed
To a soul, I surmise, that is stronger than mine;
And more gentle, it seems, than the best I could be,
Or at least than the best I let both of us see.

I suppose that this love of my life really knows
How I cared, how I felt, though I never could say.
And I'm certain that this was the cause of farewell,
Was the means of destroying our magical spell.

I dream that the love of my life gets a gleam
In her eye, or a start at the tone of my name;
And, remembering me fondly, suppresses a smile,
Recollecting the flame we had shared for a while.

But soon, realizing my love honeymoons
With her mate, though I wish it were me in his stead,
I return from my fancy content with the fact
That at last she's found joy in this marital pact.

Delight's the emotion we try to ignite
Every time that we love or we care for someone.
It lasts but a moment, or spans untold years,
And only depends on how love perseveres.

Steve Boone

SPIRIT O' JONATHAN

He begins:
"I was a champion, a victory of any feat
That I and my trusty bow and arrow would ever meet."

He shares:
"One day at the park, while I was alone, and free to roam,
I was greeted by a young kid whose name was Jerome."

He inspires:
"All my friends who are your new friends chipped in . . .
To show that we do have good will," Jerome said, with a grin.

He challenges:
"It (the bobcat) leaped down with a fierce roar . . .
And fell to the ground as a bleeding gore."

He remembers:
"In a matter of time the creature had died . . .
With a gold-tipped arrow in its side."

Seek him, watch for him, and he'll tell you his story.

Darren Dorsey

OF THEE I SING!

Behind your bright green eyes, what secrets lie?
How can I know what myst'ries therein dwell?
So deep within your soul, my black cat sly.
One thing I know, for sure, you'll never tell
Of how you steal my heart, and weave your spell;
You have so many things to do each day,
My curiosity you'll never quell,
Why do you go across the street that way?
Do you run there to frolic, steal, and play?
Who are the "cat-pals" that you go to see?
Sometimes, at home, you think it's best to stay,
On patio you sleep so happily,
And there you gather strength for your next fling,
My enigmatic cat, "*Of thee I sing!*"

Georgiana Lieder Lahr

ANTS

I fought them on the floor.
I fought them on the wall,
in the corners,
in the hall.

Wherever any small insect can go,
in the pantry,
jam,
or Gaul.

With soap, water, pepper,
chili, Black Flag spray,
I fought them all.

They are to be admired,
for their persistence,
their work's outside, I think,
a scourge beside the kitchen sink.

Helene A. Donohoe

TEDDY BEAR

Teddy bears are warm and fuzzy,
With lots and lots of fluff.
They're there to hug and cuddle,
When your mind's too full of stuff.

Teddy bears and canine pets
Are both in great demand.
The purpose both them serve so well
Is to always be on hand.

If I promise never to demand,
And not to squeeze too tight,
Would you consider my dilemma?
(I may learn not to bite!)

They're soft and gentle, loyal, true,
They give you tender, loving care.
I have a dog, I don't need that,
But could you be my Teddy Bear?

Sandy Hearn

DO YOU HAVE ONE?

Fairy godmothers are special people,
Who grant another's wish,
They labor long with little pay,
In this something you kapish?

My wand goes limp from time to time
From constant overuse.
I let it rest a little while . . .
Recover from abuse.

It doesn't take it all that long
To stardust and grow strong,
And then we're back in business,
Singing our special song.

The one I sang to you last night,
Was a message strong and true.
However busy we may be,
Fairy godmothers have needs, too.

Sandy Hearn

MY PRAYER

I take this time before I rest
To bow my head and pray
That I am chosen of the few
To see another day
If I am, Lord, make me wise
To learn what I must know
To pick the right path I must take
To go where I should go
If I am blind, I pray for sight
To see what I must see
If I am weak, please give me strength
To be how I should be
If I am humble, give me pride
So that I can stand tall
Help me struggle to my feet
Whenever I should fall
If there's a choice that I must make
Lord, show me wrong from right
When evil stands before me
Show me how to fight
Bless me, Lord, this night I pray
Upon my bended knee
Of all the prayers you hear this night
Please lend your ear to me

Veda T. Harris

PEACE UNDER GLASS

Have you seen a tiny village
encased in a crystal ball?
You can turn it upside down,
and watch the snow fall.

I dreamed once I was in one.
I was dazzled by the town.
Icicles hung from rooftops,
but the snow was soft, warm down.

I asked about their warm snow,
and of frozen icicles too.
The steeple bell rang out to me,
''This is where Harmony grew.''

''Warm and cold live together
underneath our little glass dome,
as do many opposing forces,
this is their home.''

But I was only dreaming
nothing this good could be,
and the bell rang out again to me,
''It's all in how you see.''

''The glass dome over Harmony
is your eye, for heaven's sake,
and if you vision peace
you'll be here when you wake.''

M. Catherine Bunton

THE POET'S SONG

I strive to make my words sing,
my sentences melodies,
my stanzas, sonnets, near as can
to the Portuguese.

Each letter written on a scale,
timed by metronome,
phrases meshing into song,
like bubbles in sea foam.

Will the song of a poet long endure
like an aged and yellow score?
Or like music on a cruising ship
gently fade as it leaves the shore?

If classically my pen creates,
a verse to touch a heart,
then evermore my words will sing
this song of my sweet art.

M. Catherine Bunton

BASTA

I have firsthand information
from a priest on sabbatical
that the infamous Contras
are more than radical.

Freedom fighters, think of it,
work against oppression,
whereas the Contras are
a cesspool of aggression.

So what is U.S. interest,
but accessory slop,
where the cream once rose
we're now the scum on the top.

Like the sepulcher
who rides the fence,
woe to false patriots
at people's expense.

As the priest prophesied
in his Latin lingo,
when the Third World rises
God help the gringo!

M. Catherine Bunton

GOOD ADVICE

Be still my heart, don't tremble so
For everyone to hear
Your breathless beating in my breast
The moment he comes near.

Be calm my heart, control, control,
He's only another man . . .
It can't be true, he can't be real,
Don't let yourself get out of hand.

Be silent now, cease trembling,
Take one more big, deep breath . . .
It's only love, what does that mean?
Just the difference in life and death.

Sandy Hearn

FOURTH OF JULY IN OELRICHS, SOUTH DAKOTA

or, A Walk To Moscow: Part One

Topaz sunlight
filtered through the birch leaf screens
as raccoon cat slinked out
from under green asphalt
sliding board/porch roof in
Spark Shower Metropolis, South Dakota 57763.
Green headlights
hauled orchid incendiary parabolas
across the midnight celestial inkwell,
etched with billowing shreds
of aluminum foil detritus,
solar receptors of the enormous
birch boughs crowding this outpost's
town rectangle. Innumerable
detachments of ants promenaded
across the acreage
of broken windshields and serrated weeds.
As fiery missiles roared and whined
in simulated Doppler effects,
the exoskeletal tunnel construction brigades
intruded en masse into the nylon
cocoons of intercontinental peaceniks.

Stephen E. Tustin

SARA IN THE MAGNETIC FIELD OF BIRD-FRIEND

or, A Walk To Moscow: Part Two

Rosebud Lakota ceremonial staff
ricochets through Bonesteel, South Dakota 57317,
as Celtic protein strands of fiery appearance
flap in the breeze of dehydrated cornstalks.
Decapitated eagle crown,
the pride of aboriginal taxidermy,
scans the emerald expanse that undulates down
to the Omaha Indian peyotists' bastions.
Empowered by the locomotive
energies of this ally, its youthful wielder now
arrives at macabre commemorations
of Hiroshima's stellar
eruptions of villainy. She quakingly
Questions Authority
when a bailiff complains
that the green spears of vegetation
on a Sarpy County, Nebraska
median strip have been
infringed upon by those
who publish pleas to disarm the dragon
that is ready to
exhale into our Ectoplasmic Ellipsoid
its blinding infernos of nuclear fission.

Stephen E. Tustin

ANTI-NUCLEAR RERUN

or, A Walk To Moscow: Part Three

Brimstone municipalities belch noxious hydrocarbons
onto infinite asphalt. Transcontinental perambulator,
inching through East Chicago, Indiana 46312,
picked up endless trails of aluminum cans,
encased in the choking charcoal of industrial offscouring.
Lost in a rural labyrinth
of sand dunes and secondary roads,
he beheld the flames
of iridescent rose petal and tangerine
air currents/molecular vapors
being ignited over Chicago's erector set mirage
on the northwestern horizon. Nightmares of steel mills
rode a spiral arm of artificial luminescence
into the zephyrs.
The spiritual blue bus loomed out of a
midnight pine forest,
as the selenological illumination
bedazzled the midwestern whitecaps.
Electronically modulated radiation at Notre Dame broadcasted
this band of gypsies' melodrama for a nuclear freeze.
The same epidermis was willed
to be technologically transmitted again
over the edge of the Western World, when the Life Forces
stabbed the monster in Livermore at its heart.

Stephen E. Tustin

HUNT WORN

In the Amazon Jungle on a warm summer's night;
Where the wooded land was at its gruesomest height;
And the Macaw's cry was all that really mattered;
In this place that leaves a man destitute and tattered.

The moon stood full nightwatch in the jungle sky;
Pierced by leaves of palm and rosewood that tie.
The footlights were set by the firefly's beam;
And the Io moth danced and fluttered a dream.

A Cumanagotos man looks pleadingly into the trees;
Spear in hand he drops to his knees;
Praying to his God that the hunt is good;
So he guides his dart as a shining rood.

Silence is broken by a crackling twig;
The wheel has stopped, cold as a trig.
With the screams of monkeys and the flamingo's flight;
Shaking the jungle and breaking the night.

The sun slashes the darkness as the Quetzel sees;
The passion flower weep and the pouting of bees.
A Margay sits on a limb, looking at him below;
A broken man and spear where a God said, *No.*

A tear shining on his cheek he looks to the sky;
Fearful yet wondering why his God didn't try.
So the wind whistles above the leopard's head;
And his children tonight go hungry to bed.

Mark Allen Atterson

SO ALL ALONE

My mom lives here
My dad lives there
I feel like I
Live everywhere

I wish I knew
What I could do
To make them see
They're hurting me

Was it my fault —
Am I to blame?
I wish all this
Was just a game

So it would end
We'd all go home
I'd never have
To cry all alone.

Sally Kickham Brocato

REMEMBER THE
ABUNDANCE OF GOLD

When life passes by
with love hurting you
and you finding yourself
hurting love

and the days grow dark
between losing love
and finding love

try to remember
the abundance of gold
we amassed while loving
each other, try to

remember
a certain winter day
that we spent in the
high grass on the shore
of a sapphire lake

with the swan couple out there
hardly moving at all in the
fire of the high noon, we

just watching, and
remembering nothing of future
or past, just happiness, only
here, and forever.

Renate Potjan

BLACK CAT

  Roaming around on Halloween,
Ol' Midnight makes the haunting scene,
Rats and mice, better beware,
Or Midnight will give you a deathly scare!
Bats and ghosts are his favorite people
As he prowls near the old church steeple,
And through the town, looking mean,
With witches and all kinds of fiends,
When the autumn moon shines bright,
You'll see Ol' Midnight by its light!

Betty J. Silconas

FORGET ME NOT

As I sit here thinking of you,
I realize the pain you must be in too.
Through time we've become
  the best of friends,
Getting to know each other
  and never wanting it to end.
But then there's a time
  when we have to say good-bye.
I know it's only temporary,
  but I still can't help but cry.
The times we have are
  special and few
And I know these moments
  can only be shared with you.
You're someone who's really
  taught me a lot,
So please, do me a favor
  and forget me not.

Melinda Wells

PATIENTLY

As I watch,
    patiently,
the water twinkles,
the waves turn,
    white foam teases the sand.
Sparkling crystals,
    millions of them,
    hugging the water
    waiting,
    patiently,
for their turn to move,
  to drift away,
and seek another person
    waiting,
    patiently.

Debbie Jaramillo

PLATEAU

No one comforts as
  this plateau state
    wears thin —
  the while I wonder if
    the fire again
      will glow

This idleness speaks not
  of love or a land where
    dreams are made —

Would I could say, as one
  poet said so long ago —
'All I seek (is) the heaven above
  and the road below me.'

Verna Lee O'Brien Clark

KINDERGARTEN

To kindergarten I was sent
  one fall day with
no idea it was for play.

Days and weeks went by —
No sign of progress came
  home with me at
    close of day

At last my dad could hold
  his peace no more and said,
"What are you learning?"
  Oh, nothing, I glibly say —
  *We sit and draw a while
  then go out to play!*

Verna Lee O'Brien Clark

THE MASSES

He stood on a remote hill
Away from what he felt was a
Cruel and self-indulgent world

The masses spied him and
With fear and envy
They shouted:
The fool, drag him down too!

James T. Forrest

JAMES TAYLOR FORREST. Born: New Castle, Indiana, 1921; Married: Suzanne de-Borhegyi Sims; Education: Hanover College, Hanover, Indiana; Indiana University; University of Wisconsin, Madison, B.S., 1948; M.S., 1949; Ph.D., 1951; Occupations: Professor of art history, University of Wyoming, 1968-85; currently, Director, Brinton Museum, Big Horn, Wyoming; Membership: National Writers Club; Comments: *I have written poetry since I was a student in high school, but I have not even submitted these mind-wanderings for publication until very recently. And I have been quite surprised that anyone would take such writing seriously enough to publish it in a book. I have published articles on art, artists and history in major publications, however, such as* American Heritage, American Art, *etc.*

ECHO OF FAITH #2395

If all things that we know, we perceive *evolve* from their own species,
their own kind in refinements, variations, multiples *within* their own
Circle of One . . . are we not then but a *Refinement in Process,* a
Graduation in Time from our *infinitismal beginnings* of fertilization to
become what we are in our *station* of time . . . and yet, in *relation* to

eternity . . . where are we on a scale of 1 to 10 . . . *to what power* . . . are we
less than 3, than 2 . . . *because* as yet we have failed to develop our
spiritual fruits, our *charity,* our *loving kindness* but in ignorance,
in greed, in lust for power, wealth, fame, possession . . . we have corrupted,
desecrated and polluted our planet and our brothers . . .

We have made *great strides* in *science, medicine, technology* . . . we have
through the ages developed our *creative talents,* our *genius* . . . yet,
how many minds have we wasted, how many people have we hurt, beaten,
starved, betrayed, corrupted, desecrated, murdered in the *name of* **God,** of
progress, through the hypocrisy of Satan and the Beast . . . *what advanced*

civilizations would befriend us *until* we have finally *grown up* . . . we are
still naughty children; rebellious, arrogant teenagers; disillusioned,
cynical, Godless adults . . . yet, we are learning . . . but will we ever
advance enough here to be able to *communicate* intelligently, *honestly* with
our brothers *from other worlds* . . . *who are perfected refinements* of us

spiritually . . . and have found *the peace that passeth all understanding* and
the goodness, the Godliness of their immortal spark, their link with
The Eternal . . . they are a 10 but we fluctuate between a 3 and a 0
in *the family of the universe* . . . our link with **The Divine** . . . until?
What shall our destiny be . . . **the choice is ours** . . .

Barbara Louise Martinez-Piligian

BARBARA LOUISE MARTINEZ-PILIGIAN. Born: Astoria, Long Is-
land, New York, 3-23-31; Married: George Alexander Piligian, 4-24-54;
Widow since 2-7-84; Occupations: Homemaker, Mother of five, Psalmist,
Poet; Memberships: International Society for the Advancement of Poetry,
The Academy of American Poets; Awards: 7 Golden Poet Awards, 1985;
Writings: 'Echo of Faith #1868,' *Moods and Mysteries,* 1983; 'Echo of Faith
#2077,' 'Echo of Faith #271,' *Our World's Most Beloved Poems,* 1984; 'Echo
of Faith #1143,' *Our World's Most Cherished Poems,* 1985; 'Echo of Faith
#2422,' *Peace Anthology,* 1986; 'Echo of Faith #2532A,' *Pauses in Time,*
1986; Comments: *Echoes of Faith were begun 1-1-79 as a gift of Love to
Honor God and show Him I would try to help myself rise above my pain by
concentrating my thoughts on Him and honoring Him with something I do
best even though I needed Him to help me bear my pain. Since then, I have
written over 2,697 Echoings of Faith. Some are short, others very long. All
contain God as a central or underlying theme. I still live daily in great physi-
cal pain but my mind has grown greatly in Peace and Strength to bear. To
please Him and help my fellow man though I but sit and write (I find walking,
climbing stairs, even sitting and standing can be very painful) are the dearest
treasures of my heart. I find geat solace and joy of heart in being able to
write my Echoings of Faith. My Gift of LOVE to honor GOD has now become
His gift of love to me and you!*

PEACE

Since the beginning of The Fall, mankind has searched
for peace. People everywhere long for wars to cease.

Man of old, in the Holy Book, we are told, sought
for peace of torment of dreams, and sin. Not knowing
that peace must come from within.

Glory to God in the highest on earth. Peace, good will
toward men. This song heralds in the Prince of Peace.
The one of whom would bring all wars to an end.

Still mankind was blind, and could not see, that
peace must be proclaimed, and received in Jesus' name.

For, wars by guns, bombs, and swords is not what is
destroying and killing. It's the wars in each one
and bitterness and coldness of heart, that is chilling.

Thus, unbelief caused them to kill the Prince of Peace.
They knew not what they had done. Thus through Christ's
death, and life, that peace was won.

Jesus is the Prince of Peace. He will make all wars
cease, and free us from without, and within. And there
will be peace among all men.

When the Prince of Peace dwells in the heart of all men,
then, and only then, will all wars end. And there will be
peace in one accord, when all mankind becomes one in the
Lord.

Dorothy J. Jones

SEVEN WORD BITS

Poetry is a strange vocation:
it pays one richly in beingness,
but not in money.

A gun barrel is the most ferocious of gavels.

A child is a poet's most uncritical audience.

God dissects our motives like onion cells
being split under a microscope.

Even Adolf Hitler had to get his sleep.

Good poems are iron beams that resist
Fashion's attempt to reshape them.

Man is the only creature who prays in a morgue one hour,
and then guns down his fellow man in the next.

Donald McCants

LIFE IS A JIGSAW PUZZLE

God gave me a mind and a heart to keep it working
May I use it for good although evil's lurking
So many little pieces to put together
Some are difficult to lift, others light as a feather
By the time everything fits and I make sense of it all
Life will be finished, when I hear the call
Though everything's together they will scatter once more
So someone else can search and find when I close the door.

Louise McPhail

IN TIME

Speeding hours are a drifting cloud
Whenever you've gone away.
They hurry along in a pointless way
On a search as old as time.
Or jumble together in a crowd
That keeps your love from mine.

On a happier day and better time,
There's a promise of sunnier skies
Deep, deep within your eyes.
A look in them is pure magic,
A promise of love that's mine,
In time, sensuous and esoteric.

John I. Hancock

ME

In and out, here and there
It's always near, it's everywhere
Sometimes I have it, then I don't

That someone who is me
I want to go, I will, I won't
I want to leave, I do, I don't
Is it I don't want to be

That someone who is me
I give and take, I cry and hate
Enclosed within myself yet free
I am blind and just can't seem to see

That someone who is me
Why is it that I even care
To have and share what might be there
Maybe it's just meant to be

That someone who is me
Somehow I feel I really know
That there's nothing there to see
That no one can be everyone
And I can just be me

Veda T. Harris

YOU AND I

Smile and I am happy
Cry and I am sad
Curse and I am angry
Laugh and I am glad
Leave and I am lonely
Stay and I'm content
Love and I'm yours only
Tire and I am spent
You are my beginning
And I must be your end
My mother, brother, father
My lover and my friend
Without you no tomorrow
For there would be no day
No music for the songs I sing
No words for me to say
Stay with me till morning
That we might wait for light
Walk with me through sunshine
And hold me through the night

Veda T. Harris

you can laugh at the sunrise
   crush snow into the rain of spring
To me, you will always be the stranger
   Look not for the pity of men
   We all have a right to sing

   but your lips spoke only lies

you can welcome winter and the night
   invite and embrace the cold wind
To me, you will always be the stranger
   Look not for the pity of men
   We all have wayward been

   but your face turned away from light

you can journey in silence, meet only skies
   drifting upon storms at sea
To me, you will always be the stranger
   Look not for the pity of men
   We all have a right to be free

   but you greeted us with good-byes

Debra Gasthalter

Against the sun-baked wall of stone
   chained by copper waves of heat
Upon this ledge I stand alone
   the sea cascading at my feet

I taste the salt of tears and sky
   while far below the waves resound
The barren wind is loath to die
   three tow'ring walls my shelf surround

The falling sun gleams fiery red
   how close the rising waters sweep
Upon this ridge a warmth has bled
   its tears to drown me while I sleep

My skin is bronze, my blood is gold
   my soul and his will soon be one
His burning love I must behold —
   I am the Chosen of the Sun

Debra Gasthalter

MISSING YOU

The silence, it's become so loud,
Even sunny days are darkened with clouds,
I'm missing you, my dear friend,
Unable am I to pretend,
I feel so lost, so lonely are my days,
The emptiness stays,
I've loved you for so long,
Without you, I don't belong,
There is no safe place,
And how I wish I could see your face,
Frightened by the distance between you and I,
Lord, how I hated to say good-bye,
I miss you!

Randy B. Aron

PLAYTHINGS

Some people play . . .
With people's lives —
Like playthings.
They take away . . .
Your dignity.
Tampering with your mind —
And try to gain control.
They grasp you . . .
In their hands —
And squeeze you . . .
Like a rubber toy.
Clutching at you . . .
Until your life is spent —
And then go on . . .
To someone else . . .
And begin again.

Marilyn Gold Conley

MARILYN GOLD CONLEY. Born: Nebraska City, Nebraska; Divorced; Education: University of Omaha; Major, art; Minor, English; 1947-49; Occupations: Professional freelance artist, Poet, Collector and skiptracer of delinquent accounts; Awards: Golden Poetry Awards, 1984-87; Writings: 'Tame That Horse,' unemployment crisis, *Most Beloved Poems,* 1984; 'Mama,' *World Poetry Anthology,* 1987; 'Profile of Dr. Higgins,' *Poetry Lovers Collection,* 1987; 'The Safe Ocean,' *American Poetry Anthology,* 1987; 'Fools Rage,' collecting of delinquent accounts, *A Flowering — A Festival, Vol. V,* 1985; Comments: *I write to inspire other people and to enrich their lives. When something stirs me up I can write on any subject. . .joy, or tragedy. I just hope that I can bring joy and happiness to other people through my poetry.*

He walks through the shadows of his mind
Searching for God
Real or not he believes
The mighty belief destroys the fear
And he walks on
But search isn't over
He looks again inside his mind
He must believe but the doubt persists
Tomorrow has begun
And still the faith has grown stronger
For his search is over
For he has found his God

Marty Hanes

STORM

Clouds
like tall ships
    sail
with large white masts
    collide
      then turn grey
        then black
with silver lights
    that illuminate
      their hulls
dark clouds blend
    into one
    long pout
      then cry over
        the wind-tossed sea
wave after wave
    with large
    white spraying caps
    that reverberate
      to the ends of
        the heavens

Cranston Sedrick Knight

TIME STOOD STILL

I was on a ship in the middle of the ocean, afraid at first because
I didn't know what my reaction would be,
  I had never been on a cruise before

The feeling I got standing on the deck,
  the wind blowing through my hair

Was a feeling I had never felt before, a feeling of awe

It was like there was no one else in the world,
  just me and the people on the ship

Everywhere I looked, there was nothing but
  miles and miles of water

It was as if the ocean and the sky were one, nothing in between

A feeling of being born again, a new place, so fresh and so clean

No worry of time, it was as if time just stood still

The water so blue with the waves lashing
  at the sides of the ship

A feeling of warmth from the sun,
  a cool breeze from the ocean

Everything else blanked from my mind,
  as I enjoyed the beauty around me

Knowing this could only last for a few days,
  then reality would set in

That we would be on our way home, back to
  the world the way it really was

And this would be an experience I would remember always

A special place, where time stood still

Mary P. Criniti

UNTOLD WEALTH

I am blessed with wealth I must confess
With a family, a home, and not loneliness
My riches are many, too numerous to mention
My husband and children have all my attention
Two grandchildren now and another on the way
My heart filled with love that I give every day
A husband that is caring, no need to feel blue
With a home and a job, I have plenty to do
Sometimes in my spare time I write me a poem
There is never a time that I feel all alone
My health, a family, and a home filled with love
All given to me by the Lord up above
The way that I feel, I cannot say out loud
I write it in poetry, and it makes me feel proud
Like the waves in a storm that hit with a surge
The thoughts in my head just seem to emerge
I am blessed with a wealth, I must confess
I never have to worry about loneliness

Mary P. Criniti

I HAVE LIVED BEFORE

I have lived before a long time ago
The where or when I do not know
I feel I have lived on the Royal Scene
I might even have been the Royal Queen
The color purple just moves me so
It was a part of me a long time ago
I love to wear diamonds and plenty of gold
It is still a part of me as in times of old
Where do I come from and who was I then?
Who can help me to remember again?
Is there someone out there who can help me find?
Just what it is that is on my mind!
Was it a Lady in Waiting, a Princess, or Queen?
That made me belong to the Royal Scene!
Who can help me I need to know!
Who was I then, a long time ago?

Mary P. Criniti

SOLITUDE

Would you know what to do if you were all alone
Without a T.V. or a telephone?
There would be no problem if we could use it
To develop a thought or think a bit
Just spend the time in quiet reflection
Resulting in productive introspection
There should be no desperate emptiness
No self-pity or hopelessness
As we welcome the chance to make or create
Something useful or beautiful we find innate
To living in uninterrupted solitude
And forget the pain while reaping the gain
Of a peaceful interlude.

Louise McPhail

THANK YOU

We've been through some hard times,
Some sad times, and glad times.
We've even had a fight or two.

But no matter how rough the road
Seems to get;
You always kept your faith
For me and you.

We've been through the gossip,
The lies, and deception.
And learned what people do
Out of spite.

Yet, it didn't seem to matter.
You paid no attention to them.
For in your heart you knew
Who was right.

We've learned many tricks that life
Has to offer;
And learned how to handle
Each one.

What I'd like to do now,
Is to thank you for you.
Because without you it would
Have never been done.

Lisa Cates

PICKING THE POCKET OF LIFE

Hard work!
Picks the Pocket of Life.
Laziness!
Picks the Pocket to nothing.

Hard work!
Success! It makes.
Laziness!
Only failure awaits.

Picking the Pocket of Life isn't
brief.
You! Shall find.
Hard work!
Creates! Patience! Every time.

You aren't Picking empty Pockets.
Put forth the effort.
Pick the Pocket of Life.
A Penny . . .

Hard work! Picking the Pocket of
Life.

Theodore Clay

Seeking the treasures of this earth,
I've passed many a soul.
Each time I learn and grow.
If we could all give love,
the world would be a land of peace.
I pray to the heavens above,
cleanse my soul and let me befriend
anyone I may pass on this road.

Becky Corica

O'ER THE CANDLE'S GLOW

Of the elements we come all
God's creatures great and small,
Sparks of creation's flame
Endowed with given name . . .
None so great, separate from He,
Cause of all Causes, we to be.
Holy of Holies, Beloved One blessed,
Flame bestows your Love caressed . . .
My prayer chanted o'er candle's glow,
A gift of praise I may show
To reveal inner glory in part,
We share the Fire within Your Heart!

Sylvia Rosalita Katz

SYLVIA ROSALITA KATZ. Pen Name: Svetlana; Education: Monroe Business School, Bronx, New York, 1953; Occupations: Secretary, Painter (100 paintings in lifetime); Awards: Golden Poet Award, 'Of Worship'; Honorable Mention, 'The Master Magician'; Poetry: ''Svetlana's Poetry & Songs,'' collection of 70, 1987; 'Love's Lament,' *Treasured Poems for Young and Old,* Cambridge Collection, 1987; 'My Captivation,' *Reach for the Stars,* 1987; 'Time Flies,' *American Poetics,* 1986; 'In Fixed Orbit,' *Dreams & Wishes, Vol. III,* 1987; Comments: *In poetry, I render my vision of the world religiously; also I give vent to emotions of love, both lost and found. Generally, I write occasional novelty poems and idealistic themes, usually in the wee hours. . .*

THE DREAM

As a young girl I dreamed of how it would be
To know of love complete and passionately.
So closely I held my dream to my heart
Impatient to let love have its start.
Then boys came around the older I got
But I held to my dream, and rejected the lot.
They didn't seem right, it didn't appear
That any of them could ever come near
That dream that I held safe within my heart
Of how it should be or how it should start.
Then you came along with quiet and strength.
My dream fell apart for you wouldn't relent.
I mourned its sweet passing, its innocence lost
To leave me alone and by passion be tossed
But you held me close, you anchored me here.
Then I realized my dream didn't disappear.
For you and the dream are one and the same
And love unawakened can never be named.
So softly I hold my dream in my heart
When love lets passion play its own part.
That's how it is, it always shall be
Whenever you call to set my dream free.

M. A. Donnelly

MY PROLIFIC POETRY

Whenever you erupt
from my essence,
gushing unrestrained
from the wellsprings
of my innermost soul

I cannot even suppress you —
let alone control you
(even though you originated
within me somewhere —
despite my repressed imagination)

I could no more envision
not creating you
than I would consider
abortion

For you are
the children of my mind:
You will live
forever . . .

Betty Kormick

THE BIRTH OF DEATH

Alone, so alone, am I dreaming?
The black swirling chasm surrounds me
Should I be overwhelmed with exhilaration
Or should I be engulfed in terror
Have I taken leave of my senses
I feel suspended in air hovering, floating
What state of mind be this?

A light, far away, but, am I moving toward it?
A sensation of spinning, closer, ever so slowly
Thank God! I want out!
Again! This has happened before
But when? I remember now
From the darkness I was swept
They called it *''birth''!*

What now, can I be born again?
Moving once more toward the light
What's happening?
From the darkness I am swept
No more fear, no more pain
Blissful happiness, relief, peacefulness
What calleth you?
They call it *''death''!*

Patricia Kelley Johnson

OWL

Go away, owl! Do not roost in my tree
Watching me! Do not stare at my house
Or ask, Who? Who?
Find another place to scowl.
Fly to the barn: Catch a mouse!
Soar to the field: Scare a grouse!
Or teach your timid fledglings to screech.
Just go on your way, owl,
This wasn't my day!

Thelma Dorris Karcher

A GREAT LIFE

Caviar would ne'er grace a man's dish,
If 'twere not for the salmon and the sturgeon fish.
So here's to the Alewife,
And to 'em all, for they give us in countless ways, a Great Life!

Just as James Bowie, as an adventurer and pioneer, became famous,
A legend of the American West came about from his ''Bowie'' knife,
And many a babe would ne'er been born alive,
'Twere not for the midwife.
So here's to the pioneer wife,
And to 'em all, for they gave us our history, a Great Life!

Just as the hunter, fisherman and the whittler placed value
On their personal pocket-knife,
'Twas true, with the Indian and his bow and arrow
For his daily needs were provided from his hunting skills
Of all manner of wildlife.
So here's to the jack-knife,
And to 'em all, for they surely did and still do,
Give us our necessities, a Great Life!

Just as we're promised a mansion in the sky
We can have peace within our innerman,
Yes, be in harmony with our Creator and our fellowman.
So here's to wildlife,
And to 'em all; for
''The child shall lead the wolf that dwelt with the lamb''
Since we'll all be free from strife,
Oh! What a great life!

Tonie Marie Hill Roberson

THINK

Human thoughts and infinity are the same.
Some people think but never proclaim.
Others just think and never refrain.
When thoughts are spoken others will defame.
In effect, their thoughts and your thoughts are not the same.
When one wishes to engage in battle, just proclaim
your thoughts in prattle.

Bert

LEAVES FROM A DYING TREE

What is this strange mood which afflicts me this day?
Thoughts of the future are clouded by skies of gray.
Joy and happiness seem like empty companions as I go my way,
And I wonder if I shall always feel death in my bones,
              as I do today.

I try to think of what I will be,
But a polluted river is all I can see.
My body is cold and stiff and I struggle
              to just be.

The I that I am, once so prominent,
Can no longer be taken so seriously;
Because the life that it led was a lie.
It was dull, misguided and empty.

This cold, biting and continuous wind gives no meaning,
As these thoughts of mine drift out to sea
Like leaves into a river, blown from a dying tree.

Michael Reno

IF I HAD KNOWN

If I had known you were going away
What would I have done that previous day?
I might have been unusually kind
        Perhaps I was
Then too, I would reaffirm my love
        I hope I did
There was a reason that bleak November day
Why I didn't know you were going away
Such a wonderful life we'd had together
Both good and bad like the changing weather
The piper was paid, the songs were sung,
Our sons grew up — then suddenly gone
With lovely families of their own
Through all the years your courage kept me going
Now there's only one thing that I'm knowing
The earth is warmer where you've lain
To gather the sun
To welcome the rain.

Louise McPhail

WHEN I LOOK IN YOUR EYES

When I look in your eyes I see myself
    staring back at you

It's no surprise to see that we've tried,
    and that we love to

Our hopes, our dreams, our strengths, our means,
    they are around us

With the help of the day, the light of the way,
    our love surrounds us

You're a light in the dark, a mind, a spark,
    that sets me on fire

Lightning strikes in my heart, eternal start,
    in my desire

I see you everywhere, anywhere,
    you're right beside me

I have you in my heart, in my mind,
    you're all that I need

What we feel in our love, there's so much of,
    it grows each day

What we know in our mind, we have in our time,
    and know every way

You're a burning flame, sparkling rain,
    you fly all around me

You're the night, the day, the hope, the way,
    you shine bright, inside me

When I look in your eyes I see us together, forever.

John Holton

MIND-LEAVES

My mind is not a leafless plain,
  Although the leaves that do grow there
May meet with naught but your disdain
  And, when fallen, leave my mind bare.

In this book for your inspection
  Some of these leaves are on display.
I don't claim for them perfection;
  They're just leaves that are grown my way.

They're grown from the thought-seeds started
  In mind-soil adosculated
By pollen that has imparted
  Thought-colors for which they were fated.

Some tree-leaves turn yellow and red;
  So some Mind-Leaves turn brightest hues,
Evoke bright thoughts when they are read,
  And so perchance your heart imbues?

Some may please and some may offend,
  So make a bonfire if you will.
Either leaves or bonfire might send
  A spark to warm a heart that's chill.

Carol Boyer Mitchell

HANDS THAT HELP

Hands that help are holier
  Than the lips that pray
God smiles when you lend a hand
  I'm glad it's that way

For those who care and help
  God has the greatest love
For to reach out your hand
  Takes a lot of love

Hear not evangelist
  For words are empty hands
Don't mail your money away
  For those in other lands

Look for need in your family
  Then look to your friends
Then to people you work with
  Then to whom God sends

It will be a miracle
  And you will be best
Aid someone who is in need
  And you will be blest

William J. LaSalle

MIDDLE AGE

I try to remember
  The flushed moistness
  Of the wild rose,
  Running untrammeled
  Under the chokecherry bush,
  Reeking of recaptured innocence.

I cannot recall,
  Slashed as I am
  By the clean elegance of frost
  Quieting the impassioned field grass.

Judith Gross

GOOD QUESTION

Is this happiness I feel,
or am I just delirious?
Is my position stable,
or is it precarious?
Am I finally growing up,
or am I just getting older?
Is my heart getting warmer,
or is it getting colder?

Good question.

Is this tranquility I feel,
or am I just numb?
Is my mind finally at ease,
or have I grown dumb?
Is this love I feel,
or just extreme friendship?
Am I really getting over her,
or do I desire her kinship?

Good question.

Robb Allan

I PAINT PICTURES WITH WORDS

I paint pictures with words
to show the world what happens to me.
It is my wish to let the world see
what this world is doing to me.
Not only does it help to express
what I feel inside,
but I hope it helps all those people
who feel the need to hide.
I paint pictures with words
in hopes it will benefit all.
I paint pictures with words
in hopes it will help others
cope with a fall.

Robb Allan

THE CHANGING OF THE SEASONS

Old Table Rock is white with snow
  That makes the winds blow cold.
The littlest month is almost gone,
  But spring is never bold.

She whispers in the March wind song
  And peeps with violet eyes;
She hides within the swelling buds
  And waits for bluer skies.

She tiptoes through the tulip beds
  And cries a soft, slow rain;
She's getting all things ready
  To paint the world again.

Pauline Wilson Hill

FOREST FIRES

The air is full of blue smoke
Of distant forest fires.
The sun rises dim and red,
And sets in an amber sky.
Distant mountains are not visible.
The sky is white.
We are too far away to see the flame.

The wind blows, lightning flashes.

No rain.
Only dust, dry dying leaves,

And oppressive heat.

Marie Wills

REMEDIES FOR BOREDOM

When life seems depressing,
Think of something good.
Get out and go for a walk.
Call up someone and talk.
Do something different.
Find a book you'd like to read.
Go away for a day,
Somewhere quiet and restful, and relax.

Shop around a used bookstore,
Or a thrift store.
A yard sale can be fun.
Some people just like to lie in the sun.

How about the old family pictures?
The good old days
When you wished
You didn't have so much to do.

And your diaries?

Write a book.

Marie Wills

THE CONSTITUTION

Was not written by an angel hand
but by man
filled with inspiration of divine decrees
that humans
like trees
grow best
uncrowded
and free
given
light
and
space
to be i
to become
unlike
any other
one.

Linda M. Mertens

WHO BOWS TO BEL

With birth comes the curse. A promise of
equity, to all brought forth here within.
Yet many have relished not, the joy of
mere acceptance, by national citizens kin.

Heavy burdens in life must they bear, tired bent
grey bodies, and the world seems not to care.
Still they strive with pitiful prayers and undying hope,
that not in vain do they grope, for rights that all may truly share.

But know this, king rulers, the oppressions and
wrongs you now inflict, will surely someday pass.
And remember from holy writ, that they who are
first, will surely someday, also be the last.

Aware, aware, oh brother, oh sister, set your minds
and conscience clear, and stop this damnable Hell.
How blindly you go, so to and fro, driven by deceit
to lie and cheat, unaware that it's you who bows to Bel.

Lonnie Louis

FADING FOLLIES

Oh! sweet friend of folly, first joy to all,
and opposite to old.
How once I viewed thee, through limpid eyes
and unstained soul.

Harkening to thoughts, of fair sweet play,
With tender young maidens dare I lay.
Unaware that times with fray, would waxen dim,
the glow of youth's fiery display.

Though now I moan and sometimes groan, of
worldly worries, still I know, I'm not alone.
For long ago I met joy, a gift from throne,
once in the heart, is never gone.

Up! you may bid. I fear to flee from takers of
peace and decadence free.
'Til set instead, divine rule of glee, that future
babes, may it, per chance, to see.

Full trial of years, and mind gathering sage.
Keeps my morrow come, with a welcoming old age.
So, I fear not life's next page, for I have bosomed,
the sweet folly of youth, upon this, our bless-ed living stage.

Lonnie Louis

LONNIE ROBINSON. Pen Name: Lonnie Louis; Born: Fordyce, Arkansas, 11-30-34; Education: Lassen College, California, A.A., 1955; U.C. Berkeley, California, SDS Credentials, 1975; Occupations: Computer Specialist; Employment Development Specialist; Memberships: The Planetary Society; University of California Alumni Association; NAACP; Society of Technology and Culture; Biblical Archaeology Society; Comments: *I write due to forceful urges, to personally show worldly inhumanities, and what seems to be man's unsuccessful and relentless search for true origin and peaceful co-existence.*

AMERICA, OUR GOD-GIVEN LAND

The dearest things I have locked within my heart,
are my love for my country, my God, and my man.
My parents came from across the sea, but here in
America, I was born to be free!
If ever you think you have it bad, try living your
life in another land!
Not being allowed to pray as you would, or living
your life as you should!
A military man I wed, and travel we did, from land
to land!
I learned so much in those twenty years:
The love of my God, my country, and my man.
In living abroad, I got to see how lucky
we are, in this land that is free!

God, forever bless America.
Amen.

Dolores Rey Partie

THE NIGHT

The long gray shadows of evening stretch across lonely
streets as thoughts of the day steal away
in the dwindling light.

It's as though the threat of darkness has its impact on
all nature. People close their doors, birds fly to their
nest and the bear returns to the den.

The sun makes a final strain to stay in the sky but its
fight is lost to the oncoming black of night.

As this darkness falls around me I find myself growing
weary and like the other parts of nature I seek the shelter
of my room and at last sleep, alas, another victim of night.

Warren Gwynn

THE SITAR

Flowing, shimmering sounds taking the crush of survival
with small regard.

The fine fibers of the mind blend curious themes
of earthly ambition and saintly humility
as you listen with entranced thoughts
of what was and what shall pass in time.

Ragas that gather and yield sounds in a huge, deep sea
wealthy with a glowing love of all.

An uncharted, broken inner release of physical and mental spirit
do but cut the haze of all senses
from the pounding living can entail.

Dear, sweet instrument of old,
do but come and welcome my ears
with a subtle grace
rich in inner peace!

Carl Cassner

LOOKING UP YOUR BALCONY

Looking up your balcony,
I can see you're looking too.
But what could we say more
than hi.

It isn't easy to feel what
we feel, and never get to
let it show.

Though I know you love me, too,
and I know how you feel when
you only say hi, and good-bye.

Why can't we say and do what
other lovers do?

Is it because you're so high
and I'm so low?

Is it because what we feel is
so strong?

Or is it because we are afraid
to say and express what we feel?

Zurisadai Perez

THE QUEEN OF MY HEART

To my wife — 11-26-54

I love you more from day to day,
  My heart is true when this I say;
It matters not what the times may hold,
  As long as you in my arms I fold!

I love you more, and my thoughts of you
  Grow precious as the day wears through;
At evening when the sun is low,
  My love for you is still aglow!

I love you more, as the night shades close
  Their panes of darkness in repose;
And when the still of night is vast,
  My love for you is most steadfast!

I love you when the day breaks through,
  And the grass is wet with the morning dew;
When the rays of the sun begin their chore,
  My love for you grows more and more!

I love you more, though the heat of day,
  The rain or clouds may hold their sway;
When sorrows come and joys decrease,
  My love for you will never cease!

I love you more, because I know,
  The *love* of God doth make it so;
My love is whole and not in part,
  For Christ and you doth share my heart!

John Popovich

THE ELEMENTS

Two hydrogen
  one oxygen
    and a little salt thrown in,

Gather them together
  keep them together
    but the flow begins,

Get rid of them fast
  wipe them away
    hide them from sight,

Just a few elements
  thrown in together
    hide them with a fight.

Emotions run wild
  then the elements show
    slowly they
      begin
        to
          flow.

LuAnn Glaser

A SPECIAL DREAM

A special dream that a person sees,
  Is one of millions of masterkeys.
One is all a person needs,
  To open doors where wisdom leads.
Those who use their masterkey
  Find their own identity.

Helen Broberg

EVERYBODY FLIES

Everybody flies today
(Not only witches)
And who said Satan was
The only jetset traveler
There are plenty today
Who complain of jet lag

I can't disappear
Though, at times
I wish I could, and find
Vanishing into a crowd is easy
'Cause everybody looks alike
In a mob of shoppers

O God I'm sick of people
Who proclaim themselves
Holier than the next man
And hide a multitude of sins
In the closet and in drawers
They take off and put on
But since they're so saintly
Nobody ever notices their faults
(And we all have them)

Never said that I was perfect

It would be rather futile
To declare perfection
In an imperfect world

Gretchen B. Leedy

LYING THROUGH DYING EYES

Slowly dying, day by day.
Tell my kid nothing is wrong, go and play.
My condition gets worse. I have to rehearse.
Acting as if all is fine is not
that easy with pain devouring my time.
So every day I say everything is O.K.
But I keep slipping further away.
The time has come. I'm passing on through.
I should tell my kid the truth.
But it is something I just can't do.

Chris Drury

THE MARVELOUS DREAM

The sky is semi-dark, I know
the time is right, I'll put my faith
to the test, and put my soul in flight.
  Where am I going? I know
not where. But before I leave, I'll
say one quick prayer.
  Then I am gone,
racing with the wind. Going where no man
has ever been.
  But suddenly a horrid thought
comes into my mind. What if my way
home I can never find?
  Then I awake, body and soul
intact. I have lost that marvelous
dream, I wish I could go back.

Dawn Stanton

COWBOY

Cowboy, cowboy
Last of a breed
Ride the pages of history
Blown with the tumbleweed

Lonesome nights without your gal
Longhorns stir and coyotes howl
Head on your saddle, curl next to the fire
Curse the damp and stare at the stars

Morning brings breakfast
With biscuits and beans
Lots of black coffee
Cause you're feelin' mean

Time to ride, don your chaps and spurs
Boot in the stirrup and head for the herd
Long hard ride to the cattle town
Hope you make it before sundown
Cowboy, cowboy
Your legend lives long
Deep in our hearts, our books and
our songs

Rose Brandon

SINLESS THROW FIRST STONES

Pure cream rises . . .
    Election of 1809:
Mud taints in Douglas' surprises . . .
    Hate assassinates
        Honest Abe Lincoln

P.T. boat heroes Jack . . .
    Election of 1962:
Mud-slung debates reel black . . .
    Hate assassinates
        Honest John Kennedy

Rockets star our universe . . .
    Election of 1988:
Mud-fuels of electioneers' press reverse . . .
    Hate annihilates
        Honest-idealist Gary Hart!

What freedom licenses any foreign-parted . . .
    To mind-bind our beloved nation's residents
To demand perfection? All are clay-footed and clay-parted . . .
    America's lovers love flesh-headed presidents
        Honest but free of clay hearts!

No ''real'' youth will volunteer or win . . .
Too terrified they might have human *sin!*

Sister Phoebe Passler

WHAT DOES ALL THIS MEAN?

Where have we been?
Where are we going?
How will we know when we're there?

You go through life day to day
In your mind you find the words to say
What do we do from here? Where do we go?
Something only your mind and inner soul may know

Each day holds all your moments your thoughts
Only you can decide to give and share those parts
You may not know what to do or say
You can only let yourself be guided in your way

What does all this mean?

Jamie Marie Lee

TO MR. B.

To my ex-stepson, whom I lovingly call 'Mr. B.'

So many times I've wished that you were living here with me.

May you keep growing stronger and wiser with each day,
I know you're getting bigger and will be a man someday.

You think I don't miss you, but in this regard you're wrong,
'Cause each day and night I pray to God for you in song.

So keep your spirits high and remember God loves you,
Although I am not with you now, God will see you through.

Sally Kickham Brocato

STUDENT WINNER

When you are drowning in ideology books,
When computers keep on giving you dirty looks.

When your mind figures metrics into inches first,
When by sheer frustration you are ready to burst.

When your habit of racing from work to school,
Makes you show up by mistake on Sundays, too.

When you tell your kids that if you don't come
        back,
To write on your grave: ''She died trying to pass.''

Student winner, don't let the stress break you now,
Just keep giving all and you'll make it somehow.

Sally Kickham Brocato

EAGLE'S FLIGHT

If I could spread my wings to skies of blue . . .
To see the world among the clouds . . . 'n . . . sun rays . . .
As an eagle's flight . . . in search of prey . . .
Over snow-capped mountains . . . I'd search for you!
    . . . I'd search for you!

To be higher . . . 'n . . . faster
    . . . in the turbulence all day.
For to be travelin' on . . . travelin' on a jet stream
. . . could serve me too.
Find the treasure . . . with an eagle eye . . . and I say . . .
For determination
    . . . 'n . . . perseverence . . . 'n . . . love for you!
      . . . perseverence . . . 'n . . . love for you!

My prayer goes travelin' on to an eagle's prey . . . the day . . .
A hungered heart . . . swoops down upon . . . the hunting's through!
        . . . the hunting's through!
Those claws of love will succumb you . . . the prey!
For the distance . . . shall be overcome . . . 'n . . . I say,
''I love you!''
With hopeful heart . . . I want the reward from whom I pray . . .
. . . This, the priority of my life . . . your love . . . it's true
        . . . your love . . . it's true

A. Gary Knapinski

2 A.M. (ALONE)

Do you know how it feels?
Alone in the night
at 2 in the morning?
Knowing that the one you love
is five hundred miles away.
Knowing that it may be
another week or two
before you feel his touch again.
Or hear him whisper in your ear ''I Love You''
in the middle of the night,
when memories of broken dreams are making you feel
alone.
So I sit here waiting for your return.
Knowing that you're sitting somewhere,
wishing you were here at 2 a.m.

Carolyn J. McMahon

DELAWARE WATER-GAP, LOOKING SOUTH FROM SHAWNEE.

EXPRESSIONLESS FACE

Expressionless face
I wonder what's on his mind
The sea . . . the stars . . . infinity
I wonder if there was ever a time when there never was
I wonder if there will ever be a time when there no longer is
I like my life without emotion
I like my life without tears
I like my life without smiles
I used to be quite an athlete back in my day
But the game has changed so fast
They're bigger, stronger, run faster, jump higher
Sometimes I wonder where my wife is
I wish that I could have died first
My job is my life, there is nothing more
For animals life is survival
I am merely an animal, born only to eat and make love
Perhaps I am something more
I would like to solidify and become one with the mountain
I would like to liquify and become one with the ocean
I would like to gasify and become one with the sun
I would like to be a part of the beauty that surrounds me
As opposed to being a mere observer
I am most happy in my simplicity
My simplicity was achieved
It was not always there

Steven McGill

COLLEGE

The party has ended
The drinking buddies have all gone away
To look for somewhere else that they can play
And here she is at her desk
Alone, with a couple of books in front of her
Study hard babe gotta get that degree
So everyone will be proud of you, everyone except me
"When do you love me?" I love you when your mind wanders
When you dare to be irrational
But don't mind what I say
Once I'm gone I'm gone to stay
Horizons are limited options are few
If you're not drinking or studying then what do you do?
You inquire, you contemplate, you sit in the chair
You climb the sky mountain and breathe in the air
If living and existing are one and the same
Then the hell with this life please withdraw my name
A shot in the arm, a mere transfusion
Such life is not real but only illusion
Empty of substance I search through the shelf
Dust-filled, forgotten, I find my true self
This water needs action this water needs waves!
Fluidity of motion, motion that saves
Motion that saves a starving heart
Once together we're never apart

Steven McGill

FORMOSA TREE

I am the lonely, sad-eyed man
No one knows where I am from
I am sitting on the floor in the antechamber
Waiting for my time to come

Life comes late for me
I am the last to arrive on the scene
I am like the formosa tree
When the rest of the world has turned to green

My difficult past is not known by any
Except for the butterflies who float and shine
No, my difficult past is not known by many
The butterflies are very dear friends of mine

Butterflies will wander and butterflies will roam
Yet that is no cause for anxiety or fear
In my sweet leaves they'll always have a home
The butterflies are always welcome here

Steven McGill

THE BELEAGUERED JACK-O'-LANTERN

Our jack-o'-lantern wishes he'd have reprieve
From scary spooks on Halloween,
So many monsters, flaky and weird,
Gather here once a year,
Like three witches who argue and fight,
'Neath the eerie moon that night,
About which one is the fairest,
But I think they are all quite scary,
A bat with an allergy
Sneezes all night in the trees,
And ghosts of a deathly pallor
Talk about the funeral parlor
And their new recruits
Donning the flowing suits,
Then Wolfman begs for dog food so
From our astonished pooch,
And Frankenstein gazes in a mirror,
Admiring his new-grown beard,
This pumpkin says in great dismay,
"Am I s'posed to scare such spooks away?"

Betty J. Silconas

I HAVE FOUND

I have found that the human race
Lives in such a hurried, jumbled pace
That it becomes very hard for them to face
Their own shortcomings in their own space

So very quick to put down all others
Knock their fathers and not praise their mothers
Sisters are wrong — just like their brothers
Always bad talk starters — until they smother

Should they ever stop and work on their own failings
There would be no extra time for their bad schemes
No time for daggers — nor sharp bee stings
No time for gossip — nor belittlings

Life would be flourishing in good health and love
No more blues sung in songs by our turtle doves
Joy and sunshine would fall from above
I close this now — with all of my *love*.

Hetty M. Schroeder

REFLECTION

Is time curved or flat, I wonder —
Like the sky or like the sand?
Has time a color? Gray or blue?
Does time contract, expand?

When the rain falls, I wonder:
How far has rain to fall?
How high are clouds and rainbows?
Are they really there at all?

Which things are chance, I wonder,
Design or accident?
Are the patterns of the ocean
Happenstance or meant?

Where is the wind, I wonder,
When it isn't blowing here?
Does the wind have a place to live in?
Is it a voice of fear?

What is an echo, I wonder?
Is an echo like a call?
Does an echo bounce or fall or shatter?
Is an echo short or tall?

Am I alive, I wonder?
Am I still, or thundering?
Whichever way things are or aren't,
I'm tired of wondering.

Dorothy H. Elliott

SEARCH FOR ANSWERS

What is life?

When I grow up
  I shall know
    everything.

When I grew up
  I knew
    nothing.

Why sorrow, sickness, death?

When I grow up
  I shall have
    all the answers.

When I grew up
  I had
    no answers

Where are the answers?

When I sought God
  I found Peace, and
    through His Son, Jesus Christ,
      Life!

I found my answers!

Margaretbelle Bonham

APRIL IS A CAPRICIOUS GIRL

April is a capricious girl
She first appears in whirling skirts
and dances through the air
whistling and a shuffling with not
the slightest care
Suddenly she appears
in verdant scented grass
laying a carpet for all who pass
blushingly in buds on every bough
and bush she's seen
with tiny quivering leaves in between
Quizzically she scowls a frown
her skirts now ribbons of gray
She washes everything in sight
until it's sparkling fresh and gay
Gloriously while sunshine plays
on purple hills
April spreads a patchwork quilt
in myriad colored daffodils
bordered by blue bells chiming
among the purple hills.

Louise Shannon Monteverde

LOVE

Life's little things
Get braided together
Tied in a tight knot
That binds forever

Words unspoken
Feelings unfelt
You touch not knowing
A heart to melt

Blind eyes that see
Deaf ears that hear
The call of a heart
To the one so dear

Open up your senses
Tune in to your need
Let down your defenses
Let emotions breed

An overwhelming rush
To feel at ease
To look into your eyes
And only want to please

Feelings of contentment
With me loving you
Feelings of fulfillment
If you love me too

Roger D. Lee

MAMMA MAY I

Just a little girl
Unsure of her way
Struggling for identity
She dreads each day.

She's happy when she's active
But sad when she's still
Does anybody love me?
Is life really real?

She wants to be special
Have dreams to the sky
With love and attention
"Mamma May I?"

She seeks your approval
You love to win
Show her she's right
And she will do it again.

Help her be happy
Let her know she can
Always be loved
Even if she doesn't understand.

Give her your attention
Until the day you die
Never make her wonder
"Mamma May I?"

Roger D. Lee

DOCTOR

The patient looks up
To the doctor with trust.
Make me feel better,
Do whatever you must.

I can't even work.
I feel awful today.
So please, doctor, please,
A pill if you may.

The doctor proceeds
To examine with care,
To find what is wrong
As the patient sits there.

Convinced it's a virus
A shot he prepares.
The patient, instantly wary,
At the needle he stares.

Oh, doctor, it's gone!
I feel wonderful now.
Whatever was wrong —
You've made me well somehow.

Frances P. Brown

How swiftly Death hath brought them down
        all young, intact
           hands clasped
      communion of souls
of green meadow born
          a colorful pride
        turned flaccid
          and brown

   Shallow rays risen from sleep
walk forth in a dream
whispering wind-drift swept through lone reeds
        communion of souls
      soft faces bowed
         a circle of children
          to tremble
           and weep

Daughters of love, I embraced and kept all
Storm-winds of man, the fury I have borne
     desires and dreams he hath
     torn from this garden
        communion of souls
        dissolve, leaving one —
          the flower of hope
        to wither
          and fall

Debra Gasthalter

I AM YOUR SHADOW SIDE

I am your shadow side,
Your eclipse away from brightness.
I touch you always
And follow you forever.
Even if you disappear completely
A trace of me remains behind.
I shelter you from the sun.
I am your shield.
I protect you from your enemies.
I hide you from fear.
I cover you with my cloak of darkness.
I am your veil and sometimes your mask
When you want to be concealed from people.
I am also your loneliness, your sadness,
Your other side, your suspicious, questionable nature.
Yes, I am your other self
And God loves your shadow side,
Because He made it to go with your sunny side!
Together one, united!

Donna Zeihen

BILLOW

Her skin is sleek and smooth, yet weary and worn
She sways, then serves, unsure of her bearing
Beneath a painted smile, her marred soul mourns.
With arched back and battered heart flaring,
She builds a hollow tube and coughs up mist
Belching bitter sobs while whirling around
Then folding over, she forms a huge fist
With unbared fury and a rumbling sound.
To rapid rhythm, round the rocks she weaves
And in heroic verse, pours forth her lore
Slowly stretching her body toward a reef
Relaxing her arms, then hugging the shore.
The sun magically makes her glisten
She whistles softly, bewitched I listen.

Fernanda Mascarenhas

CURIOSITY SHOP

My mind is an old Curiosity Shop
  Containing rare treasures, precious stuffs — and rags.
Sometimes one and then another is on top,
  But they are not for sale; they bear no price tags.

There are harmonies, colors that ring like bells,
  Sweet melodies wafting from loot-laden ships,
Echoes of rolling ocean waves from sea shells,
  Thrilling chords at the strum of my fingertips.

There are visions of people, their passions, souls;
  Visions of the country, the woodlands, and streams;
Visions of horizons and of far-off goals;
  Visions of worlds to conquer. Wonderful dreams!

There are memories of arrowheads, pine cones,
  Canyon echoes, silver spurs, and wagon wheels;
Memories of corrals, of saddles, and roans,
  Of the cowboys singing at their campfire meals.

In my Shop-mind is the scent of the pine trees,
  The pungent aroma of smold'ring embers,
The odor of sagebrush wafted on the breeze,
  The smell of fresh-cut timber one remembers.

My mind is an old Curiosity Shop
  Containing all of these useless wares — and more.
If you ever pass by this way, won't you stop
  A little while and browse with me in my store?

Carol Boyer Mitchell

SADNESS

Did you ever hear someone exclaim, of a man just home from war,
''There goes a boy who grew up here — he doesn't smile much anymore''?
Did they ever stop to wonder why that smile was seldom seen;
Or why he had that lonesome look, and what that look could mean?

Perhaps if they could get a glimpse of the world from behind his eyes,
They might understand just a little bit, how his heart,
   a little each day, dies.
The things that once were funny lose their humor when you're sad.
And loneliness cannot be shared with those whose hearts are glad.

The sadness might have started with some buddies who were lost,
And few would know how much was bought, or how much
   those lives had cost.
Or maybe he remembers reading of the draft cards that were burned,
And remembers fallen comrades, and how their honors, earned.

Maybe he remembers how he prayed each day for mail,
Of all that they had promised on the day that he set sail.
Just a little scrap of paper that takes so little time to write;
But that same small scrap of paper could make everything all right.

When his loved ones could go shopping, visit friends,
   or laugh and play;
But didn't have the time to stop, and drop a line or two each day.
Many things could make him bitter, and many things could make him sad,
But those things cannot be shared with those whose hearts are glad.

To those he loves, he cannot share the misery he has felt;
Just smile and make the best of things with the cards
   that he's been dealt.
But deep inside, the hurt is there, and sometimes, it must show;
So always try to understand; some day your own might go.

Les Jacobs

MY OLD TREE

A lone cottonwood tree — very old,
Long limbs gnarled and slivered,
Proudly stands, stately and tall,
On the bank of the Brazos River.

Perhaps Indians fought near here . . .
Rode the river in canoes;
Brave warriors without fear
Free to fight, win or lose.

A trailmaster proudly drove his cattle,
Lumbering, thundering, pushing for speed;
Watered them here, gave them feed,
Left with billowing dust and tumbleweed.

Wagon trains set camp nearby,
Forged the river — do or die.
This old tree provided shade
For these brave men, history made.

My stalwart old tree
Many a sight did see.
Such consolation it will be,
A source of peace and joy to me.

You, dear tree, belong to me.
I'll sit under your shade
And dream of things that you did see
While history was being made.

Frances P. Brown

CYCLES

Autumn sun,
golden-colored,
blue-edged,
pulsates with the chorus of insects.
Marking time till limb and stem
freeze in a mirror of action.

I, as the director of this scene,
order weeds out,
the disruption of homes,
and the trimming of growth.
An unended task frozen in time.

Later, beyond my view,
I know seeds sprout,
insects stir,
and the sun rises higher each day — on cue.

Bonita Dostal Neff

When the fight is over
 it is just beginning
My anger is strong
With nowhere to release
So I remain silent
And the fight continues
No end in sight
My anger grows
Why now are the thoughts
In my mind with no answers
And the anger grows

Marty Hanes

ROSIE HERM

We made a bet
 With Rosie Herm,
That she wouldn't eat
 A live worm.
Kids gathered
 From all around,
Lenny Grump
 Brought his hound.
We caught a worm
 And got the quarter,
It had to be swallowed
 Without any water.
Kids cheered,
 Rosie was set,
Worm disappeared . . .
 We lost the bet!

Richard L. Sartore

BABYLON

Hanging out in unknown quarters. Catching
walks with friends who'll go unnamed.
Penniless and often guarded with the way
you spend your money and spend your day.

Shaking your hips all the while until a
sudden revival had you changing your
style. You're tempted by a foolish tease,
who appears to be exactly what she seems.

If you're not impressed with the worth
that you see, take me under with you
when you feel this sweet sanity. In
suspicion you reign. Often reigning the
hard way.

Watch out when you're blowing low. Need me
high and need me low. In between you ought
to know, my forecast saves your vocal tone.

Yes, they rued the day when Adonis is what
they saw, upon the face of someone I called
Babylon.

Virginia Battalio

DESERT LIFE

The Desert is a busy place
Where Rodents and Rabbits run their race.
Where Prairie Dogs dig tunnels long and deep
And Snakes in cool dens go to sleep.
Where Coyotes prowl and Jackrabbits thump,
And big Owls perch on a deadened stump.
Where Cacti bloom in colors gay,
And Black-Eyed Susans gently sway.
Where Ants form armies and build a fort,
And all the day food is sought.
Where Hawks soar high to spot their prey
And down below small Mice play.
The Desert is quiet, but so alive,
A place of beauty where things thrive.

Joan M. Lacey

PETER, MY LOVE

Someone said that "to be true
to one woman, one must be false
to all other women," and Peter,
my love, I am glad that you
agree with this idea.

Joan Danylak

JOAN DANYLAK. Born: New York City,
Brooklyn County, 2-3-43; Married: Peter
Danylak, 8-29-80; Education: University of
Arizona; Double literature major — English and
German; B.A., magna cum laude, 1969; Addition-
al undergraduate work, Harvard summer school;
Occupation: Housewife; Memberships: Mensa,
Channel Thirteen PBS, Friends of the New York
Public Library, Friends of Central Park; Com-
ments: *I am grateful to my wonderful husband,
Peter Danylak, for his continuous emotional sup-
port.*

INNER PEACE

Go placidly, poor pilgrim kin,
 Amid the noise and haste,
The sham, the drudgery that make
 Your world a lonely waste.

On every side, you see the great,
 Hardhearted without ruth;
The money-mad who live their lives
 Without regard for truth.

The inconsiderate, the brash,
 Vexatious one and all,
Would disenchant you with the world,
 Make you a soulless thrall.

Surrender not to hopelessness;
 Be inwardly serene;
And Buddha-like observer be
 Of this fast-changing scene.

Who made the universe has care
 Of you as well as they.
Some have their Heaven here, on earth;
 Some in a better way.

Everett Francis Briggs

FIFTY-FIVE

In twenty-one days — I'll be fifty-five
Yes I am still very much alive
With hurts and pains more than I care to know
Like a downpouring rain just before the snow
With everyone expecting the best out of me
To listen and care for them with a calm dignity
But it is a great struggle to keep me in true line
My health, and my home, and me be on time
With so many clinging vines to detour me each day
With so many different paths that I could stray
Plus a husband who is ill and is slowly declining

Into a a huge vast world of undefining
Until he merges into a paralyzed state
Where no matter what? it is far too late
He will then not know anyone — and not even care
And with you and me — he will never again share
He will not be strong — but he will want to roam
Until he does rest in *his Master's home*
Lord, please shower him in *love* — give him back
His dignity
And when his time comes — take him home to live
With Thee.

Hetty M. Schroeder

HETTY M. SCHROEDER. Born: Eureka, California, 9-25-32; 7th of 9, reared on a cattle ranch in the mountains of Showers Pass, went for 10 years to a one-room school there; Married, age 17, for 12 years, five children; 5th marriage to Alfred William, 12-28-84; now have 4 step-children, two grandsons and 9 step-grandchildren; Occupation: Housewife; Comments: *At age 44 I lived through a brain aneurysm, and relearned how to live. Al and I have lived through a lot of pain and illness, so I write to try to understand what I hear, see, and feel.*

A HOUSEWIFE'S SCHEDULE

What are you doing at nine o'clock tonight?
What are you doing at eight o'clock tomorrow?
If you know, then borrow someone else's schedule.
Change the week's menu around; have Monday's
Menu Thursday; then Saturday go out on the town.

Up at six, out by seven, at work by eight; lunch
At twelve, off by four, out the door; hustle,
Hustle, rush, rush, rush; rush-hour traffic
Bumper to bumper.

Watching the time, want dinner as usual, promptly
At six, control your temper.
Home again, home again all in one piece.
Dinner on the table, dishes to be done, kids
With homework, no time for fun.

Kids in bed, house is quiet all by ten I wish . . .
Time, time to think; think of all the things . . .
I missed hour by hour.
Oh! I forgot Henry's waiting — my night to perform
My wifely duties.

Mattie M. Butler

ALL MY LOVE

This poem is written with all my love,
I believe we were brought together by God up above.
We've been through a lot these past sixteen years,
And we've seen each other through a lot of hurt and tears.
We've changed a lot together,
But it seems to have made our love stronger and better.
Though sometimes I get frustrated and angry,
I know you'll still be here with me.
And If I'm troubled, you always seem to know it.
Sometimes you'll even hold me
And give me a kiss.
This poem holds all my love,
The feelings and words
Are hard to come.
My feelings for you run so deep.
My heart is yours forever to keep.

Barbara Mooney

NOBODY IS UNIMPORTANT

There once was a guy who with all his effort would try.
Doing things right seemed to pass him by.
No matter what he did, it always went wrong.
Had to settle for a poem, when it was really a song.
He tried to help some people on earth.
But zero is what his existence was worth.
He wanted to leave this planet behind.
But a voice from above said it was not time.
The torture and pain started to drive him insane.
Suddenly he realized his thoughts were in vain.
He wasn't on this planet for himself at all.
He was here to help people till he did fall.
So down and out people he went to go see.
Those people did realize they were better than he.
He was never convinced that he did any good.
But until he died he did the best he could.
Nobody respected him and never would.
But at least he cared, as well we all should!

Chris Drury

AT THE BEACH

Blue sky, blue sea, blue day —
White winter sun glares down upon the ancient, whitened sand,
The frothy foam licks idly at the seaweed, limp and brown,
And gently lifts, lays back a single strand.
Far out the gulls wash softly to and fro.
Ride neat against the rippled blue,
And flying wings thresh dark against the sun,
Across the sun, beyond it, too.

The sparkling breakers dash themselves against the shore,
And, spent, close touch the sand, roll back to ocean as before.
How near the water hugs the shore!
Why is there no meeting of the mind and heart in me,
Like the meeting of the sand and sea?

Dorothy H. Elliott

AUTUMN

Now, when autumn is here, I will be
satisfied merely skimming the surface of
life, I will be satisfied watching others
do the things I used to do, to see them
repeat the mistakes I have done.
I will be satisfied now to be an
onlooker to the follies of others —
because I
have lived good and well.
I became acquainted with the night,
walking through rain and snow,
it was all there for me to see.
But I have also walked through flower beds
filled with sunlight all throughout the air,
and have been blended by the
beauty and innocence of others'
stare.
I was left no poorer for it.

Gunvor Skogsholm

KANSAS

Where you can stop out our door
And see *God's* sunset.
Kansas is a wheatfield at sunrise,
Or a friend that makes your spirit fly.
Kansas the *sunflower,*
Or KU Memorial Tower.
Rock, Chalk, Jayhawk, KU!
Danny Manning coming at you!

Kansas is beautiful
Whether rain or snow.
In a horse's grace
Or in your pet's face.
And in the beauty of nature.
In Kansas you can remember,
The way it *was, is*
And the *future to be.*

Kansas is beautiful to me.

Larry Grogan

SPRING

A lovely time of year is spring,
So colorful are the flowers she brings.
Her magic touches the barren trees,
Bringing forth buds and new green leaves.

Purple Crocuses I have found,
Poking their heads above the ground.
Daffodils next will be here,
Then Tulips and Hyacinths appear.

Lilac trees will bloom in May,
As will Lilies of the Valley by Mother's Day.
They both have a perfume wonderfully rare,
And their sweet fragrance soon fills the air.

Yes, spring's a lovely time of year,
For them the miracle of Easter is here.
And all the loveliness of earth,
Is soon released in a wondrous rebirth.

Mary Louise Brooks

VACATION PRAYER

Thank you, God, for mountains high,
For lovely clouds that are in the sky.
For waterfalls majestic heights
And stars that shine so bright at night.

Thank you, God, for oceans blue,
And for the lovely rainbows too.
For streams that bubble along the ground
And follow mountain roads around.

Thank you, God, for all of these,
Especially for the Redwood Trees,
They were here when Christ was born
And have withstood both fire and storm.

For sunset red and dawn of gold,
For lakes and valley with loveliness untold.
Thank you God, for all this beauty,
It enriches our souls and teaches humility.

Mary Louise Brooks

FEAR NOT

The fishing boat put out to sea;
Its sails began to fill rapidly
With a mighty wind.
As the sky suddenly grew dark
And the waves lashed over the sides
The boat pitched up and down.
The crew feared they would surely drown,
As they called to one
Who asleep did lay.
Master! Master!
Save us from the storm, we pray.

He arose and chided them,
For their lack of faith
When close to Him.
Yet, He raised His hand
And in a voice gentle as could be,
Said, ''Be Still,'' to the wind
And calmed the sea.

Tho this happened long ago,
For those who do believe
Have but to ask Him,
He speaks,
And we receive.

Margaret Stagg

WHY ALWAYS?

How cheap is life we throw away
    And never try to save?
The countless men we send to war,
    The children of the brave.
But why right now, you ask of me.
    Why beat us to the ground?
For freedom and for liberty!
    (Besides, the Market's down)
Without a war, we can't be free.
    Why, any fool knows that!
But you must come home conquerors
    For us to tip *our* hat!
So wage a war, go out and kill.
    Our honor you must save.
Is Liberty the tainted soul
    Of the dead . . . but very brave?

Linda P. Romig

QUIET AND STILL

Quiet and still
The nighttime is
Quiet and still
The mood is his
The moon is full
The stars are bright
It stirs within me
Myself I fight
Yet dawn is near
The morning bird calls
The sun is rising
The moon slowly falls
Yet another midnight coming
Where will I be
I look in your eyes
Maybe I will see
For in your eyes
The crescent moon tells
And in my mind
You cast your spells
What will you teach me then
To look above, beyond, below
And to remember where I've been.

Coralee A. Mollner

TENDERLY, WITH WORDS

We know words live and burn
    while bodies soon decay;
Our fusing thoughts can soar and
    climb like flying birds . . .
So look upon my love for you
    without dismay
And let me sometimes love you
    tenderly, with words.

Ethel Case Cook

TATTERED OLD MAN

Man on the street
It's a damn shame.
Clothes are tattered
His legs are lame.
Turned out on the streets
Alone to die.
No one still hears
His silent cry.
The streets are bustling
During the day.
People walk by where
This man lays.
The people are angry.
They chase him away.
''It's your own fault
You ended up that way.''
In the winter it's so
Ice-cold.
The shelters just can't
Handle the overload.
Many will die on
The street tonight.
All alone so ghostlike.

Nancy Parker

THINKING ABOUT THE WORLD

The world is so full of love and fun to encourage its people
   when the work is done
But sometimes we all get very tired, and our enthusiasm
   is really mired.
It seems as if the things we do in hope of joy just
   don't come through
With anything that's just worthwhile. Sometimes it's even
   hard to smile.
For some folks seem so greedy for just themselves, no help for needy.
They only try to steal, rob and take everything to make life a fake.
But there are so many people who are kind and true
And the greedy ones are the ones who do
The mean things that are so very bad, but when we see one, once
more we're glad.
And one among a thousand men will make us all start out again.
Thank you, God, for the kind true men who do so much
   and again and again
Bring joy and peace and kindness too in all the happy things they do.

Bernice Dennis Baker

YOUTH AND AGE

Life plays such crazy tricks on us: when we're young they always say,
"You are too young to understand — you'll surely learn someday."
And soon there come the trembling hand, the wrinkles and gray hair.
Then,"You're too old," some people say.
   "What are you doing there?"
I sometimes wonder sadly, when will life stop playing tricks
And give both young and old a chance to take the time to fix
The wrongs of life, the poverty, the people with their sins
Or will this kind of thing keep on so no one ever wins?
If you try to keep up with the crowd there are always some who say
You do not have experience, or they know some other way,
So it really works out unfairly — you are always in a group
That does not know or understand — go to some other troupe.
But the days go on and we are glad for honors that we win.
We must stay from the heartaches and keep away from sin.
If illness does not come to take our days in fear,
If people do not act like fools and rant or give you tears,
If everyone would only use the golden rule to live,
What a wondrous world this one would be in which to work and give.
If you have a lot of money that you earned by your own work
Keep on and watch your assets — help those who do not shirk.

Bernice Dennis Baker

SLAVERY

The dispute over slavery became a national question.
   The slave economy was detrimental to the South.
The great cotton belt was drawn into slavery.
   England was the best customer for trade.

The feud between the North and South became stronger.
   The slave states believed they were justified.
In spite of protests from the North,
   Slavery became predominant in the South.

The North believed they would break with the South.
   Negroes were bitter against the slavery.
Street demonstrations occurred against the issue.
   The slaves were seeking freedom.

Slavery will bring dollars to the owners.
   The emergence of a new type of machine,
Will create a mass market for products.
   The invention of machinery eliminated slave labor.

E. Saltz

A DREAM

A dream is shared by you and me,
   That will remain forever.
It is the hope man will be free,
   That peace will reign for eternity.

I dreamed the world would awaken,
   To a new dawn of plenty.
Where there is poverty, there will be wealth,
   That all would share in the earth's bounties.

I dreamed of heaven and God above,
   Of angels flying with a message of peace.
That God was near and would share,
   That all my desires could be fulfilled.

The dream man had of a better world,
   Has vanished into thin air.
The war had devastated the land,
   Brought misery and suffering in its wake.

E. Saltz

ELIZABETH SALTZ. Born: 6-15-30; Married: David, 9-63; Education: Queens College, B.A., 1979; M.A., New School for Social Research, Psychology, Philosophy; Occupation: Social worker; Memberships: Queens College Alumni Association; Philosophy Club, New School; Awards: Golden Poet Award, 1986-87; 25 Award of Merit Certificates; Poetry: 'Muslim vs. Christian,' *New Voices,* 1987; 'Greek Independence,' *Hearts on Fire,* American Poetry Association, 1987; 'The City,' *Mustard Seed,* 1987; 'Revelation,' *World's Most Cherished Poems,* 1987; 'Truth,' *Words of Praise, Vol. III,* American Poetry Association, 1987; Comments: *The senses perceive objects which lead to ideas. Knowledge is gained from ideas. All knowledge can be verified. False cannot be true beliefs. Cognition is knowing truth, which is the basis of rationality. Empirical science is rational — it investigates and exposes. It brings facts.*

LOVING WIFE

Darling I love you
And my love for you grows stronger every day
Even though we have just been together a few years
I love you just as much
And even more than that wonderful day
When we first did meet several years ago

In those few years
You did give to me
Four lovely children with faces all aglow
And as much love as any man would need

Yet our lives together have just begun
How lucky a man I am to have you
And now four children too

Truly it is a heavenly paradise on earth
That I will share with you and the children
For many years yet to come

James Lowell Schultz

LIFE'S TROUBLED WATERS

Day by day I've traveled on
   along the Path of Life.
Some days were very beautiful
   but some were filled with strife.
However dark the days appeared
   I found God's Blessed Love
Which came to me across the way
   from Heaven far above.

I know God followed day by day
   to ease my troubled heart
As throughout these many years
   Life's sorrows soon depart.
The darkest clouds all fade away
   as the sun shines far above
For Angels sing across the way
   of God's most precious Love.

As I look beyond the span of time
   to realms up in the sky
I find sweet Peace is promised
   beyond the clouds so high.
Life's troubled waters will flow beyond
   the Path of Life I trod.
As the Gates of Heaven will open wide
   and I'll be face to face with God.

R. Hazel Storm

WHAT A PRIVILEGE TO SHARE!

As we travel down Life's Highway
   sharing Love from day to day.
What a privilege we've been given
   looking through the clouds of grey.
Day by day we're being tested
   by our Saviour far above
Have we shared with those who need us?
   Have we shared His precious Love?

After years and years of travel
   down Life's valleys far and wide
Did we comfort those in trouble
   or just close our eyes and hide?
Now some days I stop and wonder
   just what God expects of me.
Have I been the kind of person
   that He expected me to be?
Did I share of Love to others
   bringing comfort, easing pains
As we journey up toward Heaven
   where our Loving Saviour reigns?

R. Hazel Storm

AS I GROW OLD

My steps are growing slower
   as I walk across the floor
My hearing's growing dimmer
   when there's knocks upon the door.
My hair has changed to silver
   while the years have rolled away
And my face is full of wrinkles
   caused by cares from day to day.
But my heart is full of happiness,
   for the friends that I hold dear
So many new friends I have found
   along life's path each year.
So many sorrows I have shared
   and blessings found each day
All prove to me my faith in God
   helped guide me on Life's Way.
So, "Thanks Dear Lord," for precious love
   I hold within my heart
For my Soul is full of Happiness
   So life's sorrows soon depart.

R. Hazel Storm

REBECCA HAZEL STORM. Born: January 16, 1900, Moultrie County, Illinois; Moved to Shelby County at age 6, has spent her life in Windsor and Ash Grove Townships; Married: A.R. Storm (deceased 7-27-76); Together they built and operated a country store for 15 years in Sexson, Illinois; One son, William Edward Storm, diagnosed with tubercular meningitis at 16 months, lived to be 56 years old; Education: Eastern Illinois University, acquired Teacher's Certificate by Examination at age 18; Occupation: Elementary school teacher, 25 years, retired 1961; Poetry collections: *Climb that Mountain*, 34 poems, 1980; *Across the Valley*, 45 poems, 1981; *Through the Years*, 70 poems, 1982; *As Days Go By*, 58 poems, 1984; Has written many verses for greeting cards and over 200 poems since the 1930s; Receipts of sales given to Central Community Church, Mattoon, Illinois; Comments: *Her family church is the Ash Grove Christian Church near Windsor, Illinois, and her loved ones are buried in the beautiful Ash Grove Cemetery. She doesn't need to buy greeting cards. She just writes them, having sent 100 Christmas cards some years to family and friends.*

DEAR LORD

Dear Lord, you have been with
Me over the years,
Through joy and happiness,
Through heartache and tears.

Through happiness and gladness,
All along the way,
Through heartache and sadness,
Through a lot of days.

You have always been my strength
As I struggled each day.
You have always been my guide,
Showing me the right way.

You are a shining light,
That brightens my day,
A ladder to climb
When I am on my way.

Dear Lord in Heaven,
Thank you, I humbly pray,
For blessing me thus,
Each and every day.

Willie Johnson Cummings

HAPPY BIRTHDAY JESUS

December 25, 1981

Happy Birthday to Jesus,
Born to be our Lord and King,
Died on the cross for my sins,
Glory to God! Hallelujah we sing.

Thank you for the blessings,
Bestowed on me each day,
For the sacrifice of your life,
When they crucified you that way.

So, Happy Birthday Dear Jesus,
So very much of the time.
We forget it is your birthday,
That is the reason for this rhyme.

As when you were born
The gifts are like frankincense and myrrh.
Born in a manger in Bethlehem,
Some two thousand years ago.

Christmas is a Holy time,
Let us this fact never forget,
For it is the birthday of Jesus,
And let us keep it like that.

Willie Johnson Cummings

PRAIRIE WHEAT

The silvery moon shone down on the banks,
    It was summertime in Mississippi.
The clear blue sky lit up the day,
    Steamboats plied the muddy waters.

The railroad tracks gleamed in the sun,
    A bird flew past the speeding train.
The wheat swayed in the wide fields,
    Ready for harvest and the market.

The town knew many depressions,
    This was the worst, as they mowed the hay.
The rugged old barn creaked with age,
    The timbers were worn and hinges rusty.

The old kitchen stove was aglow,
    Waiting for the guests to arrive,
The tables were set with party snacks,
    The great moment arrived for company.

The old town has seen better days,
    When the corn was ripe, it paid.
The market was waiting for wheat,
    Slowly, it was stacked for export.

Rising resentment against low prices,
    Forced the farmer to burn to the city.
Factory pay is better than the drought,
    Migration to the city had emptied the town.

        E. Saltz

TOES AND OTHER LUXURIES

My toes splay out on the warm floor beneath me.
Such wondrous, comforting and enduring devices,
These very ordinary feet of mine.

But the travels they have made . . .
Down through the warm velvet dust of a summer's road
All those years ago,
My sister's larger prints side by side with mine
Like the protection of her quiet presence
Much of my life . . .

Or the trips they have taken alone
Up the stairs to the podium,
Squeezed into shiny black patent
For the sake of some arbitrary voice in my head,
And wriggling their way free
When safely hidden from public scrutiny.

More like the true me, perhaps,
Than any other part,
The feet speak of service in the cause of
  curiosity,
    or love,
Or simply a passion for being me.

        J. Quaytman

THE LITTLE STATUE

There is a little statue in my house.
It isn't mine, it belongs to my spouse.

This statue is only three feet high and made of wood.
I'd put it outside if only I could.

This little statue is an Indian chief, colored dark brown,
With little beady eyes and a mouth large and round.

His nose is broad and looks punched in his face.
I wish I could put this little creature some other place.

His legs are short and his feet are funny and small.
He doesn't look much like an Indian chief at all.

Sometimes I look too long at this critter and I get a wild notion,
To load him in the car and let him take a long swim in the ocean.

Whatever my feelings are, my husband's aren't the same.
So this little wooden figure will have to remain.

Perhaps within time I will learn to like this little piece of wood.
For my husband adores it and would give it a mate,
If only he could!

        Debbie Hestand

THE UNIVERSE

Things are so far out of reach.
So near to us, yet so far from others.
Why do you hesitate so?
When you can reach out and take the things that others live
        to just see.
Man's ability has no end.
Now the moon, next year a whole new universe much like ours.
Not yet known to us, just as we are not yet known to them.
How do we know that on the other side of the moon,
        there may be yet another flag?
Only they know that their flag is waving.
They do not know we exist.
They did not see our flag, just as we did not see theirs.
But someday, we'll find another,
And maybe become friends.
Life out there is a whole new world,
Waiting for me, you, us.
Let us hopefully soon find out.
For each day we grow farther apart,
This other universe and ours.
So let us now begin the search for this other universe,
So close to ours, yet so far away.

        Rida Milbach

If by some essence of the dark, your face
Could press upon the window of my night,
I then would know the motion of your grace
Caught lonely as a single bird in flight.
Shall I consider you upon a stone?
Or hold some troubled, drab, uncertain clay?
The one already formed as with a bone;
The other seeking light as with a day.
I cannot think or turn the question 'round,
Your lonely beauty is no stone or soil;
I lie upon the cold and shadowed ground
Where memories like a snake about me coil.
  And yet like sudden swells beneath the sea
  You can with wind and wing be wild to me.

Leo Kartman

''I have no value to anyone else,
till I find the value in myself.''
I must challenge, test
and learn.
Fall down,
get hurt
but get up.
I must let the child in me
feel free to dream.
While the adult
tries to realize those dreams.
For me to be
all that I can be,
respect me,
but
most of all,
Love me.

Teresa M. Brown

A GENTLE WAY

For Lisa

A feather's touch with a pen;
Hands — gracious, fair and soft;
Tender reticence overcomes her;
— A gentle way.

Walking quietly as a sea breeze;
A fine, warm and distant island;
Seeking true love and sweet comfort;
— A gentle way.

Eyes so at ease as to be disturbing;
Something special is within her soul;
Not American, but of the universe;
— A gentle way.

Please do not crush her delicacy;
A beauty that is all too rare.

Michael Allport

COURAGE

The neverending courage of a dying man.
Though time is slipping past,
This man of peace is still steadfast.
He has yet to reach his goal,
As life has many things that are left undone.
The unity of many is still a far-off dream.
The neverending courage of a dying man.

Judith A. Marsh

GOD CARES

When Adam and Eve fell from grace
And had to leave that lovely place,
  God did not from them turn away,
  But for their sin they had to pay.

When wicked men at Noah raved,
He and his family were saved
  From the flood Jehovah sent
  Because mankind would not repent.

On Abraham God placed His hand,
And led him to another land,
  And promised him a multitude
  Of children, and God's word was good.

Old Moses, as God led the way
Through the Red Sea on that day,
  Knew God had for them a plan.
  Still God reaches out to man.

God cares. He spoke in many ways
Through prophets in the ancient days.
  For our well-being still concerned,
  God pours out blessings rich, unearned.

He gave a Book explaining all.
He stoops to lift us when we fall.
  Once, reaching out to everyone,
  God sent to earth His only Son.

Alta McLain

TO THE EARTH MOTHER

Oh Mother Mentor — torch that set my
Soul aflame.
Unformed, you saw in me
A kindred soul
Whose passion at a sunset
Overwhelms the man of ledgers.
Like a dragon, you spit fire
But my sharpened third eye
Saw the overwhelming tender rose.
Yet I could not speak, so in awe
Was I.
When tongue I found, you were
Dancing on a star somewhere
With Fred Astaire.

Cheryl Trulen

OUR HONOR TO YOU DEAR MOTHER

Our honor to you dear Mother
This day is yours alone
It's set apart from others
To express our love, each to his own.

No home is complete without you there
To guide the feet of those nearby
No teardrop will fall that you don't share
The hurt, the sorrow, the bitter cry.

Your life is filled with courage rare
Your love can heal a heart and mind
And no greater leader anywhere
Could be found through the pages of time.

You work and toil day in, day out
While starting each day anew
Tiring duties on your shoulders mount
Cheerfully, you do them till each is through.

Dear Mother, God's sweetest blessings
Upon your day and you
With loving thoughts, our hearts caress
In honor, the heart and life of You!

Willa Elliott

EPITAPH

I have seen the power of God alive
And speechless, I was bound by fear:
Muted are they who walk dead upon the earth,
Voiceless are the wise that only hear!

Lynn Geralds

SNOW UPON THE ROSE

The house wherein the spirit dwells,
May be falling apart at the seams.
The plans made in youth may have vanished,
In a sea of empty dreams.

So many schemes have gone awry,
Earthly fortunes have all passed by.
The wealth and the fame we visioned,
Were but castles in the sky.

Though the outer cover changes,
With fashion winds that blow.
The price of things and children,
Seem the only things that grow.

Of all the many treasures,
Garnered amid toil and pain.
Unlike the changing seasons,
Some will forever remain.

For inside this seemingly empty shell,
Beats a heart that is living proof.
That love and warmth are still inside,
Despite the snow upon its roof.

Clara G. Stinson

ABANDONED

A child abandoned and alone — 'cause Mommy ran away
from home — away she fled without a trace, unable
to look back upon his face.

Could she have loved him any less?
Maybe her life was one big mess?
Could it be a sacrifice or leaving him here to live
a better life?

Does she know what she has done?
Is she happy on the run?
Does she regret being gone, not knowing a thing
about her son?

To do the best for all concerned motherly love she
has to learn.

Running from the truth will never last — for the
rest of her life, she'll be haunted by her past . . .

The question is no longer, *how?*
But how is our child doing, *now?* Happy and loved
he is at home — with Grandma and Daddy he's never alone . . .

Gloria J. Burns

WILL I DIE KNOWING

Will I die knowing if I was right for this world
This place, this time.
Will I die knowing my accomplishments meant something
Poems, letters, the odd jobs people call "work"
Will I die knowing (that) they were referring to me
They know who they are
Will I die knowing my shrink was after the 45 dollars
And only that
Or will I die knowing as I do now —
Confused

Tom Bisker

IF

If you try to live beyond your income
You steal from your tomorrows.
If you don't take advantage of your opportunities
You stunt your growth today.
If you save everything for your tomorrows
Your life will be stunted, short-sighted, today.

If you live to the fullest each and every day,
Accepting each opportunity or challenge as it comes your way,
Never trying to live beyond your means,
Never living with self-recrimination for your yesterdays,
Praying for understanding, courage and strength,
You will live closer to your potentiality. At length
This will carry you far and bring contentment in your old age.

Annetta C. Stanton

A POSTAGE STAMP MARKED "LOVE" DOESN'T HELP

Sometimes
I hate my words.
that strange appendage that
grows on me and greets you
before I arrive.
it shakes your hand, your heart,
with a shake that is not my hand-
stroke.

To say hello is to bring you in
with the turn of a word — and you are in me.
but not in my grip.

and the vapor of syllables feels like betrayal:
I want you.

I love you.

I miss you, thou Other,
whose body is my breath —
    the hot steam I feel rising (from nowhere)
    the back I slowly caress
    as I feel the proud weight of your chest
    (on my breast) Oh God how tight is the

perimeter of words. It feels like iron.

I'll be home soon.

Marianne Fulop

RHAPSODY IN SWAMP

Night-things slither and creep, while Day-things peacefully
Sleep, deep in tall marshy grasses. There the swamp is alive
With all kinds of jive 'til pitchy-black nighttime passes. Then
Dawn blazons in on dew-jeweled flowers and Day-things awaken
And start their hours with tremolos and trills and concerted
Singing and daedal winging for their kind of thrills.

A Mantis is praying for what the day's bringing: an anxious
Bee humming; a Mosquito bungling; a traveling Gnat coming,
Wending its way toward the Mantis' Trap — then wham! Zap!
Mantis enfolds and holds his Gnat up to heaven, giving thanks for
His catch of the day, and like any gourmet diner, he's never
Felt finer as he devours his delicious prey.

Glistening Beetles and Devil's Darning Needles lurk near
Green-watered places, there Grasshoppers chew and leap and spit
Into myriads of rowdy Wasps' faces. Poised Dragonflies, jet-winged
And swift, chase afternoon Butterflies who float and drift on
Sun-sweetened breezes, while sashaying Moths hide away from their
Foes, who are stalking there waiting until daytime goes.

Crickets are cheering the night coming on, and Day-things are
Fearing who slithers along through the swamp's marshy grasses, to
Creep in menacing masses, 'til Fireflies blink the way for
Night-things return to wing and sing in discordant pitches, while
Day-things are going to sleep again until another darkled-night
Time passes.

Thelma Dorris Karcher

THE COLD MAN

There is no love within his heart,
Only ashes gray and cold,
Only mists of memories fading out
And a face grown stern and old.

A smiling face belies the truth
That he so falsely claims:
To him all men are fools or worse —
Or other hateful names.

There was a time when his world was new,
When youth and love were real.
Because of the strife of the ways of life
He's forgotten how to feel.

He walks alone in his cold dark world
Though his face may wear a smile.
His spirit is filled with a bitter hate
And his soul is weak and vile.

He may own the world or the universe
And all that gold can give.
But his loveless heart is a lump of lead
If he can't love or forgive.

Louise M. Donahue

A HEAVENLY INSPIRATION

A heavenly melodic choir
Rehearses in a cherubic soul,
Chanting out its praises
In a bell-appealing toll;
When a heavenly inspiration
Heralds in another poem,
A writer will be in heaven
Although he abides at home.

Peggy L. Dudley

GRANDMOTHER'S BUCKET

Off I went with Grandmother's bucket;
A five-gallon bucket to boot;
To fetch some water for Grandmother,
Thinking there was nothing to it.

Now being as I was small,
Twelve cups it would have to be;
The amount of which I could handle,
So Grandmother could have some tea.

As I departed the old town pump;
I indulged in a healthy sup;
As I staggered along the way
I would slosh another cup.

I sloshed a cup over here;
I sloshed a cup over there;
But in struggling on I thought
I really was doing quite fair.

When I arrived on Grandmother's porch,
My bucket had lost some more;
But bless my Grandmother's heart,
She loved the cups that now were four.

Peggy L. Dudley

THERE IS A REASON

Don't ever think life is foolish,
For it has a reason no doubt;
I think we are here for the reason
Of finding out what it is all about.

We are here to learn our lessons;
We are here to find our way;
Even if we don't know the direction,
Or know what we are supposed to say.

We are here to leave a footprint;
Where is the question of mind?
Or perhaps it is the *how to?*
Or maybe it's really *what kind?*

We know we are here for a reason,
As we sift and sort it about;
I wonder when we are leaving
If we ever really figured it out.

I'm going to continue doing;
Whatever I can for a clue;
Of learning whatever is the reason
For doing what I keep trying to do.

Peggy L. Dudley

PEGGY LOUCELLE DUDLEY. Pen Name: Pennetta Penn; Born: Valley City, North Dakota, 9-2-43; Married: Larry Dudley, 2-2-61; Education: High school; Occupation: Secretary; Poetry: 'Seasons Come,' *Impressions*, 1986; 'I'm America,' *National Poetry Anthology*, 1987; 'Imprints,' *Kids, Cats and Puppydogs*, 1988; 'Love's Fury,' 'I Love You, Mom,' *Hearts on Fire*, 1987; Themes: *The common theme in my poetry is love: love of life, love of nature, love of family, love of God. My poetry is the best way to leave behind me a smile, a laugh, and loving thoughts, it's my contribution of love to humanity.*

CRAWFISH

Mud bugs — red devils
Emerge with the rains
Hard times and they take over
Living in the darkness
Waddling in the dirt
Thus it is that evil exists

Watch out for their pinch
Boil them alive
You devour them
Their big heads . . . empty
Aggressive claws
Black guts

Linda Joyce Pace

FADING IMAGE

If I could have just one more day
To imprint again in my mind
Before the image fades away
And memories are no longer there to find.

Time don't let them slip away
They're all I have of yesterday.
Renew the hurt and let me cry,
Let me keep my days gone by.

I want no place I've never been
Or the touch of other men.
I know I can't go home again,
So let me keep my hurt within.

The time is drawing near,
I can feel it in my soul.
My memories will disappear
Leaving nothing of him to hold.

Ann Thomas

THE LADY INSIDE OF ME

I wish I knew the lady
Who lives inside of me
Just when I think I know her
Another side I see

At times she is like a fortress
Standing strong
And without warning
She feels so alone
She can find such pleasure
In the smallest of things

And still her nights are haunted
With unpleasant dreams
At times she has faith
That all will go right
While her fear is hiding
Just out of sight

She used to know what made her tick
But life was cruel, it played a trick
Someday the pieces will come together,
And for it all she will
Be so much better

Ann Thomas

Resting,
Now, in God's arms, she
Feels secure. We grieve, but know
She is safe. No longer suffering, only
Happy times await her for all
Eternity. We love you,
Grandma.

Jill Eitel

A LETTER FROM HEAVEN

Dear Son,
You are doing fine the way you live and believe
because you have given your life to God so you have Heaven to receive.
Up in here are golden streets and mansions to see
and everybody is as friendly as they can be
and when our Lord comes down to earth
and gets everybody who has a second birth
I know that you will come because I know you so well
that I have no fear that you will enter Hell,
because I know, "The devil you hate, and the Lord you fear."
So some of these days we will meet up here.
So don't ever get sad, and don't ever get bored
but always be happy and praise the Lord.
Up here we all have mansions and there are too many to number
but they're all made with gold and none made with lumber.
We have angel bands and saints all about
and the Lord is the light and he never goes out.
So it is always a day and we never have night
and the beauty is things that are always in sight.
I can't keep from being happy with everything so fine
and someday we will both meet again and then we can recline.
But you stay down there in the world's stormy weather,
until the Lord says we can get back together
because I know you love the Lord so I want you to stay nice,
until we both meet up here in the Lord's Paradise!

From, Dad   *Matthew 22:32*

Joe Dunkin

BABY JOSEPH

All my life I have wished for diamonds,
a house.
I have wished for love,
and God.

Through strong emotion love appeared
tenderly placing a diamond inside my womb.
As time became future my diamond matured
into a ten-pound fragile gem.
A glimpse at the mirror, I envisioned my house.
And my house was full of love.

It was Christmas day that God
I saw.
He placed that precious diamond into my arms.

And now I have learned that diamonds are priceless,
houses are big,
love is inside you,
and God is real.

Tammy Lynn Bryce

TAMMY LYNN BRYCE. Born: Chicago, Illinois, 9-3-64; Married: William Bryce, 7-3-47; Occupation: Former model; Comments: *To me, being a poet means more than just your thoughts, but looking at any object or situation and being able to envision it in a lot of different ways.*

DON'T TOUCH ME

Don't touch me, I can't stand the pain,
Don't kiss me, I've loved you in vain,
All the while that you smiled, you were fooling me,
You never really loved me, set me free.

Don't hug me, I'm too blue to care,
Don't hold me, I don't want to share,
Any lies in your eyes, I might happen just to see,
You never really loved me, set me free.

Don't help me, I just want to cry,
Don't fight me, just tell me goodbye,
While your lips were on mine, devils played within your mind,
You never really loved me, set me free.

C. K. Klinkerman

A CHRISTMAS POEM FOR MY FAMILY

Does Christmas seem to be not quite so bright this year?
Does money seem to be not quite as much this year?
Do cherished friends and loved ones seem oh so far away?
Then think of Baby Jesus, he's here with you today.

Happy Birthday Baby Jesus, born in a stall,
We thank you for our babies, so sweet and so small,
Because you were so poor, rich they'll always be
And live with you, the King, in heaven eternally.

Christmas is for caring,
Christmas is for sharing,
The love the Father gave.

Who needs earthly presents,
Money, wealth or fame,
When we call Jesus brother, and
God calls us by name.

Thou who gave us Jesus knows our every fear,
Knows about our worries, sees our every tear,
Feeds and clothes and loves us, no matter large or small,
Teach us then, dear Father, to share this love with all.

Merry Christmas

C. K. Klinkerman

GONE FROM ME

My darling, you are gone from me, and I dare not to complain,
For God in his wisdom took you to sing his sweet refrain,

The world called you many things, Grandpa, and friend and Dad,
But I called you Honey and Lover, and the husband who made
     my heart glad,
The one who held me and kissed me and kept me from all things bad.

Your smile and your love made me happy, and your hands with their
     gentle touch,
You saw only beauty in me, you never saw wrinkles or such,
You thought me eternally young, and for that I loved you so much.

You jumped anyone who abused me and you dried each tear as it fell,
You pampered and care for and loved me, you really were quite swell,
If my life must go on without you, I will never live quite as well,

And my heart will remember you with love for as long as it beats.

C. K. Klinkerman

AN OPPOSITE POEM

Hate,
I hate the word hate.
Maybe, dislike, disconcern,
Lack of confidence in a
Person, but hate.
What an abrupt word!
A final word!
A despicable word!
A disgusting sound
Of a word.
Hate,
I hate the word hate.

Love,
The direct opposite of hate.
Now that's a super word!
Concern, feelings, caring;
There are so many meanings
Of love that it's difficult
To write them down.
Besides, love is in the heart.
It is not a word to be
Bounced around,
Scrambled, or
Talked about lightly.

Marie Valeri-Gold

WHAT I BELIEVE

At the time of my death
    does time stop?

When I "pass away,"
    where do I pass to?

Will I know, remember?
    does it matter?

We are told
    "You will be transformed."

This I believe.

My sins are already forgiven.
    Amazing grace.

What a comforting blend
    of belief and faith.

No fear of what's coming,
    But anticipation,

And a surety that
    All is well,
    And will be.

Cyril R. Mill

SUMMER MORNING

pink in the east
and white in the west
the morning breeze
shattered the petals
of the rose
thrushes exchanged
their silver flutes
and dewdrops wept
cicada helicopters
in the crowns of trees
did not begin
their daily din
no lawnmowers
cut down the grass
it stood tall
and quiet still
in reverent praise
of the Sunday dawn

Vera Borkovec

OPPORTUNITY

To each being God has given,
Much opportunity,
To find the joy of living life,
With hope and dignity.
And as we go along the way,
There comes a time to know,
When the path no longer goes,
The way we want to go.
Exalted mute ambitions,
Thwarted hopes that fail,
Should sometimes be discarded,
For things that serve us well.
And if indeed we really look,
Each one will surely see,
All the many worthwhile fruits,
Of opportunity.
So do not feel vexation with,
An old and tainted star,
But be prepared to see afresh,
The dreams that really are.

Hilda Sanderson

MY NINETIETH BIRTHDAY

Oh! What a beautiful day this is
    I'm floating on air today,
For you, the nicest people on earth
    Are all coming my way.

My heart is full of love and joy
    Because you came this way.
I bow in humble gratitude
    Because you're here today.

My love is more than I can tell
    I bow my head and pray.
I thank my God, for friends like you
    On this twelfth day of May.

You fill my heart brimful of joy
    By coming here today,
To help me celebrate on this
    My ninetieth birthday.

Andy Powers

LIFE IS A METAPHOR

Life is a metaphor
An open door
Left to explore
So as not to bore

Life is a metaphor
With similies galore
As symbols implore
The creation of more

Life is a metaphor
That some adore
And some deplore
As ancient lore

Life is a metaphor
A bird set to soar
To a distant shore
Not knowing the score

Linda Joyce Pace

SEA BREEZE

To be free
Free as the wind rustling through the trees
Free as the gull gliding on the breeze

To be wild
Wild as the gale blowing through my hair
Wild as the waves splashing everywhere

To be mellow
Mellow as the calm when stillness abounds
Mellow as the hush when there are no sounds

I am kin to the wind
I am wild and free
I am mellow as the sea breeze

Linda Joyce Pace

INVISIBLE BONDS

The mind can be a prison
My sentence has been years.
For me there is no escape,
Not even through my tears.

The world is ever changing
. . . moving right along.
I'm keeping with the paces,
But always I'm alone.

Let me out, I've cried.
I need to live again
And though I've tried,
The bonds are strong, they keep me in.

Once I thought I could be free
For in my heart I felt a yearn
But this was not to be
For fear made me return.

Ann Thomas

44

EVERGREEN LANDING.

WHITE HEAD.

PORTLAND HEAD LIGHT.

PORTLAND HARBOR, AND ISLANDS.

PLACE OF MY DREAMS

Nestled in the valley
Where the wildflowers grow
Beneath the trees
Where the wild birds sing
Is a place I'd love to be
When I know I'm growing old
A place forever in my dreams.

A little log cabin
With a sun porch for two
And a kitty for the window sill.
My home, sweet home; the shadows of night
And the voice of the lonesome
    whippoorwill.

Old grandfather clock
As he ticks away the time
To remind us of memories held dear,
Telling of a place where I long to be,
When my heart is free from all care.

The old rocking chair
With you there by my side;
And the sounds of the waterfall stream.
Yes, my home, sweet home
Where I long to be
In the log house of my dreams.

Nevelyn Glenn

ALADDIN'S LAMP
Or: On a picture which
once belonged to my grandmother

To my grandmother, "Sissy."

Aloof she stands yet poised with discreet grace,
Her composure simple yet the style refined;
With what exquisite finesse she embodies
  the artist's own soul or dream
(As the Aladdin's lamp she holds
Itself the sleeping Genie's abode),
Or source of inspiration and beauty.

There in the common marketplace
She, alone, seems to understand its secret
And poised in time seemingly
  for a moment suspended —
Her eyes gaze downward at the lamp
  she holds outward;
Upon her head she wears a silken turban
Of purple, yellow, and vermillion stripes,
And in her dark tresses white flowers.

Her pale cream muslin dress is doubly entwined
  with her lavender-blue sash,
And on each foot she wears no sandals
  but with feet bare
Seems to tread not on earth
But, instead, upon thin air!

Derek A. Wilson

PEACE

A little stream ran down the hill
  Searching for a place to go,
Led by strength and forces of time
  To places far below.

It bathed the rocks
  And sparkled the sands,
It watered the roots and trees.
  It formed a place called, waterfall
A place of Love and Peace.

It rained its waters over the ledge,
  Down through the ages of time.
It formed a place —
  Deep within my heart;
That gentle place, that waterfall,
  Wonderful Peace Sublime!

Nevelyn Glenn

APPLE BLOSSOM AND
DEWDROP

In the midst of the garden,
  Stood a lovely apple tree.
It blossomed most delicate and sweet.
  A tiny dewdrop —
Had hung from its petal.
  Not anyone passing
Could be free of the fragrance
  Of the lovely apple tree.

Stricken with years
  The lovely old tree
Withered and dwindled away.
  The dewdrop vanished,
Her delicate blossom faded,
  And I shall never forget,
The beauty I beheld — the admiration,
  Of a tiny dewdrop, that had hung,
Falling from the lovely apple tree.

Nevelyn Glenn

NEVELYN ONEITA GLENN. Pen Name: Sissy; Born: Gaston, South Carolina, 11-9-37; Married: Thomas C. Glenn; Education: Eighth grade; Occupation: Housewife; Membership: Mt. Pleasant Baptist Church; Poetry: 'Wedding Band,' 'Crossing Paths,' 1983; 'The Fancies of Little Plain Jane,' 1984; 'A Place In Life's Dream,' 1985; 'A Mother's Love,' 1986; Themes: *Friendship, courtship, love, marriage, breaking the reins of home, the depth of a mother's love, searching for a Love that slipped away early in life.*

COLLEGE

Exciting, but scary
Confusing, but fun.
On some days there're problems
And on others, there're none.
The pressures build up fast
The homework list grows.
You think you're alone now
But everyone knows.
You like someone new,
You miss your best friend.
The days just get longer.
Oh, when does this end?
Then finally one day
The confusions all fade.
You get your degree —
Then you've got it made.
Only to realize
Your life just begins.
No one really loses,
But no one ever wins.

Jill Eitel

EVERETT GOES KA-BOOM

From 'Labor's Log'
For my sons, David Luke and Kevin
Scott Yoakum

The old men talked on the corner,
Boards beneath their feet
Of bad times and good times
And of the greater times ahead,

While small girls were dancing,
Pantaloons and pinafores and pigtails
Joyously jumping in breezes
Rippling cares and frights away,

Ladies rustling in long lines,
Skirts touching, brushing dust
In particles about for hooves
Of horses, trampled to the eons

In herald of other celebrations
Other times of generations who
Would holler and throw flames
And carry torches into the night.

Would it be that banners
Long forgotten would wrinkle,
Even moulder to make
The passing of shouts and

Echoes of marching feet
A monument of memories to the past?

Little boys laughed
To see such sport
And the rockets ran away to the moon!

Carlottadean Yoakum

OUR HEROES IN SPACE

It takes a lot of courage to explore the unknown, the whole
world was saddened when the Challenger's dreams

Were lost in a second of time. We had seven brave heroes whose
qualities reflected integrity, courage, and strength.

They were full of hope in their new adventure, and full of
anticipation of what they would learn

And bring back to share. Their dreams must live on. We will
always remember their spirit, bravery, and courage.

The hope for the future, life is full of chances that must be
met, so that we can grow, expand, and broaden our horizons.

There is so much to learn and uncover in space; faith, fortitude,
and unity will help us to forge on.

Elizabeth Cotton

IN MEMORY OF JIM HUTTON

He enjoyed his craft, acting meant so much, he was always
prepared for any part, he realized the heartaches and the
happiness connected with his profession.

He played a variety of parts, light comedy being his favorite,
enjoying each moment with such pleasure, and deep satisfaction
at doing what he loved best.

He left us a legacy of his work, my favorite being Ellery Queen,
my favorite detective with his nice blue eyes, and his funny hat,
his winning smile, with his niceness shining through.

He lives on in our hearts and our memories, and through his son
Timothy; he must be very proud knowing that his son is such a
success at doing what he loved best.

Elizabeth Cotton

WHAT HAVE I DONE?

What have I done?
I sit by the phone. Why won't you call?
You said you would call. What have I done to anger you?
You didn't call. I called you.
You weren't home. You didn't return my call. What have I done?
I told my friends I liked you. I told them I knew you liked me.
Was I wrong to tell them?
Was I wrong to expose your feelings?
I felt proud saying I had you. Is pride a bad thing?
Was I wrong to be proud?
I wanted to tell them how I felt.
Was I putting them down by telling them I felt good?
Was I bragging? Why was I bragging?
I want to see you again.
Or do I just want to say you're mine again?
I want to hold you in my arms again,
And tell you how I feel about you.
Why won't you call?
My friends joke around with me. I talk about you.
I tell them I like you, and want to see you again.
I feel proud. They make me prouder.
Why won't you call?
Why should you call?

Because I love you.

Stephen Kalandros

A MOTHER'S MESSAGE

A message from heaven to my children on earth.
To whom I love and gave birth.
I lost you to the welfare in 1934.
I have never felt such pain before.
I wanted to tell you before I died.
This opportunity I was denied.

I know there's a lot you don't understand,
But I would like for you to forgive me if you can.
I'm sorry for the pain you had to endure.
Nothing has changed my love for you.

Thanks for the beautiful way you fixed my grave.
I look down from heaven each day,
And give you a big wave.
I failed as a mother and I feel so ashamed.
I wish there were some way to change everything.

Through tons of heartaches and millions of tears,
I send my love for 53 years.
Hold to the future, forget the past.
Finally I'm happy at last.

Mary Ware

TODAY

Days filled of nothing.
I want to live, not just vegetate.
I'm here to stay and yet I don't know why.
To record, report what?
Nothing!
I still hope that something more than nothing will happen.
What, when?
I read about AIDS in Houston — nothing happens.
More homophobia is rampant everywhere.
I read about the Paris Fall Couture collections.
Ruffles, embroideries, waist on place, minis . . .
They were popular in the late sixties!
The price has changed.
Now a dress like that is $30,000 — $50,000!
Money has no value — it seems to me that we are only adding zeroes!
It's a total isolation, total annhilation!

Vittorio Maria Arimondi

I AM

If you want to know me then love me you must,
And make it very quickly before I turn to dust.
For life is so uncertain and there is so much to learn
So accept me as I am and from me do not turn.
If sometimes I appear foolish or seem to be weak
This is not all of me, there is so much more to seek.
So remember I can be distant and keep myself afar,
And then I can change and be as bright as a star.
I have so much to offer you which the surface does not show
And if you give me half a chance this you'll surely know.
All I can promise you is I'll be your friend,
And if you but love me as I am it will be to the end.

Joan M. Lacey

ASHES

Fame and fortune, in a flash,
Appear
As if in a gorgeous dream.
Joy and sorrow,
Success and failure,
Interact
As swift as
The sweeping stream.

Understand life better,
Whether sweet or bitter.
Enjoy life greater,
Whether sad or glad.

The thought of impermanence
Inspires
The sense of awareness.
Man comes from ashes,
And
In the end
Returns to ashes.

Christina Ching Tsao

MAY OUR DREAMS

*Dedicated to Mr. & Mrs. Bob
Decker, Sr.*

May our dreams be dreams of visions.
Know thyself, as one would say.
For God our heavenly Father
Can lead us on our way.

May our dreams be dreams of visions;
For to do the right in all our ways;
To revere and respect with kindness
Can assure our better days.

Verna S. Shellenberger

MY FATHER

My father is weakened by age
and disease.
He is a shadow of the man
he once was,
a victim of time.

When his soul sheds its
delicate casing,
he will become part of
the infinite universe.
I will remember him
as I remember the sun.

I will feel his presence,
always.
His image will be
in ripples and clouds,
and I will hear his voice
in the wind and rain.

Mae Sue Leslie

TAKE TIME TO SMELL THE ROSES

Take time to smell the roses,
Blooming 'round you so near;
For soon will come the autumn,
Later on winter and the start of a new year.
Sometimes I almost wish
The summer didn't need to go,
And there wouldn't be any winter
With the blankets of snow;
But there are many gems
We may gather from God's bountiful hand;
So why should I try to change
The blessed way He planned?

Think of the pink, wild roses,
That blossom along the way.
Their thorns may not seem so annoying,
When we see their glorious array.
And after the winter is over
And springtime comes once more;
Perhaps it is time to remember
To smell the roses like before.
And maybe venture on farther
And with a little bend,
Stoop and kiss a wild, wild rose.
Maybe — now and then.

Dorothy Klingler

from GOODBYE, BELOVED THUNDERBIRD

How many spirits are in the wind
tonight?
Do they watch over me
even though my skin
is white,
and my eyes are blue?
Do they stand just beyond
my sight
to keep me from harm?

I wish I might know
who they are!
Are they far removed in time?
Do their drums beat a rhythm
I cannot hear,
even though I'm certain
that they're quite near?

Oh gentle wind,
blow through that curtain
of years that have passed —
that vast veil
through which I cannot see —
and thank them
for me.

Doby Leuch

from GOODBYE, BELOVED THUNDERBIRD

Misty was my lovely Siberian Husky

Ohhhhhhhh Misty,
we're so very rich today!
We have more diamonds
than the wealthiest of men!

Even though they stay
for just a little while,
tomorrow morning
they'll be back again
sparkling on the snow,
catching the sun
and playing with its rays.

Crystals of frost
tossed each night
to delight our eyes at dawn
with darts of red
and green and blue,
orange and violet too
shifting as we run.

What have we done
to be so fortunate?
I wonder.

Doby Leuch

FOR MY PERSECUTED BRETHREN

My brother in tattered rags, sits writing
with the door and windows locked,
shades pulled; the precious papers hidden
in that secret spot,
he prays they will not find.
Waiting till the middle of the night
with one half-used candle, hoping rays aren't
too bright. (Exiled from family.)
He hurries to write what all morning
was in his mind.
Formed with no luxury of paper
to guide the story by.
His mind is quick-practice-patience-
persecution — he knows not, nor does he
try to understand. These questions are for
free minds to consider . . .
He does what he must — no more — but no less
My brother, *my pride!*
What do you write, oh brother of mine?
Who tells your story?
Owls in the night, 'tis true they are wise
and free to fly.
When will you find your wings?
When will you find your wings?

Pamela A. Nichols

MEMORIES OF MY GRANDMA

Grandma, you have been gone 3 years now, and I still feel so sad
But when I think of you being with Jesus, it's not so bad.
I loved you so very much, Grandma
And I have such sweet memories of you
I try my best not to be so sad and blue.
Down thru the years when I was a child
I could always go in at your house and find a smile.
My precious old Grandpa was always there too
He would always grin and say, "What can I do for you?"
As I grew older and the years went by
I would look at Grandma's stooped shoulders and cry.
She finally got where she could hardly see
But when I'd say "Grandma," she would always know it was me.
I stopped by the "old place" today and had a look around
The grass was all grown up, and there was no one to be found.
It seemed so lonesome, so cold and bare
Just thinking about you and Grandpa not being there.
It seems almost like yesterday when we all gathered 'round
To have our reunions and "dinner on the ground."
My childhood memories of her linger still
Her being gone just doesn't seem real.
You can search the world over thru millions and millions
But you will never find another like "my Dora and William."

Evelyn White

MY GRANDDAUGHTER'S WEDDING

The music, soft and romantic, had begun.
The peach-colored bridesmaids came, one by one.
And each escorted by a solemn, tuxedo-dressed man.
A flower girl dragging a reluctant ringbearer by the hand.
The frightened little boy pulled loose at the aisle's end,
And ran screaming to his grandmother, his friend.
The bride came limping down the aisle,
Her face frozen in a nervous smile.
And why did she limp? you ask.
It was because her leg was in a cast.
The groom, dressed all in white,
Stood waiting to the right.
The vows were said, the rings given,
A kiss then sealed this match made in heaven.
The music swelled again, loud and clear, to usher all
The people going to the hall,
To eat, to dance, and to have fun,
For a brand-new marriage had begun.

Marjorie B. Young

SPRING THE LOVER

Old Man Winter he finally went,
now renewed hope is at the rainbow's end.
Heavenly magic fills the air, a feeling of spring
is everywhere. Spring, the servant of God,
The lover of the universe, with the sun at his side,
he comes down those golden stairs, his breath a kiss
to every sleeping tree, to every bird he is a
happy melody. A friend to lovers, he is Cupid in
disguise, he transforms a barren winterland
into a wondrous paradise. With mysterious powers
so divine and so great, a landscape of beauty
he paints, no eye can escape. His coat of plenty
lovingly covers the land and life is forthcoming,
when caressed by His hand. For one glorious season
his reign is supreme, then summer comes and
continues his game.

Ursel Blanco

THE SWAN REVISTED

From the Lori Chronicles

When the swan glides into the dining room, all the guests
Assembled there are riveted upon her.
In her pretty pink dress draped down to her slender ankles,
She smiles and speaks with much animation to her relatives
Gathered there. Silently her hand settles upon mine
Under the table and I grasp it firmly, for I am mated to the
Swan for life and love her fiercely. I want to grab her
In a tight embrace but must wait until a suitable moment when
We are alone. The swan dominates the room with all others
In attendance. Soon we leave the guests behind and drive
Back to the swan's nest, where we can hold and fondle each other
Under her wingspan as much as our heart's desire.
Who could not love the swan?

William J. Galbraith, Jr.

IS THIS ALL THERE IS?

Is this all there is, this life we live now, or have we perhaps
Lived five, ten or a hundred times before? Have we been a king,
A warrior, or a serf in ages past? Whose hand guides me now as
I pen these lines: Yeats, Whitman, Shakespeare, or an anonymous
Poet? Why have I feelings of another life, of tumult and of
Testing? Will this be my swansong, or will I appear ages
Hence as another character upon the universe, forgetting then
Most of my present existence? My pen has stopped, my mind
Slows down. What hand of antiquity has led me on this discourse?
Do I have any power over it, or am I led by the hand of another
To put these lines to print? By God, let me alone ye
Demons of the past. Hark, let me decide my own destiny.
Begone ye spirits of yesterday, let me make my own tomorrow!

William J. Galbraith, Jr.

BISMARCK

Bismarck, my tomcat, slinks in through the door,
He arches his back, he sniffs at the floor.
He walks with his tail held high in the air,
Somehow he knows that strangers were here.
He refuses his food the entire day,
Could it be there's a thunderstorm coming this way?
He frolics, he leaps, then curls up in a chair,
He mews and he purrs and grooms up while he's there.
He sprawls upside down while he's napping and dreaming,
Now he awakens, wily, and scheming:
He's decided to sharpen his claws. He has found his T-bone,
He gnaws and he gnaws. Then he washes his face with
His gray-velvet paws.
He watches me watching him when he's through with his bath,
With outrageous rascality that each tomcat hath,
He slinks through the door into ecstatic night.
Meow, that's my tomcat, Bismarck, alright.
I watch misty moonbeams dance through his fur,
While he thinks I don't know he is waiting for her.
Kristilla, his new friend, the girl-cat next door.

Thelma Dorris Karcher

from GOODBYE, BELOVED THUNDERBIRD

Desert raven
with blue-black wings
how you soar
and turn,
now the wind sings
in your feathers.

How do we seem to you,
we white humans,
foolish
cruel
uncaring
unwilling to share
even the sky,
if sharing
stands in our way?

Would you let me fly
with you
in spirit?
For just a little while
let me stay with you
and be a friend
in this endless desert blue.

Doby Leuch

DOROTHY VIRGINIA LEUCH. Pen Name: Doby Leuch; Born: Milwaukee, Wisconsin, 12-20-19; Comments: *Now and then, though we appear to have a choice, it seems that the ultimate decision is almost predestined. I had no intention of writing a book; but for some reason (I don't as yet know why) I must complete* Goodbye, Beloved Thunderbird.

BICYCLE BUILT FOR THREE

Three rode on a bike because of th' War
Had impelled us all to work for peace;
To make use of our own elbow grease,
And to honor the flag with many a star.
Two wheels were used in place of th' car,
For tires and gas were on the decrease;
October hailed the flight of the geese,
And ration stamps provided the lard.
Ladies rolled bandages, one with another,
No problem for them to share a carpool.
''Did Ruth become a Gold Star Mother?''
Father was first out in th' morning cool,
Ready to pump little sis, brown-eyed brother;
Three on a bike, on th' way to school.

Tillie Read

THE CEILING'S SUN

Under the ceiling's sun
of white copper nails

star lipped crabs
ride horses of red light.

John Svehla

WHITE SHADOWS

Timber weed grass
through blue smoke
white shadows dream
along the road
in lost highways
of the summer fields.

John Svehla

IN THE SOUTH BERRY FIELD

In the south berry field
a yellow grasshopper lid
flies off into white seedless
waves

across the green swallow land
onions lash
white knuckles of steel
against the drowning frost.

John Svehla

JOHN J. SVEHLA. Born: North Platte, Nebraska, 7-4-46; Married: Sharon Lynn Rubenstein, 11-12-76; Occupation: Senior typist, Secretary; Awards: Honorable Mention, American Poetry Association, 1986; Finalist's Award, *Negative Capability,* 1986; 2nd Prize, California Federation of Chaparral Poets, 1977; Honorable Mention, Tie Award, Pennsylvania Poetry Society, 1977; 3rd Honorable Mention, Pennsylvania Poetry Society, 1981; Poetry: 'Planet Years,' *Wide Open Magazine,* 1987; 'Two Broken Horses,' *Poetic Symphony,* 1987; 'The Nation's Sun,' *DeKalb Literary Arts Journal 3* and *4,* 1986; 'A Shuttered Breeze,' *Wind Magazine,* 1986; 'Ships,' *The Poet,* Winter, 86/87; Themes: *I am putting forth a new idiom in nature poetry.*

NEARLY NINETY

My grandchildren think I am poor and old,
but the wealth of the world is mine;
when the years of my life are counted and told,
I'll drink to my past to the dregs of the wine.

When I wake from a dreamless sleep of night,
I welcome with joy the advent of day,
from my windows I can catch the sight
of mountains dappled with blue and grey.

This world, this earth and the sky above it,
all, all of it seems to belong to me,
maybe it's only because I love it —
this land, this sky, this sounding sea.

Never has life eluded me — much sorrow
has come but also much pleasure —
I have faced without fear each tomorrow,
held out both hands for joy without measure.

Much have I traveled in younger years
to London, Athens, and Istanbul,
sometimes with faith, sometimes with fears
but always impulsively, never by rule.

Nearly ninety now and in a wheelchair,
I live in my memories of family and friends;
uncertain the future, certain only I dare
to live life fully until life ends.

Margaret Bland Sewell

SPRITES

On the coldest day the sprites converged,
Metal and flesh jostling in the streets,
Sparks flew where icy fingers touched,
And bristling nylon fabrics were revenged.
I loved this city once, before the cold
Descended, I loved the poetry, the warmth,
The quickened sense of time and place,
The crazy-quilt of people and ideas;
Then something died, no Prospero stirred
New resonances in the mind; I felt
The cold convergence of metal and men's lives,
Congealed like fingers on a slab of steel.

George N. Braman

A CHILD WINS

A boy looks into a mirror.
He is searching for the man
  he someday hopes to be.

A man searches his reflection.
He looks for shadows
  of the child he never was.

Staring out of the silver-backed glass
is a dream . . .
  a dream of a child
  who became a man
  before the man could be a child
    . . . but no reflection.

The manchild lay forever silent.
The boy had searched too hard
  for the man he never would become.

Tiffanie L. Rogers

THE DAY

The soft eastern light
  Pries gently open the lids of night.
And as the sad and reluctant darkness rolls westward,
  Trillions of tiny throats float murmurs of welcome to the day.
I wade through countless beads of diamond dew,
  Revelling in the warmth of the slumbering earth beneath my tread.
The sunshine, in slow motion, cascades down the length of me,
  Peeling away the skeins of my sleep.
And now as the rest of the world awakes,
  The human sounds thread through the air,
Bring a mosaic of voices, bells, clops and chocks and screeches,
  Javelins of thought, riding black webs of wire,
And the air is filled with billions of invisible words and pictures
  Streaking silently to spiky antennae, perched precariously.
The long shadows shrink, then grow again in a new direction,
  Soon lengthen and slowly fade
As a filmy rose warmth replaces the golden glare.
  Soft feathered wings draw the blanket of night over an earth
Now nodding anew.
  Sound fades as the world becomes the dark unconscious focus of an
    infinite
And distant glittering audience which guards our slumber throughout
    night.

Joel Taylor

JOEL A. TAYLOR. Born: Rector, Arkansas, 2-16-22; Married: Joan A. Taylor, 1950; Education: Harvard University, B.A.; University of Geneva, Switzerland; Occupation: International Business Development.

LONGING FOR HEAVEN

My heart is longing for that beautiful place called heaven.
Sometimes it seems I can almost see Him,
As He sits on His throne in His glory.
Our fellowship sweet as I sit at His feet,
Leads me closer to that Beautiful city.

It is wonderful to know as I walk here below,
I have You, my Lord, to walk with me.
Thy grace is sufficient for each trial that I have,
And Thy love I more than I hoped for.

Oh, blessed Lord, I need to know more,
That I can enter that city.
That I, too can stand on that blessed day,
Clean hands and pure heart in thy presence.

To think of that day, what more can I say?
Dear Lord, I don't want to miss it.
So teach me Your will, and keep me, Lord,
Still under the blood of my Saviour.

Vivian Martin

YOU'RE IN LOVE AGAIN

I thought it could never be true,
  here I am, falling in love, with you.

I can't forget you, a street or someone has your name,
Since we met, my life has never been the same.
  You're In Love Again.

When I look at you, you say, my eyes tell you,
  what you, don't want to do.

We say good night, with just a shake of hand,
  will this always be,
You don't know, what you do to me.
  You're In Love Again.

Why won't you let me, kiss you and hold you tight,
Is it because an old love, didn't turn out right.

Make my wandering be through,
  say, you love me, as much as I, love you.
  You're in Love Again.

Robert L. Willyard

COUNTING THE RAILROAD TIES

Counting the railroad ties,
  remembering all your lies.
You say you've changed,
  the railroad track is taking me back.

Engineer ring the bell, toot the whistle, keep up the steam,
  they'll be no more broken dreams.

No matter what you say or do.
  I guess I'll always love you.

I'll forget the past,
  give me a love that will last.

Be at the station, I need a hug and a kiss.
  Hurry train, I can't wait for a love like this.

Engineer don't let the train jump the track,
  I want my honey baby back.

Robert L. Willyard

MY "GOLDEN LANTERN" IN THE SKY

The hour is nigh, Time approaches;
The mounted steed, with wide reproaches,
Comes to carry me, way-on-high;
Beyond the "Golden Lantern" in the sky.

But before it robs the heavenly space
And the blue of the sky, its panoramic lace,
I'll befriend the Zephyr; its gentle winds,
And listen to the brook's chatterings;

Then, I'll hover about yon sacred valley
Waving "adieu" to each hill and quarry,
And with a sigh and a tear, I'll move away
Towards that aurora's golden ray.

And, just before I close mine eyes to die,
I'll have seen my "Golden Lantern" in the sky.

George Malouf

CONTROL

In our modern society
Neither piety nor sobriety
Are words that we live by today.

The buzzword is *control*
This must be our goal
It's the good old American way.

From *mind* to *body* to *rent* to *birth*
From *arms* to *cruise* to *pest* to *girth*

From *traffic* to *tartar*
And don't be a martyr
"Take control of your life," we say.

Mary Bunker

THE POET'S FAME

Writes the poet, slow burning stall,
Creation's sting a heeding call.
Emit, commit a thought from my mind,
The birth of which no one can bind.

Erupting forth from creation's light,
Rhyming words a wondrous sight.
From where be born thoughts that come to me,
Demanding birth from my mind break free?

Still later, as I read in awe,
How from me, thoughts transcribed from raw,
Was I able to Creation touch,
And from it all, write so much?

Thanking Forces that did me incite,
To allow creation a thought to plight.
That I, insignificant, inspired and unsure,
Will perhaps forever after, renown endure.

Dianne Bahl

LITTLE CUB

I am little cub, very curious, very serious.
I live in a cave, a hole in the wall, very safe.

I am friend of the wolf and eagle.
The eagle guides me.
The wolf protects me.

I rise to meet the morning sun, to meet the
    deer,
there at a stream very near.

As the rabbits come out to greet me
so do the birds want to meet me.

I am little cub, son of the bear
with black Indian hair.

Made from his pride and blood he
called me little cub.

Henry Guzman

JUKE BOX

Thanks, you said,
I needed that.
I felt like a waitress
in a roadside diner.
Everything served up speedy
undercooked or overdone.
Killing appetites to
quell the hunger.
I'd aimed to serve you up
on a silver platter
but found myself looking
for love songs on the juke box,
unrequited for a quarter,
but still
a two-bit whore.

Barbara Noll

MY SECRET FEELINGS

As I waited by the phone for you to call,
I realized I was living a world filled with
fairy tales and fantasy. I know I was
wrong to fall for you. I couldn't prevent
love from happening. You only liked me
as a friend, but my feelings were
different from yours. Love seems so strange
to me, it's like a dream. I hoped
you would understand how I felt, I
did my best to try to understand you. I
only wish we had more than three
months together. I felt the pain when
you left to go your separate way. You
will always be special to me, even
though you didn't know how strong
my feelings for you were. I don't
blame you, I blame myself. For
not telling you how I did feel.

Connie Lynn Gates

NOVEMBER FROST

Always I remember
When dawn
Frosted earth
In November:
Air was razor
On gray
Grass whiskers,
And trimmed
Corn-tassle beards
Of frozen morning;
Lone birds sliced
Through air
Now partly iced;
And woods,
Frost-cheeked,
Faced lowlands
Where fog reeked;
My lungs arose
In tingles;
And on their wings
I breathed
The beauty of things.

John A. Downes

INFERNO

Feel the fire,
how it warms your frozen heart.
The soul burns on,
in passion; so powerful.

A kiss in the dark,
starts it with a spark.
Then bodies move, holding one another;
adding fuel to the growing flames.

Lips tenderly consume one another;
in search of the key.
Looking into each other's souls;
open window are the eyes of Love.

Emotion rules out hesitation,
feelings take control.
Souls find the key,
and open the door to become one.

Drunk on the moon's fullness,
anything is possible.
The fire blazes on in the night's storm;
life is long, the fire burns strong.

Beatrice I. L. Martin

BEN HECHT

A kiss, a hug — do not abort
What little there I ask of you —
Eternally, "Wandering Jew."

H. T. Brohl

ANGELS

Little angels all around
Some were flying
Near the ground
Sending sweet secrets
Of love everywhere
Showing everyone
They really cared.
They were so beautiful
Flying around
Flying everywhere
Without any sound
Trying to show
That they are a friend
To everyone who
Will love them.
So look up toward
The sky
You may see one
Flying by
Sending love like
Never before
And watch out
One may be knocking
On your door.

Naomi V. Osborne

IS MY RING, STILL ON, YOUR FINGER?

Remember when you said, ''I do,''
  Now you say, ''I can't stand another day with you.''

You said, ''You'll stay with a friend,''
  Is this the end?

Is my ring, still on, your finger?

If you go to a dance or two,
  Will you try to find someone new?

When the bands plays, soft and slow,
  Remember you're still mine, do you want him to know?

Is my ring, still on, your finger?

This is what I want you to know:
  Memories of all the good times, will never go.

I'll stay and wait for you,
  No matter what you do.

Is my ring, still on, your finger?

Robert L. Willyard

ENWRAPPED BY THE GOLDEN-VEIL OF DEVOTION

We are here, as one in spirit, you and I;
In some ways diff'rent, yet in others alike.
While neither's an epitome of purity,
In toil, we plow our share for humanity;
Enwrapped by the golden-veil of devotion.

As if engulfed by harmony, we exist;
In youthful love and endearment, we persist.
We try, so hard, to live as the few have lived,
And love, we do, as the trifle group has loved;
Enwrapped by the golden-veil of devotion.

Yet, in the obscure darkness, we see visions;
As, in the soft of silence, we hear echoes.
And, in the shadows of light, we bear witness
To life's nature, its beauty and sacredness;
Enwrapped by that golden-veil of devotion.

Soon, like the short-lived, spewing flashes of spark
Above the aural glow of a fire at dark,
We'll be snatched by the winds of eternal gale
Into the abyss of oblivion, to sail;
Enwrapped by that golden-veil of devotion.

George Malouf

JULY 4TH, 1987

I'm not a super patriot, but in my humble way, I honor our
America, and I do it every day. For on a little signpost
That tells the number on our street, two little flags are
Flying, and each morning sun they greet. But on national
Holidays, the neighbor's flags are flying, gigantic pendants
In the sky, I guess they think that they are trying to bless
Our freedom that will never die. But on the morrow, the fifth
Of July, there's nary a banner to be seen on high, save my little
Emblems flying every day, to signify the dead who have fought
For freedom's way. So fly your flags, my neighbors, fly your
Flags so true, fly them every day to honor the red,
  the white, the blue.

William J. Galbraith, Jr.

GROWING OLD

The tablecloth of my desire
Was hemmed with violets and yellow yearning daffodils,
While I ate the boyish dinner, knowing
Nothing changes except
The hem.

Running wild with roses
Now, the hem went all unnoticed
While I ate the young man's dinner,
Knowing nothing changes except
The hem.

To blue-eyed asters now, and
Purple plums on branches
I ate the man's dinner, knowing
Nothing changes except
The hem.

Strange, I did not think of hems
As anything important until the day
It ran a solid white
As I ate the toasted bread in the winter of
My being.

John P. Clark

DREARY DAYS AND NIGHTS

The days and nights run together,
Through sunshine and through dreary weather.
I go to work and come home to more,
The same today as the day before.

The dreary days go on and on,
We reap the seeds that we have sown.
Some flowers bloom as the days go by,
Some birds sing and some just fly.

Time passes and another year is here,
Lonely for those that I hold most dear.
They are gone to make a home of their own,
Reaping the seeds that they have sown.

Minutes, hours, days, weeks, months, a year,
Lonely as always for those most dear.
But happy that they are happy and content,
And glad of the life that they have spent.

'Blessed are little children,' and big ones too,
So God, give them your love, I ask you,
You are supreme, and the King on high,
Waiting to welcome us all in the sky.

Willie Johnson Cummings

LOST BEGINNING

Have you not ventured beyond your garden's gate
Have you not seen the possibilities outside your domain
It's a pity, for you have wasted a lifetime in a day
You have missed the new sights, sounds and feelings
Of what could have been a new beginning

Peggy Tesch

WILD GEESE

As heralds sound honking horns
To the promise of March,
The threats of November . . .
Clockwork miraculous motion
The V formation's aerodynamic perfection
In constant correction
Gliding swiftly o'erhead
With coordinated pull (no call, no fame,
putting skulling crews to shame.)
Familiar honk-bark reminders
Of seasons slipping by
Leaving us earthbonded
As they pass.
We, beasts of no aerodynamic thrust,
Admire free easy grace, and
Admit to awakened wanderlust,
When heralds' honks
Sound in the sky.

Lisa da Cunha

JACK IN THE PULPIT

Has nothing to say.
Quietly the spring
Ushers it in
Without word or din,
No reference to devil 'n' sin
Heaven nor holy
Without, within.

Jolly packet
Jack-in-a-jacket
Dewdrops for tears
Evolved o'er years
Evidently,
Successfully and,
Silently.

Lisa da Cunha

RELIGION!

Mo Slem
Ortho Dox
Is Lam
Hind U
Pres By Terian
Mor Mons
Bap Tist
Cat Holic
Met Hodist
Pen Tecostals
E Pis Copalian
Shin To
Luthe Ran
Budd Hist
Reform Ed
Quak Er
Juda Ism
Men No Nite
Angli Can
Con Gregational?

H. T. Brohl

MINIONS

Aggregate lives into one
huge afterglow.
In a flutter seeming ageless
one can know,
that uniting on occasion
can be aimless or have a true goal.
All the minions in a crowd
form their own groups in time.
It is hard to spot the good
and
much too easy to see the slime.
When one straggles away
that one sunders in his or her
own path.
As the puss or blood spills
from the Wheal, the pores
do not laugh.
Unutterable are some feelings
one can feel,
when too shy in a crowd, of minions
to point out what is real.

Darlette Clarice Knox

SWIMMING FOR
THE FIRST TIME
(ALL OVER AGAIN)

Babies swim because they don't remember
lifeless stones
sinking
or tales of kittens unwanted and drowned.
Their shudders come from cold, not fear.

You don't shudder, love, your voice
betrays no memory: it's flat but pleasant
like postcard Iowa.
I hear dishes rattling as you talk to me.

You're back on real land —
it's an exile I can't blame you for and
I like the idea, anyway,
of something cast out
on strange waters
returning to me,
a new baby
treading water,
prepared to memorize
(however all that works)
its own first infant trembling.

Larry Johnson

DREAM ME AWAY

I fall asleep,
You dreamed of me.
I'm over a pit,
And falling in.
You reach out
And dial a phone,
But Death's too busy to answer.

Bill Rae

INTERACTING

To Grievers in Toledo

The primal mother showed us a way
through speaking eye and slipping ear
to inter-act
to inter-play
from our crib
to — their grave.

Then teacher Jane
— lost her breast!

She shut her lips before the end.
But opened doors to keener minds
that *spoke* in sips
though *talked* not much . . .

Jane wanted to teach that bubbling breed
— surrounding her by day and night —
her final lesson of simple deed:

*No vital discussions
belong to talkative
percussions!*

Romuald J. Orlowski

THIS IS JUST TO SAY

I esteem you more
Than any treasure
Or riches.
You are pretty.
You are witty.
Your dexterity,
Your vivacity,
Your sensuality and sexuality
Intrigue and entice.
If joy and sorrow Candide
Found in Lady Cunegonde,
In you I found love, hope,
A best friend and good humor
To make a pleasant journey.

Rinkart Eze Okorie

THE DREAM

I dream.
Seeing your face.
All sense of reality and time,
fades away.
Taken by your smile.
Your entire being.
You are so beautiful.
I reach out my hand,
to touch yours.
Then it all fades away —
I suddenly awaken.
But I am still sure,
even faced again with the reality
of the morning sun —
you really are the best.

Victoria Anne Keck

OH MY EARTH, THE HEAVEN I REMEMBER!

I've watched the clouds as they floated away,
Like a distant ship on a summer's day,
Sailing the great breadth of your shoreless sea;

They would hover beyond your lofty mounts,
As if to kneel down on some sacred mounds,
Revering God's green pastoral-valley.

And, how oft, I heard the enchanting tunes
Of a shepherd's reed, in a moment's blues,
Caressing you with that tinge of glory!

And then, I glimpsed the serenading wind,
As it embraced each dancing branch and limb,
Whispering away life's secrets, softly.

Oh my earth, the heaven I remember!

I have beheld the lambs and goats, in herds,
While they munched away at your country herbs;
Hiding, sheltered, in a nearby quarry.

And I saw the stars, flickering so bright,
As they grazed away in the field of night,
Praising the Lord for his plentiful bounty.

Then, I viewed gypsies, bereft of raiment,
Outside the entrance of their goatskin tent,
Dancing, with upheld arms, so joyfully!

They had claimed refuge in your soaking rain;
As they trod the soft carpets, your terrain,
Dwelling, forever, in meadow's beauty.

George Malouf

GEORGE MALOUF. Pen Name: Ghassan; Born: Jerusalem, Palestine, 8-3-46; Married: Panayiota (Viota), 1-3-71; Education: Texas Tech University, B.A., Major in French, minor in Italian, 1970; Occupation: Merchant (Western store owner); Memberships: International Platform Association (American Lyceum), Maloof's International, Panhandle Writers of Texas; Awards: Key to the City of Birmingham, Alabama, 1987; Golden Poet Award for 1985-87; Several Certificates of Merit; Poetry: *The Lovely Blue*, book of poems, 1975; *Ethereal Moments of Truth*, book of poems, 1985; *The Pebbles of Time*, book of poems, 1988, pending publication; Poetry included in *World Treasury of Great Poems*, 1980; and *Words of Praise*, American Poetry Association, 1984, 1986; Comments: *My style of writing is an incorporation of the free style and the iambic, deriving from my memoirs and observations of the happy as well as the sad moments. In my writings, I address humanity to remind it of the beauty of nature, and to turn a leaning eye to the heavens to ask for our Lord's guidance.*

I HAVE . . .

The quietness of my room to enhance my dreams.
I have the light of the moon to bathe my night
to a beam of channels my mind is always fluid.
I have the music to take me anywhere my hopes
now set forth for me.
I have love unlimited in its focus.
I have the comforts of home in my heart.
I have an ark that is crowded with all the things
yet to do.
I have an Adam and Eve adventure yet to be done.
I have an index yet to finish starting with yours,
mine, and ours.
I have feelings for life as never before this as
the shadows show me the trees, the leaves, shapes
that have been left behind me.
I have a stillness as I walk the beach in the sunshine
and finally see a real sailboat.
I have everything my eyes desire that can be found free,
and spirited.
I have special things hidden away for rainy days.
I have all this, *God* gave me all the haves as I give
Him all the sounds of my happiness.
Life is all the have nots of yesterdays.

Charlotte Bell

I'd love you coming through the dark
Your body blossomed new and sprung like leaves
Upon a vine; a night of storm so stark
Your breath a tongue among the silent eaves.
I'd love your body cloven, spread with thighs
A lane between a lilac and a rose;
O Aphrodite, goddess of my skies,
O Grecian temple, warm where summer blows.
O girl, O nymph, O woman of my fate
In beauty burned and body known before,
A love apart that treads no other state,
Restive at your breast my greying lore.
  And now the pebbles of this unbelief
  Are granite grown against tomorrow's grief.

Leo Kartman

How much to take of beauty and decay?
How much of time before cold snow of death?
How much of permanence? Can we say
There is but change in every loving breath?
What falsehood sleeps within your violent truth
To touch my willful taste for grace?
What silent sobbing in your pallid youth
Is salt within my lips upon your face?
I cannot make a judgment of your love,
But take and use my lust or charity;
Against all time there is the gentle dove
Of trust, and all the light of clarity.
  Your beauty tombed within my winter's rhyme
  must by a summer skill unlock its cold and mine.

Leo Kartman

ANGELS PRAY

Hands reaching for you in the dark
Trying to find a soul barren and
unmarked
Angels pray for you, for you
to keep
Protecting you in your slumber
and sleep
Lights surround you keeping your
face aglow
Remembrance of younger times
a debt to a very old soul
Your eyes reflect the spirit inside
But God's keeping this child in the
shadows to hide
Something so in innocence washed
by the master's hand
As white and pure as known
to man
May immortality keep you the same
For death, my darling, does not
know your name.

Margo Singleton

REASSURED

You know that pillow I hug
every night when I go to sleep,
well,
I don't need it anymore —

Pamela Y. Tagami

ONE FLESH

Eyes meeting in laughter.
Quiet, jubilant voices.
Strong hands unclasping and clasping.
Bright reds and dark blues.
Fire and stormy ice.
A trembling fear in constant joy.

Minds yielding, changing, joining —
Separate; yet, inseparable.
Eyes solemn, wondrously still.
Hands gently calming.
God has somehow joined us.
This is our love.

Bodies familiar,
Known and unknown,
Given to belong to one another.
Cleaving together.
Inseparable.
God designed us so.

Spirits joined, multipled
Rising together in joy
Strengthening in sorrow
Completing one another
Laughter
And dancing feet
We are one!

D. L. Owens

WHERE IS THE DAY

have you seen the day lately
you know
that part of it called morning
where dawn begins to appear
develop
to begin to be clear to the mind
daybreak
the beginning of something

or the middle part called noon
that time before dusk and elsewhere
darkest part of twilight and
dimness
where subdued light struggles for sunset
and slides into dark

perhaps if not it's then
evening that you've found
the last glimpse of light's boundary
stretching the limit to finish
conclusion of the last part of anything
a ceasing to exist
in this unsettled condition
named day

Junesharyn Maguire

GEESE IN FLIGHT

Like little jets, geese in flight
with crackling voices winged on high,
In V formation underneath an azure sky.
They swiftly left the cold Northwest
For the Southland they knew best,
That in wintertime would be kind.
The snow-capped mountains lay behind.
Myriad geese dropped out of line,
They made another V formation.
Many were making their first flight,
They were learning orientation
Before the curtain call of night.

Edna Dewberry

THESE THINGS I LIKE

I like the simple things of life:
  A daisy on the lawn,
  A violet by the garden gate,
  A breath of air at dawn.

I like the lovely things of earth:
  A rainbow in the skies,
  A row of purple irises,
  A pair of beaming eyes.

I like the solid things of earth:
  A firm and rugged tree,
  A mammoth boulder on the hill,
  A mighty ship at sea.

I like the lasting things of earth:
  A faith that conquers strife,
  A love that brothers humankind,
  A strong and worthy life.

John C. Slemp

PLAINNESS

Unceasingly it beats and beats
The heart that lies within my breast
As the one word my lips repeat,
A word I must and will suppress.

The poor on earth are pitied much,
The lonely cheered or cast aside,
And beauty claims our praise or touch —
But plainness — oh, what road you ride!

You bloom; you fade; and later die
Unwept or missed by most of men,
They know not of the heart that lies
In loneliness, or why, or when.

You wish to be expressed and heard,
But beauty comes and beauty stays
Vainly clouding your charm, your words,
Though you strive alone and unafraid.

Oh heart please stop! Oh lips suppress
The word I love and long to hear.
'Tis not for plainness, happiness —
'Twas taught to me by hope and tears!

Erselia Monticello Barton

COLD NIGHT AT THE CABIN

Circling the door frame, Winter,
like a white wolf, blows its breath
beneath the sill. Frost paints
the window panes with crystals.
The pot-bellied stove roars;
regurgitates heat it cannot store.
It gobbles most of the woodpile;
there's no satisfying its craving,
so we crawl under thick quilts
and sleep in cape and footsocks.
Save body warmth with ''woolies,''
but exhale frosty breaths.

Dora K. T. Smith

INDEPENDENCE

I taught you to walk,
And cried with each of your falls.
I taught you to talk,
And gave you what knowledge I had.
I helped you to grow,
And be strong against life.

I taught you to fly,
To be on your own,
Knowing that someday
Your wings would expand
Into swift flight,
And leave me behind.

I taught you so well,
Your wings held so steady
As you took to the skies.
Now what do I do
With this void in the nest,
With this pain in my heart?

Elizabeth C. Cantu

THE HARVEST IS RIPE

The harvest is ripe — the workers are few;
Jesus is calling — how about you?
Let's bring them in — from the fields of sin;
The harvest is ripe — but the workers are few.

Let's throw out our lifelines — someone is drifting;
Could be a brother — let's help him from sinking.
Let's lead him to Jesus — Oh hasten I pray;
We need more workers in the fields today.

Let's work for the Master — in sowing good seed;
Let's help the wand'ring ones — Jesus they need.
We'll reap what we sow — wherever we go;
Workers are needed — A Golden Harvest to show.

Elsie Bergen

A LETTER SENT TO THE LAST BELIEVERS

The power of the spirit is like a mountain
It prevails with those who travel to it
But the world distant from it fades from these travelers
And sinks from sight to fade and die.
I once found a lightning bolt left in a desert
That a thunderstorm used to write in the sky;
I send its message to the Last Believers
To take with them to the sky:

"A flash of lightning can kindle a dry forest
Into a hundred little fires
That turn the forest into an inferno
Which toward a city drives
Shall the spirit be weak that it, like lightning,
Can burn the world aflame with a firestorm of truth?
— For all the wicked who live work to exhaustion
To try to quench those firestorms set by bolts from the sky!"

Lynn Geralds

HERE MY SECRETS ARE HID

Kept are the evening stars
Beneath the vast, star-struck mantle of God
Again, as all the planets sing
All the morning stars shout His glory
Here my secrets are hid
From the comets that visit from afar

Although my soul is lame and stupid
To the unheard secrets whispered from Venus to Mars
Should I be taken, then soon I say
May I as lightning go
To "all the morning stars that sing together
And the sons of God that shout with joy"

Lynn Geralds

I MOVE WE ALL ADJOURN

I move we all adjourn to the patio. Just look at that
Sun and that sky, blue as any blue can be. If we all sat

Out there like we were in a meeting or something, no one would
Question us. We'd sit out there and soak up some rays and we could

Say we were doing an experiment. Yeah, that's it. To see
If the sun and the blue sky would affect our ability

To perform our jobs in the highly professional manner
Our clients have become so used to. Yeah. And to see whether

Or not our thinking becomes muddled and our speech becomes slurred
From prolonged exposure to fresh air. Yeah. Out there by that bird,

We'll sit at the table, in those chairs, with one of us keeping
An eye out for the boss; the rest of us, talking and laughing

About what we did over the weekend, can concentrate on
Gossip and rumour spreading. Those colors — the green of the lawn,

The sidewalk's gray, the yellow sun, and the blue, blue sky — are
All calling us to come out and play. We can't disobey their call

And stay in here, can we? Nay, I say. We've been given a choice
To make and now's the time to . . . "What are you doing?" A gruff

Voice! Crap! "Quit staring out that window and get back to work!"
Oops. The boss man! That old fuddy-duddy. He still thinks bow ties

Are a fashion statement. We should still adjourn to the patio, though,
And talk about getting that guy to lighten up. Gotta go.

Stephen T. Keeran

YOU KNOW HOW IT IS

You know how it is, when you get a song
Going through your head and you hum along
To the words and you can't forget it for
Nothin' and so it bugs you even more;

When you can't think of something, and then you
Can't think about anything else and two
Hours later you're still muttering, "Why can't
I think of that?" like it's some kind of chant;

When you have an old beat-up Ford that went
Through Hell and didn't get a scratch or dent
And then you buy a brand-new car and get
Hit when you've not even gone a block yet;

When you take great pains to keep a picture
You bought for your mom from getting wet or
Smudged or ripped and it's still perfect when you
Get home, then you lay it down in some food;

When you're outside and you hear the phone ring
And you rush in, dropping what you're doing,
And you're about to break your leg on the chair
And then it stops ringing when you get there;

When absolutely everything you do
Goes wrong and you're wondering if it's you
Or is the whole world against you today
And if it is, boy, is it gonna pay!

You know how it is.

Stephen T. Keeran

PRETTY PLEASE

Will you please
Walk with me
We will dance
Around every tree
Pick some flowers
As we go along
And together
Sing a song
We will climb
Every hill
What we see
Will be a thrill
Hand in mind
Watch the sunset
Beautiful sight
You can bet
So my honey
What do you say
This stroll should
Make our day

R. W. Champion

MY ORDEAL

Fell right down
Off the log
On top of
Mean old hog
He took off
With a squeal
Was for me
Some ordeal
Stopped so sudden
I fell flat
By the legs
Of a bobcat
It scared him
You can bet
No hair nor hide
Of him yet
You can say
I'm on the beam
Cross no more logs
I'll wade the stream

R. W. Champion

I need a little space.
You're too protective of me.
It's like you've shut me in a case.
I try so hard to please you.
All my efforts seem to be in vain.
I don't know what else to do.
You expect so much of me.
A perfect little picture in your minds.
No matter how hard I try, it will never be.
There's not much for me to say.
Nothing will change your feelings.
I just wish you'd see it my way.

Samreen Malik

GLORY

White threads twisted
Into a pattern of cobwebs
Bedeck the sacred table:
On each side of the sacred table
Candle holders, in their coppery cast,
Sparkle forth their fake gems.
Nearby, angels kneel
In lasting meditation,
While Mary, overlaid with Jesus,
Looks longingly at Joseph,
Who stands across the room
In his mildewed collusion!

Marge Hallum

PEACE

To the dawning of each new day
I yield to smiles as serenades
Intense moments upon my face
Blessed loved ones so full of grace

To the closing of each new day
I yield to strife . . . Oh, come what may
Time passing has its own meaning
Blessed loved ones so full of grace

Slumber, yielding my soul awake
Rising to a new day to make
My prayers He did not forsake
Blessed loved ones so full of grace

Dee Hedenland

DAROLYN ANN HEDENLAND. Born: Milwaukee, Wisconsin, Married: Lloyd D. Hedenland; Occupations: Homemaker, Retired office manager, Retired boutique shop owner, Songwriter, Grandma; Memberships: New Horizon Poetry Club; Oregon State Poetry Association, The Family of God, Thousand Oaks Toastmistress Club, Thousand Oaks Women in Business; Awards: Honorable Mention for 'The Prince of Peace,' International Poetry Forum, 1985; Certificate of Merit for 'The Prince of Peace,' *Voices in Poetics, A Modern Treasury,* 1985; Inclusion in: *International Directory of Distinguished Leadership, Personalities of the Americas, Community Leaders of America, Five Thousand Personalities of the World;* Received the Key Award; Other Work: 'My Temple of Silence' read at International Poetry Reading, Whipple Center, Las Vegas; Las Vegas High School; Indian Springs Prison; Produced demo tape for Nevada State Council of the Arts of "A Rainbow Connection," radio poetry show; "Hallelujah," album, features 'The Prince of Peace.'

CANTO THREE

The relationship of Man to Heaven
Is both the daily dawn and Death:
He knows not what dawn means
Nor the other; this is the firmest test.

To build a place within the mind
Where both dawn and Death are Kings
Puts a man within his place
And farther Heaven brings.

Jean Candee

SON

"A jolly child," they smiled,
"A Raphael, a Michelangelo baby,
Straight from the Sistine Chapel.
A classic!" they said.
And they were right.
Great dark, hooded eyes, full of mirth,
Skin like glowing bronze,
Amazing micro-masculinity
Of stance and gait.

The mother looks
at the man
as he sits,
unaware of her,
lost in the fictional reality
of the bright box in the corner,
still beautiful,
a classic,
Yet out of place, somehow
In twentieth century settings.
A Raphael seeking tickets to the Super Bowl,
A Michelangelo at the laundromat,
A Leonardo waiting for the tip.

Ann Hill Beuf

PRETTY PATTERNS

Their history could be known,
But then would end imagination,
From special clay each a clone,
United or separate — a generation.

All with signs of being tough,
Coarse whites — tremendous heat,
Each shows its history so rough,
Tied with mortar lines very neat.

They never touch but they share,
Each has an equal load to bear,
Yet, for the other there's no care,
Patterns creating a pattern rare.

From Created substance out of time,
Formed into shapes in this time,
Crumbling one day back into time,
Pretty Patterns lost — coursing time.

Kirby Joe Godwin

DO YOU REMEMBER . . .

Do you remember . . .
The nights we walked along a moonlit beach,
With ocean breezes caressing . . .
Holding hands . . .
Talking, laughing, kissing.

Do you remember . . .
The sharing of heart and soul . . .
The intensity of feelings, when words were
not needed . . .
You and I and this oneness we shared . . .
Lost in complete silence.

Do you remember . . .
The nights we loved,
Scented candles burning slowly,
Making shadowed silhouettes against
the darkened wall,
Lost in our moment of eternity.

Do you remember . . .
The day you said goodbye
Promising to return.
Months, that turned into years . . .
Met new friends, new loves . . . leaving behind a
broken heart, stranded in complete desolation . . .

Do you remember?

Glenna Gardner-Wimett

GLENNA GARDNER-WIMETT. Born: Norwich, Vermont; Married: Robert Wimett; Occupation: Bookkeeper at B & R's Garage, business owned and operated by my husband and me; Memberships: Poetry Society of New Hampshire, New Horizons Poetry Club, Creative Enterprises International Poetry Society; Awards: Honorable Mention/87 Creative Enterprises; Golden Poet Award, 1985-87; Poetry: 'Seasons,' *The World's Best Poets 1987;* 'Life's Moments,' *Selected Poems of 1987;* 'This Moment in Time,' *Bluebells & Other Dreams,* 1987; 'Chapbook of Poetry,' *Heart Cries,* 2-88; Comments: *Poetry is my one great love, both in writing my poetry and in reading the beautiful works of others. I hope my poetry will touch the hearts and souls of others, as I continually strive to write about life, in all its many complex forms. "Poetry is my photograph of the soul."*

FOOTHILLS

the circle of the earth contracts and humps
heavy like a great egg proposing birth
(it is hard to climb these pages)
my feet are weights but I am sitting still
 under the steel canopy only the road in motion
my book is carefully prefaced
I am waiting for an explosion/expecting a mountain

    foothills my father said
    but I saw no imprint
    where were the visible signs
    the toe and the turned heel
    mountains I discovered creep up on you

Ann Watson Barnard

THE PERFUME TREE

I walked by an old lady's house one day,
and saw a tree in glorious full bloom;
the banana smell from the tree caused me to stay,
the old lady saw me from her room;
I was looking at the small cream blossoms,
and she came out for a while to talk;
she spoke, saying, Feel free to take some,
when I was young, we girls used to walk;
on our way before a barn dance,
we'd stop and put these sweet flowers in our hair;
for to buy perfume, we had no chance,
and we used what nature generously provided there;
I could see her envisioned in my mind,
so very long ago, in her very best;
I'm sure the boys did find,
she was wonderfully perfumed and well dressed.

Geneva Jo Anthony

CHRISTMAS

Rejoice! Our gracious God gave the human race
        A precious gift, amazing to trace.
        With guardian Joseph by her side
        Virgin Mary brought Christ to reside;
        A revered love child of destiny
        To give the world Christianity.

Renew! The spirit of Christ's nativity
        Seems lost in gay festivity.
        Decorated green trees in our house
        Displayed red and white wrapped gift arouse
        Families gathered from far and near,
        All united with great joy and cheer!

Reach out! Soon there dawns a New Year
        Anticipating no fear.
        The spirit of Christ is near
        To all who hold him dear.
        Resolve to strive for ardent giving,
        Our universe for better living.

Eleanor E. Austin

A PROMISE OF EXCITEMENT

When I first saw you and you held me in your arms,
Your eyes told me of a promise of excitement ahead.
I followed you into the good times,
And stood beside you in the hard times.
I gave you all my love,
And you gave yours to me.
Our love gave us our children,
And together we did care for and love.
They have grown now,
And we are alone once more.
And as you hold me in your arms,
I see the excitement in your eyes is still there.

Carolyn

THE CONSTITUTION

Brave words written by our Forefathers
Have withstood the test of time
By each generation in all of the words so sublime
They fill us with thoughts of perfection
For a country held in great affection

The love of Justice and Liberty
Will forever hasten us
To answer any call
To bring Peace and Tranquility
For us all

So we Salute
The Writers of the Constitution
On this 200th year
Of its inception

May Peace reign forever,
And forever guide us all
In the right Direction

Rose Mary Gerlach

THE THINGS WE DON'T DO

As aging's despair sneaks upon us
We contemplate and brood o'er the mirrored stranger
With fat protruding here and wrinkles of disgust
Our minds cringe in defensive anger.

So we bargain with ourselves that we can change
As we start a ritual and daily routine
We bend and twist in hopes to rearrange
The cellulite pouches and middle fat ring.

We run, we walk, we talk losing weight
As higher we kick and further we roll
We dance to the music and set another date
For our fervored efforts to take their toll.

Still, we persevere with our elusive dreams
Lifting and stretching through the exercise boom
Splashing on gallons of youth-secret creams
And expecting a miracle to circumvent our doom!

Willa Elliott

WHEN GOD'S SPIRIT MOVES

When the spirit of God moves, let self step aside
When His pure waters flow, let no man stem the tide
Lifted up, higher and higher on his wings of peace
Running springs of ecstasy boundlessly increase.

Felt are His presence and the fire in His love
As His spirit draws us toward our Master above.
No greater thrill, no depth so deep
As His poured-over joy from our head to our feet.

Strangely warmed, my heart grows wild
In anticipation of His loving smile
As He longingly looks into our lives
While we gather miracles, He alone inspires.

Consumed by His power and divinely given grace
My greatest desire is to see Him face to face
But how real, oh, how real, as I reach out from within
I'm embraced with His sweet love again and again!

Willa Elliott

THE "PERFECT" LOVE RELATIONSHIP

Dedicated to Jay Zimbelman

We talk of loving each other,
and yet,
how is that possible?

You talk of marriage and loving only me,
and yet,
how many other girls did you think you felt
that way about?

How do we know that what we think is real,
will last forever?
Will we live "happily ever after"
together?

How many times must our hearts break,
how many tears will we shed,
before we really have the "perfect" love relationship
we always believe we have?

My love,
I believe our quest for the "perfect" love relationship
has ended
with our love between us.

Please, help me to prove I'm right.
Let's be friends and lovers
forever.

Elise R. Jacobson

LOVE OR DECEIT?

Dedicated to Jay Zimbelman

I think I'm ready to take the next step,
continue onto the next page,
or perhaps, the next chapter.

Are you leading me in love . . . or deceit?
Oh, how I wish I could believe it was deceit.
I am so afraid of real love.

You are a mountain I never intended to cross,
an ocean I hated to swim,
an experience I never wanted to confront, and yet,
I love you more every day.

The doubt is still there . . . sometimes,
but, the love and happiness supersede
and the doubt melts away a little each day.

Each time you hold me close,
each time you kiss me and make love to me (as you do so well),
my solid, concrete walls break,
a little at a time.

And, with every crack, every inch of wall that deteriorates,
my fear of real feelings expands.
But somehow, for some unknown reason,
I feel fairly safe with you;
safer, more protected than ever before.

Please don't disappoint me,
just love me . . .
for today.

Elise R. Jacobson

UNPREDICTABLE MICHIGAN MARCH

On the warmest days of March
When the sky is azure blue,
The sun is unmolested
By clouds of darkened hue.

Then are the signs of spring noticed:
Little children skating by,
Boys are playing marbles,
And kites are flying high.

The people in the city,
Still clad in winter clothes,
From store to store they scurry,
Each with spring fever woes.

In the country the anxious farmer
Awaits to use his plow.
The days are getting longer, and
There's so much work right now.

I believe the long days of summer
Were planned ahead by *Him*
To help the weary farmer
Get his crops all in.

Much colder dawns the next day.
Snow begins to fall.
Folks sadly settle down and say,
"Just a few more weeks, that's all."

Evelyn L. Lyons

INTRODUCTIONS

Singles bars and night club scenes
Did bring to life a new scheme
Whereby computers provide the means
To find that person of your dreams.

Laborious days, lonely nights,
Tired of seeking one who's right?
Advantages the backers recite,
Busy types meet with delight.

But, I'm in no hurry — you see,
I have my life before me.
Refusing to perch upon a stool
In a crowded club looking cool,

Take my chances a different way
While going about my hectic day.
Chance encounter sparks introduction
Evoking interest, initial foundation.

Eye-to-eye contact, chemistry,
Making a decision intuitively
To extend an invitation.
Taking time for socialization

One on one, you and me.
And if it is meant to be
You and I will surely know
And the relationship can grow.

Johnnie Sue Zimmerman

ONE-SIDED LOVE

The love I feel for you is so real
My love has not been revealed

But still it's felt
This one-sided love.

You only know me as a friend.
If only I could tell you

Things might be different.
Still, I tell myself, you
could never love me as I love you.
My one-sided love.

Holly A. Hudson

IN MEMORY OF MY DAD

I'm sorry we had to say good-bye that day,
But in my heart you will always stay.
I was hurt when you were taken from me,
For I thought you'd be here eternally.

You listened to my deepest fears,
And watched me shed so many tears.
When you left it really broke my heart,
For I never thought we would have to part.

When will the sadness ever cease,
Would you tell me, could you please?
For I have such a heavy heart,
And I need to make a brand new start.

I need a life full of happiness,
And full of love I must confess.
I know it is out there someplace,
In this world called the human race.

So as I keep on yearning,
I must thank you for my learning.
I know that we will meet again,
And you will take away my pain.

I know somewhere that you are listening,
And your tears too are glistening.
There is something for which I'm glad,
I had you to love and call my "Dad."

Karen L. Simms

CRAZY

I think I'll still get in the gate
But I don't think normal is so great
'cause it don't feel so cool
to follow the crowd and act like a fool

And if you ask me it's a bummer
to say what is expected to prove you're
        no dummer
Ya I don't mind if they call me
        crazy
'cause to me normal is a little bit hazy

so I'll say what I feel is right
and I'll do my thing
'cause that makes me sing
'cause those normals can stay in their rut
    I like being a nut

Dolly Vrudny

COLORS

When my color was green
I found it hard to appreciate the scene
then I met a girl who was slightly
        orange
she helped me feel reborn
my color was red for a while
perhaps because I was just a child
Many girls cared for me as I
        went along my way
doing the duties that were called
        for in a day
These girls helped me become the color
        pink
Thank you all for being my shrinks

Dolly Vrudny

FLASH FLOOD

Ghosts jockey waves raping wind,
how to swim through wake's chagrin?

Horsemen resurrect bloodletting flood
Woe upon woe tracks sliding mud
Scales bewail Goddess' arrest
Dolphins prophesy sea's transgress

Spirits break allegiant ties and tales
Poesy's hands wing time's travail
    Iris melts bow —
        buoyant spring bouquets
    Fates embrace willow
    lo, ambrosial cascade

Behold! New design from light year's star
Twelfth planet crossing Jupiter and Mars

Marie C. Andrea

MY MOTHER

She's considerate and caring,
A friend to all humanity.
But something more than that,
A very special friend to me.
She's my mother.

She's shared so much of her knowledge,
And patiently helped me grow.
So lovingly she's listened
To every childhood woe.
She's my mother.

She loves me selflessly,
Her devotion never wavers.
And for her family,
Cheerfully she labors.
She's my mother.

So now I pay this tribute
To this one so dear to me.
For her love down through the years
Makes it very clear to see —
She's my *Mom!*

Marilyn Morris

WINDOW OBSERVATIONS

As we gaze out our window a wee bit South of East —
We're greeted by colored plants on which our eyes can feast.
This wet Memorial Day peonies bow their heads.
Two colors under the green yews show in pinks and reds.

A lone flicker has knocked his head on the walnut tree.
House finches, robins, gold finches fly like on a spree.
Beyond the blacktop, the bronze beech is a bird refuge.
This colorful haven handles flocks by the deluge.

Four-legged animals abide in this luxuriance.
Squirrels, rabbits, groundhogs, and cats observe with askance.
We humans continue to change and improve this view,
In order our deep aesthetic cravings to imbue.

Ev'ry day, this window view fills us with ecstasy.
It's just a sample of *God's Nature* for us to see!

Mervin L. Schoenholtz

MAKE MARRIAGE A SUCCESS

Son, for new poem material, we were near a loss.
Now, you're married, plenty subjects on us do descend.
Whene'er any problem rises, don't rant, rave or fuss.
Better to sit and each item thoroughly discuss!

Dismissing or shrugging off e'en a minor problem —
Begins a good marriage contract early to un-hem.
Often, a troubled marriage rises from, ''Who's the boss?''
Try on your hearts, minds, and souls, *Partnership* to emboss!

Another major contest that's not one bit funny —
Many a wedding vow's shattered because of money.
Together make out a *detailed* list of priorities.
Well-thought-out budgets keep passing fancies from sorties!

Use your brains to save your marriage from utter defeat.
The *rewards* of *marital success just can't be beat!*

Mervin L. Schoenholtz

LEON'S LUCKY LAST LUNGE

In early spring of 'eighty-seven, golf ''bugs'' were out.
'Bout Leon's score up through seventeen holes, he'll not shout.
His puttering on the stick greens, you would call just that!
And his chipping — well, no one had once to doff his hat.

During first nine holes of play, his score made him wonder —
''Who was helping, the *Man upstairs* or one down under?''
Bogies peppered his score card as though it had small pox!
Lots of drives died fast, much like balls were encased in sox!

Chapel Hill Course back nine in spring is often quite damp.
Longer the yardage, harder Leon his clubs did clamp!
Score to eighteenth was even fifty, *Hail Mary!*
Prospect for high fifties loomed for Lee as quite scary.

Now, a golf trophy on Leon's desk, one will stun!
Lee's scorecard tots fifty-one! He shot a hole-in-one!

Mervin L. Schoenholtz

HOUSE OF THE SUN

White alabaster fire
                upon the sun of the moon
Golden fire of eternity
Thou innermost fire of a hidden sun

Upon the moon thy wind of fire
And the endless stars of akashic rhythms
Thy breath upon an endless sea of stars
Thine eye the heart of an inner sun
Thy voice the heartbeat of the moon in a
                night of fire
Birth of the sun, death of the moon
Rhythm of cycles
Light of eternity
In the voice of God
Birth of the moon, death of the sun
Rhythm of cycles, light of eternity
From age to age
The same voice of God
Upon the sun the wind of the moon
The waxing and waning of eternal rhythms
Lunar cycle, death of the sun in the
Shadow of the moon
Solar rhythm, cosmic breath
Death of the moon in the shadow of the sun

Antoinette Voget

DECLARATION

Tonight I listened to a woman sing and play guitar in the Metro
Although I knew no French I understood her perfectly
Her playing was beautiful
Her voice inspiring
And she made me realize how much I wanted to sing
But I don't have the voice to sing
And I cannot play the guitar
But I do have the desire to share my joy
So my words will be my voice
And my pen will be my instrument
Just as the paintbrush was Vincent's
And I will sing
I will sing of the spirit of the soul
And I will sing of life and of death
And I will sing of order and disorder
And I will sing of nature and the sea
And I will sing of slavery and fear
And I will sing of the tormented souls
And I will sing of beauty and hatred
And I will sing of freedom and pain
But I will sing
And I will sing until all of my days are gone
And if my singing helps but one person to sing
That is all that I ask for; that is all that I need.

Mark Rifkin

HELPMATE

When dishes pile up in the sink
And his TV goes "on the blink!"
  (Just before touchdown)
All he really needs is . . . me!
When his clothes get crumpled and worn
And the Frig starts to get warm
All he really needs is . . . me!
When his "special deal" falls through
And a tire on his precious car just "blew"
All he really needs is . . . me!
When at every turn there is a "burn"
And he knows *not* which way to turn?
What he really needs is . . . me!
This can go "on and on" . . . the big "hurt"
Until a thought is born
Just when *all* seems lost
And *disaster* strikes me down!
He suddenly *realizes* and appreciates . . . too!
What he needs now *more* than *ever* is . . .
    You!

Mabel Lagerloff

RELATIONSHIPS

upside down images mirrored on the wall
split/shattered seams of cracked glass
reflect miraculously, myriad faces
distorted, deriding one another

my mother, your mother, mothers-in-law
my sister, your sister, sisters-in-law
my brother, your brother, brothers-in-law
twisted and rolled together
between the seams of glass
laughing at one another

while children's faces
watch, wearily,
learning how to hate

Angelina Rossetti

O CHRIST, WHO DIED

O Christ, who died upon a cross,
My soul attests your sharpest pain:
'Twas not the spikes in hands or feet,
'Twas not the spear thrust in your side;
These were but instruments of death,
From which your spirit never winced.
No, Lord, the sword that thrust you through
Was in the hands of faithless friends;
Their gross indifference to your fate
Was sharper than the keenest blade.
To know that those you trusted most
Had failed you in your darkest hour —
This was the stroke that pierced your heart
And brought release to death's grim power.

O Christ, whose cross is ever new,
Alas, it must be so today,
As friends of yours still stand apart
And let you die with bleeding heart.

John C. Slemp

'TIS TRUE, MA NEVER LIED

Trudging along the dusty road,
A few pennies clutched in my hand.
Headed toward the little white church —
Not by choice, it was Ma's command.

The soles of my shoes were flapping,
With every step I took.
My clothes were worn and faded
How dreadful I must look.

But, Ma says God loves the poor.
And for us, he'll provide
Food, warmth and tender care.
'Tis true, Ma never lied.

As I walked, I remembered
The time our larder was bare.
A knock came on the kitchen door.
It was the answer to Ma's prayer.

There stood a kindly neighbor,
Holding a basket piled high
With vegetables from his garden.
I thought Ma was going to cry.

Oh, the faith and trust she had in God,
With me they now abide.
She's in heaven and we'll meet again.
'Tis true, Ma never lied.

Norma K. Shea

PHOTO SYNTHESIS

Ethel is like
A plant —
Delicate,
Earthy,
And a flower,
She has power
Of love,
Like a turtledove,
She grows on you,
In darkness
Or in light,
She is bright,
Like a statue
At night.

Alfred Elkins

THE KNAVE

The Knave of Hearts has stole away —
Into His well-kept lair —
I'm sure he's looking each Heart-shaped Day —
For another queen to snare!
Perhaps I'll be the lucky one to win his heart —
Who knows?
But I'm still wishing — wondering —
    longing —?
Who sent this long-stemmed rose?

    (The Knave?)

Mary Marjorie Terry Dubach

I'LL WALK ALONE

As I stroll alone along the winding path
that goes over the top of the hill,
my thoughts are of you, my beloved one,
when we walked hand in hand, to view
the setting sun's blush on the distant hills,
as shadows of the night moved in.
Today the skies are grey and a hushy lull,
pervades, as my thoughts take to wings.
Since you went away, to distant shores,
to a land where eternal waters flow,
where blooming flowers never fade,
where dreams are dreams no more,
precious memories have not faded away.
When the stars dim in the skies,
and the sun no longer shines,
my love for you will never cease, and,
the song in my heart never die.
Until the day we meet again, my love,
I'll walk alone.

Madge R. Close

SPRING IS

Spring is
Singing birds
Pretty flowers
Green grass
A blue sky
Bright sunshine
And blossoming trees!

Spring is
Playgrounds and
Lots of children
Laughing and jumping
Skipping and running.
Spring is
Everyone
Having fun!

Staci Ellen Grogan

DREAMS

Through many dreams
I have lived other lives,
Or so it seems.
I have been happy at times
And I have been sad, too.
Then I am glad
That my dreams are not true.
During my dreams
I come within a feeling
That sometimes leaves me
Staring at the ceiling —
Remembering the scenes
From life-like dreams.
Yes, I *have* lived other lives
Through many dreams,
Or so it seems.

Staci Ellen Grogan

GOD SPEAKS QUIETLY

God's handiwork is done in silence, majestically.
Tranquility is won as God speaks quietly.
Things that have most merit spark the least commotion,
Tune out turbulence of spirit, clatter of earth and ocean.
Apple blossoms, pink and white,
Exude sweet fragrance in the night.
Gentle winds sigh through the trees
Blowing petals in the breeze.
God speaks softly; snowflakes whisper,
Dawn breaks, daylight wakens,
Sun glides east to west, clouds scatter,
Night falls, moon brightens.
The morning dew a-glistening, as the sunlight catches fire,
Whets the early thirst of plants and trees in morn attire.
New-mown grass springs upward,
Flowers break through ground,
Stemmed florets lean sunward
Following the light around.
Then God will paint the sunset in silent awesome wonder.
As we live each day beset with miracles and gifts, we ponder.
With the gift of life, the power of love
And endless sanctions from above,
God speaks gently to soul and spirit
That everlasting life we all may merit.

Lillian C. Marcoux

THE TRAIN

For but a moment, the steel and concrete towers claim their piece of sky
And then are lost, as the train speeds on through tunnel and glen,
By highway and country lane.
A ribbon of blue, red and silver, the train winds on,
Toward other regiments of brick and glass, toward signal lights
And factory signs, past startled pigeons and graffitied walls,
The mighty cars slowly screech to a halt.
Reflecting in station windows, its passengers depart,
Leaving the sleek, silver cars that slowly embrace the rails
And again glide out toward trestle and hillside,
O'er river and highway, to the wooded fields beyond.
Past farms with pastured cows and waves of grain, the train
Streaks on, too fast to tame, between the towns,
The places all called home to those who know, so well, their own.

Dorothy Holcombe

I am . . .
    Many-friended yet friendless,
Knowledgeable yet more confused daily,
    At home yet constantly lost,
Full of freedom yet trapped,
    Open and talkative yet hidden and secret,
Unique yet horribly average,
    Many companions yet lonely,
Fulfilled yet achingly empty,
    Sensible yet abstract,
Compassionate yet ever unfeeling,
    Satisfied yet full of unquenchable desire,
Contented yet unhappy with being,
    Tenderly sensitive yet cold and frostbitten,
But mostly, forever changing.

Julia Smith

COMPETENT KITTENS

Tenured household tenant shows discontent
High-pitched voice might frighten a marten
Consistent potential sounds unpretentious
No tenor — our tenth competent kitten

Disheartening tendency to quickly fatten
Inattentive to tenderloin or gluten diet
Tender tench — catty countenance does brighten
While retentive stomach distends, the area's quiet

Unfastened tennis balls create intense attention
Pushed, beaten with an extended white mitten
Hastens and straightens our unintended tension
Happy playtime tends to sweeten and soften hypertension

Our nighttime pretender has not forgotten
Daylight maintenance is non-existent while asleep
Intensification of energy obviously lightens, heightens
The tentative rest time that we humans keep

Days of real contentment are often tenfold
Potent poetry in typewritten sentence —
Does not smarten kitten worth more than gold
She's persistent but lacks literary competence.

Gwendolyn Trimbell Pease

HE'S EVERYWHERE

When darkness comes and it's time for bed,
I like to look up at the stars overhead.
I go to my window and look at the sky,
And think, God loves me . . . I wonder why?
Isn't it amazing, as great as He is,
That He cares about us, and says we are His!

When I see how the moon sends its silvery light,
I'm reminded once more of God's power and might.
He rules all the world, the stars, moon, and sun;
At His command the streams and rivers run.
The winds and seas are at His call,
And the animals, too; He created them all.

The mountains proclaim His majesty;
Their splendor and beauty are for all to see.
The fields and flowers with perfumes rare,
Tell us God loves us; He really does care!
With this reassurance that He's everywhere,
I go to bed happy knowing God's always there.

Imogene S. Swearingen

FLEAS

I'm sitting here watching my dog scratch fleas.
She's scratching from her head all the way to her knees.
Now it's a misnomer to call them fleas —
They're "Dracula's Beasts," if you please!

When one leaves my dog and gets on me,
I can't move fast enough to catch that flea.
He jumps so fast that you can't even see,
And you wonder wherever that flea can be.

Now I'm sorry for my dog when she starts to scratch;
But my feelings for her are not even a patch
On my feelings for me, when a flea starts to latch
Onto me like Dracula. Whoops! I've got to scratch!

Imogene S. Swearingen

A QUESTION OF FINALITY

Working measure after measure
   patiently with care
Enhancing and refining what
   was originally crude and plain
A theme whose essence
   is examined continuously
Phrase after phrase
   line after line
Against a melody expanding
   musically and mathematically
Taking each cluster of notes
   apart one by one
Time and time again
   to put them back together
So that each single note
   performs a logical role
In the continuum of time and space
   upon that score
So written
   over and over again
Until one moment
   locks a door
Placing double bar against
   a final measure

J. V. Presogna

OUR OWN RAINBOW!

Whenever we sight its magnificent
Colors and its harmony in view,
We sigh in touched amazement!
   God, couldn't You send a *daily*
one, just for me and You?
   We search, we aim and often
For the wrong *goal!*
   Our rainbow is right nearby,
In the spiritual awakening —
     Our soul!

Kurt Mueller

LAST DAY OF MY LIFE

In honor of Yvonne

If today were the last day of my life
   I'd use my voice
   In Him rejoice
Sing praises to my King
   To be ready
When the Hallelujahs ring
I'd vision my Lord on
   The right hand of God
   Be glad for miles trod
If I had enough time
I'd write a little story
   of Heaven's glory
In Revelations I'm told this
Heaven will be all bliss
I'd hope to tell more sinners
They can be winners
If they confess their wrong
   and for Him
     live strong
I'd bid my family farewell
Hoping they will witness for Him
Until they join me, one by one
Where there will be no setting sun.

Rowena Bragdon Holt

   Once
My once black hair
   now laced with gray
My arthritic hands once
   tickled the piano keys
My knees knelt at night
   to thank God for a day so bright
My arms stretched around
   a family with love
Seeking guidance from above —

   Now
I have other hands to help me
The knees some day will bow to Him,
My Saviour's outstretched arms
Waiting to guide as I enter in
To claim a mansion He went to prepare
So I could in His glory share —
   Forever

Rowena Bragdon Holt

NOT IN VAIN

Fragmented dreams marked the
   knight's erratic course from
     idealistic youth to gnarled age.

Dejected, he sat amid dragons of
   prejudices not slain and victimized
     women not rescued.

His broken spirit, darkened by failed quests,
   sank into abysses too
     deep to measure.

Powerful and majestic, an ethereal voice
   startled him from his
     deep pit of humiliation.

"Your dreams were not in vain.
   You sowed the seed. The vision
     sprouts in another."

Aileen L. Myers

MY SPECIAL FRIEND

My special friend, I miss you.
My life is not the same.
You loved me more than anyone, I am the
one to blame.
Though rich in love, my pockets poor,
I couldn't care for you.
They left you in an open field, no home,
the rent was due.
I never saw you leaving, I don't know where
you are.
I only know in both our hearts remains the
unhealed scar.
Just know I've always loved you, you are
my "little love."
And for our time we had to share, I thank
our God above.

Beverly Bonneau

THE CHOICE

There is something in me that
Loves the openness of space and sky;
Blue-tipped clouds
And sunsets tinged in pinks and golds.

The dazzle of the ocher sun
Through fallow fields, rich
In harvest colors,
Delights better than the
Rosy-brilliance of marbled-columns
And silver-tinted monuments
Along the Golden Mile.

My family finds this preference suspect —
As though these simple pleasures
Were too far removed from pragmatic schemes.
But I am not the native daughter
Of immigrant dreams —
To build upon their cornerstone of enterprise.

And yet, the glitter and the whirl
Of their bright world touches too my
Venetian soul.

How do I reconcile these dual roles,
So much a part of past and present:
The yearning beauty of horizons lost —
The gilded tapestry of tomorrow's hand.

Mariann Kirkpatrick

YANKEE STAY HOME

We should be careful *whom we fight.*
Enemies buy everything in sight.
   I'm speaking of *after the war,*
   When former foes flock to our shore.

Robert Emmett Clarke

IN SEARCH OF MY LOVE

I walk alone
A shallow stream
In search of my love
That no one see
Water runs
Between my feet
Warmed from the sun
I frolic and leap
As times goes on
I start to sing
A melody —
For my lover to be
Birds start to chirp
With harmony
Leaves start to sway
To the song of thee
I walk alone
A shallow stream
In search of my love
Some privacy

Margaret Purificato

HOW MUCH DO YOU LOVE ME?

A yellow moon lit up the sea as I embraced my love
While watchful were the winking stars so happy up above.
I asked her Was it truly love there lighting up her eyes.
Delightful was her answer which so took me by surprise!
"Can you count the grains of sand you see here shining on the shore?
And all the drops of water there to make the ocean roar?
Add all the seconds of time past and all which lie before . . .
That much, times all those stars above, I love you, dear, *and more!*"

I asked her if her love might fail and fall in disarray.
Then with a smile she told me how her love was there to stay.
"If every hundred million years you took one ounce away,
The universe would disappear some dreadful distant day.
Now if you timed it carefully 'til all was gone at last,
When measured 'gainst my love 'twould be *a single second passed!*"
We sat in silence for a while to drink the moonlit view.
Then with a hug I whispered, "Wife, I love you that much too!"

Billy R. Zimmerman

OH SIS, WHERE HAVE THOSE DAYS GONE

Ode to suicide and the pain it leaves

Girl:

Dear Bro; I thought I'd write
Thought of you late last night
How I used to wait by that old silver gate
Hoping the school bus wouldn't be late

Mom got a letter from you the other day
She said you felt so empty and cast away
Because our father had left (you) that way

Oh Bro! I cried and cried last night
Mom said you had tried to take your life!
Who gave you the right to hurt me so?!

Just because you felt so cast away
I lost a father, too, you know
But I remember he chose to go
How could you leave me and hurt me so?

Boy:

Oh Sis, where have those days gone
When we could ride our horse all day long?
Catch tadpoles in our Issaquah pond?
Oh Sis, where have those days gone?

Oh Sis, I wrote to say,
I'm sorry for hurting you that way
Mom made me see the goodness in me
Our father's suicide has nothing to do with me

I'll arrive home from Korea and I won't be late
I can just see you standing by that old silver gate
Oh Sis, I can hardly wait!

Eliane Burnside

GOLDEN DAFFODIL AND SNOWDROP

Said the Golden Daffodil to the Snowdrop so dear,
"If you weren't so very small I would kiss your little ear."

Said the Snowdrop to its suitor, "How great and grand you'd be
if you'd bend just a little I would kiss your knee."

Neither told the other no ear or knee to bend
so without communication — no love could begin

Daffodil stood sturdy and tall
Snowdrop stayed pretty and small

Then came the day God called them home
Each wanted God to tell them their repentance to pay
"There is none," God said on Judgment Day

They looked at each other and wondered why
Then God came with His reply —
"You both paid the price on earth you see
Because one had no ear and the other had no knee

I gave you each other to have and to hold
with no communication love could not unfold

To wait until Judgment Day, to see you both set free
seems to be punishment — enough for Me!

Eliane Burnside

MURDER FILLED MY SOUL

*Dedicated to my beloved father, Francis Burnside,
who was killed by a drunk driver.*

In the bar you drank and laughed with your son that night
Your bumper from your old beat-up pick-up truck
        dug deep into my father's skull
dragging his young dead lifeless body some one hundred feet,
dropping it in the roadside dirt

Meanwhile splitting my mother's skull
        and tearing the flesh from her leg,
leaving your tireprints in her bleeding flesh —
        leaving her a cripple

You *murderer,* you drove off leaving them both to die!
Did you even look back — did you even cry?

Mother wiped the blood from her eye,
        just in time to see the medics place
her mate's dead lifeless body in a black plastic body bag

For this murder you received,
        three-hundred-dollar fine and thirty days in jail
Rage — Revenge — Murder filled my soul!
I could feel my long fingernails tearing deep
        into your flesh of your throat
and your warm blood ooze between my fingers
        as I pulled your windpipe out

My mother's soft voice and tender hand reached from her wheelchair,
"It's OK, dear, what man does not tend to — God will!"

Two months later police notified me,
you, the *murderer,* had died of a heart attack.
God had evened the score and removed murder from my soul.
As the police walked away, my mother's words soft and tender
        echoed through my mind:
"What man does not tend to — God will."

Eliane Burnside

LIFE TREASURES

Treasure we find
inside our mind
brings us joy
to the heart of mankind
Creativity has been found
poetry or music
the arts are around
Everyone has it
a valley of streams
See life treasure
behind the dreams
These are the riches
that no one sees
Beauty lies deep
behind the scenes

Margaret Purificato

DYING TREES

We learn compassion
from dying trees
We saw the greed
among lying thieves
These were a few
that stood between
dead leaves
Take away the beauty
that once was seen
Beautiful clothes
A diamond ring
Take away the beauty
among the greed
Those that hide
behind the leaves
All that was left
Was Adam and Eve

Margaret Purificato

BEREAVEMENT

My pillow was wet from crying,
I knew I must keep trying
To reconcile his dying
Here in this lonely room.

I felt so stunned and shaken,
alienated, and forsaken.
Impelled to reawaken,
and face my life of gloom.

Condolences came flowing,
Sincere and true and glowing.
I felt thy love bestowing,
And I knew I was not alone.

I came to thee to ease my pain,
To give me hope to live again.
I sought thee, Lord, and not in vain.
I found solace in serving others.

Clara Hill

WHY?

Desire for the meal in my mind
became such a propelling force
that the aroma filled my nose,
and the flavor pleased my tongue.

Why?

Reaching for a skillet to cook,
I was magnitized passed the new,
picked the old without gleaming grooves.

Why?

Every bite was a taste delight,
boasting flavors above the new.

Why?

Dorothy Randle Clinton

DOROTHY LOUISE CLINTON. Pen Name: Dorothy Randle Clinton; Born: Des Moines, Iowa; Married: Mose Clinton; Education: Drake University, B.F.A.; Occupation: Retired government worker; Awards: Listed in *Who's Who in U.S. Writers, Editors and Poets, 1986-1987;* Two Clover Awards for 'A Cruise,' 1974, and 'Clouds,' 1975; Poetry: 'Snobbery in Nuance,' *Magic of the Muse,* 1978; 'Ascending Line,' *Carousel Quarterly,* 1978; 'The Look and the See,' *Carousel Quarterly,* 1979; 'Memory Lapse,' *Lyrical Treasures,* 1983; ''The Bridge is a Mirage,'' brochure of poems by the Iowa Poetry Association, 1979; 'Black Dignity in Marsh,' *Testimony;* Comments: *I would like to see the love and interest in poetry extend. I think this appreciation could be achieved by education if critics and publishers would realize good poetry isn't mawkish, vacuous utterances, nor merely a cerebral exercise, but an enriching experience both emotionally and intellectually.*

SHIPS AND RIGS
AND WHIRLIGIGS

I dream of seas and ships and rigs
Masts and winds and whirligigs
The quiet calm before the storm
Rolling waves the calm had warned.

The brig . . . tossed aloft, then down
    down
     down
      down.
Not a trace of her is found
  The sea is calm.

Mabel L. Bowman

NIGHT OF THE MAPLE MOON

A bright golden sphere
Hanging listlessly in the
Blackened sky
Smiling softly
On nature's shoulder
Careless winds
Sneaking through the trees
Twinkling eyes
Speckle the horizon as
The city sleeps
Under a maple moon

Russell W. Black

MUSING

Within blue walls I found home hope
Time was no longer a foe
Boredom could find me no home
When in my room I shut out prose

Women and men talk all day long
And in my mind let no thought grow
But within these walls I find my home
And from that love I'll never roam

Since I could I just as soon
Be a lover to my muse
Than to hear words that go ''boom!''
And still lie in solitude

Men and women talk in screams
To me to me soft poetry is the cream
If I want to be believed
The exclamation point is all I need!

Percie Blue

OBSTACLES

She walks past you, unaware
The light stings your eyes
The sound of birds and things
That nature springs
Echoes endlessly.
You call after her
The sound that springs from her casual tone
Is like metrical illusion.
The well-thought-out words
Grab you by the throat
Nearly strangling.
You start to follow
And the ground like quicksand
Swallows you whole.
If you struggle to pursue
But only sink deeper,
Defy them no longer
Obstacles are there for a reason.

Percie Blue

THE CHALLENGE

A house is never quite a home with shutters closed all day
And children in a Day-care; the parents both away
Nor, is home in those mansions where youngsters dine alone
And wait for Jet Set parents to keep in touch by phone.

A home is sacrifice and joy — love's most ingenious plan
For nurturing with watchful care to meet the needs of Man
From birth to death; in childhood — on into feeble age
Home is a sanctuary on the journey through each stage.

Throughout evolving history women kept the homefires bright
While men, facing awesome danger, founded nations of great might
Then the Women's Lib wrought changes in our lifestyles, and today
Houses are in favor but homemaking is passé.

In this Era of Achievement when the scientists are elite
Let us beware lest our triumphs harbor seeds of our defeat
Lest another civilization crumble into dust and fall
Lacking some cohesive factor that is vital to it all.

And that factor is — *A New Man** knowing kinship with the Whole
Radiating love and wisdom; using strength within the soul.
Home is where this work should focus — *calling forth the Man within*
From Ephesians comes our challenge and in Faith is power to win.

* *Eph. 4:24*

Verna Eppley

. . . RETROSPECTIVELY SPEAKING

Dedicated to L. D. Wilder

God, it seems that I've made history
Whereas before all things was a mystery
Now, I've been put in complete control
And I offer you my ever-creative, righteous soul

It's true, I have come a mighty, mighty long way
Experience affording me the intelligent things to say
I've employed experience as my private tutor
Turning my back on more than one ''overly qualified'' suitor

I've conceded, the Truth is the Light
And that glorious light has restored my foresight
I confess, I'm truly afraid of the dark
But like Mother Theresa, I strive to make my mark

Before your return, there's much to be done
I've faced challenges, been defeated and still won
Because I was ignorant, I've broken your commandments
Taken many falls and have had to make as many amendments.

You seem determined to make me a success
Thank you for enabling me to surpass the rest
Retrospectively speaking, before I do, each word I weigh
Silently praying for something wise and enlightening to say.

Rev. Dr. Patty A. Price-Lee Futt

MY ONE AND ONLY BILLY

Three years prior, same six in attire. Sat in the first row.
They came to share with their best friend the joy of wedding glow.
Tuxedo bound their fellow hound, pronounced till death do part.
And what once was joy among these men, now pierced the center's heart.

Just months ago with tappin' toes, they stood beside the groom.
And now again with tears in eyes, they stand beside his doom.

My thoughts now have turned to the day of their wedding.
The magnificent church, the future bright and burning.

Their daughter Lorisa, how grand her birth.
The miracle of their love, a sample of their worth.

Now leaving the land of Brigadoon, my heart heavy here in this room.

We still faced the casket they insisted our friend.
Still we prayed it a mistake and with morning's nightmare end.

Except that the room rang out with truth.
God stole not only Bill, He stole our brother, stole our youth.

Once again my eyes find his brothers as they mourn.
As I try to find God to confess of Him I scorn.

For if He were so mighty, so knowing, so wise.
Why could He not change things and hear our pleas and cries?

Did He know how Bill was needed, and that he had plans to keep?

Couldn't He see that the chain that these men formed,
Now lay broken, in a pile from the thief who snatched a link.

And if in fact you are up there and needed him more than us!
Please treat him kind and take care of our friend.
For we traded you light to receive from you dusk.

Jill Campbell

CHRIST LIVES ON

As I work in my garden of roses, the thought comes to my mind
When God gave us their sheer beauty, did He leave the thorns
                          on the vine
To remind us of how Christ suffered, the crown of thorns He wore
                          that day
And the color of red, for the blood Christ shed, that we may
                          live and come to realize
All living things in life, have a true meaning of love,
                          honor and strife?
The pasque and passion flowers we know, point out the wounds
                          there to show:
How Christ suffered so long, long ago.
The sand dollar, the perfect shell, tells again the story well.
Our orange and fruits with skin bitter like gall, also grow
                          thorns.
While our morning glory goes to sleep at night and awakens
                          refreshed on the morn.
The pansy has a pretty face, smiles with happy mirth.
Just seems to say it's happy to live on God's green earth.
The white dove flies gay, birds in the trees sing happily to say:
''Christ is truly here to stay!''
The traveler's palm gives water to the traveler on his way
Just as the palm path was laid for Christ on that holy day!
The Easter lily pure and white blooms at Easter time
To prove again, the pureness of:
                  The story so sublime!

Georgia E. Kavanagh

TO MY SWEETHEART

There are stories in the Bible,
Of friendships and of love;
There are wonders, there are miracles,
There are blessings from above.

I alone am very mortal,
Living under skies of blue;
But I'm blessed by all the angels,
All because they gave me you.

When I rise up in the morning,
It's your face I always see;
When I dream about the future,
Life's companions we will be.

We'll explore the far horizon,
Gaze into a deep blue lake;
Hand in hand we'll walk the mountain,
What a fine pair we will make.

We will pass our time together,
We'll grow young, and we'll grow old;
But our love will live forever,
The greatest story ever told.

Duke Tyler Scott

FISH

We entered with the women,
our hands already
broken from the scales.

Such sacrifice:
from two days' work,
we carried
the burden of numbers
within us.

Lifting a knife and
splitting them,
lopping off the heads
behind the gills,

our hands digging
for air sacks,
so slimed became
counting

(muscular bodies
glazed, unseeing eyes).

"Do you know what I'd like to do?"
you said to me at lunchtime
over soup. "I'd like to quit."

That night I thought of it,
soaking in the tub, it seemed
the stench would never go away.

JoAnn Gardner

when
i
looked
out
at
the
world
as
a
child
my
eyes
felt
old

Bev Kelly

MY BEST BOUQUET

"Mommy!" he called,
One time, then two.
"Come and see what
I have for you!"
A handsome pride
In his voice rang out,
And quickly I answered
His vigorous shout.
With a smile that would make
The sunshine blush,
My three-year-old came
To my side with a rush.
"These flowers I found
In the yard for you —
There are some more —
I'll get them, too!"
He hurried back
To the dandelion patch,
For blossoms that never
A florist could match.
There are orchids and roses,
Choose what you may.
But, dandelions make
My Best Bouquet.

Genevieve Sandifer Goodnow

EARTH, WIND, AND FIRE

You are the elements of my universe
Yours is the light that shines on me,
To show the way. And for this, I thank you!
You are the ground that I walk,
And the air that I breathe.
And I was surely blessed
The day that you came into my life.
For your love sparks a flame of passion!
That burns deep within my soul!
And that passion sustains me.
Oh! How I want you, every waking
Moment of every day!
And if I were to lose your love,
For any reason,
I'd surely lose my purpose for existing!
Because you are the elements of my
Universe.
You are my Earth, Wind & Fire!

Carter Mitchell

GOOD INTENTIONS, COVERED WITH DUST

Good intentions, like the leaves in fall,
Cover the walks of our lives.
We "meant to do it" one and all,
Becomes our battle cry.

We meant to spend those hours
To show our family true devotion,
We meant to send those flowers
To a friend on their promotion.

We meant to send that birthday card,
A delinquent letter to enclose —
Sympathy letters come so hard,
Especially that prose.

We meant to buy that baby gift,
(We try to keep abreast!)
We meant to call and give a lift
To one who's been depressed.

But when all is said, and little done,
We come to the end of our days,
Our good intentions, never begun,
Were just imaginary plays.

Carol G. McCann

A BRILLIANT SUCCESS

A newborn child, her small eyes bright —
Her mother's pride so real.
A host of firsts, first steps, first words —
Encouragement aiding maturity.

Older then, the child now runs,
With thoughts and dreams her own.
Her mother's there, but on the side —
Still thrilled with her creation.

And now the child becomes adult —
But Mother's the first she tells
Of accomplishments and dreams fulfilled —
She basks in the biased pride.

But something's missed, or something's lost,
The pride should go both ways —
The child forgets her mother's need
To have the praise returned.

So, Mother, for the things you've done
and all the things you do,
I tell you now, "I'm proud of you,"
And want the world to know.

Carol G. McCann

Oh guiltless guilt!
  Oh pain of the soul!
My corrupted innocence . . .
  And disheartened attempts in seeking
  What I cannot find
In places
  I know not where to go!

Christine A. Pitt

COME LET US GO SEE DIAMONDS

Come let's go to the diamond fields
Come visit with me see Guyana
Guyana has plenty land, with diamonds and gold
Real beautiful diamonds, found in Guyana

Diamonds and gold minerals untold
We need tools to select the wealth of Guyana
Come let's go to the diamond fields
Come visit with me, see Guyana

Bauxite, diamonds and gold, Guyana stronghold
Come see all mining areas of Guyana
I invite you to see wealthy mining lands
Where gold and diamonds are found in Guyana

Come, if we go together to the diamond fields
You'll see how we dig up to get gold and diamonds
Diamonds are found by shaking from our sieve
The sand. Then real diamonds. Take a visit to Guyana.

Percy E. Holder

PERCY ALEXANDER HOLDER. Born: Guyana, South America, 9-20; American citizen; Widowed; Education: High school, Georgetown, Guyana, South America; Occupations: Minister of Religion; Memberships: Church of God Within Positive Believers; Indept Associate, Jesus the Prince of Peace; Awards: Nashville Songwriter Award, 1979; Poetry: 'Hold Me Close To Your Heart,' 'Kiss Me And Say I Love You,' 'Where Can We Go From the Presence of God,' 'Dancing On The Brooklyn Bridge,' 'Moses Crossed the Red Sea'; 200 other poems; Comments: *I began writing poetry as a hobby and for amusement, and inwardly I gain joy from it. For over forty-five years I have been creating and writing poems. I have spent thousands of dollars having many of my poems set to music. So poor is their music when set to my poems that my songs never move on.*

I HAVE NO TEARS LEFT

Oh, life is so full of such joy and good cheer,
Why do the teardrops come ever so near?
Why, when I'm laughing hearty and long,
Teardrops start falling, now what can be wrong?

I cried as a baby, for love and for food.
I cried when my dollies looked sad and not good.
When puppy love came, and it's bound to do,
There was time for laughter and many tears, too.

As I grew older and saw children at play,
So happy and loving and bright as the day,
My eyes filled with teardrops, and do what I might,
The teardrops splashed over, that was my plight.

Beautiful music starts teardrops to flow,
And melodies bring memories of long ago.
When loved ones depart, casting gloom over all,
'Tis then that the teardrops profusely do fall.

But as the years pass, the wiser am I,
Sharing kindness to others leaves no time to cry.

Olive Hickerson

HAPPY ANNIVERSARY

A toast to the most wonderful years.
I'll always cherish and hold ever so dear.
We never had much to offer each other, but our love —
It's the most valuable thing I can think of.
We were too poor to afford a glamorous life —
But love made us appreciate each other as husband and wife.
Things seem so hard sometimes, but we made it through.
We've come a long way together . . . me and you.
Rich with love, yet short on funds —
Living in a four-room home, raising our little ones.
We got through the rough spots —
Picking up the pieces in our lives when all else failed —
Struggling to make it down life's lengthless trail —
It's that special bond that holds us together —
A mutual commitment that we'll share forever.
We've got something so valuable, even money can't buy —
And that's love, that will endure, until the day we die.
Though trials and tribulations will sometimes abide
Only the strong are fortunate to survive.

Charlotte Henderson

LOVE

Love is a wonderful word, which doesn't
  mean pain or hurt.
Love means caring and sharing feelings
  for one another.
Love is a word like no other.
Love is something you feel for your
  family or friend
And will always be in your heart till
  the end.
Love can be expressed by a kiss, hug
  or even a smile.
With love in your heart, you've got
  a perfect style.
Love is for a friend who is feeling
  down or sad.
You can keep this person from feeling bad
  by letting them know you'll always be
  there, and that you really care.
Love is feeling some of the pain, and
  sharing their tears.
And with your ears, makes the rain of
  tears, disappear.
When you've taken away the rain, and the pain,
  show them the sunshine in your smile,
  and make a rainbow a mile long.
As you brighten each day with love,
  you fill your spirit with the
  greatest gift of all.
And as love glows brightly in your eyes,
Someone, someday, who is looking
  for a little love,
Will find you flying like a dove,
  spreading joy to ones in need.
So when they find you, they've
  found a friend *indeed.*

Robin M. Kingbird

TEARS

When you leave, please don't cry
For when you do it will cause
The love I feel for you
To start falling in the form of
Tears.
When you come back, hold me
In your arms until the tears
That fell, fall no longer.
In their place you will fill
A sense of loss in my heart,
Causing me to kiss you harder,
Hold you tighter, love you
Longer.
When you leave, don't say good-bye
For it will cause me to cry
My tears forever. I don't want
That sense of loneliness to overcome my
Heart.
When you come back, and are
Standing on my doorstep,
We will relive our memories
And create new ones
Until the next time you leave.

Susan Schumaker

NO HURRY

The world's poor will just have to *wait*.
Until we have time to debate.
  Maybe we'll *find time after lunch*,
  While waiting for our golfing bunch.

Robert Emmett Clarke

QUIET TIME

Here — in the dead of night —
Death haunts the air . . .
Yet — peace is here — and — fright.
God is here — gentle in his care . . .

Solitude . . . so peaceful —
With the wind drifting by —
I try to catch my fill
Of serenity — then sigh . . .

For I want this peace to last —
Morning not to rise.
For with it casts . . .
Hell upon my eyes.

The pettiness of man —
His cruelty and pride.
The destruction of our land —
And nowhere to hide.

The serpent towers over — watching
Every evil by & by —
And he begins again to sing —
As humanity continues to die.

My time is at an end —
For as the sun set — it will rise.
O Lord — to me — please send —
The strength that within you lies.

Monica Slowick

MARRIAGE

Modern man has practically destroyed
The institution of marriage.
And the family life —
Is a thing of the past.
As we progress in some areas —
We regress in others.
This great strive for success in
Business — is destroying us all spiritually.
The togetherness of marriage in
The old days — has vanished from our society.
If we are to endure at all as a family,
We all must strive for truth.
For every marriage consists
Of a husband and a wife.
But in every marriage —
Where is the partner?

Monica Slowick

IF

If I could meet a friend today
or guide a poor soul on his way
my life would not be in vain
If I could end the suffering and the pain
If I could touch someone unloved
and say I love you
and help someone less fortunate
and know just what to do
If I could say, don't be lonely
then I would not be lonely too
If wishes were riches
I would be rich indeed
My wish for you
is sending you God's speed
It's true we walk together
in the glory of his love
until we meet together
in the glorious heaven above

Hazel Carestia

I PROMISE!

I'll participate in missions
  To the glory of my God,
And secretly do workings
Caring for my charges well
  Both with kindness and with patience
Showering hearts with hopeful thoughts
  The lighted lamp of Christians
Flows to one and all alike
  Pushing back drear darkness
Opening new channels
  For trapped and lonely people
Crying, "How long, oh Lord, how long?"
I'll travel someday to holy places
  With angelic song and band.
Lord, bring us back to Thee!
  I plead Thy grace to do.
Oh blessed lamb of God!
  Lord, I come; Lord, I come.
And may this rough old world
Come to its knees
  In deep repentance.

    Amen.

Iva C. Bird

LAMENT

Night's endless hours,
Heavy as a rock pushed up a hill,
Harsh as a sunburnt field,
Loneliness, as stark
As a mirror's image of you.
At dawn, your eyes search
For your other half,
In the clamor of human sound,
In the company of friends,
In familiar cafés,
Incessant movement
That uncovers every corner,
In vain, he is nowhere
But in the rhythm of your heart.

Georgia Kollintzas

H. T.

An almond tree in bloom
Has turned to oak,
Scorched leaves about the field,
But the fruit remains intact,
The heart a diamond's lustre.
From afar, a whisper
To give and give
And never empty
Your life's mission.
A higher law's demands
You followed
Faith, your best companion,
Your strength,
A love as perfect as dew.
Supple in changing times,
Always self-sufficient,
Even now, like lilies of the field,
A burden to no one.

Georgia Kollintzas

Long after
  the mug of
    steaming tea
  has quelled my need
    to taste
    a soft
    and honeyed
    breath of warmth,

The memory
  of your kiss
    sings sweetly
    on my lips
  in lingering
    hushed
    and gentle
    tones.

Trish Kaspar

WALTZ OF THE FLOWERS

Love, give me Carnation & beauty, the Rose . . .
Here giant Laurel, there odorous Heliotrope . . .
Perfume and grace, Nard Tuberose . . .

I desire money, money, Poppy . . .
I beg health, beau Easter Lily . . .
Salutes to Bougainvillea, singing to Morning Glory . . .

A travel to the Sky, Pelican . . .
And the triumph to White Lilac . . .

Joy and glee, Chrysanthemum . . .
Exuberant like Gardenia and as Geranium . . .

Belle existence, Hydrangea and Campanile, Bellflower . . .
Purity, ask you Gladiolus & belief, earring flower . . .

Dancing with Iris Fleur de Lis . . .
Ice skating with Jasmine and Hyacinth . . .

Prestige & fame, Magnolia . . .
Smiling with Azalea & Camellia . . .

Give me faith and hope, Orchid . . .
My golden Narcissus & my luxuriant Tulip . . .

Friendship, Daisy, as inconstancy, Violet . . .
Aren't sad, Pansy . . . farewell, Forget-me-not . . !

Greeting and kisses, Christmas' Poinsettia . . !

Gustavo A. Aguado

THIS IS MY DREAM

'Tis a sad song I sing
'Tis a sad story I tell
As I am born to breathe
So is my breath taken away.
I am of flesh and blood and soul
Yet I am less than human.
I was born out of slavery
And now am I free?

What is freedom?
To be told where to sit when I am on a bus.
To be told where to eat when I am hungry.
To be told where to sleep when I am tired.
To be told what work I can do.
To be told! To be told! To be told!

Oh Lord, this is my dream.
To live in a world where men are brothers,
To be accepted as I am, for what I can do, for all I can give.
Where peace and harmony reign above all else.
Where the road of life is made easier by a stranger's smile,
    and a neighbor's hand in friendship.
Where man is man above prejudice, hate, greed, and fear.
Where God is love, and love of God brings peace.
This is my dream.

Dorris J. Avner

ROOTS TO REALITY '87

As I climb through the clouds . . .
  My heart races with the sun.
As I pass through the darkness of time . . .
  I will soon enter a new dimension.

Looking back into my past . . .
  Looking forward to tomorrow.
Finding out who I really am . . .
  Reaching for the distant stars to another land.

Searching for my roots on an island of jade and pearl . . .
  I look forward to the laughter and cries;
Of my friends in the orphanage . . .
  Waiting to be found; like I was.

Remembering the struggles of yesterday . . .
  And the dreams of today.
My soul yearns to break open the dark past . . .
  To find my mother and father, brother and sister.

In my dreams they are lonely and far apart . . .
  Through my journey I will find them.
Through the pearly white mist of the unknown . . .
  We will drink and dance with the dragons.

We will play with the pandas . . .
  Together we will drink the waters of life.
And journey through time and space . . .
  To reach a new beginning.

Kim Hardiman

KIM MARGARET ANN HARDIMAN. Pen Name: Shek Ying Ying; Born: Hong Kong, China; Education: C.U.N.Y., Hunter College, M.F.A., 1985; S.U.N.Y., Stony Brook, B.A., 1982; Teacher's College, Columbia University, 1983; Occupations: Art; Creative writing; Poetry; Jewelry and enameling; Teacher at the ''Door,'' an alternative center for youths in New York City; Memberships: College Art Association; Organization of Independent Artists; Poetry: 'Song of Ch'i,' *American Poetry Anthology,* 1986; 'Aloha,' 'Distant Friendship,' 'Roots To Reality,' 'You Are A Timeless Feeling On An Endless Beach,' *American Poetry Anthology,,* 1987; Comments: *I am a poet, an artist and a teacher. My poems express my feelings toward life & people I meet, my experiences of traveling to many foreign countries, my hopes and dreams of tomorrow. I dedicate my poems to my wonderful students, friends and family. Thank you for inspiring me to reach for the stars.*

SOCIETY

Society is a courtly dame,
Who weds the elegant and bluntly shuts the door,
To gather her servants and fill her courtly frame,
With tears and toil of the desperate poor.
Society is a ruthless dame,
Who knows no scruples, only lust,
To rent the spirit, she knows no shame,
But to tread the lowly, is her shameless game.

Frances R. Smith

Let me
   grow
   like the pussy willows —
   roots
   running deep,
   dipping down
      to sip
      the earth's
      sweet wetness
         and draw strength,
   while eager limbs
   stretch lithely
      up and out,
      bearing soft
         and
            cozy
            catkins
   from the heart.

Trish Kaspar

Like icy rain,
   thoughts of you,
      sting
         and
      chill,
And I am
   buffeted
      by the winds
         of your
      taut
   words.

Trish Kaspar

MY LITTLE DADDY

My Little Daddy, a voice so deep and strong,
Your sweet and gentle manner,
That taught me right from wrong!
Mapping the road of life's long way,
There are lines of wisdom on your face,
Your hair has all turned gray!
I'll never be too old or proud,
To sit upon your knee!
I'll always be there for you,
As you've always been for me!
Though you have a fiery temper
'Twas never used on me!
'Cause you're "My Little Daddy"
For that's what you'll always be!

Sherrie Lynn Mantooth

DEPRESSION

I let out a sigh,
My mind went blank,
Into depths of nothingness,
My broken heart sank.
I'm so tired and weary
Why should I go on?
I no longer want to be here,
Then on comes the dawn
As the salty brine trickles
Slowly down my cheek.
Why do I let it get to me?
Why am I so weak?
I now start to wonder
What's left worth living for?
Then comes my answer
A "wee" knock upon the door!

Sherrie Lynn Mantooth

LETTING GO

If I could see your face again,
But, if only for awhile,
To touch and hold you just once more
Just to view your precious smile.
I know now it's not in the cards,
Your heart's no longer mine.
The hardest thing for a mom to do
Is not to become a clinging vine!
I realize it was inevitable,
As you grew you'd go on your own.
But you've always had a friend in me,
You don't have to face the world alone!
As you travel down life's long journey
'Twill never matter how far you roam.
You'll always have a place to come back to!
The place you once called home!

Sherrie Lynn Mantooth

YOUR BEAUTIFUL SMILE!

You showed a smile only recently,
   I must say:
It really made my day!
   Your eyes were shining,
Your face was all aglow!
   Your gorgeous smile can do
So much!
   Do you realize how many
Downbeat hearts you can touch?
   So practice it, you see:
It'll do wonders for all the
   Others, as it did for me!

Kurt Mueller

YOU ARE SO BEAUTIFUL!

You are what a symphony is to
Music.
A newborn star in the sky!
   You look like a million dollars,
I'm telling you no lie!
   When God created you, He
Showed His master skill!
   For you to be happy and
Loved, believe me, is *His will!*
Now keep on working on your
Inner beauty, then look in the
   Mirror and see:
You'll be amazed what's staring
   Back at you!
Now, I'm complete and: Is
   That really *me?*

Kurt Mueller

ENJOYMENT

Joy, Joy, Joy, Joy,
How can you employ
A rhythm to destroy?

Love, Love, Love, Love,
How can you employ
Anything, but from above?

Happy, Happy, Happy, Happy,
How can you employ
An action that is scrappy?

Life, Life, Life, Life,
How can you employ
A force that has strife?

Labels, Labels, Labels, Labels,
How can you employ
One with a meaning to enjoy?

Elbert R. Moses, Jr.

LACK OF SELF-RELIANCE

Modern man has built a car —
But has lost the use of his feet.
He is supported by words —
But lacks so much of their meaning.
Many fine watches he has —
But fails to understand the
Importance of time.
He has built an airplane which can
Cover much distance in little time —
But has failed to see the beauty of
The land in that distance.
He has ventured far out in space —
But has forgotten about the earth.
He has freedom, but doesn't appreciate it,
For he has never been deprived of it.
In every war there is a soldier —
But in peace — where is the peacemaker?

Monica Slowick

CAYUGA LAKE SCENERY.

HARMONY

Isn't it striking to think of our universe
As a structure that is not diverse?
There are climate, ecology,
Solar energy and biology,
All working together to form
A perfect haven
For mankind to live in.

The problem is that
Mankind is out of touch
With the natural forces
That would aid his action courses.
Mankind has to come to grips with ecology,
If he plans to survive
In harmony with biology.

Man, remember there is room for all
If you plan aright;
And allow each of the species
To settle his own plight,
With the help of him
In arranging what is right.

Our universe is not man-made;
Man is the converse.
Our time clock is running out,
While man has a great deal to think about.

Elbert R. Moses, Jr.

WISHES

Our glances crossed,
a clumsy parry
suddenly dropped,
and I unravel the weave
of my thoughts.
Words refuse expression,
scattered by the heedless rush
of emotion,
and I wonder
if my wish to touch you
is carved upon my face —

Robin Perry

SIREN CALL

I squandered the smile
you gave me,
spent it prolifically,
never dreaming
of this bitter ending
to our tale.
You left me
wondering,
screaming into the emptiness
of my soul
for answers,
echoing the rhythm
of death's siren call.

Robin Perry

THE UNKNOWN LAND

Far away in a land unknown
there is peace
there is no pain
people are laughing
there is no war
no crime
Everyone is happy
racism is unknown
there is no starvation
Everyone is everyone's friend
This land is beautiful
without pollution
or trash amongst the streets
This land will never become known
Because of the way the world is today.

Tammy N. Ayres

A GLORIOUS PUP

The puppy is a perfect waggler.
Ours happens to be an Ardsdale,
With the saddest brown eyes,
Rough coat and humorous pivotal tail,
Hardly moves himself without a stir,
Loves us greatly, being given bones,
And for fresh air expressing his trust,
In all dogs and people.
Life is one happy adventurous territory.
When failing to persuade is downcast,
Craving to join the family at church;
Anxious to escort us to a dinner dance.
Then he cries, laments and shakes,
Even remorse has a naïveté;
Honesty that is akin to gladness.
On occasion, fumbling at the latch-key,
The sound of urgency is heard,
This moaning behind the door.
Leaping about, and what is as such
Unbelievable shapes, curling his body,
Whilst wrinkling the rug Ken plays.
The part of his funny face
Is a pleasing fit to fuse the heart
Of the stoniest cynic that is seen around.

Rose Mary Gallo

LOT'S WIFE

The desert city is a
fine place to
  die
the old ones said.
Look back!
for fire to quench
a vision of life,
for blood to turn
to salt and
  lye
and the promise
to shrivel from green
to powder brown to
  cry
to Sodom
where no one's voice
will hear or care to
  try,
Look back!

Anne Wallace

CAMOUFLAGE

The water closes around me
and I am the predator, watching
pipefish sway at being reeds;
they blank their eyes to my shadow
    . . . cannot hurt you
    . . . not good to eat
and I remember, a child at five,
reading aloud, faltering
over a word I knew,
I coasted the beam of the bully's stare,
funneled down to the pool weeds
where anything different was killed at once.

The water closes around me
and I am a mote in a giant's eye,
trying to hide but distorting your vision,
refracted, remembering,
    . . . please don't hurt me
    . . . not good to hurt
I didn't mean to hide the truth,
or cloud your world with my pain;
I looked for my truth in your eyes,
but I found no mirror there,
and you are far too close to ever know me well.

Anne Wallace

ODE TO A MANNEQUIN

Grandmother was printed on onion skin.
She stretched and wrinkled
but she didn't rip when she had
a smooth glass baby in 1910.
She was tough. She grew
new skins, and died a crumpled
brown bag full of sweets.

The baby with the amber hair
in the hands of the blower was
melted down and remoulded large,
a translucent beauty with
bottle breasts and mirror eyes
and no spots on her milk glass hands.

    (They hired her at Gimbel's
    to pose in the window
    in an artful arrangement
    of creamy white cribs
    and galloping wallpaper,
    selling nurseries and
    marriage at bargain prices.)

In the Christmas Pageant she was
always the Madonna, almost as good
as the marble ones. She was lovely,
they said. Even while she was giving
birth she never moved once.

Anne Wallace

POLICE REPORTER MEMORY

One robbery in three is fake.
Someone inside is *on the take*.
  Veteran cops will tell you so.
  And I think that they *ought to know*.

Robert Emmett Clarke

ON TRACK WITH THE SPINNING WHEEL

If life
Be just a careless whisper,
Then I am old and trite already;
Such be the dirge of a lowly song
Sung to one of the absent senses.

Nice haze,
Never fitting the gentle scene.
Obscurity has a long but tender hold;
Once I dreamed of it hiding in the woods,
Marching beyond unimaginable mountains.

So long,
Perhaps, too long, is better stated here;
But then, can it really be used as a measuring of time,
Which has no bearing on itself alone;
Eternity waits not for mortality.

Ah bliss,
When it leaves the emotion seems lost to memory;
Its presence can certainly be thought of as love;
But for truth, this cannot be said,
Nor can definition explain what must be omnipresent.

James Wesley Duren

DISINVENTION WITH NAILS

It still writhes and wiggles and whispers,
despite the cool steel driven through
its fleshy-colored, hard-bound cover:
playing dead; but not dead
on the shelf where I hammered
the holes meanly through.
Wood to wood. Object to object. Stay put, dammit.

And it does stay (as does any pretentious good book)
until I wander too far away,
become preoccupied in, well, something else:
some other story, say, some simple conversation, some bad dream.
Then, here comes — intervening always quietly
to tell me in casual conscience,
with solemn sameness, the connection
and the allusion without fail.

Like a skilled carpenter I take another nail
and through the spine this time fix it —
once again — until the next intervention,
until the last nail,
until the meaning and the memory's gone.

S. Hines

POINT OF NO RETURN

You're traveling through the ''Point of No Return.''
Where does it lead to.
You're taking a chance that comes in 1:1,000,000.
How will you know you have arrived at the Point.
You take yourself and others to the Point,
That will not return you or the others,
Those people who stood by your side have disappeared for
good.
Dreams have been shattered this way many of times.
So why do people take a chance going through the,
          Point of No Return.

Farzin Sherkat

THE WORLD

While I watch the clouds go rolling by
I think of this world and begin to sigh:
Why is there so much hatred around?
I look at the sky, and hear the wind with its sound
Everywhere I turn there is hatred indeed
Will people ever read the bible and take heed?
What are they doing? Why are they so bad?
I can imagine our Creator looking down and feeling sad
What is wrong with this world? Have people lost their minds,
Or maybe what they're doing, they think they're doing so fine?
There is hatred, jealousy, killings and lust
What happened to their morals? Have they all turned to dust?
So with a tear in my eye, I sit and cry
And ask our Creator who lives up so high
''Help me, dear Father, not to become very weak
Help me to always be humble and meek
To be meek, humble and have morals that are fine.''
I know many will think I am out of my mind
Let them think what they want, I really don't care
As long as I love you and know you'll be near.
So always be with me and help me to be nice
And maybe my reward will be living in the new paradise
I love you.

Rita Pires

HUBBA HUBBA

The shopping cart she pushed along the street, was
Filled with bottles, rags and treats, so neat.
Her tiny bowed legs pushed with all their might, and
When I looked at her as we passed by, her smile
And her eyes were brighter than the stars at night.

One windy day she pushed her cart off the street to
Let us pass: I looked into her happy eyes, and said
''Good morning.'' ''Hubba Hubba,'' she replied, to my great
Surprise.

We laughed at this, and my husband said, ''She's Chinese,
And these words are all she knows. Learned from our
Army perhaps from some far-off shore.''

Elaine Bianchi

HUMAN CELLS

That which transpires coming from within the human cell —

Origination, but with modification commencing immediately upon release

To conscious or unconscious thought or forcing prompt action physically,

Must still be assumed to be individual responsibility

Regardless of hatred or darkness as reflected in outside occurrences,

And absorbed equally by the human cells of being and awareness and sensitivity.

H. T. Brohl

DISCOURSE ON BEAUTY

you shall look deep into this wood
the forest is always failing
under the changing stone
at the bend of the desecated river

the eye of the improbable butterfly
professionally interested in the flower
you will welcome in its season
your concerns are not the same

eyes with odd consequence
delight in fables and in waterfalls
meantime caught in a mind's flash
disarmed the stream pursues its way

she stood apart from him/her season
not his or the butterfly's or the waterfall's
she stooped and cupped in the palms of her hands
cones of the starcrossed tree

Ann Watson Barnard

LOYAL FAITH

A half moon hovers over
the closest to your eye spotted star.
The one in range of your vision
from that distance it appears not to be far.
But as you reach up with your arms
and stretch your fingers toward the sky
you suddenly realize how small you are,
compared to that star on high.
The moon, though, it glows
and that star, it does shine.
Someday, well, who knows,
the pair could be mine.
No obstacles bear in mind a clear path
for those who dare give try to an oath
for whosoever attempts a climb of faith
shall and can be guided by that
    Half-moon hovering over their own star of truth.

Darlette Clarice Knox

ACT II, SCENE 4

The stage is set,
The performers arrive,
The jesters, the fools, the harlequins of the gods.
They perform,
   Bow out,
      The curtain falls,
         The lights die.
They are forgotten
As a new stage is made ready
And new puppets arrive.
But all is not lost,
For the stages never change,
The scenes are redone,
And the performers begin anew,
Controlled by the gods which pull at their strings
Unwilling puppets
Come back again and again.

Bill Rae

THE FOUR SEASONS AND LIFE

Life is just a dream or rather just a smoke ring.
For in nature's wonderland, it connects us with the four seasons.
Springtime is our childhood, full of love and wonder at every turn.
Summertime is our youth, the electric energy of life.
With many roads to choose from, we have success, failure and
    hardship.
For *Youth* is full of restlessness and a passion to conquer.
Autumn is nature's gathering harvest.
Here we gather the fruits of our success or failure,
For these years are the best of one's life;
Rich with the knowledge of wisdom, and very colorful.
   Humor and *Understanding* add to the way of life.
Winter is mellow like wine, sweet, gracious, cold and refreshing.
At this point we have learned to live with our pains, heartaches;
Fighting loneliness with various elements of discontent.
The friends that are sincere and true have become few, indeed!
Age recalls thousands of memories; toil, tears and joy.
Like millions of different tiny little moffets of snowflakes.
We have set a pattern of our own, in beauty or disgrace, clinging
To life for another chance, or to get another ''peep'' at *Spring*.
We blow smoke rings in the air which form a silver cloud and passes
by and beyond the horizon.
Yes, indeed, *Life has ended its four seasons,* after a year-long trail.

Marie V. Spadaro

MARIE V. SPADARO.

CLASSICAL SONNET
THE ETERNAL MUST

There is no doubt that somewhere I shall wake
   Once more, and as I open eager eyes
   I'll sense the azure glint of summer skies
Reflected from some distant mountain lake;
   But when I rise again, I shall forsake
   The clutching fingers of those mortal ties
Which bind me now; for that in me which dies,
   Is not the part which lives without a break.

That ''I'' goes on, ignoring death and birth,
   Observing with a gleam of rueful mirth
      The eons as they pass. Yes, I go on
   Though constellations fade and turn to dust;
'Til earth and stars, and sun alike, are gone . . .
   Yes, ''I'' go on and on because ''I'' must.

Barry Green

DEAR MOM, FROM CAMBODIA, WITH LOVE

Some say the ignorant
are truly disadvantaged in life.

I say yeah.

Maybe.

Raw nerves, naked endings,
devoid of bone and flesh.

Empirical;
and crude.
Instinct over will and mind.

The beautiful sun in the morning
after last night's torrent raining.

A shred of hope.
An ounce of motivation.

God . . .

I pray this is my last day seeing the son of a bitch.

Welcome to reality.

From Cambodia
with love.

Mark

Donald M. Cline

SEEKERS OF KNOWLEDGE

Ever-watchful with a wondering mind,
Seeking ever into the universe new things to find,
Youth; the vessels that must contain the things yet unknown,
Knowledge that springs forth to meet the challenger,
The desire for it carries new generations on.

Youth; perceptive, inquisitive, exploring new territory of knowledge
Where no one has ever gone,
The backbone of generations leaving a foundation to stand on,
Daring to move ahead to horizons seemingly so far away,
Yet, the brilliance of only one mind could save the world one day.

Willard Lee Skelton

COMPETENT INCOMPETENCE

From the tunnel of darkness the world turned a night,
Awakening in anticipation to the realization of what might,
The first day of still a journey into the yet unknown,
Storing into the cobwebs of what has already gone.

The four winds howl the echoes of many a mother's cry,
The sons of all the many that in their graves now lie,
From the battlefields of many wars all over the land,
Yet the weakest no less the soul of any man.

The armour not made of steel; yet frail it must stand,
The likeness of many from which comes the inheritance of man,
With feelings of incompetence, most competent shall the gaunt pretend,
Our freedom prevails becasue of the many just such men.

Willard Lee Skelton

THE HUNGRY ANIMALS

Croaky old bullfrog sitting on a log,
Don't look at me with your bulging eyes,
I cannot help you, catch your own flies.

Someone else's cat, don't look at me like that,
I wish you'd stop scratching on my door,
Go on home, I've told you before.

Little gray squirrel sitting in that tree,
Why are you always looking at me,
Looking at me that way, I'll feed you today.

Old stray dog, don't you have a home,
I'll look around, maybe I have a bone,
Then go away and leave me alone.

Hey all you birds! Why don't you fly away,
I think you've eaten enough for today,
It seems to me that you've come to stay.

I'll feed you all I guess, or do my best,
When I look in the cupboard to see what is there,
Like Mother Hubbard, I hope it won't be bare.

Willard Lee Skelton

UNDERSTANDING

Living in such a complicated world today, understanding
Is greatly needed. Sometimes patience is the key to
Understanding.

In this day and time, understanding seems to have run
Astray. Almost forgotten is the true meaning of the word.

If we would only take the time and try —
We might just see the world in a better light.

Holly A. Hudson

FORGOTTEN FAMILY

When I was born didn't you say,
You would love me forever and a day?
Didn't you say you would always be,
There to always take care of me?

And when I was young did I ever say,
I want to live on the streets someday?
Did I want to be in the cold and rain,
And have no one to help ease my pain?

Now I spend all of my time,
Wondering where I will get my next dime.
Trying hard to understand,
Why you're not here with a helping hand.

Did you forget I was once like you,
I had dreams and ambitions too.
Something happened along the line,
And now they are forgotten dreams of mine.

It is unfortunate that we didn't make time,
For each other more than we do.
And it is a heartbreaking crime,
When your family forgets about you.

But maybe that too was a dream,
Trying to pretend it was true
But family it would seem,
Should always be there to love and take care of you.

Karen L. Simms

SHAKING UP THE BEST

Sometimes the hand is quicker than the eye
The careless speech is faster on the sly
A casual acquaintance
Can be more than meets the eye

Your words and actions differ
Are they meant just to disguise
The blast of icy examination
There is nowhere to hide

Your assumptions are misleading
On these the judgment depends
Searching for a common bond
You can't believe I'm me

The change perceived can't be believed
As nothing is the same
At times there is so little of me
I can't survive your needs

Bonnie Zaborski-Beck

PEACE

If we could grasp the meaning
In the Cross of Calvary
Appreciate the beauty
Of our Gift from Galilee
Grow in love that would end karma
On its slow, snowballing spin
Understand ''The Shroud's'' strange imprint
Baffling all scientific men.

If we could see the pathos
Needless tragedy of man
Wrought by stubborn arrogance
That scorns God's helping hand
Disbelieving man's true essence —
(Not a dust-formed hollow clod)
But immortal, glorious Spirit
In the image of his God.

If we could know the value
In heart-felt visual prayer
And picture loving harmony
With mankind everywhere
''His will done in Earth and Heaven''
See it and give thanks; Ah! *then* —
Hark! The sound of smashing weapons
Hail! All Hail! ''Peace Unto Men.''

Verna Eppley

DENIAL

The heretics arrive
  In shapes and forms I do not know
Gathering in my path
Chilling my spirit
Reminding me
Reminding me
  of my imminent destruction
Yet I walk
  Cautious — anxious
With an impassioned denial of fear

Catherine Kiernan Flynn

STARS

Stars fill the sky tonight,
Turning darkness into bright.
They speak of home across the sea,
Where I know he waits for me.

Stars, you know of life around us,
Out on other planets.
Yet, on earth it seems we must
Live our lives alone.

Does he stare at stars at night
With questions on his mind,
Wondering what else is out there
Stars, what will we find?

Are there secrets of the mind?
Is that what we will find?

The night sky holds the mystery.
The story of our soul
Lies above among the stars,
Just waiting to be told.

And yet as nighttime turns to dawn
We face another day alone,
Always searching for the one who
We can give our heart and soul to.

Stars, are we alone?

Carrie Powell

RAINWEEPER

Heavy-lidded, heavy-hearted,
A poet grieves where gray rain falls
Without ceasing on roofs and alleys
In this city of unvoiced woes.

Ambushed by what hateless treason
He cannot tell, but mourns alone
Summers and autumns too soon gone
To earth, like these drops that flow

Crisscross on leaded windows
Glazed as the eyes that know
No cause for the tears that well thus
Other than the seasons' blues.

Peter Thomas

PICNIC ISLAND

Two Greeks and a young boy
Took us to an island with no name
Where we had a cookout and drank wine.
No, there was no resemblance to an
Outdoor barbecue back home.
On this island poppies grew, and something
Like a passion flower. The sea was
Beating all around, and as we looked through
Hollow rocks at the froth it made, I
Thought, it's hungry too — Poseidon
Must be fed. All the while
There were laughter and gay spirits
I could feel, as the darkness fell,
That something was waiting for its share,
Sheathing and unsheathing with the pulse
Of the sea.

Patricia McRaven

sing my body to freedom
rejoice my soul in rebirth
color my days
shine through the haze
as i become one with the earth

mind: the music of wisdom
heart: the beauty of love
color my world
as i am unfurled
with warmth of the stars high above

joy to life that surrounds me
tear to the sad that abides
color in wonder
prepare for any thunder
if lightning should strike i won't hide

journey to what life awaits me
follow the roads i must go
color directions
in a mirror of reflections
a colorfully painted rainbow

Amy E. Turner

HURRICANE KATE

Say! Have you met Hurricane Kate?
  A lady she sure ain't!
She came roarin' out of the Caribbe
  Dumpin' water to our knees,
Knockin' down our beautiful trees.

Now she's prowlin' out in the Gulf,
  Takin' aim on the Deep South.
She's buildin' strength with ease,
  Wants to knock us to our knees.
A lady she sure ain't,
  This late season storm,
Hurricane Kate!

Sandra A. Madsen-Camil

VISION OF GOD

Shooting star — falling star
Did God let Heaven's door
For just an instant go ajar
Permitting its light to crescend
Night's sky
Might it be His mirrored floor
Reflecting some of His Glory to descend
And be caught by the human eye
Then might those souls of His Creation
Be awed by those heavenly lights
Yet God perceives both days and nights
To Him no darkness ever deceives
For He has an all-seeing Eye
From which His Creation does often sigh

Richard D. Cagg

MESSED-UP HEAD

They told me to stand on my head
  but I stood on my feet instead
They said do it this way
  but I did it myself okay

I'm tired of being told just what to do
I'll put my left on my right shoe
The doctor said I was confused
but I'll do it the way I choose

Life seems a little bit muddled up to me
  and everyone wants a large fee
Pay me and I'll make your brain a copy
       of mine
Forget it I'll just stick to wine

Won't someone say you do what you think is best
wouldn't that make an interesting test
I want to see the people who are well
that's what would make me rejoice like hell

Bell hell well, well bell hell, my doctor says
       I'm confused
I think it is a case of brain abuse

Dolly Vrudny

REMINISCING

Can you remember
  The long walks in the park,
  Our serious talks after dark,
  When we were both young and free . . .
  . . . dreaming about what we wanted to do and be.

Can you remember
  Listening to The Pretenders in the rain
  The enduring ''good-bye'' at O'Hare which left us tear-stained.
  Then we pledged our love will never stop . . .
  . . . first find success, then meet at the top.

Can you remember
  Such a time when we were so naive
  That we would actually believe,
  That time and distance had no effect on a relationship . . .
  . . . these feelings could never slip.

Can you remember
  Your first taste of success,
  And how that tremendous feeling was not any less
  Because we were apart . . .
  . . . success has nothing to do with the heart.

Can you remember
  The one that got away.
  I can.

Barbara Lue-Hahn

THE ETERNAL DESERT

How like the nomadic tribesman are we,
Ever roaming in our pursuit of that Oasis
Fertile in each our mind.
Myopic prejudices and unkempt thought
Carry us as though we ride a blind camel,
Struggling through each day over the arid sand,
Thirsting after what pleasured mirage,
Plodding, plodding, over the eternal desert.

Joseph Frankel

SHARING THE DAWN WITH YOU

To share the dawn with you each day, dear heart,
  is my idea of bliss —
Until that time when we will have to part,
  we shall seal with a kiss.

Beyond the distant parts of this our earth,
  the true God rules supreme;
We strive today, tonight, to prove our worth,
  so this is no mere dream!

Ridgely Lytle

R. RIDGELY LYTLE III. Born: Philadelphia, Pennsylvania, 1931; Married: Ruth, 1960; Occupations: Stationery company records clerk; Memberships: National Writers Club; Awards: for ''Three Days,'' short story, 1949.

A WORD FROM THE FATHER

Did not I tell you I would come again?
Did not I tell you My Love is not as man's?
My caring is not a spark which you must fan.
It springs outward spontaneously again and again.

Every time you think you have lost;
Think of Me and how I came not counting the cost.
Then you will know My Love for you is embossed.
Think of Me every time you think you have lost.

Always I am there by your side.
I will never leave you, in you I'm inside.
Remember this, my child, with you I do abide.
And I will be with you always, whatever betides.

Don't forget these things I'm telling you.
Don't forget My Love, and then carry through.
Remember My Love for you in whatever you do.
I love you dearly, and will stay with you too.

Good things come when you trust in the Father.
Good things will come to those who will with Him bother.
Gone is the one who can go with you no farther.
But God is there, the Holy Spirit, and the Son, my brother.

Only when you remember Me,
And let me cause you to see,
The wonderful things that will be,
Will you remember that you will be with Me eternally.

Alice May Shutt

SOMETIMES

Sometimes quite suddenly
    I am terrified.
Terrified of being alone, terrified
    of not being alone,
    of dying, of living —
Of walking along some precipice
    with darkness all around.

I'm terrified of loving, of hating —
    of feeling anything at all,
    of feeling nothing.
A tear starts to fall —
I heard somewhere that only the strong
    can weep . . .

Nancy Cassell

CHANGES

As we open to the flow of all Life:
Pain brings understanding,
Grief breaks our shells
    so that we grow through
    vulnerability and danger —
Loneliness brings tears,
    tears that wash and cleanse
    tears that water and seeds of Love.
Frustration gives birth to patience,
Loss signifies a gain,
And death is merely another beginning.

Nancy Cassell

I WISH

I wish that you could know me —
The me I've become this year
Through sorrow, success, growth and tears.

I wish you could know me —
The me who tries and knows she can win
Through the dark nights of doubts and fears . . .

Most of all I wish you could know the me
Who laughs and loves — and
Lives with the joy of having you for a Friend.

Nancy Cassell

THE ARGUMENT

If it were possible
To eliminate
The tangible space which separates us,
The comic form of dust
That isolates our breached souls,
I suppose
Our words, like evil wardens,
Would erect black iron walls
To keep us in the proud Bastille
Of our discontent.

Cathryn Warren

ON AWAKENING AT 11:30 P.M.

Frightened, hazy, I sought your face
Quietly etched with unchanged grace
And found you were not in your place.

I turned, expecting you to greet
'Twas no-man there who called me meet
Faint warmth left from your soothing heat.

But hark, what sound is this at sink?
Our kitchen holds a thief, I think.
I jump — it's just you with a drink

Of lukewarm water from the tap.
I laugh at thoughts of thieves which cap
Phantoms that tore me from my nap.

You comfort me from dreams undone,
"Come back to sleep, night's just begun."
Soothes, I return to sleep's dimension.

Jenny Jamison

FOR KIT

I stood on the mountaintop and
Imagined I saw you soaring;
Your silvery plane knifing through
The billowing clouds,
Tipping your wings to me.

"Welcome to Colorado"
I strolled the streets
And felt as tho' my footsteps
Were walking the paths
You trod before me.

Sipping my tea
in the small café,
I could almost hear
Your laughter
Reverberating from other mornings.

I was here;
You were not.
You left eleven years ago.
You didn't know you wouldn't
Be back. (Or did you?)
I came here not knowing
I was going to find you.

You were waiting for me.

Mary C. Mc Dyer

SAN FRANCISCO — 1981

Young faces . . . old faces
Sitting still or marking paces;
Faces glaring . . . faces staring,
Looking for someone who's caring.

Face with painted, mournful eyes;
Trumpet blaring . . . woeful cries.

Tourist faces . . . happy faces
Wand'ring through these saddened places.

And then . . .
Forgotten.

Mary C. Mc Dyer

GRANDMAS

Grandmas are for story telling
Of things they did when small;
And they capture the attention and
Imagination of us all.

Grandmas are for shopping —
If only on a little jaunt;
But they have a way of buying
Just the thing you mostly want.

Grandmas are for secrets,
Especially at Christmastime.
They wrap and hide small presents
And make them hard to find.

Grandmas are for squeezing —
For they are so soft and round;
And their laps are meant to sit on,
And none better can be found.

Grandmas are for loving,
And they have lots of love to give;
And they'll share that love with you
For as long as they shall live.

Grandmas are for comforting —
For they know much about pain;
And they can kiss away small hurts,
And make life worthwhile again.

JoAnn Wollam

THE SEARCH

Somewhere within the depths of me,
There burns as tho' with fire,
A never-dying languished sea
Of unfulfilled desire.

It roves the caverns of my soul;
It clutches at my breast;
It beats its wings in frantic flight;
It seeks to find its rest.

It reaches up with hungry heart;
It cries as tho' in pain;
It pleads with anxious, searching eyes;
It weeps, then weeps again.

And somewhere too within my soul
There also burns with fire,
The knowledge that I'll ne'er attain
This innermost desire.

Fore'er on earth, this deep desire
Must wander to and fro,
And never find its place of rest —
For God has ruled it so.

But when at last I leave this earth
And enter Glory Land,
Long-lived desire shall find its rest —
God's will I'll understand.

JoAnn Wollam

THE CIDER MILL

As I circle the dirt road
that borders the stately red structure,
I hear a sighing, bubbling noise
penetrating the old mill's walls.
The door creaks on rusty hinges and latches;
its windows clacking like old bones.
And its planked floor resists
the weight of 100 years of guests.
The machinery of rollers, grinders
and chutes is thrust into motion.
A maze of huge belts, chains — all
linked as one — create the tangy flavor,
sweet, yet tart and sprightly to my tongue.
Its amber color sparkles as I lick my fingers
where the moist juice trickles to the floor.
Entranced, I saunter up to the dirty
stained window at the other end,
and press my hot face against the cool
glass — and see the wooden wheel
that powers the mill as I treasure
the fragrance of autumn's first October morning.

Denise Martinson

DENISE ANNE MARTINSON. Born: Detroit, Michigan; Married: Michael Ray Martinson; Education: Institute of Children's Literature; Newspaper Institute of America; Occupations: Freelance writer; Memberships: *Who's Who in U.S. Writers, Editors, & Poets,* 1987; Society of Children's Book Writers; National Writers Club; Awards: Honorable Mention, *Wide Open Magazine,* 1986; Finalist in *Midwest Poetry Review,* 1987; Poetry: 'Terminus,' *Today's Modern Poetry,* 1987; 'Shipwrecked,' *Odessa Poetry Review,* 1987; Other Writings: ''For Pete's Sake,'' *Living With Children;* ''Word-Speaking Experience,'' *Primary Treasure;* ''My Friend,'' illustration and paper doll layout; Comments: *Besides poetry, I love writing for children. They are the most fun to write for. It is a highly specialized field. And yet, it is the most difficult type of writing to do. You must not write down to the child; rather, you share what you have to say with them. I am also writing my first children's book,* The Heart Run Hero.

GOLDEN PETAL

A golden petal lay dormant in the sun,
Somehow on its own climactic run.
It didn't have legs or any real emotion,
But it struggled along its own path with devotion.

And while it contemplated its quiet doom,
It filled the loneliness within this room
With a warm and softly radiant light
Reflected from golden skin and its inner might.

I laid down my pen and thought of the flower,
Of how we shared some softer power
Within us, as we pondered our fate,
To still help another open the gate.

Dennis Dwyer

PRECIOUS FUEL

The only *authentic* fuel we have
We derive from *love*
And this *direct* from *heaven* above!
If we *deny* it, our *motors* soon start sputtering
And many of us end up groaning and muttering!
However: *If we* and (*if* is half of life)
If we fill our tank(ards) with *love*
Our bodies will soon reflect on this condition
Thus *aid* us to fulfill our *earthly* commission!
We can *run . . . life's* race to reach our *eventuality*
And this in confidence and reasonable health!
Although many of us are *materially . . .*poor . . .
And lack any great wealth
We can use this ingredient — *love*
For what it was *originally . . . meant! Then,*
Your *life* will be . . . *well spent!*
So . . . gas up with this *precious fluid*
Love not only yourself, but your neighbor . . .
     Do it!

Mabel Lagerloff

OUT OF SIGHT

Ten years ago, I wrote a ditty
Eulogizing a *celebrity,* a little out of pity
His *fame* and *fortune* reached *colossal* heights
He *broke all records* — truly, out of sight!
They said it was OD, took him away . . .
Yet, his songs played on and on . . . *to stay*
I repeat breaking *all* records . . . even . . . *today!*
Impossible . . . you say? *Not so!*
It shows us all what *true* love is all about
If it is true love . . . born of a *broken heart*
Then *it cannot end . . .* it sings on and on
To *heal* and *mend!*
'Tis a *legacy* to *mankind* from a dear, departed *friend!*
He may be dead, but he cannot *hide* this *gift* of *song*
Just because he died!
He'll live on and on, of that I'm sure
For *he* once said which describes him to a ''T'' *perfectly*
''Without a *song . . . there is no me!''*

Acts 20:35

Mabel Lagerloff

OLD WARRIOR

Only yesterday, Old Warrior proudly stood.
Nature's masterpiece in massive wood.
Tender teardrops twinkled down each leaf.
Farewell to the forest folk brought Warrior grief.
Feathered friends who found a place to nest,
Weary travelers who sought his shade to rest.
The raging winds who wrestled this tower.
Downed by muscled limbs who proved their power.
He strew acorns for furry friends to carry away,
So they woudn't hunger on a wintry day.

Chosen the sign board in days of yore.
Clad with maps, news and posters galore.
Tales of settlers, Indians and a hanging or two,
Secret meetings of lovers and soldiers in blue.
Now, being robbed of these treasures and his crowning glory,
Ends the saga of Old Warrior — an unwritten story.
I wept! the pangs of death I could feel.
As Old Warrior fell by blades of steel.
Oh, why this ruthless trait in mankind?
The lust for money has made them blind.

Norma K. Shea

MAGIC

The joy of knowing you
Is one of life's wonders,
My heart I give to you
Nothing tears us asunder.

The pleasures which we share
Bring me so much happiness,
Our love is gently shown
In a tender loving caress.

A call from you so far away
Means the world to me,
I hear the warmth of your voice
And I smile so happily.

We're told to smile
And the world smiles with you,
Thoughts of our magic
And I smile too.

Karen Sri Kartomi

A SHELL

Peace is in a shell
when you hold it up
to hear a swell of
Love within.

God's eye
murmurs

I am, I am,
I am.

Tricia Hart

games

why does she lie to me always
 is it because she fears reactions
  or honesty
   which may reveal her as being human
    and therefore vulnerable to pain

her eyes give away her deceit
 and i see
  but she does not know truth
   so is unaware that i could verbalize
    the games she plays

even when i make up stories
 she agrees they are so
  not wanting to appear forgetful
   people thinking
    ''perhaps she is getting old''

yet this total untruth
 exposes her
  to all that which is
   and will forever be
    because we are
     after all the games
      what we are

Laura Lee Ames

NYPL

Feline patience guards marble halls
 Fixtures seething with wisdom.

Your people were a strange convoy
 of madmen, nomads parading
 through the streets and in the end
 passing unfiltered through your doors.

Patience and Fortitude, your names
 are well given.

To deal with insidious plots
 and endless conspiracy

To work and perhaps hold your sanity

To lax and learn the wrath
 of your figureheads

To serve, to live, but in the end
 work and die.

So the circle spins and spins
 until dizziness finally creeps in.

Angel Pagan, Jr.

A LOVE ODDITY: FOR
HARRIETTE E. KOHLMAN

Lost and Lust are by definition
two unlike things
Yet they exist in Nature
Siamese in their needs and wants
Each fills the empty soul
like a cup filled with zestful life
The drink: Sweet nectar from
her matted loins.

Deep ambrosia clouds the mind
dulls the senses.

Love is exclusively human
Rising above the primordial night.

No, we will not lose again
living alone, life a certain doubt.

Groans, moans
Sex becomes a cinema event
Choreographed and limited by the twins
Taste and Style.

I will not falter.

We are imprisoned by the drives
of the jungle.

Angel Pagan, Jr.

KEEP IN LINE

Unfinished meals rot with appeal,
In an amusement park house.
Trails full of trash linger like hash,
Smoked only seconds before.

Dark-colored nails drip on the snails,
Under a carpet of thorns.
Pipes full of oil puncture the soil,
That forms inside of a brain.

Kids go to homes and get bruised bones,
Because they can't comprehend.
Parents on trial bring out a file,
To prove they are innocent.

Ray Walker

ANIMALS

Tortured and abused,
Homeless or confused,
We all are beings,
In this world of a zoo.

Hungry and alone,
Poor or on a throne,
We all have feelings,
Stay true and let them show.

Marching for a cause,
Or walking down a street,
Driving to the market,
Or getting beaten with rubber whips,
One thing is true no matter what,
It is sad when your friends have to die.

Ray Walker

The name is Valerie.
But I guess it does not matter now;
It isn't really important.
I have felt and tasted of you,
Succumbed to the joy of your presence,
And drowned myself in your eyes.
I have caught the whisperings
Of your voice
And breathed the ecstasy of
A moment.
But all this is locked in my heart,
And will live on forever.
Times of recollection will bring
The tenderness of your eyes,
And the gentleness of your touch.
The smile upon my lips will be
A fond memory.
And this is what really matters,
Isn't it?
That I should remember what you are?
But even so,
I think I shall always remember your name,
Even if you forget mine.

Valerie M. Deen

ANGER

I came to the shore to cast my cares o'er the sea.
But, found the waters were angry and roared at me.
Donned in a drab and dark drape of gloom,
It dispatched its course with destruction and doom.
Small crafts were lashed and brutally battered.
Bit by bit, their broken pieces were scattered.
A wild pack of jaguars, baring jagged jaws,
Jeopardized the jetties as they pounced the shores.
Debris, the swells swallowed, cluttered the coast.
The hazy horizon became a giant gray ghost.
Above, a dragon flashed its flaming breath.
Whipped its tail and sent gulls to their death.
A message unraveled, as I witnessed this behavior,
Forgive us our debtors — vengeance belongs to our Savior.

Norma K. Shea

MY DEAREST GODDESS OF LOVE

Dedicated to my darling mother,
Mary Elizabeth Peck Terry,
Born 3-10-1892, Died 9-1-76

How could I not love and adore you — my sweet Goddess
of Love? — silken hair — gentle voice — discerning
caring eyes — sweet perfume of love surrounded your
whole body. I lay at nighttide talking about my
problems on your tender arm — you, too, shared with me
your inner dreams and sorrows, sublime — I cherish all
our memories — special sacred moments — Dearest Goddess
of Love — Oh, gracious, special, tender Mother of Mine!

Mary Marjorie Terry Dubach

THE DREAM

I dreamed I met a young girl the other day.
    She asked me to take her hurt away.
I asked her why the hurt was there
    But she just looked at me through a misty stare.

In her eyes I saw a secret shame,
Experiences buried and frozen in pain,
A little girl caught between father and mother
Obeying one but angering the other,
Of love just beyond her reach,
The lonely echoes of a windswept beach.

When she finished she turned to me
    And asked me to explain reality.
I asked her to come the following day
    But she just smiled and ran away.

When I woke I thought I heard
    A little girl's voice echoing each word.
In the mirror I saw the face of a stranger
    The manifestation of rage and anger.
And then I knew and screamed to see
    That the reality of that dream was me.

Mary E. Dyson

NIGHT TRAIN

Far off in the distance I can hear a tiny sound;
Almost like a whisper, it's so slight;
The sound becomes a hum, a thumping, rumbling roar;
A shrill and piercing whistle splits the night.

Off and on the whistle shrieks,
Discordant moan and beep;
Through little towns where people lie
In warm beds fast asleep.

The roaring thunder hurtles on —
On up the valley wide;
Deafening echoes rock the air,
Re-echoing side to side.

The whistle screams, it blares and toots;
The crashing blasts compete;
Iron on iron the wheels grind
Their clacking rhythmic beat.

Then the roar drops to a hum,
Growing fainter down the track;
The howling of the whistle fades —
The sound comes trailing back.

I hear the lonely wail of the whistle on the wind;
Like a soul that has been lost along the way;
It whispers to my spirit as the dying whistle fades,
Growing faint and fainter still, and far away . . .

Delphine LeDoux

COME WITH ME

One night as I lay dreaming, the Master took my hand;
I went with Him on a journey into sweet Bethlehem.

He said, "Come with Me to the manger; see My humble bed.
A King am I, but I chose to be the Servant of all instead."

We walked the roads of Galilee . . . I saw the blind and lame;
I saw Him heal them one by one, and they praised His holy name.

Then He said, "Come with Me to the Garden . . . there I was betrayed.
For thirty pieces of silver a trade for My life was made."

I saw Him carry that heavy cross along the narrow path.
I saw Him stumble and slowly fall . . . I saw His bleeding back.

Then He said, "Come with Me to Golgotha; let Me show you the tree
Where I suffered, bled and died . . . died to set you free."

I saw Him close His eyes and die; the sky grew black with gloom —
Then I saw them gently place Him in the borrowed tomb.

Then He said, "Come with Me to the empty tomb . . . see the stone
  rolled away.
Death and sin were defeated . . . Victory I won that day!"

I saw the clouds receive Him up to Paradise again.
I saw Him gently smile at me — my Saviour, Lord and Friend.

Then He said, "Come with Me to my heavenly home; I've prepared
  a mansion for thee.
The table is set and ready . . . come now and sup with me."

Then I awoke and knew for sure that all my dream was true;
My glorious mansion is waiting . . . is one waiting there for you?

Joann Benfield

HEAVEN IN YOUR EYES

I can see my heaven in your eyes,
Such a beautiful love, in your eyes,
I wish those beautiful eyes could see,
How very deeply you are loved by me.

But I'm far too shy to tell you so
And full of fear that you might say no.
So I'll try to write what lips can't say
With hope in my heart, about that day

You finally read the words I write
That will make my feelings come out right.
And on that day I will try to win
The heaven that I know I saw in

Your eyes.

Allan Davis, Jr.

I TRIED

I tried to write a love song
But I could not find the words
And anything that I could write
I bet you've already heard.

So I tried to paint a picture
Of the things you mean to me
But when the colors mixed in with my tears
It was a sorry sight to see.

If a picture paints a thousand words
And a poem says as much,
Why can't I tell the way I feel
Every time we touch?

I tried to show you how I feel
And I tried to read the signs,
I tried so hard to be with you
And I tried to make you mine.

Allan Davis, Jr.

Why all your hurt
For I also hurt
In many ways more
Than can be told
For it's hidden
Deep within. For
In you I see
Myself in a memory
A painful memory of
Being left and taken
From me a part of
Me that can never
Be replaced. In your
Eyes I feel the hurt
And see that part of me
Which long ago was taken
From me so cruelly

James R. Hayes

Alone without being lonely
Apart from the others yet there
Floating along a lazy river
Seeing nature in her purest forms
Waiting only a second yet years
For no limit or unit of time
In the vast regions of the mind

James R. Hayes

SNOWMAN

The snow sifts through our rising thoughts
And falls about the streets of cities
To be mixed with shapes of concrete buildings
And our footprints

There is a snowman
Fighting off the sun
He knows the meaning
Of the lines of water
He came a winter's eve
And fears the Saturday warmth

He laughed with the crowds
But the laughter was
More intricate
Than joy or oblivion
It was a noise of passing
With grace
To end a brown puddle
That ruins inner soles

Rithia McGlaun

ENIGMA

Like the sheen of crystal autumn
Like her change in style of hair
Her moods in shifting patterns
And the dresses that she wears

A puzzle rimmed with riddles
A mystery enclosed
Within her eyes, enigma hid
For is she thorn or rose

Her petals' nectar brimming sweet
A desert bloom at dawn
Her fragrance soft in velvet waves
In ripples when she's gone

I've forgot the prickle's hurting
And the pain I felt inside
But can't forget the flowers blooming
Flowing with the tide

M. Dwight Hurst

THE PARROTS

Distant birds in blues and greens
Pastel parrots, still-life scenes
Feathered heads together free
In some exotic jungle tree

My gift to you, would it were more
To cause your spirit free to soar
For chains to bind could never you
Your dreams unfettered, dancing new

Yet knowing I must stay below
My spirit longing, feet so slow
Perhaps in yet another time
Our hearts as one will wing in rhyme

M. Dwight Hurst

KNOWING HER

She's hard to know
But the learning's worth the cost
She teases with her loving
When she melts the morning frost

She touches me
As no one has before
And I am drawn concentrically
To beg her love once more

As slowly she reveals
Her hidden self to me
I revel in the knowledge gained
That she could really be

She's sultry, happy, moody, sad
A rainbowed soul in hue
A bit like flint but soft as silk
In pink and aqua blue

M. Dwight Hurst

PRINTED PORTRAIT

A shadow hovers and lingers,
Feather-light on the rim of my consciousness,
Its edges so gently merged
From imagination into reality
That I cannot discern
Its beginnings or ending.
And, as my pen journeys
Through thoughts without inhibition
(As with an old friend),
I see before me, not a picture
Neatly framed upon a printed page,
But a human warmth that reaches out,
Somehow alive, even in its stillness.

Nancy N. Sipos

SHE LOOKED LIKE AN ANGEL

She looked like an angel
Dimpled cheeks, lots of black hair
Skin so soft, hands so dainty
We loved her as she lay there.

I held her in my arms,
Happier than ever before
She lay quietly with her charm
And I loved her more and more

My thoughts went to Job 1:21
"The Lord gave and the Lord hath taken away."
Very vividly the verse came to me
God revealed His will the next day.

He called her home to be with Him
To wait for us in that lovely place
Little angels are needed in Heaven
Good-bye, till we meet face to face.

Rowena Bragdon Holt

ROWENA F. HOLT. Pen Names: Rowena Bragdon Holt, Robert Endicott Bragdon; Born: Merom, Indiana; Married: Louise J. Holt; Occupation: Homemaker; Memberships: Community Concert Association; Awards: Golden Poet Award, 1987; Honorable Mention, 1987; Poetry: 'First Winter on Charlotte Rd.,' *Best New Poets of 1986;* Nine poems, *American Poetry Showcase,* 1985; Six poems, *Masterpieces of Modern Verse;* '50 Years of Love,' 'Bells Will Ring,' anniversary poems, *Hearts on Fire: A Treasury of Poems on Love, Vol. III;* Comments: *Nature, religion and love are the themes I usually write about. Through the years I've enjoyed reading poetry of others and now I'm writing and hoping my poetry might give joy or comfort to others.*

GREEN GRAPES

. . . Into the crackle of fire
that played along the horizon shift
of cloud-like shape . . .
the air was alive with squawks and squeals
and the water moved across in swells
of constant sparkle —
and boy, that was one superb green grape.

So blinded was I about matters of light
along with other viewers,
that just for argument's sake,
and far beyond me, of what I now know to be
the spectrum incarnate — I could not help,
in flamboyant array; I could not help popping
this tender and cool, wet green grape.

Well, there upon the scrap-pile heap
the butterfly's slash in one clean cry
leaves only a steely wake,
and the planet gropes to claim its note,
and here I sit with the lady bright
watching the smoke bend away from a distant stack
and we break off from the vine two more green grapes.

Tom McGirl

RESCUE FROM TUMULT

A wave of fear has covered the land,
has crashed on the shore and covered the sand.
The voice of confusion cries out for control
hands reach for the vessel, eyes watch the seas roll.
The command of the tide is far beyond man,
he stands in derision, on his own, cannot stand.
A shout from above sends the lightning and rain,
it floods near the hills and over terrain.
A river comes forth from heaven above,
from out of the throne, freely spills out in love.
An ensign of peace, not created by man,
has come forth from the stream, that no wall shall withstand.
A power from heaven has reached out to earth,
to draw in the waves and give us new birth.
We can't stand alone on this ocean of life
in a world of confusion, death, fear and strife.
The ships that we build with our imagination will sink,
as man, by his own imagination does think —
that this life is his and by his own human skills,
has mastered the earth with all of its ills.
There is One who is greater than earth, land and sea
This God in control is "*I am,*" that's He!
A rock for the anchor to keep us secure,
in life we can rest as His peace does endure.

Lois Krafsky Smith

THE COQUETTE

Pondered pensively the poet-proser composing stanzas of
     prose-quatrains of poetry
  Betimes it all is exactly as so it but merely seems . . .
Of life-love-romance-realities
  Of pretense-mockeries-deceits-delusions-treasons become the jaded
     fading dreams
As pondered a soul alone of wisdom-virtues-dignity-integrity and pride
  Being beset of loneliness in mankind's Big Wilds (large cities) of
     the 20th century
The modernites concrete neon wilderness

Strolling leisurely along the boulevards around town . . .
     seen across the street . . .
  A lovely young lady in a beautiful lavender gown
Twinkling as a star agleam . . . full the moon in the Heavens High
     and its silvery light
  did shine . . . as I decided that the lovely lady in the lavender
     gown . . .
Would one day be mine

Modestly — I was sure I could woo and win her in but time and a
     little while . . . but
  Alas alas the Loner — the Loser (me) that was not to be
As sophisticated-suave fine friendly fool had wooed and won her . . .
     so I say . . .
  And say again miserably — O Fate O Destiny what fool could have loved
     her more . . . or . . .
More better than me — what fool could have loved her more-or-more
     better than me

So soft and waving her hair and so demure-enticing her beguiling smile

Yet — as she was departing smiling . . . she softly spoke to me . . .
  O Loner O Loser remember (as coquettes are known and wont to do)
     that . . .
When the rhubarb blooms again in Bella Vista Heights, Arkansas . . .
     perhaps . . .
  I shall return to you

Yohauen Austerlitz

FAITH

I have learned through experience
I must have trust, love and faith
To help me through this agony of defeat
To lose a son, I loved so much
A part of me, whom I have brought fought
Through childhood, teen-ager and adulthood
Suddenly, he is gone through illness
I see him now and by evening he is gone
The sadness and grief, cannot be replaced
With words of kindness and sympathy
It is like a limb, broken off me and not
Being able to be replaced
I look up to heaven and speak to my God
Asking and praying for guidance
My trust in God, who made the choice
To relieve my son of his agony and frustration
God loves him, He gave me my son
For such a short time and took him back
I am trying to rejoice his happiness
Relieving him of his sadness and loneliness
Believing, Faith, Trust and Love of God
Have helped me through this crucial time

Mitsue Kubojiri-Mahi

PLAYING THE GAME

I watched the boy as he played,
I did not know his name.
He did not win but a loser was not
Because he played the game.

Why is the winner so important?
Why should he have all the fame?
If the loser had not played his part
There would never have been a game.

Don't fret when you don't come in first.
Here's a fact you will always find;
For someone to be ahead,
Someone must be behind.

So remember the guy behind you
Though you may not know his name.
He may be small or six feet tall,
But he's in there playing the game.

Marie Jenkins

WHY?

When we were born into this world,
It was not of our own will.
Maybe we were a product of a perfect love,
Or maybe a slip of passion's thrill.

Then as we came, so shall we go
Into that ''Great Unknown,''
If we have acquired great riches
Or if we have nothing of our own.

We hope. We pray, a week, a month, a year,
Because it seems he doesn't hear.
Then our hearts break, as our hopes flee.
But as it is, so must it be.

We weep until we can weep no more
And we stare with eyes so dry,
Our souls then fill with dormant anger
As we wonder: ''Who calls the shots and why?''

Marie Jenkins

UNTITLED

Broken is the heart
Forgetful is the mind
Torn is the world
For others yet to find
Though buried face
Reveals such measures
Endowed is the love
Which yields much treasures.

David A. Mills

THE PROPHET

caught in a curious rapture
  where truth vitiates
all previous confidence
this man known to few
finds himself chosen
  a man of God
filled with the sorrow
only the righteous may know

it is a sorrow for life
traduced by sin

even still for him
  the Prophet
there is joy
a joy for the service
to Almighty God
Creator of all virtue

destined to this service
his beating heart is pacified
despite fears of the gloom
a sinful crowd might proffer
in not glorifying the prophecy
but stilling the word
  of God
with the sword's edge

Thomas Kennedy

HOLLYHOCKS

Hollyhocks bloom at mid-age of the year.
When winter's cold has gone,
their roots enlarge earth's form
processing strength for plant
to burst out from the soil.
When spring's fresh winds command
and slanting sunbeams woo,
the rapid child-like growth
hides underneath its stem
small buds that very soon
will evidence themselves
in adolescent time.
When heaven's straightened rays
pour forth increasing heat
and summer's thunderclouds
bring down the needed rain,
blossoms then erupt,
not simultaneously,
but as our children spaced,
that in his time each child
might have sufficient note.
Then Mothers Earth and Plant
are fully satisfied.

Marjorie Glasgow Smithson

CRUEL WORDS

Words that should be spoken,
kept within,
yield festered mind,
perverted will,
and sickish soul;
and it may mean
eternal loss to one —
or more.

Marjorie Glasgow Smithson

ETERNAL SPEECH

Speak not of skies
and earth
and seas;
these
are obvious.

Speak not of courts
and kings
and priests;
these
are oblivious.

Speak of His hour
on Cross,
our Savior,
He
is marvelous!

Marjorie Glasgow Smithson

REMEMBERING BRODIED HERNDON

Our Poet

We see him walking still
Down beaches of the streams
He loved and weaving verse
With dipping gulls and dreams . . .

The waves still toss their foam
More gently where he stepped
For herons, winds and tide
His memory has kept . . .

Here through the summer days
He bore his net aloft
In search of butterflies
Or some rare winging thought . . .

We hear his laughter still
Where waves and winds have leapt
And search for signs of him
On sands his thoughts have swept . . .

''The loved we do not lose —''
He told us once in talk
And now we know it's true
As down his beach we walk.

Agnes H. Ware

TO THOSE IN PAIN

Pain reared its head, twisted, and stabbed me like a knife;
Then, slowly and unmercifully, robbed all my joy for life.
Even stronger, unrelenting, pain tore on to its goal;
It won battle o'er my body and now headed for my soul.

Pain filled my cup with anger, then tried to drown me in despair.
As life went on all around me, pain still held me in its snare.
Though friends and family stood nearby and tender love was shown,
Pain's unceasing rude reality was a trip I took alone.

Pain kept stabbing, robbing, stealing — till I had no more
     to give;
Then plunged greedy hands through my sore heart and took my will
     to live.
Exhausted. Defeated. I knew I couldn't face another day;
I felt God's presence near me, but was just too drained to pray.

Then I felt His hand enfold mine and His strength ran through
     my veins;
He said, ''My child, just lean on Me, I know your every pain.
I'll walk with you and fill your cup with joy from up above;
Give me your broken heart and let Me fill it with My love.''

God didn't promise painless days before He calls us home,
But he said He'd comfort us and we'd never walk alone.
So, when I feel discouraged and I'm just too weak to stand
I'll bend my knees and lift my eyes and take the Master's hand.

Jacquie Rodgers

ANOTHER MACHINE

Dreaming of glories to be won and victories to be gained,
The invincible human machines of war pushed over
Shallow streams, war-scarred mountains and
Lifeless bodies, grotesquely sprawled over
Silent plains.

Powerful in resolve and strategy, the robots of war,
Humans conditioned to inflicting death without
Conscience, descended into the abyss of horror beyond.

Shouts of attack and confidence jellied into shrieks
And defeat. Bigger and more numerous machines of war
Fulfilled their own dreams of glories to be won
And victories to be gained.

Aileen L. Myers

AILEEN LIPE MYERS. Born: Stanly County, North Carolina; Married: Dr. G. Harold Myers (minister), 7-22-47; Education: Catawba College, B.A., 1947; Occupations: Teacher, high school English, 31 years; Memberships: NCAE; Poetry: 'Brief Limelight,' 'Stitches,' *A New Day,* 1987; Comments: *Only recently have I tried poetry. I had done short stories, but could get none accepted. A book of farm parables is now being reviewed by the United Church Press (drawing morals from actual happenings).*

CAN YOU FORGIVE ME?

I loved you once, far too much.
I tried to force my love.
I showered you with loving praise,
small gifts, and cards, and such.
A limo ride, and roses too, a private room reserved.
My heart and soul in pure silk truth,
the best that you deserve.
I didn't mean to make you mad, rejecting
me, my heart.
I asked forgiveness, no reply.
Of me you'll have no part.
Every night, before I sleep,
I say a little prayer.
That somehow deep within your heart,
somehow, some way you'll care.
Enough to just forgive me, I feel my heart
will break.
I came to you to love you, I didn't come to take.
I didn't come to con you.
I didn't come to steal.
The love I once did offer was true and very real.
So on my knees, once again, I ask God above,
That you'll forgive me in your heart.
Please? You, a man of love.

Beverly Bonneau

LOVE, JOY, FAITH

Christmas is a time for sharing,
a time to give; one-to-another.
Time to share our Love, Joy, and Faith,
whether it be a word or a gratuity.
A token of Love, only comes from within,
family, friend or foe — it matters not.

Christmas is a time for Joy.
The Joy we shared in times gone by;
so shall we have in future perfect.
As you give Joy, one to another,
you shall receive tenfold . . . untold.
Though it may be a helping hand or bent ear.

Christmas is a time for Faith.
The Faith we share with one to another,
for the things past and the things unforseen.
For Faith comes from our conception or mental creations,
we can work with it for good,
or toss it aside and have emptiness.

Love, Joy, Faith.
We are nothing without it.
Christmas is a time to thank God;
for the birth of His son Jesus.
For all these things are impossible
without Love, Joy, Faith within *Him.*

     Amen.

Jessie Stinson

WHAT WOULD YOU DO?

What do you do when your greatest love turns away from you?
What do you do?
What do you do when your family shoves you aside because you
    are not like them?
What do you do?
What do you do when you are so unlike other people and you
    do not fit the mold?
What do you do when the country changes from a deep-seated pride of
    tradition to a fast-paced superficial fast-food economy?
What do you do?
What do you do when it is in in to be *Macho,* greedy, square,
    shallow, two-faced, and stone-faced?
What do you do?
What do you do when it is ''cool'' to be loveless, hard, cruel,
    and composed?
What do you do when intelligence, and emotion leave and man no
    longer is a spiritual being, but a greedily lustful, carnal mind?
What would you *do?*
What *will* you do?

Lynn Patricia Pisula

PAINTED BUNTING

Who has seen the painted bunting with its rainbow-colored wings
Close inside the swampy thicket where it perches as it sings?

While mosquitoes hum in chorus with spring peepers in the creek
Why need such a beauteous creature hide itself in shadows deep?

For the world could use its color and the music of its song
Yet we only catch brief glimpses in the murky dusk and dawn

Any seeker who would view it makes a long and tiresome search
And on more than one occasion all his efforts in the lurch

But perhaps there is a lesson in the way he hides his light
In a world that's filled with dimness, search for beauty, ban the night

Still hold your given secrets, all your talents on the shelf
Unless someone comes a-seeking keep your gifts unto yourself

As a treasure sent unbidden is a gift perhaps despised
So ne'er unveil your essence to a pair of stranger eyes

Who has seen the painted bunting in the shadows where it dwells
Or the music and the beauty hidden there inside yourself?

Kenneth A. Cyr

The agonized strait-laces of society
And the plaints of Plath
Decorate my friend's life with razor motives
Her heart in a maze
And I am terribly afraid to take one step inside

Imagine — women's hips entwined
And their warm red understanding every month
Which keeps her bi-sexual, and
            desiring it as she desires life.

Jenny Jamison

THE MIST OF LIFE

Our lives are but clouds that wander in space and feel
            but the brim of creation,
            yet bask in the brightness
            transcending the globe;
            just mergers of atoms
            that drew but a mist of
endless arrays, unique to the heavens and all;
            the thin veil of breath that
            twirls with the storm and lights
            with the coming of stars
            to question the purpose
            of being and life;
the pliable mass that lingers in darkness
            and waits to transform
            through the coldness of light
            and the thunder of hands
collecting the price from the start of the breath.

Antonia Zapata

SOMETHING GOOD AND MINE

If I carry this calmness within my heart, then it must be
because I am a part of something wild, humble, strong, and free.
That tells me quietly and boldly that salvation through my
judgment is right for me.
Others seek it and want it, but they just don't have the key.
This trip is mine, and my path is wide and long, yet it
still guides me.
Envy me, if you must, if I accomplish my worldly goals; for
that is really all my future holds.

Joel C. Jefferson

TROPIC NIGHT

The glaring sun has crept away to take his daily rest
The wilting heat is dying — now comes the time that's best

No more the sun draws forth your life in beads of energy
The fire is slowly blown away by rising ocean breeze

The crickets in some arbor home are tuning up their song
As brown erratic bats embark to sail the whole night long

The moon with Oriental face smiles down from above
While katydids are trilling forth their eager song of love

Exotic everbearing blooms spread perfume on the wind
The smell of distant cooking fires — it's tropic night again

Amazing little creatures sally forth into the dark
Were you to see them in the light they'd give you quite a start

Grotesquely molded beetles and geckoes upside down
Go marching through the shadows when humans aren't around

Giant water beetles bump against the merest light
Vast hordes of moths on powder wings are swarming through the night

But sometimes things aren't so serene, the gusty monsoons come
And torrent rain and raging wind upon the thatched roofs drum

Yet when the storm has swept away, the pale moon shows her face
Though sometimes hiding shyly behind veils of soft cloud lace

And then the air is cool and clean and everything seems new
As sparkling raindrops linger — waiting morning's rendezvous

Kenneth A. Cyr

A WEDDING PRAYER

Together forever
  Is so much to say
Yet we'll say it and do it
  Beginning today

Two separate people
  Who join now as one
Pledging our love
  Before Father and Son

As you take my hand
  I will help you along
Dry all your tears
  And join in your song

With a title of friendship
  And love as the theme
I will help write your story
  You will help build my dream

May the love that we're feeling
  Grow again and again
And tomorrow reward us
  I love you, Amen.

Samuel M. Myers

THE FOREST OF DREAMS

Walking through the forest of dreams
Knowing life's not what it seems
It's a fool's game to be played
The winding road is a masquerade

Don't fall down the hole that's made
Everyone knows it's a big charade
Keep up your guard, don't fight back
You'll always lose on the twisted track

When in need, draw your bow
If you're sure, shoot your arrow
Keep your pistol at your side
Let your instinct be your guide

The different figures tease your eyes
From anyplace the Demons will rise
Defeat them all and you will win
But when you sleep another game will begin

Irene A. Peto

MY GOAL

A poet laureate?
Not me.
A Maya Angelou I'll never be.
But through this gift
of expression God has given me,
it is my goal
to touch a lost,
confused or troubled soul.

Dorothy Hemphill Edwards

EARTHBOUND

Without a chime at a special time
  Before an early dawn
The world so still in a midnight chill
  As night gives way to morn

His sound is heard, the song of a bird
  As he greets a bright new day
The message he sends to all his friends
  It's time to be up and away

Sweet, Soaring Bird, flying so high
  Take me with you across the sky

I see him ascend and I pretend
  I'm with him on his flight
I try to see the things he sees
  But he's gone from out of my sight

I want to be free, as free as he
  But I'm left here on the ground
While he flaps his wings and sings and sings
  As he travels the world around

Sweet Soaring Bird, flying so high
  Take me with you to the heaven in the sky

Judith LuBow

QUARTER NOTES

Damp root roused,
Twisting its crawl.
Blossoms quiver . . .
Pollinating sprawl.

Sun burns proud,
Great boulders broil.
Basking snakes slither . . .
Liquids steam and boil.

Dark wool clouds
Blanket to lull.
Flowers wither.
Resplendent leaves fall.

Deep white shroud
Stings numb the soil.
Tender seeds shiver . . .
Gnawing worms recoil.

Ian Russell Ayres

IAN RUSSELL AYRES.   Comments: *I live in thought.*

THE MIRROR AND "I"

The never-changing "I" inside,
Feels the same now as it did then,
Always there, deep within.
I stand facing the looking glass
Blindly staring eye to eye,
Reflections from the mirror
Embrace the "I" inside.
A memory takes the place
Of the lighted empty space
Between the mirror and I
Seeing a little girl there
For a moment, am not old.
Blinking, breaking the stare,
I am aware of fingers
Reaching a jar of color
To cover the surface
Suddenly greeting me there,
Between the mirror and "I."

Lynda B. Barnett

DIVULSION OF THREE

He stained It.
Now he came to take
the very thing he stained,
like taking the chair from the table
or the hutch memories are stored on.
In its place
he left only a void,
and in return
nothing was received
but stainless memories.

A closer look
would show how hard, how brittle,
the surface had become.
Like the hutch memories are stored on,
It was frayed.
One could get splinters
from the rough edges.

Oh, what hope
he would see this
and not take It,
but word had been given
that he could,
so now he removed
the very thing
he stained, It.

Lynda B. Barnett

STEF

And when you came that
Sunday afternoon,
I could see the feelings
written across your face,
eyes; a space . . .
A space that a dancer
Leaves to the audience who
Remembers —
        how to dance

T. D. Hamrah

GRANDFATHER MOUNTAIN

Grandfather Mountain his shoulders stooped 'neath Carolina skies
Cries with tears of purest dew, the mournful wind's his sigh
He's sat there lo these ages long with cloud beard white as snow
While driving rain and chilling frost have aged his countenance so

And yet he sits and does his job of holding up the sky
While days and years, centuries and eons all pass by
His cracked and wrinkled granite face grows thinner with the years
As sunlight, wind and tempest assault his eyes and ears

And yet he sits, and still he sits, and occupies his place
So man may marvel at his nerve and wonder at his face
He's just an old worn mountainpeak, I seem to hear you say
He's lost the vigor of his youth, he's seen his better days

And yet he sits, and still he sits, though elderly and pale
He sits there persevering all attacks and mean travail
What good is he, you might retort, a mountain old and gray
A thousand grander summits have long since washed away

A thousand lofty mountaincrests eroded down to sand
Who needs this weathered mountain, too old to proudly stand
And yet he sits and decorates the Carolina soil
And reminisces of his youth, the centuries of toil

— And he'll be sitting there e'ermore you've long since
    passed away
Reminding all that hearty youth is one day old and gray

Kenneth A. Cyr

THE TWO SURVIVORS OF FLIGHT 255

They boarded the flight in such happy delight,
As they chatted and greeted each other;
Flight 255 was ready to fly, as they longed for
Their loved-ones at Phoenix Sky Harbor.

But the flight was cut short in the craziest sort
Of a way that challenged the mind to unfold
Logic and reason for such disposition
Of burnt metal and bodies . . . a sight to behold!

There were cries and explosions, mixed with prayers and emotions,
While the firefighters risked their own lives;
Now the smoldering life of Flight 255
Was another statistic in Aircraft Archives.

It was gone like a sigh; but, wait . . . there's a cry!
A survivor in the midst of such spectacle?
So a search was begun with doubts even among
Those who believed in a miracle.

They raked and they clawed through rubble and sod,
Till they found one live being . . . in the arms of another,
A child suffering pains 'neath her mom's charred remains;
Two survivors they found, *Cecilia* and the *love of a mother.*

Bob Robles

LET THE BELLS RING AGAIN AMERICA!

Once it loudly pealed
to proclaim liberty throughout the land
it tolled the death knell for the colonies
to herald the birth of a nation grand.

*Through sacrificial deaths came victory
a glorious resurrection set men free!*

Now it lies silent
reposing in the old State House hallway,
since it tolled for Chief Justice Marshall,
*hallow was the 50th year that day!

*Did it forsee the civil strife ahead
and mourn for those who were of noble mind?
Does it await to hear their likes again,
Godfearing men who gladly served mankind?*

Let the Bells ring again, America!
Liberty waves its '87 torch
to celebrate its Centennial year
proclaiming liberty, freedom for all!

*You must hallow the fiftieth year by proclaimin'
liberty to all the inhabitants of the land!*

    Leviticus 25:10

Joseph H. Avellone

GOD'S SANDY BEACHES

When I walk not alone, but with you,
My Life slips past as the sand sifts to the sea.
I look to Heaven and see God's temple of blue,
And the brightness of it nearly blinds me.
I wonder if we'll walk the beaches of that temple,
Hand in hand, heart to heart.
Will life beyond be that simple?
The look of love lingers, and I see we could never part.
For when our bodies lie cold and still,
Our souls will race as do the balmy breezes.
Forever knowing it is God's precious will,
For true loves to walk his *sandy beaches.*

JoAnn Crittenden

THE SOUND OF GLENN

He was born in Iowa in 1904,
It was destiny that he became a musician galore,
An arranger, a trombonist and a leader of a band,
His hits swept the jukeboxes of the land,
Moonlight Serenade was his theme song,
With such beauty he could not go wrong,
Little Brown Jug, In The Mood and *A String of Pearls,*
Were equally popular with the boys and girls,
In December 1944, Major Glenn Miller boarded a plane,
Never to be heard from again,
But the sound of Glenn Miller has become a legend,
And we can be thankful that the sound of his music
Has not come to an end.

Brad Lee

A NEW YEAR'S PRAYER

May this year be filled with contentment,
  Sowing many seeds of love.
Giving ourselves with joy,
  And blessings will come from above.

May this year be victorious,
  Standing faithful for right.
Bearing one another's burdens,
  Helping others to see God's light.

May this year be growth in knowledge,
  Of God's word each day.
Our thoughts be for others,
  As we kneel to pray.

May this year be a daily understanding,
  Of God without inward strife.
Each one looking to Jesus,
  For we have accepted eternal life.

Charlene Carpenter Acker

THE FALL SEASON
IN EAST TEXAS

The flowering dogwood trees are full
  of bright, red berries.
The bluebirds are finding a delicious
  meal that looks like cherries.

There are sumac bushes along the
  fence rows.
They are the first leaves to turn
  red as we know.

The quails are disturbed while
  eating seeds.
A hunter's dog is creeping through
  the weeds.

This season of the year has a
  crispness in the air.
When the wind carries the clouds
  away and the day is fair.

The fall season is a great time
  of the year.
To be thankful for all our blessings
  for Thanksgiving is near.

Charlene Carpenter Acker

SEND-OFF

Throwing seeds into the creek
ripped from weeds easily, casually
starting over
down and beyond shady groves

If only, (I could)
I would shrink myself
down
ride a seed until it docked
at fertile valleys we're both
seeking

Carol Exton

SUNSETS

A beautiful sunset in all its glory
  Is truly a wonder to behold.
It's like a fascinating tale
  With its embellishments to unfold.

We savor its every phase
  Hoping it will leave us never;
And we are sad when it sinks
  Beyond our sight forever.

A sunset is truly the Creator's masterpiece.
  It brings us into His realm
And convinces us, without a doubt,
  That He is the Captain at the helm.

Alice Ekern Sulzdorf

A GOOD FRIEND

A good friend
  is a most valuable treasure
One we don't constantly
  have to measure.
They know when
  they are sorely needed
And they don't
  turn away when they aren't heeded.

A good friend
  seldom displays jealousy.
They know that
  loyalty isn't just a fallacy.
They want the
  very best for you,
A characteristic
  possessed by very few.

A good friend
  is extremely hard to find,
For there has to be
  similarities of the mind.
Once you've found this treasure,
  never let it go.
This is a cardinal rule
  we all should know.

Alice Ekern Sulzdorf

CONSTRUCTION OR
DESTRUCTION?

As the ball of fire fades toward the west
I stand in quiet, as nature's guest
The city lights, the city sounds
Man has destroyed nature's grounds
We hope one day to bring it back
Try somehow to stop our attack
The soft pink sky, as sundown falls
Takes eyes away from man's bare walls

Jodi Lee Ramseth

COME WITH ME

Come, my love, come walk with me
Walk where mountains meet the sea.
  Follow the trail
  of the deer and the fox
  Palmprints of possum,
  pigeons in flocks.

Come, my love, come listen with me
Listen to nature in harmony,
  Follow the song
  of the lark and the thrush
  Hawk in the sky,
  quail in the brush.

Come, my love, come stay with me
Stay on my mountain beside the sea.
  Follow me now
  to the highest peak
  And there in my arms
  find the love you seek.

Barbara S. Weppener

LIFE'S LEGACY

I opened my eyes on a winter's day
  and there in Mother's arms I lay.
She rocked me with the rhythmed rain
  and lulled me with an old refrain
Of fairy tales and lullabies
  and angels watching from the skies.

I blinked my eyes on a winter's day
  and in my arms *my* girl-child lay.
I rocked her slowly to and fro
  and crooned those words of long ago
Of fairy tales and lullabies
  and angels watching from the skies.

I closed my eyes on a winter's day
  and in *her* arms *her* baby lay.
She rocked her gently on her breast
  and whispered stories *she'd* loved best
Of fairy tales and lullabies
  and angels watching from the skies.

I shut my eyes this winter's day
  and as I rock alone I pray
That fairytales and lullabies
  and angels watching from the skies
Will still be heard when I am gone
  and part of me will thus love on.

Barbara S. Weppener

I cry out —
  but no one hears . . .
they don't know that the globe I throw
is not a ball for play —
  but rather my fragile world.
Fragments cascade
  over the dying ground as the sun bursts . . .
and yet,
  I look unto the one who destroyed my world
  and see only my own hand.

Veronica Birmingham

YET ANOTHER SPRING

The tree had but one leaf
When the spring met it at last
And sprayed it with its sorrowful dew
And one rose sprang, and then two

And all that was anguish seemed to pass
Children played, elders stared
Lovers with a grin and a blush robbed
Yet another rose and yet another sprang

Not so painful to the unsuspecting leaves
Who thought that Fall wouldn't come
But came with such a shock
As if Summer was not vast

Yet to the prescient tree who knew well in advance
That Spring had not come to last
Had suffered all the while
When it was coming, when it came,
While it was there and when it left
And all the while it would pray
Yet another Spring and yet another came

As children stared in disbelief
Through the windows of their dreams
Lovers parted, elders died
Yet another Spring and yet another at last.

Percie Blue

SOMEONE HELP ME . . .

Someone help me . . . I've lost my way.
I walked this street just yesterday.
When I got tired I sat on a step, alone
A policeman came and took me home.
But he took me to a place that is not my own.
Somehow I am missing something that has slipped on by.
Not so long ago but now . . .
No one seems to hear my cry.
And strangers whom I do not know
Stop and smile at me. They take my arm
And try to make me feel
That what's around me is quite real.
I try to accept what they offer me
But I long for those arms that comforted me
And somehow kept me from the cold.
Now young ones tell me I'm getting old.
Dear God somehow again I've lost my way
And I was home just yesterday.

Elinor Shurtleff Churchill

AUTUMN SONNET

*Written September, 1985, in Liberty Park, Salt Lake City
as I looked at all the beauty of sky, clouds, trees.*

Wooded hill — lush greenery! Yonder trees of beauty —
Sweet symmetry — a bit of gold — a touch of red —
Autumn is here — Sky, Cloud, Earth and Tree are wed —
Who can look on this fair scene — and not become calm —?
God-like serene? He touches us to make a king or queen
of all these — His bounties you and I survey. Could we
ever create, you and I, such a glorious autumn day?
Oh, magnificent autumn day!

Mary Marjorie Terry Dubach

RHAPSODY ON WORDS

Comfort me with words.
Inebriate me with them.
Words are my life.

Words are immortal.
David and Solomon
speak to us out of the past,
singing of man's ancient wisdom,
and wrongs;
Sappho, Alcaeus, Horace, Catullus,
speak to us with divine songs.

Where do they come from, words? How was silence first broken?
By what incredible powers have Dante, Shakespeare, and Milton spoken?
Words are music, love, law.
They are our transfiguration and our strife.
Comfort me, inebriate me with words.
Words are my life.

All my days and my nights I have labored with words,
waiting for something illusive
to pour out like rain.
Words have brought me excitement,
exultation, and pain.
Admit me into the company of singers,
and fill me with the glory of words.
Speak to me, write to me, sing to me with words.
Words are my life.

Beverly Boyd

GOOD MORNING

Good morning, world, how are you today
another day your wonders to survey
Good morning, children, hope you find your way
Good morning, sun, hope the rain is done
I wake to the sound of migrating geese
All the wonders of nature, will they ever cease
The glory of the Lord came down
and now appears in leaves so red and brown
They transform the landscape of town
and the countryside shows nature's lovely gown
another season is here, another time to cope
as the colors appear they give us blessed hope
we know our lives can change like the seasons do
there always is time to start our life anew
to add more color, as nature's vivid hue

Hazel Carestia

THE PAPAL VISIT

Two hundred fifty thousand strong they came,
To see the Pope.
Eight hours and more they waited by Lake Ponchartrain,
To see the Pope.
They stood the heat, the storm, the rain,
To see the Pope.
And when he came, with awe and love,
They stood and cheered,
This man from Rome these people so revered.
Rain ceased, the wind then pushed the sun,
Behind a cloud, to cool the crowd,
When *John Paul* spoke.
No greater love could any other man evoke, it's true,
Than *John Paul Two.*

Beverly G. Ales

95

SOCRATES

In memory of my dog, Socrates

He sat alone, so very still
Beside the trail, on the side of the hill.
Why had he stopped — what did he see?
Why had he walked away from me?
As he raised his head to the freshening air
And autumn breezes roughed his hair
I ran to him with arms spread wide
And pressed him close against my side.
I lay my head against his ear
To catch the sounds that he could hear.
I tried to see in the valley below
What was the spell that held him so.
Was it a dream of another place?
Is that what put the smile on his face?

Then — a smell in the wind, a distant sound
And he left my side in one great bound.
Antlered deer trailing crimson oak
Latent memories awoke.
Nose to the ground and flag-high tail
A spirit freed streaked down the trail.
Sound of the hunt — the chase was on.
Before I knew it, he was gone.

I let him go, 'twas just a game.
He'd come back to me — if I called his name.

Barbara S. Weppener

FATE

How fragile is a life
Cradled in time.
Breathe softly e'er you step.
Be it coin paid for that bought,
Be it alms given for that sought,
Be it ear lent to wisdom taught,
Fate will respect naught.

Joseph Frankel

OLDER MAN IN REVERIE

How shall I deal with you?
What will appeal to you?
Shall I be abstruse,
A bit foggy,
With a nebulous cast to my eye?
Should I be simplistic,
A bit naive,
With the ingenious gaze of a virgin shy?
How can I relate to the inner you?
How can the antennae of our minds attune?
Listen to me for I am Truth.
I am Faust and you are Youth.
Given back the years, my audacity,
I would teach you my love's ferocity.
Oh — my dreams!
I gather my desires in this way
To sweeten the ever-lonely day.
And in this, the marathon of time,
I listen, always, for your step.

Joseph Frankel

THE DOGWOOD

I stood and viewed a Dogwood flower
On the limb of a springly tree
My somber mind on thoughts of love
The Dogwood made me see

I saw a Cross, and skin so bare
Writhing in pain for you and I
Broken hearts, and distant stares
The Father's son, returns to the sky

Four petals on this flower
All white and streaked with brown
In the middle of each one
I spotted this tiny crown
Gently falling like rain
Shining like a pearl
Came the bitter teardrop
Falling on the flower.

Eula G. Cochran

O' QUIET WATERS

O' quiet waters on a bed of time,
Drift with me, other places find.
Barren, silent tree standing tall and free,
Stand with me in the silence to see.
Cool, brisk breeze playing through the trees,
Speaks a message to me from thee.
Radiant sun glistening through the silence,
Warmth I feel, with you an alliance.
Sands of time, upon you I stand.
What secrets do you hold from this man?
As a stone within quiet waters,
I, too, find starters.

Henry Bingham, Jr.

LOVE BLUESETTA

10th Anniversary

when she lost his ring
she knew he'd be mad
and never speak to her again
but of course . . . he didn't

and when she got drunk
and embarrassed him in front of his parents
she was sure he'd hit her
but of course . . . he didn't

then when he found out she'd had an affair
with his best friend
she knew he'd leave her
but of course . . . he didn't

his love was her strength
and she knew she had let him down
that was all right though
she'd make it up to him
when he came home from Vietnam
but of course . . .

R. David Howell

FOR ANNA

As I pass my time thinking
Of these feelings so true
My thoughts and dreams crowded
With visions of you
I find myself anxious
To hold you so near
I will always be with you
Of that, never fear
For, I will love you forever
If given the time
Content with the knowledge
That you're by my side . . .
I can tell you this now
Though you've known from the start
These things I have said here
Come straight from the heart
How has all this happened
Since two years gone by?
My dreams have come true
I dare not ask why . . .
You're the one I have hoped for
To love and to care
The one who I hope for
These feelings to share . . .

Shawn P. Madison

UNITY

Was not expecting anything
a friend pointed the way
across the darkened streets
to where life was dancing
in the light

Recognition in the shadows
the closing of a circle
which became an illusion
as the unity cracked
and the pieces fell

The rain came
and washed the pieces away
leaving only memories
empty as a bottle in the street
abandoned

Momentary conjunction
orbits intersect
the planets continue to wander
across the void
continue to wonder

Silence of years
louder than words
turning to thunder
between souls
sharing the sky

Chris Young

PERSONAL VIEW

I rode a train across the Great Northwest this year,
Vacationing.
The scenery unfolded before my eyes bears
Reckoning.
The beauty of this nation is unbounded.
I saw the pristine elegance of the timeless mountains,
Surrounded by great cities' ever-changing skyline,
Lakes and rivers resplendent in their brilliance,
Venturing ever into the verdant grandeur of the woods.
As I gaze upon this grace, this charm, this beauty,
Unadorned, I say,
This is good! *God* is here!
I'm glad I came this way.

Beverly G. Ales

BEVERLY GLORIA ALES. Born: Laplace, Louisiana; Married: Dr. Warren Vincent Ales; Education: High school, Business school; Occupations: Artist, Homemaker, Student of children's literature; Memberships: President, Metairie Art Guild; Board member, New Orleans Art Association; President, Le Petit Art Guild; Poetry: 'Untitled,' 'Joan,' 'Different Strokes,' 'The Papal Visit,' 'Personal View,' *American Poetry Anthology, 1987;* Comments: *Generally I like to write contemporary humor; then there are times when I am inspired to write more serious poetry. I have been painting professionally for over twenty years and was director of my own gallery in New Orleans. Now I have decided to give my all to poetry and short stories.*

CHRIS

I met him the summer of nineteen and eighty;
Beside the pool when swimming in my bikini;
That was the summer I became alive again;
And, I fell in love with him;
Our romance lasted throughout the year;
And ran through the spring of 1982;
Then, in the summer of 1982;
He fell in love with me, too.

But he didn't know my love for him was deep;
And he drifted away from me, away like sleep;
Then, I saw him again, in the beginning of the spring;
When the buds were on the trees;
And the butterflies chased each other in the breeze;
He told me he loved me, yes, he told me in the wintertime;
The wintertime of eighty-three;
Then, I decided to make him mine.

He wanted us to marry; that was in December;
I said, ''Yes, I will,'' and set the day;
My wish for love was happy, so;
I let him taste my love, and he would not let me go;
Not a tear did I cry;
Then why should I;
Because this was happiness;
And I thanked God for giving me Chris.

Laurie Anne Mach

SHOULD LIFE BECOME AS BLACK AS NIGHT

Should life become as black as night,
Your presence, like a sunrise, shall shine a
New light to see in the darkness, deep
As a bottomless, unscalable pit.
Orange rays warm the pitch of chilliness of
Shadowy night, when poem flowers shut,
Animals must sleep, to shield from callous
Cold, omnipotently evil, night's great curse.
Radiance of your golden eyes cover
Damp night smoothly, soaking up dark drops of
Dew, wetness left by pre-dawn's cruelty, its
Touch reshaping the clean earth, bright and warm.
  When life enters the cellar called night,
  Dawn can break the wretched trap with her light.

Robbie Bignell

A FRIEND LIKE YOU

You've been a piece of my life
That has been there through the happiness and sadness.
You know some of my darkest secrets,
You've learned my weaknesses and strengths.
Most of all you know the genuine Julie.

When I had my pneumonia,
You showed me concern and called to see how I was doing.
When I was unbalanced emotionally over a certain person,
You would give me advice and get me back to reality.

Throughout the years our friendship has grown,
That's because we didn't let it die.
You've given me support by just talking to me and being there.
And who can forget all the laughing fits we've had together,
Which caused us to have hiccups and teary eyes.

Lynn, you are a friend who is hard to find,
I'm grateful I met you four years ago.
Even if someday we have to go our separate ways,
In spirit and in our memories we'd still be together.
A friend like you makes life a little easier,
And makes the phone bills a little higher.

Julie Lachman

The penetrating cold
              outside
        does not
            pierce
            so deeply
    (nor chill so thoroughly)
    as the
        corners
            of your voice
    when you
          speak
          to me
          from the turret
        of your self-imposed
          walled castle
    on the other side of town.

Trish Kaspar

MOVING DAY

I am moving deep inside myself today.
Since here in this horrible, always
put-down place, I must stay.

I am always trying to do the best I can.
But on my feet I cannot stand.

So here I am trapped, in this place.
The future I am to face.

Digging up old bones, is a no-fun game.
Some like to play it just the same.

Growing old is not so bad.
Wanting to be young, is what makes it sad.

Looking back into the past. Reliving a life that
could not last.

Before me — perhaps it is best, pretending
I do not exist, or ever did.
Maybe that is the test.

Anyway I am tired. So I am moving deep inside
myself today.
Here I believe I can stay.

Inside myself I am free.
Just to be *me*.

Vel Randolph

VELMA LOIS RANDOLPH. Pen Name: Vel
Randolph; Born: Roswell, New Mexico, 2-16-30;
Married: Troy Dawn Randolph, Sr., 7-10-48;
Education: Roswell High School, 1947; two years
of business college; Memberships: YWCA,
Easter Seals, Vice President, Lubbock Stroke
Club; Poetry: 'Sean the Seagull,' 1985; ''North to
Alaska,'' short story in rhyme, 1987; Comments:
*In 1974 I was confined to a wheelchair, due to an
airplane crash. I write about places I've been, na-
ture and feelings. I illustrate my short poetry
stories because I've always liked to draw. Now I
have time.*

THE FRAGILE EDGE

Grey lines of crimson thunder clouds
Rise thickly over the fragile edge
Of the harsh orange horizon as the wind
Shears the final lights from the empty fields;

Damp silhouettes of purple haze,
Tense masses of rhythmic shadows
Vault across the sharply sutured spaces
Shattered by diaphanous silences.

Hugo Walter

NAVIGATION

Alone wayward cloudship
Drift voyage blue main.
Somewhere this wide trip
Will strive homeward wane.

Broad sail at adventure
Or chanty heard bell
Sing heroes venture
Let song wisdom tell.

Down fathomed rainfall
Deeper than dream
Which poets recall
Rainbows are steam.

Hear thunder ahoy pour
On crops below there
Anchored by fence more
Strict waves unbare.

Orien Todd

WHAT DO I OWE?

''What do I owe,'' my child may ask,
  ''To you who've given me birth?
For all the years of love and care,
  How can I count its worth?''

''You do not pay in kind, my dear,
  To those who've done for you,
But spend a life of service for
  The souls God gives to you.''

''What do I owe,'' my child may ask,
  ''To you who've given me birth?''
''A life that's wholly yielded to Christ
  Will amply pay its worth.''

Ruby Gray Young

LIFE, LIBERTY, AND THE
PURSUIT OF HAPPINESS

The men wear wigs,
  with trousers too.
Wear fine tweed coats,
  with imported silk shirts.

Each has a personality of his own,
  some are happy and gay,
    others are sad and grey.

In each hand is a black ink quill,
  with which they sign their own names.

The huge white paper with a bunch of words,
  was which they personally signed.
Soon it became a new beginning
  of the U S of A.

It is called the Declaration —
  the Declaration of Independence.

Tracy Cervenka

NOW MR. CAT

The wind and the rain.
I climb the stairs.
The dreams have all
been sorted out and
tied up in bundles and
put in their cubby holes.
Time for bed. But first
one last cigarette. The
smoke goes up and
drifts away. Now
Mr. Cat shall we get
into bed and shall we
lie together in the
dark and listen to
the wind and rain.

Mark Arvilla

LITTLE CHINA BABE

Little China babe,
Well-boned face,
Exemplary of your race . . .

You are a branch,
To a limb,
To a trunk of a tree
Deeply rooted in the good earth.
Let your leaves shimmer
As you grow tall;
Then the world will know
The wind is passing through.

August in Alabama,
The month of your birth;
The myrtle tree is blooming,
Flower pones hang loosely,
Rose and pink and white,
Old-fashioned like;
A beautiful sight.
In celebration of your hour;
I claim them
As your birthday flower.

Jesus, sweetest name, special of births,
Peace and love crest the surf;
Seek him, in your trek on earth,
And quest for life eternal.

Jessie Butler Jones

TWO BUTTERFLIES

Once I saw two butterflies
Floating in a verdant glade
With sunlight bright upon them
And every leaf and blade.
Soon, each one found a flower
To sip the nectar sweet;
Then would flutter here and there
Before they chanced to meet.
Twirling like a shiny top,
Winged lovers danced with blissful grace,
As I stood sadly by the trees
O'er which they rose without a trace.

Frederick S. Crafts

SUCCESS

Are you prepared for the trials that confront you;
Or are you one who dallies,
While others are giving their all,
To make their dreams come true?

My advice is to take
The trail that few have tried.
The climb may be steep;
But the rewards are great.

Elbert R. Moses Jr.

DR. ELBERT RAYMOND MOSES, JR. Born: New Concord, Ohio; Muskingum County, 3-08; Married: Mary Miller Sterrett, 9-21-33 (deceased 9-9-84); Caroline Mae Entenman, 6-19-85; Education: University of Pittsburgh, A.B., 1932; University of Michigan, M.Sc., 1934; University of Michigan, Ph.D., 1936; Occupation: Professor and retired LTC in Army Signal Corps; Memberships: American Speech and Hearing Association; Phi Delta Kappa; Life member, Association of Former Intelligence Officers; Board of Governors, American Biographical Research Association; Awards: Prose, Joseph Posik Award, Veterans' Voices, for "An Adventure Given by the Army," 1982; First Place in first World Institute of Achievement Literary Competition for essay entitled "Good Communication," 12-85; Poetry: 'Make Us Pilgrims of the Cross,' *American Poetry Anthology, Vol. 7, No. 2,* 12-87; 'Life,' *Poetry of Life: A Treasury of Moments, Vol. I,* 3-88; Other Writings: *A Guide to Effective Speaking,* book, 1956; *Phonetics, History and Interpretation,* book, 1964; *Three Attributes of God,* book, 1983; Comments: *My basic reason for writing is to uplift humanity. Listed in* The Writers' Directory for 1984-86 and forthcoming one. Comments on writing: Good expression-life philosophy; good use of language.

DERIVED FROM NATURE

Evidence shows the world is mystic,
Unfurled with beauty in the skies,
The glory of day, portions of hours
Like kind all in the sun.
There is the tending moon,
As a prophet of storms, orbs of the night,
The dispenser of dew,
Bringing a dream of twilight and music.
How well pictures of the heavens,
Ornament the earth.
Guides for sailors who compass the stars,
Moonbeams of love rendering a verse.
Opposed reverses in the air,
Bearing forbidden fruit,
Implications of the waters, dryness of breath,
In place is a tuneful respiration.
It is scrawled in the winds,
That which has borne and yet must bear.
The changing of the mighty hurricane
Hither and thither of shifts renew.
When the engager of plants,
Fettered on this universe,
Meets the frost numbing our feet,
Astronomically from the coldness to recoil again.

Rose Mary Gallo

DECREE OF THE RAIN

Sorrow's tears betray not the slumbering eyes of
brother's and sister's cries — need not the thunder strike
twice the heart that would be love's friend to the
end for somewhere in the dominion of love needs be to
mortals more than friends.
Shining brightly though silent in dismay sometimes
for some to see brotherhood awaits each in call
to heart in many and varied away, steadfast with
arrow-like lightning the haunted plea does stay
ever near beyond the unseen view until
mortals' needs find the heart of you and guide
anew to the seeking good deeds to do
somewhere in undone deeds the dominion
of love has brothers' needs written in the
decree of the rain.
Decree of the rain love's own call finding brothers'
in spirit is but one with all where tears among
brokenness shine unspoken in sufferings as even
the mighty fall to tie the heart to the all-time
call of brotherhood for such heart's tears call
all and the dominion of love a holy fall its
lightning speed tells some to see, what to
be in the decree of the rain.

Patricia Ann Grossie

You are unchanged by time —
  For what season can diminish light that emanates
    the tender Heart of God?
You are as dear to me this morning as on every morning past;
  The mirrors of reminiscence radiate
  The fervid passage through our many years, and we are bound,
  Not be coercion,
  But by the communion of our lives.
Respectful of our differences,
  Yet we are one in our diversity;
  Embracing separate triumphs as shared accomplishments of all.
I am the child of your influence and the student of your wisdom;
  The happy beneficiary of your goodness and your grace.
But though the years seem shorter and too precious moments
    lost in haste —
  I long to hold the flowers in my heart again . . .
    and capture in a photograph
  The magnitude of yesterdays,
  Resplendent in the virtues of your sweet bouquet of gifts.
You are the guardians of faith, and this faith survives the tumult;
  By this nurtured strength of spirit
  You have led me on the quest for everlasting joy, and when in heaven
  I shall come at last
  To know the Heart of God,
There shall I find these gentle faces
  In the reflection of His own
  Forevermore.
    . . . I love you, Mom and Dad!

Christine A. Pitt

SCREAMING EAGLES 101 AIRBORN

To those who died
While keeping peace.
We honor you,
Each and every one!

We will not forget you,
Or what you have done!
We will miss you,
But we will *never*
Forget what you worked for!

You represent us
And our hopes.
Someday soon,
We hope and pray,
Peace will come
To the entire world!
When this day arrives,
For I believe it will,
We will remember and praise you
For all you did to bring
This wonderful change to us all!

Evonne R. Mohring

SPECULATION BY P. J.

As I sat upon a reef
And gazed out at the angry sea,
A sea gull landed at my feet,
To rest.
I listened to the angry sea,
As the wild wind whipped it to a creamy froth.
I put out my hand to touch,
The sea gull at my feet
And I speculated.
Why had the angry wind and the angry sea,
Brought this creature of God to me
And laid it at my feet?
The gull responded to my touch
And our eyes met.
For one fleeting moment we communicated,
He spread his wings and flew away.
The wind died down,
The sea calmed,
Infinity was mine.

P. J. Dick

XIPE TOTEC

In the spirit of one
Known to some
As Xipe Totec
Of Nahuatl legend
And tradition
From notoriety
Of those yet remembered
I herewith accept my fate
In all due humility
And respect
Because you all want me so
This is the way I must go
In this way I am
To you my people
Your fearless, shameless
And sacred sacrifice.

V. Fourwinds

GOD WILL PROVIDE

It amazes me, as I look back.
  How far I've come along the track,
    of life.

Feast your eyes on your surroundings,
  And see the Grace of God, abounding,
    amidst your strife.

The world is cruel and full of sin,
  And beckons with its clamoring din,
    you've failed.

But praise Almighty God on High
  We have a covenant in the sky,
    He has prevailed.

So, no matter what your circumstance seems,
  Never give up on your precious dreams,
    God will provide!

Billie Gourley

BURNING THE MIDNIGHT OIL

Powerful in words written
With drawn pen
I burn the midnight oil again
Wishing made known
The truth I see
Instilling in hearts the flame
To care and arise
To something beyond all
The enemy can offer
When all the tricks
Are exposed
To spark the dying ember
Into a prairie fire
Driven by the whirlwind
For which I am sown
Because for the tree
To arise
It is written the seed
Must die
And I do this myself
A remnant of the sun
So that brothers you may
Live
As libertines of honour
Like an age ago.

V. Fourwinds

EMPTY CHAIR

Day after Day — I look for you there.
But, all I can see is an empty chair.
Your face, I cannot see, for memories
are all I have for me.
I know you are gone
I know not where.
But memories, I still have you
  in that empty chair.
Someday, I hope to see you
just somewhere,
and leave behind me,
  that empty chair.

Mary A. Wagner

VEXATION/SALVATION

''You can't go home!''
The devils say
They must be lying
In their nature's way
Deceptive spirits
That they are
I don't believe them
So I might yet be blessed
For I don't love
A single lie that's made
Truly though it may be
Of my own making
Whether or not I know
In this I yet find hope
And consolation.

V. Fourwinds

VICTOR DISMAS FOURWINDS. Born: Lebo, Kansas, 1948; Education: Vocational Certificate, Native Culture, Alberta, Canada, 1979; Occupations: Artist, Gardener; Memberships: Alberta Metis Association, National Rifle Association, Roman Catholic Church; Awards: $25 for poem published in *New Breed* magazine, 1985; Poetry: 'Native Brotherhood,' *New Breed,* 1985; Comments: *Most of my writing carries a message which is prophetic in nature and morally honest to a fault — sometimes brutally so. At times I feel this sadistic drive to make the reader hurt — using the truth as a two-edged sword.*

SALLY IN A CANOE

You up front
Back to me
Oracle, siren, child.
Strongly stroked
Over the infinite lake
Toward the eternal horizon.
You said,
  ''I won't let myself get close.''
With the same determination
You used to pull toward forever.
Being there,
I had to follow,
To listen,
For your wind voice words
Speaking separate destinations.
As we pulled away,
Pulled together.

James Wolfe

Wasteful, worthless
Shambles of mind; what terror defines
The trek of your soul?
What morbid condition; reacts of contrition;
To juggle and tumble and wriggle and fall?
The truth of the knowing is running away . . .
Hidden in secret
With no place to stay . . .
The fact that I'm empty and filled with despair . . .
The madness that covers it all.

Christine A. Pitt

BEST NEW POETS OF 1987

America is lifting Hope's Lantern . . . brushed of sun . . .
  (God's messenger-seer's Own Psalm: John Paul II had come!)
    In robes of peace white flowing
      Staffed with Christ's pure glowing . . .

Among Worlds' best new poets: His Holiness brings Light . . .
  And Truth: small peoples faithful, best poets are who write.
His arms bestow the masses, his lips divine Earth's prayers.
  Nor storm, nor heat erases His Kingdom's holy heirs!

A glow beyond all seeming . . . dwelt long in hearts of men:
  In workers' hands preparing, in writers moved their pen!
If Eighty-Seven wrote one (. . . best poets' songs in Man) —
  'Twas surely by God's Own Son . . . as Dawn lit Pope Paul's clan.

Some waited long in raindrops who knew of Mankind's pain.
  The Popemobile in stopping, it stirred forgiven Cain.
Our shining new of poets went crowding up that Knoll,
  Some touched the Hems of God and penned Man's candled soul.

If through the mists of Mem'ry . . . down all the years to come . . .
  We would but seek such Coming and wear God's Crown of Sun!
What glow beyond all seeming . . . would touch us all again . . .
  Yes, Eighty-Seven wrote one: Christ's new songs in Man!

Val Rogers

THE ADDICT

He was a boy turned Man
reality unfaceable

and then, *that crutch*

Life's beauty can be seen
still unreachable

oh, that *crutch*

Visions, Visions
coming closer, reaching
still untouchable

clutch, *that crutch*

World, his world,
spinning, turning
reality coming close, closer
almost faceable

away, *that crutch*

Now, his body, reeking, fearing, shivering, screaming
reality uncontrollable

Oh, *that crutch*

Roslyn D. Smith

DREAMS PAST AND FUTURE

It is cold and dreary as I sit, dreaming of that which
has gone before, and that which is yet to come.

The future assumes no reality, and though it hurts to
live in the past I prefer it so.

Now I am beautiful; in my prime;
Laughing, crying, hoping; and still the future comes.

I sit and dream, dreams of my lost loves, my found love —

And the: — The Pain!

And now I sit, sit forever in my chair on wheels; dreaming —
of a darkness, which never comes.

Roslyn D. Smith

A SONNET

I'm writing in rhythm to challenge my brain;
It's dying from stagnant disuse.
The words on my paper are coming too slow;
The strain shows apparent abuse.

If I were a student of science or math,
If I were a teacher of art,
I'm sure that my efforts would not be in vain . . .
Ideas would flow free from the start.

But since I have wandered in fields far from ''home,''
And since I've neglected my ''trade,''
I'm destined to suffer from bouts of despair
And sleep in the bed I have made.

My story is over; my tale has been told.
'Tis time to get back to my talents of old.

Mary C. Mc Dyer

ME

A book my life could be, with chapters very long;
some sad and unrewarding, some happy, filled with song.
How I wish my life had been an easier one than this,
but would I have realized so much, could even reminisce?
Supposed I'd never married, or had a family?
I would have missed so many things which were absolutely free.
No, I guess I would not change it in any other way,
for if I did, I might have lost a very precious day.
Now as my life gets shorter, there are things I can recall,
that made it all more beautiful than anyone's at all.
We seek things that are difficult to do or even find,
if only we'd be satisfied in body, soul and mind,
with every day and what it brings to each of us, you see;
then life might be a time of lovely mystery.
No, I don't think I will change a thing, because in any case —
God knows what he is doing with all the human race.
He put us here to work and play, to be what we might be,
with proper wisdom, useful lives and great humanity.
My book of life is closing, the ending all too near,
but if I've left someone happiness, there's nothing I will fear.

Jeri A. Wilson

THE SANCTITY OF LIFE

"Let the children come to me, and do not hinder them; for to such belongs the kingdom of heaven."
— Matthew 19:14

Impassioned words of Christ
Resound from centuries
Ago when He rebuked all those
Who did not understand
That children were concerns
Of God — and their neglect
By callousness brought reprimands
To stanch their apathy.

The sacred family life
Which builds society
Is dying, spawning human ills
Of monumental size.

Our current way to solve
Neglect through agencies
Is not a substitute for home
Where parents guide their young
Responsibly in ways
That Christ, through love, has taught,
Till they become God's instruments
Which further truth and right.

E. Ruth van Appledorn

VILLANELLE

Their trust and faith in God sustained
The wearied Pilgrims, long at sea,
  And law through Compact was attained.

With democratic ways acclaimed
The body politic felt free,
  Their trust and faith in God sustained.

By firm resolve and strength regained
They bested new adversity,
  And law through Compact was attained.

That winter they were not detained
In founding Plymouth Colony,
  Their trust and faith in God sustained.

With tribal help and knowledge gained
They furthered their agronomy,
  And law through Compact was attained.

A celebration was proclaimed
For thanks and geniality,
  Their trust and faith in God sustained
  And law through Compact was attained.

E. Ruth van Appledorn

LOVE

Strolled alone through a fallout zone
and I am calling one last time
just cannot face myself alone
but not saying to change your mind
'tis good to see your smiling face
all above the mists of sorrow
your heart so beautiful of lace
for the times we had to borrow
strangers now but lovers at night
and love is here and now to bring
memories of unlawful fights
with happiness of joy to ring
our love cannot tear apart
now it is just a start.

Lisa S. Eland

THE BEACON OF YOUR LOVE

The beacon of your love
steadied me
someone close was so far
but the beacon of your love
guided me
'neath your wing
my cares were not echoes
for someone shared in my pain
the beacon of your love
so warmed me
to the coldness
that so surrounded me
gently caressing
so aware of the fragile shell
that nestled me
so touched I've been
for the kindness you've shared
so portrays
the beacon of your love

Vinicia Martinez

SPOOKIE

Spookie, my cat
  is charcoal black.

She gazes at me
  I gaze back.

Topaz eyes — opened wide
  Paws curled in
  side by side.

She twitches her tail
  forth and back

Then bows her head —
  'tis time to nap.

Valerie Cummings

CONSTANT CHILL

There is snow all around us,
There is ice in the trees,
And the wind is blowing,
Feel the cold, cold breeze.

My world seems so hard,
I really don't understand,
Can someone please tell me,
Am I a boy or a man?

Although I can see,
I often feel blind,
I'm always searching for something,
That something I'll never find.

Cold, unclear thoughts,
Not doing what I was taught,
Just doing what I thought
Was the right thing.

Is there someone who knows?
Knows how I feel?
Is there someone who can teach me?
Teach me what is real?

Is there more to my life?
More than I feel?
Is there a way to defrost?
Defrost a constant chill?

Dan Davis

THE WAY OF LOVE

Depend on me
I'll hold you tight
cradle you in my arms
when you cry in the night.
Touch your smooth skin
stroke your soft hair.
I'll care for you.
I'll always be there.
When I grow tired
we'll not play.
You never fuss or interfere
by night or day.
Shining glass eyes
that do not see
you are a toy,
alive only to me.
I am so angry
that I box your ears
because you do not listen
when I have fears.
Lord, show me a better way
of love when there is life
to share, care, give, and trust
with a child, man, or wife.

Pamela B. Harris

hermans

wide-mouthed jars sat
fat
with candy — colors matching clashing a neverending
diffusion of hues and tones blending — blurring my vision —
inside my cheeks droplets of anticipation
multiplied messages sent to my brain

two please i told herman the pennies i extended wet
with sweat
two please and hurry i thought or i would die
he made me wait smacking his lips — silently i screamed
dont dont please dont —
give them to me
cant you see i am in agony

he laughed and dropped the sweet delicious treasures
into my outstretched hand he seemed far away
behind the counter — so big and tall
and me so small but i didnt care the candy was mine

i ran outside and did not hear the tinkle of the bell
on the door it was just me and my treats so good
in my mouth as they bumped against my teeth my tongue
such fun — then they were gone — i turned and heard the bell
tell herman i was there where wide-mouthed jars sat
fat
with candy and i had — oh wonder — two pennies more

Laura Lee Ames

FIDDLE MAN

Fiddle man, put your fingers on the strings.
Play the Westphalia Waltz for me to dance,
So I can close my eyes and remember Daddy standing there,
Putting every foot, cripple or not, out on the dance floor.

Just like you, Daddy had a special thing with music.
When he picked up his fiddle, it was to give his heart.
He would play that fiddle for days without stopping.
There was no advertisement then, just word of mouth.

Being the musician he was, trouble was his constant companion.
I saw my mother's jealousy, she had the right.
He was her man and everyone knew that.
Daddy never told Momma, but he loved to see her dance.

He stood on the stage the same way you stand now,
With rosin on his bow his music captured every heart.
Although it was Daddy's fame that broke up his and Momma's marriage,
He loved my mother with all his heart until the day he died.

Amanda Marie Stone

WHERE ARE WE?

The meek are not weak, and the weak are not meek.
To be weak is to be cowering, capitulating, compromising,
  and conforming.

To be meek is to be controlled, channeled, curbed, chaste,
  and courageous.

None of us are either, or
But a combination we explore.

Edith Chenoweth Stribling

WHILE THE BOYS PLAY

Woman is never given credit for all
The pains of life she must endure,
From birth till she's old enough to run,
She is taught motherhood with toys,
"While the boys play"
Then she's taught cooking, dressing, and cleaning,
"While the boys play"
When she approaches her teenage years
And becomes aware of boys,
She is given rules by her parents as guide,
In what to do and what not not to do,
"While the boys play"
When marriage enters her life
And she thinks that all the pressures of life
Are behind her,
She soon finds out she's wrong,
Even the pains of childbearing are not shared,
Or the endless nights of a child's needs,
And she soon finds herself,
On a merry-go-round of life,
"While the boys play"

Alejo Rodriguez

PEACE AND REST AT LAST

On the 8th day of December, God called you home
Peace at last, no more to roam.
Fighting Viet Nam and fear of killing, many others went
But not too willing to linger there with death so chilling.
Ah! For you Christmas Eve was so hard to bear,
When you think of the blood shed over there
And for what? You say, "Is there no peace anyway?"
The River Patrol was a weary task
Up and down the river searching out the enemy as in the past
A machine gun run, taking them captive at last.
People, thought to be enemies, line the shore,
Cut down and their bloody bodies placed on the boat floor.
Trying to forget is so hard to do,
Always the haunting memories make you so blue.
Driving you, nearly losing your mind
And how people could be so unkind,
Knowing not the horror left behind.
Back in the States there was little care
'Cause this was one war no one wanted to share.
A war without cause or honor, some say,
But to the men over there it wasn't that way.
So let this lesson to Americans be,
Thankful that we're still in a land that is free.

Winifred S. McClung

DON'T BE AFRAID

Drops of Burgundy splash on the pavement,
While a broken bottle strikes a man's head.
The laundry has fallen into the drain,
As the princess of a land goes to bed.

Twirling strobe lights and antique wooden stairs,
Are seen through the glass near a pool of wine.
No one was arrested and convicted,
Because no one would say they saw the crime.

Pieces of bright colored burlap and silk,
Dry in a kitchen under a cool plate.
The cherry pie is cooked and then eaten,
As the victim's wife locks years in a crate.

Ray Walker

THE CARDINAL

God knows I love the cardinal, so
  He sends them by my way.
Just to stop outside my window, to
  Brighten up my day.
The cardinal seems to say to me,
  ''God sent me with His love,
To remind you He is looking down,
  From Heaven up above.
Forget the problems of the world,
  You're a pilgrim passing thru.
For someday Heaven will be your home,
  When He's all done with you.
But while you're living on this earth,
  Always share God's Word.
For there are people everywhere, who
  Have never, ever heard.''
Then the cardinal says, ''So long,
  I'll see you another day.
Whenever you are lonely or blue, God
  Will send me back your way.''

Susie Joyner

ONE MORE DAY WITH MOM

If I could share with Mom, just one
  more day,

There are so many things I'd do and
  so many things I'd say.

I'd pick her up, we'd go shopping, and
  even stop for lunch.

I'd tell her how I enjoyed her company,
  and loved her, oh so much.

I wouldn't say, ''I'm too busy now, I have
  a family all my own.

No, I can't come visit, but maybe we'll
  talk later on the phone.''

See, Mom is gone now, and I'm not
  busy after all.

I have lots of time to visit, if
  only she could call.

Mom is in Heaven now, and she's not
  lonely anymore.

She's visiting with the angels, and
  Jesus Christ the Lord.

If Mom could come back for just
  one day,

There's so many things I'd do, and
  so many things I'd say.

Susie Joyner

BEING JUST ME

Someone told me once that there is
  a person inside of me.
They said I have her trapped and
  she needs to be set free.

How did she get there, I wondered,
  how can I let her go?
There is no magic door to open,
  the way out I did not know.

Now I know that I am that person,
  trapped within myself.
Instead of just being me, I've tried
  to be someone else.

Somehow this person trapped inside
  is starting to appear.
I think I've found that magic door,
  it was always very near.

I've decided to accept this world,
  however it may be.
I no longer want to be someone
  else, I've decided to be just me.

Susie Joyner

APRIL IS

April brings the thirsty earth fresh showers,
April wakens the early buds of spring;
Opens ground for fields and hills of flowers,
The trees' first leaves, insects and birds to sing.

Mother Earth and her daughter, Nature, glow
In their lovers' warm tender embraces,
His kisses bring to life the fecund flow
Banishing the fears that all life faces.

April is the month of fevered romance
When virgins taste the pungent smells of lust,
When men and maids begin the mating dance,
Heeding the earth's birth pangs as all life must.

One smell above all scents is first to please,
The Mother God's sweet breath is in
  the breeze.

Joseph E. Barrett

THE BOBWHITE

On spring mornings calmly born
In dewy fields of grass and thorn,
Rings a voice so clear and bright
With vibrant phrase — ''Poor Bobwhite!''
And when wind, only, fills the nest
And summer's mood puts most to rest,
Although no singer can be found,
Bold whistles charge across the ground.

Yet, why does this bird
To us proclaim,
With loud abandon,
Its perfect name?
After all, 'tis just a quail —
Like one flower, sweet and frail.
Perhaps for love or place unknown
The Bobwhite pleads his case alone.

Frederick S. Crafts

THE LINK

My blood feels the excitement of a
creature that waits for the stretches
of night,
Longing to search the forbidden
places, it seems all too right.

This kinship that lurks inside makes
me love the earth and sea,
Yet there is a desire it cannot
fill in me.

I think of things far beyond, and
when the first was started,
Of things now, and yet to come,
and others already parted.

Of a being so full of love that I
must feel the bond,
With justice, power, and wisdom,
of these I am too fond.

Now the darkened animal roams my
soul, but the lighted spirit makes
me think,
While part of, yet no part of
two worlds, I am still their
link.

Candy Campbell

CELEBRATION

Sway, green brethren,
To the wind's rising song.
Dance, winged friends,
To nodding blooms.
Sing, feathered cousins,
To the beauty of wild places.
Run and jump, my brothers,
To freedom's call.
Swim up, fair sisters,
To the promise of light and air.
Celebrate, everyone,
But give thanks, also,
To earth, moon, sun
And all the stars.

Frederick S. Crafts

BROWN EYES

We
are the sum
of that
which is left
in a smile
or the path
of a long
lost tear
that finds
no rest
no place
to hide
a drying
badge
of self
despair

Gary C. Shukis

Black River, near Elyria, Ohio.

THOUGHT BASES

With all the fears
within me
yet lurking
close beside

There lives a touch
of greatness
that cannot
be denied

Illusions
delusions
or can it
really be

A force that cries
electrifies
and whispers
to be free

Gary C. Shukis

THE MIRROR AND MIND OF LIFE

When we call upon the eye
    The mind is in command,
The eye cast red as we cry
    Flushing a tiny grain of sand.

The eye is a mirror to capture a view
    The mind will call a name,
An object old, an object new
    Another will do the same.

Another will view from their direction
    As mind and mirror combine,
The mind and mirror are your protection
    For love, dance, and dine.

When mind and mirror separate
    There may be a wrong decision
The mind alone will translate,
    Or fall from a collision!

When the mirror of life is broken
    The mind will linger on.
When words we use to see are spoken
    The mirror of life is gone.

Ed Lewis

SHARING

I want to be able to
speak the truth,
be a success in my work,
dress the way I want and
yet share my days with you.

I want to be able to enjoy the activities I like,
adhere to my own values,
act the way I feel and
yet share my nights with you.

I want to be able to be myself,
I want you to be able to be yourself and
yet share our lives with each other.

Kathleen L. Spicher

APT TO CHANGE AND FREE TO FLY

Love
Cannot be captured:
It is free and
Alive on wings
In an undefined sky.
When it finds two hearts
One that needs the other,
Love works like magic
Waving a wand of dreams.
Love is immortal
Yet, it is not concrete.
It is much like the life
Of the little caterpillar;
Apt to change and
Free to fly.

Christine M. Goldbeck

CHRISTINE MARY GOLDBECK. Pen Name: Amber Hues; Born: Pottsville, Pennsylvania, 3-20-66; Single; Education: Completion of Writers Digest Fiction Writing Course, 1986; High school, 1984; Occupations: Freelance reporter, Poet, Social secretary; Memberships: National Writers Club, Pennsylvania Poetry Society, Schuylkill County Council for the Arts; Awards: Golden Poet Award, 1985-86; Honorable Mention for 'Loving Shores,' 1985; Honorable Mention for 'Preservations,' 1986; Poetry: 'Self Portrait,' *Impressions,* 1987; 'Loving Shores,' *Our World's Most Cherished Poems,* 1986; 'Preservations,' *World Poetry Anthology,* 1987; 'Feelings Captured,' *Best New Poets of 1986;* 'Rapture's Tears,' *Independent Review,* 1987; Comments: *Love is a universal word, an emotion known to all living beings. Through communication we express this feeling, whether it be with a smile or a tear. Writing love poetry is my means of communicating my feelings, and I enjoy sharing this with others.*

SONG OF THE STATES

Work, work, work, work,
That's the Song of the States,
Work, work, work, work,
Those are words I just hate;
And they said in the U.S.A.
Automation had won the day,
But to my horror I find and I find,
Work is still the same weary grind.
The gadgets I've tried are a countless score,
But behind them all I still have to go.
Oh, for a gadget that will work by itself,
And do all my chores while in bed I just rest.

Lulu Hazlewood

THE DRUNKARD'S DILEMMA

He was so very properly scared
For he thought his foot had spread,
And with a fright he did shout:
"Oh, Good Lord! Have I got the gout?"

But his friends roared with laughter
When they saw what he was after;
For on the foot already shod
He was trying to wear the other odd!

For a lark they put him to bed
With ice packs on his head;
Then they said; "Don't worry, Jim,
This will cure your swelling limb."

But the poor man began to groan
With imaginary pains in every bone;
So his friends with cheerful glee
Left him to recover from his drunken spree.

Lulu Hazlewood

BARGAIN DAYS

I don't know how and why it is
    But this is what I find,
I never am the shape and size
    For all the bargains advertised.

Another thing that's very strange
    And needs psychiatry,
Is why I buy the things I do
    Their uses for me are so few.

But then again the reason is
    Not so hard to find,
It's in the advertising, it has a
    Potent effect on the human mind.

So bargains come, off I go,
    Rushing to the department store,
Trying to find what isn't there
    It's very tantalizing, quite unfair.

Lulu Hazlewood

When it rains outside I wish
you were by my side to share
my thoughts and feelings — to
feel the cool breeze of the rain —
to smell the freshness the rain
brings to everything — to feel the
warmth of each other's bodies —
to hear the silent pattern of raindrops
on the cars, plants, and concrete —
to listen to the few cars come
and go — the silence the rain
brings is comforting and helps me
think — the breeze brings only a
slight chill and has me wanting
you all the more — only when it
rains the wanting and need are
stronger than ever.

Ann-Margaret Tebbe

THE FACE OF DANVILLE — EVER-CHANGING

Woodland Indians followed the river to a buffalo wallow.
Hunting buffalo was great in murky waters so shallow.
The Iroquois Nation; Piankeshaw, Kennekuk and Kickapoo
journeyed for many a moon to camp at a nearby salt lick too.
Intrepid explorers, hunters and trappers were next to arrive.
They were followed by river boatmen —
      the town would soon come alive.
Dan Beckwith surveyed the scene, decided to stay, built his town.
And as others concurred, it flourished and acquired great renown.
Abraham Lincoln and Uncle Joe Cannon both gained national fame.
Stars Helen Morgan, Gene Hackman and Dick Van Dyke also did the same.
Waves of European miners came when soft coal was discovered here.
The town's personality kept changing with each succeeding year.
Big corporations — heavy industries were the next to arrive.
The economy and population boomed and then took a dive.
Midwestern economic recession had made some people fear
that all the residents would be jobless and have nothing to cheer.
Others were trained to become management in Leadership Danville;
producing new entrepreneurs, effectively using their skill
to conquer new horizons with their talent, fresh ideas and grace.
As in the past, this adaptation required a new change of face.

Elaine Peterson

SCULPTURE CLASS

It doesn't take much to provide for a heady caper.
A base of wood, a pile of clay and lots of old newspaper.
Crush a newspaper armature in the shape of a head.
Cover with wet, kneaded clay placed on a wooden bed.
The newspaper turns into a sort of papier mâché.
Assess all of the features and reproduce them in clay.
Don't allow the marked reservations of a doubting spouse
discourage your ambitions and creative instincts douse.
Unexpected, artistic accidents can drive you wild.
They can totally frustrate and leave you completely riled.
Be persistent and on a convenient and boring day
knead and punch the air out of your flexible, molding clay.
All students are told to mold the features the way they grow.
Models' criticism may make the progress very slow.
Measure every inch of the model's head and take great care.
It's so easy to thin out the clay and make a tear.
Too soft an armature resulted in eyes that caved in.
It required five eyes to finish and wore a grin.
The mâché was removed and the extra eyes cut out.
When it finally was finished I wanted to shout.
The surprised model was handled his head on Father's Day.
The problem and demands of this hobby may turn one fey.

Elaine Peterson

PERFECTION

Graceful is every movement that flows smoothly within
A radiant appearance rare to its true form
Timing of perfection as solid as bronze
Relating intellectually that which one wishes
Physically structured around a blemish-free garden
Total self-control within one's own thoughts
Born into corruption from a destructible tower
Never to be uprooted from its mantle
Hours of pure dedication soon reveal its treasurers
Hidden amidst the unknown gems of fiber and muscle
Only one secret to each shall be obtained
The gift of perfection is to be received by many
He who has the will to achieve shall acquire his perfection
Cut flawless as a diamond is pure.

John H. Young

FIFTH HORESMAN OF THE APOCALYPSE

The first horseman surveys the field
with bloody sword held high.
He sees the ruin of his passage; his name is War.

Close at hand rides his ally, chained captives dragging behind.
Slavery enjoys the additions to his realm.

Famine roams far and wide, his torch flaring and smoking.
Starvation is his goal, but blighted crops summon his brother.

The pale white horse moves slowly on, carrying the rider
who fears none.
He brings death to thousands with a touch, and bears
the name of Pestilence.

As they crest the hill, a fifth figure is seen,
silent, gaunt, malevolent
Who bears aloft a ragged standard. This is the herald of the Horsemen.

His steel-gray mount creaks as it walks, and breathes
an acrid, odorous smoke.
Its iron feet tread crushingly on the skulls of innocents.

His iron jaw, worked in a death's-head grin, makes no sound
as he approaches the battlefield.
This is the Fifth Horseman of the Apocalypse, the herald of the rest.

His name is Technology.

Allan Davis, Jr. and Shelley Cornish

CHILDREN

How tall?
  just look at the wall.

The marks will tell,

  like a disease they spread,

  around and around,
  higher and higher,

then over your head.

Basketball stars
  practicing slam dunks,

Spatterings here and there
    of all kinds of junk.

So out with the paint,
  to brush them away

trapping their energy between thin films,

  at least for today.

A time will come when they won't come back,

  like lost hair on my head,

such a disappointing fact.

In silence,
  I'll watch the mirror and the walls for a change.

Old pictures and memories will be all that remain.

Robert J. Waldon

Home is where one is
happy. As I wander
the empty hallways,
stopping by each door,
I think of all the
memories that shall
never be. I'm going
away for an indefinite
stay. All the time I
will be thinking of
home. The world is
one big grey blur.
Shadows form into
my face and the eyes
of the dead stare back
at me from the mirror.
The tears that should carve
valleys in my face
won't come, when I think
about the warmth and
love I'll miss out on!
Visions of me will
fade with time, like rocks
which erode to dirt.
Home is where I'm happy!

Krazy Kevin

Inspirations seem
to elude me, while
the dreams of the
twisted bounce around
my head. Then I came
across a treacle for
dispelling grey clouds.
It was as green
as emeralds and
sweeter than ambrosia.
Most would try to
possess this magic,
not me. I refuse
to corrupt beauty!
If I should ever
need to partake of
its healing graces,
may it still be
readily accessible.

Krazy Kevin

NIGHT WALKING

I spoke to my father
But he did not care
I spoke to my God
But He was not there
I spoke to my son
But he did not hear
Now I speak to myself
As I sit here and stare

Gary C. Shukis

JESUS SUFFERED*

In the garden at Gethsemane,
Jesus suffered deepest sorrow;
He prayed, ''Father, let this cup pass,''
For He knew what He must do, tomorrow.

I know that Jesus wept,
For sweat like blood did fall;
The knowing that on Him,
Would lie the sins of all.

The agonizing thoughts of separation,
For One who knew no sin;
The humiliation and the dying,
The only way to save men.

Jesus humbled His body into subjection,
For He would drink this cup of pain;
Jesus was born to endure the cross,
To redeem the world through His name.

Stop and think —
What if it had been you?
Could you have suffered death —
For a world that didn't love you?

* St. Matt. 26:36-46
St. Luke 22:39-46
Hebrews 2:9-10; 5:7-9

Barbara L. Settlemyre

TAKE HOLD OF YOUR FAITH

Genesis 17:18-21

God hears our prayers
And He answers them
He shows He cares
When the outlook is grim.

When God says no
We don't understand
It may be so
He can work out His plan.

He's not willing
For us to have second best
His way is thrilling
Yet, we'd settle for less.

Knowing all along
He sees the outcome
Afraid to trust He who is strong
Our hearts grow cold and numb.

He has the power to melt
The coldest of hearts
What joy is felt!
Once submission starts.

Take hold of your faith
Realize the solution is on its way
The Lord will lift you up
When you get down to pray.

Wayne Stedham, Jr.

TIME'S DISTANCE

Winter's afternoon
against the terrace stones
where a cliff is breathing
the dim parade of ghosts

from the empty shore
love waves fallen arms
glances of the hour
burn in time's distance.

Sharon L. Rubenstein

FOOTSTEPS

Lost in distance
summer's wave goodbye
where love waits sullenly
against the dark terrace

Vagrant children
against a neighborhood
where winds have fallen
through the wall's footsteps.

Sharon L. Rubenstein

TIDE

Love breaks distance
against the fallen children
where sirens cry
in the tide's midnight

the desert moon is dreaming
of snow's thin windows
and voices of torn eyes
treading over a forest.

Sharon L. Rubenstein

SHARON LYNN RUBENSTEIN. Born: Los Angeles, California, 8-30-45; Married: John Svehla, 11-12-76; Education: Pierce College, 2 years; Occupations: Legal secretary, Word processor; Awards: Feature Poet, 'Broken Streets,' 1985, 1987; Feature Poet, 'The Poet,' 1984; Poetry: 'Summer Neighborhood,' 'Waving,' 'Echoes,' 'Lost Winds,' *Broken Streets,* 1987; 'At Shore,' *Prophetic Voices 8,* 1987; Themes: *My poetry is about love, youth, neighborhoods.*

EMBRACE FREEDOM

Don't smile and say "That wrong is right"
Don't walk away when you should stand and fight.
Bury friendships when they die. Let the heart
Cry out in pain. Weep bitter tears. Let them cleanse the soul.
Don't stain clean soft memories with unburied carrion.
Try not to resurrect that which no longer breathes of
Love and life.
Cast away that which is no longer yours.
Release, unbind, amputate that part of your heart
Which belonged to the person
Who has walked his mile with you.
Breathe deeply the sweet fresh air of freedom.
However painful it may be, it will forestall the mold,
The dust, the dead leaves, that gather around
The clinging vine that refuses to let go, until it falls
Into utter decadence.

Marie Jenkins

INEVITABLE

Power and Knowledge allied.
Together they've ruled,
Since man's first weapon and tool.
Mustering through fraudulent timestorms.
Coagulating in forces joining.
Dark knowledge. Polarizing.
Patiently awaiting in revolution,
The twilight of its sun.

Our children sleep safely. In silos.
As sleeping beauties awaiting,
Their awakening kiss of M.A.D.ness.

Ignorance, once realized, propels knowledge forward.
Bounding and chasing, with aims of replacing,
Faster and faster with computerized speed, reinterpreting reality.
An abstruse outlaw on the run,
Never escaping the world of one.

Evoking the truth of Eden;
Knowing nature as pure and good.
But only through the forbidden fruit,
Has the truth of life been understood.

Robert Sciba

CHIMERA

An omen I have had about this day,
A day when love should be all for which I care.
I fear that at day's end within your lair
I will find I have truly lost my way
And then what might occur I cannot say.
The moonlight shines through windows to compare
This night's chimera to this 'noon's affair.
My eyes like my enemy do betray.

With sunrise, I find a new state of mind.
Is this love, this confusion and this fear?
There is no turning back once you have made
The choice to leave the world you hold so dear.
New things I hope for him to help me find
Now that I am sure love will never fade.

Elizabeth Whitley Fickling

AUTUMN

No artist can on canvas portray
The fullness of the beauty of an autumn day.
The heat of summer is then gone,
And "Jack Frost" appears with the dawn.

The honking of wild geese can be heard;
To seek a warmer clime they have been stirred.
'Tis a sure sign of cold weather
When birds fly southward together.

The trees wear leaves of red and gold.
Chrysanthemums in bloom are a sight to behold!
Pumpkins are ripe on the vine.
The glory of autumn is yours and mine!

Halloween is fun for a kid;
"Trick or Treat" is a familiar bid.
Cemeteries are beautiful on "All Saint's Day,"
In memory of loved ones passed away.

The time is here for Thanksgiving.
We should express gratitude by "thanksliving"
For many blessings, both great and small,
Which our Creator bestows on all.

Kathleen Hicks

COCOONING IN THE BIG APPLE

An advertisement for Shakespearean theatre
Said, "When Shakespeare comes to New York,
All New York's a stage." Well, if that is the case,
Then many New Yorkers are suffering from stage fright.
A supermarket newspaper reports "a nationwide trend
   called *cocooning* —
Staying home where you're safe . . . "
Somehow I feel that cocooning has more to do
With the big city rather than the small town.
New York is a raw kind of place — the Big Apple,
Where a subway ride to a Broadway show or the Ringling
   Brothers Circus
Holds its own peculiar share of indignities to be faced.
New York is a hard place "to find oneself," and I experience
A Sehnsucht, a yearning for a quieter lifestyle away from
   the crowds.
Although I've been to Europe and even to Asia,
It's just much easier to stay home with the radio or the VCR.
However, since I expect never to learn to drive a car,
It is most likely that New York remains my town.

Joan Danylak

THE VIRGIN QUEEN

There never was one lovelier than you
Heart-pure immaculate as winter snow.
Each creature pales before your mantle blue;
Voiced angels chant your beauty pleased to know
It is God's Mother chosen from above,
Right owner of the "Fiat" thus to be
Grace-touched conceived by Shadowed-Spirit-Dove:
Incarnate Word, her Saviour-Son born free.
Not ever would a generation pass
Queen blessed that great things you could do by Might
Unto that Calvary, the Living Mass,
Entwined with Resurrection — Victory's flight.
Elected truly Queen of heaven and earth,
New Life begun with "yes" to Saviour's Birth.

Robert Carmen Angle

BRIGHTER DAY

Somewhere the sun is shining
Somewhere the birds are singing
Up in the heavens so blue
Somewhere the voices are singing
In the land God knows
Where never no night
And sun shines so bright
Somewhere in the heavens so blue
God watching over you

Glenna Jaeger

When walking the lonely country roads
Through the dark night of the soul
Learn to follow the stars
And the scent of those dearest blossoms
That show their faces only to the moon
And when the dawn is nigh
The night will be its darkest
Learn then to use the fires within you
To light your path
Until, at last, you knock on the gates
Of the palae of the sun
And, entering,
Become a dawn unto your own day

Barrington King

CHILD OF GOD

Child of God, Son of Man,
When will you come this way again?
Or did you stay within our hearts,
to calm our fears as love imparts?

You showed the way for us to live,
the love we feel to freely give,
to all mankind, his voice so clear;
Upon our hearts that we may hear.

So open our eyes that we may see,
the love of God, so let it be.
No thought of man can ever sway
the thought of God that's here today.

So let us join our hearts in prayer,
and God, our life, will soon be there;
To put the tortured minds to rest,
with only God, we will be blessed.

Barbara Powell DeMunbrun

HOLD ME IN YOUR HEART

Hold me in your heart forever,
With a love time can never sever;
So that no matter what may come and go,
In my heart I may always know
That you are always with me,
With a love that will always be.

Sheila Leyde

REMEMBER THE MAGIC

When dust settles on my memory
And you can no longer my face recall;
When your life is all you want it to be
And you think you are past it all;
Take time to remember for a moment
That magic that once held us spellbound.
Remember how much it once meant —
That special magical love we found.

Sheila Leyde

I HAD A VISION

God gave me a vision
A rainbow in the sky
And what He made was beautiful
And you cannot buy

He showed so much love
That I could sit and cry
He showed me my babies
As they looked up at me
In my arms they did lie

God said no one can do this
It's my miracle of life
In my mind gave me this
And I was so amazed
At the vision He gave me
I would sometimes gaze

The love of one another
That's important to God
And the vision of the cross
Is the love God gave
To accept Jesus and be saved

Mary Meadows Waller

A HOUSE FOR ME

A small house, just for me
A place where I could independent be
Somewhere, where I could see
Through my window a lilac or a tree
Maybe even a little garden
To have grown
Enough vegetables for a salad of my own

Oh yes, I am an independent cuss
Not willing to have anyone wait on me
I would not care for too much fuss
But like a tree
Live each day, happy and free

Whenever I pass a Senior Center
I shiver at the thought
That through their door
I may have to enter
No, no, no, I do not wish to go to the Center

Only let me live free
Like my big, big, tall tree

Rose Mary Gerlach

IN MY DREAMS I DANCE

Though I am but twenty-eight
And to many still quite young
The many tragic years of fate
Have taken my youth and spun

Now the years that are not many
And the list of pains still rise
Leaving me alone and empty
That fills the tears inside my eyes

If only that I had a chance
To prove to those who care
I'd show the world at a glance
And prove to those who'd dare

But that is what cannot come true
And I know I've not a chance
So when I dream, I make it count
And in my dreams I dance.

Jenny Moline

FRUSTRATED CHIHUAHUA

I lie at your feet, yours to command.
Faithful, obedient, I kiss your hand,
Bravely defend you with all my might;
Fierce as a lion, I bark and I bite.
I'd give you my life, wishing more I could give.
My whole heart is yours, else why would I live?
I'd do anything for you, anything at all,
But I have a problem: I'm but six inches tall.

Carol S. Meyer

WHISTLES IN THE HILLS

In my heart I feel today
A longing for my yesterdays,
To live again the simple life.

Zesty living, long since gone;
The air was cool and clear at dawn,
Shrill whistles echoed in the hills.

Big red thrashers sent their calls
To come to work, each one and all;
The shocks were standing golden brown.

Hayracks rumbled on the roads.
The neighbors came to fetch the loads
Of sheaves to thrashers in the lots.

Daylong toil then had begun.
My tasks would not soon be done;
I'd work all day to wait on them.

But I would surely thrill again
If I could serve God's noblemen,
And hear the whistles in the hills.

Carol S. Meyer

WORDS OF PRAISE

We set our hearts and minds to praise Our God
On bended knees with hands that gently fold.
Rich words of praise with sight and heads to nod
Declare His mighty acts with Love untold.
Sweet Precious Lord, Our Saviour, and Our Rock,

O fill our souls with grace, our very being;
Forget-us-not to ask, to seek, to knock,

Proclaim your glory, Faith to heal for seeing.
Remember not the transgressions, but praise
And love we daily pray to you, O Lord;
Incense our temples and our spirits raise
Secure in yonder Kingdom heavenward:
Eternity with Father, Spirit, Son
. . . the Undivided Trinity in One.

Robert Carmen Angle

TO MY COMPLEX HUSBAND

In the year of forty-nine and we were thirty-five,
Neal and I were in love and very much alive.
We bought our little home and united our lives.
Two strong personalities to become one we have strived.

Our Father impossible situations He does take
So our lives He continues to mold and to shape.
In due time two sons came to our family to bless
Our home with the love and joy of real success.

As our sons grew and alternatives took shape,
Through the church and camping we decided to take.
Fifteen years God's creations and man's we explored.
Our fond memories and pictures we have in store.

To our family was added two lovely daughters-in-law,
A granddaughter and grandson, to that God saw.
Now as we come to the last bend in the road;
My husband's tender loving care does lighten the load.

Edith Chenoweth Stribling

YOU I REMEMBER

You I remember as an infant just born that day.
Gordon Gray your name; sister Grace had taken me away.
There you were with mother, all cuddly and warm.
A handsome little lad our home to adorn.

You a little boy, roly-poly, and dear.
Too soon mother left us; how do we comfort and cheer?
Our loss so hard to explain; yet she was Heaven's gain.
Her family united with her will be prayers attained.

You I remember as you too your fortune came to find.
It was nice to have you around and to visit and kind.
Uncle Sam called; to the railroad station we went.
Proud, but confident, God would return you whom He sent.

You I remember as Gladys and you were wed.
When Dad needed care, "I will go" you said.
With a lovely family you have been blessed.
These are all factors of real success.

Edith Chenoweth Stribling

THE MAN BY THE SIDE OF THE TRACK

For the homeless:

The man by the side of the track.
Something keeps drawing him back!

Is it a plea for help?
Or a desire to help?

In any case, he touched my heart,
in a warm way,

and caused me to say,
to give, a friendly *hello*.

Inside, I love him so,
because, I know,

In any case, he touched my heart,
caused me to feel,

Lets me know, Love, is real.
Helping others, helps us,

to trust,

to Love!

Bearded, dirty, ragged, and yet I saw Love inside of him,
Love, reaching out, for the Love inside of me.

He, and his kind, deserve to be helped.

Margaret C. Moore

NOT MINE BUT THINE

I asked the Lord to make my life a blessing;
That those I meet could see His grace in me.
I felt a Holy Presence drawing nearer,
And thought my prayer would shortly answered be.

But it was not the answer I expected!
Instead of joy unbounded there was pain;
Instead of bliss great tempests swept my being;
Instead of smiling skies came chilling rain;
Instead of flow'r-strewn fields my path ascended;
The jagged rocks assailed my weary feet;
Instead of heaven's blue dark mists enshrouded;
Instead of balm I felt the furnace heat.

"Where art Thou, Lord?" I cried aloud in anguish.
And then I felt His Hand so strong and warm.
He said: "This is the answer to your prayer, child;
Be not afraid! Your Father rides the storm."

Oh hallowed thought! His Presence was beside me,
And through the din I heard His "Peace be Still!"
I bowed my head in humble adoration;
I knew at last the glory of His Will!

Hazel T. Lynn

WHAT OUR COUNTRY NEEDS IS NOT

A good ten-cent cigar,
Nor lower priced motor car;
Not a higher recompense,
Higher budget for defense,
More freedom of the way we live,
Less concern for that we give,
Protection for convicted thugs,
Legality for the use of drugs,
Free abortion on demand,
Free admission to our land,
More laws to guide us to perfection,
More ways to perform inspection,
More ways of punishment infliction,
More ways of personal restriction.

Any of the above someone will please,
And remove bits of others' ease.
We each need to be less dense,
And merely use our common sense.

William W. Dillinger

WHERE ARE YOU WORKING?

There are people working in our town.
Some building up. Some tearing down.
Some willing to build at others' expense.
Some wrecking for no recompense.
Some building for the good of man.
Some tearing down just the weaker span.
We need be sure that those who build
Are skillful members of the guild,
And those destroying are equally good.
Removing only that they should.

William W. Dillinger

HAUNTING MEMORIES

Why must memories from the
   past keep coming back to me?
Why do they haunt, why can't
   they just let me be?

Those ghosts from the past
   flit in and out,
Making my troubled mind
   shriek and shout!

They hide in my malingering
   subconscious,
Just waiting for a chance
   to be obnoxious.

I seek help to conquer
   these demons from the past;
I cry out in desperation for
   peace of mind that will last!

Yet, these haunts of yesterday
   keep closing in on me;
Obscuring the present
   with what used to be!

C. Dian Worley-Chambers

RECIPE

Take a thimble filled with gladness,
A bottle cap of hope,
And if you have it, little girl,
A leaf of heliotrope.

A chipped plate with some trust on it,
Some plantain stems of mirth,
A clothes pin sprayed with fairy dust —
Rain, twigs — a penny's worth.

A modicum of eagerness,
Done up in a wrinkled glove,
Add petals from a dandelion,
Pretend they're hours of love.

I knew you slightly, little girl,
Your mixtures made of stuff;
And even now that you're grown up,
They still are good enough.

Dorothy H. Elliott

AN AMBITIOUS ROBIN

I want to get a ladder
And had a great surprise,
Five robin nests all in a row
On it, before my very eyes.

The ladder hung upon a wall
Underneath the doghouse eaves
A cozy place to build a nest
So very safe from thieves.

Now did the robin start to build
And not know when to stop,
Or was she just a fussy bird
Whose nest must be tip-top?

So I can't use my ladder
Until her young have flown,
But I don't mind, because I've had
An experience few have known.

Edna Dame

THE STRUGGLE

Lord, grant me the strength
   To fortify the family,
      Through the breath of happiness!
Lord, may the love within radiate
   And cast a protecting shield,
      Lost among the darkness of Eden.
Lord, the fellowship among the kin
   Shall rejoice in somber tears
      For the unification of Your love.
Abba, the plight forthcoming, the cliffs
   Ragged — the summit overlooking
      The valley of destruction —
      Shout the triumphant blow!

Christopher C. Smith

OUT OF THE DARK

I wanted to be alone in my world
But before I could put up a fight
Into my life you were hurled
Making me see the light
I came out from the darkness
Letting you steal my heart
Yet love can never be painless
This I knew from the start
I did not want to let my mask down
But it was not up to me to decide
In your love I began to drown
And was swept away with the tide
I hope that you do not use my love
And then just throw me away
But even if my world falls from above
I am out of the darkness to stay

Erika Rick

ADIEU . . .

Set me asail, on a quiet shore,
   leading out to sea . . .
      Light a candle for the darkness,
build the raft, of pitch and reed . . .

Send the vessel out at twilight,
   do not do this in the day . . .
      For in the dawn yet coming,
my soul shall pass away . . .

Say these words, in soft whisper,
   "For, My Love, I set you free . . ."
      Then turn, and look no more,
as the light sails out to sea . . .

Set me asail, without question,
   of what I ask of thee;
      Our souls shall meet again, my love,
somewhere, in eternity . . .

L. C. Katz

BLACK-EYED SUSANS

Look at all the Susies! I love them so!
My yard is just aglow!
Brown eyes popping out of faces of gold,
Swaying in the breeze, so bold.
They grow in vast profusion
Which makes but one conclusion,
God must really love them too
For He kisses each one with the morning dew.
They, in turn, nod to Him in praise
As they follow the warm sun's rays,
Turning their heads from east to west,
Giving to Him their very best.
These myriads of brightly colored flowers
May be trying to tell us of God's great powers.

Eula H. Johnson

TO SHARON

Written on the birth of my niece

To think that we who walk the common way;
Comprised of that which makes humanity;
Who, finite, grope along from day to day,
And view, as in a dream, infinity —
  Unable now to comprehend that One
  Who from His Fingertips flung stars in place,
  And stretched a heavenly canopy of blue
  As cov'ring for this systematic maze;
  Who, reaching out His Hand, made storms be still,
  And wind and waves obeyed His Perfect Will —
Have joined with Him to bring to being you,
O miracle of love's origination!

. . . we stand with bended head.

  Hazel T. Lynn

TO ALAN

I chatted with Cupid, told him what I wanted,
He smiled, he winked, and left — nothing daunted:

A trace of orange blossom, a smidgen of lily,
A whisper of roses; oh, heigh dilly dilly.
A scent of the lilac with morning breeze mellow,
The kiss of a violet, and daffodils yellow.
Wrapped in fern fronds and sealed with the dew,
Some of the things I am sending to you.
Sprinkling of rainbow, a dusting of starshine,
A frosting of snowflakes with God-wrought design;
The peace of a woodpath, the brush of a wing,
And beautiful music to make your heart sing.
The sough of a pine tree, the song of the bees,
And acres of moonbeams right up to your knees.
With strings from my heart enwrapping this treasure,
I send you my love in fullest of measure.

  Hazel T. Lynn

WHERE ARE YOU GOING?

I can write a poem a day
And never run out of things to say
Each day promises treasures untold
Some I spend, some I hold
Some I give and some I take
Some are given and some I make
How can one say, "Is that all there is?"
Seems to me their life has no fizz
Existing in the netherworld of work and woe
Facing each dawn not above, but below
Serendipity is unconceivable
The only thing that is believable
Is more of the same
They smile on the void with a plastic grin
"That's life," they say, "the trick is to win!"
Racing in circles against the clock
"Got to keep movin'!" they're one of the flock
Scared to look back, dreading what's ahead
Reaching their destination only after they're dead

  J. Kenneth Ezzell

WHEN I WAS THREE AND TWENTY

With apology to A. E. Hausman

Way back — when I was twenty-three
I envisioned the perfect *He:*
Tall, dark, and handsome he must be —
A man of perfect pedigree
Preferably, with a Ph.D in Physics, Math, or History
A perfect build, and perfect health
And, of course, possessing, *enormous* wealth!
Neither of us would e'er be ill —
That would be far too bitter a pill.
I, in turn, was very slim,
My waist was thin and hips were trim —
The perfect Her for the perfect Him!

Now, that I am forty-five
And grateful to be well and alive,
And both my waist and hips have spread,
The sort of man I want instead:
Is one who'll tolerate my ills
And help me pay my dental bills.
A man who's thoughtful, sweet, and kind,
Who's interested in what's on my mind —
Such a man, to me, is a *real* find!

Today, in my maturity
It's easy to look back and see
The banal triviality
Of my "perfect man" — at twenty-three!

  Audrey Mae Luban

TRANSFORMATION

The sky is overcast with low, gray clouds.
Light frosting on brown grass and trees relieve
Somewhat the drabness of the winter day.
We travel westward down the winding road
And see the clouds ahead grow brighter as
They slowly part to let the sunshine through.
The sun reveals the frosting to be ice
Encasing every bush and fence and tree.
The landscape is transformed into a scene
Of sparkling beauty bathed in radiance,
Like light-reflecting diamonds everywhere.

Searching for guidance through God's Word,
Man travels Life's uncertain, winding road;
Relentlessly, each moment of each day,
It leads him westward toward Life's final hour.
And when the hour comes, he sees the clouds
Of sorrow, grief and toil lighten and part
To let Eternity's bright light shine through.
The weary traveler beholds the light
Of endless day; and hears his Saviour say,
"Well done, thou good and faithful servant. Come,
And share My joy throughout Eternity."

  Iva A. Rensink

DAY DREAMS

I like summer mornings,
  And the canyons at dusk,
On a cool desert night,
  With the smell of musk.
To see the new gold of sun,
  Or the glaring neon lights.
Bright moonlight glowing,
  On stars in the night.
A pretty mountain lake,
  In which to go swimming.
And drink cold lemonade,
  And eat with fancy trimmings.
Hear summer thunderstorms,
  And the sound of a train.
Or the strumming of banjos,
  Above the patter of the rain.
And eating cold apples,
  On the new-fallen leaves.
With frost on the windows,
  When it comes Christmas Eve.
I like the smell of perfume,
  And the light in your smile,
As I go drifting off
  In a dream for awhile.

George S. Foster

GEORGE SIDNEY FOSTER. Born: Rantoul, Kansas, 8-24-26; Education: Rantoul High School; Occupation: Maintenance engineer; Memberships: National Academy of Songwriters, Top Records Songwriters Association, Nashville Songwriters Association; Poetry: 'A Life Time,' *Moods and Mysteries,* 1986; 'Doughts,' *Midwest Poetry Review,* 1986; 'Flight Of An Eagle,' 1985; 'Friendship,' *Best New Poets of 1986;* Comments: *I love to write poetry and songs. It is the one way that will let a person feel free to go beyond reality and capture fantasies of one's imagination and to place it in print for the whole world to enjoy.*

TO THE RESCUE

I was too tired to laugh,
And I was too tired to cry;
I just kept on "trucking" when,
Lo and behold, into my life, you came by!

I didn't know then that you would be my groom
And that I would be your bride;
Life's weather includes both ups and downs,
But now at least you're by my side!

I'm not always on a pink cloud;
Today, I happen to be blue;
But Peter, I know that
My life has improved — thanks to you!

Joan Danylak

I TREAD SOFTLY ON GOLDEN LEAVES

I tread softly on golden leaves
Among the tall, majestic oaks,
A holy peace reveals to me
A second coming in the shade

Of silent murmurs' soothing chimes,
I hear a prayer slowly rise
From the moss-darkened evening glade
To meet a prayer from the sky

Falling in pale-white, red-sheathed shrouds;
The saffron wind carries the prayer
To the last showers of the clouds
And to the shrill-green veils of night.

Hugo Walter

WIND

Who, what is this elusive wind?
With power to lift and tumble men.
Could it be this is God we see?
Blowing his power through yonder tree.
Could it be? Could it be so?
That the wind is here to let us know?
That here exists an invisible force,
With power to bend and change a course.
Where is the fool who shouts, "No God!"
When the wind has blown him good and hard?
Cannot he see that he can't see
This power that blows both him and me?
That mighty roar outside the door
That when you look is there no more.
That invisible push that all men feel,
That lets you know, unseen is real.
Just like the Lord, our God, it's true.
An unseen force with power, too.
An unseen force that changes ways
And whisks away our cloudy days.
With power to touch, to warm, to lift.
To let you know that God exists.

James T. Glover

TIME

I think of memories, the gentle breeze of time that has passed me by. Not long ago, in a world past me now, I would run, sit in the sun, or just listen to an eagle cry.
My youth is almost behind me now, I feel it slowly descend. Don't leave me now, on what else can I depend?
The chains of time are bound around me, refusing to set me free. How can I help what I feel, when one look in the mirror will reveal? Youth must be in the heart and mind, even after our beauty is behind. We are still prisoners trying to break free, to a life of eternal rejuvenation that can never be.

Kelley Prosser

I dress
myself in
oblivion
and eat
up
all
the stars.
Would you
like
a
bite
or dress
yourself
for
an eternity
of nothing?
Maybe you
already
have.

Cheryl Cruz

BALLAD OF AN INTROVERT

I came across a woman, beautiful to behold,
A divine sight.
She did not speak nor smile at me — silent
As a cat waiting for her prey at night.
Love at first sight!
No harm shall come to her, while I am near.

But it is because I am shy, I am
Silent about my feelings toward her.
What shall I say to her if she comes toward me?
She is coming toward me!
She greets me with a smile,
And praises, and so much more she gives to me.

We felt the ice breaking between us.
Now I know what is meant to be loved,
And to love. I don't want to leave her,
I want to be near.

Now we only pass each other silent,
Not even a smile do we make or nod.
Remembrances of happier times we did have.
I came up to her and gave her a hug.

Thomas R. Boughan

LOOK NOT BACK

Look not back at things past and gone forever.
Don't dwell on errors made long ago, as Life's too short.
Greet each day as a new adventure — one of challenging endeavor.
Keep alert for someone who may be in need of your support.

Look not back on things you cannot change, no matter how you'd try.
Don't make the same mistakes again.
The ones already made — just try to rectify,
If they caused someone pain.

Look not back on things that were of the Devil's making.
Don't let him trap you with his crafty ways.
God's love is yours just for the taking.
To *Him* ever give the praise.

Look back only to recollections of happy memories,
Dwell on those that bring the most joy to you.
Let your relaxing moments be filled with these.
Keep going 'til the dreams you had, have all come true.

Look not back at all the years that have sped away.
Don't waste sadness on what might have been.
Keep looking to that bright future day,
When your goals set — you finally will win.

Eulaliah T. Hooper

WOLVERINES

Many a night would see me cry.
Alone I lie, a sheet covering partially.
A boy in his room trying for innocence,
Shadows putting nightmares into dreams.

I'd close my eyes whispering, God, take me away . . .
And he would.

Then when I was a man lying on a beach
In some far-removed land across a yellow sea,
Fighting wars for those with a pedestrian vision
Of some valiant persecution of the enemy,

Shadows twisted from youth to manhood,
Images now reality, blood covering harshly.
I squeezed the rifle tightly in my hand and screamed
When blood met blood and man met man.

A friend lay fallen at my side, no motion,
His breath deep and rapid, body spread upon the sand.
He begged me kill him, the shadows closed.
I laid the barrel to his brain, pulled the trigger,
 eased the pain.

Many a night would see me cry.
Alone I lie, a sheet covering partially.
A man in his room trying for innocence.
Shadows putting nightmares into dreams.

I'd close my eyes whispering, God, take me away . . .
If only he could.

Dennis Dwyer

ONE DAY AT A TIME

One day at a time, I know that He is mine.
I know He is mine, and my way I can find.
One day at a time, each day of the year;
I know my Saviour goes with me, and I have no fear.

One day at a time, each day of the year;
My Lord is with me to wipe away my tears.
He helps me, and guides me, and conquers my fears.
One day at a time, each day of the year.

What more could you ask for?
What is there to life more?
Who else is a more true guide?
Who else is there in whom you can abide?

No one else could give such love as He.
No one else would die for one such as me.
No one else could open my eyes and cause me to see.
To see what I am missing without His true liberty.

Yes, one day at a time, I know He is mine.
Each hour of the day, a new treasure in Him I find.
Each day of the year, one day at a time.
Each hour of the day, I know He is mine.

Alice May Shutt

THE DOOR

Here I set, right at the door.
Here I set, and yet I need much more.
I need to get up and go through that door.
For there I will get what I need to heal a heart that's sore.

Yet still I set here day by day.
Wanting and needing something more.
A gentle hand, and a kind word you would say.
But I won't get up and go through that door.

I wonder how often I have come to that door,
Seeking for the help, and kindness and love within,
Only to set and look longingly at the door;
Not realizing that to receive what I need, I must go in.

What is it that keeps me setting here looking at the door?
What is it that I fear? Why won't I go in?
Can't I realize that Christ is the door?
The door to Heaven and all I have to do is just to go in.

Oh, dear Father, help me I pray, to go in.
Accepting from You Your cleansing from sin.
Knowing that Jesus is my Door.
He gives me the kindness and love and even more.

Now I no longer set looking, longingly at the door.
I have gone in that door, receiving so much more.
Love and joy, and salvation from sin.
And the Holy Spirit to keep me clean from within.

Alice May Shutt

MY CHILD BEYOND HER YEARS

The look in her eyes so saddens me —
As I feel the tears I try to hold back.
For I, as a mother, should have the knowedge,
At times, I do so lack.

Yet here she is:
My gift from above.
This child of only eleven years
Knows the words I need so to hear —
To stop my flow of tears.

For you see; it is a muscle disease I have.
No more the strength, the energy
To do for her as once I could:
Yet she has always understood.

As I have become much weaker,
I've watched my special daughter
Become stronger within.
And when I am down and very ill,
This special angel, with such a strong will;
Does not let me give-in.
Yet gives me the strength to fight on.

Even with the tears and the fears,
It only takes the love and strength
She does bring;
To once more make my heart sing!

Glenna Montgomery Reames

LIFE IS A BUBBLE

Your life is but a bubble,
  The shell of your soul,
Which our Great God forms
  In His huge pipe's bowl.

He admires your growing beauty
  As He fills you gradually,
And gently blows you upward
  When He sets you free.

You're composed of all the substance
  Of the beauty of the earth.
He frowns when you're in danger,
  And when safe, He's full of mirth.

He loves to see you floating
  Long in life's atmosphere.
Let your beauty shine on others
  As you wander far and near.

When the pressure 'round about you
  On the earth becomes too strong,
When you strike some dangerous object,
  Or the course you take is wrong,

Then your shell is burst asunder,
  And it melts into the sod.
But the thing that sent you floating —
  God's breath — returns to God.

Rudy Loeffler

WHERE DID THE SUMMER GO?

The beaches are empty now
of summer lovers
and worshippers of Ra . . .
dark, but not Egyptian.
The gulls circle forlornly
sensing winter's approach.
How much easier
to catch peanuts in the air
than to forage along sandy stretches.
The boardwalk bustle
is all but gone, too.
A lonely hotel room
holds few summer memories . . .
just endless canvasses
reflecting your face
and sheets
still smelling faintly of Aramis.
We said it was more
than just another summer romance,
but summer's wine
makes us all a little mad,
and at the end of May
summers looms forever.
Suddenly it's September.
Where did the summer go?

Perry Richards

LORD:

  Hold me close and hold
me tight
  And never let me fall
apart again
  Right now I am running
scared
  To a direction I am not
sure of
  My fear is taking over my
heart
  I know I should slow
down
  But I find I am unable
to do so
  Dear Lord I am scared
help me
  find the right road
to take
  I need your strength to
go on
  I am in a hole need a
helping hand
  To find my way out in
the open
    Amen.

Sandra L. Condon

THE BIGOT

That man there can't come in
Why? because his lip's too thin.
That man there let's treat unfair
Why? because the length of his hair.
That man there has no brain
Why? because the way he spells his name.
That man there he's a creep
Why? because of the religion he keeps.
That man there is a Communist spy
Why? because of the slant in his eye.
That man there let's hold him back
Why? because his elbow's black.
That man there let's keep him down
Why? because his fingertip's brown.
That man there, he's never right
Why? because his forehead's white.
That man there is a sneaky fellow
Why? because his ankle is yellow.
That man there don't let through the door
Why? because his family is poor.
That man there is as stupid as can be
Why? because he don't think like me.

Michael L. Mills

LIKE FATHER — LIKE SON

Beside the old front steps at home
My little ''Small Fry'' stands.
Determination on his face
His hammer in his hands.

His mother writes, ''He builds a boat
To sail across the sea,
Since Daddy's slow in coming home
O'er there with you he'll be.''

How many ''Small Frys'' there at home
Are building little ships
Across the mighty sea to sail
Upon their tiny trips?

How many GI ''Pops'' o'er here
Have thought, ''I wonder why

I cannot build myself a ship
To see my own Small Fry?''

Keith S. Kirkham

KEITH SPERE KIRKHAM. Born: Lehi, Utah, 10-22-16; Married: Isabelle; Education: University of Utah; Occupations: Tent maker, Welfare services director; Poetry: Wrote for the Army newspaper in World War II; Comments: *I like to write about the things I see. Nothing abstract.*

RAIN

Softly and tenderly it beats,
  Down upon the heaven-scented grass.
The soft puttering of drops fall upon a blade,
  Just barely touching,
    Before —
      Splash! Splash!
One little drop is destroyed,
  Merely by a single touch.

How could such a soothing vision,
  Be destroyed in such an instant?
How can something so harmless,
  Possibly destroy:
    Crops,
      Futures,
        Homes,
          and
            Lives?

Tracy Cervenka

LITTLE GIRL IN CAMISOLE

Little girl in camisole,
Sweet, not yet sixteen;
Seeks the garden, a quiet place,
To dream and dream and dream.

The topiaries guard the walk,
Fantastic shapes, trimmed so neat;
Camel, giraffe and elephant;
Birds, clipped and shaped, complete.

The chameleon scurried among and between,
Thrusting the tongue rapidly in repeat
As it grasped, it would cling and coil
Changing its colors, an amazing feat.

The gardener, beyond the gazebo,
Was working in the vineyard;
Digging near the roots. His next move
Would be to the aromatic plants, the spikenard.

Walking near the creekbed,
She lifted the hand to shield the eye;
Spied the sealskin-stretched frame, the kayak,
A-coming and watched it as it glided by.

Little girl in camisole,
Sweet, not yet sixteen,
With imagination roaming free, wandering on;
Left to dream and dream and dream.

Jessie Butler Jones

NOTE TO THEM

I stand here in my tower looking out upon the sea
Lonely hours pass in trivialities.
The mist shrouds my time of life and death, yet
I only think of wanting you to be the ghost of me.
As echoes of the waves repeat the cleansing of the shore,
And whispers of some windy lips pronounce forevermore,
So my mind is free to grapple with what others would deplore.
And come to find a different me,
It's you I knew before.

James Wolfe

MY CHILDHOOD PAST

It seems like only yesterday
When I was a child of five
I worked so hard at all my play
To make wishes and dreams come alive

I'd build huge castles made of sand
Pretending I was a knight
I'd get a stick to be my sword
And defend it with a fight

Perhaps I'd be a princess
With skin and hair so fair
A prince would ride up and give lots of kisses
And my dreaming would stop right there

When I climbed up our tallest tree
I was never Tarzan or Jane
I'd hang upside down screeching *OOO OOO OOO EEE!*
And drive my poor mother insane

Sometimes I wanted to run away
So I jumped into my box
Once I gassed up and drove all day
And came back with the Chicken Pox

Yes, life was hard in my childhood past
I think of it now and then
The years fly by but the memories last
I can dream I'm five once again

Michele M. Evans

WINNIE'S FAREWELL TO NELSON

You know in what manner I have loved, ever since we met!
I loved you with all humility, through Times we will never forget!
I kept back nothing good for you, I swear by God above!
Oh, let us come together, and enjoy once more Our Love!
. . . But no, they come! You must go! You know where!
I know Pain awaits in that Prison, I know what will happen there!
But you fear none of these though assailed by every strife!
God, let us finish Our Course! That is more Precious than Life!
And, now, my dearest Nelson, I can be with you no longer! . . .
Remember we never stepped back! I pray God to keep us stronger!
We coveted no one's silver or gold! Our hands provided our needs!
And now if War must leave its spoor, I hope for the Poor it bleeds!
But I can say no more! Just let me touch your face! . . .
Nelson, My Love, I must leave you! . . . Oh, How I'll miss your embrace!

Martin J. O'Malley

SELF

Self, Janus-like, tempted from Adam's time,
Struggling with two heads vying for primal dominance
  While facing opposite ways:
One would prize the distinction merit brings,
  Desirous of notoriety that crowns achievement
  With worldly praise;
Unremittingly the other, understanding why God condemns
False pride and all self-centeredness tearing one
  Ruthlessly from God,
Would pause to reinstitute mind and heart with Christ,
  Strengthened through His love.

E. Ruth van Appledorn

HEARTACHE

The heart breaks, the heart mends
Covered by leaves of pain
We struggled through each busy day
Never again the same.
''We have forgotten,'' we proudly say,
''That was another life, another time.''
A snatch of song, a face in the crowd
A memory accompanying rain
The tears flow, the head is bowed
It begins all over again.

Dorothy Reed

Thumbing through the scrapbook of my mind
I found a face
    Forever etched upon my heart;
I heard the whisper
    Of a favored voice —
Echoing through
    The hallways of my mind;
I felt the smiling
    Eyes of love
Warming me to
    The depths of my soul.
I paused a moment in the hour of my life —
    And remembered.

Anne Macko

MAY '79

On my way
to the same old place
people's glances get left
unanswered.

You,
as always
in your tattered denim jacket,
smoke surrounds your tired face
I slip my arms around your waist.

You go on playing
the silver ball
bouncing from light to light.

Silence
You turn and walk away
Leaving me wondering.

Diane Arlene Marks

GENESIS

A pail rainbow
Arches
Billowing thunderheads.
Crisp gold leaves
Dance to sunny whirlwinds
Across a November highway.
The Lord of the Dance
Renews His covenant
With this Day of All Souls.

Nancy M. Ryan

FAREWELL ULYSSES

Ashore I wait for you to swim,
Are you listening dearest one?
How could my song go unattended?
Please do what I bid done.

You're there aboard your lifeship,
Bound hand and foot against my song.
It isn't death that awaits, it's me.
And it's with me you belong.

Above the sounds of the waves I hear
Your soul's silent sound.
You do love me, how could you not?
I feel my heart begin to pound.

What will be done? I know not.
At least my dearest you've heard.
What I cannot do in fact,
I'll try to do in word.

My love for you has no conditions.
At last now I am whole.
For all my life I'll remember
Your imprint on my soul.

Nancy Sutton

NANCY JO SUTTON. Pen Name: George Stratton; Born: Dansville, New York; Single; Education: University of Redlands, Redlands, California, B.A., Management, 12-81; Mesa Community College, Mesa, Arizona, A.A., Business, 5-73; Occupations: Executive secretary, Business instructor; Memberships: Association of Information Systems Professionals, Vice-President, membership, 1984; Writer's Group, Dansville, New York; Poetry: 'My Soul's Caress,' 12-27-86; 'The Heartlight,' *American Poetry Anthology*, 12-27-86; Comments: *My poetry concerns lost love . . . written in a positive way. I like to get across that life is so very exciting, one must write about the most meaningful parts. My poem, 'Farewell Ulysses,' is about a love that cannot be. Their destiny is to part and they both know it. An ending takes place before the relationship begins.*

I LOVE THEE

So do
I love thee!
Morning glory,
You are as precious
As a
Sunlit morning.

Carol L. Oliver

IF I'VE MONEY
TO LEND OUR LORD

If I've money to lend the church,
    Then there is more I must give.
What I have . . . first came from the Lord;
    'Tis shown each day that I live.

If there should be no family,
    Then my pockets would be dry.
Coins and bills . . . could stay not within;
    Momentary things are why.
If there were no friends around me,
    Then vultures surely would come.
The battle . . . could be no battle;
    Their strength is greater than one.

If I've money to lend our Lord,
    Then replace it with my gift.
Two of us . . . have been made happy;
    Neither God nor I get ripped!

H. R. Krauss

NOT ALL OF GOD'S PLANS
ARE WRITTEN IN INK

Not all of God's plans are written in ink,
    Some have been penciled in.
It happened with Moses in Exodus
    As good gave way to sin.

Some of God's children do have restrictions,
    One has to do with robes.
Such plan may have been written in pencil —
    Yet to be changed in droves?

Our sins are another good example,
    Some turn more than the cheek.
God the Father will do His erasing
    If from the hearts we seek.

Say not that His plans are less than pure gold,
    Check both love and reward.
Not one time does He use the eraser —
    Changeless marks for our Lord!

Not all of God's plans are written in ink,
    I'm glad He writes this way.
O that the eraser He used for me
    Is new on Judgment Day!

H. R. Krauss

WHAT IS MAN?

What is man?
A noble creature
Wandering the earth
Looking for home
Everywhere
But within oneself.

Carol L. Oliver

ECHO OF FAITH #1455

I sit, and all I can do is write while all around me men die from
hunger, disease, war — I sit, and all I can do is write while all
around me children cry in pain from abuse and neglect. . . . And yet
I serve as I am called, *I voice His words* anew and I *Re-echo
His song* again to men.

I stir the Heart, the Mind, the Soul through *Love of Him.*
I renew Faith, rekindle *Celestial Fire,* light *the Way.*
I bear the Torch, the Shield of Righteousness, the *Sword of His
words, His echoings* of Faith. I wear the Helmet of *Salvation
Shining* . . . Bright Lights of Salvation's Calling, Paths of
Righteousness Renewed . . . Faith Flowing with Celestial Fire —
Inspiration's Holy Ghost Cometh . . . The silent, patient accepting,
waiting, trusting, being, doing, voicing, echoing; seeking, praying,
"Come, *Holy Ghost,* inspire! *The serene coming, filling, hearing,*
Melodic Whisperings, Peaceful Strength and Contemplation, Humble,
Devoted Loving.

To *overcome,* to stand fast, to emerge, attain, *Be* . . . as it
pleaseth *His will* . . . the Beauty of the *Lord, His* Reassuring
Presence, *His* Peace . . . I sit, and all I can do is write —
and yet, I serve as I am called, *His voice* to listen to, *His Will*
to be *obeyed* . . . that men should *hear,* should *listen,* should *obey*
and *grow* in the *Spirit* despite disease, starvation —
that from abuse and neglect — Love and *Faith* groweth as blooming
cacti in the desert — Mute Testament.

And those who work to help their fellowman *shall have* an *inner peace*
that calleth on the *Lord* in *faith* and desperation . . . Satan may rule
the land, we may starve in vain to help *Mankind* — but each rose
the blooms brings pleasure . . . and each Soul we save, each pain we
soothe, each mouth we feed, body we clothe or make well, we do for
all Humanity. One Good Deed, One Seed of Love sown may give rise to a
Tree of Life, a Source, a sheltering for *all the world* —

I sit and write — you listen and do —
together we help to Light the World *anew.*

For God's Honor and His Glory . . .

Barbara Louise Martinez-Piligian

ECHO OF FAITH #1912

It is not the quantity of time we have together here upon the
Earth that matters most — It is the quality, the communication,
the reaching out and touching, the transmitting of the thought,
The feelings, the love of *God* in what we do, we say, we strive to be
and to attain . . . the brief minute, the flickering candlelight . . .
one moment here upon the stage of life lived in and with

True Virtue's Essence, substance, budding, flowering *fruits* of
the *Spirit* which are Honor, Duty, Courage, Loyalty, Moral
Excellence and Chastity, the ethical discrimination
Between right and wrong, the striving to do, to be the Best that
we can be that we may better serve our fellowman . . . but
most of all our *God.*

To suffer without complaint, to exercise great self-control, to be
indifferent to pleasure or pain . . . that they should not rule
our lives, weaken our character . . . yes a fragrant flower
Of *Virtue* is to endure pain or hardship without complaint . . . and
another is to enable, to dignify, to make worthy, to refine our
Mind, our character, our behavior, our heart and soul, the
Celestial Fire of our substance that we should become an
exalted carrier, a worthy, a lofty towering *Messenger*
of our *God* . . .

Yes, the Tree of Life holds many Budding, Flowering, Fragrant
Fruits that we should desire to cultivate, to refine as
a Gift to *God* . . . Do you? . . . Do you? . . . Do you?

Barbara Louise Martinez-Piligian

ECHO OF FAITH #2450

Don't blame *God* for the bomb . . . Man made it — he took *God's*
Gift of Creativity and used it to destroy life, to control for wealth,
for power, for fame — or was it to protect his way of Life,
its Goodness from evil . . .

Only *God* can *Judge* in *Truth* for *He knows* who listened to the
temptations of Satan's sweet snares and succumbed to evil's many forms
of corruption.

Don't blame *God* for Man's inhumanity to man — *God* allows man *Free
Will* to listen to *His Words, His Commands* or to be tempted by Satan
and the Beast . . . *for Earth is God's testing ground of Eternity.*

God gave man a Beautiful Earth as a Glimpse of Paradise . . . and
also of Hell. A Promise . . . and a Warning. *God* doesn't want your
selfish, pride-filled prayers — your complaints — your
arrogant, graspy, greedy bargaining . . .

God wants Unselfish Loyalty and Devotion *no matter* what the
circumstance. *He wants* your Love without thought of reward — for
the *Lord* giveth, *He* maketh, *He* taketh away *according to
His Desire, Will, Grand Design.*

God wants us humble *for he wants* no more Lucifers in *Paradise* . . .
We are here to prove our worth to *Him* . . . Are you ready, World, to put
Him first — to make Earth a Paradise, to live in Peace and
Tolerance, to make yourself worthy to be received in
His Heavenly Home . . .

It is you who need to repent before it is too late *and* in stiff-necked
arrogance and stubborn pride you turn Earth into *another* dead planet
revolving around an insignificant *star* in the *galaxy* called
Milky Way . . . You are *not* unique, you know —
Just a Grain of Sand in the *Vast Desert of Eternity* . . .
God's Creation of *Forevermore* . . . Are you listening, World?

Destiny awaits . . .

Barbara Louise Martinez-Piligian

RATIONAL I

We two, a cynic and a spirit,
Both searched the silent lights
And darkened void of evening.
Our feet, scared by the same stone, dangled in limpid liquid.
While watching face reflections, for hints of what might swim
Below our shallow image.
Listening in the vague illumined morning,
For a mystic subtle sound
That foretells rising of the sun.
We questioned poets, prophets, books, and fools,
Taking notes on our palms
Which soon sealed our ears and eyes
From the echoes and shadows of their mad answers.
But in a sudden niche or tick as we sat transcending nothing
You saw a flash I missed. My gaze was not directed.
Advancing or retreating, you the spirit swaying slightly
Drifted onward and softly
With a flying, feathery, farewell grip,
You told me you knew your duty,
Then overtly disguising a spot now anchored
Begin to contemplate the beginning and end.
You sit now in solitude
Found alone, as it must have been fated.
Waiting for your essence to go swirling; toward; nirvana.

James Wolfe

FALLS OF MINNEHAHA.

FRIENDSHIP

What is a friend?
Is it someone you can trust,
  Someone who is honest and just?
Is it someone you can go to in need?
  This is, a true friend indeed.
A true friend, I have in you.
  You make me happy when I'm feeling blue.
The little jokes that you say,
  Seem to brighten my whole day.
You listen to my problems without saying a word,
  When inside you think the whole thing is absurd.
You're there, when I have no one else to turn to,
  You help me to see my problems through.
That's why now, my friend, I tell you,
  How much I love and appreciate you.

Sandra Lynn Smith

I sit and I wonder, and I wait for the day
For my mind to be free, and for my heart to play.

To be free of this memory, so hard and so wrong.
Will this day ever come, I have been waiting so long.

I want to escape, there is only one way.
You carry the burden all the way.

You dream and you write, and you sleep and learn.
And in the end you give up everything you have earned.

My mom and my father, my girls and their brother.
Please dear God, let there be another.

Give me a chance for what I have learned.
Return me my mother, and my father, my son, my girls.

Ruth Wolf

I am but a child, yet I have three.
I don't want this for them, what has happened to me.

Something very special has been neglected from me.
I have been taught wrong, it's so plain to see.

How can you teach and how can you grow, when you have
    missed something,
  the finest thing you will ever know.

The warmth of another, warm flesh with a nice glow.
Nothing sexual, you see I don't know.

I am all grown up, with breast so small.
My feet are fast, I don't mind at all.

It's like living in a house, with a fence so tall.
No gate, no crack, no way out at all.

Ruth Wolf

VELVET RHYTHMS

Velvet rhythms of evening poppies
Flow across moist, salmon-green fields,
Blue vapors spill from cold silences,
Heavily torn with golden light.

Shrill sapphire sycamores exhale
Maroon breezes in gnarled shadows,
Softly twisting toward the pale horizon,
Consumed slowly by the warm crucible of night.

Hugo Walter

YOU AND I

When I closed my eyes last night
A memory floated by
A boy and girl so much in love
They looked like you and I

They were holding hands and laughing
And looking into each other's eyes
I couldn't hear what they were saying
But they sounded like you and I

They laughed and kissed and picked up a bucket
Strolled on down the winding trail
At the spring on the hillside
They stopped and kissed, then filled their pail

Hand in hand they climbed the hill
Pausing once beneath a tree
And as he gently bent to kiss her
I knew those kids were you and me

Many nights my dreams are haunted
By a pair of loving eyes
And when I awoke with my lips burning
I knew those kids were you and I

So many years since our last meeting
So many memories stored away
I often wonder where you are
And if our memories come your way.

Ruby J. Turner

LADIES TOWN MEETING

The geese are gathered 'round the font
  I now perceive what I've been missing.
Chance to get in a word, is nought
  amid the gabbing, honking, hissing . . .
My old cronies still 'round about,
  did I *really* think that all'd be changed?
I watch each goose. Without a doubt
  not one tittle has been rearranged.
Yes, the geese have gathered in the square.
  Among them, Aunt Bell and sister Sue . . .
Did they not know I'd sure be there
  and that their dirty tales, they'd rue?
This goose returned — is honking, still;
  can't allow the herd *their* talking time,
a point to make. Yes, I would kill
  if need be. And it would not be in mime!
Be gone, you hissing, gabbing geese —
  E'en your beaks are like those nosey birds . . .
Just give we normal mortals, peace —
  We'll make *our* noises with kinder words.

Elsie Ruble

FLEETING MEMORIES

Fleeting memories!
Come and go.
People living in their past
With no room to grow.

Fleeting memories!
Of childhood fantasies
That were once important
Still haunting their being.

Carol L. Oliver

ANTICIPATION

When the air glows with anticipation
Sparks fly, lighting the imagination,
Quelling thoughts tinged by trepidation,
To stimulate this tedious life.

The mind explores its outer limit
Seeking unknown shores as requisite
To drink a sip of the infinite
And hide a moment from storm and strife.

Awaiting events that bring pleasure
Becomes its own juncture to treasure,
Bearing sweet rewards without measure,
Enriching the enchantment of life.

Helen L. Gillies

FOR ELIZABETH

April morning, winter cold
tender green, twisted gray
coiling, pointing
silently touching
shadow to shadow
root to root

as petals fall
the sun returns
new leaves open
petals fall faster
the song of a swallow

remembering,
slowly remembering
another spring . . .
the laughter of crows
filling the sky
a breaking branch
cutting

turning to face
a sunless sky
swallowing tears
of life and death
knowing a mother
will never forget
a mother's love

Will Mooring

BLUE MELODY

Searching back in my faded past
The memory of her still wants to last

I'd like to go back
And do things differently
And have her in my life again
To be a part of me

When we were together
We shared the simple pleasures
And an enchanted joy and happiness
That was difficult to measure

Now that we've been apart for so long
The best I can do is to recall it all
With a blue melody and a song

Gil Saenz

WONDERING

In the night air
Of the warm spring
My imagination
Keeps on wondering

Will I find
The right love for me
This year
Or will she be
Just another wrong choice
And insincere

I just can't quit the notion
That there is a certain
Someone who is right for me
Somewhere in the vast
Earthly ocean of humanity

Gil Saenz

THE ANNIVERSARY ROSE

It was only a tiny rosebud,
But it meant so much to me,
Because it burst forth in bloom,
On our wedding anniversary.

The bush had been gradually dying,
But then came back to ''life''
And as it is less than one foot tall,
I call it my ''mighty mite.''

There had been no buds upon this bush,
In over two or three years,
So imagine my surprise,
When the little rose appeared.

My love always gave me flowers,
On our ''special day'' in June,
And I was really delighted,
When I saw this small, pink, bloom.

Was this his way of saying,
Here is a remembrance from me,
As I cannot be with you
On our forty-second anniversary?

Mary Hamilton

FRAGMENTS OF A POEM

Blessed are the poor:
for they are crucified by society.
Blessed are Superpowers:
for they have the tools of destruction.
Blessed are modern Evangelists:
for they are accountable to no one.
Blessed are arms makers:
for they know how to trick us into war so
as to make a living.
Blessed are colonialism and imperialism:
for they led Africa into a beggar status.
Blessed are elephants:
for they trample ants with impunity.
Blessed is Nigeria:
for she turned her ''oil boom'' into ''oil doom.''
Blessed are African leaders:
for they have beautified Africa with poverty.
Blessed are poets:
for they teach us how to see, ''by throwing a
bucketful of light onto the commonest things.''

Rinkart Eze Okorie

GOD'S WORK

Life is like a flower —
It opens up . . .
Into a pattern . . .
Of intricate designs.
Heartaches and joys . . .
To carry us . . .
Through the night . . .
Bringing reality —
Into focus . . .
Of a bright new day.

Marilyn Gold Conley

YESTERDAY'S DREAM

I am not my body, the inner voice echoes
but my pain-strained brain says Yes

Cool blue waters soothe not
   The heat inside of hell
Prison of pain, let me dwell
In yesterday's dream turned upside
      down
Oh tell me please —
This is not what I think it is
Release my heart to soar in peace
I am not my body: throbbing, pounding,
   resounding in battle
   once won in power
Oh, death, emerge to set my spirit free
Let me dwell in yesterday's dream

I am not my body, this thing, infernal
I Am Not My Body
Oh yes, indeed, you cower
The Voice says, *No!*
Keep still, and you will know . . .
I Am Not My Body . . .
I *am* the *now,* Eternal

Phyllis Ferraro

MOONDREAMS

Tonight stars are bright, the moon aglow,
Globe astray in heaven's array, casting beams below.
Silence gold its wraps unfold, no breath nor sigh,
Attune your ear and you may hear a wisp of cloud go by.

Star bright, diamond light in hair of night is spun,
Night's ebon hair which everywhere will fall with rising sun.
Milky Way, spangled ray, guardian of the sky,
Silver arc which in the dark will watch the evening die.

Now to bed to dream instead, bring you into mind,
Eyes so bright with starry light in silken hair entwined.
The night should be less bright, the day not come so soon,
You'd be with me eternally and share with me the moon.

Samuel Wallace Magill

CLASSROOM LOVE

Across the crowded room a penetrating eye
requires a glance,
a subtle smile,
a concentrated stare,
no one else is there.

The long, long class is done, nervous fingers touch,
the thrill is there,
warmth within,
heartbeat pounding in the ear,
everyone can hear.

The brief walk home, weightless books,
no task too great,
no path too long,
at least throughout this day
love is here to stay!

Samuel Wallace Magill

SAMUEL WALLACE MAGILL. Born: Ashtabula County, Ohio; Married: Bea Magill, 5-15-62; Education: University of Maryland, B.S., 1961; Boston University, M.A., 1965; Occupation: U.S. Military Lieutenant Colonel, retired; Memberships: International Platform Association; American Chamber of Commerce, Munich, Germany; Awards: 1st Prize, John C. Klein Literary Award, 1977; Honorable Mention, American Poetry Association, 1985; Writings: "White Gold of Odenwald," article, *Lapidary Journal,* 1964; "Crafters, Craftsmen & Cameos," article, *Lapidary Journal,* 1966; "The Story of Bad Tölz," article, *Gazette,* 1985; "Let There Be Light," article, *Gazette,* 1983; "It's Time To Roll the Barrel," historical article, *Gazette,* 1982; Comments: *I believe that poetry should have both rhythm and rhyme. It should also be informative. It should be as a lady's skirt, long enough to cover the subject, but short enough to be interesting.*

MARTIUS

The Mother God's sweet breath is in the breeze,
Enchantment to the nose at break of day;
The clouds turn white, sap rises in the trees,
The ice and snow turn liquid, flow away.

Rome named the first month for the God of War,
Well named because this is the border land,
The Marches and foul winter's conqueror
Where Ice Gods make their last fierce futile stand.

But Roman Gods can't make or stop a change,
An older God called Demeter's to blame,
Her lover's kisses all her body range
As she rotates no kisses are the same.

Her lover brightens up the winter sky,
His kisses quickly make the Ice Gods fly.

Joseph E. Barrett

MAIA

It's May and flowers dress the fields and fill
Each moment with the scent of life's rebirth;
Each chuckling brook, each skipping dancing rill,
Sing contra-puntal odes to Mother Earth.

Bees hum in tune and dance each blossom's taste,
While pollen fills the air and blankets all,
Seed to spill, seed to plant and seed to waste,
April was gay and bright but May's a ball.

Two girlish names behaving like two girls,
One leggy, coltish, stormy, not quite sure,
One knowing, wise, with a lustre like pearls,
Or diamond dewdrops glistening and pure.

Both fair and smelling fresh as new-mown hay,
Enchantment to the nose at break of day.

Joseph E. Barrett

SNOW

The hush of the softly falling snow
Paints the barren earth with a white glistening glow.

Enfolding the naked branches, and blanketing the fallen leaves
Hiding all the hurts and wounds of which our earth grieves.

Sunbeam and shadow play a symphony of reflections
As clouds move about, splashing lights on various sections.

Flawless, beautiful and cold it appears
Covering all the deeper characters made throughout the years.

Peace and solitude seem to reign —
Thawing from the warm sun's rays will bring life back again.

Elizabeth Borselli

THE LILT OF YOUR LAUGHTER

The lilt of your laughter
Was there from the start.
Whatever possessed me,
To drive us apart?

The lilt of your laughter,
Brought sunshine through rain.
Oh, how could I shower,
Those eyes with such pain?

Oh, how could I stray,
From a love that was true.
For better or worse,
Meant something to you.

I'll never repay you,
I'll certainly try,
For the lilt of your laughter,
Brings tears to my eye.

And if you'll forgive me,
You never need fear.
As long as *God's* willing,
I'll always be near.

Carol Jelinek

LOVE

It can't be bought at any store,
Once lost, it's hard to find.
It can't be leashed upon a chain,
Only held within the mind.

It's something given freely,
A hard thing to define.
And yet it's all around us,
With it, you walk the line.

From *God* to man, to those who know,
It fits just like a glove,
Warming all within its grasp,
This priceless gift called Love.

Carol Jelinek

WHAT DO YOU HEAR?

My words fall on ears that can't hear.
Or, could it be those that don't listen?
I speak, and the words float aimlessly,
Not being heard.
No, not just words.
Feelings, emotions pouring out.
Listen to me, please.
It's not easy to say what I'm saying.
Emotions kept deep within my soul.
Feelings seeping out slowly.
Needing, wanting to be heard.
What do you hear?
Words, just meaningless words?
A desperate cry.
The sound of my tears falling into the pillow.
Hear me, please just listen.
The words so simple.
What do you hear?
I said ''I love you.''
Did you listen?

Donna L. Hellman

SANCTUARY

Where the sun glows red-gold
like the dying fire's embers
and star-speckled black
edges the azure blue,
this the place
to which my soul flees
when the day's tasks are through.

Myrtle Morrow

ONE BY ONE

I gathered
  the haunting scent of wood violets
  nested in crushed ferns,
  the swift blue flash of jays
  gossiping in the pines,
  the shrills of eagles
  soaring above the cliffs
  dueted with the splash of acrobatic bass
  cleaving a placid lake surface,
  the humbling quiet of deep woods
  broken only by rustling in the undergrowth;
Moistening them
  with crystal river water,
I bouqueted my gatherings
  to store in a potpourri of memories.

Mrytle Morrow

VIEWS FROM PROPHESY BRIDGE

Gaze young lovers
at your entwined reflections
mirrored in the placid water;
Suppress your shudders
when a breeze ruffles the calm surface,
seeing yourselves twenty years from now
need not repulse you;
Please! do not draw apart
those were only ripples in the water.
I gazed also
but had no reflection
those were only ripples in the water.

Myrtle Morrow

GOD'S LOVE

Though we may express ourselves
We must not have fear
For God is always near
He helps and guides us
And shows us the way
If we but pray each day
He will bless us
On this earth
And hold us close to Him
As He did before our birth

Rose Mary Gerlach

CAPTURED BY TIME

We prayed the night
'Til it was dawn
We prayed 'til all
The stars were gone
We felt the surge
And held the power
Up into
The waking hour
Seeing fire
Seeing rain
We closed our eyes
To all the pain
And when we woke
To catch the sun
We knew that each
Of us had won
For as it lies
Within our hearts
We understand
Its separate parts
Into all we see and do
And captured by the time

Sonya Eileen Lenz

LOST

Have I forever lost
  the peace I've strived so hard to gain?

I've fought for many years it seems
  and yet no closer have I come,

To finding that elusive dream
  I dream about most every night,

Peace.

While smiling in my dreams at night
  I wake to see the morning light,

And hoping this might be the day
  that peace will come to me to stay.

I scramble out of bed to hear
  the strident tones of battle near,

And longing to escape again
  from all the things that's held within,

I turn to seek my bed and dreams
  when from below I hear the screams,

And standing it no more I go,
  to try and settle with them the score.

Peace, it is no more.

Via M. Cross Comrie

STAR OF THE EAST

As you gaze up in the Heavens
Do you see a star up there?
Does it try to tell a story?
Of its message are you aware?
Did you ever stop to consider
That it once guided both rich and poor
To the feet of our Salvation,
To the gates of Heaven forevermore?

As you gaze up at this star
Do you think of a night and land afar?
Do you wonder at the chagrin
Of innkeepers who hadn't let Him in?
And the animals He blessed
As He lay in their feed so poorly dressed?

The poor shepherds and rich wisemen followed this star
To see God's Son, their King and Saviour — they traveled far.

What blessings — what love —
Sent to all of us from God above!

Elizabeth Borselli

A CHRISTMAS WISH

May the Prince of Peace, with His halo bright,
Shed His love on you, and yours, tonight.

May Mary's love and prayers for you
Give you comfort all year through.

May God, the Father, hear your prayer
He wants you for Jesus, so do take care.

Celebrate His birthday, in a very special way.
The gifts He'd have you give for Him
Are sorrow for your sins within — and to our Father pray.

All have a happy, holy holiday — as you celebrate His birth,
And may His peace enfold you, every day you're on His earth.

Elizabeth Borselli

LOVE IS A GIFT

People show love in unusual ways,
It's not always pleasant, as in the old days.
Though some times are precious, as others are sad,
We all must accept the good with the bad.

Love is a gift that not all receive,
Only love can survive, given strength to believe.
Love is not perfect in every way,
But honest and happy, forever love stays.

In depths of our hearts, love pounds with each beat,
You know it's true love the first time you meet.
No need for a word to ever be said,
When love is true love, the heart will be led.

To know is to love, this phrase fits so well,
If love's what two share, no words can tell.
With people in love, one thing is for sure,
She'll love him to death and he'd die just for her.

What he and I share is true love, I can say,
That expresses more strength, with each passing day.
Our love is a gift, sent from Heaven above,
Through rainbows and comets and snowy white doves.

Deedie Macon

ANGEL ON EARTH

*Dedicated to Kimberly McCollum
on an anniversary of our being together*

I thank God for your love every night.
You entered my life when it seemed my only
friend was the Lord
Alone, I had lived day to day doing what
I could do to get by, none of my music hitting
the right chord.

But now that you're a part of my life for what has
just passed month seven
I am now sure not all of Heaven's angels
are with God, because He sent me one here on
earth, and when you stand next to me, I thank
the Lord for His gift who stands five feet seven.

Kevin D. Cooper

THE ARRIVAL OF PEACE

As the dew from all the ages past evaporated from the dawn of
Today . . . I realized that all the palaces of yesterday have already
Been trodden with sandaled feet . . . His!
The minutes grow late . . . not many places left to walk . . .
I look up . . . I see jets . . . screaming in mid-air . . .
People race . . . onwards toward deeper unrest . . .
Many choose not to see . . . care . . . I look around . . .
People running . . . clamoring for more power . . . wealth . . .
They are cold . . . they have no smile.
Many tears stream my face . . . don't you care? . . .
I touch an arm . . . they pull away . . .
Children in the gutters . . . no one picks them up.
Babies buried in the trash . . . no one prays for them . . .
No time . . . I cry . . . I sense this to be
The richest desolation in all the earth.
I stop . . . I wonder . . . are you still there? . . .
I wait . . . then . . . I hear it.
The rustle of your robe! Sounds as a soothing breeze.
But wait! You are changing . . . the robe is off . . .
Replaced by your holy armor . . . ready for the battle . . .
Yes . . . it is time . . . peace must now begin . . . here . . .
And over there . . . everywhere . . .
Look! It is starting to rain. The dew is back on the leaves . . .
The leaves of the book are anointed . . .
They whirl in the wind . . . they stop . . . high, high up . . .
All can see . . . they read: "Thou *shall love* one another" . . .
Too late . . . we acted not in time . . .
And thus the Lord doth return to earth . . . peace has arrived.
        It *will* reign eternal.

Linda Hinds Peterson

LOVE THINGS

Black-satin nights in spangled lace,
Harvest moon-face with polka-dot dippers,
A wild sun ending safari and bluing the landscape,
Leaping deer bound in bitter brush,
Flowers making rainbows in mountain meadows.
Embarrassed leaves waving to Autumn soon to be clad in ermine
Changes weather for seasoning.
All love-things etched in feelings, I find.

Raymond Befus

I love
Your baby blues
Wide-eyed wonder
In shifting hues
Of grey and green
Sweeping vistas unfold
A panorama of sights
Untold
I long for the surprise
Of seeing me
In your eyes

jet

John T. Enloe

TO KATHARINE HEPBURN:

What can be said,
That has already not,
You seem to have done it all,
Though I'm sure you have not,

You're witty and charming,
So perky and bright,
You seem always cheerful,
But, I'm sure that's not right.

Your eyes, they do sparkle,
With mischievous delight,
Your hair is a frazzle,
But, oh what a sight.

You're bold as brass,
And so full of sass,
I wish to be like you,
You're my favorite lass.

F. Vadnais

VIEW FROM THE TOP

Uncomplaining
at rigid
attention (facing northwest)
the wind spinning
three-armed
giants
stand watch on the
mountaincrest
as valley bovines
browse among
green grasses
and golden poppies
fold sun-warmed
petals while a lone
mallard contemplates a
late swim in spring's
fading lake.

Frances Johnson

SOMEWHERE FAR AWAY

Somewhere far away,
  there's a land of great beauty,
    where a slippery slope
      reveals the work of the sea,
        sculptured by the winds.

The sun conspires with the moon
  to make the tides rush
    against the weakened land,
      claimed by the raging sea,
        etched by windblown rain.

Beyond the chalky cliffs
  sweeping steeply upward
    with silver stripes
      like windy castles in the air,
        wooded land is pinned.

The birds visit some flowers
  and sing love's refrain,
    and the array of colors
      is beyond compare
        and dazzles the brain.

Josephine Bertolini Comberiate

JOSEPHINE B. COMBERIATE. Pen Name: Jay Bee C.; Born: Washington, D.C., 3-11-17; Married: Michael Bruno Comberiate, 11-25-45; Education: Honors in piano, harmony, academic studies, 1934; Honors from Comptometer School, 1935; Strayer College, Secretarial/accounting, 1937; Catholic University, 1930; University of Maryland, 1977-79; Occupations: Piano teacher, 1934-44; Composer, Author, Publisher, Poet, Pianist, Organist, Grandmother of 12; Memberships: American Society of Composers, Authors, and Publishers; Awards: Gold Watch for safety slogan, National Safety Council, 1955; Commendation from Pope John XXIII for Hymn, 1960; First prize for baby slogans, Banister Baby Enterprizes, 1963; First prize for song, Chapel Recording Co. and Talent, Inc., 1986; Certificates and awards for various courses and club memberships; Poetry: *Love, Life and Liberty,* music book of 139 own songs, words, music and harmony, photo collages; Self-published, 1979; *Love's Story — Life's Glory,* own anthology of over 630 poems, verses, lyrics; Other works: Almost 200 songs, record albums and other recordings, greeting cards, published poems; Themes: *Love, life, liberty, religion, creation and nature, family, friends, babies, animals, music. Published poems have appeared in poetry books, newspapers, magazines.*

AGELESS REFLECTIONS

I sit by the mirror and reflect
while staring at my reflection
thinking back on my past
and of my future direction

How could time pass so quickly
and the years add at such a pace
as to leave so much grey in my hair
and lines etched so deeply in my face

Then I think of my children
and all my years as a wife
and I know at that certain moment
that mine is a very good life

Now I can see my hair is not grey
but more like a silky silver crown
and the lines in my face are caused
more by smiles than ever by frowns

Jan L. Dosch

SILHOUETTES

I looked out on the frozen world
and the pristine mantle there,
the giant trees with arms unfurled
were silhouetted everywhere.
Like schemes and plans on solid walls
are drawn in clear design, and
march like sentries in hallowed halls,
reminding us of fleeting time. And
the disillusion lurking there
behind each effort we neglect,
which watered down to Spartan bare,
in time becomes a silhouette.
The years that rob our pristine plans
and hike us down from vaulted hill,
chip at shaky walls of sand
to captivate the soul of skill. And,
obliterate with dread report,
which turns the turnstile of regret,
and hampers ethereal thought
so life, becomes a silhouette.
Dream your dreams and carve your thoughts
on solid ramparts where they'll shine!
Till you exhaust the time you've bought,
and leave your mark on the walls of time!

Peg Scanlon

the small slick pleasure
of new tapes sliding tightly
out of cellophane wrappers
unmarred cases snugly
wound silent audiophiles
stacked beside faded colored
boxes of music
saving the still-squared hulls
like the locust casings i carefully
plucked from walnut trees
and hoarded as a child.

Charlie Shells

SANDALS UNDER THE CROSS

His pain has begun. His sandals are off.
They shall walk no more after today.
His bared, bleeding feet shall trudge that
Broken cobblestoned path to the hill of
His death. His sandals wait there.
His burden is at its heaviest now, for,
He carries us with Him to that place of pain
And tears. We are heavy for Him, yet He keeps
To the path, and for our sake, does this
Gentle man never once run away.
He fulfills his destiny, and gives us ours.
His tears are falling, we know not if they
Are tears of pain or of relief.
Still He is quiet, and now as the hill looms
Into vision range, he relaxes his heart.
It's over. Soon He will be with His father.
He has won the victory for us. Prophesy fulfilled.
Tell me . . . did He die in vain? . . . Did He?
Then rise up . . . put on your sandals . . . continue the
Walk.
For He is back . . . He is alive . . . not just a man tho' . . .
For now He is Lord. He has His sandals on again.
We must walk with Him . . . now . . .
It is time.

Linda Hinds Peterson

THE CABIN

I know of a cabin in the remote woods and
   wilderness, just off the shore of a lake.
My family and I like to sit on the porch
   and talk and laugh all the laughter we can take.
And early in the morning when the sun has just risen,
   the birds chirp while you are hardly awake.
This cabin of which I speak has brought me
   lots of happiness and joy, I can't wait to see how
      much more it will make!

Catherine Rogers

BAPTISM BY FIRE

All roads lead west.
All roads lead to the sunset.
All roads lead to the golden city.

Roads white and shining
Streak to the city in the clouds.
Auto lights blink along the way like dazzled moths,
A myriad of fearless fireflies drawn
Beneath the city's blackened spires and leaping bridges,
Drawn to charred mazes
Where wild music gushes from bright doorways
Enticing me to enter, to indulge, to enjoy
The wine and the dancing.

I feel the force of the firelight
I trace the patterns the feet beat into the rubble,
Feeling the pulse from the hearts of the black buildings,
From the warmth of the wine
And the warmth of many hands and many faces.

I turn again,
Born again
Eastward
To the chill of new morn,
To wait again
Until the city calls.

Theodora Fair

HAND IN THE CLOUDS

As I gaze upward . . . thinking . . . I see:
One cloud . . . the shape of a ram,
Another . . . the size of a mountain.
Both moving rapidly in the same direction.
At first glance the mountain is moving faster than the ram.
Then before mine eyes the mountain stops . . . abruptly.
The ram hits . . . head on . . . the mountain absorbs all the ram.
I weep. I am the ram. The mountain is my life. But wait!
The mountain begins in motion again. The ram has reassembled.
Yea . . . suddenly! Another cloud from higher up.
Larger than all others. Like a hand of force. Great power.
It reaches down . . . quickly . . . quietly.
It scatters the mountain deep 'cross the span of the horizon.
Now . . . I look . . . I see the sun where the cloud was,
There are new small clouds resting about . . . gathering.
They will to form yet another mountain . . . but wait!
There waits the hand . . . waiting to smite again . . .
And look . . . there is the ram . . . only this time it is not
Butting . . . the horns are evaporated . . . it is being led
By the hand in the clouds . . . the ram is at peace . . .
For the new forming mountain shall not conquer . . . ever again!

Linda Hinds Peterson

LINDA JEAN HINDS PETERSON. Born: Portland, Michigan, 2-20-48; Married: William, 2-14-83; Education: Life, the best teacher of all; Partial high school; Occupations: Wife, Mother, Grandmother, Writer, Christian; Memberships: U.F.W.; Writings: ''Rag Tag Tillie,'' short stories, 1986; *Ribbon in the River*, collected works, 1984; ''Sleep On My Children/Day Is Dawning,'' recording, Rainbow Records label, 1987; Themes: *How real (I saw him) God is. How kind and compassionate, how he really does deliver the poor, the oppressed, the ugly (in sin.) He keeps His word. How patient he is. He is no fable or image of a disordered or messed up mind.*

SPEAK SILENT

Spellbound your gaze held me helpless to escape,
Frozen within the hands of time.
Frightened and confused I stood,
Listening to your eyes speak.
Silvery starlight holds hands with the velvet night
Dancing across your face.
Haunted eyes veil their pain,
Yet never waver in their intensity.
Unspoken promises spill forth
In the splash of a teardrop
As it caressed a path to your lips.
No words passed between us,
No betrayals, nor secrets unshared,
For all spread before us open and naked,
As understanding dawned with the light
Laying bare our human souls.
Locked together our eyes embraced
Witnessing the oneness we've become.
Fear and uncertainty melted away
As we gave ourselves to the magic.

Linda Piscitelli

ECHOES

In the cloisters of my mind,
you dwell, in the silent
syllables of devotion.
Echoing, ever echoing,
twenty times over,
again and again,
in passive rapture.
Once consuming my days,
new, with eternal whispers
of past enchantment,
reverberating
with insistence, and
holding me,
to promises long interred.
In the reality of a famished soul,
as long, lonely hours
gobble up the days, and days
gobble up the years,
in the endless parade
to immortality.

Peg Scanlon

GOD IS WONDERFUL

When I look back at my life
    I realize I've been blessed.
Man can sometimes disappoint,
    But in You I find rest.

Through faith I moved those mountains
    I thought I had to climb,
You've given me so much joy,
    And shown Your love, so kind.

In so many ways You've helped
    Others just like me.
I'm a witness to this truth
    Because I see them free.

All I have to do is pray,
    And leave the rest to Him.
He can do the same for all.
    We have to let Him in.

Diane L. Clark

CELESTIAL BEING

Clouds form in such a way
Enticing dreamers to dream all day
Like a pillow floating in the sky
Encouraging the faithful to give life a try
Silver linings that cannot be seen
The dark clouds sometimes seem so mean
Inspiring are those angelic puffs of white
As they pass through the dark of night
Like a ball of smoke they come and go

Bringing ideas to thinkers below
Each and every cloud I see
Instills new hope in the likes of me
Need you to know that when a cloud floats by
God is dreaming in the sky

Norma Neiman

MONUMENT TO LOVE

Majestically rising
separating itself from the earth
Labor of love, for love
Shrouded in mystery, forgotten knowledge
Science, more
in a line
planets, the sun and moon
Weight alone baffles, Degrees
a single ordinary? man
Time predicted, finds
accuracy in antiquity
Beauty unfolding, sensitivity
Nature's playground accepts
the challenge.
one piece,
I can feel the magic,
its energy coursing
20 feet above,
rocking without sound
Stepping stones
in *perfect* balance
the Why? was personal.
the How? is only lost,
to the mind that cannot see.

Aven R. Baral

MOONSONG

Pale rays of golden hue
Ride the glow of night
A vision of spectral aura
Finds my floating consciousness
Merging along the plane of light
Each has something to give
Paths of reality
Perspectives of change
Quiet, peaceful, loving
Looking up, unaltered
Listening to the moonsong.

Aven R. Baral

LISTENING

Sometimes I feel we judge only by
    what we see;

And;

Sometimes I feel we judge only by
    what we hear;

It is the one who can bring the two
together, that will feel no need to
    judge at all;

For they will have come to understand,
    what it means;

To judge.

William Arthur Shoemaker

MUSIC

Free from time,
My life is now mine,
Where will you find me, now?
Lost among the stars,
Can I travel that far,
No limits put upon me?
With no beginning or end,
My spirit I send,
To all who can hear its song.
No longer alone,
I've found my home,
In the hearts of those who love me.

Philip A. Meade

COPPER HARBOR TRIP

A cool breeze sweeping across the land
Trees swaying and leaves blowing
No bright sun today
Rain clouds high above

Small group of people gathered on hill
Don't fall, it's a long way down
Rocks became a fence
A lake in the distance trees

Barbecue aroma in the air
Talking and laughter by the tables
Children getting dizzy on merry-go-round
Aging gray cabins far away
Audible songs of birds

Debbie L. Budnick

JESUS SAVIOUR

You asked me why I love Jesus?
He's my Saviour, my guide, and my Friend.
He's waiting with God up in Heaven.
But one day He is coming again.

If you tell someone you love Jesus,
Do you show it by the way that you live?
Do you treat others with love and affection?
Or do you expect more than you give?

If you don't know Him as your Saviour,
If you've never been saved from your sin,
Just ask Him today to forgive you,
Then open your heart and let Him in.

He's the Son of my God up in Heaven.
He's the Saviour of a world full of sin.
He's the light in a world filled with darkness.
And oh how He wants to come in.

Don't you know He will love you forever?
Don't you know He'll forgive every sin?
He's waiting at the door for your answer,
Oh please won't you let Him come in?

Virginia K. Hutto

THE SONG LIVES ON

As one life is bound to another, the Song lives through us.
It derives life from us and seeks comfort
In its message of joy and laughter and love.
Like a haunting refrain, its melody fills the mind
And invades the soul with its silent peace,
Only to touch the heart, the Song lives on.

Like the sun's protective warmth is boundless
    and rain's tears plentiful,
As nature's parade of mysteries and beauty surpasses
    the tragedies of life
To fill the air with awe, so does that one solitary Song,
As it touched the soul of a world in a rhapsody of unselfish love.
And now, even though the last strains have been played,
The echo of its recurring melody will continue.

It can be heard in the rhythm of every raindrop
And with each new birth of day.
It has come to us on the travels of a summer breeze
Or on the wings of a butterfly in flight.
Yes, the Song lives on, it can never die,
For as long as we love, as long as we share,
We will the Song life.
Listen, hear its gentle voice building, building until
    it possesses us.
It has touched our lives, it has kissed our souls.
The melody returns and the memory of that Song will linger forever.

Linda Piscitelli

MAGIC

Eyes burn hidden fire, tiny flames dance within their depths.
Motionless you tower before me, silent and majestic as the night.
A glance offers its wordless command, my will suddenly grows weak,
Drifting aimlessly a prisoner of your thoughts, trapped
    in a sea of your choosing.

A smile shares a secret with your eyes, as the tilt of your head
Draws me closer into the crystal maze, called your world.
Your voice spins music around me, a cascading waterfall of song,
As moon and stars caress the sky, I fall captive
    to your circling arms.

Royalty King, come lead me home, weave your magical spell.
Be you mystic or magician, what is this power you possess?

A bittersweet melody catches my heart as stars glitter
    on velvet satin.
Bathed in one golden moment, dissolving the boundaries between us.
My steps fall in line beside you, lost in the memory of your touch,
Mindless of the path you lead, I follow in silent consent.

Treasures you offer, your kingdom as prize,
Shared evenings spun in valentines;
A canvas of diamonds you paint in the night,
All these to be mine to stand at your side.

Royalty King, come take my hand, forget your magical spells.
My love I offer, a gift set free, will release this power over me.

Whisper low, words unspoken, eyes deliver crystal gems.
Two hearts dare to reach beyond different worlds.
Asking for so little, we've gathered the prize
As we realize true magic lives within us.

Linda Piscitelli

DIAMONDS

God gave me a diamond in a world of stones;
He gave me a diamond, so I wouldn't be alone.

This diamond dazzled along a dark road,
Offering companionship, and sharing my load.

The words this diamond spoke still shimmer in my mind:
''Cast your cares upon God, and He will dry the tears of time.''

Then God sent me on a journey, with the end hid in the night;
He blessed me with His Spirit, and this diamond to shed His light.

I fell, but God lifted me up, and again made me a wife and mother;
He said, ''Now — take time to lift up your sisters and brothers.''

God gave me a starburst of jewels in a rainbow of colors;
He told me, ''Write a message of my love, and share it with others.''

I cry as I think of the side of me that helped put Jesus on the cross,
And I can't be satisfied, until God's message is shared with the lost.

God gave me radiant silver in the stars, and mellow gold in the moon,
And as I look toward Heaven, I know Jesus will be coming back soon.

God's been so good to me, tho' the battle is not yet through;
God gave His love, God gave His son, and a friend such as you.

Now as I search my past — God has opened my eyes to see,
All my beautiful friends, and they have all been *diamonds* — to me!

Barbara L. Settlemyre

CAN YOU IMAGINE

Can You Imagine if it were always dark, always night?
If you never saw a flower or the dawn of the morning light?

Can You Imagine if the moon no longer gave its golden glow?
If the stars ceased to shine and the day was as dark as the sea below?

Can You Imagine if life were an empty void, with
    no sun, moon, or stars?
If nature's beauty couldn't be seen, and love,
    and peace were totally barred?

Can you imagine yourself in a deep, dark dungeon of space?
If no longer any laughter rang, and you saw no smile,
    and no other face?

Would you wonder then about God? who He is? and what He's done?
Would you take the time to think about life? its purpose?
    and God's only Son?

Would you stop and realize that you've wondered much too late?
For The End has come, and no amount of praying
    can change the date.

''Be Ready'' is my fervent plea, for *now* is the time
To accept God's gift of life for eternity.
Before you meet death, and your stars no longer shine,
And life as you know it — ceases to be!

Barbara L. Settlemyre

A VISITOR

You forgot something
When you left.

I chased you in an
Attempt to return it.

It took me two whole
Blocks just to catch up.

Then I found out,
I was chasing someone else.

Henry W. Butler

INEVITABLE

The only being
Who is growing younger,
Is Merlin the magician.

He will eventually
Die of his youth
And fade into oblivion.

Let us enjoy
The age
We have reached,

While we are younger
Than we will be,
When tomorrow comes.

Henry W. Butler

THE DEW FAIRY

In the early morning light,
I saw the dew a-shining bright.
Later after, I looked again;
I only saw drops now and then.

And later on in the day,
All the dew had gone away;
I wondered where it did go,
But, I never did get to know.

After night has fallen dead,
And everyone has gone to bed;
Something strange happens then,
About half a past ten.

There is a fairy that comes,
And with her she does bring,
A group of her fairy chums,
That laugh and play and sing.

There is a fairy that I love most,
She is as white as a ghost.
If you don't know her very well;
These words, I will tell,
She is the Dew Fairy!

Etta Person

EVEN NOW

Life is not to be defined.
Listen, it will speak; grab, and it flees;
Motion is the essence, yet only a vapor
Of space, and what you see, its vacancy.

Life is in the existence of the earth
Whirling. It is itself in its continuity.
Observe, and it amazes; enter, and it is you
Who in the forgetting of it, make it whole.

Matthew Weiner

I'LL ALWAYS BE THANKFUL

God gave to the hunter his skill with a knife.
God gave beauty and kindness to the mother.
And He gave to the husband and his wife
Eternal and undying love for each other.

God, with all His mercy and wisdom,
Gave birds wings and to the fish, the sea.
He gave to the king wealth and a kingdom,
And made the sun so the world could be.

I looked at these things, then I thought — why?
A feeling deep within me, a feeling of doubt
Made me wonder, and I looked to the sky.
Has God forgotten me, has He left me out?

Then God gave me you with beauty so fair,
And now I know I've got more than my share.

Etta Person

THOUGHTS IN THE NIGHT

I felt a distant memory,
Of love lost long ago.
A feeling of the way it was,
Has made a mark upon my soul.
I sense a warm summer day,
Of many years gone past,
When we were young and full of life,
And knew our love would forever last.
You come at night upon a dream,
To remind me of the days,
Of making love and laugh along,
In the quiet morning haze.
A gentle warm and tender touch,
Of bodies in loving embrace,
Calls upon my memory,
To find what's lost without a trace.
Many years have past since I knew of,
Your warmth, your love, your plight,
I cry sometimes to think of you,
These thoughts come to me in the night.
I leave you now with this my love,
A thought from a foolish heart,
If once again we could revive,
A love, a dream — so far apart.

William Joseph Martinson

BENEATH A WILLOW

Bury me beneath a Willow
  to cool me when I rest.
Bury me beneath a Willow
  to join the choir's nest.

Bury me beneath a Willow
  plant a white rose bush
so love may always blossom
  above my grassy bed.

Bury me beneath a Willow
  beside a crystal lake
to greet the weary travelers
  who pass my humble place.

Maria L. Canales

THE LORD'S EYE

Colorful memories of a rainbow's prism,
Seem to illuminate the air,
The climate is so fair,
Beautiful luminous clouds decorate the sky,
Feelings and emotions so high,
Sea gulls' flight, so free,
Clear sight to see,
The Lord is on my side,
So I must abide,
In his truth and in his spirit,
Echoes of peace and mind soar,
For I am whole in his Word,
Gentle breezes surround me,
Still waters run deep in my mind,
I have finally discovered that great find,
The Lord's Eye, so kind,
That I rejoice and say Amen!

Shira Yael De Llano

FAREWELL

Life interrupted —
  Dreams of you and me always —
    Death shattered reality . . .

Dale Behrens

LINCOLN

Melancholy seizes me
as I contemplate the
intrigue, deceit, greed
and strife designed to
undo what our
forefathers so valiantly
fought to preserve.
How will it end?

I stand in the East
Room and watch as
citizens of these newly
re-united states weep
beside my dead body.

Joan Bushno

THE MOON IN YOUR POCKETS

In the beginning, which is today and tomorrow
When the waves dropped upon the shore
Until the underlying pink became a chestnut brown
You were there with those eyes and that face branded in memory
It was the mask put over, Become Reality!

And a me, I did some actions
I love, you, all
Like the first spark become fire
About which we gazed
And through it saw our Holy Father
It is silent, still
The playing music
I pretend
But it is His face
You pretend
And then it is alright past posing
That we were the tentative ones
Flickering in darkness
And we poor men
Want to come back from these hunts with *the* face
Like the moon in our pockets
Sometimes it hurts
Walking with the knowledge you gave us
More precious, invisible
You stronger in the traveling, happy darkness

Philip M. Zrike

ALAIN, ADIEU

For Allen Truett

Do you remember so long ago,
  when I first began to love you so?
It was on that day, I found, you were the one
  who, from my heart, my love had won.
And I love you now just as I did then,
  so, why do you ask my love should end?
Is it not strong enough, the love I share?
  Is that why you ask that I cease to care?
Tell me, don't you believe,
  in all the love from me that you receive?
Don't you see how hard it seems,
  for me just to throw away my dreams?
And how hard it is to tell you good-bye,
  knowing we weren't together, you and I?
Maybe I was truly wrong,
  waiting for you for so long,
But, that was the promise I had made
  that my love for you would never fade.
Now I know, since I have found
  you were the one I built my life around,
That to live my life without my love for you,
  would mean to build my life anew.
And since your love wasn't meant for me,
  this is the way that it must be —
  Now I must bid to you, good-bye, my love, Alain, adieu.

Tracie L. Runyon

TRAFFIC JAM

Bumper to bumper, face to tail,
Most human tortures in comparison pale.
You may be outside, but you're also in jail.

Your eye follows the highway, dune to dune,
There's no indication you'll be moving soon,
As the radio plays your least favorite tune.

Though your car's capable of running with God
You must be content to trudge, grind, and plod,
If you don't overheat or perhaps throw a rod.

And those miles-per-hour your speedometer measures
Are pipedreams merely, not present pleasures:
You move inches-per-eon; **those** are your treasures.

Over your shoulder a truck driver frowns;
Some man shakes his fist, a cabby's horn sounds;
Hate proliferates, ill-feeling abounds.

Man has done wonderful things with his brain.
He can fly to the moon; he can predict the rain.
Too bad he can't improve on the wagon train.

John Mumma

BIRD RIVER

Canadian geese cloud a river-reflected sky
In T-formation.
Flooding the air with sirens of screech.
Leader controls his command knocking furiously with
Wings of steel any competitors craving to challenge.
They drop as fallen angels
Into their liquid restuary.
An uninvited intrusion to a river
Feathered-white with gulls.
Extended vacation warming weather to permit.
Mallards, black and white to season surroundings.
Ducking in and out of ever-flowing stream. Seeking fish
A treat to eat quickly before hungry predators overtake.
Winged messengers squeaking, squalling,
A change of weather to inform.
Seagulls, Canadian geese and mallards —
A peppered backdrop for an autumned sky. Fluid motion
Of feathered creatures back-pedaling every cherished
Moment before frozen sunshine descends sending them southward.

Mary Frances Hayes

OBSERVATION MIRRORED:
ABSTRACTION TO ACTION

A sheet of sun-tanned newspaper
Danced crazily across the ripe grasses,
Clicking its own castanets!
Animation contrasted the net-wielding scoop
Of a man cleaning his swimming pool.
But, tenacious winds worked
At staging their scene, by flapping hair and shirt and net!
I mentally queried, "Is life granted so, about me?"
If answer be, "Yes,"
Then 'tis I who must observe, to live!

Raymond Befus

SOMETHING MAGIC

Above the house, from the sky
The moon is hanging, shining
And smiling, almost talking
One young at heart would say.

The early autumn breeze,
Clear has kept the sky,
And the shy stars dare
Show their trembling dim light.

Something magic keeps
The trees so still, and proud,
The still tender grass in harmony
With them, and makes the crickets
Sing so softly, so sweet.

They quietly seem to applaud
The bright full moon,
That salutes and embraces them,
With the ocean of its rich light.

And gracefully the branches
The tall planetree sketches,
To catch the golden beams
Coming from the disk in streams.

Nike Kotsalos

NIKE KOTSALOS. Born: Palama, Lamias, Fthiotidos, Greece, 3-5-49; Married: Efthimios Kotsalos, 6-23-74; Education: High school in Greece; One year of college in Toronto, Canada; Occupations: Housewife, Formerly clerk; Poetry: 'Mikri Mou Yparxi,' *Proini, 4-7-79;* 'Ta Prospa,' *(The Faces), Proini,* 5-10-79; *Amples Psihis,* collection of poems, *National Herald,* 4-26-79; Other Writings: "Xenitemos & Seperation," short story, *Proini,* 4-7-79; Comments: *I write both in Greek and in English. I write of feelings, of events, of relationships between people and generally of people and life, and of their inner and outer beauty, and certainly of their pain and sorrow, for without them the cycle of life would not be complete.*

A KOREAN VILLAGE

Misty mornings
and a silent breeze,
as we walked through the
village, beneath the trees.
And you were beautiful
for I will remember my life long,
how we sang that lovely melody
in that beautiful morning calm.

Marcel Holloway

WIND OF COURAGE

The eyes wide open!
How they long quite often,
To embrace the charm and beauty
Of the great masterpiece!
Sea gulls they wish they were,
Chased by angry waves,
And lulled by calm oceans.

Ulysses' ship though the heart is.
In Charivde's mouth it got lost,
And in Hade the soul went,
And came up alive!
Still, the cloud of suffering
Is there, and marks of wounds,
And stains of bitter tears shed.

Strong wind of courage heads her ahead,
Pulls her onwards, as the master
Pulls the horse by the reins.
To reach Ithaka, where the dream
From sprout becomes a tree,
The hope a living truth.
Can a dove with its eyes open,
And broken wings, win the Universe?
Can a bleeding heart
Win anything at all!

Nike Kotsalos

OUR SWEET LIBERTY

Our Sweet Liberty, how firm she stands.
Watching the harbor to a promised land.
Our goverment knows, as well as we,
She is the symbol of a land that's free.

Oh my! Oh my! how proud she stands,
Lady of liberty sent from another land,
Gleaming and bright when first she came,
Standing proudly, through wind and rain.

One hundred years has taken its toll,
Shrouding her in a dingy stole.
"Restore her we must," was the cry.
Ringing over the states far and wide.

The hearts of this free nation,
All raised up without hesitation,
Churches and schools, industries too,
Pitched in to restore Sweet Liberty like new.

On her birthday the Fourth of July,
Liberty will look as she did in years gone by.
Proudly looking out to sea,
Lighting the way to the land of the free.

You and I can stand proudly too.
We helped to make her look like new.
For we are the hearts of this promised land,
America, for which she stands.

Elizabeth G. Brown

THROUGH AGES AND STAGES

Through ages and stages,
From the first shaft of light.
I helped write the first pages,
Deciding what was wrong or right.

Many miles I have walked,
Only to have my path washed away.
In many languages I have talked,
So few things are permanent today.

I unlocked ancient mysteries,
Washed the highest mountaintops,
Into the depths of the sea.
In Egypt I met with Cheops,
And cured the land of leprosy.

Through ages and stages,
Through many eyes I have seen.
Locked inside human cages,
To many galaxies I have been.

Many years I have spent,
Are buried beneath the sea.
Mostly I came and went,
Each time with a different key.

I'm as old as the wind,
As elusive as the air,
For those who have been,
Drifting from here to there.

Mary Cross

ETERNAL LOVE

It's not so hard to understand,
That Father God became a man.
To comprehend His eternal love,
Through His son sent from above.

Only Jesus Christ can set us free,
Break sin's chains and live eternally.
Into our hearts we ask the Lord,
To unite us all in one accord.

When our old ways we forsake,
Our broken lives He can remake.
For our wrongs He took our place,
Someday we'll see Him face to face.

He knows who are truly His own,
Soon He'll take all His children home.
Straight is the gate and narrow is the way,
Eternal love is found in His word today.

So serve the Lord with all your heart,
He promised He would never depart.
His yoke is easy, His burden is light,
His Holy Spirit will lead you right.

Mary Cross

THE WISPY FOG

The wispy fog is making a blanket against the sky,
Masking the rolling hills, the trees, the town; and my —
So pleasantly blending all as one. And, glancing 'round,
How a quick survey of the ground
Calls attention to tiny creatures hurrying,
Scarcely making a sound with scurrying.

Buds and blossoms nod gaily in an airy breeze,
Giving the impression of being slightly teased,
To awaken from some deep slumbering trance.
Flightless birds appear awaiting some happen-chance.
Yon, joyous sounds of church chimes somewhere
Are suspended high in the misty air.

Slowly emerging through the haze,
Rather dominating the plays,
Bold branches on lofty trees look stiffened —
To anything that would listen
Seemingly trying to beckon:
"Wait! Something glorious is to happen."

Then, suddenly in one corner, as if torn
From some forbidden delicate form,
Comes the sun peeking through,
Dispersing the wispy shadowy fog as dew;
Revealing a mass of vibrant hued background
For one to encounter breathless beauty all around.

Lou Eldridge

THE BRIAR AND THE ROSE

No greater story of desire has ever been foretold,
than how the lonely briar became the perfect rose . . .
As evil is, as some believe,
the manifest of our souls,
so was the passion of the briar,
in creation, of the rose.

    There speaks a flame in each man's heart,
    of conquests, words, and deeds,
    so was within the briar's bowels,
    brought forth from hence the seed.
    Blown by the wind, the flower's breath,
    touched, and became entwined,
    and left its seed to do the work,
    destined, within the vine.

And so the tranquil flower grew, entangled by its fate;
the briar swore to ne'er let go, until it was too late . . .
Never before had evil known,
such beauty could exist,
and though the rose cried out in pain,
such love would not resist.

    Therefore the story must be true,
    each time we prick our thumb,
    of how the lonely briar,
    and the rose, became as one . . .

L. C. Katz

FRIEND

Oh, thank you for being my friend,
I thought you should hear it again.
Just thank you for being my friend, my friend.

The times that we've shared have been fun.
I've wanted to tell everyone.
The times that we've shared have been fun, each one.

I tell this all to you.
What am I gonna do?
I tell this all to you, just you.

Now, what do you think of me?
You're the one who holds the key.
Now, what do you think of me? Let's see!

Gail L. Hofer

THE WILD GEESE

The lake was a mirror reflecting the trees
Standing gaunt on her shores, bare now of leaves.
All was serene on that wintry morn.
Migrating wild geese were sounding forlorn.

In familiar formation they hurried along,
Inconceivable grace aloft in the dawn.
A hunter's gun spoke from a blind on the shore;
A beautiful goose was to fly nevermore.

She fell to the bosom of the blue lake,
And floated there sadly, a small crumpled shape.
The gander then followed her from high above,
Eloquent proof of his sorrow and love.

Forfeiting place in the flight for her sake,
He descended and folded his wings on the lake.
Gaggling in anguish, he swam by her side,
Trying to comfort her there as she died.

Huntsmen, beware bring down the sublime
To satisfy cravings of base humankind.
Ours are not solely the hearts that can break
When circumstances cruelly destine our mates.

Carol S. Meyer

THE HILLS

Of all the places in the world, I know I love the best these hills
that I call home, that God has surely blessed.
These hills offer beauty, and strength for each new day, when my
soul is tired and weary, and cannot find its way.
With a little stream that gently flows to some far-off place,
the water seems to call to you to slow your hurried pace.

The beauty all around me lifts my spirits and fills my heart with
song. I give thanks to God for those hills of mine, these hills
that I call home.

In the evening I watch the sunset sink slowly into the west, taking
away the cares of the day bringing peace and rest. I hear the
plaintive call of the whippoorwill as the day slides into night;
its mate's answer, echoing from the hills, fills me with delight.

When my time draws to a close, and my life has ceased to be,
I leave no mark upon these hills, but they leave their mark on me.

Betty Calton

RAINBOW HARVEST

The golden lights of sky
Shine into my mind,
And visions of blue waters
Float upon my soul.

Scents of evergreen and
Berries fill my empty senses,
As crisp winds caress
My skin gently and fully.

Sharp images of colors
Flash as prisms before
My eyes seeing only color,
And tones within structure.

As one unto the plains,
The breezes gently sway
My body within the wheat,
And rebirth unto transcendence.

Edward D. Broyles

love is
intangible
yet real
fleeting
yet everlasting
hard won
but easily lost
once tasted
never forgotten
once held
never forfeited
love is
you.

Angelia M. Clancy

ENIGMATIC

She came into my dream.
And brushing the dust of ten thousand years
From the silk of her flesh,
And driving the ache of ten thousand fears
From the mist of her soul,

She stepped across the line.
Speaking in a voice that seemed familiar
In the halls of my mind,
Telling me it shouldn't seem peculiar
That she lived in my heart,

She said I must be brave.
And singing the hymn of ten million choirs
In the heavens above,
And playing the tune of ten million lyres,
And of God-given love,

She said I must be strong.
Living in a world which craves destruction,
And will have what it asks,
Learning from the ones who need instruction,
I must give what I have.

J. R. Ping II

ANGRY MOONLIGHT

In the moonlight, angry moonlight,
Shadows stab me in the back.
In my conscience, never silent,
Voices of my will attack.

Yes, you, my angel,
Have led me astray.
My beaten morals
Had nothing to say.

I have argued with my conscience,
Told Him what was wrong and right.
I have vict'ry and dishonor,
Winning, I have lost the fight.

Yes, you, my angel,
Have led me astray.
My beaten morals
Had nothing to say.

In the darkness, blinding darkness,
You were all that I could see.
Was it moral? Was it evil?
''Right for you is right for me.''

J. R. Ping II

CEMETERY

I am alone,
Except for the graves,
And my thundering thoughts,
And the devastated dreams of the dead,
And the frozen fire of forgotten feelings,
And the pervading presence of passion,
And the lingering love,
And the past.
I am surrounded.

J. R. Ping II

I HAVEN'T GOT TIME TO DIE

I haven't got time to die
  There's too many mountains to climb,
Just to see the morning sun,
  As it climbs into the sky.

There's too many things to do.
  I have to look at the blue, blue sky.
And trees with branches stretching high.
  I have to stop and smell the roses, too.

I have to feel the rain against my face
  And I have to pet the puppies, too.
And kiss the kittens when they cry.
  So you see, I haven't got time to die.

I have to feel the summer breezes
  Blowing through my hair.
There's too many babies I have to kiss
  Too many sunsets I don't want to miss.

But most of all I have to find the time to say:
  ''Oh, how I love you today.''
All of these, and many more are all reasons
    why,
  I haven't got time to die.

Ida Rasch

THE POET CAFE

Menu

We have burgers for Papa,
and even his spouse.
When you start to eat them
they melt in your mouth.

We have french fries or
chips. Whatever you like.
There is even a burger for
your little tyke.

We have milk shakes and sodas
and coffee with cream.
There are strawberry sundaes
that look like a dream.

Our cook fixes the order
with his special blend.
Then the waitress will serve
you. With a darling grin.

Karen Buak

GOOD FRIEND

I have been blessed with
a very good friend.
That will stick with me
to the very end.

A friend can be so very
dear.
Mine is always ready to
lend an ear.

Good friend thank you
for standing by.
You always listen when
I cry.

Karen Buak

THINK TWICE BEFORE YOU WALK

It is so easy to walk out
  and not look back.
    The hardest thing is for you to
    stay on the right track.

You could end up in a messy
  divorce.
    Find yourself going way off
    course.

Then jump in the frying pan back
  in the fire.
    Finding this life is not what
    you desire.

So sit down and talk. Then try to
listen.
    You might find your life may
    even glisten.

Karen Buak

Arched Rock.

F.W.QUARTLEY Sc.

AMERICA IS GROWING UP

America has come through the infant stage
Of demanding and taking with pleasure,
The childhood stage of "I, me."
Blind to its faults beyond measure,
The adolescent stage of seeking, searching,
Rebelling. Answers? Knowing them all!
The mature stage of seeing its faults
And admitting them, hoping to recall,
Get rid of the wrong in our country,
Hold fast to the right, we yearn,
Combining a love of our country
With a broader outlook of concern
For all the world and its people,
Knowing each individual has rights.
America, there is hope for you yet
To grow from darkness to light.

America, you are growing up
And I think that we will see
You right the wrongs, keep the good,
Be the great America you can be!

Ruby Tippit Peacher

A SMALL POET SPEAKS

What is thunder, Mother Dear?
 Listen close and I'll tell you.
It's God's great voice when he speaks
 Away up in the blue.
And lightning's His big searchlight
 That helps angels find their way
To children that they guard at night.
 They never lose their way!

The rainbow, Mother, is a path
 The angels all have made
On their way down to our back yard.
 It doesn't really fade.
Sometimes we can't see it
 But when the sun's just right
It makes a bridge across the sky
 That looks so wondrous bright!

The night is God's sleep blanket
 All pinned with jewels that gleam.
But they're not really jewels, Mother.
 Do you know what I mean?
Stars are peepholes into Heaven,
 And that's the gold you see.
The twinkle that I saw just then?
 An angel passed and peeked at me!

Ruby Tippit Peacher

Where is the end?
i sought; i cannot see
the one that comes
too soon for me
to save the soul i lost,
 and when
comes it at last for me
 the time we have
 is past the hour of
 eternity.

Tamara J. Bohn

AS THE CURTAIN FALLS

Flamboyantly costumed
in folds and folds of crimson
She screams her protest
in a magnificent, bloody aria
to eagerly straining hearts,
spending herself —
collapsing —
exhausted —
as the last notes turn
and pierce Her final expiration,
leaving the silence stunned,
overpowered and
speechless with horror
as the curtain falls.

Tamara J. Bohn

FEELINGS

What do we do now that we have touched
Each other's hearts?
We have led each other into waters so deep,
And far from where we felt it was safe to love.

We have touched each other's souls and risen
To new heights of feelings and passion than
We had ever felt before.

So beautiful and intense is our love,
Bringing waves of awe and fear as we
Journey into depths unknown.

Let us not be afraid to love.
Take my hand and let us venture together,
Into the most beautiful adventure of all.

And if along the way we should have
A trace of doubt, or fear,
Let us find peace, and strength in a love
So strong that it cannot be weakened
By oceans of tears, or lifetimes of years.

Lourdes M. Estrada

REFLECTIONS

I look in the mirror and I see
Your eyes.
You can see my soul,
Indeed at times you know me better than I.

I feel so at peace by your side.
I need your wisdom to guide me through
The confusions dreamt up by my mind.

Your love is the light that shines on
The darkest hours of my life.
I can feel your breath warm on my body,
It heals the aches felt by a lonely heart.

I hear your heartbeat in my sleep,
It beats to the same rhythm as mine.
I know you are a part of me,
Two hearts bonded by destiny and love.

I am yours until forever,
Until forever be mine.

Lourdes M. Estrada

A SONG FOR ALEX

Why do I love you so?
Is it because I believe in love because of you?
Is it because I can see God in you so much
 easier
Than I can in myself?

Am I trying to find myself in your eyes?
They've a depth which erases all track of time.
Two cool pools of love that melt my heart.

I know now that one can live or just exist.
Love vibrates through every fiber of my being,
And I know that I am alive,
I know that I am in love.

Why do I love you so?
The answer rings clear through my heart,
And through my soul.
You are love.

Lourdes M. Estrada

A ROOM FOR THE LITTLE ONES (PARC AUX PETITS)

Every Saturday night the Cajun mothers
Put their babes and children down
In parc aux petits   dormir
            shh hhh
 sleep go to sleep mon petit babe
 sleep go to dream Minette kitten

And while little ones slumber Maman
 will dance the gavotte with Papa
 who gathered moss or trapped all
Week to buy that accordion that soothes
 cries
    avec douceur
 sleep go to sleep mon petit babe
 sleep go to dream Minette kitten

Rest precious souls here in a place
 for angels till our musicians fire a
Shot into pink dawn crying, criant,
 Le Bal Est Fini!
 fawns   we will gather you in our
Arms heading home en haut up the bayou
    triangle violon have
    quieted . . .

Jessica Freeman

MY EARNEST PRAYER

Father in Heaven — Blessed is Thy
Sacred name — O, Jehovah
Thou who showest me tender mercy and
Loving kindness in the hour of sorest need
Ever is Thy wing ready to cover me
Thy hand outstretched in infinite compassion
The breath of Thy love is as sweet
Music in the still hours of the night.
My praise of Thee is honey on my lips.
Dear Father in Thy unbounding love and
 abiding charity
Grant me the grace and worthiness
To love and serve my fellow men.

Helen deLong Woodward

THE IMPOSSIBLE DREAM

Many people don't dream the impossible dream.
They say that it is hard to do.
They refuse to believe in it
And their dreams will never come true.
But I find it easy to dream the impossible dream.
Dreaming means that I'll have you.
Living means that I never will.

Some people won't dream the impossible dream
And lose their faith and will to live.
Going solo, never on a team
No capacity for giving love.
But I want my chance to dream the impossible dream.
Dreaming means that you I'll love.
Living means that I always will.

Many try to live the impossible dream.
They give up or die trying
To wade the waters of the stream
Made of their tears and their crying.
But I don't want to live my life the impossible dream.
Dreaming is life redeeming.
Living means onward we go.

Jim Heald

THE VANISHING CHILD . . .

The child learns to comprehend
  The world as a multitude
    Of inter-connecting facets.
Within the midst of feelings,
  The child loses the control of identity.

An integral part?

        The identity
Of being lost within the realm of existence
Becomes the echo in the caverns.
  The light shining with an intensity
Less than the square-root of the
  Reciprocal of the age.

The path, so absurd, that
Leaves lose their color in the spring.
  The child searches for answers
Within the myriad prism of the calculating age.

The forbidden rivers flowing in a parallel
  Away from the understanding
Of the bay.
The child begins to dig within the shell,
Crumbling the litter of the past.

The youthfulness melting into the core!
  The fantasy lost, life lost:
    Adulthood begins?

Christopher C. Smith

MARGARET

I looked at your face and saw a beauty
That, even though imperfect,
Was enough to hold my attention
And more than enough to earn my admiration,
For there was more to see than just another pretty face.
I asked you for your permission but I was denied.
My heart gave into temptation
And we gave into each other
For one second's worth of pleasure in a kiss.
What I did defied my code of honor
And altered my feeling of reality.

Why I let it get to me, I don't know,
This worthless dream so full of glory.
It tugs at my heart and runs through my mind.
These thoughts don't bring me any comfort.
Yes, it was a fantasy, it was shadow,
So much form without life
But the pain of the memory is sharper than a knife.
I'm haunted by an event that never occurred.
It intrudes on my thoughts,
Defiles everything I've been taught
And mocks me in the still of the night.

What happened that night never was
But I pray that it does.
Both of us knowing what we do.

Jim Heald

JAMES F. HEALD. Born: Dayton, Ohio, 9-26-64; Education: Ashland Community College, Law Enforcement Major; Occupation: Mailroom worker at *The Daily Independent;* Memberships: National Rifle Association; Gun Owners of America; Citizens Committee For the Right to Keep and Bear Arms; Comments: *To date I have written over 50 poems. They are primarily concerned with dreams and my feelings regarding them. When I use the term "dream," I am talking about rapid eye movements (REM) that occur when sleeping. 'Margaret' is the name of a lady I work with and is based upon a dream I had about her.*

A LYRE UPON THE DISTANT WIND

A lyre is heard upon the distant wind which blows
through the corridors of time.
Within, there are Dorian melodies and voices which murmur the love
songs of Olympus and the tragic requiem of those who fell heroically
on the Mound at Thermopylae; reminders of our ancient past.
Though as diverse as love and war may be,
the span of ages has shadowed their reality.
To us who live there is a haunting romance in both.
And to those who will in future ages stand where we stood, love and
tragedy will be one in the same, silhouetted by the imagination of our
descendants' dreams of what reality was to us, to what they conceive it
to have been.

Scott Arminas

THE LOST WATCH

It seems it all started
On a sad day in May,
Who could believe
Who conceive
That things would develop this way.

The only item wanted
Was a gentle man's watch,
A sentimental keepsake
Not a materialistic cheap fake
The timepiece he loved so much.

Due to irresponsible actions
And lackadaisical deeds,
There is family separation
Strained communication
Totally disregarding people's needs.

Future generations have been cheated by this
Doesn't his family care?
This special treasure
That kept time to full measure
The damage can we ever repair?

Mary Mar McCuen

A SEASON INTERLUDE

The Autumn sunset so brilliantly
 Has touched the forest green.
And instead has hued the woodlands
 Into a golden Autumn bronze.
While the northern winds around my house,
 Not to gently toss the falling leaves.
To make my carpet green a carpet brown,
 Rake, oh! rake those fallen leaves
That gave you shade in the summer's heat.
 There! it just fell in the heap of leaves,
A robin's nest so neatly woven.
 It withstood the summer storms,
And now it makes its farewell to summer.
 And as I hold the nest I can see,
The love it took to house the blue eggs three.
 Rake, oh! rake those bronze-colored leaves
That gave you shade in the summer's heat.

Josephine Sadowski

THE FOUR SEASONS

Solemnly towards winter's sky
I thoughtfully cast a glance:
Will I be here when it returns
A part of life, its game and chance?

Sprouting flowers and coming spring
And streams that reach the sea —
Will it be then that I must leave
While you come on incessantly?

Or summer in your leafy green
With flowers bright and clear,
Will you still blossom on and on
When I'm no longer here?

Colorful and fruitful fall
Harvest time of year —
Which season will it be for me
When reaping time draws near?

Erselia Monticello Barton

LIFE'S EDGES

There are thoughts that come with twilight
Mellowed by the glow of dusk
They soften sharp and pointed feelings
Smooth rough edges deep in us.

There's a time for retrospection
In the calm of even'light
And the pause for deep reflection
That one feels when comes the night;

When the errs of early morning
Though unimportant they seemed then,
Come to us as timely warnings
From that world of might-have-been;

When our love is of the purest,
Strong our faith in mankind, too.
When our dreams stand out the surest
In all things we plan to do —

But when night rolls up her blanket
And the dawn breaks cool upon us,
There stands life with all its edges
To be faced again at dusk!

Erselia Monticello Barton

CEOL

life
ceases to exist
beyond the crowded pub
when Irish music
casts
its happy spell

enchantment reigns
and
magically
the charms of lilting tunes
draw hands together
each to each
to count
the lively beat

toes tap too
as fingers dance
across the singing fiddle
and
driving rhythms
leave no one
but
the dead
unmoved

Kathleen P. Mallon

LONELY BIRD

Lonely bird of dusk
Take flight
To a warm haven
Before your paradise
Goes its earthly way.
Soon summer's love
Will fade to
Winter's chill
Shattering your
Spirit of spring.

Martha Mae Martinson

FIRE AND ICE

fall's fiery colors
invigorate
the spirit
before
the black and white
of winter

golden mirrors
on the ground
stare back
at outstretched branches
and
reflect
the regal,
though temporary beauty
of
autumn's glorious glow

soon
they'll turn to starkness
when
winter winds whip
whiteness o'er the land
and
the calm of cold
claims control

Kathleen P. Mallon

The sea has a million faces
It shimmers in the sun of seekers
And shouts out false freedom
Caressing the senses

The sea is beyond controlling
A million bodies are lost to it

Reach out for a reasoned realm
Yearn for a sturdy anchor
But the sea goes on unheeding
And a million faces stare
Without comprehension

Doris Beausoleil

A POEM FOR MICHAEL

Michael's aura is laughter and love.
The beauty of innocence in an
exceptional child.

My nephew is three,
he reaches for stars . . .
catches them too,
they twinkle in his eyes.

Michael can make a dreary day bright.
A smile from him brings sunshine into my life.

Here is the best gift your aunt can give you,
a poem written from the heart,
with love, for my nephew.

Linda Carapella

IGNORANCE

"What's wrong?" she asks,
    "What's wrong?"

            "Nothing," I murmur,
                    "Nothing."

    If she only knew.

Her stare lingers
    then slowly turns away

            And my heart becomes a
                    deeper shade of blue,

    If she only knew.

She sits in her ivory
    tower, so ignorant.

            My mind's eye sees
                    her and weeps.

    If she only knew. . .

Elizabeth Berlie

OUR FRIENDSHIP

Friends are the silken strands of life that entwine into threads,
To be woven into the fabric of our existence.
Each strand has something to contribute whether it be color,
Length, strength, size, sensitivity, or endurance.
A cloth can be no better than the thread from which it's made,
And a garment no better than the cloth.
The most rare and artistic tapestries owe their beauty and endurance
To the materials involved as well as to the artist's talent.
Such are we as individual strands of humanity;
Strands of lives. Those are our lives
That are much akin to each other in hope, aspiration, and expectancy.
We may be entirely different in capabilities, methods, opportunities,
And performance, and yet so entwined in comprehension, appreciation,
Attraction, and concern, as to become a strong bond of affection
That will endure time, trouble, trials, and separation.
Just as the quality or content of thread is ofttimes
    the act of nature,
So our lives are many times directed by God or Divine Providence.
Our lives sometimes seem to be affected by mere happenstance, but
With proper meditation, culminate beyond all expectation
Into pleasurable circumstance.
Such is the nature of *our friendship*.

William W. Dillinger

Constantly on my mind, the joy of hearing your voice,
    seeing your beautiful eyes in smile
        simple pleasures yet so immense

    Oft severe demands of the human condition
    occasional tensions dissipated in giving to each
        supporting, touching — love as giving

Wanting to be understood, loved at the deepest levels
    wanting to touch, hold and share
    love never cheap — yet to behold as the greatest joy

Kerry McGeath

END BURN

In days gone by, when wood was king,
Warmth to homes Round Oak Stoves did bring.

With numbers raised, each stove was dated;
On the side of this stove they were located.

On cold winter days people would stand
With back to the stove, the heat was grand.

In a short nightshirt Grandfather stood
Soaking in heat from his hard-earned wood

When on the floor, a tiny dime spied
He bent over to get it; "Ouch!" he cried.

To the Doc we rushed him to treat the burn
He looked at the damage, then looked real stern

And said, "Why did you come for help so late
When your accident happened in ninety-eight?"

Since back to the woodstove is now the trend
Watch out! and don't get burned on the end.

Edna Dame

OCTOBER AERIAL GRANDEUR

Sunshine highlights nature's beauty
    as cloud-curtains roll back.
Looking from miles above, 39,000 feet up in fact,
    man-made concrete highways seem to "just ribbon along."
On this flight we're surrounded with skies of blue;
    nary a cloud obscures such splendored view.

Winding rivers and streams, forests, fields, plains, farms,
    valleys and towns stretch — a crazy quilt of pieces
    — all patterned by God's plan.

As we cruise along at speeds unheard below,
    the scene slowly changes, but before we go,
    notice that "speck of lint" moving along
    on the "highway ribbon" — is it a semi-truck?
    that "grain of salt" behind it, a passenger van?

The cottony clouds drift by lazily;
    clarity fades along with fall's beauty
    where yesterday's snow covers the ground
    like chocolate and whipped-cream topping.
Less and less is visible of town after town.

Our plane switches to a northeasterly course;
    the pilot announces how soon we will land.
While cloud formations gather, our panorama of clear sky
    and fall-colored scenes vanishes
    and a touch of winter blankets the ground.

Elsie V. Alfrey

POETRY WORKSHOP

You flew to us
on fearful wings
to lead the waiting
old and young;
— the anadromous
hopeful scribes.

Our renitence flooded exedra
forgetting dues and expectations;
— arresting bellies
— moving declensions
— freezing ideas
— heralding dross.

Then waiting hopefuls met again
fetching the fodder
of simple words:
dropping defenses
getting applaud!

Your lurid lips
pronounced attainment
of our goals beyond Prospectus;
through worsted tamis
of drabby workshop
we sapped papyrus
worthy of crowning
Homo Erectus . . .

Romuald J. Orlowski

STRONGEST QUALITY

Sometimes it comes in subtle ways
other times well known.
It can be very soft in thought
or sometimes strongly shown.

It is willing to be open
in any form or way
and it only wants to grow
getting better every day.

It can give encouragement
or a kindness undeserved
while it hopes for only good
and shares a friendly word.

It has so many uses
and fills our life with awe.
Being absolutely free
it's the greatest gift of all.

Without it hearts are lost
because it is our best
human attribute
overcoming all the rest.

It can only be one thing
and it proceeds from God above.
Our strongest quality is what
the human race calls *love.*

Denise Hayden

SILENCE

Silence is just as pleasing
as the chirp of a mockingbird
just as sweet to my ears
as a raging river heard.

Silence is just as soothing
as the rustle of new-fallen leaves
just as warm to my thoughts
as a fast but soft-blowing breeze.

Silence is sometimes a blessing
as the stir of new life around
just as welcome in my heart
as raindrops that fall to the ground.

Silence is sometimes a wonder
as the night when sounds don't occur
just as happy to my day
when all sounds suddenly stir.

Silence can be so calming
as the waves that roll to and fro
just as pleasant to my nerves
as a friend I've come to know.

Silence can make me happy
as a mountain stream crystal clear
just as lovely to my soul
as any sound I may hear.

Denise Hayden

JUST IDLE HANDS

As you walk along life's road,
While you make your numerous plans,
Are you working for the Lord,
Or do you have "just idle hands"?

Jesus came, he made the way,
He broke the shackles and the bands
While he walked and preached and prayed,
He didn't have "just idle hands."

Paul and Silas, Peter, Luke,
They all traveled many lands,
As they spread the words of Christ,
They didn't have "just idle hands."

What are you doing there, my friend?
Are you walking by His plans?
Or are you slothful, slumbering, sleeping
With just a pair of "idle hands"?

Peace and joy that reign within,
Smooth out all life's shifting sands,
He did a work beyond compare,
Christ did not have "just idle hands."

Silver nailed him to the cross,
There made a record that still stands,
Deep within my heart I'll share,
My life for Christ, no "idle hands."

Glen R. Buck, Sr.

BLUEBIRD

Bluebird, make a nest in my tree
Bluebird, do not fly away —
Raise your babies here in my yard —
Never, never go away —

Happiness will ever linger
Right here in my own dooryard —
I would fight the storms to save you —
It wouldn't be ever hard.

For you bring a world of gladness
When we see you fly around
Sing your songs so sweet and tender —
Peace and pleasure will abound.

Your name stands for what we all seek
In this grim old world today
Stay around and just remind us
To help you to keep it gay!

Marjorie Hennigan

LOVE'S LIGHT

Love's light unfolds.
The clouds are a window
   of its reflection.
Dancing in the daytime,
   holding peace,
and clinging to the evergreen.

Love's light is brightly lit.
It does not hurt to look inside.
Its pathways are a mirror
   of every answer
a man must look for.

Love's light is steadfast
   in knowledge.
Forming rainbows from
   droplets of water,
giving heat to the warm heart
   that has been shivering for so long!

John Moran

MOON SHADOWS

A day world of devils
Had scratched at my brain;
In the evening
When the trees danced in the starlight
And moon shadows softly swayed
In the whiteness and quietness,
The secrets of my soul
Mingled with them
And they took my cares away.

Martha Mae Martinson

SHHH

A barren desert she roams — a no-man's land she walks alone
I watch her through a sheet of glass —
    through which my tears for her cannot pass
Her body numb. Her shoes are worn —
    she drags the tow. She's dressed in thorns
Time heals one and hurts another —
    a wound breathes when it's uncovered

Restless nights I'm all alone — an empty aching in the bones
Under my ribs I feel the cut — a bed for two but there is one
Priceless things. This time with you —
    glass sheet between us I want truth
In a pit of snakes she makes me burn —
    something here for me to learn

Don't let go now we're almost there —
    a humid night something shared
Sun drips through the blackened cracks —
    lifting shadows off her back
We rocked each other gushed in the clench —
    was there heroin in her kiss
A pool of tears I watch you shake —
    let me suck the poison from your veins

Now I touched your lips can I touch your soul —
    you've been hurt once so you withhold
In your eyes I see the fear — so like the sea I learn to yield
You drew a line you can't erase —
    that crooked line expressed your strength
Don't return unto that place — up the road it becomes straight

    Uh-huh . . . Shhh. Uh-huh . . . Shhh Uh-huh Diane.

    Howard Dantzler

A STATUE AT MEISENHEIM

In a courtyard by a park
On the verdant grounds
Of the Klinik Meisenheim
A stone statue stands.

Three naked little children reach up to hug their mother.
She looks down and smiles
At the bare babe on her arm —
Reaching for her waiting breast.

Inside the four-storied building many rooms look out
At the hills over old Meisenheim.
In spotless corridors, lined with pictures of the English hunt,
Doctors, cheerful nurses and their helpers move busily about.

Patients, for the most part, are ambulant.
They're walking wounded still —
Evidence of nerve damage
From operations at other times and places.

At Meisenheim, they make people whole again.
It's a mighty task to put damaged nerves on track.
The mother in the statue knows about these things.
She prays that her children never are botched-up.

    Royston W. Donnelly

A CHRISTMAS MEMORY

I stood in line with other shoppers,
On a busy Christmas Eve day.
The sound of jingle bells filled the store.
Of shoppers there seemed to be more and more.
I grew tired of the colorful display.
In memory I went back to a long-ago Christmas Day.
There was a new-fallen snow.
I walked with other villagers to church in the twilight glow.
All was quiet; then I heard a little child say,
''Mother, the stars are so bright.''
The mother whispered, ''Thus it was the first Christmas night.''
We entered the little church lighted by the candles' glow.
The villagers had made a crèche,
A village girl was the virgin, a doll the babe of long ago.
The villagers knelt, their eyes held reverence,
The village girl was Mary, meek and mild,
The toy she held, the Jesus Child.
Softly, the stooped old organist with gnarled fingers began to play,
Silent Night, Holy Night, the soft music filled the air.
I bowed my head in reverence — I knew God was there.
''Your change, Madam,'' I heard a salesgirl say.
I gathered my packages and hurried on my happy way.

    Susie Katherine Smith

HIS LAST HOME RUN, PART I

He stands there posed, the pitcher throws —
What might be the score, home run, suppose?
We wait in silence, every one,
All that is needed is a home run.
Slightly bent, he gives a powerful swing,
That ball soars high, like an eagle flying.
He throws down his bat and starts to run,
'Midst the roaring of the crowd cheering him on.
He picks up speed like a bullet shot from a gun —
He made it, he made it, he made a home run.
And I, his mother, with pride, overcome,
Whispered softly, ''Well done, my son, well done!''
Now that he's gone, I have sweet memories,
With his old uniform across my knees,
Knowing in my heart, he made it through,
The pearly gates up there in the blue.
I used to sit after day's work was done
And stare into the sky toward the setting sun,
And to Jehovah, our Father, in heaven say,
''Why did You take my son away?''
I know he was ill and was suffering pain,
But You could have made him well again.''

    Nelda Wilson

LIFE

The sun in all its radiance brings forth a new morn.
An old man is dying while a child is born.
I hear people at work and children at play.
I see persons rushing to and fro on their way
to destinations; I know not where.
Perhaps they seek pleasure or fortune there,
but an outcome that's bleak waits many or few.
The future lies waiting to unveil its plan.
Am I the wrinkly new child or the wrinkled old man?
I'm afraid to ask! Aren't you?

    David Wayne Perry

MANHATTAN

out
out
shout
shout
some distance
between
cars
some space
away
away
from the heart of
Manhattan
into another world
still steel
still rain
still trucks
skyline
behind
smoke stacks
scattered
smattered
smog

Martha Mae Martinson

MARTHA VENNER MARTINSON. Born: Batesville, Arkansas; Married: Harald Edward Martinson; Education: Stephens College, Columbia, Missouri, 1942; Huntindon College, Montgomery, Alabama, 1960; Hagerstown Jr. College, 1984; Memberships: Daughters of the American Revolution, Fountainhead Garden Club, Officers' Wives Club; Awards: First, Second prize, 'Lonely Bird,' 'Moon Shadows,' Hagerstown Jr. College creative writing contest; Themes: *Nature, other environmental influences and experiences, religious, personalities. Images in words are emotionally felt.*

CHILDREN OF GOD

Children of God,
That's what we are.
We all have fears,
But we've come so far.

To find the trials
And joys we're given.
Our test is to realize
They are sent from Heaven.

To overcome problems,
As well as temptations.
To make each day brighter
And finally defeat Satan.

Jan Kimball

HUE OF LOVE

''Shh!'' the storm is loud.

Love reflects from the clouds
and a rainbow reaches down.
Touch the colors of the 'bow
penetrating through your soul.

Blue, violet, yellow, green
flush into a crimson stream.

Rushing, pumping through your blood
floods into the hue of love.

Then rises up into the bow
arching over the storm below.
And rushes back into the clouds
of the heart that love just found.

''Ahh'' the sun is out.

Julie Meador

BEAUTY'S TRUTH

for Charlene

There is a beauty that lies deep within
a given few divinely touched
That captures the soul and sends
a radiant image of sculptured love.

The senses crave the pleasures of lust
but the heart aches with splendor
When beauty from within is thrust
from a soul strongly tender.

Outward beauty flees with age
few know beauty's truth:
Inner beauty never fades
for it's the only begotten of youth.

Julie Meador

IN MY DREAMS

We were supposed to get together
To take a midnight stroll
Along the beach,
To caress and please.

I was told you'd already left.
I headed for the beach
Not knowing where you'd be
I followed my instincts.

Back, back to where we had lain
The night before
But all I found
Were your sandals in the sand.

Returned to my room
Was tired, fell asleep
But, I finally caught up with you,
In my dreams.

B. J. Lisatz II

THE TEDDY BEAR IS DEAD

The Teddy Bear is dead,
What an awful shame.
He had such a good home,
It will never be the same.

But no one wants to realize
His life could have been spared
If some would have opened their eyes
And showed they really cared.

Teddy died of lonely tears,
It's sad but very true.
As happy as the bear appeared
No one could see through.

People are too busy,
Concerned only for themselves,
They couldn't see his insides
Crying for some help.

The game of life is hard to play,
And it hurts for me to say,
It was a shame, everyone cried
The day that Teddy died.

Linda Carapella

GREAT-GRANDMOTHER BROYLES

In her 90's, Great-Grandmother,
An invalid, relived the past.
She told of Civil War days and
About hiding in a haystack.

Union soldiers came marching through
Their large farm in Monroe County.
She hid with Grandpa John, a boy,
While the soldiers took their bounty.

Then she lost her power of speech,
Her lovely red hair had turned white.
One evening she became restless,
Wanting to smoke her corncob pipe.

Uncle Ovie's Minnie asked her
If she wanted up in a chair.
She nodded yes and Aunt Lize helped
To put her in place with great care.

Aunt Minnie filled the corncob pipe,
Lighting it and taking a draw.
She carefully placed it firmly
In the old hands of Great-Grandma.

Soon there was a billow of smoke,
Aunt Minnie said, like a brush fire!
Great-Grandma enjoyed her last puff,
Then she slumped over and expired.

Eileen B. Perry

HIS LAST HOME RUN, PART II

But today, dear Father, I know why,
When I called, You heeded not my cry,
And why, by You, my weak judgment was spurned.
My life's lesson is now well learned.
For in Your great love and wisdom, You could see,
What was best for my dear son and me.
You caused me to venture into a lovely dream.
You placed me in the grandstands again.
Row number one, cloud number nine,
I could see well, dear son of mine.
He stood there so straight and tall,
No defects, none at all.
I could hear angels cheering him on
As he flew through the gates on His Last Home Run.
Then and there I knew it was true,
He was well and safe in the arms of You.
Now I can see Your plans are right
From that beautiful dream I had that night.
What seemed reproof to me was love most true,
You did what any loving father would do.
You healed his wounds, took away his pain,
You made him well and whole again.

"Now I lay me down to rest
Thank You, Father, you know best."

Nelda Wilson

TO THE VIETNAM VETERAN

It was many and many a month ago,
in a land beyond the sea,
where fields of soldiers, some you may know,
survived, died, and fought for victory.
Who went as a boy, and left as a man,
in this land beyond the sea.
Those we loved with a love, a glorious love,
deeper than the sounding sea,
the ones who fought for you and me.
And this is the reason that many and many a month ago,
in this land beyond the sea,
there came to be names, and names of men,
placed on a monument in D.C.
Every winter, summer, spring, and fall,
Mother Nature falls upon the stone,
and each name, each man, each soldier there,
may in Heaven roam,
for hell was in Phu Bai, Mai Lai, Da Nang, Quang Tri,
and at the DMZ.
And so all the men who once were there,
in the land beyond the sea,
are loved with a love, a glorious love,
deeper than the sounding sea.

Peggy Kendrick Clements

GOD'S CHRISTMAS TREE

God has a Christmas tree
Whereon He died for you and me.
He brought us back what Adam lost.
Oh! It had to be love to pay that high cost.

Under the tree you can see
The gift of peace for you and me.
As we look at his marred face
We can see the access to the throne of grace.

There is another gift we call hope and it's for all.
This holds us up when we are about to fall.
Triumph in trouble is under the tree.
That is another grace for you and me.

Love is there for me and you.
That causes us to be faithful and true.
The gift of the Holy Spirit surely stands out.
He will lead us and show us about.

Deliverance from wrath don't you overlook.
We are his children, and our names are in his book,
Another gift for you and for me
Which reads Joy, this you must see.

These eight gifts are yours and mine.
God has displayed them so true and kind.
So don't forget God's Christmas Tree.
There he proved his love for you and me.

Troy Lee Walsingham

GOD'S PLAN FOR MAN

God's plan for man,
Is to redeem him if He can.
God reaches out everywhere,
But man keeps on as if God didn't care.

God's plan is in the hand of man,
To carry it out the best he can.
If men would only answer the call,
The job would be easy on us all.

There are just the few who will take the stand,
To carry out God's master plan.
God knows the horror at Judgment Day,
When people stand before Him with nothing to say.

We open the church doors to God's grace,
That men may be saved no matter the case.
There is no excuse that God will accept,
He knows us all, we need His help.

Man's plan is to do the best he can,
God knows then he will miss the promised land.
Let us forget the plan of man,
And listen to God's master plan.

Oh, God, here I stand,
Lost and helpless as a dying man.
Forgive my sins that Christ atoned,
I accept Thy plan and make Heaven my home.

Troy Lee Walsingham

BLIND AS A BAT

Dedicated to victims of epilepsy

Blind as a Bat!

That's what the man said.
Before the townspeople
put him to death.

A change of view,
or a different idea
is a crime against our way of life
that will not be tolerated 'round here.

One dimension people
tunnel vision disease
frightened of opinions
or different beliefs.

If I have to live amongst ignorance
I'd rather be dead
so go ahead and tighten the noose
sitting on my neck.

You can't kill everyone who's
different than you.
There will be others comin' soon.

I have lived a full life, with no regrets,
hurry now and complete your task.
It's just sad you people are alive,
yet you were born dead.

Linda Carapella

LINDA MARIE CARAPELLA. Born: Brooklyn, New York, 8-28-56; Occupations: Accountant, Computer operator; Epileptic; Poetry: 'Soul,' *Impressions,* 1987; 'A Daughter's Regret,' *Award,* 1987; 'Talk to Me,' *A New Day,* 1987; Comments: *'Blind as a Bat' is dedicated to victims of epilepsy. They are a group of intelligent people who are deprived of jobs, who fight with medication, are misunderstood by the criminal systems, and above all are misjudged by the ignorant people around them.*

AN ODYSSEY

It is not so much the sadness
    of the night
And the loneliness of the sea
That cut deep through
    the heart
As it is the memory
Of a tenderness now turned
    to spite
A devotion now turned
    to indifference —

Concordia B. Braña

IT'S UP TO YOU

I am a man
with only one heart

It can never
be replaced
if torn apart

Be very careful
or yes,
you may see
this man turn into
one

two

three

Craig S. Moore

MRS. DUFFY

It's so peaceful here with you
A nice and easy, quiet life
No surprises come to shock me
Since I have become your wife

You're always home at night for dinner
While other men stop at the bar
Other women wait and wonder
At five fifteen I hear your car

Our days are planned out by the hour
Rise at six — in bed by nine
The checkbook comes out to the penny
Each Friday we go out to dine

Our shoes are lined up in the closet
All bills are paid the day they're due
Our pictures hang there straight and even
No crooked lines to spoil the view

We choose our friends with quiet care
There's not a rebel in the bunch
We all share much the same opinions
Each Monday we go out to lunch

From all life's troubles I'm protected
Because I'm always here wtih you
I've everything I've ever wanted —
I wish I was in Kathmandu.

Deanna Williams

AYE AYE

Listen to a sunset.
Catch a falling star.
Ask yourself the question
Do you know who you are?

Dive an ocean deep.
Climb a mountain high.
Ask yourself the question
Do you know who you are?

Attitude without purpose.
Reason without rhyme.
If only for a moment
you become lost in time.

Ask yourself the question
Do you know who you are?

Craig S. Moore

ONE DAY OLDER

Was it an earthquake
that stunned me awake
at daybreak?
No, in seconds, I realize it was heartache
listening to the sound of my own heart break.

I wish to drift upon a quiet sea,
old memories clothed inside of me.
Not to think I'm a divorcee
drifting fancy-free,
to a degree, as an absentee.

I feel so afraid.
God knows I've prayed.
My debts seem overpaid
trying to persuade
these many tears to fade.

My children are all grown
with children of their own.
Leading lives apart from mine,
why do I feel so empty inside?
God, I've been so blind.

Tomorrow is another day.
This, in fact, I must never betray.
Life does go on.
This, I must see
and continue to believe.

Rose Marie Ruth

BLACK

Black invades my yard by night
with long, soft brushes.
Just before black paints my place
it always presents me with colors
of unimaginable beauty
splashed across the evening sky.
Then slowly black creeps in
decorated with shining jewels
that lets you know all is alright
to close your eyes.

Pam Niskanen

THE FLAG

The flag stands for many things to many people.
But to me it gives a message like unto a church steeple.
Its colors I admire as it waves high in the sky.
It seems to say on me you can rely.
Red to me is Sacrifice, Love, and Power
For God's people to live victories every hour.
White is for Purity, cleansed and redeemed,
That Holiness, Justification, and Rededication can be proclaimed.
Blue is for Heaven where the Savior is so true,
Sitting at the right hand of God making intercession for me and you.
So you see the flag and its colors mean much to me.
For it reminds me of Redemption, Purity, and Heaven
Where I will one day be.
So let us fly it high and proud.
Proclaim its message and proclaim it loud.

Troy Lee Walsingham

THE CHALLENGE

In a beautiful dream last night,
I visited a land of pure delight.
There I walked upon streets of gold,
and basked in the radiance of untarnished souls.
I conversed with angels, talked at length with Abraham,
and then I stood face to face with the Lamb.
His countenance indescribable, His presence thrice blest,
just to stand before Him brought all my turmoil to rest.
I wanted to stay, but He bid me go.
I had to return to this world below.
I asked, Lord, must I go back there?
to streets with potholes and crime everywhere,
where there is sickness and hunger and no justice can be found,
where the good is downtrodden and evil renowned?
He answered, ''My child, you must fill the potholes,
and crime you must defeat.
Share that which I have given you that the hungry might eat.
If concern for the sick you truly feel,
you must tell them of My love that will completely heal.
Your challenge, My child, along with the entire human race,
is to make your land a better place.''

Dorothy Hemphill Edwards

THE CALL

Lord, you have called me from a world of limits,
to a consciousness beyond earthly bounds,
to that realm of the Kingdom of Heaven,
where perfect peace and contentment may be found.
Although I now see its beauty dimly,
and its scope I do not fully comprehend,
it is changing my life daily,
leading me to a future without end.
Lord, you have called me from a world of limits,
to a consciousness full and free,
leading me to complete expression
of my image and likeness to Thee.

Dorothy Hemphill Edwards

HARLEM

Harlem, home of the spirit.
Can you hear it?

In the bars, in the cars,
In his vein, in his pain.

Hey, Harlem. Say dignity.
Say pride. Don't hide!

I danced with the souls of my ancestors
On a stroll down Adam Clayton Boulevard.
They jazzed me back to their time.
A time when men weren't allowed to be men.

A time when Billie bluesed and gay was cool.
And black was not and jazz was hot.

Hey, whispering horn, here you were born.
To swing, to croon, to fly me to the moon.

Hey, Harlem, I say, will you live another day?
Will you live if we pray to dance again the night away?

Your lies and your truths
Have escaped our youth.

Giving you no reason why,
No reason for . . . no reason!

King heroin still blows in the wind
And clouds of fluffy white cocaine
Still leave us in the sky.

Your life, your music,
Your existence . . . why?

James T. Glover

AIN'T YOU TIRED?

Oh, whiteman, ain't you tired yet?
How long will it take before you forget?
All those boogeyman lies that your father told.
And that slavish thinking from days of old.

Oh, whiteman, ain't you tired yet?
Hey, don't you feel the least regret?
It's been over a century since you knew my name.
But what you call me is still the same.

Oh, whiteman, ain't you tired yet?
Do you get pleasure getting me upset?
Does it make you smile to make my mother cry?
Or watch my father's dreams fly by?

What vain pleasure do you get from this?
What's the joy in these chains around my wrist?
What you fear I don't understand.
Don't you know that I'm just a man?

And now that you've heard my mournful song
And now that you know I've suffered so long.
How can you continue, how can you persist?
How can you treat a human being like this?

James T. Glover

REMEMBERING DICK

Dedicated to Gina, Dick's wife;
Betty and Don, his mom and
dad; Bill and Brenda,
his brother and sister;
my son, Kevin, his best friend;
and all of us who loved Dick.
Dick was one who found a time for
everything.

The death of a friend
left us with a hole
that will never be filled.
Dick is gone, we are here.
Turn! Turn! Turn!

We continue with life
knowing something important is missing.
It will never be the same.
Dick is gone, we are here.
Turn! Turn! Turn!

Goodbye, dear friend,
we surrender your body,
but we keep the beautiful
memories you left us.

Lynda M. Gallup

LYNDA MARIE GALLUP. Born: National
City, California, 9-30-37; Married: David, 3-7-59;
Education: U.C. Santa Barbara, B.A., 12-11-76;
California Lutheran University, Teaching creden-
tial, 8-21-87; Occupation: Teacher; Memberships:
National Council of Teachers of English; Poetry:
Poem, *American Poetry Anthology,* 1985; Other
Writings: "Career Profile," article, technical
publication, 4-82; Comments: *Dick's favorite*
song was 'Turn! Turn! Turn!' (the Byrds' 1965
rendition of the full and complete philosophy of
life described in Ecclesiastes.), and it expresses
the complete person that he was.

WANDERING MIND

The sky was clear and so very bright.
My mind seemed to wander through the night.
Will tomorrow be another yesterday?
When I lost you somewhere along the way.
I go on searching and praying and trying to find
Somewhere on this earth peace of mind.
So many yesterdays have come and gone.
I can't help but wonder where I went wrong.

Nan Blackshire-Little

COMFORTABLE

Comfortable with you
with my face in the morning
my hair with no fluff
my middle-aged self
wrapped in pine-green robe!

Comfortable with you
while cleaning our house
wearing worn shirt and jeans
or while exercising on the floor
with my white clay clown-face!

Comfortable with you
when we make love
only now and then
or step out to dine
but are back home by nine!

Comfortable with you
as the years come and go
sharing joys, sharing tears
through all things always
how wonderful to be comfortable
with someone so dear!

Song of Solomon 2:16

My beloved is mine and I am his!

Sharon J. Daley

WRITTEN TEARDROPS

I don't want to cry anymore over you
I've cried a million tears
seeing you, not having you
has caused my endless tears
There is no end to my loving you
I'm hopelessly in love
I sit alone and start to write
I'm writing down all my tears
I've cried enough, dear, over you
waterfalls of tears
If I should keep on crying, dear
I'd drown in my own tears
So, if ever I should see you
and should you glance my way
I'll be writing words on paper, dear
writing my teardrops away

Mona F. Lundell

FEELING

Never had this feeling, this
feeling is sublime.
Never had this feeling, now I
have it all the time.
Never had this feeling, it is
totally new.
This feeling I have is reserved
for a few.
Never had this feeling, I know
not from whence it came.
Now that I have this feeling,
I don't feel the same.

Frederic Exume

WON'T YOU BE MY LOVE?

I have a song I'd like to sing
I think, I'll tickle the ivory,
And let the bells ring.
Oh, just take me under your wing.
If our love gets strong,
I will never want to depart.
I think, this is where I belong.
Oh, please, don't say I'm wrong.
Just hold me tight.
Kiss me with all of your might.
You know, tonight could be the night.
So, please, take me by your side,
And whisper words of love I can store inside.
In your love, I can abide
Because my love for you, I cannot hide.
Won't you be my love?
Help me find my true identity.
Take me home with you and love me.
If I'm not smart,
I'll let you dance into my heart.
My love for you is real
Can't you see? Oh, can't you feel?
Oh, won't you be my love?

Mary Elizabeth K.

LIFE'S PROSPERITY

What are we all struggling for
Peace of mind, wealth as of yore?
 Waiting for the pot to boil
 Our efforts it does always foil
Being too eager for riches return
Prevents recovery for that which we yearn
 Let's walk away from the boiling pot
 Try to be useful while it slowly gets hot
Life is like that
If we forever sat
 And life rolled easily by
 There would be no sense in living
 We must struggle and try
To keep the pot just hissing
Although the wealth is missing
 Life's prosperity, we must struggle till we die

Pearl Van Slocum

YOU MADE ME REALIZE

You made me realize, it was you I was meant to love and adore
And as time goes on, I have even begun to love you more and more!
It's like being in an enchanted garden, fairyland has come true,
And everything in the world seems to have become all sparkling new!

The silver glow of the moonlight, and the golden glory of the sun,
Seem to have gone back in time, it is like the whole world
    has just begun!
The beauty and wonder of love are surrounding me everywhere —
All because I know you are there, and that it is for me you do care!

Even the trembling flower petals that are falling down at my feet
And the tiny rosebuds just opening up seem to smell twice as sweet!
It is like lovely, glittering stardust has fallen down
    from the skies —
Pouring out bright, dazzling color, and opening up our wondering eyes!

All because of you, this mantle of magic has fallen — around me!
The feeling that you truly adore me seems always to surround me.
You made me realize it and now I know I won't be without you!
I know it's you I adore, and I love everything about you!

Kathleen Lyon Vaughn

WHERE THE LANDS HAD JOINED

Floating into the darkness toward the bright light Mecca in an abyss
of tranquil energy. The summit now reached on Zion is indeed
a promised oasis, where the lands had joined in solemn prayer and
meditative reflection on Thee, oh God, my God forever and ever.
In the Elysian fields there is a tranquil village which sets itself
upon the banks of a flowing river. Within, there is joyful clamor of
jubilant souls which dwell on the threshold of eternity.
Oh song of the Pharoahs, the search for Olympus brought thy children
to sacred gardens laurel where bloom the ancient flowers of Babylon.
Here, the mantric chant echoes from the lips of the Wise Man on the
Holy Mountain, a haunting ode to Gilbran and The Prophet and
memories of a contemplative Merton nestled in a wooded hermitage,
reposed in angelic visions of Thee, oh God, my God forever.
Why?
It is for the Paradise remembered, for a moment, where the lands had
joined both Heaven and earth.

Scott Arminas

SCOTT ARNOLD ARMINAS. Born: Staten Island, New York, 2-12-60;
Married: Dr. María Basora-Arminas, pediatrician, 9-12-87; Education:
Brookdale Community College; Rutgers University; Occupations: Laboratory
technician, Revlon Research and Development; Memberships: M.T.F.D.,
1981-1986; N.J. All Shore Jazz Band, 1977; Middletown Reformed Church
Choir, soloist tenor, 1981-1986; YMCA Scuba Diver; Poetry: 'Weeping for
the Children,' *Best New Poets of 1986;* 'The Edge,' *American Poetry Anthol-
ogy,* 1982; 'The Focus Homeward,' *Words of Praise, Vol. III,* 1986; 'The
Inner Temple,' *Words of Praise, Vol. II,* 1985; 'The Promise of Delphi,'
American Poetry Anthology, 1983; Themes: *God and His Kingdom I try to
reflect in my writings.* Comments: *For years when I was a musician I used
my talent for God's glory. Now, as a writer, I try to do the same. In 1985 I
finished a poetic volume with the central theme focused on finding God. Still
awaiting publication,* A Quest For The Ancients Rhyme.

ONLY GOD'S BIG ENOUGH

In the beginning God had a plan,
From the dust of the earth He made a man.
He breathed in his nostrils man became a living soul,
Man's wonderful shape from his head to his toes.
So with our eyes we can plainly see,
That only God can make a tree.

The birds that fly so high in the sky,
And the song they sing is a lullaby,
The sun that shines on us each day,
The moon and the stars at night display.
As we travel far to a distant land,
Have you noticed the mountains how tall they stand?
The streams that run in the valley low,
The grass and wild flowers how they grow.

All these things above and below,
Were in God's Plan He made it so.
And then God left it up to us,
For only God is Big Enough.

Emma Burress

DISABLED VETERAN

  He's awake, discouraged, *alone,* in a bright hospital room
Soldier of our country fair, who lost *both* arms, ''over there.''
Without hands or arms — how endure? His darling 'Ann,' how tell her
    can't take her in his arms again,
    can't walk *a-hold of her small hand!*

This stricken warrior had hope stirred
  Hearing promises from God's Word.
  ''Be thankful for *everything,*'' the Apostle said,
    (Paul's beaten back was bloody red).
The Master spoke courage, helped him too!
    As he looked beyond self, to God, — hope grew! —
      He accepted his fate!
      And mechanical arms might compensate!
  He learned their use, did his best:
  God blessed his efforts — gave Peace and Rest!
    Hatred, and worry gone — real Joy was given.
And 'Ann,' God's dear child, is united with him.
  The destroyed arms she tried not to miss:
  No sacrifice — just *reality of life* this.
    They are walking along together
      Growing in God's Grace!

  Someday —
    They'll
      Enjoy Eternity
        Out there in space.

Alice Cummings

ALICE ATKINS CUMMINGS. Pen Name: Alice Sea, Birdie Ben Bow;
Born: Roberts, Illinois, Ford County; Married: Max Edward Cummings, 2-
18-25; Education: High school, 1921 (valedictorian); Teacher's training,
1921; Occupations: Teacher; Nurse to mother who died in 1924; Farm wife;
Farm hand; Mother, Gardener, Canner; Awards: Honorable mention.

CLASSICAL CATS: THE SECOND CLOWDER OF LIMERICKS

EXPERTISE

The pianst cat Goudonovsky,
Was a master at playing Tchaikovsky.
　　But when his wife tried,
　　The Maestro cried,
"Of Tchaikovsky my dear please lay offsky."

Said his wife, "Very well, sweet bublitchky.
Suppose you and I were to switchky?
　　Could *you* cook with spice,
　　And prepare curried mice?
Or pink salmon Paprika Kouchitchky?

JUST FIDDLING AROUND

The great violinst Pussarius,
Played a concert on her Stradivarius.
　　She performed In the Mood,
　　Turkey In The Straw, and Hey Jude.
The audience thought it hilarious.

Said the Maestro Klozzwald Van Vlassiks,
And the harpist Miss Kit Katzenbrassiks,
　　"My dear in all truth,
　　Such a stunt is uncouth.
You really must stick to the classics."

Maria Amhara Yemariamferé
(Philogyne)

BREAD OF LIFE

This recipe for life is free.
The ingredients — just five;
But if you follow faithfully
You'll truly be alive!

The prime ingredient is love,
So use abundantly.
Add some faith in God above;
'Twill bring consistency.

Now stir in hope, ingredient three
For when you're feeling blue.
Compassion, next, that you may see
And help the needy through.

Forgiving others is the last,
Though surely not the least;
For if you can't forgive what's past,
You bake without the yeast!

Richard A. Duro

THE WHISPER

I thought I saw a whisper today;
But how can anyone see a whisper, you say —
O, it was there all right, it followed me
Deep into the night.
It crawled up and down my spine
Like a piece of twirling twine.
It spoke a little too, I guess,
Told me whispers were meant to bless.
It talked in my native tongue;
Hard to understand a whisper softly wrung.
Gave me a wink, pinched my cheek;
Made me feel kind of weak.
Then it smiled and I felt at ease;
It left as it came — on the evening breeze.
So you see what I saw; what a nice thing
A whisper can be; especially —
When it says that you love me.

Ronald Russell Enders

RONALD RUSSELL ENDERS. Born: Hartford, Connecticut; Married: Nancy Messenger, 4-12-86; Education: University of Hartford, B.A.; Syracuse University, M.A.; Comments: *My mind is a fathomless abyss of creative thoughts that allow little time for sleep. The power of imagination surfaces and finds its way into my novels and poetry. It is my inner voice longing to be heard.*

Y LA LLUVIA CAE DEL CIELO

The stars take a slumber
Mr. Moon don't know why
But lately it seems
Mother's starting to cry
"Perhaps it's an illness"
Says Neptune to Mars
Hear rumb'ling agreement
From their fellow stars
But I know what's causing
Her anger and fright
The illuminous fire
That lights up the night
It's a hurt that's so deep
Which no one can bear
A feeling that comes
When nobody cares
So, now moon and stars
Have figured out why
While the pain just goes on
She continues to cry
Y la lluvia cae del cielo.

Annmarie Pacchia

DARK

It was the first day of winter
A December day when the air wasn't cold.
The only coldness I felt
Seeped from his heart
Leading me on
Only I knew better from our start
I always thought this guy was too nice
My dreams of men never come my way
Dreams of him never would arrive
Then that December day
Dark
He began a deadly drive
This jerk convinced me he was
a different type of fellow,
to give him a chance and
my judgment fair
Alone, dark, cold on this day
She knew they were a completely different pair.

April Lee Holguin

THE POET

Inside of everyone there lies
The desire to be a Poet.
And surprising as it may be
Everyone is — but some just don't know it.

For truly isn't Poetry
Nothing more than verses written out,
Expressing someone's inner feelings
On different things they think about!

Now sometimes the verses may rhyme
And then again they may not.
But regardless what it does
It's still someone's Thought.

So it can be said without a doubt
That everyone can be a Poet —
It's just that some are better than others
And you and I know it!

Cora Lee Fuhring

NEW ENGLAND WOMAN

　And by years of discipline
New England women develop
a more incisive simplicity.
Drawn as by way of example from
their ever-so-sensible calves.

　The possession of minions
no doubt,
　these women
launder their wisdom,
walk their spaniels

Managing their days' accord
to twelve's perfect obedience.

Shana M. Olson

A 20/20

For all of life's so tempestuous days, remains a calm of far
    easier ways;
"Hold on so, oh fairest one, so God may grant your life a "song"!
Today, you now have "one-score years" . . . not so many, but are
    my cheers —
"Joyous rewards for your 'well done'; continue on, it can be fun!"
Our goals should not be to attain, just "material blessing" that
    we gain;
For friendships, should our hearts abound, and "Higher Thoughts"
    so profound: Of faith in God to guide our way, and propose this life a
    "happier stay."
May you find joy in knowing me, that my friendship . . .
    lends "maturity";
And, I too, might "borrow some" of your youthful zest, that I
    do become —
A "vigorous cause," so down the road, for you have eased my
    "menial load"!
All in all, may God so see . . . our mutual friendship, so to be . . .
Pleasing most, His "purpose first," avoiding guise that may
    be cursed.
Thanks again, oh Kirsten dear, . . . you could not have made me
    Happier!

Arne Maurice Simonson

THE SCHOOL BUS

I like to watch the school bus coming up the road;
It stops close to my doorstep and takes on a merry load.
There's Jack, Jeanette and Joe, Everlyn, Jane and Mary;
They pile in to take their place in a bus that's clean and airy.
They talk about mathematics, an exam they'll have today;
Make plans for their noon hour; where they will go to play.
They notice Jim is missing and wonder if he's ill;
That Martha has a new dress; a new fall hat tops Jill.
They talk and joke and laugh and sing and soon at school are they;
For a crowd of eager youngsters the doorman now makes way.
And when the day is over; a little more they've learned,
They're eager to get home again for a rest that they have earned.
Again, I see the school bus coming down the road,
It stops again near me to discharge its weary load.

Dolly Ziebarth

ROSE GARDEN

How like myself, these flowers here —
Some, their youthful soft skins of blushing pink
Betray a belief in their own eternal lives,
And the deep scarlet red of others imply themselves
Capable of unchecked passions.
Neatly arranged in a pattern, they move about
All day in the wind and rain and sun,
A never-changing routine of budding, blooming, fading;
Yellow for my grown-up years,
And finally, white: pure, refined, aged, dying.
I wonder if they look at me,
Softly nodding to each other, sighing,
Whispering wisely as to why
I stealthily make my way here so often to watch them,
And asking, as I do,
"How soon shall I return to earth?"

Colleen E. Hansen

PRINCE OF DREAMS

Prince of Dreams
with the aqua eyes
and the crooked smile
    dance with me awhile.

Tell me of beautiful cities
in faraway lands
where crystal-clear water
slowly washes the sands
    and the moon shines white beams
    on the face of my Prince of Dreams.

Dance with me —
Dance with me —
Spin me around.
    My heart beats a beautifully rhythmical sound.

Clouds, so soft
catch me
as I fall from your embrace
only to land in a more familiar place
where life is what it truly seems.
    Yet, in my heart
    you remain forever
      my Prince of Dreams.

Diane Arlene Marks

THE ANCIENT ONE

Once on life's sweet note of melancholic humor
Traveling through this incessant life
Singing to the break of endless dawns
A journey of a million years
Ever since our first few strands of time were sewn
Knitted in rows and clumps of scenic clandescent patterns
We were thrust into the whirlwind of revolution
Once we built our world in the shadows of immortality
We danced in the winds of creativity and evolution
We flew among the ranks of the most divine conceptions
Yes we even moved with bands of sovereign unity
Our liberation, pride and joy
Were caste in statues standing high and bright
Even when starry-eyed skies were wrought in distress
Even with trembling hearts and faltering souls
    Pulchritude — was still created by our searching minds
And even after our ashes were strewn in the dying wind
We lived in our memories
We lived in our hopes
    that we once had
      and will forever have
        of the great Continent, of the great times
          hurtling into the second millennium
            the Ancient One —
              Africa.

Alawode D. Oladele

A TIME OF INNOCENCE

Ah, I remember a time of innocence,
The kind of innocence that exists no more.
The days of summers that rang with laughter
Among the sand dunes on Lake Michigan's shore.

And I remember the simple evenings
We played before the radio on the floor,
The drone of voices in soft conversations
Still sate my mind with ideas to explore.

How I remember the tears I freely shed
For a president and fathers lost to war,
Not understanding that all such innocence,
The world's and mine, was now lost forevermore.

Today there remains no time of innocence,
The atom's split, and fear stalks us to death's door.
Technology has reared its hideous head,
Bringing us clean destruction with bloodless gore.

Who then can recall such simple innocence,
Before the alphabet bombs loomed at our door,
When easy discourse served as recreation,
Those ''screens of life'' showed no scenes we now abhor?

Oh, I remember that time of innocence,
The kind of innocence that exists no more.
I envy not the youth of this angry age,
For I remember when innocence could soar.

Helen L. Gillies

LITTLE SISTER

You are a treasure from God above.
You make this world brighter, and you sow love.
Your love is as pure as a white summer's dove.
But, fate continues to give you a bad shove.

Your surface reflects happiness and joy.
Your sadness you hide behind a sweet warm smile.
Still waters run deep, and sorrows flow.
Your sadness is wide, as deep as your soul.

I am older, you are younger,
I see your deep inner hunger.
I hurt for you, I even ache
Your greatest pain I would gladly take.

With ten years between us, I've been where you are.
I stumbled, mumbled, and blundered through.
What advice I give may not be wise,
For you were always purer than I.

There is an answer for every question you ask,
Be still and listen to your deep inner self,
Discover your source of sadness, bring it into the light,
With strength and help from above, you will find happiness in life.

Carolyn C. Blackwell

HOW WOULD YOU LIKE TO FARM?

You have to milk them, or I'd love cows,
I like little pigs, but they grow into sows.
Horses are nice, you train them or ride,
We had a pretty sorrel once but he up and died.
Soft downy chicks I adore, to watch them grow is fun.
But feeding, watering and getting eggs keeps you on the run.
Goats and lambs are playful, they also make money,
But when you aren't looking, bang, they bump and it isn't funny.
Turkey, geese and ducks are awfully good to eat.
But the way you have to feed them, you earn your meat!
I guess it doesn't matter what animal you raise,
They all are a lot of work without any praise.
There's never any dull time so farming can be fun,
Something's always happening to keep you on the run.
The cows are out or the pigs need feed,
The corn grows so fast it's time to go and weed.
The horse has got a spavin, the pump needs new leathers,
It's time to run to the brooder the chickens are picking feathers.
The new expensive pup is tearing clothes off the line,
You have to rush there first, so dinner isn't on time.
Oh boy! it's a merry-go-round, this farming the soil,
But no matter what your work, you always have to toil.
And so for my money, I'll be a farmer's wife,
And stay on the farm for the rest of my life!

Dolly Ziebarth

THE HORSE

The beast who stands tall and bold,
Serves man with pangs untold.
Whose heart will grow, when work unfolds,
The horse, a legend of brawn and beauty to behold.

A Neanderthal descendant holds pure to heart,
Of harmony's brief journey, emblazoned to soul's armor.
A God-blessed sojourn between man and animal,
A sacred bonding of brain and power; equestrian might.

This creature of flesh and muscle,
Bore my body, winged flight my soul from earthly bustle.
A mortal heart of sapien, pierced by thorn of Thistle.
Then cradled, spiriting my soul's tortured mass to rebirth,
with sinewy, equine muscle.

The musty scent of sweat-foamed leather,
The journey through pine boughs and heather,
In dark of night and pall of weather,
I plus horse will eternally remember.

Of swine and bovine it can be told,
A favor when eaten by man, I behold.
But when time for equine earthly bond to take flight,
Not man should order horse to death's dark light,
Only to deity belongs the right.

Thomas H. Nonemacher

AND SHE IS MISS CONGENIALITY

I have conceived a pure, pure soul,
It emerged on the feast of
  St. John, the Baptist
And presented on the feast of
  St. Andrew, the Apostle —
I very fondly called it
  'Andrew John'
It came into being . . .
A very lovely child of
  the Universe — now —
    ''Rowena Jean.''

Beloved Corazon

AN INDIAN PRAYER

Oh, Great Spirit!
whose voice I hear in the winds
and whose breath gives life to all
the world,
hear me!
I am small and weak, I need
your strength and wisdom.

Let me walk in beauty and make
my eyes ever behold the red and
purple sunset,
make me wise so that I may
understand the things you have
taught my people.
Let me learn the lessons you have
hidden in every leaf and rock.

I seek strength not greater than
my brother, but to fight my
greatest enemy, myself.
Make me always ready to come
to you with clean hands and
straight eyes,
So when life fades as the fading
sunset,
My spirit may come to you
without shame.

Sidney Brown

Communication need not be
long conversation
nor the sound of voices

I hear you with your caring
follow your expressions
understanding your thoughts

Answering with
a simple smile

The beauty of unspoken words
is love expressed silently

Love that builds
our harmonious home
unites our family
and makes it complete

Rose Teresa Guyott-Avitia

THE FINAL DARKNESS

Where does this folly end
The tide goes out
And washes back in
And the madness of adversaries
Clash in repeated refrain
As they wail like fools

Why must we be this way
Asserting the same points
Which were rebutted yesterday
Clamoring through dull minds
Madly propelling finite souls
Through impenetrable darkness

And where does it end
To the night we are born
And live until death sends
Us back to the night
Against our will
Under a bed of black dirt

Why, we cannot know
It is the destiny of mankind
Which makes life so
As we clash in repeated refrain
And clash again and again
Until consumed in a final darkness

David M. Hargis

WHO IS MORTAL MAN?

Isn't it a shame
how man plays God's game, trying
to improve on God's perfections?

He annihilates the Jews
to build a ''Master Race,''
then develops robots
to take a human's place.

He ruins the air we breathe —
the soil and water, too,
then tries to make the world
into an artificial zoo.

He's made artificial sun
and artificial grass,
artificial flowers, and
even food — how crass!

Wouldn't it be nice
if man would one day see,
how God so loves us all;
He made this world to be.

''That every good and perfect gift
comes from our Father above,''*
and man, though very knowledgeable,
can't improve upon God's love.

* *James 1:17*

Myra Moore

ANGELS AND MEN CRASHING

Life can be expressed in simplistic verse
Omitting the course designed by the soul
Ignoring the veil of the intrinsic curse
That haunts mankind and extracts its toll
As we write of flowers, and castles, and kings
And evade the glare of death,
Of broken wings
On angels
Crashing

Poetry flows in a regurgitated stream
Most often as idle platitudes
Hollow, repetitive as though they seem
Engorged in exaggeration which exudes
Blithe verse, blind hope, and faith
Ignoring the stench of betrayal
And broken dreams
Of men
Crashing

David M. Hargis

BABY TEDDY BEAR

I remember long ago
when I was just a boy
I was feeling very blue
needing a little joy

My mother found me hidden
and crying here and there
And noticed I was wanting
a baby teddy bear

She picked out the clothes he wore
and stitched him up with care
With some yellow yarn atop
to give him fuzzy hair

Toward the evening I soon found
for no reason at all
A present marked with my name
which left me standing tall

No one cared about my bear
they all just said ''that's nice''
But my heart, true happiness
my bear was without price

And to this day I've not found
a better one than he
Loving . . . Caring . . . in that bear
my mother made for me.

Phil A. Pickard

OH TO BE FREE

Just as free as the breeze are
nature's creatures

Squirrels gathering nuts along the bowers.
scampering and hurrying along the path.
 lost in solitude among God's animal kingdom.
 the cat with her shining coat of hair
  hasn't seen a bird flying in the air;
 the dog more submissive has grown lazy,
 by comparison he is man's guide and pal.
 the ducks swimming in the lake are a gorgeous sight
  in the evening dark.
 come as you are and enjoy all that's glorious
 the sun and flowers and every breath we take
  angels in heaven and every silvery strand
   we are but children in our youth and years.
 all escapes as we strive to find the perfect answer.
 known God in our carefree freedom
 only we know the joy of the glowing fires
 that God has gracious generosity.
  oh to be free and sail the ocean blue
  as a sailor lost at sea on a raft.

Margaret Jonas

QUESTIONS

One day I saw the sun and the next I saw none.
What happened to the world?
Today or was it yesterday?
Did I ever see the sun?
Now there is nothing
Except vast fields of dirt and sand.
A few scattered buildings and one small church.
What happened to it all
Between two mornings?
Was it the Armageddon
Or just a bad dream.
I'll ask the priest.
"Father. What has become of our earth that was so
    full of life?"
"Son, it has not changed."
"Why is the world so dim, so lifeless? Nothing is
    left and there's nothing worth living for?"
"My son. Death is a sad thing, but one cannot stop life
    because you are mourning for another."

Janeen Steel

LOVERS

My heart is lonely,
My arms are empty,
My room is dark and gloomy.
But then, the 'phone rang!
Across a thousand and twenty miles
A sweet voice calls my name,
And, in an instant, life comes back to me,
My heart leaps for joy,
My arms reach out to hold,
The only true love I've ever known.
Across a thousand and twenty miles
Two hearts race to meet,
And, in meeting, merge and blend,
Bringing sweet memories of a thousand embraces,
Uniting once again two lovers,
    You and me,
    In ecstasy.

Vincent Foo

INCHES

Walls all around me,
I count your inches!
12 feet on one side,
144 inches. Times four,
576 inches!
They close me in these inches,
like tucks in a gown.
My seams. Protecting me
from the drafts of life.
Secluding me, yet cramping my style.
I wish, they were 20 times these inches.
Then I would have 11,520 inches as my space.
I could have a party! Invite friends!
Decorate these inches with my art!
And let beautiful music echo through their seams!
Write a poem for every inch!
Dance, and sing, to the rhythms of my soul!
In fantasy, my walls are as those
of castle ballrooms, and I am the
Cinderella of the fairy tale.
When the inches shrink back to reality,
I am the Cinderella of the hearth.
Friendly inches! Meager but warm!
        My inches! *My* space!

Peg Scanlon

RANCHLAND MEMORIES

 An old ranch house sets there, out on the Nebraska
Prairieland, and it sets not far from other sheds, and an
Old red barn. Cottonwoods wave, and the box elder shades
The place from the winds that blow the whole year long.
 All the buildings are in need of repair. Their empty
Windows stare out at you, and beckon you, to come, and to
Stay a while, just to look around, and to leave your
Footsteps there. No happy feet run, to and fro, where once they
Skipped so gay — for silently, they all slipped away, and left
The old ranch all alone.
 Tall grass has taken over the orchard, where once the fruit
Trees stood so proud — laden with fruit, in the summertime.
 And the few apples that grow, now all fall to the ground,
And are eaten up by the birds. We kids used to get sweet
Juicy apples from those trees, and big red cherries, from these.
 We filled up, on mulberries, in June and July, and on the
Plums and currants, from the old north thicket. Mother made
Us pies from that fruit and nothing can beat the smells
That came from her kitchen oven.
 Dad planted that old north thicket, for a windbreak from the Cold
Northwest winds and blizzards, and wintry gales, that
Sweep across the Nebraska Prairie lands, in the wintertime.
 The land is alone now, and it's grown up to tall prairie
Grasses, that slowly dry, and grow brown — nobody cuts the grass now,
You know, and so — there are no mowing machines heard anymore.

Annette N. Ashbough

FRACTIONAL JOYS

We live by fractional joys,
are made whole by minute sums,
healed by small ingredients
which transform the whole.

In certain clear and pure moments,
lives can be saved:
by mythic dreams,
by truth which lies in art,
by love that holds fast,
by flickering blues and greens
of this earth's tilting mysteries,
by all that swims and lives
in the holy seas
and in the forest's heart.

Like fishermen, we sail
through whispering dark,
through little worlds
in phosphorescent tides,
our eyes on the seeded stars.

Jean Musser

AMOUR, AMOUR

She makes me love the snow,
  She makes me love the winds that sing.
Just having her to love
  Makes me love everything.

I used to pass the flowers
  And never see the rose,
But now I love the ground
  Where the lovely flower grows.

I could have met her before
  In my early spring;
But I could not love her more —
  She is my everything.

I stand upon the walk
  In the morning sun
And look for her, my love;
  Look for my only one.

We go out in the evening
  Maybe to dinner and a show,
Or just go anywhere
  Where we want to go.

Just have her to love
  Makes me young once more,
Makes me love my loved one —
  The one that I adore.

Orlie L. Brannaman

FATHER DIVINE

If you could self-inflate
  And swell up like a toad
You might claim divinity,
  Outer space as your abode!
You might walk on water,
  Have Holies worship you;
(When they don't understand,
  That's usually what they do.)
Because of your light weight,
  And freedom from gravity,
You'd float like a balloon
  And be an abnormality.
You might even start a cult,
  Become a creature mankind owed
A debt for its existence
  As Children of the Toad.

Orlie L. Brannaman

THE BELIEVER

His brain is rooted in granite
  New ideas die at his gate;
He tries never to learn anything new,
  New discoveries are obviate.
Wherever he lives science
  Is something taboo on his horn.
When he dies he will probably be ninety
  As ignorant as the day he was born.
If he had a fail-safe shuttle,
  One that would go up through space,
Would he stuff it with food survival
  And go up his Creator to face?
Would he, would he, we ask you,
  Take a chance on living again
Would he rather be in his Gold Heaven,
  Or spend more time among men?
If he really believes in his God
  When a friend dies why does he grieve;
Why does he fight hard to stay alive
  If his faith is what he'd have us believe?

Orlie L. Brannaman

PASSION

My heart so sweet
  Will tenderly soothe
My heart so fragile
  A whisper moves
I long for passion
  I give the clues
I wait in fate
  There are no moves
You nudge you snuggle
  And turn out the light
Then roll over and say
  Good night

Adrienne E. Townsend

A BIT OF MORNING SPLENDOR

Good Morning Glory, my gladden
That glistens of morning dew,
And grants your gracious greeting
Of bold bounties in pastel hue.
To chase the gross of glooming
From warm sun's splendid view,
Your beauty adorns my garden . . .
My dowdy fence makes blue.
Invites tender touches and glances
As thick mists warm breezes ensue.

I welcome your generous garnish!
Flitting friends, attending . . . a crew.
Your silent beauty, demandingly, shouting
In the grandeur of nature so true.
Your trumpeted form . . . so regal, unfolding,
Announces the day in preclude . . .
"'Tis morning! Come dreamers . . . awaken!"
Here, hazed, where hot breezes once blew,
I enjoy your vista of splendor!
The whisper of daybreak . . . your cue!

Clara Mays Benson

CLARA MAYS BENSON. Pen Name: Rusta "B"; Born: Darby Township, Pennsylvania, 2-3-32; Married: Dr. Floyd Stephen Benson, 12-20-58; Children: Stephen Eugene, born 3-68; Education: Philadelphia College of Art, B.F.A., Education, 1954; Temple University, Tyler School of Art, M.Ed., 1962; Fitchburg State State University, Certificate, Art Supervision, 1975; Occupations: Mother; Homemaker; Educator; Artist; Writer of children's stories and plays, articles, short stories, poetry; Freelance photographer; Memberships: Delaware State Education Association, Philadelphia Art Teachers Association, Pennsylvania Education Association, Massachusetts Association of Craftsmen, Harvard Craftsmen, Nashoba Art Association; Awards: For drawing, painting, sculpture, macrame, ceramics, pencil, pen and ink; Poetry: 'Creativity Rebukes Ignorance, Waste and Bigotry,' *American Poetry Anthology,* 1985; 'Serernade,' *Hearts on Fire,* 1986; 'A Meal Grace,' 'Monolithic Exultation,' *Words of Praise,* 1986; 'To Docile Minions of the Mimosa,' *Best New Poets of 1986,* 1986; Other Writing: "Professor Higgins Joins The Space Race," 1965; "A Gumper Christmas," 1966; children's plays; Comments: *The many issues of grave concern to us all in today's current events not only affect our behavior but can absorb much of our time and energy. Though awareness of such issues can remain constantly a part of our lives, deliberate withdrawal to enjoy the beauty of the many natural environmental gifts can be quite rejuvenating. Assessment of these simplicities often helps us to check our goals, rearrange our priorities and adjust our perspectives. We find, thus, along with a purpose in life comes a life with a purpose.*

NEW-AGE THOUGHT

The Cut Version

Here we go again
Like tears in the rain
A déjà vu
From memories of long ago
Flashing in my mind non-stop
Silent questions uncut
A crying child awakes near
Not here, nor there
All the impulses
Where have they gone?

Psychic sources spinning in my brain
Storing the many lives of my soul
Storing the many tales of my lives
Flashing back and forward
I try to decipher the memory
The memory of those haunting seconds
Seconds of instant Karma

A kiss of Karma has touched me
A kiss I won't forget
The union of Yin and Yang
The perfect fusion of body and soul

Reborn to live many lives
Reborn to love many times
Like tears in the rain.

Andrew Dazz

WIND ON MY FACE

Cool is the breeze,
whispering to me.
''Rise, rise my child
and sail with me.''

Cool is the breeze,
whispering to me.
''Come, my child, be with me.''

On we soar, brothers with the wind,
higher and higher,
I fly with thee,
leaving behind all sense of reality.

Stars as our guide,
over hills and valleys,
oceans and streams,
''Come and sail with me.''

Feel with your heart,
what your eyes see,
all that is meant to be,
''Come and see,
as you sail with me.''

Charles Starkweather

BLUE TERRA

The Big Bang Theory
Gave birth to this brave New World
The history of the world?
Starts with the experience of the Greeks
Followed by the rise and fall
The rise and fall of the Roman Empire
The Age of Belief
The Age of Adventure
History takes a turn
Creating the prophecies of Nostradamus
Spinning, spinning, the turning world
With the Age of Reason
The Age of Enlightenment
The Age of Ideology

And analyzing the Age of Analysis
They have all come and gone
A new front cracks the evolutionary earth
Bursting out with the New Age
The New Age comes of age
Reaching the year 3796
Bringing the end of time
Time as we know
And beyond?
Only the spirits know.

Andrew Dazz

ANDREW DAZZ. Born: La Havana, Cuba; Single; Education: Rutgers University, B.A., Political Science; CUNY, M.A., International Politics; Occupation: Bohemian; Memberships: ACLU, USA-United Nations ASS, NAM-MYOHO-RENGE-KYO, American Way; Poetry: *Third Wave Images,* book, Vantage Press, 1987; 'The Look,' *American Poetry Anthology,* 1986; 'Dazz Blue,' *Bohemia,* 1986; 'The Age of the High-Tech Man,' *Hearts on Fire,* 1987; Comments: *When a subject arouses my interest — I write. When my soul is full of joy — I write. When I find myself in deep sorrow, I write and to cut a story short: I began to write to mend a broken heart and since then I haven't stopped.*

POLLUTION

As I look upon the rivers,
With their beauty and such splendor,
All at once I visualized,
I saw the fish and heard their cries.
Save us from this awful fate,
Believe me friend, it's not too late.
Give us a chance to breathe again,
Or take one last look at what might have been.
For through pollution, which we can't stand,
We'll have to die, thanks to man.

Edward W. Green

BULKHEAD TO DEMOCRACY

The bulkhead stands, weathered by time,
persistent, a wooden wharf
separates public from private beaches.
Crevices are worn enough to admit
wash from a boat's wake. It is a
token gesture.

When the river is quiet, traffic lanes are
clear, the bulkhead reigns as a solid
reminder of things that tear asunder,
that keep inequality constant as the
classes of society know their places,
so residents do not overstep territories.
They accent boundaries.

When there is plenty, the water is
turbulent. The waves crest high and break
against the generous bulkhead. It is
a symbolic sacrifice, river water
momentarily contaminated by debris
ridden brackish elements from the
other side. It is a gesture to keep
the fires of hope burning. Just enough
to inspire the next generation.

Dr. Lois H. Young

LOIS YOUNG-TULIN. Pen Name: Lois H. Young; Born: Mt. Vernon, New York, 7-1-40; Married: David P. Tulin; Occupation: Executive Director of PRONAC (Professional Organizations for Nuclear Arms Control). For over 10 years she was Program Administrator at Antioch University where she was named the University Scholar in the Teaching of Writing for 1984-85. She earned a Master's degree in Creative Writing and a doctorate in Educational Administration. A prolific writer of fiction, non-fiction, and poetry, her work has appeared in such publications as *International Poetry Review, Bitterroot Magazine, Muse's Brew Poetry Review, Letters Magazine, American Poetry Anthology,* and the *University of Pennsylvania Literary Journal.* In addition to teaching literature and creative writing at Antioch, she has taught writing courses at Drexel and Temple Universities.

FUTURE PLANS

Someday I plan to have lots of time
I'll have loads of energy and be in my prime
I'll contact my old friends and tell them hello
I'll buy a big Singer and learn how to sew
I'll make all my own clothes from Levis to silk
I'll locate a dairy and milk my own milk
I'll have people to dinner — I'll write to my dad
I'll admit to my sins and have time to be sad
I'll read lots of poetry, write a great book
Crochet a lace tablecloth, learn how to cook
I'll clean out my storeroom
   and polish my house
And immediately after — embroider a blouse
I'll open a bank account and I'll save a dime
But I have to go now — I'm all out of time!

Deanna Williams

TREK

Engraved in human destiny
The golden thread that lures
The Marco Polos of the world
To follow ridges that have led
To hidden valleys
Such as Kathmandu
Reveals only to the bold
The chiseled ranges
That reach up to Himalayan skies,
Where millions
Lost in wonder and in worship
Of the Machapuchare peaks
Are shifting
Like the Annapurna snows
And searching
Through the sunlit mists of Dhaulagiri
In rhododendron frame of old Nepal
To view, to understand
The mystery, the alchemy
Of One to one.

Emily Brueske

THE SEA OF GALILEE

Oh, how I yearn to walk
Beside that beautiful Sea of Galilee;
To sit there and contemplate,
The serene face of my Master, so dear,
To — mayhaps — catch some of the thoughts,
He taught, while — in person — He was there,
Beside that beautiful Sea of Galilee.

Joy S. Pearce

ALONG THE AHTEL

Still, often running or
even wandering to new places.
Only to find my 'last time' tracks
and a comfortable way to stand again.
And never alone in this home
where hearts and souls
always seem to know so well,
along the Ahtel.

Steve J. Matty

MORE MILES

Like a road often travelled,
I've wound my way for a thousand days.
Through quiet towns
past parkside benches, and
the old men with the missing dreams.
And not unlike some mountain trail
secretly breathless and hidden
among fallen wood.
Along edges of earth so far below
to watch the ways
and lovers grow.

Steve J. Matty

LAST MOMENTS

What is this tiredness that I feel
Creeping over me like a shroud?
The eyelids heavy, heavy, droop and stay.
Tiredness envelops my aching body.
Control is slipping away. Sleep persists, insists,
I succumb . . . in this my final defiant sleep.
Weary, creaking bones, brittle, fragile,
No longer struggle to support me.
Sagging muscles loosen and meander
Only to abandon me in my trustful moments.
Breath moves in wisps and thins.
I make an effort to rouse myself, but all in vain.
No laments. Do not weep. My time has come.
Palm moves toward palm in final meeting
Prepared to pray. My mind's at rest . . .
Tranquil in these last quiet moments.
My spirit soars, encompassed by celestial music
Of unbelievable exquisite beauty.
I yield to a Higher Power, my last breath,
My soul's release . . . 'Tis sweet! 'Tis Sweet!

Mertie Elizabeth Boucher

WHEN ONCE . . .

When once I was so very young
The world seemed all so new,
When once I was so very young
I dreamed of much to do.
When once an adolescent grown,
The time to speak seemed mine;
When once an adolescent grown
My thoughts — they seemed to shine.
When once I was a young adult
With flag of Truth unfurled,
When once I was a young adult
My thoughts turned to the world.
When once I had of age become
Humility I had claimed;
When once I had of age become
I youthful follies tamed.
When once twilight began to set,
Grew wisdom into song;
Yet once twilight began to set
My youth and voice had gone.

Robert E. Jones

MEDITATION

The roll of waves speaks soft to dreams
In bold expanse the beauty beams
A rainbowed mist's sunset/sunrise
Calls witness songs as viewed of eyes.

Robert E. Jones

MY LOVELY WIFE

And now her short life is ended
All trials and temptations are o'er
She has returned to her Maker
No hardships for her anymore.

How short was the time she was granted
To live on this Earth here below
How happy we both were together
Her death was a terrible blow.

She was a most wonderful lady
So graceful, so sweet and so kind
A mother, there was just none like her
A wife as no other you'll find.

She has left me to be with her Savior
A place where she longed to go
She is waiting for me there to greet her
When I too must leave here below.

God loved her and that's why He took her
From me in this valley of tears
It will not be long till we're united
Forever, not measured by years.

C. H. Willke

HARVEST

Sown in winter's cold
   my little seedling
   lay quiet . . .
Until in springtime's warmth
   it slowly stirred.
In June an outline
   betrayed its presence.
By July it tickled me
   as if to share
   a private joke,
No longer one by August;
   it punished me
   with kicks instead.
In September my restless roomer
   denied me sleep
   until one October night
there came a steady knocking
   at the door
   and Nature opened it.
Into the waiting world,
   with all its wonders,
   our son arrived —
Demanding to be heard,
   hungry for Life
   and Love.

Dorothy H. Starzyk

DREAMS OF REALITY

Listen to the man try to justify his life.
Babbles to his woman, babbles to his wife.
Talks in garbles, making no sense at all.
Poor ole man.
Poor old soul.
He speaks of someday making something of himself,
though he knows he'll never come close.
His children talk, he doesn't hear.
Son of his dreams, children of his nightmares.
His hard luck stories are all around.
He knows he's not the only one in town.
Still people listen, pretending to hear.
They only listen, they don't really care.
The man comes crying.
No one's there.
He hums songs from days gone past,
though he knew they would never last.
He wastes no time to get nowhere.
Hurries fast, but no one's there.
He thinks he's figured what life's about,
yet as he speaks there's room for doubt.
But no doubt should there ever be,
if he's mastered the illusions in his dreams of reality.

Virginia Pounds

THE LIGHT OF YOUR LIFE

Cast upon the stone of wisdom
Listening to a paraded thought
Not knowing where it really comes from
Until — until one day you use the words of its sort
They keep repeating themselves
And then you feel like you're not alone
For you to start all over again and again and again
So this time you won't pretend
While taking down the bars
To give yourself another chance while reaching for those stars
The passion you receive through the dream lets you know
That you just haven't listened to the words
But will use that plan when your eyes open wide to see those
    glowing stars mend
Helping you keep that promise to not just understand
Piece by piece the light begins to unfold, while a sacred image
    comes to life
And out of that sacred image —
You will see that its always been you — wanting to fly free while
    making another stand —

Lori Richardson

URIAH

Flee! Prophet, flee to just Osiris' breast!
Leave everything, deny your lids their rest.
"The lion roars, the land lies desolate!"
Your regal enemies with blood lust foam;
Into Egypt their sinister shadows flit.

Oh, has the mighty Nile no clemency?
Is there no refuge for a refugee?
They bind your hands and bring you to their king:
"Let him taste the sword he prophesied!"
Into a common grave the corpse they fling.

Augustine Ephrem Valentine

AS I STOOD THERE, FOURTEEN

Early morning as the blue mist of the mountains
lingered thinly about the air,
I witnessed the beauty of birth and the ugliness of death.
As I stood there, fourteen.

The sounds of nature were numerous that day.
A small animal, perhaps a rabbit, scampered across the dirt path.
Then, I heard a thin chirping coming from amidst a shrub.
Although avoiding frightening them, I witnessed a quail's young taste
their first morsel of life on the outside of their shells.
As I stood there, fourteen.

I had never known such beauty existed in the world.
Looking through the trees, I spied a group of deer lavishly drinking
cool water from the slow moving river.
Then it happened.
From an unknown source, a bullet carrying the name of death plunged
into the side of the buck, who undoubtedly was the leader
of that small, unharming group of deer.
As the others fled, the buck fell.
He quivered and his hind legs kicked, as the last bit of life left
the motionless body of beauty.
As I stood there, fourteen.

Nikki A. Morin

SOPHISTICATED LILACS
ODE TO MOTHER

I dream of days when mauve tulips
arise from nature's seasonings into your heart
freeing you from yesterday's leftover blues

I relish thoughts of blue, marine octopuses
swimming through your dishes of sorts;
crab legs, chicken breasts . . . *spinach?!*

Always on a "bandwagon," uptown = downtown
"or is it?" . . . "Oh! I'm so confused"
Yes. But I've always admired you in colors
or rather your flair for fashion
which makes it altogether unique

All seasons come to an end
but rain or shine,
all of Nature's trimmings shall be devoured!

Arnold Forson

ARNOLD FOSU FORSON. Born: Accra, Ghana, 5-10-68; Education: Xavier high school, currently attending School of Visual Arts; Poetry: 'Twilite Time,' *American Poetry Anthology*, 4-1-87; Themes: *My themes generally deal with memorable real life experiences. My greatest recollection is of my poem, 'The Answer,' which my mother found so overwhelming that it brought tears to her eyes.*

CHRISTIAN BELIEF

If I go through this world a believer
This large and beautiful world,
Life also can be a deceiver
If against temptation you're hurled.

If you see how people are spending
Their days from morning till night
Some have a terrible ending
For refusing to do what is right.

They looked for but never did find it,
Love, Honor, Power and Wealth
They ended their days disappointed,
Perhaps even losing their health.

There is an answer for sinning,
For the poor disappointed heart,
It could have been had at beginning
If they had believed from the start.

There is relief for the weary,
For all who trust in the Lord
Who laid down his life just for us
On the Cross at the Golgatha ford.

C. H. Willke

CLARENCE H. WILLKE. Born: Anchor, Illinois, 12-14-1896; Married: Alvina Frasking, 2-24-20, deceased; Helen Bane, 1-2-70, deceased; Dorothy Gash, 9-17-83; Education: Browns Business College; Occupations: Chick hatchery worker, 1920-36; Grain and lumber dealer, 1936-62; now retired; Other Writings: Three church biographies; two family histories; poems, mainly to express praise to my Lord Jesus Christ for all the blessings received during my long life of 90 years and helping me to survive the hardships I encountered during my productive years. I also enjoy telling others how wonderful it is to live a Christian life; I hope that my writings may acquaint others with our good Lord, while they are still on earth as they will eventually meet Him in Eternity.

it's because i love you

i can fly and i do
it's because i love you
i ride home through the stars
in the nest of your arms

Stefan Pasti

AS A BLIND MAN SEES

I feel and yet I do not cry.
I know and yet I question why.
I hurt and yet I feel no pain.
I want things to be the same.

I do not know where it went,
the beautiful gift that God had sent.
It has been ignored and shoved aside.
Yet my love it could not hide.

My love bloomed in darkest night,
as shadows fell and dimmed my sight.
Your hands nurtured my wilting leaves
and made me feel as a blind man sees.

Please don't let this slip away.
Don't walk away from me.
Don't let the sun set on this day.
Come with me and soar.
I'll make you feel as a blind man sees.

Stephen J. Schlager

COINCIDENCE

If through the forest of time we go
and look to know what is there in
the chancing of events we see
the way we sift the evidence.

Stefan Pasti

NUCLEAR HEAVEN

Womb tomb
World
Catacombs of bombs
Orchestration for annihilation . . .

Alberta Anna Hannaman

ALBERTA ANNA HANNAMAN.

A WEEK ON THE AVON

Flow gently on sweet Avon,
Gently down to the sea,
With Captain Mike to steer the locks
And Richard to serve our tea.

Flow gently on sweet Avon
Through Evesham's lovely vale,
With Jonathan to guide us
And Flo to gourmet-dine us
As we paint our own "Winter's Tale."

Arlouine G. Wu

LIKE A SEAGULL

Like a seagull
cries in the oceanscape, I cry.
Out in the dewy air
"Lyric" and "Tune"
mix in the salty water.
My thought
        Seagulls.
My wings, the eagles.
I shall be more passionate,
than any mothering bird.
Long since my raw birth,
I choose to fly.

Ling Wun Wu

LOVE

My utmost love to a man
who made me his newly married,
my unearthly knowledge
to know the reality,
the purple lilac,
the sheer ivory chess,
love in a sunny plateau
singing in the garden
where all things
are equally desirable,
each moment as pointed light.
Loving him
as in thought,
philosophy opens my heart,
music be our oath,
while space moves.
We are in a night world
while time moves,
made beginning to our life.
All mine are yours,
a secret lamp,
the first innocent truth
a forbidden language, the myth. Yet
here is sacred water,
drink and be *whole* together.

Ling Wun Wu

ANGER'S BILL

The silent echoes are heard in the devastated towns.
Echoes of terrified women and children
Paying the high price of their fighting men,
The price of the catastrophic wars men fight to no end.

If only the kings and politicians would listen to reason,
Precisely put forth by the sound of the doomed,
The cry of the dead, and the call of the desolate.
Brought on with feverish ecstasy by men at war.

But lo, the day is coming when humanity shall find the way,
To settle our disputes in the Paradise of Peace.
For Anger's Bill carries not the seal of justice,
And is paid with hatred and murder.

There is hope for those who wish to promise peace to their children.
Though only God's Will determines whether they too pay Anger's Bill.
But such horrors cannot endure forever.
Only until time shall be no more.

But while the Day of Anger elapses,
A man must maintain his morals,
Lest he and his own are sundered
By Anger's Bill.

Wilford Fraser

IN THE FOREVER FOREST

Oh Holy Light
In infinite sight
In the Forever Forest
Where an angel's chorus
Encompasses the celestialized globe
In the spotlight of Holy strobe.

Vibrations of sound blend into vibrations of light
As infinite time undulates softly by, like a quivering kite.

A daughter who died young
Views the peacefulness of green
And remains forever curiously serene
As her ancestors and posterity
Gather one by one around
In waves of victorious sound.

Ancient trees remain passionate
As their web of life claims internalized fate —
The fountain of life,
The kernel of greeness,
The cradle of productivity.

Oh beautiful age
And Holy light on a Forever stage!

Eleke

LIFE'S EBB

What is the metal of which you are made?
Is it bronze, steel, or ore of another shade?
When things go right and one is riding high
The world is your oyster and there is no need to sigh.

But life in its ebb doesn't always flow thus.
The peaks and the valleys are necessary to us.
The vales make us stronger as they test our true being.
What the future holds there is no way of seeing.

Shirley B. Firebaugh

CONFERENCE OF THE BEARS

They convene at meetings
Called, not to be purposely mean,
Polite, suited, some casually muted —
To the psychological occasion to get down to the business
Of city development, water control, university policy,
P.T.A.'s, teacher's meetings, a card party or afternoon tea.

The bears represent different points of view,
Which united in relativity
Could produce a future rainbow of some kind of beauty.

Certain objectives proposed are catalytically new.
A new world of meeting inference lies unexplained.

In conference the dualism of day and night
And of an inner consciousness bound tight.
What seemed so simple
Has suddenly become a tangled system
Of complicated concerning features
For all the participating present creatures.

Suddenly, the natural, mindless reared its head,
Like the modern commentators tearing the flesh of a man's mind.

"Nature red in tooth and claw," Kipling said —
Mouth too all bloody with psychological gore
And brute force of muscles up front
Winding up the participants as though
They were some kind of a natural stunt.

Eleke

DIANA, GODDESS OF THE WOODS

Diana, Diana, oh dear phantom lady of ancient saga,
Not Icelandic nor Nordic, nor Arthurian,
But a holy apparition to the Greeks and Romans,
An artful Artemis, a lady of religious blessedness.

Artful Diana, Goddess of the woods,
You bared your breast to the breeze
As you chose to protect lost baby creatures
Lying left alone by a dying mother among the trees.
You looked after human maidens, tempted and worry-laden,
Inspiring their virginity as a godly purity.
You were always there to care for a young mother
So surprised by her impregnated and growing size,
And soothe her anxious concern
When her life brought forth the time to learn
That parturition with its dramatic hormone change
Would cause her child to burst forth
From its inner cradle, the womb,
Down the vaginal canal with anticipated smile,
And with a gasping first indrawing of air
Into wet, new, never-before used lungs,
And into the world with your first strong wail.
Here one must learn how to cry.
It's just as important as to learn how to smile.

In the ancient minds, oh sacred Diana, you were a mother god,
The virginal model for Christ's mother, Mary.

Eleke

IN LOVE WITH YOU

I've often been
    in love with love
And when I did
    soared like a dove
But now I know
    in fact I'm sure
That not with love
    am I in love
But with just you
    forever more.

'Tis really true
    I'm sure you know
I am in love
    with none but you
But if you doubt
    my feelings, dear
Do not forget
    our days of cheer
I truly love
    just only you.

Daisy I. Infante

ADORABLE

Shyly shrug your shoulders,
who seek to hide your smiling face,
and I smile, looking down.

Curl up on my bed to rest,
tired — very tired — and groggy,
slurring your words like one
who's had too much to drink,
and I am intoxicated
with observing pleasure.

A child — yet not a child —
inside a woman's body:
excited at the coming of Spring,
your face blossoms
like the flowers you see.
And I want to hold the flower.

The gentle wind that is your soul,
like a breeze across a lake
on a hot summer day,
compels me to say, ''I love you.''

Tim Frink

GOODBYE

Subtle whisper — maybe wind —
slightly moves your hair
as you stare at moonlit blades of grass
in your backyard.

It seems so hard to breathe a sigh,
to unlock the gates within
where flowers and thorns
and tie-died stains remain.

Your toes are moistened as you move
toward the house by fallen dew.
On porch-way steps you leave wet prints,
fading near the door.

A quiet creak lets you in
as you switch the kitchen light.

Tim Frink

MOONLIT MAN

I turn out the lights
and turn to go to bed.
As the blackness fades to light,
I discern a form — a man.

The moon beams through the window
to his body pale-ish blue,
and highlights his white underwear,
his stomach, his dark-haired chest, his face.

I see his eyes
following me as I approach.
By the time I'm there
there's room for me beside him
and he's beneath the sheets,
his clothes beside mine on the floor.

I fold away the covers,
settle my body next to his
and place the covers on my breasts.

I feel his hand at my neck,
and then his arm
pulling me close to someone warm.
I smile calmly
and know I'm satisfied.

Kassandra

FRIENDSHIP

Nature is my friend.
My Love for her
    will never end,
I Love to live within her hair
With all the animals
    with which to share;
Her fruits and drinks will never end
My Love for her I'll always send,
Because she is surely my true friend
My Love for her will
    never end.

John Dowdell

UNTITLED

Droll & dreary
    mist of morning
Rise upon the night.

Change from daylight
    into twilight, then turn
    into night.

Neighs & whinnies
    horses cry;
Intense agony
    the animals die.

Emerge from your cave of darkness
    witness the day's beginning;
And enter life,
    with head spinning.

John Dowdell

MYSTERY

Shadows flicker on the ceiling
And across walls
As the lamplight expands, attempting
To fill the dark room.
Remembering, that once this was enough,
I am content
And thrill as the thunder
Seems to shake the house to the very core.
Somehow, in the darkness,
Excitement for life revives —
Progress is once again
Concealed in formless shades.
Behind the lamp, I catch a glimpse
Of the dark secrets in your eyes
And I remember
All that we have shared.
I reach for your hand
And with your grasp
I'm caught wondering at the mystery
Of eternal love.

Jo A. Hughey

WHO'S ON THE OTHER SIDE OF THE DOOR?

Who's that knocking on my door?
I can't pretend to ignore
Who is knocking on my door
When youngins' crying — all four —
He ain't no deaf man I bet.
Is he friend or foe I've met?
Bills ain't been paid I confess.
Dirty dishes — house a mess —
I sure would like to know more.
Who's that knocking on my door?
Now a fly I'd like to be.
Setting on the door, I'd see
Who's that knocking on my door.
Who's that knocking on my door?

Juanita McIntyre

MELANCHOLIA

When gulls are calling and night is cold
The wind goes forth in an angry mood;
He cares not at all for the cache of gold
That man in his fancy might collude.

And little he cares for the ailing child
When gulls are calling and night is cold;
The wind is cruel and it's howling wild
And tonight a woman of thirty grows old.

A woman who feels that her life foretold
The melancholy she feels this night,
When gulls are calling and night is cold;
For her little one's fever is high in spite

Of bathing she gave throughout the day
As in her fear she tries to hold
Her much-loved child lest he fly away
When gulls are calling and night is cold.

The wheeling gull cry in the night
And the wailing wind grown old
Deny the fateful, unreasoning fright
When morning sun shines bold.

Regina Golden

THE CRUEL DESTINY

In rare mood of gladness or by fickle fancy *The Destiny* has thrown our
paths to cross once more; thus — we have met in our time of crisis
     And promised not to part forevermore.

She evidently knew not what this meeting started; in distrust we kept
our love affair private, secretly secured; *She* probably forgot us with
the years and seed *She* dropped has grown, blossomed and matured.

She shared misfortunes, grief and losses; the Life's best pleasures we
enjoyed — just you and I; in loyal trust the bond between us tightly
woven we needed one another more and more with years
swiftly rolling by.

The happiness is brief uncertain fragile. In mood of violence and
vengeance *destiny* came back; *her* voice harsh and loud, words —
menacingly dreadful: ''You stayed together far too long.
It's time to part.''

''I will not let you do that'' was my answer.
''I cannot give her up, ask anything but that.''
And with the hostile, rising fury *she* repeated:
''This is my warning: be prepared. The time is up for you to part.''

From that moment on my days were growing darker. I stubbornly resisted
cruel, fateful force; I pleaded, prayed, protested, asked for grace,
for mercy, I fiercely fought the battle with *The Destiny*
. . . and lost.

*   *   *

To whom I now tell how much I loved *you* or who can understand
the empty feeling in my heart?
You only *you* could give me *your* unlimited devotion
     Intense, complete and noble from the start.

In times of loss one should not be resentful; for fourteen years *Lord*
has given me the right to be with *you; you* left the memories for me so
rich, my little darling, my most beloved friend, my one and only
               Shaggie little doggie, *Cindy-Sue.*

Claudia Stoop

CINDY-SUE.

I feel lonely even when I'm surrounded by people.
It's like being far off on a mountain steeple.
I'm the only one who can feel
The wound in my chest that will not heal.
I'm the only one who can see
The fog that is engulfing me.
I'm starting to slip,
Into a pit,
Way down there,
Into despair.

Glenda Davis

TO ELLEN STOLPE

Honoring her 91st birthday, 9-11-81

Your childhood was not picnic fare, you were the first born of the clan.
Family was growing with years and you became
your mother's helping hand.

The household was bustling busy. The brothers — six of them —
came one by one; in vain you wished for sisters — helpers,
they took their time, they would not come.

Like river's water years swiftly flow; each day was filled with
chores — to scrub, to bake; so many shirts for boys the mother
had to sew; the buttonholes and buttons were for you to set and make.

With father boys had their work in garden, repaired fence, fed
cows, chopped the wood; all family attended church on Sundays;
affectionate devotion was your rule, conduct and mood.

And with more time it came to happen: like softest breeze, like
gentle rain, the precious little sisters — Ruth and Elsie —
desired much and long awaited for — at last they came.

As priceless gift the tiny moppets came from Heaven, they finished
and completed perfect score, they were delightful wonder, they were
pleasure to love, to cuddle, to adore.

By now you became a pretty maiden; with school diploma, charm and
manners measured best, so well rehearsed in parents' home
you were prepared to build your own little nest.

And it was natural and normal for man to see in you the excellence
of match and mix; you liked the man, agreed to marry, made home
and raised with him the family of six.

Amazing is your simple story. You worked with *love* each day *to give.*
We honor, we salute you, *Ellen Stolpe,* you did not waste your time,
you *lived.*

Claudia Stoop

GREAT LIFE

To Dr. M. L.

Alluring, forceful, fascinating *life* leads us through the
curves and bends, majestic, powerful but fragile
     In mystery *she* starts and ends.

She measures happiness with prudence, instructs to treasure
what one gets, in troubled days of pains and losses
     Directs to wisdom from regrets.

She sprinkles punishment with kindness. One morning bright
when sky was blue *she* guided me to doors of healing
     And introduced to all of you.

Young handsome doctors, charming ladies — Pat, Gerry, Nancy,
Maggie, Sue, Hope, Kerry, Bernie, Bill and Eric
     And music — loving doctor — *you.*

In clear voice *she* was saying: ''Remember, you are given best.''
To precious *life* I gave my promise not to forget that I am blessed.

     If over struggle for the *living*
     Destructive forces win the deadly strife,
     If pearl of planets — *earth* — should perish
     Could *life* be saved? Can *she* survive?

     Creator great in spare light years
     By sifting ashes and the sand may find
     The priceless remnants worth redeeming.
     Will *He* restore the *universe* to cherish
     The love, the music and *great life?*

Claudia Stoop

161

SPRING UNFOLDING

Based on sun,
Swallows return
Adders count the sunny days
Move, when the sum's enough.

A slow succession,
Light, plants, animals.
Longer lighter days.
Wild geese depart . . .

Life giving sun, silently
Promotes the run, North.

Lisa da Cunha

ELIZABETH HERRALA DA CUNHA. Pen Name: Lisa H. da Cunha; Born: Deposit, New York, 8-22-34; Married: Dr. Carlos E.J. da Cunha, 1960; Education: State University of New York at Geneseo, New York, B.S., Education; Indiana University, Bloomington, Indiana, M.A., Bio-Anthropology; Fordham University, New York City, currently enrolled in doctoral program of Arts and Sciences, graduate school; Occupations: Teacher; College Professor; Wife; Mother; Peace Activist; Memberships: Kappa Delta Pi, National Honor Society in Education; N.Y.S.T.A.; Amnesty International; Awards: 1st Prize, Spring Nationals of Poetry Connoisseur for 'Barbed Wire Beds,' 1985; Bradley English Prize at graduation from secondary school; Poetry: 'Autumn Leaves,' *Interlaken Review,* 1951; 'Oh, To Be A Teacher,' *Lamrom,* S.U.N.Y., 1955; 'Barbed Wire Beds,' *National Anthology of Poetry Connoisseur,* Spring, 1985; Other Writings: "(Hiroshima) One Day at 8:15 a.m. the World Changed," *Social Action Newsletter of U.U.A.,* 1984; Themes: *Nature: trees, rivers, flowers, animals, seasons; social criticism, to create a greater awareness of social problems; and poems to illustrate the devastation caused by wars.*

AND WHAT?

And what is the wind but running feet?
And what is life but a city street?
And around the next corner we may meet —

What is night but a lonely moon?
What is love but a mocking tune?
Oh, pray, my soul, to end it soon!

Tonight the world is darkly blue —
My heart is looking through and through
The wind and life and the night and you —

Doris E. Woolley

MARRIAGE, A NEW LIFE

Dawning of a new age,
Beginning of a new life.
Two to share
In *all* they have.
Marriage.

Words whispered in sweet ecstasy;
Tender surprise,
Joy and heartache
Go hand in hand.
Two care deeply,
One for the other.

New at first, maybe old later —
But love renewed day by day
As God leads both along
The fleeting flight of life in this world —
Eternity lies beyond.

John T. Barton

TWO ALONE IN THE TWILIGHT

So alone you stood on the hillside,
A still, still, figure enchanted, apart,
You, such a stranger to stillness,
Carelessly holding my heart.
Softly I moved and breathless,
At last you did comprehend,
This then was the beginning,
That a moment before was the end.
The stars swung low in the twilight,
And the trees whispered pleading things,
My body was singing and thrilling,
My soul — took wings.
Wonderingly I crept forward,
Abruptly you turned your head,
"Oh dear, oh my dear" I whispered.
"Shall we dance tonight?" you said.

Elizabeth S. Benoist

DEPOSITION III

Release
Him gently
From unyielding
Wood and iron nails

Nor jolt
The Body;
Patiently
It bore the sin and shame.

Lay Him
Down with care.
Remove the thorns
Tangled in His hair.

Love Him
Whose spirit
Rested lightly
On us, burdenless.

Regina Golden

A BOX

Fear builds
itself a box,
one wall
at a time,
then pulls them in,
close.

Donice M. Palmer

SOMETIMES IT MAKES ME WONDER

Sometimes it makes me wonder
When your eyes look up to me
The feelings that you're feeling
The man you try to see

Do I meet the expectations
Of the little boy you are?
Will I always be your hero
And help you reach your distant star?

Do I answer all the questions
That a little girl finds to ask?
Am I still your knight in armor
And will I be, without the mask?

Sometimes it makes me wonder
When your questions reason why
And the feelings that you're feeling
They just won't pass you by

Because, I'm here; and always will be
And, as you lean on me
Stop; to think and wonder
Of your feelings that flow free

Sometimes it makes me wonder
When your eyes look up to me
The feelings that you're feeling
The daddy you try to see

Lucky Rimpila

VALENTINE TWO: A NEW YEAR'S RESOLUTION FOR BILL

I want to know if
We are privately engaged, or if
You're still thinking through the newness
Of the offer you inadvertently let slip
(Two years ago when I grabbed, hog-tied and
Pinned down the surprise as a
Veritable Prize, and/or
Badge, of high quality
Fashion/glory.)

When do I get my
Ring?
Both on the phone
And on my
Finger —
So that we can
Run off together, in haste.

Love-in-good-heart,
I'll see you soon — as
My "person."

Geneve Baley

GRANDMA

There are not enough words to describe all Grandma could be,
The warmth I felt, sitting in her lap, her arms sheltering me.

She loved children around her, entertained them well,
Weaving tales so interesting, had us under her spell.

An adventurous spirit her ancestors had, a love of liberty,
Signed the Magna Charta, Constitution, fought to make us free.

Like some of those before her she lived to a ripe old age,
Known for her clear mind and memory, a truly judicious sage.

She was a friend to all in need and had the healing touch.
From doctors in her family tree she had learned so much.

Compassion she had, and fairness, courage and wisdom galore,
A love of her Bible and nature, a sense of humor — much more!

I hope that some of these traits have passed through her to you
And that I have them in my being, remembered for them, too!

Ruby Tippit Peacher

RUBY TIPPIT PEACHER. Born: Indian Mound, Tennessee, Stewart County; Married: Joseph William Peacher, 6-13-36 (deceased 1976); Education: Bachelor of Science in Education, 1958; Austin Peay State University; Occupations: Elementary school teacher (now retired), Indian Mound; Reading teacher, North Stewart; Memberships: Retired Teachers Association, Stewart County; Historical Society, United Methodist Women, Stewart County Library Board, Tennessee Library Association; Poetry: 'Spring Is A Child,' *American Poetry Anthology,* 1987, APSU Newspaper, 1935; 'Family Tree,' 'My Sister,' *American Poetry Anthology,* 1987; Other Writings: ''Acadian Accents,'' genealogy, history, *Our Family History, Book 1,* 1983; ''The Seay Side,'' genealogy, history *Our Family History, Book 2,* 1985; Comments: *Appreciation of our heritage and inspiration to do our best are the themes of most of my writings. I have more poems written, but I have not tried to have any published until this year. I feel honored to have some included in this book. I am now working on short stories based on my childhood. I was chairman of* Stewart County Cemetery Book, *helped produce* Our Heritage *by Stewart County Historical Society.*

MEANING

Listening through the darkness to the clock tick on the wall,
Have you ever stopped to wonder what's the purpose of it all?
Watching fading sunsets paint the storm clouds crimson red,
Have you ever stopped to listen to the things that He has said?
Looking past the heartaches to the joys you knew before,
Has your heart become so hardened that you cannot see there's more?
Hearing more than nonsense in the speeches of the meek,
Has your ear become so deafened that you cannot hear Him speak?

Lewis E. Winkler

THIS ISN'T AMERICA

This is not America — the America I read of in books;
It was a land of love and patriotism found under God.
Sometimes I wish I could get lost in the pages of history
because this is not the America our forefathers dreamed it would be.

The men from the colonies who gave their blood to fight;
to fight to give us a land with freedom's ringing bells.
Our ancestors found desire in their hearts to be a nation under God
and yearned for peace and liberty while singing their praises loud.

I see our *flag* that waves so proudly through thick and thin;
But as a nation we don't see that glory:
For drugs and liquor are used to escape life's problems
and when spouses are bored they find secret lovers.
We steal and we kill and disregard ruining other lives
because we hate and deceive and lie and worship greed.

It is the United States of Adultery or
It is the United States of Crime for
it seems to be the United States of No Morals.

I call Mr. Lincoln, Washington, Polk and the others to help us see —
because this is not the America our forefathers dreamed it would be.

Jim Harris, Jr.

THE ART OF ANGEL GLIDING

I fell upon the white clouds while lost in my dream
but there I saw my dear brothers Bob and Steve.

They were with other angels flying about
it seemed they were playing some game jumping cloud to cloud.
But when my brothers saw me they rushed on over
and a tear streamed down my face when I saw Steve smile at me
while Bob patted my back assuring me they were alright.

They each took an arm and took me up into the blue skies.
Bob held me up while Steve showed me a gentle stride;
a gliding horizontal permeation through two soft clouds
and when he came through he smoothly thrusted back up to us.

Bob gave a forceful but graceful rush through the air
and stopped before a cloud and calmly drifted back.
I saw some angels watch as my brothers showed me some moves —
the simple ''Vertical float'' and ''Downward drift.''

After a while they took me down to the cloud and gave me a hug.
They waved good-bye and I watched them glide through the Heavens.
The next day I woke up in bed but knew it wasn't really a dream.

Jim Harris, Jr.

SONG OF THE RIVER

Let the river flow my love
And let yourself flow with it
No matter where its winding path will take you
Through twists and turns and hurdles it will pass
Giggling, gurgling, swiftly swirling
Then pausing to reflect . . .
And gently guide you to a newer undiscovered path.
Stay your course and seek your virtues
Hold to all the best
And bring about that lovely glow
That surely is the test.
Oh, grateful mind for letting go
And great the mind that does it
For as the waves move high and low
You're sure to rise above 'em.

Saundra Fields Collins

AFTER THE SYMPHONY:
THE CAR-CHASING SEARCH

Row upon row of cars,
Lane upon lane of cement
Winding up, down and across
The great cement encasement
Providing parking space for
Several cultural events taking place
As in Lincoln Center; (New York, New York)
Simultaneously.

Traffic cops stand injudiciously
Here and there, sparsely; in this vehicle
Maze of nonentity; monotonous, continuous
Sameness of car-parked design.

How did we find our
Mid-size compact after midnight closes the
Hall of the Houston Symphony?
(In the wrong lane, and on the
Wrong level, looking for
Our transport-home, identity?)
Pure luck, pure chance, pure
Trial and error, work!
On and of, the car-chasing search —

Geneve Baley

I BELIEVE IN MIRACLES

I believe in miracles
And pray, my friend, you do —
For if there were no miracles,
There'd be no me nor you!

I believe in miracles
All through the day.
I believe in miracles
As to our Lord I pray.

I believe in miracles
From the first crack of dawn.
I believe in miracles
Till the setting of the sun.

I believe in miracles
In life and in death.
I believe in miracles
With each gasp of breath.

I believe in miracles
And pray, my friend, you do —
I believe in miracles
For I believe in you!

Waneta Wells

SNOWFALL

Silent, peaceful, quiet snowfall
Snuggling 'round the trees and plants,
Slowing outdoor activity.
Then emergencies arise forcing mankind
To contend with cold and exhaustion
Helping the young and the elderly,
Often too ill to enjoy the beauty of the scene.

Arlouine G. Wu

UNTIL I SEE YOU

Excitement fills my heart
waiting to see your face

You, the one who made me
feel like a man so proud

I bask in the radiance
of your pretty smile

Every time I look in your eyes
life becomes a grand celebration

I can feel the soothing
touch of your creamy skin

All these emotions are ready
to erupt; showering you

Cooling and comforting the precious
heart burning with love.

David Spriggs

FOREVER

In the days of old when knights were bold,
And the world was fresh and clean,
Beneath a bower, in the shade of a tower,
Two lovers met, unseen.

A vagrant breeze caresses the trees
And the green grass at their feet.
Where the flowers grew, both red and blue,
That kept the air so sweet.

Through the years, both smiles and tears,
With children numbering four.
No angry shout, no childish pout
Shrouded this castle by the shore.

Centuries pass as through the glass
The sands of time do fall.
Years of weather work together
And the scene is beyond recall.

The heaps of stone are overgrown
With flowers of red and blue.
Yet from somewhere on the perfumed air
Come the words "I love you."

Marie Morse

LONELINESS

When I walk the streets
All I can do is be me
I see people walk with their friends
But my loneliness
Has never ended
All of them look so happy
They make me want to cry
When they walk on by
they don't say *hi*
And all I can do is walk on by them
And cry
'Cause hopefully my loneliness
Will end someday

Renee Mindt

WHEN

When you can hope when there
is no help
When you can wait when there
is no time
When you can cry when there is
no more tears
When you can think over all your
pains
When you can talk when no one
listens
When you can't move because there
is no place to go
When you can fly and can't get
up
When you kneel and lift your
head and pray
Then the answer will come without
delay.

Mattie Wright

OVER THE HILL

Last night in my dreams
   I walked Over the Hill,
to the sound of the voice
   of a whippoorwill.

Tall, leafy cornstalks
   swayed Over the Hill,
rustling and crackling
   in the evening still.

The silos stood silently
   just Over the Hill,
at the barn a lazy kitten
   in the windowsill.

Summer sun was sinking
   way Over the Hill,
I heard the folks calling me
   and then time stood still.

Last night in my dreams
   I walked Over the Hill,
to the sound of the voice
   of a whippoorwill.

Theresa E. Erickson

THE PRETENDER

The first impression
   he was handsome and stately
with a commanding voice
   which coupled successfully
with his facial expressions.

His attire displayed impeccable taste
   a "Mr. Esquire."
Love had escaped him
   like a slippery eel.
Caught off guard
   it was discovered
he had been camouflaging
   his exalted ego.
He was a pretender.

Jay Hugo Forde

Old Furnace, at Kent Plains.

WORDS SPOKEN

The word spoken
   goes forth with power
and cannot return void,
   but must prosper.
Born to consciousness
   it is eternal, indestructible.
It casts out,
   rejects and destroys
the lie and the liar.

Jay Hugo Forde

MORTAL MIND

There is a mortal mind
   with avenues
through which it can act.

There is a mortal mind
   that has
activity, power, influence.

There is a mortal mind that has
   an object
upon which it can act
   as law, rule, desire.

That mortal mind
   and its activities
have a past, a history.

Jay Hugo Forde

HUGO J.C. FORDE. Pen Name: Jay Hugo Forde; Born: New York City; Education: New School for Social Research, Drama Workshop, 1947; Writers Institute (N.I.A.), Journalism, 1975; TV/Playwriting, 1977; Memberships: The Dramatists Guild; The International Society of Dramatists; The Authors League of America, Inc.; The State Island Council on the Arts; The American Legion; NAACP; AARP; NMRA; ART/NY; Poetry: 'A Summer Breeze,' *Visions of Mine,* 1986; 'Soliloquy at Dusk,' *Poetry of the Century,* 1986; 'Life,' *Masterpieces of Modern Verse,* 1986; 'The New Me,' *Best New Poets of 1986;* Other Writings: 'The Beginning and the End,' 'Turkey in the House,' 'Maylee,' 'The Open Door'; Comments: *Through my poetry I sincerely attempt to convey to my readers my thoughts and feelings in their most direct manner.*

MY PLACE

I have a place nobody knows
   deep, deep in the woods,
It's always back near my yard
   where trees cover like hoods,
There's a battle back there an' bullets soar,
I'm a general — I win the war —
I protect my country of rocks an' things,
An' run for cover 'fore a bumblebee stings.

Sometimes I sit on a great big stone,
An' pretend I'm a king — on a golden throne,
My servants are ants an' bugs alike
An' a chariot, that's really a bike,
My castle's gigantic — it's real true —
My carpet is green, my ceilin' is blue,
I'll share a secret thought with you —

My light is high, and shines real bright,
Needs no switch to go out at night.
But when it starts to get real dim
I leave my throne in the woods within —

Out I come from my 70-mile hike,
That's me an' my 50-speed bike.
Then I'm home in my great big bed
With that shiny moon beamin' over my head —
An' I listen — an' I listen — an' I hear it say —
I'm watchin' your place for another day.

Marge Doran

MARGIE M. DORAN. Born: Jersey City, New Jersey, 8-24-42; Married: James K., 11-18-72; Education: Nursing, Medical Tech, 1962; Occupations: Nurse; Medical Tech; Memberships: Natural Childbirth Association of Hudson County, 1961; Worked with T.B. for 8 1/2 years with the doctor who invented cure for T.B.; Poetry: 'Child Abuse,' ABC Eyewitness News, 1976; 'What Kind of Life,' *New York Anthology,* 1986; 'When Did This Happen,' 'Not Old,' *California Anthology,* 1987; Comments: *At the moment I am writing a book on education. I have been working on it for the past two years. Poetry is my love and amusement, it is my way of sharing life as I see it, and love, a language all can understand.*

ARE YOU MISSING SUMMER FUN?

Oh! the world is missing out on
the wonders of our times
the air of early morning —
and such beauty oh sublime!

Mother Nature's done her part,
but we've left her very sad —
the stars are shining teardrops,
and the moon is downright mad.

What have we done?
to mar our summer fun
we disrespect each other,
and our work is never done.

Some snort cocaine and dope
they just don't seem to care,
and looking over things out there
it doesn't leave much hope.

So stop! dear hearts and analyze,
the good Mother Nature's done —
I guarantee you'll stop those habits,
and enjoy your summer fun!

Joyce W. Giles

LATCH KEY CHILD

What dastardly deeds we've done
our example to the young,
slip of the lip, bad action —
and vile language from the tongue.

Eerie a darken latch key
to open a dungeon doom,
only to find the otherside —
an empty, lonely room.

Oh! let the television greet them,
to calm the eager heart —
for there's no parental guidance,
to play a loving part.

Who's to know what ails thee
Who's to know your pain
Who's to answer all the questions
Who's to kindle love's flame?

The parents, and the teachers —
have a continuous role to play.
Loving, training by example,
each child along the way.

Joyce W. Giles

VIOLETS IN THE DESERT

Violets in the desert
Are only doomed to die.
While cactus by a bubbling brook
Beneath a leafy sky,
Will lie among the lushness
And die among the leaves.
For every climate casts its own,
And only some can leave . . .
And only some can leave.

Sally Irene Davis

SUNSET

Did you ever watch the sunset?
  At the end of a perfect day,
When the golden sun meets the earth,
  And the cares of the day give way.
I pray, do watch it some day,
  For its beauty cannot find known words.
And you'll find God's gift at sunset,
  Is one of His great mighty works.
I wonder at this greatness,
  This mass of pure round gold.
So many miles above us,
  And yet it meets the earth.
Sometimes a cloud divides it,
  A strip of some dark blue.
Then slowly it changes to a deep purple hue,
  And then the gold keeps fading,
To a bright and burning red,
  Till the trees look as if they were ablaze,
But only touched by the sunset rays.
  I can only see the tip now, of the burning sun at rest.
And the purple hues of the evening,
  Are now taking their place.
The evening shadows are falling,
  The night clouds are almost here.
Thank You, God, for a sunset
  That is bringing a new day near.

Josephine Sadowski

JOSEPHINE SADOWSKI. Born: Chicago, Illinois, 7-16-19; Education: Grace Street Grammer School (now called Canty), 1929-36; Steinmetz High School (College Preparatory 2), 1936-39; Art Institute of Chicago, scholarship, 1938-9 (eye surgery in 1939 required giving up anything that would cause eye strain, unfortunately); Occupation: Retired, previously four years of medical work, 17 years of clerical work office work, 10 years of analyst work/medical papers, 15 years of teaching Sunday School; Memberships: Grace Evangelical Free Church; Directed two Christmas pageants during the 1970s, completely designing costumes, programs, etc.; Always active in church choral groups; During World War II, was given the War Manpower Commission, training people within industry; Awards: Honorable Mention for eight poems appearing in *Important American Poets and Songwriters of 1947*, Valiant House Publishers, and two poems in *Talented Songwriters and Poets of 1947*, Heaven Publishers; Poetry: 'Autumn Scenes,' 'First Snow,' 'Amber Skies,' 'Ode to the Oceans,' 'Little Fisherman,' *Important American Poets and Songwriters*, 1947; 'When Springtime Comes Again,' 'Play a Symphony to Fall,' *Talented Songwriters and Poets*, 1947; Comments: *A person can learn much from poetry. I write by inspiration. My themes come easily and vary somewhat. I like to write about Truth, and the four seasons. The desire to write has always been with me. As a child, my first poem,* The Beauty of Spring, *appeared in the school paper. I have done a lot of writing through the years. Since I have retired, I am trying to finish much of my manuscripts. I have always had a busy and very active life, and I only wish I could do it all over again — however, now, at 68 I can look back and like the life I lived walking close with God; the beauty that's left is in the heart. I was born of Polish parents, the seventh of nine children.*

HOLD FAST YOUR DREAM

In ancient days a ruler lived in state
Of Oriental splendor, holding life
And death of all his subjects in his hand,
A monarch loving arrogance and strife;
Yet he awoke in terror, summoning
Soothsayers to his couch. In agony
He cried, ''Interpret ye my dream; and tell
My dream, as well; for it has gone from me!''

Do you remember happy days, and bright,
The time of dedication, days of youth
When there were dreams of conquest and power,
With gleaming sword of righteousness and truth?
Oh, have you guarded well your shining dream,
And kept it clean, and free from stain of earth,
And held it close against your heart, in love
Enfolding it, deep cherishing its worth?

O friend, hold fast your dream, the splendid spark
Immortal, born of glory and of fire.
To bless your joy and suffering, to light
The gloom of all the world, your heart's desire.
''Tell me my dream, for it has gone from me!''
This bitter, heart-torn cry through fading gleam,
This deep, despairing cry burns down the years
Even to you, O friend. Hold fast your dream!

Jennie P. Thompson

LOON SONG

From depths indescribable you bring a long tone,
Drifting on evening air, sad and alone.
You hauntingly echo between northern pines,
Crossing the barriers of modern times.
You send oral missives throughout the dark night,
Speaking the truths of your ancient insight.

Lewis E. Winkler

HEROES OF THE CHALLENGER

The call came to challenge a project in space,
  The bravery of their hearts shown in the bright smiles of their face.
Oh! Poet, how can you write of such a flight?
  When your eyes want to cry for what to write.
Write I must, we grew fond of them all,
  They were to represent the Greatest Nation of All.
Into that beautiful Spaceship they went,
  We watched their valor, that became the Blast of Sorrowed Fame.
That instant, that moment when all life ceased,
  And now forever the Flags of Courage fly,
Fly high for those Americans who died in the sky.
  All men who build remember always the great task you have,
For, in the palms of your hands you hold
  The future beats of the hearts; when they go, will they come back?
Challenge, Courage and Space, the Wonder of it All.
  So great the hearts that gave to human man their Sacrificed Call,
Perhaps, was this God's plan how man should die?
  Now Heroes of the Past, who left with us their smiles of Great Hope,
You were fine, you were brave, you made a Hero's choice.
  Oh! Poet, how can you write of such a flight?
Yes, God only knows it; America, you must fly high
  the Flags of Courage,
  God must have blessed their Souls in this Treasured Memory.
To the Families and Friends and Children,
  To the People of the World, this Poet with tears has written
Of the Valor that went with the Challenge, Courage and Space.

Josephine Sadowski

TRUE BEAUTY

Are you one who sees the beauty of
Each thing that you pass
The beauty of the lakes and trees
Or in the tall cool grass
Colors that will bring to you
Their every rainbow hue
Of the flowers crowned in glory
The ocean and its view
Beauty comes only within the eyes
Of the one that sees
A mother with her babe in arms
Will never cease to please
Of all the beauty in this world
Above any other
Will be the loving tender eyes
Of my dearest mother

Robyn M. Rogers

TREE OF LIFE

When you are young and oh so eager
Exploring things you see
The joys you share the carefree days
Until you've reached puberty
School days soon gone first signs of love
Then marriage and all your dreams
Two darling children one boy one girl
There's more to love this means
Then as you pass those wedded years
You find time repeats again
A grandchild in his early teens
To tell stories now and then
The years pass quickly one by one
As the petals start to fall
You'll know you're getting on in years
Father Time too soon will call
But when the tree and the limb of life
Bends as the Maker calls
He'll guide you to your eternal rest
Just as that last leaf falls

Robyn M. Rogers

THE SOB-SIGHS

Many, many years ago,
When you left and abandoned me,
To live and survive on my own,
How many tears did I shed!
How much human sufferance
To experience the hard way!
How much sobbing
For the loss of my love!
The sobs that resulted
From heart-breaking cries,
Have never left me,
Thirty years later today,
Which have become sob-sighs,
Unperceivable to others,
And unpredictable to myself.
A constant reminder of
Those painful days,
Unerasable to this day,
Will most probably stay,
Till the end of my day.

S. L. Yen

FOOLS SUCH AS I

The night is but a billion
Starry eyes
Looking at us mortals
From out the skies
Now our earthly mortals
Look back to see
Heaven's rainbows blending
Harmoniously
Spring days with flowers
Scattered here and there
Young maidens running
With bouquets in hair
Watching young baseball teams
Is such a joy
Seeing young parents rooting
For their boy
The miracles happening
On this earth
New father watching as his
Wife gives birth
Beauty is everywhere
That you can see
Urging "fools like me"
To write poetry

Robyn M. Rogers

PAIN

I fell down the stairs last week,
and I may appear very weak.
Yes I may seem that way,
for now I cannot sing hooray.

The doctor says I was lucky
since I only broke my toe. I'm not stubby.
I could have broken all my bones
and then I would have yelled a lot of tones.

My brain could have been splattered,
I say now would it have mattered?
Most likely I'll fall again,
next time there will be other pain.

Elvira Wells

Death:
You are a savage King!
I hear your last gurgle then the
Pain and the
Silence left to
Fill a void.
This vacuum gorged with
Tears that stain and sores to
Reign as monarchs of my
Wounded world.
Once your child filled my empty
Womb. All your tomorrows were
Here, too soon; yet
Morning comes for a rising
Sun. And your boldness looms in
Defeat and peace.
Oh Death —
Wipe away your last tear!
I see your empty tomb.

Sally K. Wheeler

THE FAMILY DOCTOR

He treads a precarious path
Between sickness and health;
Indeed, at times,
Between life and death itself.
Upon his diagnoses depends
The salvation of his patients.
Upon his wisdom and compassion
Depend his relationships.
Attention to his own health
Determines his length of service.

He is pressured constantly
By time and stress.
Interruptions beset him;
Quick decisions face him.
He must force himself to listen
Despite a crowded waiting room.

If you have found this perfect
Family Doctor, cherish him,
For he is an American Treasure!

Virginia E. Cruikshank

WHERE IS THE LAUGHTER?

What purpose is there
For a child to suffer
An adult battle with death
And no way to buffer
The pain or the fears?

Where is the laughter
I thought I would hear,
The learning, the triumphs . . .
Yet I only see tears?

Naive, and so valiant
For someone so young,
How to understand
Why cancer's among
Our children so dear?

Barbara A. Dailey

LADIES BEFORE SEVEN

Where are the ladies, small and old,
Who climbed the hill before seven?
Plodding to toil with bags they hold
Like birds of blue, brown, gray leaven,
Bright of eye and bobbing of head,
A summary of years gone by,
A comma after past life led,
Dreams over and plans gone awry.

And what are they seeking ahead?
After they cook, clean, put away,
Or coax babbling babes being fed,
A small wage at the end of day?
The long years have left them alone
Bereft of family and friend,
Now, shadows of what was once known
Portend their own approaching end.

Grace K. Pratt-Butler

THE STATE OF AFFAIRS

should we plunder until there is nothing left to plunder
should we kill until there are no more to kill
the earth is full of parasitic bloodsuckers
their habitation is in the hospitals
supply and demand it's what makes things cost how much
power hungry people with nowhere to go
they thought they could get us above the heavens
into the realm of the stars! you've seen the movies
we work and we toil and nothing follows us into the grave
do you suppose the earth will become a desolate wasteland
nobody is getting off this planet
we went to the moon but it doesn't harbor life
the source of oil is supposed to be a bottomless pit
and yet the resources vanish away
what do you suppose will happen to our children
all fighting to survive and a place to live
it's cutthroat you know and i guess it always has been
this merry-go-round is supposed to go on forever
but people still die
we're in need of a resurrection when power follows after but nobody
wants to pay the price
and what do you suppose the price is?
it's a godly life i imagine

Mark Wilhelmi

HEARTBEATS

Written to my wife

Absence makes the heart grow fonder
Makes our union knit much stronger
Oh hasten hours and days and weeks
While in my dreams my love I seek

The heart through absence fonder grows
For one whose love alone I know
That special gesture, word or thought
In days gone by I oft had sought

When through absence the heart strengthens
Without you close the days do lengthen
Oh days, go speedily rushing by
That I may to my lover fly

The days, the hours, the moments linger
For time with you, a real bell ringer
I watch and hope and yearn and pray
For you dear heart, every day by day

Glen R. Buck, Sr.

TIME IS NO STRANGER

Time is the shadow of its own lingering memory.
It is a tapestry of remembrances;
Too many to weave.
It echoes in its endless hall; it shouts,
It whispers and calls
To ancient gods and mysteries yet unseen.
Time is the threshold
Of all that has been or will be —
It is Cassandra, Moses and me.
Great thoughts were born in its hallowed womb,
Countless loves lie buried in its dark tomb.
Time is no stranger to us all,
For we are her children — her soul.

Ronald Russell Enders

FOR ME AT CALVARY

At Calvary He gave His life, my sins to atone,
At Calvary He suffered and bled and died alone,
There they crucified the blessed Son of God,
As He hung there His precious blood dripped to the sod.

Jesus bravely walked the road that led to His death,
He carried the cruel cross that took His very breath,
On the road that reached the brow of Sorrows Hill,
He went there to fulfill His Father's Perfect Will.

They took Him down from off the cross, His work was done,
They carefully wrapped and laid Him in a new hewn tomb,
There he broke the bands that held Him to this earth,
He placed high the cost of what a soul is worth.

We can look back at what took place that bitter day,
If I ascend, I will come back that very way,
Keep your eyes upon the signs in the skies,
One day I'm coming back to claim my glorious bride.

At Calvary, at Calvary, at Calvary, at Calvary
Jesus paid the awful price,
The day they crucified my Christ,
And He did it all for me, at Calvary.

Glen R. Buck, Sr.

SIMPLY OF LOVE

Today was the day the story began,
The maiden, the prince; when he took her hand.

Happily ever after so the story goes,
But so much more that no one knows,

The trials, the pain, the love and the tears,
To build that kingdom we'd dreamt of for years.

We had no big palace nor riches of gold.
Our treasures were of nothing to hold.

Our money was our hearts and of it we spent,
Upon our children; there was no lament.

The best of our love, in them we grew.
The happiness we shared, and we never knew,

That we'd see the love that we once sewed:
That is worth much more than riches of gold.

And now we've watched our dreams succeed,
In those once so vulnerable seeds.

We survey our kingdom, the love and the smiles,
That have consoled our hearts over hundreds of miles.

And no million miles did we have to own,
Just ourselves, our children; we were our home.

Today we gather to celebrate those years,
And in memory of times, we shed a few tears.

No stones to build kingdoms, nor towers above,
For we've built our kingdom, simply of love.

Lisa Fisher-Hiller

LIFE TRIUMPHANT

Death's brown cloak majestically swirled
Like huge wings tumbling to my chest,
Smothering me as it unfurled.
Neither icy nor cold, but warm
As nature, blanketing her child,
Brings earth heat softly in its folds.
Trumpets neither blared nor choirs filed
Regrets, to nature's warming work.
Soft, my heart nearly stilled its beat
Beneath the cloak's ebbing motion,
But life, not primed yet for defeat,
Pierced the cloak, triumphant once more.

Grace K. Pratt-Butler

YOU AND ME

Love is like a speck in time
Easy to lose and hard to find
Two aimless lights in a sea of dark
Touching together, and then — apart

Where does love go to hide in the night
The sweet scent of you —
    these embers so bright
Drifting alone in a people-tossed sea
What are the odds of you and me

Specks in time, lives that rhyme
Yours with mine, for all of time
With so many lights adrift you see
What are the odds of you and me

Who made the rule that keeps you from me
Apart in all, but my fantasy
For all of time, if we aren't meant to be
What were the odds of a you and me

Phil H. Garton

MOTHER, FOR A MOMENT

A beautiful dawn approaches
Announcing another full, long day;
Yet deep, heavy clouds come between us,
My heart and its Father of hope.

Oh, how many sunrises missed I,
For a few extra moments of sleep?
Now, painfully, called to observe it,
I'm so torn inside, I can't see.

Lord, I beg You for strength and endurance
To face what I seek from this day;
If a new life inside must be taken,
Give me purpose to follow Your will.

And protect me for future creation,
That one day I may marry again
A child who is truly as special
As this one You're recalling today.

M. S. Berger

HER TOUCH

Ever since I can recall,
I need not medicine to make me fine.
When fever comes I've always known,
The ever-present voice benign.

And when at times I hurt
I trust to feel less pain,
She's always there to give
The best of care I can obtain.

For when feeling so bad
Is when you see what you got
And finally realize
How simple love can mean a lot.

Thank you ma . . .

Victor Lopez

VICTOR LOPEZ. Pen Name: Adam Softer; Born: Cuba; Single; Education: Miami Dade College, A.A., Business Data Processing; Occupation: Department Coordinator; Poetry: 'Travel,' *American Poetry Anthology,* 1987; Comments: *I see poems as containers, inside each is a part of my life. Whenever I care I open one up, and feel what I felt at the time I wrote it. It's how I remember yesterday.*

ADVICE OF TEARS

Advice, did you ask
For advice,

Why ask me?
One that sees yet
Sees nothing,

The fool's paradise,
Where all have steps
Built upon me,

Ships sail far just
To take leave on the
Island of one who is so blind,

No, ask not advice of me,
Nor any other who sits
Alone upon these steps,

Your advice shall be
Gained from the tears
You shed.

Michelle L. Hall

MUSE IN GLUON

Cells dictate my height and race,
  man judges my worth.
  I am made of

the building blocks that
  jostled in the beginnings
  of the universe.

The same within a distant
  night's star, and around
  it, an unnamed cousin

life form viewing mine in
  its sky. Eternal matter,
  neither created nor destroyed.

There is no
  black or white,
  Jew or Gentile,
  Capitalist or Communist!

We are the body of God! Forever
  fighting for that which we do not own,
  cursing what we do not understand.

We are both great . . . and insignificant.

Reginald L. Goodwin

TIME

Time is a gift to all mankind.
To each goes a certain measure.
Some squander it ever so carelessly;
and some each moment treasure.

Time is the present in which we live,
And the past we can review.
Time is the future mysterious unknown —
Where dreams we make come true.

Time is the second in which we are —
Whatever we chose to be.
Time is all we have and yet —
It is absolutely free!

Time is a word that measures only
What goes on within our lives.
Time is the savory sacred sacrament
Within which we live our lives.

Clara Hill

TORN LOVE

A rose, a heart;
Shall never part,
Its beauty disguised;
Covering lies.

A heart, a rose;
Together love shows,
Its strength, its thorns,
The heart it has torn.

Gwen L. Bond

MY PRAYER OF THANKS

Thank You, O Lord, for answered prayer
Thank You, dear God, for being there
Thank You for answering our call
And for giving us Your all
For giving Your life for the lost
That sinners might live without paying the cost
Thank You for blessings from above
Thank You, dear Lord, for abundance of love
Thank You, too, for patience given
Thank You for my home in heaven
Help us, O Lord, to be worthy of You
We can never repay all that You do
Lord, may others see Thee in me, by the way that I live
And I daily pray to Thee their hearts they might freely give
Talk to them daily, Lord, I pray
Before it's too late, show them the way
Help us walk closer, dear Lord, with Thee
Grant, Lord, we'll be what You want us to be
Draw us so near we can feel Thy touch
O Lord! Dear God, we love Thee so much
Give us boldness to witness for You
Be with us, Lord, in all that we do
Go with us, Lord, over all of the land
Help us, Lord, to take our stand

Millie Poletto

MILDRED PAULINE POLETTO. Pen Name: Millie Poletto; Born: Jeffersonville, Indiana, 12-21-24; Married: Wallace E. Mathes, 1943; 7 children, 4 boys, Wally, Tom, Bill and Mike; 3 girls, Bunny, Wendy, Barb; divorced, 1970; Married Henry J. Poletto, 1972; 12 grandchildren; Education: High school, 3 years; Occupations: Salesperson, Soap inspector, Butcher, Salad girl; Memberships: Tabernacle Baptist Church, Christian Women's Club; Poetry: 'Your Gospel Train Leaves Soon,' *American Poetry Association,* 6-87; 'The Six Days of Creation,' 1984; 'A Tribute To A Fallen King,' for Elvis Presley, 1977; 'What America Means To Me,' 1972; 'My Prayer of Thanks,' 1974; Comments: *All of my inspiration to write my poetry is given to me by the Lord, this is His will for my life, and the way He wants to spread His word to many others. I am only His instrument. He is the one who deserves all the credit for any poetry I write. The American Poetry Association is the door the Lord has provided for me.*

SUDDEN STORM UPON THE LAKE

Mad Lake, an hour ago you were serenely calm
Heaven lent earth golden sun for balm
  Over the mountaintops the sun streamed away
  A swingy breeze with the trees began to play
  Blowing over the lake she seemed to say
Romp with me
Exercise like a mighty sea
  One by one the raindrops fell
  The lake was playfully mad, we on land could tell

Pearl Van Slocum

THE REASON FOR ALL

Standards are set, with many designs,
To eliminate negatives of various kinds.

Someone must begin, to define the goal.
And make conduct clear, in the proper role.

There once was a man, honorable and good,
Who gave us the way to be loved and understood.

He said many things, until then unheard,
Those He converted, knew He was "The Word."

Perfection divine, He maintained the peace,
Those imprisoned in self, He did release.

Some possessed of devils, He also made free,
Blind of head or in heart, were able to see.

The standard He gave, touched every man,
To the quick and the core, with God's perfect plan.

Who could it be, unchanging, always the same,
The Son of God for sure, and Jesus is His name.

Ken Possanza

IT'S YOUR OWN DAMN FAULT

Prices are up; salaries are down.
Po' working folks go 'round and 'round
Just trying to make ends meet,
Hoping they don't end up out on the street.
Doing their best to keep their heads above water,
But the President says they ain't doing what they ought to.
If they just try hard, it'll be all right.
It's their own damn fault they're out in the night.

Tell that to a man who's out of work with no place to go.
Tell it to a mother with a child at her breast and no milk to flow.
They've worked all their lives for the American dream.
Now they've learned it's not what it seems.
We're all equal; that's what they say.
You take that to a bank one day.
They'll say to you — Who are you, you Bum you?
Why didn't you manage better?

Eunice Fox Fontenot

THE UNTOLD STORY

I look at this ring, gleaming of gold,
Clasped in my hand, its story untold.
The times of the troubles with poverty near;
The times of sadness, pain, and tears.
It tells not the glory, when all was fine,
Our struggle together, with your hand in mine.
I remember the day our new life did start;
We took the vows, "Till death do we part."
It tells not the sadness my heart did endure
The day that you left me for Heaven's pure.
I lay down this ring, in velvet box;
My time has come, on Death's door I knock.
Good-bye to my family, my friends, and my foes;
I leave you not knowing of my story untold.

Michelle L. Brauer

STAFF AND BAR

The rhythm of the heavenly orbs,
Encompasses the universe,
Galaxy after galaxy,
Like the unwinding tail of a kite.

The woods re-echo the surging seas,
Bumble bees buzz and bird song
Interlace the symphony
Of its antipodal tune.

Ethereal, unkeyed mystical music,
Swelling into a sensual chorus,
Of muted thunder that divides
The globe into its spheres.

Then sing inside our answering bodies
A song, frail as swirling echoes,
That muffle the beat of our bloodstream,
Birth and death songs mesh,
Into a vast and voiceless serenade.

Irene C. Hypps

PANIC ON THE PODIUM

Ode to Toastmasters International

"*What* am I doing here?"
    A questions sagely asked
Of those who confidently claimed
    "This club is quite a blast!"

"What *am* I doing here?"
    Reiterate again
For usually the spotlight's beam
    Glows against the grain.

"What am *I* doing here?"
    Most inappropriate one,
Who would rather slink in shadows
    Than brave the glaring sun.

"What am I *doing* here?"
    With stumbling halting speech,
Stuttering and spluttering
    And puzzling all and each.

"What am I doing *here?*"
    Where least desired to be,
Every major point forgotten,
    All instincts dictate "*flee!*"

Virginia F. Brown

THE FOLLOWING QUESTION

Many rose, many fell.
Many will rise, many will fall.
So who will we follow,
The ones who rise and then fall,
Or the One who fell and then rose?

Steven Michael Hall

All any of us
    really
want or need
    is
to have others
    think
us to be worth the
    trouble
we cause.

William C. Rice

WILLIAM C. RICE. Born: Westwood, Lassen County, California, 1-5-37; Married: Joan Cannon Rice, 8-26-60; Education: Brigham Young University, B.S., Psychology, 1962; Penn State, M.S., Child and Family Studies, 1966; Brigham Young University, Ph.D., Psychotherapy, 1971; Occupations: Psychotherapist, University Professor; Memberships: AAMFT; Other Writings: *Notes From Happily Ever After,* 1987; Comments: *My poems are usually about everyday family; relationships and parental struggles and good times.*

SEVENTEEN

Today I saw
seventeen,
it passed me
quickly and effortlessly;
it was loud
and strong like
the early morning
rooster's crow;
its body was
well tuned, and
its gas tank
was on full;
it was 7:45 a.m.
and ready to go,
just on the brink
of new beginnings

Donice M. Palmer

OF REPAYMENT

An old man sits by the river,
With his speech, Afflicted.
Perhaps, an earlier transgression.
A slip of the tongue;
That has later become due.
For the early years,
Were filled with folly.
And who could pronounce woes.
Wasn't I clever?
Wasn't I brave?
Wasn't I bold?
But time and eventuality,
Have become one.
For the lives, of the many.
For the lives, of the few.
For the life, of the Son.
And so there he sits,
With his speech, Afflicted;
Engulfed, in his dreams.
A silent word,
Twenty years ago,
That was heard;
And, remembered.

Robert K. Walcott

THE BLESSING

May your life unfold, in glory,
With the destiny of your choice.
And may all the wisdom, of Solomon,
Become the ring, of your voice.
For life, indeed, runs a short course.
And the fool, perishes quickly.
For a man, devoid of understanding,
Brings the rod, very swiftly.
May your prudence, always guide you,
That you find mercy, and favor.
And may diligence, become your motto,
That you bear fruit, in all your labor.
May your knowledge, and understanding,
Reap the rewards, of a king.
And may your Grace, and Discretion,
Preserve your life, in the end.

Robert K. Walcott

COLD RAIN

Boisterous thunder.
Angry lightning.
It is a cold rain
that falls from the sky
when you're alone and unloved.
The winds are rising,
the clouds are forming.
It is a cold rain
that falls from the sky
when you're alone and unloved.
The sprinkles start
to fall on my face.
It is a warm rain.

Arthur Slate, Jr.

(I WOULD LIKE TO BE THAT)
SOMEONE SPECIAL IN YOUR LIFE

Could you ever dream of
Holding someone so close
Without touching them at all.
To share your deepest and darkest
Inner thoughts and secrets
Without feeling inferior.
Someone who cares enough to pick you up
When you are feeling down.
To help keep you on the straight
And narrow road, no matter what it cost.
I would like to be that
Someone special in your life.
Could you ever dream of
Someone walking into your life,
Telling you that you are beautiful,
Just to brighten up your day.
Even though that person might be feelin' down themself.
A person who does things for you
Who watches over you like a guardian angel,
Never to ask for nor expect anything in return.
I would like to be that
Someone special in your life.

R. E. Lunt

THE FLIGHT OF THE PIGEONS

Upon the housetop where I look down
The roof of a private dwelling in the midst of the town
    Each and every morning at the strike of seven o'clock,
    One splendid pigeon arrives from a flock
For a moment he sits upon a chimney top
Soon he starts to hop hop hop
    Another bird flies to the scene
    Before five minutes have passed hundreds out of the air have come
    From my window I do lean
Gazing upon their graceful lustrous beauty
Just a flock of pigeons, but they perform some daily duty
    Their leader like a teacher in a class
    Conducts what I call the pigeons' mass
To each other *good morning* they do nod
    Quickly they all take flight
'Round and 'round in a circle they approach the sky, as if to God
    Back from their heavenly flight they swiftly fly
Perching themselves all in a row
Along the ledge of a lofty roof for ten minutes or so
    Holding a conference with each other
    Closely together they hover
As if by magic they disappear one by one
    Until the following morning
Loyally they return to awaken me at the rise of the sun

Pearl Van Slocum

DELUSION

In your eyes I don't see me anymore. Could it be the love, want,
    and feelings are gone?
Has someone else taken my place? And this is why I'm no longer
    in your face.
Ha, oh yes, I saw it fading for some time and couldn't quite
    picture it in my mind.
I have faded far out of view, to the point of no return.
I can't recapture what is gone; to you I was never born.
Perhaps I was never there . . . Delusion.

Nan Blackshire-Little

I'M DELIGHTED

Oh, Lord, My God . . .

I delight mineself in Thy Word.
Thy Psalms speak to me.
They flow through me a blessing.
They give me hope, courage, happiness, strength,
And safety in my mind.
They give me joy, peace, comfort, and a calm
Assurance in my heart.
Therefore, I have a new song to sing.
You are my confidence and my help in time of need.
You brighten my darkness and keep me warm
In your arms of Love.
I open mine eyes before Thee,
And I open my mouth for giving thanks.
I abide in your present shadow,
And I put my trust in Thee.
When my soul was wounded,
You were there,
And were merciful
Because you care.
The beauty of the earth overwhelms me,
Thy kindness surrounds me.
How can I stray from your spirit?
How can my thoughts stray away from Thee?

Mary Elizabeth K.

THE DARKEST ANGEL

Sadly,
  The Darkest Angel stood apart
    And mourned — because He knew
  The anguish & the grief He'd bring
    If He took one such as you.

But God had said, "There's suffering, Death.
There's pain in every tiny breath."
    And He sent Death after you!
Then I cried, "Lord, forgive me —
    I can't accept this thing you do."

Forlorn,
  Death's Angel held my Darling tight
    And wept! (To see *my* pain.)
  But the child clutched the Angel's Robe,
    And she was made whole again.

Dear God, quench this anger, make me brave,
Let me recall the joy she gave.
    Please still these tears that fall like rain
Give her back when life is o'er,
    And in Death's arms I, too, have lain.

Sally Rickerson

ON GUARD

He spoke softly and called my name; saying he loved me so very plain.
He seemed so for real and sincere; I tried hard not to show any fear.
My body seemed to tremble when he touched my hand.
I wanted to run as fast as I can.
I have been bitten so many times; this I've got to keep in mind.
I feel I can't and won't ever love again; it took too long for my heart
    to mend.

Nan Blackshire-Little

THE WORLD WHERE I WANT TO BE

The world where I want to be
 has perfect harmony.
The world where I live today,
 there's turmoil constantly.

This place where I want to be
 has everything for me.
Somehow, though I work and play,
 I find no jubilee.

The world where I want to be,
 all souls are one and free.
The world where I now survive,
 I live so hopefully.

In this great infinity,
 I see such ecstasy.
To some degree, here I see
 a sea of misery.

The world where I want to be,
 there's peace eternally,
And it is mine, if I find
 in me, God's harmony.

This world of love I foresee
 was made by God's decree,
And it is here within me
 if I but find the key!

"If it is to be, it is up to me!"

Josephine Bertolini Comberiate

HEARTBEAT

Adrenaline's flowing destination heartbeat.
Through the corpus callosum to the brain.
That has two hemispheres.
To the heart that has four chambers.
The right hemisphere and the
left hemisphere.
Both hemispheres which are
used in childhood.
The right hemisphere is creative.
The left hemisphere is dominant.
The upper right ventricle.
The lower right ventricle.
The upper left ventricle.
The lower left ventricle.
Through the veins all through
the human body.

Heartbeat, energize and, activate me.
Effectively, positively, psychologically,
and successfully.

Charles S. Walker

As a freeless love turns
 to rage;
A wild bird is forever
 caged.

Gwen L. Bond

THIS STRANGER

The day was dawning when I was awakened,
From a blissful sleep through the night,
While rubbing sleep out of my eyes,
The stillness was broken I was alert!

Alert and active to a knock at my door,
A knock so strong it should have broken,
The door was there when I held the knob,
Opening the door to this unusual stranger!

This stranger was kind and O' so lovely,
Blue blue eyes shining as the seas,
Glowing hair hanging about his shoulders,
A handshake that was gentle and firm!

Love was flowing from this stranger,
In my mind I knew him instantly,
His beautiful words left no doubt,
This was Jesus knocking at my door!

O' my Lord why have you honored me?
Honored me with your presence today,
You are welcome only come inside,
All I own belongs to you my Lord!

Yes, my friends the thought is beautiful,
Only wish this really had happened,
Let's have faith and trust in God,
So in the future this will occur!

Doris Burleigh

DORIS LAVERNE BURLEIGH. Born: Robertsdale, Alabama, 8-14-27; Married: Norman Burleigh, 6-8-45; Education: Junior high school and self-educated with complete study of God's Holy Book; Occupations: Waitress, Food co-ordinator, Homemaker, Nurse's Aide; Memberships: Madison Avenue Baptist Church, Albany, New York, writer for Manna Food Bank, Pensacola, Florida; Poetry 'Peace Between Nations,' *American Poetry Anthology,* 1984; 'A Bride in White,' *American Poetry Showcase,* 1985; 'A Treasure,' *Words of Praise,* 1986; 'I'd Swim the Tides,' *Hearts on Fire,* 1986; 'Life Is,' *Best New Poets of 1986,* 1987; Comments: *Love and peace are the needs of all nations —love of country and love for all the people with less prejudice in our societies! More love instead of more money worldwide! More understandings under our caps!*

DUMB LOVE

In today's sleazy sexual scene,
One simply has to learn not to feel
Except with the nerves in one's ass,
Maintaining a heart of cold steel.

Disposable partners, easy to spurn,
Blazing new trails of self-doubt and fears,
Of memories that scar and burn,
Sad characters, subject to smears.

This time, it's me, the one disposable
Almost paralyzed, helpless from fears
While my love seems uncontrollable,
As inconsolable as my tears.

I tell myself, "You're an entity,
Not a throw-away paper doll.
So, go seek your true identity
Before you heed any mating call."

"Somewhere there's a lover able to see
Inarticulate love trapped in me,
Still able to trade need for need,
Caring enough to follow — or lead."

Dorothy Cariker Cart

DOROTHY CARIKER CART. Born: Kingston, Arkansas; Married: Ken Cariker, deceased 1970; Bob Cart, 1974; Education; McMurry College, Abilene, Texas; University of Oklahoma, 1971; Occupations: Editor of house organ for Humble Oil for 13 years, Freelance writer; Memberships: Oklahoma Writers, Screenwriter's Guild; Poetry: 'Token of Lost Love,' *Best New Writer of 1986,* 1986; 'Housewifely Hazards,' *American Poetry Anthology,* 1986; Other Writings: "How I Got Investigated After Kennedy's Assassination," *Chicago News Service,* 1965; "Knight in Overalls," short story, *Hi-Call Magazine;* Comments: *I have written eight novels, a novella, a screen play, a teleplay, twenty short stories and innumerable poems, including several others published by American Poetry Association. My last novel is based on my experience in China-Burma-India, in World World II. Most of my novels and poems deal with ordinary people caught up in life's problems.*

WASTED TIME

My baby crawled to me
Her eyes full of tears.
I told her to just let me be,
I don't have time for all your silly fears.

I have to scrub the floor,
Do all those dirty dishes
Plus a lot more.
I have no time to fulfill all your wishes.

But she was too small to understand
That I had no time to give her a hand
So she just sat on the floor and cried
And life just kept passing us by.

When she was sixteen on a nice day
She packed a bag and ran away.
My baby is now gone
She must have felt like she didn't belong.

If only it was a bad dream
For my house never did seem
To ever get very clean
And all my baby did was scream.

So leave your house chores and go out into the sun
Just close those dirty doors
And have some fun
Just you and the little one.

Kerri Higley

DEATH IS NO FRIEND

Death is cruel even if its intentions are best,
There is no peace in eternal rest.
Hamlet's fears carry through the years,
For though he is gone, his anguish lives on.
Mothers crying, infants dying;
What blessing of heaven can displace the tears?
Where in the great design was room made to comfort
those left behind?
Sons slain in war, an enemy begging for more —
Disease settling the score.
Who ends the pain; what really washes away in the rain?
Mourning and woe is what death tends with his hoe.
Sorrow remains, minds go insane — all in vain.
Where is the promise? Is it far in the clouds,
Or is it lost forever in funeral shrouds?

Ronald Russell Enders

THE GOLDEN AGE OF SCIENCE

Whether deductively or inductively,
humankind has never thought so hard about reality.
The very hinges of the past rattle.
Gods are destroyed by the tens of thousands.
Whether peering through an electron microscope
or rocketing into the very heavens,
humankind's perception of the cosmos has changed;
and
unless some foolish war or pestilence,
we will never peer with the same naiveté
as our ancestors.

Les Amison

HUNGER

Hungry people want food, for Body and Mind.
And for each of us, there is a different kind.
Hunger for love, Hunger for riches,
Hunger for knowledge, so they won't have to dig ditches.

Hunger for pleasure, that gives full measure.
Something they will always treasure.
Hunger for friends to help, when they're down,
And Hunger for city life, when they live in town.

Yes, Hunger for a life that's free
From strife and responsibility.
Now which is the one that you would choose?
Pick the right one, so you don't lose!

So before your life ends you can say,
I'm happy I choose to go this way.
But the Hunger we all share, is for Peace,
Which will be satisfied only
When all the Wars cease!

Ruby M. Olson

BOOK OF LEARNING

Our life is a Book of Learning.
 Each day a thought.
 Each week a phrase.
 Each month a chapter,
Of good and bad days.

Each year a volume,
 Filled with problems we overcome,
 And hope that the next one
 Will give us less pain.

So study, work hard and share,
 The lessons you learned, with those who care,
 Life gives us all joy and sorrow.
 So live for today, don't wait for tomorrow!

Make each moment count,
 And you will find,
 That life can be good,
 If you educate your mind.

Ruby M. Olson

DAMN LAZY MAN

Damn lazy man talented and true,
But it looks like society has put a damper on you.
Naturally vibrant, you could have been a big success,
But you were overwhelmed by laziness and you settled for less.

Overflowing with potential you could've had the best,
But you allowed the scars to overpower you and you failed the test.
You could have been at the top, that indeed was your rightful spot,
But you did not believe in yourself and you started taking pot.

Instilled within you is a valuable commodity to produce for mankind,
But you had chosen something else, totally out of line.
Oh how I wish you would use that brilliant and fantastic mind,
But instead you've chosen to live like you're blind.

Damn lazy man, I still believe in you,
Stop feeling sorry for yourself and do something true.

Tonia Watson

THE LITTLE BOY WITH THE STAND-UP HAIR

What words can I write
To help you to see
The little boy with the stand-up hair?

Books are his Magic Carpet
He is the hero in every tale.
He has traveled to far-away places
On animals great and small.

His eyes sparkle with mischief
Loving the excitement and fun of it all.
His smile is so disarming
When dimples slowly appear.

Did my words
Help you to see?
This little boy with the stand-up hair?

Dorothy McGaughran

RIPPLES IN MY HORIZON

I see ripples in my horizon;
As I dream in the early morn;
I see ripples in my horizon;
For soon, I will see a new dawn;
Ripples in my horizon;
I saw them when you held me tight;
As I lay dreaming;
Dreaming of you last night.

The ripples in my horizon soon;
I'll no longer see;
I know that I'm going;
To the place I want to be;
For, these ripples are in my horizon;
The horizon is within my grasp;
Pretty soon, I'll be there;
The ripples are traveling fast.

The horizon is changing;
The ripples are strong;
See how they ripple;
As I come closer to the dawn;
I can see you in the morning light;
And, I run to meet you; for soon;
You will hold me tight;
My horizon is you.

Laurie Anne Mach

MY CHRISTMAS SONG!

Christmas Day that is what I'm wishing for!
To build a snowball just right,
To see the stars at night.
Christmas Day that is what I dream about!
To be with my family who loves me,
To see the presents around the tree.
Christmas Day that is what I'm asking for!
To play with my friends in a snow mound,
To see the wonders of nature that are around.
Christmas Day that is what I pray for!
To get a new bike and new toys,
To see the world with hope and joy.

Mark Haines

MY FRIEND, MY YOUTH, MY DREAM

Into the Valley of Death I wandered
  and search I did in vain,

For something lost yesteryear,
  for which I have no name.

All at once I heard a familiar sound,
  a whistling through the sky it was

Artillery shells exploding
  upon the valley green,

And shrapnel searching through the air
  to end somebody's dream.

The machine guns' rapid fire,
  and the rifles' steady beat

Increased with tremendous volume
  as the battle reached its peak.

And in the distance you could
  see the tanks, and

Hear the roar of motors, and
  clanking of their tracks

As the Infantry rode into battle
  upon their iron backs.

Then all at once the valley was calm and serene,

And now I know what I had lost,
  "My friend, my youth, my dream."

Felix Otero

TIME STANDS STILL FOR NO MAN

Time stands still for no man,
A man who is running from a gun,
Time stands still for no man,
Whenever, he's on the run.

He's been flirtin', you can tell,
By the way his eyes would look at Maybelle.
He's been flirtin' with a woman,
Who left her lover for him,
Now her lover has a gun and
He is hunting for him.

He's gonna run him down,
Put him 'neath the ground,
That'll be the last time he'll ever make a sound.
He's gonna' gun him down
With a long cold gun.

Time stands still for no man,
Who is runnin' from the gun,
Yeah, he is hurtin', that's for certain,
And, he's been drinking, like a purple martin.

Time stands still for no man,
A man who is runnin' from a gun,
Time stands still for no man,
A man who is runnin' from the gun.

Laurie Anne Mach

THE TREE

The seed was planted — and sprouted life.
The tiny plant grew to a tree
  and at the outset none could see
  for just what purpose there would be.

Through years it grew high —
  as high as the sky.
  Yet, none of the passers-by
  ever searched within themselves — why?

'Til one day when such purpose came —
  a man of innocence would suffer shame
  and take upon him man's sin's blame.

That tree, high and strong
  waited with such patience long;
  realized now what was going on.

"Cut it down," the cry shouted —
  and in a moment was the tree crowded
  with men, as the tree silently pouted.

For it knew now its solemn role —
  the son of God to die upon,
  that he might save each man's soul . . .

Gregory Seewald

ABSURD

I searched for a word
  to rhyme with 'absurd'
but 'absurd' I became
  to find such a word.
For in searching I've found
  that there's just but one word
to be rhymed in a sentence
  with 'absurd' as the word.
Now, the word is a mystery
  to some (it is heard) —
and revealed in a poem
  has it only occurred.
So, if anyone claims to have
  heard this strange word,
you can be sure of this one thing —
  the word is 'absurd.'

Gregory Seewald

Born in and for the dead of night
Ancient lover of her sacred beauty
Asking now my birthright
Give to me the ability to see
All that which is my reality

'Tis for you I am obsessed
How delicate your moonlight seems
I've always been yours possessed
Finding gleams the meaning of my dreams
While my intuition grows as she deems

Somehow I know we'll never forget
All that we've shared throughout eternity
I now surrender all I am without regret
Dwelling in your amity is forever my destiny
For within our love I've found serenity

M. W. Maccree

ODE TO HARRY TRUMAN

Here's to a big man, just an ordinary man,
he wasn't known to the world,
as such was our late President Truman;
but we was just as noble and human.
He stood tall, and strong in his beliefs,
he spoke freely of his thoughts, our freedom of speech.
He was true to his land, to the end, freedom of rights.
He was faithful to his wife, till death do us part.

The mountain rumbled, and the mountain roared,
people laughed, and people scorned,
at that senile old man of the ravishing mountain.
He was as true an American
as any man I hope to know.
As he stood for what we all take for granted,
and proudly lived by every day of our lives.
The freedoms of speech, belief, and rights,
and the pursuit of happiness.

Harry's spirit will live on
in the generations to come.
And in the hearts and minds of us
that had the privilege to have known him.
I salute you — Harry Truman, man of the mountain.
A Great American as you were.

Jessie Stinson

CALL OF THE BLUE JAY

A saucy young blue jay hopped about for food
And if one didn't know his ways
You would think him bold and rude.
Our feeder is his table, he does not like to share
And to a guest the cardinal, he really throws a scare,
Some folks think the blue jay is troublesome and mean
But his plumage is so beautiful he really is supreme.
It's nice to hear his cheery call so early in the day,
He seems to like our garden, perhaps he's here to stay,
His love life is his secret, for we seldom see his mate
And when we do she sits alone on our garden gate.
I'd like to know his secret thoughts hidden deep inside,
But blue jays are so bashful, they too have family pride.
Fall leaves turn all colors, plants settle down to sleep,
Feathered friends fly south, but our memories we must keep.
That saucy young Blue Jay has answered the call of friends,
Perhaps he'll come back again, when the winter ends.

Elsie M. Westrick

THE OLD WINDMILL

A backdrop of an autumn golden hill,
Stands an old weatherbeaten windmill,
The bright and shiny silver wheel,
Either turning or proudly standing still,
According to the wiles of the wind that blows,
For the faster it blows, the faster the mill goes
Bringing up the fresh water from God's green earth,
Cool and clear, to quench any thirst,
Through winter storms and summer rains,
Standing so solitaire in the valleys or plains,
It's such a sight for sore eyes
As you wearily stand and scan the skies,
Just to see that silver wheel,
And to hear the creaking of the mill,
Thanking God for the guiding hand,
Giving the ability to build, by an ingenious man.

June Cooper Wristen

STREET LADY

She had bravely walked the lonely stones of hurt
And quietly washed her eyes with tears each night;
Never saw the moon-glow in the eyes of others
Or heard a sweet song of love, by candlelight.

The mattress was dented, on the floor where she lay,
As the sputtering candle gave a misty glow.
The street lady knew it was time for drifting
And the path was dim, as if covered by snow.

In a whispered voice: "Read a poem of love, my friend,
Yearning words, since youth, I have wanted to hear.
Life is seldom kind to the hurting mind
And withholds its music from the lonely ear."

The good friend slowly opened an old leather book
To read a poem of love, to a once lovely Miss.
But, Death that had winked a few moments in jest,
This time, sealed her unpainted lips with a kiss.

Poems are only words and lines in a book
Arranged to rhythm and music by someone's mind;
But, for the lonely heart and beggars of love,
A gift of sight, for a world that is blind.

If you listen each night by low candlelight,
In a tumble-down shack near Third and Vine;
Another lonely friend opens the same worn book
To read a poem of love, from page one forty nine.

I. J. Evans

THE LAST NUGGET

Lovely women are first in some men's dreams
And religion in others, who are not so bold.
But, the desert is filled with a savage of life
Who exaggerates dreams and lies that are told.

Sixty years, for the precious metal, he dug,
Where silent sidewinders wrinkle the sand;
Faith and persistence were his only nuggets,
Matching calloused scars that showed on his hand.

Each petal of fate hung on a slender stem
Where minds of men pricked the vein;
Coffers they filled from the pock-marked hills
Wrote a story that was never the same.

Three things were the code of the old miner's life,
"Put first things first, faith and persistence," he said.
He gasped three times in the stifling heat
Then, losing a last bold effort, dropped his head.

He knew there is a time when one must succumb to dreams
And become a part of the mist of which they fill;
Securely pull covers of life over the head
And become a part of the weeds on the rising hill.

A lonely buzzard circled the small desert shack
As his young partner did as he had been told;
Picked up his shovel, to put first things first,
But, this time, it was not to dig for gold.

I. J. Evans

FEEL THE LOVE

Feel the Love.
Feel the deep, deep Love.
Set your heart
  on the goodness of *God*
  and all that your Soul's
    been dreaming of.

Seek the land that never ends;
  that only Faith can see.
For now (though it's hard)
  his visage is still marred,
  and his Glory shall always be.

It's a hope with Love entwined;
  for the Master both gentle and kind . . .
  . . . feel the love —
    that love from above;
    . . . and discover the Master's mind.

Gregory Seewald

GREGORY MATTHEW SEEWALD. Born: Phoenix, Arizona; Education: Westland College, Fresno, California, Certificate of Completion, 1981-82; Valley College of Medical and Dental Careers, Studio City, California, Diploma, 1987-88; Occupation: Respiratory therapist; Poetry: 'Close the Door,' 'The Clock,' *American Poetry Anthology,* 1988; 'My True Love,' 1984; 'Come, Lord,' 1986; 'The Time to Know,' 1983; Comments: *Poetry, to me, is a gift from God. Sometimes I've abused it, and written silly things, and sometimes I appear to write inspired things. But the gift is still there, and I want to bless people with my poems. My personal favorite is 'The Tree,' which I've included in this book. I pray that it touches your heart, as it did mine.*

A BRUSH

There once was a time . . .
  places, and people, and things,
  that are no longer.

An illusion is spell-binding . . .
  see the surroundings;
  the air you're breathing!

Woodland, field, and barnyard . . .
  water pumps, and tree-swings,
  plow blades a-rusting,
  main streets of dust and you see?
  The Grace of God —
    like the stroke of a brush.

Joseph F. Hauch

MY SON

My Dear Son I love you
Just how much you will never know.
You are very precious and mean so much to me
That's why I love you so.

Sometimes you may wonder
Just how much I really care.
You are always in my heart
And always in my prayers.

God gave you to me for a purpose,
Which is plain for me to see
Not so much what I did for you
But what you did for me.

Now you are grown and have gone
And it seems we are far apart.
Remember we are still together
Because you are always in my heart.

George Kingery

FRIENDS THROUGH BROTHERHOOD

The friendship through brotherhood
is knowing and doing what we should.
Doing what we could is not enough,
because then we always say
I should have done this or that.
'Cause being friends should be no bluff.
There are many wonderful things to do for
one another to become friends.
Like to tell a brother to get high
you must have wings. To tell a sister
you miss her. To tell a brother to start
going to church, and level with him
that it really won't hurt.
I want all you to hear this brother.
Being friends don't make us a lover.
To be honest with you, and to level with you.
It just plainly and simply helps us to
understand one another. My friend,
trusting in one another is no sin.
It's brotherhood and that's good.

Clarence Gantt

BENEATH THE SURFACE

I dive beneath
the surface
of the lake
into a world
which seems separate
from that which
I have come to take
— for granted.
No longer do
I carry about the weight
of any role
which has been cast
upon me.
For now I'm free,
swimming with the joy of life
as the fishes do,
welcomed
until I return
— renewed.

Olivia McCormack

THE CLASS REUNION

The people are gone
but the room remains
still filled
with suspended emotions,
still crowded
with stirrings of youth
impaled in the past.

The people are gone
but the tension of expectancy
still hovers,
the strain to recall
the familiar still lingers,
hangs nervously
between old dreams and frail future.

Not here, the best known
best loved,
they are gone —
their absence makes more silent
the room still filled
with the bonding of youth
that was better then.
The long ago camaraderie
so intently sought,
is no more binding now
than a casual introduction.

M. Norris Stanton

IF I WERE AIR AND YOU WERE SUN

If I were air
And you were sun
What would there be
That must be done

You as the sun
And I as the air
Could shine brightly
And blow a breeze at the fair

You as sun
And I as air
Could be the hot and the cool
Near every pool

If I were air
And you the sun
There would be all of the children to watch
Which of course would be fun

If I were the air
And you were the sun
Oh, so much
Would need to be done

Bryan J. Bouchey

MIND IN A MIRROR

You slipped the paper canvas behind rubber rollers
  and set the margins for the proper space.
Your dancing fingers pounded words into lovely concepts,
  as ink-hungry pages kissed the jumping keys.
You guided beauty, love, inspiration and power,
  through the tangled map of uneven lines.
Carbon ate your flowing sentences, as staccato of the
  ringing bell denoted, musically, the end of each precious line.
Seeds of thought sprouted into words of love,
  then, grew into power, like a river of life energy
  flowing through the fluid of your magic fingers.
Whimsical thoughts of your magnificent brain dimpled the printed
  page, as you struck the final period.
Drained, exhausted and exhilarated, as one who has reached the
  peak of the highest mountain, you pulled the printed thought
  from the clutch of the mechanical keys.
There was a brief moment, almost a silent prayer,
  as you slid the beloved manuscript into my trembling hands.
But, a curtain was drawn, as I queried, —
  "If only I could read?"

I. J. Evans

CLASSICAL CATS:
THE FIRST CLOWDER OF LIMERICKS

IF THE SHOE FITS

The ballet cat Rina Belfosco,
Was taught by the great Madame Kosko.
  When she danced in Swan Lake,
  The Bolshoi did ache
With such envy they went back to Moscow.

OOPS!

The baritone cat Purricato,
Starred in the opera Donato.
  Tripping on a loose board,
  He fell on his sword.
Now he's singing soprano castrato.

SHE'S ALL THE RAGE

The opera cat Golda Von Glurk,
Performed a Wagnerian work.
  Her voice so delighted,
  So thrilled and excited
The audience they all went berserk.

CRITICS! WHO NEEDS 'EM?

An opera cat named Balestracci,
Once sang the lead role in Pagliacci.
  But the audience jeered,
  And the critics all sneered,
Remarking: "His technique is botchy."

Maria Amhara Yemariamferé (Philogyne)

CLASSICAL CATS:
THE THIRD CLOWDER OF LIMERICKS

THE CAT AND THE FIDDLE

Signorina Felina Cattati,
Played her violin made by Amati.
  Paganini on hearing,
  Cried, "Bravissima!" cheering
this virtuosa from Stellati.

SUPER SOPRANO

The soprano cat Trilla Di Miura,
Is renowned for her vocal bravura.
  Though it may seem strange,
  Her voice and her range
Is a five-octave coloratura.

TRILLY WILLY

The world-famed Katwillader Klute,
Is more skilled than Rampal, more astute.
  His performance is always
  Much finer then Galway's.
This cat who can play on a flute.

HE DOESN'T PUSSYFOOT AROUND

At the debut of Tomsky Katchinsky,
A ballet danseur from Zarinsky;
  Baryshnikov boggled,
  Nureyev simply goggled
When Tomsky leaped higher than Njinsky.

Maria Amhara Yemariamferé (Philogyne)

THE SAILORMAN

In a vacuum there lived a sailorman,
Who tipped his hat and played his hand,
For he had met the fairest maid,
And was to pay the heaviest price he had ever paid.

Her eyes were green like emeralds,
Her lips were ruby red,
Her hair was thick and auburn,
And her thoughts were strikingly far ahead.

With her misty eyes and her warm heart,
The sailorman knew he could never depart,
Because her beautiful smile brightened his day,
And he could live only as if to say,

"Why, God, oh why am I to face this fact,
I have traveled, I am weary, I can no longer act,
Tell me why do I have to function in this hell,
Why can't I live happily, this story I must tell."

But he couldn't and he knew because he was wise,
He knew because the sea had unmasked his disguise,
He knew because he knew that she could never understand,
That basically inside he was just a sailorman.

He lost his love, he lost his heart,
He lost everything because soon it was to part,
His ship was lost in a sea of strife,
And soon afterward he eventually lost his life.

Ronald Bissland

YOUR NEVER-DYING LOVE IS ALL

Dedicated to my mother, with all my love

A gift so pleasant, the silence of a dream many so
    unspoken moments, i ponder — if there be a
    god, then to he i must give praise, for in
    his perfection he has given you to me / only i
    can see how blessed i have been

Your love gifts its many riches to my soul, as if night
    & woes are never to come / and O so beauteously a calm
    of brilliance, as i look into your ever-understanding
    eyes / and i know, your never-dying love is all.

Richard O. Rodriguez

RICHARD O. RODRIGUEZ. Born: Saint Helena, California; Single;
Education: Napa Valley College; Occupation: Youth counselor; Poetry: 'To
The Lily,' *American Poetry Anthology*, 1-18-86; 'Immured as the Walls of
Hades,' *American Poetry Anthology*, 4-21-85; 'Through The Eyes of a
Child,' *Words of Praise*, 9-13-85; Comments: *I would like to become a be-
havioral therapist. I like to work with teens, although this has not always
been one of my lifelong dreams. I want to help them make it in life. I feel I am
able to understand their feelings — and also not get taken in by them, which
is very important. It makes me feel good that I am doing something that may
change someone's life.* Themes: *My poetry is mainly about life itself, beauty,
happiness, love, sadness, death, hatred, and sorrow.*

WHISPERS

The wind whispers to me and the snow is light.
The sky is black and it's late at night.
Your eyes speak to me so green and bright.
You make me feel good, I'm feeling all right.

Let's go inside and sit by the fire.
You can almost feel my passion, I'm filled with desire.
Please stay with me all through the night.
Even you know that the time is right.

Your body grows tired, your eyes, they grow lazy.
How can one woman make a man feel so crazy?
If I ever hurt you before, let me say that I'm sorry.
You've conquered my pride and all my raging glory.

Look out the window and see the newly-fallen snow.
Your cheeks are so red and your eyes are aglow.
I love you so much that it's impossible to measure.
I will take good care of you — you're my most precious treasure.

Bradley S. Martens

WE NEED THE RIGHT MAN

I've been in your jails and institutions.
You've violated your own Constitution.
You've taken away some of our homes and put us out on the road.
You've taken some of the poor and left them out in the cold.

The poor are dying from starvation, but you won't send them money.
The rich just get richer, it seems kind of funny.
We don't take care of our poor — Most are mistreated.
What's causing these problems? It's the way our leaders are seated.

You can't blame one man, it's really not fair.
Other government officials have all done their share.
It's a case of, ''You scratch my back and I'll scratch yours.''
But this won't feed the hungry and it won't clothe the poor.

I hope we find a man who we all know is right.
Someone who understands all of our plights.
Someone who gives it all and a little bit more.
Someone who feeds the hungry and takes care of the poor.

Bardley S. Martens

ONCE I WAS SLEEPING IN MY BED

Once I was sleeping in my bed
I awoke from the sound of raindrops falling over my head
I was dreaming of a lady I once knew
I thought it was her but my dream didn't come true
Once I was sleeping in my bed
I heard a voice whispering over my head
I thought it was her calling my name
When I awoke it was a dream of the same
Once I was sleeping in my bed
I felt a gentle kiss upon my head
It was so soft and sweet
When I awoke it was only in my sleep
Once I was sleeping in my bed
I felt a woman resting beside me in my bed
I felt her breast up against my chest
I felt her warm and tender skin rest against me
    time and time again
Once I was sleeping in my bed, Shara

Dennis Humphrey

TO FADE OR LAST

You shine in my eyes like the stars in the sky
such familiarity
I feel so far, to know you so shortly
You seem, almost heaven-sent at times
Were we meant to be to seek out life together
or just pass in the night
I've heard it said if another time or place
it would have been different
I'd say, ''We are afraid to touch the emotion we feel,
we both know it's infatuation,
'tis not eternity but our friendship
could be our only destiny, because I'd
rather hold your friendship and we will
not be passed by! To fade or last.

Diane Henning

A POET'S PRAYER

''Lord, let me never fail to see
A chance to write a poem, for Thee!
Let me not miss, a single word
Or an idea, from things I've heard . . .
As source of inspiration for
A poem .. . never known, before!

Not in mine own eyes, can I see . . .
The things, which I should write, for Thee.
For in this busy world of ours
Where there are never, enough hours . . .
It's easy, to not recognize
A poem, there . . . before my eyes!

A bird . . . a tree . . . or Springtime flower,
Or foliage in . . . some woodland bower!
Or clouds . . . or wind . . . or shining sea:
Or many other, wonders, that be!
There is a wealth of things untold,
That should be shared, a thousandfold!

Lord, may I help to bring some cheer
Or bring a smile . . . to one, who's drear.
And may I help, someone to see
The joys of Life . . . which come from Thee!
And may You always show to me . . .
All these . . . a Poem . . . yet to be!''

Beatrice Drummond

EMOTIONAL PAIN AND NOT PLAIN

Black moods cloud rivers of loneliness
Pitiful and pitiless — a screen of ill-fate
Tears of linear, perfect rage
. . . they bestill the space I possess . . .

Naked thoughts bound accordingly
Pain so painful that it leaks invisible blood
Mirages the senses to a slur blur
Paralyzes the heart apart

Iron gates rusted through to the dead bones
We have all been here before
The icy halls of hell in lost love
Breakups and divorcing calls of falls

    Passing through and through
    Lessons hardly ever learned — ?
    When it starts in a seep
    Pain Pain to Creep Creep

And night always leans to dawn
Rebirthing like the gentle fawn
Though wind and rain carve the land
Dust removes the sand,
Reign of pain never lasts forever
To living love — an emotional endeavor
Maturing and always trying again today
Will never lead the victorious soul astray —

Chris J. Nielsen

YOU

The happiest moments of my life
are spent with you
I love you more
than life itself
You are my dream
of the future
And I want to keep
that dream alive
For I cannot
be happy without you
To hear your voice
and your heart
beating against mine
is all I need
When I look in your eyes
and see that you love me
I melt beneath you
and love you even more
as our moments together
pass by.

Danyelle Lynn Solomon

I NEED LOVE

When I look in your eyes
I am drawn to you
And I envision the world
of love shared between us
I have never been
so much in love
My love for you
is limitless and unending
Growing stronger every day
I sometimes feel insecure
Separation from you
would leave me
feeling empty and neglected
Silence of the heart
I admire your individuality
I want to give you
your freedom
But it comes natural
to want to be with you
Your love is vital to me
I need your embrace
Every moment I spend with you
is memorable
and I would sacrifice anything
to be with you forever . . .

Danyelle Lynn Solomon

SOFT TALK

We move as one
embracing the stillness of the night,
fulfilling a love we could never live
    without.
Within each heart a pledge
lifted up together in perfect song.

Marilyn Joy

CROOKED PATH

I was meandering along
On the crooked path of life.
The path was full of detours.
Failures and disappointments were rife.

In the midst of the confusion
On that lonely, dusty trail,
My gaze focused on a bridge ahead —
An archway to help me over the bale.

I crossed the bridge hesitantly —
Prudent of things unknown —
And when I reached the other side,
My miseries had flown.

For before me was Eden;
A paradise of dreams.
Goodness was flowing everywhere.
There were no malignant schemes.

Then, I looked back at the bridge —
On which I did depend.
But I was once again on the crooked path —
Standing before me was a friend.

Anne Patricia Knyff

THE OCEAN MIST

Black cat stalking prey at night
I looked away, and lost the fight
And now the mist falls on my face
The ocean waves cannot replace
The sounds and smells of love, so clear
The ocean mist turns into tears

Dead of winter, frost and gloom
Cold dark night, no flowers in bloom
Shadows falling within my heart
Dark nights alone, torn apart
Castle walls tower above
A heart imprisoned, no love, no love

A heart cries out alone and torn
Prince of light, remove the thorn
Prince of light, give me the kiss
Release me from this dark night mist

Shadows in my heart do fall
Casting silence on the walls
A breeze of light I think I hear
As it falls dark upon my ears
And the ocean mist turns into tears

Janice L. Piercey

A REFLECTION ON MAN

There are no great men
But only great challenges
That ''authentic'' men must meet
To overcome
Not only personal fears
But also
The dread of that unknown reality
Which manifests those challenges
Through which they become great or heroes.

Franco Boni

THE MEANING OF LIFE

The meaning of life can be heard to speak
    The strong do surely prey on the weak
    And the lion does not lay with the lamb
    And men blindly kill
    Swing swords of steel
    And mate with the snakes in the ground

And life itself may sometimes cry
    Everything born will someday die
    And you and I can watch it pass
    Together, or alone
    As if we had not known
    That anything never begun can never last

Or the meaning of life can be heard in a song
    As two people learn they cannot live alone
    So worlds must end and form again
    Like ocean waves
    With spray that bathes
    The sand and leaves it smooth and clean

And the meaning of life may then be known
    For a few short moments until it is gone
    From the minds which perceived and condoned it
    The thoughts, the pain
    Of continuous change
    As life draws its meaning each moment

David M. Hargis

DAVID MICHAEL HARGIS. Born: Warren, Arkansas, 2-10-48; Occupations: Trial lawyer, Investor, Writer; Other Writings: Numerous legal articles; Guest columnist, *Arkansas Gazette;* Co-author, *Quality Assurance in Health Testing,* College of American Pathologists, 1986; Comments: *There is no bad poetry. It always results from a human effort to express or create, and that should be encouraged. It is best, however, when it results from a spontaneous eruption of the soul.*

A TOAST

Here's to the life that every man seeks,
To the goals which set gigantic peaks,
To the men and women who finally reach the top,
Who hover about not daring to stop.

Here's to the joys of days gone by,
To the relentless sadness we know with a sigh,
To the future that before us uncertain stands,
And to the past we leave with broken strands.

Here's to the life that we all must live,
And to the love that we all must truthfully give,
Here's to the hearts that so broken cry,
Their endless yearnings to a clouded sky.

Here's to the present, future, and the past,
To the wonders and fantasies that rarely last,
Here's to the people who strike out at their fears,
Because their courage far overcomes their tears.

Ronald Bissland

THE DESERT OF FORGOTTEN DREAMS

Somewhere in a rich and abundant land,
There lies a desert full of restless sand
With large gray rocks scattered 'round about,
The barren mountains scream from drought.

Silence, silence not a sound is heard,
Except for the rustle of some large black bird,
Nature's hideous serpents scatter to and fro,
Leaving not the slightest trace of where they go.

But this land once rose high and clear,
Filled with precious hours wondrously dear,
Its beauty rang out for miles around,
And its fertile valleys, full of sound.

Then the winds of time and the breaks of change,
Hurled their wrath with a creeping mange,
Slowly and with purpose their teeth did tear,
And no one noticed and no one cared.

But for you and I all goes well today,
Tomorrow will come and maybe we'll pray,
For nothing is quite like what it seems,
Except in the desert of forgotten dreams.

Ronald Bissland

SAY I LOVE YOU

Learn how to say *I love you*
So many people don't
Learn how to say *I need you*
So many people won't
Though it's what we're meant to do
And what forever is about
Learn how to say *I love you*
And you'll never be without

Learn how to say *I love you*
Bring a friend some laughter
Learn how to say *I want you*
Maybe then you'll find what you're after
Time doesn't always heal, the wounds of fate
Learn how to say what you feel, before it's too late
Say *I love you* with bliss, don't be a fool
I wouldn't be telling you this, if I didn't love you

Richard Clark

ALL THINGS — TO HIM WHO BELIEVES

His Promise broken? Never!
Always His Promises are forever — But —
Let no man deceive you, dear seeking one;
That road Heavenward, is not always smooth.

Can you imagine, what weaklings we would be,
If all our problems were solved for us — eternally?
The storms must come, to help us grow: But,
Blue skies — which follow — His great Love doth show.

So, my dear ones, fret not, over problems without answers;
Put them — lovingly — in His hands, He will send responses,
For "whatsoever ye ask, in my name — *Believing*" (Mark 9:23)
You are now — without any doubt — *Receiving!* (Mark 11:24)

Joy S. Pearce

GYPSY HEART

You roam around, the midnight hour
Forgetting our love, as you prowl
Hear the tears fall, rain hits the ground
I'll never be free, love torn apart
Bound to you, and your gypsy heart

You roam around from door to door
Seeking new love, you haven't had before
Through your midnight eyes, I loose control
Love so blind, it tears me apart
Bound to you, and your gypsy heart

And like a gypsy in the night
You spread your wings, and take the flight
But soon you'll return, come to mourn
When you feel the sting of the thorn
And you hear the spell, cast in black
The shadows falling, on the moon
Darkness is coming, coming soon
So close your eyes, hide from the dark
Run for your soul, and your gypsy heart

Pain I feel, through your midnight eyes
Tears at my heart, and takes my pride
You shattered my love, put me down
Still I'm bound inside, and torn apart
Bound to you, and your gypsy heart

Janice L. Piercey

I'LL BE YOUR FRIEND

He looked so lonely sitting there,
  The young boy asked him, "Why?"
"Because I'm old, I don't walk much
  For my legs won't comply.
But I feel younger since you came;
  It's fun to chat with you
For it reminds me of the days
  I did the things you do.

"Back then, I'd run a foot race
  And the spectators would cheer;
It was said, I ran as fast
  And as graceful as a deer.
I walked three country miles to school,
  Lived by the golden rule.
The creek that flowed behind the house
  Was my swimming pool.

"In days of old, my life was full;
  Now I'm alone and weak."
The young boy said, "I'll be your friend,"
  As he touched his wrinkled cheek.
The old man said, "Because you care —
  Seems I could run a mile."
The young boy smiled and said, "I think
  I'd like to sit a while."

Bessie Lee Anderson

HAPPY MEMORIES

This special poem to you, my Son,
  Is meant to tell a part
Of the happy, love-filled memories
  I've kept within my heart.
I still recall the dandelions,
  Wildflowers in your teens,
And later still, the store-bought flowers,
  Sometimes beyond your means.

Your friends that seemed like family,
  Your kind and loving ways,
The confidential talks we had
  I'll cherish all my days.
And when you'd say, "You're special, Mom,"
  And kiss me on the cheek,
I knew you'd be the kind of man
  That gentleness bespeaks.

Now, you have children of your own
  So you know how I feel;
And Son, you know my love for you
  Is warm and deep and real!
And so I want to thank you, Son,
  For loving, close-knit years;
Your gifts of happy memories
  Are treasured souvenirs!

Bessie Lee Anderson

ELECTRICAL APPLIANCES

So well connected to
that cord, but one
pull and the vibs cease
with the incompletion:
A close association indeed
as in most phenonomena
the plus and the minus,
The embrace and collaborative
satisfaciton of incompletes,
Who will stand alone?

Dr. Christopher G. Jesudason

JOHANNA

Glittering stars of sunlight dancing
On long scarlet hair.
Bows of lace like butterflies
Perching here and there.

Beams of happiness sparkling
From green and golden eyes.
Random freckles dot the space
Above an ideal smile.

Sounds of laughter tinkling
Like crystal through the air.
Head thrown back in joy
As the wind fans her fair.

Her soul is love and music,
She's my heart's daily manna.
She's always been, and will remain,
My own, sweet, Johanna.

Pamela Luter Simmons

I WONDER

Some time
    before eternity
    got started
God
    the inconceivable
Diffused
    itself

Into
    sea
    sunbeams
    mountains
Fish, birds
    mammals
Star-worlds

And us.

Oh, how
    will
Its ultimate
Be attained?

Dorothy A. Meyer

AUTUMN THOUGHT

Cool woods
    are orange bright
    with October,
And I am wafted
    on a slide
    of leaves
To where a crow
    caws meaning
Into my silence,
And a lone duck's
    flapping.

We all are one,
    duck,
    crow,
    leaves,
    trees,
And I,

Linked by old,
    faint memories
    in forgotten time

Of matter,
    simple,
    unevolved.

Dorothy A. Meyer

THE STAGES OF LIFE

*Dedicated to Janet Dickerson,
professor at Swarthmore College.*

Everyone experiences pain and sorrow.

Some people accept the fact that being
   hurt is a part of life, and keep
   thriving for their purpose of being
   alive.
Others let grief destroy them and die a
   life, which they lived in vain
   forevermore.

In times of despair most of us become bitter,
   but the smart ones remember the times of
   being blessed with good fortune and happiness.

Life has its ups and downs.
Its moments of pain and sorrow.
Its moments of joy and happiness,
   and its moments of doubtful unawareness.
But if you're strong and you realize this
   and accept life for what it is and not
   what it ought to be;

Because life is only stages of emotions, which
   tend to vary endlessly.

Sandra M. Gildersleeve

JERUSALEM

For Roger Johnston

I am no longer a woman, I am a city.
How many men have walked these streets,
  worn down these paths,
  watched their faces in my windows?

I am a city.
I cannot love one man for he is never you.
So I love an endless succession of men
  finding part of you in each of them —
A city full of men who together cannot be you.

I am a city with a city's memories.
At night I am filled with the ghosts of each and every man
  who has known me
  held me as I moved beneath him
  looking up into dull eyes that did not contain that vision.

I am a city who dreams in fragments
  all turned toward you as the one bright center.

I am a city and you are the sky.
I shall never contain you the way I am contained by you.
Only your winds shall blow through these empty streets
  trodden by others who can never be you.

Theresa Rasmussen

MARCH MAGIC

*"The stormy March has come at last, with wind,
and cloud, and changing skies." (Bryant)*

Against the lowering dismal skies the maple shakes her shaggy locks
   and stands aghast,
   bared arms akimbo in the cutting wind,
And window panes are streaked with sudden tears,
   while autumn's leaves, like impish brownies,
   swirl, leap, and cavort in frenzied dance.

Now comes the sun, and slashing through the gloom
   it brightens woodland paths with sudden fire
   and sets the treetops blazing in its wake.

The rain-tears check their racing flight down glassy cheeks
   and halt in frozen, rounded crystal drops
   to watch the fleeing whitecaps roll across the gray.

From brilliant splashing gypsy shades
   the western sky fades into deepening dusk;
   the wind mounts high and ruffles scattered clouds,
A husky Hercules, it whistles shrilly, like a rowdy
   at the timid dark.

So March, that artful showman, gives a varied pageantry
   of sun and shower, of warmth and chill,
She runs the gamut from deep snowbanks piled
   along the creeks to violet gay
   and robin's cheerful trill . . .

And then, to add the climax to her show,
   tossed from her hat, a mad March hare
   goes skipping down the lane . . .

Ruby A. Jones

MOISTURE WHIP

Rubbing on the Maybelline Moisture Whip
Reflections deceive
"It will make you look younger too," Oil of Olay —
Touché! You didn't work, Germaine Monteil,
"Actually helps to prevent new dry lines from forming,"
But there they are, those awful lines . . .

You lie, making me soak in each hopeful phrase,
The lines can't be felt under the layers of oil, but they're
Still there, never to be gone again.
I am old, but you say old is ugly, unfashionable,
Maybe I look great without your potions, you'd never know . . .

Who are you to tell me how to look and feel?
I am not an object, I am human and I won't oil my face anymore.
I found I like how I look without the Moisture Whip —
I know growing old is beautiful.

So, I toss the Oil of Olay into the trash,
Crush the Germaine Monteil into pieces,
But I'm going to keep the Moisture Whip, so I'll remember;
And your words will fade from the page.

Jamie Nathanson

185

ONLY ME

Accept me as I am —
  A human being who makes mistakes.
Let me be me —
  Not having to pretend or be a fake.

Be there —
  when I need someone to hear me.
Support me —
  even when I might be wrong.
Help me —
  when I'm learning from my errors.
Love me —
  when my patience has all gone.

Laugh with me —
  when I need a little humor.
Hold me —
  when I need a special hug.
Protect me —
  when I feel the world surround me.
Back me —
  when I need a push or tug.

Accept me as I am —
  A human being not always on my best.
Let me be me —
  Not having to be like all the rest.

Dee Ann Snider

MY BROTHER'S FIRE

My brother, one of honor,
  Among the homeless cold;
He had no one to turn to,
  No place to call his own.

He encouraged me to build a fire,
  To light our lovely home;
With hope, peace, warmth and love,
  We could always call our own.

Now that he's no longer with us,
  I see his face among the flames;
Encouraging me to warm my hands,
  Feel his presence once again.

He had no place of refuge,
  This poor and lonely soul;
Except the haven of our hearts,
  And of our happy home.

A memory I will always have,
  Of a flickering flame;
And a boy who turned our lives around,
  In an instance of a day.

The world may never understand,
  Why his life turned out this way;
But, he'll know that he was loved,
  Among the honored graves.

Hazel Mae Parron

A SIMPLE ANSWER

Now I'm just an ordinary woman
And may not amount to much,
But I do a lot of thinking
About world conditions, freedoms, and such.

And I had an inspiration
Perhaps from up above,
There's an answer to our problems
It is called ''brotherly love.''

We Americans take for granted
That our rights are here to stay,
But I'm wondering about the future
Will our rights be taken away?

Why do we persecute each other
When we know that it is wrong?
Why do nations fight and argue
If united, we could all be strong.

Jesus gave us the perfect answer
When He gave us this command,
''Love Thy Neighbor As Thy Self''
It could work in every land.

It is just a simple answer
And time we all should start,
To say it with our mouth
And mean it with our heart!

Vonda Blum Wyatt

TO HELP MAKE TIME PASS EASIER

Delivering a child, is to help make time pass easier.
Attending a learning institution and gaining knowledge,
  is to help make time pass easier.
Making friends, is to help make time pass easier.
Playing a game to amuse yourself, is to help make time pass easier.
Working to support yourself, to have a place to live,
  is to help make time pass easier.
Taking a vacation from work, is to help make time pass easier.
Going on a trip during your vacation, is to help make time pass easier.
Growing older and becoming more experienced,
  is to help make time pass easier.
Dying and having your soul go to heaven,
  is to help make time pass easier.

Being born . . . helps in making time pass easier.

Darrel-Jay Tedeschi

HEARING . . .

It's hard to figure where to start
  without some peace of mind.
And have you felt that much before,
  or haven't you had time?

So very strange to write a thing,
  how wonderful to chat.
O, please stay on, and know the fun
  of hearing ''where-it's-at.''

Allow that I be to the point,
  and let the thought unfold.
It's bound to be a lovely poem,
  and good for young and old.

For lots of things are on your mind,
  like girls, and girls, and girls:
the way to start to fall in love,
  is with a prayer, my friends.

Joseph F. Hauch

THE MIRACLE MASTER

My *Lord, God* is my miracle
He is with me in each day,
He leads me and *He* guides me
And *He* helps me make my way.

He helps me when I'm up
He helps me when I'm down,
When I get into deep waters
He won't let me drown.

Sometimes the day is bright
Sometimes the day is dim,
But I'm sure of making it
Because my *miracle* is *him.*

Christ Jesus the *master*
He performs the greatest *miracles*
That were ever performed,
He wears the greatest crown
That was ever adorned.

Helen T. Barker

MAMA'S HANDS

The hands that rocked the cradle
Are the hands that made the bread
They are the hands that cooked the meals
To keep the family fed.

The hands that touched the forehead
When the fever it runs high
Are the hands that soothed the sick one
And dried the tear drops from the eyes.

The hands that changed the sick bed
And their job they never shirked
They do just about everything
That is the hardest to work.

Every wrinkle in her hands
Is worth the purest gold
For the Lord God made them
With His special mold.

Helen T. Barker

THE LONGHORN LEGEND

In Mexico, the landscape belonged to the rawboned,
their colors melding into a rainbow.
A blending of creams, browns and golds.
Then the creatures of white,
the two-legged gods, descended
transporting the rawboned to a land unknown.

A land which was as varied as the rawbones' shades,
as vast as their horns.
A land
sometimes docile, more often fierce.

For centuries freedom was theirs.
Freedom to roam, to graze
to remain of pure blood.
Until, once again
descended the gods
attempting a new creation, a new breed.

This century's turn brought a new breed
of white.
Freedom prevailed
and the cream, the brown and the gold hues
remained the true creation
and the Texas longhorns feared no more
that their legacy was to be a legend.

Ellen Black

DROUGHT

In shades of blue and gray,

Under still nights and deathless days,

They raise their parched faces to Heaven and pray.

And the messenger of the wind carries
their words scattering the meanings
in a thousand different ways.

The animals stir in endless need.

Dying golden stalks, withering brown,
kneel helplessly on the ground.

Mother Earth wordlessly asks why her children bleed.

The willow ceases to weep and listens
to the silence of sound.

Yet the complacent clouds sleep lazily,
and refuse to see the ruin below.

The river in its unsatisfied thirst,
lies choked and dry on the eternal stones.

And the soulless sun rages in
anger for an answer to a question
no one could know.

In the last moments of terrifying
calm the cumulus opens his eyes,
and cries to the yellow orb as he
looks in mortification upon the
utter desolation of the sun-
bleached boned.

Robin Larsen

THE AGGRESSIVE INTRUDER

Kudzu at my window; kudzu climbs the wall.
Vine and leaf keep climbing . . . might enter the center hall!
Have yet to see its flowers; the vine's still in its prime!
What growth! . . . how fast it inches . . .
    the flowers a matter of time!

Thrash that vine down quickly; burn the clusters . . . now!
Scatter its leafy twinings; put the sprawling bandit to plow!
But wait! Is that a ''find'' there, yonder, where stately stood
    a grove?
Where twining once plowed under, unearthed, have we a trove?

My word . . . it is a treasure; a ''find'' more precious than gold!
Amid the kudzu shreddings, a toy from youth, grown old!
And near my treasure . . . seedlings, now gaining ever strong.
Thrusts out all competition; and grows in mighty throng!

I'll not permit nor ponder the advance of my infringing foe.
I'll arm myself for battle, and strike a mighty blow.
So once again I trundle with tiller, scythe and saw.
Assault the vain intruder! My choice of green, the law!

Clara Mays Benson

THE DARK CATS OF EIN GEDI

Nothing can bring two beings closer
Than sharing dark unknown together.
What lovers reveal by proud daylight,
Shy souls tentatively show by night.

Two of us, different as night and day,
Shared an experience in crannies of Ein Gedi;
His calculating mind, gauging nature at a distance,
By sunrise had warmed to my receptive sense.

''We know their ways and paths they follow;
When they eat, have sex, in what pools they wallow.''
By moonlight, his gaze beamed a mental excitement.
Surely, mystic cat was more than creature of habit!

Came dawn again, a kittenish face
Bore down on us, whiskers spiked like rays,
Flecked fur tiered behind sharp ears; necklace
Flamboyant as sun's rays, ruffling last shades.

On her irises! Sparkling as Ein Gedi's falls;
Green light dancing, animate, radiant.
She tripped down muscularly; almost flawless.
Paused, snarled, hump-backed, impatient.

Glowed a moment with light born out of darkness.
Berry-black rosettes exploded on a downy mustardness.
Then she was gone, halo'ed by a sole epiphany.
Leaving us the dying embers of a fleeting memory.

Mike Scheidemann

EPIGRAM I

When a stone falls
On a person's head
He certainly knows
How deep is the pain;
But when an idea falls
Into his head
He never knows
How deep is the pain.
Conversely, if an empire's walls
Always start from within to fall,
Then it is rather droll
That a man should be looking at from without
What he should be looking into from within.

Franco Boni

DADDY'S DO CRY

I remember sitting on my daddy's
   knees
And the words that he spoke to
   me
When I asked, "Daddy do grown men
   cry?"
He said, "No sweetheart, they keep their
   feelings inside."
I know my brothers they all
   cry
I guess as they grow up their tear ducts
   will dry.

Then today my grandma
   died
And I saw my daddy wipe tears from his
   eyes
I didn't understand how this could
   be
I still remembered the words he spoke
   to me
But I guess there is still a boy
   inside
Because today I did see my daddy
   cry.

Linda Miller Whitener

RACE:
MALAYSIAN STYLE, 1981

Each throb, each breath pertained
to the externals.
Eyes flicker and glint in friendship
or hostility or both, without paradox.
Each soul with the almighty
dollar tagged,
Like bricks, they become
objects in national-building
maneuvers.
And rigid haunting structures
prevail, deadly cold, unmoved,
irreversible, reflecting the echoes of
past, present and future dreams
they come hurtling back
at one and remain whims
confined and encrusted
in private beings.

Dr. Christopher G. Jesudason

EGO:
ORGANISMS TO
SUPERPOWERS

Turn to Me, and feel the pain
of tortures, of time lost and
opportunities missed.
My Lord, I know Thou hast forsaken Me.

So, like a self-imposed demi-god
I will impose My plans,
My omnipotent will
— so swears the new-found God to Himself,
for I have wormed myself,
like an impotent, creeping, lowly thing,
to exaltation, within that moment
when eyes were closed.

Now, My exaltation is complete
in its infinite form,
and the re-enaction of My
unfortunate past will be seen,
in My will.

So understand My sufferings,
O little mortal things
for the Lord hath forsaken Me.

My love gushes out like
blood in my former afflictions,
— give Me some of yours,
give Me some of yours, lest
I die.

Dr. Christopher G. Jesudason

CAGED

   In a quiet Garden
Surrounded by a wall,
   A lonely bird sat caged
And sang its gentle call.

   All the trees and flowers
Rejoiced in what it sang,
   And all the Garden basked
In those sweet notes that rang.

   Still its song was ringing
In hope that there would be
   An answering song beyond
That then would set it free.

   Singing all alone in
The Garden it held fast,
   But then one day it knew
Its Spring would never last.

   So it sought to flee from
The prison it had known,
   And found against the bars
How feeble it had grown.

   Then the Garden watched as
It fluttered to the floor,
   And all the Garden knew
The lonely bird would sing no more.

Walt Summers

IMPOSTER

Time — you phony!
Parading 'round as some
Important aspect of a
Person's life;
Pretending endings
And beginnings —
Giving the impression
You and Fate
Are in collusion —
When, in fact,
You're not reality
But an illusion!

Sharon Rudolph

SHARON LaVERLE RUDOLPH. Born: Erskine, Minnesota, 12-12-42; Married: Joseph Rudolf, 5-19-67; Education: Moorhead State University, two years; Occupation: Housewife; Awards: Golden Poet Awards, 1985-87; Poetry: 'Silence,' *Our Western World's Most Beautiful Poems,* 1985; 'Surprise,' *Wide Open Magazine,* 1985; 'I Am Your Friend,' 'I Am,' *Twilight: A Collection of Verse,* 1985; 'Where Is The Child,' *Impressions,* 1986; Comments: *As a firm believer in reincarnation, the power of Positive Thinking and dreams, a lot of my poetry is written on time-lessness, faith, hope and joy in being. May everyone share in these!*

LEGEND OF ROBIN
REDBREAST

While on His way to Calvary
According to a legend it is said,
A robin mercifully picked a thorn
From the crown on Jesus Christ's head.

As the bird flew with the thorn in its beak
Way back to an unfinished nest,
A drop of blood fell down from the thorn
And landed on the pious bird's breast.

The blood stained its breast, thus dying it red
As the legend goes may it ever be,
Robins will have a scarlet breast
From then until eternity.

Alice Charpentier

INVITATION TO A FEAST

Crossed the Lord's path in the truest wrath,
A prayer of unmeasured thought,
In return the value it brought,
Of endless inspiration with unbounding innovations,
To the soul bringing joy,
A prayer overflowing with overjoy,
In answer of faith's reflection,
Under the divine protection,
The prayer of invention,
In return a prayer of invitation,
Of the Lord's creation of priceless mention,
Being blessed with hope of fruitfulness,
So precious the thought so precious the memory,
So beloved the thought,
That the prayer brought,
So beloved the memory,
Of the rare prayer of oratory,
With a vivid view of life's birth,
In hand with joyous mirth,
With emotions of a value of the Lord's grace,
That should not be feared when faced,
The Lord's gift of intuition,
With the best in reason,
The Lord's answer,
From a prayer of refer.

Anthony Pace

the scarfers

except for one small puerto rican
most of you were big enough
to be professional football players

i would watch you with your twenty pound
oxy-acetylene torches march up and down
those steel billets washing the slag
from the surface with monotonous skill

there was always something lunar to it
— you dressed in your silvery aprons
to protect you from the sparks and heat

and it was never pleasant
during the winter there were extremes of heat
as you would warm yourselves by the gas furnaces
while in the summer it was one hundred and twenty
degrees no matter where a man stood

since it was an incentive job
you were always calculating what
so much work would net you
and then
you would always count on me to add a little
to keep on good terms with this hell we were in

les amison

ODE TO OUR FRIEND

Lo! there the rosa cheeks blossom like flowers,
    Beautiful friend Ella, fair, disappears,
Enclosed are my lengthy expectations in hours,
    And awakens the blue rose without fear!

The heart's lover prays she never knows,
Conclusion to the poet's Christian note,
    The final loneliness of dreams:
Truth, seemingly forever like the sky,
Bending like into a mirror one can try,
    Hoping her friendship continues to flow.

Where'er she walks in the light
    A brighter sunshine,
Where'er he tossed and turned
    She still made her flight,
While he would wait with life's link
    Her heart and mind made children think
    (At least inclined to God's constant state)
Now vain this 'Knight's' armour,
Now show, how both love Jesus,
    How wonderful our 'King' of man is great!

Bennett Carson Ritter

FOR JEAN

God, how much time is allotted to me?
How many beautiful things can I see?
Is there time to travel — to laugh — to sing?
Will I have enough years to do everything
I want to do? Will You give me the chance
To sing my songs — to party — to dance?
Can I have a child and watch it grow?
There are so many things that I need to know.
Will my life be long and full to the brim?
Will I fall in love and grow old with him?
Each day's a miracle and life is so sweet.
There are so many friends I have yet to meet.
Your world's full of wonders for me to treasure
With feelings and passions too great to measure.
But You've never promised how long I can stay
Please help me to live as if there's only today.

Deanna Williams

NATIONAL AUDIT, 1979

How many times do you have to be told
Of the times and ways you've often been sold?

The times and ways I'm talking about
Are the ways and times that you've been sold out.

To any high roller, and more often the low,
Just hand them some money and they won't let go.

Our Congress will kiss, and much more than the hand,
All of the hustlers that abound in the land!

What we need is an accounting wall,
There is no need for it to be tall,

And certainly no need for it to be wide,
But the trip to that wall should be a very short ride!

Jack Kimbrough

STARBURST

There is a *love* in you
  I do not understand;
Beautiful little boy,
  Before *this* life
Did you hold me — by the hand?

Assisting mommy
  When she gave you birth;
Forgot the world — a miracle!
  Such sweet — mirth.

Only *hours* old, you earnestly
  Gazed upon my face;
Did you know me then?
  Do you — remember this place?

Anxious to hold — cradle you,
  Spellbound beyond belief;
A new throbbing — breathing life
  Yet a part of "us,"
A part of me —

Love I give you
  From the depths of my soul,
And a meager bounty;
  Not a saint — nor strong as Hercules
I just *am;*
  My dearest *jewel* — my *poetry,*
I'm just a *man.*

Peter Moser

PETER B. MOSER. Born: 1949 (Scorpio); Married: Trixie, 1981; Awards: Golden Poet Award, 1986; Poetry: 'The Bubble Century,' *Wächter und Anzeiger,* 5-10-85; 'Pedestal Shattered,' Spring, 1986; 'Visions Manifest,' *The American Poetry Anthology,* 1986; 'Quasar,' 1986; 'Rebels of Mortality,' *Best New Poets of 1986,* The American Poetry Association, 1986; Comments: *My efforts span numerous themes. They reach for color, emotion; depth and ambiguity.*

NATURE'S SORROWS

Rapid waters;
Rushing falls,
Season changes;
Nature's laws,

Winter's cold;
Lives claimed,
Nature's beauty;
A bitter shame,

Danger passes;
Survival for few,
Season changes;
World is new,

Life continues;
Grassy greens,
Nature's surface;
Colorful scenes,

Life so strange;
Now seasons change,

To a blackened season
  as whiteness falls;
Sorrow beneath beauty,
  nature's laws.

Gwen L. Bond

I WONDER

I wonder sometimes
What sounds must be like.
The sound of a car
Or the sound of a bike.

Do snowflakes and raindrops
All sound the same?
I wonder sometimes,
It's almost like a game.

In my silence I ponder
About the leaves as they fall.
And I wonder . . . I wonder . . .
Do they make sounds at all?

I watch a dog barking
At a cat in a tree.
Would they sound both alike
Or similar to me?

To see a child laughing
Or singing out loud,
Does it all sound the same
When I stand in a crowd?

I haven't an answer
To these questions I raise,
For I have not heard
Any sound in all of my days.

Esteva Lee Westfall

CIRCLES OF GOLD

True love is as
Of fairytales old;
The rose that grows
In circles of gold;
To have and to hold:

The jewel in a gentle
Dawn, after the sunset
Of agony's passionate
Storm:

With castles and courts
For knights today to
Share with ladies fair:

Joy of time alone . . . in
The sweetness of a quiet
Enchanted embrace:

True love is as
Of fairytales old;
The rose that grows
In circles of gold;
To have and to hold.

Doris Jackson Reynolds

WHY?

Why am I here,
Year after year?
Is life worthwhile?
Sometimes I only smile,
At the irony of it all,
I took 33 hours to be born,
Puny, whiny, sickly.
I've been through a fine childhood,
A sad adolescence,
A worse marriage and divorce,
Had 2 girls without remorse,
Sold, wrote advertising,
Did Avon and civil service,
And wasn't too enterprising,
Saw one girl married,
She had a baby girl,
The joy of life's swirl,
I've written poetry for years
And mostly it's been laughs and tears,
If I were to die
Tomorrow,
Who would sorrow?
But I didn't do too badly (sigh)
So this is my answer to *Why?*

Jacqueline Miller Adam

190

THE BUCK

You came from South Mountain, fearing the motorcyclists,
who brrred their way through your feeding ground.
On the north slope of the river you find 721 Central Blvd.,
where the mulberries ripen in thick summer heat,
where the grass is lush,
and where, except for my prowling dog and an occasional
hunter spotlighting for easy meat,
you can rest hurried limbs and forage for a meal.

Each season you are here you give me solace.
As I watch you feed on fallen apples,
you note me peering through the window, give an easy
two lopes toward the stand of mulberry trees
to pause transfixed, thinking yourself invisible
to this morning observer, and thinking correctly
that your quick hoof-fall is master over my leadened gait.

We achieve a mystical transference:
— you, a true vegetarian; I, trying to imitate your ways.
— You, possessing a beauty of stance that even in old age
counters my middle-age rattle.
— And finally, with this season's hunt, it is a question
of survival . . . you, me, and with an awkward leap, America.
No soapbox this, but the interlude of democracy having
seen so many winters.

Les Amison

A BOX OF TWELVE CANDLES
ISN'T ENOUGH ANYMORE

Brendan turned thirteen today . . . the cake is ready, chocolate,
his favorite, but . . . a box of twelve candles isn't enough anymore.
I look at him . . . his shoulders overpowering the new puppy, "Max" . . .
His cheeks still twelve-year-old rosy . . . is there a suggestion . . .
a wisp of a moustache . . .?
His laughter rings out . . . pre-teen, raucous, lively sound . . . but . . .
He's thirteen-year-old solicitious of Grandma . . . I'm waiting on
him and he notices. Then, Happy Day, gleefully: "Can I lick the bowl?"
A box of twelve candles isn't enough anymore . . .
Thirteen now . . . and one to grow on . . . isn't he yet the child who
asks: "Can Max come in the hot-tub with me?"
The grown-up one assures me: "He'll be OK; my dog can swim already!"
. . . The child who used to kick the ball around now puts a
steady, unerring foot on it . . . and trips on his untied laces . . .
The teen-ager, all-knowing, helps Grandma put air in the tires . . .
He can, if I let him, drive better than I . . . But . . . leaves the
car window open a bit . . . "My stomach is whoozy . . ." . . . Too much
junk food . . . maybe?
The younger grandson still hugs Grandma without restraint . . .
Oh, the joy of his embrace . . .
But . . . please remember . . . don't enter his bedroom unannounced . . .
. . . Today, my grandson is thirteen . . .
A box of twelve candles isn't enough anymore.

Rosemarie Werkman

HOME AGAIN

. . . She is Vice-Pres. of *this* . . . Co-Chairman of *that* . . .
Coordinator . . . Re-Vitalizer . . . Busy Work . . . Busy Work . . .
But, when Cassidy was missing and her grandson's voice cried out:
". . . He's been gone since Monday . . . My dog's my best buddy,
Grandma . . . I can't live without him . . ."
She became Italian Grandma Extraordinaire!
. . . The calendar was cleared . . .
She and he drove for hours; they tramped the woods . . . Bren and she . . .
They called his name . . . rode . . . and dwelled on the 'good times' . . .
The road workers would watch for him . . . "Yes, we saw him yesterday,"
They encouraged . . . "A yellow Lab, right?"
Our spirits soared . . . "He's probably playing and forgot the time . . ."
Cassidy would come back . . .
. . . He returned! . . .
The conquering hero came home! Dirty, tired, but triumphant . . .
Smiling . . . accepting the *Love* . . .
And Grandma stayed on to cook the victory supper . . .
". . . Thanks, Grandma, for going with me . . ."
. . . She has a special glow about her now . . . returning to her
V.P. of *This*, Coordinator of *that* . . .
Cassidy came home . . . and so did Grandma.

Rosemarie Werkman

WE WON!

He was bent over amongst his spring plants,
blues and yellows.
Then he stood as I waved to him on this familiar drive
from village to home.
I beeped the horn, he turned and waved in the same motion,
knowing it would be a friend drawing his attention.
. . . And then I saw, for an exquisite moment of youth, not
the middle-aged man, but a young one . . .
Wearing school colors of blue and gold; he turned, rhythmic,
arm up, making a perfect lay-up shot.
And I am in blue and gold . . . cheering . . . we won!
We won the game!

Rosemarie Werkman

ROSEMARIE A. WERKMAN. Born: Washingtonville, New York, 4-21-26; Married: Henry J. Werkman, deceased; Education: Several writing courses beyond secondary education; Occupations: Receptionist, advertising agency and school systems; Assistant-Librarian; Clerk-Typist, Doubleday Publishing Co. and Stern's Department Store, New York City; Memberships: Vice-President, Blooming Grove Chamber of Commerce; Trustee, Blooming Grove Historical Association; Trustee, Theatre of Hudson Highlands; Member, Orange County Council for the Disabled; Ad hoc committee member, Revision of Blooming Grove Master Plan; Awards: Recognition for poem 'Twilight Time,' in *Hearts on Fire, Vol. IV*; Poetry: 'We Won,' 5-86; 'Home Again,' 10-86; 'A Box of Twelve Candles Isn't Enough Anymore,' 5-87; Other Writings: "Mrs. Corradi and Skeesix," short story, loving account of a neighbor and her young friend (the author), published by local newspaper; "A Stone's Throw From Heaven," manuscript, story of Love, War and Family; Comments: *The themes of my poetry and writing are often inspired by the occurrences of family members, friends and myself . . . or by the sights and sounds of the natural world around me.*

MINIMAL CAFÉ

For Cynthia

Different people follow different changes
I need something I can follow also
Sometimes I wonder exactly what I'm thinking
I just know I have something to do

If we have the time
We'll stay right here
We'll cry for you
We'll laugh and cheer
For this is the place we spend our lives

Faces follow faces through the open door
Where they come from I don't want to know
Just to have them in here
    is good enough for me
Come on in, stay a little while

If we have the time
We'll stay right here
We'll cry for you
We'll laugh and cheer
For this is the place we spend our lives

Chester D. Sherman

INTO ETERNITY

Into Eternity,
    is that where you went?
Did you enter the other world
    or are you waiting yet?

Are you caught in a fantasy?
Or a part of my dream,
I just can't imagine
the fate of this scheme.

Can you tell me, tell me the answer?
Can you give me, give me a sign?
Did you do it on purpose,
or was it just your time?

    In a vision, gazing,
looking down on this world's crazy theme,
    Do you know now of its mysteries,
or are you in between?

    Are you near or far,
    Can you see me now,
    I wish I could touch you,
    I just don't know how.

Can you tell me, tell me the answer?
Can you give me, give me a sign?
Did you do it on purpose,
or was it just your time,

Teeka Lynne Stevenson

ERIN

It came upon us suddenly
as the wind swept through the sky
filled with fear and hatred
I saw my brothers die
the men fought bravely
their eyes were wide and bold
but they ran to the hills
the wind blew hard and cold

they burned our homes
then gave us promises

Our fathers owned this land
as their fathers did before
we shall be returning
to take it back once more
many lives were taken
and shall be once again
as we decide our fates
we watch the falling rain

they burned our homes
then gave us promises

Chester D. Sherman

SONIC WHISPERS

Boy, to be insane again
Velvet sofas are all mine
all in the game when
she offers to be fineness.

Whispers consume my life
I live and breathe finitely
to survive means strife
yet I feel mighty.

time spent day and night
velvet softens the plight.

what can whispers and velvet be
when the mind sees?

Maureen Kearney Jones

NEED TO ESCAPE

Pressure mounts.
The world hurries faster.
No time to relax,
Sunk in a pool of problems.
Try to beat time.
Speed fast to success,
There may be no tomorrow.
Work harder
And be swept in a tide of stress.
Don't be pushed aside!
Tension is driving you mad.
There is a need to escape.

Jessica D. Bayliss

MY DOLLY

I have a pretty little dolly
She is as cute as she can be.
She was given to me by Santa
He hung her high on the Christmas Tree.

I just knew she was my dolly
As soon as I saw her there.
But she was hanging up so high
Could I reach her by standing on a chair.

I pulled the chair over to the tree
Then standing on tippy toes
I lacked a lot of touching her
My! how my excitement grows.

I place a bucket on top the chair
Then climb on top of them.
By stretching oh so tall
I can almost touch her hem.

I gave another long hard stretch
The bucket slipped, the chair tipped.
The tree came crashing down
But I grabbed the dolly tightly in my grip.

The noise was loud as thunder
Sounding throughout the house.
My parents both came running
I told them it was only a mouse.

Ardith M. Reed

STANDING AT THE DOOR

The fog hangs heavy
Thick and grey
Keeping the sun
From shining all day

The snow has fallen
All over the ground
Then frozen so hard
It makes a crunching sound

The water still runs
In the creeks and streams
But ice is forming
'Round the rocks in rings

The north wind
Whistles and blows
Making deep drifts
By blowing the snow

Old man Winter
Has come to call
Arriving this year
Early in the fall

But there is beauty here
As I explore
It's not so bad
If I just stand at the door

Ardith M. Reed

WHEN MY FATHER SPEAKS

Oh, when my Father speaks to me,
My heart comes alive — gloriously —
Oh, when my Father speaks to me,
I know His love is mine — eternally.

Oh, when my Father speaks to me:
He tells me of a beautiful life — yet to be.
He tells me of happy dreams — yet to come true;
He tells me of iridescent skies, all shining blue.

But, He also tells me of darkly clouded skies;
Of rolling thunder — and lightning — away up high;
Of torrential rains, filling our earth — all of this
To give us a magnificent Promise: A rainbow has its birth!

He assures me of love, of joy, of peace;
He tells me of the freedom, which will never cease.
He tells me of happiness — yet to be.
All of this, for you — and you — and me.

Joy S. Pearce

QUEEN ANNE'S LACE

Today I saw a field of Queen Anne's Lace,
nature's crocheted bedspread.
A French-blue sky, dappled with clouds,
boldly boasting, "Here I am, the perfect canopy!"

Dare I throw myself on this stately bed,
and snuggle its tiny snowflakes to my face?
Dare I saunter with wonder, and
childishly think of those candies, non-pareils?

Shall I, with apology, gather a few,
and tenderly arrange them in a country pitcher?
Would you say I was wasting time,
because I made so many trips to my kitchen,
to "wolf" down the prim magic of Queen Anne's Lace?

What a glutton I am for nature's work!
Today, my eyes and soul have feasted.
Mother Nature crochet on,
cover me with Queen Anne's Lace!

Jane Marrazzo Tortorello

ANTICIPATION

There he stood looking deep into the pool;
A spring-fed grotto amid natural rock, desert palms,
Flowers, and grasses green and cool.
His gaze intense, yet pleasant, full of confidence.
Perhaps he'd made a wish, or come to a decision.
A young man with a dream; his pose that of self-assurance.
The spring gurgled and spurted in the soft lantern light,
Bouncing off the rippling surface in golden droplets
Reflected in the clear water.
Silver and copper coins scattered below, glinted and sparkled
Like jewels, twinkling in answer, as fireflies on a June night.
Distant strains of music from the calliope,
And wafts of perfume from the night-blooming blossoms
Permeated the air.
I stood entranced on the footbridge, as he straightened
And turned. The lamplight glow revealed the happiness
On his face. His eyes danced. He smiled.
A young man with a dream and a purpose.
Truly, an enchanted evening
Here at this oasis of magic and mysterious promise . . .

Mertie Elizabeth Boucher

THE PENCIL

Phone jangling
Voice urgent
Pen wandered off again
My fumbling.
At last
Deep in a cluttered drawer
A jot of pencil
Chewed wood, green paint, gold letters.
Business completed,
And the phone resting again upon its cradle.

Then
Rolling the pencil
In my fingers
Déjà vu!
Daniel's name
Recalling years when
Stockings always needed stuffing
With rulers, whistles, pens, and other elongate equipment
Since baseballs never fit.
Remembrance of Things Past!

"Danny, come here.
I have something for you.
This used to be
A pencil of your Dad's."

Joanne D. Denko, M.D.

LOVE DEFINED

Love, too, is a fragile thing.
It thrives on deeds of kindness, trust,
Believing in the good, and hope — that all tomorrows will bring
Less pain, more solace, understanding, brotherhood and peace.
Love grows with the giving, with care about our fellow man.
It grows with tolerance and forgiveness
Through the elusive substance of *God.*
Love endures the elements of time and space.
It requires a searching — a belief that it can be found.
It is found close by. At home. Within, in the depths of the soul,
Within the being that is attuned to *God.* For *God* is *Love.*
Love is a circle that spreads and encompasses those who find it.
Neverending, always returning to the sender; always sparked by *God.*
Love comes from *God;* flows through one being to another;
Electrifies the air. Never dies. Always here within us.
Love is the thread of life that binds all men together,
And man and *God.*
Love is the magic key that opens any door to life.
Love is such a fragile thing. Yet strong . . . Love endures.

Mertie Elizabeth Boucher

SILVER DREAMS

Me alone, so it seems.
Dark is the night yet still light,
By the midnight sun's silver beams.
Searching and seeking
Every corner of my mind,
Releasing secret dreams within that hide.
Their beauty captured within the glow,
Dancing and swaying in the silvery snow.
They move with style, in such grace,
Within the light they softly embrace.
I awake from this dream, this beautiful dream,
Searching and seeking the silvery beams.

Michelle Cox

Well my Darling, it's finally here.
Imagine this, it's one whole year.
It was a year from this day
that you asked me to stay.
A year from this date
we decided our fate.

Being with you is like a spell
that will never be broken.
Anything I say or do will
be such a small token . . . of . . .
showing you how wonderful it's been,
going through life with this stupid grin.

I keep your picture on my desk,
and look at you when I'm depressed.
There you are smiling at me.
Now I can finish these dirty deeds.

Debra Ascot

TO MY UNBORN CHILD

You bring so much love
Into our hearts.
Happiness fill the air.
The pride in your father's eye.
You're still too new to understand
All of this
But I know you
Can surely feel
The joy you have
Created in our lives.

Tracy Highberger

I DO NOT WANT TO WISH

I do not want to wish
That you were mine
Or that my dream of you
Would be all that endures
I only want to wish that you
Would want and pine
To wish and dream
That I were yours

Jerry Martinez

THE MOON

How mystical it is to see
The wonders of the moon
To see its full face all aglow
Like the sun shines high at noon

It illuminates the sky at night
While soft clouds drift close by
Its glowing beams of light shine
So stars twinkle in the sky

It radiates the evening as
The sky shines bright and clear
Its beauty takes your breath away
As it strives to draw you near

I close my eyes to feel the moon
So full with realms of light
It heightens all within its reach
Shining through the darkest night

I gaze about the lighted sky
Searching far and wide
To find its brilliance glowing
All around me from all sides

As I stare into its lighted face
A wave passes over me
I feel my soul's in unison
In peaceful harmony.

Donna R. Sims

SMILE

You have a smile
that's bright and gay
When you smile, you
show no hate.
Although your smile is
sometimes fake, you still
refuse to show hurt or hate.

It's a smile that makes
you look great, it's a smile
that will take you a long way.
It's a smile that will
certainly brighten up the day.
So smile whether there's hurt
or hate.

Lenesser Massey

JUST ONE LOOK

Just one look, that's all it took
And I was in love with you
Just one smile you flashed my way
And it took my breath away
You touched your lips to mine, a simple kiss
And in heaven I knew myself to be
A gentle touch of your hand, a slight caress
And I wanted to feel your touch
You held me in your arms as we danced
And I wanted you to hold me forever
I feel so good loving you
I'm so happy all the time
You've gotten me enchanted and captivated
I can't imagine life without you
I've got just one love, and baby it's you
Just one life and I want to spend it with you.

Andrea Raymore

THE LAW OF SUCCESS

If you would just believe
in the one that created us all.
And understand the power of thought.
Then you will begin your way on the
path of success.
Even when you fail
you should always arouse determination.
Analyze yourself.
Even if its good or bad.
Know what you need
and who you are
and what you want to be.
Because your habit of thought
will control your life.
Power is in the divine will.
It will work through laws known
and unknown.
Always keep faith in our creator.
Learn the way of meditation.
When you have happiness,
there will be success.
Know and understand the power of God
and put His power behind your efforts.

Harrelle Felipa

FALL DAYS

The crickets sing
Wild geese are on the wing
Leaves of red and green,
These are fall days.

Tiny animals frolic through the leaves
Crisp, cool days and a slanted sun
Time to finish what summer had begun,
These are fall days.

Charcoal skies carry fat, puffy clouds
Nature's song is humming out loud
And beauty covers the land,
These are fall days.

Days of flaming trees and pumpkins
These are fall days
When the earth goes into repose,
And waits quietly for spring.

E. Filchock

DRIVEN

She wore ambition as a cloak,
Desire was the girth about her waist,
Gentleness became as impudence,
And sullied her fair face.

Consumed by flame of self,
There was no need of friend,
Hearts were her stepping stones,
She gave no quarter; nor would she bend.

When at last she reached the top
At center stage, she wondered why
No one was there — she was alone,
And no one listened when they heard her cry.

Barbara Shreder

The Merrimac.

COURAGE

Courage is more
Than the sudden surge

Of emotion that
Motivates some heroic act.

It is a
Built-in capability for

Facing up to
Any situation, no matter

How bad it
May be, and despite

Pressures of peers
And others, to do

The right thing,
At the right time,

No matter what
The cost may be.

Arthur A. Wood, M.D.

PATRIOTISM

My love of my
Country stems not from

Flag waving, sabre rattling,
Hero worship, or even

"Of thee I sing."
It comes from a

Sincere sense of gratitude
To all those Americans;

The magnitude of whose
Sacrifice; the steadfastness of

Whose purpose; the constancy
Of whose vigilance; the

Judgment of whose vote;
Has kept us free.

Arthur A. Wood, M.D.

MANKIND'S HARVEST

All human progress
Has resulted from
The planting of
Seeds of discontent
In the fertile
Soil of man's
Mind; the watering
Of it with
The enthusiasm of
Active desire; and
Its cultivation by
The persistence of
A strong will.

Arthur A. Wood, M.D.

SNOWPLOWED MAILBOX

Snowplowed mailbox
a victim of the weather
crushed flat recently and
holding no package or letter.

Our poor friend afield
with mouth opened wide
nothing but cold snow
can be found inside.

Monster highway machinery
meeting less than his match
moved fast through the scenery
leaving behind his catch —

Awaiting the warm spring, now
green grass and days all sunny
our snowplowed mailbox
found winter was not funny.

Gwendolyn Trimball Pease

I dreamed of my wedding
And something was wrong
For there was another
Standing where you belong

I looked at his face and
I saw love and trust
Then I heard you crying
And my heart turned to dust

Then I sent a prayer to
Our Father above
To please put me back
In the arms of my love

But I had a feeling
My prayer had fell through
So I just stood there quietly
While my heart went with you

And if I live forever
I'll never forget
The hurt in your eyes
And my tears of regret

I won't mail this letter
What good would it do
Oh! *Lord* please forgive me
My dream was all true

Dollie Jones

SMILE OF A CHILD

Given my choice of gold or the smile of a child,
I'd think quite a while,
  ere I'd choose the gold —
As it soon would be gone
But the memory lived on
I'd have the rare treasure
In my heart all the while
To examine at will
The sweet loving smile!

Marjorie Hennigan

QUEST

I crossed the golden shifting sands
Soft fleeting tide by tide.
I sunset-watched a silken dawn
From driftwood's smooth carved side.

A seabird flashed on gliding wing
Past wave-tossed tumbled shore,
While on my age-carved piece of wood
I touched my quest for more.

The shadows grew to deepest red
While rising white-tops flamed
As I, beneath the fired sky,
Knew stars were still untamed.

M. D. LeDoux

DEW DREAMS

Many were the tears that
Fell upon the ground last night.
Some elfen maiden
Empty wept her heart . . .
I saw her tears like diamonds on the grass.
I found her gossamer wedding dress
lying across the leaves.
I found her silken clothing line
Left unused,
Waiting . . .
In this morning's light
Her grieving tears were
Starfire.

M. D. LeDoux

AFTER THE SOLDIERS

Marching miles of marching men
disappear around a bend
floating dust weighs the air,
they once were there.
Tiny figures scramble out
from hidden hollows 'round about
the thirsty road.
They stand and stare.
Gentle silence . . .
Where's the violence?
We need some rain.

Cheryl Ann Fitzgerald

YOUR DREAMS

I charge you,
To diligently follow,
The footsteps you have laid.

A soul with clipped wings,
Needs only to have patience.
For time will give it,
A broken flight,
And it's by far better,
Than a crash landing.

Karl Scott McDaniel

OUR MORTAL LIFE

Why don't we rememeber how fragile this life
When we think of sickness, trouble and strife,
How soon can be ended all pleasure and fun
How uncertain we are, if we walk or we run.

Not long ago our parents were here
Death mowed them down, we stood at their bier,
They had the same wishes, their hopes were the same
And we'll go the same route with no one to blame.

We have the same thoughts, we wish to remain
Alive and well, our folks did the same,
We cling to our lives both young and old
But death takes us quickly, when living does fold.

We have the same hopes, we have the same aim.
We live in their dreams, we feel the same pain,
We have the same joys, during sunshine and rain,
We loved as they loved, our plans were the same.

They died, yes, they died, we will die too,
None will remain here not even a few,
Then why are we proud and think we are just,
When we know for sure, that we'll turn to dust?

Why not shun our pride and think of our end?
Why not live wisely, as our life we spend?
For we go to Heaven or we'll go to Hell
Where forever we'll be there to dwell.

C. H. Willke

ALWAYS IN A HURRY

People always seem to be in a hurry to get things done —
Each day is rushed in order to have time for fun.
Hurry to work, eat, always worried of being late —
Only to find, hurrying gives you more time to wait.
Rush, rush, rush!

We have microwave ovens, TV dinners, and instant drinks,
Drive-in restaurants, quick diets, and no reason to think;
Drive-through funeral parlors, banks, and prefab homes,
Hurry to use charge cards, and let your kids roam.
Hurry, hurry, hurry!

Wanting more time for jogging, shopping, and biking,
Fishing, hunting, vacations, and hiking,
Visit the family bar, watch TV, party, or sleep late,
Sit, smoke, and talk on the phone, or date.
Fun, fun, fun!

You can't hurry for a newborn baby, death, or seasons,
Growing up, war, education, whatever the reason,
Becoming an artist, writer, make movies, or dance,
Train dogs, grow a tree, or kill pesty ants.
Time, time, time!

Yet — no time for saying "I love you," or a child on your lap,
Helping with homework, calling Mom, or taking a nap,
Give compliments, write your congressman, or vote,
Go to church, or care for a friend who cannot cope.
Shame, shame, shame!

Hope Marie Maki

MEMORIES

Tonight I am remembering when you first learned
Our dream was coming true, our love to be fulfilled
        In our own child.

I told you right away, as soon as I was sure, for
Well I knew you yearned, as I did, for a small one
        Of our very own.

This is a happy memory, almost a humorous one, for
You became so careful of me, so tenderly cherishing me
And our child-to-be, as though we both were made
        Of fragile glass!

How happy we were as we planned and dreamed of our little one.
I asked you once whether you wanted a boy or a girl. I have
Never forgotten your loving reply that you would adore either one,
And so you did adore our baby girl, all the short ten months of
Her life, such adoration that when we lost her something in us
Both died with her, and you could not face her loss
        Even with me.

And now you two are together in the other world, and I am
Still alone, needing you both so much that when illness and
Pain torment me I fail to be brave, and cry frustrated tears and
        Sobs of loneliness and sheer rebellion.

Dear God, forgive me and help me bear what must be borne!

Frances R. Brown

THERAPY

So many years the loss was locked away:
Babies avoided like the plague, puzzling friends until
They thought me cold, unfeeling, since I would not say
Why their little ones could not bend my will.

Fool that I was not to admit my pain,
Not to seek help, but mask my loss within
Academic pedantry, ignoring what might gain
Surcease where flesh and blood had been.

Such wasted time until the day a son was put into my arms
Where no small one had lain for more than fifty years.
Later, to scotch the hurt and stifle my alarms,
I held another baby boy, in spite of unshed tears.

But this older one, though weaned, had well remembered
Where breasts were, what happiness they brought.
He tried so hard to get what he wanted, while the December
Lady holding him longed to be able to give him what he sought.

His struggle ended with a frustrated howl in which I, bold,
Wanted to join at the irony of it all — an eighty-year-old
Woman with painful, swollen breasts and eyes full of tears,
Transported back in time near sixty years!

Frances R. Brown

TO MY CHILDREN

I know that you want me to be a friend,
But as your Mother, I cannot bend.

Live your life with fun and joy,
Just don't treat life like a toy.

Life can be fun and sensible too,
It all depends so much on you.

As you complain in your wrath,
I must guide you to your path.

Life has so many glamorous ways,
I don't want glamour to lead you astray.

God gave you to me in His trust.
I must raise you, true and just.

When you have needs you want to share,
Always remember that I am there.

Dorothy M. Aikin

SOUL FELT SYMPATHY

There was such happiness and joy in your life,
The day that you both became Man and Wife.

But there is nothing that is quite so sad
Than to lose the wonderful son you had.

In your pain and sorrow, it is okay to cry.
You know it is alright to ask God, *Why?*

Let us comfort you and ease your pain.
Think of the love you have yet to gain.

Think of your son with warmth and love.
Just turn over his soul to God above.

Share your grief, for it has its place,
And look to God for mercy and grace.

Dorothy M. Aikin

BETWEEN SISTERS

To my sister that I love so much,
Our common grief helped us to touch.

In our pain that we have to bear,
We found so much that we can share.

In the ones of whom we love,
We are bound together by God above.

He has given us a common goal,
To share and to preserve our soul.

No matter what tomorrow may bring,
We praise the Lord and together sing.

As we find strength in each other,
We are closer than any sister or brother.

I love you sis, I'll not pretend,
In you I've found more than a friend.

Dorothy M. Aikin

RELAY

The fountain
said to the wind:
''Catch!''
and flung out
its tears.

Most of them
floundered
in the gusts
and dried to death.
A few bled
anonymously
into mud.
But one
went a little
sideways,
landing eventually
on a sunflower seed.

K. Margaret Brown

VOYAGE

*Dedicated to Chris Maziarz, who
died on 10-2-87.
He is loved and will always be
remembered by our family.*

Have you had a child?
Vomit, discomfort, veins, fatness
A special life inside
Nine months later — outside
Screeching, eating, sleeping, wetting
Two against the world
Legs, long and straggly
Hands, football size
Dreams racing
Everything so little, yet — so big
Been told — babies are gifts from God
On loan — for how long?
Enjoy the moment
Forget messy diapers, spilled formula
They *don't* matter
Cries, smiles, gurgling, cooing *do*
Mud from cleats can be wiped
Spots cloroxed bright
Only you can laugh and
Make the winning touchdown
You're in the satin coffin
Eyes closed, hands crossed
The flowers weep
I stare and wonder
Chris, I love you

Suzanne Fortune DiGiacomo

DREAMS

I hear you. I hear you.
The sun went low behind
the gray-streaked birch tree.
Its limby arms, a straight
pointing path to heaven.
It would be so easy to give in.

Suzanne Fortune DiGiacomo

CAROUSEL

The carousel goes 'round and 'round
filled with kids and me
My happy horse goes up and down
It's lavender, pink and blue
Candy colors shout at me
brilliantly bright as I like
With one stirrup I ride
I see my image in the mirror
Everything is a gingerbread house
'Round and 'round I go
And one woman furiously snaps
picture after picture of just me.

Suzanne Fortune DiGiacomo

ONE DAY HE JUST DISAPPEARED

I'd tell myself I'm here
To serve God not man
Instead of giving
My husband a hand
I'd demand
He was to dry each one
Of my tears
Even if he didn't
Put them there
But I hardly took interest
In his ailments
He never hinted
It wasn't fair
One day he just disappeared

Sherrie Rini

STOMPING THROUGH PUDDLES

It's raining outside
And my soul feels every drop,
As it crashes to the ground,
Gradually forming puddles,
On sidewalks.

Nobody will ever know,
The destiny of a raindrop.
The mouths it will wet.
The gutters it will run through.
The rivers it will form.

Joining with its brothers,
To fabricate,
An army of raindrops.
Such an undefeatable force,
With a marvelous battle record.
Until now . . .

Technology is the cancer,
That eats to the heart,
Of this world's greatest army.

Karl Scott McDaniel

A CHRISTMAS REMEMBRANCE

So many times in recent weeks and months
I've written to or about my precious baby girl,
Too often mourning her loss instead of joying
In what I had and cherished for so short a time.

Today, the anniversary of your birth so long ago,
My thoughts flair out in fine thin wings to that same
Christmas season when, for the only time in many years before
And since, I did not sing ''Oh Holy Night'' as the solo at a service.
I literally could not do it then so close to your own birth,
But I remember singing it softly to you as you
Lay in my arms in that hospital room, with
You and your father as my only listeners.

I remember so vividly that you looked at me with
Those wide blue eyes as though, tiny as you were,
You knew and understood what and why I was singing that
Beautiful carol of the Saviour's birth. It was His
Birthday as it had just been yours, and so my
Heart was full of love and joy and peace.

Dear God, help me keep remembering that scene and
Not that my baby's life was shorter even than His
Who has her now in His safekeeping.

Frances R. Brown

RECURRING AUTUMN SPECTACLE

How proudly each holds up its head,
Splattered with gold and shades of red,
With patches of pristine green peering through!

Erect as soldiers the trees do stand,
As though waiting to march to the tune of a band,
Resplendent, ready for a final review.

Once they lined an unpaved road
Where plodding horses pulled their load,
As pedestrians plowed their way on the sod.

Now, as speeding cars whiz by,
The trees still blaze with beauty on high:
Spectacular masterpieces of God!

Elsie Walush

A QUESTION OF OWNERSHIP

There's something sad about a house alone,
Forsaken by the only family it has known:
Vacant it stands, a forlorn shell,
Yearning for the folks it knew so well,
Silent, apprehensive, awaiting its fate,
Consoling itself with mementoes of late.

But there's something smug about a house alone,
Somehow aware it will ever own
The family which deserted it after many years,
For a finer place, to keep up with peers:
The deserts will nowhere ever find
The parts of themselves they have left behind!

Elsie Walush

TONIGHT

Tracy's Poem

You have made me believe in the powers above,
a million emotions on the wings of a dove.

A skyline of lights in a city of shadows,
the fog lifts with a touch of your kiss.

The moment we've shared will never fade.
Not one will surpass what together we gave.

My love for you will never again be bound.
For my heart, a resting place has found.

Your most tender moments to me you've shown.
My love for you has done nothing but grown.

I will never forget what we've shared tonight.
I open the cage and let my dove take flight.

Stephen J. Schlager

THE VOICE

When the phantom of realities ravaged my body,
When all else no longer meant a thing to me,
A sweet soul-entrancing voice ringing in my ears,
Touched my deepest, a nectar to my very soul;
A beautiful flower blooms in my heart,
And spreads its lovely fragrance around.

S. L. Yen

THOUGHTS OF YOU

I was sitting alone in my own quiet, little world
when these thoughts leapt to mind.
Thoughts of caring uncertainty;
thoughts that are frozen in time.

Thoughts of freedom and captivity.
Experiences of pain and euphoric fun,
thoughts of all the happy times
that are yet to come.

Feelings of loneliness
and a hollow life.
Thoughts of happiness,
thoughts of strife.

Now I turn to define what I think,
and put terms to what I do.
No words leap to mind,
only thoughts of you.

Whether they run shallow or deep,
I am yet to know.
But to a state of confusion,
I am sure to go.

I know nowhere my thoughts lead
and feelings lead.
I only know that my heart, it bleeds.

I know, in time, my life will again be mine
I only hope that you will be there to share that special time.

Stephen J. Schlager

I gave to you my
    most treasured possessions
and you took them
    with pride
I gave to you my secrets
    locked deep within
and you hid them
    within yourself
I gave to you my
    friendship
and you took it
    with no questions
and now I give to you
    my love
take it
use it
and return it
    nourished
I give to you
    all of me
    undemanding
    take me.

Michelle E. Barra

TOO DIFFERENT

We are in love with each other
But we cannot get along.
Our minds are compatible
But are we that strong?

I watch the sunsets
You will watch the dawn
You like the canaries
I would prefer a swan.

You like the freedom
I love the companionship
You want to be more than friends
But what kind of relationship?

We are too much in love
To argue so much
We cannot give up the feelings
Because we care too much.

You say I cannot shut you out
I say you cannot box me in
I cannot let you lose
And you will not let me win.

Kathy Menninger

SAMPLERS

The future
    opaque coordinates
of visions boiling to a degree
    of refinement.
As one stores the untouchable
    virtues
still yet in the making
    of what total DNA exchange
will carry to its next point
    of inherited love —
and sampled in the surprise
    interface;
the corridors of one's
    heart's production!

Patricia Anne Solek-Fritsche

NIGHTTIME

It's Nighttime
I feel the closeness of you
By my side
I reach to put my arm around you —
As I do,
I caress the beauty of your face —
As the night wears on —
We hold each other
And love into the wee small hours —
What happiness we have known.

Jo S. Reynolds

TEARS FOR ESTHER

Tears for Esther,
No, not tears —
She gave to those
That she held dear.

So much to offer
In so many ways
So many talents,
Most were amazed.

A woman of intrigue,
Sensitive and kind.
Such a person of depth
Is hard to find.

Her striking beauty
Was an enigma to all,
Her mystic world
Held most in awe.

The memory of Esther
Will be sustained
Etched in the hearts
Of those who remain.

She is at peace now
There is no more pain
For Esther Mae Williams
Our love we proclaim.

Jo S. Reynolds

THE ULTIMATE BOUQUET

I dream of a bouquet,
too beautiful to be sold.
A splendid sight for the
heart to behold.
I see the children of the
world playing together happily,
oh what a heartwarming sight
to see.
A glorious array of colors,
in their native dress.
Singing together,
without worry or distress.
How wonderful my heart would feel,
if this elusive dream were real.

Klara Farnum

FOOD FOR ETHIOPIANS

Who knows why the food sent to . . .
The Ethiopians was burned by rebels?
These starving people waited . . .
For the trucks to come.

The convoy doused with gasoline . . .
Shot up into flames —
Leaving 45,000 people . . .
Famished and starving . . . and dying.

Oh, God, please hear my prayer . . .
My heart is breaking —
For these lost souls . . .
God's children . . .
Who only wanted to eat.

Marilyn Gold Conley

IT IS THE LAST CALL

There it was so I heard,
    Known as the last call.
Like a porter on a train,
    Last coffee for one and all.
So the season says it,
    There it is — the Fall.
Then without uttering a sound,
    A swift windy wall.

It is here — whispering,
    Softly saying,
The call is coming,
    And seems to be waving.
Cheerfully yet dolefully
    The sound is weighing.
As clearly as any train whistle,
    The last call is fading.

Capitola Paxton

NEW FRONTIERS

Our founding fathers
    came to new frontiers —
with high hopes
of building a better culture,
to reap
the blessings of prosperity.
This move was a reality.
There were no egotists
in that era of need.
It was time to pull away
from the illusionary culture
of old world frontiers,
but their progeny
strayed backward.
They crossed cultures.
Our founding fathers
blazoned the trail.
They showed us how to survive
in new frontiers —
an example for us today
to embrace truth
and come out of the world
of confusion.

Frances Garner

FOR THOSE WHO LIKE RIDDLES

it is something that comes from before time.
it is always here (no matter where that is), and it is always there too,
even though sometimes it seems like it must be somewhere else.

it does not go anywhere, but we think that it does.
it does not do anything, but we think that it has.
No matter how many different ways we describe it,
    it stays the same.
Yet when we look around, we think it has changed.

We make interpretations.
Sometimes we think that we need it,
    imagining that we do not have it.
Sometimes we think that we have lost it,
    imagining that we forgot where it is.
These entanglements are interpretations.
it does not depend on how we look at it.
it is the source of interpretations.

We use it even when we are trying to figure out what it is.
When we know what it is, we are it.
it depends on how we look at it.

What is it?

Stefan Pasti

CAPTIVES OF SPRING

Bleak winter now has passed, and we are caught
In the old rhapsodies, the webs of spring!
Bright bands of marigolds will hold us fast,
While daffodils assist. We have not lived
Until this longed-for hour! How sweet the ties
Of fragrant turf and soaring, singing birds!
Wood violets weave a chain of amethyst
Around our hearts in fragile symmetry,
And spider-gossamers in early mist
Entrance our thoughts into their filament.
Warm dawns envelop us — and ropes of rain!
A glistening net of dew, sun-shot, is laid
To keep us here, with spring, and who would go?
We are the eager captives of her whims!

Sylvia E. Niemi

IMAGES OF LOVE

If I should see reflections of your smile
Caught in the eyes of children at their play,
Or mirrored in some joyous incident,
You would be near, in vibrant memory!
If I should hear your voice, as in a choir,
Or whispering angelic tones of peace,
I would rejoice! These February snows
Would melt and gush as in an early thaw.
If I should touch the semblance of your love,
Held by a shining strand of happiness
On agate beaches, where we sometimes strolled,
My joy would be complete, reflecting stars!

Sylvia E. Niemi

TO A BELOVED BROTHER

The skies of silky blue still shine above
Wide fields where goshawks gently dip, then pass,
And where the bob-o-link sings to his love,
Perched on a stem of wild canary-grass.
The sunshine follows rain, just as it should,
And larks sing just as sweetly as before.
The mourning doves coo from the pasture-wood,
As though awaiting your approach once more.
A quiet kind of healing now pervades
Each changing season as we think of you.
Our sorrows leave us as the winter fades,
And summer comes on wings of peace, anew.
    Your spirit hovers near . . . alive, serene,
    To bless us still at each familiar scene.

Sylvia E. Niemi

                The date is today and I sit here alone
            Not sure what to feel but I know what is gone
        The spirit of life and the things that go with it
                    Like the smell of the flowers,
                        The blue of the ocean

                Now it's tonight and I sit here with you
                My body's alive but my soul is dead, too
    Like the spirit of love and the things that go with it
                        Our silent romance,
                    Your ever presence . . .

Candace Coalman

MISERY

This feeling of uncertainty makes my
    heart sick.
I wonder . . . is it plain jealousy . . .
    or is it in some way founded?

Why this irrepressible impulse to cry . . .
    To weep . . . to be sorry for having
Fallen in love?

Is it because of dissatisfaction?
    Or is it because of inconfidence?
Or a deep fear of his insincerity?

And if so . . . why still love him? Why,
    dear God, do I have to love someone
I am so unsure of . . . someone who can't
    prove his professed love except
Through sensuality . . . through his carnal
    desire to devour me?

And what more . . . why do I love him even so . . .
    Despite the fact that all his deeds
Hurt me . . . And his words much more so.

Am I a masochist that I readily accept this
    punishment . . . that I allow him to
Disrespect me and say unworthy words of me?

Why am I so dumb . . . so tonguetied? Why can't I holler back?

Oh! Love, can thy name be Misery?

Then, Misery, Come to Me!

Daisy I. Infante

DOUG . . . LINDA

I am a father
  I have silver hair
    And brown eyes . . .
      With face serene.

I look around
  And see my son . . .Doug
  And the girl he loves . . . Linda

He is handsome
She is lovely
Both are beautiful people.

They are looking at one another
  With soft eyes . . .

He takes her in his arms
  And they kiss

Soon they will be as one
  And there will be

  Joy and Festivity

He is no longer a little boy
She is no longer a little girl

God bless these two people

Douglas A. Rofrano

DOUGLAS ANTHONY ROFRANO, M.D.
Born: Brooklyn, New York; Divorced; Education:
Springfield College, B.S.; Georgetown University
Medical School, M.D.; Occupation: Physician;
Memberships: AMA; American College of
Physicians; Connecticut Medical Society; Con-
necticut Poetry Society; Waterbury Poetry
Society; Awards: Golden Poet Awards, 1985-87,
9 Honorable Mentions, 1984-87; Poetry: 'Nickel
Pickle,' *World Poetry Anthology,* 1987; 'Fishes,'
Our Western World's Most Beautiful Poems,'
1985; 'Rain,' *World's Most Beloved Poems,'*
1984; 'Cheesecake Lady,' *Family Physician,*
1986; Themes: *My poetry is simple word-
photographs, touched with humor. Also a number
of nature poems and play-on-words poems like
"Trible, Trickle, Trickle,"* etc. *I like to write
poems of recollection, as well as spiritual.*

YOU LOVING HER MORE

*In dedication to all siblings of a
favored child.*

Mama, I'm tired, so tired of suffering,
For you loving her more.

Yes, she is my sister and you're just,
Jealous, I don't want to hear any more!

Growing up was a shame, I was always,
The naughty one, and she was your dream.

No matter how I try, it will always be,
Her you're proud of, not me.

But Mama, I want you to know what you,
Loving her more has done for me.

You gave me a life of insecurities,
Unable to feel at ease.

You gave me this feeling of having to,
Prove myself constantly.

You gave me bitterness, that now hurts,
The people who love me.

You gave me impatience, after all,
That's all you had left for me.

But most of all, Mama, you gave me an empty,
Impression of what a mother should be.

So you see, Mama, I'm tired of suffering,
For you loving her more.

Tina Gropper

THE DOOR

I have tried
To build our love
As carefully as if I
Were building the first tree.

Here is something for you and
Here too.
Continually we grow
Into the world that is
Nearest us.

In your love wrap at night
I have dreamt, and yet
I know the soft night —
An opening, like into
The vastness of another room,
Your room, yourself.
All of that must be
A place for me.

And yet the morning, like
A door I don't want to
Go out of.

Thomas Dates

THE OLD INDIAN

I can see
The old Indian, ice
Fishing on the lake —
His hole in the ice
Not big enough for
The monster
On the end of his fishline.
Was it the size of
The hole?
Did he really want
That monster?
No, I think not.
Much too much
For his clan and the tribe.
So he cut the fishline,
And had nothing.
Went fishing in the stars
Of all souls known.

Thomas Dates

WALK IN THE SPIRIT

*If we live in the Spirit;
let us also walk in the Spirit.*
— Galatians 5:25

Let the Spirit of the Lord
be with us.
Let the Spirit dwell
within our heart.
When you seek wisdom
and study the word
of God,
wisdom will come within our souls.
Where there is faith,
knowledge in the Lord,
wisdom will come
and the Spirit of God
will dwell with us forever.

Zora B. Fetner

THE BLACK AND WHITE OF IT

Magpies are you and I,
Ash and ember, a shadow and a star
Under fluorescent lights;
Inertly, we avert Argus-eyes.

Strange it is that you
Of subtle shade and hue
One of Nature's rarest jades,
Must endure criticism undue.

Irony it is that I
Find no quiet night in which
To set my song upon high,
No night in which to shine.

Magpies we are,
You and I,
External opposites,
A shadow and a star.

Sont

CHAIN OF LOVE

Love is a word profoundly felt.
Love is a mystery inspiring dreams.
Love is a dream wished reality.
Love is a life of heavenly bliss.

Love is a possession we long to share.
Love is a responsibility to sacrifice.
Love is a lover who gives his all.
Love is the beloved of all mankind.

Love is an encompassing virtue.
Love is a virtue void of vice.
Yet Love can be vicious and so untrue.

Love is untrue when ego-bred.
Love is selfish when I-oriented.
Love is self-motivated when none else is in view.
Love is a view of disappointments, too.

Love unifies man with everyone.
Love is everything good and sometimes evil.
Love is a representation of the nature of man.

Love is a beauty of unexpressed emotions.
Love is an emotion of variety.
Love is a series of necessities.
Love is the need for companionship.

Love is attachment to friends and relations.
Love is a marriage through eternity.
Love is a chain binding man to man.

Daisy I. Infante

DAISY INOCENTES INFANTE. Born: Philippines, 8-3-46; Married: Rosben R. Ogbac, 1-30-87; Education: Fairfield University, M.A., Communications, 1971; University of Santo Tomas, B.S., Psychology, Magna Cum Laude, 1966, B.A., English, 1965; Occupations: Real Estate, Insurance, Travel, Employment Executive, Waiter, Inventor; Memberships: National Association of Female Executives; American Society of Professional & Executive Women; Lions International, 1977-78; Philippine Chamber of Commerce Secretary, 1985-86; Feature writer & columnist for newsmagazine, 1975-76; *Phillipine News,* 1978-80; VIA Times, 1985-86; Poetry: *Poems of My Youth,* collection, 1982; Other Writings: *My First Twenty Songs,* melody & lyric compositions, 1981; Themes: *All three poems I'm sending are about love and the different feelings that come along with such emotion.*

TO THE SEA

To the sea I go whenever I feel the need. The sea calls to me.
In the darkest of nights, I find its shining lights.
In the harshest of storms, raging strong, I find its quiet strength.

And whenever my heart is sore and aching I turn to the sea.
The sea comforts me.
— In the gentle slapping action of waves touching shore.
— In the salty breath of the sea air.
— In the calming vision of fishing vessels,
  proud navy ships and rowboats drifting by.

To the sea I go to reaffirm the harmonizing ties of birth,
  life and death.
To the sea I return to discover my regeneration and rebirth.
And to the sea, I flee to revitalize my batteries.

And, time and again, I rush back to the sea
  to restore the inner peace lost to me
  but locked inside the treasured depths of the sea.
Thankfully, the sea holds the key to salvation, waiting, just for me.

Dianna Asserson

ALONE

Alone, all alone in the middle of a crowd
Of people scurrying on their self-appointed errands.
"Sorry I'm so rushed but good to see you."
"I'm late for my meeting. Call me tonight."
Brief encounters that cannot pierce the loneliness.

Alone, all alone in the middle of a room
Of friends and acquaintances mingling drinks and gossip.
"I hear the new director is expected tonight."
"Isn't our hostess stunning in red?"
Short encounters that cannot pierce the loneliness.

Alone, all alone in the middle of the forest
Of birds and animals foraging for a livelihood.
"Phoebee, phoebee. Chickadee-dee-dee."
"Cheers. Cheers."
Unintelligible encounters that merely soften the loneliness.

Alone, all alone in the middle of the night
Surrounded by memories and books.
"Open Sesame!" And the King's Treasures appear
To please, to entertain, to inform and console —
Timely encounters that quickly disperse all loneliness.

Arlouine G. Wu

UNTITLED

I've already written everything there is to write —
This I call *the poet's fright.*
I sit & think of an inspiring thought,
a dream escapes & another is lost.
The void of space is vast with knowledge;
But knowledge is often vast space,
  that is void.

My mind is empty, I think of nothing;
I tap my pencil & await for something.
The noise of silence kills my ears,
This I call *the poet's fears.*

John Dowdell

WHAT A WAY TO START

I've never lived in your world,
You've never lived in mine,
Yet it seems somehow I've known you,
In another space and time.

You've said I'm too young for you,
Or that you are too old,
But is that the way you really feel?
Or just what you've been told.

You asked if I'd be habit forming,
I must admit I am,
And have been dropped like a bad habit,
Time and time again.

You say it's just a game to me,
In a way I guess you're right,
The object is to make you feel,
You've made the right choice for the night.

You say I'm a devil,
A wizard's more what I am,
For stars, sparks, and fireworks,
Are there at my command.

And I can make the clock stand still,
Stop its very hands,
And leave you smiling breathless,
When I lead you through my land.

James R. Peterson

THE WAY ONWARD

The road is dry,
The sun is high,
I walk onward.

The air is hot,
Focus on one thought,
Must move onward.

The sky is clear,
Not a sound to hear,
I march onward.

The wind is brisk,
The sun an odious disk,
I go onward.

I walk toward the setting sun,
My journey just begun,
Always moving onward.

Matt Zuck

IN HOMAGE

To Scharansky at the Wailing Wall

I could not admit
such joy to my pen
but you cross the bridge
on your own two feet
two hands for an embrace
the handshake of freedom
reminds one just how far
and honest hope can go
and that a desire fulfilled
is a tree of life.

Zenas

NOTHING NEW

Listen now, as I weave
A yarn as time sifts through the sieve.

On a stormy night as the darkness set
In my bedroom I was met
By a revolutionary revelation.

There I sat immersed in thought,
When I realized what I before had not —
My thoughts were not new!
How could they be?
Out of five billion people
There must be someone else like me!

And so with this thought,
Out went my pride,
For in your own mind there is no place to hide.

Matt Zuck

WALLS

Walls of old anger
Rise like the spectres of dead souls
Who have found no rest
Only calling out at intervals
Across the veil of time . . .
We here remain
Far from any finer world
Encased always in what was
Lost in visions of what cannot be,
We are bound in paper chains.

Mary-Elizabeth Epstein

MY SLEEPING FLOWERS

I'll bank my flowers deep in their beds,
Their nodding, glowing, petaled heads,
Will feed and cover snug with straw,
Where they'll await the spring's warm thaw.

They'll deeply sleep in this dark place,
Hiding here their patterned lace,
Will rest themselves through winter's snow,
Emerge in spring's awakening flow.

I've known their sweetness in the spring,
Their fragrant summer blooms that sing,
And fall's gold, russet colors loom,
That lit a path through winter's gloom.

Who tip-toed in with blanket white
And covered deep their beds so tight,
While lulled to sleep they waited here,
Until the touch of a new year.

I wait in breathless wonder still,
Until they raise their heads at will.
The riot of their blooms, I know,
Will set the waiting earth aglow!

Lucille M. Kroner

DRIFTWOOD

The Sea of Confusion
Rocks me from side
To baffling side
Sloshing, swirling
Tossing me
Against the jagged edges
Of all that I try (to)
But can never hope (to)
Understand
I am the Driftwood
An aimless piece
Of nothing
Guided only by
The Sea
Confusing, always confusing
Aimless me

Stacy Lawson

DEAR LORD

Dear Lord I pray
Bless me this day.
May each hour pass
Brighter than the last.

May everything I do
Be acceptable to You.
In life may I take the right path,
May evil never enter my heart.

To others may I be good and kind,
To their failings may I be blind.
May I learn to give, not only to take
And all that I do be for Thy sake.

May all evil be far from me,
Only the good in life may I see.
Joy may I to others give
Doing all the good while I yet live.

Roslyn Aaron

GOD IS THE ANSWER

When things go wrong
And you feel like crying,
Have faith in God
And keep on trying.

When troubles come
Which you can't take,
Just try to bear them
For the Lord's sake.

When you feel helpless,
Helpless as can be,
Remember the Lord is there
To help you and me.

When you're miserable
You don't have to despair.
Just open your lips
And God will answer your prayer.

Roslyn Aaron

SUICIDAL? DON'T DARE DO IT!

Depressed, feelings of guilt, anger, hurt, suicidal and lost hope?
Don't let the Devil destroy you with His venomous fangs of dope.
Say "No," to all drugs and driving drunk which is like a loaded gun.
Flee temptation and resist the Devil that your battle be won.

Do not let the Devil trap you in a cocoon of self-murder.
Your life is God's precious gift to you —
    not to take by self-murder —
A death so unnecessary to leave behind those so lonely
And sad at heart in a world of emptiness you can fill only.

Open up your Bible and read about sin and Satan's wages.
Do you know that it is written in the Bible's Holy pages
That the very hairs of your head are all numbered? God does love you!
Fall humbly on bended knees and talk to the Lord, for He loves you.

Juanita McIntyre

A PRISONER'S DREAM

Behind these cold, cold iron prison bars is such a lonely place,
But prison bars can't stop me from dreaming of your lovely face.
Oh, how I long to hold you once again in my arms tonight,
Though I know you're far away from me except in dreams tonight.

My only escape from behind these bars is dreaming of you.
Lost in my fantasies of dreams, I will bid this world adieu.
Darling, hand in hand we'll climb the Golden Stairway to the stars.
Then for tonight, I will be free from behind these prison bars.

We'll walk in the beautiful star-lighted Heaven high above.
While passing by the Big Dipper, we will stop and sip of love.
You will be my angel veiled in stardust from the Milky Way.
Cheek to cheek in each other's arms we'll dance 'til the break of day.

Too soon will come the dawn of light that will steal away the stars,
Steal away my dreams, and leave me behind these cold prison bars.
I'll always have your memory of a precious star so bright
That will linger in my beautiful Heaven every night.

Juanita McIntyre

IS THE WORLD A KALEIDOSCOPE
TO ROSEY, THE BAG LADY?

The eyes of the world see a plump girl sad eyes looking around,
But the Blindman knows she's a dreamer with ideas way deep down.

Then they see her friendly smile, uneven teeth and skin,
But he knows she's someone trying to bring light from outside in.

They see reflections of an awkward walk, funny shoes and feet,
But he can hear her paddling to life at another beat.

They see gestures, arms crippled with unexplained motion,
But he feels her palms reaching out with signs of devotion.

They see clothes that must always be yesteryear's design,
He thinks her poverty sounds colorful and only costs a dime.

They see tears and insecurity in her dark pensive eyes,
But he thinks she is brave to be revealing her insides.

They see a girl worn and thrown out to the light of day,
He sees her like jewels in the light giving everything away.

Marcella Ann McDonell

ANTIETAM

The bloodiest battle of the Civil War
Fought at Antietam in three days
Twenty-three thousand lost their lives
Of both the Blue and the Gray.

McClellan discovered Lee's orders
Which around some cigars were wrapped.
Had he acted with vigor and dispatch
Lee's forces might have been trapped.

The Union Army attacked at Bloody Lane
Antietam Creek ran red.
A.P. Hill's arrival was almost too late —
And twenty-three thousand lay dead.

It was here the "Angel of the Battlefield" came
She tended the wounded — Clara Barton, her name.
She rolled up her sleeves, tucked her skirt
    in her waist
Went into the fields, the dying to save.

Many Sharpsburg citizens fled their homes,
Others barricaded themselves in,
To brave the storm of shot and shell
Praying and aiding both sides to win.

Lee's army was forced to retire
A Union victory was won.
As a result of the now-famous battle
The Emancipation Proclamation was done.

Joanna McFarland

A DOG NAMED RAGS

Rags belongs to a man named Ed;
He always goes wherever Ed's led.
Ed is a fisherman tried and true,
And Rags — well, he goes too.
Rags is at home on any boat,
That is, if it's a boat that can float.
He always picks a place to rest
Where he watches the fishermen doing their best.
He chuckles sometimes at the men on board
As they try for the chance to catch one more.
He just lays back and sometimes grins
At the terrible mess their lines get in.
As the boat would pitch, and toss, and turn,
Rags would lay there unconcerned.
For he knows that Ed will take good care
To see that he is happy there.
Whenever he barks they all take heed
To see to Rags and his every need.
His life is easy, and full of fun,
But he is always happy when the day is done.
Rags, in his dreams, sometimes laughs within
As he thinks — "It doesn't take much to entertain men!"

Delva L. Wolfe

I WANT TO BE REMEMBERED

I don't crave a lovely mansion.
I don't care for silver and gold.
I just want to be remembered
When I'm lying dead and cold.

I don't want the tears of thousands.
Of a hymn I'd love the sound.
Praising God while I'm being lowered
Right onto the muddy ground.

And when people talk about me
Let them say I didn't look for gain.
I just lived to thank the Lord
And my life was not in vain.

Roslyn Aaron

ROSLYN AARON. Born: Rangoon, Burma, 10-23-36; Education: Loreto Day School, Matriculation Examination, 1952; Occupation: Secretary, Paul Baerwald School of Social Work, Hebrew University, Jerusalem; Awards: Merit Certificate, Honorable Mention, Golden Poet Award, 1987; Poetry: 'I'll Trust in God,' 'My Family,' *New Voices in American Poetry,* 1987; 'Think and Give,' 'The Bright Side of Things,' 'Don't Walk Alone,' *American Poetry Anthology,* 1988; Themes: *My poetry flows from happenings in my life like religion, love and family, from which I derive much satisfaction.*

A PRAYER'S ANSWER

Dear Lord, help me to write a poem
  To my husband of many years,
To tell him that I love him
  Much more than it appears.
You do not say, I love you, Hands —
  I love you, Eyes — or Knees,
Yet he's as much a part of me
  As any one of these.
You do not say, I like you, Month —
  I like you, Day or Week.
With him not there beside me
  Time's meaningless and bleak.
You do not say, I need you, Sun —
  I need you, Rain — or Air,
And yet the greatest need we have
  Is for someone to care.
And so I'm asking You, Dear Lord,
  Before my lips, one day, You seal,
Please help me to convey to him
  The depth of love I feel.

Louise Grimmett Doughty

HAMMOCK TIME

In my hammock — down by the sea,
  All sorts of thoughts occur to me.
I can become an ocean wave —
  Rising, falling — loathe to behave.
Perhaps I am a cloud up high,
  Drifting lazily through the sky —
An autumn leaf blown by the wind,
  Oblivious to my journey's end.
Oh! the thoughts — the fantasy —
  In my backyard hammock — far from the sea.

Louise Grimmett Doughty

MY BANKER AND MY BROKER

I wonder if they know
  How dear they are to me.
My sons — now all grown up —
  No longer two and three.
Thank Goodness for the memories
  In my heart — now tucked away,
Including all the priceless things
  Little boys do and say.
If I had known the time would fly
  As fast as it has flown,
I would have hugged them twice as much
  'Cause you can't when they're all grown.
I can but watch and beam with pride —
  And that I surely do —
My Broker and my Banker
  No longer three and two.

Louise Grimmett Doughty

LOUISE GRIMMETT DOUGHTY. Born: Buckhead, Georgia, 9-21-19; Married: David Winston Doughty; Education: Mercer University, Macon, Georgia, A.B., 1941; Occupations: Teacher; Homemaker.

MANIPULATION

You arrange it so that no one
else can do it but me.
You arrange it so that if I
don't do it, I'll feel guilty.
Why do you do this to me?
Why must you do this at all?
You say you love me, but I wonder.
You wouldn't do this if you loved me.

Ann J. Rutledge

NOCTURNAL MEDITATIONS

I long to have her in my arms
  The way it used to be;
To melt in her embrace, again,
  And hold her endlessly.

I worshipped her from afar
  Until, at last, we met;
The way I felt when she was close . . .
  I never can forget.

Although I knew my love would last,
  I had to take it slow;
Time would prove that it was true
  And, then, the world would know.

The callous hand of destiny
  Has led her far away;
Many empty years have passed.
  I love her still, today.

I wonder if she, too, despairs
  That we must be apart;
I hope she knows that she, alone,
  Can soothe my aching heart.

Paul S. Strauss

FADE OUT

Love was in the air
A small burning fire
Ignited by fate
A chance to make
Something to last forever

Clouds came in too fast
With strong blowing winds
To put the fire out
And fate passed us by
Without a chance
For us to give it one final try

Fear of being hurt
And losing once more
Gave you all your reasons
For pulling away
And staying apart

The fire is out now
And fate has gone
Alone and confused
I must travel on.

Lisa A. Wehrle

THE TWILIGHT YEARS

Age is akin
to old silver,
Worn a bit,
Perhaps flawed
and tarnished,
But much loved,
Hand-rubbed to
a new lustre.
Elegant and refined
with a beauty
that has weathered
many years.

Barbara Shreder

THE KILLING WATERS

November 5 of '85 is a day we'll remember the rest of our lives!
Torrents of rain fell, rivers — enraged
Overflowed banks on a killing rampage
Ravaged, destroyed, ripped apart, tore asunder,
Moving all in their paths — up, over, under.

Train tracks — like pretzels — twisted and torn;
Homes moved from foundations, wind-carried, thrown.
Trailers disappeared — later were found
Severed and sheared — in trees, in the ground.

Rivers changed courses, topsoil was gone:
Huge rocks where rivers once did run.
Broken concrete, piled in disarray;
Bridges disappeared, found every which way.

A father and son spent the night in a tree;
A car washed off the road — killed were all three.
Hundreds of thousands of animals drowned;
Loved ones swept away — some were never found.

A dam broke, hundreds fled for their lives
A husband, in the water, lost his hold on his wife;
Twin brothers caught on their way home from work;
Four others died there, by a cruel fate's quirk.

Mirrored in every face were shock and disbelief.
Stunned expressions, senses numbed, hearts burdened down with grief.
West Virginians will forever recall
The black Killing Waters of that terrible Fall.

Joanna McFarland

JEALOUSY

Black clouds gathered overhead
Hate and jealousy felt once before had returned
I guess that it had never really left either of us
But now it had risen to the surface

Pounding! Pounding!
Rain hitting the black ground
Splashing down as steam rises, clouding our minds

Hearts unwillingly beat
To the music in the background
As two young females silently stare ahead
Knowing just what the other is thinking — and why

Each wanting the same thing
The one thing neither of them could get
And both thinking the other had it

Accusing words
Long-forgotten sins return
The sweet pain of hate that we all crave
Filled us both

Something that we had built up so very big in our own minds
Had killed a love so strong between friends

It has been so long
The desire has now faded
But silently, silently, the jealousy burns on

Jody Blaney

ON READING JOHN KEATS

But is Beauty Truth?
What am I to think today, my dear John?
Thou who art so far away from the ugliness of
Dirty, tangled hair and bare feet.
Of raucous screamed obscenities, of clenched fists
And ribald laughter.
For these are truth they shout.
Though I prefer your Grecian urn
Oh what am I to think?
When everywhere I turn
That which was wrong is now considered right
Delicacy in love is talked as shame
You are a pretty fusty dame
Who blushes at first kiss
When kisses are what handshakes used to be
Yet I do prefer your trees that never shed their leaves
Your maiden caught by time into eternity
Always her clear shining form
Shall be — my norm
Though modern youth doth take the world by storm.

Elizabeth S. Benoist

NOT EVEN EINSTEIN

Oh man made in infinitesimal image of Almighty God,
Questioning, reaching, fumbling from the sod.
So restless, never satisfied.
At ease.
The world, though beautiful, seems not to please.
Spite of many ventures to be done,
Ignored by you,
As you go wandering through space,
Seemingly successful with agility and grace.
Oh, stay awhile,
Explore no more
For your humanity will shut the door.
In spite of your intelligence and strides
In spite of overwhelming pride
As yet you are but finite man.
Return I pray from afar
Not even Einstein could create the smallest star.

Elizabeth S. Benoist

ELIZABETH SMITH BENOIST. Born: 4-8-01; Widow; Occupation: Writer; Comments: *I really specialize in prose. I have written 4 books, the first of which was "The Dish Ran Away With The Spoon," a cook book. And it seems Silhouettes were quite a recipe in the Middle West.*

YOUR DREAMS

You always hear *If you believe in your dreams,
they will come true;*
but why doesn't it
seem that way to you?
Your dreams are yours
to keep, and you think
they only happen in your sleep,
but that is not always true.
They can be true, if you
just believe in you.
Your dreams are your
future not yet lived.
But will be lived if you
don't let them die.
People always say *Be realistic;*
but your dreams are
from start to finish.
So just remember
your dreams are yours,
and cannot be
anyone else's,
so just believe in your dreams,
and they will come true.
It happened for me,
and I'm sure it will for you.

Amy Barnwell

OUR FRIENDSHIP

Here we are
together again.
We stick by
each other,
through thick
and thin.
By this I know
we are truly friends.
We were apart
but faith brought
us back together
and with that
I know we are
here with each other,
not just now,
but forever.

Amy Barnwell

THE CALL

I dial your number
you're waiting for
my call.
I turn the corner
to sit in the hall.
As you answer
with a polite hello,
I remember all the
love I found for you
so long ago.
And as we talk
the time flies by,
from the first hello,
to the last goodbye!

Amy Barnwell

TO MYSELF I OWE THIS DAY

*Written one lonely Sabbath after
the death of my dear friend,
Mildred.
I had no one to talk to.*

I heard someone softly say
''To myself I owe this day.''
Then I mused in silent prayer,
Dear God, there's suffering everywhere!
When Jesus walked this earthly land
He always gave a helping hand —
In the Bible we cannot find
One single passage or a line
Where Jesus ever turned away
From needy souls He met each day;
The only passage in God's Word
Is when He went alone to be heard
By God, the Father, and for power
To face the ordeal of that hour.
Not one Disciple stayed awake
To help Jesus, and as He spake
''Could you not watch with me one hour?''
In human weakness they began to cower,
And I can almost hear them say,
''To ourselves we owe this day.''

Blanche Bradford Harryman

FOREVER TO BE

Soul is searching to discover, the unique
And oneness of its proximity —
Never quite attaining the totality of sublimity.

We have the majestic mountains to wander —
Deep vast oceans to ponder —
The eternal search for God's meaning —
Man is but a million thoughts —
A millennium of dreaming.

We pass a million souls, and then —
Journey back — to pass again.
Call it fate, or destiny —
This need to set one's own soul free.

Life is but a brief moment in its span —
Encompassing the whole of the universal plan.
To live — to die — and yet! Then —
To live — to be — *just be* — again . . .

Constance (Arthur) Bennett

JUST A LITTLE BIT OF SUNSHINE

Just a little bit of sunshine,
Came in the door today,
It was your smile came shining through,
'Til my heart didn't ache away,
Adoring again and again,
'Til all the ache did melt away,
And the love felt ten times ten,
Glowing like the sunshine,
And our mergered forms did blend.

Janice Wagner Richardson

YOU ARE THE STONE BY THE RIVER

You are the stone by the river
That never washes away.
You are the American flag,
Sign of freedom night and day.

You are the humble oyster
Whose treasure lies within.
You are the inspiration I need
In order to begin.

You are the mountain's highest peak.
You are the fresh, fertile sod.
You are the mystery of one's lifetime.
You are God.

Elizabeth Fugiel

CHAPEL IN THE HILLS

Come take my hand and go with me,
Oh, weary one whom tempest fills,
In search of sweet serenity
Within the chapel in the hills.

What harmony to worship brings!
My longing heart with rapture thrills
As unsung hymns all Nature sings
Within the chapel in the hills.

No temple or cathedral's tower
Compares to God's sweet daffodils.
Tranquility is waiting there
Within the chapel in the hills.

When I'm beset by doubt and fear,
I seek Him by the trees and rills.
His presence always seems so near
Within the chapel in the hills.

Joan Cissom

THE SILENCE OF GOOD-BYE

The silence of good-bye
Lies heavy on our hearts
The darkness of the night
Whispers as we part.

Our dreams now are withering
In the salt of my tears
I can picture all the memories
We made throughout the years.

My heart begs the night
That you will never leave
Please let us continue in the past
In a spell of make-believe.

But I can see your shadow
As you walk across the floor
I can hear the silence of good-bye
As you gently close the door.

Evelyn Dacunha

WHO GAVE ME LIFE!

Some thoughts on paper for my mother
because she means this to me.

To the one who gave me mornings
I am so pleased to gather in the dew
To touch the coolness of an autumn's moment
To wake and breathe in a sunrise;
To linger in thoughts of a day's past;
To the one who gave me my afternoons
Where I can longingly stretch with a warm summer's wind
Where I can witness the season's bounties
Where I can play in the sounds of a mid-summer's folly
To taste the sweat of brow from hard work;
To the one who gave me my evenings
Where I can melt into a sunset;
Or be swept away with a winter's storm
Where I can share the sounds of nature settling in
And capture my day in poems and prayers
And reflect against my own shadows
To the one who gave me my nighttimes
When my heart opens to blossom and bring in the darkness
The sounds are your comfort; the memories; your rock
To know that morning is on its way to chase this solitude
To the one who gave me my life
To live my mornings, my afternoons, my evenings and my nights
I give back to you the best of any of these hours
My gift; to say thank you and I love you;
For giving this all to me . . . who gave me life!

Lucky Rimpila

TURN IT INTO SOMETHING ELSE

Somewhere in this life of mine; through the windows of my years
Someone once said ''hold it back''; for nothing comes of tears

I played this game that hurt so; the feelings couldn't hide
They tore and ripped and washed away, this sense I knew as pride

Can I be true to others, when I stand and lie to myself?
Of feelings that don't show easily; locked upon some shelf

Turn it into something else; easy enough to be said
I just might turn it around; and let the feelings all be dead

Then, you can sit and hold your tears; if there are any to hold
And I'll lie back in open space, and watch to see how bold

I despise this hurt inside me; I hate when it can't be used!
Leave me alone, to one who's my own; as these feelings become abused

In this life which I so cherish; it's me and whatever is mine
I now know a truth; I now know a friend; it's sweet life that I find

You consider me a failure; for giving to emotions so fair
Someday look back, consider the fact; a failure because I care

I can leave with this feeling; a feeling not from above
A feeling we must give ourselves; to share with those we love

I back from you into new life; stand tall and swallow this pride
Turn and walk from you proudly; with tears on my cheeks from inside

Lucky Rimpila

THE BRIGHT, GOLDEN, TOMORROW OF FOREVER

What is the color of your eyes (and
   Don't go to Europe on business before
We say, I love you —)
Too many years lapse;
Of confused segments, into maturity.

The sailing ships of time
Pass us from that day, with your brother, we met
And were younger than we are (— at 52/53 years —
As serious parents; respecting marriage —)

Now is the today of our contentment
And we made the commitment of
Desire (in mutual empathy of
Direct contact enactment, integrity.)

The years together will bring us the
Months that betray our hope for each
Moment in aspiration where
The transparency of the future
Ages symmetrically, for the older, yet
Bright, golden, tomorrow
Of forever.

Geneve Baley

IT

The Mystery of Love

If one can't define ''it''
Why should its power be illustrated?
All we fell for its pit
Since the arcane world was for it created.

What pristine Eve embraced but forbiddenly bit
Theorists ravaged with a mystery of their wit
Since Satan rebelled against its divine writ
And the Lamb made human atonement for it.

Where the wild Adriatic washes the dormant skulls of old
And yields Rimini's shore radiant of gold
The genial stroke of the love-besotted Francesca
Restored its status quo *di novo moto*
Crying not in a sheep's clothing vendetta
But with the storm and stress of the romantic motto:

Why that which is the source of so much joy
Becomes the cause of so much deep sorrow?
Knowing no way out of this existential decoy
Except ''learning to love'' being the measure to follow.

This is the activity which destroys all anxiety
For separateness is the ruin of all humanity
Keeping love from bearing men's harmony
And then their ultimate union with divinity.

Franco Boni

Anthony's Nose, from Iona Island.

LOVE IS UNIVERSAL

We celebrated 31 years of married bliss on 7-15-87.
He died on 8-3-87 from a massive coronary.

Love is universal from your heart to mine
I'm glad you love me for I love you all the time
We may have our quarrels and spats as all lovers do
But when we make up I love you more it's true
I wouldn't want to be without your love
A love that was meant to be
A universal love God's given us, a love for you
and me
So I send my love this Valentine's day to my love
Who was created by God above
This man who loves me in his own way tho'
Impatient at times
I wouldn't want anybody else, Paul Whaley you are
mine.

Betty R. Whaley

MY EVERYDAY VALENTINE

I love him in my heart as a special person
For whatever he does, he does it with a purpose.
In the night, sitting at his side in the dark
He's the one who has my love, as I give him my heart.
I'll love him, forever, as my very best friend
As this lady will always be standing behind him.
In the arms of one another as we hold each other close
With a tender kiss, a gentle hug, as whispers are spoken.
Bonded by the trust, we talk and share our deepest feelings
Love has taken the hands of two human beings.
In the dreams of the rainbow, we are everlasting lovers
For he is the man I'll forever cherish like no other.
As the hopes of tomorrow, we take today as it happens
Believing as one, for togetherness, is the song sung within.
In the eyes of God, His magical words are spoken
As the mysteries of life endure, never to be broken.
The candlelight softly reveals as he makes love to me
Finding my pot of gold, being filled with peace and serenity.
In my eyes, tears fall, as one plus one equals us
He means more to me than anything ever thought of.
I love him for the love he gives is all mine
Cupid made my baby an everyday Valentine.

Debra R. Moellers

COMMONWEALTH AVENUE — 1930

The pulse of the city beats more leisurely here,
Along these rows of fine old houses
Where one meets a faded sort of gentility —
These walks and rows of trees between the ways,
These shining cars and liveried escorts,
These dignified stone fronts
And windows like sightless eyes —
No blaring note of youth — no clashing cymbals
Shatter its unruffled calm;
Only an old man sitting on the sunny sidewalk,
With pinwheels turning in a basket,
And gay balloons float stiffly from a fence.

Doris E. Woolley

LEGACY

A heartbeat day by day, the breath that is here
for such a short stay

In so little time with much to do, living and
experiencing life before we are through

For what we do while we are here, will help us
learn year by year

And when the beat stops and the breath is gone,
there will only be the memory of us that continues on.

Andrew L. Phillips, Jr.

ANDREW LEONARD PHILLIPS, JR. Pen Name: Ieom; Born: City of Yonkers, New York, 11-11-46; Married: Patricia, 1-17-87; Education: Westchester Community College, Criminal Justice, 1975-76; New York State Bureau for Municipal Police Academy, 1982-83; Occupation: Law Enforcement Officer; Memberships: Federation of Police; Putnam Valley Police Benevolent Association; Served with the United States Army, 1966-69; United States Air Force, New York Air National Guard, 1981-87; Honorable discharges from both branches; Poetry: 'Patient Steps,' 'Muse,' 'Forbearance,' *American Poetry Anthology,* 1988; Themes: *Themes in my poetry come from every aspect of life, from the simple beginning to a most infinite growth. For that of past history, present accomplishments and futuristic goals. But, including our own personal wants, needs and desires.*

THE WORLD

I dread to think of nuclear war,
    Which will end the world to nothingness.
If we are smart to make thermonuclear bombs,
    We should be smart not to end the world.

We have explored the world as beautiful,
    And have safely landed on the moon.
We are sending space probes to other planets,
    The last frontier of our constant exploration.

The world is our home,
    Beautiful to look at from space,
Where we shall build a space station,
    And even colonize the moon.

Our exploration rewards us with scientific wonders,
    We all reap its material benefits,
The harvests of our minds are not denied,
    So we shall have the abundance of our lives.

But for the sake of peace and love,
    And harmony in our human relations,
Let us tear down the barriers dividing us,
    And perceive the world as one home under God.

Rolando L. Boquecosa

WEDDING DAY

The love between you and me
Is as great and mighty as the sea.
As long as we have each other,
We'll never need another.
Oh, how those wedding bells tell
Of our special feelings that swell
With every breath that we take
And each move that we make.
Brightly does shine the sun
As you and I become one.

Beth Hamilton

APOLOGY OF LIBERTY AND JUSTICE FOR ALL

Dedicated to all martyrs through the ages in our U.S.A.

What are my friends in good ol' U.S.A. . . .
Liberty and justice for all,
It's the blood and sweat of many a good name
During hardships of weather, they stood tall . . .

Yet, why martyrs fight and stand
To keep our banner clean and honest.
Liberty and justice must demand
That we honor our ancestors best.

They fought for this good land,
Let's not stain these garments brave,
Breaking golden rules, making it sand,
When such hearts brought us to save.

So give to all those who work hard.
Their just banner in our land,
Sweet rewards of what they want,
Liberty and justice for all, we demand.

Alfonso Te Rodriguez

The Hon. Seaman

ALFONSO ENRIQUE (TE) RODRIGUEZ.
Born: Mayaguez, Puerto Rico, 2-27-36; Married: LuCena Avis Rodriguez; Education: High school graduate; Military courses 1956-1960; Reflexology, 1973; Scientific massage, 1975; Occupations: U.S. Navy petty officer, 8 years; Warehouseman; Memberships: U.A.W., 23 years, General Motors Parts Division; Awards: Letter awards from Mayor of Baltimore and now Governor of Maryland, William D. Schaefer, 1984-1987; Poetry: 'The Gift of a Mother, 'America's Rat Race,' 1984; 'Apology of Liberty & Justice,' 1985; 'A Sailor To Be,' 1987; 'Thanksgiving Anthology,' *Veterans Publications,* 1985; Themes: *I like to write poetry that is logical, based on experiences since my early youth till my late years.*

PRECIPITATION

The spring rain soaks into my soul
As I walk in the April showers
Of my mind.
The worms lie at my feet,
Drowning in their own stupidity;
The new leaves have turned
Their backs to the world;
And I am drenched
To the skin.
I shiver in the breeze,
Longing to be wrapped in
My childhood securities.
Mother, hold me to your
Warm, gentle heart,
Ease my sorry state of mind
With your milk-and-cookie love.

Nancy Martindale

IMAGES AND IMAGINATION

Lost in the twilight
Of my mind
Searching for a secret
I'm just hoping to find.

Sitting in front of the mirror
Looking for a friend
I look into my own eyes
And I start to pretend.

Caught in a dream
I wish that I could stay
But down come my tears
And all my dreams are washed away.

Standing in the tears
Pooled around my feet
Running from my fears
I'm just hoping I will meet.

Still comes tomorrow
And gone is today
I will go on living my life
As just a character in a play.

Evelyn Dacunha

YOUNG ARTIST

Recognition . . .
 I need it!
Oh, to hang my work
 in fame . . .

While "every art museum"
 . . . dusty
 . . . old
 . . . musty
only holds
 Rembrandt!

Linda G. Rhea

WARTIME SPIRITS

Secrets ride the storm
As Johnny grabs his gun
The summer was mighty long
But Johnny didn't have any fun.

No answers are hidden in the wind
All is over and done
No reasons could be found
As Johnny laid down his gun.

The silver bullet
Marks the end of pain
Johnny has laid down his life
His blood, sweat, and tears are mixed with rain.

Johnny's not coming home alive
His name has been added to the list
Lost in the hell of war
He sure will be missed.

Silence can be golden
And rules are often broken
As Johnny's casket is lowered
No words can be spoken.

Brother Billy cries the night
Mama, she suffered an attack
As I look out the car window
I see Johnny coming back.

Evelyn Dacunha

BIBLE HISTORY CLASS NOTES

How can I sit here and write
As if this were an ordinary night?
You kissed me!

Suddenly, at a most surprising time and place.
Tonight you appear so calm, composed,
Attentive and normal, at ease.

What are you writing, thoughts like these?
Are you thinking how you kissed me
Or are your thoughts on history?

You look so calm, so stable.
I'm so shaken emotionally, unable
To turn my thoughts to the Pharasies.

Does my heart beat audibly?
Now the thrill of it must show
If they look at me now, they'll know.

It's too soon
To shake the magic of a moonlight night
That came on a windy afternoon.

You've kissed me many times before
But it was fantasy
Oh the difference and delight of reality!

This time it was me!

Betty B. Pruett

AUTUMN

When leaves are ablaze with colors
Russets, oranges and gold;
And trees stand out in the skyline
Tall and brave and bold;

When squirrels are hurrying, chipmunks scurrying
Among the fallen leaves,
Gathering nuts and berries
To store against winter's freeze;

When the sun begins its northerly path,
A round harvest moon turns orange,
A million twinkling stars array
The sky in heavenly plume;

When Jack Frost starts nipping at the vines,
And pumpkins strange faces wear,
Autumn has arrived at last,
And winter snows will soon appear.

Joanna McFarland

AND FOR ME, YOU DIED

I picked up a card Lord, and as I read its
reply, how You stretched out Your arms, and
for me, You died!
Overwhelmed with much sorrow, I cried out
Your name, Lord, forgive us! We caused You
much pain!
How much do You love me? This card implied.
This much, You said, and stretched out and died!
Whenever I look at the cross, Oh Lord, my
reply, the immensity! Your love, I can never
deny!
A reminder, it be, of Your love for me! Shall
I display of the cross, for others to see!
Remember shall we, Your love not to hide, display
of the cross! And for me, You died!

Carleen Y. Atkins

THE WISHING PLACE

Far beneath vast heavenly skies in shades of powder blue
  Fleecy soft and light in the mist appears a cloud or two
Our warm sun reflecting light in his own time and way
  Spreading light an eternal distance creating a bright day
Sunny rays of warmth reach out reviving gardens we grow
  Yards of greenery impressing beautiful blossoms we know
Thriving for perfection with rain and gentle drops of dew
  Tender care makes a garden grow, reaping what we sow is true
Delicate miracles relate to the splendor of nature's view
  God given beauty to precious plants that we all love so
An assortment of colors with fragrant flowers so sweet to smell
  Surrounding and enhancing the mystery of our old wishing well
Encased in faded red brick with a shingled worn roof to match
  A rope frayed with age although existing waters still deep and blue
Memories of wishes gone by reminds me proper credit is due
  So if you'd like, choose a colorful bouquet to bring luck to you
Then drop a coin in waters of blue and make a wish come true.

Lee Dennis

THE DOLL MAKER

Pretty dolls of all kinds sit happily and politely in a row
  With smiles of pink, eyes so bright and faces all aglow
Beautiful hair softly shining with braids and gentle curls
  Waiting quietly and patiently for the touch of a little girl
These beautiful dolls are so precious, especially made you see
  By a doll maker that put her complete heart and soul in these
Love was tenderly placed with every stitch in every single doll
  Gentle patience and timeless hours generously shared with them all
One doll dressed in overalls with love left over in her to store
  A surprising delight to the cute little girl that lives next door
Angelic Cupid dolls with dimples, dresses, lacy bonnets and bows
  Delivered to Santa himself for little girls to cherish and know.

On holidays all the girls in the family received a pretty doll
  Repeating they're never too old for dolls, they treasure them all
These range from Wee Blinks with a cute little turned up nose
  To Oatmeal Cookie, Watermelon Slice, Candy Cane and Mandy Jane
From dolls of Cupcake Corner to all the cuties from Lollipop Lane
  With a few exceptions of all the dolls that gladly wait in a row
The doll maker adopted the first one made and the collection did grow
  Crystal Lee adorned in peach with party bows in her long brown hair
Vanilla Jean in shades of pink, soft blonde hair and oh so very fair
  Grape Jelly decked out in purple and green, top seller a few weeks ago
With love on their faces they share a secret only the doll maker knows.

Lee Dennis

THE EPITAPH

Down in the land where men are men, and lonely rides alone,
Upon a creek bank, dusty dry, I found an old tombstone.
The summer sun and winter cold, had made the letters fade,
And wind blown dust, from somewhere west, half hid it where it laid.

I sat beneath a cedar tree, and thought of times gone by,
And of the man, down in the ground, and how he came to die.
The dirt and dust I brushed aside, and read the faded poem,
The message there was crystal clear, a story told in stone.

''In this hard rock country, lies a man who's buried deep,
His hat's still on his bald spot, his boots still on his feet.
This man was not an outlaw, nor famous, so to speak,
He was just a cowboy, who drowned in this creek.''

''His old friends put him in this grave, dug it six feet deep,
Said some verses o'er him, then laid him down to sleep.
A man judged by his cared-fors, not by his defeats,
Was this well-liked cowboy, who drowned in this creek.''

I sat the stone upon the grave, and slowly walked away,
Soundly sleeps, the swimless one, awaiting Judgement Day.
Will any cry, when I shall die, when Death my soul shall keep?
Like this simple cowboy, who drowned in this creek.

T. R. Stephenson

PAUSING TO WONDER

I pause on a rock, as a waltz of leaves
Rustles and whispers through my thinking place,
Where, I wonder, why can't a world that grieves
Give each identity and strength to face
What is, as those in the velour of night
Await the choir for their Requiem Mass,
Then seek Resurrection's promise to light
Stumbling steps down the road where all must pass,
Stripped, humble in petitioning array,
Pleading God's grace for everlasting day.

Grace K. Pratt-Butler

213

YOUR SECOND LIFETIME

Your second lifetime! Oh how blessed
    To be among your friends.
How glad I am you passed that crest
    Where many another ends.

If I could give to you long life
    I'd add a touch of bliss,
With work to do, but never strife.
    Just diligence. Take this.

I'd give to you a life that's gay
    The merriest on earth.
Reach out for it and it will stay.
    For happiness, take mirth.

Had I but known you long ago
    When you were still a boy
I'm sure the twinkling eyes I know
    Were laughing then. Take joy.

Faith, truth, and beauty never wait
    Upon a foreign shore;
When love lies waiting at your gate
    Love's plentiful. Take more.

It's not within my power to give
    The things I wish to see.
If all my wishes are to live
    Oh love, I pray, take me!

Betty B. Pruett

JUST YOU

I've been waiting to meet just you
For an eternity
I never did go out and look
I knew our time would be.

I used to ask the Lord above
How will I know it's real?
The answer was as silent as
The knowing that I feel.

But what if I love one who's cold,
Who's too afraid of pain,
Afraid to love because he fears
His heart will bleed again?

You do not question butterflies
Within a safe cocoon.
You do not ask the sunset now
If there will be a moon.

As surely as you know a heart
Can see and hear and think,
It feels and tastes, and it will know
When thirst is quenched by drink.

You'll know when God has answered you
And these two hearts have met
They cannot fail to recognize
His perfectly matched set.

Betty B. Pruett

NO POT OF GOLD

A pot of gold
    was what I sought,
My bare feet chilled
    By the cold wet grass;
On the meadow's mist,
    Hung the rainbow's arc;
My eyes peered back,
    Like mirrored glass.
This spectrum, is just
    A dream, I thought;
My heart's hope sank,
    No pot of gold!
The colors danced
    A widening path;
Not leprechauns,
    As I had been told!

L. D. Moore

HIDDEN FOOTPRINTS

I saw a man's firm heelprint
    in the soft earth
And felt inconsolable grief,
Beside it the starkest
    daisy lay,
White, against the brown leaf.
Center of yellow, bright
    as the sun; and
Tears flowed, like riverlets
    from a fathomless spring.
I wondered even then,
What is this hidden
    personal pain?

L. D. Moore

LOVE SONG

His love doth adorn me from head to toe.
He's wrapped me in fine linens with
sandals on my feet. He plaits my hair
upon my head and kisses my cheeks of
rosy red. His glory shineth upon even
me. The love of my life he shall be.
His love is like the mountains high
and as swift as the rivers nearby.
In the valleys is his love nest, for
it is fertile and bringeth forth good
fruit. There his seed is cast and
brings forth fruits meet at last.

The seed springs forth and gives life
new of course. He holds me near upon
his breast and whispers of love, I am
blessed. My lover saw me in my
distress and cast his love of righteousness
in warm caress and did not detest,
but lifted me in favor for all who
might test. My shame is gone, replaced
with righteousness from his throne.
My lover saw me in all of my distress.
Instead of scolding me about this
worldly mess, he drew me to his breast,
and whispered gently, ''You are blessed.''

Jan Brown

THE LAST RAIN

Crops had been buried where planted,
No funerals required,
A falling twig's small puff of dust
Punctuated finality.

Farmers' prayers . . . curses . . . silence.

Noon became night.
Cumulo-nimbus clouds clapped hands:
Boom! Vroom! Babba-boom!

Plish-plosh, ploop-sloop, splish-splash,
And the rains came.

Ta-ta-tum, ta-ta-tum, ta-ta-tum,
How the rains came!

Countless emissaries of changing shape
Merged into a shapeless change.

Ta-ta-tum, ta-ta-tum, ta-ta-tum,
Ta-ta-tum, ta-ta-tum, ta-ta-tum.

This *splitter-splattering,*
Pitter-pattering
Drumbeat of devastation
Transformed arid anguish
Into sepulchral slime.

George B. Williams

YOU AND I

You splash your face in sunlight
To set your heart atune.
I bathe my face in ebon night
Beneath a gibbous moon.

You traipse in a lonestar day
For one & all to see.
I flit in shadows gone astray
From any company.

You are friend so often to many,
Either at work or play.
I, for friends, just haven't any
To lighten up my day.

People polkadot your landscape,
While mine's a barren stretch.
You frolic with many a form & shape,
And I am a lonely wretch.

George B. Williams

DEATH

Death is black
It tastes like whiskey
It sounds like a soft breeze,
And it smells musty.
It looks like an empty chair
And it feels like a broken heart.

Jacqueline Wirtz

214

COUNTRY BOY IN CONCRETE

A full moon rises, over trees, where sleepy birds sit quiet,
Up in a charcoal sky it shimmers, casting down its light.
A luminescence circle round, its full face crossed by clouds,
And somewhere on a mountain path, the hunting cry of hounds.

Of course the arc lights hide from me, all except my dreams,
The only sky I see is steel, a rusty faded creme,
And bars of steel, divide my moon, and cast a shadowed stripe,
Across a moonface, wet with tears, without a cloud to wipe.

Oh God, I miss the mountains and the rivers and the creeks,
The armadillos, rattlesnakes, and turkeys when they cheep,
Red granite rocks, caliche dust, and limestone's snow white chalk,
My body's here, my soul is there, where lonesome spirits walk.

The sparkly stars are there I know, although to them I'm blind,
On steel strung stalks, the arc light shines, while beauty hides behind.
When locked doors slide and flashlights pick, my body for their count,
They do not know, I've slipped away, I'm hunting with the hounds.

T. R. Stephenson

STRANGERS

One day I met a stranger in a wood;
A man with signs of age upon his face, his hair like snow.
Dark glasses hid his eyes. He held on leash a shaggy dog,
His other hand a pipe with fragrant smoke.

I leaned against an ancient oak and wept —
For days of flying feet that always ran;
For perfect legs, for friends who'd turned away,
For dancing nights that would not come again.

"Why do you weep?" I heard, and turned to go.
Then glanced up at a craggy face, lean muscular physique,
And two strong legs. He raised the hand that held the pipe.
"May we sit down?" I nodded, then sat at once upon a log.
He too; the collie lying quietly at our feet.

I smoothed the skirt which hid my bandaged knee and ugly braces.
We sat in friendly silence for a time. Then like a springtime flood
I poured out my unhappiness and grief. He listened silently,
With now and then a word of sympathy. Then said,

"You have no cause to weep. You see the sky, the ocean spray.
You watch the colors of the sunset glow, but I . . ."
I gasped, and touched his hand, made all aware that loneliness
And need, a mutual love of nature, had brought us to this place.

At last I understood. No longer strangers now, we walk together,
Loving life. For I can use his strong, straight legs —
          And he my eyes . . .

Vivian S. Flannery Dees

ANALOGY ON LIFE

We are spindles spinning in a lathe,
Suspended between live Heaven and dead earth.
The Machinist knows that tools are sharp
Of edge to turn the spindles true,
Checks the length and sets the template,
Forming us to His blueprint.
But if the spindle-forgings are of
Stronger temper than His lathe tools,
Disaster comes and we are lost.

John F. Koons

LORD THEY ARE ONLY WATCHING ME

No matter how much you dance and shout
  our friends will see what it's all about,
They never read God's word you see,
  Lord they're only watching me.

The lost and the lonely are there
  some are hungry with nothing to wear,
They never heard salvation is free,
  Lord they are only watching me.

The lady at the well never thirsted again
  Jesus wrought miracles they could not explain.
Those around us want to believe,
  Lord they're only watching me.

Edward Hogendorn

SHOUTS OF HONOR

        I'm on the brink of all the worlds.
Things they rise to the occasion
And let all those who stand in God's grace
Remove themselves from the wars that we wage.
        Divide and conquer the romantic fools
Who hope that one day the meek shall triumph.
Coming forth in all their glory, shouts of honor, manly claims.
And inherit the Earth.
        I never ran away from words
That made my will bend to the thoughts
That would have shadowed a glowing spark.
Inside myself a burning passion fire.
        I need a friend who won't be long
In coming to the rescue of a falling form.
But who to the good, resemble traces,
With bright grasping hands.
        I love you all, I cry aloud
To everyone, who has lost their way.
And thoughts become so crystal clear.
On hallowed ground, I tell you now, I love you all.

Anthony John Ciccariello III

GRANNY

There's no one quite like my favorite granny
Memories of a lifetime in every cranny
A houseful of kids and nary a pot
Just Doris and Norman, Wayne and Dot
Herbert and Kenneth, Mona and Fred
Keith and three or four to a bed
Depression stew to clean the fridge
Couple of squirrels from up the ridge
Plates full of biscuits that vanish from sight
Kids with fever through the night
Houseful of boys in a time of war
If you counted just money they'd come up poor
But the hand of the woman who taught them life
Through ninety years of work and strife
Shaped their minds and guides them still
Through lives that began in the Ozark hills

Phil H. Garton

THOUGHTS ALONE

Mem'ry's upstairs windows
Open too easily.

I conceived, believed, achieved
Total aloneness.

Perhaps I see it in the daring darts
Of a reckless skylark,
The pale plumes of a distant chimney,
The utterly peopleless landscape.

Perhaps I smell it in the faint aroma
Of the newly mown hay,
The pleasingly sharp odor of cinnamon
From an untended kitchen,
The haunting fragrance of early lilac
From a singular bush.

Perhaps I feel it in the rough texture
Of my window sill,
The gentle caress of a vague zephyr,
The coolness of a lonely tear
Coursing down my cheek.

Perhaps . . .

George B. Williams

TWO TURTLEDOVES

Two turtledoves were sitting in a tree,
Talking a language of their own,
Discussing the fact of true loves,
Discussing the fact of true freedom!

Yes, ''We're so lucky with our love,''
''No responsibility as God feeds us,''
''No cage of bars to confine us,''
''Gives us freedom to fly forever!''

Two turtledoves flying from tree to tree,
Landing for a moment upon a limb,
To pick a leaf and pick their feathers,
Before their journey to another county!

Two turtledoves all preened and ready,
With no school and with no meetings,
With no clothes and with no laundry
Find only happiness on four wings!

Two turtledoves with four wings,
See the cities with all their people,
''Why we wonder are they so busy?''
''Leaves no time for feeling free!''

Two turtledoves taught us a lesson,
To respect God and to find time,
For relaxation and feeling freedom,
As four wings go sailing by!

Doris Burleigh

THE TEST PILOT

Look out Sky!
I've got wings and I like to fly.
I want to explore that ocean of blue
To see if what I heard is true.

Today I left the earth behind
Wondering what I might find
As I sailed on silver wings
Dreaming of a hundred things.

I danced between fingers of sunshine
As I continued to climb and climb
Leaving the clinging bonds of earth
Passing future worlds in birth.

With the clouds I played hide-and-seek.
Passing upward I took a peak
As I shot like a bullet from view
Where never even an eagle flew.

I slipped into the chambers of space
Leaving a trail of snow-white lace.
I topped the windswept height
Into a world filled with light.

I felt — Free! Free! Free!
Then I wondered where Heaven could be.
To reach it I must choose the better part
Heaven begins in each willing heart.

Dr. Charles Haggerty

CHARLES EDWARD HAGGERTY. Born: Fairmont, West Virginia, 9-8-13; Married: Lenore Dowden, 1979; Education: Brigham Young University, A.B., 1939; M.A., 1945; University of Illinois, M.S.L.S., 1949; Ph.D., 1950; Occupation: Library administrator and consultant, Genealogist, Historian; Memberships: American Library Association, Illinois Library Association; Poetry: *I Remember,* 1975; *I Am Law,* 1987; 'How Precious,' *American Poetry Anthology,* 1986; 'These Things I Hold,' American Poetry Association, 1987; Themes: *Love and home, nature, spiritual, inspirational, philosophy of life, children, history, social problems*

AWAKEN

How many live without living,
Without dying they die.
They see without seeing,
They do not hear. Do they try?

Their eyes are not open,
They miss the beauty of earth.
Their spirits have not awakened
To the symphony of birth.

Life can be full of joy,
Even death has much to give.
The challenge of life is to awaken
And really learn how to live.

Dr. Charles Haggerty

MARCH

March comes racing
Across the land
With great gusto,
Tossing sky high
The startled birds,
Tangling streamers of sunshine
Among the swelling buds
Of golden forsythia,
Sweeping away the cobwebs
Of languid winter,
Teasing the sleepy trees
To awaken,
And, parting the clouds,
Lets earth behold
The sun and sky
Looking at her with
Smiling eyes of blue.

Dr. Charles Haggerty

THE SON OF LIBERTY

She was the Lady Liberty
Built by the French for
The land with an island
Off the coast of New York
What a statue she was
Standing in the new world
Passing greetings to the
Viewers with the hopes of
Space to live and green
Grass to play in for the
Young and old
Years of life for the Lady
Had passed when a boy was born
As he grew
He began to look like
His mother's son and
Stated with his success
It could be done with
Hope and hard work
And the birth of new ideas
So, blue suede shoes was
One of Elvis Presley's songs
''The Son of Liberty''

Grave Yard Moss

THE RIVER

Where rock and water oft collide, and cool mist fills the air
Reckless men do pit themselves 'gainst the river's dare
Where peaceful calm can quickly change into a swirling rage
And trap an unsuspecting man within her frothy cage

Why is it men feel they must, force the river's hand
Leave their wives and families, the safety of the land
Drive their rubber chariots through jagged rock and foam
Dashing thoughts of all their cares, kids and jobs and home

Life is like this too, you know, like the changing stream
Changing from a restful sleep into a frightening dream
Hurtling down between the rocks, that tear now at your flesh
Changing back to peaceful calm, where rock and water mesh

I think men seek, at times the gorge, the power of its white
To make their lives seem smooth and calm, against the river's might
To make each day an eddy, apart from raging stream
Drifting them back to start anew, breathing life into their dreams

Phil H. Garton

PHIL H. GARTON. Born: Twin Falls, Idaho, 9-16-46; Married: Maureen Hayden, 6-27-70; Education: University of Arkansas, Air Traffic Controller; U.S. Navy in Vietnam, 1966-68; Occupation: Owner, insurance and investment company; Themes: *I like to write about the outdoors. I am also very interested in characterizations of people, and am currently working on a collection of these that is a composite sketch of the many interesting and humorous people in my community.*

SWEETNESS

You once possessed an undying love for me
But somehow . . . I was too blind to see
For, your love was quite genuine and true
Being too stubborn to admit that I truly loved you too

Due to an unborn child, I caused you humiliation and great pain
Gave no support of love and no financial gain
I robbed myself of the joy of a birth and the care of infancy
A loss I shall regret with great intensity

But alas, I came to the realization
That God's gift of life is truly a compensation
My heart finally opened to express a multitude of love
That which God intended from heaven above

However, my desire to love and care came a bit too late
Now, someone else has the keys to my gate
I can only cry tears of sorrow because of my great loss
And just maybe, I can help someone else from paying this terrible cost

But I pray every day that my family returns to me
For, I would love and cherish them throughout all eternity
I know that to love someone who truly loves you
Brings peace, joy, love, and understanding that will always be true

Larry E. Watkins

THE MAN ON CALVARY

With worry and distress in my pathway
 I could not find a real purpose in life,
danger at every bend in the road
 my every effort brought strife.

Everything in nature wanted to speak
 my heart was heavy and hard as stone,
voices everywhere tried to be heard
 bitter tears came, I felt so alone.

In despair I came to the end of each day
 I stood trembling, my heart full of fear,
suddenly I saw footprints in the sand
 drops of blood on the pathway everywhere.

On the brow of the hill gathered a crowd
 loud voices filled the air, *crucify, crucify,*
helpless to raise a hand in his defense
 accepting the penalty he chose to die.

Sin in my heart lay bare at his gaze
 my heart was overwhelmed as he spoke,
I fell on my face, a heart full of remorse
 I heard words that gave me hope.

I heard another voice, *remember me* he cried
 the answer was like music in my soul,
this day in my kingdom thou shalt be
 spoken by the man *Jesus* who died on Calvary.

Edward Hogendorn

THOUGHTS ON POWER OUTAGES

Power outage, not an uncommon thing, yet, the rhyme, or reason
can scarcely be explained.
Someone, somewhere with a pen and a form decided that today would
be a day to conserve electrical energy.
Without choice you save energy too as you sit in darkness.
You are all alone, alone with your fears as every noise is magnified.
The only saving force is the light from the outside sun.
Its beams trickle in and fill your soul with warmth
as they dance about the room.
As minutes and seconds pass away, each seems like hours.
No television, no radio, now it is only you, you and your conscience.
There are rooms too dark to explore, and happenings not questioned
yet hardly understood.
This forced darkness seems evil, there is virtually nothing
you can do but sit, sit, sit, and wait. Wait for what?
You chose a window seat, for this brought you more in tune with
the outside world, and its saving sun,
Yet, now the beams are dim, and unceasingly fading away, ever away.
The day will soon be evening and your living world will die again,
and fade away to sleep.
It is now time you do the same.
Drift away to a slumberland,
a land that is only filled with your thoughts,
your visions and dreams as lofty or as low as they may be.
In your dreams, if they are like mine,
you will probably see a brighter sky,
a fun-filled day with voyages and visions yet to explore.
Never again in this terrifying darkness,
for as long as you shall sleep.

Cynthia L. Gardner

JUST ME AT MY POETRY

Again it is time.
A penny for your thoughts, you say.
But inflation, I laugh.
Now they are a dime.

You shrug as if to say Who knows
As I pace about the room.
But in my mind ideas are forming.
Shall it rhyme or be polyphonic prose?

Sweet inspiration
I do call unto thee.
Why so slow?
Such hesitation.

Finally I sit,
Pen poised to strike.
In my mind the words emerge,
But how do I make them fit?

A whistle cuts the air,
And I glimpse your questioning movement.
But I make no gesture that I will fetch the tea,
So you stalk away, hands thrown up in despair.

When you return, at me you scream.
What's with you? Can't you hear?
But you should know my habits well.
It's just me at my poetry.

Michael Crouthers

OFFICE ROMANCE

Oh, how we've heard it all before.
You two should be together.
Yeah, yeah, we shrug.
But in our eyes there is a twinkle.

You know you want to, we then hear.
The office is not the place, we protest.
And we are not compatible.
On this there is agreement.

For a while it stays this way.
Our differences discussed.
Then a new cry is heard.
You could try and prove us wrong.

It would be a waste, we state.
It is clearly defined.
We are not suited for one another.
Why bother to play this game?

The discussion's finally dropped,
As we leave for the day.
We wait patiently by the elevator.
We sure have them fooled.

Michael Crouthers

MY COUNTRY, RIGHT

Oh Fran, I say,
How can you speak that way?
In your truth I cannot believe.
For it is not my country, wrong or right.

Do not holler and say I'm not patriotic.
Our points differ. That is all.
When America entered that war
It was wrong, my dear Francesca.
It was wrong.

America decides for itself,
As every country should.
And when we were split in half,
There was no ally to join the fight.

During that long past war
My people's lives were changed.
Had there been an ally,
We might never have been freed.

The other war was the same,
But to us it did not belong.
That is why we paid such a price,
Why our loss was so great.

Even now countries are split by strife,
But America must know,
They must decide in their own turn,
As we did when it was ours.

Michael Crouthers

LOST TO A LULLABY

Alone in the surroundings of
people, drawn by a song of silence.
   The only person I see is one,
a figment of you and me.
   Remembering a time, a solemn
forsaken promise, a golden memory.
   All around you an eye paved glow.
   My eyes, only two, have
been deceived. I believed I was to
share love with no one but you.
   A last glance,
the last taste of our bitter romance.
   A silver lacing of a tear's tracing;
a stolen forgiveness, and a past
resemblance.
   A tried smile to overcome the
mysterious chemistry workings of us,
me and you. Given the chance
you would enhance the two.
   Suspension of being in a trance,
looking as a lonely cry;
placed as a fortune in a lullaby.
   You have lost what we were,
   saw no risk,
   took no precaution.

April Mari Bottomley

GOODWILL TO ALL NATIONS

Will there ever be peace between . . .
The nations?
Are their personalities so different . . .
Than ours?
There is only one God to direct us . . .
On the roads that lead to Friendship;
Love and Peace.

Why can't we agree with each other . . .
And create a link in the chain?
Are our beliefs so different?
Will the issues always be United Nations . . .
Vs United States?

Yes, there is only one God to direct us . . .
As the United State tries in vain . . .
To capture the Friendship, Love and Peace . . .
Of people within these nations . . .
Who cannot see beyond their dreams.

Marilyn Gold Conley

LIFE

As we go through life,
As we know how hard it gets.
How confusing.
But each day we must take a step
Further.
Even though that step might be
Bigger
Than we could take.
We take it little by little.
Soon we will make it.
But I can't take that step right
Now,
But someday I will.

Jacqueline Wirtz

EDITORIAL

Life is a mystery. A gift sent to us from God
With every sunrise — who can understand?
Knowing God created us and in so doing He
planted the seed of love in our hearts that we
might multiply and replenish the earth. Falling
in love then is a natural thing to do, and
no one should interfere in the lives of others.
Why pay interest on trouble before it is due?
Love always grows where the sun shines, no
one can reach their highest potential until they
have experienced the deep true beauty of love.
It's a shame we have to live a lifetime before
we really learn to live and to know that
death is also a part of life.

Christine Howard

DAUGHTER OF EVE

A soul refuses to yield
To be overcome, to be worsted
By the indigent surroundings of its human host
It rises above the adversity of its circumstances
Refusing to be put to its last shifts in spirit or
in reality
And so it soars, above the vicissitudes of its life,
And it creates laughter, and it dances;
It refutes its impecunious existence
And remains indomitable in the face of the providential
and auspicious fortunes of others.
It is a keen, bright, strong flame
Burning with an esoteric reality
In the mind of a little girl.

Lisa Wanzer

THE DARNING NEEDLE

Look up, Luv, from your tapestry entitled

Anamorpho, Sis . . .

   Like a Genus Castanea
Again It's Christmastime

Anonym Chrysanthe *mum*

No points scored yet in the ballpark played

Utensils all and trees, for shade

   Hippety-Hop Oletta — A new place, letter fly
Train whistles railroad tracks wood piles — *Aye.*

I'll mail you a postal with my picture

Next Fourth of July.

Nadia Lorraine

AGAINST ALL ODDS

And the battlefield, of life.
To the victor, goes the spoils.
To my right,
Stood the *Lord,* the Most High, in all his majesty.
To my left,
The glory of *He,* who has dominion.
In front of me,
Stood Satan, with his mightiest warriors.
And he fought valiantly.
With confusion, stupidity, and ignorance.
And the battle became heated.
Indeed, it seemed as though they had won.
Then, I heard a voice.
"Get behind *me.* Till I make your enemies,
Your footstool."
And the mountains, roared.
And the earth, shook.
The sounds of screams,
Could be heard, for miles.
And when the dust, had cleared,
The Sons of Satan, had fallen.
And there, alone, stood Satan.
And he looked at me, and frowned;
And, was gone.

Robert K. Walcott

THE CONSTITUTION
ON ITS 200TH BIRTHDAY

The Constitution governs the United States,
Proclaiming the freedom America contemplates.
From the thirteen states, delegates were selected,
When the Annapolis convention said they must be elected.

Some of those men were opposed and some didn't show,
But the constitution was signed, even though.
Thirty-nine delegates agreed and thus signed,
While the others remaining politely declined.

On September seventeenth, it was finally complete,
And sent to the states to accept or defeat.
It took quite a while, but now we can say:
We have freedom and justice in the U.S.A.

America means a lot to me,
The country where I can be free.
I can make my own decision,
It's my very own choice of religion.

I get to choose what I want to learn.
Since my education is my own concern.
Something I want, the career I choose will be,
But whatever it is, it'll be up to me.

Whatever choices I'll decide to make,
The consequences, I'll have to take.
But, whatever decision that comes to be
Will be my own because in America, I'm free.

Tiffany Mano

For Mama Everly and Baby Rhodora
A Letterpoem . . .

   With peace be this morn, an inspiring morn
wherein the fragrance of blooming phalaenopsis
bathe the thin air. Now I again speak as I
remember your good memory.
   Here is the moment of worship and the
teaching of our souls. Until now I am still
a wandering spirit woven in the knowledge of
quiet. Since I am still looking for the reasons
why of all this emptiness.
   In these moorlands I still have long miles
to wander. It seems I am now tired. What is the
purpose then of love?
   In the moments that we live I come to speak
and you listen. As you end-up listening you also
speak — which is the language of love. Your words
strengthen my hungry soul. They move my wings
to cross again in the vastness of life's mysteries.
You give me your fruit, I drink from your glass,
and I can feel the sweetness of your lips as I
wrap your body with my flesh. Now what will I
share? I share the soul of life with sincere prayers
and good praises to sustain the majesty of our love.
   Tears now are welling in my eyes. Yes, I will
always remember a sincere human, a lovely smile,
      a beautiful soul . . .

Elmer Omar B. Piso

WE WERE SPECIAL

We were special, sad we'll never know —
too frightened to let our feelings flow.

Being in your arms was a place I never knew,
not even with a chosen few.

Your words were all so right,
then gone like a broken string kite.

A perfect place to be in my dreams,
waking up to reality is harder than it seems.

Time molded us together very slowly,
now I am empty and lonely.

No one is to blame,
our past has left us slightly insane.

We were so special, sad we'll never know —
too frightened to let our feelings flow.

Sondra Brody

MY COFFIN

Deeming that I was due to die
I framed myself a coffin.

So full of graveyard zeal was I
I set the folks a-laughin'.

I made it snugly fit
My jointering was honest.

And sometimes in it, I would sit,
And fancy my great fit.

I stored it on my cabin shelf,
Forever to remind me
When I was tickled with myself
That death was close behind me.

Let's be prepared, I used to say,
E'er in the dark we launched us
And so with boding day and ay
I kept me coffin-conscious.

Then winter came dark as doom,
No firing wood had I,
My stack was icy as a tomb
And I was set to die.
But e'er the losing of my wits
I saw that coffin there,
So smashing the damn thing to bits

I made a gorgeous flare.

Edd David McWatters

Hollyhocks will
bloom and die
and bloom again
But I will die forever

Eleanor Robertson

SOLDIER OF LIFE

When life is full of sorrow and care
and your burdens are too heavy to bear
march on, little soldier, march on
When your eyes are tired of crying
and your body's tired of trying
and all that you think of is dying
little soldier of life
march on through pain and strife
Remember, anyone can give up and die
but it takes special courage to stay and try
The cross may be heavy and the way is long
but you must be strong and march on
Yes, in spite of all, you must stand tall
even though you may stumble and fall
Your battle will be won
when you see what you have done
You'll be a hero to others
and inspire your brothers
Then a new day will dawn
when the shadows will be gone
and you'll be very strong
and in your heart you'll know
it was overcoming pain that helped you grow
Now a new light shines in you
because of all that you've been through

Yvonne James

THE JOURNEY

Gliding on an unending Journey
Along the outskirts of Reality
Reflects the thought as well as
An inspiration to the seeker
Of the oblivious destination, home.
Pondering the inevitable wild goose chase
Yet, yielding to Euphoric Bliss.

Brenda Mixon

BRENDA JOYCE MIXON. Born: Texarkana, Arkansas, 6-19-56; Education: Henderson State University, 1975-79; Occupations: Library technician, Volunteer as emergency medical technician; Poetry: 'In Hope,' *American Poetry Anthology*, 1986; Themes: *Nature, life.*

FALL

Orange, yellow, red, and brown,
See them come tumbling down.
Mother Nature's done her best;
To keep her children dressed,
All in bright gay colors.

Just see them flutter, here and there
Like fairies everywhere.
They seem to fly and swing up high,
Before they come tumbling down.

The wind that carries them to earth
Just blows them all around.
Then gently puts them down to earth
So they are homeward bound.

So Mother Nature's quite the gal;
She gives us pretty colors.
And dresses up her children dear,
With all those gay bright colors.

Christine Weum

IT'S A GREAT LIFE!

Infinite happiness, joys and delights,
Truly enhance all our days and our nights,
Serenity and peacefulness on the ascent,
Abundance of good things keeps us content,

Glowing with brightness wherever we go,
Raising the hopes of all those we know,
Eagerly encouraging our cares to descend,
Always prepared to assist every friend,
Taking each day with comfort and ease,

Loving and caring and aiming to please,
Insuring our problems will greatly appease,
Family and friends sharing life's pleasures,
Enjoying our days to the fullest of measures.

Ruth J. Colella

WORLD

golden beaches with orange sunsets
the roaring waves flash
  upon the sand
cool breezes
  caressing the shore
alone
  with God
mighty trees with cathedral branches
the yellow sun dances
  among the leaves
swaying branches
  shadowing the earth
alone
  with nature
alone
  to wander the earth
  to walk the paths
  to dance in the sun
  and to watch the stars

Mara W. Cohen

SEASONS OF LIFE

From darkness and desire, I came into this world;
  like a bolt from the blue, there I was — a baby girl!
I gazed into the light, and I found gladness there —
  I had nothing to wear but had someone to care!

The darkness filled with hope, and the light filled with joy.
  My parents loved their girl as they would have a boy!
Minutes became hours, and hours became days;
  weeks became months and years, sparkling like the sun's rays.

My early days were like the sounds of Spring
  echoing all the joys that childhood brings.
Like the Summer sun and stars burning bright,
  my young years of love yearned day and night!

Just as my family has come and gone,
  colorful crowns adorn each Autumn's song.
The chilling sound of Winter's melody,
  like senior years, repeats it rhapsody.

Now, these final years, beyond all reasons,
  both present and past, are like all Seasons!
And Springtime's, Summer's, Autumn's, Winter's strife
  resolve and transform to all Seasons of Life!

Josephine Bertolini Comberiate

TO THE HIGHEST BIDDER

Old Roy spits, squints at the threatening skies,
''Gonna rain like a cow on a rock,'' he prophesies.
''My pasture done all died.'' He snorts, ''Stinkin' drought!
Now my damn foreclosure sale probly git rained out!''

A mother cow runs Ole Roy's fence and cries.
May, his wife, has tears in wrinkles beneath her eyes
As bawling hand-fed calves are hauled away,
Bound for city slaughter-pens this awful auction day.

Stetson-clad, tanned men in manure-caked boots
Shrewdly survey the auctioneer's advertised loot —
Knowing bankers have closed their mothy vault
To debt-ridden farmers likely to default.

Cowboy auctioneer sing-songs another spiel,
''Folks, want a cedar-churn-planter? Let's make a deal!
Came on a covered wagon in the early days;
Seen a hundred years of churnin' at Ole Roy's place!''

As the hoarse huckster shouts, paces in the yard,
Roy scratches his white thatch, adams-apple bouncing hard.
Then Ole Roy out-shouts the last loud bids,
''I'm keeping' that bloomin' churn for my kids!''

''My mama sung me to sleep to its beat,
As our big ole fireplace crackled and hissed with heat,
Pa's daddy passed it on to him with this land;
Losin' it all is about more'n a man can stand!''

''Too old to till the soil, to feel the beat
Of earth's ole heart beneath my failing legs and feet,
I'll feel it still in this churn's cedar
That the Lord sent 'fore any of us could need her.''

Old Roy stroked its red cedar and brass bands,
Crying with the rain torrents now drenching his lands.
''Mama,'' he choked, ''the Lord'll send a better day,
And we'll *own* our memories 'til He calls us away.''

Dorothy Cariker Cart

WHISPER ON THE BREEZE

Hear the sound of the horses' hoofs, on the crest of the air
. . . It steals
Listen to the sounds of long ago, the rumble of chariot wheels

The wind last night carried the thud of ten thousand warriors' feet
Shields glistening in the sun as they marched against the Crete

Hear the wheels of the caisson roll to the rear of the steed
See the chosen few of Caesar, now proudly in the lead

The rattle and clank of armor echoes over the land
The desert air is filled with blinding, choking sand

An endless column of bodies struggling in the sun
Reflecting in their thoughts the many wars they've won

The warriors that are waiting are shrouded in terrible fear
For they know that ''Spartan's'' best is drawing ever near

Oh, Oh . . . Did I get carried away again,
  dreams programmed to tease
Or are they really sounds from Rome, whispered to me on the breeze

William K. Brobst

DADDY'S SHOES

When I was just a little one
Mom would let me go with Dad —
And he took me everywhere
I remember the fun we had

I walked in his footsteps everywhere
And I loved it all so
This was the best time I'd ever had
But that was many years ago!

He was on his horse one day
And we were playing hide and seek
He was chasing me through the woods you see
While behind this tree horses' hoofs passed by me

That's when my mom stepped in
I no longer was Daddy's little girl
She said: ''This is the time
For you to become a young lady and big girl!''

Now Daddy wears the shoes I gave him
And they fit my feet too
Yes, Daddy wears the shoes I gave him
Daddy wears them every Sunday!

Laurie Anne Mach

LITTLE ONE

Eyes of blue that sparkle and shine
tender lips shaped so fine
little hands that hold on tight
from early dawn to late at night
skin as soft as the petal of a rose
from the tip of your nose right down to your toes
from a world of being all alone
to a place where you belong
so hush little baby don't you cry
Someone's watching over you from up high

Denise C. Schoemer

IN LOVING MEMORY

i can't believe that you are
gone.
   i put you to rest in this green
lawn.
   Your voice will never be heard.
   i can't think anymore, not even
a word.
   i have to put you behind
me.
   i have to let your spirit
be.
   i can never forget the love
you gave.
   As i stare down at this cold
grave.
   So good-bye for now until
tomorrow.
   All i have is time to
borrow.
   i say you still live in my
heart.
   Someday i will make a brand new
start.

Charles Maier

FARM LABOR LOST

The Tillamook Cheesemakers
Took on Seaside,
Fans cheering after the little slippery ball.
Meanwhile
Out on the highway
Fog rumbled in on the fierce Northern wind,
Obscuring the pines
And their fallen needles
Just south of the deserted farm.

The ragged buildings sleep,
A tiny lost village,
Resting after a long haul.
Panes cloudy, unseeing,
Boards warped like aged bones,
The paint blistered,
Peeling,
Shutters atilt,
Crying out with each gust

Good-bye.

Norma J. Stiritz

CONTRACTS

Matrimony.
Alimony.
An end to wedded bliss.
A testimony —
For palimony
Has loving come to this?

Melinda Maybruck

JUMP CUT

lapped
cool waters
breeze across Great
Tetons dis
tract the heat concentric
light transport us to
places cross prairies
deserts bottoms of ancient
seas reefed in lime and
sandstone
erode at leisure to
forms long familiar and
light dis
sport us foreground
framed against
the aeons' relief
sculpting

Michael Zucaro

WISHING

Sitting here on a rainy
Day
Wishing that I
Had taken a different
Way on this
Road we call life;
Not that I could have
Changed anything,
Necessarily,
But maybe it would have
Had a better chance
Of working out
For you and me.

Maybe if I'd been more
Elusive, less eager to
Please,
You might not have
Eased yourself out
In such a grand
Way.

But wishing won't change
It, will it?

Rose Hodges

ROSE MARIE HODGES. Born: Fort Plain, New York; Education: Ithaca College of Fine Arts, Ithaca, New York, B.S.; Occupations: Former school teacher, Presently professional songwriter; Awards: Lyrics for some songs on records in Hollywood at Sunrise Record Co. and Hollywood Artists Record Co. in 1987.

MAKE ROOM FOR GOD

When circumstances irk you,
And someone has you "in a stew,"
Do friends seem only a few?
Make room for God.

Do you feel as if you are dragging a chain?
Don't surrender to weakness and pain.
Struggling to live, God does not ordain.
Make room for God.

Does your mind carry thoughts that please?
Is your heart heavy and ill-at-ease?
Don't be loaded down with any of these.
Make room for God.

Throw out each ugly thought;
You know the pain each brought.
The battle of decision has been fought.
Make room for God.

The future will look bright;
Darkness will become light.
Troubles will take flight
When you make room for God.

Betty C. Baker

CO-CREATION

Ofttimes past,
When I would sit
myself into a quiet moment
with plume in hand and
poems in mind,
and oft thought to be
between corner and lamppost
in my thinking,

Let reason go;
circles
inward
commanding me . . .
I must obey.
I am
commands
must transcend into time spiral,
losing time
for all time.

I write the lyrics
and
He writes the song.

William Thomas Sly

THE ONE SONG

I used to spend great times
contemplating the mysteries
of the universe,
until it was revealed to me
that there were no mysteries . . .
only the Uni-Verse.
So I fired my guru
and hired a music teacher
and life has been
a wonderful sing-a-long
ever since.

William Thomas Sly

THOUGHTS AT RANDOM

Running water beneath green trees,
Birds with feathers ruffled by a breeze,
A child's warm firm grip on your hand,
Waves softly breaking on a pebbly strand,
Clouds forming odd shapes, away out of reach.
All these are things that can teach
That loveliness is not to be bought;
Each moment has to be a memory caught.
These precious pictures cannot cause litter,
Stored in the mind, they help erase anything bitter.
Oh how bleak is the wintry scene!
Trees so bare that once were green,
Yet their very bareness seems serene,
Sleeping they are remembering what has been.
Snow and ice have a gift to bring:
They make us seek the warmth of home and shelter;
Make us thankful for a haven from the helter skelter;
They form patterns of beauty that make my heart sing.
My strength is renewed when in my mind I can recall
Random thoughts that become pictures which Nature
and Life gives to us all.

Kathleen Potterton

BUT WAIT . . . WHAT ABOUT PEOPLE?

I love . . .
The blue of the sky in Jerusalem.
To feel the morning dew beneath my bare feet.
The sudden unpredictable offsprings of nature.
The strange yearning escalated by the scented grass.
The sun-ray caress on my face.
The lullaby of the birds.
To lose myself in the rainbow.
To tease the stars,
And flirt with the moon above.
The charming command of the rooster, "get up!"
The complaying rustle of falling leaves.
And respect their crumbling under my feet.
The monotonous sound of rain.
The whispering of insects, in the stillness of the night.
To become ecstatic, at the sight of a lightning,
And shriek, by the following thunder.
To feel along with the outraged raving ocean,
And seeing it become spent and gradually subsiding.
The nostalgic feelings generated by the moaning winds.
And the notion to climb to the top of the Himalayas.
To understorbingly express it all to the Creator.
But wait . . . What about people?

Paula Cytryn

AWAKENING ETERNIZING LOVE

Awakening through your eyes seeing eternizing love
Touching your skin velvet breeze that glitters when touch
Your facial lips are a mystery of silence
Your nose is the breath of inner consciousness

Your laughter reminds knowledge of a baby understanding
Your hair shows that you care
Your hands were created from a thought
Your arms hold patients

Your shoulders and neck hold together here and now
Your breast feeds earth desires
Your secret lips hold the doorway between what is and what is not
Your legs hold the form of night and day
Your feet and toes are egos of today and yesterday

Melvin Sykes

PEACHY DAYS

It's Sunday Morning; I've come down the little
flower-lined path behind my marble mansion, to
    my Peachy Everything.
I fit into my peachy abode like Eve fit into the rib of Adam,
    reluctant to leave for anything.
I'm home in my Garden of Eden, the Queen of Peach Cosmetics.
My Peachy Days go on, and sometimes way late at night,
    with the moon over Miami.
I'm in prime of my peachy ideas to come up with new ways
to immortalize my King of Fruit on this reconverted hunk of
    Florida everglade land.
Once infested by snakes and crocodiles until ten years ago,
my pioneer folks came and planted the first peach seed,
    that started it all.
I'm no longer Mama's little peach picking peddling gal who
invented her first elegant bath toilet water at age thirteen.
I'm the Peach Empress, who like Mama like daughter believes
peaches are the "Sugar La Creme" of life that builds marble
mansions for two under aqua-hysrilla shade trees to stay.
I've come up with everything from peach shampoo to peach lotion
to perfume the world, still wanting to be left here one day,
a gray-haired grandma, wondering why a peach rots, falls to ground.
Though I've saved my peachiest idea yet for a rainy day,
I await my hero knight to rescue me from this golden cage
    of Virginity.

James W. Ayers

Dear Vet . . .

How do we say "we're sorry" for your sweltering pain
For failure to listen when battle dreams came like rain
For giving you 365 days on the job training for experience,
    in total fear
Only to come home to a hypocritical world
    that didn't dare understand or care
We now know how you could give up on a young man's dream
How you lost your inner curiosity and outer youthful gleam
Now we wish not to forget you, or the over 58,000 that didn't return
After years of denial, I now have questions, please help me to learn.

Dear World . . .

You still have a chance, take time to know these women and men
For they have returned out of the pits of hell, we call Vietnam.

Denise C. Schoemer

MOTION OF PERPETUAL EMOTION

Cool wintry passions of a misty eve
Fall perpetually on a dimming heart
Tearful raindrop laden with heavy emotion
Of a blissful life in constant motion

Clouds in the evening sky
Disperse with shimmering rains
Fog lit distance crowned with distant ships
Dark, furtive, and pitiless are the high seas
A Captain's order — a mate's reply
Soon Man will be able to fly

Sea gull screaming circles around the moon
Grey angry clouds blanket the sky with a cover
While whitecaps of the ocean speak their own sly phrases
God's proof of His own Eternal Emotion
Of many blissful lives in constant motion —

Chris J. Nielsen

THE INFINITY

The vehicle of Death
  Carried in the sullen shadows
Brought to the burrows of men — Death
And brought in such multitude
  The couriers of Lifelessness
Swarming like a lethal brood
Darkened whispers of violent slashings
  A funeral pyre of auto's crashings
Immolation in the human realm
Death looks at these with morbid laughter
  Awaiting there in the ashes
To take what it is after
Swallowed through a blackened portal
  Of infinite and unending depth
The souls of all those mortal
  Taken by their human death

Christopher Comfort

UNTITLED

*The inspiration for the poem came
in March or April, 1981*

Once again my heart will know
The hopelessness of spring
And turn away from promises
It always used to bring
That soft and lovely time
Of blossoms that renew
But soon the angry summer sun
Will burn away the dew
That lies like gentle tears
On the flowers we once knew

I turn away my listening
From the sound of morning's birds
Making promises with song
I never heard in words
And looking back through clouded years
To springs of long-lost time
I cannot see the new-leafed trees
Only hills too high to climb

Were all the joys of spring a dream
Were they never real
Is truth the way things really are
Or truth the way I feel?

Eleanor Robertson

ALWAYS

It turned out to be monday
Wouldn't you know it
  just like the last one
They don't seem to change
  always end up the same
I seen the sun rise
  into a tuesday dawn
Feeling the same
  there just does not
  seem to be any change
And the video plays
  again and again
    again and again
While the audio
  echoes within this dream

Billy Mac

THE SOUND OF THE MOON

Crooning softly, rolling on edge
Between nebulous layers of clouds,
The light-hearted lady on the lunar ledge
Gathers her voluminous skirts, proud
Not to brush off the bright points
Of several of the newborn star crowd.

Serenely moving to her heights,
She seems to be planning her nights,
Casually noting the stars of the morning.

Her voice, like a melodious flute on high
Carols a greeting to the star-kissed sky.

Then, her colors fading along with her tune,
She greets the new rising sun soon,
Blaring its trumpet, red gold and bright.
Lady Luna's waiting, waning light
Slips silently, setting behind a heathery hill,
Subsides and is still.

Dorothy Landry

REFLECTIONS

What profits me my life
If I did not touch your hand,
Brush the tear from your cheek
To let you know I understand?

Along life's way are many snares,
And paths that are not true.
Discipline my course with right
In whatsoever I may do.

For like a stone cast into the pond,
Life is but many reflections,
Circles spiral — ripple softly,
Reaching out in all directions.

So let me walk, but not alone,
Unto self I must not be,
Rather open to another's heart,
Only then will I be free.

Barbara Shreder

REALITY

Life is not real.
Reality is the mind.
Perception of what is real comes from
fading back to black, and projection of
fading forward to blue.
In the end "reality" is unimportant.
When the mind ceases to interpret its
Reality we should keep a knowing smile —
for we are innately aware that *then* is
the time to start anew with a virgin Reality.

Mary Annah Hoey-Alemán

Don't you believe that the greatest intellectual
sin of our time is a fear of the obvious?

Mary Annah Hoey-Alemán

Life was but a blood tear in Time.
I sighed, I cried, I died.

Mary Annah Hoey-Alemán

MARY ANNAH HOEY-ALEMÁN. Pen Name: Maya: Born: San Antonio, Texas, 3-6-36; Education: University of Texas at Austin, 1954-56; Incarnate Word College, San Antonio, Texas, 1955; Universidad Iberoamericana, Mexico, 1956-57; Alliance Française, Mexico, 1966; Goethe Institute, Mexico, 1973; Centro de Arte Mexicano, AC, Mexico, 1981-82; Universidad Internacional de Mexico, Mexico, 1983-84; Memberships: Junior League of Mexico City; Theatre Workshop; The Mexico City and the San Antonio Panhellenic Associations; El Comité International Pro-Ciegos; Delta Delta Delta Alumnae Association; The American Society of Mexico; The American Federation of Astrologers; Amnesty International; The American Benevolent Society of Mexico; Southwest Craft Center, San Antonio, Texas; Awards: Recital of poetry, *Poesia Metafísica y Mística,* at the Casa de la Cultura Oaxaqueña, Oaxaca, Mexico, 2-15-84; Mary Annah gave a poetry recital at the "Sunday Afternoon Readings in the gardens of El Circo" in San Miguel Allende, Guanajuato, Mexico, 9-28-86; Poetry: *Leaves from the Memory Tree,* 1987; Mary Annah was honored by the Panhellenic Association of Mexico City on their twentieth anniversary with an autograph-signing brunch for *Leaves from the Memory Tree;* Poetry has appeared in *New Voices in American Poetry,*1986; *Best New Poets of 1986; Hearts on Fire, Vol. IV,* 1987; *Words of Praise, Vol. III,* 1987; *American Poetry Anthology, Vol. VI, No. 4;* Themes: *My thoughts regarding love, its emotional impact, and its inevitable revolving destiny, are the principal themes of my poems. The essence of love's fulfillment beyond the physical presence; the ever-knowing that nothing in this tangible world is static. The truth that our personal desires do not coincide with our fates and that we must learn — in the Zen sense — "to let it be."*

Smuggler's Notch.

THE MEMORIES IN THE MIRRORS OF MY MIND

I am too young to have lost so much
memories of a mother's caring,
a father's loving touch, a brother's
protection, a great-niece's loving affection.

Life is short, somewhere I've heard,
Shorter for some, so I have learned.

My heart was heavy, until I thought it
would break, the pain and tears
I could not shake.

I heard time will heal a broken heart,
and drive the tears and pain away!
And fill your mind with memories of
happy yesterdays!

When I ask, tell me the day!

Time has passed, I sit and think
of each loved one I have lost.
My heart swells with pride, as I reach to
touch the memories in the mirrors of my mind.

The tears still flow down my cheeks,
but now have found a smile to greet.

Lord, I thought you took my happiness away,
but with time, I see you left behind,
many happy yesterdays found in the
memories in the mirrors of my mind.

Christina Grisco

OUR JOY FULFILLED

In secret His Word counts for nothing
But when declared in Spirit offers cleansing
Through Christ shall all be made alive
Trusting Jesus to make sure we'll survive.

After sinners have believed this true story
Everyone around them will behold Jesus' glory
The Words of Scripture are not bound
Upon God's promises there is solid ground.

Christ declared Himself the Son of God
With sinless life having endured the rod
Salvation from Jesus makes your life new
Your joy none can take from you.

Having studied with reverence from our youth
Believers will be sanctified with the Truth
Faith the evidence of things not seen
Trusting Jesus' blood to make us clean.

This holy man was crucified for the people
Our risen Saviour is our precious gospel
They shall see greater things than these
Invite Jesus to control your life please.

Having given all things into His hands
Upon God's Holy Word our faith stands
While we have our Saviour in view
Nothing will by any means harm you.

Paul O. Carlson

IN COMMEMORATION OF THE CONSTITUTION

''We, the people of the United States,''
Was the phrase coined by the delegates
That placed power with the people's vote
Pledging general welfare to promote.

Thirty-nine staunch men were on hand
To sign the ''supreme law of the land.''
Justice and liberty were the goals
Of those able patriotic souls.

While the nation's fate was decided,
George Washington proudly presided,
And James Madison's contribution
Was ''Father of the Constitution.''

This brief document was intended
To plan for change and be amended.
Government by ''Republican Form''
Was to help new states weather each storm.

Hamilton and Franklin played a part
In the 1787 start.
September 17th is the date
Our nation needs to commemorate.

Shield of democracy was the call
Of the men in Independence Hall,
Who by their unanimous consent
Approved our Constitution's content.

Lura Louise Hanson

CONSIDER THE LILIES

Lord of the fragrance of these moments
Thy glory spreads from seed to flower!
Creator God! Refreshing Spirit!
Such scenes of beauty and of power!

Thine are the flowers in all their wonder
Which blooming scent the morning air.
My heart's enchanted as I see them
For Thou art known in all that's fair.

Along the hillside Thou hast painted
Meadows in bright and happy hue.
Father of love! Author of beauty
In fields and trees and azure blue!

O bring unto our souls desiring
The joy we see so full and free
Bursting before us in the flowers —
Such joy that comes through faith in Thee.

O keep us praying as we see them,
Praying their faith may be our own —
Humble and pure, trusting and simple —
Such faith as is by nature shown.

O speak to us in meditation
That we may know Thy caring love
Is watching daily, blessing ever
With gifts that come from heav'n above.

Robert A. Happel

GOD'S BOUQUET

I cannot feel your feelings
     But I can share your grief,

And pray that God, will comfort
     And time will bring relief.

A child is like a flower
     It starts from a seed and grows,

From a tiny bud it blossoms
     And goodness overflows.

With each unfolding petal
     Comes beauty, joy, and tears,

Bringing us a happiness
     That lasts throughout our years.

And though we tend these flowers
     Each one must go their way,

And some I know the angels pick
     To brighten God's bouquet.

Violet D. Stout

THE BUSY FARM WAVES GOOD-BYE

America's heartland needs a new job
It won't be waking up the sun anymore
It quit involuntarily

Strike the words from the song
No more amber
. . . America the less beautiful
Yes, the farm with the house down the road
The one we used to love
Is waving good-bye
The cement silos are calling

Richard Bretz

SIMILTUDE DEFENESTRATION (LIKE BREAKING A WINDOW)

The see-through wall cracks
Letting your blue eyes pierce
The outside air for your convenience

But don't lose yourself
In the acid clouds

When it seems your window
To the world
Is cracking
And the final blow is near

The satellite gods with
Their dancing wavelength advice
Should be feared

Remember
Believe in yourself
Or turn to Oprah

Richard Bretz

UNDER ARIEL

Undome!

Under this "Dome!" It is once that was begun; Now —
   it's done, it's been doing, and it's done —
     Now, it's "Dome!"
   Now, and if so, and then: It's "Done-By-Me!"

We have still to see, but always, also what we've seen,
   coming, to the ceiling; over the fall to this —
the fly — this, to this — inward, in this sky!"
     It's "Dome!" *The Dome!*

It's, as if it wills its way on its own will — Is this,
   then this is this — so far-low, to the blankets:
   or, the falls, where — low-far, low-farther, far,
and low, so-so, is this!"

This much doesn't matter, so much, Oh "Mater!" Not so as much,
   as it's "Dome!" Or where and as it should be.
But, where or whence have I, or we? I've — reached-off!
I? I've reached to *Ariel! Ariel! Ariel! Ariel!*
"Speak!" "So, You Are, So!" — "So, under this Dome!" Of
   Tome! — Is It so Dedicated: "To Me Alone!"

   Yes, But still so — So Nice — Yes, and,
   still yes so light it — Or, then, so Light it —!
Yes, it's, Yes — "It's the real "Tome!" Or:
   "Undome, Far Beneath Me!" I am as she is, *Now!*

It is how is it, that it does, a snow's blanket warm,
warmly falls, and falling! Yet, So only smoothe:
of the soothes crystalline, in the lie, of poems!

   Robert S. Cassidy

SYLVIA TOME

"How is this, this, "Dome?" Tome, opened —
Said she: "Tome!" — "It's, on & over, & under,
but, through — of a round Noble's table: the sables, once
known; are he's grown! No sable, not yet; no sable,
   No, none. No, none! But, yes, while looking —

It is, "Tome;" "To-me-alone!" for, because, it, it,
sees from ways to all of me, and through, and through —
then, through it alone: "It is, It is!" I would see it!

"So, and, how is this "Done?" Well — "Dome?" Is it — still?
Yes, it's quite quiet, quite, & yes, still still, so still —
No, it's not that I'm alone — but it's alone — Yes, I am, and yes
so, are we: For each whom sees that I am, through what I am,
So sees Sylvia Tome!"

"I am sometimes someone else — now, I'm the painter, with
my own brush, in yellow oils — singing: alightly —
He's leading me, he is — the canvas with my face —
This, would he call, for me, Tome — and pronounce it, in
my name, in mine — Sylvia!"

"Yes, knows, then, it's so — that "Dome" someway
   is song, carrying on —
It is also always Unsong, or Not Song —
   "Leading is, it, is — Leading is, it, is —
   Leading is, it, is — Leading out, and in;
   Seeing out, brushes; No, so much in a brush;
   Nor, into, but through, down and under and out, again!"

   Robert S. Cassidy

ARIEL (CONTINUED, PART II)

3rd Test To the Poesies Texts

"Speak!" "Three, Colassalls!" "Three, Colassals!" "Colassalls,
Threes!" "Three Colassalls!" "Three, Colassals!" "Colassalls!"
"Colassalls, Speak!" "Speaking Collossals, Three!" "Colossals!"
"More again, Speak!" "Speaking, Of Me, Speaking Collossals,
Threes!" "Collossalls!" "Collossalls!" "Colossalls, Threes!"

And, they in the Collosseum, "They, go, to come, and to go,
so would we know, they know!" "So, then:" "Thee, Colossal, Thee —
Walk Of The Wait; *or:* 'Pater-noster, & Mader, It's what it
seems seemly, to be!" "Then so it is, Gentle, White, So Slow,
   Gigantus, and Giganteen!"

   So, reach us, Reach, to me — I'm ever so lowly, down ye,
so below of you! "Then, reach out, To Me; "Reach from-highly,
to-go-fro-so-lower!" So, she'd reach us, Reach, to me — Then,
   but holding up three, Colossals!" They would, of course
on the ways — But see the smile, of your eyes, and you, on me!"

   And, spoke He: "I reach, to You, whom you are, or —
Thinking, or thoughtful that perhaps, you have been, so much —
ponding, or pondering, then, that, having been are, Now —
Not so — 'like' no, you, No — But, 'like 'me' they, yet —
So! You are again, as I! You then my breathe, most needs!

And, then are the fires, these of his imaginations: From where?
Further, whence sounds are silences of the carrier from here,
so slowly, Slowly Giants! Why? Thee! "Thee, Colossal, fought —
I'd had to see You! To know breathe fire, none, so I sat!

   But my final words: "Colossal — To your knees again!"

   Robert S. Cassidy

THE JOYS OF BEING
PART OF A FAMILY AGAIN!

On a very cold, windy, rainy morning in November
The new neighbors moved in next door.
There were two young children, a boy and a girl,
Also a small baby possibly a few months old.

With so much confusion, I hesitated to go over then.
The next day I felt was the time to welcome them.
I was greeted very cordially, and we seemed to like each other at once.
The baby, a boy, three months old, stared at me with big laughing eyes.

It was just before Thanksgiving, the father
Had gone on his annual hunting trip with his friends.
Loving children as I do, I was very happy to have them next door.
By Holiday Time they had decided to adopt me, since I am all alone!

In a few years, a delightful little girl was born.
She was fun to be with, liked to dance and sing as she grew.
Late one night they called —
   could I come to stay with the children?
Early the next morning the father called, they had a healthy baby girl!

She was a beautiful blue-eyed, blonde child
Always ready to be cuddled and played with and loved,
While her sister had never wanted to be held at all.
But the little blonde cherub enjoyed attention, hugs and affection.

Now all these wonderful children are growing up too fast!
It has been marvelous to share this part of their lives —
   and still is!
The whole family has given me love and understanding —
The Lord has blessed me in bringing us together,
   I am part of a family again!

   Mildred A. Martin

To Justin and Grayson

He brings the morning sunshine
   Before the breaking dawn,
Unties the golden air waves
   And puts the music on,
Gives us the latest data
   That brings the world in touch.
He gives us news, time, weather,
   Sports, temperature, and such.
He brings us morning brightness
   In his own special way
And gives us inspiration
   To make it through the day.
Restores our sense of feeling
   And clears our sleepy eyes,
Debugging all the defects
   From ground to dawning skies.
Ad-libbing through the program
   A single person cast,
Welcoming the latest and
   Remembering the past.
A voice that offers friendship
   A gift we don't repay.
Yes, I'm speaking of a dee jay,
   K S U E's Hugh Hardaway

Violet D. Stout

ALWAYS

*To Victor D. Bouchard, my
brother-in-law*

There's always a flower
   For someone,
There's always a place
   In a heart,
There's always a sunbeam
   Of brightness,
There's always a new
   Way to start.
There's always a word left
   Of kindness,
There's always a song
   In the air,
There's always the time if
   We take it,
To tell Someone Special
   We care.

Violet D. Stout

EASTER SUNDAY

Redeemed through victory of our risen Lord.
Every believer to worship with one accord.
Saved by the shedding of Jesus' blood.
Under His Spirit then apply this flood.
Reassured by Jesus rising from the dead.
Real life is ours Jesus once said.
Enter now into the Kingdom of God.
Claim for Jesus, ground you have trod.
Trusting the promises recorded in His Word.
Inviting others to share the gifts offered.
Of Jesus' triumphant life, not some other.
New life proven one saint to another.

Paul O. Carlson

LOVE GIVING PEACE

Faith in Jesus breaks the eternal day
God of love has prepared the way
Stand before God by grace with prayer
Assured of salvation with love so rare.

Are you the soul of Jesus' heart?
Accept His gift to do your part
The promises He gave then are yours
All His riches on you Jesus pours.

Having all power to obtain this goal
With love giving peace in our soul.
Ecstasy with faith shows love to amaze,
Your lovely voices are filled with praise.

All believers will rise into the air
We'll leave the ground caught up together.
God be praised we love Your creation
Jesus' triumph over death, our true salvation.

Paul O. Carlson

PAUL OSCAR CARLSON. Born: Aurora, Colorado, 6-28-09; Married: Lovina May; Education: Bible schools; Occupations: Electrician, Superintendent of Union Pacific Railroad Depot; Memberships: Electical unions; Bible schools; Awards: Awards of Merit, 1986-87; Golden Poet Award, 1987; Poems used by many pastors; Poetry: 'Power To Attain,' *Poems of Praise,* 1985; 'Infinite Forever,' *Poems of Praise,* 1986; 'Enjoy Forever Now,' 'Bonds For Peace,' *Poems of Faith,* 1985; Comments: *God is using me through the inspiration of poetry, and His spirit to convey the good news of the gospel, to save the lost, and to comfort all believers and to praise His name with hallelujahs.*

IMPRESSION

fields of snow
  a white canvas
s-t-r-e-t-c-h-e-d
  on the
easel of nature . . .
   being filled with
     People,
     Red,
     Green,
     Color,
Splashing from the
brush of humanity.

Painting and signing
a valued reflection
  of life!

Linda G. Rhea

ON VIEWING A STATUE OF GEORGE WASHINGTON

Is this the hand that raised the sword
That set our country free?
Is this the man who signed the scroll
That gave us liberty?

Is this the commander who led his troops
Through battles far and wide?
Is this the patriot who suffered so
When his comrades bled and died?

Is this the statesman who led our nation
Toward our chosen destiny?
Is this the president who governed
With such integrity?

Is this the American who did
What no other man has done?
Yes, this is the Father of our Country,
This is George Washington!

Henry O'Grady

BY THE SEA

Oh what a pleasure to live by the sea
And watch its ever-changing face,
One day so placid and serene,
Next day a violent storm takes place.

Most people like the sunny days
With balmy winds and deep blue skies,
A day to watch the many birds
And silent sailboats gliding by.

Or take a cruise out on the deep
And see the porpoises at play,
Perhaps a picnic on the beach,
Or just go fishing in the bay.

But there is something frightening and exciting
About a storm at sea,
When sailors quickly reef their sails
And guess how fierce the storm will be.

Sometimes a monstrous hurricane strikes,
With screeching winds and mammoth waves,
Often we leave for higher ground
And pray our cottage will be saved.

Yes, there are many differences
In living by the sea,
But one thing I truly understand,
It's the right place for me.

Henry O'Grady

RELEASE

Only let me show thee, here
Within my warm embrace,
With what humble power I love, dear,
Is written on my face
Yet read within my impassioned heart
Love's height, love's depth, love's peace
And find, in each poetic part,
pain's tenderest release

Sharon Kessler

TEARS OF SORROW

A man is slowly walking towards me, His arms outstretched to the sky
He doesn't ask for much, He only comes to cry

He is one only I can see, I am only too familiar with Him
Often does he come to me, when the mortals sin

At first He only looks real sad, and He mumbles a little prayer
For they all did Him wrong, and His love he wants to share

I am prepared for what comes next, and my body starts to crawl
As I move closer to Him, I see the first tear fall

I slowly wash over His feet, and then I back away
He cries a little harder now, and His body begins to sway

I come at Him now, with a stronger force, and now He's on his knees
His hands cover his paining face, because they ignored His pleas

This time I am stronger yet, and further down He'll go
The tears are falling harder now, and only I will ever know

Now His sobs rack His body, and I am at my peak
I crash down heavily upon Him, now He's very weak

I ebb back gently now, and take with me His tears
As I have always collected, all throughout the years

He is now done His cleansing, and He stands and backs away
He did not grant me a voice, so there is nothing I can say

But He will come to me again, when the world is filled with wrong
Until I see Him again in time, I the ocean, am calm.

Betty Ann Clark

BETTY ANN CLARK. Pen Names: Beeann, Elliott; Born: Potsdam, New York, 11-28-68, Thanksgiving Day; Education: Massena School of Business, Steno-Secretarial Diploma, 6-11-87; Occupations: Secretary; Awards: Honorable Mention for 'My Love, My Rosebud,' 1987; Golden Poet Award, 1987; Poetry: 'Hand In Hand,' *American Poetry Anthology, Vol VII, No. 3;* Comments: *I write on love, in love and out of love.*

VISIONS

Flames through a glass — dancing, speaking to me —
''To what will be'' —
I held the glass slightly higher in the barroom mirror,
And drank the wine.
''Winner take all''
''To the winner belong the spoils.''
And what of the losers — broken, laughable,
Forever crushed?
Not so —
''The world shall hear from me again'' —
And again — and again — and again.

In despair, there is hope —
In losing, peace —
My enemies damned me — I never said a thing!

Wulf D. Kort

PEACE AND STILLNESS

Restless yet wary with cares of the day,
My mind was unsettled, determined to stray;
I lay in the darkness but sleep would not come.
I rose from my bed; I was feeling quite glum.
Out on the balcony, the stars were so bright
Their twinkle and sparkle gave light to the night.
The moon casting shadows from over the trees
And caressing me gently was a warm summer breeze.

As I stood in the silence, my mind finding calm,
I drank of the splendor, cleansed of my qualm.
How majestic the beauty of all I surveyed
In a silence not present in the light of the day.
Oh! I felt a bonding of heaven and earth;
God's infinite mind had created its birth.
Then soothed by the beauty, I lay down my head;
Peace had consumed me and restlessness fled.

Bessie Lee Anderson

THE ONLY WAY

Have you found the Way the Truth and the Life?
Then you have found Jesus Christ our Lord.
You will never again be lonely or be alone
Nor never again be bored.

If you ever sometimes think you feel lonely
And it seems there is no one to care.
Remember Christ will never leave you
For He is always there.

If your burdens sometimes seem too heavy
Then go to the Lord in prayer.
For He has promised to allow
No more than you can bear.

You will never again lose your way
Through all struggle and through strife.
Just remember Christ is with you always
For He is the Way the Truth and the Life.

George Kingery

AS I AWOKE

As I awoke this morning, I thought am I all alone,
Does anyone really care?
Then I heard that still small voice whisper
God is always there.

I prayed Dear God please help me
That I get through another day.
Then Jesus said, ''Fear not for I am with you
And I will lead you all the way.''

Then I felt light and complete
As if I were flying through the air
And on my way to Heaven
With my God taking me there.

It seemed I had left the whole world behind
And had gone to meet my loved ones and friends who had gone before
Where there was only Love, Peace, Joy and Happiness
In Heaven with God forevermore.

George Kingery

THE MIRROR

Someone stares back —
Someone with brown eyes —
Someone resembling myself,
but, oh, so wise . . .

Someone has wrinkles —
and long snow-white hair —
Someone is waiting . . .
and right over there . . .

Someone is smiling —
a sympathy smile —
Someone's been calling
me for a long while . . .

Someone, who are you?
Someone-kind of elf?

Someone, I found to be . . .
my future self.

Linda G. Rhea

WASTED YEARS

What can I do with this life,
That God has given me?
To live up to his expectations
Will be the best that I can be.

What does life have to offer?
I shall find out if I can.
I would like to play a vital role
In God's eternal plan.

God gave me the breath of life
Many years ago.
I wasted precious years
Doing what? I do not know.

Now that I see the light
There's breath in this lifeless form

Now: the flame is brighter
Than the day that I was born.

I gave my life to Jesus
For guidance along life's way
My outlook has been brighter
From that very day.

Helen Olivia Hodge

I am a parasite, I feed
    upon your body
I am a parasite, I drink
    in your life
I am a parasite, I bask
    in your love
but, I give to you
    unselfishly
    my life, love, body and soul
take them, feed upon them
    and never let them go
and together through life
    we will continue
    as one.

Michelle E. Barra

A VICTORIOUS DAY

A late day walk through wooded path
Inhaling deeply now and then
Where air and forest shared a bath
And droplets swarm on brown and green

A fresh invigorating stance
Uplifting nerves with every step
An abundant exercising prance
In tune with nature in spirit and hep

How great the feeling, the exciting pace
The thrill lights up a shining face
Reality triumphs throughout the set
Another day: no cigarette

Jerry Martinez

JERRY MARTINEZ. Born: Baytown, Texas, 9-30-28; Education: R.E. Lee High School; Honorable Discharge, U.S.A.F., S/Sgt; SW Business University, Houston, Texas; Father of Eloisa Maricela and James Edward; Poetry: ''Tenaltic I,'' ''Tenaltic II,'' ''Tenaltic III'' booklets; Poetry published by *Port of Houston* magazine, American Poetry Association; Themes: *Trying to liberate the good locked up within us.*

YOUR LOVE WOULD BE HEAVEN TO ME

The birds o'er the meadow are singing,
The sky is so tranquilly blue —
But sadness to me still is clinging
Because I am longing for you.

I'm longing for you all day long dear —
I dream of you all the night through.
Your love is my heart's only song dear
My hope and my happiness too.
Oh say you will love me forever,
That truly my own you will be;
Then joy will depart from me never
For you would be heaven to me.

I thought dear I never could love you
Though you were so sweet and so true
But now there is no one above you,
And how I am longing for you!

I'm longing for you all day long dear —
I dream of you all the night through.
Your love is my heart's only song dear
My hope and my happiness too.
Oh say you will love me forever,
That truly my own you will be;
Then joy will depart from me never
For you would be heaven to me.

Christine Howard

UNCONSCIOUS PURPLE

Fearing — yet, unconscious of
    The reason why;
Driving her home — his quaking insides
    Started to *die.*

He'd miss her — journeying to far-off
    Uncertain *lands;*
Waltzes in — The Sea of Passion —
    Quieting touches of Tender —
Now befouled by
    Whispering sands.

Aged — silhouetted memories
    Visiting in fragments,
Can no longer — sustain his days;
    So he beckons, ''Sweet Night — hurry!''
To dream of her — and, her ''loving'' *ways.*

Hitherto — Cupid's arrow struck them not
    And as it screamed past ''their world'';
Triggered a wake that tripped their souls
    Scraping Mars' jutting sword.

Thus — blood dripped unto the sun
    Eclipsing ''their world'';
Two wounded souls searching,
    Thoughts pass — *shine on them Lord.*

Peter Moser

FOR JEROME

The pages of my life keep turning
All those words gone by of
All those times with you
    Before —

I never read between the lines
Everything was so black and white
Our love was so defined.

And now the chapters aren't so clear —
    Too many spaces
    In between the lines

I want this part to end
    Missing you —
    And still loving you.

I thought by the end
There would have been
Another part with you in it
Maybe just one more page
Before I closed the book.

Laura Tevoli

STORM SKY WATCH

the roaring rolling thunder
sky watching with the lightning
my goodness — it's frightening
abstract streaks through the sky
landing close by with a boom
the blast-off of nature
    the storm
on an august morn
the rain white washing
the grass, flowers and trees
the grey blur of fog rolling in
the tall pinoaks soaked in rain
the ground drained with mud
the ground breaking footprints of the mailman
after sailing in the driveway in his cart
darting through the storm
the yellow slickered visitor during the downpour
the cars start moving — splashing water on the street again
    the rain halts
    the fog lifts
the sun shines through the clouds
the summer storm gently roars in the background
    mystical and proud

Carolyn Hasselle

MARY CAROLYN HASSELLE. Born: Memphis, Tennessee, 5-21-43; Education: Rhodes College, B.A., 1966; University of Aix-Marseilles, Certificate of European Studies, 1963; Occupations: Artist, Poet; Memberships: National Writers Club, National Association for Female Executives, Charter Member National Museum of Women in the Arts; Awards: *Soul Poetry,* book of poems, 1982; Poetry: 'Angel Sunset,' *American Poetry Anthology,* 1982; 'Snow Bank,' *American Poetry Anthology,* 1986; 'Chagall's Lovers,' 1986; 'Snow Blanket,' *Best New Poets of 1986,* 1986; 'French Park,' *P.E.O. Record,* 1982; Comments: *Most of the inspiration is from nature, change of seasons, snow, autumn leaves, the advent of spring, and the lush green and flowers of summer — how they relate to the experience of the author's personal life and associations.*

WISH UPON A STAR

If the brightest star were within my reach,
I'd take that star to treasure and hold tight.
Though my wants are few and my future bright,
I'd keep a small part of that star for my wishes,
the remainder of that very bright star, I'd give to you.
For all your dreams, all your plans to come within your reach.

Carolynn Ward

AFTER THE STORM

I went out where the rain was falling,
not like silver needles but soft
words or little kisses. A fur
cloak of silence mantled the city air that was
once again like the breath of tiny cold streams,
for the cars were too timid to growl
while the sky sternly brooded.
In the gentle garden, flowers
nodded to the water and laughed at
those who cringed.

The storm had flaunted so gaudily
its slashes of paint glaringly silver,
and the dark-voiced thunder that gripped frail souls.
The wind had urged the trees to frenzy,
raving with their stale brown arms.
The storm had withered slowly, and left.

I paused there, a moment,
to listen to the crooning of corpulent drops.
I returned to the dry warmness and noise
my senses lingering in remembrance of
serene coolness and perfumed pastels,
and the rain dripping like jewelry.

Jeannine Hall

HIGH SCHOOL SWEETHEART

You will always be my high school sweetheart,
    You will always be the one that I love;
        And it's not puppy love anymore,
            This I'm for sure.
We're beyond the stage of going steady,
    Things are serious and I know I'm ready for
        Just your love —
            And yours alone!

I won't rush you man, but I won't slow you down. You've got to keep up a pace if you want me to stick around. Just a glance from you or a touch of your hand — you don't have to say a word, your appearance shows, that you are my man.

All you've got to do is tell me so, and I won't stick around. Although it's true you know, you're the handsomest man in the town. Just to hold me in your arms or to kiss me once or twice — you are my tower of strength, you make everything seem all right.

    'Cause:
    You'll always be my high school sweetheart,
        You will always be the one that I love;
           And it's not puppy love anymore,
              This I'm for sure.
    We're beyond the stage of going steady,
        Things are serious and I know I'm ready for
           Just your love —
             And yours alone!

Hazel Mae Parron

TO PAY A KING'S RANSOM

My heart weakens every time, That we pass;
My heart can break, I know that it's not made of glass;
Yet, my pride and upbringing, Make it seem I'm made of stone;
Why is it your pedestal, Seems to be a throne?

    You wear a crown, you know that you,
    Have been made King;
    I am just a nobody,
    The mild, the meek.
    I am silent, you are silent,
    We do not speak;
    You must think lowly of the person,
    From the other side of the street!

It's a battle whenever I see you, At a glance;
You realize, you hypnotize me, And mockingly laugh;
Your haunting eyes talk, Even when you don't speak;
You're vision plagues my dreams, While I sleep.

    Time will tell, I'm under a spell,
    And you've made me weak;
    One day I will crumble,
    As I turn the other cheek.
    I don't mean to disgrace or discredit,
    Your divine majesty;
    You'll never find a more loyal subject,
    Than the day you over-looked me.

Hazel Mae Parron

HAZEL MAE PARRON. Born: Norfolk, Virginia, 6-15-56; Married: Norman Rogers Parron, Jr., 11-4-77; Children: one daughter, Jenny Lynn Parron, born 12-10-83; Education: Professional Business Institute, formerly of Norfolk, Virginia, 1974; G.E.D., 1975; Central School of Practical Nursing, Norfolk, Virginia, 1977; Attended Hampton Institute of Hampton, Virginia for continuing education classes in nursing process and written care plans, 1979; attended numerous continuing education courses through Humana Hospital Bayside, Virginia Beach, Virginia; am currently certified in Cardio-Pulmonary Resuscitation; Occupations: Licensed Practical Nurse, presently employed at Humana Hospital as a staff nurse, 1980 to present; also former nursing instructor for Professional Business and Medical Institute; former employee of Lafayette Villa Health Care as a nursing assistant, 1974-77, and a charge nurse, 1977-80; Awards: Golden Poet Award, 1987, Honorable Mention for 'Life's Best'; Poetry: 'Dreams and Fairytales,' *Best New Poets of 1986*, 1986; 'Life's Best,' 1987; 'Child's Prayer,' *Words of Praise, Vol. III*, 1987; 'Caroling Messengers,' *American Poetry Anthology, Vol. IV*, 1987; 'A Letter to my Daughter,' *Poetry of Life, Vol. I*, 1988; Comments: *Family, friends, true to life feelings, and God inspire me to write my poetry. I enjoy writing about life itself, whether it be good or bad. If someone can read something I have written and say, ''Hazel Mae Parron, wrote it and it was good,'' then I feel I have brought pleasure to at least one person's life. 'My High School Sweetheart' was written sixteen years ago, for my husband, Norman, to whom I am now married. 'My Brother's Fire,' was written especially for my brother, when he was going through some rough times and was trying hard to be accepted for the person that he is; and was written with a meaning only he will understand. ''To Pay A King's Ransom'' was written with the ''poor'' in mind; that are loyal and deserving of the work they do, that is often overlooked by superiors.*

THE PRISONER

This is a poem for you, my son, Christopher.
You are locked up in a prison that you do not understand
And of which you are completely unaware.
I have often wished that I could visit you
Within that prison, understand and share with you,
The bars of frustration and the restraints of anxiety.

I have ached to be able to know what you must feel and think.
I have anguished at the absurd hope of one day
Slackening your shackles and releasing you to life.
I have despaired at the lost promise of the unlocked, barred cell.
I have long since abandoned the belief of the optimist
To ever hear the childish question, ''Why?''

And then . . .
I look in awe at you, my small son.
You smile at me and I see shafts of sunlight
Pierce the clouds and brighten my day.
You are six years old and, though autistic,
You are also so alive.
You are happy and sharing and giving of love;
Unaware that you even have a problem.

This, then, is a poem for you, my son, Christopher.

Michael W. Lee

THE BURNING BUSH

When Moses tended sheep, and saw the burning bush,
That burned incessantly nor was consumed,
He fell upon his knees in consternation
And awe — to see the miracle.

    Through many years and climes
    The burning bush had come to earth —
    A bush consuming woman, man, and child
    Upon the fiery faggots of Inquisition;
    And in the wars of conflagration.

But recently, the burning bush fell into evil hands,
To swallow father, mother, child
In crematoria.

    And following this evil,
      the mightiest burning bush of all —
    Nagasaki —
    Burning hordes of humans into cinders;
    Then was itself consumed!

O grant us, God, the world may never see
Another burning bush!

Mary Schulman

LONELINESS, FREEDOM AND HONESTY

Sometimes the loneliness
of this life
gets to be a little too much

Like too high of a prifce to pay
for my freedom

Like the price you pay
in this world
for being honest

Freedom and honesty are
such sad things to have alone

Craig Deem

WISDOM OF THE CROWD

Wisdom of the crowd

Looking for a sign
Got to match the mood
Check up on the times
And then you make your move

The wisdom of the crowd

Look right past the truth
Live a lie to make the grade
Check up on what's new
And your values you can trade

Follow the wisdom of the crowd

Find out who they like
Find out how they rate
And then you can sell yourself
You can seal your fate

Just follow the wisdom of the crowd

Don't know what to think
Don't know what to do
You've got to ask 'em
Ask 'em what's really true

Wisdom of the crowd

Find out what they like
Find out what they hate
But you'll never find yourself
Never at this rate . . .

Craig Deem

HAIKU

It's early morning,
the sun knocks at my window.
I open the blinds.

The bamboo thicket.
Birds sing to greet the new day.
Sunrise on the lake.

I drop a nail trace,
from above, down to your face.
You snuff it away.

Phil Angell

YOU ARE . . .

You are the warmth that I remember
When I wake on a cold morning

You are the smile that I give
When I feel I've none left

You are the song that I sing
When it comes from my heart

You are the light that I see
When darkness covers my dreams

You are the peace that I feel
When I lie awake on a summer night

You are emotion that I see
When restless tears fill your eyes

You are silence that I need
When I lie asleep in your arms

You are my lover
I will be there close to you
I'll always be there
To take you in

But I'll also be there to share
The simple things
Leave a little space in between
'Cause you're also my best friend

Craig Deem

CRAIG DEEM. Born: Columbus, Ohio, 5-2-61; Comments: *Someone once said that to become a poet, a man must be in love or miserable. I've spent my share of time in both areas.*

FRIENDS

The cold air bites and the wind blows strong;
　We are strangers.
Our bodies move close for keeping warm;
　We are shaking.
Our bodies touch — we ignore the storm;
　We are calm.
Sunbeams shine brightly this freezing morn';
　We are happy.
White clouds block sunlight, but not for long;
　We are trusting.
The wind settles down — birds sing their song;
　We are friends.

Debra J. Barba

HEARTACHE

Life has his torn or heartache
that no one can deny as winter
turns to spring and tears want
weep no more than laughter
come show us the way to land
where freedom lay to guide our
mind we want be blind

Teardrops from my pillow
heartache in my mind let me in
so I can grin and leave all
things behind

Rain fall down my window that
dry my heartache tears now I can
feel the precious being that I
once never felt
and what all to do to me my life
is yet to come my heart want run
just normal hum! now all my
heartache little ones my dreams
just smiles right in to be along
where I have gone my life just
walk right in

Eloise Bass

ELOISE BASS. Born: Panama City, Florida, 8-2-35; Married: Willie Fred Bass; Education: High School, Blountstown, Florida; Occupation: Housewife; Membership: Church; Awards: Golden Poet Award for 'In Time,' 1986; Golden Poet Award for 'No One Lives Forever,' 1987; Several merit certificates and honorable mentions, 1985-86; Poetry: 'Kind Lady,' 1985; 'I Thank God for America,' 1986; Comments: *Quitting is failure and determination is success. I love the country, the bees, the birds that sing where the treetops swing. I enjoy writing and I thank God for my given talent!*

DEVIL'S LAMENT

I fantasize and dream,
I plan and I scheme,
But man rises not to the bait.
They scream and they yell,
Those few dragged to Hell,
For the rest I know I must wait.

My complement is small,
Only a few dare fall
From the grace of the one they love.
And I sit here below,
The first one to know,
The wrath of the One up above.

Lee W. Kelley

FROM BABY TO TEEN

He doesn't need comfort for hurt knees that are sore,
Not one tin soldier or bear on the floor.
He doesn't need propped up to set tall in his chair,
And he doesn't need help to comb his hair.
No tying his shoes, no blowing his nose,
Where did the time go, do you suppose?
He grew from *baby* to *toddler,* from *boy* to *teen,*
Overnight he grew up into a macho machine.
But he still kisses good ole Mom bye,
And tells me his problems with girls and junior high;
He still needs me I know, especially at night,
To pull up the blankets and turn off the light.
He's growing by day into a fine young man,
He won't need me long to hold his hand.
But I'll always be there for him I pray,
And the memories I have can't be taken away.
For when I am old and he has grown,
I'll remember his little hand in my own.
I'll smile and be happy, for I will see,
What a really nice man he turned out to be.

Faith Cole

THE WRETCHED WENCH

Who is this wretched wench, that stands behind the picket fence?

Faintly sweating beneath the noontide sun
Thinking of the time that her years were young

Life was hers to choose at will
To drink of life's never ending still

A statue of beauty that stood before
A choice of suitors at her door

A genial smile beheld her face
The whole woman an air of grace

An inspiration to all who did see
She was every women wish to be

The wrought of life she did choose
To be a wife and a mother too

Forgetting about the woman inside
Giving her all to be a bride

Now a hoary halo she wears
Only a faint sign of her dusky hair

Her face is lined from years of strain
And her body is writhe with pain

Her children have since left
And the husband that she kept

For he has gone to turn back time
To once again stand in line

Yes! Life was hers to choose at will
To drink of life's never ending still

Linda Miller Whitener

A PRAYER IN WESMINSTER ABBEY

Oh Lord, my prayers go up to Thee, with words of gratitude,
That You have brought us safe to London town.
I feel the presence of my lost love, as I hear the
Restless stirrings of his son kneeling beside me
On the cold smooth stones.
For twenty years we saved and dreamed of such a trip,
To see the past unfold itself before our eyes;
And now the twenty years are gone; death took my love,
But proof of love remains and kneels beside me
And our prayers go up to You and bring us closer.
These silent stones have heard so many prayers
Their mingled pleas must form a steady stream
To God on high; So I, too, express my gratitude
In simple words, Oh God, I thank You for this gift so rare,
To cross the seas and look upon the land from whence
My forebears came, I look with double sight, one for myself,
And one for you, my love, whose presence seems so near.

Mabel R. Bennett

BEST FRIENDS

To Anney,
with love always, April

Friends, everyone has them, but is
Any as special as your best friend?
Well, mine is the best, she is always there.
She always has a shoulder for me to cry on.
I tell her all I fear and all I hope for.
We share our secrets and our dreams.
I would never turn my back on her.
She may do things to me that I don't understand
But they always seem to come out right.
I just hope she never leaves me, because if she did,
I don't think I could go on.
Love ya Anney, remember that always.

April Bosworth

AS WE GROW OLD

Some people say that growing old
is not so great and so I'm told.

Some people say we must be bold,
but others simply just grow cold.

As from the beginning, we are born in a state of void.
So does it end when our time comes, that
 from whence we came we come again.

And, from the beginning we know of nothing.
Some seek out knowledge while others merely play along.

And, in this world of question and uncertainty,
Who is to say which path a man will take?

And, in this world of mystery and awe,
Who will believe that there is a God?

Some wonder if there is a purpose to life,
While others continue to struggle and strife.

And, who is to say that there is no purpose in death?
And, who is to say that our lives are not pre-ordained?

And, who can say when looking up above,
That a presence is there and much beloved?

Yvonne G. Engel Davis

MY AWNING

When I feel defeated,
and mental fatigue takes "control,"
when dredge overwhelms my soul,
your love takes my hand and
lets it take hold.

Fatefully you are my rock.
Your ability to predict my need
is no mystery to me.
You are my justice and order
bringing me back to reality.
You are my guide and defender!
With calm reassurance
you bring me back to the basic.
I can feel your love and understanding,
as I speak to you honest and sincere.

Sophisticated is no longer in form.
I give to the unseen and
            surrender.
    We are one!

Jeri Lea Golden

THE WILD ROSE

You don't ask who I am and I don't need to say.
But, for the sake of sanity,
I need to speak it today.

I have my own style,
At my own pace.
Everywhere and always.
Forceful, delicate and free.
Survival is my soul.
Tranquility is my goal.

You may admire my outward glow.
For only a short while.
But, shun my thorn: it stings.
Disturb my balance, then you will know.
This wild rose with wings.

Jeri Lea Golden

LET GOD

Life is such a mystery;
    We do not understand
The workings of Almighty God,
    Nor the reason for His plans.

We fuss and stew and rush about
    To work things out just right
Forgetting that He's able still
    Our battles all to fight.

When all the while He's waiting
    Our burdens all to bear,
And if we'll only let Him
    He'll show us how He cares.

So let's just look to Jesus
    And give to Him our all,
Knowing He is listening
    When on Him we do call.

Hope Scott

SPIRIT OR MATTER

Some say, "Spirit created matter";
Some, "Matter created spirit";
But the wise say, "They coexist."

The advocates of spirit remember God
But do not act.
The advocates of matter act
But do not remember God.
The Wise do the both.

To live life is to act, and
Is both spiritual and material;
this, the Wise knows.
He works out both,
Gets the proof for his say
And continues to live.

"To remember God and act
Is to work out both,
Is to get the proof
And is to live."
Everyone understands sooner or later.

Ganesh Lotu Bhirud

I NEED YOU, LORD

I need you, Lord
    like flowers need sunlight
    like the tide needs the moon
    like the beach needs sand
    like life needs breath
I need you, Lord.

Kathleen Eastman

WALKING THROUGH DARKNESS

To My Companion

the demons in my mind — no judgment —
with breath and beating of the heart
in the still night of my darkness,
Listen.
there is a small voice within my heart
that i will allow
to burn —
heartflame —
until all that is
in darkness
surrenders
to lovelight.

the beating of birdwings
violet and yellow
humming
birds
in flight
full of laughing grace,
then perched on telephone wires
and cocking their heads,
looking curiously at me —
relaying their message
of my questioning
a celebration
too dear to forget.

Julie Weiss

RAISING THE DEAD

down in the alley
of strange dis-ease
in a marvelous world
of make believe,

she wonders
if anything she does
thinks or says
is not distorted or
beyond change;

she
wonders
about
the impossible —
a change
in the weather.

Julie Weiss

THE GREAT MYSTERY

within walking
  is the movement of the soul —
  so perceived
  a heartbeat may fill you
  with your sweetest dream.

within any gesture
  so flourishes the soul's desire
  to be known
  in the simple rhythm of being
  human.

this is a nightmare world
  we are told time and time again.
yet see the magic in your movement,
  embrace all that you feel —
  and you alone
  have saved the world
  time and time again.

Julie Weiss

THE DIVINE UNION

The bridged light dawns
    On an open field.
Love and friendship
    This union will yield.

A harvest comes
    On a whisper spoken,
Of hearts entwined
    And souls unbroken.

The divine spirit
    Is witness and judge,
For through peace and despair
    These two will trudge.

Combined in spirit,
    Combined in heart,
The church bells sound:
    Not 'till death do they part.

Rebecca Hurst

MEMORIES OF HENRY

My heart is filled with joy and sorrow,
When I can only think of yesterday and not tomorrow.
My memories are always with me of you,
Your face, your voice, your tenderness too.
I miss you more than words can say,
For all these years have not waned away.

You were always there when I needed you —
I remember the night, I called your name,
And with little sleep, you came to soothe my pain.
Twenty one years have passed, my life has changed.
I like to think that you have been here to
     encourage and help me gain,
The courage I lacked to grow and become,
The woman, you always believed in.
I am now a wife, and a mother too,
But I owe this all to the love from you.
You will always be with me —
My shining example of goodness, charm and
     intelligence too.
To my Father, Henry . . . *I love you.*

Carol Goldman

RETURN

Dreaming about banshees colouring the night sky
Taking away the fears that live within our hearts
Someday we'll return to all the good things we remember
Someday we'll return to the firelight

Don't turn away from darkness, there could always be a way
Dreams that dwell in the daylight aren't always painless
Someday you may see that the colour of the night sky
Can be the sweet serenity in your mind
We will return to all the good things we remember
We will return to the firelight

Standing on an open plain somewhere in the country
There was not a single cloud in the sky that day
What does it mean when the dawn comes too early
What does it mean when the dusk seems late
We will return to all the good things we remember
We will return to the firelight

Dreaming about banshees colouring the night sky
Taking away the fears that live within our hearts
When will we return to all the good things we remember
When will we return, where's the light

Chester D. Sherman

HAPPINESS IS — SUMMER

I step softly and listen —
A hush of freshness walks on the air,
Blue-birds shimmer, hills kindle green,
Light casts shadows slantwise — a golden stair
Of yellow reflects on the dandelions.
The air is electric with motion, whispering
To the wild roses bowed with fresh dew.
The chatting brook is merrily chuckling,
Dancing over the glimmering rocks.

I lift my face full into the soft breeze,
I listen to the chatting brook moving;
My own flesh and I are snug and laughing sisters,
I know we are forever mingled with the winds' pulse,
And the golden sunlight.

Dolores R. Patitz

LIFE'S ORCHARD

The fruit trees are laden with a plentiful supply;
The shiny red apple seems to catch your eye.
Great pear trees and plums, you are so overbearing,
With branches bending low, filled with fruit you're wearing.

The orchard's overflowing. The fruit is all around,
Covering the trees, and even spread on the ground.
Everywhere you look, the coloring is vivid;
With yellows, greens, reds, and some too, are livid.

It's a garden of plenty, to taste at your will;
To crunch the sweet flavors, 'til you've had your fill.
Then pick a bushel for you to take home;
Gathering so carefully through the orchard you roam.

Gather the fruits of life in just that same way;
Pick them, and taste them, don't let the good get away.
Gather them gently, and be filled one by one.
That's what is meant by, "Thy will be done."

To be done on earth, as it is written in heaven.
Pick life's fruits tenderly, be it one or seventy-seven.
That's what our life's story on earth is all about.
So take a visit to Life's Orchard. Take time out.

Florence Klabunde

LULLABY FOR THE UNBORN BABY

You will come to us
like a snowdrop
which foretells a joy of spring sunlight
in whiteness of our lives.

You will come to our world
which is vast like the universe,
and little as a toy
in your hands.

You will see on your ways
huge ancient ruins, startling modern paintings,
interior of the atom, and everyday griefs
of plain men at dusk of their days.

You will experience in your life of adventure
enchantment of voyages, fascination of exploration,
never-to-be-forgotten places, countless faces,
nights, roads, and ideas.

We welcome you to our busy days
under the sky full of clouds of incertitude,
and to our hearts
warm like a small sparkle which lights a fire of love.

Tomorrow, you will fulfill
secret hopes of many human hearts;
Today, sleep joyfully
under the heart of your mother.

Eugene Joseph Kucharz

MELLIFLUOUS MASQUERADE

Sitting in my room again,
   the rain outside beats down.
Strangely now, I feel secure
   staring at my clowns.

Their cheerful smiles remind me of
   happy times I've had.
They always bring joy to my heart,
   making a sad day glad.

Their painted faces mask the lore
   of passive inference.
They watch in silence, speaking naught,
   smiling their innocence.

Words are not always requisite.
   They mutely sympathize,
Communicating compassion
   through their twinkling eyes.

The Pierrot with pensive face
   sentiments can't hide.
The understanding empathy
   spills over from inside.

My clowns, each one is special.
   A prize treasure all hold,
For underneath the costumes
   beat hearts made of pure gold.

Kimberly Finley

MULGROVE HILL

The stars come out on Mulgrove Hill
And beams of light bounced from marble stone
And I'm left here with knees bent down
To mourn the one gone on alone

Oh, I hold no stored up anger
Not to God nor Satan's 'count
For I realize a time's appointed
And on ebon' steed we mount

And that day I look back upon
The flames of life low in her eyes
And how I drew her closer to me
And wished death would loose its ties

Its ropes, its bonds, its tight fit noose
And strength would lift her frailness there
And blood flow and fill her tauted lips
To kiss away my deep despair

But death held on and was the victor
And a voice said *time to go*
And I heard the sound of hoofbeats
In the valley far below

And now the church light playing games
I see her likeness stay
And as I draw close unto her
I hear those hoofbeats ride away

Lonnie Collins

NIGHT VANDAL

Vandal,
Crashing through the fence at night,
Ripping shingles off my roof,
Dumping garbage on the ground,
Then rattle-rolling empty trash cans
Down my drive,
I know you . . .
I recognize that jeering whisper as
You tap tap on my door;
I know whose fingertips come scratching,
Snatching out some way to
In.

Cold-hearted prankster,
Clatter-banging at my window,
Rousing me from sleep,
It's useless . . .
I'll not let you in!
Whimper whistle whine your best, you,
Rattle rap bang as you please!
My house is locked and barred against you,
Vandal . . .
Nasty noisy prankster wind.

Dorothy G. Leuser

TRAVELING ON

I find myself so often
Living in the valley low
And I know that if I'd conquer
To the mountaintop must go.

There are many different roads
Upon which I have to tread
Some are paved with happiness
Some of them I dread.

Without the shield of faith
I would not dare to go
For I am weak and fearful
My steps are very slow.

But I have a guide called Jesus
My Saviour, Lord and Friend,
For everything that's needful
On him I can depend.

There's a road that's full of music
Where happy voices sing
Owning their allegiance
To Jesus Christ the King.

When my traveling days are over
Then the way I'll clearly see
Where the mountain meets the valley
And God reaches down for me.

Blanche Simmons

MY NEED

Lord I need you once again today
Everything's all wrong
Troubles all around me
Have robbed me of my song

Why can't I learn the lesson
Worry never pays
I've let fear and doubt and bitterness
Ruin so many days

When I look back I plainly see
That you were always near
To rescue me from every snare
To heal, to help, and cheer

I may fail another day
I may slip and fall
And yet I know most surely
You'll be there when I call

I'll try to do much Lord
I've said it times before
But what I need is more of you
More and more and more.

Blanche Simmons

FOLLOW THE LORD

Seek and ye shall find
Find and ye shall follow
Follow, follow, follow the Lord.

Follow where He leads you
Through each path and bend.
Follow where He leads you
To life's journey's end.

Seek and ye shall find
Find and ye shall follow
Follow, follow, follow the Lord.

Follow Him through green meadows
And to the mountain heights.
Follow Him through dark valleys
And on to celestial lights.

Seek and ye shall find
Find and ye shall follow
Follow, follow, follow the Lord.

Kathleen Eastman

TRAVELING THROUGH THIS LIFE

I'm traveling through this life
I'm walking with my Lord.
I'm believing in His promise
Glory, hallelu.

I'm trusting in His presence
I'm listening to His call
I'm singing to Him praises
Glory, hallelu.

Kathleen Eastman

INTRUSION

The guns are done in Lebanon tonight.
No child's wail will rise above the plea
Of human pale inherent in the agony
When peace had gone to serve Religious Right.
Just silence now; and horrid is the sight —
With which sad eyes of all are dashed who see —
Of Sisyphistic fate of the cedar tree
When peace had gone to serve Religious Right.
The child at last beneath the earth's undone,
A cedar sapling cut before its time;
And close laid waste the old, the young, the prime
Of straight and stately trees of Lebanon.
Some say the cedars fell from cult disease.
I say: locusts . . . from other shores and trees.

C. Coolidge Wilson

CEILING SHADOWS

Before the brightest ember in the fire dies,
I'll lie alone with you in shrouding dark to see
Among the ceiling shadows caught by passion's eyes
A hint, a glimpse, a fraction of eternity.
Some sombre shadows tell a tale of mystic woe
Within the heaving breast of love's propensity,
Like spring's first crocus snipped in winter's loitering snow
A wisp, a thought, a vapor of contingency.
These dancing shadows show the blush of passion's heat
By which the night of Plato's cave could burst with light,
By which the primal din of solitudes could greet
A taste, a truth, a tremble of Faust's delight.
My glutted rapture, surfeit in your castellan-charms,
The ember spent, now welcomes sleep in vigilant arms.

C. Coolidge Wilson

THE WALKER . . .

He walks heavily, head bowed
Against the boisterous surge of wind.
Sand too wet to blow is dimpled by pebbles indug.
The flow of departing floods leaves the foam
Like summer lace to dress the sand.
He wearily drags the netted bag
That almost topples him on the knoll.
And pauses there to catch his breath.
Sun rims beneath the clouds
That twist themselves like smoke rings roll.
Along the horizon that feels the whip
Of rising tides. He trudges through
The whipping marsh grass to the high beach, beyond.
His mother's apron so loosely tied
Flutters as she gathers sheets from the line.
They fold her in as she pulls them free.
Holding the basket of wash between them
They walk against the sheltering wall.
Wind roars full of laughter towards the sea.
He pauses to watch the white crowned waves
As they pound against the steep stone-clad beach.
He is home again.

Elinor Shurtleff Churchill

SPENDTHRIFT

I am profligate with me, and spend myself
As drunken sailors spend their pay.
I fling my love in all directions
As bread is cast upon the waters of the sea.

In widow's weeds I pace the walk, the
Spyglass of my anxious eyes sweeps endlessly,
While overlooked upon the shore, the stoppered bottle
Bobs and floats and bears your love to me.

Patricia Bowler

WORLD WIDE GAME

Why do you talk while other people are praying?
Why don't you listen to what others are saying?

It's fine to have your own opinions, most people do.
But when you force on others your beliefs, it's hard to get through.
You're as kind as anyone can be, giving all that you have.
But thrusting your condescending mentality makes objective victims mad.

Why do you talk while other people are praying?
Why don't you listen to what others are saying?

Yet on the other hand, I understand in which the situation you live.
You keep good humor during it all, your country being supportive.
But stereotyping different nationalities just isn't right;
You must give each individual a chance to put up a fight.
And in the end, you'll find that no two people are the same;
That it's a much bigger contest, called the World Wide Game.

You're a very funny person and good at heart
Which was one thing that was apparent right from the start.
So please understand and don't take this the wrong way.
It's just constructive criticism; it's only fair to say:

Why do you talk while other people are praying?
Why don't you listen to what others are saying?

Catherine McCarthy

SOMETHING TO HOLD ON TO

Something to hold on to: my mind races forward
        my heart beats fast, it
        pounds against my chest.
        time passes with every
        tick of the clock.
Something to hold on to: in the middle of the night
        as sleep passes by me, tossing
        and turning on my bed of discontent.
        chasing my tail, as round and around
        it goes.
Something to let go of: like scales falling from my eyes
        my heart silent, as time passes: unnoticed.
Something to hold on to: peace quenches my thirst like fresh, cool
        water rolling down my back, it cleanses my soul . . .

        Something to hold on to . . .

Carl Evans

FOREVERMORE

All the glory that was mine;
Now at last, has become thine!
In the heaven in my heart —
You've become, at last, a part!

When I gazed into your eyes,
I saw a light, like a sunrise!
Bells, a song of love, rang out —
Prove to me, what it's about!

All really that's worth giving,
Is this moment, we are living!
All rapture, sweet and tender —
Ours, if we but surrender!

Because, way deep within thee,
Are dreams of love, heavenly!
And these, I know, will be mine —
When we lovingly entwine!

All the beauty, deep in me,
I would like to give to thee!
If our future does come true —
I'll always feel, love for you!

Like a sparkling ray of light,
That shines in the darkest night,
Our pure love, points out the way —
Into love's eternal day!

Come with me, where ecstasy,
Is part of life, sun and sea!
And where waves upon the shore —
Whisper, *Love's Forevermore!*

Kathleen Lyon Vaughn

WAR AND PEEPS

The cat I love
My bird does not.
In truth, he'd sooner
See him rot.
A shame it is,
It could not be,
These two could
Live in harmony,
But cats, as cats,
See birds as prey,
So Tolstoi stalks
By night and day.
And though I think
It safe to say
He'd hardly make
A canapé,
Ever-wary little Peeps
Keeps one eye open
When he sleeps.

Jack Lynott

MOURNING

No parting words spoken
yet silent good-byes echo
cool and still the air
 ''morning''
star shine

Denise Michele Keppel

THE ADVERTISERS

So many raucous voices
Shouting in my ear,
Stretching on their tip-toes,
Shoving from the rear,

All demand attention,
Wild things running free,
Who opened up the madhouse
And set them loose on me?

Jack Lynott

A SMALL VOICE

Have you learned any lessons today?
Is the dark turning slowly to grey?
 Are you closer to truth?
 A bit less uncouth?
Were your efforts rewarded today?

Did you manage to add to your store
A scintilla of scholarly lore?
 Did you husband your time?
 Did you painfully climb?
Did you suffer and come back for more?

Are you burning your candles at night?
Are you yearning for more and more light?
 Are you training your mind?
 Are you mad? Are you blind?
Is the end that you seek out of sight?

Is your intention to keep me at bay?
Are you bored with the things that I say?
 Though I poke and I prod,
 Do you drowse? Do you nod?
Would you rather I just went away?

Jack Lynott

THE TEARS IN MY EYE

My tears I held inside for so long,
it is now a whole year since you've
been gone.

When I think back to the good times we
used to share, I feel so much pain that
you can sense it in the air.

One night, the tears came down like rain
from the sky. If you could've seen this
grown man cry, well, you wouldn't believe
your eyes.

It seems that our precious love has come to
a bitter end. It's like living, then dying,
and then back again.

I believe you would know how much you've
hurt my feelings & pride, if you'd just
turn around and see the tears in my eye.

Lavell Dwayne Bailey

GRANDMA'S WAR ON THE HOUSEFLY

Grandma hated houseflies,
 on that you can rely;

They jumped into her buttermilk,
 and nibbled at her pie;

She couldn't stand their buzzing,
 nor the mess they always made;

They even tried to bite her nose,
 as she drank her lemonade;

She tied cotton balls on screen doors,
 to scare the flies away;

This was long before someone,
 invented insect spray;

She waged her war both day and night,
 against those little pests;

Stopping only now and then,
 to get a moment's rest;

Her strategy was very well planned,
 and as hard as she did try;

She lost the mighty battle,
 against the common fly;

Grandma is resting now in heaven,
 I wonder what she would say;

If she knew those pesky little pests,
 are still flying around today.

John T. Hudelson

TRACK AND FIELD

Track and Field are very great.
A lot of people run a race,
With a lot of grace and win every race.
It don't matter, if you are small or great.
It's how you run the race.
If you lose, it's no disgrace.
Everyone don't run a perfect race.
It's just the same in the field.
Just do your best, what can anyone expect.
It sounds like a race that no one will regret.

Mr. & Mrs. Henry Case

BASEBALL

The pitcher's mound is very round.
They say, ''The pitcher is the best all around.''
The catcher backs up the pitcher.
The pitcher backs up the catcher.
Then, the pitcher backs up the first, second
 and third basemen.
The fielders' got a place of their own in the field.
So, you see the pitcher can't do it all,
But needs them all, just the same.

Mr. & Mrs. Henry Case

OUR CHRISTMAS TREE

We're going to have a Christmas tree
Green and tall as it can be

Ornaments and lights so bright
We're going to do it up just right

You're invited one and all
And we hope that you will call

He'll be coming pretty quick
Bright and jolly old St. Nick

While we plan the days to come
Friends who'll visit, joys and fun,

We'll thank God that we are free
To gather around our Christmas tree.

June Staudte

MEMORIES IN DENIM AND LACE

*Written in honor of my parents,
D. K. and Margaret Morehouse.*

They lived on the land and tilled the soil,
Whether years were good or lean.
They kept a home through labor and love,
And we learned to hope and dream.
Wealth possessed was not silver or gold,
Nor baubles held in the hand.
Our riches were caring, sharing and faith,
And love for our fellow-man.
No soul in need turned away from our door
Of the old house there on the farm,
But love reached out to lift and sustain,
In friendship true and warm.
The years rolled away, youngsters grown.
Still they trod with slowing pace,
While the pen of time kept writing
In lines of life on each face.
Weddings widened the circle,
And 'round the fireside glow,
To a third and forth generation,
Their love continued to flow.
With all their labors ended,
Our parents had finished their race.
At Home Over There, they left us
Memories in denim and lace.

Reva M. Smith

TIME HEALS

I felt so weak, so terribly weak,
    I was sure I could not cope!
So many sad, sad moments
    Had robbed me of all hope.

Each day seemed, oh, so weary!
    No smiles, just tears, I knew.
And though I sought the sunshine,
    Nowhere would it shine through.

But "Time" came to my rescue,
    It healed me — made me whole.
And once again my God I thank
    With body, mind and soul.

Pearl Sandahl

SHIPWRECK

A ship of dreams rides at anchor
In the harbor of memory,
It became a ghostly galleon
Tossed on a stormy sea.

The course appeared well charted,
Allowing for winds of doubt.
Reefs of tears were expected,
Brief gusts of dismay without.

All else seemed right for sailing,
Skies were blue above,
A stalwart captain at the helm
To guide this ship of love.

But dark clouds rolled, a hurricane raged,
And the captain was swept away.
With none to stand alert at the helm,
A broken craft returned to the bay.

The ship now rests in the harbor,
'Though time has made it a wreck,
Unused, her cargo of golden dreams,
A captain's memory still walks the deck.

Reva M. Smith

RAIN

Rain, rain, coming down.
Bouncing on and off the ground.
Your perfect rhythm is a tune,
To this wet weather we've had in June.

Dancing raindrops on my sill,
Come in my open window.
Tapping, skipping, slipping, until,
Through the screen they go.

Flipping, falling, on the floor,
Creeping, crawling, toward the door.
A puddle here, a puddle there.
Rain comes in without a care.

Rain, rain, come down in vain.
I love your sweet melody.
Until you return again,
I'll crave your tranquility.

Karen Aileen Libero

THE BUTTERFLY

Golden in the sunlight . . .
    resting on a rose
Fragile wings a flutter . . .
    as into the wind she goes.
High in the blue sky . . .
    she flies to meet her mate.
Gracefully she flies . . .
    for butterflies are never late.
We see them now among the flowers . . .
    see their golden wings.
They are nature's masterpieces . . .
    so very beautiful.
Even the north wind sings . . .
    Spring is here.

Doris June Winkelman

HOPELESS vs HOPEFUL

The lady had a problem —
    "It's overwhelming," she did say.
It gave her only heartaches —
    All seemed hopeless day by day.

"I think I cannot cope," she said,
    "When things so hopeless seem;
Depression's robbed me of my worth
    And of my self-esteem."

"O Lord, my blessed Saviour,
    Please hear my humble prayer;
I so badly want your guidance,
    Your vigilance, your care."

And soon the *hopeless* problem
    By prayer was eased away,
And in its stead a *hopeful* trust
    Ensued without delay.

The lady still feels problems,
    But now she can endure
Because *Hopeless* turned to *Hopeful*
    And of God's grace, she's sure.

Pearl Sandahl

The last word, the last say.
A vocal victory,
Have it your way.
You have gained nothing by claiming all.
I have lost nothing
By conceding the same.
One heart, then two,
Now one again.
You played the game
But you didn't win.
The conqueror defeated by a heart denied.
If victory is yours then why must you hide?

David Cook

THAT I MIGHT SEE

You are not, Oh Lord, just "from the sky,"
For everywhere, You so imply . . .
Your "wondrous works" of Majesty,
That, I your "image" might humbly see!
Yet, carnal mind eludes Your way . . .
So, must I kneel to penitent pray:
"Guide my path each day in Thee,
Show me Lord, that I might see."
For no thought I bring to bear,
Ere escapes your "listening ear."
Cleanse my guilty, blood-stained heart,
That Thy Son so may impart . . .
A "Crown of Life" so surely be
A reward of faith in trusting Thee.
Lord, lead me on to greater heights,
Ease my fear of earthly frights;
Secure my soul, Thou gavest me . . .
Forever, now and eternity.
"Guide my path each day in Thee,
Show me Lord, that I might see."

Arne Maurice Simonson

SUCH A SPECIAL GIRL

Such beauty in your eyes, there's so much beauty,
it can fill the skies.
Such tenderness in your touch, a man can love you,
oh so much.
Such happiness in your smile, makes my whole life
worthwhile.
Such beauty as you can see, my love for you is now
reality.
Love, John.

John C. Eisenhower, Sr.

DREAMS HAVE NO BOUNDARIES

On one quiet cool summer night:

For we are united together again,
    as one until the end of time.
For we share truth,
    in our daily life together.
For we are one with each other,
    in our love, honesty and trust.
Come my love,
    let me hold you in my arms,
Come and lay down beside me,
    on the cool sheets.
Let me feel your soft, silky,
    body next to me.
For we know each other,
    better than someone, who knows himself.
For there isn't anything,
    we don't know about each other.
For we spend our time together.
    and time apart for ourselves.
For as long as we have each other,
    then dreams have no boundaries.

All is quiet now, except for the birds singing outside the window.

Marcia Randall

OPENING LAIR

Expressing things inside your mind, in words of
    mazing games.
Memories seem compelling, to he who all
    complains.

When many do not wonder, of one who
    understands:
He shall start to ponder, with what he can
    withstand.

Now with his learning ways he knows, that soon
    he'll comprehend;
That there's nothing he can't conquer, no one he
    can befriend.

Doujhe Dragnist

ILLUSION'S

As the elegance of nature's secret visions —
carefully begin to unfold,
Our heart of hearts, mysterious Destiny.
Unforetold Dreams to behold.

A long unwinding road,
A path which we must all take,
Enclosed with *Illusion's,* hopes and mistakes.
Silently the north wind whispers —
to our starlit Heavens above,
Revealing our innermost feelings,
Secrets of a heart, my Love of Loves!
'Bout wishful thinking carefully wrapped with care,
Unforetold feelings, a heart full of despair.

The delicate nature of one soul,
seems to determine, whether we shall — stumble or fall.
The fullness of one's heart —
and awaited dream —
Overflowing with Ideas, bursting at the seams!

As silence rejoicingly encircles the earth's hemisphere,
Delivering an unspoken *Peace* —
To all who Dare!
Receive her smile and shake *Illusion's* hand!
To gain the understanding,
of Nature's Generosity of Giving —
the gift of life — *called Living.*

Zenobia

EMERGENCY CALLS

In the quietude of the night visitors slowly walked out.
''I'll see you again,'' they said.
Onward home they went.

The doors closed to the atmosphere unlike home.
All who remained felt very much alone.
''Here we must stay,'' they seemed to say.

The lights flashed at all hours of the night.
The signals were for the ones dressed in uniforms of white.
Many were the emergency calls throughout the night.

''Help!'' was the yell that didn't disappear.
The voice continued until someone appeared.

''I wish my arms could stretch to help simultaneously more than one.''
That was what was said, as one rushed to someone's bed:
The urge to help could be felt.
They often eased the pain and fear.
Everywhere they tried to cheer.

Busy was the night shift while the clock moved to morn.
Help didn't cease when their duties came to an end.
Others in their place ambitiously spread.
Like the clock that doesn't stop, the work doesn't end.
On their duties all depend.

In giving praise we thank those in uniforms of white.
They are at the emergency calls day or night.

Frances D. Rosenthal

MY SON OF TEN

I bore a son
In the month of May.
You came to me
On a special day.

You struggled hard
To make your way.
A little help from me
And then you came.

Your voice rang out
To let us know.
You were alive
And doing alright.

I've cared for you
All of ten years.
I look to see
If you're still real.

For in my heart
I can't believe.
You've come to me
Even as I speak.

The joy you've brought
Words cannot express.
The love I hold
Dear to my breast.

Bobbie J. Brown

SHE CARED

Will we remember
All those things.
She gave to us
Those passing days?

She gave us love
Along with hugs.
And kisses so sweet
That made us blush.

Of all the tears
She wiped away.
And all the cheers
She gave each day.

For our goodness
As well as our bad.
The lessons she taught
And spankings we got.

Only to remember
With all our hearts.
When no other was there
She cared.

Bobbie J. Brown

BESIDE YOU

Every soul must choose a path
Facing life; its joy . . . its wrath.
Whether the wind blows foul or fair
God and I, your friends are there.

Delores Hendricks

NUCLEAR PEACE

A blinding light
a deafening roar
a violent rushing wind

Buildings shattered
trees turned to ashes
shadows burned in stone

Then, sudden silence
no more screams
all hearts stilled

The chill of death
land without life
earth without form, void

No more leaders
no more protests
no turning back

The end of war
all is at rest
a costly peace

Denise Jean Ford

MY CORNER OF THE WORLD

I've always heard the world was round
But surely that's not true
'Cause I keep finding myself in corners
In so many things I do.

I paint myself into a corner
Twenty feet from any door
There I sit for hours
'Til I can't stand it anymore.

I creep across on tiptoes
Not leaving many marks
And then a door swings open
Letting in a dog that barks.

I swing my arms and yell at him
He comes running in alarm
I'm flung in another corner
That damn dog on my arm.

The next house I buy
I'll look it over good
To see that there's no corners
Around in a square neighborhood.

Renna Gillespie

TIME

Time is an empty cup
Tied with an ebony ribbon.
It offers us nothing
But a measured cadence
To which we march out
Our lives.

Lynn J. Ducote

MEETING

atoms move asunder into oblivion
or is it eternity?
with unfathomed speed of light
and glacial slowness.
their legacy is our universe,
this mysterious world
whose secrets cannot
reveal themselves to humans
and whose rituals will not
touch their souls —
except yours and mine.
when all the colors of the universe merge
into the white eternal light
we, too, are part of this miracle
but for a brief forever moment.

Ggisela Nass

IS MY NAME WRITTEN THERE

Lord, I don't care for riches
Or silver or gold
I just want heaven, to be my new home
And someday, to enter thy fold

To be by your side
In that heavenly place
And abide with you father
And see your sweet face

In the book of thy kingdom
Of that city so fair
Oh sweet Jesus my Saviour
Is my name written there

Emma Collins

DID HE KNOW?

Did He know?
    From the moment of His birth,
    What His life would be on earth?

Did He know?
    In His manger in the cave,
    A like place would be His grave?

Did He know?
    Was He carefree as a child?
    Him — on whom our sins were piled?

Did He know?
    As He helped friends tend the sheep,
    People's souls were in His keep?

Did He know?
    Did He learn to work with wood
    Knowing His would be the rood?

Did He know?
    Just how old that He would be
    When He'd die upon that tree?

Yes, He knew, my soul, He knew
From the first breath that He drew.
Double burden! First, the knowing —
Then, the paying — for our owing.

E. Maurine Rathje

ENCOURAGEMENT

"Send me a poem," is what was said.
It came from a poetry editor I never met.
I had no poem, so I got my pen.
But, with no paper, the poem would be dead.
The thoughts would stay in and nothing would be read.
So, I bought a book for poems to be written in.
Finally, I had a poem that I was glad to send.
It went to the poetry editor.
He sent me a letter again.

"Congratulations!" Your poem will be in the book to be read."
That's what he said in the letter he sent.
Few were the words, but they brought me joy.
They made me wish to write poems some more.
I got so busy with more poems in my head.
I never thought I would write so many poems with my pen.
My pen is getting used to writing more poems that are getting read.

"Congratulations," You have been selected as one of our
  Best new poets for 1987."
Those were the words that he said, in another letter he sent.
This time his words brought more joy than ever before.

What could I write for such a book to be read?
"Anything you like," is what he said.
Here I am writing how it all began.
With one poem many more spread because of what was said.
Enjoyment comes with what I write and wish the world to know.
Soon I'll have a manuscript of poems that I wish some day will be sold.

Frances D. Rosenthal

NOW AND FOREVER

Now and forever, remember the words of my heart are always true,
and continue to love me as much as I love you.

Now and forever, even if it doesn't last,
I'll always have the memories of the past.

Now I have the good times and the bad times too.
And Forever, I'll have the beautiful thoughts of me and you.

Tina Kossmann

MOMENTS GONE BY

To walk barefoot on a lonely beach
Sea gulls soaring within my reach
Water lapping against the shore
My thoughts are blurred, time is gone

A ten year old and her Dad, hands held tight
Catching the sun on the water as it rushes in
Running so not to get soaked
Laughing, not to have a care in the world

Bringing back those memories in my mind
Helps me understand how precious love is
To store in a magic corner
There, when you need warm feelings to hold on to.

Carol J. Parker

As a sign of danger vents its nervous exhaust,
There is the sign of the sun,
Chanting his song of yesteryear.
How high upon the skies divided,
Can the heavens remove the harp.
They struck the thundercloud.
They hold human abbreviation of birth under a seconded tree.
Upon its beloved spouse's care,
It rests eternally well,
Above and beyond the bliss of a spiritual poet.

Beyond the golden crossed, it is glad to have a true shower,
Paint the earth with gold beyond referendum.
It is with the flute, beside each gain, that have eased,
The sisterhood of a life burgeoning with excess delay and delight.
It is within the midst of these ambrosial wings,
That doves take lost, over in well-controlled flight.
To penetrate its harp's visage,
The contemplation of a penetration in a morning glory,
In likelihood, erases the mind of a poet,
And a poet's life in derivative,
It is held in poet's delight of a camisole comradery.

Lisa Miller

WINE TO REPLACE MEMORIES

Just like the strains of a haunting refrain,
That glass of wine takes away most of the pain —
Those haunting memories that still fill my mind,
Like those haunting melodies, it will end in time.

Why didn't I love her so very much more,
Instead of the wine that I bought at the store?
She came second place with me all of the time —
For the first on my list was that bottle of wine.

She was always there, helping carry the load,
But I took her for granted, little kindness I showed —
But for that wine I'd do most anything,
And through it all, she made me her king.

And now I'm alone, with only my wine to hold,
But the warm feeling it brings, soon turns cold —
Why does a man leave his kids and his home,
Throw self-respect away, just to drink and to roam?

Some will fly kinda high, others end on skid row,
And wherever they end, it's a piece of hell, you know —
They go down that road, where there's no turning back,
For their great desire, is that bottle in the sack.

Phyllis Morton

That faith of our fathers that led them through trials
Over trails that were hard to be crossed
That helped them fight Indians, storms and hot suns
Kept their minds and their hearts embossed.
Did they give up and say, God, I'll never get through
Though at times all their patience wore thin —
And their bodies exhausted and ready to fall —
They passed on great heritage to their kin —

Marjorie Hennigan

ACCUSATIONS

He was crucified!
He bled, and He died —

And we're quick to accuse
Those self-righteous Jews
Who yelled, "Crucify Him!" —
And not one stood by Him —
Still, the lips that are bruised
Say, "It wasn't the Jews."

"Well, then, Rome did the deed
With its hate and its greed;
They scourged Him with scorn,
And crowned Him with thorn." —
Yet, a hoarse voice — half moan —
Says, "It was not Rome."

"Oh, it was God's plan
To reconcile man.
It was foretold by seers." —
Then His eyes fill with tears.
"Don't you see?" He implores,
"I gave My life — for yours!"

E. Maurine Rathje

LOVE'S HOPE

*To my beautiful wife, Nona,
for we have found Love's Hope*

Love, that precious oil,
    that brings forth healing
when life has delivered
    a crushing blow.

That balm that lifts
    from the dregs, that human,
defeated, battered, beaten down
    and bathes away the dirt.

That tender gentle touch
    that encourages, endures
until the shadow has turned
    into the substance of life.

Love is the promise, the hope
    the crying need of every human being
to be held, to be needed,
    to respond.

Willard E. Toller

THE TRUTH

They told me it was wrong
they told me you would hurt me
they said you would leave me
they said you did not care
you told me not to believe them
but I was torn in two
I did not know whom to believe
but now I believe in you
I ask you to forgive me
but if you don't, I'll understand
I was mean to you
because of a foolish heart.

Amy Kathleen Westerhoff

GENTLE BREEZE

The beauty of autumn
Is like no other,
As I walk through fallen leaves
There's a quiet place
Within my soul,
As the soft wind's gentle breeze
Caresses my tender heart,
Uplifting my spirit.
This autumn scene, painted so perfectly
By the great master of art:
The golds, the browns, the reds and oranges
Brushed by Nature's hand,
Colors of autumn trees will remain
Forever in my mind,
And of the rustling leaves
Upon the ground,
Swishing and swirling all around.

Teri Payne

TIME FOR ALL THINGS

A time to smile, A time to cry
A time to live, A time to die
A time to be happy, A time to be sad
A time to be grateful, A time to be glad.

A time to keep silent, A time to speak
A time to mourn, A time to weep
A time to embrace, A time to love
A time to give thanks to Elohim (God above).

A time of war, A time of peace
A time to plant, A time to reap
A time to love, A time to hate
A time to be patient, A time to wait.

A time to sing, A time to pray
A time to talk to Elohim (God each day)
A time to thank Him for all He's done
For the precious gift He gave us
His only begotten son.

Hattie Martin

You know
So much about me
I will never know . . .

The color of my eyes
The instant I wake
The way it feels to hold me
Or be held in my gaze
The way I breathe
When I'm asleep
The damage my words can do
The surprise of my touch.

No wonder
You can hurt me.

Carolyn Coffee

DESCENT

A journey by elevator
Downward plunge
Shadows and bloody images
My soul on ice

Blood washed from my hands
Whoever you are
Whatever you stand for
Go away . . . please

Steel bars descend
A fearful stupor
Clanging and banging resounds in my soul
Damnation awaits

Katherine M. Allen

EXCITEMENT OF TIME, PLACE, AND PURPOSE

I love to keep old photographs within my reach
And this one is special
It has everything I need and more
Honesty
Love
Raw courage
Memory of autumn winds
Banner stretched from here to eternity
Anger
Devotion
Determination
Honesty of purpose
Memory of autumn leaves
Excitement of time, place, and purpose

Katherine M. Allen

UNSUNG

I'm an unsung lover
You're my unsung friend
It seems I've blown my cover
No fences left to mend

Who's the unsung savior
On whom we all depend?
We feel his goodness everywhere
His ready ear to lend

You're my unsung hero
I could have been your friend
But I saw it once; I saw it twice
And then I saw it end

You're an unsung lover
I'm your unstrung friend
You've gone and blown my cover
No friendship left to mend

Katherine M. Allen

BARNWELL NURSING HOME

Because daily health care has potential
Around this aging neighborhood
Readjustments in living are essential —
Next changes could easily be good
Wellness is often a state of mind
Even when the body hurts and aches
Leveling off is hard, we find —
Long, lasting actions are what it takes.

New health concepts come and go
Using modern terminology, just so
Recycling what we already know
Seemingly clarifying our technology
Investigations prove the attitudes wise —
Nowdays total care can be a reality
Great care-givers of every sex and size.

Having both quantity and quality style
Overview — good care is readily seen
Making the whole human effort worthwile
Everyone's involved, with the staff in-between.

Gwendolyn Trimbell Pease

THE ONLY STAR OF EVENING

'Twas the only star of evening ashining through
  the night.
'Twas the only star of evening that assured me in
  my plight.
Surrounded by the darkness, akindled by the
  night,
Yet the darkened reaches of evening could not blot
  out its light.
Surrounded by the darkness, akindled by the
  night,
Yet the darkened reaches of evening could not
  blot out its might.

Ruth Goldfarb

LIFE BEGINS ANEW

How does one deal with sadness that becomes a soul-gripping,
  heart-wrenching ache?
A melancholy so large as to take on life of its own,
  threatening your heart to overtake?

Lord, I'm weary of this sorrow, this emptiness,
  this void which robs me of vitality;
Was not the hurt, the heartache enough?
Do I also have to suffer emptiness & self-pity?

But wait — could it be that I'm wrong
  and the void is not at all complete?
For, if I feel pity — rather than nothing —
  then the void may be becoming obsolete.

It's time to get on with this business of life
  and love and full living
And forget the sadness, self-pity and again
  learn to be good and giving.

Although life may be different now, it still can be real good
If I hold my head up high and think positive like I know I should.

And perhaps I'll be a better person now,
  more compassionate & understanding
Since I've experienced pain, loss, emptiness, and, finally, expanding.

Sharri Sanders

STUDY IN CONTRAST

Self Portrait

I teeter on the edge of decadence,
4-letter words erupting as from a volcano
When the occasion arises . . .
Or dependent upon whose company I'm in.

On the other hand, I feel a deep faith and
Am strong in my belief that the Lord will
Watch over me and mine.

He has seen us through so much —
Never failing to give the needed strength.

I've been able, in part, to pass that strength
On to others in need —
Firmly believing *for* them that He would lead
The way — seeing them through — and feeling
Total confidence that it'll be o.k.

So, why do I have this fight within . . . this ability
to talk — and think — like a heathen, a wretch?

Which side will win out?

My faith tells me He will — and I'm ready!
Feeling almost homesick for Heaven, I wait —
With open arms — for Him to cleanse my mind
and purify my heart —

For I cannot do it alone.

Sharri Sanders

SLIPPING INTO THE VOID

Have you ever had the feeling that nothing's left
And you're not quite sure what it was,
But whatever was there is gone now
And you start looking for something to be part of.

I want to climb across the red-tiled roof
And jump into the azure sky;
To find what I can before I splat.
It's the time I feel locked on the ground
That I really want to fly.

There's times when I reach down deep inside
But what's there isn't where it used to be.
I sit on my sofa with a dull face on
Looking into space to find what's lost.

I've been looking through a window to my heart
But what's inside is clouded by the dun.
When I look in after the rain falls
I only see the glare of the blinding sun.

There's something inside me that's slipping into the void,
So I'm grasping at the shadows it might be,
But if this darkness keeps falling over my eyes
It won't be long 'til there's nothing left to see.

So slip away; whatever it was I could never find.
It's hiding in another place or time
And I'd give up searching if I didn't have a reason
To seek the sky on this upward climb.

Gregory J. Borden

GRANDPA'S PRAYER

The old church is quiet now;
The congregation has gone away.
The door is locked and boarded
So no one comes to pray.

Only a few in the town remember
The faithful of long ago.
Their deeds of kindness hidden
As grass 'neath winter snow.

If only the old walls
Could speak for a change,
Perhaps they'd tell me
How grandpa's life was rearranged.

They'd tell me how
He got down on bended knee
And asked God to save him
For all eternity.

His simple words uttered
In a moment of time,
Changed grandpa's destiny
And also changed mine.

Judy A. Deeter

FRENCH CURVES AND MARBLE CHIPS

Across the street
I watch you as you tend to cuts of green,
You taught to root
In pots of clay, and cedar box.
I watch you coax each one to reach
Toward the sky, to grasp the rays,
The giving lines the sun casts down.
I see them stop along the way,
To kiss red brick,
Or dance upon slate stepping stones,
And marble chips.
Young birds appear in frantic moves,
Replaying their templated tunes.
I turn to be the passing wind,
Tracing french curves,
Past the softest skin.
I feel the warmth within you
Turn the cold stone, of the city,
Into a growing new projection of love.

Robert F. Vitalos

A CLOCK WITH NO HANDS

I once heard of a deer
with two heads
so afraid of life
it leaped from a cliff

I wonder what it thought
standing there on the edge of awareness
must have spoken to a man
with no heart
about winding a clock
with no hands

Ronald Anthony Browne

ALL ABOUT BABIES

All about babies
how they were created;
through a commission of love
where two people related.
A bond from baby to mom
but at any rate,
I'm so glad that men don't
labor through this fate.
Time is true trauma when
birth draws near;
healthy was the answer
I wanted to hear.
Now the parenting is essential
it begins with you;
because kids watch every move
then do as you do.
First teach love and respect
when you're not there, that
they'll go to the Father
with an earnest prayer.
Let them know that
whatever comes what may
that they are important, special
and in your heart they'll always
stay.

Wayne Lytle

CONFESSIONS OF A YOUNG MOTHER

Dawn till dusk,
belaboring this stifling existence
a quiet moment to contemplate,
a change so desperately needed.
The silence is shattered
by that familiar hark — *Moom!*
i must go on again
securing life for this day
while dying a little more.
Oh but for a fleeting moment —
i fiercely wish no other existence,
for all is rather perfect,
yet i spend light and darkness
in this dreary brooding
my query for meaning
consuming my every emotion
millionary *whatif*s —
distanced by the unimmortal interruptions
of my own flesh and blood —
the innocent eachness of all beauty
though regrets beyond conceiving
can scarcely dare to meet
death's heartless beat
but gives me courage to receive
life's greatest dream.

Johanna Fisher

FUTURE PERFECT

This will never change . . .
Your hand in mine
Through all the years . . .
This chanting in our hearts . . .
This will always be.

Vera Current Thummel

FLYING

Behold the toy earth at ten thousand feet!
Tinker's dream,
Dollhouse world in patchwork perfection.

I glide, dip and soar, eagle-free, eagle-me.
My metal wings cleave cotton wisps
That melt as fast to mist.

I float along on molten blue,
Embracing the sun-fired, ice-crystal sky.
A paradox?
So too the earth!
No longer cruel at ten thousand feet.

Nancy L. Williams

NANCY LOUISE WILLIAMS. Born: Seattle, Washington, 6-6-42; Married: Terrence C. Williams, 12-1-62; Education: University of Central Florida, B.A., Anthropology, Summa Cum Laude, 1984; Occupations: High school English teacher, Creative writing teacher; Memberships: National Council Teachers of English, Florida Council Teachers of English, Phi Kappa Phi (National Honor Society).

CUMBERLAND

Long and shady, peaceful walks;
Bent and gnarled old trees —
Sea gulls flying lazily
To the rhythm of the seas.

Climb the sandy dunes and feel
The freshness in the air —
This island will make you feel
As if you've never had a care.

Ocean waves of deepest blue
Trimmed with snow-white foam —
The gentle lapping on the sand
Says you've at last come home.

The warm and sandy beaches
Strewn with multi-colored shells —
Sand dollars lying in the sun;
Oh, what a story it tells!

There are very few places
Created by God's great hand —
That give us so much beauty
As our gracious Cumberland.

Sheryl Funderburk

BONDING

We are nature.
We are living matter with the urgency to *possess!*

With the loving desire to *caress*
To *coalesce!*

When we love, we *bond*
It is something we attach our love *upon!*

In this *bliss,* we experience happiness
In all *this!*

Bonding is love
We bond when we *mate!*

We bond when a child we *create!*

Florence Dora Rapp

FLORENCE DORA RAPP. Born: On a farm near Ramah, Colorado; Education: Miami High Graduate; Colorado University, Boulder; Drama, Voice, Piano, Art, Typing, studied at Denver schools; General course graduate in Graphoanalysis, 1959; Occupations: Avon representative for 28 years; Pioneered the El Cañon Motel, Glenwood Springs, Colorado; Memberships: Arizona Authors Association; Order of the Eastern Star, No. 12, Denver; Poetry: 'Glenwood Springs, Colorado,' *Glenwood Post,* 1970; *Outbursts of Thought,* book of poems, 1975; 'Vigorous Youth,' 1978; *Love In Its Many Aspects,* book of poems, 1979; *Eve's Rib,* book of poems, 1985; Themes: *My poetry takes in a variety of subjects: Science, Religion, Philosophy, Works of Mankind, Social Problems;* Comments: *I have a strong urge to reveal to the world, reality and truth as I see it. I hope fresh insight can be gained from the readings of my poetry.*

PERHAPS ANOTHER TIME

Perhaps another time when one of us can listen
Perhaps another time when one of us can hear
Perhaps another time when resentment turns to kindness
Perhaps another time when we both let go of fear

Perhaps another time when the pain is not at surface
Perhaps another time when we care to understand
Perhaps another time we can witness buried feelings
Perhaps another time we can give what we demand

Perhaps another time when one or both are empty
Perhaps another time when one of us is free
Perhaps another time we can give the other grace
Perhaps another time one or both of us will see

Perhaps another time we will grasp the whole illusion
Perhaps another time we will realize we're the same
Perhaps another time or if not, another lifetime
Perhaps we'll meet again sharing love instead of blame

Arlene Singer

AT THE STATION

Soft, pitter-patting taps of rain descend,
To wave in gentle curtains with the wind;
The man in the empty station 'waits its end,
Or else awaits a worse storm to begin.
He scarcely feels the trickle down his back,
And emptily observes the barren track;
The minutes turn to hours in the rain,
Well past the passing of the midnight train.

Long searching in the hollows of his heart . . .
He stares into the mist as into time . . .
He juggles the absurd with the sublime,
And dreams of hopes new vistas may impart . . .

But laughing softly in the lamplight's gloam,
He rises and begins his journey home.

David B. Hawthorne

AN AUTUMN MEETING

As the twilight falls and shadows deepen,
Brisk winds spinning whorls of leaves across the avenue,
She walks with purpose in an aimless circuit,
And prays with fervor that the morning will bring something new.
The summer's languid pleasures are forgotten,
All swept up by the urgency of Autumn's chilly clime;
Unwanted vigor chases empty hours . . .
The lonely heart is not renewed by undistracted time.

From a window floors above the concourse,
Watches one with heart and eye enjoined with quiet longing;
Sheltered from the vagrancies of Nature,
He cannot find relief from fears that keep him from belonging.
She flips around a corner, thoughts still churning;
He turns away and lays aside the hopes he dare not muster;
The orange leaves fall down between their parting,
And blow away, like meetings never chanced, in Autumn's bluster.

David B. Hawthorne

DIMINISHED

At times I diminish
thoughts of you.
Though they follow endlessly
chasing
backing me into a corner,
the compelling will of so many varied voices
forcing me to confront their existence.

I am not a diminisher by choice
Only when the fear becomes too intense to hold back.

At times I do fear.
Not only love
thoughts of you
or love diminishing,
I fear
I will diminish
in your love.

Kimberly Hix Trant

RONDA

One of the best presents
Mom and Dad ever gave me
Was you

With Steve I found laughter
In Mark I find strength
With you I find compassion
Un-ending width, un-ending length

You always see the diamonds
Never focus on the flaws
You don't love me ''even though''
You love me just because

And that's the beauty of
Your gift, unselfish love
Without an end

What a treasure I have in you
My little sister
My loving friend

Karen G. Adams

KAREN G. ADAMS. Born: Modale, Iowa; Education: Currently enrolled, University of Nebraska at Omaha; Occupation: Administrative Assistant, for a large insurance firm; Poetry: 'Childhood Memories,' *Make A Wish,* 1987; 'Grammy,' *American Poetry Anthology,* 1987; 'Micheala,' *Chasing Rainbows,* 1987; Comments: *My poems are simply a gift from me, to my family and friends, with love.*

OUR TERRY

Life hardly seemed worth living
When you first went away,
By living our lives, one step at a time,
We made it through each day.
In our love we had forgotten
That God gave us only the loan of you,
And that He had the right to take you
Whenever He wanted to.
We had to learn that the sun still shines
And that flowers still bloom in the spring
And that little children still laugh and play
And that birds still know how to sing.
We had to learn to be thankful
For the time that God did allow,
Though we wanted to keep you forever,
You are ours only in memory now.

Catherin Eblin Hatton

REMEMBER ME

Remember how the air feels
On an early day in Spring —
The way the leaves turn green
And the little sparrows sing.

Remember in the Summer,
The stillness in the air —
The sound of the whippoorwill
On an evening soft and fair.

Remember when the Fall turns
The leaves to red and gold —
An evening by the fire
As the night grows crisp and cold.

Remember deep in winter
As you're trying to stay warm —
Hurrying to the fireside
Before the first snow storm.

Among all your memories,
Please leave a place for me —
And remember us together,
Just the way we want to be.

Sheryl Funderburk

OUR TREASURE

Oh, Love, I need to hold you
And feel you close to me —
You are the very strength I need;
My life you'll always be.

I only want to be your love,
To never leave your side —
So take me deep into your arms
And from this world we'll hide.

Only when I'm with you
Am I happy and at peace —
Only when you love me
Do I know such sweet relief.

Loving you is easy,
You're such a gentle man —
But no one else could love you
In the special way I can.

So take me to your heart
And always keep me there —
For our love is very special,
It's a treasure that we share.

Sheryl Funderburk

THE SEASONS

We *Spring* into life preparing ourselves for new things to come daily.

We see the task before us in beautiful things accomplished in *Summer's* time flowering.

In the *Fall* we look forward to a new harvest of wonderful ideas.

We cherish in the *Winter* solitude lovely things accomplished in our *Seasons.*

Doris L. Brown

DAWN NICOLE

A solemn beauty in repose,
With features fair and hair spun gold.
Her mother's eyes . . . her father's smile,
The best of both . . . reborn a child.

Attentive now, she runs to me,
With dancing feet.
And now I see . . . a smile
That lights the darkest day
And hugs that make me want to stay
And watch her daily as she grows
With freckles on her upturned nose.

A temperament that wants to please.
Yet clearly capable to tease . . .
The cat . . . or pink bear for a bit,
Before she gives them each a kiss
And tells them both how much they're missed
Each day as she goes off to school
To learn to live by other rules.

I pray she keeps that child-like charm
And grows up safe . . . away from harm.
Happy and loving with cheerful soul.
These things describe my Dawn Nicole.

Joy Thomas

FOR WANT OF A POEM

Charley loved to read.
  He also read poems.
One day Charley looked about —
  Where is the poem?

What poem, his sister asked.
  Why, my new love poem
  of course, Charley replied.
Silly goose, his sister replied.

You have twenty-one poems on
  victory and hope.
What need have you of a
  poem on love?

Oh, love is fun.
  It can make you warm
    on a cold night.
It also is a warm companion.

Silly goose, his sister again
  replied.
Here is your poem entitled
  ''Romance.''

And Charley took the poem
  and ducked down
    under the covers.

Natalie C. Yopconka

CHRISTMAS PRIMER

There was a star,
  On a winter's night
    And shepherds' tender care.

Still shines the star
  And all men's hearts
    Kneel by the manger there.

Vera Current Thummel

NO WORDS

When a man of words knows of none
To express the warmth that grows within
Each time your fingers lie on my skin,
Your lips brush my mouth,
Or your eyes melt the shard over my heart;
When this man takes silent pause to linger on a trail
And meander through the melody of you,
Of the light of love that shines yet brighter
With each moment in your company;
Then must you listen to the silence
For the unspoken joy of newborn emotion.

Gregory J. Borden

WHEN IT'S TIME

When it's time for one of my loved ones to die,
although I may rant, rave, grieve, and cry,
   Lord give me the strength to carry on.
When it's time for the children to leave home,
to search out a life, a time, a place of their own,
Heavenly Father make me strong enough to accept the change.
   When it's time, and the loving has ceased to be,
   the person I deemed my life has left me,
   Dear God, be my refuge.
When it's time for friends to become enemies,
cutting me deep like a knife,
invading my world with misery, pain, strife,
Lord be my comforter. For Thou art the best friend.
   When it's time; depression, evil thoughts invade my soul,
   leaving me blind, desolate and cold,
   please God, wrap Your protective arms around me.
   Shield my entire being from that which is not of Thee.

Lillian A. Christian

LILLIAN ANN CHRISTIAN. Born: Kansas City, Kansas, 5-9-46; Married: Glenn Edward Christian; Education: Metropolitan Business College; Penn Valley Community College; Occupations: Hospital Nourishment; Factory worker; Hotel maid; Night club singer; Pre-school teacher; Secretary; Poetry: 'Love Aria,' *American Poetry Anthology*, 1986; *I Have Something To Say*, book of poems, 1987; Themes: *The ideas for my poetry and short stories come from the life I live and people I have been blessed to meet, good or bad. All has been a teacher, in this vast world we live in. Furthermore, I'm happy to share with others, what God has shared with me.*

HEAR THE RAIN SIR WREN

Someone help my heart, it has been hurt again
Someone help my soul, aid me please Sir Wren.
Take me on your wing, cover me with love
Hold me in your heart, change me to a dove.
Show me to blue sky, let me be so free
Give to me your world, to you I will give me.
Life is but a puzzle, to break and harm one's brain
Your life it is so easy, you never hear the rain.
God bless you dearest wren, your little wings I'll save
For now a gun has gripped you so, I'll show you to your grave.
The sky will miss you dearest wren, you were a gift of love
You needn't worry about false pain, you'll hear no rain above.

Unique Schreiber

PREACHER BOY

In the 1950's, while completing Senior College days,
I was also a local preacher, first at Slagle's Chapel half-ways
Between Elizabethton and Watauga,
   northeast Tennessee between pristine
Doe River (covered bridge) and Watauga River with bridge, ravine
And large grist mill. I rode buses, hitched rides. I mean
Many times, the three country miles from Elizabethton to roam
On Sunday morning. Gracious members, after church service fed me
Home-cooked meals. Sunday evenings were visiting times. My endeavor
Was somewhat successful, but inexperience was plainly seen. Later, ever
Moving ahead, I was assigned to Tazewell, Southwest Virginia, near
My uncle's pastorate. He helped me a lot to visit, preach, music. Here
I bought my first car, traveled many miles between churches for a year.
Mount Pisgah Church, located in a grassy valley. Behind white mere
Wooden fences, a delightful quest, sheep grazed in green fields. We're
Next at Pleasant Hill, glistening white on a hill. The choir
Performed a beautiful Christmas Cantata. Back at home water pipes dire
Froze and burst. Mount Pleasant church, block style by highway higher
Than a wide river which flowed below. A water mill was nearby. Desire
Of the prosperous farmers —
   to enjoy social, spiritual blessings prior
To beginning each week at church.
   But I was yet unmarried, a breach —
An unpardonable sin in the pastorate.
   My uncle's daughter suddenly died
By auto accident. A boy shot his father (abusing his mother) beside.
Gradually, I knew I could serve God better as teacher. I have tried.

Cleveland C. Matchett

THE LEVERS OF MY MEMORY

   I must have pulled the right lever in the sea of my
memories today.
   It's been a while since I thought of you. And I wanted
you to go away.
   But a crack in the web of life's lining, let you float
through my conscious mind.
   And now that you're here, so is the pain I thought I'd left
behind.
   I loved you. And I lost you. My uncaring wisdom knew the
fault was all me.
   You were good, and I was bad. From my pedestal, this much
even I could see.
   Time is lost. But memories are full of levers.
   If I pull the right one, just maybe! You will be with
me forever.

JoAnn Thomas Tanner

FEELINGS

I hunger too:
I thirst too: *For*
I refuse too: *Better*
I love too: *Knowledge*
I hope too: *How*
I sympathize too: *To live*
I realize, too: *In*
  I cry out   *This*
  too!   *World!*

Doris L. Brown

GREAT WORLD

As time goes on — it is a phenomenon —
That the wise and the good —
Have either to hide —
Or swallow their pride —
Or glide — into oblivion.

Our beautiful world —
Great — wide and precise —
A former paradise —
Has not enough room —
For the good — the strong — the wise —
As they are forever a sacrifice.

And strange as it seems —
As life goes on — the strong grow meek —
The wise grow weak —
While the brutal become great.

And so the wise, the good, the strong —
Have seldom room in our world —
And are accused to do wrong.

Halina de Roche

DIVINE THINGS

It's fun, fun, fun
To run, run, run

In the Sun, Sun, Sun
Seeing God's Divine Things on earth in Birth!

How about that Lady Bug?
Did you get your daily hug?

How about that Spider's Web?
Did you get caught inside instead?

How about the Honey Bee?
Did you see the flowers and the Honey Tree?

How about our Butterflies?
So colorful as the Rainbow skies.

O Lovely sun, sun, sun
Dries us off after a summer's swim
Keeps us fit and trim.

It's fun, fun, fun
To run, run, run
In the Sun, Sun, Sun.

Doris L. Brown

GONE IS MY LOVE

My love wanted to be as the wind blows free,
Gone is my love, and forgotten me!
Gone are the dreams of life's happiness,
Lost are the sighs of a tender kiss.
Linger yet, the sweet memories of yesteryears,
As the cold wind dries the bitter tears,
Gone is my love, and oh so free,
Gone is my heart, he's forgotten me!

June Cooper Wristen

SPIRITUAL BURN-OUT

Are we in a spiritual desert,
Our souls as parched as sand?
Or sailing on a troubled sea,
None charting us toward land?
Are we confused, depressed?
Not knowing how to cope;
Or face despair without someone
To offer comfort, hope!
If we have lost our vision,
And our faith seems dull and dim —
We will find a bright new haven,
If we only look to Him,
Who took our sins upon Himself;
Now waits upon the shore!
Though we keep ''log'' of all our sins,
God remembers them no more!

Opal DeGrote

ICE-STORM

There is beauty in the aftermath
  of a winter's ice-blown storm;
For each object that it touches
  assumes a lovely form!
A tree becomes a fountain
  sending out a myriad spray,
And it twinkles like the diamonds
  through a large plate-glass display!
We hear tinkling sounds like ice cubes
  in a crystal goblet, rare,
As we walk beneath this icy dome
  with some wariness and care!
The grass is a fairy castle
  we've seen in a childhood book;
And a woven fence, or tree stump,
  now earns a second look!
The air is crisp and heady,
  like a wine that's aged and clear,
And there is an air of fantasy
  in this crystal atmosphere.
We are awed by this wondrous beauty
  that the ice storm has unfurled;
For our landscape seems a palace
  in this ice-encrusted world!

Opal DeGrote

LOVING

Loving is the essence of life.
Life is the essence of being.
What is life without seeing?
It's a world of sounds,
filled with gorgeous meaning.
And what is life without hearing?
It's a masterpiece of colors beaming.
Without either it becomes
a world of dreaming.
But life without caring
becomes daring.
And what of life without loving,
this cannot be.
For loving is the essence of life,
and life the essence of being.

Patrick H. Ehrsam

LOVE

Love is special.
Love is kind.
Love is more than
A picture in your mind.

Love is caring.
Love is right.
Love doesn't mean
You have to spend the night.

Love is strong,
And love is caring.
But most of all —
Love is sharing.

Sally Ann Byrd

THAT SOMEONE SPECIAL

You're the center of my circle.
You're the apple of my eye.
When people ask me who I like,
I say there's just one guy.

His name is Someone Special.
He's as sweet as sweet can be.
When I get to see him,
It's so very plain to see.

Look in my eyes — they sparkle.
They glow when he's in sight.
When he comes near and touches me,
I become filled with fright.

I want him to love me.
I want him to care.
I long for the warmth
of his tender stare.

He likes someone else.
That's easy to see.
Maybe in time,
He'll be with me.

Sally Ann Byrd

OUR HOME

Our home is not a grand mansion with crystal chandeliers.
It's only a modest house that we have lived in for many years.
Our happiness does not require the splendor of marble halls.
We have no luxurious furnishings, or valuable paintings on the walls.
Our dear relatives are a great source of our happiness.
We value our friends for the integrity they possess.
We've seen the wonders of London, Paris, and Rome.
To us, the most wonderful sight of all is our own cherished home.

Olga Krawetsky

WHAT IS THE YMCA? GLAD YOU ASKED!

It is a London clerk, George Williams, who wanted to spread —
  for duty —
Christianity to young men.
  Or a Chicago shoe salesman, Dwight L. Moody,
Who started Sunday Schools, YMCA activity — citywide crusades, too.
It is the USO, service to armed forces — Civil War to World War II.
It is William G. Morgan from Holyoke who invented volleyball —
Where players hit a ball back and forth across a net with hands all.
Or a James A. Naismith of Springfield who invented basketball,
Played first with soccer ball and peach baskets on the wall.
It is where we come to learn about swimming skills that improve
Heart action, blood circulation, firm muscles, water safety moves
And lifeguarding to save lives. Also, children's programs with camps,
Indian Guides. Too, Hi-Y in schools, or International Academy revamps
Springfield College where students come from many lands, training high.
It's Norfolk "Y" that rents modern resident rooms
  to single men who vie with women.
Or in Rockford, try Faith & Fitness Aerobics — by
Gospel music and prayer. Chattanooga "Y" encourages church groups'
Use of new facilities for meetings. In west New York City, is news
The "Y" provides affordable rooms for chemotherapy patients' views.
Anaheim "Y" Senior Citizens produce shows that feature costumes,
Scenery and music for all.
  Shelbiana, Kentucky, Railroad "Y" has rooms
For residence — 24 hour food service.
  Duluth implemented basketball
Program in local schools. San Francisco "Y",
  women first accepted all
For membership (1874).
  Portsmouth "Y" sponsors Diagnostic Wellness call
For health habits in a Christian atmosphere. And, on it goes to convey
That we are in the people business. Keep the tradition. Join today!

Cleveland C. Matchett

EMPTINESS

  Sadness creeps into my heart silently.
Always there. Waiting, violently.
  No emotions are unleashed. A nothing kind of feeling
as if my life has ceased.
  The joy has gone out of my body, of living.
Like an empty shell so tired of giving.
  There is no peace or calm in sight. It's just gone,
and I no longer can fight.
  I'm so tired I just want sleep. But I can't. Over
my body the emptiness leaps.

JoAnn Thomas Tanner

FATE OF THE CHILDREN

  With rivers of tears rowing across their land.
Unclothed babes weep in the chill of the sand.
  In their faraway world they live in despair and
doubt. Help! Don't let God's children go without!
  Racked with the fever of hunger they do not under-
stand. A world reaching out to us with drowning hands.
  Where are you? Who will take a stand?
  Their crying please do not ignore. For if you do,
soon, there will be no more!
  Hurry today, for tomorrow is too late. Help the
little children, for you are their fate!

JoAnn Thomas Tanner

FOR MY LINDA

I've been through sorrow and pain
Looking for sunshine, just finding more rain.
Thought life had taken all I had to give
Took all my strength to keep wanting to live.
It felt that I carried the whole world on my back
Just wanting fulfillment, but finding the lack.
Then you came along with your kind words and sweet smile
Suddenly every moment for me is worthwhile.
You picked me up gently and turned me around
Took the load from me, put my feet on the ground.
The sounds of your laughter, the light of your smile
Carry me softly across many a mile.
You make me fly higher than any bird's ever flown
The more I am with you, the more my love's grown.
I've changed my whole outlook, and from my point of view
The world is much brighter since I met you.
Now I see no more darkness, I feel no more rain
'Cause your smile is like sunshine, your touch stops all pain.
I love you so much, more than words can say
My life, like a pathroad, your love lights the way.

James R. Peterson

RETROSPECTIVE INTROSPECT

Call it fantasy if you like

I met a man in white robes, glowing like the sun.
He talked to me of past lives, and things that I have done.
There was a reassuring kindness, in his eyes of aqua blue.
But I could not keep from asking, just how these things he knew.
He said, "Close your eyes and relax, on a journey we shall go,
And when the trip is over, you will see how it is I know."
So I closed my eyes and relaxed (it seemed strange, I know, but true),
And felt an eerie feeling, as through the years I flew.
I saw a mighty warrior, in polished brass and steel,
Who cut a path through armies, to make the foe king kneel.
Not one could stand before him, at arms he was the best,
But the life he led was lonely, his only friend was death.
He showed to me a wizard, dressed in black and gold,
Who strove to find the secrets, the universe did hold.
A man well versed in powers, of the planets and the stars,
Who advised the fate of princes, kings and queens and czars.
He showed to me a farmer, dressed in the deepest brown,
Carving cropland out of wilderness, by laying tall trees down.
His arms and back were knotted, there deep lines on his brow,
From years of heavy toil, with axe and trusted plow.
And when we returned the old man said, "You asked me how I knew,
You see the wizard and the warrior and the farmer and me, were you."

James R. Peterson

SASSY JAZZ

Sassy jazz, sassy jazz,
My eyes have seen,
My ears have heard
The syncopated beat of
Notes sublime.
I love to hear that sound
When I dream.
Sassy jazz, sassy jazz,
The beat, the beat,
When I move my feet
To the rhythm of sassy jazz.

Anne Burwell Harris

A MOTHER'S LOVE

I write this poem to you for
I love you true.
While I watch the sun setting in the west,
I hope that you will always do your best.
I watched you grow from a little baby into
A young lady.
You will soon be on your own and
You will find that life is not always
The way you want it to be, so
If you find that you are going astray,
Always remember
The little things I used to say.

Anne Burwell Harris

THE CHAIR

I've sat in this chair for what seems an eternity
Listening, hoping, crying tears of love's lament
Innocently longing to be a part
    of someone's life
Under the pretext of being heaven sent

Many moments spent in a dreamy state of mind
Question the motives and quality of one's being
Sorting out the errors of wasted time
Ignoring what was real — and not really seeing

The view from the chair
Seems like a puzzle in disarray
One or two pieces are always missing
And they usually fall where they may

So much for promises — on the wane
There's no time for a second chance
The stars won't capture your feelings
When you're dealin' with romance

Once in love — always the gambler
I watch as dreams go by
Pardon me — for the way I've mistaken
Love's reflection in your eyes

Jim Ingles

JULIETTE AND GRAM

As I held her close and rocked her
And looked at her sweet face
She peeked at me and dropped her eyes
Down to her secret place;
A pocket where her treasure was,
A soft, blue piece of clay —
A ball of many wondrous tricks
That we learned, just that day.

As she held it in her dimpled hands
It became so many things:
Only she could understand.

But now, a weary baby was thinking of her day,
How many times the little ball
Had seemed to fly away, a butterfly
A little worm and many other things.
Then as she pressed it on her nose
I whispered softly to her,
"I love you, Julie Rose."

June Clogston

SPRING SONG

Spring, you lusty wench,
Bursting forth with muddy hem,
With lace of snow in your hair.
We skip ahead to hold you.

Enough of Winter,
Your senile old lover.
Take care, lest, because of your
    amorous desires, he may return;
For, the pulse of you
Is in forest and meadow, on lake
    and stream.

No mock modesty here, away from
    Winter's icy blanket.
The Bridal Bower is everywhere
For your new love; on leaf, on branch
    and in water.

The miracle of life unfolding —
No straining, no birthing-stool.
The ancient insistence on survival
As, when the God of creation, "Brought
    forth."
Songs of joy are carried on the
    cool, fragrant winds.
Spring, even as youth is to life,
Too short a season!

June Clogston

TELEPATHIC DREAMERS

Whispery wings of midnight touch her soul
Propelling his psyche into her dreams
Soft shadows shimmering beckoning her come
Drink deep the fruits that are her lover's
Endless energy send sparks igniting
Two twilight souls to horizons unexplored
Pristine promises perpetrate the dream
As feathery fingers finely mist the vision
Dawning distance does not exist for them
These telepathic dreams are always as one

Lorey Umberger

Step inside your vestibule
    to the room beyond;
Tables and chairs and furnishings —
    a lamp that bathes
    the spaces of eternity
Only to diffuse upon the walls
    of finity.

Soon it all crumbles
    tumbles
    and falls,
For none of it can stand upon its own
    to compose,
A separate identity.

Steven G. Czarnetzki

MY LOVE

As the beholder, never
    letting go
for my life is fulfilled,
    a dream 'tis not.
Like the Great Walls of China
    a neverending relation . . .
    . . . ours shall be.
A love for you, so deep
    down inside
cannot thy deepness
    burn thy feet;
with the feeling of joy
    flowing through thy blood.
I visualize your face
    so gleaming and bright
such as a sunset, beautiful
    and still.
Forever I shall cherish the
    feeling I have
only for you my love . . .

Carol A. Marino

THE WEDDING RING

*Composed for the Golden Wedding
of Mr. & Mrs. Zeng*

This ring you gave me five decades ago,
At our wedding as you know I know.
My love for it few people understand,
It grows and grows with running of the sand.

My companion, my love, my life, my hope,
In times so hard that we could hardly cope;
Your gift, your trust, your love, your memento.
For half a century in weal and woe.

Its shape, equator of this ceaseless earth,
Bears no start, no end ever since its birth;
Its essence, durable as its solid face,
Defies the boundaries of time and space.

Z. Lite Cai

THE SWIRLING AGES

Mystery heard the winds of His breath blowing
  through the swirling ages

They blew about expanding the Universe; the force
of their passing still rages

They empowered the galaxies

And delivered no fallacies

The great, awesome thrust of might and liberation
  filled the void with sound

Engendering acceleration in luminous clusters
  momentum was newly found

Mystery's presence followed in its wake

Essence made manifest for all to partake

Cora Mendeola

THE BEGINNING

Mystery's shadow falls upon swirling matter
Nothing escapes its touch
Nebular materials compose a thickening batter
Drawing in the elements they clutch

No echoes are heard in forming canyons
Soils know no shooting pines
No descending limbs of banyons
Life shows no promising signs
Land is subject to harsh heat, harsh cold
And is molded into spheres undone
Tales of its glory are yet to be told
Fierce radiation leaves the proto-sun

Mystery and matter embrace through milleniums
And many children are born of this union
One child speaks after a myriad of aeons
Telling the tale of glory and communion

Cora Mendeola

FRIEND OR LOVER

Death is not my friend.
Yet always I await her arrival:
A lover who whispers sweet nothings in my ear,
Consuming like fire,
Leaving the ashes of time passed.
She takes one after another,
Friend and foe alike.
She lies with us
A frail lover more permanent than mother or wife.
She courts every man.
We struggle with life's passions in her arms
Until finally we are weary and welcome sleep!

Mary-Elizabeth Epstein

QUIET HEART

I am content in this existence.
I do not wonder at the weeks passing by.
I watch life as one watches the boats on the river
Passing down to that great ocean
Whose life our tears and this river nourish.
At our last supper we feed on this wonder-full sea of time;
Our nourishment is our communion;
Our very lives bear the message
That is the succor of the disciples,
Giving meaning to life that feeds life.
In the caress of rain upon my face
There is joy beyond our fleeting hours.

Mary-Elizabeth Epstein

THANK YOU WILLIS

You never announced your comings or goings
Like an angel you appeared
And with lotion and salve
You anointed my friend.
Just as softly and tenderly
You came each day.

Somewhere, suspended between heaven and earth
Between life and non-life
I believe my friend could not distinguish the touch
Of an earth angel from that of a heavenly happening.
At transition, something beautiful happened to my friend
And I thank you for it.

Mary Susan Smith

MARY SUSAN SMITH. Born: Bermuda; Occupation: Nurse; Memberships: American Nurses Association, Bermuda Registered Nurses Association; Poetry: 'To Merlyn,' *American Poetry Anthology,* 1987; Comments: *Willis is my daughter. She visited Gladys (my friend, her aunt) each day during her final illness and I, among many others, wished to thank her for her loving attentions.*

LONGFELLOW'S RESIDENCE

CENTRE ST

BROOKLINE

CHESTNUT HILL RESERVOIR AND DRIVE

BOSTON SUBURBS.

THORN IN YOUR SIDE

Dedicated to Joyce Agostini,
who'll always be a part of my success.

The only one person for me is you
Simple math means one and one is two
Accidents happen without control
From the constant fear taking its toll

The second planned meeting was another mistake
The imagination of one is becoming opaque
My knees need shoes 'cause I have to be crawling
While New York keeps on timelessly calling

I'm the thorn in your side
From the rose you can't smell
I'm the thorn in your side
And it's hurtin' like hell

We should have stayed in our own worlds, Honey
Now there's no such thing as two jobs and no money
Pushed into the upper from the lower class
With some elbow grease and unleaded gas

Happiness is the world of the first pioneer
With a wife by his side, it's cash and cashier
And while the earth keeps on revolving
The thorn in your side is slowly dissolving

John Cichoski

BREAK FREE

The limousine's coming and I'm ready to ride
Playing hide-and-seek with nothing to hide
I'm breathing comfortably and not afraid
Even though tomorrow is an invisible blade

My flesh is the prison in which I dwell
A nightmare of truth, forbidden to tell
Now is the time I'm uninterested
For being an adult and getting arrested

Break free of the chains I must leave behind
Break free for all the gold I must find
Break free, it's time to open up my soul
Break free and let the half man become whole

There's no use in heaven for fighting the air
There's one man on earth and one woman will care
Taking for granted nothing I own
It's a long walk to freedom walking alone

Time passes carefully blinking your eyes
And destiny for two will materialize
Break free and have the future polished
And let personal slavery be abolished.

John Cichoski

EVELYN

Evelyn was beautiful the night of the Valentine Dinner.
Her white suit, red blouse, and red and white pin
Set off her brown skin, her dark hair, and her friendly smile
To perfection.
She was, herself, a valentine of distinction in the candlelight.

I kept seeing her in my mind's eye
All the next week.

Juliet Ashley Lesch

A LOVE POEM

Through closed eyes, I see a terrific hourglass with much sand
at the top.

Grain by grain the sand descends, further fortifying an already
venerable foundation.

And, through that foundation, there grows a singular, beautiful
tree.

It grows as one for a time, then splits into two great limbs, as
trees are wont to do.

Each limb reaches higher, seeking its own source of light,
finally blooming, and adorning the tree in brilliant majesty.

Through open eyes, now, I see the hourglass, and that glorious
tree.

Still the sand falls, the limbs growing, apart, but never apart.

For, ever, joined at a powerful base, rooted to a strong
foundation . . .

And, without either of which, the tree would die.

Paul S. Strauss

EPILOGUE

Love is immune to the perils of change!
    Manifest by time, sanctity is sustained.

Fate may reveal the course life will take,
    Sooner or later; for now, there is faith.

Then one day, perhaps, the outcome is clear,
    Rewarding one's faith or confirming his fears.

But, unresolved, the time has to come;
    The old book must be closed, a new volume begun . . .

For, while more may be written (only God can be sure),
    To dwell in the past forsakes the future.

Paul S. Strauss

A FATHER'S PRAYER

May this little hand — holding my thumb so tight
Never hold a gun to fight
Never pull a switch to eliminate
His fellow man in a death state
Or press a button and start a fiery hell
Causing all living life to fail
May he never rape — causing pain and agony
Nor to rob another's home — invading privacy
May hit and run never be his game
Nor do drugs or cause family shame

But to take this feeling as I hold him tight
Loving him fully with his future in sight
Where he will always feel my love
And pass it on with faith from above
Giving hope and compassion to all in need
To pray — to help — to heal — to feed
May he recognize the good in his fellow man
And make this world safe as this moment stands
Me holding him close — our love bonded with care
May this moment be shared — with all he holds dear
    The world's future is in his hands.

Valentina M. Panzone

In my dreams, a kind of passage
winds me down to unknown thoughts.
I say 'unknown' because I mostly
forget them all and bring them naught
back with me. 'Tis a pity—
I lose them on my way back home.
But, I do feel almost fearful
when the passage begins dividing;
then, choices taken by me seem to
matter little in abiding;
(needs do not come easily to
one who's lost on their way home.)
I remember only snatches:
a broken promise on the rocks
takes the image of some spirit
whom, when living, had me locked
up inside my bedroom crying.
No pity have I for them, now.
No wonder I forget them when I
leave them chained below so long.
It's easy to forget a voice when
no one down there sends a song,
or, even screams, or, moans within as
I pass by on my way home.

P. B. Quinn

FAITH

Faith
is like sunlight
sprinting past primeval boughs
into forests of fantastic fears.
Faith warms the face and
dries up all the tears.
A spirit
dressed in flowing blue,
she's only visible to fools:
fools with eyes that always see
everything where nothing is
and positives for negatives.

Faith
is like moonlight
pouring past a passion-kiss
into hearts of timid hopes.
Faith calms the sea and
swells up grateful notes.
A spirit
robed in silver-red,
she comes to us, the living dead,
with eyes that always resurrect
those from pits where negatives live:
transfiguring them to positives.

P. B. Quinn

ON HOLD

Wintry woods waiting just like my heart
Bare barren branches hoping for warmth
Sun shining starkly amid icy feeling
Where is the spring to thaw us both?
Gone into hiding until the old season passes
And love's rays can once again shine free.

Lorey Umberger

SMILE, PLEASE

Those mental-midget-tricksters
who crowd around our door: —
why must I be exposed to them,
and why their uncouth uproar?

Now I see why you hired me:
to be your bodyguard—
to head-off vagrant vagabonds
and tinkers in the yard.

This ain't my job — but, I'll do it,
and won't expect no thanks for it:
take your advantage of me now:
tomorrow, I might love another.

Do you favors? — sure, I will:
this and that — they're all the same:
I want to be your friend today
and make you laugh and smile at me.
For when you smile, you're Cupid's sister:
and when you don't, I really miss her:
one smile a day can make me stay
the strength I need without you.

P. B. Quinn

NO GREATER LOVE

Thank God for His love
For undeserving sinners
Thank God for the way that He made
For He gave to us His Son
The Pearl of great price
To purchase our lost souls
With the greatest sacrifice
For they opened up His side
and He purchased the bride
By the blood that flowed from His heart
He bought her soul from bondage
And gave her a wedding gown
Of the purest white linen of great price
In great love He sought her
And with His blood He bought her
With the greatest riches in the kingdom
of our God
And stretching out His arms
He gave His life in love
That she might be with Him
In His Father's house above.

Odean Warren

AMERICAN GOLD

Whitman would have loved the Olympics
Sandberg would have cheered.
However —
Emily,
That dear belle of Amherst,
    Might have been saddened
    By the lack of attention
    Given to those
    For whom the gold
    Still resides at rainbow's end.

Doris M. Compton

OUR GOOD SAMARITAN

Jesus like the good Samaritan
of the parable that He told.
We the strangers by the wayside
no one cared for our souls.

Thieves had stripped Him of his clothing
naked in his blood he lay.
Wounded and dying they left him
as they went upon their way.

There were those who looked upon him
and passed by the other side.
With no compassion in their hearts
they were lifted up in pride.

Satan is the thief who robs us
leaves us dying in our sins.
We are helpless and defiled
and left without a friend.

But thank God there is another
with compassion like a mother.
He became our elder brother
Jesus Christ the sinner's friend.

Odean Warren

THE FAVORED PLACE

On the bosom of the Father
closest to the Heart of love
rests the head of our dear Saviour
in that favored place above.

We as sinners saved by Grace
and moved in that wondrous place
not by works that we have done
but by the grace of God's own Son.

When he took on Himself our sins
and died upon a tree
He gave to us His righteousness
this favored place to you and me.

Then let us accept this wondrous gift
and not insult the Saviour's love
but rest our hearts upon the bosom
of our Father's heart of love.

When we accept this gift by faith
He moves us into this favored place
what a joy to rest in Him
to be free from all our sins.

Odean Warren

THE PAIN

Of all the pains in the world
the one that hurts me most
is knowing that you are not there
to hold me ever so close
and never again will I see
that wonderful face of yours
or feel the love that you have
for those who loved you too;
to let you go has hurt me so
a pain that will never heal
and the memories will never fade
because of my love for you.

Amy Kathleen Westerhoff

MY STRANGER

His eyes were cold and unknowing, as they led him down the hall
He then looked back — right through me, a stranger —
   no recognition at all

For seventeen years he seemed so happy, he never shed a tear
He was so pleasing and responsible, so loving —
   to those he held dear

How can a mind so normal, crumble up so fast
Under the influence of some drugs that erased his loving past

As the drugs loved and embraced him, he became close
   to their harmony
They fulfilled and released him, at last —
   mind and emotions were free

My son became a stranger, frightening those who held him dear
Pent up words and emotions, he screamed — for all to hear

I struggled hard — tried every way, to break up
   the drug's embrace
He had to walk down that hall, only therapy could help him trace

All those facets in his life that a mother can't fulfill
Only confuse him and shut his mind,
   fears — I didn't know I instilled

But as he walked down the hall, to his life of therapy
I knew in my heart — sadly, that he would never need — me

Valentina M. Panzone

VALENTINA M. PANZONE. Born: Canonsburg, Pennsylvania, 2-14-22; Married: James V. Panzone, 1941 (deceased); Education: Macomb College, Warren, Michigan, A.A.; Wayne State University, Detroit, Michigan, B.A.; Eastern Michigan University, M.A., Ed.S.; Occupations: Retired; Special education teacher, 1950-1982; Counselor; Psychologist; Awards: Golden Poet Award, 1985-87; Poetry: 'Approaching the Statue 1919,' *Best New Poets of 1986;* 'Cycle of Love,' *A Treasury of Love Poems,* 1987; 'The Parting,' 1986; 'The Empty Chair,' 'Voyage Home,' *The Poetry of Life,* 1988.

IN WATERTON LAKES NATIONAL PARK

When we got out of the car at the lake
A gray jay flew down and lit on my hand.
He wanted food.

There was food in the car we could have given him
But I didn't dare to move or to speak
And so the moment passed and he flew away.

This is something you see pictures of
But it had not happened to me before.

The thrill of his trusting closeness
And the feel of his dry little feet on my hand
Were an experience I shall not soon forget.

Juliet Ashley Lesch

MY SISTERS — TERM AND MERK

When I open my book of memories,
I so very often find —
The most pleasant thoughts are of —
You two sisters of mine.

We have shared so much of life — in so many ways —
Now, I'm recounting all the special days.
I am recalling both laughter and tears —
The sad and happy times — down through the years.

I think of your always cheerful smiles —
Your willingness to walk those extra miles.
The warmth and joy, togetherness brought —
The many times, we've shared the coffee pot.

On these magic memories of the past —
We built something good, that forever will last.
There is no tie that binds, that will live longer —
No strength to hold, that will be stronger.

They say "In life — if you find *one* friend —
You are truly blessed — till the very end."
So, I consider myself "well blessed" . . .
Because, I have not *one* but *two* of the very best . . .

Constance (Arthur) Bennett

TOMORROW

When tomorrow comes, smile and do your very best,
Trusting in God to help you pass life's daily test.
Be kind and considerate, saying words to cheer,
Leaving unsaid thoughtless things that could cause a tear.
Remember yesterday's friends and instances shared,
Which will forever be a part of past dreams dared.
Work today and from life's experiences borrow
Knowledge and courage to reach your goals tomorrow.

Lura Louise Hanson

CHERISH THE LOVE YOU SHOW

For Della

Cherish the love you show,
To people who you meet;
    You are always willing to extend
    To others your arms of open love.
The time you spend with us,
The things you do for us;
    The meals prepared in love,
    The watchful eyes so wondering;
Wrapped in warming concern,
For the very loved one.
    The tears that you wipe dry,
    The conversations of encouragement,
The support you are constantly giving,
The friendly fellowshipping.
    And God blessed you, O yes,
    He made you a glorious mother!
We cherish the love you show,
We love you very much so;
    We cherish the love you show,
    And not just only for your family!
We cherish the love you show,
Because you give it also to others;
    Yes, we cherish the love you show,
    Because you give it to all who you know!

Paulette Speights

WINNING LIFE'S GREATEST FIGHT

When you feel like cursing, son,
Put a bridle on your tongue.
Bid unkind thoughts arrest,
Which arise within your breast.

Unkind thoughts and anger are,
Poisons, which your life can mar.
While the others loudly talk,
Go aside, son, take a walk.

Silently, His help, entreat.
He will not only guide your feet;
But He will guide your thoughts aright,
And you will gain strength, in His sight;

Gain new strength, to conquer wrong,
Strength, which makes you feel so strong,
That you will know, with thoughts aright,
You are winning life's greatest fight.

Jennie W. Madsen

JENNIE WEBSTER MADSEN. Born: New Hampshire, 7-26-09; Married: Harold J. Madsen; Education: High school graduate; attended Concord Business College; Occupation: Formerly had a school of home cooking; Sales work; Poetry: *My Favorite Recipes with a Variety of Choice Poems,* book; 'Changes, Since the Days of Long Ago,' 'Apollo Eleven,' 'Where Are You Going, Dear Youth?' 'What's Happening Out There, Gram?'; Comments: *I write a variety of poems, both for adults and children, some religious, some with a little humor, some serious, etc.*

SPACE HERO REQUITED

I must journey to the farthest stars
Keep my bed warm, I'll be home after Mars.
Encapsuled in armour with metal bright
I sleep through most of this endless flight.
Distress call comes through headphones clear
I've a feeling disaster is drawing near.
Computers adjust our free fall through space
As we head towards an enemy with a nameless face.
Battle engaged, a hit at point zero
Ship explodes! Now I'm only a lost hero.
Curious! Body gone, but I still feel alive
As the universe bends to my will to survive!
Don't grieve for me for I'm with you still
And I'm happier now as I go where I will.

Lorey Umberger

PICTURES

We have five pictures on our wall
Each of a little boy
And each one in his special way
Gave his parents lots of joy.
Each boy was different in his ways
But things worked out just fine,
And they went to church and Sunday school
Which helped them stay in line.
They all went on to college
To help prepare themselves for life.
Now the first four boys are on their own
With children and a wife.
Our hearts are filled with humble pride
As we see our pictures there,
We think of how they each turned out,
And they know how much we care
About each one and his family
And that we love them, one and all,
Our fifth boy lives in Heaven now,
So he did the best of all.

Catherine Eblin Hatton

MUSIC

Beautiful music has a master's touch
Because in it, he truly lives the part,
As those lovely, resonant strains come forth,
Straight from a full and understanding heart.

When I hear music, that beautiful kind,
I forget my sorrow, forget my pain,
My soul fills with sadness and joy combined,
Which, try as I may, I cannot explain.

It seems that birds are sweetly singing,
That peace and joy are hovering around,
Silvery bells are sweetly ringing,
All that I see is beautifully crowned.

Then, finally, the music ceases,
And from that world, wonderfully serene,
I arouse, awake from my reverie
As one awakened from a golden dream.

I return again to reality,
Yet with heart and soul impressed so much
That life seems sweeter, having listened to
Music with a master's inspiring touch.

Jennie W. Madsen

THE SILVER LINING

There is a rainbow in the sky,
When the sun shines, as it rains.
It is so beautiful to see;
Until the clouds cause it to wane.

And if we have understanding
And patience along the way;
They bring sunshine within the home,
Even on a cloudy day.

Oh, life is so beautiful,
When there is kindness in the home,
When *True Love* abides therein,
And by actions, it is shown.

It brings so much happiness,
Yes, so much joy it does bring.
Having *happiness* in the home,
Is such a beautiful thing;

Then, when the clouds come along,
With any pains, which we must bear,
We can see the 'silver lining'
As we kneel to say our prayer.

Jennie W. Madsen

SOMETHING THAT HAPPENED IN OCTOBER

Luke 8:45

He heard me
Someone finally listened
Someone finally cared
The years of pain and tears
Were just His lessons
And He teaches still
I didn't know it then
No blinding flash of light
No angel wings
I just went in the water
To pick up one gull's feather
But something happened then
Perhaps He said
''Who touched me?''

Betty Fossing

ACCOLADES FOR MY HUSBAND

Robert A. Bennett

I see you toiling for our good
I know that oftentimes I should —
Tell you what you mean to me
Tell you all the good I see.

Climbing up a ladder, with paint brush in your hand
Or chopping down the weeds that would over-run our land.
Then stoop to pick a yellow blossom with gentle loving care
Place it eagerly in my hand — God's gold with me to share.

Always so thoughtful, with a helping hand to lend —
Or your love to add to a letter, that I'm about to send.
Paying all the bills when due —
Never leaving much for you!

Though you are often not rewarded
For the nice things you do and say —
Somehow, you go along undaunted —
In your jovial, happy way.

I do appreciate your efforts
To provide nice things in life —
Although I rarely say it —
I am proud to be your wife!

Constance (Arthur) Bennett

OF COURSE IT WAS
ONLY A DREAM

In my dream we sailed to far foreign shores;
Strange scenes, exotic faces, odd scents and more.
We stacked our baggage in a pony cart
And climbed aboard for a new start.
Along narrow winding lanes we saw the sights:
Crowded markets, profuse flowers, old gas lights,
A bakery shop, fish for sale, by the pail,
Portrait artists, maids in grass skirts, cats with no tail.

Suddenly we are in a Rolls Royce car,
Being whisked in style to the villa afar.
Our chauffeur is awesome in his skill,
Weaving between handcarts and bicycles at will.

We marvel at the smoothness and comfort of the ride,
And we feel grateful to be on the inside —
When sudden drenching rain comes down.
We see no more sights, only rain, soon it is plain,
We can go no further in this downpour.

slands,
Dined on ambrosia and food so grand,
Oh, I hope I can dream it again!

Dorothy Landry

LADY

Rich lady of passion
    give me a sparrow
    to fly along the jeweled lake
It's a beautiful day
        Thank you for the sun
    you said the iris is beautiful today
Oh yes, the sparrow melts in the waves
    crystal wings and indigo clouds
    you said the yellow mustard is beautiful today
Oh yes, the sparrow is spicy fresh in its stems
Yes lady it's a beautiful day
        Thank you for the sun

Stephanee Pagano

SKUNK CABBAGE

The skunk cabbage does not have a pretty name
And later on it smells faintly like skunk,
But it brings us spring.
Its bright yellow spathe
Curved around its club-shaped spadix
Bright against the brown earth
Makes us shout for joy.
Spring is here at last.

Deer like the roots. (The tops are harmful to them.)
Bears eat it in the spring after their long winter hibernation
And humans can use the roots, dried and ground into flour,
For emergency rations.

Before the bloom is gone
The green plant starts growing
And becomes big with immense long leaves,
Its summer garb.

Then winter comes
And old and tired it disappears unnoticed
To become again a fresh bright yellow
Exclamation point of spring!

Juliet Ashley Lesch

AUTUMN PORTRAIT

The winter sun
    is like the dying weeds
That droop in the mud of a sleazy pond,
Where frogs croak and
    mosquitoes whirl in ever-thickening circles.

The birds no longer drink
    of the rain-soaked water,
And butterflies soar far from
    its brackish scent;
Only the rushes keep up their lively rustle
Sawing against each other in the chilly breeze;

Even this rasping sound is in tune
With the season.
Autumn sings a reaper's song,
Of gathered grains and golden
    sheaves of wheat.

Irene C. Hypps

SMALL WORLD

Today

It's I —
Not we —
Not you —
Not they.

Somehow my world
  Is first person
  Singular.

I wish it weren't.

A world of one
  Is
  Very
  Small
  Indeed.

Doris M. Compton

FRIENDS WHO CARE

Friends who care make life worth living,
Friends who live their life by giving
Comfort to their fellowman,
Spreading good where'er they can.

God sees, he knows, when we really care.
We may entertain angels unaware!
To turn away a lamb in need,
Proves a heart that's full of greed.

Our Christ was turned away at a door.
This misdeed was done in days of yore,
Testing mankind for charity of heart,
Mankind failed this test from very start.

Cathy Campbell Jacques

ST. ANDREW BAY

Long ago and far away, tho to me it
  seems like yesterday,
We spent many an hour on St. Andrew Bay.

We swam we fished, and went scalloping too,
  Sometimes were found enough clams for a
  stew.

The water was fresh and clean and pure,
It was great for swimming,
  that's for sure.

Yes, many an hour on St. Andrew Bay,
  The years of my childhood were spent
that way.

Now the crabs, scallops and clams
  are few,
Barely enough to make a stew.

Cathy Campbell Jacques

COURAGE

What is mankind wishing for?
Always after a distant star?
Hopes and dreams all crash around,
While man dumbfounded makes no sound.

Are we just puppets on a string?
Are certain ones to be a king?
Are our fates set at our birth?
Let's chart our course upon this *earth!*

If we are buffeted in the wind,
Like a pine tree let us bend.
Then our spirit will never break,
Though hell tries our *soul* to take!

Up we'll rise to fight again,
Then our battles we can win.
Courage is the name of the game,
Without it a spirit is quite lame.

Cathy Campbell Jacques

**MARY-CATHERINE CAMPBELL JAC-
QUES.** Pen Names: Cathy Cambell Williams,
1961 to 1-64; Cathy Campbell Jacques, 1-64 to
12-87; Born: Port Saint Joseph, Florida; Married:
Vester Adam Jacques, 1-12-64; Education: Bay
High School, graduated with second diploma in
business/stenography; Gulf Coast Community
College, Panama City, Florida, 32 credit hours in
education and arts (mostly nights), 1961-81;
Sherwood Music School, Chicago, Illinois, exten-
sion piano, theoretical studies, Extension piano
diploma, 1980; Occupations: Civil service
stenographer, permanent status, Navy base and
Tyndall Air Force Base, Panama City, Florida;
Affiliated extension piano teacher, Sherwood
Music School, 1977-86; Luzier Cosmetic Consul-
tant, 1969-87; Homemaker; Memberships: Order
of Eastern Star, St. Andrew Chapter No. 223, Na-
tional Guild of Piano Teachers, Austin, Texas;
First Presbyterian Church; Poetry: 'Love,' Gulf
Coast College, Fall, 1980; 'Distant Star,' 'True
Beauties,' 'Feelings,' college poetry paper, *Sex-
tant, Vol. Five, No. 2;* 'Hands of Time,' *American
Poetry Anthology, Vol III, No. 1-2,* Spring/Sum-
mer 1984; *My Inspirations and Reflections in
Poem,* collected poems, 30 pages in booklet form,
unpublished except for 'Sands of Time,' 1987;
Themes: *Love of beauty, family, God and nature,
treasures of friendships, joy or pain of love and
life, always searching for hope and beauty in
despair, and courage to go forward with life.*
Comments: *I have written since childhood, but
didn't save until a college professor told me I was
gifted and should pursue and share. The poems
come rapidly and inspirationally, usually in the
still of night, so I write in shorthand to decipher
later for my collection and to share. Some of them
are about the beauty of our bays and gulf
beaches, or about the snow white sand that
abounds this area and which I love.*

TROUBLES

On the sinking Titanic,
There arose a great panic,
And my mother-in-law made her a clone!
All my friends had deserted;
Sort of "windwardly skirted,"
And old sows thought me one of their own!

Yes, the world passed me by,
And I wondered just why
I was shunned and rejected and banned,
And my old nanny goat
Sang a joyous note,
As she ran up and licked at my hand!

It was nearly a week
That my wife wouldn't speak;
She's a woman of taste and discretion.
I was lonely and bored
To have been so ignored;
Just me, my pet rock, and Dalmation!

Then one day, as I feared,
My old sinuses cleared;
'Twas the day that our freight train derailed.
There just wasn't a doubt,
As the switchman passed out,
For I knew, my deodorant had failed!

Willard Silvey

DARKNESS

Dark is the night over
The dark, clear, starlit sky,
The leaves on the tall trees
Make quiet lulling sounds
Like the little brooklets
Running over the ground.

Sad is my heart, and as
I look at the night sky
I keep asking myself
Why, why in this wondrous
World of the day and night
Life has to be to us

Such a turmoil and plight,
As darkness and sadness
Seem to have come our way
Turning our days of light
Into the darkest night.
Yet the sad darkness might

Have its own beauty too
With twinkling stars and the
Light of moon, though lucent
And faint gives pale outlines
To surrounding scenes as
In an ethereal dream

Elspeth Crebassa

THE COVER KING

A fear of becoming a part of untold myth; beholding my heart, I wish for introduction to the person within you.

I am questing ground to find the opening; and feel your heartbeat with my welcoming.

Though in ways I can see through you, your world within lies dim.

In my sight; my vision clear, I am blind looking into your eyes; before me, to see beyond the boundary.

With time, and a book unread, chance is desire, and hope to never let you feel misled.

April Mari Bottomley

THE BOUNDARY

Relieve yourself, and embrace my smooth silk hands, follow me as we journey beyond the boundary.

Swallow the scent of bubbly champagne, and our bodies entwined.

With one tantalizing glance, and exotic movement of steamy hot lips, release yourself into my world; candy love.

See the sheerness, feel the caressense, live with me, and my luscious.

Every door opened taste the sweetest, any given moment share the tenderness.

Feel, and love the shimmers. Dream, and fly beyond the wettest.

With every gracious touch you can't resist me; covered eyes, and dramatic body movement in revolving mist.

Touch, and share the hottest moments of your loneliest nights.

Journey beyond the wildest with your sugar-coated mischief, indulge yourself in our passionate last night.

Grasp the image of love where there remains none.

Hear the motions of whispering; the silence of our breathless fight.

April Mari Bottomley

ESCAPE

I wanted to escape from all the pain
That seemed to circle inside.
The time we spent together,
When we both felt alone.
Wondering what to say next.
I wanted to escape,
When I liked you for more than a friend.
When my feelings were tangled with my childhood.
Wondering which way to turn.
And I seem to be still wanting to escape.

Jacqueline Wirtz

RECOVERY

Insight and fantasy. Dreams and probability
Rekindled hope. Nay more!
Not tomorrow on a faraway shore
But here and now!
How splendidly I realize
I'm alive and warm.
My heart in fact was not cut out of me
Or scarred and torn.
My reason is intact, it merely skipped a beat
Like being struck by lightning when I didn't see the storm.
I labeled that interlude, tripped over my ego and called it defeat.
My reason did not intrude. But now! What sweet recovery.

I'm functioning. The cold and bare significance
Of that brief flash in the night
Took hold and dared magnificence
To reveal more than light
In the splendor of a thunderstorm.

Not suddenly, not brief,
But with both feet on the ground
There is earthshaking beauty beyond belief
With vision clear and thinking sound.
I view it not by chance.
A panoramic view of life

Not a glimpse if a circumstance.

Betty B. Pruett

SOUNDS OF SILENCE

In sounds of silence you've handed back my heart
   More than slightly broken.
      Thanks for the token.

Our problem, you said, was my reluctance.
   To make a commitment
      Thanks for the remitment.

You ardently pursued until I fell at your feet
   And ended your fervent chase.
      Thanks for the race.

You built the fires of love then left me
   Alone on a griddle.
      Thanks for the riddle.

Were you shy, timid and proud, or
   A determined entrancer?
      Thanks for the answer.

You wanted to tell me how you feel in a letter.
   What thoughtful divesture!
      Thanks for the gesture.

Your silence has been as kind as death,
   As honest as treason.
      Thanks for the reason.

After the agony and ecstasy of our romance,
   Plagued by inconsistence
      Thank God for distance!

Betty B. Pruett

MY LOVE

If ever I thought
such a beauty would come
She would kiss me softly
and make me numb.

She would steal my heart
her love would make me blind
She would be very special
A one of a kind.

I feel for her
a passionate touch
She is always thought of
and loved very much.

I thank God
for such a perfect gift
I thank Tyra
for giving an emotional lift.

I have everything
I've ever desired
I have Tyra
Nothing could lift me higher.

Benjamin Shaw

COME IN AND STAY AWHILE

Taken by the wind . . .
  Swept up through the trees
    hollowed out conversations
      arrive muffled,
        soothing

To rest gently by my window.

  Ah! Sweet Company,

Come in . . . and stay awhile!

Michael A. Fazio

MICHAEL ANTHONY FAZIO. Born: Bronx, New York, 9-11-58; Comments: *Capturing a scene or feeling in my poetry gives me great satisfaction as I hope it does others.*

HEARTS ON FIRE

Hearts on fire
Hearts of loveliness
Heart's desire
To know love's caress

Hearts reveal
What cannot be denied
What they feel
You cannot hide

Hearts awaiting
Passion's sudden flare
So elating
Lost in its glare

Hearts are wise
Dark and knowing
No disguise
When love is growing

Hearts consume
They will capture you
One must presume
Hearts are always true

Evelyn Judy Buehler

REALITY

You told me that you loved me
But when I fall you walk away
You said you cared
But when I am in trouble
You are not there
You said you would not leave me
But now that I need your love
You are not here.

Amy Kathleen Westerhoff

AMY KATHLEEN WESTERHOFF. Born: Hammond, Indiana, 2-25-73; Education: Freshman at Tolleson High School; Occupation: Student; Poetry: 'Farewell,' 'Your Eyes,' 'A Change,' all *American Poetry Anthology, Vol. VII, No. 3, 1988*; Comments: *My work is based on my thoughts. I write about how I feel at the time or things that have happened to me or to my friends. My poetry is special to me: it's my way of getting through life.*

EVER AFTER

We were footsteps apart in a
world full of sorrow;
hers, a lost childhood
and mine was tomorrow.

Hers, showy parties and money
and laughter;
mine, always hearing the
words "ever after."

She died young and lonely
for our steps weren't as one
and when it was over
she left me her son . . .

Phyllis A. Kuligowski

ANGEL'S PRAYER

Little angels new to heaven
Pray that you should not be lonely
Down on earth, since they have left you.
You will feel their love forever.
Do not grieve, but listen closely.
Listen to their love and caring
Sending you God's special blessing.
We will bring you comfort, cheer you.
There will be great peace within you.
Here they know no pain or sorrow.
They are happy here in heaven.
Wish to comfort and to bless you.
Life on earth and life in heaven.
All of us with God, together,
Life eternal, love most blessed.

Dorothy E. Smith

NOTWITHSTANDING THE MANY NEBULI

Notwithstanding the many nebuli
Of the spacial scheme waiting to be discovered
Of the countless numbers of galaxies
Hidden in heavenly array.

I cannot possibly tackle all of space
With all of it invariable and infinite
And there is not a thing in the race
To the stars for they are happily in place

Doing what stars do in the suspension
Of night between them with a comparison
Of this, whatever this ethereal phenomenon
Can we pose the question, What is space like?

'Tis something we live in and would not beg.
It is not like asking a fish what likens to water
Or to a bird what is liken to air
Nor a bat what is liken to darkness.

Space is a monopoly of the greatest dimension
For taken to night is a small intention.
To waiver to the higher being looking down
Upon us is indeed being held in a microcosm.

Herbert V. Short, Jr.

EMPTINESS

Emptiness is just a word
A soul in torment is never empty
   It is
Full of words and music,
Full of sweetest odors,
Of light and longing, of embers of a
   Blazing love of life still remembered.
Memories of tenderness and of fears,
A life not mercifully
   Ended in a moment,
But ever so slightly deprived of food and air and light
Until suffocation and hunger in their turn
   Grow cold like the light that will not burn.

Moments to remember, too delicate and cherished to share
Cannot re-light ashes remaining there.
Thumping, pounding,
Gnawing torment deep within,
   I know not where,
Nor why it stays and grows
Until my blood turns colder
No longer warmed by memory
Of every hope and dream fulfilled
For just the briefest moment
   Less than one grain of sand
A desert upon eternity.

Betty B. Pruett

THE JOURNEY OF COMPLETENESS

You have become a man now
You have become a woman
You have found you both have love in common that leads beyond yourself
You have discovered that in becoming one you are beginning to feel complete
Now it seems that the world is an easy street

As you go on, you find you have differences and this may make you a little bitter and you grow apart
Then you feel a sense of loneliness but the love you have keeps you searching for the part of you, you think you have lost
Then you realize it is the differences that keep you constantly discovering each other and making you grow strong to know that the love you have can allow some differences and working together can remove the trivial ones and *life goes on*

Now in knowing the difference between the two of you, you now feel life is complete
Then you discover there is a world out there that might not relate to yours
It pulls you both in different directions and you are wondering can you survive it all
Then you realize what effects you effects the others so you pull together and become strong

Now you know what it is like to become complete
A man and woman becoming one

Celestine J. Custer

CHRISTMAS POEM

Christmas is like a child's fantasy
   that lingers in adulthood,
But remember it is for Jesus,
   which is not always understood.
It shouldn't be that way,
   but who's to say why man seems
   always to turn away.
And the few are faithful to the end,
   and some pretend,
And some have no will,
   they're looking for a Jesus thrill!

And Jesus highs can fall to Jesus lows,
And Satan waits to run the whole damned show.
But we are not the ones who pull the strings;
So let's have Christmas and sing
   a carol for the one who presents bring.
Remembering our miseries are part our own,
But who would ever make us fully atone.

Merry Christmas.

Dan M. Nance

GOD SAVE OUR CHILDREN

God Save Our Children
First, free their minds from the old webs of lies that have bound man from the beginning of time
God Save Our Children
Give them a world of dreams of sugar plums, and fairy tales that keep their spirits free from adult hells that stomp their growth into the spirit world
God Save Our Children
Create some guidance to help show them the way into a world of morality and dignity and with love that is meant to stay
God Save Our Children
Send them teachers to teach them Your ways, and leaders who live Your ways day by day to keep Your presence forever in their lives and to let the children know that without You in their lives they can never grow!

God! Please Save Our Children!

Celestine J. Custer

AREN'T I BEAUTIFUL

I loved you more than I loved myself
Aren't I Beautiful!
I gave you more than anyone else could give you
Aren't I Beautiful!
I gave you life that I could not give myself
Aren't I Beautiful!
I built you up when your world was falling down around you
Aren't I Beautiful!
I gave you my life and now there is nothing left of me and
   I still love you
Aren't I Beautiful!
It is because of you my soul is lost and it can't be found and I
   wander from town to town and
I still care about you
Aren't I Beautiful!
And now the end is near and looking over all my years I found the beauty that I was looking for in you inside me. Now I do not feel betrayed by you anymore because you did not see in me the beauty I saw in you. Now I know, I am beautiful because I could give life you could not give.

Yes! I was truly beautiful!

Celestine J. Custer

I JUST MET YOU

I just met you
And what do I do
One wrong word
Or one wrong act
That's what I am afraid of
Having to go back

First to say something
New, exciting and different
To ease you
But confidence of the mode being right
The way being true
Is easy to say
But so very, very hard to do

But the moment is near
And the time is nigh
I have rehearsed it time and time again
But what it all comes down to
Is to be yourself
And whatever happens
And whatever you do
Remember I'm always with you

Bryne L. Garrett

A WOODEN HEART

A wooden heart that says "I love you."
Faded words on worn-out paper.
Pictures in my mind.

Pleas we've made and shared for the future.
Little presents given each other.
Memories in time.

Songs on the radio that tell our story.
Serious talks while holding hands.
Memories of you.

Picnics at the lake, lunch at "our" place.
Snowball fights that I'd win.
Things we would do.

Everyday problems, worries and hurts.
The joy of being together.
Thoughts of the past.

Our simple cabin up in the mountains.
The happiness of one day.
Things that didn't last.

Pictures of you yellowed with age.
A wooden heart I always carry.
Things always with me.

You there with your life; me here with mine.
Years and miles separating us.
The way it has to be.

Roberta A. Walker

OH LORD ABOVE

*Dedicated to my beloved
husband and my family*

Oh Lord above, hear me this day,
That i might walk the Heavenly way,
Somehow that i might know with you,
Holding my hand, will see me through.

Dear Lord in this old sinful world,
I pray that i may never fall,
Away from you and all your glory,
To be your child is my one desire.

If in this world of sin and strife,
There are some pleasures in this life,
It's knowing you, our Lord and master,
Gave us a gift of life hereafter.

So when temptations come our way,
As they surely will each day,
I pray that i will sin no more,
And then i will enter that heavenly door.

Oh Lord hear me this day,
That i might walk this heavenly way,
Somehow that i might know with you,
Holding my hand will see me through.

Jean Reed

JEAN REED. Pen Name: Jeanie; Born: Corning, Arkansas, 2-2-32; Married: Gerald Reed; Education: Sheridan High School, Medical Office Receptionist School, 1973; Occupations: Housewife; Poetry: 'Going Home to be with Jesus,' 1986; 'Troubled Waters,' 1975; 'Friends,' 1987; 'Never No Never,' 1979; 'Oh Lord Above,' 1955; Comments: *In my poems I hope to reflect my love for my Lord Jesus Christ; my poetry is the words that He gives to me. I pray they will be a blessing to someone somewhere.*

ALLEGRO FOR THE MOON

What is it
keeps me coiled on this
fine white web of memory,
is a binding thread
my captor on this dark mantel —
a layer of dust, my ashes?

Once, to escape,
I hung from my window
the moon as my ally.

Today a child blocked my way home.
Her eyes as glossy as a clock face.
And I could not brush past her,
suspended again, on my window ledge:
face frozen in the same motif
till she let me
pass, burning the sidewalk
as I raced home.

Because the moon forgave me:
I'll dust the mantelpiece
and turn the clock
to the wall.

Janis Gillespie

THE LETTER

Sadness came in the form
   of a long solemn letter
   its cold words printed
   on icy white paper

The person who wrote it
   hid . . . beyond reach
   of this painful message

It's much easier to send
   a cruel blow with
   the aid of a stamp
   and not be there
      to,
   witness its excruciating pain

Matteo Jannicelli

BLACKBIRDS

A beautiful sight of the blackbirds walking,
   walking outside my window.
I saw them today out on my lawn feeding,
   feeding outside my window.

I heard a *chirp chirp* outside my window,
   outside my window today.
A spark in my eyes lit up as I took a peek,
   took a peek outside my window.

I love to hear the cool refreshing nature's call,
   nature's call out my window.
It seems to soak me up in its welling wall,
   welling wall out my window.

I heard a *chirp chirp* outside my window,
   outside my window today.
A spark in my eyes lit up as I took a peek.
   took a peek outside my window.

Glenda Faye Hendrix

I am husk and you are whole
the intricacies of my intellectual armour
betray in like degree ever-deeper wounds of fear
over which are knit loops and pearls —
the philosophies of a thousand wondrous worlds
of the thinker's crochet of living.

Now you stand beside me
at the bare bier, gaze at the blanched face that reflects our own

and speak to me of God. Your eyes   soar with faith
while I from my imagined superior height
dove-tail turns of speech and mind
then drift simply down
as an autumn leaf
on a lazy lost wind —
feel an early winter
settle on my soul —
which now too long has been filled
with Platos and Marxs
has forgotten the unbounded world
the universe of the whole,
which now
you've found,
oh soar! unbound!

Diana Cardenas

RESERVATION BAR

wooden slats run the floor
cracks fill the spaces
but no one notices
as the clouds gather outside
and rain begins to filter through the roof
the buckets on the floor fill
but they do not notice
another round is poured
everybody drinks
and the child at the end of the bar sucks happily on its bottle
and no one notices
the crowded room makes a tough pool game for two
    beer-saturated patrons
fishermen, probably
but they do not notice
as they swallow down two more beers
my, but the whiskey tastes good
as the woman behind pours another
and lets her mutt in from the wet
but i do not notice
it is getting late now, time to stumble out the door
but the barkeep shouts one more
and everybody notices
except the dog, who sleeps in a corner.

Bill Buseman

MY FRIEND I LOVE

My friend, I loved has turned his back on me,
The hurt I have in my heart, will never set me free,

Dear God, I pray if I have faltered along the way,
I hope he has forgiven me, and we can start over, day by day,

There is not too many years, in this span of life,
And may we forget and forgive the bit of strife,

We must cultivate, our love and lives each day,
That we can know God's loving way.

Willa V. Hartschen

TWO MEMORIES

Long ago life held great promise for my husband and me.
Our minds, hearts, and bodies were young and supple.
We walked with spritely steps, heads held high,
willing and ready to face the trials and tribulations of the future.
I didn't know there would be lusterless days of heartbreaks, sorrow,
and loneliness.

Yesterday, a blustering wind blew the brilliant leaves from the trees
leaving branches naked and dark, reaching to the gloomy sky,
symbolizing the passage of time.
Time brought love again to me and my new friend who was also
    old and lonely.
We walked hand in hand on the leaf-strewn path into the silence of the
autumnal ravine, broken only by the song of a lone bird and the ripple
of the creek rushing to the river.
The sun shone through the bare branches on us touching our souls and
hearts, awakening love, as we sat on the gnarled root of the old tree.
The joy of living came to us again for a short time until my friend
too became a memory. And now I must relearn the subtle hammerings of
loneliness.

Florence Jobe Kuhn

MY HUSBAND

I love you when you dress for church
Seeing you are so trim and neat,
But when you are all soiled from work
Our love is just as complete.
I thank you, dear, when there are gifts
You toil to buy me other things
Though, when you're ill and cannot work
My true love always remains.
Your beauty, dear, I now adore
Your wavy hair, your shiny eyes
I'd love you still if bald and grey
It's our shared love I prize.
My love you have so many skills
Your talents make me proud of you
You love to work, make use of time
If skills were less I would love you.
I love you always — my love is the same
In sunshine and rain — if talents be great or small.

Ruth Middleton

QUEEN OF THE MAY

On the first day of May, is a day of festive rejoicing.
The awakening of earth's rebirth of a long winter's sleep.
A renewal of nature's fertility, a new day of spring.
As the young maidens that dance around, an erected pole,
with long streaming ribbons, of the colors of Spring, are
making May anew!
They come from far and near.
Such are the selected few, as the fairest of the day, as
the Queen of the May.
The rustic morris dancers, with flourished flowers and
hawthorne branches, upon their heads.
Rejoicing, making merry, of the mating rites; unlike that
of the hobby-horse and a fool.

Dennis Macedo

MY MOTHER'S VOICE

Will heaven ever be tranquil again
Now that my mother has taken residence
There these last few years?

Here on earth, a continual torrent of
Advice and admonitions flowed from her
Lips into my ears.

It was *Don't forget to put your boots on,
Eat your dinner, Lock the door,* and
Save the money that you spent.

*Do*s and *do-not*s preceded me no matter
What I did and followed me whichever
Place I went.

These directives never ceased, and it
Mattered not that I was seated in the
Senate or that I reached the advanced
Age of sixty-four.

Even visiting ambassadors were interrupted
By my mother's voice cautioning from a
Nearby room or from some far off floor.

Time was I would thrill to soft nocturnes,
Canaries' songs and trills, a lion's
Thunderous roar.

But now she is gone, the only sound I long
To hear is my dear, sweet mother's voice
Once more.

Allen Glass

I STILL LIVE

Take this forgotten book
Of poems from off the
Shelf and hold it tenderly.

There you will find what
Once was my heart and my
Soul, all that remains of me.

No need to wonder what
Kind of person penned
These lines of poetry.

Here in your hands is
My quintessence. What
Matter all the rest of me.

What matter my stature,
My resonant voice,
My countenance, discerning
Eye, or any corporeal entity?

You need only read my poems
To cause a breath of life
To stir again in me.

Then when the last
Leaf has slowly fallen
I will come alive and
Be with Thee.

Allen Glass

A TIME TO LOOK FORWARD

You are coming to a new start
With many unique unknowns
A testimonial to your years of smart
And how much you have really grown

Time now moves to be on your side
As you take a quantum leap
And forward your Be-longings with pride
Moving on to new tasks to complete

This day of your birth
Is a moment so rare
A time to validate your own worth
And lavishly bathe in self care

Opportunities lie before you
As you see how far you have come
Looking outward, to another view
And contemplate the yet undone

Happy Birthday
With wishes for the best
May each tomorrow enrich you in every way
And give life all you've got with zest

Jeanne Faust

ENDLESS WINTER

Looking through the window pane,
the snow falls heavy like the rain.
A white blur, starts to appear
and with a blink it disappears.

The cold radiates from the glass,
bringing back memories of the past.
The wet springs, hot summers, cool falls,
they never seem to last at all.

The winter is here as if to stay,
nothing but bitter cold, day after day.
Turn up the heat and close the blinds,
nothing can help except the passage of time.

Kenneth F. Leck

COLORLESS SHADES OF GREY

Colorless shades of grey,
cloud my mind,

While the presence of time,
rolls silently by.

One day ends, another begins,
then back again.

Colorless shades of grey,
fill the sky,

While the clouds move in,
the rain begins.

It is hard to concentrate,
without the light.

Colorless shades of grey,
pass on by.

Kenneth F. Leck

SING OF PEACE

The jittery cactus wren screeches
atop its perch of stately saguaro,
warning others of its desire amidst
the throng of paraded desert trees.

Do you see me?
Can you hear me?

He calls,
searching the windy canyons
for something or someone to understand.

The endless environment echoes
the sound,
vibrating his vantage point,
craning his neck
while he sings.

And sings.
And sings.

Suddenly there is silence.
The wren's distinct voice can be heard no more.

He has gone now,
but will return and charm the desert in song.

For those who truly listen,
there is peace.

Lynne Armstrong

MYSTERIES OF NATURE

What mysterious treasures
  does the endless sea hold?
What secret truths are there
  that remain untold?

What artifacts remain from
  our ancestors long ago?
What ancient secrets are there,
  hidden way down deep below?

Why do birds fly south for the
  cold winter season?
Who can explain this; is there
  a reason?

What makes the thunder roll so
  very loud?
What makes the uniqueness of
  each and every cloud?

What makes a rainbow appear and
  then go away?
What brings the beginning of
  each new day?

What makes the stars above
  shine at night?
It is the mysteries of nature;
  do you think I'm right?

Denise Comb

THE ANGELS

As the twilight descended, a vision appeared,
  It was the Angel of Mercy.
Calling to her people to have no fear,
  Like a vision, she appeared, holy and true.

I blinked my eyes as she appeared,
  I saw the Devil arise from the underworld.
He was clad in a black cloak with dagger,
  He strolled nonchalantly by her.

But she saw nor heard, so engrossed was she
  With other affairs, she hardly saw.
The chorus of angels appeared again,
  Chanting melodies to the earth's inhabitants.

God appeared on high with his message of faith,
  He blessed the people of the earth.
They had gone astray and now must repent,
  He forgave them their sins on earth.

The angels heal the sick and wounded,
  Care for the poor and indigent.
The ascent to heaven is a glorious journey,
  Descent into hell is a tortuous ride.

      E. Saltz

HUGS

Hugs are very nice.
Better than good advice.
Give more hugs, there is a need;
As good as doing a good deed.
Hugs can relieve a pain;
Help composure to maintain.

Hugs can relieve depression.
Learn to share this expression.
Hugs make the secure even more.
Share those hugs; give hugs galore.
Hugging is an exercise;
One you might not recognize.

Hugs make the healthy healthier, the happy happier.
Hugs make one feel good and steps are much snappier.
Benefits are too numerous to mention.
Hugging feels good and eases tension.

Hugging is a stretching exercise, if you're short.
This exercise is easy, to this one, you can resort.
It's a stooping exercise if you're tall;
But not too much to do, not at all.

Hugs make impossible days possible.
And make uncrossable bridges crossable.
Hugs make happy days happier still.
Share your hugs today, if you will.

      Betty C. Baker

THE MOVER OF MY HEART

Dedicated to Michael Joseph Imbruglia

My heart is star-struck and bewildered; yet it beats,
Rhythmically, to a voice from within.
My soul is receptive to sounds of atoms crashing amid the din.
The dove is resplendent in the light, which brings peace, and
  I will remember;
As the Age of Aquarius slowly fades into radiant splendor.

There's no distraction so evident, as an arrow traveling
  through time and space,
And as it falls upon a barren place,
Upon it blooms an eternal garden of saving grace;
To what end — surely, His plan will show its face.

The moon's influential façade adjusts an emotional ebb and flow,
Which provides the music to which we dance to and fro.
Destiny intertwined though translucent truth prevails,
And the mover of my heart is mindful of such tales.

In the star-struck twilight, the heart feels and the soul knows
Of what He proposes.
Reality based on facts in the mind disposes.
The journey of the soul streaks across the sky;
The mover of my heart understands the reason why.

      Elizabeth A. Wolasz-Ruhland

STILLBORN

Desolately I sat, a mangled corpse
  Listening to the abandoned night
As the droning pattern of acid rainfall
  burned straight through my failing sight

Dazed memory of shattered dreams
  Their broken shards lying contortedly about
Dull points sharpened by a frozen wind
  to cut the groping wrists of those without

Over and over the dregs' echoing cry
  ''Doom'' crept up on those about to die
Once their desperate pleas met with callous sneers
  While the turbulent waters of chaos rose drowning the tears
  the shadow of annihilation silencing their fear

Helpless in the Apocalypse's grip
  Hell is seeking souls to claim
    Our consuming hatred kindling the Holocaust
      with no one left to blame

Darkness' descent into the heart of a dying earth
Drawing taut around its throat as Lifelessness is given birth

The destruction is consummated with the last breath
The remains settle slowly into the dust with tortured thoughts
  of a painfully final death

      Christopher Comfort

HOMECOMING

I walk down the road tired and weary.
　One could say I've walked my last mile,
But I know my mother is waiting,
　so I'll push forward with some style.
My back and I will hold a bit straighter,
　and the sun will not once dim my sight.
These Tennessee bones will be rested
　when I see my mother tonight.

The old house is now barely standing,
　but the front gate is pearly white.
And the dim glow off in the distance
　I know is my old bedside light.
The old dinner bell's ringing busy;
　Mom's most beloved child's coming home.
The same bell will echo tomorrow
　for little sis as she drives in alone.

Mary Ann Taylor

THE SET OF THE SAIL

How beautiful the pleasures
Played upon our minds,
Like the glare upon the
Windswept sea of time.
We are all on the same tact,
Yet going in different directions.
Wisdom upon the crests,
Bares no witness of youth —
Suddenly, tempest roaring
Of scudding waves!
Mother cries, ''Drop the sails!''
As the force of the gale
Played havoc until our calm.
A child lost then found —
Our day,
A reminder, God is alive
He is speaking and moving
Upon the face of the deep.

*Dr. Mark Montgomery
& Debra Kirkham*

POETRY'S PASSION

　　poetry's
passion irritates

long after
the orange sun
slides
beneath the western sea

the irritation
sticks.

and soon
and sooner still

midnight's oracular
touch

secretes
　　the pearl.

Richard Alan Bunch

HIS MEMORY

The story my friend
Doesn't have an end
It has few words to be told,
It represents my love for one,
Who's gone from this earth to behold.

A rainbow goes forever,
With its colors all of cheer!
It represents my love for him,
And carries me on — with no fear.

The butterfly is forever free
With wings that soar him high
The tear-drop has entrapped him,
As it fell once from my eye.

And Dad, you know
What you meant to me,
And I know now that you are free
And within this emblem I carry
Forever your loving memory!

Dawna Barker

ST. PAUL'S VISION OF THE CHRIST

Who is this man —
of whom I tell —
to those in my world —
this product I sell?
This man with thoughts so fresh and new —
whose love as sweet as morning dew —
His life I hear so much about —
His light I never live without —
am I to write his life, per se —
as others did along the way?
There's nothing new, it's all been told —
the stories now, they're all too old —
my destined purpose is all too clear —
to write of his bright promise dear —
His ugly death I must reveal —
and from his blood our souls are sealed —
Who cares about the life he lived —
this life strained through the mortal sieve —
His death does bring us life anew —
in Him I declare victory to you.

Larry G. Gray

LIFE

The mystery of life
is so deep-rooted
so beautiful created
that only God knows
　　about it

In happiness and sufferings
we all are involved
　　the rich, the poor
have tasted it all . . .
but nobody knows
when the end of that life,
in form of a cloud,
folds its hands,
　　and says . . . Good-bye

Antonia Fernández-Corcino

SCREAMS

Silence,
Quiet hounds of hell
Pad the jungle trails.
Fear,
Stabbing at my gut,
Burning through my mind.
Sounds
Explode from every side,
A madness in my ears.
Blood,
Soaks into the ground,
Paints the foliage red.
Screams,
From men and boys, from me,
I scream myself awake.
Sweating,
I sit, the nightmare gone,
And I am still in Hell.

Lee W. Kelley

REST

The leaves of bull rushes
Whisper softly in the dawn,
As the sun shyly peeks
Under curtains night had drawn.

Tide, almost unnoticed,
Slaps against a blue-grey bow.
An old man sits and thinks
Of yesterdays and now.

Watching the new day begin,
He finds comfort in a thought.
Yesterday's marvelous dreams,
This peaceful rest have brought.

Lee W. Kelley

LEE W. KELLEY. Born: Pasadena, California, 4-27-43; Married: Virgle, 6-16-61; Deceased 10-27-79; Education: Graduate, Writer's Digest School of Fiction; lifetime of education through observation; Occupation: Bookkeeper for patent law firm; Memberships: AAAS; National Writer's Club; Planetary Society; American Federation of Police; Marine Corps Association; Poetry: 'Dust Dream,' *American Poetry Anthology,* 1985; 'Catch The Moment,' *The Art of Poetry,* 1985; 'Silly Dragon,' *Best New Poets of 1986,* 1987; Other Writings: ''The Giving Stone,'' Christmas sci-fi for radio, DSA Radio, 1985; Comments: *I've been a Marine, gas station owner, horse trainer, dog trainer, ranch hand, and bookkeeper. I'm also a mother with two fine grown sons. Through it all I've been a writer, avid reader and people watcher. My short stories are sci-fi, but my poetry may take any form. Currently writing a sci-fi book.*

Brewer Fountain, Boston Common.

TESTIMONY OF MAN

Is everything perfect again?

Before I open my eyes
and fully realize
the burden of my actions
tell me; am I forgiven?

Am I absolved of guilt
Am I purged of sin
Have I silenced the din
with the screams of my repentance?

Is the sky still blue
Is the world round, too
Does the earth yet
revolve around the sun?

Just let me know
Before I crawl back out of my hole;
Is my innocence restored
and the universe set back in order?

I promise I'll be as good as gold
I promise I'll be the "me" of old
Just don't make me
            face her judgement

Christopher Comfort

IF YOU FIND THE LIGHT, LET IT GLOW

It matters not the color of your eyes, skin, or hair—
How smartly you dress; the jewels you wear —
It does matter how you think and feel; it's the
Beauty inside that shows —
If you find the light — and it glows!

It matters not where or when you were born —
If you're Irish, German, or Jew —
It does matter if God's love's in your heart —
If there, it'll shine radiantly through!

Don't be obsessed with your dress, speech,
Position, and such —
If you really love God, He'll love you as you are —
Love you so very much!

But, you can't fool God; you can't fool yourself —
If it's there, it surely will show —
So, find the light, keep it bright, and forever
Let it glow, glow, glow!

Vonda Blum Wyatt

HIDDEN LOVE

My past existed no more.
  Life's light, to fade through time's door.
The final words of mind had passed.
  Lips were quiet — sealed fast.
In life, feelings were not to be said.
  You feared to hear them — commitment — a word you dread.
And so, ever so quiet,
  Hearts' words held silent.
With no one to hear them,
  The walls shant reveal them.
Last and parting thought was of you.
  These words whispered at last:
      I love you —

Michael V. McCann

THOUGHTS

I spoke to you of loneliness and of my dying thoughts
Perhaps surprised or just bemused
You asked
Are you thinking of dying
Ah no I said not dying but my thoughts are dying
Dying from being turned over far too many times
Examined held up to the light
Worn from too much handling
But only by me
For no one else can know them
Thoughts of what I wanted once and thought I'd want forever

Thoughts that lie quivering on the floor of my mind
Afraid to form themselves and live
Afraid my love would never be returned
Thoughts of what were cherished dreams
I knew could not come true
Thoughts of hope of changes still to happen
To make all things good
Thinking thoughts so dear to me
Long years ago would blind my eyes with hope
Shining too bright to last
And tears would soon replace with their warm and bitter salt
The smile I saved for you

Eleanor Robertson

SUMMER IS OVER

Seeing the leaves change with the
  waves of time.

Yet the warmed is still here in the heart.

So pleasing to the eyes to see the many
  wonders of fall coming in.

Some waiting for the sound of the winter
  wind in the air.

Trying not to think of vain things like the
  z-persons do.

School is here/the winter wind is a step
  away.

The seeds will have to know the school lesson
  and the false realities.

Some learn of Ism in ways wrote, some not wrote
  down.

Something changing in the learning/to live through
  their life every day on Ism earth.

So much time spent on hollow things.

School has started, the time has come to meet
  new seeds and learn the meaning of man's reality.

Yet summer fun is over/now it's time to get back to
  ink pens, paper, books.

Felix Louis Wicks

OH! WHAT A MAN

Oh! what a man, my Lord Jesus; Oh what a beautiful man.
Yes, I mean Mary's baby and my Father had a plan.
Lived thirty-three years as a human, knowing all the while in the end,
His people would try to destroy him, no one would be there to defend.
All his disciples in fear of their lives; their lives saved from
                         sin by *God's* grace.
Would suddenly flee, leaving my Lord alone, to bear thorns, nails, spit
                         in his face.
Ridiculed, scourged and derided, told to save his own soul;
He asked his father to forgive, for this was not his goal.
Bearing the whole world's sins along; meeting death on its own
                         stamping ground.
Snatched the victory away from the grave, making love and faith by
                         Grace abound.

Don Dixon

FROM THE EYES OF A CHILD

Talking bears,
         crawling bugs,
And Daddy dressed as Santa Claus.

    No school because of snow,
      faces at the kitchen table all aglow,
      and my new baseball mitt I've got to show.

Timeless moments,
      some captured,
             others repeated but not
with the same feeling.
          Child crying,
           parents rush and soothe with a pacifier,
wish the world's problems could be just as easy.

Frank F. Atanacio

THANKSGIVING ANTHOLOGY

Dedicated to our nation,
the good old United States of America.

We raise our hands oh God!
Through all these years of grain and bount'
And many of us and others of years ago,
Have gathered to thank you for love so sound.

We raise our hands oh Heaven!
And pledge some words of deep gratitude.
For all the centuries and goodly brethren,
That brought us strength and brave, our fortitude.

We raise our hands oh skies!
And render thanks for liberty and test.
And bless the lands of others in their plies
Crying in their hearts to get life's best.

United we dream and work for peace,
This is a time for us to wholesome give.
United we sing and thank God for these,
Blessings of land and gifts here we receive.

Alfonso Te Rodriguez

DREAMS

You took my hand
    We walked
    We talked
    We were silent
Enjoying the peaceful feeling
    Of just being alone
    If only for awhile.
The fog thickening . . . we did not notice
    Our eyes unable to see anything
    But our hearts going out to each other
    As has happened so many times before.
I need your presence in my life
    To regain my calm
    To keep my peace of mind.

When I awake, I am fresh and ready
    To face what this new day brings
    Because I have once again
    Spent time with you . . . if only in my dreams.

Judene Johnson Ainsley

I NEED YOU

"I need you, another Ezekiel, to sit with the captives,
and to speak to the whole house of Israel.

I need you, another Ezekiel, to inspire Israel as one nation
again, the Spirit of God having come on the dry bones.

I need you, another Ezekiel, to prepare Israel for her
Tribulation.

I need you, another Ezekiel, to sound the clear trumpet warning
of war from the Gentile nations, against Israel in this
latter day.

I need you, another Ezekiel, to weep, and fast, and be
dumb before Me.

I need you, another Ezekiel, to speak for Me on end-time matters.

I need you, another Ezekiel, to hope for the Messiah
to come again.

I need you, another Ezekiel, to save my people.

I need you, another Ezekiel, to live, and worship, and pray.

I need you, another Ezekiel, to speak, and give, and love."

Conclusion: Ezekiel was among the greatest of the prophets
of Israel, with knowledge, service, experiencing great suffering,
and captivity, and he was a writing prophet. Ezekiel was a
priest in Israel, continuing to serve off the land during part
of the Babylonian Captivity of Seventy years under Nebuchadnezzar.

Estella M. McGhee-Siehoff

THE DEAD IMPENITENT

I am seventy-one years old, and a widow of
nine and one half years, and it comes as a
shock to me to know that people do die impenitent.

They really do.

They will not repent, even with death impending.

They hope to live, and if sick, to get better.

They want food, and shelter, and medical care . . . free.

They want life after death, if they believe in it,
with no accountability for this life.

God owes it to them.

They believe this, and will die this way.

Any other way, they will not listen to.

It is the shock of my life, after so much love
given to them they die defiant and ungrateful.

Impenitent through their deaths.

Lost.

Hell's fires await them. They would not repent,
even under conviction, with saving knowledge.

God cuts them off. Would you like a few names?

Estella M. McGhee-Siehoff

THE PERSECUTION HAS TURNED
INTO INQUISITORIAL PURSUITS

They cannot stop the flowers from
Growing on my grave,
But they can pick them . . . all of them,
By siphoning off every thought in ridicule.

They cannot stop the flowers from
Growing on my grave,
But they can pick them . . . all of them,
By engaging in willfully destructive begging,

For their comfort and enrichment,
At my expense,
With no thanks, or gratitude,
Or any kind of payment, just begging.

They cannot stop the flowers from
Growing on my grave,
But they can pick them . . . all of them,
By invention and mischief in evil words and deeds,

With pure joy,

In the flesh,

From Satan's inquiry.

Estella M. McGhee-Siehoff

SANDS OF LIFE

The words I wanted to write
Are scattered along life's highways,
Like some of the things I could have said
And chose not to say.

And the dreams I dreamed
Are still floating around in some distant sky,
Like the chances I had for riches and wealth
And let them all pass by.

But deeds can't be measured in dollars,
Nor values in nuggets of gold,
And the dreams we dreamed when very young
Shouldn't bother those getting old.

For life is constantly changing
As the sea shifts the sand on the shore,
And the things we once thought we had to have
Don't intrigue us at all anymore.

So live for today and be cheerful.
Don't worry about things you can't change.
Plan, if you will, for tomorrow,
But tomorrow will not be the same.

Help others less favored than you
Even though some are much older.
And soon the golden butterfly of happiness will come
And light upon your shoulder.

Henry O'Grady

ATOMTRONIC

Five years retired
Five years for playback
Five years, to feel the impact
from sixty years of the fast track

Who were they, the achievers
that progressed living standards
from knowledge of the electronic phase
to develop the technology
for today's neutronic maze

Who were they, since the thirties
that took technology from centuries peaked
to scope the furthertronic haze
and prove economics has no peak

Who were they, the achievers
to have no name, have no face
No recognition, in history's time phase
when the atom, became the furthertronic to space
"That infinity of knowledge for the achiever"

As the people mover rotates
$H = HsL^2$

James M. Andary

CHRISTMAS IS TO ME

''Christmas to me is just another day,''
A high school girl was heard to lightly say.

Not seeming to think
Of peace to men on earth,
Or love so infinite
As to give men second birth.

But Christmas is not
Just another day to me.
It's a day to be kept holy,
And humbly bend the knee.

Before the loving Father
Who gave His only begotten Son.
And bowing thus, remember,
That Gift and the Giver are one!

Agnes Angel Stiles

THE STOCK-LAW GATE

Living on a mountainside when I was small
Seems more a gift of God than a trick of fate.
The fun I liked the best of all
Was riding on the Stock-Law Gate.

This big gate which was across the road
Had wooden hinges that creaked and bent
When sleds, or wagons with a load
Or oxen, horses, or people came and went.

I felt safe atop that big gate
From the bull that would snort and paw,
The big horned cow that grazed so late,
And wild hogs . . . which I really never saw.

Agnes Angel Stiles

DOES IT MATTER?

Raindrops fall on a country pond,
 Little fingers in the batter;
Man and wife pledge eternal bond
And to some it does not matter.

The wind blows dead leaves through the air,
 Stirring spices into the brew;
Acting like they no longer care,
Forgetting a love they once knew.

Unrelenting heat of the day,
 Incandescence under the pot;
Without thinking of what they say,
Saying things which really are not.

Elements in the world we know,
 Ingredients cast in the stew;
We reap the harvest which we sow.
Tell me, does it matter to you?

Christopher Jennings

IT COULD HAVE BEEN

It could have been so
different —
 If I had let God
have His way.
 If I had lived to please Him, as I lived from
day to day.
 But now my life is over —
and I face God's judgment throne.
 What will be said of me —
when I reach my final home?
 For life is but a journey.
We know we cannot stay —
 Is there *one* life
made sweeter — because I
passed their way?
 Or with tears of bitter
sorrow —
 ''It could have been
you know.''
 If I had taken just
a moment — a little love to
show — just a little visit —
just a flower or two —
just a moment spent in prayer
was all they longed to hear.

Lillian W. Payne

WITH ALL MY HEART

I dance and sing
With all my heart
For all that never was
For all that could have been
For all that is lost
In the sudden chill
Of fate's wind

I dance and sing
With all my heart
For all the tears
Wrapped in fears
Hidden quietly
In the passing of years

I dance and sing
With all my heart
For all the lives
I might have known
For all the blessings
Of joy and pain
For all of life
And nothing less

More reasons now
To dance and sing
With all my heart

Kerry Ann Shields

I LOVE YOU

Have you told someone
today — ''I love you''?
 I'm sure if they were
sad it made them glad.
 I know it made you
happy when they said —
''I love *you* too.''

Lillian W. Payne

A CHILD OF WISDOM

Old Man do not leave
Alone, with no one
Without a spoken word
Nor gesture of kindness

For over the years
Your eyes reflect
You've come to know
Life's depths — its secrets
Within your heart

Come . . . walk with me
Along the sea
Together with the wind and sky
To feel once more and to see
Their majestic elegance and beauty

To rest again in the hand
Of their silent friendship
To listen for their unspoken words

Before returning again
To be so very alone
Inside a capsule
Of our modern age
Shut in, isolated
In four walls called home

To write, to ponder in silence
A child of wisdom

Kerry Ann Shields

STAINED-GLASS TEARS

Listen — to the laughter
Is sorrow smiling?
In the freezing winter's snow
Reflections can be beautiful
Like a stained-glass tear . . .
Magnified like raindrops
Flowing down cheeks and hills
Empty into endless oceans
Within me and you . . .
Memories of my mother
Special gifts she just had to bear
And she said my ''hands felt like
Butterflies''
And ''love is eternal''
Oh, but I miss her now . . .
Listen — can you hear laughter
Could it be sorrow smiling?
In the freezing winter's snow
Reflections can be beautiful
Like a stained-glass tear.

Shelley E. Frick

I have a dream
of becoming something
you already
think I am,
and because of
your faith in me
it has become possible.

Carol Gross

LITERACY

History molds a nation with scope
Literacy is tomorrow's hope
Illiteracy famed, the immigrant slang
Illiteracy today, molds the degenerate gang

To miss the achievements of history grand
Cycled by print, with the constitution grand
Freedom for knowledge, shall rule the land
Freedom by literacy, shall set her trend

Yes! this nation, where God laid his hand
'Stands Miss Liberty,' with three words in hand
''We the People'' have the freedom to speak
Freedom for literacy, for minds to peak

To coin Kate Smith, in song of fame
''God bless America,'' where literacy makes fame.

As the people mover rotates
$$H = HsL^2$$

James M. Andary

WISDOM GAP

In defense of knowledge, from history's view
In defense of wisdom, when nations grew
In defense of logic, from cycled phrases
Technology grew, from history phases

It's there, from the frequencies of time
The ups, the downs, from societies in time
The people, the proud, the weak, the strong
That progressed life, knowing right from wrong

To the young, with a generation gap
To the young, caught in the negative trap
Let your prime emotions hang out
Let your prime emotions give you clout
For education is history's theorem
To a life that can be supreme

As the people mover rotates
$$H = HsL^2$$

James M. Andary

THE FLYING GEORGIA BOY

Dark clouds drifted, as lightning clashed, and flashed across the sky
Troops scrambled and marched to battle with the rising sun
Brothers of a race, destined to fight, face to face
Battlelines formed and bugles sounded
Chenault saw the stars and the moon and the rising sun
He knew war was soon
Troops amassed, cannons and mortars boomed
but his vision came from the skies
A lad from Georgia had a dream about a flying machine
He had tried and failed, but never again
He tapped the wing of that monstrous thing, climbed into
the wind, climbing faster, diving, and rolling
He flew his machine against an enemy he had never seen
Flying and fighting with friends and saw some meet a bitter end
His country was behind him, but where and when?
Scotty came back again and again and he knew he would win
because ''God was his co-pilot.''

Edward A. Hawkins

THE BATTLE OVER

Let's go for one drink you once said to me
Now, many years later, they say you are free
The drinking is not your main thing in life
Everyone is behind you in your struggle and strife

You had us so worried, so sick, and so mad
Now we're proud, quite exhausted and strangely sad
To wonder if truly you finally won
The one thing most wanted by everyone

Now we are the struggling which you left behind
Now we are the problem, the stumbling blind
But you are our hero and we know what to do
It is worth everything to be sober like you

Jerry Martinez

WINTER IN MIAMI — BACK WHEN

When you read about Miami, and its sunny southern clime,
Where the flowers are ever blooming, and it's always summertime;
Don't forget, we too have winter oh my friends, to you I plead;
Please don't send me dogwood when it's firewood that I need.

Yes, the skies are always sunny, and the months are always June,
But you'll find a fur coat welcome — underneath Miami's moon.
This is but a friendly warning — and I hope dear friends,
     you'll heed;
For you will not yearn for dogwood when it's firewood that you need.

Once you've visited in Miami, and the sand gets in your shoes,
Well, there just ''ain't'' nothing like it! that can chase away
     your blues.
At the first approach of winter — you will beat it back
     with speed;
But you won't be seeking dogwood for it's firewood that you need.

Here the birds do double duty; for they sing throughout the night,
And the horses, dogs and season make money vanish from your sight.
Oh, there's sports and entertainment but you'll feel an urgent need;
To return, to — not the dogwood — your home fireside's
     what you need.

Christine Howard

THIS LOVE HE GIVETH ME

I saw it in His eyes that day; In His smile as we met.
I felt it in His tender touch; It's a day I'll never forget.
It came so soft, so warm, so free; It cleansed my soul from sin.
It filled my heart and let me sing; This love He left within.

Oh, Jesus, Lover of my soul; Who saved a wretch like me;
You shed your blood to make me whole, when You died on Calvary.
Sweet Spirit of the Living God; Fall fresh upon my way.
Teach me Thy everlasting love, and how to live each day.

This love, O love; This love so free;
This love of Christ divine;
This love, my hope; this joy is mine;
This love, He giveth me.

Eleanor S. Follmer

MAN WITHOUT WOMAN

Little flower,
Fairest in all the fields,
Blow thy petals into my garden.
I will gather them up one by one
And make a sacred book of enchanted pages,
Each one a poignant moment of beauty
To decorate my solitude.

Little flower,
Messenger of light and spirit,
Loose thy girdle
And drop thy loveliness in my lap.
A cold north wind has swept down
From the mountain through the vale
And killed the last chrysanthemum
By my cottage door.

Little flower,
Child of love and life,
Fair daughter of spring and summer,
Blow thy lovely petals over the walls of time
Into the garden of my heart,
That my soul may awake and live.

James Sexton Layton

APPRAISAL

In olden times when skulls were thick
And heathen passions ruled,
There was a method sure and quick
To deal with love that cooled.
When their dear ones grew worn and numb
All wrinkled and a bore,
They hit them on the cranium
And then they were no more.
But, now, we're made of sterner stuff.
We'd gaze in righteous rage
At methods that are crude and rough —
In this enlightened age!
Now, when loved ones are old and grey,
All spent and out of breath,
We simply take our love away
And let them pine to death.

Colleen Barton

A JUNE NIGHT

To write a poem in December
Is to remember
The sweet roses that bloom
In the month of June
We can't forget the bright moon light
That shines on a warm June night
And the twinkling stars
That look like the Christmas tree
Though they be as far as Mars
I'm still happy that they shine on me
So December too is fine
Because it is divine
For it is the time
We celebrate
Our dear Lord's birth
All over, His wonderful Earth.

Rose Mary Gerlach

DID YOU THANK HIM?

Just a year ago today
someone stopped
    me on my way
Did you see him —
Did you say;
Thank you God
    for life?
For happy children
    voicing cheerful
Sounds as they play?
Thank you
    for each bright day
For the simple
    things in life.
Take our luxuries, if
    you must —
For you are the greatest;
The One we love and trust.

Claudine L. Evans

CONFIDENCE
(AND WHAT IT MEANS)

*Inspired by the book
"Jonathan Livingston Seagull"*

A ship without a rudder
is a sorry sight indeed
for it is actually going
    no place, don't you see?
But someone who is lacking someone
To whom they can go in confidence
    is a sorry one indeed,
for without confidential words
    with one who cares
problems can become *nightmares*.

In summation
There's seldom a ship without
    a rudder — no never
and seldom one without a *real*
    close friend — if ever,
for that isn't the way God
    meant us to be
When he placed us in his great
    creation
Don't you see?

Claudine L. Evans

SEA STORM

The clouds walked low on the water,
Lightly treading a pewter sea,
The gulls flew back to the shallows,
And the seals hurried home to the lea.
Black shadows stalked the clouds
O'er the waters,
A windy white mist moaned in from the sea.
We were alone, for a moment
Alone we three,
Alone in a misty white world unknown,
Outcasts from an angry sea,
The gulls, the seals and me.

Martha E. Gosnell

THE LAST DAY

My heart raced, come forth my tears,
the news, I knew was bad.
Message received, would alter years,
disrupted the good I had.

The words, were like the smell of Nam,
etched so nothing could take its place.
Deep, no one friend or foe, could give
a damn, if you awoke again, from sleep.

As I stood, near the fence with clenched
hands, mind wandering, *Oh God*, why not me,
to give my soul to my country land, to
keep her, ever free?

The choppers were hovering overhead,
though silence inside me known . . . Arthur,
was truly dead, I needed not, to be shown.

Stanley A. Marquette

WHAT MAKES A POET?

Why do poets sing?
Do they hear bells,
That do not ring?
Do they see light,
Where none is supposed to shine,
    Or behold tantalizing rainbows
    In their nonexistent wine?

What makes a poet strive to rhyme,
Rosy dreams of space and time?
Now tell me, please,
The answer to such things as these.
    And set my tortured mind at ease
    Tell me at once,
    So I will Know it.

    What makes a poet, a poet?

Martha E. Gosnell

APRIL

April is a fickle lady,
A willful, woeful lady,
Torn between joy and pain.

A lovely, lovely April
With long dark locks of driven rain.

Her eyes are twinkling dewdrops,
Her smile a thousand flowers,
The morning mists her garments,
Her feet are trailing showers.
She taunts and flaunts
The sun her lover.
She's foolish, vain and proud
For she hides from him,
Her charming self behind a purple cloud.

Martha E. Gosnell

IN MEMORY OF ANNE FRANK

Behind a closed door, in a secret hiding place,
Eight souls, crowding together, found refuge to keep safe.

It was a time when family life of Jewish faith
Was cruelly shattered by Nazi terror, torment and hate.

Hidden there, in those days of the Holocaust,
Was Anne Frank, a child of war, innocent, lonely and lost.

In the early bloom of youth, shut away
From all the joys of youth's sweet carefree days.

Her heart longed to see the sun, the blue sky,
A bird in flight, the trees, the grass, a butterfly.

Her thoughts, her hopes and dreams of being free,
Were confided each day as she wrote into her diary.

Writing was her gift revealed her daily life,
Writing helped to free her spirit, to keep faith, to survive.

Until sent into the *Bergen-Belson* camp of death,
Her courage and spirit endured with her last breath.

Anne Frank's diary bore witness to those fearful times,
When the world was silent, blind to Nazi crimes.

A young girl's diary, written in those evil years,
Opened the eyes of the world, and moved each one to tears.

Too late, the world would understand the past, the shame,
Too late, the loss of the innocent millions, who perished in the flame.

Anne Frank's story has become a living memory;
That will never let the world forget the darkest page in
human history!

Rena L. Rosenzweig

A CHILD I KNOW

The inquisitive child
Loses a direction on the path
Where the infinity machine makes snow fall there

I cover my ears
When the sun sets
Do you hear it?

The children have nothing to do
The electric iridescent key opens the gate
Winter is such a playful time of the year
Especially for toboggan rides

Parents close their mouths
When they speak of love, sometimes

It beckoned
They said
They laughed
They sneered
They died
And before

They said we're all adults here

This is a child I know

Richard Bretz

YOUNG CARPENTER

There once lived this young carpenter
Who dwelt on this earth
This pure young carpenter
Who came to do his father's will

He came unto his own
And they received him not
This pure young carpenter
Who came to give his life
That his father's chosen children
Could have everlasting life

But they pushed him aside
And plotted for his life
Though he healed their sickness
And gave sight to their blind
This pure young carpenter
Who came to give his life
But they cried out the more
Each miracle he did
Away with him! Away with him!
And rejected him as their king

But God in His wisdom
At the beginning of time
Had drawn His master plan
That through this pure young carpenter
We all might have eternal life.

Doris Marshall

MOTHER

I went to the gravesite of my mother
For it was time to rake the leaves
As I knelt to put fresh flowers there
A longing took hold of me
Oh Lord, why did you have to take my mother
She meant so much to me — just her loving voice in joy
In woe — was such a comfort to me

I heard a bird singing in the distance
That brought memory to my soul
Of the sweet, sweet way that she sang to thee
Oh Lord, did she have to go
For her place here is so lonesome without her
And her house, it will know her no more

Dear Lord, did you need her in heaven
To put a bright star in the sky
For whenever twilight was falling — and darkness was near
Just her presence would brighten the night

Now Lord I know your judgment is true
And forgive me for questioning your motive
Only I miss her loving arms around me
Oh Lord, take care please of my mother

Doris Marshall

SOLITAIRE, 3:30 A.M.

She sits alone and shuffles the cards,
For, you see, she cannot sleep.
If she would allow herself
She would lie abed and weep.

Why does she sit and shuffle the cards?
Why lie abed and weep?
Why in this lonely nighttime hour
Is she not fast asleep?

It is not for a love that is lost
Nor for a loved one who has gone on.
It is not for a death she mourns.
She is wondering about her own.

Two years ago this very month,
When the roses were in bloom,
The surgeon said just one short word.
A word which oftimes means doom.

She knows there are medical miracles,
And that the surgeon's knife is sure.
But, for that diagnostic term
She knows there is no sure cure
    For Cancer.

Anna E. Hayes

BEAUTIES NOT SEEN BY MAN

My God, my God, Creator of the Heavens;
My God, my God, Painter of the Sky;
The brilliant blue, the whiteness of the cloud.
My God, my God, in all this autumn splendor
It makes me almost cry aloud.
My God, my God, all this autumn splendor;
Not just this year but year proceeding year.
Since you are master of all this beauty,
Please tell me what I have to fear:
When I put on the raiment which is eternal;
When I pass into a more splendid sphere.
I may be saddened for my friends at parting;
But, I'll meet friends too, on the other side.
And, Jesus my mediator will show me
Beauties never seen by mortal man.
He will hold me and he will love me
Now I can almost feel his hand.

Anna E. Hayes

MIGGIDO

Hear, and hark, the rumble, rumble, rumble,
Over desert, hill and plain.
Hear the screams and groans
See the crimson stain.
That is not the footsteps of a baby.
That is not the rocking of his chair.
The Beast. Has it awakened?
Is it stalking from its lair?
Is it marching now in unison
With the angels in the air
On their way to Miggidare?
Have the fowls been invited
To that ghoulish feast of flesh?
Is the bridal chamber readied?
Is the bride awaiting, dressed?

Anna E. Hayes

AN IMAGE TO BECOME

Sculpted on the cloistered mind
A graphic figure stands,
Draped with dreams and hopes to find
Fulfillment of one's plans.

Childhood fantasized its strategy,
"When I become a man,
I'll be rich and sail the sea,
Find treasure all I can!"

Unglamorous, though, the tangled strain
To find one's niche in life;
A target set, a goal to gain,
Unflinching face the strife.

Pursue your course, 'gainst rival strong,
Through trauma's pulsing fears;
No passing trivia e'er belong
To ravage life's few years.

The tyrant deep within your breast
Is bursting to become
That image which will stand the test
When lesser dreams succumb.

Relentless, then, without regret,
Your maverick rhapsody;
Dare until desire is met
To be what you should be.

Wendell K. Babcock

TIME

Time drags his feet on my sidewalk,
    And pulls at the hem of my skirt.
He stifles the hands of my timepiece,
    And endlessly counts every quirk,
Leaving me apprehensive — and tensive.

Time rushes blindly past me,
    And scatters my thoughts all awry.
He laughs at my work all unfinished,
    And finds me more tasks to try,
Leaving me weary — and teary.

Time eludes all my questing,
    And doesn't hear when I call.
He's never around when I need him,
    And has no compassion at all,
Leaving me sad — and mad.

Time hovers just past my doorway,
    And waits for the end of my race.
He settles his wings on my shoulders,
    And deftly absorbs all my space,
Leaving me cold — and old.

Joyce Wallace

Herder
Sheep's guardian
Caring, guarding, protecting
Enduring Nature's various faces
Loner

Martha Janette Dorsett

FRIENDS

I wandered by a bubbling brook
    Turning and churning,
    As the warm earth shook
Gently, beneath my bare feet.

    I gazed into the hazy sky
And watched a flock of birds fly by
Flapping their wings and crying
    As far as my eyes could see.

I found a swarm of honey bees
    Near the top of an apple tree,
    Buzzing and humming,
    Busy, as only bees can be.

    I sat upon a fallen log,
    And whistled to my little dog.
He came running and licked my hand,
    Happy, as usual, to be my friend.

Faye Teague

STOUT BY THE RIVER

Stout by the river
you shining cottonwoods grow
and mingled in your brave assemblage
are smaller lesser growths
with fine names
some called
lilies of the field.

But now
let silent river flow
along determined way
to show us more
of nature's bounty.

The fields nestle
caressed by new growth
in river bottom
may all seeds fall
and blossom.

Thomas Krische

FIRST SIN

The first sin's committed by the heart,
All others by the flesh.
With ease,
Like sound upon the dark.
Yet
As I watch the morning come awake,
I have seen reflections
Of the resurrection
In my eyes.
While memories of stars
Ran
Through a bitter sun.

Robert J. Pluss

THE WAY OF ANOTHER LIFE

My Lord sat about on teaching me — the way of another life
It's not here you see — I wonder what it shall be like
I read of walls made of pearls
And streets made from gold so pure
A river and a tree of life
When I make it to the other side
It makes me want to sing and dance
But yet it scares me too — the way of another life

He says there will be no sun there
For he will be the light
He says there will be no flesh or blood
No corrupt thing you see — as he teaches me
The way of another life

He says the church now is within me
As he comes in to sup with me
The bread he gave to strengthen me
As he teaches me — the way of another life

So I'm beginning to feel like a stranger here
And I want sometimes to run and hide
From the different philosophy here
Go this way! some say — No, here is the way — another says
Though I read someplace where his words have said
Unmerited grace — not of me — but he
So I learn as he teaches me — the way of another life.

Doris Marshall

DORIS MARSHALL. Awards: Eight Awards of Merit Certificates, 1985-87; Three Golden Poet Awards, 1985-87; Golden Poet Trophy, 1987; Poetry: Three poems published by the American Poetry Association, 1986-87; Other Writings: *Work and Play,* children's book, 1987; ''A King's Love,'' song on the ''Hallelujah,'' album, Rainbow Records, 1987; ''Sun Set,'' song, Sunrise Records, 1987; Themes: *My common themes and ideas in my writing and songs are to teach and inspire others in those things which I have learned.*

JUST TO KNOW

I've dreamed, until my mind no longer knows the truth.
And now, my dreams abandon me —
as did my fleeting youth.
My heart is flooded with unbidden memories
that seem to reach and tear at me.
They seem to taunt and tease.
Is there anything for me? The questions come and go.
A touch? A thought? A glimpse of love?
My heart cries out to know.

Carolyn J. Carruth

GO DOWN MOSES

This Hebrew baby Moses — raised as the son of an
   Egyptian princess so fair,
   Never forgot his roots or the God of his people there.
Instead of enjoying the pleasures of sin for a season,
   He chose to endure hardships with his people; and love was the
   reason:

Moses settled in the desert of Midian and cared for his father-in-law
   Jethro's sheep.
   He and his wife Zipporah had two sons for whom his love was so deep.
Moses fled to this desert and lived for forty years in obscurity
   and peace.
   He didn't know that God had chosen him, *his* people from
   bondage to release.

One day when on *Mount Sinai,* he came into the path of a burning
   bush so tall
   That was not consumed by the flames — and not singed by the
   heat at all.
God spoke to Moses out of the bush and bade him his feet to bare;
   For the ground on which he stood was *Holy Ground* there.

When God left Moses, He had given him a great command;
   ''Go *down* Moses and free *my* people, way *down* in Egypt land!''
This story of the miraculous deliverance of the Israelites we all know,
   For God's ultimatum to the Egyptian Pharoah was, ''Let my people go!''

Moses became the leader of God's people as they journeyed to the
   Promised Land.
   For one disobedient act he received God's stern reprimand.
He climbed upon Mount Nebo so that he could really see
   The land flowing with milk and honey, at last God's people
   would be truly free!

Then Moses with his ancestors at last lay down to sleep,
   In a grave God dug for him in the heart of the earth so deep.
No one knows to this day the place where Moses lies,
   But we will surely see that great leader some day,
   ''when morning gilds the skies.''

Carolyn LaVonne Carroll

CAROLYN LaVONNE CARROLL. Born: Sylacauga, Alabama, 10-18-30; Education: Bishop College, Marshall, Texas; Occupation: Former substitute teacher; Poetry: 'Thinking of You,' 'Be a Role Model,' 'The Gift of Life,' 'Love Is A Flower,' 'My Heart Cries'; Comments: *The goal of my work is to touch hearts and minds with the reality of spiritual truths and explore the vast world of love — romantic and spiritual. My desire is that my poems will give emotional satisfaction to each reader as these truths are related to daily experience, leading one to joyous and victorious living.*

STREETS AND SATIN SHEETS

I met a man in a honky tonk bar.
He was playing on an old guitar.
He once played in a traveling show.
 I asked to sit and we talked a bit.
Then his finger began to twitch,
and I knew it was time for me to go.
 He picked a little then strummed a while.
On his face he wore a smile.
He said here's one my daddy sang,
 he started singing with tears in his eyes.
It was then that I realized,
where his destiny lay.
 He sang about streets and satin sheets,
beautiful music, the people you meet.
He sang about every man's dreams.
 He sang about love and about sorrow.
You only live once but it's a life you borrow.
He sang about you and about me,
 the song was over and so was he.
Fate was his destiny,
playing in a honky tonk bar,
 nickles and dimes, sleeping in a barn,
old whiskey bottles have lost their charm.
He once was a pop rock star.

Richard La Roy McPhee

SAIL AWAY SWEET SISTER

 I was riding my bicycle
when you were riding your tricycle.
I loved you then and I love you now.
 I said I could look into the sun.
You said I was the only one.
Now I'll tell you how.
 We are a little older now.
A little smarter, a little bolder now.
So listen to what I have to say.
 You're my sister, I'm your brother.
Both gifts from our mother.
That's the way I hope we'll stay.
 So sail away sweet sister.
You only have to whisper.
My heart will always be with you.
 Go ahead, look into the sun.
Someday you will find someone
to love you half as much as I do.

Richard La Roy McPhee

HEAVEN UPHELD

In Big Sky Country
you can see the horizon
in every direction,
with no hills, no mountains
no buildings to block the view.

I imagine that the sky is dome-shaped,
rounded by the curvature of the windshield
and the safe limits of imagination.
It is dizzying to face the truth —
that the sky is endless . . .
no limit has ever been discovered.

Deep blue sky: the ultimate argument
for the existence of Heaven.

Deborah Newton Cooksey

RAINDROPS

 I looked out my window,
raindrops fell before me.
How can you be so beautiful
and yet make me so lonely.
 Raindrops please quit falling,
you make me want to hide.
Can't you hear me calling,
you're locking me up inside.
 Raindrops rolled down my window,
I asked myself why.
Raindrops can't hurt you,
but they can make you cry.
 Raindrops please quit falling
so softly to the ground.
Can't you hear me calling,
through your thundering rain sound.
 Raindrops streaked my window
as if they know their way.
They may make the world greener,
but I hope tomorrow dawns a sunny day.

Richard La Roy McPhee

MIRACLES OF LIFE

You held my hand all through the night
I squeezed it hard and oh so tight.
The pain was bad, I had to scream
Hoping I'd wake from a terrible dream.

The night went on with you by my side
The fear in your eyes you were unable to hide.
Finally it was time and they wheeled me away
Morning had broke to a beautiful day.

Delivery was easier, it didn't take long
Her first little cry was a beautiful song.
Now it's no longer just you and me
Life's little miracles just made it three.

The pain is all gone and so is the fear
We did it again in less than a year.
Now we've decided to have no more
Our beautiful family, our family of four.

Michele A. Johnson

ECHOES

A romance cherished by both, silent,
no bounds, yet no sounds.
Invisible violets they share, the
scent from petals lost, may
someday give them away.
Timeless moments they embrace,
crystal teardrops descend from her face.
Trembling fingers as they touch,
their silence whispers so much.
A voice stuttering emotions,
mere echoes of the soul.
Loneliness of their distance,
no one to console.

Linda Colliér

JUST FRIENDS

Friends,
Just Friends,
is all we are.
That is so much.
You touch my life,
the pain the loneliness the empty spaces
and find Me.
I laugh in anticipation
of what funny thing
you'll say next,
all the while knowing
you are serious,
serious as two blue eyes
following the sun's red yawn
and wondering
in an off-the-cuff manner
what strange new thing
I'll think of and not say next.

I crave you
because only you
above the rest
were willing to karate chop the world
to walk with me,
listen to me sing off key
and be Just Friends.

Deborah Newton Cooksey

RESTLESS SOULS AND DESPERATE HEARTS

My eyes have heard the news
That life is cold as steel.
And everything's so obvious,
And I don't want to see your tears.
But late last night
You were the nicest lie
That I've been told in years.

I think I should be flattered.
You seem so damn impressed.
I'd like to share a chocolate bar with you.
I'd like to watch you get undressed.
But then, somehow,
You'd be allowed
To get real close to me.
Did Jesus Christ
Give you the right
To know the way I feel?

Well hell is simply nothing more
Than a self-inflicted place in time,
Where every heartbeat is an hour,
And every footstep is a mile.
So there's nothing left to speak of
Except what appears to be the truth,
— Restless souls — desperate hearts
And no one plays the victim quite like you.

Robert J. Pluss

THE LOVELIGHT IN YOUR EYES

When I look fondly into your luminous eyes,
    The lovelight I see there is not feigned — nor is it a disguise.
Your eyes are really like the night.
    Dark and brooding pools of light.

I look deeply into your eyes and find
    A reflection of your heart, so pure and kind.
Ne'er a one so pleased my mind, I breathe for you a longing sigh.
    And I will love you oh so dearly, 'til the day I die!

Carolyn LaVonne Carroll

LORD SAVE OUR COUNTRY

Lord save our country, so large and so grand
    With all its fine houses and rich, fertile land.
The cornerstone of all our freedoms great,
    Is found in these United States.

The Statue of Liberty gives forth her light
    As big ships dock into port at night.
''The Lady'' welcomes each weary soul
    Who enters onto our vast threshold.

When huddled masses reach our shores,
    We still offer them refuge as in days of yore.
''Give me your tired, your poor!'' is ''The Lady's'' impassioned cry,
    As the majestic eagle soars over the big blue sky.

To remain at the pinnacle of greatness is our nation's goal.
    They fought to win the prize, those for whom the bells toll.
Fulfilling the dreams of all brave men,
    Lord save our country and bless Her again.

You have promised that if we turn from our wicked way,
    You will send us a new and brighter day.
And Lord if we pray and seek your face,
    You will heal our land with greatest haste.

I love to hear our American songbird, the meadowlark, sing
    As I shout Hosanna to our wonderful King.
Let us share with our neighbors the gospel story.
    Lord save our country 'til we all live in glory.

Carolyn LaVonne Carroll

A SOLDIER'S LEGACY

A soldier boy lay wounded, in a jungle far away
When the enemy leaned o'er him, this is what I heard him say
There's a letter that I carry, send it to my folks back home
And I pray someone will read it, to my son when he is grown
To my son when he is grown

In a distant city window, I saw the mother rock his son
As she read this soldier's letter, tears fell on the little one
As she drew the infant to her, pride was written on her face
He would grow to serve his country, serve with pride and not disgrace
Serve with pride and not disgrace

Tonight I saw a proud young soldier, standing 'neath a spangled sky
He had grown to serve his country, and as he watched Old Glory fly
One could almost hear him thinking, Dad, I still don't understand
I'll defend that flag, Old Glory, but you're still in Vietnam
But you're still in Vietnam . . .

V. Jene Lindaman

LOVE IS SCHIZOPHRENIA

Metamorphosis has begun, when her absence behind the sushi bar made into a drowning wall invisible. She creates predators tormenting the victims of those who I am. To make love I have wondered at her image flowing in the silent dreams locked within my bed, melting into sheets, besides windows of filtered light's lament.

Illusion has begun, dissipating into dark brown skin, knowing its perfumed madness, so sick of love songs hidden in pretense. In greed I bathe in traps, forming impressions with threats that cut my vision in half. Psychic impressions follow a form of madness, numbing madness, like jealousy so erotic in become a voyeur in its giving grasp.

Divided within the city I have known, yet I know nothing, within rage of guessing her next move, seeing only my movement, feeling a test that may be no more than an empty classroom. Will I meet her touch in death? I wonder: emotions scattered in envy. A popularity test that she has won, she, knowing kisses far more than I am the misfit of my own existence.

Joe Castillo

A WRITER'S CAGE

Ink blot memories drag upon every wall testing sanity.
    Every image a bar through the science of dark times decay.
Erotic stains that form my mind, reflected upon unwashed walls that trap existence.
    Smeared ink on paper visions of words flattened to give birth to love other than sounded meanings. There, ink blot predators prey on such, waiting for the fool to publish my blood, perhaps to sell my soul: there which writer's *heaven* becomes a title desired, and hell to pay when one lives in a cage.
    A high price for freedom is also printed, but in green, whilst one looks upon its crime abstracting sanity with each dying breath's struggle. Agencies form the phantoms that control those whose life is to sell, as judges that read us, haunt us in our sleep, crawling into dissolving corners in weeping shadows lay, casting sinister spells upon our beds, surviving our rest.

Wasted words become dust, so we blow away with the invention that is part of us. Therefore as deadly as the flesh, 'til transmigration of the soul, whose actions we write down, as I write myself to capture what we are.

It's ink we bleed upon our hidden dream: you and I become one, you and I in different worlds before a stained-glass design sunrise; behind no recognizable form awakening to an unknown parallel.

Joe Castillo

MYSTERIOUS YOU

You are like a cat
With your dark mysterious past
One of which I know little of
Secret you possess only a few been told
Of the ones I know are ones you wanted me to share
You are a beam of sunshine
Which stands out in the black stormy sea
You are a breath of fresh air
In a city of foul air
You are a person who calms a stormy sea
With a voice as sweet as honey
You are these and many more
You are a friend
A friend who will all ways be in my heart
You will always be my love
With your dark mysterious past

George Irl Angell

AT DAWN

I caught your kiss in my hair
this morning —
you leaving for work —
then got up to put on another blanket.

When you go
another blanket is always needed,
a dark wool one
like your hair I stroke smooth
until it ripples in waves beneath my fingers —
a blanket dark and bristling like your mood
when you're in a deep funk, ruffled.

I close some windows to keep the air out
and leave others open to let it in.
It is not the cold
as much as it is our response to it
that counts.

I snuggle in arms of wool
and let blood drops make children
where we lay at dawn
touching and leaving and saying hello.

Deborah Newton Cooksey

DEBORAH NEWTON COOKSEY. Born: Houston, Texas, 6-24-52; Married: Ricci Elden Cooksey, 3 children, Sybil, Nicole, Austin; Education: Pomona College, B.A., 1974; Claremont Graduate School, M.A., Education, 1976, M.A., English/American Literature, 1987; Occupation: College English Instructor; Memberships: National Education Association; California Teachers Association; Martial Arts Club of Pomona; T.G. and the Halloween Band Club; Awards: 2nd place for 'To The Lonely Artist,' Mt. Sac Writers Contest, 1985; 1st place for 'Black Eye Blues,' Chaffey College Contest, 1986; 1st place for "Love Without A Smile," short story, from Mt. Sac Writers Contest, 1985; 1st place for "The Riot," autobiography, from Mt. Sac Writers Contest, 1987; 1st place for "'No' Was Never So Hard," short story, from Chaffey College Contest, 1986; Comments: *For me, writing and living vitally are inextricably connected; I cannot conceive of doing one without doing the other. For that reason I am not "a person full of stories and poems," rather I am a living collage of the writing I produce.*

HAIKU

Proud morning glory
Prince of dawn, master climber
Conceals its crutches.

Barbara Nell Lamb

MY EYES, YOUR EYES

Your eyes hold my fortune
  a wealth of unbelievable gold
My winters made comfortably warm
  as you have whisked away my cold
As we danced our ballroom dance
  you held me nearer and near
Finally my tormented sky has changed
  to a soft blue crystal clear
When you held my hand
  and softly caressed my cheek
I found my heaven on earth
  I reached my mountain's peak
As I gaze into the days to come
  we are as one and one only
And I cry tears of joy for I know
  we will never again be broken and lonely
Your eyes light the way
  as I follow close to your lead
As I see your eyes
  I tell you your love is what
    my eyes need

Michele Rae

MICHELE LAUREN RAE. Born: Pittsburgh, Pennsylvania, 11-11-68; Education: Hillsborough Community School, Tampa, Florida, 1986; currently attending Bauder College, Ft. Lauderdale, Florida; Occupations: Care Giver, Children's Academy of Brandon; Care Giver in the private sector; Memberships: Word of Faith Outreach Center; Awards: Honorable Mentions for 'For the Love of Children,' 'Our Joyous Rose,' 'Hold On,' 'My Lifelong Friend,' 'Angel on the Ledge,' 'Love and Blessings'; Golden Poet Award, 1986, 1987; Poetry: 'For The Love of Children,' *World Poetry Anthology,* 1986; 'These Teardrops,' *American Poetry Anthology,* 1987; 'Our Joyous Rose,' *Great Poems of Today,* 1987; 'I Know Where I'm Going,' *Poetry of Life,* 1988; 'Her Blade of Death,' *Best New Poets of 1987;* Comments: *I believe God loves all of his people no matter what color they may be. I feel very strongly about equality for all Americans and I hope to denounce racism through my poetry now and in the future.*

WHO DOESN'T

we peek under walls
of restroom stalls

to see whose feet
ours will meet

Craig Andrew Wassel

INNER MIND

Listen my children
I have some good news!
This important information
I am sure you can use.

Christ's Pure Love
Patiently waits
For you and me
At heaven's gates.

Christ you will find
In the kingdom within.
That is where
You must begin.

Deep in your heart,
The subconscious mind,
That's where you start
The spirit to find.

Listen quietly
To your inner mind,
His comforting spirit
There you'll find.

Worth M. Jones

CHRIST'S ELECT

God's Holy Word
Shows Christ, the Way.
We should study,
And follow each day.

Accept the Savior,
Confess your sins,
Tell Him you're ready
Now to begin.

Working by day
For His perfection.
Trying to be worthy
Of His election.

Praying by night,
And dreaming, too,
To find insight
And guidance true.

The day will come
When we shall see
The mansions He's made
For you and me.

Worth M. Jones

INTERLUDE

High in mountain meadows wild and free
A canyon breeze unseen by you and me,
Animates the lifeless scene and leaves
The aspen dancing, wrapped in golden sleeves.

One day as it passes leaves will fall
'Twill seem as if they never waltzed at all,
And someday it will dry the tears of those
Who weep when I am gone, and so it goes . . .

Barbara Nell Lamb

SOCIETY MUST CHANGE

Where are we going with our wasted society?
Nuclear waste, pollution and garbage.
Men competing with women.
Women competing with men.
Aren't we one?
One world.
One soul.
Why must we destroy, ruin and molest all good?
There is time to save us.
And so we should.

Our children are chemically dependent.
The adults are drug induced.
They ask what is there to believe in?
What do you say?
Or how can you.
In your state of mind.
There must be a change in law and order.
Are we willing to accept doom?
The great blast.
The big boom.

Jeri Lea Golden

GRANDPA

You lie so motionless
Eyes closed and in a different world
Hair gray and skin wrinkled from hard-working years
Your lips pursed as if to speak
Yet your body lies motionless.

Only yesterday it was you scolding me for
Smashing down the garden vegetables
And running me out of the garage
So you could find those ever-helpful tools.

You gave me wisdom for my life to come
Things to think about and do
To enrich my life and others' lives.
You gave me the strength and courage to fight on
And the insight to look down the road.

You always had faith in what could be done
And you did everything to perfection.
Nothing was finished until it was done right
And work was never complete until sundown
With an early start in the morning.

Your working days are over now
Only the hard times are left to be conquered,
And that you've done so well in the past.
Now you await the green pastures in the sky above.

Thomas L. Trail

A SOUL IN SEARCH OF A DREAM

Every once in a while you find that you are so alone
that surely no one can ever find you there.

Just when all hope of ever having a close relationship
has all but left your dreamscape,

There appears far out on the horizon a drifting soul
in search of one such as yourself.

And in the greeting there is a realization that for
you both the hoped-for dream has come.

Barbara L. Holder

WISHES

I only wish to be free.
I picture myself on a park bench
    the splashing of a fountain
        only a short distance away.
Children feed quacking ducks,
    an older couple smiles.
All I have anymore are memories
    and my prayers.
I feel pain,
    I run frantically to all parts
        of my room,
            looking behind the walls.
                I only wish to live in peace.

Craig Stephans

THE GIFT

There is a gift we all must have I know with
'cause I was there. You have it too my dearest
friend, for we were all and bare. We had our first
breath of life, that day we knew they cared.

We closed our eyes for just a trite, and now
we are in the midst of life, the gift, all tattered
and wared, but if you lose this precious gift, you're
back to where they cared.

Over, and over, and over again life's Love
we all must share, sometimes I'm sure I must have
seemed mean but that's only because I care.

Often your Love is like a fresh breath of air
is to a newborn lung, and even though nowhere is
hard to get we must be on our way, for all that we
are is the presence God and the wisdom, therefore
we keep trying, if only she knew just what I'd do,
anything for the gift of Love she has and even though
she'll feel it too, it will feel like the very
first time. God is not just a he or a she, therefore
they are in us all. This is the true gift to all
with Love, and a promise to share.

Thomas Wm. Gales III

AS THE CLOCK UNWINDS

Hardened time as life unwinds leaves stories
untold, but yet we are as the days unfold, and who
are we to say of this truth in the wondrous passage
of all our time? So as that shadow creeps by
with his hook that weaves, he blinds, as does the
trueness of love in the days of our prime.

When the bolts in this clock become loosened
with age, the spring you can't hold as it shoots
through the days. A killer it's not, though for some
it may be, we talk of this time as if it's been used.
If it were us we know what we'd choose.

Memories of men that have long passed by,
their greatness of soul leave thoughts that are torn
and wanting to cry.

Thomas Wm. Gales III

CHRIST, THE WORD

The best control
This world has known
Is the spiritual love
That Christ has shown.

He is the Way,
The Truth, and the Life.
He is the Answer
To earthly strife.

I've won your pardon,
Paid your fee,
"Take up thy cross
And follow me."

Be ye transformed
By renewing of mind.
Love your neighbors,
To all be kind.

"Heaven and earth
Shall pass away."
Only Christ, the Word,
Is with us to stay.

Worth M. Jones

SAIGON

With the taste of brutal hatred
Just three angstroms long,
Your force extends beyond infinity
By the horror you impose.

I've felt the touch
Of your artillery love,
The heat of your napalm kiss,
Yet within the war,
Within our hearts,
Your tasteless rage breeds death.

And avenues flashed randomly
Against perforated walls
That held my brain.
Red tail lights tipped
 To meet the sky,
As we choked on blackened rain.

Robert J. Pluss

QUIET TOWN

A quiet little town,
The Salmon River the only sound,
And those who live there,
Have quiet minds and souls serene,
And plenty of time to dream and dream.
To fish to their heart's content,
And ride their horses homeward bound.
After they have done the town,
There is very little stress,
But when there is,
They head for the river,
On a rock they rest.
If you are not content with where you live,
Just head for the river,
Peace it will give.

Peggy Start

UNLIKELY HEROES

Men I have seen; I'm no liar,
Who, in the prime of youth,
Quailed not before enemy fire,
Risked their all for country and truth.

Every day, these same men I see,
Still paying with their health,
Facing decay just as stoically,
Self-respect as their only wealth.

Who can measure the courage needed
To hurtle through enemy skies,
Or charge, enemy fire unheeded;
Accept — when life's promise dies?

It takes as much man not to weep
When his mind makes bold plans
His older body cannot keep
As to charge danger, gun in hand!

Unlikely heroes are these men,
Some in beds, pale and weak;
Some cannot see; some cannot speak,
Yet most face the day with a grin!

Dorothy Cariker Cart

RICH MAN, POOR MAN

The rich man lives in luxury,
 in this walk of life.
The poor man begs for bread,
 along a lonesome road.
The rich man in his worldly pride,
 turns his head as the poor man cries.
The rich man holds his head up high,
 the poor man's is bowed low.
The rich man does not need the Lord,
 the poor man always does.
The rich man trusts in his worldly goods,
 the poor man trusts in the Lord.
Tell me, who really has more?

Roseanne McMillan

REMEMBERING YOU, MOTHER

So many times throughout the day,
I recall the things you used to say.
Your face I see as if you were here,
I turn and expect you to be there.

Sometimes I'm bewildered with unbelief,
trapped with emptiness and grief.
I've never felt this way before,
my life won't be the same anymore.

The day I had to say good-bye,
a tear fell from your eye.
I wiped it dry and ran from the room,
knowing you would be gone soon.

I can't reach out and touch you as before,
and I won't see you in this life anymore.
But I'm remembering you with tearful eyes,
wishing I never had to say good-bye.

Roseanne McMillan

O FOOLISH HEART

O foolish heart thought
 thee to find,
a perfect love as told
 in rhyme,
only to find when thee
 did look,
it doth exist but
 in a book.

O foolish heart be
 not despaired,
what is found be good
 if it be shared,
if it be thine
 O foolish heart,
do not pine for what
 it be not.

Mary D. Welker

GAMBLE

Various kinds of races and cards, roulette
and craps, slot machines, and the lottery
are some of the types of gambling people do.
Some try many ways of gambling, others
try just one or a few.
Some people gamble too often, others gamble
some of the time and some think they
never gamble, that I am speaking of in
my rhyme.
However, to me, all people gamble, throughout
their life,
when they do such things as find friends,
pick a career or choose a husband or a wife.
In fact, to me, life is a gamble.

Judith Friedman

MY EYES

Deep within those
beautiful eyes, is
a cavern way down
deep inside.

Here lies the soul
that few can reach.

Unseen by many and
touched by so few!

Naked and fragile
and in need of care
never a mask or a
sheath to wear.

Suspended in life
like a picture in
a frame.

Yet, deep within those
cavern walls this
soul remains . . .

Unchanged!

Arika Dark/Ann Lasley

Mountain House.

REJOICE!

Rejoice! Spring is near,
Evidence is everywhere.
Children, out-of-doors at play.
Rejoice! It's a joyous day.

One does not live in spring always,
Winter, fall, summer's hot days;
The seasons of life remain.
Blessed are they who recognize change.

The warmth of sunshine, God's love,
New life, like spring, he gave from above;
Bursting forth, pure joy in spring,
Coming of fall, a sure thing.

Colorful trees, all colors and sizes,
Remind one of, fruitful lives.
Fresh crisp autumn breeze,
Leaves, when brown, fall free.

Ah yes! Winter; long or short,
Must be faced with a joyous heart,
This time of rest and reflection,
Turns one's life, in God's direction.

Josephine S. Brown

MEMORIES PATHWAY

For my sons Mike and Steve

There's a secret meeting place
Hidden deep within my heart.
I call it Memories Pathway
A place where fears depart.

This pathway is lined with roses,
Nourished by countless tears.
There's always an endless rainbow
The sun never disappears.

Two special people meet me there
They were called by the Lord above
But they're alive on Memories Pathway
Where they left a lot of love.

When twilight spreads its misty veil
And I'm lonely beyond compare,
I walk down Memories Pathway
They're always waiting there.

Faye C. Barber

ON A SPRING DAY

Spring is watching children
play,
On a warm and sunny day.

Spring is trying to catch a
butterfly,
That wants to fly away.

Spring is running through a
flower field with fragrance
of delight,
And saying in my mind this
is a wonderful sight.

Meridell W. Merritt

A MAGICAL WELL

Your body was enhanced by that dress,
I could never have known such happiness.
When I think about you, all I can see
is the natural beauty that surrounds me.

With each step, my heartbeat quickened,
and my consciousness grew without end.
The moon's presence lying low in the sky,
is felt when I see that sparkle in your eye.

A magical well of genuinely deep emotions,
is influenced by a moment's expressions.
The memories won't let me get away,
they bring me closer to you each day.

In your arms I enter this threshold,
and the mystery of our fantasies unfold.
You give me the courage to open this door,
in your smile I see the excitement in store.

My heartbeat awakens emotions that say,
your smile is the rising sun each day.
To know the love you have to give,
is to have found all I need to live.

Albert Duran

THE SHORES OF ECSTASY

A new horizon rises in your eyes each day,
and our enchanting dreams are here to stay.
The sun now lies low in the western sky,
and this light of day stirs in me a sigh.

I hold the essence of this moment's rapture,
and my heart, your magic spell did capture.
As a captive of this path in my destiny,
time caresses the heart that holds the key.

To reach the shores of ecstasy we've won,
our heartbeats suddenly became one.
You fill a void in emotions I believe in,
and stir a presence in me from within.

No page will go unturned for you to see,
since you became a part of my destiny.
Each breath crested as a sigh in this potion,
and I surrendered to this stimulating emotion.

A tear is a pearl of warmth in this venture,
and joy is the fulfillment of this treasure.
From the depths of my heart comes a tide,
and the need to hold you comes from inside.

Albert Duran

THE RIVER

I listen to the roar of the river,
As it tumbles over the rocks,
It says to me, I'm free, I'm free,
I need not conform to the city's ways,
I'm free to be me,
I'm free to be me.

Peggy Start

TREMBLING LIPS

Tenderness leaves nothing to conceal
as a feather's beauty you see and feel.
Your love reaches out to break my fall,
and every waking moment you have my all.

The darkness fades from this dimension,
as our senses reach passion's creation.
The virgin shores of my defenses
caress the surrender of your kisses.

We savor the allure of our fate
as our trembling lips separate.
Two worlds meet in time and space
to become one for us to embrace.

The flames flicker into the night,
and its warmth invades the firelight.
You are the essence of life I cling to,
and the link in evidence it holds true.

I was immersed in this eternal fire,
as I yielded to the will of desire.
I see dreams that lie so deep
filled with peace as you sleep.

Albert Duran

FAMILY

Way out in an unknown field
Stands a big oak tree.
It's tall and straight and beautiful.
It's all alone and free.
Then somewhere along the way,
Another starts to sprout
And grows next to the big oak tree
With certainty, not doubt.
Soon there's three and four and five.
What a gorgeous sight.
They're happy as a family.
There is no dark, just light.
Now the trees are growing old.
One dies, the others fall.
They fall into their separate paths.
They each hear their own call.
Sometimes they stretch their branches out
While they move through life.
To feel that closeness once again
In good times and in strife.
They all seem to be happy
In fields of their own.
But never will there be a place
Where the oak tree stood alone.

Joan Voltz

GATHERED HARVEST

Wheat, gold etched on
A dusty Kansas plain
Huddles wig-wam fashion
Yellow sheaves hugging
Each other in Thanksgiving
As God's people rejoicing
  At Eucharist.

Bette Armstrong

TO A LITTLE BOY'S COACH

When you start building up your team
Don't do it at the cost of shattering a little boy's dream
Remember, the boy with the limp may not run very swift
But he may have the courage that will give the team a lift

And should you overlook the weak ones for the strong
The victory of winning will not last very long
For somehow in the future it will surely cross your mind
To leave out the less fortunate is not so very kind

I've seen so many little boys not chosen for the game
I've felt the breaking of their hearts and my heart filled with shame
To think that mortal man could find such joy in winning
While causing so much pain

Blanche Simmons

BLANCHE TOMANY SIMMONS. Born: Wausaw, Wisconsin, 5-17-09, daughter of John Steven Tomany and Mabel Amy Keithley; Married: William L. Simmons, son of Lyle Simmons and Grace Dye Simmons.

SNOW DUNES

Snowflakes jump sky high
buffeted with rambling blows
to turn noon into early dawn.

Graced by streaking flecks,
mounds ld sturdy momentum
i
u
b
to push over a winter's edge.

Shimmering crystals
reveal form over matter
to dominate a changed landscape.

Dynamic duos
of wind and white pul-ver-ize
reality's drift into dreams.

Blizzard conditions
seeking scenic finales
settle d
o
w
n to trackless wonders.

Solveig Larson

GLENDA

My daughter, not just my child,
    talks all the time.
        She dips and dances past,
chattering away.

And sometimes she sings words that
    must be unknown
        except to her. She laughs,
enjoying the day.

She goes to school with others.
    Nevertheless,
        she's all alone. Somehow
a private person.

Jumping, dancing with delight
    in her own world.
        With light, quick steps, she's now
filled with pleasure.

Paul M. Lamb

TIME IS THE MEMORY OF YESTERDAY'S PAST

Time is the memory of yesterday's past.
    More real than today in our mind.
Would that the days fleeing backward could last.
    Binding two lovers entwined.

I'd stay here forever to be by your side.
    Tomorrow a dream in retreat.
'Til the end of the world, 'til the last lapping tide,
    'Til entropy's day is replete.

But memories fade like the cells they imbue,
    With a life that is sere and alone.
And the love that is ours now can never pursue
    Bright yesterdays' memories gone.

So now for the nonce, live the love that is true.
    Tomorrow will bring what it may.
I promise to promise you, promises few.
    And to live and to love for today.

Paul M. Lamb

THE THRILL DIVINE

This is "The Thrill Divine," knowing you are mine.
The birds trill it, angels whisper, that I am thine.
    Like gypsy ancestors, I have "second sight."
I know love's there, you care, whatever my plight.

So glorious is that love, that's in my heart —
I hope from it's joy, that we will never part.
    Like a wild bird free, your heart's calling to me.
Like birds mating on wing, my heart clings to thee.

Lonely like echoing of whippoorwill's song;
Ecstatic, like spring peepers humming along —
    This is the greatest joy you will have ever,
Except in heaven, where joy is forever!

We are in paradise, it lies before us.
We'll hear angels sing out, in one grand chorus!
    This is that "once in a lifetime only" — when
"The Thrill Divine" — will never happen — again!

Kathleen Lyon Vaughn

THE MAGIC DIES
(FOR A CHILD OF OLD)

how quickly does the magic die
when childhood wonders are gone by
with cautious hands and curious minds
but not knowing where to look to find
fast searching for the answers to
the questions which their minds run through
in years — in eyes — the world seems to change
becoming more so ever strange
reality grooms in different truths
outside of clouds above smoky roofs
those around seem not so tall
a world becoming more ever small
the secrets behind the magician's cloth
mysteries gone when his cloak is off
as each one is unveiled and shown
we long for what was once not known
how quickly does the magic die
when childhood wonders are gone by
the magic dies for a child of old
to whom and why is that magic sold?

Craig Andrew Wassel

SPECTRAL WEB OF LIFE

Strange strong palpitations
beat within me
I reach
down
to touch the power of earth
— it is at once within me
and I
reach
screaming for the sky
the open triumphant blue
all of that openness
also pours into me.
I become an alchemistic
draught
of heaven and earth.

Gwen Williams

OUR DREAMS

The heartache to create the dream
Those long and desperate hours
All the times you had to scream
Just to build the smallest towers

The struggle just to make it real
To bring the dreams alive
To give it everything you feel
Then left empty and deprived

You simply must keep trying
In order to succeed
There is no sense in lying
Just be honest of what you need

You only live one lifetime
Try to be what you want to be
No one will hear you if you mime
They'll only stop to see

Tamara N. Wagner

DUST STORM LULLABY

Hush-a-by, baby,
Be still don't you cry,
And Mother will sing you
A dust storm lullaby.

The daylight is dimming
Soon 'twill turn dark,
So hush-a-by, baby,
It's all just a lark.

The sandman is coming
(No fairy tale this!)
Be still and you'll feel
His harsh gritty kiss.

He'll throw sand in your eyes
And cover the moon,
So hush-a-by, baby,
It'll be over soon.

The windows are sealed.
The curtains are drawn,
So hush-a-by, baby,
Did I hear a yawn?

Marjorie V. Slater

THEY DID IT WITH MIRRORS

Everything seemed so quiet and serene
nothing to interfere with the beauty
you were on the other side of the screen
and the walls did their duty.
Every movement was so graceful and precise
the sheer elegance of the moment was not lost
who knows what the device
was or what was the cost?
You were engulfed in a cloud
I could see your figure
as it disappeared in the crowd.
I was left to try and figure
out what had come to pass
once I saw you floating on air
such a sweet fair lass
passing through life without a care.
I thought I saw your face
but it just confirmed my greatest fears
that you had never been near the place
they did it all with mirrors.

George Hull

Cast in the shadows
  Of self-induced anxiety,
Is the image of a lover
  Who waits to take form.

Is it my future that I see
  In the mist of uncertainty —
  Or has my imagination
    Exceeded the bounds of reality?

I reach out to you,
  In the hopes that you are mine;
To take my future into my own hands
  And make a reality out of this dreamland
    Into which I have journeyed.

Adrian F. Schleis

MATURE ADULT

My eyes opened at dawn's early light,
I stretched and curled my toes
Consciousness returned to sway what goes.

Grateful for life, I arose with a jump
But moaned as my body spoke woes
Saying, "Now that was not really very bright."

I thought I could and so I would control
Mind over body and hold her steady
I'd just remember to be ever ready.

And so when the sun sank in the far west,
I knew that my determination won.
I sat contented now, I wasn't wan.

I knew I could crawl into bed this night
Uncurl my toes with glee
Drift into dreamland knowing, God's with me.

L. Lasher

THE DEPARTURE

I saw you yesterday
  and there were tears . . .
like often of late.

We reached out to each other —
  and found the other
    reaching too.
I was reluctant to let you go,
  you were reluctant to leave . . .

You held me close and kissed me —
  said you still loved me
    and then
I watched you drive away
      to her.

Jeanne McClintock

SCARECROW LAMENT

Scarecrow, standing solemn there
With arms outstretched and not a care.
Your job secure throughout the year;
For all the crows, they vanish at your sight.
I sometimes wish that I, like you,
Could stand around with naught to do
And let the days and nights just drift on by.
But, somehow, as I contemplate
Then place myself within your fate,
I wonder just how well I would endure.
For to savor of your lonely self,
Devoid of all that God hath given.
I, too, must then relinquish something more.
And that, my friend, I cannot do,
That thing that makes me human, too.
And that, Old Scarecrow, is my sacred soul.

Robert Weetman

FACING FIFTY FEARLESSLY

What's this I see? Another gray hair?
A new wrinkle so faint and fine?
Bless my soul, this can't be so . . .
not when I'm *just . . . thirty nine.*
Crying won't help — and believe me, I know!
I tried *that* as a last resort.
So, with a smile on my face, I'll act nonchalant,
and try to be, just another ''Good Sport!''
They say a good wine, just gets better with time,
and that *age* makes it mellow and smooth.
But . . . after imbibing said bottle of wine,
it gets hard and harder to move.
Your memory goes first, so I'm told.
But I can't let that thought bother me.
My memory may go — but, gosh, look what's left.
I'm footloose and fancy free!
So, now as I glide through my 'golden years,'
I'll enjoy my life with a smile.
If my memory hangs on, and my body holds up,
I'm ready for that last . . . long . . . mile!

Carolyn J. Carruth

OH! GRACIOUS LORD!

When the Sun overshadows the darkness of days,
The Lord seems to smile on our Face.
Though, dark and dreary it all seems,
His smile is all I truly need.
To keep me strong and full of strength!
To bestow upon me his never ending Grace!

Oh! Gracious Lord,
You who are so magnificently divine!
How can I thank Thee, time after time.
Your never ending affection, which meets —
Immeasurable bounds,
Gracefully unwrapping a spirit of dismay —
A new inspiration, an enchanting day.
Delightful visions of Joy, secretly revealed to me —
A contented heart, a soul at Peace,
A splendorous *Love,* a Love cherished and sweet.
Eternally indebted to you, I will be,
Forever written on my tear-stained face,
Affectionately yours in every way.

Minus you, I just seem to Drift —
Without you, I float amongst Confusion ship.
The joy I receive when Blessed from above,
Constantly assures me of your so precious, ''Love,''
When the Sun overshadows the darkness of days,
The Lord seems to smile on our face.

Zenobia

STARLIGHT

On a grand evening many years ago,
Summer stars put on a magic show.
Gods and goddesses from years gone by
Made an appearance in the dark, black sky.
Old Aunt Marie told story after story
About how gods and animals became heavenly glory.
And the reason, she said, stars send to earth a glow
Is so the great God of heaven can just say, ''Hello!''

Judy A. Deeter

SEE THE TEARS OF JESUS

See Him hold the little baby in His loving arms.
See Him love the young child on His knee.
See the face of Jesus as He pleaded with the throngs;
See the tears He shed for you; for me.

See Him heal the crippled man so he could leap and run.
See Him making eyes again to see.
See the precious hands of Jesus touch the soul of man;
See the tears He shed in agony.

See Him feed the thousands on the hills of Galilee.
See him calm life's fears and set us free.
See the feet of Jesus as He walked upon life's road;
See the tears He shed at Calvary.

See the crown of thorns they made and placed upon His brow.
See the stripes He bore to set us free.
See the nail-scarred hands and feet; Jesus took our place.
See the tears and blood He shed for thee.

Oh, see the tears of Jesus flowing to the heart of man.
See them cleanse and bring new life again.
Oh, see the tears of Jesus, shed on Calvary;
See the tears He shed to set you free.

Eleanor S. Follmer

ALWAYS

Twisted arthritic fingers of ice cling to windows
  midst the dormancy of winter nights.
January with its tenacity holds us in her grasp
  while nature's elements keep us prisoners in our
  abode.
We can dream and we can scheme of future days untried
  and new, knowing that spring will come at last.
This season as all, ever changing yet always, just
  as you and I.

Mildred Schlagle

THE COUNTERPART AND I

She used to be dying back there in country wood.
She really was dying and often felt she should.
Life had been robbed right from her youthful prime.
She really was aging and still there were no signs.

You know the signs, crows feet and the like —
She decided it was high time she took a hike.

The lady had a vision —
Yes a pining dream —
To clean out all his sewage —
And spiritually heal her stream.

Divorcing her burden, man was his claim —
Packed up her mind all but insane —
Left with her tears, her fears and her pain —
And became her own bus, boat, train and plane.

Beyond the divorce I twice gave birth —
Adams was second but Todd was first
I am now a mother and forever remain —
My Counterpart and I are one and the same.

Nic

NECESSARY TRIPS

Frequently of late
I find myself walking on a thin line.

Compelled down the
    pillaged and ravaged back roads
      of consciousness,
I find the path deserted.

The silence reaches out
    and clutches at me from the shadows.
Everything is grey matter
    and the horizon cannot be found.

Hopelessness closes in
    and replaces the chilling numbness.
I feel the pain of a jagged edge
    of my broken heart.

Accidentally I stumble across
    a fragmented memory —
        and I cry.

Needful,
    albeit temporary,
        relief.

Jeanne McClintock

JEANNE RUTH McCLINTOCK. Pen Name: Ima Brick; Born: Terre Haute, Indiana, 2-1-42; Occupation: Medical office manager; Awards: First prize for 'Reality,' April in Paris Show, 1985; Poetry: 'Chastisement,' *American Poetry Anthology*, 1987; Comments: *Most of my earlier poems were composed in the aftermath of divorce. My first book,* Threads in Weaving *(yet unpublished), deals solely with that topic. I have started a second book of poetry which I hope to illustrate as well. The thought of writing a novel intrigues me more and more, as does writing children's stories for my grandchildren.*

THE HIRED MAN

''The brandts are flying tonight,'' he said
Without feeling or design,
Jaded syllables from his lips like
Unwilling fledglings from a nest.
No romantic foolishness, this.
Nothing of wonder, beauty or song
Neither dreams nor delight of soul.
Only a simple statement of fact.
Just his annual implication
That November's due again.

Vera Current Thummel

INNOCENT LOVE

Take me into your arms
with the same candid love
as you praise the Lord in church . . .
Let it be an innocent love . . .

Please, hold me very close to you.
Kiss me and let me dream
within the horizon . . .
Let me hear again
your love songs.

Our kind of love
is very special:
Your dedicated soul
has been chosen under the stars . . .

Your soul touched my soul . . .
Your mind touched my mind . . .
Your voice touched my senses . . .
You showed me the way . . .
You showed me the stars
I should follow through . . .
let it always be
an innocent love! . . .
I will always love you.

Alice Levy

ALICE C. LEVY. Born: Havana, Cuba, 3-8-43; Married: Arthur S. Levy, 7-20-73; Education: Vibora Pre-University, Havana, Cuba, B.A., 1961; English and business courses at New York University; American Language Institute, New York University; Graduate of Broward Community College, Tourism, 1986; Occupation: Accounting clerk; Memberships: Academy of American Poets, National Writers Club, The Cousteau Society, Florida Lions Eye Bank, DAVA, Republican Presidential Task Force, Republication National Committee (life member); Awards; Special Award for 'Loving and Missing You,' and its Spanish version, 1985; Poems: 'True Love,' 'Forgiveness,' 'Your World,' 'Dreamlife,' 'Sorry!'; all American Poetry Association; Comments: *My poetry is a reflection of love's feeling in different phases: joy or disappointment; excitement or pain; compassion or dismay. I write because I have feelings and ideas within myself that must be expressed somehow. It is just natural to my kind of personality and background. I have always admired the art of poetry, and I love to write and recite different kinds of poems. My work is a product of a true love for the arts.*

YOUR BEST FRIEND

The best friend you have is your mother
So treat your friend right while she is here
For when she is gone no other friend
To you will be so dear.
She always stands beside you
Whenever you're in right or wrong
And she tries to plead your innocence
Even though you're the guilty one.
She is always ever by you
When you are sick and lie in bed
And always seems to know what to do
To ease your aching head.
She never tells your secrets
And when your heart with sadness swells
You go right straight to Mother
And the whole sad plight you tell.
When the world seems oh so dreary
And friends to you grow cold
Still your mother patiently waits you
To soothe your cares with hands so old.
So while these silver threads are shining
In her hair which once was gold
Please remember your dear mother
Even though she's growing old.

Harriet Elizabeth Stauffer

ELIZABETH STAUFFER ASHCRAFT. Pen Names: Harriet Elizabeth Stauffer, Elizabeth S. Waltman; Born: Rogersville, Missouri, 12-8-1898; Comments: *Elizabeth Stauffer Ashcraft began writing poetry at the age of twelve for classroom assignments while attending schools in Springfield, Missouri and then moved to Muskogee and Tahlequah, Oklahoma. After marriage and moving to Pine Bluff, Arkansas in 1927 she continued writing poetry as a hobby while raising four children. Now residing in Fayetteville, Arkansas, she ''keeps in practice'' by occasionally writing poems and quotations.*

ON MOTHERS

God knew what He was doing
When he gave us mothers;
He knew the times unnumbered
When we could not be calmed, by others:
And so he allowed special women
To bear the trials of birth;
Just so we could have
One good thing from this earth.

We thank this Lord of ours,
For the glorious gift that towers
O'er all others:
The grand and wonderful blessing
That we now know as mothers!

Eula R. Henderson

HOME SWEET HOME

A home is somewhere you hang your hat.
It's a place, you can go and set down
In your easy chair and prop your feet.
There's no place like home, when it gets time to eat.
You can do just about anything at Home,
Even invite your friends over, play cards or checkers,
Whatever the mood strikes.
When you are sick, then it's no fun.
You have to turn your friends away
And tell them to come back some other day.
But, a home is not all fun and games.
There is a lot of responsibility.
There's always things to do, wash dishes, sweep
And mop floors, take out the garbage,
Wash clothes and vacuum rugs.
That seems like part of life though.
It's a never ending job.
That's just Home Sweet Home.

Mr. & Mrs. Henry Case

THE GLORIOUS SUNSET

Above the horizon, the sky was aglow
With hues of red, reflecting in the clouds to show
The glorious sunset. The rays of the sun,
Bursting forth with color, so very awesome.
Each person, seemingly, spellbound
In the quietness, so amazing.
Not an utter, not a sound.
Only reverence, as each one stood
On the mountain's edge, gazing
In the distance as they understood,
The picture painted in the sky,
By the Master Artist from on high,
The creator since the world began,
Alpha, Omega, Beginning — End.

Mildred Quine Dennis

COULD I BUT . . .

Could I but write one line, one gem of wisdom
    That would live on long after I am gone;
Could I but lift a wary friend's stiff burden
    And make his shadowed cares seem not so long;
Could I but love my neighbor as my brother,
    Help him to hope and trust and, yes, to pray;
Could I but smile and spread a ray of sunshine
    And make life a hopeful journey day by day.

Could I but feel the Everlasting Presence
    When the weary, toil-worn days are at a peak,
Could I but lose my worries and my heartaches
    And give them to my Lord for Him to keep.
Could I but place more trust in Christ my Saviour
    And thrust away my qualms, and doubts, and fears;
Could I but learn to seek and, yes, to listen
    To that still, small voice whose power can dry my tears.

Could I but do all this in one short lifetime —
    In the span of years that I this road must tread.
Then life for me will know complete fulfillment
    And at its end no grievances I'll dread.

Pearl Sandahl

ODE TO GRANDMOTHER

Grandmother, Grandmother, what are you to me?
To me you are what no other could be
Nor could another be what you have been
Like a lifeguard, a second mother and best friend.

When I'm down and out, life having gone astern
For love, reassurance and guidance, to you I turn.
When the pains of confinement transverse my spine
The sound of your voice brings me peace of mind.

Wisdom is your words, healing is your touch
Your caring and understanding have meant so much.
Whenever there is a problem, situation critique
No matter what the subject, to you I can speak.

About your trustworthiness, can a world be told?
In your keeping's caress I'd trust my soul.
The faith you adhere to, like feathers on an arrow
That road you travel, the straight and narrow.

Were I to mention all of your qualities, I'd be giving you your due
But if I entail them all, I'd never get through.
So to say it all as I impart in the best that words can say
Grandmother, in the galaxies of my heart you are the Milky Way.

Carlos Johnson

ADMONITION

Be not I *Eagle,* soaring o'er the heights!
Mightiest to remain of winged, with piercing eye to discern —
Yet, precarious I be too . . . of "nature's balance frights"!
Harken my cry, Oh American, for I "call" to be stern:
I am *Eagle,* symbol of an awesome nation be . . .
So blest of God, to heed the cry of humanity.
My sons have died, near every side . . . to stay our shores secure.
Hold to thy pride . . . of former . . . God . . . Blest . . . *Fear!*
Has it not failed "in times before," tallying man's "powers" to be
Above God's so "patient Hand," and rendered all to calamity?
Thus, *all powers be,* and nay alone, of our own "recourse,"
For schemes the "bold-one," so to stealth at every source.

Statesmen, and all, so sworn thy duties to perform . . .
Even yet, consider the lowly-plight of some of our aged be;
And, "tear our hearts" at "young up-starts,"
    who are so often "shorn,"
"The common-chance" to so "fence" . . . in "land of liberty" —
Their "drug abuse," to so induce . . . of ruinous "nation's prime"!
It so *is* "evil forces," at the "sources" . . .
    it *must* be "stemmed" in time!
God grant us "favor" to perceive, beyond our "nose's length";
On "bended knee" do bow our heads . . . and, plead anew *our strength!*
I am *Eagle,* symbol of greatest nation be . . .
Blest of God, to "hear the cry" of all humanity.
Too, my name means "strong as an eagle, brave . . . strong,"
And, you now have . . . "just heard my song"!

Arne Maurice Simonson

YOU AND I

As we walk life's path together
  For better or for worse,
The better things we will treasure
  And the worse ones reverse.

As we strive to help each other
  Walk through life hand in hand,
We'll be each other's comforter
  In times of great demand.

As we shed some tears of sorrow
  With people we hold dear,
Let's think of how this makes us grow,
  Bringing us ever near.

As we walk farther down life's lane
  To our sunset of gold,
Let our memories entertain
  All those fine thoughts we hold.

As we view life in retrospect,
  Eyeing the path we've led,
May our feelings always project
  Those wedding vows we said.

Lou Roberts

VIRGIN INFIDELS

bitter winter monuments
to the stark deep blight
              of final mind.
. . . Idols of the hissing Silo . . .
buried in the balance
above the abyss
where nullity sleeps
              . . . stillborn . . .
in lethal dreams
      of inanimate Oblivia.

Brian Bywater

L IS FOR . . .

Lyric for Silicon Valley

L is for L.E.D.,
  which rhymes with dead,
And so does lead
  that fills my head,
Or feet, or a —
  (when "out of gas") . . .

I think I'll pass
  from this morass —
From fen, from bog,
  away from smog
And traffic clog —
  quiet as fog
Out o'er the sea
  'n earth's greenery:
Ah-h-h, that's for me!
  (L is for F.R.E.E.)

Richard Alan Rieger

THE BRIGHTEST STAR
IN THE SKY

The brightest star in the sky
On Christmas Eve it's said,
Sprinkles Heavenly Stardust on
Little children's heads.

It is a glorious night in the heavens
The celebration of birth,
And the brightest star in the sky
Sprinkles peace over the earth.

Jarie Lee Waterfall

THE OLD CABIN

Down a lonely valley
Back against the hill
Over behind the bushes
Near that large old oak tree

The cabin is old and battered
Its windows broken out
The chink between the logs, gone
The door is not around

The path is overgrown
The grass is high and wild
See the vines along its sides
The moss upon the ground

The chipmunks make their home here
And, yes, field mice too
Sparrows in the rafters
And bees along the eaves

No one lives here anymore
No one lights the fire
The battered old cabin
Just sits alone and sighs

Charles Rockyvich, Jr.

SECRET LOVE

I want to do so much for you
And make your dreams come true
I want to shout to all the world
About my thoughts of you

I think of you each day
And dream of you each night
I think about the way you smile
And make my days so bright

Even when the sky is dark
And troubles plague my might
I need just think of you
And everything seems so right

You mean so much to me, my dear
But there is no excuse
To tell you of my love
And let my feelings loose

Oh! I wish you were here with me tonight
So I could feel your touch
And hear the softness of your sighs
To tell you, dear, I love you very much

Charles Rockyvich, Jr.

FIRST SORROW

He was only a wild baby rabbit,
A sweet tiny cottontail,
Daddy found in the hay barn,
Huddled behind the hay bales.
He rescued him from a black snake,
And brought him to me in his glove.
Hoppie sucked milk from a bottle,
How he thrived on clover and love.
Long hours we played together,
Me, and my cottontail friend.
When Hoppie grew tired of playing,
He cuddled to sleep in my hand.
But, one evening as we were playing,
Hoppie came to a very sad end.
Daddy buried him under the peach tree
And I showered peach blossoms on him.
Then, I ran to the arm of my mother,
And cried and cried and cried.
How I loved my little wild rabbit,
But my little wild rabbit had died.
Sometimes I rest 'neath the peach tree,
Close to his little earth bed,
And I think of my dear little Hoppie,
And of all the fun that we had.

Flossie F. Gregory

LAUGH

Don't laugh at me
if I don't talk as you
Don't laugh at me
if I don't look like you
Don't laugh at me
because I struggle trying to achieve
Don't laugh at me
Don't laugh behind me, you don't understand
Don't laugh at me
Don't underestimate me
Only estimate your laughter
For God created me in His own image
Are you not laughing at Him

Sharon Ford

GORE MOUNTAINS

From the train window

When the train tracks wound
'Round your body, at times
Train almost meeting train
We first saw you
From our window
Our eyes scaling up
Into your unexpected heights
We were not prepared for
Pinnacles and summits shaped
By wind and rain
Or evergreens and aspens
Green dots on
Dark red rust earth,
Your garment,
Enhancing your
Your bouldered shape
Not yet spoiled
By towering condominiums.

Constance Quarterman Bridges

ALL ARE BROTHERS!

There is a rhyme and a story I'd like to tell
I hope you like it and think it's swell?
We need lots of laughter, also some mirth
Right down here on our good green earth.

All children and parents and those without
We all can do it if we don't fall out
Each people on earth such as those we see
Have something to offer for you and for me.

Yet some will holler and some will shout
Because they simply don't know what it's all about
They say they don't like a certain people there be
In the many ways over as many do see.

For many are the colors we have of paint
Just touch them up and now some just ain't
So we mix up the colors of all on the earth
To enjoy them much for they all have their worth.

Just remember it kids, you parents and all others
We all came from the one and that makes us Brothers
The whole world of mankind is just like the flowers
Some simple, some pretty, some plain but they're ours.

A small boy's pet frog, a little girl's doll
Will be there for you, for me and for all
Remember this story, this rhyme and feel tall
To be one for *many* and the world for *all*.

Rick Arnold

BARN AGAIN

BARN AGAIN big red letters shout
BARN AGAIN, FINE FEATHER FACTORY,
Big red letters scream out to the highways, over cudzu covered
rolling hills, and in smaller letters, *BIGEST BARN HERE 'BOUTS,*
LEST WAYS WITH NATIVITY SCENE AND MANEGER. ALSO, PEACANS,
AND PEANUTS.

The pear wood nativity, life-sized figures, life-sized manger, hand
carved and built by the late Mrs. Fibber Fine stands early fall to
January 25th, always to the right of the barn's front doors, in the
middle of a fine-mesh wire fence, feathers deep, like banked snow.

Umpteen billion geese feathers and down, drifting floating about, mostly
upside down inside wire, waiting to be ticking packed and hauled.
Big, double-tin, treasure house barn full to the top. At the bottom
of Baby Hollow, wild dogs from the old woods, bark at the tame,

imprisoned geese. Mr. Fibber Fine's twenty hunt-guard hounds rub
against preacher's legs, when they arrive by buggy and autos. The
nativity draws them? The pecans? The peanuts? Preachers glance
around for the child. Hidden, away in dark shadows, the child kneels

knee deep in down. "Christ'an life ought'a cheer me," she whispers,
listening to the winter wind shake the tin walls. She listens to the
sermons on the radio, when Mr. Fine spends week-ends in Burntcorn.
The sermons talk of love, and the warm comfort of kindness. And in

the summer, when quilted darkness falls, the child holds tender her
corncob doll. She smiles, humming, climbs high, and rests her
questioning hymn-filled head against apple boughs — as safe as
golden oats, she's cradled within God's arms.

Jean K. Bruce

THE DESERT

Inscrutably,
    The vast and silent desert lies surreal —
    Its heat waves dance and shimmer in the sun;
    Mirages form and disappear like phantoms
    Before the brain identifies their shape.

Impassively,
    It stretches out to all infinities,
    And calmly bears mankind's infringements;
    And, just as calmly, thwarts each plan to stay
    With too much heat, and not enough water.

Inexorably,
    It overcomes man's wit and will and wisdom,
    Dishonors dreams, and batters hope and pride
    Until a man must choose to stay and die,
    Or leave and live — and that is not a choice.

Impartially,
    It alters alien and native forms alike —
    Bleaches all shards of wood to desert silver,
    Rusts metal parts to seven shades of sandstone,
    And all of it becomes the desert panorama.

Relentlessly,
    The searing sun makes kiln-like the vast wasteland,
    The parching wind blows harshly here and yon,
    The fine-grained desert sand both bares and buries,
    And Today and Yesterday seem all the same.

E. Maurine Rathje

THE TEENAGE YEARS

There comes a time for each of us when we reach the
"dreaded age," where we are judged by our peers
like puppets on a stage.

Our parents start to worry, have they done the
right thing? So they put us to the test and
start to pull our strings.

Our friends at school influence us as to what we say
and do. The "social scene" around us now seems more
important too.

The boys now like the girls and the girls they like
the boys. The cars we drive and the music we play,
to our parents, make too much noise.

We can't wait to grow up, yet we want to remain young.
We are torn between responsiblity and still wanting
to have fun.

At times we'll be so happy and at times we'll be in
tears, but they say it's all a part of growing, through
the teenage years.

To help relieve the pressures and quiet all our fears,
we need our friends and families to get us through
these years.

When we've made it through this time, we'll look back and
see the importance of the teenage years in our book of
memories.

Alice Langebartel

COLORADO RIVER

River, I first heard
of you in a classroom
and filed you in
a dusty corner.
Then
I hadn't grasped
the grandeur
of your crimson waters.
Now
I gasp looking down
at your clear, sometimes
muddy waters.
Forgive me for not
knowing you sooner.
I think on seeing you
there should be a monument
to your special splendor.
Then I see
in your twisting currents,
which flow like blood
through the valley's veins,
floating debris
discarded empty cans.
Is this our monument
to you?

Constance Quarterman Bridges

DIARY OF A RIVER

From tiny spring a trickle born,
  In rocky heights and earth's first dawn.
Bubbling forth on distant morn,
  This singing stream goes dancing on.

Slipping, sliding, now go gliding,
  To sterner, steeper slopes below.
Always leaping, whirling, crashing,
  Smashing onward, ever dashing.

Through deep dark canyons I will soar
  And shoot the rapids with a roar.
Foaming, swirling, geysers fountain,
  Now far away from lofty mountain.

A quiet eddy now and then,
  A time for rest then on again.
One thousand miles I've stretched my length.
  Now great and wide but losing strength.

I'm slowing now, water's dropping.
  My waves are trembling, feeling fear,
But I know there is no stopping,
  And surely now my end is near.

Then what is this? oh joy, what bliss,
  For this is not the end of me.
Not an ending fate is lending,
  But happy blending with the sea.

Harold D. Gascoigne

GLENWOOD CANYON

"Majestic mountains shelter me."
Black voices of spirituals
heard in countless churches
echo in my ears.
My black blood of Africa
mixed with red Algonquin
forces my eyes upward
into your pock-marked face
your rust-grey granite
through rocks
trees force their way
pointing proudly
triumphantly heavenward
clouds are wrapped carelessly
'round your head
like dirty bridal veils.

Did my Algonquin fathers
crouching in your bowels
cry out, "Great Mountains
shelter me"?

Constance Quarterman Bridges

CONSTANCE QUARTERMAN BRIDGES.
Born: Plainfield, New Jersey, 10-22-30; Education: Philadelphia Community College; Atlantic Community College; Attended Charles Morris Price School of Advertising and Journalism, Philadelphia, Pennsylvania; Occupations: Retired from Internal Revenue Service; Freelance writer; Comments: *My themes are varied. A creative writing instructor inquired, "How do you see yourself as a writer?" My reply: I am a vacuum cleaner in the hands of an indiscriminate housekeeper who sucks up bits and pieces of life. The housekeeper is also very lazy, so the bag is large and never needs emptying. So I sift through the bag making discoveries which I share in the form of poetry.*

GREATNESS

How great men live,
How they forgive
  like Bible seers.
The spirit draws near.
There loves knee heaven.
The magic number seven.
They hold the seven stars
  in their hand.
Their offspring numerous as sand.
They like a guiding light.
Keep heaven in their might.

Joan Johnson

SURE DEFEAT

Who sits and waits beside
The road for safe passage through
His life.
  With thought the world owes
Laughter omit all stress and strife.
  Who knows and holds a love
So rare yet does not give his all.
  Who walks this tightrope
Without care thinking love won't
Let him fall.
  Who builds his selfish small
Small world denies all others
To repeat.
    Who? The biggest
Fool of all to ask the world
For sure defeat.

Bonnie N. Anderson

THE LIMIT

When you hit a limit
On the Richter scale

Listen to your heroes
That teach you so well

Think about a being
Who loves you so well

Think of me for
I love you so

Amo Cheesh

ABRAHAM EMILE CHOOKOMOOLIN. Pen Name: Amo Cheesh; Born: Hawley Lake, 1-25-47; Married: Gladys L. Chookomoolin, 3-28-87; Education: University of Guelph, 1969, 1974-75; Fanshawe College, 1975; Northern College of Applied Arts and Technology, 1980; Occupations: Translator, Reporter, Librarian, Guide, Broadcaster; Poetry: 'Princess,' ' Whiskey Jack,' *American Poetry Anthology,* 1985; 'That Fall,' *Freighter,* 1985; 'Nishawbeski, Tribute' *Wawatay News,* 1982; 'LaLull,' lyric, *Nashville Co-writers' Plan,* 1984; Themes: *Love, spirituality, nature;* Comments: *In quietness and confidence comes renewed strength for the body and the soul. This poem I wrote after my first wife, Margaret, died on May 16, 1986, in the great flood at Wiwisk. The poem is 'The Limit.'*

NO MORE FEAR

A world without fear and one without greed
Is really the one that all of us need.
A planet without war and that lives just as one
That's the hope for the new, that's the way it will be done.

If ever they stop and if ever we learn
The people want peace, that's what we all yearn.
So put up the bombs, gather up all the guns
It's these we'll destroy and not our young sons.

Tell the leaders to cease, call an end all the killing
Rid the earth of all violence, for that all are willing.
Someday it will come the true way of peace
And nevermore to hate, all the past is to cease.

There comes us a lesson and while it does rhyme
All mankind on earth will agree it's about time.
If some think it's too hard their way to bend
Just think of it this way, it could be our end!

The only way left to stay on the top
Is be willing and able to end it and stop.

Rick Arnold

HER DADDY'S LOVE

At this time, she is only but a child, with her daddy's
loving face and sweet, charming smile. She brings to
her daddy's life bright sunshine and blue skies, by the
twinkle of mischief that shows in her eyes.

She's at the age when learning really can be fun and if
anyone can teach her, her daddy, he's the one. Oh, he
can teach her the basics of ones, twos and threes and
he can even teach her her all the a's, b's and c's.

But the love her daddy has for her and the caring ways
he shows will teach her so much more of life than we
could ever know.

It's a love that will nourish her and help to make her
strong. It's a love that will teach her what's right
and what's wrong. It's a love that brings her happiness
and though there may be tears, it's daddy's love that
comforts her and drives away her fears.

As time goes by and she grows up, she will surely see
that it's the love her daddy gave her while she sat
upon his knee that taught her what she needs to know
and how her life could be and to his heart, she only,
holds the magic key.

For whether they be together or a great distance apart
she will always be daddy's little girl in that special
place, locked deep inside his heart.

Alice Langebartel

WHISPERS IN THE RAIN

In each and every lone drop of rain, there lies an answer to our pain.
Each minute droplet has a name and purpose.
Each drop whispers, whispers its message.
The rain's orchestrated music gingerly wafts to the ears of our being.
Oh God, you must listen
For only she is the music meant.
For only she can really hear this message to her heart.
How sad if these capsules carrying joy, love,
    and peace must fall in vain.
There is hope you see!
For once the droplets fall from the sky,
    their wisdom pierces the earth.
From her each living thing drinks with thirst,
    each living tree, plant, and animal;
Hence, the wisdom, the key, is drawn within.
When the wind blows, the snow falls, or the rain tumbles,
    this knowledge is merely knocking at your door
        begging to be acknowledged.
So next time you distinctly hear golden leaves rustling
    outside your window,
Or a *drippity-drop, drippity-drop* outside your window
    on a calm grey day,
Listen, for you will hear a whisper so gentle at your inner door.
Open it, don't be scared.
What will you see?
A reflection of you, and in her hand a precious golden key.

Heather Gard

DOUBLE BLESSING

In memory of Sandi and Sheri

There's nothing like a mother's heartache
    when God calls her child away;
But, recalling all the happy memories,
    she knows an angel passed her way.

Just remembering all the sunshine they would spread,
    where ere they roamed,
And the joy they brought to loved ones,
    helped to make our house a home.

Many times as "mother" held them,
    back when they were tiny things,
She would kiss them as they slumbered . . .
    their face was soft as angel wings.

The smiles they wore as they grew older would set an entire room aglow;
If they once had cause to worry, they made sure "mother" didn't know!

You see, I'm speaking from experience,
    for God called my twin girls home;
And though, sometimes, I feel lonely,
    I *never* really am alone.

It pays to keep our mind on Jesus; lean on Him in time of trouble;
He oft requires a lot from us, but He also blesses double!

I've had many, many blessings, and I remember when I pray,
To thank God *especially,* for two angels sent my way.

Lovingly, Mother

Rae Martin

IN THE BEGINNING

Someone else will listen to your love words
And be caressed by their softness,
But I heard them in unpracticed passion,
In stammered worship.

You will kiss another endlessly,
But I remember when your lips were startled
By the sweetness of my mouth,
When you were drugged
With only one intimate moment.

You were mine when life was new,
When sensation was fresh and wondering.
Your eyes lingered on me
When they were seeking the desirable one,
Your hands touched me
When they were reaching
For something precious to hold.

I was first,
And whoever may come after me
Cannot have what I have had.

Annie Ruth Waldsmith

WILL AND TESTAMENT

When I am dead
I would have cremation for my body,
My body, ever redolent of you,
Ever scented with attar of your nearness.

I would not have it rot
In loathsome stench
Or shrivel to a mummy.

My hands have touched your hair,
And in their cells are stored
The perfume of those moments.
You have kissed me,
And my lips and face
Will never lose
Their flower essence.

When I have died
I would lie
Silver ash of incense,
Dust of fragrant memory.

An urn made of Earth's riches
Will hold the siftings of an odor-sweet love,
Earth's most precious treasure.

Annie Ruth Waldsmith

Airy, fleeting, floating thoughts
    swirling through my brain;
there, and gone, like wisps of smoke
    never holding still;
a rainbow burst of color
a fireworks display
a multi-hued soap bubble
    filled with thoughts of love
        — for you.

Cynthia K. Chapman

WHO AM I?

Once I had a name, now
I am a 'Dot' in a computer.
Like a robot I walk to the sound
of bells, signs and colors.

I am a number on a tape, I talk
with and to machines.
Dehumanized, I am in limbo.
Without a number I am a nothing.

How strange these days of my life.

Hilda Adams Bonebrake Suter

BALLOON RIDE

Up above the clouds so high,
soaring across the big blue sky —
floating like magic through the air
without a worry or a care.

Like a free spirit that has no bounds
we listen for nature's delicate sounds —
over the fields and mountains we glide
on a breathtaking hot air balloon ride.

Like a magic carpet on a clear day
the gentle breeze carries us away —
on a brief adventure until we land,
we know not where — it isn't planned.

We pass over the treetops, so leafy and green;
Words cannot describe this beautiful scene —
the world is a painting on display
as we casually sail up and away.

Alas, our journey must come to an end, and so
we travel down to the ground below —
like birds we flew across the sky
on a balloon ride, my baby and I.

Jodi Lynn Meyle

LOVE IS HARD TO UNDERSTAND

Why do people fall in love
For so many different reasons?
In love forever, or so they say —
But how long is forever?
I always thought forever was eternity;
But, I've yet to see a love to last that long.
Always and forever —
These have taken on brand new meanings
For lovers only
Isn't love supposed to be
Overflowing everything a person does?
Very seldom has it happened
Quite that way. Who can truly say,
''I understand love''?
Is love meant to be
Understood? I wonder . . .
Love is hardly ever
Totally understood.
Yes, I'd say that
Love is hard to understand.

Lisa J. Shaw

NO PAIN WANTED

The lifegiving flow trickled from the inner part
Like a baby fawn, when hit with a dart,
He was young, but he wasn't blind
For he knew my kind of woman
    was hard to find
On a velvet cushion, he brought it back,
With each delicate part much intact.
I gave it a toss, and cast it away
To a mermaid, who caught it
Like a bride's bouquet
''You can't do that,'' I heard a fisherman say
But I've never had a heartache to this day.
(She has no heart.) Aha! Aha!

Mina Huffman

AWAITING DESTINY

You came along, it was too late
My hand was taken, a trick of fate.
I loved you then, I love you yet
The glow in your eyes, I can't forget.
'Twas long ago, you entered in,
It was true love and not a sin.
For your abode, I set apart
The secret chamber of my heart.
To you, I cannot be a wife
I can't untangle the threads of life.
In darkened silence there you wait
Till when — another trick of fate.

Mina Huffman

SHOW ME THY SIMPLE WAY

As I tread the narrow way from day to day
Dear God, show me thy simple way
''To lead erring souls to the right
To win them from darkness to light.''

As I sing thy praise from my heart
Dear God, help me to do my part
In leading others in thy throng
To sing the old familiar song.

As I come to thee in prayer
Dear God, may thy presence be there
To hear my humble petition to thee
Expressing in a simple way, my plea:

As I'm trying to lead a simple life
Dear God, in spite of pride and strife
To hold out faithful to the end
And show thy simple way to a friend.

Mina Huffman

SOUTH AMERICAN DELIRIUM

Long ago in clouds of time there was a place of peace
Where everyone and everything bade any work to cease
 Great lizards bathed in warmth and light
  while winged ones danced aloft
 Lush plant life never was so thick with leaves both full and soft
The water steamed at midday while huge dragonflies few by
And mammoth beetles congregated in the reeds nearby
Nestled far from shore the giant lake dwellers would eat
Of water greens and creatures on the floor beneath their feet
In early eve the rhythm of the daytime crowd's retreat
Was met by nighttime's countless numbers wakened by the beat
 In the darkness of the night all steamy waters waned
 Yet cold and damp did not exist for night life warmth remained
Snakes that never seemed to have an end to all their length
Would linger in the pools and sometimes swim with all their strength
Gentle giants — mute and languid — heard the din of talk
From many creatures in the night while going for a walk
No insect brave in horde or hive aroused those placid beasts
As they lingered dining freely on their leafy feasts
Monstrous moths and swarthy bird-bats played their games of stealth
 Amid green vegetation's splendor flaunting all its wealth
And man they say was never there — it was so long ago
Yet footprints next to footprints seem to say it wasn't so

Cora Mendeola

EARTHQUAKES AND STORMS

Country living with all of the thunder
makes me sit here still and wonder
How I'll do in one big quake if it should really come?
All the world thinks we're silly living here where it's oh so hilly
Saying all the hills will flatten out for sure.
We just keep right on a-living while the quakes keep on a-giving
With their rolling rumbling jolts with no quick cure.
We're as happy as we can be for to us there will never be an end
of mountains valleys rivers or the land.

All the eastern folk think that their norm is better still
with all their storms
Yet to us it's better here than on the sand.

In the middle sittin' saddle among all the herds of cattle
with winters cold to freezing don't you see?
We feel we're better off dear with all these saying quakes here
will cause the state to separate or sink.

Just ponder over troubles as volcanoes with their bubbles
'cause few will leave here no not me.
If you should feel like coming you'll find us really humming
'Cause all of us are really in the pink!

Rick Arnold

ANGEL

 Guiding spirit of influence, producer of my day.
Natural loving being, drove all evil away.

Greater than human power, supernatural good.
 Silver-grey-haired figure, delicate example stood.

 Epitome of intelligence; innocent, beautiful, and good.
Archangel to my dragons, supported more than money could.

Set of wings and halo, messenger of God.
 Kindly moment in life, preciousness made proud.

 Saucy set of limpid eyes, argument never given.
Fabulous soother of soul, Grandmother now in heaven.

Ric Filip

THE SEARCH

In these moments that we've shared,
Passion gained in the moonlight.
Love, painful, yet gentle, breathes life into my body.
Slowly, my eyes open to a new day,
My spirit still clinging to the image of you.
The pretender, believer, defender.
Compliments of golden, sunlit hair, strength upon you.

Given the power to be all, and the love to be one,
I close my eyes in search of you.
Vanity beseeches me on this quest,
And no longer are our spirits engaged.
The intensity of the bright, yet emotional dream,
Soon fades into just another,
Yet I still gaze at passers-by hoping the magic of my dream is reality.

Mary M. Feyereisen

And woman said in plaintiff tone,
"I wish I had those things possessed by man,
 which up to now escape me,"
Said man, "Take all, take all, both good and bad,
The burdens of uncertain life, shortened oft by sudden, violent death,
The pestilence, the constant strife, and stress of life,
Competing ever with fellow man and Nature,
The grinding toil, the guilt over things beyond control,
The constant effort to excel and build, ambitions run unchecked,
Amassed wealth earned, and stolen, and pillaged from friend and foe,
Alone, alone, among God's creatures, always alone,
For biologic necessity has placed this load upon my back, unwanted,
To be released from all of this, would be the greatest gift,
That God could give to me,"
Said woman now in subdued tone,
"I think that I shall keep those things,
Which currently I possess,"
Things oft seen from distance great,
 look not so fine when seen up close.

David E. Carson

NONA

She sat on the side of the bed,
 her comb gently stroked her golden hair.
Her voice hummed softly the tune to "The Way We Were."
 I watched her shoulders with one thought in mind.
 How could love that burned so bright, so long ago;
smoulder so deep and constant after all these years?

 It seems like a millions years ago,
  though it's only seventeen.
 I can't remember when she wasn't a part of me,
 it's so natural to touch her, to have her touch me.
 Most of all, it's moments like these that tell me,
 eternity isn't long enough, life will too soon pass,
and that a stop action begins whenever I take her hand.

Yet, the time seems to announce that once again, we must be apart,
  together, for we are one;
  You see, she is my wife.

Willard E. Toller

NO LIFE

Another Man.
A Soldier.
This one's asleep,
on train car seats.
 Face
 so dusty,
  it blends in with his gray
army coat.
Unlaced sneakers, bare legs,
ripped cuffs.
His shirt,
Also gray,
No Life.
No Happy Fellow,
A Barren Tree
in a field of apple trees.

Rhonda Desilus

I WAS BOUGHT, A WAY PREPARED

Hope and love in ashes lay, the world suddenly
turned dark and gray, as on Calvary hill they
killed our blessed Saviour that day.

As for me the ransom paid was far from being
an even trade, for on this earth I have no
worth, not even enough to justify my birth.

And yet His blood has set my soul and spirit
free, no greater love will this or any other
world see, this is what my blessed Saviour did
for me.

No longer will the slings and arrows of this
world torture me, from these things of this
world my God in the end will set me free.

On this earth I never at peace can be until I
too have conquered death and my spirit at last
He has set free, then from this world my spirit
will soar to be with Him forevermore. Amen.

Leland D. Wertz

FATHERS

I was a little girl in a foreign land,
And my earthly father took my hand;
He taught me all the words to say,
And also how to sing and play.

I'm a little girl in a foreign land,
And my Heavenly Father takes my hand;
He listens to me day by day,
And hears me as I sing and pray.

My earthly father was good to me
And loved me very tenderly;
My Heavenly Father supremely gave
His Son for me, that I might live.

Janice R. Meyer

WONDERCOLORLAND

 Colors are rosier,
Sky forever azure.
Even when storm darkens to gray
Smiles still carefree; fairyland.
Witness to golden benches
Lining the pathway leading to
Endless bliss;
To children, smiling faces,
Skipping to the beat of their
Ruby pith, cheeks rosy, warm.

The yellow brick road.
Returning Dorothy to Auntie Em.
Goldielocks, comfortably sleeping,
Her head cushioned by curly locks;
Warming her toes beneath
Red plaid comforter.
Cozy in the bronzed bed,
Antique wood chipping from wear.

Brighter than the reality of the gray storm
clouds passing over me as I dive into the
pool, only to crack my head on the shallow
bottom, painted sky-blue to look never ending.

Mary Beth O'Hara

MARY BETH O'HARA. Born: Detroit,
Michigan, 7-2-63; Education: Michigan State
University, Journalism and English; Occupations:
Writer, Waitress, Bartender; Poetry: 'Dancing
with a Pregnant Woman'; Comments: *Writing is
my life, literally, and I plan to make my writing
part of everyone's life.*

BREAKUP

When good comes to end,
There's nothing left to mend,
No secrets left to share.

No more flowers left to send,
No convictions left to bend,
No parts of your souls left to bear.

Your love remains still,
Yet, no voids left to fill,
But, continue you try and try.

Not a stone remains unturned,
Not a candle unburned,
 And to go on, you ask yourself *why?*

It's time now
To say goodbye.

Paige Levin

MALPAIS!

Tortured, twisted river of silent rock.

Mute testimony to liquid fire, belched
 from the Mother Crater,
Conceived deep within the subterranean
 womb,
Born in an angry maelstrom of smoke
 and ash,
Ordained to an instinctive flow
 downward,
Swallowing forever the earth, consuming
 greedily all it encompassed.

The molten river coursed furiously,
Scrambling into crevices and illuminating
 its path with electric red fingers.

Vegetation wilted, bowed down, and was
 covered with the black shroud.

Terrorized younglings and slow-footed
 creatures were engulfed and lay
 beneath their igneous headstones.

The offspring expelled, the Mother
 Crater fell quietly exhausted,
The explosive child cooled.

Tortured, twisted river of silent rock!

Maggie Ramsay

WE HAVE OUR GIANTS, TOO

I can imagine how David felt
as he stood before his giant
trembling, yet trusting in his God,
when everyone behind him was telling
him, ''You can't.''

But like the faith of an innocent child,
he went with his sling in his hand.
After picking up five stones from a stream,
he replied to Goliath, ''Here I stand.''

And he stood before his enemy, in the name
of the Lord.
This impossible battle to fight,
but with his weakness, God added His Grace,
and David won it because of God's might.

We, too, have our giants today.
Though they may come in a different shape.
They may be of a physical, financial,
spiritual or mental nature,
or just something or someone we're trying
hard to escape.

But like David, we can fight our giants.
Like him, we need God's grace.
If we have enough faith and trust in God
Our Giants, we, too, can face.

Quincia Clay

WONDERING

Why couldn't you have told me, and spared me all this hurt,
Why bring me to the altar, when there was nothing there,
You had no heart, no feelings from within, because you never
    would have let all these things begin.
Now our love is gone and the feelings from within,
Are all swept ashore and nothing left for indemnity,
You took a job out of town, driving trucks to and from and all around,
When the weekend came rolling around how would I ever suspect
    that you were out painting the town,
The shock of it all was hard to endure, because it all came
    about in no time at all,
The Lord only knows the ache in my heart, but furthermore he
    made me get smart,
As times goes by and your mind gets a rest,
You can see things more clearly and at their best,
The Lord inspired me to enjoy life each day,
And not to look back on bygone days,
Sunshine and rainbows follow the rain,
And it will remove all the stress and pain,
It's never the end of this big world,
And a new beginning is always there.

Margaret Freije

THE MARCH

The old soldiers marched slowly down a sunlit street
With their uniforms well-pressed and shiny boots on their feet.

They'd gathered to remember a long ago war
And friends and companions who existed no more.

A flag was held high as they sang loud and strong
About far away places and caissons rolling along.

In each of their minds, old memories awoke.
They heard long-forgotten screams and saw dark pillars of smoke.

They felt bullets rushing by the tips of their ears
While down from their eyes streamed rivers of tears.

The crowds nearby whistled, clapped and waved
For the service they'd given to the ''Home of the Brave.''

But silence filled the air as they marched up the Allentown Grade,
For it was the end of the 29th Annual Memorial Day Parade.

Judy A. Deeter

PREFERRED MODEL

I claim no greatness from within —
I am lowly, not exhalted;
But supposedly a freed man.
Believer, unbeliever, a sinner, a saint;
An all-in-one man,
My soul is not free from taint.
I think and feel as others do,
I plan and build and hope and pray;
and curse my heritage, day by day.
Countless golden idols do I woo,
I've cast my lot with those who bray.
My image is the likeness of God,
Though my actions suggest I'm in the devil's pay;
This and more of me is true,
Yet — I am but made of clay.
And, so are you.

Eula R. Henderson

IN APPRECIATION FOR LOVE

Only you see the rainbow in our minds, only you have the
Understanding of a clock spring as it slowly unwinds;
Remember farming in Colusa, a sky filled with ducks and

Geese; remember Thanksgiving and Christmas and children
Round a tree in peace; remember the turkey and yams
And the pies with a scoop of homemade ice cream on top,
Nothing dims those memories, like the love of a single dew-
Drop; there will always be a garden with vegetables and
Many flowers in bloom, there will always be the smile of
A grandma with the warmth of a summer's afternoon;

Grandkids, great grandkids and great-great grandkids, the
List of a great family tree; the gatherings bring together
A happening of five generations in harmony; come
Dream with me of a time before the airplanes flew, when
Youth was the symbol of courage and bravery, when the
Sun dried clothes on the line and we were only two;

Come walk with me on golden pathways in the twilight
Of our years; come gather stardust and moonbeams and
Forget about our fears; sit beside me in the meadow in a
Forest of long ago, when rivers ran free and clear and were
Made from the melting snow; hold my hand and feel my heart
And know your granddaughter is my wife, there is one
Name we will all remember, it is you who give love and life.

John B. Passerello

SPRINGTIME ON THE PRAIRIES

When the springtime comes back to the prairies
    And the flowers are blooming again
With the sun shining bright on the desert
    And no clouds in the skies to descend

There soon I shall be a going
    For to see all my dear loved ones again
As I travel over the prairies
    O what a beautiful sight there to see

Our God He made all of this freedom
    He gave it to you and to me
It seems like the garden of Eden
    So quiet so peaceful and serene

Down through the mountains and canyons
    And on to the desert that ends to the skies
Soon God in all of His Kingdom
    Will reclaim all this land by and by

As I wander this vast land of beauty
    Far over the great divide
Where the doggies they used to wander
    With the cowboys that rode by their side

O God bless this land of America
    The pride of our forefather's time
O God protect our America
    And may forever freedom's Holy light shine

Myra M. Williams

GILBERT LINKOUS

Dedicated to the principal at Gilbert Linkous,
Mrs. Doris McElfresh

Every year it's a new beginning, like the opening of a new book,
With time to learn and discover, what takes place inside.
It's a development of growing, of excitement and fun,
A great time for sharing, with each individual one.
Here the children learn the colors of red, yellow, blue,
Using their own imagination, of knowing what to do.
They paint their own originals, with shape of different kinds.
A creation from the back of their minds.
Like the fairytale of rhythm, and rhymes.
With arts and crafts, fish and birds.
Learning the meaning of their names.
Of letters and different words.
The children spring forth new ideas, like the shining of a star,
That you can see lit up, coming from afar.

Gilbert Linkous now closes the end of its page,
Like the drawing of a curtain, when you are on stage.
The children are helped by the faculty,
Making their dreams become a reality.
Hoping a door will be open,
To each one that holds a key.

Nancy Armstrong

NANCY LEE ARMSTRONG. Born: Pulaski, Virginia, 5-4-45; Married: David Armstrong, 8-11-46; Education: High School diploma; Occupation: Schoolboard staff, Gilbert Linkous Elementary School; Memberships: Mountain Brook Baptist Church; Awards: Silver Poet Award for Christmas poem, 'Jesus Was Born'; Golden Poet Award for 'Gilbert Linkous'; Poetry: 'Gilbert Linkous,' *News Messenger,* Montgomery County, 11-7-86; Comments: *I am an inspired writer with an ambition of becoming a songwriter. I've been writing since 1968. I now have a demo record, recorded in Nashville and being played on country radio stations.*

A LIFE MAP

What fun! I've always pondered, to chart a life as on it wanders.
Like a river . . . ever bold; what similarities unfold.
Both begin . . . from deep within an apex old as time unseen
And both take shape from some unknown and question not . . .
 but strive to be.

Both course their way from that beginning toward an ocean far away.
The travel takes them to distant places, touching others in their sway.
A stop at times might be made, to stay awhile . . . and play awhile.
To mingle and merge . . . perhaps submerged, then slowly,
As a river leaves a lake, assuming motion,
 touching people in its wake,
Meeting new friends . . . going new places,
 tasting; hearing; seeing new faces.

The lucky of us seem to share that surge toward an unknown lair.
With active minds and senses keen to explore the places yet unseen.
How sad to know you are deprived when old you grow
 and you arrive at ocean's edge,
And then to wonder what could have been . . . and what was squandered.

Joy Thomas

THE TRIATHLON

One hundred of us now compete to be the top triathlete.
Endurance plays the major role of who will stay and who will fold,
With aching arms and shoulder pain, I struggle now . . . just to gain
Another yard toward my goal, with one more mile to swim I'm told.
Ignore fatigue and muscle ache . . . I'm in the lead, so I feel great.

A change of clothes . . . a quick rubdown,
 I'm on my bike to Provincetown.
I start out with a burst of speed, with strategy to keep the lead.
The weather's mild . . . the roads are fine,
 it seems as though I'm making time.
I'll concentrate and see it through . . . to do what I set out to do.
No stops until the winner's gate . . .
 I'm in the lead and I feel great.

The hardest part is yet to come with more than twenty miles to run.
Around the bay of old Cape Cod to sandwich town where pilgrims trod.
I've run this race before today and know the pain it takes to stay.
But greater still . . . the pain to stop
 and never know what might have been.
Our dreams before us yet unfold of winning now that trophy gold.
Some call it luck or maybe fate that I have won . . .
 but I feel great.

Joy Thomas

JOY THOMAS. Born: Seguine, Texas, 1943; Married: with two sons, Scott, age 15, Chris, age 22, and one stepson, Robert, age 26; Education: Attended Del Mar College in Corpus Christi, Texas; Aviation training school and Central State University in Oklahoma; Occupations: Oil and Gas Accounting; have real estate license; Co-owner along with husband of ten years, Chesley Thomas, of custom design jewelry business; Pilot of non-commercial airplane for pleasure only; Awards: Have won prizes and recognition for numerous poems since 1984; Comments: *My poems, like my interest, and my life in general, are so diversified that I can hardly claim a common theme. Perhaps because my accounting work is extremely structured, it allows my other interests and ideas to take flight.*

LITTLE THINGS ON A FALL DAY . . .

Cobwebs wafting in the wind . . .

Ancient spirits lingering in my presence
Fingering my heart while telling of truth.

Crispy fall leaves colored with fire and honey
Sighing as they are carelessly juggled in a breeze, unnoticed.

The sense of being, of belonging for an unaware moment.

Cool, gentle transcending communication with nature's plane of being.

Flashes of childhood delight, of childhood tenderness . . .

I see for an instant what my heart longs to see.

Heather Gard

ACCUSATION

Beware the pointing finger;
  It could be a gun,
Aimed to take away your life,
  When life has just begun.

The pointing finger accuses,
  Though a man be guilty or not;
He could be the scapegoat,
  Victim to someone's plot.

Behind the pointing finger,
  Can lie a viper's tongue,
And it's often so deadly,
  A man is quickly hung.

Many a man is wrongly accused,
  Marked for life as it were,
And he lives in infamy,
  Though history will not concur.

Luke Nathaniel Baxter

LUKE NATHANIEL BAXTER. Born: Van Buren, Arkansas, 9-12-15; Education: Tulsa Central High School, 1933; Occupations: Retired Poet, Painter; Awards: Over two dozen honorable mentions, 3 times Golden Poet award, 1985-87; Themes: *The humor, pathos, and tragedies of life.*

AMY

As I look back to what I was
And what you made of me,
I thank you.
I envied someone who could cry without shame,
The feeling of release.
To bow my head to your shoulder,
And let my tears flow and to be held,
Knowing it's alright for a man to cry,
With you holding and comforting me,
I feel secure in your arms,
You taught me to show my weaknesses,
So I didn't have to be perfect.
I can show love and fear,
And still be loved, no matter what.
This is why I fell deeply in love with you.
As each minute goes by.
That's why I smile with pure joy
At the mention of your name,
When I see you smiling at me
My heart beats faster in my breast.
I'll never let you go.
What is life without love?
It's dark and dead.
That's what I would be without you.

Mark Jorgenson

LIFE

Like a tender bud life begins to open
into the vibrant bloom of spring;
exciting new life and beauty
soaking up the sweetness
of new experience —
then as a dragon's breath
summer winds breath upon the tender part
bringing a new maturity,
but still a gentle heart
hides beneath the wilting petals —
The beauty of autumn brings a calm,
soothing petals that were burned;
they cool and start to fade —
The days grow shorter
until winter's chill drapes a shroud of snow
adding a majestic beauty to the wilted rose,
a last bit of glory
before it falls softly away
onto the earth — to decay . . .

Donna Taylor

LOVE'S SIGNET XXXI

I see you shining from afar;
bright, lone firefly
amid a field of midnight blue,
through sunset steaks
of magenta and azure
I see you winking.
Our personal communication.
Winking in harmony
soon,
very soon
I will be with you.

Steven Richard Robinson

ROBINSON JEFFERS

headlands
of the Big Sur
restrain searching salt
fingers of the Pacific.
stone tower.
acid-
bitten metal,
those lines carved in a face;
embodiment of sentiment,
measure

of wit,
ironical,
violentissimo.
the conscious lyric physician,
controlled;
haggard,
like digging in one's
heels, trying to harness
cloud rivers of fog flooding
through canyons.

E. L. Kelso

SECRETS

Moments of loneliness spun into golden hours
of memories,

Dreams — re-dreamed, re-newed, and re-lived,

Youth — gained long enough to taunt our
groundless fears,

Mind — lost to another time, another age,
another you,

And then returned to know the *Whole*.

John R. Chiesa

JOHN RICHARD CHIESA. Born: Chicago, Illinois, 7-6-24; Married: Frances, 1-22-48; Education: St. Joseph's College, B.A., 1965; Northern Illinois University, M.S., 1969; Occupation: Disabled; Poetry: 'Grandpa's Quandry,' *American Poetry Anthology,* 1987; 'Commitment,' 1987; 'Calm,' *Many Voices/Many Lands,* 1987; 'Now,' *On The Threshold of a Dream,* 1987; 'Indelible,' published by the 802 Tank Destroyer Battalion Veteran's Association, 1987; Comments: *All of my work is directed toward a loosening of the emotional tones within the individual. My efforts are to provide the doorway that releases the tossing, surging sea of emotions that requires relief from within the body and mind.*

WHAT IS LIFE?

What is life?
And what does it mean to us?
Do we plan our future or destiny,
Or does it just happen along the way,
Like the starting of a brand new day?
Do we instantly know what the future brings,
Or do each of us have secret dreams or
Secretly plan our goals in life?
Should we get depressed when life's secret
Desires do not go as we wish?
Should we cry when we feel sad or hurt
Over things we cannot control?
And dare we be completely different from
Each other, to find we are just the same
As our parents or grandparents before us?
Not as sure of ourselves, nor of them,
As we would like to be.
Our lives would be so much better if we
Take the time to look around us!

Michele Roy

MIKAL

The most angelic face in the choir has decided to move
South and retire.
We will miss her with all of our heart. Of us, she will
Always be a living part.

Househunting and moving is no thrill, she says she doesn't
Like it and never will.
Of course, when all is behind, a completely turned trick,
She'll rest in the sand of the beach at old Brunswick.

Her children think this move is yucky — leaving behind old
Hometown and friends not ducky.
Starting in a new school, being new kid on the block, isn't exactly
What makes them feel like a solid rock.

Promotion for husband, job-hunting for wife. Dear Lord, do you
Know you're shaking up her life?
"Of course, but precious Mikal will take it in stride, her
Magnificent faith tells her I am at her side.

Like Ruth of old, she will be her husband's pride even if life
Provides a rough and rugged ride.
Whither thou goest there go I. It's her style. Thy people shall
Be my people forever, not just awhile.''

So long, not good-bye, sweet Mikal! We love you!

Ric Filip

TEACH ME

Lord, teach me to pray,
That when I wake to the light of dawn
I remember to thank You for another day.

Lord, teach me to pray,
That when I recite the *Our Father*
I lack not sincerity when I say . . . "Thy will be done . . ."
That I may fully understand my dependence upon You
    in asking . . . "give us this day . . ."

Lord, teach me to pray,
That my heart be truly repentant as I ask . . .
    "forgive us our trespasses . . ."
Full of forgiveness when I say . . . "as we forgive . . ."

Lord, teach me to pray,
That I may come to You not only in pain or sorrow,
Also to share with You moments of happiness,
    my love for You and Your love for me,
To abide in You now and forever.

Lord, teach me to pray.

Elia Vann Colmenero

BITTERSWEET

Old falling leaves of amber, yellow, green and gold
You hurry past my window before the winter's cold
Beautiful to watch but with sadness to behold
The dreary sight of stately trees so naked and yet so bold
Awaiting winter's wrath with dignity and cold.
How can you bear the chilling climes of deadening hope untold
Yet plan spring's abundance, her beauty to unfold
Whisper now your secrets long waited to be told
For wan and tire and weary I too am growing old.

Clay Kershon

THINK AND DO

We become what we think and do.
For everything there is a price.
We work for good, we work for evil,
And we get what we ask for. How nice!

To act is to ask and thus to receive.
But if we don't ask we better believe,
A universe full of free things,
Like them or not, we still shall receive.

We cannot change the consequences
Of the free things we receive,
Unless we act swiftly and firmly
And ourselves do not deceive.

So we don't stand about and do nothing.
We'll be struck by natural disaster, a shrew.
Remember? We can alter the outcome of our life
With innovative thinking applied to what we do.

Ric Filip

DICK ZUFELT. Pen Name: Ric Filip; Born: Moab, Utah, 12-20-20; Married: Sally M. B. (Filipova), 7-10-63; Education: Brigham Young University, 1939-40; University of Georgia, 1951-52; University of Hawaii, 1956-57; University of Omaha, 1959-60; University of Georgia, 1968; Occupations: Military, Private to Lieutenant Colonel, World War II, Korea War, Vietnam War; Businessman; Public relations; Cemeterian; Teacher; Lecturer; Writer; Poetry: 'Why I,' American Poetry Association, 1984; 'Life's Piazza,' 'The Door of Life,' 'Living Power,' 'Passage — Here To There,' *American Poetry Showcase*, 1985; Themes: *I write philosophically about lifetime experiences: love, adventure, creating, recognition, security — the five great needs of mankind.*

BATTLE ON THE MOUNTAINS

An eagle, great winged bird of the sky, his wings are that of sails,
a sailor riding the sea of winds.
Above hills and canyons he flew, the wind his motor,
instinct his pilot, what was to keep him from flying higher yet?
Flying high in the sky, his natural right,
hunger directed he find something nice to bite.
On a mountainside, what a sight! An apple tree, fruit fresh and ripe!
Good enough to satisfy his appetite? Just right!
On his way down, what did he see?
A brown hawk in the tree, just as hungry as can be.
The hawk, flying up to protect leaf and fruit,
not to mention a most satisfactory roost.
Beak versus beak, like swords swung in anger,
no one yet the victor as the air grew darker.
A talon came down, the hawk did strike,
muscle, wing and feather were crushed with bone-shattering might.
To the Earth the hawk fell, too scared, hurt,
or confused as to what to do.
The eagle flew down, the fruit its prize,
victorious at the battle on the mountain, but tasty besides!

Daryl Ortmann

FOR MY SON

I wish that I could ever see,
The world as black and white as thee.
Your little eyes could never know,
How complex life can be.

Autumn S. Demuth

ME 'N' RUBY

Bundled and delicately wrapped;
I saw her!
As she fluttered
And nestled
Into a quiet corner
Of my branchless heart.
And, I felt her soft, warm heartbeat
Within mine.
Then . . .
She spoke!
And from a thousand
Timeless black-tanned echo chambers
Of her entire being,
Came velvety soft paindrops
And I remembered her;
The Pyramids, the Nile,
Her eyes . . .
Misty and warm, they were,
Whispered to me . . .
"I appreciate you too!"
And for a little while,
I took an angel's arm
And we walked across the night;
Me 'n' Ruby . . . *Tugetha!*

David I. Johnson, Sr.

DAVID ISREAL JOHNSON, SR. Pen Name: Soulghost; Born: Columbia, South Carolina; Divorced: father of two children; Education: University of Illinois, M.A., Art Education, 1968; Drake University, Des Moines, Iowa, B.F.A., Commercial Art Education, 1962; additional study at University of South Carolina; Occupations: College Art Educator and Musician; Memberships: Omicron Delta Kappa, Drake University, 1961; ROA (USAF Reserve Officers Association); AOPA (Aircraft Owners and Pilots Association); NAEA (National Art Education Association); Poetry: 'Charles Towne, S.C.' 4-87; 'Apartheid,' 1-85; 'Power by Sunbeam,' 2-57; 'Warm Ice,' 3-64; 'Mushroom Cloud,' 2-61; Comments: *In my work, I seek to "conjure-up" passions for "caring"; as though along a rippling, roaring river of emotional sound and sensation, through rhythmical alliteration and picturesque metaphor; until beached upon that climactic stillness of each unique experience.*

I WONDER

When there is nothing but the
Night outside my door,
I think of you and how
Things were before,
And wonder if these words
Would have a different sound
If, perhaps, you had loved the
Drifting clouds a little more
And I had kept my feet
Upon the ground.

Roseann Rutz

SILENCE

You left my life as you entered —
Without a word.
Silence
Draining me empty of
All but pain.
Day turns into days
Days drag into years
Yet the soothing balm of time
Lies impotent
Upon wounds too deep to heal.
Can I never be free of the
Relentless question,
"Why?"
Please, I pray, break this vow of
Silence
And set me free.

Sharon T. Winn

TO KATHY

I know the pain,
The anger, the anguish.
My heart and soul
Are with you
Every minute you
Breathe and I am
Holding your hand.
The minute, the second
It gets harder and
There are tears
I am holding
All of you
Close to me.
For I have been
There. With the same
Emotions, different
Circumstances.
So know,
I am with you
Truly always.
For the only healthy
Medicine is time and
You, my friend, have
All of mine you need.

Rosann Claeys

SOLITUDE

To be at peace
With one's self
And surroundings,
To have the
Strength to *not*
Be fearful of
The aloneness,
To enjoy each
Breath like a
New experience,
To have the
Wisdom to know
It is choice,
To be in
Solitude
And not to have
It be
Something
That is
Wrong.

Rosann Claeys

FEAR

Deceiving —

Laughing at you —

Deluding —

Bamboozling —

Holding you back —

Stopping you in your tracks —

Governing your every moment.

Is it worth stopping your life
To listen to it?

Rosann Claeys

ROSANN CLAEYS. Born: Newark, New Jersey, 7-27-59; Married: Henry, 8-20-83; Education: B.S., Mechanical Engineering; Occupations: Engineering Supervisor, Writer, Poet; Memberships: Society of Manufacturing Engineers, American Society of Mechanical Engineers, Pennsylvania Poetry Society; Awards: Golden Poet Award, 1987; Poetry: 'Mind,' *Great American Poetry;* 'Thank You,' *The Poetry of Life: A Treasury of Moments;* 'My Love,' 'Gratitude,' *Hearts on Fire, Vol IV;* 'Being Human,' *American Poetry Anthology;* Comments: *The goal of my poetry is to reflect people's ambitions and innermost secrets in such a way which frees or stirs something in them never seen before.*

THE MASTER OF ILLUSION

He is the master of illusion
and the secret of illusion
can be found in self-confusion

Listen to him speak
till you're knee deep in the street
chocolate-covered candy or sugar-coated treats

He's almost out of time
like you're nearly out of rhyme
nothing will effect him if you would just elect him

He's so well steeped in his confusion
that he's fooled by his own illusion
truth is just a victim of his pomp and circumstance

If you ask for understanding he'll just run and hide
like the truth deep down inside you
he can't be caught inside a lie

When I'm trapped in by confusion
in this world of mass illusion
I come to one who is the master

He is the master of confusion
at the art of self-illusion
and the secret of confusion
can be found in self-illusion

Ronald Anthony Browne

YE ARE NOT YOUR OWN

Dedicated to Jan Stone

I am the habitation of God,
   My body the Holy temple —
      Created by Christ Jesus,
         Where within lies His Kingdom,
Directed by the Holy Spirit,
   The Comforter left by Christ,
      Who leads me beside still waters
         To meet my Father.

Jeri Jo Wade

LITTLE GIRL BIG MOTHER

As a little girl playing with her dolls, she was their mother,
Yet in her make-believe way, taught them love for each other,
She would play house or school, with serious teaching given to no end,
And also very strict in demanding obedience and attention from them.

But only too soon her dolls and toys were put away,
As she grew into womanhood with each passing day,
She took her marriage vows, with such great pride,
Standing there in white, with her husband by her side.

Always so very devoted to her family and home,
Also a wife and mother, solves her problems in a pleasant tone,
Has love and respect for both the young and old,
And her words are warm and friendly, but never bold.

So from a little girl to a big mother she has grown,
Holding her family together with love, in a happy home.
She is the perfect example of what a wife and mother should be,
And many are still around waiting, for you and me.

Louis D. Izzo

UNTITLED

1. the process had stopped
2. and there was no desire, no way to really leave.
3. sirens blared in the streets, "overstimulation."
4. he couldn't do it because of fear
5. and it was fear that someone else had put there.
6. it wasn't his fault. "it really wasn't,"
7. he pleaded to himself aloud.
8. the sure-footed drums were playing the congo beat
9. on that day, "over and over," they said
10. there was nowhere left. "there wasn't anywhere left,"
11. he screamed. hard on that day
12. the rock fell from the cliff.
13. the man blared from his place on the street
14. sirens jerked as if they couldn't hear
15. particles of dust swirling their designs.
16. "it was as if they couldn't hear him,"
17. he screamed, as if it were sirens
18. and fear, a fear that told him,
19. "that there was really nowhere
20. left to go."

T. M. Spina, Jr.

THE TIME FOR JESUS

The time for Jesus, to begin the long, long weeks,
The time of pain, humiliation, and disbelief,
The time of "prophets of old," the word to descend,
Time for God's promises to be proven to men.
A short time for Jesus to heal, a new love to teach,
Only to be betrayed by kiss upon the cheek,
The time they bound his hands,
In the garden, where he prayed,
They spat upon my Savior, and mocked his holy name,
The time they nailed him to the cross that day.
The time of darkness! The temple veil was rent!
Proving this "son of man" was heaven sent,
Time of three days, and the stone was rolled away!
The "Son of God" liveth! to appear another forty days,
Time for God's plan to be finished, with salvation free,
The time the "Lamb of Calvary" died for you and me,
Time to believe the "gospels," this chance to you is given,
A ransom paid! for everlasting life in God's heaven.

June Cooper Wristen

THE WHISPERING TEAR

Her hair was light, streaked with gold
Those eyes so blue, the gaze was cold
They can always see through thoughts untold
And if your view is extremely clear
You'll be allowed to see her whispering tear

Once passion was given with such delight
A voice so soft you'd have to fight
To make yourself try to hear
A quiver, a sign of her secret fear
And perhaps on occasion you'll be allowed dangerously near
To witness the demise of her whispering tear

The days have been dark, without light from above
To brighten those eyes with the gift of true love
So widen the distance, as those did before
See all the warning of a dark corridor
Or she'll pull you in closer, to absorb all her fear
You'll be lost if not guarded from her whispering tear

Eileen Erwin

HAVEN ON THE HILL

Somewhere up on that hill
Is my house,
Where western windows
Shine golden in departing
Rays of day.

White stucco with arched porch,
Red floor and foundation,
A new steep dark red colored roof
Flanked on both sides and rear
By gables — five in total.

It is a mammoth house,
With large rooms —
Made for a family.
And I wish to share it
With a wife and our children:
One, two, or three
Would be this poet's dream.

But, for now, when long shadows
Of evening crawl like spiders
Up the wall,
I feel my aloneness
And seek someone
To talk to —
My haven is left
For another day.

F. Richard Dieterle

THOUGHTS

My mind is drifting into space,
Thinking of your lovely face.
My thoughts are on you all the while,
I wish I could see your warm sweet smile.
It doesn't matter if you're near or far,
Your face is shining like a star.
Whatever distance you are away,
Your thoughts are with me night and day.

Kevin L. George

RUTH II

This isn't a comedy
Or even a spoof
I met a nice girl
And her name is Ruth.

I like her immensely,
But this really won't do,
For alas she is married,
And I'm in a stew.

Her eyes are so big
And the bluest of blue.
She has quite nice features
You would think so too.

Her figure is shapely
And proportioned just right.
A wonder the men
Don't all have a fight.

Ruth is so pure
Asleep or awake
Only her husband
Would be on the make.

F. Richard Dieterle

WATERLOO

I envision you —
Eighty years old,
Cloistered in your kitchen,
Stirring broth,
Sipping herbal, honey-laced tea,
Surrounded by marble and porcelain.

Alone.
Leather, supple, but not
like skin.
Marble, unforgiving and rigid,
nonconforming to the curves
of your limbs.
The gleam of polished wood,
not like the warm glow of love,
radiating from someone's caring eyes.

Your conquests — all pieces of alabaster
for your display and amusement.

You, who had always pursued
That elusive demon —
Perfection.
Never settling for
"Good enough."

I tried to warn you,
Long ago.

Mary L. Bates

A WIDE EYEFUL

She so would call
the buttercups to play
with her golden blonde hair
though the flowers
would thrive in the thicket
she would pluck
not one but the many
that shined as her hair
when I would find me
there to call to the buttercups
to sing
to the buttercups given
the tears a wide eyeful

Michael Kingsley

DROWNING

Grasping for breath
Reaching for shore
Clutching on to life
Though I have it no more

Entangled in the current
Pushed down to the sea
Praying for forgiveness
Yet, no one hears me

Wanting to start over
Yet, caught up in the tide
Fighting Mother Nature
Yet, all breath ripped from inside

Torn between living
Or accepting my death
Should I fight for survival,
Or sigh, and take one last long breath?

Paige Levin

ESCAPE TO REALITY

Into my bar one damp and misty day,
Limped a dirty one-legged man.
I'm sorry sir I cannot pay,
But help this veteran if you can.

Some wine, some wine! he cried aloud
With piercing, pitiful, pleading gaze,
I hand him jug, but not so proud,
To see him sink in wine-soaked haze.

Then into Bacchus land he drifts,
Once more he's whole, no longer begs.
For in his mind the whole world shifts,
To the time of youth and two strong legs.

I see him there in full command
Say come on lads lets give them hell!
And I think, now I understand.
I pity him then and wish him well.

Now when he's sobered up again,
Fear-filled eyes and feeling pain.
Knowing the man he might have been,
I fill his glass with less disdain.

Harold D. Gascoigne

IN MY HEART

In my heart,
Wells up a pool
Of thoughts, of feelings,
Of sadness.

I miss you,
I love you,
As my life
Quickly crumbles in.

I am sad.
I am lonely.
I have nowhere to turn.

I have not the strength or
Clearsightedness to push out
Those now pushing in.

I feel as though I will collapse.
I am sad and aching and yearning.
I am wishing for that which never was
And never could be.

I am wishing for what is right,
For what feels good but cannot be.
I am sad.
Please love me.

Paige Levin

MY PEN

My pen is the one I use.
What I write is confused.
It's simply to amuse.
I love different inks.
Blue, black, red and shades of pink.
Bic bananas stink.
So without a doubt
I write and write about. Then
My pen runs out.

James H. Nelson

MOTHER LIVES

Mother lives through me, my children and theirs.
Though her body is returned to the earth
and her spirit is in the heavens
her blood, her love, her brilliance live
within me and my children and theirs.

Though body and soul are gone from me,
Mother lives, her image, her love.
The memories the beautiful things
I have within me live forever.

Though I shall miss dearly her being,
the warmth, the loving, the place in my
heart where Mother now lives will always be.
Mother shall live forever through me,
my children and theirs.
To Mother, I love you yesterday, today and forever.

Patrick H. Ehrsam

SUMMER LOVE

These days of summer have flown by fast,
But my memories of you will always last.
I'll never forget the first day we met.
I looked in your eyes and my mind was set.
You were the one I'd be with forever.
I thought we would spend our whole lives together.

We love each other and that isn't a lie,
But at this point in time we must say good-bye.
Our love for each other comes from the heart.
Now that this summer is over, we must depart.
I love you so much — I don't want summer to end.
But I know that in time my broken heart will mend.

Sally Ann Byrd

QUESTIONS

Shining black granite holding back the earth
Unfeeling stone emblazoned with 58,000 screams
The silent shrieks blast my eardrums and sear my lungs
  with their cold fire

Who will hold back the earth from the black hole they have
  laid him in
I see the brown clay falling, I hear the thud as it covers
  his dreams and smothers his spirit
The crumbling mud sealing forever his smile and his love

Who will hold back the earth
Flowers, teddy bears, a winning baseball lay at your feet
Are you an idol of war or a cry for peace
Will the leaders understand
Will your unyielding defiance disarm them
Will your perpetual stone remind them of their responsibilities
  to humanity
Or must we wait for his infinite voice to come rumbling
  from the black thunder clouds
Over the precipices of doom and into the valleys of death
  "Who will hold back the earth"

Marie Randazzo

WHOM GOD HAS JOINED

Ah! the mischievous — and dancing eyes
  of a thousand and one inquisitive "whys"

Their zest for life — and all things good
  butterflies — rainbows — toys made of wood

Bouquets of dandelions — on the window sill
  playmates at the door — with tummies to fill

Teddy bears covered — so they won't catch cold
  their make-believe world — and kittens to hold

Warm summer wind — and sun in their hair
  times they cry out — just to know we are there

Brushing away — the tears they shed
  wishing their hurts — were ours instead

Bedtime stories — and kisses good night
  the joy in our hearts — as we turn out the light

Watching them grow — day after day
  till the tiniest freckle — has faded away

Sharing their troubles — heartaches — and doubt
  talking things over — and working them out

Then — suddenly it seems — they are fully grown
  anxious — to face the world on their own

We laugh — and pretend — though a part of us dies
  when they're ready to go — and we've said our good-byes

But no matter how long — or far they may roam
  the road they love best — is the one that leads home.

Marilyn Jimerson Brewer

LAURA, A THREE

Well, to the couch she's headed;
Her arms are full of books.
If looks could shatter
But it really doeesn't matter at all
For everything is ready,
I can no longer stall.

She points out every tiny bug,
Each little, bitty mouse
And follows up in some detail
About the mousies' house.
"Oh, yes that is a birdie a-singing in a cage."
Then, with great deportment, demands, "Turn-a-page."

This turn-a-page goes on and on
Until at last I see:
She's reaching for another book
And looks right straight at me.
"This is Dr. Seuss," she says, so to engage
And I am really ready, when she says, "Turn-a-page."

Now there is a little book, I know,
Where little girls were all just so,
With ribbons and lace and each little face
Is fat and blank and round.
But not so saucy Laura, example of, Her Age
For there is no hesitation, when she says,
"Turn-a-page."

June Clogston

THE CHANGING OF OUR TIMES

We're living in a time of change,
Although love is the answer,
Still many remain the same.

Each time the wind blows, it brings
About a change, and the many smiles
We see, are not really smiles, but
Reflections of the hidden rains.

To be caught up in the times,
Where giving up is so easy,
When no one seems to care.

To see fear so prevalent in many faces today,
And still to find so many speechless, without
Constructive and unselfish words to say.

For the lands over to be stricken, by a
Hunger for love and companionship,
Is the type of famine in the end,
That will destroy us all.

The winds are blowing,
The change is here,
Try to remember to love and share,
The choice is up to you.

Wanda J. Pugh

BEWARE! SADISTIC RUGS

A trip — a slip and down I went.
Felled by a scatter-rug event.
Why can't it stay a welcome mat,
Unwrinkled — then I won't fall flat?
I'd pulled a "something" in my back
Which pinched my sacroiliac.
Today I move less chipperly,
Why chance another slippery?
Sadistic rugs enjoy my flips,
To hear my snapping bones and yips.
My accident creates such hob,
I need a reassembly job!

Margaret R. Otis

A FRAGILE LEAF

I am a leaf
yes!
that fragile!
I'm floating in the air.
I left the tree
I'm falling down
and all I see
is the
cold
ground.

The ground is very
dangerous
a footstep's all it takes,
and I'll be crushed forever . . .
Is that to be my fate?

Barbara Bell-Teneketzis

THE FAULTFINDER

I vow to always wear a frown,
And look for someone to run down.
No situation can exist
That I can't give an ugly twist.

If I see someone who is glad
I'll find a way to make him sad.
I punch and probe. I stab and pick.
That is how I get my kicks.

I frown all day — I frown all night.
I find what's wrong and hide what's right.
I carry a chip on my shoulder
And it grows as I get older.

Very outstanding you may be,
But I'll find plenty wrong with thee.
Good deeds you may ever do,
But I'll make them look bad on you.

I find fault with everything.
I'd find a flaw in an angel's wing.
I don't know why the world can't see
That all are out of step, but me.

I hope someday to find my way
Up to the pearly gates
But I'll lay odds of ten to one
The pearls are not in straight.

Flossie H. Smith

FLOSSIE HATFIELD SMITH. Married: Joe R. Smith; Education: Concord College, Athens, West Virginia, B.S.; Themes: *I have written about 20 poems. They are the humorous type. Several of them are about occupations, especially teaching school.*

MY SISTER — MY FRIEND

You have a heart made of gold
It can neither be bought or sold
You have a sympathetic ear
Never prejudging what you hear
I tell you my troubles at length
To me, you're a tower of strength
You're like a breath of fresh air
Always calm, always there
You're like a rainbow after a rain
Always consoling others in pain
You're my sister, my best friend
On whom I can always depend
My love for you goes beyond today
You're special to me in every way
For that, I thank God every day.

Ann E. Abrams

THE FARMER

I go walking by clear waters
Where spring's gentler breezes blow
With an eye upon the otter
Speckled tadpoles cautiously go
Willows' lashes weeping down
To rest upon the river bed
If indeed they weep, they've found
A home here by the river's edge.

Amid zigzagging split rail fences
And ancient barns now falling in
The farmer's face has no pretenses
As he tills the land again
Perhaps this season shall be good
It's all in chance he's understood
From the day he first began
To trust the dark and fertile land.

When I was a child I dipped my toes
Down where the soft green willow grows
And took for granted all my corn
Knowing not how just one storm
Could leave so many empty plates
But now I can appreciate
The places I have carelessly been
And the farmer called "just Jake" back then.

Julie Markham

LAY TENDERLY THE FRAGILE TIMBERS

He had no cathedral to show —
 no stained glass, steeple.

His congregation was small, poor —
His community changing, transient.

He felt his ministry something less
 than a pastorate.

But unwittingly he told of true success:
 of winning a desperate young divorcee
 and saving her from prostitution —
 of teaching a tall man to read,
 taking away his embarrassment
 and turning it into dignity and strength.

Lay tenderly the fragile timbers,
 O my brother,
For you build the true temple,
 the very house of God —
Your building will stand
 when the cathedrals are gone.

Francis Marquis DuBose

STARTING OVER

You can mend a crushed leaf.
 But will all the pieces fit
exactly as they were before?

Barbara Bell-Teneketzis

Night falls, the sun slowly sets in loneliness.
Heavy silence fills the air, a dim lamp lights the room.
How many nights has he sat there,
Tears slowly rolling down his face?
How many nights has he rolled over,
Just to find an empty place?
He knows — she's gone forever.
The house is cold. The nights so long.
He has nothing to hold on to.
And when the day finally comes,
The sun alone cannot enlighten him.

You awake to a day clean and rosy.
Busy feet, happy smiles
To share and greet.
You have no fear of the cold around you,
Because your spirit is jolly.
And even though your tears do fall,
That will never compare
To the lonely stare, that is always there
Before he turns the light off.

Kristen L. Marsh Anderson

MOUNTAINS

There once was a mountain I could not climb,
and a river I could not swim.

There once was a morning I could not laugh,
and a night I could not dream.

There now comes no more empty days and nights,
for the void that once could not, is gone.

It died once upon a dreamless night,
when rivers flowed and mountains rose.

When mornings entered, instead of dawned.
When nights came with black, that shed no light.

For now I have found me a man, that calls me wife.
Together we dream of forgotten dreams.

A birth has taken place;
The universe sleeps on.

Elizabeth A. Cornele

I WOULD — IF YOU WOULD

I would move the world for you and hold back the depressing rains
If you would but be honest with me and stop your foolish games.

I would be wise and have the Midas touch to turn your dreams to truth
If you would but be my own true mate and stop acting so uncouth.

I would brighten your darkest mood and bring on the cleansing rain
If you would but trust in me, my love, and stop this torturous pain!

I would be all that you could wish, stand strong and calm at your side
If you would but show the love for me you so desperately try to hide.

I would, my love, if you would.

Lorey Umberger

OUTGROWN LOVE

Where is the love and laughter we knew?
When did it leave? Where is it it flew?
There once was another place in time
Where things had meaning, rhythm and rhyme.
But we grew differently, you and I,
And somewhere along the way love died.
Now we're two strangers in the same house
Maybe it's better if you're no longer my spouse.
We both might be happier not to mourn love lost,
Rather get on with our lives and absorb the cost.
We're no longer the people we were at the start
Can't we be friends though our lives must part?
Let's remember the love and laughter we knew
As we both start over our lives anew.
Don't let bitterness, anger or pain
Thwart you from your future gain.
For what you once gave me, I wish you the best:
Success, love, happiness and a life filled with zest.

Lorey Umberger

TO MY SPECIAL FRIEND

May the happiest of birthdays be yours this year
May the road you follow always remain clear.
For what you've given me, thank you isn't enough
And finding words to express my feeling is tough.

You've stuck by me through bad times and good
You've given me support when no one else would.
You've gentled my soul and made me trust again
I've untold wealth with you as my friend.

You gave me truer words softly spoken
When I was down and my spirit was broken.
You've given me strength, happiness and hope
When I'd have given up, you taught me to cope.

You're a special person, a special friend indeed
Who always seems to know just what I need.
And for your birthday I wish you untold
Success, love and happiness returned tenfold.

Have a super wonderful birthday!

Lorey Umberger

THE ANGELS

Have you seen angels treading on this land?
Why — you haven't? Come and look over there —
Those three figures beside the corner stand
Behind the pile of clothes and food to share.
Whom can it be that they down there await
In such a time of year with Christmas near?
Whom but the tramps and those in needy state,
Whom in their hearts they hold equally dear.
For what do they give up their cozy home
And choose to share the cold with those low-down,
Who through the dirty gelid snow-mush roam?
For money, medal, honor, or for crown?
  True angels don't descend the world above;
  True angels live in us with care and love.

Z. Lite Cai

BOOK OF LOVE

In my book of pages,
Stuck together with some glue,
I tried to place each precious thing
That I have known with you.
Like cards, and poems, and flowers
All pressed into their place
I've found a memory for my mind
That time cannot erase.
I cannot press a phone call, or
The places we have gone,
Or your touch that means so much.
I could go on and on.
I cannot press the tears I've
Shed for times we were apart,
Or the love within your eyes
Or the pounding of my heart.
I'll pack away my book of love
To start another new,
And fill it like I did the first
With all my love for you.

Bonnie N. Anderson

TOTAL BROWN

What keeps these people living here
in a world of total brown
even the greenest shades are stained
like old army tanks coming down.

A green front lawn is laid in squares
purchased from the nearest town
but within the next few weeks
it too will earn a shade of brown.

Is all Nevada shaded brown
by tones of dirt and dust
painted by the hand of *God*
so many shades of rust.

Could be these people living here
stay to fill their cup
with the beautiful sight at daybreak
when the mighty sun comes up.

I for one would like to see
a far more beautiful day
when the snow will blanket this valley
in *God's* picturesque array.

The living can't be easy
in this valley of shaded brown
but the rewards I know are many
when the quiet is tumbling down.

Don't tell us about your cities
paved and dust free within your reach
of buses, trains, planes and people
we won't listen to you preach.

These are neighbors helping neighbors
to carry out *God's* simple scheme
with room to grow food or person
life is more than just a dream.

Bonnie N. Anderson

THOUGHTS OF YOU

Sometimes when I'm alone,
or sad and blue,
I take a few moments,
to think of you.

I think of your body —
your face and your mind.
Your thoughts and your feelings,
that stay on your mind.

You're always so happy,
cheerful and free.
Your thoughts and your feelings,
mean a lot to me.

So whenever you're alone,
feeling sad and blue,
Please just remember
I'll always love you.

Michele Lopez

ARE THE COMPOSER AND THE PIANIST THE SAME PERSON?

My mind keeps returning
to the picture of your face.
(Stripped of the superfluous flesh,
it had taken on the luster
of polished marble, and you were,
like some modern-day David,
statuesque, immobile, and nearer
perfection in the encroaching nakedness.)
I was struck by the beauty
of your dissolution.

I'm talking about the place
where a person stands, forever
anchored in tangible space.
How long can the question remain
poised without at once recalling
the familiar reference point
of a word, a name, a picture . . .
a face? This shadow falling
upon the ground is mine, not yours.
(My mind keeps returning.)

Tom Bruhn

HEARTBREAK

The hard cement numbed through my coat
As the January wind blew by.
He leaned up against the wall
Trembling at the words I spoke.
My thoughts came out as ice-cold breath
And shivering I took my hand from his.
Warm tears ran down my face
As I stared at the starlit sky.
"But you said you loved me."
I turned and saw his shadowed face
Then looked away again.
"I'm sorry." I wiped tears away
And left him there alone.

And people passed by, laughing, on their way.

Jane Marchant

I WORSHIPED HIM

I loved him more than I can tell.
His gentle smile I knew so well.
His kiss, as soft as falling snow,
Always gave my heart a glow.
He'd hold me close and calm my fears,
I had his heart for many years.
With his tender touch and loving care,
I worshiped him beyond compare.

I gave to him my girlish heart,
We laughed to think we'd ever part.
His love for me was strong and true,
The years flew by but our love stayed new.
He was my lover and my friend,
We never dreamed our love could end.
But he left our world and my heart died too.
I worshiped him, my love so true.

I've learned to live again and yet,
Though my tears have dried I can't forget
The nights, so filled with grief and pain,
When I ache to see my love again.
To see his face and hear his laughter,
And I pray we'll be as one, hereafter.
He comes back to haunt my dreams, and still
I worshiped him and always will.

Helen Ramsey-Wilder

HELEN RAMSEY WILDER. Born: Washington, North Carolina, 7-1-22; Widow; Occupation: Retired and doing lots of volunteer work; Memberships: Palm Springs Writers Guild; Navy League; Retired Officers Ladies Club; American Cancer Society; Eisenhower Auxiliary; Awards: Golden Poet Award for 'Seasons of Despair,' 1987; Poetry: 'What You Mean To Me,' *American Poetry Anthology*, 1987; Comments: *I'm writing some children's poems. I plan to have my grandson do the artwork for them and put them into a children's book. Also doing a series of prose on the life of man — from birth to death!*

SPUN

Around we spin,
Spinning 'round the sun.
So little gained,
So little done.

Danny O'
(Daniel Harris Hellman)

BRAND-NEW BABY

Grandpa's sitting in his rocking-chair,
  has room for a new grandbaby on his knee.
Tiffney and Zandra, twin sisters, helped with
  household chores, just awaiting for me.

Jason Ryan, my brother, chose blue booties for me;
  friends gave bottles, blankets, and toys,
My parents read stacks of books, searching
  lists of names for girls and boys.

Telephone message: "A bouncing baby boy!
  8 pounds, 5 ounces," related with joy.
My name, Jesse Brandon, fits me to a tee;
  October 20, 1984, a birthday just for me.

Aunts and uncles cuddle me, and
  comfort me each time I wrinkle my nose,
Cousins Jody and Lisa think I'm grand,
  and giggle when they tickle my toes.

Grandma says, "God made all babies look so sweet,
  helpless, soft and small.
Little messes really, voices loud and squeally,
  with tantrums, no manners, no shame at all.
Moments spent with little ones
  can't be bought with silver or gold.
They're from the storehouse of God;
  precious memories can never be sold."

Juanita J. Wallis

PROFESSIONALS

Many would-be professionals think
  they'll set the world ablaze,
But in time only a flicker
  is detected through the haze.

Professional life seems so easy,
  applying all that skilled know-how;
Easy as a cowpuncher's life when he's
  breaking a bronc, or trailing a cow.

True, professionals also have heart-
  rending problems once in a while,
But so often are unselfishly set aside
  as they walk the second mile.

The cowpuncher and me know a professional who
  uses latest skills and tools of the trade;
Interested in saving teeth, and with the help
  of Mother Nature he's got it made.

It takes patience when you have patients
  (when the appointment book's full)
Who telephone a message: "Tell Doc
  I've a tooth to fill; one to pull,
And tell Doc I can't pay my bill!"

The professional we know has patients,
  and patience either way we look;
A dentist from Clovis, New Mexico,
  by the name of Dr. Jerry W. Crook.

Juanita J. Wallis

WOES OF THE BEEF PRODUCER

The image of the beef producer,
  or at least in the public eye:
"Cowpunchers are a stubborn bunch
  who dream of pie-in-the-sky."

Nobody cares that cattle ranchers are
  independent, and just as soon be left alone,
True, nobody's concerned about the cattle industry;
  they just want their Ox-Tail and T-Bone.

Often our children need an interpreter
  when we send them into town;
City cousins don't understand our lingo,
  they scratch their heads and frown.

New York bankers, politicians, and futures market
  created problems for beef producers years ago,
Now, the dairy "whole-herd" buyout, and
  hundreds of bureaucrats need to go.

Cowpunchers don't care what the public thinks,
  producing the best "Beef" consumers can buy
Is the reality of the independent cattle rancher,
  and dream of punching cows 'til the day we die.

Juanita J. Wallis

DAISY JUANITA WALLIS. Born: Jordan, New Mexico, 10-10-29; Married: W. J. (Bill) Wallis; Education: Self-educated; Occupations: Cattle rancher, Cow-calf-yearling operation; Awards: Golden Poet Award for 'Peace on Earth,' 1986; Honorable Mention for 'Mama's Wood Cookstove,' 1986; Poetry: 'Stars and Stripes, *American Poetry Anthology,* 1987; 'Life Compared to a Rose,' *Best New Poets of 1986,* American Poetry Association, 1986; 'Signs of Winter,' *American Poetry Anthology,* 1987; Comments: *I write New Mexico history, cowboy poetry, ranch life, and stories for children. I also write season's greetings and scriptural verses.*

INITIATE SUCCESS

I see a vision of the future that is clear.
It is a winner's plan of life. Success is drawing near.

The path is steep and rough and calls for courage keen.
Enthusiasm paves the way. Bright hope is ever seen.

The picture is indelible and it will stay
A charted map upon my heart. It is as clear as day.

By visualizing such success, I now have run
Up that wild path with confidence. My victory is won.

Dorothy E. Smith

RELEASE

Have you ever wondered why
The many passers-by
Both old folk and young
Strolling sweethearts and joggers too
From that limb that hung
From that tree, across the path
Simply could not resist
To snatch a leaf to twirl
Or give some twig a twist?

There is magic there I see
It does the same to me.

Evangeline Aten

BELONG

Jesus said, help me to live.
To live one must forgive.
To love and help each other,
and always love your brother.
A person in need,
is a friend indeed.
One to count on,
and help you see the dawn.
Jesus he died,
and we did cry;
for we could finally understand
he was more than a man.
So if you get low,
search deep in your soul;
look for that trait
that kept him narrow and straight.
Jesus, he walked
and Jesus, he talked.
He tried to show us right from wrong
and how everyone, can belong.

David Hartman

YOU NEEDED ME

A fragile flower
choking with life's thorns —
You stooped and cleared the tears away
and gave it room to grow.
You missed a fragrant rose in bloom.
You needed me.
Love is like that, they say.

A baby bird
having fallen from its nest —
You bent and gently cradled it
in your dear calloused hands.
You longed to hear a robin sing.
You needed me.
Love is like that, they say.

You needed me.
And, oh, I needed to be needed so
in your kind loving way.
For you I'll bloom my brightest hues;
for you I'll sing my sweetest songs
because you needed me.
Love is like that, they say.

Joan Cissom

DISCOVERY

We were both in the world
Yet out of the world, lost,
In our shadows of solitude
Until at last we were
Together

Then a new light
Illuminated the shadows
And a new love
Softened the edge
Of despair

And we found ourselves
Back in the world
A world that was there
No longer

Evangeline Aten

BURIED ROADS

The snow will bury roads,
that I have traveled.

Please hurry glorious winter,
the time is short.

You will be my friend
and help me forget.

Your blankets of white,
will keep me warm and safe.

Safe from the memories
of those traveled roads,
that you will soon bury with snow.

Mitzi J. Bartée

MITZI J. BARTÉE. Born: Northville, Michigan; Education: Student of registered nursing, Kettering College of Medical Arts, Kettering, Ohio; Diploma in Medical Assisting, 1983; Memberships: Student Nurse Association; Poetry: 'Restless Hours,' *American Poetry Anthology,* 1987; Comments: *Having a 12-year work history in the field of health, I've had opportunity to witness much human suffering, the worst kind of which I believe to be emotional. My hope, as a nurse, is to contribute to my patients' emotional well being, as well as their physical well-being, by allowing them to vent their feelings. One of my own releases is through writing poetry.*

CONTINUITY

The beach stretched,
long and white,
then curved —
questioningly —
into the sea;
and the sea —
indefatigueable —
flirted with the land,
swelling and shrinking
upon the shore.
Amid laughter
and a search for shells
we laid footprints
in the sun-warmed sand
until insidious waters
jealously blurred —
then erased — the mark
of our finite passage.
And, once again,
the beach stretched,
enduring, timeless,
and curved —
mutely —
into the sea.

Gail V. Baker

THE MONTH OF THE PINK MOON

Come walk with me through the woods
in April
The month called the month of the
pink moon
So named by the Indians of long
past ages
For the mystery and the magic of the
moon-song eternal . . .

Come walk with me, wear soft moccasins,
carry a bright feather
Walk lightly over the tender, fresh
bed of spring
Drink with me at the fountain of rebirth
of all nature
And revel in the magic of life's
silken wonder . . .

Remember the fragrance of the locust trees
rampant with blossoms
And if you remember, perchance a yellow
butterfly
Will lift its wings over a buttercup
before you
And you will walk forever through the
month of the pink moon!

Evangeline Aten

All I can do is my best
All I can be is myself
All I can share is my love.

Mary Ellen R. Calitri

STRANGER IN THIS WORLD

I'm a stranger in this world and feel so out of place.
One day I shall leave it to again see the Master's face.

Deep within the caverns of my soul is a mysterious non-consuming
    burning.
I have set forth into this world on a pilgrimage of learning.

I linger but for a time here to absorb all the spectacular reds
  and golds of a crisp October morn.
Time and time again, I stand in awe of new life being born.

As the seasons change, rain and water turn to snow and ice.
There are such intricate complexities and yet they're so concise.

The trees will sleep in winter and blossom in the spring.
There's a variety of creatures, some of fur and some of wing.

I'm longing to go back there, to the world whence I came.
From experiences in this one, I know I'll not depart the same.

I long to return to my Father, to His world beyond the moon.
I'm anxious for my journey's end. It could never be too soon.

Sandra Higley Scott

THERE IS NONE

  What do I need?

Freedom from pain! And there is none.
Recognition, for what I can do! Not what I've done . . .
And there is none.
Healing for my muscle disease! And there is none.
Finances too, but there is none.
But there is one thing I do have!
Faith in God and hope . . .
This I have! And then some . . .

Sue Naylor

THE LOST DREAM

Today i found a dream
i know it's a dream
because i felt the clouds
so intense drifting by . . .

This world of reality
is petty-pitty
nothing has caressed me
My mind and mood were steady!
Where did i go when
i wished it would happen; into the sea of you and me . . .

There's a deep-colored cloud in the way
all i see is a long dark bay
the sky shaped as a heart . . .

. . . of what do i want to see?

Why are things so blind
can we not see far behind
blindness is now on my mind
for you . . .
    for me . . .
        for *loving* . . .

No one really knows how to feel, there are many layers to be peeled
soon — you should not feel; fears or tears
go away with a pride that is guilt; just a lost dream barely built . . .

Deborah L. Sorgani

A LOVER'S FORSAKEN JOYS

I wanted to watch the sun rise on an early summer's day
Thinking that it would drive all my sorrows away
I wanted to walk past the beach, barefooted in the sand
Imagining the two of us walking hand in hand
I wanted to feel a cool breeze capture me by surprise
To help me imagine the sparkles of love in your eyes
I wanted to hear the birds sing in harmony
Creating sweet visions of you and me
I wanted to reach out to you in your times of need
Hoping to put you and your pains at ease
I wanted to openly give you the key to my heart
Without the fear of having it torn apart
I wanted to share all my secrets and desires
But I was afraid to get burned by the lover's fire
I wanted to share all the joys of love with you
But I was afraid that you didn't want me to
I wanted to feel the gentleness of your lips against mine
Tasting the sweetness for the very first time
I wanted to watch the sun set beyond the ocean's bay
Knowing that you and your love would be mine someday
I often looked to the stars at night and said a little prayer
Hoping that it would increase my courage to say, ''I care''
There were so many things that I wanted us to share
But we have lost them all because I was afraid to say, ''I honestly care.''

M. G. Mitchell

A PAGAN'S DREAM

'Twas a pagan's dream that stilled a storm.
In the old church tower
    The dream played chimes,
    Once, twice, and many times.

'Twas a pagan's dream that sang with the wind.
At the dust of a form
    A dream made love
    One, two, three stars above.

'Twas a pagan's dream that shown on the moon.
As the form was kissed
    The dream played chimes.
    Once, twice, and many times.

Eileen Bates

THERE'S MORE TO THANKSGIVING

There's more to Thanksgiving than gobbling the gobbler
There's more to Thanksgiving than heaping the plate
There's more to Thanksgiving than gobbling the gobbler
There's more to Thanksgiving than how much you ate
There's friendship and sharing
And caring for others
There's cousins and uncles, sisters and brothers
There's friends and neighbors, fathers and mothers
And stopping to think of the plight of others
There's parades in the streets with bands of all hue
Majorettes and drummers and funny cars too
There's floats and animals, the policeman and the clown
And on this day Santa Claus comes to town.
There's more to Thanksgiving than gobbling the gobbler
There's more to Thanksgiving than heaping the plate
Give thanks to God for what He's given you
Give thanks to God for what's on your plate
Remember the pilgrims and what they went through
Give thanks to God it didn't happen to you
It all started with the pilgrims and what they ate
Yes, there's more to Thanksgiving than gobbling the gobbler
There's more to Thanksgiving than heaping the plate.

Leo Feebish

NOSTALGIC INTERLUDE

An old book was dusted
And from between the pages
Ashes of roses fell at my feet

Memories so faded and rusted
With years that seemed like ages
Again caused my heart's quicker beat

But like visions of dropping dewdrops
Swiftly disappearing in the sunlight
From the leaves before my eyes

So the last vestige of an old love
With the faint aroma from the pages
Soon melted in the air with my sighs.

Evangeline Aten

EVANGELINE ATEN. Pen Name: Evangeline
Rayworth; Married: Robert G. Aten, Sr., 1969;
Education: Texas State College for Women, 2
years; University of New Mexico, Albuquerque,
Special Art Student; Occupation: Artist & Designer, ''Patio Fashions''; Memberships: National
League of American Pen Women; Creative
Writers Group of Las Cruces; Poetry: 'Old
Baldy,' 1954; 'An Adventure,' 1986; 'Another
Dedicated Man,' 1985; 'Mirage On the Mesa,'
1967; Other Writings: ''Wiggle,'' children's
story, 1949; Comments: *My educational preparation and my work have been in fine art and
design. However, from my high school days I
have loved and written poetry, as well as a few
children's stories. Most of my poetry resulted
from notes made while I was experiencing intense
emotional states; sadness, exuberance, extreme
joy and anger. I have completed 30 to 40 pieces
of poetry of varying lengths. I presently reside in
New Mexico, where I have found once more the
sunshine of my youth.*

Who is she?
Who smiles with me.
Her every movement
Is of graceful design
A greater gentleness
Gives her body-line.

There she goes
A gentle rose.
Have I been
With her before?
I feel it gently
In my inner core.

Alois Fersching

POWER LOVE

Words of power, words of thrust
Thoughtform of love, sent on waves of lust.
You push, I pull
Trying to change the here and now.
I turn you
Turn you on
Turn you into — my ideal love.

You're a new acquaintance,
With fresh seed to sow.
I'm a good friend lying here,
You've never had before.
You push, I pull
You turn me
Turn me on.
Turn me into — your ideal love.

Laura Irene Ernst

PARAMETERS

We are not bound
  to any time or place.
Spurred by imagination
  we are propelled
    into exotic lands
    or borne forward
      into space.
Cued gently by scent or song
  we transcend time —
    in laughter or in tears —
      reliving life's rare moments.
Fired by inspiration
  our thoughts leap forward —
    in anxiety or in joy —
      toward all our dreams design.
We are not bound
  to any place or time.

Gail V. Baker

WHITE DRESS

Just to let you know,
I didn't spend all
the money, dear,
On milk, e-g-g-s, et-cet-er-a.

Instead I found
a white wool dress,
at Jacobsen's downtown.
It's not too frilly,
not too simple,
just right.
It doesn't just hang,
it clings
in all the right spots.
It feels soft and silky,
in a woolly sort of way.
It will go with everything.
Jackets, scarves and hats
will make it posh,
A simple strand of pearls
will make it elegant.

Please understand, dear
It is me.

Nancy L. Williams

QUIET MADNESS

This quiet madness,
No one knows.
It steals upon my mind.
Sanity's thief or sanity's relief?
This quiet madness becomes complete.

This quiet madness,
Don't you know,
First fills the form, then breaks the mold.
This quiet madness
Takes shape of its own.

This quiet madness,
Like a subtle storm,
Blows the mind and blocks the norm.
This quiet madness
slips sanity's crown.

Laura Irene Ernst

MIND DESIGN

Turning on dead-end corners
In the maze that is my mind.
I find the past my only hold.
The present too hard to find.
I'm terrified of leaving this space,
'Cause, to all but the sane,
There is some comfort to be found
In familiar, oh too familiar, pain.

My soul lies —
In puddles of yesterday's dreams,
Floating on my fear, breathing
The breath that is the past.
Not knowing how long this existence will last.
Too afraid to shake the labyrinthine daze.
Too weak to break out
of my cocoon of pain.

Laura Irene Ernst

FIRE

A tiny spark, will soon ignite.
The twigs within, its fiery site.

To set ablaze, my heart's desire.
Fulfill with warmth, and awe inspire.

Your roaring flames, now rising high.
Competing with, the starlit sky.

It seems are there, in brilliant flight.
To capture my spirits, and make my night.

Just like the stars, up in the sky.
As clouds will hide them, floating by.

Your flames will cease, coals whistle and cry.
Then to smoke, you will turn, and slowly die.

But in the morning, I'll wake you up.
Put on some coffee, and fill my cup.

Phyliss Estrada

CAPE HORN

WINGS OF LOVE

Forgotten names,
Long lost streets,
Fallen dreams . . .
Harmless wanderers
Who occupy park bench seats.

Soulless spirits,
Widowed monks,
Lonely travelers . . .
Motionless human beings
Who sleep beneath silent tree trunks.

Let all equal men
Who destiny hath failed,
Through the cold cruel swallowing blow
Caused to the shattered
Freedom's dove,

Be touched by the graceful
Resounding brotherhood of man,
Pledged through the "Wings of Love."

Douglas R. Haney

Where do we,
People of my generation,
Look to find hope and sweet inspiration?
With this great world, as it is today,
Does one still truly believe in,
The good ol' American Way?
Homeless, living in the streets.
Children who know only of defeat.
Have you yet one of those faces to meet?
Nuclear weapons by the millions.
What if they should destroy our heavens?
Politicians who hold the future in their hands.
Who can't remember.
Who don't understand.
Teachers who guide our upcoming voices.
Have to make sacrifices and limited choices.
Disease that is spreading faster than we realize.
Innocent are dying.
Is there even a glimmer of hope in their eyes?
I find comfort in my memories.
In the music that I listen to.
In the heroes of yesterday.
In my friends, that are true.
With the love of my family.
What about you?

Gina M. Scabet

LORD GIVE ME BACK
MY HEALTH, I PRAY

Hallucinating isn't fascinating
When struggling to hold onto life
No control — Of your very soul
Just eternal strife.

Fighting illusion to a sad conclusion
Of a real-life play
That was me — as I was there
Yet oh! So far away!

Give me back my health, I pray

Emily B. Green

BAND OF RED

The Band of Red that we wear
Shows all others that we care.

POWs, MIAs are alive in a foreign land
We must show them we understand.

Each Red Band is for one who fell
He is spending his time in hell.

Trying hard not to let others know
Our tears we try not to show.

The pain we feel for those we lost
Hardly anyone can know the cost.

Our time and lives are spent
To Viet Nam we were sent.

A lot of our buddies are still alive
By their guts they survive.

Waiting and hoping they will be free
We are left with the memory.

Once again return we shall
We all have spent our time in hell.

Joanne Cara Myers

YESTERDAY

As I sit here all alone
Reality soon evades me
Memories and moments of time ago
Here once again to see.
So I escape to that time
Of you, of me, of us
I feel you holding me closely
Leaving my fears in a rush.
Caressing my body with softness
Whispering lovely words and more
Making love so gently with me
It was I that you adored.
Tenderly kissing me goodnight
Lying naked in the breeze
All these things cloud my mind
And for a moment, I believe.
Then I awake, tears burn my eyes
The time has slipped away
And I remember only then
Those times were yesterday.

Dea Bishop

IN MY HEART

I wish I had a way to say
The love I have for him today.
It's something that I've kept inside.
I thought I would before he died.

I hope that it is not too late
For me to say how he's been great.
From 25 to 87,
I hope he's looking down from heaven.

So please, dear Lord, lend me his ear.
It's the only way to dry my tear.
Sorry dad, I thought you knew,
But if you're listening, *"I love you."*

Victor Lopez

SOMETIMES . . .

Sometimes I am afraid . . .
That you might go away
Leaving me only your memory
Your face, your voice that way.
Sometimes I am afraid . . .
Our someday may never come
You'll be taken away, my dreams will die
Touching you will be done.
Sometimes I am afraid . . .
My star will fade in the sky
And when I look to see it shine
My only vision will die.
Sometimes I am afraid . . .
That life won't let me see
The warmth and surrounding beauty of
Love with you and me.

Dea Bishop

THE RAIN

It's raining now —
And I've fantasized about us
Making love outside
With the cool rain beating down.
It's late at night —
And I'll dream about you
Caressing me
So soft and gentle, but passionately.
It's become dawn —
And I don't want to open my eyes
For you've left now
And won't return for quite some time.
It's striking noon —
And my thoughts begin to wonder
If you think of me
Or ever could the way I do you.
Now the rain's stopped —
And I wake up to reality
But thoughts linger on
Of my most precious times of day.

Dea Bishop

WONDERING

I sometimes wander off
And start to think of you,
Whatever are you doing
Could you be thinking too?

There are mistakes we've made
But that's the way life goes,
Where will we both end up
No one really knows.

Life never gives a second chance
We live and learn each day,
So if we ever met again
Would there be much to say?

So think of all the good times
We surely had a few,
And maybe you can smile
'Cause I'll be smiling too.

Regina Jones

FAIR?

"It's not fair!" you hear the irate child
Screaming and stamping, oblivious to words
Of reason and solace. The spoilt brat. The un-preferred.
Revenge takes root. Does it die or grow in a soul-gone-wild?

So . . . it's not fair, you say,
That man kills man, be he murderer, terrorist,
Vigilante, veteran, drunken-driver, idealist
Or teenager, desperate to having his own way.

Neither is it fair that little creatures
Are caged and abused in the name of science, to aid
In the search for cures of diseases . . . some man-made
Through selfishness . . . but who listens to preachers?

And is it fair that many of the handicapped
Suffer stares and arrogance from those who can?
Can what? Move, go, do independently and
Still complain that life's not candy-wrapped.

So you laze while another enthuses;
You accept today while another grabs the chance
To fulfill a dream, to reach a potential, perchance
To succeed. But is this fair while another loses?

So . . . what *is* fair? Who defines 'fair'?
Some things may seem unfair today but in retrospect
Are proven fair. And tomorrow? Expect
To be the un-preferred. Who cares? If Man will not respect
And obey the Golden Rule, then Life can*not* be fair.

Cole Bourne

SOLITUDE

One night I went for a walk along on the beach.
I remember how sad the sea sounded —
How hauntingly different it seemed from that earlier place
That had been alive with color and the playful screams of children
When the sky seemed white with the brightness of the sun —
But it was the same. Only time had changed.

I slipped one shoe off and took a step. The sand was cold
Where only a few hours before it had burned so hot
That the soles of my feet had danced to gain relief.
A shudder overtook me as a sudden breeze
Shot a cold spray into my face.
I hugged my shoulders tighter under my shawl and looked up
Into what seemed a million blinking eyes.
And standing there on that selfsame shore
Where once I had felt so warm and contented,
I knew for the first time in my life —
Absolute Solitude.

The sea is all around me now, as I sit alone inside this room.
I hear your laughter mingled with the children's voices —
The waves are sighing their night-sombre song;
I see your paints, books and brushes strewn carelessly about
   in the fever of your work —
The ocean breeze blows its chill right down to the depths of me.

The room is the same. Only time has changed.

Donna Blois-Johnston

LET'S YOU AND I BE PROUD

Let's you and I be proud of our country
Let's you and I be proud of our flag
Let's both you and I realize we've got to back our guys
When they go off to fight a foreign war

Let's you and I be proud of our country
Let's you and I be proud of our flag
Let's you and I remember from January to December
We're living in the land of the free

Let's you and I be proud of our country
Let's you and I be proud of our flag
Let's all get together and unite
And do the things that we feel right
Let's make this land a better place in which to live
And ask not what to take but what to give

Let's remember those who fought in foreign wars
And lie buried now on foreign shores
They died for you and me, they died to make us free

Let's remember the red, white and blue
Memorial Day and Veterans Day too
Remember the Alamo, Pearl Harbor and Flag Day
Let's all make the 4th of July our day
Let's give thanks to God for what we are
Let's give thanks that we are free
Let's you and I be proud of our flag
Let's you and I be proud of our country

Leo Feebish

LEO WALTER FEEBISH. Born: Wilkes-Barre, Pennsylvania, 11-8-30; Parents: Leo William Feebish and Ada Elizabeth Tewksbury; Married: Margaret; Education: High school graduate, 1948; Occupations: Hod carrier; Stockboy; Forestry worker; Gas station attendant; Relocation director, urban renewal, Dearborn Heights, Michigan; currently a sales representative; Memberships: Holy Spirit Catholic Church; Jaycees; Boxing Club Coach; March of Dimes Captain; Poetry: 'Christmas is Here,' 'Just a Phone Call Away,' 'Santa's Snowmobile,' 1975; 'You and Me,' 'The Most Beautiful Sound,' 1978; Themes: *I write what I see and feel and I try to express my feelings in my poems. I write for pleasure, not for judges, and I have written over 100 poems to date. I plan to publish my poetry and write an adventure book.*

WINTER SHELTER

Trees are now unclothed of the colorful dress once worn;
All except the pine, whose greens shall always adorn;
It stands mightily 'gainst the others less pronounced;
Protection from the cold is powerfully announced;
Winter friends gathering 'midst the boughs of greenery —
Chattering, chirping, 'bout the snow-white scenery.
Below the deer make use of the sheltered bedding ground.
So respected is the pine by all who shall be found.

Debra J. Barba

WHY? OH WHY?

bayonets in earth so soft
red with blood of
men so bold,
upright rifles
stocks splintered and worn
where hang the helmets
limp and forlorn,
they lie so still
with open eyes
as if to ask the
heavens high;
Why? Oh Why?
the brooding skies
do not reply,
the spectral visions
of the
lake of fire
appear in shadows
misty and cold
to quietly unveil
the shades of below, of
Erebus, Avernus and Zamiel too
and now unblinkingly, the eyes
reveal the answers true;
Why? Oh Why?

Maxwell C. Kaufman

FLIGHT OF LOVE

Come, spend the night with me.
Let me take you into eternity.

We'll fly there on Cloud #9,
And stay there for all time.

Now that our flight has begun,
Is it all right if I call you ''hun''?

On the wings of love,
We will soar above.

Holding hands all the while,
We travel mile after mile.

My heart begins to race,
As we start to embrace.

Our kisses fill the air.
God! You really *do* care!

Merla Cumbow

THE SPIRIT OF LOVE

With His gentle hand He guides me
And showers me with His mercy.
Though I oft forget His ways,
He waits for me with patience,
And smiles, when again I find the path,
And take His hand to steady my steps.
He fills my spirit with His Spirit,
And His loving-kindness wells up in me;
A brook of pure spring water.
His love is a flowing stream of light
That never fades away.
Though the world will pass into darkness,
I will abide with Him always,
In the light of His glorious Love.

Ellen Feller

ARE YOU MY FOREVER LOVE?

You have become a part of my life,
A very special and important part.
You bring me love and you bring me joy.
I treasure the moments we spend together.
It is my hope that as time goes by,
Those moments will expand into days,
The days will grow into months and
The months will melt into years.
I want to know you and be with you
For a very long time.

It was not I who planned our chance meeting.
I was not looking for love
   when I found it in you.
Perhaps someone greater than both of us
Planned it all along, and with His guiding hand
Will help us to bring all our hopes and
All our dreams to fruition, as we grow
In our friendship and love for each other.
I pray that what has begun to grow between us
Was not planted in vain, that we may
Continue to love one another.

Ellen Feller

ELLEN ROSE FELLER. Born: Grand Rapids, Michigan, 7-17-51; Education: Ventura College, Ventura, California, A.A., general liberal arts and sciences; Occupation: Full-time student at Fresno City College; part-time Rainbow sales representative; Poetry: 'Into the Jade,' *American Poetry Anthology,* 1986; 'Silent Surrender,' *American Poetry Anthology,* 1987; Themes: *I write a lot of love poetry, but I also write poetry about my relationship with God, friendships and nature.*

A LONE ROSE

The moonlight's silver-tipped fingers so bold,
reached down for the lone rose below,
its petals newly opened from the fold,
awaiting the new morn's glow.
The night, racing toward the dawn's light,
with the drops of dew,
kissing the lone rose so lightly,
its petals barely opened and new.
The dawn onward rolled
bringing the daylight,
shining down on the lone rose, like gold
And making the dew's gleam so bright.

Edna M. Crunelle

WHEN WE KISSED

When we kissed, electricity went through us and entwined our bodies.

It always amazed me how close spiritually one can get through something as simple as a kiss.

Through every kiss wishing the moment would never end because the grandeur of it was so intense.

The happiness inside me filled me up so much that I felt like a hot air balloon about to burst.

And then after the feeling of ultimate ecstasy fades I settle softly in a period of relaxation — like falling softly on a petal of roses.

Shiree Dandridge

ODYSSEY

And I looked up
   and there were stars
stars so bright that
   they shine over my body
illuminating me as if
   I was one of them

How my spirit was cast
   out of my body floating
as no glider has drifted with
   the wind, as no bird has
flown the heights, nothing brings
   me down, no wind is calm

Up is all I go, higher
   higher, where no other has
been or breathed, seeing
   through one-way glass windows
which are the eyes of my mind

Complex, far-fetched, sci-fi
   adventure that is vast, timeless
intriguing, oh how I can't bear
   being separated from this peacefulness
how harsh and lonely life can
   and will be without dreams and
hopes such as these.

Shiree Dandridge

CRYSTAL PIECES

Counting moments on one hand,
Like the crystal pieces of sand,
These tiny fragments of time
Steal away moments of crime.
Like the slam of a door
Or the feelings of being poor,
Because one didn't want to say,
''I'm sorry for what I did today.''

Patricia A. Newgaard

HAPPY DAYS

The lights are on, a new day has begun
It's 7:45, I must run.

The boss is yelling, the workers are busy.
Here comes the coffee girl . . . Miss Dizzy.

She sees me, oh no!
Nowhere to hide or to go.

Walking to my desk, she slips, what a mess.
She's done it again, dropped coffee down my dress.

Hands me a towel with a sad little smile,
then tells me, "Don't worry, that dress was out of style."

Nighttime has come, I'm no longer on the run.
As there is nothing to do, I watch the dying sun.

The peace and quiet is what I love best,
fed my pets, now it is time to rest.

But then, the morning comes once more,
with the mailman at the door
dog crap on the floor
the building in an uproar
and me, almost sure
that this will be a happy day once more.

Martine Germain

MARTINE EUGENIA GERMAIN. Born: Brooklyn, New York, 11-25-65; Education: Brooklyn College, B.A., 1987; Occupation: Elementary teacher, chapter one mathematics; Memberships: The Sunshine Club, Sewing Associates; Poetry: 'Hell's Mirror,' *Levington, 1983*; Themes: *My poems are an expression of my feelings and an important part of who I am. Writing is freedom and freedom is joy.*

BECOME AS ONE

Come and listen to how it is done, where land and sea become as one.
    Come and listen to how it is done
    ocean symphony muted by fog-dimmed sun.
    Hear the whispered music of watery reeds
    accompanied by notes of the mating grebes.

Come and listen to how it is done, where land and seas become as one.
    Come and listen to what sea sirens say
    "Come dance with us, join our aquatic ballet."
    Hypnotic music of crashing wave
    has lured many a seaman to an early grave.

Yes, come and listen to how it is done,
  where land and seas become as one.

Charlene W. Villella

PROGRESS

The old man with gray in his braids and pain in his eyes
Spoke of ancient ways; days when a man could be proud to be a man.
When he could hunt and fish to provide food,
When he could accomplish his coups with great pride.
When inside each brave there could reside both the bear and the eagle.
When there was laughter in his eyes and on his lips.
When each was allowed to choose his own way.
When names had great meaning, Sitting Bull, Cochese, Crazy Horse.
Now a brave has become a squaw, and worse his mind has become idle.
He has no dignity, he has been turned into a beggar.
He must beg for his food, his clothing,
His very way of life.
All in the name of white man's progress.

Charlene W. Villella

DREAMSCAPE

Old ways hidden deep inside modern man surface in dream wishes.
Campfires burn inhibitions and ancient chants come unbidden
to silent lips.
Feet feel rhythms of echoing drum beats,
    bodies sway to forgotten dance rituals.
Eyes shine with rememberings of past lives.
I walk in the land of my ancestors, head held high with pride.
Braids sway in time to songs sung in lost tongues.
Beads click softly on ceremonial dress as
Mocassined feet walk dance on wind whispers, Goldfeather is
Recognized as becoming a woman and walks into a dream.

Charlene W. Villella

LEAVIN'

The doctor said I was to die so Papa built my coffin.
My mother rung her hands and cried, "She's visit me quite often."
My little sis just looked at me, "This old toad you won't be needin'."
Brother took my shoes away. I told 'um, "I ain't leavin'!"

The preacher even took a stand, now the angels they are waitin'.
I bet they won't know what to do with my wings they are creatin'.
My aunts and uncles always hated me, now they're pretendin'
  to be grievin'.
I grin at them like yesterday and tell 'um, "I ain't leavin'!"

Now Scarlet lives just down the road, never once did she speak freely.
And now she comes with teary eyes. I show my coffin just to please me.
And Granny? Oh, my little granny! I tell her, "You ought not be
  believin'
The sorry tale they tell on me, 'cause Granny, I ain't leavin'!"

The neighbors, they come on tippy toes, they never liked me either.
Now they stare and touch my brow to be sure I have the fever.
The ugly teacher that I have always swore I was deceivin'.
I know she thinks she's rid of me, but, "Teacher I ain't leavin'!"

All this attention was mighty fine till my dog lay by my coffin,
Then all night long it ran through my mind, one doesn't die and die
  very often.
So guess I'd better tell you all I switched blood to get even.
It happened when Doc's back was turned.
"So tell me, Doc. Who's leavin'?"

Mary Ann Taylor

THE LATEST NEWS

Most of the news,
Is read over the breakfast table.
That's just a glance,
For many of us the only chance.

We read, about two giants,
Who signed an alliance.
Or the army took over to rule,
Because the former leader was cruel.

It might be, that after much damage
And noise, there was no other choice.
In spite of sitting for hours at the table,
Some governments are still not very stable.

We read, how the rich nations
Eat too much and too good,
That's why the developing countries,
Don't get enough food.

Or, instead of trying to work better
And harder,
Some think of nothing,
But filling their larder.

Helena M. Jones

A NURSING HOME: THE CHRISTMAS SPIRIT

Where rests this Spirit?
I can hear it:
Rolling softly through these Halls;
Teardrops rolling from these Walls.
Gnarled fingers, clutching Holly;
Deck their brows in weary Folly.
Waiting underneath Mistletoe:
There is no one to kiss them.
There is no one to show
Their Salvation Army presents to.
And so, they are hidden carefully,
As a pleading glance toward anyone
Such as you: upward, longing . . .
Knowing no one shall ever
Truly look and see
Where rests this Spirit.
Oh, but I can hear it:
Rolling softly through these Halls;
Teardrops rolling from these Walls.

Jingle Bells
Jingle Bells
No One Tells

Andrea M. Tait

HYMN TO AMERICA

America, of thee I sing —
I let thy praises gladly ring.
Land of grandeur beyond compare —
I sing thy praises without spare.
Rising from the firmament
Hope of all — anent!
Starry flag and blue sky,
Broad prairies rich with rye,
Rushing rivers, mighty oaks,
Beeches, birches in numberless hosts,
Swift-flying eagle, mighty and proud,
Laurel-crowned above the crowd!
Liberty's dream!
Yet shaken by furies that threaten the dream!

Rise above! 'Tis dross — not turf!
You are chosen of the earth!
Lead mankind afar — above!
Teach the world to love! — to love!
Meet your destiny firm and strong.
Do not fear the blight of wrong!
Mankind tortured, shackled, bent —
To your torch seeks hope of relent!
   Beauty springs from liberty.
You alone can set men free!

Chester Michael Matzner

SONG OF BIRMINGHAM

Slam, clang — slam,
Song of Birmingham!
Hammer, tongs — anvil,
Muscle, brawn — shovel —
Vulcan's flame and smoke —
Mountain, lime and coke
Slam, clang — slam,
   Song of Birmingham!

Muscles of the South
Sinews of Dixie's Youth —
Vital, clanging, strong —
With no sense of wrong —
Crackers pouring in
Brawling, whoring, hustling
With no sense of sin.
Slam, clang — slam,
   Song of Birmingham!

Working, whoring, hustling
With great iron muscling
Slam, clang — slam,
   Song of Birmingham!

Chester Michael Matzner

TYPIST'S LAMENT

Type, type, type —
Nothing to do but type!
Keys, jam, slam!
Nobody gives a damn . . .!
Since I came from Alabam!

Type, type, tripe —
When will it ever end?
When will I ever see
The steamboat 'round the bend?

Type, type, type —
   Soon I will have to scream!
Soon, unable to dream —
Sleep, sleep, sleep —
My soul creeps to the deep.

Type, tripe, type —
Swirl, curl, hurl —
My head is in a whirl!
Window open wide —
Out of it I will glide!

Fly, fly, fly —
Fly, fly, far away —
Into a land of play,
   My soul will drift away!

Chester Michael Matzner

THE EMERALD FOREST

The enchanted wood.
Gentle, peaceful
enhanced by an ethereal splendor.
Here
the sun never ceases to shine
spreading its golden blanket over
the emerald forest.
When I enter my secret haven
the lime-colored reflection
casts an hypnotic spell
that fills my whole being.
The emerald trees
provide a natural roof for my comfort
in slumber, I lie tranquil,
but in my unconscious
I search for that precious gem
that gave the enchanted forest
its name.

Lucia Figliomeni

TO BE SO BLESSED

For Marge Foley

While others feverishly chase rabbits
and rock their boats with every changing cry

you translate goodness into deeds
and spread your karmic blanket across the stars

and find easter in each blade of grass
and poetry in the hummingbird,
haikus in the poppy's eye and aging
wisdom in listening to mountains grow.

no wonder you are so laughingly, so humorously, so
young

Richard Alan Bunch

SO PRECIOUS, MY JEWELED MEMORIES

Ah . . .
Rubies and diamonds and sapphires have I,
Glinting like stars in the distant sky —
Memories of yesteryear.
Precious these jewels in their golden box,
Yet never a need for key or locks,
For what are they but memories —
Memories of a childhood slipping by,
Dreams of a girl whose love is nigh,
Moments of laughter mingled with patter
       of tiny feet,
Sylvan scenes of crystal streams
       and leaping deer,
Of wild birds soaring far beyond
Cattails growing in their hidden pond,
Of saffron sails in the sunset's gleam,
Awaiting the moon's first silvery beam —
Poignant dreams and memories,
These are the jewels I hold so dear,
As evening shadows draw slowly near,
And darkness begins to fall.

Laurene G. Charlebois

LAURENE G. CHARLEBOIS. Born: Houston, Minnesota, 8-18-13; Married: Leo Charlebois, 1940, Widowed; Education: St. Olaf College, B.A., magna cum laude, 1936; Metropolitan School of Business; American Institute of Banking; Occupation: Escrow officer; Memberships: St. Olaf Honors Society; St. Olaf Alumni Association; Business and Professional Women's Club; Awards: Various college scholarships; Poetry: 'To Stacey, A Tribute,' *Best New Poets of 1986;* 'House of Memories,' *The Art of Poetry,* 1985; 'Eternal Love,' *Hearts on Fire,* 1985; 'To My Daughter And To My Son,' *American Poetry Anthology,* 1983.

SIMPLE EVIDENCE

Deadly bored
from hours of computer-processed paperwork
and numbers spewed from a calculator
to prove I-don't-know-what
(it still wasn't right)
I looked up from my desk this morning
just in time
to see through the office window
a white butterfly
alight on a broad green leaf
to bask in the June sun,
and I was blessed by the brightness of its wings
and the delicate beauty of its flight.
That such a small and fragile thing could
in a split second of effortless perfection
stir my heart to life
is proof enough of God.

Donna Blois-Johnston

SILENT FORTRESS

I thought of you tonight
and how there're too many ways
that we don't touch.
Nothing seems so real to me
as the way we do, when we do,
and in those moments when you look at me —
really look at me —
I see worlds in your eyes
spinning out to infinity . . .
But the memory isn't enough
to last me through the silence.

I will no longer so fear the broadening moat
that I charge the walls of your fortress,
heedless of the bricks with which it has been built.
I can only bloody my bare fists
and avail no entry
until you willingly, peering out at me
from the cold safety of your watchtower,
decide to open the gate
and let me in.
Are you so afraid
we might become inseparable?

Donna Blois-Johnston

MY MIND UNWINDS

In my most comfortable clothes, I am bedecked
There is so much to see, so much to inspect.
I find a place for my chair, then go on my way
Stop to chat with a child
    and watch the tide of the day.

I take a long stroll with my feet in the ocean
And watch sea gulls fish as they cause a commotion.
The wind is just right for kites high in the sky
'Tis a wonderful place to watch boats passing by.

Some people take pills for their mind to unwind
My medicine for stress is a more natural kind.
As I breathe the salt air,
    my mind clears and becomes free
All the tension of the day
    slowly flows forth from me.

Joan W. Schatzberg

PLANET EARTH

Listen!
What do you hear?
Just what do you fear?
Is it the footsteps of some unknown?
Is it the cry of an eerie moan?
Why do you hide your face?

Listen again!
You have little to fear.
The wind is playing tricks with your ear.
The footsteps are your own.
The moan is your own.
There is no need to hide your face!

Be strong!
It won't take long.
Dawn is here.
There isn't any need to have fear.
The day can be bright
    and full of light.
Act now — and do not procrastinate —
    before it really is — too late.

Glen R. Anderson

GLEN ROBERT ANDERSON. Born: Chicago, Illinois, 4-20-52; Education: Senior at University of Wisconsin, Stevens Point, European history major; Memberships: The Honor Society of Phi Kappa Phi; Poetry: '1986,' *American Poetry Anthology,* 1987; 'Our World,' 'Life,' *The Poetry of Life,* 1988; 'All Eyes,' *American Poetry Anthology,* 1988; Comments: *We, as in the human race, like to think of ourselves as intelligent beings. Yet, many of our actions only articulate our stupidity in world affairs and our insensitivity toward our environmental problems.*

THE MELODY

The walls around me could not be penetrated,
For a lifetime I concentrated,
On shutting people out,
Until love came in and erased all doubt.
The world is in and I am free,
Wonderful dreams appear to me,
This is what the world can be,
When life becomes a melody.

One day you start to believe,
For so long, you could not perceive,
What others tried to show,
You've faced the dawn, now you know.
Wonderful dreams you will see,
When the world is in and you are free.
This is what the world can be,
When life becomes a melody.

Penny Pigman

THE PEAK

I've climbed to my feet,
Come up from the bottom to meet,
A new-found spirit flowing through,
Allowing me to go and do,
I've reached this place by following you,
And make the decision to start anew,
I'm touching that part of me,
That for so long I could not see,
I've found the spirit that has to be,
Soaring free, endlessly.

We touched for an instant in space,
And now carry the spirit we embrace.
We must go to seek and find,
Separately but of one mind.
We take a new philosophy,
Spreading love to humanity,
As I touch that part of me,
That for so long I could not see,
I have found my spirit has to be,
Soaring free endlessly.

Penny Pigman

LOOKING FOR A MEANING

With the stroke of a word —
sometimes fiery, sometimes deep
painting pictures of passion
(the poet   . . . speaks).

Face to face, cheek to cheek —
searching for truth
(the poet   . . . sees).

Heart to heart, soul to soul —
images of unseen life
(the poet   . . . shows).

Destinies and yet unknown prophecies —
looking beyond
(the poet   . . . seeks).

In pursuit of truth, love and life —
looking for a meaning
(the poet   . . . writes.)

Gael Shytle

REFLECTIONS OF YOU

I saw within your eyes,
The reflection of my soul,
You believed in my being,
As I had only longed to,
And you saw within me,
All that was good,
When my tears were moist.
You held the tissues,
You never denied the pain that I felt,
Though I know, at times, you wanted to,
You helped me to see the world with new eyes,
When I failed to let down my walls,
I looked for your smile to brighten each day,
And somehow you never let me down,
Though now, miles will come between us,
Good-byes are so very hard to say,
A part of you will dwell within my spirit,
We will always be as one,
For you are my friend . . . and I love you!

Gidget Friedley

HARBOR RISING

Astoria,
An ancient quality, wrecks dot the capes.
Rimmed by the bold Columbia,
Fettered with clapboard-sidinged dwellings
Of sea captains
And dentists,
Carpenters,
And all their long-dead friends;
Ruled now
By renovation
That chips
And stains,
Glimmers under the eaves
In whimsy,
Outlines the past,
Freezes it, glowing,
Resplendent.
Frilly,
At last real.

Norma J. Stiritz

RAPIDS

Up, down, swiftly slicing salmon runs,
upstream, down-ledge splitting sun-circles,
I swiveled high on a dawn dream.
The thrust of it booming toward.
Canoe-bark in full wedge,
I went head-on over sedge, my eyes open,
my skull soaking in parka cap,
too strong to quit rapids.
Up me I was too light to go
tumbling down on shale-plates
to earnest with the elements.
Booming upon some God-muscle,
I opened to a banked copper-coil,
and blinded myself under doom.

David St. Lawrence-Blaisdell

HEALTHY RELATIONSHIPS

Perhaps the most ingenious thing
One can say of the dread word "relationship"
Is
"Just don't make a habit out of it."

*Debbie Fredrich
and Dennis Brotz, Jr.*

SLOW AFTERNOON

Airplane droning
Somewhere in the sky
My soul red-shifts
Temporarily
Airplane, heard but not seen
An aural ghost
Whispering of people, places, things
Its voice a physical but intangible link
Between the world and me

Lily Principe

THE RACE

This day I would remember there are races yet to run,
And many dreams of splendor still waiting to be done.
I would quit the familiar haunts and forsake the beaten thoroughfare,
To take the lonely path and dreams of glory dare.
I would tread each mile with courageous heart and strong,
And seek only truth and justice and to rectify all wrong.
I would brave the sleet of winter storm or the wind of summer hurricane,
And although battered and worn, rise to run again.
I would not deal thoughtlessly for victory's sake,
Nor in my quest for success, bitter adversaries make.
I would no doubtful actions take nor ascribe to deeds untrue,
Nor with the crowd, any compromise pursue.
I would chance the loss of the cherished prize,
Than to win by the methods which honest men despise.
I would see with dreamer's eye beyond the weeds, the rubbish,
   and the grime,
And remember that around the bend blooms the rose of summertime.
I would seek the company of those of valor and hold my honor dear,
And when adversity arises, I would persevere.
I would pledge in every circumstance to give my all,
Whether I win with the great or with the broken fall.
I would know the peace and joy that comes when the day is done,
To the hearts of those who keep the faith
   and the race with patience run.

Billie Jean Henry

LOST AND FRIGHTENED LADY

The night is dark and lonely,
And rain begins to fall.
This lost and frightened lady, hears
That beckon call. She cries with full
Emotion, and of deepest despair.
Oh, God! She cries, *Please hide me anywhere.*
But the night is dark and very lonely.
And oh, so very cruel. She finally finds
A car without any fuel. But desperation
Leads her back into the wilderness of
The night. Where she must remain until
The morning light. Oh, lost and frightened
Lady, you walk in the shadows of the past.
You know that your destiny really wants
To last. You can't escape the horrors
Of which you came across. And no one
Knows about your hidden fear, except
God up on the cross. Oh, lost and
Frightened lady, your fearful spirit
Roams. I guess you shall always
Remain a fearful spirit all alone.

Barbara Wirkowski

ABANDONED?

Where is the man who stands so strongly tall
He overshadows all reality?
Where is the man whose daring heart knows mine
As if he had been born a part of me?
Where is the man whose arms are gently strong;
Who fills my mind, lives in my heart each day?
Where is the man who makes life pass too fast
When near me, yet drag slowly when away?
Where is the man, the only one for me?
I do not dream. I know that he is near
And he is real. But I miss him so much
I question everything without him here.

Colleen Barton

ODYSSEY OF LIFE

Priceless is the fragile frame of life,
   Microcosm of unfolding hope,
Foisted on the tyranny of strife,
   Traumatized, e'er struggling to cope.

Stalwart 'gainst torrentious pulse and tide,
   The fledgling proves his power to survive;
Focused on his mecca deep inside,
   He wisely charts his course to thus arrive.

Syndrome of both triumph and disdain,
   Man with lavish instinct seeks to find
Answers to alleviate his pain,
   Randomizing from both God and mind.

Jocular, he hears applauding fans;
   Expertise in business brought him fame;
Plaudits gained, though granted only man's,
   Encourage honor for one's family name.

Think great thoughts and dare to stretch afar;
   Faith demands unselfish goals to reach,
Unsullied as the Pleiadean star,
   Though bosomed fresh upon a typhooned beach.

Enigma, this terrestrial, transient trail,
   Polarized by dynamic and defeat;
Foes oppose and closest friendships fail,
   Sifting till life's odyssey's complete.

Wendell K. Babcock

MY DAY AS GOD

If I were God of China, I would be
A photographer, and go around and make
Pictures of the folk of China, and show
Them that their oldest gods are still alive.

If I were the God of India, I
Would wander through jungle and countryside
Once in a while, and take a look at my lost
Fertility, and I'd put on new clothes.

If I were the God of Africa, I
Would mask my eyes with tom-tom drum, and ride
A midnight moon over the crawling rivers
To Kilamanjaro's unmelting snow;

There on its alabaster western height,
While the moon was behind the clouds, I would
Revive the frozen leopard, and keep it
In the House of God near me, for my pet.

If I were God of Greenland, I would be
An iceberg, white and silent and austere,
For the most part concealed, and I would share
The unrelenting doom of those I ruled.

And if I were Great God Himself, and had
All the things on my mind that He has, I
Would rest, and I would come down to the world for a while,
And wiggle my bare feet in the bare earth.

James Sexton Layton

I DIDN'T SEE THE SUNSHINE

To Jim, with love

If you would give me another chance
I'll tell you what I would do.
I'd take my heart, and soul and love,
And give them all to you.

I'd tuck them in a great big sack
And tie it with a string,
Then I'd grasp it in my hands
And give it a little fling.

I'd throw it in your direction,
Hoping you'd catch it by the top,
Keeping all the contents in —
Not letting any drop.

For if the string should come untied,
And my emotions all fell out,
You would never know, my love,
What my feelings were all about.

So, if you still care for me,
And you want to start again,
I will open my arms real wide
And let the sun shine in.

Sondra Middleton

MASQUERADE

You can't believe in love
    with your emotional blockade
Impossibilities arise
    in a silly masquerade

Release your seasons for love
    and uncover your mystery
Surrender the condition of your heart
    and I'll be part of your history

Efren Sablan, Jr.

LADY . . . WOMAN

To think of her, satisfying
I think very hard and very deep
That this woman I see every day
May be a *woman* full of joy
Or she may be a *lady*
Filled with emotion

As I see her, she's a *woman*
Funny and full of laughter
She's strong and she's proud of her
  beauty
This woman I see is exciting
Overwhelming, and full of pleasure.

But as I dream of her, *lady*
So exquisite and full of beauty
She's affectionate with understanding
This lady in my dream is the center
  of my life
I adore this lady but want this woman.

Efren Sablan, Jr.

THE TWO OF US

What will we do, the two of us?
Shadow lovers
hidden behind locked doors
sharing clandestine embraces,
forbidden love
secretly breaking
society's unwritten law.

What will we do, the two of us?
Hapless lovers
sharing one last embrace,
aching as we tearfully part
unable to
publicly challenge
society's unwritten law.

What will we do, the two of us?
Hopeless lovers
searching in approved arms
for the love we secretly shared,
wishing we had
boldly rewritten
society's unwritten law.

Barbara Brown

EHIND THE FACES

The smiling faces in the pictured pose
Arranged by the photographer,
Display exterior
And studied poise for all
The paper's daily readership
To scan among the blocks of printed prose.
And in those smiling faces nothing shows
Of doubt or apprehensiveness,
Relinquishment of dreams
Or painful yesterdays,
The clutching hand of loneliness
Or every life's free-flowing highs and lows.
But thoughtful readers pause between the rows
Of words to eye the faces there,
To muse on parallels
Between each span of life
And ponder on the darknesses . . .
Behind each face . . . that no one ever knows.

Mauricia Price

THE HOUSE OF MY LORD

The doors to the house of my Lord
Swing open to all who will come.
It matters not how heavy your burden,
Or how near or far you've come from.
This house is a place of worship,
A place to praise, to sing, to pray.
'Tis a place of sweet remembrance,
Of what happened on Calvary one day.
In this house I know I am welcomed,
With arms that are opened so wide.
In this house I can't help but be thankful,
That for me, Jesus suffered and died.
Yes, it's here that my heart is happy,
And my soul finds peace and rest.
For in this house I'll find the answers,
To pass life's difficult test.

Yvette I. Shelton

I'M LIKE A CRAZY QUILT

I'm just a healthy little boy
  But I'm awfully hard on clothes.
It keeps my mother busy
  As she sits at home and sews.

It seems she's always busy
  Sewing patches by the score.
And now I'm wearing patches
  Where I had pants before.

The rips and tears I often get
  Have quite the oddest tilt.
When Mama gets done patching
  I'm like a crazy quilt.

Emily B. Green

EMILY BERTHA GREEN. Pen Name: Ahtreb Yeniw; Born: Lodi, Ohio, 3-2-17; Married: Charles Lloyd Green, 4-21-35, widowed; Education: High school graduate, 1935; the 101st nurse to receive waiver LPN license in 1950s; Occupation: Licensed Practical Nurse; Memberships: B.P.W., V.F.W. Auxiliary; American Legion Auxiliary, R.S.V.P.; Awards: 1st place for book of poems, Senior Citizen Fair, 1978; 1st place for 2 songs, 1978; Poetry: 'Being Friends,' card and booklet company, 1974; 'What's Right About America,' poem and song, 1976; Other Writings: ''Reflections,'' weekly column; *Chaffee Signal*, started 12-20-67; Comments: *The life of a poet has brought happiness to my life and the greatest time was when I worked through the schools playing novelty instruments and encouraging the children to work collecting to help the handicapped of Southeast Missouri. I did this work for nine years.*

FULFILLMENT

In the midst of evil
Of horrors uncontained
Peace is to sleep
To dream

To feel the soul rise
A cool breeze
To smell the sweet aroma
Of flowers yet to bloom

To gaze at a life that's passed
With no regrets
With no sorrows
And feel contentment . . .
That was life

Mindy DeBaise

A MOTHER'S PEARL

A sea-wind swells along the coast with white
Gulls gliding, swirling, diving through bright plumes
Of spray breaking against a thrust of rocks
Innumerable. Hand in hand with destiny
Hard gray shells brain and writhe mud to pearl, that's cast
Upon the shore, where the waves meet the land.

Do you know what it is to swell and swell
Until you can no longer see the shape
You used to be and knew? That's where I live,
Growing for my time, waiting for the tide
To throw a mother's pearl upon the sand
Of love, giving my Stranger back to me.

A road passes by my house, between the house
And the sea, stretching, winding along the shore,
Indelibly drawing my sometime course;
Where it begins and ends, I cannot tell;
Some say it goes 'round the ocean, all the way,
And comes back home. Of that I do not know.

Sometimes late I hear a dog bark, far off,
The cry of a hawk, or a lonely gull;
But no soul travels the road by my door,
Though I'm on it all the time, looking out
For the sails of the Stranger to come in sight,
Who wisely put this load upon my heart.

James Sexton Layton

JAMES SEXTON LAYTON.

NIGHT SEA

From a cottage in dunes near the sea,
The townsfolk say:
"If you look to the beach when the mid-summer night
     is moonlit and calm,
The soul of a man can be seen."

A man walking by the sea,
Walking in a night like silver day.
He is searching, walking slowly,
Watching waves shatter to mirror foam upon the shore.
He stops and stands still, hearing a silent call,
Watching the silvered ocean, held by another will.
A splash, sliding, the crest of a wave surges,
Leaving the Silent on the shining surface.
The Silent lures the soul on the shore,
Does she wish to draw the last of a man to the sea floor?
To take him down into her realm of moon-bleached blue,
Past ramparts of weed and coral, in dream shapes each a different hue?
To the soul on the shore, can he not see?
How beautiful and perilous this ghost light can be!

Byron Z. Willard

THE LIGHT OF MY NIGHT

*Written for my husband, David Leinard,
as we prepare to renew our wedding vows
in celebration of our 16th anniversary.*

David, I married for the rest of my life,
    To have and behold as I became his wife.
A simple existence, it seems very clear
    Wife and children, he holds so dear.

A gentle spirit that only I can see.
    Warmth and tenderness hidden to all but me.
He's misunderstood by most in view;
    But deeply loved by the genuine few.

Despite my faults, he still loves even me.
    I don't have to pretend on who I'm to be.
He accepts my shortcomings — my temper so hot.
    He overlooks with his heart the things I'm not.

A house he has built out of love to provide,
    Made into a home with his tears and pride.
He does what he can with strength from above,
    Husband and Father, God's gift to love.

Whenever I stumble, David's there by my side,
    To keep me uplifted, to help and to guide.
With another anniversary just in sight
    I'm proud to share it with *The Light of My Night.*

Kathy Bess Thibodaux

KATHY BESS THIBODAUX. Pen Name: Chicky; Born: Amarillo, Texas, 2-5-53; Parents' Names: James Pete Petropoulos, Tennie Katherine Nix; Married: David Leinard Thibodaux, 9-13-71; Children: Joseph, 7-1-72; Kerri, 5-1-76; Jason, 9-9-73 (deceased); Education: Santa Fe High School; Albuquerque TVI School of Nursing, LPN, 1983; Occupations: Wife,; Mother; Hospice nurse; Emergency medical technician; Student for health social worker; Memberships: American Business Woman's Association; Red Cross Disaster Team; March of Dimes; Sweet Adelines Barbershop choir; Berean Baptist Church; Awards: American Business Woman Chapter, Woman of the Year, 1985; Poetry: 'It's Difficult to Say Goodbye,' *Best New Poets of 1986,* 1987; 'Going Home,' *American Poetry Anthology,* 1985; Other Writings: *His Tender Touch,* collection of 20 poems that have been used as greeting cards, church bulletins, funeral masses, and in Ladies Christian Fellowship meetings; Themes: *As I grow and mature in my physical life, I tend to write about the growth and maturity of my Christian life. My poems show the hopes, the joys, the trials, and the tribulations that I've encountered. No matter what may be ahead of me there is a sustaining faith that encourages me onward and upward.*

FAITH

Life is sometimes agony.
Life is so unfair.
When these shadows hover about
and you feel that no one cares
Look up to the sun
and realize the controlling hand.
The beauty in all of nature
wasn't made by man.
God does not ask of you
anything that you cannot do.
When the road grows long and cold
Follow what your heart is told.

Jerrie Poindexter

JERRIE MAE POINDEXTER. Born: Yadkin County, North Carolina, 1-8-62; Education: Forbush High School, East Bend, North Carolina, 1980; Occupation: Customer representative, Duke Power Company; Poetry: 'Even Though,' *A Vision, A Verse,* 1978; 'Daydreams,' 'Autumn Drive,' 'Time,' *American Poetry Anthology,* 1987; *Sea Chanty,* 1987; Comments: *Having grown up in the country in North Carolina with strong family ties, I write about things that touch me emotionally. For instance, 'Forty Years' is a poem I wrote for my parents' 40th wedding anniversary, which is very rare these days. Also, being situated between both the Appalachian Mountains and the North Carolina Coastline, I have many secret places that inspire my writing.*

REFLECTIONS

My thoughts . . . My harmony
My pain . . . My comfort
My sorrows . . . My joys
My dreams . . . My aspirations
My fantasies . . . My realities
My tears . . . My laughter
My struggles . . . My endurance
My changes . . . My growth
My father . . . My heritage
My mother . . . My hope
My brothers . . . My boldness
My sisters . . . My charm
My companion . . . My friend
My son . . . My gift
My God . . . My life
My life . . . My blessing
My faith . . . My strength
My love . . . My peace
My spirit . . .My eternity
My memories . . . My reflections

A. Mozelle Michaux

THE IMPASSIONED I

I write I;
I Cannot write
of anyone Else.

first person Plural
many persons Singular.

I write I
for All the I's
Around me.

Joan M. Schumack

JOAN MARIA SCHUMACK. Born: Province of Messinias, Greece, 11-4-53; Education: Marquette University, B.A., Journalism; Course work completed for an M.A. in Journalism, Marquette University; Occupation: Freelance journalist; Memberships: Milwaukee Press Club; Women in Communication; Wisconsin Single Adoptive Parents; Milwaukee Art Museum; Milwaukee Symphony Orchestra Friends; National Federation of Local Cable Programmers; German Language and School Society, 1971; National Council of Teachers of English, 1972; Awards: Quill and Scroll Award for High School Journalism, 1972; Society of Professional Journalists Mark of Excellence, 1975; *Who's Who in American Colleges and Universities,* 1976; *Who's Who in the Midwest,* 1987; Comments: *To the adage, ''Art imitates life,'' I would like to add the postscript that art can lead life. In my essays, I take a pronounced feminist stance, which paints the picture of a world that could be, if only someone pointed the way. My poetry reflects a strong, positive ego: my sense of self projected onto others makes me sympathetic to people whose actions or attitudes frustrate me until I imagine myself in their circumstances.*

HOME

I found myself in the middle of a field
Gazing up unto the sky
When a sudden flash of reality come upon me
And I saw my life before my eye

The clouds embraced my gentle soul
Carrying me far away
And I found myself at peace
At home
This is where I wish to stay!

Mindy DeBaise

HAPPIER THAN YOU ARE

I'll sing in the sunshine
 Follow sunbeams to no end,
And gather loads of sunglow
 For my dearest friend.

I'll walk on a rainbow
 And paint its colors fair.
I'll gather colored ribbons
 And tie up my hair.

I'll fly in the moonlight
 Whisper fun things to a star,
And dance on a moonbeam
 To wherever you are.
I'll sing you a love song,
 And make you happier than you are.

Virgie McCoy Sammons

OUR LOVE

For Kenny, I love you

I feel like I have known you forever
Even though we've only just met
Needing you to be, all you are to me
Our love I will never forget

I remember when first I saw you
And your eyes burned through my heart
Heated by the passion of love, for you
I know we shall never part

I fantasize about you in my dreams
Ours together to bring true
The future eternally before us
Thoughts and feelings of loving you

Mindy DeBaise

MINDY ANN DeBAISE. Born: Staten Island, New York, 7-16-64; Occupations: Bookkeeper, Bartender; Poetry: 'Alone,' 'The City,' 'The End of a Day,' all *American Poetry Anthology,* 1987; Comments: *I have been writing for over 10 years, usually writing about depression in my poems, and horror in my stories. I'm inspired more by others than myself. To T.J.R. and what could have been, R.I.P. Thanks to Mom, Dad, R.R., S.R., P.M.R., K.C.R., M.P., C.L., M.M., K.D., G.R. and to all that has been or will ever be.*

REFLECTION

I don't want to reflect on truth again.
Truth, while it blesses, also brings great pain.
Loneliness, misery, are death to dreams
When the bitter tears won't flow, nor will screams.
So those who rightfully rebel at night
Must seek a new solace and fresh insight.
To those who have known distrust, I say this:
Build a chest of iron, gray like the mist,
With a lock of strong steel, black as new coal,
And there place the dreams of your heart and soul;
The beliefs in elegant, worthy lands;
The delights that desert tightly clenched hands;
The wishes that are made on a bright star;
The longings to linger in lands afar;
The need of music to enrich the heart;
The yearnings of the mind, hope to impart.

After these treasures are safe in the chest,
All neatly labeled and silently blessed,
Lock it tight, hide the key, ignore the pain,
And you won't reflect on truth again.

Colleen Barton

On that island, bare and boundless
    rain falls sleeting, free and soundless
        walking in wonder
        hopes retracting
        standing asunder
        our world defeating
On my island, sweat and sensation
    sun shines strong, no thought realizations
        watching in wonder
        moving emotion
        sleeping asunder
        surrounding my ocean
On your island, calm and collective
    wind blows timeless, strong and respective
        waiting in wonder
        searching a reason
        sending asunder
        changing in season
On our island, rant and reality
    water flows quickly, some stalk congeniality
        wanting the wonder
        restless frustration
        serving asunder
        unvowed situation

Shawna Lee Benson

NEW BEGINNINGS

The baby lay kicking upon its bed.
"Beautiful and healthy," the doctor said.
    Only a short nine months ago,
    She was but a frozen embryo.

    The parents filled with ecstasy
    Ponder, what her name will be.
    A special name for a special girl,
    One born in thirty, in all the world.

Faye Teague

A STITCH IN TIME

A stitch in time — is a neat little rhyme
    But, what will it take for me to define
All of life's worries that need mending today,
    As I watch this grey morning slipping away!

Yesterday, I shared coffee with a friend and read
    her my poems —
Reminisced about past times, our children and our homes!
Today — she is leaving! Yes, she's moving away,
    Another stitch in life cannot be delayed!
Like the wind that blows free . . . changes its
    course, endlessly!

A blend of materials chosen with care, have been
    sewn together and stacked on a chair.
The assortment is varied, with gifts to include
    A new little baby in life's interlude!

An afghan, a sweater that took hours to make
    Has stitches of love for a little one's sake!
A letter to write — a prayer to be sent
    To remember a friend with a life to mend!

The list is endless of things to be done —
    Including prayers for our ailing loved ones!
If all of these stitches arrive in time —
    My heart will be filled with a joy that's sublime!

Clara E. Schauman

WHY ME

Sometimes I sit and wonder,
    what makes people treat others the way they do.
When people lose their confidence and self-respect;
They always ask, *Why me?*

When they try so hard to please everyone,
They eventually get hurt themselves in the end.
They always ask, *Why me?*

When throughout life others keep telling them how they can't do
    things, instead of how they could.
They start doubting everything they do,
    so when they are asked to do something.
They aways ask, *Why me?*

What gives people the right to pass judgment,
    when they start to notice changes?
Why do people set guidelines for others in their minds,
    so that when changes do come about they start to gossip?
It makes you ask, *Why me?*

What people forget is that everyone has feelings.
They should find the positive traits and accentuate them.
Help others through the hard times,
    so they don't seem so bad.
Always help them to build confidence and self-respect,
    instead of destroying it.
So they ask, *Why not me?*

M. Kendra Turner

GHETTO CHILD

Ghetto child
dark and strong
ripping off the neighbors
just to get along.
Ghetto child
strung on drugs —
calls himself a Warlord,
cops call him a thug.
Got into a gang fight —
tried to help a friend.
Ghetto child stabbed in the back,
left dead in the end.
Next day in the paper
this is how it read:
''Rumble over Warlord turf —
Ghetto child is dead.''
Ghetto mother speaks,
her tone so strong yet mild:
''He may have been a hoodlum
but he was my ghetto child.''

Cynthia Renee Highsmith

AWAKENING

I bare my soul
A window you looked through
Shades pulled up
Exposing all inside
When we met
There were the eyes
Of a woman-child
Burning with hunger
Brimming with innocence
The years have passed
As we now have
So has the child
Leaving shell intact
What has emerged
A person — individual
Scared and scarred
Strong and resilient
In herself finding
The person
She wanted most to be —
Me.

Kim Law Porec

TEARS

O Lord, I cry unto You.
O Lord, my eyes are blurred with tears.

Now, at last, I see
how even one selfish thought
offends Your loving generosity.

And now, with sorrow in my heart,
and renewed resolution,
I beg forgiveness.

My tears have turned
into signs of joy.
My God has drawn me to Himself.

Mary Frances

LABELS

What is life but
an array of beauty
    which through one's
senses can be absorbed.

    The colors,
    The textures,
    The tastes,
    The sounds of life,
    The most complex; the most simple
        of forms.

    What is death but
an unknown concept
    which is labeled to a corpse
when one's senses have come to an end.

    The darkness,
    The numbness,
    The deafness of death,
    The most simple; the most complex
        of life begins.

Cindy Robinson

MY BROTHER

Precious Lord, I have a brother
who needs Your help.

You know his need, Lord,
even better than I do.

You know best how to help him.
O Lord, hear my silent prayer for him.

Guide me in the way I talk with him
and in the way I listen to him
and in the way I let You
reveal Yourself to him.

Please, Lord, let me help,
but help me let You
draw him to Yourself
in Your own loving way.

Mary Frances

THE ONLY WAY

O Lord, You created me.
And You created my brother.

I am Yours,
And he is Yours.

That is why I love You
and why I love him.

Grant that my brother
may love You
because You created him,
and love me
because You created me,
and because You love us both.

Mary Frances

SNOW FEVER

Cocaine tragedies within many nations.
Rapid mental deterioration and hallucinations
Fixation.
Human tragedy in the making.
Crystallized power for the taking.
Drug disaster in several years.
A gift for mankind many tears.
Cocaine craving and momentary delight.
Speedily you pass through day into night.
''Coke Cold La'' will make you a slave.
Leading you directly to your grave.
Cocaine addiction, it's no joke.
Seeking yelp you're no dope; there is hope.
Call #1-800-Cocaine you can cope.

Judith St. Vic

FORTY YEARS

In another time
some forty years ago
you took your wedding vows
and love began to grow.
The roots were firmly planted
coming from strong family minds.
A seed of love soon sprouted
new life upon the vines.
Then another and another,
still another making four.
And with each of us brought
the love out even more.
Through the years of parenting
how did you find the chance
to slip off and just be a couple
searching for romance?
All the kids have moved away.
You have the time alone you've missed.
The house is much quieter now
and you don't need mistletoe to kiss.
Remember back through all those years
and how much in love you've been.
All of your seeds were nurtured by this:
The love that has no end . . .

Jerrie Poindexter

TRUE FRIENDS

You talk to me
And I to you,
We really understand one another
You and I.
Secrets told and secrets kept;
No criticism or condemnation
In any way.
Sharing and caring
Is the order of the day.
Effortless acceptance and help;
Socially as well as spiritually atuned
You are indeed special to me.
I'm so glad you're my friend,
And I am free to be me.

Annethea Anderson

AUF WIEDERSEHEN

Throughout the world there are many languages which enable
    people to communicate different sentiments.
No matter what language you use to say *good-bye;*
    It is never easy to say.
Some languages make *good-byes* sound romantic;
    Others give it a harsh sound.
Good-bye in French is *au revoir* or *à bientôt;*
    While in Latin it's *valé.*
Germans say *auf wiedersehen,*
    Italians use the word *ciao* or *arrivederci.*
Sayonara in Japanese, even though you can't read it,
    still means *good-bye.*
Music, the universal language, has its own way to communicate
    good-byes such as a thernody or swan songs.
While *aloha* is the universal greeting in Hawaii.
The language someone uses to convey the message doesn't matter;
    Good-bye will always mean *farewell.*
Remember when someone says *good-bye;*
    Someone else is ready to say *hello.*
Auf wiedersehen.

M. Kendra Turner

SIC ITUR AD ASTRA

Crisp, cloudless stellar blackness
    novas shining in nebulous never-neverland mist
gingerly peeling back the Milky Way gauze
    starspun zodiac nursing, examining, blowing off the cosmic dust
on gangrenous, but healing tender Gehenna-sores
    soaking up the stars and gegenschein
maudlin reminiscing about what might have been,
    but wasn't, and isn't
but is real presently if tuned to Andromeda dreamland.

Mark E. Durand

DAYS AND DAYS OF FOREVER AWAY

Lingering mini-eons of abject boredom, and dull gray blandness,
    piqued with interludes of twisted panic, and the horrors of the dark.
Ticking away the days and days of forever as seconds.
    Exuding apathetic nonchalance over mere hours passing.
The core of obsession is alive, and seeps through the slow frustrating
    death of the foggy months.
    Hope is continually reborn by the tearing and crumpling of calendar
        pages,
and the thousands of tally marks uniformly carved,
    through the slime in graffiti-covered granite,
by grit, force, and chipped, tempered fingernails.

Mark E. Durand

SNOWBLIND

Snowshoeing towards, the solstice snowblind.
    Lazer-slanted squints, wince on winter star.
Rabid, mad shadows, lay twisted behind,
Snowshoeing towards, the solstice snowblind.
No fell thoughts jade mind, tensions, doubts unwind.
    No white burning scars, black bruises bizarre,
Snowshoeing towards, the solstice snowblind.
    Lazer-slanted squints, wince on winter star.

Mark E. Durand

FOREVER FRIENDS

There was a constant hum of idle chatter all about us.

We were each in our own private, little worlds, gazing out
    a restaurant window, eyeing the flocking, rushing traffic.

We both sat so still, we were ever so silent.

''A penny for your thoughts,'' you said.

''Considering the rate of inflation, it'll cost you a
    dime now,'' I said.

We both laughed, and cried, and at that instantaneous
    moment, we touched each other's hands, the way that
good friends do.

We let our eyes, hearts, and souls speak their own
    private language.

You, my friend, are the bridge — leading from the path
    of who I was.

You are the artist, who is moulding and shaping me
    into the person I am and the person who I
may yet come to be.

You share with me your wisdom, your laughter, dreams,
    your devotion, your loyalty, your sensitivity,
    yourself.

You are warm, tender, and loving.

God could give me no greater gift than your friendship.
You are my teacher, my confessor, my confidant,
my best friend.

We are now and always, forever friends.

Mary Ann Taber

GOD'S EVERLASTING LOVE

Do not feel sad, because I no longer walk upon the earth.
Shed not a tear for me, after all my searching
has finally come to an end.
In life I struggled from day to day
To find the gentle Love, that never passed my way.

Upon the earth, I walked weighed down.
My spirit became heavier than I could carry.
My mind so confused no longer clear.
As often I found myself shedding another unwanted tear.

A heart, a mind, a soul.
Carried in a body, that just grew too old.
Then I heard a voice, I had not known,
that is, not since I was fully grown.

He talked for only a short time,
Then laid his hand softly upon mine.
God's words hung gently in the air,
As he spoke these words, ''Someone does care.

Yea, I have loved thee with an everlasting Love.
Therefore with loving-kindness have I drawn thee near.
Fore Love comes to you, as your searching ends,
Come kneel beside me, for now your living begins.''

Izella Jean Morlan

SCENES IN AND AROUND ALBANY.

HER MAJESTY

For her I looked so very long to see —
I resigned myself that extinct she must be.

When I had almost ceased the search for my lady fair —
Suddenly there before my eyes she did appear!
Draped in black hood and cloak —
Wearing a strand of white pearls at her throat.

Perched there with queenly grace —
Peering straight into my face.

For one celestial moment — elated!
Our eyes met — our senses communicated.
Though neither of us a sound did utter —
The lady took her leave,
And into terrestrial flight did flutter.

I was sad to see her fly away,
For fear that she would not return another day.

If herself she does not again to me reveal —
In woodland or park.
To see her — I have only to look into my heart.

Virginia D. Morgens

VIRGINIA DARE DAVIS MORGENS. Pen Name: Virginia Dare: Born: Del Rio, Tennessee, 10-09-34; Education: Fulton High School, Knoxville, Tennessee, 1955; Occupation: Disabled retiree; Memberships: AARP; NAPPS; Smithsonian Institute; City News Service; Songwriters Club of America; Awards: Production contract, Broadway Music Productions; Commercial recording contract, Tin Pan Alley Records, Inc.; Lifetime membership, Songwriters Club of America; Poetry: 'Strolling,' *Words of Praise, Vol. III,* 1987; Other Writings: ''Blood Shed On The Mountain,'' ''Little Johnny McCall,'' ''The Farmer's Plight,'' ''The Doctor's Ultimatum,'' songs, Tin Pan Alley Records, 1987; Themes: *People, nature, occasions, events, values;* Comments: *I am currently devoting what time I am able to my manuscript and film script. Both of these are a continuation of the song ''Blood Shed On The Mountain,'' based on a true experience.*

DAD

I think of you each passing day
The things you did in that special way.
Always remembering the love we shared
Knowing always how much you cared.

It doesn't get easier as the days pass by
It helps a little to sit and cry.
Those special times can make it so tough
Memories are beautiful, but they're never enough.

I know I'll see you again some day
To you and the Lord each night I pray.
Living my life to the fullest 'til then
Loving you always, until we meet again.

Michele A. Johnson

TURBULENT SEA

I'm deep like a well and broad as the sea.
I look down into the well, but cannot see my face.
I look out to sea, and don't reach my self.
I'm calm within me like a lowly water spring.
Impulsive I am as turbulent sea.

How bloody are the battles
held inside ourselves
behind the dense ramparts
of the anatomy!

How bloody are the battles
held inside my self!
Neither blasts
nor cries are heard.

Everything seems quiet
as you glance at the siege:
like a soulless body
or something extinct.

How bloody are the battles
held inside my self!
Soul of mine, dismaying,
be courageous again.

Everything looks quiet
as one looks at the siege,
but within my soul
is a turbulent sea.

Ernesto Oregel

ALONG ROCK CREEK

The headstone said he died in 1883.
But in this age-old cemetery, he's still alive to me.
I feel his presence all around
In this little graveyard, I have found.
Across the path the post office lay
Though mail hasn't been there in many a day.
The building is gray and broken and small.
After fifty-odd years, it still doesn't fall.
Down the road and over the hill
Is a swinging bridge to a once busy still.
The still, like the man, has long gone away,
Yet all the relics you can still see today.
Back in these mountains you go back in time,
Godfearing people and coffee a dime.
You drive down the road with bait and your pole.
To catch a trout — look out! There's a hole.
A narrow bridge made of logs
''Coal'' dead trees in miniature bogs.
The people are gone and so is the mine,
Yet, there in the splendor, a tall green pine.
A history lesson for all to share,
Nostalgia, dreams, for those who dare
To see this place as a temple of wonder,
Not as a plight of coal-mining plunder.

Mary E. Stephens

FOR I SAY

What universal law exists today?
Heaven and earth have not passed our way.
Teach right from wrong every hour and day.
Stay on the right path.
For I say!
Ignorance is man within vain sin.
Heaven and hell shall have no end.
Nature tradition go hand and hand.
The ultimates are children's in no man land.
There're crystal temple made for man.
Application for citizenship with heavenly sand.
Glorious time with ''Lord of All''
No one here shall never fall.
Orientation on the light within.
Rise up with power your beginning no end.
For I say!

Judith St. Vic

JUDITH ANN SAINT VIC. Born: Manhattan, New York, 12-8; Education: College of Staten Island, B.A., Psychology, 1986; Occupations: Actress, Artist in fine art, Designer, Perfumer, Songwriter; Membership: Staten Island Council of the Arts, Pyramid Art Gallery; Poetry: 'Song of Love,' 'The Last Word,' 'Reflections,' *The Poetry of Life,* 1987; 'All for Me,' *American Poetry Anthology,* 1985; 'Intoxicating,' *American Poetry Anthology,* 1986; Comments: *My expression and ideas are of the Guardian of Faith, The All Seeing, The Source of Peace, The Mighty, The Creator.*

COMA

I gently stroke her furrowed brow,
And caress her withered hand,
While trying quietly to comfort her,
In this frightening, unknown land.
It's so unfair that life has dealt her
Such a cruel, hard blow.
It's not easy for me to hold back
My tears that are begging to flow.
She cannot see or hear me,
Or feel my loving touch.
She doesn't hear my aching heart scream,
For the mother I love so much.
A coma has paralyzed her life,
And trapped her in its tomb.
She cannot awaken nor does she try,
To escape its suffocating womb.
A coma is holding her hostage,
So I pray, on bended knee,
Dear God above, rescue her with Your love,
And bring my mother back to me.

Helena B. Schildknecht

SPIRIT

The house held spirits.
Surveying the unbelievable.
Surveying the fears of the lonely all
alone.

I have seen them.
Somewhat like a shadow.
And as erect as the fear.

It is an evil.
As the devil himself.
A threat of hell,
as departing from the body
of a person at death.

Seen as a treak.
A well-known reason.
Death before you and maybe
someone else.

How long are they to be in sight,
in this supernatural house.
''Take them back!''

To make the mind clear at the
gaze of them.
''Take them back!''

Edna Harris

LET ME NOT COMPLAIN

Let me not complain, Lord,
When things don't go my way.
Instead, may I appreciate the
Gifts You send today.

Forgive me if I grumble because
Life seems difficult, once in a while.
Remind me that others have problems too —
Help me face tomorrow with a
Cheerful smile.

Open my eyes to the wonder of
Nature, the flowers in full array.
Teach me to love my neighbor, to
Listen to what he has to say.

Give me patience and understanding,
Lord, especially when I'm under stress.
Increase my faith and endurance,
So I can give You my very best.

Let me not complain, Lord, or distress
You with my whining.
For every cloud that rains on us,
You send a rainbow to keep us smiling.

Pat Rath-Sanchez

GOOD NIGHT!

Her velvet voice so sweetly sings
A lovesome lay on winsome wings,
And wafts the threads for dreams I'll spin
On words which quell the daily din.

Charles J. Lumia

MY BLUE LAGOON

I knelt beside the blue lagoon,
Therein to view, my youth, my bloom,
To see the magic, to feel the power,
Of youth's sweet song, to unfold as a flower,
To revere my reflection, and languidly dream,
As I yield to its flow, its chant, its theme,
While the wind breathes, in a whisper unique,
With my very thoughts, so poignantly to speak,
Of this grand retreat, my very heart,
With my image of youth, never to part,
But, the clock ticked, and the years advanced,
The eye of my soul, no longer danced,
My face now infirmed, with lines of wrath,
A menacing blunder, to an unknown path,
How would I fare, where would I go,
Without the essence of my glow,
I must with psalm and song, my way outline,
I must be loved, and somewhere shine.

Irma Schwartz

THE MAGIC OF THE SEASONS

The magic of the seasons
Brings changing color, changing scenes
For eyes that see and
Wonder evoke.

The beauty of summer will
Prepare to cover herself with
A new cloak.
The budding flowers and trees
Will slowly dwindle, and so
To a quiet sleep.

The birds will leave their nests
To seek another home.
The winter's chill will wait its turn,
Making ready to blanket all with
Its soft white glow.

Sheila Wolf

LOVE IS

So many definitions, expressed
In so many ways.
A gentle touch, that certain
Smile.
The lingering look, no words
To say.
A warm embrace, the joy you
Feel.
The tenderness, that shows with
Caring.
The closeness, that glows with
Sharing.
A promise made, for that special
Day.

Sheila Wolf

OUR MARRIAGE

How do I explain the way I feel
When sometimes my life just doesn't seem real?
We always have good times, but some times are bad
We're always so happy, yet sometimes we're sad
Our lives are so different from others we know
Our love never dies, it just seems to grow.

Why can't everyone have it this good
If they'd only try harder I bet they could
They always wonder why ours is the best
Why we seem happier than all the rest
It's not always easy, sometimes it's tough
But never stop trying, it's never enough.

Sharing our feelings each passing day
Always knowing the right thing to say
Saying ''I love you,'' helps so much
I think that's what gives it that special touch
Maybe some day others will see
It's easy to be happy, just like you and me.

Michele A. Johnson

WINTER JOY

When it becomes the days of winter cold,
I love the joy I hope to behold,
Meeting the children bundled in scarfs and coats,
Seeking the love every smile denotes,
With the brightness of every rosy cheek,
That is shared with the friendly warmth I seek.

When it is the days of winter snow,
I love the joys the children show,
As through the snow in spirits bright,
They trample and tumble in delight,
Filling every heart with love to share,
That a frequent glance of smiles declare.

When I see the signs of winter everywhere,
And I sit about in lonesome care,
I wait and listen for the children around,
To cheer my heart with joyous sound,
When I see by footprints in the snow,
The children are leading the joyous way to go.

Anthony S. Goss

WITHDRAWAL

Grotesque thoughts of insanity and death
Mingling in a dazed mind and alcoholic breath.
Rage turned inward to a helpless self.
Empty bottles, hidden on a shelf.
Agonizing pains of alcohol withdrawn
Sleepless nights and long coming dawn.
Nerves, like snakes, winding and squeezing
Breaths in gasps and muffled wheezing.
Hating self, while blaming all other,
From overweight wife to long-suffering mother.
Knowing that death waits down the path
Lying there drenched in a sweat-soaked bath.
Wanting to pray, but not feeling able
To presume that God would sit at my table.
Defiantly trying to go it alone,
Stubbornly refusing to pick up the phone.
Pray for me wife, mother, and friend,
To find some peace before life's end.

Mary E. Stephens

BATTLEFIELDS

On the battlefields of war, broken bodies lay astrew.
With blood and guts and moaning, of not a simple few.
A shattered leg, a broken arm, and, very few who met no harm.
We cry, we scream, we feel their pain,
And the fields are red with blood's own stain.
But, with the help of God, and caring, solutions come, with
  courageous daring.
Medical help to mend the holes, and God's own grace to heal
  the souls.
But, other battles, of a different kind, shatter the trust and
  bitter the mind.
There love and hate and bitterness dwell, there anger, hurt,
  and pain just swell.
This battleground is in the home. Where words and deeds like a
  pestilence foam.
Here angry, bitter words are spoken, and, hearts and feelings
  soon are broken.
Here retribution becomes a game, and, right and wrong become the same.
Here, no one gives a fleeting thought, to the terrible destruction
  they have wrought.
The screaming and yelling and bitter tales, drown out the hurt, and,
  soon love fails.
Where is the peace and love and caring, when all these hurts
  we're angrily sharing?
Where are the bands and the medals to give, to the winner whose
  scars will forever live?
Why do we do it again, and, again? When will we learn to live and
  let live?
Peace will not come, nor, love endure, 'til we softly and quietly
  look for a cure.

Mary E. Stephens

SILENT VISITOR

I know not what had called to me in
what was the darkest of dark nights,
and led me to a window to see, and it
came swift, the brightest of bright lights.

Something from somewhere came silently,
something massive that lit up the night,
disappearing as rapidly as it had come, seemingly,
to sink into the earth as the end of its flight.

Often I wonder what had awakened me
and taken me to that window that night,
that brief spectacular display to see,
to watch that parody of the sun in flight.

Mary D. Welker

WHEN MORNING COMES

Model of Perfection, Lover of the Cross, pierce with
the sword of patient endurance. Fasten us to Your heart.
Stay with us *When Morning Comes*.

Defender of the innocent, guide of pilgrims, lead us
to the Father. Transform our leopard spots. Separate
sheep from goats. Wash in blood of the Lamb. Stay with
us *When Morning Comes*.

Sanctuary of Understanding, chamber of commerce, world
traveler, give us a new lease on life. Place our feet on
holy grounds. Hear the voice of Jesus say: ''Behold the
tabernacle of God with men, and He will dwell with them.
And they shall be His people; and God himself with them
shall be their God.'' Stay with us *When Morning Comes*.

Muriel R. Wiltz

HOLD ME GENTLY

Hold me gently
Speak softly in my ear,
Whisper the words of love
So that I may rise above
To heights without fear.
As we touch, should me mind
Swirl and swirl like the
Spin of a top
Oh, that the feeling would
Never stop
Hold me gently

Sheila Wolf

BRUNETTES

Their lustrous locks evoke the night
With shooting stars of transient light,
As nimbi drift through tufted threads
Eclipsing moons in ebon heads:
Where raven hairs, refined and chaste
With wafts of midnight's fragrant taste,
Imbibe their drinks of solar heat
Which warm their chill when day's complete.

Profoundly rich, romantic dreams
Are weirdly wound in foggy streams
Aflow through silken, runic strands
Of braille we stroke with loving hands.
And Sibyl's most clandestine truth
Discreetly dwells in tawny youth:
To spurn, for mystic shades ignored,
Each worldly blonde so much adored.

Like cozy hearths that thrill the gloam,
Each sober tress embodies Home:
Domestic warmth in dusky dark,
Precursing love's nocturnal spark.
For if the flaxen hold the claim
To fanning passion's fiercest flame,
They're nearly spent — these ashen girls,
While fire's presaged by smoky curls.

Charles J. Lumia

LOVE

Love is caring and sharing.
Love is laughter, grief and pain.
Love is forgiving one another
Over and over again.
Love is tasting the sour,
As well as the sweet.
Love is getting the despondent
Back on his feet.
Love can be happiness,
And love can be kind.
Love can give one insight,
And sometimes love can be blind.
Love can give one courage,
And love can give one hope.
And when problems arise,
Love can give one the ability to cope.
Love can be madness,
Love can be sadness,
And love can bring sorrow,
With little hope for tomorrow.

Jacqueline C. Graves

THE APPOINTMENT

Ring! Ring!
she sang in my hand
as the stiff stuffed chair turned 'round
Then, Bong! Bong!
against my pane
the bristly burly arm put down
Ash! Ash!
Puff! Puff!
Cough! Cough!
Hello!
Anxiously I repeat my address
Then, Click! Click!
Bustle, tussle, toss and tumble
Minutes expire
while ''In a few'' nulls in anger
Then, Ring! Ring!
she rang in my ear
as the stiff stuffed chair turns near
Beep! Beep!
the taxi blew
Ash! Ash!
Cough! Cough!
Hello!
Click! Click!
Bustle, tussle, toss and tumble.

Jeff Herald

MY LADY, MY WOMAN, MY LOVE

In the mist of mysterious dreams
My heart embraces one possession
The reality of my loving schemes
Is you, sweetheart, my only obsession

Where I search to find paradise
A lonely heart knows you are needed
A simple look into those wondrous eyes
Sweet thoughts are never unheeded

Guided by the thoughts of her
The goodness she has always shown
A patient wait only to prefer
Being together through love alone.

As sunshine brings the morning dew
And beautiful dawn beckons within
Refreshing breezes remind me of you
Our love commences to begin

Happiness abounds within my heart
As precious thoughts are only of
My beautiful work of lovely art,
My Lady, My Woman, My Love

Earl Howes, Jr.

STORMY NIGHT

You came to me,
upon a stormy night.
Filled with laughter,
fun and tears.
As the clouds cleared up,
the sun once again,
beat upon my shoulders.
As I followed the rainbow,
to the deepest end.
Only knowing over the rainbow,
there lies another stormy night.

Christina McCoy

SUMMER ROSE

I was your summer rose.
You treated me like a delicate petal.
You watered me every day,
with warmth and love.
You kept me trimmed,
with kindness and gentleness.
Then you stopped watering me,
and you didn't trim me anymore.
I slowly dried up,
and piece by piece,
my delicate petals,
fell to the ground.
Until there was no more.

Christina McCoy

REFLECTIONS OF SARA

As I looked into the mirror this morning,
 I saw myself in you.
Your reflection brought back memories
 of when I was your age.
As I combed your hair
 and put the ribbons neatly in place,
. . . you smiled.
 Your eyes sparkled as you admired yourself
in the mirror, you giggled and proudly said
 ''Thanks Mom!''
You looked one last time and walked away.
 As I stood by myself,
I looked again at my own reflection,
 thinking, how much we really are alike.
Oh, how blessed I feel at this moment,
 to have a wonderful and beautiful
  daughter like you!

Jeanine Shaner

THERE'LL BE NO FORECLOSURE IN HEAVEN

There'll be no foreclosure in heaven
We'll all have beautiful homes.
They'll all be gifts to us,
We won't need to make any loans.
We'll eat the fruit from our own vineyards.
No one will need to beg, borrow or steal.
There'll be no floods or dust bowls.
They'll all have perfect appeal.
Perhaps it will always be summer,
No cold to freeze the fruit buds.
No extreme heat to burn up our gardens,
No temperatures to drop with a thud.
We'll not have to move for not paying the rent,
Not cut-off notice for lights will be sent.
No doctored-up water, it will be sweet and clear.
No hunger or homelessness will we have to fear,
For God will be our light.
And of food there'll be plenty for all.
And Satan won't be there to hurt us
He'll be left down here on this caul.

Marcia R. Morris

EARTH'S MOIST ESSENCE

Wispy drifts in Earth's heaven
    Frequently exceed seven.
Every bulged and blackened can
    Spills moisture on land and man.
Sky's flashy night and daylight shows
    Cause chills and thrills from head to toes.
Sun glaring from above Earth's grand gate
    Lets opaque wetness evaporate.
Where Rain, Hail, Snow, Frost, Sleet, Ice . . . have been,
    Nature's prized dampness could come again.

Joyce Bravo

CIRCLES AND LINES

the turtle sees as he walks the shore
never wishing to return
to where he passed before
alone in his way
for he wants to forget
what his mind retains
his heart regrets

    the otter swims circles just as before
    wishing not to see
    what he missed ahead on shore
    playful in his way
    for he needs to belong
    feel his choices
    were not the wrong

        under their sun's certain rays
        each in his way
        survives tomorrow's
        yesterday

Craig Andrew Wassel

EVEN THROUGH YOU'RE NOT THERE

I'm looking back at what used to be
I realize just how much you mean to me
    And I'm loving you
    Even though you're not there
    And I'm holding you
    Even though you're not there
    And I'm missing you
    Even though you don't care
        anymore

I'm smiling at all the times we shared
I'm finding out just how much I really cared
    And I'll dream of you
    Even though you're not there
    And I'm touching you
    Even though you're not there
    And I'm kissing you
    Even though you don't care
        anymore

I have you in my thoughts
It's as real as it may seem
If I can't have you physically
At least I have my dreams
At least I have my dreams

William D. Waag

HOPE

Christmas brings us hope,
When a little bit of heaven comes down to earth,
The world was never the same,
When the Blessed Mother gave birth.

The Baby Jesus brought salvation,
To a lost and weary world,
Christmas is the great ovation,
For the Prince of Peace,
Hope will unfurl.

Peggy Start

KNOWING

Today I looked upon the skies
I could hardly believe my eyes
I saw you there in all your wondrous glory
Knowing I no longer need to worry
Your hand pointing in one direction
Showing me the way to protection
I promise to follow the path for me you have chose
Knowing in the right direction this path goes
Feeling your presence at my side
Knowing you will walk with me at my stride
Watching over me as I sleep
Giving me dreams that are mine to keep
Helping me to find the light
Guiding me to do what is right
Bringing light into my darkness
For this I give thanks unto you my Lord Jesus Christ

Donna Davies Dominguez

TIMELESS THOUGHTS

Thanks for those
beautiful summer days
we had together.
It feels good
to think back
on memories like those.
Because, somehow,
it makes it seem
as though it was
only yesterday.

Jeanine Shaner

ONLY IN MY DREAMS

In the shadow of darkness
you stand before me.
I see the outline of your soul
from the light in which
you stand in front of.
I reach out to touch you
and my hand feels
the warm air . . .
Nothing is there.
It's so lonely in the dark
of the night,
I've wanted you so badly
that you haunt me
in my dreams.
I want to smell and taste you
to feel your body next to mine,
but, I know this will never be.
Because for now and forever,
you're just only in my dreams.
. . . Only in my dreams.

Jeanine Shaner

MY FIRST LOVE

When we met, I was in love.
You were all I could think of.
You came into my life, time after time,
and faded out again. My emotions went
soaring, growing deep within, but
after a while that would all end.
You went your way; I went mine,
but I will never forget our many
special moments, now lost in the
sands of time. The memory of you,
my first love, will always be there,
and so will the love we once
shared. For us to be together was not
our destiny, but if you ever need a
friend you can find one in me.

Vickie Cerrato

LITTLE OLD TREE

under the water
you can see the sky,
its reflection so deep
and never to lie.
the outline of the clouds
clear as can be,
can be seen beyond
that little old tree.
its leaves are green
with a touch of gold,
it's full of pride
and ever so bold.
the trunk is dark
with a rigid touch,
seemingly sincere
as a love is much.
with this little old tree
in the middle of the clouds,
it adds a special touch
that could never be loud.
under the water
you can see the sky,
with that little old tree
standing ever so wry.

Lisa M. Laratta

TODAY

Today is a day
  that will always be here,
  until it becomes a yesterday.
Then, and only then,
  can today become a memory.
A memory of love
  and a memory of tears,
Remembering life's joys
  and its many fears.
Today can be happy
  or today can be sad,
It can bring to you good things
  and also bring you bad.
Today can bring mystery
  only when it's a tomorrow,
But beware of that mystery
  for sometimes it brings sorrow.
Today is a day
  that is remembered by yesterdays,
  and thought of by tomorrows.
But yesterdays are forgotten
  and tomorrows never come.
So live your life happily and free,
  just one today at at time.

Lisa M. Laratta

WHAT IS A BROTHER?

(or sister)

A brother is a playmate in childhood
A friend and protector in your turbulent teens
A counselor in young adulthood
A great strength in maturity
A treasure of memories during the golden years
The hand of Love and Mercy outstretched —
Forever — across the Universe of Humanity.

Florence Carpenter Janis

JEINA

Innocent, yet mysterious,
Her auburn hair falls below her shoulders,
Accenting her universal eyes,
  which have a life of their own
  . . . another world it seems.

They are so deep and entrancing
  pulling you in with wonder.

Deeper and deeper into her world,
Her world of make-believe,
  her world of childish dreams.

So secure, and yet not a care.

She plays in this world,
  deep in her eyes,
  so gentle and sincere.

Yet still — her youth is only beginning.

Lisa M. Laratta

IN HIM WE MUST TRUST

It's such a happy feeling
To wake up in the morn
To look out the window and see
A new day being born
To see the curtain rising
On God's great stage
To know that we are part of all
The creation that He made
He sets the stage for the day
In all its brilliant best
And with the splendor of it all
We are truly blessed
And then in the evening
As darkness unfolds
The curtain closes and rises again
More beauty to behold
So God in all His wisdom
And love for each of us
Sets the stage for all things
In Him we must trust.

Virginia Robinson

I REALLY BLEW IT TODAY LORD

I really blew it today Lord
I really lost control
My emotions just boiled over
And Satan took a-hold
I said some things that just weren't nice
Not pleasing to Your ear
I know You'll understand dear Lord
And wipe away each tear
This makes me so aware dear Lord
Of just how human we are
It's so very easy to sin
And our souls so easily mar
Forgive me Lord for unkind words
That we so easily said
Help me to think before I speak
And say kinds words in their stead

Virginia Robinson

I ASK OF YOU

Come and take me by the hand
Show me the ways you have planned
Give me strength to pass each dawn
Watch over me as the doe watches her fawn
Teach me all I need to know
Show me knowledge so I may grow
Give me courage to seek what I must find
Help me to pass through all sorrows
Give to me hope of tomorrow
All of these things I ask of you
To guide me in all that I may do
Through you is how I live
It is you who taught me how to give
I am one of many daughters
But you are Father of all fathers
You are Father of heaven and earth
It is you who truly gives birth
I will walk my days on this earth
Following you my Father to my place of new birth

Donna Davies Dominguez

UNREST

You look around to see the people
Wandering into the nearest building that has a steeple
Still feeling turmoil and unrest
Looking east and then west
Looking everywhere with eyes that are blind
Following an empty path to seek what you need to find
Standing before a window looking for a place to hide
What is this shining light that stands by your side
Putting one foot in front of the other to step forward
When you hear the loving voice speak, fear not for I am
your Lord
The voice came from the shining light and said, You were
blind and could not see
because you looked everywhere but unto me.

Donna Davies Dominguez

POLITICIANS PLEASE

Why can't we make our politicians see
That truth and honesty could do more to
Make our country shine
Than all the dough and wine?

Some try to hide their sins behind closed doors
And some laugh about the many tricks they play.
But people do discern
For them that's real concern.

How pure and simple it would be if they
Could but realize where their duty lies.
It's to people and God
For the approval nod.

Apathy, irresponsibility,
spending above income, padding pockets
Damages our image.
That must be presage.

So merciful Father above, let them be fair,
Bow in reverence and I pray, Let them
Portray our nation free
For all countries to see.

L. Lasher

PEACE

Today I shall go up into the high mountains.
Higher and ever higher the road wound through the deep green forests
where the pines lifted their heads, searching for the sun.
Near the summit of the peak, the trees gave way to an endless
vista of deep cobalt blue, accented by dreaming, drifting clouds.
In the far distance, as if in a half-remembered dream, rose
the almost unbelievably massive pinnacles of the mighty
Snagre De Cristo range, seen as far away as 50 miles.
Unseen dwellers of the mighty angelic kingdom, with the aid of the
wind, had gathered great masses of clouds to hover near the peaks,
doubling their height to afford greater protection from storms, and
to enhance their breathtaking beauty like frosting on Mother Earth's
birthday cake.
Here, near the fragrant pines, I silently spoke words of
the ancient rite:
 "Earth to earth, ashes to ashes, dust to dust,
  Eternal peace grant unto her, oh Lord, and may
  light perpetual shine upon her."

How she loved this place of utter silence and beauty,
crowned by the glory of the snow-covered mountains, blessed by
the warmth of the mystic sun, and by a myriad of gleaming stars, seeming
close enough to touch — in the velvet nights.
And a symbol of neverending life, the soft and gentle
winds blow . . . forever free.

Sibyl Michel

A STRING OF PEARLS

*Written in loving memory to my mother
who taught us all she knew and understood
about love and life.*

A string of pearls on my mother's dressing table
Laid there by her aged wrinkled hands
Oh! The stories they'd tell — if only they could
Of her life — most reverent and sweet.

I'd like to go back to the spring of her life
And walk arm in arm with her then
To admire and to love the things she knew
To try and to understand.

The pearls on the table are a loving reminder
Of the life she willingly shared
The hardships she hurled, the things she loved most
Are the things I'll always treasure.

She never questioned how tough life would be
As the tasks of her life lay before her
She never doubted that loving and caring
Could any more righteous be.

Her pearls of wisdom she taught us each day
To love and respect one another
To diminish the span between sister and brother
'Tis her story of complete love and devotion.

Except for the love I had for my mother
And the things she stood for in life
Few things are loved more by me today
Than Mother's pearls on my dressing table.

Joan Lee Schetter

GLIMPSE

I stepped outside
I thought it dark
I saw the flight
Of bird — a lark
Swoop toward the trees
Clumped close en masse
On guard they stood
For what might pass
My eyes surprised
Drew to a part
Of sky encompassed
Piece of art —
A brush of paint
Had touched that spot
With rose — with purple
Melting pot.
A gasped! A beauty
Seldom viewed
My fascinated
Stare stayed glued
Until the colors
Dimmed from sight —
The sun was kissing
Day — good night.

Lavona Bunting

TREE OF LIFE

Flow on crystal river
With your abundance of pure water
The roots of the *Tree of Life*
Hold firm into your banks.

Leaves softly rustle
On the branch
Waiting for spiritual love
To come and pluck them from the stem.

Medicine is being made
For the healing of the *nations*
The sound of the dove is heard
Throughout the land!

Florence Carpenter Janis

TOGETHER

Let each kiss be a special treasure for you
to keep and hold.

Always share and trust each other and together
you will grow old.

Listen to your love and hear not the wind,
one is external and the important is within.

As you reach out to each other, may your love
bond you as one.

Let your journey into forever be both exciting
and fun.

Jacques Russell

A GARDEN

Dig deep, O God, within my heart,
the root of sin destroy;
Dig deep, O God, within my heart,
restore to me Thy joy.

Uncover all the ugliness, reveal
sin's awful blight;
Let the seeds of Thy love germinate,
restore the awful site.

Dig deep, O God, within my heart,
please control my life;
Dig deep, O God, within my heart,
to end this awful strive.

Dig deep, O God, within my life,
down where I begin;
That I might shine forth the reflection
of Your sweet life within.

Let my heart become Your garden,
watered with love's sweet dew;
May my life be Thy rejoicing, as
I bring forth the ''fruits'' of You!

David Rymer

A TOUCH

Lord you've been so good to me,
you've given me so much;
You've given to me life itself,
thank you for Your touch.

A joy, a home, a family, serving
You is grand;
I'm rich, and blessed, and happy,
I'm a humbled, joyful man.

Heartache and joy, comfort and
cheer, home, and love, and land;
These are the blessings that
You give, by Your extended hand.

Love, joy, and blessed peace, the
things we need so much;
the blessings we need so desperate,
come from the Master's touch.

I thank you Lord for loving me,
I thank you O so much;
For your great loving-kindness,
and Your sweet, gentle touch!

David Rymer

QUIET MOMENTS

The rain is softly falling,
the wind doth kiss the trees;
The meadow lark is singing,
flowers blown by gentle breeze.

The cattle on a thousand hills,
a babbling, laughing brook;
The rustling of a billion leaves,
the mountains stand and look.

The quietness of the morning,
the stillness of the night;
The voice of Thy creation,
in Thy presence they all delight.

All Thy worlds shall praise Thee,
Thy creation shall bow its knee;
Thy praise shall sound so awesome,
like the fullness of the sea.

The saints shall worship in Thy
presence, we shall feel so grand;
we shall abide forever, in that
glorious, glorious land.

David Rymer

LOVE

I'm not a religious person,
But I know that God is there;
For where else could I have gotten
So much love to share?

I give it to my family.
My children, I adore.
I give it to my husband,
And yet, I still have more.

I give it to my parents,
Who've done so much for me.
My brother and my sisters,
I give it happily.

And there are many others.
They know how much I care.
They make it oh so easy
To give them each a share.

And when the load gets heavy,
And it's hard for me to see,
I think about the ones I love,
And they give it back to me.

Julia Eddins Fisher

YOUNG MAN BLUES

What a troubled young man you really must be, never knowing where
  you're going or who your friends truly must be.
Suicide has been a comfort to you, but not fully touching your heart.
Just another passing thought.

What a troubled young man you really must be,
Society knocks at your door and the dogs are barking at your heels.
You wrap the leash around their necks until they lie limp in your hands,
And you cry in self-pity for something, even you, do not understand.

Well you already know that life is strange, and those strangers have
  almost made a home in your bed.
You shout your frustrations and vent your anger at those four walls,
While you reach for the whip and throw in the towel.
There is no solution for what you want to do, I just hope it doesn't
  end up costing you.

What a troubled young man you really must be,
All those flies that swarm around your head, make it rather difficult
  for you to see.
Bite the chains that seem to only bind you young man and reach for
  what you believe.
We're here to lend you support while you battle society and social
  disease.

Cathrine Christine

LETTER FROM A FAN

Dear —
    You know me not, I'm just another pretty face in the crowd,
jumping up and down, dancing to your music like a stimulant in my
brain. When at last the night is done, I go home and go to bed alone.
    No tears stain my pillow.
    We've all got our dreams and Tinkerbell does exist for those of
us who believe. I always wanted to be a big-time writer . . . books,
maybe even songs, but I'm a poet instead; I guess that isn't half bad!
    I'll remember you at Christmas and again on your birthday. I'll
send you a card or two like I always do. And if you're sick, I'll still
think of you.
    This isn't a letter of love or worship. Some of us know when
fantasies begin and where reality ends. Society has already crucified
me for my beliefs; they'll one day know what it is like to die hanging
from a cross.
    Next time you pass by, through this little town, be sure to look
me up. I know where you'll be staying, even though the hotel has changed
its name. Who knows? Maybe we'll have a hot cup o' tea and some good
conversation.
    Best Wishes Always.

Cathrine Christine

CATHY CHRISTINE HOUSE. Pen Names: Cathrine Christine; K. C.
Whitefeather; Born: Slidell, Louisiana, 1962; Single; Education: Adams City
Senior High, Commerce City, Colorado, 1980; Barnes Business College,
Denver, Colorado, 1980; Occupation: Data entry; Awards: Honorable Men-
tions for: 'A Warrior Called Death,' 1986; 'Who is to Tend My Grave?''
1986; 'The Writer,' 1987; Golden Poet Awards, 1986, 1987; Poetry: 'A War-
rior Called Death,' 1987; 'The Book,' *American Poetry Anthology,* 1987;
'Touch Me,' *Remembrances of Love,* 1987; Comments: *Death, as morbid as
it is, I am rather fascinated with it and just as scared. Originality — a must.*

THINKING

You were my friend when I had none . . .
  You thought you were weak,
    but I knew you were strong.

Life has taken another turn . . .
Another lesson, I supposed . . . to be learned.

Wondering now if there will be
Another being like you, who sees
        me for me?

I never knew you looked up to me . . .
    A heroine, you thought and believed
    I *was* . . . and *Am.*

Sitting and thinking of moments that are past . . .
    Contemplating, Life.

Andréa D. Arnold

BUTTERFLIES

When diamonds on black velvet
    was my Indiana sky
I had to turn away before
    you saw moisture in my eye —
When your arms encircled 'round me
    as your lips caressed my hair,
And the place was Fairbanks Park —
    it was there, it was there . . .

Your soft words of reassurance
    stirred the slumbering cords once more
And those dead forgotten feelings
    began to rise and soar,
I first began to realize
    (praying not to be a dope),
That perhaps my face
    could smile again
And my heart could dare to hope.

Jeanne McClintock

HAPPINESS

Happiness comes from within
It starts with a prayer, knowing
God forgives sins
Happiness can come from a friend or loved one
Happiness is more than a feeling
It is a constant struggle
Sometimes our emotions get in
The way of happiness
We feel depressed or angry and
We don't know why.
Happiness is the foundation of
All emotional strength
In order to be happy you must love yourself
We are never happy all the time
As we get older, we learn from our experiences and grow spiritually
We are all striving to become mature, responsible human beings
Most people want to be in charge of their lives
The losers are content to remain lost,
And the winners keep on working at it
Love is where you find it — it is
what makes us whole

Chapin Field

FOR CHIP

Once upon a time,
I wandered through my life;
Searching, ever searching
For a world more free from strife.

I wandered through a tunnel,
So dark and full of woe.
I wandered through a forest,
Where nothing bright could grow.

I wandered up a hillside,
So steep and hard to climb;
And thoughts of ''Is it worth all this?''
Kept running through my mind.

I looked down in a valley,
A safe harbor for the soul.
I knew that God had been there,
And I had reached my goal.

I saw love and peace and sunshine
And flowers of each kind.
I knew that I would be all right.
That valley was my mind.

Julia Eddins Fisher

THE CANCER OF THE EARTH

Sun sets his eye on her glamours
The Earth displays healthy colours
Blue waves, green waves of the forests
Wide poles of ice, sharp biting crests.

Sometimes his rays burn his old love;
Planes have drilled holes in the ozone;
Drops of the sea they can't remove,
A film of oil spread on a zone.

New suns shaped like orange mushrooms
Bruise the rich bosom of the Earth
Still young after five billion births
Of human ants piling up rooms.

Ants who don't store their rejections
But dilute them in air, water
And soil, poisonous pollutions
Of the ants planning the murder.

Early ants took care of the Earth,
Coloring the fields with flowers,
Tapestries of gardens, pickers
Of fruits, not Cancer of the Earth.

Emmanuel Pierreuse

SAD, PRETTY

I've been sad in Tokyo,
Sad in New York City
So many girls I've seen
Look so pretty

Don Mac Laren

DUNKERQUE

Church in the dunes, fishing harbor;
Both French and Flemish are spoken;
Streets, American names given,
The wounds of history are still sore.

Dunkerque, your Leughenaer Tower;
Leughenaer, Flemish for liar;
Your clock says a-quarter-to-four
Any time I face the harbour.

Dunkerque, your ''Minck,'' your fishmarket;
Silver of herrings, venal girls;
In a bar, jazz of a trumpet,
Drops of rain, your refreshing pearls.

Baptism of the sea, sailing
To Iceland, women waving
Their handkerchiefs of lace, their man
Will disappear or fill the pan.

Dunkerque, bridge over the canal,
Shipbuilding, fusion of metal
In the blast-furnace of courage.
Workers deserve a better wage.

Dunkerque, alive are your legends
In my exiled heart; one attends
Your carnival with excitement;
Throw of fish, colorful giant.

Emmanuel Pierreuse

TIME TO BE STILL

Constant searching for the place
    Where time stands still.
Unnoticed recognitions
    Of movement on a hill.

Developed senses flourish
    As the sun delivers night.
Uncompleted thoughts
    Complete with blossoming delight.

Curing anxious wounds
    Enables grief to safe restore.
Soothing comforts rest
    As the clouds begin to pour.

Windy meditations
    Find the answers once unknown.
Questing love awakened,
    Peaceful visions finally shown.

Inspired by the silence,
    Conscious efforts go unheard.
All listening time surrenders
    When God's breath reveals a word.

Sheryl Lynn Porter

FORGIVE

Old friendships reminiscing
    Tempting weeds of scornful past
To encounter painful moments —
    But this time won't be the last.

For hatred never waives
    Upon its rightful place to live —
In heavy thoughts of fury,
    Those refusing to forgive.

While dwelling on this anger
    Tearful wounds can only pour —
Some words of poisoned venom,
    Causing spite to burn the core —

Of endless reasons pondered,
    Building layers to remain —
Upon the heated coals
    Within the one who holds the pain.

So why continue hating
    And refusing to forgive —
When all revenge must die
    For any peacefulness to live.

Sheryl Lynn Porter

MORE THAN A PRAYER

Too many Americans when put to the test
Are self-seeking persons who hope for the best.

The creme-de-la-creme seems to be their goal
A philosophy of humanism, avoiding all toil.

In attaining the line of least resistance,
Helps in some ways to shorten the distance.

One minute in heaven, an eternity in hell,
No need to ask for whom tolls the bell.

The very fiber of this great nation
That in the past caused jubilation,

Is rotting at the very seam,
No longer claim we the American Dream.

Never having reached our apogee,
It's downhill now day-by-day.

It's depressing what our selfism has wrought,
To our very beginning, we are now brought.

The big lie in Eden would make you a God
All it did was cause a great sob.

Dear God we plead in penitential gloom
How have we come to this sorry doom.

An answer comes to us from within
To help explain our New-Age sin.

When good men do nothing and evil men dare
To change the world takes more than a prayer.

Katherine Bieluck

MY SHADOW

My shadow is a part of me
that lives inside myself
If you know my shadow, you know me
It knows no evil, and stands tall in the late afternoon
It is my constant companion and allows me to feel good
In the nighttime it goes to sleep
It is like a mirror that reflects
all the love you feel inside yourself
Sometimes I wish it would just
go away and leave me alone
Other times it is an inspiration,
which carries me through the day
When the sun shines, it is always there
All you need to do is look for it
I love my shadow and it loves me
As long as I am alive, my
shadow will be with me

Chapin Field

LOVE IS JUST A
FOUR-LETTER WORD

If life were a bowl of cherries, we would all be rich.
But we must accept the unfairness of life and care about other
people besides ourselves.
If you allow people to love you,
you will find that life can be beautiful.
You don't have to be the immaculate conception,
you can just be Chapin and people will like you.
Don't blame God or other people for your problems.
The situation is never hopeless
no matter what people may say
Freedom *is* just another word for nothing left to lose.
Hang in there and ride the wave to the best of your ability.
Soon the ride will be over and the wave will be just a memory.
Value your life, because it is a gift from God.
It is ok to be cool and Communist, but don't let it go
to your head.
Keep thinking positive and then good things will happen.
There is so much to learn about
and do in a world that wants to know.
And I am the focus of everybody's attention.
I guess I like it that way.
It hurts a little, but at least I am not lonely.

Chapin Field

TO THE DOLLY VARDEN

In crystal waters cold and swift, you fought
And won a thousand battles, denying man
His trophy sought; you swam in raging mountain
Streams against the rapids, gave no thought
To failing, so you won! — and, time became not
Friend but foe; a prize far grander than
The rest you did become. With tail held high and
Proud you basked in glory! — but, freedom's lot
Is fragile; and mighty warrior, lightly taken,
For you 'twas lost forever. A tear did fall
Upon my cheek today, remembering when
You wore the victor's crown; oh well, 'tis all
For naught — dreaming of what might have been,
Me on my bed — and you upon the wall.

Barbara Nell Lamb

THE CLOSE OF DAY

The sun is slowly sinking behind the mountaintop
The children from their playing now must stop,
Their voices are hushed till rosy morning.
Now they are quietly wrapped in bed
While the stars and moon shine brightly
In the sky above their head.
While the day is closing
And shadows fall in the forest and around the garden wall,
The lonesome owl the whippoorwill too
Have come from their nests
And are singing to you.

Harriet Elizabeth Stauffer

THE EMOTIONAL NUCLEICS
OF THE HUMAN REACTOR

Motor throat.
Oil machinery speaks
open/closing . . .
Each word slithers,
                reptilian,
like droplets of liquid metal,
                smoke/hissing . . .
scent and sound
somehow guilty in the sunlight.
Emotions . . . reaching . . . critical . . . mass . . .
molten lava/blood of fire
the squid-tentacled brain
                suction/spiked
erupting volcanic cactus flowers —
!meltdown!
!meltdown!
the sky is broken!
my eyes are broken!
My tears are hot liquid prisms
                burning through the core.

Brian Bywater

HELL'S PARLOR

Werewolves lurk 'midst the shadows of night:
Goblins loom in the eerie half-light;
Gargoyles leer, partly hidden from sight:
Look into my world . . .

Satans lust for lost souls with delight;
Witches lean o'er foul brews in moonlight;
Zombies lurch from dank graves, reeking fright:
Come into my world . . .

Vampires lure virgin victims, then bite;
Monsters lunge against chains, full of fight;
Dragons lash tails that maim left and right:
Step into my world.

Warlocks leap, cutting off chance of flight;
Steel doors lock, booming shut hard and tight!
Bright flames lick, spelling doom, sealing plight:
Welcome to your world . . .

Richard Alan Rieger

THE MISSION

Ancient streets of the Mission —
Laced with lost souls,
Faces penetrate the collective muse —
Hidden in the graffiti and telephone wires,
Hidden in the blood on Twenty Fourth Street.

Ancient people of the Mission —
Turning over dreams like sliced beef,
Like sliced flesh.
Seen in the languages, the smiles —
The decay of man —
As a man lay face down on the sidewalk.
Seen in the crowned frowns —
The rebirth of mankind.

Night falls — omnipotent,
Rain falls — omniscient,
Life crawls in the Mission —
Through the sleazy bars,
In the stolen cars,
Under the rusty stars —
Of the cemetery.

Lives, life itself — melts in the Mission,
As priests bless the confessors,
And young virgins undress
The assassins.

Don Mac Laren

DON MAC LAREN. Comments: *Don Mac Laren's journey through life began about thirty years ago in Detroit. It has taken him (among other places) from San Francisco to New York City by thumb and from Fukuoka to Tokyo by bullet. At present he makes his home on a fault line.*

LARA

As natural as the Northwest Wind
Sudden happiness, from within
The wondrous gift from God above
A daughter, created from love.

Sometimes as calm as the floating sea
A lovely girl, a lady to be
Mysterious as the midnight moon
A rosebud, just in bloom.

Her face as fresh as the morning dew
Sparkling eyes of ocean blue
More precious than the rising sun
None sweeter, no not one!

Teresa Overton Chestang

MY MOTHER

Someone very special
Someone very bold
Someone as good as gold
My mother!

Someone who never fades
Someone brighter than sunny days
Someone who only gets recognized
On these special days
My mother!

Someone nice and sweet
Someone you can't beat
Someone who always takes
The back seat
My mother!

Someone to talk to when things
Get rough
Someone to lean on when things
Get tough
My mother!

Teresa Overton Chestang

WHEN WILL ABEL WIN?

After he got back from Vietnam,
We said, "He'll be all right.
He'll forget. That'll be the end of it."
Questioned, he'd only say,
"War is raw."
Except for his sleepnessness
Or his nightmares,
He did seem much the same —
A little more restless,
More withdrawn perhaps.
One thing, though.
Now he didn't want to study law.
He said he'd outgrown it.
And nothing tempted him,
Not money nor love.
As for guns, he couldn't abide them.
Sometimes he'd ask the preacher
Serious-like, "When will Abel win?
When will we be whole again?"
Then one day he was gone.
At dawn Seth found him
Swinging in the old oak
Down by the creek. We agreed
He'd just given up. Seems he'd learned
Abel never would be home again.

Deloris Robinson Mullwee

A LITTLE THOUGHT

A little thought occurred to me
It even made me shudder.
If Pasteur had invented the pill,
Would I have had a Mudder?

The thought is frightening
Very distressing too,
And even if there were a me
Would there have been a you?

Mary Christine Bowen

LISTEN

Can you hear it?
The drum beating
  out its song.
It is different
  for everyone
  but it still
    beats its
    song.

People marching
  on the forest
    track.
People marching long.
  In a
  quiet revolution.
  A thousand
    drums
  in different
    beat;
  Harmonizing.
  Listen to the
    song
  of freedom.
  Can you
    hear it?

Christine Tatem

GRADUATION

The wind blows his flowing black robe,
His mortar-clad head is held high,
Pomp and Circumstance soft beats
Are echoed in my proud heart
Just yesterday he came to us
Garmentless and crying
Now with diploma, in hand,
He goes to guide his own life.
Oblivious to the crowd, my thoughts race
To memories of a childhood spent
And tears fall softly, as time takes back
A treasure only lent.

Mary Christine Bowen

TIME TO MYSELF

I'm sorry to leave like this
The game of life is it hit or miss?
I need to understand about myself
Instead my dreams grow dust on a shelf
Memories fade like the sun.
Destiny changed and a new one has begun
Who am I? And what am I all about?
I'm full of questions, fears and doubt.
Searching for the eternal wisdom key
Unlocking the doors to set my spirit free.
Chasing rainbows in the eastern sky
Take flight and learn to fly.
Absorbing fragrant fields of flowers
Adventuring through dark castle towers.
Unfolding the mystery of life,
Learning to overcome my inner strife.
Why can't I see
What the future holds for me
To wish upon a fallin' star
Living fantasies that lie afar.

Shirley Zagorec

SMOKE

Smoke a stogie for Bogey

I love these cigarettes:
   love their ashes and flames,
   their trailing smoke and their names;
   their ashes and embers
   a universe that remembers
   the many times, many places,
   many names and many faces
   when, where, and with whom I've smoked . . .

And, as each smoke burns down
   (As did Old Londontown,
      (Old Berlin, Tokyo, Seoul, Saigon, G. I. Joe . . .),
         As each smoke burns down
            Like a bomber in flames
               (To the echoing sounds
                  Of brave men without names)
                  I take heart
                     (Like the Anglos, the Saxons, and Jutes)
                        And my American roots.

Richard Alan Rieger

AMBITION

Suspension of disbelief becomes an element essential
For the survival of adult imagination;
Recapturing for a moment or a lifetime
The childfaith that laughs at impossibility
Making all the difference, sometimes
Between a life well lived
And mere existence.

The hope in our souls drives the playthings of fancy
Through that windy summerland inside us
Our dreams are like colored flower petals
That blow here and there in our secret landscape
And a child that never died and goes by our name
Runs after them there, laughing
And sometimes gets lucky,
Snatching one from the wind on a high glorious hop.

William T. Masonis

NIGHT IS NOT DARK!

Is night to you like an inky black
   that your eyes can't begin to pierce through?
Look again! Through my kitchen window.
   You can see: the church steeple
radiantly aglow — lit by angel lights;
   the beginning of a new moon, waiting to erupt
into big and full — lighting the sky.

   When dark comes on — houses, one by one,
shine with a glow that hurts the eye as switches are flipped.
   Streets lights, all in an orderly row,
blink on steadily.
   Cars go by — two bright eyes and often more.
They cast their brightness on the endless streets.
   There is light everywhere where darkness once was.

   Electric — what a wonderful invention!
All but the moon, were not meant to be light.
   Night is *not* dark but it should be!
      Night was not meant to be light!

Joan Morrone

A WAITRESS'S NIGHTMARE!

"Oh Waitress, Waitress, come and see!
   There's something floating in my tea.
I really don't know what it is
   But something took a bite of me!"

On the other side of her, another pipes up haughtily:
   "Oh Miss, oh Miss, my coffee's cold; my ice cream's hot.
Oh, please take care of me."

Her tray is full of many things, just loaded to the gill.
   "Oh Miss, oh Miss, a glass of water fast I need —
So I can take my pill."

All day she hears this mournful song:
   "I need." and just right now!
No matter that another needs
   Just what *you're* asking for — and how!

   The waitress's question is — just how — ?

Can I — be *here* — and over *there* —
   on the other side of the floor?
   Give me a pair of roller skates and plug my motor in.
      Wind me up and let me go
      And I'll serve you with a
         G
           r
             i
               n!

Joan Morrone

WHAT COLOR IS GOD?

What color is God?
   Is he white; is he black?
   Is he yellow or red?
      Did he say one was better?
      Did he write *you* a letter
         To tell you to fight with one who is white
         Or one who is black and he mustn't fight back?
Did he say to ignore the one who is yellow
Or to chase off that red, Indian fellow?
   When you get to heaven as *you* think you will;
      (Though you didn't love your brother)
         Do you think God will say:
   You black saints go to the rear,
   White folks stay up front:
   Red man, I have a reservation for you;
   Yellow man, I'm not sure I prepared for you a place.
      God is a spirit
         Where does color come in?
         Break down the barrier.
         To hate is a serious sin.
      We are clay in the potter's hand.
      He chose to make us different.
      He put us all on different lands.
      Then to all, his son he sent.

      What color is God?

Joan Morrone

VOICE OF SILENCE

Summer called to a maiden it even hasten
to be near, as I bask in its warm sunshine
beneath me the cool earth above the
gentle air. Hummingbirds fly off in
search of nectar, while whispered sounds
that have long passed echo through my mind.
How silent the noiseless wonder that
speaks my voice of silence, my own
thoughts, my own best words to pen.
Memories that are joyful bring peace
and are without feeling of despair.

Dorothy M. Anderson

BRINGING OUT YOUR BEST

Jam session in my brain
When he speaketh to me
I never doubt as saints seem to be
With a shout with Joy pours his Jubilee
Into my body into my soul he let it be
He is further than the highest cloud
Closer than the nearest star
Why would you be left behind
Trying to master your troubled mind
When you cry and no one hear
When you are sick and enemies are there
Don't just read and listen you say a prayer
Jesus guideth you everywhere
Jesus maketh living better
With the help that in a Blessing
Don't try to prove your love is true
Love in your heart will prove you
God love cover the world it's a gift from above
I have a view I have an idea too
That some concerned person feels
What religion is for real — I say
What ever Bringeth out your Best
It is the one for you

Rosa Lee King

WHAT TIME IS IT?

To a child
   time is the spring;
   it signifies growth.

To a youngster
   time is a boiling kettle;
   it takes forever.

To an adolescent
   time is graduation;
   it's almost here.

To a young adult
   time is tomorrow
   it can always be done later.

To an aging adult
   time is an ocean wave;
   it merely comes and goes.

To an elderly adult
   time is an avalanche;
   it begins slowly,
   rapidly builds to a roaring anxiety,
   and smothers you beneath its weight
   as it passes you by.

Charles E. Stickle

ENLIGHTENMENT

Children born into this world
Know not a parent's prayer.
They rightfully take for granted
This wondrous love so rare.

Through the years my own were born,
I turned around in awe.
Just who was it that taught me life,
And God's Treasured, Golden Law.

It was Mama's hand that rocked the cradle,
Her soft voice we heard at night.
Daddy's strength was always there,
He taught us wrong from right.

With gentle tears and shaky smile
I know the truth at last.
The reason for my being thus,
Comes from a well-taught past.

If I can teach my own sweet babes
Just half as much was I,
Then they will have their wings someday,
And join us in the sky.

Billie A. Skelton

I WOULD PICK YOU

To Michael and Lynn O'Brien

If I had to climb a mountain,
   I would climb Mt. Everest.
If I had to sail an ocean,
   I would sail the Pacific.
If I needed a metal,
   I would pick gold.
If I needed a gem,
   I would get a diamond.
But if I needed a friend, I would
go no further than your door,
because I would pick you.

Michael E. Hatcher

TIME

Time flies
Time lags
Is still
Is kind
Cruel
Happy
Sad
Leisurely
Mad
Cures
Kills
Is a thief
A tell tale
A nag
Foe
Friend
A beginning
An end

Joy Jackson

MEMORIES

Memories
Locked in time and space
Bittersweet hiatus make.
Unbidden they rise
To play whimsical relays
In everyday lives.
Tread careful
With those best unaroused.
Pray
That your flights be
Fleeting, unexposed.
Return!
Mindful of your spouse,
New memories
To make
Through which to carouse.

Joy Jackson

LATE BLOOMER?

Proud Sumac
Just beyond the fence,
Convinced of early spring.
Migratory birds swoop down to rest,
And pluck the young teats
Off her breast.
Come April,
There she sits undressed,
But for the mistletoe that clings.

Joy Jackson

NIGHTTIME DELIVERANCE

Be brave my small and precious one,
As day has fallen and night has come
For many burdens will soon be gone
As the battle's ended and our war is done . . .
Darkness has drawn nigh.

Nightfall will encompass our souls
With a blanket soft as silk
Cradling us in peaceful slumber
Protecting our hearts from harm . . .
Close of day is upon us.

Throughout the umbra of evening tide
Visions of flight and fancy embrace our fantasy
Of dreamland building our castles in the air
To fill our spirits with inspiration . . .
Dawn is soon approaching.

Nighttime shadows have begun to lift;
Our dreamlike state fades softly, slowly;
Slowly from our minds, our hearts, our souls,
Vanishing, while leaving us renewed for life.
Daybreak.

Caroline Bredekamp

John Andrew & Son Co.

LOVE DEFINED

Oh, love is like a shining star
That radiates light from afar.
To some it is a guiding light
To alleviate the darkness of night.
Love is a joyful shared emotion
It is a soothing lotion, a magic potion
It makes life truly worth living
With emphasis on caring and giving.
Love is experienced more than seen
In life, it is the *reason* for *being*.
A special feeling that takes hold
And affects most everyone — young and old.
Love is a delight and pleasure
Love is discovered buried treasure.
Love is difficult to describe
Yet it makes one feel secure and alive.
Love is an inspiring melody
That lingers on — in perfect harmony.
Accompanied by heady notes — highs and lows,
From an Arpeggio to a Crescendo.
Love is like a piece of cake
That one may refuse or partake.
Whether it's frosting or crumbs one takes,
Love is determined by the choice one makes.

Phyllis Hefty

WHAT USED TO BE

The sun shone down on her golden hair
She looked like an angel standing there
She was remembering the days that used to be
Before her love set out to sea

He told her that he would return someday
And bring her jewels from across the bay
One night a storm swept across his ship
He never was heard of after that trip

The sun shines down on streaks of grey
She looks worn out and has nothing to say
She's remembering the days that used to be
Before her love set out to sea

Betty Baker

MY HERO

You are my hero,
my everlasting love.
For you're always there,
through the good times
and the bad.

You share my joys.
You wipe my tears away.
You feel what I feel,
love the things I love.

You make me laugh.
You make me cry.
And, through it all,
you will always be my hero,
my everlasting love.

Deborah Pratt

MY FAIR LADY

My Fair Lady — I
Know her form and face,
Moving where she will
In satin and lace.

Together for ages,
Distance is no bar —
Here dancing with a moonbeam,
Or swinging on a star.

Love is not exclusive —
You can know her, too,
When your eye is single,
And your heart is true!

Lillian G. Alexander

IF YOU KEEP ON MOVING

If you keep on moving
You've got to get somewhere
Don't stand in one space
And you'll keep getting near
Keep your feet circulating
In the air
If you're not going backwards
You will eventually get there
Tasks and obstacles are before you
But it's just a matter of time
Before they will be behind you
As you progress and steadily climb
If you keep on moving
You've got to get somewhere
Tomorrow's problems will soon disappear
Others will follow but they too
 will be in the rear
Just pick up your legs
Go forward — Have no fear
Because if you keep on moving
You've got to get somewhere

Bessie Frazier

THE OLD PAWNSHOP

I want to stroll on the old boardwalk
And search in tiny shops
For old dreams lost or put aside
'Midst earrings, bracelets, clocks.
Nestled there in a faded case
Is a tiny golden ball,
A triumph rare of high school days
Abandoned against the wall.
Engagement rings sand wedding bands,
Necklaces, beads and shells,
A gun or two, and a horn that blew
Gay tunes when all was well.

What is that against the farthest wall?
A baby's shoe all worn,
Preserved in bronze it nestles there,
Immortality forsworn.
You've left these dreams all here for me,
Of you they were a part,
You've left them here for me alone,
And touched my willing heart.
And if I came into this little shop,
What would the owner say
If I asked for the dreams he has on sale
For me alone today?

Lucille M. Kroner

LOVE

We often speak of love each day,
But fail to let love lead the way.
Instead we strive for selfish gain;
All of our efforts are in vain.
We do not love, share, or give.
We have forgotten how to live.
Greed has been our way of life,
Filled with envy, hate and strife.
Love must fill our hearts each day
And be our guide along life's way.
The more we learn to freely give,
The happier life will be to live.
Peace will reign and we will see
It is love that sets us free.
No matter where on earth we go,
We prosper by the love we sow.

Margaret Binnix Nevins

WISHES FOR LUCILLE

I wish for you a songbird
To sit upon your window sill,
In the early morning hours,
When all is calm and still.
 I wish for you an Eastern sky,
 Tinted with pink and red,
 To give you happy thoughts
 As you climb out your bed.
I wish for you a sunbeam
To brighten the corners of your room,
And fill them full of joy,
To chase away the gloom.
 After clouds have sprinkled raindrops,
 I wish for you a colorful rainbow
 Of red and orange and yellow,
 Green, blue, violet and indigo.
I wish for you a beautiful sunset
As it sinks slowly in the West,
Until the light of another day
May you have a peaceful rest.
 I wish for you sparkling stars,
 And may their charm, you feel,
 As if they all seem to say
 "Goodnight, sweet dreams, Lucille!"

Alice Kline

JUST A POET

When you forget to bring that pad you always tote around
To scribble down ideas that just somehow enter your mind,
Then you'll know just how a fish must feel when it is
    high and dry,
Or what it's like to be a bird without the air to fly.
Well! That's exactly how I feel when my pad is not around —
Just a poet high and dry without his verse.

Robert Weetman

OF COURSE! YOU LOSE!

Gone! Gone! Ha, Ha I can't stop laughing, Sir.
You didn't know that came?
That the fountain of youth that Ponce de Leon searched for
    is nothing more than a dream,
That the withered and tattered old look on your face is the
    expression that all of us wear,
When we finally believe what the mirror tells us? No! We
    didn't pull one over on the game.

Robert Weetman

WEDGE

The Sumac shouts a deeper red this fall
Bittersweet clings closer to the vine
Woodsmoke whispers white and hugs the chimney wall
Reluctant as the chill wind mixes it with time.

Too soon frost film is on the moss-rimmed pond
Yahweh's hourglass ''Say'' of Season's constant rhyme
Where wild geese lift to slash their northern bond
Pulses streak to keep the unknown climb.

Bette Armstrong

TINY CHILD

Hair of filmy threads of sunsilk,
Face soft with contours of questioning,
Crooked finger pointing to a bird,
Child, I wish it were true what they say.

I am told that I can make of you anything I choose,
That I can give you fluency of speech,
The artistry to shape the air
Into crafted molds of sound,
That I can make of you a writer
So that your plastic pen
Could fill the page with love's mystic lettering,
Or that I can steep you in astronomy
And teach you to look into the distant past
And glimpse your far beginnings.

I wish it were true but it is not.
I cannot go back now into your mother's ovary
And take the twisted helix from her egg
To redesign its life specks.

I must accept you as you are
And help you find that skill of hand or mind
That to you will be enchantment.

I am the one who must consider you,
Not you who must conform to my distorting will.

Annie Ruth Waldsmith

WHAT IS GROWING UP REALLY LIKE?

Joy's to teach others, where we've failed.
Achievements in whatever we do.
Not wasting time, for tomorrow may not come.

Memories of our past, will always be treasured.
Is growing up really that difficult, in facing our responsibilities?
Cherish the past, forget about growing old.
Help others to learn from your mistakes. Guide them with your wisdom.
Achievement is success, happiness, the wonderful feeling deep inside.
Each step is advancement forward, leaving the past behind.
Laughter, tears, our love are the keys to life's happiness.

Victory is yours for the taking.
Is saying I love you, Jan, really wrong?
Notice the things around you. Treasure them before it's too late.
Caring is loving, sharing, thinking of the other.
Enjoy what we have, stop trying to destroy it.
Notice who you're hurting and ask yourself why, is it worth the sacrifice?
Today is the time to say I love you, for tomorrow I can be gone.

Sandra Jean Keefe

TO MY LOVER AND HUSBAND

Saying I love you, means much more than words
spoken between two people.
No one knows what true love is really all about.
To me, it's the light on our faces that seem
to glow whenever the other is nearby.
The pain we feel when the other is hurting,
wanting to be with the other to hold, hugging
the other tight.
Just simply being there, standing by the other's side,
through good times as well as bad times.
To smile at the other and say I love you and I care.

Sandra Jean Keefe

A LEGENDARY HERO

You're a special gift, I'll always treasure.
You've made my life beautiful and pleasurable.
Each day I thank God, with every breath I take.

You spare life without hesitation,
willing to sacrifice your own.
You're important, highly in demand.
You cherish the hearts of many, capturing their souls.
You make our world safe, warm and beautiful.

The sunlight makes your shield glow.
You bring smiles from tears, a crowd to a roaring cheer.
You provide shelter, a warm place to rest.
You protect the innocent from the cruel cold world.

You're a legend that has come true
You protect others with your bravery, claiming your victories.
You're proud to stand, fighting for peace, justice, making things right.
Never backing down from any fight or situation you're up against.

You're the treasure gift from the Valley of the Gods.
Never asking for anything in return.
When your mission is complete, you just disappear.
You're just one of God's angels, *a legendary hero*.

Sandra Jean Keefe

A SPECIAL HIDDEN SECRET

You bring a shining glow to Michael's face.
A new lifestyle to Saint John's and Stringfellow's class style.
You keep Miss Joe on the go, hopping mad, and seldom free.
As well as Lock, Archangel, and Catlin, fast on their feet.

Your beautiful black shield is a sight for sore eyes.
You're like a black knight in shining armor, ready to fight.
You'll never be forgotten, for Hawk taught you well.
Now you dance on the clouds, always showing off your style.
Your speed is faster than light throughout the galaxies.
Breaking sound barriers as you streak across heaven's skies.
The silence you show, as you eavesdrop, hovering low.

You'll always be Hawk's lady, Debby's sire's offspring.
Hidden deep in the Valley of the Gods, you're kept out of sight.
A new generation has come forth, working side by side with the old.
Together they bring peace, freedom, justice in law and order.

Many will be surprised to learn the *hidden secret.*
There's more here than what meets the eye.
Every living thing continues the pattern of generations.
Even Hawk and his lady must answer to one who is higher.

Sandra Jean Keefe

A SPECIAL ANGEL'S SECRET

You keep **A**rchangel on his toes.
The **F**irm **I**nstitution on full alert.
You're always standing by, **R**eady to go.
Around the **W**orld flying Mach One,
Speeding faster than sound.
Leaving a streak across the sky,
More beautiful than a rainbow.

Only the angels know who you are,
Where you come from and where you're hidden.
Throughout the world, you're known as
Hawk's **L**ady, flying **F**ree, keeping peace.
Your famous name is -------.

The hidden underworld has given your knowledge
To the outside world, to help keep law and order.
Archangel, Saints, Angels, Strings and Great Santinis,
All keep you safe, free and secretly hidden,
Within the Valley of the Gods.
You're *A Special Angel's Secret.*

Sandra Jean Keefe

SANDRA JEAN KEEFE. Pen Names: Sandie Brown, Sandie Vincent, Kathy Taylor; Born: 10-1-49; Married: Dennis George Keefe, Sr., 7-17-70; Education: Hollywood Scriptwriting Institute, Hibert College; Occupations: Freelance writer; Poetry: 'Husbands,' 1987; 'A Special Message,' 'I Promise,' 1986; Other Writings: "A Special Stranger," script, 1986; "The Mysterious Five," script, 1985; Comments: *Being a freelance writer is rewarding as well as challenging. Especially within the film industry. It's the character's role I create from thin air, that an actor/actress brings to the screen. Making us a special team.*

MEMORIES

As I sit dreaming quietly in front of my fire, the flames dancing with a chaotic, hypnotizing grace; soundlessly the fire is replaced by a solitary figure walking a lonely road. I could feel the bitter chill of the autumn breeze as it stung my face. The mist obscured my vision; but I still knew you were there, so far away beyond my reach. I tried calling your name once, twice, three times; only to hear my desperate cries come echoing back to me in mockery.
I hastened my step in a desperate effort to reach you; but no matter how fast it seemed I was running my feet didn't move a step. Slowly you grew farther and farther away.
My heart sped up and my mind raced for the answers. "How can I reach you?" I forced myself to pick up one foot and put it before the other. To my surprise my efforts were not in vain. Slowly I walked one step at a time. Now I keep pace by your side and take you in my arms to kiss you warmly. Then we separate and my eyes open to see a comforting fire dancing in its place.
And you, though your hair has gone from an ebony black to a snow gray, your smooth face worn with age; the smile on your lips and the sparkle in your eyes say the love in your heart is still young and burns as fierce as ever.

Michael Whitmer

BEAUTY

Beauty.
Is it not a rare and extravagant gift only the blessed have and the wise withhold?
A statement used all too casually, given as a hallmark to everything fancied by the eye.
When true beauty comes from the heart which is impervious to scar, blemish, and age it has the power to bring love to the hateful and determination to the failure.
Truly I say, thou art by far the most gorgeous lady I have ever had the honor to behold.
Thou art a woman among women.
But be thee the most lovely, or be thee the most ghastly woman I have ever beheld I will love thee for the beauty of thy heart, not thy shell.

Michael Whitmer

MICHAEL SEAN WHITMER. Born: McKeesport, Pennsylvania, 7-2-72; Education: Student, Elizabeth Forward Junior High; Memberships: Elizabeth Baptist Church; Poetry: 'Fathers,' 'The Church,' 'Alone,' *American Poetry Anthology, Vol. VII, No. 4;* Comments; *I would like to thank my parents, Steven R. and Dorothy A. Whitmer, for their encouragement and support. My poem entitled 'Alone' is dedicated to a very special girl I once knew, Josie Q.*

THE CHRISTMAS CHILD AND MINE

My child, a miracle to me
   (The miracle of Mary's child),
A child I never thought I'd see.
   (Not understood, but meek and mild).
Given late in life this child of mine
   (His unexpected birth foretold);
A gift for him I hope to find
   (And honored with a gift of gold).
To show my love this special day
   (As from beginning prophesied),
In some extraordinary way.
   (A heaven's star would many guide),
But what is there that I can give
   (To Bethlehem and Mary's son),
He's given me the joy to live
   (That our Christmas be a joyous one).
A miracle that echoes time
   (A child is born to love and wonder).
God's given me this son of mine
   (A child is born to love and wonder).

Rogerleen Wiggins

CANCELLED FLIGHT

I shall leave behind the bonds
Of dark earth and wooden fences;
In icy solitude I challenge
The soaring breath that rises beneath the wings
Of every great expectation.

I watch the rain
Become a prism of splendor on the pavement,
To glorify its dream with a higher wind
Until I can embark on a journey
Beyond the realm of a distant sky.

I can vision lush acres spread out in squares;
A deep-cut red earth freshly plowed
So like the stillness of a steady hand,
Arise to the occasion of darker wine
To bring forth the glass of anticipation.

For I have found that the journey
On which life bears its flaw
Cannot consume nor defend the altitude
To which we all aspire, and later claim
That the beginning only imitates the end.

Joanne Monte

WHISPER MOMENTS

Gentle silence, whispers a moment, a slot
in time vanished from our sight. Blue and
vivid color is the sky, replace the day
to dusk, with an ending, a set of eyes
becomes night, a black so submissive and
yet an active reality. To the right a droplet
of water full of salt, a mind turning
with despair, a smile on lips and yes a
thought in a heart; eyes in the mirror
blue water to the past reveal the
situation held tight within reach.

Julie Kolodzaike

WHERE DO I BEGIN

My lioness, where do I
begin to tell you,
to tell you how I feel,
how I feel when you're
near?
I'll try with paper and pen,
but where do I begin?
I believe I'll let my soul
fumble with the words.
When you're near, just the
dancing spirit of your eyes
enthralls me.
And the unseen flames of that
spirit warm me.
I've never known one who
could touch me so softly, so softly,
I've never known. If I could
touch you this softly, this softly,
I would.
For it seems unfair,
that I have all this,
and cannot share.

John White

MY RED RUBY RABBIT

I once heard that we all resemble
some sort of animal,
I once heard that we all resemble
some sort of jewel,
and I once heard that we all resemble
some sort of color.
Just stories or proven things,
I used to wonder.
But not after seeing you,
my red ruby rabbit.
You're red, because you shock me.
You're a ruby, because it's
in a gentle sort of way.
But more than the other two,
you're a rabbit.
Not one hopping and scurrying,
but one off to the side.
One off to the side,
always watching, always from a distance.
How do I know? I think it's because,
I'm another rabbit,
off to the side,
watching, from a distance,
always, my red, ruby, rabbit.

John White

MY KIDS

Torn stain dresses
Dirty faces
Muddy feet
But the smile so sweet!

Laurie Jenkins

SONG OF MY HEART

My heart once sang for you,
But now a lonely silence
Echoes through my soul.
I had sung to the music
That your love had supplied;
Or had I just imagined its tunes?
When did the music stop playing;
Or have I sung a cappella from the start?
These answerless questions are all I possess,
Except for the memories of that melody
Of which a few notes will always linger.
You were my music,
And now that you're gone
My heart shall never sing for you again.

Crystal L. Renner

PEOPLE THAT HIDE

There are people out there,
people that hide,
hide from people.
They hide from anyone,
anyone who says,
''Maybe I'll touch,
maybe I won't.''
So they hide behind walls
that say, ''I don't care''
and dark sunglasses,
the type that say, ''I don't
give a damn, if you ever
see me, really see me,
because you with your
arrogant air, your turtle shell
attitude, and smug face,
make me feel sorry, sick,
and sad, because I know
one thing, maybe you'll
touch, maybe you won't.''

John White

PEACE?

War-torn and battle-ridden,
they cried.
Sorrow buried their gladness
that conflict had ended,
But in truth, another
conflict had just begun.
The conflict of rebuilding
towns. Lives.
The fighting was now over —
Brother against brother no
more.
Hearts hung heavy on that
dark and dreary day.
Hearts that had given their all 'til
the last measure.
Hearts that now were defeated.
Giving their colors,
they surrendered
their lives,
their cause,
and — their hearts.

Cary Mizzell

LIFE'S JOURNEY

My journey through life has not been small, I've
struggled up my mountains, yes I've conquered them
all, standing on my mountain tall, from here I can
hear my dear Saviour call.

My journey was sometimes down, my eyes always looked
up, I now know that every time I would fall, it was
because I would not hear my dear Saviour call.

In my life there have been joys both large and small,
there's been sorrow and sadness too, but the greatest
joys of all, were the times I would hear my dear
Saviour call.

I'm nearing my journey's end and through life I've lent
myself to situations of both love and hate, the good
things in life both small and great, now above it all,
I very clearly hear a loving Saviour call.

Yes my race is nearly run, I know many of the things I
wanted to do I'll never see done, that really doesn't
matter at all, if in the end I can plainly hear my dear
Saviour call.

I know that in heaven I'll be, if once again my dear
departed friends and loved ones of this world I see,
then once again I'll stand tall, and both see, and
hear my dear blessed Saviour call.

Leland D. Wertz

THE WHISTLING DELL

As the dark of night crept in, our hay wagon rocked to and fro,
Through the woods and around, a Halloween haunting we did go.

Young children in the wagon, bright-eyed but a little scared,
Listening as the driver told, of the strange whistling in the dell.

'Twas Halloween evening, we picked this fateful ride,
The moon above our heads, but our hearts fell to our sides.

As the driver spun his tale of gore, our knees began to clatter,
For tonight he drove us to the dell, how our teeth did chatter.

The wagon drew to a clearing, we all listened for the sound,
The driver was daring, he got out to look around.

''For years,'' he said, ''the whistling has appeared.
But only on this night, it happens every year.''

Just as we thought, we'd all die before our years,
A creature grabbed the driver, and a whistling appeared.

Gone was our driver, while the whistling rang on,
We finally gathered courage, to undo this terrible wrong.

Down from the wagon twelve frightened children went,
Speaking to each other, words of the capture and encouragement.

Now let me tell you people, young bones do rattle too,
Reaching the tree he was captured at, we saw laughing — *You know who!*

Yes, that crafty driver, had led us to our doom, his arm
    around his friend
The creature, on his shoulder a whistling parrot called, Typhoon.

We must have looked a bit undone, as they laughed themselves to tears.
It was a Halloween night, we'd all remember, with laughter, for years.

Rebecca Ginn Smith

A COMFORTABLY LIT CANDLE

the light in the room is dim
        yet I wonder
    whether the light i see is from
your eyes or from your
                heart
    the pictures on the wall are
            crooked
and you stare
        at the broken glass between us
    white wine dampens the carpet
            silence surrounds
it is becoming comfortable, somehow
            slowly,
        sinking deep in my chair
            i wish you would get up and
    straighten the pictures on the wall
            i realize the light is neither from
                your eyes nor from your heart.
a candle is lit in the darkness
of the house across the street
        i wish i was there
    yet you still have not
            straightened the pictures
                so i must
                        wait.

Mary Beth O'Hara

MURDERING ONE HEART WITH ANOTHER

Bloody-red screams fill the space between your heart
and mine. Filtering through the smokey air,
shooting darts through your heart;
Cupid stayed in bed today, sent me to rip and pick at
your flesh, peering at your heart through a microscope.
I escape quickly, leaving my shoes behind.
Escaping to the street
I stand, then sit under the light of the street
to the endless end of nothing I can imagine.
Over my head the June-bugs swarm,
I wonder what in light attracts them,
what attracted you.
My feet, soaked in muddy water
no shoes to protect them from broken glass,
my hands, wet with sweat.
Caking blood turning brown, left behind.
Dead in an instant.
The weapon pounding under my breast.
I swat a flying bug to the ground,
smashed against the pavement, easily.
But the blood doesn't run as yours did.
I stand, then sit under the street light,
unable to move or save myself from remembering

what Cupid left for me to do to you.

Mary Beth O'Hara

I loved you with such candor, such truth, such honesty,
that I doubt that I shall ever love again!
If you stay away: for all the rest of eternity
I shall never become so completely another,
So completely one with all of life as when we two were one.
Now, you are a part of me and when you leave —
I die!

Virginia Dalglish

MASQUERADE

The party is about to start;
You are invited to attend.
Come dance to our tunes,
Come play in our games;
Come join in our Masquerade.
Here, dreams seem too hard to follow,
And lies seem too true.
Here, reality is the chameleon,
And love is but sorrow in disguise.

The parade is beginning;
Do come march along.
Heartbreak is our destination;
The journey is not far.
Fear and confusion lie along the way.
Oh, yes, you must come;
Do not shy away.
The party has already started,
And once you have been invited,
You have no choice but to attend.

Crystal L. Renner

BUILD YOUR MARRIAGE ON A SURE FOUNDATION

Build your marriage on a sure foundation;
Everything else is sinking sand.
Build your marriage on the solid rock;
Anything else it will fall apart.
Build your marriage with Jesus as the head;
Everything else will fall in line
As you are being led.
Build your marriage on a sure foundation;
So you can enjoy God's wonderful blessings.

Barbara J. Herron

OUR BIGGEST MISTAKE

Their remains were tossed into a
Crater-like hole
As if they had no hearts or souls

Fighting the force we all know as man
Killing their own because they don't
Give a damn

We tried to see how much they could take
But when it was over
We realized our biggest mistake

The torture, the dreams
The everlasting screams
Of those in that covered-up rendezvous
We know as Vietnam

The most talked about yet never
Explained war in history
Will always be a great big mystery

Except to those who had to go through
That seemingly endless
Battle of youth

There was nothing left behind
Nothing left to take
Except the memories of the people
And of the United States of America's
Biggest mistake

Eric Howard Kline

VIETNAM REQUEIM

Monsoon reigns. I move
not for shelter but . . . contact.
Rain strikes, resolute.

I breathe waterfalls
but rain soothes enemy fears —
sodden pods half-watch.

Through torrential mesh
hot bullets cross-grain water.
Hard hits. Soft repose.

Susan L. Maguire

SUSAN MAGUIRE. Born: North Carolina, 4-17-49; Married: Steve Maguire, 1970; Education: American University's School of International Service, B.A., 1970; Occupation: Mother of 6; Poetry: 'Would I Could Get The Meter Right With A Two-Year-Old In The House,' *American Poetry Anthology*, 1987; Comments: *As mother of six irrepressible children, I'm often discombobulated by the pace they set skidding in and out of new stages. Poetry is a sane catharsis. I can figure it all out on paper if the kids haven't "borrowed" all my pens. My husband, an airborne ranger-type infantry platoon leader, led 180 air assaults in the Mekong Delta of Vietnam. Finding his realistic accounts of combat there intriguing, I am drawn to formulate experiential poetry about it.*

THE FLIGHT OF THE FALLEN

Tapping sounds from up above,
blue eggshells tumble to the ground.
Feathers fly from all around,
a chirping sound is heard.
A fallen bluebird at my feet
is nestled in a bed of cloth.
Its fate unknown to all the earth.
Cradled by a fond hand.
Nurtured in constant hope
that this creature might be saved,
but this was not God's plan,
for while the lights were out
morning came and took his soul.
Now in peace he sleeps,
no more struggle against his foe.
For though he was not fit to live,
he is safe from the darkness.
He is in the best of hands.

Diana B. Dubey

LIFE'S LESSON

Quiet is my life at last,
Peaceful are my days,
But ever I remember love,
And its ultimate betrayal
(A young woman with a heart
Crazed by the sudden sorrow
Of the beloved yearning for adventure
Not including her).
I thought I should die of it,
And yet life lingered —
I then was wanted, loved,
By a person more mature,
Excitement & joy were mine,
But duty held me fast,
Till all was lost, the second loss
Of a bewildered one,
Caught in the web of earth,
Longing for freedom of the skies —
So then I learned that sadness
Leads forth into wisdom,
Caring opens doors for others,
Despite despair there's hope,
Leading to true happiness,
A light in the darkness,
Revealing roses.

Ola Margaret James

THE HARE

The rain fell softly to the ground,
as the sun reached the horizon.
Each drop glistened brightly.

It was only yesterday,
while I was walking along the river,
I saw him, standing there, stiff with fear.

He was silently brooding
though he stood majestically.
His paws were like silk gloves.
His toes were wet with dew.

I saw the sadness in his heart.
His eyes were clear and blue.
His hair was smooth and soft.
His whiskers twitched with fear.

I took one step closer to comfort him,
and he turned and bolted like a deer.

Diana B. Dubey

RESPECTING GOD DIVINE

If my love ruled and ruled again
 I would free every pest on earth
And every pest would become a friend
 Throughout the universe

None would therefore be repelled
 Or poisoned unto death
Nor would excess go to waste
 But breathe eternal breath

If my love ruled and ruled again
 I would free things that plague mankind
And there would be peaceful co-existence
 Respecting God divine

Todd Dorian Wilson

WHAT IS MIDNIGHT?

What is midnight?
An uneasy feeling?
An electric emotion?
A tangible object?
A fleeting bit of time,
lasting but an instant,
then allowing the clock to settle?
Or possibly an invisible tsunami,
circling the globe at breakneck speed,
crashing silently into coasts, mountains and cities,
leaving in its wake
destruction of the old day,
creation of the new?

Thomas Kennedy Iovino

THE HOUSEKEEPER'S PRAYER

Dear Father,
  You gave me the privilege of coming before Your
heavenly throne as *Bold* as a child would come, yet,
I come humbly. I praise You for the *Cheer* You've
given me. It's no *Secret* that Your love has
*Caress*ed my life.

  Though the storms have raged, You've been a
Shield of protection, helping me to ride the *Tide*
and face each new *Dawn* with a *Fresh Start*! It's just *Super* knowing that I'm
saved. And an even
greater *Joy* is in serving You. I *Pledge* that as for
me and my house, we will *Shout* your goodness.
  With a *Glad* heart, I say,
    Thank you, Holy *Dove*.
      Amen.

Quincia Clay

QUINCIA RUTH CLAY. Born: Memphis, Texas, 2-19-37; Married: Otis
Carl Clay; Widow since 6-10-69; Education: Born Again; Occupation:
Registration-coordinator, Houston Eye Association; Awards: Silver Poet
Award, 1986; Poetry: 'The Hymn Book Prayer,' 1982; 'Guide Us, Lord,
From the T.V.,' 'I Stood at Calvary'; *From the Heart of a Black Widow,* and
Doves in The Window, collections of poems; Comments: *My life has been
filled with adversity, losses, heartaches, and tragedies. But through it all I
feel blessed because my trials have brought me into a personal relationship
with God. A trip to the Holy Lands and this awareness of Him have inspired
most of my writings.*

WHY ARE THE MEDIA SO MEDIUM?

Why are the media so medium, so average?
So watered down, so shallow-wrong?
On the face of it, not communication at all.
Positions, interventions, commerces,
Rather speaking-talk, messages, truck,
Patter to the Times, points of honor
To the Chronicle,
To the Examiner,
To the Broadcast,

To the News, or in that theater, a drama,
Unscientific opinions, interests,
Fictions, sometimes not even correct Who? What?
Where? When? Mental creations, imaginings, lies
Even.

When the people booed A. Lincoln at Gettysburg,
There were no engineers present
To soften the blows, the shame and embarrassments.
No reporters' strange questions, inquiring about
Adultery or opposition. Who said life was a crime?

Madison wanted their absence, always, press,
At any secret official event. There is no branch of
Government called *The Media*. Bullets always kill the
Victim. Words kill us all, unkindly cuts.
There were no producer-directors, either
To tell Lincoln where to end his huge majesty.

T. Powers

OUR FUTURE TOGETHER

The love we have for each other today
Has a potential to live with time
A love that grows stronger day by day
A love that's yours and mine

Distance has strengthened your love inside
A love we have for each other
Time has kept us occupied
Making it impossible to love another

Our relationship was chosen to be the one
To last until Lord knows when
When the infinite seas swallow the sun
We'll both know what happens then

I pray each night for *us* my love
And the Lord knows it is right
He's constantly watching us from the heavens above
And guiding us by His light

I love you more than you'll ever know
'Cause you are the one for me
Soon it will begin to show
That our love is *Eternity*

I know our love will last forever
'Cause the Lord has told me about ''Our Future Together''

Kenneth S. N. Mendiola

MY LIFE

My life is a weaving,
Between my God and me.
A pattern, for everyone to see.
My life, has the hills and dells,
And the knots in the trails.
A poem, for joy, for learning too.
A song, to sing, that happy times brings.
Music, dancing, love of life,
Unhappiness sometimes even strife.

My life is a weaving,
Between my God and me.
He sees the upper pattern,
On the upper side.
And I only see the underneath
Side of the plan.
Where the knots are tied and
It looks rough to the eye.
The upper side is a Blessing when
finished at the end.
My life is a weaving,
Between My God and me.

Betty Jean Brooks

IN THE SILENCE

In the silence,
I hear you.
I listen
to your cry.
Where do I go
from here?
I sigh.
As I walk,
I feel the
cool breeze,
but I don't
freeze.
You keep me
warm,
and away from harm.
I love your
charm.
Keep me
in your arms.

Maria M. Roman

EACH DAY IS A GIFT

Each day is a gift
From the Giver of light
Unwrapped by His hands
From the ribbons of night

Some come in sunshine
Some come in deep gray
But whatever the color
We can't throw it away

Each gift has a purpose
With a one-day guarantee
As your trials are so
Shall your strength be

If each is used wisely
Then we'll hear Him say
"Well used, my child"
As night stores it away.

Mim Cundiff-Rambo

ONE SUMMER DAY

Scrawling in the sand,
muddy water land, not so far away,
we spent one summer day.

Shaded trails of wood
filled with the silence of life,
it was all we could do
to stifle our thoughts
one summer day.

Speaking now and then,
reaching out for something
worth holding,
thoughts unfolding,
yielding hope for the future
and salvation for now.

One summer day, I turned to find you there,
someone to care,
just showing me where
peace of mind could be gained.
Tear-stained no longer.

One summer day riding on air,
floating on water,
finding faith from nothing,
made me thankful for the day
and the friend who showed me the way,
one lonely, summer day.

Pamela K. Phipps

ECHOES

*Dedicated to my cousin, Steven,
who's in the Persian Gulf,
and Gilbert, a Vietnam Vet.
(September, 1987)*

A different time.
A different place.
But the cries are the same.

Ships steaming to far-off waters,
Waves beating against the bows
As hard as the hearts beating on
them —
Each beat echoing a fearful cry
of doubt.

We have a new generation of
children
Living in the shadows of yet
another televised "peacekeeping
mission."
Children watching, excitedly, for
"Daddy's ship,"
Unaware that Daddy is watching for
mines and "in-coming."

The all too familiar sounds of the
Gulf
Now echo beside those of 'Nam.
Will they get as loud,
if not louder,
Than those of Vietnam?

Annette Burek Holstad

NEVER SAY NEVER

Please remember that never is forever;
So endeavor never to say *never*.
Never will never be,
Never will never come.
So it is very easy to see,
To use the word *never*, is nothing but dumb.

The only time to say *never* is,
Never.
Nevertheless;
Never say *never*.

Now that you know,
To never say *never*.
Never say *never* any more,
Never say *never* forevermore,
Never say *never*. Por Favor!

Raymond C. Kuehl, Jr.

RAYMOND C. KUEHL, JR. Pen Name: Zot From Zoy; Born: Wisconsin Rapids, Wisconsin, 12-30-46; Single; Education: Milwaukee Area Technical College, Two associate degrees in business management and accounting; Occupations: Farmer; Custodian; Liquor store clerk; Foreman; Office worker; Construction worker; Rewinder operator; Political candidate; Entrepeneur; Writer; Membership: Phi Theta Kappa; Awards: Presently a registered Democratic United States Presidential Candidate for 1988 election; Poetry: 'Bonds,' *American Poetry Anthology*, 1987; Themes: *Inspired by the poor, handicapped, homeless, elderly and drug users, which hopefully I can help by running for United States President, directly or indirectly, elected or not elected. I also would like to make all the United States Prison systems self-supporting and pay all the inmates (at least minimum wage) for their personal contributions so that they would be able to save for their release date, thus, giving them the financial support to readjust to society.*

EMPTY HEARTED

My heart is empty without you here
It hurts so much inside
My world is wishing you were near
To comfort me by my side

I feel so lonely each time I think of you
And when I do I want so much to cry
A subtle tear would follow through
Each time I think of our last good-bye

Memories flow when I hear our song
"There'll Be Sad Songs To Make You Cry"
My mind keeps saying it won't be long
'Cause my heart gets stronger bye and bye

I hope you feel the way I do
'Cause baby you mean a lot
And I mean that when I say it to you
'Cause in this world you're all I've got

Like the stars that twinkle in the night
And the sun that never dies
Honey you are my guiding light
And the love resting in my eyes.

Kenneth S. N. Mendiola

KENNETH SAN NICOLAS MENDIOLA. Born: Guam, U.S.A., 7-12-64; Education: Guam Community College VHS; Occupation: U.S. Navy; Awards: 'Graduation Night,' Honorable Mention, 1984; Golden Poet Award for 'Our Future Together,' 1987; Poetry: 'Graduation Night,' 1984; 'A Prayer For The World,' 1985; 'God's Universal Love,' 1986; 'The Ultimate Prayer,' 1987; all American Poetry Association: Comments: *To my mom, dad, and family, you are all my major inspiration in my work. I love you all so much.*

WHEN YOU LOVE: YOU CARE

When you really love someone,
   you care what they think, do, and say
   in a special kinda way.

When you sincerely love someone,
   you cherish what they think, do, and say
   in an intimate kinda way.

When you truly love someone,
   you care, you cherish, what they do and say,
   in an intimate kinda way.

When you compassionately love someone,
   the things that someone thinks, does, and says
   throbs your heart in myriad kinda ways.

Mercedes Barnes Thompson

STATUS QUO

I change mercurially with the seasons:
Autumn finds me: versatile, vociferous, varied;
In winter I'm hibernatious, healthy, happenstanced;
Springtime sees me bittersweet, barometrical, bright;
And in the summer I grow pensive, productive, peaceful.
Presently the mundane trivialities of everyday workability
Bore me and I long to sit rapt, resolute and readied
At my typewriter for hours on end,
To plot my plays and compose my poetry.
Will Father Time and Mother Earth accommodate my approaching
   deadlines?
Will my family and friends understand my driven writer's
Passion to succeed?
Presently I'm experiencing a semi-schizoid status quo
Of decisive age in which I long to answer the indecisive know
Of my writer's actions.
Semi-schizoid status quo: Remembering the past, meeting the present,
Preparing for the future, to answer the everyday go of my life.
Semi-schizoid status quo:
Facing it expressionistically in the 1990's:
Facing it fully, facing it free;
Facing it a feminist survivor.

Valerie M. Conti

EXACTITUDE: A POEM FOR ELIZABETH LE COMPTE

We shared an endless moment ten years ago: we touched.
You took me from behind the center of my being,
With your strong, caring arms and nestled me deep inside your chest,
Until my crying ceased and I could honestly release
The tears of my own biography.
Ohthosefathermothersisterbrother physical culture blues.
Those painful, funny, frenetic, no-money Twentieth Century dues . . .
Cleansed, gone, all-died-out-of-me:
Feminia Italia News.
Bittersweet Lady: Laugh-me-to-my-feet Lady: Lady Kind: Lady Wise:
Lady Understanding Compromise: Lady Director Nonpareil.
I appreciate you for reaching into me:
For teaching me to define my score;
For reminding me that enough is not ever exact,
And love does not ever mean more.
Exactitude: Our ten year lesson: Our endurance test: Elizabeth:
And I honor our ten year friendship and mutual careers
   expressly for that.
You are a true inspiration and role model for me
Exactitude: Elizabeth.
Yes: Adieu.

Valerie M. Conti

LEAF OF LIFE

Spring leaf flapping on the tree, fresh, green, vibrant
As one who marches with vigor while parading in the field of youth
Autumn leaf turning colors, waning as it wrestles with the wind
To stay its hold on the trough of the mother tree
Yet, yielding gracefully as nature makes the final separation
As one, weathered and faltering at the end of life's journey
Resists, not wishing to depart, then goes peacefully
With God when he makes the final call.

Elizabeth Kelly

DEATH

Lurking in the corner of my room
Death is near, I know it's soon
I feel the emptiness, before it comes
I know the impact it will have on everyone.

Death is near in the darkness of the night,
I fear not for me, but for those who survive.

I see the look upon their faces,
They think I'm not aware of why they visit.

It will be over soon, my loved ones,
The pain and agony is yet to come
The pain of knowing not that I shall die,
But the unhappiness I know you'll feel inside.

June Drao

JUNE KAY DRAO. Born: Brooklyn, New York; Occupation: Freelance writer; Memberships: Pennsylvania Poetry Society; National Writers Club; Walt Whitman Guild; Awards: Golden Poet Award, 1986, 1987; Several merit awards; Poetry: 'Scared,' *Poets Memorable Songs,* 1987; 'Christmas Time,' *Bluebells & Other Dreams,* 1987; 'Tender Moments,' *Misty Moonlight,* 1987; 'Death,' *On The Threshold of a Dream,* 1987; 'Excuse Me,' *A Treasury of Moments,* 1987; Themes: *My poetry is written from my heart. I try to capture my feelings, as well as others' who may have been in the same situation. I try to express that we are not alone in our feelings, that life treats us all the same in so many ways.*

MY MOTHER

You gave a lot of yourself
to us.
27 years of your life you gave
to us.
You gave your love, understanding,
compassion and, in times of sorrow
and grief, a shoulder to cry on with wise
and loving advice.
And when our problems became unbearable
for us to go on, your strength you gave
to us. All done unquestioned and with
love.
At times I wonder if you knew what
you were getting into when you created us.
Although we don't always show it,
we have always in the past and in the
future appreciate and love you, Mom.

Magadaline Ruth McCart

A TIME OF LOVE

Valentine is a time of love;
To be with the one who stays.
That's the one who's sweet as a dove
In all so many nights and days.

Thou art a champion and a friend:
All this world can possibly be.
When troubles come, thou art my blend;
Irremovable as a tree.

When thou first gleamed upon my sight,
Thy heart held motion, light and free.
Thy love's a phantom of delight:
The records of faith are so sweet.

Your charm in harmlessness will lay
Always like metal in a mine.
A look on your face takes more away
Than youth can conceive about thine.

Thy beauty antepost of joy above.
How great a beauty you can be.
Like the sight of heavenly dove;
It's God that made such things as thee.

Dr. Clayton Bell, Jr.

DR. CLAYTON BELL, JR. Born: Ennis, Texas, July 13; Married: Vassie, 12-4-55, Children, Michael and Angela; Education: Bishop College, Dallas, Texas, B.A., 1956; North Texas State University, Denton, M.A., 1967; T.W.U., Denton, Texas, Ed.D., 1982; Occupation: School Principal; Memberships: NASSP; TASSP; Phi Delta Kappa; RASSP; ARE; Adult Education Association.

SISTERS

One, a fair-haired princess
a dainty angel,
almost a porcelain doll.
Appearing so fragile
and yet, deceptively so.
She's strong of will and mind.

An exotic beauty, the younger one,
dark of eyes and hair
and a photographer's dream for a face.
With a sly look or a trembling pout,
she'll melt your heart.

Two sisters — two little girls
each alike, but so unlike the other.
And when they take my hand on either side
and we skip away, I know —
God has shared with me
the best of both worlds.

Susan Barichko

HEY, I LOVE YOU MOM

You gave birth to me 19 years ago.
In 19 years we laughed, we cried
and we had some terrible fights
I know at times I've caused
you great pain and sorrow.
But I hope at some time in
my life I was a source of joy.
I know I gave you plenty of
reason to regret giving birth to me.
I haven't said it enough, I guess,
I took it for granted you knew
that I loved you.
I hope you have no regrets
Because *Hey, I love you Mom!*

Magadaline Ruth McCart

WE LOVE IN SILENCE

Mutual attraction and powers allure
While antagonist forces separateness assure

Our eyes encounter in captivating stare
Hostile lords whisper ''Don't dare!''

The feel of touch, oh common delight
But something says ''You have no right!''

Oh wondrous forces coax and entice
While rival troops thwart and device

We'll love in silence till the day
The victor force his rival slay.

Irene Valeriano

I AM FREE

I'll crawl no more in shadows
But in sunlight shall I stride,
For the bondsman's yoke is broken
And his spell is cast aside.

The chains that so long bound me
Now at last are loosed;
I feel clean wind upon my face,
And I am free to choose.

I choose to live, and grow, and learn,
To walk with my head high;
I choose to love, and then to laugh,
And then, at length, to cry.

I choose to reach for mountain peaks
That lofty stand apart,
And feel the ever-mighty beat
Of freedom's song within my heart.

JoAn A. Lee

SUDDEN DEATH OF AN APARTMENT

"A fire, a fire, a fire."
Not hysterical, but strung out together like a child's voice.
Muffled in fear. Waking up from a dream and entering a nightmare:
The monotone roar of the brilliant orange waves
Beckoning me to an eternal slumber.
Everything frozen in time, except for the flames;
They were having a feast on our beautiful old woodwork.

The hallway bellied with clouds of gray.
Once again I looked, mesmerized, at the devouring torch;
Seemingly knowing of its triumph.

A sauna bath in the hallway, moving shadows.
The old tile stairs, ice cold under bare feet,
Running so fast, almost missing steps,
To the door of starting over.

Where were the hands behind me, shoving me forward?
"Michael," I yelled, the clouds overhead transforming into vultures.
"*Michael!*" I screamed.

An arm around me and out of the dragon's mouth we emerged.
Wide-eyed mirrors everywhere;
Shattered glass explosions couldn't make them blink.

For underneath, lie comfortable chairs and old photos.
Favorite jeans, and walnut desks,
    with buttons and broken lighters inside;
Letters of love, and wheat penny collections.
Tears sealed so deep inside that the mirrors took a long time to crack;
And when they did, there were never enough tears
    to extinguish the memory.

Laura Weck

ADAM AND EVE,
THEIR COURAGE AND DESPAIR

Filled with emotions of despair,
They watched a flaming sword flash, governing Eden's affair.
In the days following they became vulnerable.
As their tears often mingled, both felt responsible.

In love they awakened new sense.
In mortal moments their love became
    a treasured presence.
Their courage eclipsed fear.
In the sweetness of flowers blooming, they accepted their year.

On the day of Eve's pain Adam fled,
Coming back with animal skins, cleaned for his woman's bed.
When the light winds blew, they loved to hear God sing.
Eve remembered God, and cried out to Him in birthing.

In beautiful prayer Adam cried
For his son's release from sin; tenderly pursuing his pride.
Eve held her babe to her bosom, touching his skin.
He found food and she rejoiced in her gift from within.

I find a promise in their spirit.
In temptation, a litany for generations was lit.

They struggled with rejections in mortal breath.
Their flesh felt pain, and they were condemned to know their death.

Audrie M. Fiskaali

PRELUDE TO A POEM

Prelude

Poets are love, kneeling down to life.
Their inward greatness, gentle vision, and sparkle temper strife.
Like old wine, their maturity has soul warmth to beget.
Their intimate words of beauty, call to me, yet.

A Poem

His words were ephemeral truths in verse.
I heard blossoms blow, from a low voice, and winds call, to converse.
I heard cherished years, like soul play, tumble from his brain.
In me he gave his kindred spirit, to retain.

I felt my heart hurting in his hand.
Loving him, I quivered afraid that he would understand.
He made me watch a birth, and I was alight, against him.
In seconds, his tenderness made my anger, dim.

In, Heart will meet, his valley of care,
An enchanting paradise unfolded my love in its dare.
In ecstatic breaths, I awakened to a rhythm.
I let my words, wondering in beauty with them.

I stepped back from pearls in his praise.
Away from revealing chimes in my heart and its sudden craze.
In a black and silver night, I raced from midnight's gong.
When I fell he held me to him, with a night song.

Audrie M. Fiskaali

WHO ARE YOU?

Who are you
    Who slipped into my life
When I especially needed someone
To brighten my days
And lift my spirits just by being there?

    Who speaks with a silver tongue
Words I love to hear
Yet wonder at, for fear they
Are too good to be true?

    Who looks at me
With eyes that reveal in brief, unguarded moments
A mystery, the depths of which
I dare not to explore?

    Who fills my mind
And occupies my secret thoughts,
Penetrating my carefully laid defenses,
Demanding entrance, simply by his presence?

Who are you?
    Stranger whom I scarcely know?
    Friend and confidant?
or
    Love in faint disguise?

I wish I knew.

Sharon T. Winn

CAGED

Trapped
Caged
Moldy walls
Dirt floor
And cold, cold bars.
Identify the disease
— Me —
Isolate it
For the good
Of
''The Family,''
Put it away
Destroy it,
If you can
But don't tell anyone —
Oh, the disgrace —
Just quietly cage it
'Til it dies
For want
Of air
And light
And simple
　Love.

JoAn A. Lee

YOU LOVE ME

I'm so glad You love me, Lord,
　even when I'm bad.
Sometimes I stray and misbehave,
　and I know it makes You sad.
You correct me and chastise me
　as a father does a child.
Without Your love and mercy
　I would probably be wild.

When I lose my temper,
　and scream, and yell, and fuss,
I wonder what would happen
　if You did the same to us!
Yes, I'm so glad You love me,
　unworthy servant that I am.
Your blessings are too good for me,
　my precious loving Lamb!

Let me lean on You, Sweet Spirit,
　for more changing do I need.
I don't know how to do it,
　but Your words I will heed.
I love You, Dearest Father.
Never leave me, this I pray,
For without Your hand to guide me,
　I would die along the way. Amen.

Donna J. Nixon

A VICIOUS CIRCLE

　　Faces of my past lovers
　　float shoreward to greet me
　　mocking at my tattered heart.

I gaze away to erase my memories;
My feet avoid retracing sandprints
made by walks through each love.

　Never hurdling my past failures,
　stumbling in the shoreline fog,
I blind myself from needing anyone.

Insecurity guards new trails —
I discard offered fresh beginnings.
　Destitute, I walk in circles.

Gatekeeper of my fractured mirror
suffocates between the bobbing flotsam
desperately attempting to break surface.

Decomposing like washed-up kelp,
　my waning spirit waits to see
painful memories wash out to sea.

N. Douglas Smith

REASON

Almighty God,
　Creator divine,
Infinite powers
　Surely are thine.

Thou art the light
　I use to see
The sense of life
　Through its mystery.

I cannot believe
　For one brief day
That I at most
　Am molded clay.

I cannot conceive
　The thought that I am
Less than part
　Of some Diagram.

Hugh Miles Ray

IN MY ARMS

I hold my grandchild in my arms.
I hold smiles and charms.
I hold innocence.
I hold life's essence.
I hold a miracle.
I hold love's pinnacle.
I hold yesterday.
I hold today.
I hold tomorrow's bairns.
I hold eternity in my arms.

Virginia D. Casteel

AFTER

*Dedicated to Physicians for Social
Responsibility; all physicians who
treat victims of radiation and
chemical contamination, cancerous
degeneration, birth deformities and
genetic abnormalities; to American
Indians who reverently tended and
preserved land, water and air; to
the urgent need to develop safer
energy.*

Chernobyl stunned the continents.
Radiation poisoned living land.
People, dying, dazed and maimed
Evacuated habitats.

Vacant houses stand.

Nuclear energy — a must?
Human error lives with us,
A world gone chemical, nuclear numb
Exploding mutations — Caseium, Strontium
To luckless victims near nuclear tombs
With marrow failure in their bones.
An icicle winter is what they know,
Their lives like etchings in crusted snow.

All chemicals, and nuclear — safe?
Hideous accidents tell it all
With ills no power can dispel.
Better safe acres of Indian Love
Than Three Mile, Bhopal and Love Canal.

Reactors, thermo-nuclear-fusion-based,
Safer, perhaps, but still man-made.
Human error is un-erased.
San Onofre, Diablo plants
Are near and on the earthquake faults.
Faults lie not just beneath the earth
But deep inside of us —
After Chernobyl!

Marjorie Sandstrom

SITTING IN THE NURSING HOME

As I touch the blank wall before me,
I search for some difference
in the cold white surface.
A hand falls before my eyes,
one I no longer recognize;
for upon it time has put its mark.
Softly,
whispers fall like drops of rain in my mind
and upon the wall a rainbow of memories falls.
Soon the whispers are screams
as the tempest dances in my head,
filling the blank walls
with but a blur of color,
till once again
only the hand remains,
among the wall of blankness
and the whispers are raindrops
in the distance.

Tracy Shoemaker

SUMMER DREAMS

A Tribute to Summer

Sounds of summer's joys dancing on the wind —
amidst waving hands — and tender looks — and
hugs — and tears — saying all the things words
could never say.

Summer's dreams — some fulfilled — and some —
lingering awhile — then drifting slowly away —
hoping to be born anew.

Summer's goodbyes — promising much that is so hard
to find — meaning — we would have at a future time
— what we held in our heads — in our hands — in
our hearts — just moments before.

All — returning to our own — our own pace — our own
role — our own selves — and what each new second would
bring.

None of us forgetting — those rich — warm — rewarding
times — together — in the summer — when some of summer's
dreams could be fulfilled.

John R. Chiesa

MUTED CALL

Last of summer
Lifts its muted call,
Like Henry Bussey's
Shuffle rhythms
With muted horns
Of the Big Band era.
All are present
In the air.

   Just feel the residue of warmth
   Of late summer days
   And hear the Big Band sounds
   On a local radio station.

    Summer stretches out
    For several weeks,
    Then it yawns
    And relinquishes time and space
    To Indian summer —
    After a frost,
    Warmth will linger
    On the edge of autumn.

      Indian summer and fall
      Hold sway,

        Winter just a faint cry
        In the far distance.

F. Richard Dieterle

SHORT FLIGHT, LONG MEMORY

In the sky over Florida I saw a one minute, seventeen second flight.
Hot metal and gases became white smoke against blue sky,
Fragments of red, green, and gold shooting like fireworks and stars
provided a spectacle, a spectacle of shattered lives,
human parts, and tile pieces falling into the cold Atlantic waters.
Public eyes stared, cried.
I cried.
Children huddled, wiggled in front of TV screens, smiling,
stopped, and went back to class.
Teachernaut said,
''Ten souls will be with me . . .''
but there were at least eleven, maybe more,
because I was there, longing to be a pioneer,
exploring the frontier,
ready to take the risk.
She left behind a loving husband,
a lovely daughter, prayerful parents, a sister,
noisy students, quiet students,
traffic jams, crowded stores,
threats of nuclear war, starving children,
bigots, peace lovers, waterfalls,
smiling faces, sad faces,
cities, farms,
the whole earth,
and me.

Sherry Percic

QUESTIONS

I march to a different drummer's beat
And I listen to a strange, melancholy, haunting tune
That guides me along my way each day
As I strive to capture an elusive dream.

I dream beautiful dreams of brilliant colors,
But am constantly interrupted as shadowy thoughts
  filter through my subconsciousness
Calling for that which I know not.
Do they whisper from a previous life,
Or do they evasively promise a bright new existence in a future time?

Questions! Questions! Questions!
Who can answer them?
They float and fade in and out
And finally grow dim.
Yet, I forever reach, like a clinging vine, listening to that
  drummer's beat and that strange haunting refrain.

Mary Janeen Dorsett

FOR SIS

As the wind blows across her face
The teardrops weave into her silkened skin.
Twisting turning of the ronduress moon,
Reflects the shadow of her beautifully
defined face.
Beams of velvet blue appear in the dusk;
Their radiance enters through my skin,
Translucent into my heart!
Long beautiful brown, shelter her from the dawn.
For like the movement of the stars,
Is the movement of her soul.

Cindy L. Carlson

A NEW ROSE OF FREEDOM

I'm now free to grow
in the sunshine and rain
as a flower child
blooming bright again.

I escaped a prison of love
into the hard, real world outside
        where friends support
        and rivals fight
and time marches on through it all.
Protection is needed at times
from threatening facts that arise,
        but healthy life
        grows with the flow
of individual dreams come true.
The harder it is to escape,
more planning it takes to complete,
        but in the end
        it's all worthwhile
for everyone living alone.
New horizons now loom before
in splendor instead of in dread,
        challenging us
        with hopes and fears,
leading to eternal repose.

Cheryl L. Larson

CHERYL L. LARSON. Born: Seattle, Washington, 3-18-48; Education: Seattle Pacific University, B.S., Mathematics, Physics minor, 1970; Occupation: Mathematician/analyst; Membership: National Association of Female Executives; Poetry: 'Growing,' 'Life,' 'The Stranger Friend,' *The Poetry of Life: A Treasury of Moments,* 1988; 'The Rise and Fall of the Sea,' 'The Skeleton Of A Tree,' *American Poetry Anthology,* 1987; Themes: *Observations of nature, life and human nature.*

ODE TO A BUTTERFLY

Although there are many, many more,
Let me apprehend and differentiate four.

Black as midnight, Stygian hue,
Metamorphosis to shine as few.

Yellow as a lily in the glen,
Born to glow and glimmer in the wind.

One so white as bright as light,
Escaped from wrath and made its flight.

High above the earth to reign,
Only a Monarch dares to deign.

Leu Leana G. Baker

CONTEMPORARY THOREAU

Sitting gently, sandy hill
Zip cars passing quickly by
Find a mountain window sill
Take a look see as you sigh.

Two shoes scatter lonely streets
Red wheels raving someone sick
Tick hand closes as they meet
Freckled skin is growing thick.

Off to sea-shore greeting Palms
Tall sleek grasses slowly bend
While the blind man gathers alms
Hope he sees the wall at end.

Back with palms and silky moon
Tender caring shapely thigh
Quick lips asks me if there's room
On the lip of velvet sky.

Open hand says ''yes,'' sit there
Leaving trinkets by the door
Ask the room for breathing air
Don't let on for anything more.

Russell R. Babington

SINGING IN LAUGHTER

Hearts full in the genes of life
No one tear can be the same.
Many games that people play
To touch the mind of every day.
Soiled thoughts one might say,
But in the den of lovers
You hear singing in laughter.

Singing in laughter swept away
Touch-me-nots will come out to play.
Say to the wind, ''I love you'' today
Rays of the sun bring flowers and May
Putting on laughter by the tons
Of happiness, singing in laughter.

Daintiness and silver thongs,
Where oh where do we belong?
Up in the sky so bright
Love love in heavenly delight
The morning after, squeals of laughter
Singing singing like a pure white dove.
Singing in laughter from a song above.

Bonnie Simmons Peter

THE NIGHT COMES

Gently, ever so gently,
Darkness steals the light.
And the golden sun is replaced
By the gleaming moon's light.
Shadow overtakes the land,
And soon the sky is gray.
Midnight soon replaces that,
And blackness blankets gray.
But in between the black,
The eye will always see
A multitude of stars
Winking merrily.

Holly Cravens

COME TO ME WHIPPOORWILL WHIPPOORWILL

Lightning spit fire
Of our every sweet sweet desire.
When will we meet?
I want your heart to keep
Like a deer will you leap?
Come, oh come to me, your heated love.

Our heart is like the wind
As time goes by
Where oh where did our love begin?
Has our love passed or will our hearts
As one eloquently last?

When we first met
Together we sat in thrills,
Leaning so tall
Would you come if I would call
Like the whippoorwill
Perched on the highest hill?

Can you see, it's in your arms
Holding your charms,
I want to be
With you in a river of love
Come to me, oh come to me.

Bonnie Simmons Peter

FEATHER PILLOWS

Georgie slumbers to my left;
Johnnie to my right.
At play one day we each did heft
  Our pillows for to fight.
Shouting from our little beds,
''King of the Hill,'' with might —
Fat pillows swung about our heads.
  ''Downhill'' we did alight!

The pillows burst! Out they came,
Tumbling to be free,
Fat feathers now to join the game
  Creating silky sea.
We, quick, became great captains
On sailing vessels three,
Defending ships from pirate swain —
  While pillows pelted knees!

Mother opened bedroom door.
''My darlings, I declare!
Goosefeathers scattered o'er the floor
  And drifting everywhere?''
Up we picked them, one by one,
With Mother guarding there.
Alas, now 'twas the end of fun
  And feathers in the air.

Cameron Noonan

BRIDGES ON THE MISSISSIPPI, AT DUBUQUE.

ROCKERS

Every child must own a horse —
No, not real, but wood, of course,
Perched upn the shelf each day
Eager to transport away
    To the lands of queens and kings,
    Ships, and sealing wax, and things.

Golden hooves, bright golden mane,
Stunning horse with tethered rein,
Silent, watchful, as he stands —
Making no unjust demands —
    Hoping so you love him true
    As he guards your childhood through.

Old Man Moon creeps into view;
Rockers know now what to do,
All-consumed with pride, delight,
Watching o'er a child at night,
    Guarding to keep warm and safe
    Each and every tiny waif.

Cameron Noonan

NANCY CAMERON N. DILLMANN. Pen Name: Cameron Noonan; Born: Durham, North Carolina, 11-11-47; Married: Joseph M. Dillmann, 7-3-86; Education: St. Joseph's School of Nursing, 1969; Occupation: Registered nurse; Awards: Golden Poet Award, 1987; inclusion in *Who's Who in U.S. Writers, Editors & Poets;* Poetry: 'School Daze,' *North American Poetry Review,* 1987; 'Career,' *American Poetry Anthology,* 1986; 'The Magic of Storms,' *Impressions, Vol. II,* 1986; 'Wafting Perfume of Rain,' haiku, *Memories of the Halcyon Days,* 1987; 'Dream Hat,' *Rainbows and Rhapsodies — Poetry of the Eighties,* 1987; Comments: *Currently I am working on several children's books in verse.*

PERFECT LOVE

The only perfect love
Is one frozen in time
Receding into a dreamer's cove,
Growing more fascinating and sublime.
One not tried by sorrow or strife
Not marred by life's grime
Or touched by sordid need of daily life
Perfect love — a fine dream preserved in time.

Virginia D. Casteel

LIFE

A little twig stands on a hill
Some take for granted, she's unable to feel,
    The problems of the world they bear.
She bows her head in silent prayer.
As the years pass by, the little tree grows.
The rain comes often. The sun seldom glows.
She absorbs all that she sees and hears.
The rain is too much. She develops her fears.
She sees the love all around
Reaches, falls, hits the ground.
Reaching again, all is gone.
She wonders silently what is wrong
Soon, she cannot cope with the rain.
She feels the hate and all life's pain.
She looks at herself, a healthy young tree.
All she really wants to be . . .
        Is loved.
You see, that tree is me!

Rhonda R. Stone

ANOTHER LOVE

Distant, but so close, feelings deep
Inside cry for this distant love,
Which seems so near, yet far away.
Listening to that other part, which
Brings this love to heart. Wish there
Were two of me. Then I would be happy!
Thinking of that other love. Because
He too! I think of.

Cherished moments cloud my mind. My
Thoughts of who? this time. Memories
Linger near, as the images become clear.
That of whom I think of: is another love.

Carolyn Baptiste

NO TIME TO WASTE

A card came in the mail today
It lifts my spirits high.
The sprawling words were few but clear,
"How are you? I am great," they say.
"My grades are good. The weather's fine.
Love always," Jay.

I answered quickly and gave him praise.
Because I know
I must not lose that spark of love,
It means too much,
For he is young
And I am not.

Luci A. Yeager

UNTITLED

If you knew the tale of life,
you would realize what is right.

Our souls are locked within our
shells, because our minds just
could not tell.

We say the world is in a mess,
because the leaders have failed
the tests.

But you yourself who are just as
vile, release your heart and say
with a smile:

Lord have mercy on my soul, for
I have played a benighted role.

Waldemar Zambrano

SOMETIMES I WONDER

Sometimes I wonder
who's gonna teach me peace and happiness
with the world arguing, arguing with itself?
Raging sounds
Stifled fears
The sky is burning
A sea flame
The world's changing
I'll be the same
    tired of falling in love with obsessions
    reaching my senses and hurting my heart
Sometimes I wonder
    where do I start?
Why must my childhood end,
    when I haven't seen the innocence of man?
Sometimes I wonder
    I'm happy for the man
    remorsed by a child
    'cos it never comes back.
It'll never come back.

Gabrielle Vasquez

GOD'S GROWING IDEAS

I've taken ideas
and watered them.
I've cleared and
turned their place.
    I've believed in
almighty love
and am grateful
for my God's grace.

I have seen the
invisible
develop, and
begin to live.
I must ask you
also to *see*,
and thank God for
what He will give.

M. A. Butcher

THE BEGUILED ONES

The beguiled ones who are now lost and alone, have
nothing more to offer, but a lonely old home.

True love and sincerity we're so eager to receive, but
more often it is abused because of lust and greed.

To achieve the peace and serenity, we all seek in life,
is often accomplished from disappointment and strife.

For the harder we try, more often denied, and we
sometimes feel like we want to cry.

But we are able to overcome the obstacles of life,
because of determination and pride.

Life is a mystery, this I'm sure we'll all agree, but if
people considered one another, it wouldn't have to be.

So before I point a finger at someone else, I stop and
notice how many fingers are pointing back at me.

To climb from rags to riches in one's own life, to me,
has to come from one's heart and soul with kindness,
and without a price.

Wanda J. Pugh

WANDA JEAN PUGH. Born: Kansas City, Missouri, 12-24-35; Married: Chester E. Pugh, 4-30-78; Education: Laney College, Chabott College; Occupation: Inventory control analyst; Awards: 1st and 2nd place for poems, 1976-86; Poetry: 'My Mom,' *American Poetry Anthology,* 1986; 'Each Other,' *American Poetry Anthology,* 1981; 'Love Game,' *American Poetry Anthology,* 1982; 'The Last Days,' *American Poetry Anthology,* 1983; 'My Sister,' *American Poetry Anthology,* 1980; Comments: *I believe in God, and my writing is just one of the gifts from my father. My work is merely a reflection of my inner thoughts and feelings.*

TODAY IS A NEW DAY

I awakened this morn, and you were there by
my side. Helping me to hold on, I realized how much
we needed one another.
A man by my side, to drive all the past away, and
bring me to a brighter day.
Today is a new day, when you were there for me, to
touch, to see, to hear.
A day for all days, because you brought that
special feeling with you.
You and I know what it means, but, isn't that our
shared moment?
I love you, forever, just for being you. For us,
that is all that matters.
I'll pray to God each day, until you return; for
words cannot exclaim what my heart longs to say.

Ollie Henson-Bennett

SERPENT'S HEART

Where the marsh is murky and thickened black
The day lily (like my heart) has sprung
A brilliant bloom by such deepened contrast
I know not whether by being vain or stunned
She hides her golden face from night
And only can listen for owls' silent flight
And hopes to only not witness
The serpent leave his dark den
Endeavoring to shed his bitter skin
He crawls beneath violets' tender heart-shaped leaves
Where Cupid's darts render no defense
Upon his cold, numb heart, it seems.

Open, Lily, your face to dawn
For you visually render the nightingale's song
Feel the unicorn's heavenly mane
Slide silken by, slightly damp in dew's rain
And see fallen among the violets' leaf-hearts
Millions of targetless sweet Cupid's darts
Wake not the serpent 'neath those heart-shaped leaves
But let him sleep as in dreams he believes
He awakens one day a bright butterfly
For the heart that crawls longs *most*
                                        for
                                        the
                                        sky.

Julie Markham

JULIE MARIE MARKHAM. Born: Wildwood Road, Salem, Virginia, 5-20-57; Education: G.E.D.; Occupations: Crest Uniform Co., order picker; Memberships: Rosicrucian Order, 1981; Poetry: 'Song of the Lark,' *Impressions,* 1986; 'For a Gentle Heart,' *Chasing Rainbows,* 1987; 'To The Bird Who Lived in Thorns,' *P.S. God Loves You,* 1984; 'Because You Love,' *In Quiet Places,* 1985; 'Beseiged,' *Hearts on Fire,* 1985; Comments: *Poetry writing, for me, is an instinct: as flying south for the winter is inborn to birds. I was always a quiet and serious child and began to write poetry at age 11. I write to honor friends or any in whom I see kindness, and for personal expression.*

TO THANK THE MOCKINGBIRD

I sat outside one summer's eve, that idle hour of thoughts and dreams
When a mockingbird song filled the gathering dark,
    an ode of joy that stirred my heart.
A repertoire of sweetest sound, to bring the evening curtain down
Liquid silver melody, effusive ardent rhapsody
What is the source that so inspired, your song of such glissando fire?
Oh if I could only share your secret sung on the sweet night air!
Indeed then I would surely find no greater gift to all mankind.
And when the Lord sees fit it be my time,
    I want no hymns of mournful rhyme.
But the only sound I want be heard,
    is the sweet refrain of the mockingbird.

Nancy E. Sherman

IN DREAMS

Oh still night in silent mean
There I lie again to dream
The wind a sullen cold
Silence piercing the window pane
Steals my breath again and again
A tree sways to and fro
Wake me not, sleep oh sleep
This dream locked away for I to keep
The moon a quarter past
Still fallen rain, a dancer's tap
Gently echoes a thunder's clap
The stars in song at last
Someone whispers, the air is still
Sharp is the dew, a beggar's kill
Another sleeping soul
The storm reaps a crying child
Timeless age of cold so mild
Before me winter's snow
In early morn the dream awakes
The storm is calm, memory breaks
A child cries no more
But may I catch a star that falls
That in my dream a beggar calls
The calm before the storm.

Stephanie A. Cooley

YOU MADE THE DIFFERENCE

As I lean against the window sill
    Quietly reflecting times gone by,
I listen to the mockingbird's trill
    While watching the sheep graze lazily
Upon the hill.

I remember all the happiness
    And all the sorrow.
And as I look back, I realize that
    You were there in my life yesterday,
And you'll be there tomorrow,
    That it's you who's made the difference
In my life today.

I remember birthday parties and special days
    Scattered throughout my younger years.
It was you who made the difference
    With your thoughtful and loving ways.

I cherish those moments
    And remember now and then
Of all the love wrapped up inside of me
    Starting from way back when.

And even though I sometimes don't find
    The right words to say,
I know you made the difference
    In what I am today.

Roseann Rutz

CHESAPEAKE

We're living here where the Chesapeake Bay
    And the lovely South River meet,
For natural beauty and peace of soul
    This spot just can't be beat.

They call it ''The Land of Pleasant Living''
    And we've found that this is true,
For nowhere is the view so grand
    Or skies so azure blue.

There's something mighty peaceful
    And awe inspiring too,
In viewing God's great waters
    And man's ships — close to you.

Yes, this *is* pleasant living —
    Or working — if you choose,
A place where care's forgotten
    And there's no place for blues.

Come visit us and share our view
    Enjoy what God has given,
Yes, join us here on the Chesapeake Bay
    In the land of pleasant living.

Jean Hammerly

In the sight of man
    is a darkness.
Within the hallowed halls
    of earthly dignities
lie cracks
in the golden busts of leaders.

These are the visions
    of things
that pollute the souls of men.

Clifford A. Beck

TO MOM AND DAD

You're both so very lucky
    To have a son like me,
I'm strong and very healthy
    And cute as I can be.

Enjoy me while I'm still so small
    And I am in your power,
You have control of all I do
    In all the daily hours.

Before you barely blink an eye
    I'll dash away from you,
And climb a tree, fall from a bike
    Like Daddy used to do.

I'll want to go to ball games
    And kiss the girl next door,
Then next I'll want to drive the car
    And who knows what else more.

But you will always love me
    And I will love you, too,
And try to make you proud of me
    As I'll be proud of you.

Jean Hammerly

SECRETS

Far back in the quiet recesses of our cells
Are many great and small secrets.
Depths beyond depths there dwells
Feelings, thoughts, deeds and regrets;
Secrets that would hurt those we love
Or ones so joyful and fragile
That to share our hidden trove
Might cause their beauty to defile.

No one knows us entirely.
Secrets we always keep
From self, friends and family;
Secrets we carry to our final sleep.
Life is no story book
Revealing all of oneself
No matter how closely we look
Or how deeply we delve.

Virginia D. Casteel

VIRGINIA DARE CASTEEL. Born: Dungannon, Virginia, 12-23-26; Divorced; Education: V.P.I., Blacksburg, Virginia, 1943-46; East Tennessee State University, B.S.; Occupation: Teacher, retired 6-10-87; Memberships: Retired Teachers Association; American Association of University Women; Awards: Award for 'Mountain Heir,' 1987; Golden Poet Award for 'The Sea,' 1987; Poetry: 'The Vine,' 1987; 'Mountain Heir,' 1987; 'Many Faces of My Mountains,' 'Proud Tree,' 1987; 'Mountain Memories,' 1986; Themes: *Various themes, mostly mountains and nature.*

PYTHIAN LANE

He crouched at her feet
while his daddy rattled the facts,
calm as a serpent whistling
dixie by the silver moon.

Lying in the sofa's arms,
too tired to cry out.
Smelling her skin, long after
they had blurred into the horizon.

Later he brushed his hair till
all the tangles had disappeared,
ran off like a cat at the
supper bell, loud and clear.

Squalling in his Sunday best
low branches scrape, rip bright
buttons from his tidy vest,
falling down, moving
towards the highway, penitent.

Janis Gillespie

THE VANITY OF FASHIONABLE FLESH

In this world's theater in which we play
The fateful stage of life displays our roles
And with the advanced tools possessed today
We can sculpture our flesh, but not our souls;
And to these vanities we hold as truth,
Are themselves called beauty and eternal youth.
Fabrics distort and disguise our mortal frames
That beauty sustains and shines without
But clothes alone do not the charming name,
Nor pleasing scents that through air flirt about.
For if character walks not by her side,
How can loyal love then also abide?
The jealous woman or envy-laden man
Who wish their looks changed so to the eye appease,
Should logically look to medicine's plan,
To lure their lover with a pleasant ease,
Or for public sight to lift their social life,
By the surgeon's quick and quiet knife.
But after they pass into that breathless land
A truth they elude will in their souls speak
And echo timelessly like hourglass sand
That runs emptiless, while the light they seek
Will soon reveal themselves with eyes enthralled,
As if no surgery were performed at all.

Henry Tye, Jr.

ODE TO THE SUN

As the dawn begins to approach,
  so ended the night at its last darkened torch.
Then came the morn, warm and rich,
  slowly spreading the color of peach.

Never once had it missed the chance,
  to show her face in her graceful dance.
Through the happiness of breathing light,
  it chased away the dim, grimful night.

It supplies the earth with its warmth,
  to all things and heights and depth.
It furnishes the earth with its color,
  green, yellow, red, and other.
It shows to the earth of its beauty,
  with the silky rainbow that's huge and mighty.
It has lived long before our time,
  yet it will still live as we pass by.

To the future and challenging age,
  it casts an eye on our short and living page.
To the strength and harmony of the skies,
  it is the Sun; the opening to paradise.

Nancy Chang

LOOKING BACK

There was a young lady a few years ago, whom a young man met
and love began to show, this young man said; Hey, this love will
grow.
So you can see, this young man was in the know.
Winter passed, but the snowflakes that had fallen on this
pair were unseasonable as we know.
Wedding bells rang, vows made, hearts mingled and were filled
with budding blossoms of Faith, Hope, Charity and Love, this
pair had made a rainbow of their own that would last and last.
Just look at their beautiful lassies and handsome lad and the
new blossoms they've had.
Ah yes, this young man was in the know and this love continues
to grow.

Reva McCaig-Jones

THE MINSTREL

The metro stopped at Odéon.
The rocking carriage upon the rails
  had been a lullaby to weary passengers.

He came aboard at Odéon, a
  common minstrel of the street,
  to serenade indifferent riders
  of the rails.

I, twice jaded, in this foreign
  place, closed my ears to all sound —
  until his voice began a soft
  enchantment, in my own tongue.

I saw him, then, a fellow countryman
  in a foreign land,
  in ragged jeans, blue with cold,
  singing of home.

We were alone, there, fellows
  adrift in an alien place,
  and the sadness of his voice
  matched the tears upon the coins
  I tossed into his cup —
  a tribute for his having brought me
    home again.

Gail V. Baker

PRACTICE

My Brother Jim can neatly fold a fitted sheet.
What is this? I slit a sheet a sheet I slit?
Not exactly.
No, it's more about my brother and his
ability to figure out how to do things exactly,
and do them.
My problem is, I see no need for neatly folded fitted sheets,
but it nags at me this thought that it may be good practice.

C. E. Courtney, Jr.

AUTUMN'S AUTOGRAPH

Etched out beneath our earthen sky lies autumn's autograph,
Skillfully carved with glorious splendor to form a striking cast.
Dressed in all their finest colors stand amber-crimson trees,
Gracefully dancing to the tune of a crisp, gentle breeze.

While the autumn wind softly chants its illusive melody,
It entices clinging leaves to set themselves free.
Tumbling, swirling, gently they are led
To the earth's floor to form a soft, crimson bed.

Scurrying across new-fallen leaves, a squirrel in search of food,
Diligently gathers acorn nuts for the approaching winter's interlude.
He scampers in and out of trees while they bend and twist and sway,
Trying to lure him from his task, suggesting it's time to play.

Silhouettes of autumn's harvest stand barren in their fields,
While bins stand filled to the top from farmers' harvest yields,
And pumpkins array their bright orange faces awaiting the
  sculpture's craft,
As our Heavenly Father lovingly inscribes autumn's autograph.

Sharon Crozier Waterman

PARADISE

I know a wonderful place
Of solitude and peace;
There man's haste is lost, and
Entering all conflicts cease.

An oasis it is . . .
Which replenishes my soul;
I can rest, fish, or hike;
My reward is greater than gold!

My place has a fishing hole . . .
The "pot hole" is its name;
All you need is a cane fishing pole,
Bass and trout know its fame.

There my father would camp,
With several children along;
Pine splinters lit for a lamp;
Frying fish and singing songs.

I long for its serenity . . .
I go there when I can;
It is where I belong . . .
There I feel the touch of God's hand.

Joan Hughes Black

PAUL

Above clouds of white,
At peace with God and man;
Serene as a still, perfect night;
You reach out for God's hand.

Soaring like an eagle
You are brave, daring, and bold;
Blue skies beautiful and regal,
Engulf you in their hold.

You become a part
Of the universal plan;
Beating inside your heart,
Is the adventurous spirit of man.

Onward and upward you soar,
Sounds of angels you hear;
Reality returns as you lower
Your plane's landing gear.

With the universe you are one,
Its beauty and splendor so rare;
Surpassed only by Allen and Mae's son,
Who grew up so good and fair!

Joan Hughes Black

HUNGER CRIES

A village silent in the brush
Where laughter once rang through the day
And little feet ran in a rush
Without a care in endless play.

The laughter now has disappeared
As little voices moan long while;
Parent's hearts know only tears
As hunger steals the faintest smile.

A mother's heart cries out in pain,
As hunger plays its mournful game;
The father's dreams end all in vain
As mounded dust reveals death's claim.

Caroline Janz

TO MY CHILDREN

I wish for you . . .
In all you say and do;
To be happy with good cheer
All through the days and years.

I want for you . . .
A mountain of love so true;
Laughter and happy times
And a family with ties that bind.

The love inside my heart
Is so great we will never part!
Thank you, my precious, darling ones,
For making my life a successful one.

I am at peace . . .
And when I leave you
The best of me will never cease!
Because the best of me is you!

Joan Hughes Black

SOMEONE LIKE YOU

I've never found someone like you
I've never had thought of knowing you
Things had been so hard for me
My past had been scandalized with pain
I've been torn down, always stepped upon
The pain I got was so great
   it almost crushed me to the ground
   almost grounded me deep within it
Until I found someone like you
Somebody I could lean on
Someone so great and loving
The emotions I felt were battering me
I can't do anything about it, but try
   to accept it
Such love I was feeling was so impossible
   to hide
Too much for me to keep it inside
That I decided to tell you
I've never loved, someone like you.

Maria Loida F. Cruz

UNTITLED

Darkness enveloped me
In a cold shivering night
Wondering all alone
Frightened and lost
   Dark,
     cold,
       Alone and
         Lost
Blinded by the darkness
A night so cold
Alone in this wilderness
Wanting out, but, still lost
   Dark,
     cold,
       Alone and
         Lost

Maria Loida F. Cruz

MARIA LOIDA FLORES CRUZ. Born: Manila, Philippines, 2-17-66, to Mr. and Mrs. Leodegario F. Cruz; Education: University of the Philippines; Poetry: 'Mysterious Me,' *American Poetry Anthology,* 1986; 'Trying To Make It Easy,' 'I Still Love You,' 'The Pains We've Benn Through,' *Hearts on Fire, Vol. IV;* 1987; Comments: *For some, poetry is a fantasy world. A life full of hope and happiness. For others, it is the reality they just can't accept and face. It's a kingdom full of gay music and bright lights for others, or maybe, for the other half, a box of eternal darkness and sorrow. It's one's magical illusion or someone's move of desperation. Its colors bring life to the dying and at times death to the living dead. Either way, it's one's ultimate escape.*

THE CROSS

The cross
Inscribed on the wrist
Runs red
   Along the hand

   Watercolor
   To paint the spattered picture
   Inside the body

   Sprawled beside pillows
   With the mind
   Propped up to view

   A christ decaying
   Into the white plaster
   Of the cheap statue.

Mark Oliver

DAUGHTERS ARE SO BEAUTIFUL

If you never had a daughter, then you don't know what I mean,
To say a daughter's beautiful, is more than can be seen.

It's a feeling we all have, way down deep inside,
To know she's yours alone, is a feeling you can't hide.

A man says she's my daughter, and his eyes gleam with pride,
It's really truly wonderful, the feeling he can't hide.

He'll always have his little girl, no matter what her age,
Even when she's all grown up, and left and gone away.

To see the worry on his face, to feel his hurt so deep,
When she leaves home the first time, to go across the street.

When she goes away, to live her life, as they all do,
The tenderness he shows, will always stay true.

She will always know her father cares, no matter where she lives,
Because her father loves her so, no matter where she is.

A mother that's no different, she loves her daughter too,
But she's the one who teaches her, to cross that street so new.

She teaches her the meaning, of love that is so strong,
When daughter leaves home that first time, it's mother who is strong.

Mothers love their daughters, just as much as dads,
For daughters are so beautiful, is really almost sad.

Nancy Jensen

THE EXTRATERRESTRIALS

Perhaps there were times when our galaxy
has had 12 planets and among them there was
one giant planet with a super civilization on it
when its celestial body has been badly injured,
having ripped apart one big slice from it.
That cosmic nebula traveled many galactic cycles
till took form, till a life sprout, the future earth.

Many billions years slipped by until a post-adamic race
was brought here, in the land of the Lemurs, by the gods
from the ''Mother Planet'' and that race were sometimes
the gods' guinea pigs, who through a genetic manipulation
created munsters, androids, giants and extinct hominids, etc.

The earth too received immigrants and exiles brought here
from other planets and those space aliens lost gradually
a memory of their ancestry, yet they brought thence their skill,
their habits, tradition, their idioms, which they still preserve.
Therefore, our roots and our language are cosmic.

Afterwards, the gods brought the aryas from former planet
Pegasus and settled they on the land of the Hyperboreos,
and gathered there roving groups of Swedes and Norwegians.

The earth had always been visited by gods, even today.
Apparently, the universe and our world were created
by cosmic computer; we're programmed and reprogrammed.
If God is the Soul of life and the cosmic energy, who are
the computer programmers? Is there other God? How many?

Nicky Katzingris

FAITH

What is faith to me, the *believing* the word of Jesus Christ and God.
The strong bond I feel from knowing to be true the words of God.
The unwavering feeling of God's truth, and promise that I claim.
The feeling I get when I awake to a new day, that God has given,
That I may have one more chance to prove him and help gather the
    sheep.
That in some small way I help, that he has me do good for him.
That I will do this work till it is God's time of completion.
That I will give my all in what I do as I would for God.
That I learn to treat others with the respect I treat God.
That I will believe my life belongs to God, and I am doing what he wants,
That he loves me. This is the faith I have and will live by till I die.
But not the death that claims the end of our lives, but the death
That would certainly destroy my soul. For without God I would have
    none.
So I will keep my faith, the faith I have learned from God. Forever.

Nancy Jensen

THOUGHTS OF GROWIN' UP

To Debbie

Bright red cheeks with a ponytail,
Little blue eyes that kings would hail,
Princess in a castle daydreaming of her prince,
Thoughts of growin' up just don't make sense.

Fairy-tale kisses of a godmother's spell,
Precious secrets tossed in a wishing well,
Ugly frogs leapin' outside a kingdom wall,
Thoughts of growin' up make no sense at all!

Teddy bear pals and dolls that share,
Pretty dresses, white shoes, and shampooed hair,
Imaginary cookies bakin' with a mother's care,
Thoughts of growin' up just aren't quite fair!

All too soon the days drift by,
As tiny toys leave without saying good-bye,
And sadly the magic of youth fades away,
For thoughts of growin' up, are nature's play!

Today a proud mother stands over her child,
A newborn baby girl meek and mild,
Over in the corner lies a new stuffed toy,
Hope . . . that thoughts of growin' up, will bring her joy!

Douglas R. Haney

CLOUDS AND RAINBOWS AND CASTLES OF KINGS

Clouds and rainbows and castles of kings:
all are the stars of my childhood dreams.

Some sail aloft on the tides of a breeze,
altering form with the rustling of leaves.

Some decorate the sky at the end of storms
with promises of love and bright, peaceful morns.

Some can be found on mysterious, sunlit land,
also in picture books and on the white sand.

Clouds and rainbows and castles of kings:
all are alive in my backyard swing.

Beverly Riley

FOOLISH TEARS

Still I cry these foolish tears
  but only a few
When I think back on how it was
  how much I loved you
We could never be separated
  always by each other's side
The tears rolling down my face
  remember when I cried?
You held me in your loving arms
  thought you'd never let me go
But now things have changed
  I'm really sorry though
Still I cry these foolish tears
  I hope only a few
When I think back on how it was
  how much I still love you.

Stacey Tibayan

STACEY ANN TIBAYAN. Born: Hollywood, California, 12-15-68; Education: Allan F. Daily High School, 1987; Awards: Honorable Mention for 'Our Story,' 1987; Poetry: 'Never Could — Never Will,' 1984; 'The Way You Were To Me,' 'You & I Before,' 1986; 'Puzzle Piece,' *Best New Poets of 1986,* 'To Live in Hell,' 1988; Comments: *A singer sings a song. A circus clown will make us smile, a painter paints a picture, I've known it for a while. It's the poet who expresses, while the actor plays the role, because the poet knows the sound . . . he feels the music of the soul.*

PONDERING

Whenever I sit and think of you
It seems that you are near —
Even though you're far away
Somehow I know you're here.

Time and distance fade away
They seem to lose all meaning —
Hours too wonderful to be real
Am I awake or dreaming?

I look and see the other half
Of what's inside of me —
Tell me if I'm making wishes
Or living what's meant to be.

Still, when I sit and think of you
Deep inside I know —
As long as I live day to day
Our relationship will grow.

H. Kristina Hightower

TEARS

Tears
  Are as the dewdrop,
  That trembles on a rose.
  Glistening as a jewel.

Tears
  At times, refuse to stop.
  They are the heart's
  Cleansing, as the rain
  Washes away impurity
  From the flowers, so
  Our tears cleanse.
  They help refuel
  Our heart and soul.
  As sun follows
  The rain. Our tears
  Follow pain, in turn
  These too are followed
  By joy, for our

Tears
  Are as the dewdrop
  That trembles on a rose,
  Glistening as a jewel.

Petal A. Beebe

FOR SOMEONE

He huddled in a chair,
Acceptance seemed
His creed.
In his tired and lonely
Heart lived an ever-
Present need.
Not for food or shelter.
For someone to say
I really care.
Someone to hold out
Their hand to the
Loneliness that
Lived there.

Petal A. Beebe

SNOW

As the snow falls all around,
It makes a blanket on the ground.
The blanket stretches far and near,
And makes the day cold and clear.

It sparkles in the midday sun,
Calling children to play and run.
They roll and shape it like a clay,
''I love the snow,'' the children say.

Maybe it will snow all night,
The schools will close, but that's alright.
Faces against the window pane,
It is home they remain.
For it's another day of snow,
And out of doors the children go!

Jean Ponting

THE GARDEN

In the hazy morning mist,
I love a walk through the garden.
When all the flowers have been kissed,
With dew, as the day starts in.

A tiny spider is working hard,
On a web of glistening dew.
Is he not aware, or on his guard,
That I have a magnificent view.

And when the sun wakes to find,
The roses blushing like a wine,
The colors become so vibrant there,
More beautiful than anywhere.

Jean Ponting

HEARTACHE AND SORROW

I saw you last nite, while you were out walking
I watched as you paused by my gate
And I wondered if you were remembering
Or if the nearness ever made your heart ache

I was thinking of the times we spent together
And how happy I was by your side
I felt the deep pains of heartache
And I hung my head and I cried

I thought of the birds in the treetops
How their voices blended, with leaves of gold
And I knew they were free forever
For the branches had no bars to hold

I'm a prisoner to heartache and sorrow
And my soul is not really my own
I travel the highway of many
But I walk in the darkness alone

Oh Father let there be a heaven
A heaven somewhere in the regions above
To release this soul from bondage
And a heaven that's filled with love

Melvina Jordan

EVERYONE LOSES

Someone stopped caring
And didn't want to become involved

Someone stopped sharing
And thought their problems solved

Someone stopped bearing
The burdens of others

Someone stopped wearing
The badge of justice for their brothers

Someone is lost
Someone is broken
Someone is abused

All because someone stopped giving
The essential token
Needed for living
Love!

Vicki J. Malyurek

GOD'S FOOTSTOOL

I like to sit under the starry sky,
And marvel at the wonders up above;
   It makes me realize how lucky I am,
To be in God's great and wonderful world.

I love to smell the beautiful rosebuds,
With their sweet fragrance they so abound;
   I love to watch the fine feathered friends,
When in the air they go soaring around.

God made this great earth for man to enjoy,
Its resources He intended for us to preserve;
   But somewhere along the long, dark way,
I believe man has forgotten His word.

After God made this great universe,
He must have broken the mold;
   For its beauty cannot be surpassed,
And its wonders are too much to behold.

The angels marveled at God's creation,
For it was so beautiful to see;
   And with love in His heart,
With dust from the earth He made me.

Soon Jesus will return again,
And this earth I'll help Him rule;
   For the Bible plainly tells me,
This earth is God's footstool.

Fletcher J. Eller

THE MONKEYS' CONFERENCE

It happened way back in the jungle,
The monkeys called a conference to discuss man;
   They gathered under a large coconut tree,
And they sat down on the cool, white sand.

The reason we've called this conference,
Is it's rumored we're descendants of man;
   So before we begin our discussion,
Let's all stand up and shake each other's hand.

We monkeys don't steal from our neighbors,
And we don't covet each other's wife;
   We don't shoot each other with guns,
And we don't stab each other with a knife.

We don't beat up on our children,
And we don't take drugs and drink beer;
   We don't create a disturbance,
So the whole neighborhood can hear.

We don't bear false witness against each other,
And we don't lock each other up in chains;
   We don't go out and commit a crime,
And let another monkey take the blame.

So we're going to adjourn this conference,
For there's one thing we all understand;
   And that's for sure and certain,
We monkeys aren't descendants of man.

Fletcher J. Eller

MY MOTHER

If only I could turn back the pages,
To the days when I was a kid;
   I'd tell Mother how much I loved her,
And I'd undo some of the wrong I did.

She'd wear the same old dress to church,
So I could have shoes on my feet;
   Many times she'd say, ''I'm not hungry,''
So I could have more to eat.

Many times she kept my dad from scolding me,
By saying what I did wasn't wrong;
   Then she'd tell me of my mistakes,
When she and I were all alone.

She'd always take me to church on the Sabbath,
And I can still hear her singing those good old hymns;
   She'd say, ''Son, when we gather at the river,
I know we'll all be there with Him.''

Now she has gone on to rest,
And I know there'll never be another;
   For no one in this whole wide world,
Can ever take the place of my mother.

Fletcher J. Eller

FLETCHER JUNIOR ELLER. Born: Gillsville, Banks County, Georgia; Married: Pearl Knighton Eller, 8-5-53; Education: University of Maryland, College Park, 2 years; Sumter Technical College, Sumter, South Carolina, 2 years; Inventory Management Specialist School, Management Supervisory Course; Supply Officer's Management Course, Strategic Air Command, NCO Academy; Occupation: Retired from U.S. Air Force, 24 years in the military, 12 years in foreign countries; Memberships: ASCAP, Non-Commissioned Officers Association, South Carolina Songwriters Association, American Legion; Poetry: 'America You'll Always Be Beautiful to Me,' *American Poetry Anthology, Vol. VII, No. 2,* 1987; 'Softly,' 'The Blind Man,' 'Pretty Flowers,' *The Poetry of Life,* 1988; Comments: *To me, writing poetry is a personal expression of my innermost thoughts and feelings. It gives me the opportunity to share with others my thoughts, places I've been, people I've met, and things I've seen. It is easier to put my feelings and thoughts in writing than to openly discuss them. Poetry relieves the tension of the everyday stress and strain. Poetry makes me forget my troubles and brings me closer to my God, who made this great universe.*

OLÉ, THE CRASH OF 87

It owned the ring for several years.
Everyone took a challenge despite their fears.
Then one day the arena was packed full.
For an unknown came to challenge the bull.
All eyes were focused upon the East.
As the matador tried to tame the beast.
It was a fierce battle to the very end.
For this optimist brought wealth to many men.
With the arena still jammed full,
The crowd roared, ''Olé, Olé, he slew the bull.''

Wendell S. Hawkins

WILLOW TREE

Have you ever had the opportunity
To observe a willow tree.
To see the long flowing branches
waiting so silently
to perform its passionate dance
with nature's activity.
It only takes a soft breeze to
start the beautiful swaying in
graceful harmony
each willow branch swaying separately
ever so tolerant of raging winds
not one branch will lock together.
It perfected its technique way
back in time.
It sways back and forth in rhythm
obviously knowing you will respond.
The willow tree has made a conquest
with its serenity.
The beautiful overwhelming
dance of the willow tree.

Vivian Sprinkles Nyberg

FLAME'S BEAUTY

Come and sit by the fire with me
watch the flames so white hot.
Amber and greenish blue.
Come and feel this love I have
for you.
The flames can leap and swirl and
break away.
Come sit by the fire with me
feel the warmth and see the
beauty of the flames with me.
The fire glows as I do with this
love for you.
Come and sit by the fire with me
and share the warmth my heart has for you.
My lips a soft amber
my eyes greenish blue.
This fire I have in my heart
wants only to leap out to you.
Come sit by the fire with me
let us feel the warmth of the
flames
as they spark our love
into a melody.

Vivian Sprinkles Nyberg

PHENOMENON

So much is always written
Of the phenomenon of love,
But I'm sure I've found an answer
Love is sent from up above.

I'm not speaking of flirtations
Or the short-term games some play,
But a very deep affection
Time and space cannot allay.

A heart-to-heart commitment
Facing good times and the bad,
Whatever hand life deals you
Be they happy times or sad.

Jean Hammerly

FLOURISHING LATE

Blooming into a
scarlet rose took
years of struggle
finding my worth.

Worthy of no one
other than self I
lost track of my
worthiness in search
of myself.

Thorns laid beside
me withered I
stood, not a drop
of water caressing
my moods.

Wilted and withered
lonely I stood till
my Lord sat beside
me saying ''I knew
that you could.''

Christina Acevedo

GOLDEN NUGGETS

A piece of yourself
you gave one and
all, those tiny pieces
made us grow tall.

The ''Golden Nuggets''
helped others as well
and kept young and
old with stories to
tell.

Gallantly walking
by our ''Master,'' each
day, you failed not
to notice what
troubles passed
your way.

Few that are
chosen are exactly
like you, for God
has a purpose choosing
''Golden Nuggets,'' it's
true.

Christina Acevedo

CONCLUSIONS

Shoes, untied socks on the floor.
No one near to close the door.
Car oil is low, gee I have to go.
You said goodbye, because I said no.

It's ten-thirty my dear.
Your folks will soon be here.
After all this I must admit.
I truly truly must quit.

Deborah Adams

STAR

Today for earth
A star was born,
Thousands of light years
Away
Before little children
Began to play,
Before Adam and Eve
Lived in the garden
Of our dreams,
Perhaps,
Before the star
Of Bethlehem
Led the way
To Jesus
And the lamb,
Before God parted
The heavens
And made earth,
He gave
This young Star-planet
its birth.

Margaret Rosenborg

FATHER AND CHILD

He was tall
And dark,
His voice
Had a smile,
When he picked up
The child,
She was completely
Beguiled,
They ran together
In the grass,
Wind between them
Held them fast,
Their laughter seemed
To last and last,
She could still
Hear the sound,
Their laughter
Was a bond,
Now she was
Tall,
And he was
Gone.

Margaret Rosenborg

BLIND DATE

Affectionate movement
Arms around new acquaintance
Rocking to the humor of the moment
Laughing carelessly
Head thrown back
Sliding forward and over between the faces
Instantaneous combustion
A terrifying flash of light
Numbing heat
Singed hair, scorched cheek
Shorter eyelashes
A salty stream
Ashes on the half-eaten sopapilla.

Charlotte A. Bowlds

LOVE CAN SURVIVE

You're gonna laugh and you're gonna cry,
Sometimes without really knowing why.

Hold onto the one whose love is so strong,
For it is there that you surely belong.

There are good times yet times you will fight,
But make sure to say "I love you" each night.

Work toward that special love every day,
For it can far too easily slip away.

You must work at love and happiness,
Otherwise entering will be emptiness.

Remember that a love is very dear,
And foolish pride has no place here.

Don't lose sight of love not even for a minute,
Instead cherish love, respect and value it.

Allow love to grow —
To love, don't say no.

How very sad it would be
If you were to give up on me.

Share what you are keeping inside,
Don't be afraid and don't hide . . . Love truly can survive.

Merla Cumbow

I WOULD

Would that I had been a Mary,
To walk and think and grow,
When Jesus walked by Galilee,
Those days so long ago.

Would that His words had been poured
Upon my listening heart,
And each day's prayers, from His own needs,
Had, of me, become a part!

To see a blind man see,
To hear a mute man sing,
To watch a dead child laugh again,
To help a lost man find his way,
To share His world — more wonderful, to share His day!

To sip the waters from His Truth,
To feel the Spirit walking close,
At eventide to rest in Peace,
And find all time a sweet repose.

To teach, to learn, to pray, to sing,
To watch life bud, and bloom, and die — to bloom again!

Margaret S. Matthews

THE STARS, THE MOON AND A DREAM

I sat and watched the sunset fade,
and soon the moon was there to gaze,
the stars came out,
the darkness grew,
and out of all this came thoughts of you.

A gentle breeze whispered past my ear,
and just then I could almost hear . . .
your name, your voice and your laughter,
promising friendship forever after.

As all of this disappeared,
I looked to the moon once again,
and there I thought that I could see,
the "Man in the Moon," wink and smile at me.

Was it true?
Were you looking too,
from somewhere far away?

Maybe it was just a wish,
or maybe a scheme,
planned-out by the stars, the moon and a dream . . .

Donna Neidert-Hemminger

SHELLS

We are the sons of war —
Crossfire, cartridge, and cordite,
Flash of steel from thundering gun,
an empty shell through a barrel;
brief smoke through a hole
like the ghost of some soul.

We are the scars of war —
Pale strangers and gentle heroes,
fallen comrades in arms.
Faces that stare through bloodshot sockets,
their darkness for insight, white-eyed in blindness.
Open-mouthed, yet mute, in lock-jaw mockery;
Frozen in cynic grin.
Brave flesh, twisted in paralyzed form —
We are the hollow men, the empty men,
shells of our former selves;
scarecrows at midnight,
phantoms of the light.

We are the voices of war —
The hoarse chorus echoing the ceaseless duress;
noise like an ocean, moaning through a shell,
sounds to silence the obscenity, the same old Lie:
Dulce et decorum est
Pro patria mori.

Clifford M. Bannister

FOREST

Forest trees
Lined the road,
Fur pine sycamore
And oak,
Night dark
With starry sky
And a pale moon high,
A car sped down
The shadowed road,
Carrying a full
Passenger load,
Car lights touched
Giant forms,
Whispering of
A coming storm,
Branches reached
Long feathery arms,
Children knew
Trees meant no harm,
They sang the songs
That children sing,
Feeling the shelter
The forest brings.

Margaret Rosenborg

AND I JUMPED OVER THE MOON

I have been watching,
Waiting as our life on paper unfolds,
Noting its seepage through skinful wordings,
Into the vital dusts of the Phoenix
And winter breathing.

Within my skin,
You are everywhere,
Orchestrating,
Imploding noiselessly as God . . .
And as completely.

Now, just to laugh with you,
Or merely to eat flowers in your company,
Would be All.

I want to be with you,
As I always waiting am,
Without caution or despair.

For you will always be, at least, the Moon
And I, at least, Nocturnal.

Claire Burns Miller

S

I wish
that I could talk to you
about this fools' paradise.
Only one can win
and I'm truly happy.
Touch me Jesus.
I know myself.
Chaos is so close that
I'll never be ashamed.
Oh how love helps.

Alfred G. Rowls

TIMANDRA'S SHOES

My first winter boots
— a gift to myself —
laces and straps bind new feet
weary from treading the same
one-dimensional path.

Once, my mother
bought me boots she liked herself
for my sixteenth birthday.

Today my feet nap in rose-brown boots.
Years will stain them. Lessen, their beauty.
The salesgirl sniffs a remark of
incision. I wince as she sighs.
She bends to dust the tip —
a gesture not unlike mothering
and though I can't afford them
I do.

Because you've asked:
they're mine because you
don't approve.

Janis Gillespie

Do I cross your mind at times
  Is it me that makes you smile
Do you miss my touch at times
  When I'm away for a while
Do I stand above the rest
  Have I earned a place in your heart
Will you let me be the one
  To call you my sweetheart?

Can I place my hand in yours
  And let you lead the way
Would you ever turn to me
  In search of a brighter day
Will there ever be a time
  When we won't be apart
Will you let me be the one
  To call you my sweetheart?

When you close your eyes at night
  Am I the one you see
When I look for truthfulness
  Will you treat me honestly
If I need a helping hand
  Would you be there from the start
Will you let me be the one
  To call you my sweetheart?

Lisa Marie Villa

A CLOCK WITHOUT TIME

For Tricia:

Without the ocean there'd be no beach,
Without the future — no goals to reach,
Without each other there'd be little hope,
Without love it'd be hard to cope,
Without the circus there'd be no clowns,
Without the laugh it'd be all frowns,
Me without you is like a clock without time;
It may reach the hour but it'll never chime.

Chris Harrison

I want you with me all the time
  But know it cannot be
So the times that we must be apart
  I close my eyes to see

I see the days we've spent together
  The memories that we've shared
The times we've laughed, almost cried
  The times you've said you cared

And though I know it's just a dream
  It brings you here with me
It takes away those lonely times
  When I must close my eyes to see

Lisa Marie Villa

Another day
 Another time
Some other place
 When people are blind
When love is just love
 When we're all one kind
Another day . . .
 You and I

Another day
 When the world is grey
When black and white have
 Nowhere to stay
When people are just people
 With nothing to hide
Another day . . .
 You and I

Another day
 I'll wait for love
Another day
 For which to cry
For just one moment
 To spend with you
Another day . . .
 You and I

Lisa Marie Villa

WITNESSING FOR HIM

Dear Lord,
As a pilgrim wandering here,
I pray that I might bring some cheer
To those in need, weary and lost
And gently lead them to Your Cross.

Help me to use each passing day
Befriending sinners along the way,
Freely sharing my life with You
That they might come and follow, too.

Before my life on earth is done,
Help me touch the straying ones,
Keeping them from Satan's hold
And bring them safely to Your fold.

Juanita Caudle Crane

I WANT A MAN

I want a man who loves *all* kinds of women
 All shapes, all sizes, all colors and all multitudes of brains
  or no brains at *all*.

I want a *man* who knows he's a *man* and doesn't need
 me nor his sexual aggressiveness or non-aggressiveness
 to constantly remind him of ''Who wears the
  pants in the relationship.''
   Especially since we both do!

I want a *man* who's assertive *and* open-minded.

 A *man* who's strong yet tender
  Walks like a cool breeze
   Temper like thunder
    Heart like gold
     Skin bronze to ebony

I want a *man* who's a *man* no guess work to *it*!
 A *man* who wants a *woman*
  A *woman* like *me*
   A *man* who has *more* love to give
   And no restraints to it!
     A *man* with faith and who is faithful.
      This is the *man* for me.

Shiree Dandridge

IN SEARCH OF FELICIDAD

Her grandfather slowly rocks away.
It is a sunny day down on Chesapeake Bay.
To many, he is considered wise and is a man of integrity.
Today, Jeannie, his granddaughter, sits on the railing opposite
 this elderly man noted for his alacrity.
Jeannie, an intelligent girl of nine,
 had a question in her mind.
Grandfather, is peace not better than war?
Aye lass, 'tis for sure.
Grandfather, is it not better to help your neighbor than
 to harm thy brother?
'Tis so — we must help those who lie in the gutter.
But lass, remember this —
 the bear and her elder cubs will not give up without a fight
 and there won't be any bliss —
 if we fail to stand up for what is right.
But, never fear — for the future is bright.
We must spread the light for all to see.
The future can be pleasant for you and me —
 to include our neighbors down on the sea.

Glen R. Anderson

THANKS

Friend, I thank you for being just that,
One with whom I can always chat,
Relate the good times and share the dreams,
Endure the bad times and mend the seams.
Valuable is your love for all;
Ever is it showing via ways big and small.
Remaining by me, you neither go ahead nor behind.

Finder, you are, of positive words in a negative bind,
Receiver, as well as friendship giver;
Illustrator of God, learner, and teacher;
Encourager and uplifter too.
No dearer a one, for you I pray today and each day anew:
Deliverance from the evil one's snares and blessings beyond all awares,
Saturation with joy and peace, and happiness that will never cease.

Kathryn Lytle

ONE COLD NIGHT

There was a full moon as I stepped through the drizzle of a light mist.
I turned my ear toward the mere to determine if I could list.
I distinctly heard the soft wail of someone sobbing.
Yet — perhaps, it was just the wind crying.
I plodded over sodden ground.
My countenance held a deep frown.
For now — in the distance I could see a lady in her flowing
  white negligee.
She appeared quite enticing down near the bay.
I advanced nearer to see
  this mysterious lady down by the sea.
As I came closer I could see that she had been crying;
  but perhaps, it was just the raindrops which were not drying.
My heart pounded. My body quivered. Our eyes met!
We reached out. Our hands touched. Her hands were wet!
Her hands were cold.
I shook and I trembled beyond words I am told.
I restarted the fire and wrapped a blanket about me.
In a few minutes my lady handed me a cup of hot tea.

Glen R. Anderson

THE ONE

A new life have I begun
Due not to what I've done
But to my faith in the One
Who holds life in His neverending care;
Who is always here, there, and everywhere,
Who knows infinitely more
Than you or I could possibly store,
Who has strength so great
That all, He can overtake,
And who loves beyond the human extent,
For to pay our debt His Son He sent,
That on Him, we would believe and repent
To avoid condemnation and gain eternal life content.
I know this one so true,
Who waits for you too
To know Him and start life anew.

Kathryn Lytle

PSALM OF PEACE

For Recinda

Bring me to still waters and green pastures, O God.
I am like a doe lost in deep woods,
I am a woman in search of You.

Find me where I am
in my confusion and despair; my soul is heavy;
My soul weeps through all my days.
I yearn for Your cleansing presence
that comes as a fresh morning rain.

By the power of Your love
lift my countenance like a rising summer wind
and I will be strong once more.
Grant me Your kiss of peace,
and wrap me in garments of Your eternal light
so that others may see You and come to know You.
And let me hear again the birds of the morning
You have placed outside my window
singing songs of healing
and peace.

Cecily Markham

LETTING YOU GO

Love is hard to let go of
after you've had it for so long,
how could we have let ours end,
prevent it from going on.
We were so much in love,
nothing could have pulled us apart,
but then one day the bond
 suddenly snapped,
and now we're both alone.
Yes, I know that life goes on
and that I will forget you some day
 soon,
but letting you go was hard on me,
and I'm afraid that this
 time,
my heart just won't mend.

Leslie Makela

CHRIST'S RESURRECTION

Christ's miraculous resurrection
Conquered all of sin when in hell.
Jesus is the divine incarnation.
Thank God that our Lord is alive and well.
Christ's resurrection was a miracle.
In God only should you now place your trust.
Christ raised was prophesied by oracle.
Jesus Christ grants victory over lust.
Our sins were paid by Christ on His great Cross.
Heaven is His glorifying treasure.
Jesus Christ is our great Almighty Boss.
Praising God is Christ's marvelous pleasure.
Jesus Christ conceived by the Holy Ghost!
Lord Jesus Christ: an omnipotent host!

Timothy A. Wik

THE GUPPY SHADOW

Once I saw a whale
Quite large and fancy free,
Unique markings on its tail
Reveal the whale's identity.
This whale made a wrong turn
Into San Francisco Bay,
Up the Sacramento River,
A long, long, long wrong way.
No one had it in their memory
Of ever seeing a whale this close.
The news media named him Humphrey
The glamour whale of the West Coast.
Humphrey got confused somehow
Swam inland from the ocean,
The SPCA jumped on their boats
And made a loud commotion.
Angled Humphrey downstream again
To the whale's oceanic freeway,
With each whale passing, now and then
One is apt to hear people say:
Why there are no ifs, ands or buts,
No perhaps nor even maybe,
Doubtless my mind, it is, indeed,
There goes good old "Hum Baby."

Amy Fonda

CHRIST'S RETURN

Christ's return is our anticipation.
Thank You Jesus Christ that You will return.
Praise God for His great divine salvation.
His omnipotence You will someday learn.
Jesus Christ conceived by the Holy Ghost
Is a resurrected returning friend.
Jesus Christ, as Redeemer, is your host.
Christ's great love towards man will never end.
Christ's return is like a thief in the night.
Jesus Christ will judge at the last judgment.
Let God grant you divine spiritual light.
Christ's return will be a joyous moment.
Lord Jesus Christ is in heaven quite well!
Jesus Christ holds the keys to death and hell!

Timothy A. Wik

CHRIST'S DEATH

Jesus Christ died a miraculous death.
Jesus Christ died as your very best friend.
Jesus Christ born in a stable in Beth-
 Lehem of Judea. The Cross did send
Jesus Christ through death and hell to be raised
From the dead. Christ's reconciliation
Provided salvation as angels praised
The King of Kings in appreciation.
Jesus Christ is our great Almighty Boss.
Jesus Christ was judged at His great trial.
Jesus Christ's death was on His lonely cross.
Omnipotent is His greatest style.
Christ fulfilled heavenly eternities!
Christ's death was His spiritual agony!

Timothy A. Wik

POOR AMERICA

We try to forget it,
But it'll never go away.
There is no use trying to avoid it,
It is everywhere today.

Where can we go,
When everybody turns their backs on us?
What can we do to save our dignity
And save ourselves?

Please help us now
We'll take anything we can get,
They say this country's generous,
But for some reason I just don't see that.

Our American dream is shattered.
It's now just dust in the wind.
Our tears show our destruction.
Is this ever gonna end?

You're either over- or under-qualified.
Is there any in-between?
Just how far down must we stoop,
Before we lose our self-esteem?

Stephanie J. Yusko

SECRET DREAM

While I'm awake . . .
Miles away — is what you are . . .
Miles away — is where I am . . .

Do you know — the way I feel?
Should I dare — the things I dream?

You are the Secret — that I keep . . .
Buried deep — just for sleep . . .

While I dream . . .
Miles away — you are no more . . .
Together we stand — sharing the joy . . .

Yes you know — the way I feel!
So we love — in this dream that's real!

The friend I need — is much more?
A friend indeed — as I dream!

You are the Secret — that I keep . . .
Buried deep — just for sleep . . .

Awake once more . . .
Miles stay far and between — this I know . . .
And you'll never see — this secert that I hold . . .

So back to sleep I go . . .
For only — while I dream . . .
Does my love — become whole!

Yes you are the Secret — that I keep!
Buried deep — should anyone ask!

Tonya Ione

HEN

When I was born,
Who was it that sang a lullaby,
And rocked me so I would not cry?

When I was born,
Who sat by my cradle,
And watched my sleepy, weary head?

When I was born,
Who looked upon my eyes,
When pain, sickness, and fear made me cry?

When I was born,
Who told me a story,
To keep me in my glory?

When I was born,
Who ran to help when I fell,
Or kissed the hurt to make it well?

When I was born,
Who taught my lips to pray,
And walk in wisdom's pleasant way?

When I am old,
I will be affectionate and kind to thee,
Who was so very kind to me.

When I am old
And you are feeble, old, and gray,
It will be time for me, dear mother,
To kiss your hurt away.

Barbara Ann Caton

EMERGING

Have you ever watched a person emerge?
Emotions ready to surge,
As the joy and love merge,
And for an instant they stand on the verge,
      Of the person who,
      With dreams to pursue,
      With a life so new,
      Waits to shine through.

You wonder why the past caused such hesitation,
There seemed no resolution,
As the person waits in quiet anticipation,
For the moment of emancipation,
      Of the person who,
      With dreams to pursue,
      With a life so new,
      Waits to shine through.

You find the strength to end the fight,
You find your center, you see the light,
You have the answers to put life right,
As the person within comes into sight,
      Becoming the person who,
      With dreams to pursue,
      With a life so new,
      Shall forever shine through.

Penny Pigman

I LOVE YOU (OF 2-14-83)

for GFB

Overtones of glad giving, milk, movies,
   mesmerizing kisses blend quietly
   into spiritfood of the Day's daze,
   shining through clear sun/skies,
   and mold the best, newest me.

Sweeping playbacks of chocolate mountains
   bring your soft, repeated image
   the heated, holy smiles, easy transcensions
   cascading from these lofty rivers . . .
   and wholeness at long, long last.

Marcianna Bowman

YOU'LL NEVER DIE IN ME

My heart remembers your kiss I have never had
while I shed your warm tears I had never seen.
They're all gone! Yet they'll sprout someday
from my wounded soul and our untouched yesterday.

And as my life's pendulum will stop soon its swing
I will let the ecstasy of my karmic love for you
in every song of birds, wood's trees, each fountain,
in the spring's rainbows, I'll let my refrain.

in every song of love, from Aegean Sea's islands,
in every wave's foams, in each warm beach sands,
In every solitary peaks, in each twilight majesty
you'll be forever in my sad and silent ecstasy.

Forgotten and alone am in this blessed, weepy spring,
listening the saddest owls my funeral forseeing,
and the calls from eternity; yet I have no more fear.
I'll sit waiting for you till the time comes to go!

Eleni Tita Moustaka

WINTER AS A KID

For Ron, Bill, Don, Jerry and Terry

I remember —
Moving from the city and its modern conveniences
To the old farm house . . .
We kids drawing pictures and writing our names
On the frosty window panes . . .
Cold, crisp mornings . . .
Six children pushing and shoving for warmth
around a little pot-bellied stove . . .
Mama yelling to hurry and eat before the food
Froze . . .
Breaking ice in the bucket before we could drink . . .
Houseplants wilted and frostbitten from the cold . . .
Seeing our breath as we talked and breathed . . .
Daddy cussin' to shut the doors quickly
To keep out the draft . . .
Mama trying to heat one room by hanging quilts
To the door frames . . .
Putting up a fresh-cut Christmas tree from
The woods . . .
Hanging clothes outside till they freeze-dried . . .
My mischievous brothers shooting the frozen
Sheets full of holes with BB guns . . .
And the beautiful snows that blanketed the hillsides
Made us forget the cold inside . . .
We went out to play.

Sondra Middleton

MY COMPANION

I woke up this morning before daybreak, Lord,
Uttering a prayer straight from my heart,
But I couldn't feel You anywhere,
Were You hiding in the dark?

I repeated a prayer to You I've said many times before.
I've spoken it so often, my soul is getting sore.
But wait a minute, I just remembered,
Did I hear You speak my name —
When I was but half-dreaming,
Or was it a whisper of the rain?

I dreamed I saw You sitting
On the side of my old bed, and You
Stretched Your hand out to me
Then You gently stroked my head.

I have been so troubled, I can hardly sleep at night,
And I search for You each evening
After I turn out the light.

No, You weren't hiding, Lord,
But my companion through the night.
And in my dreams, You'll be back again,
Clutching my hand so tight,
And when the morning comes, I know,
Everything will be all right.

Sondra Middleton

Arched Rock by Moonlight.

AUTUMN FOLIAGE

They had married in middle years.
They lived a modest life,
couldn't afford very much.
They lived along the parkway.
The parkway-landscaping people
were merciful — beautiful trees.
A concrete pathway had replaced a roadway
without obscuring the trees and plants and grass.
The trees had grown with their married life.
On Sunday afternoons they walked along the pathway,
in the autumn especially.
As their affection for each other grew and deepened
they loved the beautiful foliage,
and they loved each other.

Florence K. McCarthy

WHAT IS MAN THAT GOD SHOULD BE MINDFUL OF HIM

Down through the ages man born of woman,
  And nourished from the soil like any plant or
Living organism on earth, yet man is a completely
  Different entity — even from his birth.

God's Holy Word — the Bible tells us that
  Man will continually weaker and wiser grow,
Each succeeding generation year after year,
  Tells us unmistakably that this is so.

Man's inquiring mind is ever restless —
  Like the constantly shifting desert sand,
He is intrigued by all the mystery —
  His mortal mind can't fully understand.

But sometimes his human ego leads him —
  Off intellectually into the wrong direction,
Making him feel of men through space and time —
  He alone of all of them, has reached perfection.

Ah foolish man! Your eyes are growing dim —
  For what is man that God should be mindful of him!
For from a lump of clay, God created man —
  Gave him the breath of life for life's span.

Down through the ages to this day, man lives his
  Designated three or four score years and ten,
On earth, and then again returns to clay, although
  Man's mortal remains return unto the sod, Eccl. 12:7
Tell us that man's Spirit will return to God.

Mary Sachs Zello

THE GODDESS APHRODITE

The night was warm, the moon a ball of light.
The garden was aglow, it was so very bright.
She seemed most unreal, her body picking up every ray.
There was a smell of rain — but that was yesterday.

The fog slipped in so swiftly, like a last curtain call.
The last I saw of her, she was standing by the wall.
She turned and smiled, and threw a kiss.
Then walked into a cloud of fog, disappearing in the mist.
From that night on I can say I'm truthfully blessed.
A Greek poet once wrote, "Where she walked flowers grew."
You say you don't believe in Aphrodite — I do!

Helen Pastushin

I WATCHED THROUGH A WINDOW

As I watched through a window on a busy street,
There appeared a person with very crippled feet.
She struggled to walk with crutch and brace,
And I could see the anguish on her face.
My first thought was to rush out and help.
I paused in fear I would cause her to misstep.
In her path there was a car,
No time to even run that far.
Then like a miracle the car stood still
A wonderful message I saw fulfill.
The man in the car had such compassion in his eye
As he patiently waited for her to pass by.
With beads of perspiration on her brow,
She managed to stand up straight somehow.
Her thank you mirroring a beautiful soul
With no handicapped spirit she had reached her goal.
I'm glad I watched through a window that day,
For I may never again pass this way.

Gladys A. Weidel

BECAUSE OF FREEDOM

If *this* be Freedom, give me censorship and
Dictatorship, like any literate old Greek.
What do they mean "freedom of the press?"

One painter to another, "Dowd? Where is the
Dispatch? A great conversation? More like a
Lecture!" Communication?

The facts? Who, what, where, when, why, perhaps?
The byline imbalance is truly commercial.
It is a myline madness, an unnatural suspicion.

Questions forever? There seems no sanctity of
Freedom.

Is every story economic? commercial? dialectic?
Materialism? Oh, what an awful name, *Dowd*.
Did you provide any funding, honey?
Reviewing books one cannot buy?

Uncivil civil liberties war on non-combatants.
Parents, genes, fields, conditions,
Even populations, educations, books,
Diet, everything of which one can think,
Without leaving anything out unscientifically:

Controversies and confrontations, oppositions.
It is bothersome, a ridiculous nation, USA.
So much opinion cannot in itself be best,
Or clearly expressed.
Unreasoning skeletons stare back.

T. Powers

NATURE'S WONDERLAND

Sails and vapor trails blending
The sea and sky like water-colors in the rain.
The sunshine on the hills makes the earth aflame.
I feel so small in this — nature's wonderland!

I reach out and take the world in my hands,
And then the heavens and I become one.
I'm at peace — I'm not alone!

Helen Pastushin

SUNRISE AT MIDNIGHT

XIX

Talketna . . .
  Talketna . . .
Talketna . . .
  What a nirvana
In a tent
  A book of verse
Time marching
  In polished boots
Sparks
  Of time past
Sending the soul
  On a journey
Of memories
  And passions old
Of nights serene
  And days of many scenes
Of wild dreams
  In time's beams
In a glass of wine
  Of yours and mine.

William K. Yakoubian

WILLIAM K. YAKOUBIAN. Education: Fresno State University, B.A.; University of Southern California, M.A.; Occupation: Employee of Los Angeles Unified School District; Poetry: Two unpublished books of poetry; Other Writings: "A Journey to Utopia 17," prose; A novel, unpublished; Comments: *I've tried to find some meaning to life somewhere between the serenity of the sunrise and the melancholy laughter of the sunset. Poetry, in its various forms, is a spiritual, emotional, and intellectual journey into the enigmatic world of laughter and tears, of living and dying, of time and timelessness. I feel quite comfortable with Emily Dickinson or Charles Baudelaire or Paul Valery or T.S. Eliot or Vahan Tekeyan. Very few people have heard of Vahan Tekeyan, but he remains one of the greatest poets of all times.*

NATURAL LEMON

There's something wrong, I'm sure
When lemon juice, that's real and pure
  Is put in dish detergent —
But, in lemon soda that we drink
There's artificial lemon stink —

In furniture polish too
Real lemon juice is used
  But in your lemonade
Artificial lemon goo for you.
How could we be so dense?
Why doesn't that make sense?

Dorothy M. Barkin

A POEM HAPPENED

We went to the woods at sundown,
  my dog and me.
The brambles tore my legs
And my feet sank in the sweet earth.
It was many years
  since I'd played in these woods,
And I was astounded to find it
  still untouched
  with civilization screaming
  all around.
Then I looked up and saw my old tree house
  still clinging,
  and deep inside me,
  a poem happened.

Arlene Woeckener Baldino

THE SWORD'S EDGE

My son, my darling boy
You are too young to understand
What I am going through.
But as the dungeon's darkness
Did once torment and imprison me
The chains have also bound you
Since your life is part of mine
And my living sustains yours.
In your confusion and mine —
I know your acts of disobedience
Are desperate cries for my attention.
Take my hand, child
Let not your innocence be taken
Away before its time
As mine was snatched away.
Awaken, sleeping princess!
For knights were slain by dragons long ago —
And the little prince does need his mother
To crown his life with love
During the days his youth does reign.

Juliet C. Bettencourt

MY LOVE

My love for you
  will not fade
  or wilt like
    summer grasses,
  nor will its embers
  grow cold as
  untended fire.
For the flowers
  of my heart
  bloom bright
  and fragrant
as the flames
  burn strong
  and warm.

Ondrea Jill Pehle

A ROSE WITH THORNS

A rose with thorns that
Pierce the soul
Forever to die a
Thousand deaths,
This rose that assures
To make you whole
But chills your heart
With poisoned breaths.
This rose so sweet
No sign of hate
Its petals hide
The blackness borne,
Yet once you touch it
You seal your fate
For your heart is rent
By a rose with thorns.

Monica Hafer

SONG FOR TARA

She's a little bit of heaven
That fell into my arms,
And she has captured my heart
With her many charms

Could she be a royal princess
An angel in disguise,
I know she is the sunshine
She brightens up the skies.

Tara's all the wishes
Ever wished upon a star,
Tara's all the music
In all the songs there are.

When she walks the rainbows follow
Whichever way she goes,
She fills the world with beauty
My Tara is a rose.

Jeanne Louise Morgan

LET IT BE THE BEST FOR YOU

You were the emotion I gained gazing inside
From the outside. To have the other person
Within and no female place in me, only feelings,
The spiritual openings of my male seeking life.

Until I found you, sensate pleasures, senses
All in the logical order, outside in, flowers,
Loving, loving, loving. I would be greedy,
In my other body, possessing mind over matter.
I would have loved you more thoroughly physically.

I do minister to your happiness, slave ruler,
Releasing out of my masculine charge.
It was no game. It was demiturgis as I would create
Our passion's glory, author.

But it is your body, that material form,
Holder of your slender form, delicate spirit,
Ageless as we grow older amidst the swirling loving.

There are indistinguishable things,
We seem in a mass, adrift in conflicting emotions,
Me against you, you against me. We verbalize like the
Ancients. We have seen the face, split profile: God.

The best of your life,
The rest of your life.
Joy now, happiness forever.
The sequela of your endeavor;
You are my most beloved lover.

T. Powers

IT WAS ALL WORTHWHILE!

Sometimes, I really wonder if my whole life has been worthwhile.
I wonder if I've done my best in meeting each new trial?

I really haven't done a single thing, to glorify my name
Not even a small dent in any "Hall of Fame"!

Yet somehow I know, God has helped me to be
Because he gave one great gift, to show he approves of me.

A little small bundle he laid by my side
Something very special from heaven for me to love and guide.

I babied him with kindness and taught him with truth
I was thrilled at every moment, each tiny cry and each precious
    new tooth.

Then one day at five years old
I sent him off to school.

A special time of celebration . . .
Then soon as years went by, I bought his cap and gown,
To wear at his Senior Graduation.

So, now he has reached his manhood,
To me, the greatest gift on this earth.

Now I realize, I could have done no greater thing
Than to give my son, birth!

I hope and pray, the good things I taught him
Will be engraved in his mind.
Then I'll feel all I've done, hasn't been a waste of time!

Congratulations, Son!

Love Always, Mom.

Senior Year, 1986

Juanita J. Avila

WHY CAN'T WE BE AS ONE

Why can't we be as one?
Quit the hurting that has been done.

Fighting and arguing, seems no escape
Country after country having debates.

More nuclear weapons, that's not my prayer!
Everyone says peace, yet no one seems to care.

Mothers and children in Lebanon
Suffering and hurting, it's all wrong.
They're hungry in Africa, they cannot go on.

Armed Forces fighting, gunned, and marching in troops.
We must join together, united as one in peace groups.

This is not the way God planned, his world to be.
Love, Peace and Joy, that's the way it was read to me.

Child molesting, rape, and pain.
If I ruled the world, I'd change this game.

The Lord said, and it "Shall Be Done!"
Why can't we all just be as one?

Rules, regulations, and what about the Good Book?
I think we should re-read and take a long good look!

No one's really happy, for we cannot live like this.
Let's join hands in prayer and put an end to all of this.

Love your brother and neighbor, as "I have loved you."
That's what God said, when the world first started anew!

Let us all kneel, "in prayer this be over and done."
If we ask God for forgiveness, I know we can be as one!

Juanita J. Avila

ON A FRIEND DYING YOUNG
OF A CONTAGIOUS DISEASE

His bulk loomed, immobile, huge
    (I must show solidarity),
Dare I lure the germ from its refuge?
    Tempt its power, its voracity?

I circled closely about him, dancing
    (Millimeters separated our skin),
Every move deliberately prancing,
    Taunting the creature entrenched within!

A smile broke, colossal, pleasing
    (Belying the horror devouring his marrow),
Lighting his countenance; wide; face-creasing.
    (Malignant spirit! Depart your burrow!)

Detested actions! futile and vain
    (I must show I'm not afraid!),
Wet tears glistened through the pain.
    Damn this creature of the devil's brigade!

Inevitably, fate will swiftly slam the door
    (Meanwhile he's battling furiously) —
A sadder place — he'll grace this world — nevermore!
    The creature exalts — infectiously!

Leon E. Chamberlain

THANK YOU MY LOVE

How sad and sweet it is to turn back and see
the memories of you and me.
Our yesterdays that fill our hearts with
things no one else could see.

As you turn the pages of memories you see the
love we shared, and for a moment i was young
again, with long black silky hair.

Smiling face and rosy cheeks, we never seem
to tire, to play and run just having fun with
one another.

Please let me say just one more thing before
you close the thought.
My dreams of things you gave to me i'll keep
forever in my heart, you gave to me one last
hope, of love with real meaning.

So let me share just one more care, let me
tell you never stop dreaming.

Rosalie Johnstone

ROSALIE JOHNSTONE. Born: Detroit,
Michigan; Single; Awards: Songwriter's Certifi-
cate for composing the song lyrics titled
'Shadows of a Man,' Columbine Records
released the song, 12-18-86; Poetry: 'Douga,' 5-
31-85; 'Shadows of Love,' 1983; 'A Soul
Whispers, 1984; 'My Brother,' 11-29-87;
'Broken Dreams,' 11-29-87; 'Thank you My
Love,' 11-20-87; all American Poetry Associa-
tion; Comments: *I write because there is so much
to life, that sometimes a person cannot see past
the pain that he or she is feeling, so you look for
the someone to pull you through it. With a prayer
on your lips and in your heart you say, "God
help me to make it another day." Poetry is the
very soul of a person's pain or happiness, but to
someone dear to me it is only pain. Let me tell
your story in all that I write, for your heart is
heavy but love is light. Let me love you, here is
my hand. This book is for you from Rosie,
"W.R.J."*

AN AMOEBA

An amoeba, after long division,
Made a resolute decision
To deviate from accepted norm
And keep intact his present form.

A brother not yet far removed,
In haste to show he disapproved,
Said mockingly of his endeavor,
"Hell, he don't want to live forever!"

Helen T. Widoe

GAMES FOR A SUMMER EVENING

Play a game of sunset with me,
You be crimson, I'll be gold;
Racing through a towering cloudbank,
Color riots we'll unfold!

Play a game of summer shower,
You be thunder, lightning, me;
We will rock and split the heavens,
Set the thirsting desert free!

Play a game of cool sweet midnight,
You be moon's glow, I'll be stars';
Light thus bound endures forever,
Riding space-time's handlebars!

Helen T. Widoe

The forms contradict,
Arrows point apart
In Socrates Sculpture Park.

By light of a smile
The iron-bars stretch,
Tensions in steel.

By warmth of a glance
Beams and chains dance
A turn in harmony.

My steps retreat,
My heart delights,
What your fingers touch
Springs well alive.

W. Notta

NUMBER ONE
My Wife

I passed by and looked down at her,
As she lays so peaceful there.
My fingers drop as I walk by;
Just to touch her beautiful red hair,
And for a moment linger there.

As I walked on my memories were
of the past,
When I was a young man and she
was just a lass.
I thought of the many things
that she and I had done,
And how she had become number one.

I looked back as she lays there,
So beautiful and without a care,
I think of all the good times we
have had,
And they, ten thousand times,
outweigh the bad.

Dewey C. Collier

FLASH BACK

As I sit here tonight on this
stormy beach,
I listen to the thunder and the
howling wind.
I watch the lightning run about,
I watch the frothy waves of the
restless ocean come rolling in.

The lightning reminds me of the
flashing guns that were all
around me.
The thunder reminds me of the
shells that were bursting in the
sand.
The howling wind reminds me of
the screaming of the wounded
and the dying,
As they lay in the water and on
the soil of this foreign land.

Dewey C. Collier

TRUE LOVE WRONGED

The days are so dreary.
The nights are so dark.
Since, my true love,
Your father made us part.

You were just a lass,
And I was thirty-eight.
But what the heck,
It was love on our
first date.

But your father made
certain,
That our love for each
other was through.
He wronged us both,
But what could we do.
He said you were given
at birth to another man,
And the bargain had been
sealed,
By the shaking of hands.

Dewey C. Collier

HEAR WITH, LISTEN WITH

Hear the beat.
Listen to the music.
Hear the music.
Listen to the rhythm.
Hear the children's laughter.
Listen to their joy.
Hear their cries.
Listen to their sorrow.
Hear someone's joys.
Listen to their heart.
Hear someone's sorrow.
Listen with your heart.

A. Gregory Rosario

FACELESS HEART

I felt sick as I climbed the stairs
clutching my bag
my own possession.

I was afraid on this hot July morning

sweat dripped from my brow
    down my arm   to my hand
        now frozen quick
        to the door's handle.

I can't scrape it off, only wait
until the heat rises
until it melts, and
fine crystals evaporate on tear-stained glass

or, until a stranger's hand warms my own.

I don't remember entering the room
I was just there
    lost, in a room of smiles.

Someone was singing
taking me back to a dirty town
    I tasted the dust
    smelled cheap whiskey

watched a black woman kneel
mourn for her dead child.

Women walked past, pretending not to notice.
They hid beneath layers of petticoats
and aristocratic presumptions.

Men simply tilted their hats.

But, on this hot July morning
surely they too would sweat without dignity
unable to shade themselves with their lace parasols.

A voice called my name.

Time to say good-bye
    one more time.
Time to speak with a priest
    one more time.

My slippery palms
My cold palms
could no longer feel the warm hand.

It's almost over she said
and, she disappeared
into no more than a smile.

Now it is my turn to kneel
    to mourn

      for my dead child.

Linda Born-Gibbs

DREAM VIEW

The cool feel breeze
The warm feel attracting of love

The cool clear water. Water clears freshes a fair
The rain drizzles clean the ground
The night dreams a veil of dark

The vision of day lightens
The vision of light picture its view
The cadence of the wind by the power of its travel

Adam R. Mayfield

THE GOLD OF THE RAINBOW

Folks have tried since time began to find the pot of gold,
That lies at the end of the rainbow but fail we're often told.
Their tiring search is ended and nothing do they gain,
And never know which way to go so find they search in vain.
When if they'd search right close to home, to see what was in store
They'd find the "Gold of the Rainbow," right at their own back door.

The beauty of springtime flowers and warmth of a summer day,
The changing colors of autumn, or snow for a winter's sleigh.
Each season making magic, in its own and perfect way,
Makes our whole world brighter, as we welcome each new day.
So in this world of splendor, there is much we have in store
Yes, we have the "Gold of the Rainbow," right at our own back door.

We're rich in friends and neighbors, all up and down the street
Have many pleasant hours, with which to meet and greet.
With health that's given from above, to help us daily on
And show the way to future days, that greet each perfect dawn.
No wonder we are happy. Not that our thoughts may soar.
For we have the "Gold of the Rainbow," right at our own back door.

The wealth of the day that's dawning, crowned with sparkling dew,
Songbirds' beautiful music, to start each day anew —
Children's joyous laughter, and gladness everywhere
Make us happy we're living. As we breathe a silent prayer.
We have the best in God's blessings, so need we search anymore?
When we have the "Gold of the Rainbow," right at our own back door.

Emily B. Green

THE STRUGGLE

Self-inflicted pain

Illusions shattered
The wandering mind — struggling
Anguish, depression, sight unknown
Seeking
Spritual growth
Deterred — clothed in darkness
The soul consumed — clinging
The spirit weeps
Strength embraces the soul
Breaks through the wall of iniquity
The outstretched arms
Tears from within
The outer self revealed — annihilated
Light penetrates the soul
The word is spoken — the heart listens — love glistens
The garment is shed
The atonement begins — God's love transcends
Paradise envisioned
Life illumes then ascends
The struggle ends
I am begins

A. Mozelle Michaux

WILDFLOWERS

You dapple the meadows while strewing the world
With beauty where beauty is seldom unfurled:
In shadows, in waste, by the road's dreary side,
In humblest of dwellings, you gladly abide.

Eschewing, for darkness and bogs where you wend,
The gardens your tamer relations befriend,
Your glorious mission is precious and rare:
Benevolence, brightening dismal despair.

Charles J. Lumia

WHEN I MOVED TO MONTANA BY WAY OF ISPHEMING, MICHIGAN

Fascinating to observe a man
who feigns spontaneous smiles
weakly presented to apathetic students
as he caustically shows us
how to use plastic sliderules

Bombastically he projects plastic images
upon a plastic screen
as he perambulates in his plastic shoes

With a plastic pen
he indicates specific points
on a plastic chart screwed
to an artificial wall
as he adjusts the black plastic frames
of his broken glasses

In a striking gesture
a plastic watchband leaps forward
supporting his plastic watch
protruding from the sleeve
of his plastic shirt
neatly tucked into his plastic pants
secured by a white plastic belt

Lastly, in pathetic pathos
did I glance at his name spelled
incorrectly on a plastic nametag

Michael Blythe

TO RHYME OR NOT TO RHYME

If it was good enough for Shakespeare
  It's good enough for me
It was good enough for Frost
  And Kilmer rhymed me with tree.
But, now the powers that be
  Tell us rhyming is passé
All they say is nay, nay, nay.

It's unfashionable to rhyme
  They tell us all the time
Forget the June, Moon, Spoon,
  Forget the fine, dine, wine.
The powers that be, have so decreed.
  But I tell you now, they won't succeed.

So, if it was good enough for Shakespeare
  It's good enough for me
And since I *like* rhyming poetry
  That's what you'll hear from me.

Dorothy M. Barkin

THANKSGIVING IN PITTSBURGH, PENNSYLVANIA, 1987

Thank You, Lord, for the leaden sky,
The straggly birds as they fly by.
Thank You, too, for the air to breathe,
For birth and life, and time to seethe.
For time to wonder, we thank You, too,
The wonder of love and kindness true.
We thank you for the power to feel,
A conscience that keeps us on even keel.
Thank you for the telephone wires
That connect our loved ones, as well as tires
To ride to Church on this quiet day and say
Thank You, Lord, show us the way.
This happy day, though dark and murky,
We thank You too for Julius's turkey,
For all the food banks for the unemployed,
For strength and will and things deployed.
Once a year is not enough
To thank the Lord for all this stuff —
I shall say a daily prayer,
To thank, and share, and be aware.

Dorothy M. Barkin

THE BLIZZARD

In the twilight of the evening,
The snowflakes gently fell,
Covering everything in purest white
Like the icing on a wedding cake,
Decorated in delicate lacy patterns,
By the greatest decorator of all.

The blizzard of the year,
Around us came in wintry blasts.
The wind did blow, and the
Snow did fall in huge flakes,
Wiping away the colors of autumn.
Changing them to bridal white.

While inside, all cozy and snug,
The young couple sat by the fireside.
The warm glow from the fire,
Casting a soft shadow on the room,
Like a giant hand reaching out,
To caress a loving child.

The couple sat by the hearth,
So wrapped up in each other's love.
Oblivious to the raging storm,
Which was in evidence everywhere.
It was on this celestial scene,
We bade a fond farewell.

Shirley Ann Aden

STRANGER AT THE GATE

There's a stranger at the gate
Let Him in
He holds His lantern high
Let Him in
He looks for His lost lambs
That have strayed
His lonely frightened sheep
That have strayed

There's a stranger at the gate
Let Him in
Don't wait till it's too late
Let Him in
He will call you by name
Follow Him
He will keep you safe from harm
Follow Him

There's a stranger at the gate
Alleluia
He's the good shepherd
Alleluia
We came to gather in His flock
Alleluia
He has come to lead them home
Alleluia

Jeanne Louise Morgan

I AM

I am unique
I am one in five billion
I am self-contained
freestanding
individual
My protein configurations
are specific to myself
identifiable by whorls
of fingertip skin
and by special medleys
of fragrances
emanating from my body.

I want to sing and dance and shout
that I am unique.
Love me for what I am
not for what I may become.
Dance with me in the streets
whirl with me on this earth
sing your tune and I will sing mine
and wonder at your selfness
as I wonder at mine.

Maliza Mildred Hoffman

THE HEART OF THE SOUL

*With love and thanks to my beloved
mother, Wilma R. Michaux*

I think about how much I love you, Mama
I think about our struggles for understanding
I think about the times we have shared in harmony
I think about the unfolding of our love from mother & daughter
      To best friends binding our soul from sunset to sunrise

I think about how I smile when I see your face in my dreams & thoughts
But most of all, I think about how God has endowed my life with many
Blessings but his greatest gift to me was the gift of your love.

A love so great and dear I know that wherever I may be you will come
And share the blessings of my new destiny

So, thank you Mama for being there when I needed spiritual
Nourishment and guidance — for even when you thought you had
Failed me the spirit of your love instilled hope and gave me strength
To endure all the perils and disillusions of life

Now as I meet the sunrise of each new day the love that flourishes
From your heart to mine keeps me aglow, for I know

      I am from within you
      I am a seed sown from the garden of your heart
      I am an extension of your love and life

I am the child that humbles herself and give thanks to the Almighty for
      his precious gift of your love

I am forever in prayer for your peace and happiness in this life

      For you Mama are the heart of my soul
      The light of God's love manifested

A. Mozelle Michaux

A. MOZELLE MICHAUX. Pen Name: MoAndhi; Born: Lenoir, North Carolina; Married: Spiritually committed to God, Doran Harper, and our son, Andhi DiJon; Education: Dwight D. Eisenhower, 1968; Studied Fundamental Art at American Academy of Arts, Chicago, 1986; Occupation: Office management systems consultant, Administrative coordinator; Memberships: Wilder Community School Advisory Council, Southside Neighborhood Housing Services Board of Directors, SNHS Strategic Planning & Development Committee, SNHS Public Relations Committee, SNHS Rental Rehab Committee, Early Learning Center's Parents' Board; Poetry: 'These Trying Times,' 5-10-82; 'The Rapture Of My Love,' 12-4-80; 'Discernment,' 9-82; 'The Gift of Love,' 5-10-87; 'Andhi,' 5-19-87; 'The Wandering Mind,' 7-3-85; Comments: *'The Struggle,' written 9-21-87: A spiritual message revealed from the still soft voice of Him who dwells within my soul; 'Reflections,' written 9-25-86: The consummation of light revealing the hidden self; 'The Heart of the Soul,' written 10-23-87: A dedication of love and thanks to my beloved mother, Wilma R. Michaux, for giving me love that I might come to understand the true meaning of my existence in this life. As a servant from the garden of God's love, I graciously emit His gift in all that I am and in all that I do in this life. Thank Him and you for affording me this opportunity to share this gift.*

RAIN

Into each life a little rain must fall,
I once heard a wise man say.
So, rejoice in the sunshine life will bring.
And prepare for that rainy day.
For rainy days will surely come,
When you just can't see the sun.
Just think of the happier times of life,
When your days were full of fun.
Let happy thoughts be your umbrella,
To protect you against life's storms.
And remember, that ole sunshine you're missing,
Comes in various shapes and forms.
Don't let those rainy days upset you.
We all know that they're no fun.
When the raging storm is over,
Open a window and behold the sun.

Yvette I. Shelton

WINDOWS

Have you looked into a window on a dark and rainy day,
And seen a fireplace burning and the children all at play.
From somewhere within, you hear an old folk song.
You look, even when you know it's wrong.

Today the house is dim and quiet, the room has seen a better day.
The fireplace is charred and black, it seems to mock you and say
Where are all the children, and where do they play?
You feel the coldness clutching at your heart.
You turn around — then slowly depart.
You lift your eyes to heaven and offer up a prayer.
You hope that those who made this house a home are happy —
    somewhere.

Helen Pastushin

FOR DREW

As I stepped from the Cadillac
a group of folks all dressed in black stood at the door.
They took your body in the church
and as I watched, it really hurt to see you go.

Your mother's eyes were filled with tears
as she recalled the happy years not yet begun.
I tried my best to comfort her
'cause, after all, I know you were her only son.

You looked so calm as you lay there
with not a worry or a care — your life complete.
And as I passed to mourn your death
I placed a wreath of baby's breath down at your feet.

My little Drew, as you lay dead,
I fixed your bonnet on your head and wiped my eyes.
I couldn't let it end that way
so I bent down to kiss your face and say good-bye.

Well, Drew, my son, you've gone away
and nothing that I do or say will hide the hurt.
But, darling, let me tell you this:
"In my heart, my son still exists — *You were Mommy's first!*"

Cynthia Renee Highsmith

SPAR

Pole and glide
On a powdery track
Along the cold canal.
Bare oaks
In frozen silhouette
And a blue-gray heron
At ice edge immobile;
Beside whale rocks
Under snow caps,
We push on and on
Through dusky woods:
An unmarked trail.

Pedal and coast
On a dappled path
Along the old canal.
Beeches nod
With golden bows
And mallards dive
Deep green down tails up;
Stallion walls rear above,
While patchwork canopies
Shield our spidery wheels
Over leafsilk strand:
Spinning home.

Diane Hoyer

A LOVE LIKE WOOD AND LACE

Just as though a wounded bird,
She lay across his chest
And as she softly cried to God . . .
He slipped into sweet rest.

Sobbing as a child in pain . . .
Emotions torn apart,
She held him cradled in her arms
Against her breaking heart.

His voice was like the thunder
That softens in the wind;
He wasn't just her lover . . .
He was her dearest friend.

Now she sits alone to watch
As waves rush back to shore,
Remembering her lover's face . . .
His touch to feel no more.

A single tear upon her cheek
Is brushed across her face,
As she recalls the love they shared . . .
A love like wood and lace.

She softly blows a kiss and turns
To whisper with the wind,
Farewell my sweetest lover . . .
Good-bye my dearest friend.

Vicki Williams

SILHOUETTE

So swift sail the geese
In flawless form of flight
From one point travels in somber ease
And moves across the night.

Commands of leaders to followers en route
Echo their way down to me
I hear hoarse voices cry out
If only I could see.

In reach of memory I know
That form that parts the sky
The beauty of the squawking geese
And happily I cry.

Too many, too few, never see, nor hear
Such simple sights or sounds
When up above is traveling grace
While we're here on the ground.

Mark A. Evans

MARK ALLEN EVANS. Born: Amarillo, Texas, 7-24-63; Education: North Harris County College, A.A.; Attending University of Houston for B.A., Humanities and fine arts; Occupation: Project PASSAGE/Klein ISD Vocational Adjustment Trainer; Memberships: Poetry Society of Texas, Poets Northwest, Academy of American Poets, Cultural Arts Council of Houston, Cypress-Creek Association for Retarded Citizens; Poetry: 'Illegal Death,' *Today's Greatest Poems*, 1983; 'By Choice,' *Our Times*, 2-87; 'Dreams,' *Timeclock*, 1987; Other Writings: ''Champions,'' short story, *Our Times*, 4-87; Themes: *Communication, not only mind to mind, but also heart to heart. Life is full of lessons, and we have to communicate those lessons to others, share the experience, and grow. One of the main themes in my writing is you have to live your life for yourself, not by yourself, but for yourself.*

SPECIAL PEOPLE

Dedicated to my children, Kandis and Unique.

What is it in little children
That makes them so special?
Is it their little limbs,
Soft and harmless?

Or, is it their shrill voice,
Firm, yet resonant,
Harping on the same tune,
That makes parents pay attention?

Or, could it be their eyes,
Puffy, yet majestic,
Inspecting and investigating all clues
Of love and special attention?

Perhaps, it's none of these.
It could be the total self —
Simple, yet commanding;
Sincere, yet subtle.

Yes, I think I know!
It's that lamb-like innocence
That moves mountains without words —
With a will — a belief.

I'm blessed to be part of them,
But wish I'm once again like them —
Gentle, yet firm,
Sincere, yet subtle.

Those special people — children.

Gerald J. A. Nwankwo

GERALD J. A. NWANKWO. Born: Umulogho, Obowo, Nigeria; Education: Reading Specialist Certificate; Ph.D. candidate, University of Pennsylvania, since 1981; Villanova University, M.A., Educational administration, 1980; Holy Family College, Philadelphia, B.A., English, 1978; Occupations: Reading specialist and English teacher, Community College of Philadelphia; Reading teacher, Cooke Sr. High School, Philadelphia; Memberships: Phi Lambda Theta, University of Pennsylvania, 1983; Storytellers Association, Philadelphia; Awards: *The Gem*, high school supplementary reader, 1972; 'A Song to Unique,' 1986; 'Love from Heaven,' 1987; Comments: *I love writing. It enables me to relive yesterday and begin today to enjoy tomorrow before it ever comes. It also helps me to make a public assertion of the Great Maker whose love has been overwhelming.*

GRANDMA'S HANDS

Grandma's hands led devotion during revival.
Grandma's hands never done nobody wrong.
Grandma's hands made us children read the bible;
she said it would make us strong.

Grandma's hands were real useful with a needle.
Grandma's hands sewed Max's britches when they tore.
Grandma's hands ached and swelled up with arthritis
from scrubbing those white folks' floors.

Grandma's hands gathered eggs from out the henhouse.
Grandma's hands were a blessing in disguise.
Grandma's hands came in handy in the kitchen
making cornbread and sweet potato pies.

Grandma's hands chastised all the neighbors' children.
Grandma's hands spanked their butts when they were bad.
Grandma's hands washed Momma's dress while she was sleeping —
it was the only dress Momma had!

Grandma's hands canned preserves to eat in winter.
Grandma's hands planted 'bacca in the spring.
Grandma's hands lined us up and gave us whippings
that summer we broke the brand new swing!

Well, my grandma's hands are cold now and she's not here
    to help me stand.
We're all down here on our own now and we sure could use those hands!
Every day, I miss them more and more
but up in heaven, I'll bet they're thankful for
Grandma's hands.

Cynthia Renee Highsmith

IN EXTREMIS

Far into the future I drift to reflect upon the long ago.
I encounter an old, bitter man sitting confined and alone.
His crippled shell inhales my essence and I perceive through his
            eyes — my eyes
            Cold, confused eyes.

I sense peace of a distorted nature.
Carousels of stale, brown memories revolve in his thoughts
            Over and over and . . .
        Carcinogenic fragments rule every moment.

Constant flowback into time lost recalls wavering images of oil
            Over and over and . . .
Endless remembering plagues his mind and hollows his soul — my soul
            Lost, leprous soul.

Only deep, darkened suspension can comfort us.

Affected, I realize the way to prevent the old man
        from inheriting my deformity.
I alone possess the means to banish his pain and relieve his
            life — my life
            Wretched, weary life.

Induced by my yearning, we find ourselves drifting into sleep
            Drifting far away.

Victor Griffin

TO FLY FREE

Dear Tim: I must tell you about me
Remember me, that little bird
too secure under my parents' wings
The day I met you, you filled my dreams
Prince Charming, I made you my king

I am the envy of many birds
I live in such a golden cage
I have a king who takes care of me
Material things, I am never in need

Little bird, I said to me
it is time for you to meet the world
I peeked out the door and I learned
Little bird in wisdom grew, and now I know
how the weather affects the flight
if it is stormy one cannot feel as free in flight

It is so hard for me to see
what the future will bring to me
all I know is that I want to fly free
today, as I fly you see
I carry the golden cage with me

h me

Maria-Isabel Campos

TWO ROSES OF LOVE

A single red rose given in the name of love,
The symbol for the greatest power on earth.
It is the power that moves the heavens.
Together through all time in harmony,
Forever and anon, love will be strong.
Two crimson lives joined in blood.
Red rose of prosperity, red rose of faith,
The first rose of love.

A rose of all colors placed between the broken lives.
The gestalt floundering in a sea of remorse.
Death, destruction, pain, life brought low,
Through the heart the love ran out.
Cries of anguish ring in discord
In a dark, barren landscape lost.
Blood blackening on the turf beneath a stained moon.
Black rose of desolation, black rose of death,
The second rose of love.

Eric T. Anderson

CHRISTMAS IS THE TIME

Christmas is the time for cheer
For everyone that you hold dear.
Ornaments that sparkle bright
Tree lites that shine all nite
Gifts and toys for everyone
Special dinner and guests are fun
The star from long long ago
Tells us where we're to go
We should keep the Christ Child
In our hearts — not letting our "ole"
Teaching depart
Remembering not only during this season so near
Christmas is the time for cheer
For everyone that we hold dear.

Annethea Anderson

COME UNWOUND

My mind is full
of memories
with the years
I've been around.

It seems like
only yesterday
my feet were
on the ground.

I guess I've
lived a good
life for I
feel I'm
Heavenbound.

Today it feels
so wonderful
just to sit
and come unwound.

Betty Evans

SOMEWHERE . . .

Somewhere lies the greatest Gift
That Man could ever know.
It is stronger than the strongest man
And brighter than our sun's noon glow.

Somewhere here, on earth, It glides
Between those who walk God's earth.
Stopping or going, walking or running,
But one could not call It terse.

Somewhere along the battered line,
It will touch the hardest heart.
The Gift, I speak, is Love itself;
To seize It would be smart.

Somewhere, It will touch your life
But I must warn you this:
It does not come that easily
And to look, you might miss . . .

Somewhere, though, It will come,
It is promised!

Jodi Wilson

BURRO BURRA BURRITA

''Me enamoré de un ranchero,
Por ver si me daba elotes;
Pero el ingrato ranchero
No me daba mas que azotes.''
— Mexican folksong
(El Rancho Grande)

There was a burro with a heavy load
who climbed a high steep hill
following an ear of green corn tied
upon a stick
with one end fastened to his head.

And when at last he reached the top,
his master took away the ear of corn
and beat him with the stick.

Irma Wassall

MY FRIEND

There's something I think you should know
Your friendship means much to me,
And wherever in this world I may go
You'll always be my best friend.

Friends, how would we live without them
Friends, we never could do without you.
You brighten our days in so many ways
I could not do without you, my friend.

God gave me you as my own dearest friend
To help me through the thick and the thin.
To stand there beside me,
To help lead and guide me,
Encouraging words you give,
To conquer troubles in the end.

A friend like no other
Who'll take the place of a brother,
Who knows just what I need
And when I need it most.

A friend such as you to help see me through
Since He knew I needed his presence beside me
And someone who I could talk face to face to
He included you, my friend.

Virdia Stevens

THE POMEGRANATE

Are you the fault
From the Tree of Life?
Oh, lovely pomegranate.

Oh, wondrous fruit
From the Garden of Eden,
That filled the ancients
With awe.

Secret fruit,
That holds so many treasures,
I love to behold your splendor.

You decorate the edges of the robe
Worn by the Priest.

Your stem is shaped into a crown,
Symbolic of the Christ.

You hold within
The red of precious rubies,
The likeness of the drops of blood
That Jesus sweat,
In the Garden of Gethsemane.

Are you the fruit
From the Tree of Life?
Oh, lovely pomegranate.

Jean Russell Houser

SOARING

Soaring, I'm soaring
On rivers of golden light
Continually gliding
On currents of a sun-kissed breeze
The wind on my body
My flight's speed to increase.

With powerful wings
To mount upon high
I'm climbing upward
Toward the heavens
To his presence in the sky.

To fly as an eagle
To my home on high
Over hills and mountains
To my eyrie in the sky.

Virdia Stevens

FOR GEORGE WITH LOVE

From the moment she first met him,
he took her breath away
And now she tries to say the words
she's been afraid to say.

Every day he fills her thoughts . . .
their loving warms her heart
And she can hardly bear the time
when they are far apart.

She looks into the face she loves
in sultry gray-green eyes . . .
Tonight as they are making love,
she softly starts to cry.

No other man has ever touched
her heart in quite this way,
And though she hasn't told him yet . . .
. . . she's telling him today.

Vicki Williams

OLD MAN

He crouches on a bended knee
And shivers from the cold —
His home a cardboard box and twine,
His clothes are worn and old.

He wanders through the streets at night
And no one knows his name.
He has no friends and no one cares
From where or when he came.

He watches from the shadow's edge
With tired and weary eyes.
His mind is fading from the drink
As bit by bit he dies.

The lonely heart is seldom heard
By even those close by,
Its desperate voice cries out and still . . .
A hardened world goes by.

Vicki Williams

THE WINDS OF TIME

Blinded by the youth of eighteen, Amidst unforeseen truths
    and untold dreams,
I never thought much of getting old, Promises made or visions, foretold,
Never much concern placed upon the winds of time that moved on,
The twisting vines of fate hereon have awakened my mind
To the winds of time that move on.

Intangible trusts and faces reversed to turn,
Love's healing light and its accompanying burn
Have taken my by the hand into the winds of time,
Enlightening my night with memories of a lifetime,
The strangeness in your eyes told me, That the winds of time
    had pushed on.

Different destinies taken have swept away and forsaken
The common bonds once held,
We couldn't foretell tomorrow, The precious times we only borrowed,
Now, the strangeness of our conversation has befallen the
    quest we had begun
To become a victim of the winds of time that've moved on.

And the winds of time keep movin' on,
The bells that chime keep changin' their song,
And the strangeness of your voice tells me,
That the winds of time have kept movin' on.

I can now only try to balance the scales
Between lessons learned and a dream's tale,
The battles won and the many failed,
And try to grow strong my heart's softly spoken song,
To keep ahead of the strangeness in each day that tells me,
That the winds of time will always keep movin' on.

Jeffrey Adam Sager

CHANGES

Change is just one rule of life.
Lesson is learned unfold the light.
Lashing out to each other in fight.
Eating your heart out no delight.
The practical step in lost romance.
May change your relationship go to France.
If you have outgrown this relationship by chance.
Step in two new direction and gracefully dance.
Relationship over let go do not stay.
Cling not to the past go your way.
Future possibility maybe lost in the sun.
Parting in time can change into fun.
Letting go someone means to be brave.
Set it free it's not your slave.
Forever keep in your heart a space.
Wishes are fulfilled in time and place.
Trying to get even going to the length.
Only shows weakness not your strength.
The fruit of life is within your heart.
Learn the rule of love you're getting smart.
Let go forgive and self-forgive.
You just learned how to live.

Judith St. Vic

THE SHIP OF LIFE

We journey on, the ship of life, destination unknown,
Time bringing us closer, to our eternal home,
The sun reflects upon the sea, as a sparkling guide, to our destiny,
We watch the rising and falling tide,
With a strange ambivalence, deep inside,
Feeling totally detached, and adrift,
Somehow waiting, for our soul to lift,
To rise each morn, with the blazing sun,
To be in harmony, with the elements as one,
With ascending music, clearly soft,
To soothe our way, while we're aloft,
To gain possession of that golden key,
To open heaven's gate, to glow as a star, in His galaxy.

Irma Schwartz

YOUR CHILD

Listen to the sound of laughter,
Flow deep, from the soul of your child,
Listen, to the child of wonder,
So closely, to your image styled,
Feel the rapture around you,
As your child hugs you real tight,
Spin in the realm of magic,
Kneel proudly, for your heart's delight,
Live with bliss and amazement,
As you see his body grow,
Kiss away his fears, make the light forever glow,
Lead him well to safety, should the curves become too steep,
Be always by his side, when he's made that dangerous leap,
And open your heart, with a passion serene,
Be lovingly there, to inspire his dream!

Irma Schwartz

DESPAIR

    Sun goes down,
Red hot, over blue, clear sea.
    The man, so cold,
    So humble,
Bent in spirit; in flesh; in mind.
    He does not see.
So bent in spirit, he can no longer cry.
    No longer asks why.
    No longer does he try.
His bracelets are chains,
    His houses are prisons,
His passions are sadness, and pain.
    The land from which he first breathed life,
Spews its ashes upon his tiny life, and swallows his
hopes and dreams.
    His head turns upward and toward the sun,
The sea he cannot touch, and he calls:
    "Oh, God, please take me!"

Annabelle Ambrosio

KISSING YOU

I can almost taste your lips
Wet with desire
Burning like fire.
Sweet as a honey-drip
I can almost taste your lips.

I can almost see you blush
Showered with candy
Listless with fancy.
Quake with the hush
I can almost see you blush.

I can almost feel your tongue
Tremble with crime
Colliding with mine.
Brilliant as the young
I can almost feel your tongue.

I can almost taste your lips
Thirst with shame
Thunder and tame.
Moist as a cloud-sip
I can almost taste your lips.

Connie Blankenship

SPRING

Spring
Each year
Adds a special season
To my life.

My senses increase,
Feelings deepen; I become more aware
Of the newness
All around.

With each spring
Comes April,
The arrival of warm currents,
Gentle breezes,

Bright sunny skies
Tattered with soft cotton fluffs
Hovering o'er flowering tulips
And dogwoods of pink and white.

Mailboxes
Chock full
Of newsy letters.

I missed your letter today!
Why didn't you write?

James M. Cannon

FOUR YEARS AGO

Four years ago was when it came.
Upon a man it placed its claim.
It seemed to me that it was mad . . .
And it was mean and it was sad.
It smothered him and took his air.
It gave him pain and left him there.

Yes, it was angry and it was sad . . .
That mean disease that killed my dad.

Lori Simonton

I always think about you
No matter who you're with or where
And no matter who you love,
I will always care.
I open my eyes, and still you're there
But someday I will see;
The truth that we both share
You're not mine, and never will be.
Friendship is much better, I guess
No brutal fights, and tear-filled nights
And relationships that end,
So I guess that's why I'll always be lucky,
Just to have you as my friend.

Michelle Haggy

THE CELL

When we can write its genetic code
In the simple manner of an ode
It will fill a thousand volumes
Two thousand pages each
Five hundred words to every column
Without a single breach.

Powered by the sun's radiant fire
And the precipitous waste of atomic transition
The human cell conducts life's molecular flow
In quiet, innocent complexity.
Protein and enzyme propelled,
Simple molecules are ushered to the cell
Given reciprocating affinities
They lure their electron complements
Into complex, polymeric marriages
To appease the nucleic deities, DNA and RNA
And satisfy a transient need for stability.
Transformed, they leave to define destiny
In life's innumerable, diverse patterns.
Thus, the action acted, the word spoken
The feeling felt and all things perceived
Rest with the character of a chemical bond.
A bond sustained by the intrinsic forces
Of attraction and repulsion
Like love and hate caught in a silent storm.

Hemson J. Zenon

THE NAKED HOUSE

There is a naked house
With a black roof of clouds
That lets the raindrops in
Though sunlight never enters
And in this naked house
Love and hate have learned to live together
In quiet desperation
Here's how they do it:
Love breathes a soft, warm breath
Into the frozen face of hate, and
Something natural happens:
A condensation of emotions
Into a fluid flow of passion
Which both feel they must have
In order to survive.
Thus, by this one common need
Like a thin black silk thread,
They vowed to hang together
Until dead.

Hemson J. Zenon

HAPPINESS

You took me in
 and gave me life
You provided a haven
 from unbearable strife

My one link to sanity
 companion, friend, soulmate
Bonded by ethereal tie
 heart to heart, an open gate

And more, a lover
 such as I had never dreamed
Awakening our bodies to passion
 never felt nor even deemed

Happiness that filled my Self
 so that no words could tell
Unbidden, unforseen, I feel in love
 then your mouth told me farewell

Each minute, hour, day,
 forever in my being knit
Perfection for a little while
 and I regret it not one whit

Annie O'Dunlaing

THE VISIONARY

There contains a presence.
So fond, so known, so dear.
Inseparable from the heart.
An undergrowth of the soul.
A fire lit for an eternity
Before the foreboding quietude.

Now dims its vile flame.
There is engulfing emptiness
Upon the midnight sky.
It reaches beyond forevermore.
A stabbing pierces all.
It penetrates. It pervades.
Breath . . . so shallow.
Another; creeps into grief.
There contains no beating.

It severs what was.
What might have been.
It is a grim death.
The death of two hearts
That shall never beat as one.

Janine R. Harrison

THE CONSUMER SALUTE

I pledge allegiance
 to the network
 for upgrading our
 standard of living;
 and to its marketers
 for providing status
 through image
 and products
 with labels
 but especially
 the power
 to purchase it all.

Bridgitt F. Boggan-Dunn

THE SEA OF LIFE

The ocean of life is rough, wide and deep,
  and it's a perilous journey on those quests that we seek
  And it's true, we may conquer these seas all alone
    but then if we do — no Port of Call will ever be home.
    Doomed we will be to sail over the Brine
      like the Flying Dutchman till the end of time

This mate that God gives us — may govern but must never rule,
  and those who think otherwise are nothing but fools.
  For all of the courses we chart and the landfalls we plan,
    must in the end conform to His, not her Master Plan.
    Yes, this mate can assist us past rocks, reefs and shoals
      But it's this Master Mariner — who makes the winds blow.

Barney Reilly

THE MASTER PLAN

We chart our own courses and we set our own sails,
  but without divine guidance, our small crafts are frail.
  So if ever you've floundered on a merciless sea,
    you know only too well what a safe harbor can mean.
    And of the awesome feeling that fills all of your being,
      of being saved from the sea by this Almighty keeping.

We are giving this free will and may roam as we please,
  over the land or over the sea.
  But a Log Book is kept of each journey we make,
    and entries are made of all our mistakes
    So on the final voyage — when at last we head home
      this record we made, will be all our own.

Yes — He leads and guides us, and He does understand,
  but this freedom of choice — He still leaves in our hands.
  This freedom is giving, to be used or abused.
    Final Judgment will separate the Wise from the Fools.
    And the Eternal Reward will at last be at hand,
      for all of us who at least tried —
          to conform to His Plan.

Barney Reilly

COMPANIONS

Sometimes they aren't around and your mind remembers
good times in the past.
You can feel the good vibrations and you wish they would last.
Friends are bonded by affection, trust and esteem.
We know our friendships are with us even as we dream.
As the sunrises come and go, we need to share our fortunes
and sometimes a regret.

Our work and play are important to us but the special times with
a friend is the best bet.
Who can you call at 3:00 a.m. about car trouble when it is dark
and you are alone?
When the voice answers a certain comfort relaxes your mind because
you know they care to talk with you on the phone.

You also know that a star in the sky is closer to you than a
friend in another state.
Yet when you think of each other at the same time, somehow you know
you will always have your soul mate.
Words are not enough to express this love that is embedded
deep within.
And if asked what it means you would answer:
It is someone who is my friend.

Jacques Russell

IMMORTALITY

We like old houses and the dreams that they hold.
To us old houses grow old.
We like old houses in the center a stream —
Which keeps giving life to renew love's theme.

The ages go by, each branch breaks away —
To start a new life a generation away.
Immortality from an old house which once had been new
A Nation was born — the building is you.

Florence Carpenter Janis

THE SECRET

"I'll tell you a secret," said Val to Sue,
"It's a big secret, and it really is true."
Val leaned forward and her eyes were bright,
"You will keep the secret?" and Sue said "all right."

"I'll tell you a secret," said Sue to Lyn.
"Oh, I love secrets," she said with a grin.
Heads went together, one dark and one fair.
"It is true I tell you! it is! so there!"

"I'll tell you a secret," said Lyn to Nell.
"I know you can keep it very well."
"Of course." said Nell, with a haughty air,
As she drew close, the secret to share.

"I'll tell you a secret," said Nell to Gwen.
So the great big secret was told once again.
No matter if you lived uphill or down,
By the end of that day, it was all over town.

Next day, Val's Mom said, as they walked to the store,
"Before long, our secret won't keep anymore."
From across the street came Betty Lou,
Who shouted to them, "When's the baby due?"

Mary M. Betz

BAG LADY

She scuffed along the litter-filled street,
Her face was as worn as the shoes on her feet.
The wind whispered past, lifting grey hair,
Her eyes seemed to plead, Won't someone care?

She carried two bags, one in each hand,
And on her finger was a worn wedding band.
Where had she come from? and where would she go
When the winter storms came, with sleet and snow?

She'd gone through the summer with its putrid heat,
Scavenged food from cans on city streets.
Folk scowled at her through window panes,
Children spat upon her, and called her names.

Then winter arrived and she wheezed up a hill,
She needed warm shelter, she felt very ill.
On top of the hill was the church she was seeking,
She would talk to the priest, hear a Christian greeting.

But the doors were shut, and locked up tight,
Too weary to move she stayed there all night.
In the morning he found her, too late for his advice.
Upon her face of marble were sculptured tears of ice.

Mary M. Betz

THE NEED TO TRUST

I wish that I could find the words
To make you trust me more.
To make you really understand
That of one thing I am sure.
I love you more than words could say
And that sweetheart is true.
I've had my share of fun and games,
My needs are very few,
I want to share the rest of my life
Loving and loved by you.
I need your love, I need your trust,
I need for you to see,
Your love and trust would not be wrong,
If you gave them all to me.

Andrea McDonald-Black

AVE MARIA

Ave Maria
Queen of the the Angels
Hear us we pray,
Virgin most holy
Blest among women
Show us the way.

We are tossed like the leaves
In a whirlwind of doubt
And we carry our scars
Through long seasons of drought,

Ave Maria
Mother of Graces
Christ is with thee,
Lead us repentant
Unto our savior
Ever to be.

Evelyn Pitel

DR. MARTIN LUTHER KING AND KAREN REGINA COOKE

Among the faceless, emotionless people
A voice was heard, a song was sung
Through devotion, love, compassion
The reality of King's dream had begun

Today there is a softer voice
But the message is just as strong
Only through love and humanity
Can we overcome the wrong

Martin Luther King lived for
Giving all he had to give
In Karen Regina Cooke
His dream of compassion still lives

Both, often misunderstood and overlooked,
Fought battles that weren't even theirs
Just to prove to the entire world
It has no value until it cares

In all the death and destruction
AIDS, prostitution and dealers of dope
Because of people like King and Regina
For our world there may still be hope.

Danielle D. Saunders

WILL THERE BE LOVE FOR ME?

On a starry night, not so long ago,
We first met and fell in love, just so.
The time we spent together,
Was few and far between.

We walked along the beach
On warm summer days.
Walked through the park,
Most every other day.

The love I felt for you
Was ever so strong.
But now they tell me I have been wrong.

I see your love has been given to another.
The hurt I feel is deep.
We said we would be forever together,
Now the end is here.

Our ways have parted,
I watch you from distances and wonder.
Wonder where your love for me has gone?
Wonder if there will ever be, love for me?

Edward H. Kwantes

TO WHAT COULD HAVE BEEN

Gazing into the evening sky,
I gaze up into distant stars.
Dazzling us with miniature lights,
I wonder about what could have been.

We were carefree spirits,
Our meeting each other was not planned.
But when we met there became a bond,
A bond that could have been love.

Looking back now I wonder.
Was I blind or just didn't want to see?
For now I believe that what could have been
Is forever gone.

Gone are happy times,
Gone are shared joys and shared sorrows.
The bond that could have been love,
Is shattered with doubt and disbelief.

For there was someone else more important.
Important enough to leave me.
To stop loving me and to break our bond.

To what could have been,
I cherish moments of joy.
Searching, for a new someone
To have what could have been, with you.

Edward H. Kwantes

WHO AM I

bestill my soul   you need a rest
what is it   that you are
trying to manifest   why struggle
why fight it   what is your cause
the battle ends   the cause is lost
wake wake my soul   the day is dawn
you must go forth   you must be strong
now it is time to   straighten out your back
and look ahead   here I come
I have been bending   with the breeze
            for too long
now I know   what I am trying to
            manifest
My Pride   My Culture   My Happiness
I am emerging world
to what I was   before I came —
before you took — raped — beat
killed and put me in chains

Ronald James Dessus

THE OLIVE TREE

*''But my horn shalt exalt like the
horn of a unicorn.
I shall be anointed with fresh oil.''*
Psalms 92 . . . Verse 10

The *Olive Tree* I know so tender,
God in all His Refuge.
Preservation sweeping down,
through overwhelming floods . . .
and *Mercy*.
Our Spirits unite,
Wings of terrestrial innocence,
The *Father* who consecrates,
trembling anguish ceasing its *Cry*.
The abhorrent *adversary* dispersing . . .
to the bottomless excavation.
Spiritual communion,
Immersion of oppressing *Cargo* . . .
Refreshing quiet of lily fields,
rejuvenated by mighty *Forces*,
clothed in white.
Unstained healing *fountains* . . .
this *perpetual life*,
the ultimate felicitous *Rapture*,
when the *Olive Tree*,
poured forth *oil* over *me*.

Elayne Gocek Walden

SHADOWS

Dark shadows on a cold and lonesome road
Wind blowing through the green trees and
    through the brown fields of home
Lying in the gray shades of the windblown
    trees
Lying and watching up through the branches
    white clouds moving slowly in a
    blue breeze
White lines moving on down the dark and
    lonesome road
Won't you see if the sun will take you
    home?

Larry Shuffle

DEVIL'S DOOR-WAY, DEVIL'S LAKE, WISCONSIN

ODE TO EDUCATORS

If we can make one light to shine
If we can one lost pupil . . . find,
Then this our task of molding minds
Shall not have been in vain.

If we can make one life worthwhile
By just a word, a deed, a smile;
Then all our efforts for ''the child''
Shall not have been in vain.

If we can make one day more bright
if we can shed a radiant light
That helps to set one wrong path right
Our work is not in vain.

If we have done all in our power
To make this day a shining hour;
If we have caused one weed to flower,
We have not toiled in vain

LaVerne Byrd-Smith

LAVERNE BYRD SMITH. Pen Name: Charmayne Byrd; Born: Richmond, Virginia, 12-14-27; Married: Lewis Smith, Jr., 11-25-48; Education: Virginia Union University, history/education, 1944; Virginia State University, M.S. Ed., psychology/reading; University of Maryland, Ph.D., reading, curriculum, instruction, 1985; Occupations: Classroom teacher, Education professor, State education supervisor; Memberships: International, Virginia and Richmond area reading associations; Association for Supervision and Curriculum Development; American Education Research Association; Poetry: 'An Easter Dream,' *American Poetry Anthology,* 1987; ''Pokey the Playful Whale,'' children's story in rhyme, *Popcorn Magazine,* 1980; 'Does a Dream Die with the Dreamer,' *Diamondback,* University of Maryland, 1982; 'A World Without Words,' *Richmond Afro-American,* 1983; Other Writings: ''And The Greatest of These is Love,'' article, *Good News Herald,* 1987; Comments: *Response and reactions of humans to life's anomalies and realities may prove to be a unifying thought in my poems and stories which span three decades. The tone of these works ranges from the philosophical to the ''rap'' and may include social commentary, religious, didactic, entertaining or creative content. The best exceed 25 lines.*

MAMA'S ONLY BOY

He was tall and brown
Mama's only boy
He rarely wore a frown
Mama's only boy
He cared, He dared
Mama's only boy
Swallowed up, in the streets
Through friends he did meet
Mama's only boy
Lost in the crowd
He cried out loud
Mama's only boy
Drugs, he hit the big score
Mama's only boy
He is no more

Lois T. Hordges

BLACK CHILD

Black Child, Black Child
Where is your pride
I say, Black Child
You've got nothing to hide

Black Child, Black Child
Where is your love
I say, Black Child
Where is your Love

Black Child, Black Child
Where are you headed
I say, Black Child
Give yourself credit

Black Child, Black Child
Get up and show your stuff
I say, Black Child
You haven't done enough

I say, Black Child
Black Child
Where is your pride

Lois T. Hordges

LOST SONGS OF THE SHIPWRECKED

Sailing my boat on broken waves,
steering my ship away from shore.
Mermaids trying to sing me into jagged rocks,
as I head for unknown lands.

Sailing on broken waves,
the wind catches my sails,
taking me along.
Stars look over me out in the
unknown seas, as jagged rocks call for me
just before a storm.

Larry Shuffle

A DREAM TO REALITY

I saw Lord Jesus looking sad,
Saint Peter, frowning, stood beside.
Both paced, with deep concern for lads
Fed with erroneous data slides.

Children, with darkness all around,
In silence sit as scenes they view . . .
Fire-breathing dragon rose to sound,
Forming strange planets, stars that grew!

Some cheers they gave as lights beamed low
From planetarium's painted skies!
Lodged in unconscious, seed to grow,
Misinformation and some lies.

Courage delayed . . . the note I sent
To one who leads and has control,
And asked that Truth and what it meant
Be so explained as in the Scroll.

God, our Father, Creator One,
Whose Son came down from Heaven above,
The suns, moons, stars, all these were done
For man, His masterpiece of Love.

Inday Nabor Lombardi

OLIVER NORTH

A hijacked plane with hostages,
In Grecian airport, all await . . .
Some plans to rescue with stages
So delicate, procedure straight.

Achile Lauro, hostage there
At high seas; terrorist fears steered
And killed a helpless passenger;
Their freedom, Ollie engineered.

In Beirut, U.S.hostages
With tortured nights and meager meals . . .
Oliver North soon arranges
Their freedom with some weapons deals.

But then before some success find,
The deal was made known in Iran.
Oliver North, back, in a bind
With politics, the law, the man!

He fights for freedom at some cost!
Vietnam, Granada, other lands;
To Nicaragua gave the most,
As Contras' bravest helping hands.

Inday Nabor Lombardi

THE ROAD TAKEN

It is a lonely road to go
That will not be paved with gold
But that of the gold of autumn splendor
Deep in the lovely forest fold.
Nor will it be lined of silver
Except by the silver of snow
And there may I not grow twice as old
As old winter's hair in seasons cold

George D. Scott

MOLLY JONES

One day, Molly Jones pulled something shady,
She pinched a purse from a well-dressed lady.
As she rushed up the street she came a cropper,
Straight into the arms of a London copper.

She screamed and yelled and stamped her feet,
Her language was something I dare not repeat.
He finally managed to get her subdued
The crowd gathered 'round and booed and booed.

They took her off in the black maria.
Next, to the court, where they would try her.
The judge sat up high, with a dignified air,
And a white powdered wig covered his hair.

"Mi lord, I found that there purse," she brazenly said.
He did not believe her, she wished she was dead.
They took her below to the cold dingy cells,
A place of crying, and moaning, and awful smells.

She sat on the floor of that place vile and rank,
'Twas like being at the bottom of a septic tank.
She served her time, and they let her go.
Where she went after that, I do not know.

Mary M. Betz

MAMA

The touch of an angel, I feel softly beside me today.
Grieve not for me my daughter, for I must leave you now.
As distant eyes reach beyond visionless skies,
weakness of body has translucent glow of heaven.
Within gates of eternity, soul finds peace.
You cared for me today as my body lay sick;
my weakened legs, now will walk.
For I was given to you only a moment to help you learn.
As stardust falls beneath the misty sky,
a special star holds memory once shared with you.
Far away beyond the sunset, within my father's
Garden of Eden, remember my daughter:
For you are as me, and I will always be
with you, even beyond eternity.

"There are the days I remember my grandmother,
Within my own mother's eyes."

Gayle Nicholson

PLEASE

Where is the sunshine — the laughter — the warmth?
It seems so long since I've seen a genuine smile,
    or felt the sincere touch of a hand upon my
    shoulder, or heard the sound of my own name,
    spoken with the slightest hint of tenderness.
I know I can't go back. I can't retrieve the things
    I've lost. I know that I can't live on memories,
    and that I have to move forward. I have to
    rebuild my life, by myself. I have to create some
    semblance of normalcy in the midst of all of this chaos.
God, please help me. I know that winter is near, but
    please send me a ray of sunshine. Help me look
    through the clouds and see beyond myself. God,
    help me find some hint of spring.

Julia Eddins Fisher

THEN CAME YOU

Sitting alone in a big empty chair —
Longing to find someone who really would care —
Feeling alone; and feeling blue —
Without even looking; then came you . . .

Having problems; can't seem to cope —
Looking for answers; looking for hope —
Very depressed; not knowing what to do —
But as I looked up; then came you . . .

My heart was aching — eyes full of tears —
My life was filled with many fears —
I have no answers — I wish I knew —
The answer came 'cause then came you . . .

Life isn't worth living; I don't want to smile —
But having your love makes my life worthwhile —
You are the answer; you're my life too —
I'm glad I can say, "then came you" . . .

Ruth McClanahan

TAKE MY HAND

When you are down and full of despair —
    Always remember you have me to care —
Reach out and simply take my hand —
    I will reach back and will understand . . .

I will be the friend you really need —
    My love for you will be a starting seed —
Of something that will grow to last —
    We will live for tomorrow and forget the past . . .

So take my hand, my darling and my love —
    And let's look up and smile to heaven above —
We are blessed indeed to have each other near —
    We will make it together; we've nothing to fear . . .

And when things are going to our best —
    That's when our need for each other is the test —
It's then we both reach out hand in hand —
    And know our love's the best in all the land . . .

Ruth McClanahan

DADDY'S TREASURES

So many times, I think and dream about my dad;
Wishing he were here beside me, when I'm down and sad;
To comfort me and hug me in my battle to live;
Reaping only the leftover pieces, left in the sieve.
They say, time heals, but believe me, it isn't so.
His words are tattooed in my mind, "I love my little Jo."
I look to God in prayer, to console my grieving soul;
With my head buried in my arms, filling up the hole.
Daddy gave his life for us, when I was only four;
Never again seeing him come through the front door;
Leaving me with only his treasures locked in a drawer;
Mother's old letters (the Army sent back after the war),
His purple hearts, are all stuffed in a special sock.
And in one of those letters, holds my long, blond, lock!

Joanne Landry

I MET THE MORNING IN THE NIGHT

My empty room
and cooling heart
asking me yet:
''See why so mad
and brown the moon
and iced the light?''

I met the morning
in the night.

I lost you dear.
When? Yesterday?
Your smile? Your kiss?

Oh why so hard
feeling a wooden, passing heart?

My cool tears fall . . . and run away
drop down to oily gutters. May
with empty face and bitter fight.

I met the morning
in the night.

Hilda More

POOREST ON THE VINE

What remained after you?
Yawling days, funny place
in Hollywood.

Bus stops on the Vine,
rough slaps in the mine
weeping face.

Some tears what the wind
soaks down with the mint-
colored light.

Your face vanished . . . faints.
Don't ask what remained?

I am poor.

Poorest on the Vine.
You stole all mine
rhymes away.

Hilda More

MY MOM

Mom, your hair has grown
Gray and you can't move
As fast as you could before.
But one thing is, you are
Always there when I need
You in good times & bad.
And Mom, I love you.

Alan R. Casperson

EASY-BUSY NIGHT

Waiting for you on Vine . . .
where you were mine
dearest dream;

where easy-busy night
became blue and bright
on yesterday.

Summer spoiled the way
of your kisses. Play
laid down on the sky,

pulled you up the space
where silvery lace
dreams on easy days.

I lost you on Vine.

Don't remember mine
were you once, or nine
times on the Vine.

Hilda More

IN THE MOOD FOR MONK

When I am in the mood for Monk
I don't want to hear no ''Hard Day's Night'';
It is much too hard on my ears.
Please don't play no ''Tennessee Waltz'';
It will only bore me to tears.
My ears are tuned for ''Bebop Funk''
When I'm in the mood for Monk.
Nothing else will set my mood right,
No other kind of sound will do.
Oh, no, no bubblegum — no ho hum;
Only Monk for me when I feel blue.
I want melodies that make me drunk
When I'm in the mood for Monk.

It's erroneous if not Thelonius,
His tickling the ivory will pull me through;
So euphonius is Thelonius,
His sound is sunlight on morning dew.
When I first turned on to him
I felt a joy I never before knew.
He, like a gladiator of sound,
Clears the stones from my ears' pathway
When they tire of the hot air blowing round.
I run from darkness headed for light
And I just can't stand for no junk
When I get in the mood for Monk.

Charles Henry Powell

PASSING IMPRESSIONS

Though born when different stars appeared,
Not even sharing similar thoughts,
And yet we are of kindred hearts,
With deep impressions, passion's fire.

The ardor in your smoldering eyes,
The boldness of implied desire,
Forgive me for not grasping how
To cope with — even share — your love.

Arlene D. Krueger

IF

If I were but to live a moment more;
The ecstasy of knowing your love
Would be all I'd need to live for.

If I could hold you but a little while;
The depth of your love, so precious
Would cause my heart to eternally smile.

If I were to lose you suddenly;
The pain would be too great to bear,
And I would wish to join you in eternity.

So keep my love close to your heart;
As I will keep yours, always,
Till in death we shall part.

J. R. Moses

AT THE CROSSROADS

Be strong of heart whate'er you are,
Every moment's a reality,
Make your faith and talent dare
Yesterday's haunting melody.

Thorny and rough the road may be,
Rely on yourself and be independent;
Use your faculties effectively,
Every challenge will surely make sense.

Feel not depressed, this land has good
Opportunities for your becoming;
Relate with friends, be alive in your work,
Time will make your life exciting.

Every moment in your life
Virtuous and true you should be,
Ever alert to catch up with time,
Raise up your life and feel free.

Let your days shine in the Book of Life
Ornamenting this beautiful land,
Remember you are the light,
Devote yourself to something grand.

Otilia V. Nicolas

A MOMENT OF LOVE

If only for a little while
We entertain this fleeting love,
Discover love as few before
Have ever known the passion of —

Then let that little while become
A lifetime of requited love,
A cherished passion just we two
As lovers, know the meaning of.

You are the magic of each day,
You are the one that I adore,
If I never know another,
Thoughts of you will make my heart soar!

Arlene D. Krueger

SEASOUL OF A CHILD

Do you know? Prison, stubborn forehead;
It was walking on the lake of the eyes,
A damp answer takes wings.
A wrinkle ringed in the merry silence.

I have seen! The skyline is widening.
The sun rises on a magic land.
It ripens the sleepy protected field of the dreams.
The seed is poured out, the sea bears fruits.

The child breaks the shell and savours the fruit,
This pure milk of a coconut the sea has born,
It goes to his head which turns towards the ocean
The lake of his eyes, this mirror of the child.

He watches himself living in the bosom of the sea
Which gives him the milk and keeps the salt.
The salt flows from the lake and dries up the sea
The salt has purified the undulating breast.

Emmanuel Pierreuse

EMMANUEL PIERREUSE. Born: Lille (North of France), 10-19-58; Married: Diane Mensch, 7-26-86; Education: Ecole Normale de Lille, C.F.E.N., 5-80; Certificat d'Aptitude Pédagogiue 12-82; Occupations: Teacher, currently Fine art consultant, Translator; Memberships: San Diego Mandolin Society, Singing String Bands, San Diego Folk Song Society; Awards: 5th Place, Summer Poetry Contest, American Poetry Association, for 'Loneliness'; Poetry: 'Languages,' 'The Guru,' 'Ideals,' *American Poetry Anthology,* 10-87; 'A Frenchman in America,' *Creative Enterprises,* 1-88; 'Atheistic Prayer for the Earth,' *Many Voices/Many Lands,* 12-87; Themes: *The earth, human rights, friendship, love, childhood. I also try to express my opinions about political power. I wish some of my poems would help to preserve the earth and the cultures of minorities like Indians, Bretons and Flemish people.*

ON A JOURNEY THROUGH LIFE

The subway car leaves Oakland's Fruitvale Street Station
It travels above freeways
Omniscient eyes take in the view
Graffiti-painted faces of walls of burnt-out buildings —
Sad, tired, grey, nocturnal and abandoned
Vacant faces of dark, nocturnal alcoholism — juxtaposed
With my visions
In a Spanish accent . . .
Visions of Detroit, visions of the Bronx,
Visions of the virginal Hispanic across the aisle,
Visions of peace, visions of beauty,
Visions . . . of sugarplums — dancing in their heads.
The subway car moves in a straight line
From here to there to
The lines of poetry written on the foreheads of
All the passengers
As the train moans in a low, visceral groan
Whilst red-blooded energy flows to my bones
Whilst all of us —
All — passengers,
On a journey through life.

Don Mac Laren

ADMIRATION'S INSECURITY

Little moments — treasures of big moments,
    relating sun to moon.
The sky — blue rainbow's promise.
Violet touches blood of red,
    gold ponders.

Risking green
    and watching.
Torment grows to reveal beauty and unfulfilling pain.
Love — more torment
Hate — wanting love
    more torment
        confusing each other.

Anonymous letters written in love and pain
    wanting attention.
Admiration — holding back.
Force, aggressive souls — standing, sitting
    in hunger.
Never conscious, always sleepless —
    in dreams thirsting for quench.
Response — needed for delicious reply.

Time can blossom or destroy,
    a life . . .
        waiting in anxious hopes.
Sometimes satisfied.
    sometimes not.

Sheryl Lynn Porter

IN GRATITUDE

Life is so fast paced these days
There are deadlines to meet and orders to fill
There are so many things calling for my time
It's hard to find a moment to just be still

And yet as I rush from one thing to the next
As I juggle and balance work and family
I still hear that soothing voice inside
That says, ''Take a moment and listen to me.''

I feel so pressured to do other things first
But I know the value of obeying that call
So I say no to those pressures and yes to your will
And I have no regrets, no none at all.

For you speak of things the pressures drown out
You set my sights again on truly important things
You let me see how much I need your guiding hand
And how much peace your living word brings.

So in gratitude I pause now, dropping everything
Thankful that in a world of millions rushing to and fro
I have a heavenly father that still takes time to talk to me
A father who cares so much will never let me go.

It's truly a miracle when I stop to consider it
The God who knows every thought and every deed done
Though never slighting one single person or thing
Still takes time to speak to me, one on one.

Barbara Jean Walker

MOTHER

Who keeps our home jolly and bright,
A homey place for us to start
Learning simple lessons given,
To enhance our growth and development?

Who attends to us when we are sick,
Or down in solving a problem that pricks?
She's ever there to relieve the pain
For us to feel better again.

Who keeps us cool when we're in trouble,
Around the corner, at home, or in school?
She gives us peace of mind and heart
And makes us feel big in our life.

Who makes love live for young and old
No matter what this world unfolds?
The air around us is enlivening
As she smooths rough edges of living.

What can we do to reciprocate
Her boundless love that reverberates?
She works so hard to help us become
A worthy person our world demands.

Otilia V. Nicolas

Mom said (the other day)
if a person lived
to be 100
it wouldn't be enough
time
to get everything done.

She told me she looks
in the mirror
and is surprised at how
old she seems,
while inside still feeling
like a young woman.

I stand in front
of the mirror.
I look and feel young.
Yet my mother's face
reflects behind me —

Oh,
to age in body yet
retain a youthful soul.
To weep
for time lost,
never to regain.

Patricia Sheneman

Live life to the fullest,
    until it becomes so deep
    in your soul that no one
    can take away what it has
    given you or what you have
        given it.

Angela Hertle

A DREAM

This came about unexpectedly,
A dream when I was young and free,
I'll ne'er forget where'er I am,
I keep it as a precious gem.

'Twas an orderly procession,
Composed of a large congregation,
With lighted candles lighting their way,
All walked slowly, chanted and prayed.

Enchanted looking at the crowd,
I joined the adorers unperturbed;
Amidst the throng was a row of saints,
The last in the line was Christ the King!

He beckoned me so fatherly . . .
Bewildered I approached Him reverently,
Knelt down, sobbed, and pleaded for mercy,
On my hair His hands ran down comfortingly.

''My child, I've been looking for you
Through all the years, I'm glad I found you,
Remember you're the third and youngest
Little girl of mine I've chosen on earth.''

Otilia V. Nicolas

OTILIA VILLEGAS NICOLAS. Pen Name: Laling Tillie; Born: Calaoagan Dackel, Gattaran, Cagayan, Philippines, 12-13-27; Married: Dominador P. Nicolas, 1-21-18; Education: Lyceum of Aparri, B.S., Elementary education, 1980; Occupations: Retired public school teacher; Housewife; Poetry: 'Christmas Charms,' *Rose-Marian*, 1946; 'Gattaran March,' lyric poem, *The Horn*, 1979; 'My Child,' 'Homager's Plea,' *The Horn*, 1980; Comments: *My faith in God, along with the support of my family, has strengthened my determination to carry on. I love my professon and its demands. I love my family and its future, too. Modesty aside, I always have this in mind: ''Nothing is hard when done with love.'' I retired as a Master Teacher II on 6-17-86 because my daughter and son-in-law petitioned our coming to this wonderful nation, ''America, the beautiful''!*

POT O' GOLD

Such dreams I hold in my heart,
to write, fly, travel, to laugh,
develop a growth in spirit,
challenging me to believe in more.

Visions are yours, Dad said, and remember,
you can always be,
triumphant at life, mind and heart,
in the dreams that set you free.

A guarded fire is in your eye,
a deeper gleam in the blue, he whispered,
protect this flicker, feed it and keep
the light of dreams before you.

A dream is a rainbow transformed,
to fit in the confines of my soul,
and reaching for the distant spectrum
shows yet another pot o' gold.

Ginny Lindauer

THE DARK

If when the misty moon begins its howl,
I am no longer with you,
forgive this tattered soul,
for I no more choose where I go,
than does the moon decide its nightly pass.

If when the woven winds begin to blow,
I no longer heed your voice,
note the distance between your heart and mine,
for the reach between your embrace
 and my chilly vault is great.

If when the dark embalms the light,
my laughter turns to tears and raving delirium,
hold me and rejoice in your own sanity,
for as the day sweeps away the dark,
so shall my joy sweep away my sorrow.

And when the night comes
hold me, forever hold me.
For if I see the face of night
and feel his breath,
my soul will be his forever.

Peggy Doyle-Walters

It was love.
When I saw him.
When I gave up everything.
When I ignored and overlooked.
When I built up dreams.
When I encouraged
and rallied.
When I woke up
and walked away.
I loved myself.

Uraina N. Pack

HAPPINESS

Happiness is often found through the simple things in life,
It can fall upon peaceful minds and disrupt unwelcomed strife,
One need not be a king or queen in a velvet-carpeted palace,
Happiness so lovingly dwells in a cottage free from malice.

Happiness shared will filter through the barrier of loneliness
And fade away the clouds of gloom that often lead to stress,
Good thoughts bring happiness and contentment to the soul
And incentive to the undermined to achieve a higher goal.

Happiness is a treasure to protect and wisely nourish,
It creates sweet nostalgic memories to forever cherish,
God's love shines as brightly on a meager humble dwelling
And instills in hearts happiness with bitterness repelling.

Happiness can flow as gently as a winding mountain stream
Imparting ''good sentiments of life'' for one and all to dream,
A fuller measure of life is obtained through being self-denying,
True happiness shared unselfishly is oh so gratifying.

Happiness is a blessing that entails warming responsibility,
To accept God's love prayerfully through faith and with humility.
A helping hand or a consoling touch imparts thoughts so kind
And creates a rewarding happiness along with peace of mind.

Happiness is being grateful for the serenity of dawn,
Thankful to greet a newborn day as life continues on,
Happiness combined with faith is a joy beyond compare,
How glorious this world would be with happiness everywhere.

Dottie H. Walker

OUR FAIR LADY

'Twas the year 1865 the first seeds were so profoundly sown,
Since the U.S.A.'s sympathy for France surpassed any other nation
A monumental tribute to America's dream story should be shown,
Sheer wonder of a colossal in sculpture became a realization.

''Miss Liberty'' gloriously stood on her pedestal one century ago,
Her magnificent bronze figure a symbol for the land of the free,
With her right arm outstretched and her illustrious torch aglow
Her welcoming rays of hope filter through the barrier of destiny.

Millions of awe-stricken immigrants through their blinding tears
see ''America's Promise'' towering before their weary eyes,
Her silent command fills the air and echoes within their ears,
Long-awaited dreams of liberty and freedom begin to materialize.

''Come, all you troubled and homeless, take my hand,
   Leave behind all thoughts of turmoil and strife,
   Opportunity awaits you in this great freedom land,
   A new world, a new beginning, a better way of life.''

So proudly she stands; her beckoning light a glowing invitation,
New York harbor is a haven of hope for freedom lovers everywhere,
Every race, color and creed she embraces; each God's own creation,
Our ''Mother of Exiles'' stands by freedom's door and places them
   in His care.

She gallantly withstood the storms of life coming in with the tide,
Though many years of ravaging weather have been quite devastating,
Her restoration has remarkably enhanced America's patriotic pride,
With her commemorative torch rekindled ''Our Fair Lady'' stands
   waiting!

Dottie H. Walker

OUR TWILIGHT YEARS

O God, our beloved Heavenly Father,
The years have passed so rapidly,
We're bewildered in this uncertain stage of life,
Please keep our mind and body close to Thee.

Now that we're in our twilight years,
Diminish our fear of death and sorrow,
Give us the courage to accept grief and pain
And faith to face the unknown tomorrow.

We thank Thee for the gift of life,
For the Glory of our Saviour's Birth,
We're indebted to Thee for the forgiveness of sin,
For our loved ones in heaven and on earth.

We beseech Thee to be with us O Lord,
To uplift our hearts with Love Divine,
Cleanse our soul with the comforting assurance
In these twilight years we are Holy Thine.

Redeem us O Lord from vanity and self-conceit,
From unforgivable temper and arrogant pride,
To accept with dignity the flaws of aging
As easily and gracefully as the changing tide.

O God, our beloved Heavenly Father,
Strengthen our weaknesses with Thy Love,
May we have the awareness when we leave this world
We'll unite with Thee in Thy Kingdom above.

Dottie H. Walker

DOTTIE HORNER WALKER. Born: Greensboro, North Carolina; Married: Charles D. Walker, 6-17-51; Education: Kings Business College; Occupations: Receptionist for 'Stop the Music,' Model, Secretary, Homemaker; Memberships: Active and caring member of Mt. Bethel United Methodist Church, Marietta, Georgia; Awards: 'Christmas Eve at the Walisers,' 1986; 'First Moon Voyage,' 1987; published by *Hoosier Challenger;* Poetry: 'An Antique Shop,' 'The Old Abandoned House,' 'Yesteryear,' 'I'm Thankful,' 'Mona Lisa,' Spring, 1986; Comments: *My three sons, Ty, Kerry and Wyn, were an inspiration for many poems. I love writing religious, sentimental, humorous poems — truly, most anything that strikes my fancy. I always make my own greeting cards for all special occasions and sympathy cards also. I love writing poetry as that is the way I express my feelings.*

TO A DAUGHTER GROWN

The whirling wind blew the years swiftly away,
But for a time the earth stood still!
We talked, laughed and fussed as mother and
 daughter will
And now only the memories come
To sit and talk with me,
Of dimpled hands, skinned knees and baby tears,
Pot holders, handmade cards, your golden hair and
 big blue eyes,
Of beauty, school, love and smiles,
Sometimes, so sweetly, we sit together,
Loving the years over again, memories and I.

Mary Christine Bowen

THE OLD LADY, NIGHT, AND THE WAR

The soldiers put out their fire
as the sounds of the combat draw near
An old woman wanders through the camp
wearing a cloak of mourner's black
As she walks an occasional explosion
lights her miserable way among dying men
Someone cries out in pain and anguish
and she bends down to take him in her arms
All around are sounds of agony or fear
young men are trying to stay alive tonight
The man she holds looks to her
with pleading eyes and a quiet voice
And prays to live another year
to go home to his wife and child
Then he goes limp in the old woman's arms
Youth and death no longer conflict
Tears stream down her pale face
and a cool rain falls from the night sky
Slowly she walks away as rising sun
turns the sky blood-red
And she disappears, gone with the night.

Laura A. Deerfield

QUESTIONS OF THE HEART

Where does love start? Compassion stop?
Espirit de corps fit in?
Where's the fine line 'tween the three
When around those called your friends?
Are people normally so blind
Or afraid of an open heart
That to offer trust, want togetherness
Makes them set you far apart?
Am I so strange to love my friends,
Show caring when I can?
Mere courtesy's a very cold thing
Unlike the warmth of an open hand.
People back away in fright
Once they've looked deep in my eyes;
Is my soul so dark or is it so light
They can't stand what does not lie?
Are they all alone so much
That reaching out's a thing of the past?
Must hearts be set on one person alone
In order for love to last?
Are there none left to reach in the dark
And gather my weeping soul in?
Or must my heart forever break
As truly alone my life I spend.

Jon S. Evans

INTIMATE PATTERNS

Intimate Patterns, wanting more
    Indifferent connection, our minds;
Relationship entwines souls, core
Intimate patterns. Wanting more
We probe beyond each other's door,
    Dream shattered, disillusioned, we find
Intimate Patterns, wanting more
    Indifferent connection, our mind.

Karen S. Wolff

TO GLORIA

I lay in bed with my eyes closed
And looked out at the world that I know.
I ask myself "When I come to the end of life
What will I have to show?"

I went through a list of everyone I've known
And I stopped when I came to your name.
I said: "It is Gloria and the memory of her
That I will have to show and not my fame."

"What have you accomplished?" they will cry
When I come to the end of my day.
And I will remark, "I was loved by Gloria"
And they will say "That's an odd thing to say."

As I look back over this life,
It's not the travel, the money, the fame.
It was being loved by Gloria Cutler Eversole,
It was Gloria, Gloria, that is the name.

B. J. Eakin

BILLY JOE EAKIN. Born: Staff, Texas, 10-23-29; Married: Gloria Cutler, 8-16-87; Education: North Texas State University, Denton, Texas, B.S., Business administration, 1956; M.S., Business administration, 1957; American Academy of Asian Studies, San Francisco, Ph.D., 1961; University of California, Berkeley, Associate of the National Institute of Credit, 1961; Williams College, Berkeley, LL.D. 1965; Occupations: Shipping company executive; Writer; Memberships: San Francisco Latin American Lions Club, Chamber of Commerce; Other Writings: *Poverty*, 1968; *Magic Carpets*, 1970; *No Night is Wholly Black; Blondel, Sing Again; Random Thoughts*, 1969; *Velvet Horizons*, 1971; *Shadows*, 1974.

WHISPERING WIND

Blowing so soft and low
Teasing the grass blades
Kissing the rose petals
        as you go.
Carry to him my message
of undying love
Wrap it gently round
him, warm
Brush his lips with the
kiss I enclosed
Turn his head to what
used to be
            and me.

Claudia Caldwell

LOSS OF A LOVED ONE

The sky seems barren, cold, and grey;
The space in the soul black as night.
The anguished screams of a million men
Cry "Why? Please make it right!"

An answer comes with whispering,
Not with thunder and flashes of light.
Suddenly the heart has ears
And minds make imagination's flight.

"I'm here! I'm here! Listen" it says,
"Feel in your heart and you'll know —
As long as you love and remember me
My presence will never go."

"Inside of you is part of me
All I taught and exemplified
Hold on to that and use it in love
And I'll be there right at your side."

Then the whisper's gone and
It's seen the sky now blue has grown,
The soul is filled with the stars of love
And we walk, knowing, never alone.

Jon S. Evans

LITTLE BIRDIE, SING YOUR SONG

For Julia

Where do I go when I need to hide
From the pain that comes from deep inside?
Behind my eyes there is a place,
Where comfort lives, without a trace.

There's a little birdie in a tree,
And when I cry, she sings to me.
She holds me in her arms of song.
Through her music, she makes me strong.

Please sing . . . sing all my tears away.
Why, birdie, must it be this way?
Birdie, sing all through the years.
Dry my eyes . . . I'm blind with tears.

Tears are rain from clouded eyes,
Eyes that search for a disguise.
Little birdie, sing your song,
Through the day and all night long.

Birdie, sing away my pain.
Birdie, sing throughout the rain.
For, Birdie, in your voice I find . . .
A warm embrace and peace of mind.

Lori Simonton

THOUGHTS

Whispers from my mind, go beyond the earth's confines. Silent, I listen to the words with surprise. Symbol of madness, new and welcome thoughts of the future.

Karen S. Wolff

SNOW BLINDNESS

White powdery snow fell this time,
Different from the last damp, weighty piles.
You bark and chase the drifts until the brain travels freely,
Not seeming to mind the restrictions, though you'd rather run free.
The pup's constant teasing annoys you,
Reminds me you're still a pup yourself.

I remember how you staggered home, seeking relief,
Collapsing, blinded, at my feet, your head mangled from cruel blows.
We all thought we'd lose you, your will to live might be broken.
Another unanswered ''why?'' — so many exist . . .

Learning left from right and retrieving on voice commands,
Your senses now advanced, it's a rewarding sight,
To watch you seek and find the thrown objects.
Your quarter horse turns when you hear ''Left, that's it!''
Leave us grateful for your life, and warm us through all the cold.

The sun is shining brightly and melting the newly fallen snow.
The piercing light causes me to shield my eyes,
Sadly knowing the light gives you no pain.
Snow blindness and human ignorance intersect.
When painful glare intrudes our vision.

But now, Buster, less than a year later, the ''whys'' become
    ''if onlys.''
If only the law didn't require the chain,
If only the neighbor hadn't let his dogs run loose,
If only you hadn't tried to jump over that door,
If only I hadn't found you hanging . . .

Greg Thomas

LOVE IS LIKE A ROSE

Love is like a rosebud
When nurtured carefully and tenderly
It can blossom into a perfect rose sublime

Love when handled wrongfully
It can thorn you painfully

Love can glow brightly red
Red with passion all aglow

Love, like a white rose, when handled with
Gentility and loyalty
It can be white, white with purity
And when handled faithfully
It can blossom all through the years
Into a golden anniversary

Pink is the color of love so innocent
And of a rose soft and sweet
Blue is the color of a broken heart also found in a rose
Color of the same claim to fame
Black is the color of a heart that uses and abuses
Love, black black as a midnight rose
And love when it's neglected and unnurtured
Like a rose it can wither and it can die

Kenneth D. Patton

DARE TO BE LIKE AN EAGLE

Dare to be like an eagle
Dare to be free
Eagles dare to soar above the clouds
They are what they must be
Dare to fly the winds to far and distant lands
Dare to ride on thermal currents to distant mountaintops
Dare to be like an eagle
Dare to be proud and free
Dare to be loyal — Dare to be true
Dare to spread your wings and fly above the jungles and the forest
Searching, searching, ever searching, for something you must have
Dare to be like an eagle — Wild and free
With every beat of your wings, your heart pounds
Born to be proud — Born to be free
Born to be proud — Born to be free

Dare to be loyal — Dare to be true
And when eagles mate
They usually mate for life

Kenneth D. Patton

JUST DOWN THAT ROAD

To Roy, with loving memories of Frances

Nothing fancy, nothing expensive
About that little spot of land
At the edge of the wood.
Just a snug little trailer
Inhabited by ordinary folk
And yet
I wish, I still lived just down that road
From the neighbor's place where pleasant conversation flowed;
Where I was warmly welcomed to, ''Come right in from the cold
And have a coffee, and, stay a while.''

Here was sharing with a smile,
An easing of heartaches encountered on life's lonely miles;
A giving of hope for the future, in this world that moves too fast;
An assurance of an extraordinary friendship, at last.
And the Lord only knows —
How I wish, I still lived just down that road.

Esther E. Young

BREEZE OF LIFE

      Spring was here;
   It was a girl, in a different time with different feelings.
Sweet surprise was not so slow to bud then;
but she left the girlish woes, the carefree bliss,
and . . . Womanhood bloomed for Summer's fare.

      Autumn is here;
   It is a woman, more mature; so worldly and caring.
Though at times she yearns to go back,
she knows she must wind her way through the ups and downs of life.
For like the leaves: That is the nature of things.
And so . . . The snow will surely fall to make her bed.

Sandra Vargason

MY SPRING LEAF

You are as much
a part of me
as a leaf is
a part of a tree.

As a flower comes in spring,
it was spring you came to me.
Your beauty and frailty
were as a cherry blossom on its tree.

Your youth seemed as green
and fresh as new grass;
and your glee was a sunburst,
that wouldn't set but always last.

The summer spent with you
was as happy as can be.
You were my pretty leaf
and I was your strong tree.

I knew just as the autumn
takes the leaf from the tree,
time would separate us.
It would take me from you, and you from me.

All things are temporary
that I know;
and I'll remember the green leaf
that came in spring, but in fall had to go.

Elger E. Offutt, Jr.

ELGER E. OFFUTT, JR. Born: Washington, D.C., 12-25-48; Married: Alfreda; Education: D.C. Teachers College, 1971-1972; Occupation: Telephone company frame technician; Poetry: *Dreamers*; 1986; 'Changes,' 'Letter To Myself,' 'The Conqueror,' 'Mystery Lady,' 1986; Themes: *Some themes of my work include social commentaries in poetry verse, stories of love lost and found.* Comments: *My wish is that my work enriches the reader by being interesting and entertaining. For the few who can feel the poems, I hope you feel what I felt when I wrote them.*

LOOKING BACK

To suffer
 to cry
 to feel
Life is full of pain.

To try
 to accomplish
 to conquer
Life always end in despair.

Kelly Sharon

TEMPESTUOUS WATERS

The streams of mercy
flow into the ponds

of

human infirmity —

The currents of grace
empty into the tributaries

of

fleshly preoccupations —

The brooks of giving
float into the lakes

of

selfish indulgence —

Making rivers of *Hope*, seas of *Temperance*
and oceans of *Peace!*

Patricia R. Williams

How long will I speak out
And people without spirit
Retract themselves from me,

How long will I speak out
And offenders force rocks
To block and seal my way,

I will speak out as long
Away from critical aim
Man's actions widely err.

W. Notta

Of history times that come to pass,
And men who start to quibble;
Pay close attention to the words
That I'm about to scribble.

Hondo, and *Of Mice and Men*,
All the books we read;
Caesar, then does give no help
To buy the books we need.

Our English teachers with no time
Doth give a test to score;
And then they sit and give no rest.
They make us read some more.

So listen, lads, to what I say
Be sure to heed it quick,
Fill your shelves with books to read
From the habit you can't kick.

To teachers I do give salute
From eyes so sore and red;
Please have a heart this next semester
And put your books to bed!

Angela Hertle

N'AWLINS

on bourbon street
i gave myself
to the passion
of the music
and the heat
of the nights.

lost in a dream
filled with
the echoes
from a time
long slipped
into the past.

wondering
why make deals
with the devil
knowing
because *God* does
not make deals.

why do i tremble so
i never made a deal
with him.
but i did meet him once
lost in a dream
on bourbon street.

dee Mabry-Speir

THE POWER TO AMAZE

It still amazes me these days
Your very loving, caring ways
The strength of which I thought
Could not be found or bought
And for me to be so blessed
Much more so than the rest —

Amazes me.

That someone, anyone, could care so
And for no other one than *me* — so low
I who has always felt unworthy of such love
Now feel just a bit like a dove.
You'd think my mother would be pleased
That I have finally been appeased.
How bad a person can I be
To receive such a love, given so free.
To be worthy of such a wonderful bond
Can only mean that someone is fond
 of *me*

Amazing!

Cindy L. Railine

NIGHT

Lightning flashes and illuminates a dark night
Rain pours down on a well-worn roof
Inside are people with different thoughts
Always thinking, trying to find truth

The rain has slowed down with the coming of morn
Branches slightly broken, leaving
The trees like sheep that have just been shorn
And little beads of moisture
Linger on the leaves

The hot sun changed what the night had brought
The same people but with different thoughts
By the coming of day all things are light and bright
All this changes, the sky darkens

Then a brand new night

Betty Baker

ON A MAYFLY'S WING

a pause keys the passage
from one breath to another

often static signals the ensuing birth, whereas
each life lasts for just an eternity
and each eternity is the duration of song

i live somewhere between the melody and the words
jubilant,
symphonious,
depressed or vibrant
    perpetually umbilicaled to the folk song's hymn
yet with only one passage,
i must live one life at a time

so many favored songs
they are lives put on hold
carefully stacked and arranged
protected,
shadowed and free from discord

the fantasy is to be totally immersed in song
antonymous to despair

the surest reality is to merge all lyrics into one
that i may thrive

and never pause

Randy S. Adams

LET ME LIVE IN SUNSHINE

I want to live in a world full of sunshine.
    I want to live in a world where there's rain.
I want to live in a world without sorrow.
    I want to live in a world without pain.
I want to live in a world full of beauty,
    Like the stars in the sky up above.
I want to live in a world without hatred;
    But not in a world without love.

Richard Gendek

GREEN WISDOM

The Lord formed man of dust from the ground
and sent man forth to cultivate the earth.
Man has strayed far from the green wisdom of this birth.

Gardening will mend and bring you peace.
Feel the bonding of hands and soil,
the joy of a flower after growing's toil.

Gardening will humble and inspire you.
Notice the seedling breaking free with all its might,
the striving of a vine reaching for the light.

Gardening will teach and enlighten you.
Hear the lessons the trees and plants bring,
the secrets all of God's creatures bring.

Heed and tend your garden well
for we are laid in the ground we till,
with eternity resting on our faith in Christ's will.

Tammera Lynne Foxworthy

PEACE BE STILL

When the stress of life bears in on you,
    right down there where you live
  And you're asked to keep on giving, when you have no more to give
When it seems you're barely hanging on, and you're way out on a limb
    Then Jesus whispers, ''Peace be still, cast all your care on Him.''

When you've fallen many times before,
    and now you've stumbled one more time
  And you're wondering if you should get up,
    or if it's even worth the climb
When it seems your day has turned to night,
    and life has lost its charmsn
    Then Jesus whispers, ''Underneath, are the everlasting arms.''

When life's burdens weigh you down, and no one lends a hand
  When it seems you're out there all alone,
    and you're just too weak to stand
When you've tried to do your very best, but nothing turns out right
    Then Jesus whispers, ''Take my yoke, because My burden's light.''

When life's battle rages on, and all things point to sure defeat
    As the giants move in closer, and all you're thinking is retreat
When you take that first step backward, and you cry, *Oh help me Lord*
    Then He whispers, ''I'm your buckler,
    I'm your shield and I'm your sword.''

When your confidence has been betrayed,
    and you don't know who to trust
  When the ones you counted as your friends,
    just brush you off like dust
When lonesome closed in on you, and it seems you have no friend
    Then Jesus softly whispers, ''Lo, I'm with you to the end.''

Victor F. Josi

COLOR BLIND

Lord, make me color blind to the
skin of men
To better understand Your kind
of love.
The fellowship of love You spoke of
through Your begotten Son.
Lord, You have the power and
the will
To send Him back to earth
again,
Will He be red, black, white
or yellow?
Will I see Your goodness
within
When I look into His eyes?
Or, because of His color,
Deny Him as my brother?
Lord, make me color blind
to the skin of men
That I may truly have
the right
To call You —
"Father."

Elia Vann Colmenero

IN DIRE NEED

My shoes have holes,
'cause my toes are breaking through;
I'm really growing,
just like you want me to.
My pants are short,
and above my ankletops;
and my hair just grows and grows,
I've quite a fancy crop!
I know it takes a heap of care,
just know I'm not complainin';
when things are in quite dire of need,
there could be worse remainin'.
There's always things need fixin',
replacin' and repairin';
what counts, though, most of all,
is that you keep a carin'.

Marjorie S. Carder

BLOSSOM, MY CAT

She is peeking out the window
Looking at the earth and sky,
    Wondering if the weather
    Will ever become dry;

Where went summer, and now
Winter's stormy weather,
    Blocking out the sun
    For many a moon now;

Oh, Blossom, with your
    Sparkling snowflake fur,
How I wish a little sunlight
    Could warm you
As much as your love
    And soft purrs
    Have warmed my soul
        Through winter's cold.

Pamela Delis

SHEDDING TEARS INSIDE LIKE RAIN

Look deep into my hazel eyes,
And tell me what you see,
Do you see who I really am?
Or who you've always wanted me to be?

Look carefully at my naked smile,
Do you sense happiness within?
Or is there loneliness and pain,
Behind this subtle grin?

Look closely at my tired face,
My skin, dark, leathery brown,
Do you see these lines of age?
With wrinkles so profound?

Listen to my fading voice
What do you hear in every word?
Is my speech distinct enough?
Do you really think my voice is really heard?

So many of us hurt deep within,
Feeling loneliness and pain,
Camouflaged by a smile or a grin,
Shedding tears inside like rain.

L. Joy Hunter

GLORY OF A MORNING GLORY

Mom

Like a morning glory on the vine
Wet with life's dew, as the daylight
dawns, at the sunrise, you blossom
to full bloom. But as dusk appears
and the shade of night is drawn,
you fold your arms in blessed sleep
until a new day dawns. As you
awake to a brand new day in a land
where night will never be, this
morning glory will stay in full
bloom, throughout eternity.

Peggy Duncan

DREAMS ARE . . .

Dreams are
    The fabric from which we spin
    The web of our existence;
    The reason for rising in the morning,
    To withstand the myriad
    Of dull repetitious acts
    Which consume most of life;
    The purpose behind all we do
    Which we would rather not,
    Giving meaning to all we must do,
    Providing hope for all we want to do.

Dreams are
    The force which nurtures
    The strength which sustains.

Carol Lee Witsoe

HOME TO GOD

Dear God help us to share
With our sisters and our brothers
Instead of thinking only of ourselves
Let us be reminded to help others
May the Light of Jesus shine
In every good we do
Jesus is our best friend
He wants to be yours too
An invitation is being given
All across the land
The calling of God's children
God's perfect plan
It's ringing loud and clear
And if we listen we will hear
Sinner come home oh sinner come home
Because the time will soon be here
Praise be to the Lamb of God
Who died on the cross for all
And we can have salvation
If we answer to the call
God bless everyone is what I have to say
And I hope that we are together
On that great rapture day

Irene Downey

TO POETRY

Away! Away! Come fly with me
to the enchanting land of poetry.
Writing poems is so much fun;
So, leave your cares, your woes,
and run.

Run! Run! Just be carefree
in the world of imagination and poetry.
Are you a stranger in this land?
Then welcome here, please take my hand.

Poetry! Poetry! It calls to me
to calm my fears and clear my mind.
So, travel on to heights untouched;
You'll find the natives here are fine.

Soar! Soar! We'll meet again, dear one.
In another land of rhyme and poems.
So, Away! Away! Come fly with me.

Elaine Miller Raby

Life is rejoicing
Life is wonderful
When we struggle through
    and attain our goal
Yet, love is the best of all
When we have someone dear
    to love, to cherish, to devote
Life becomes so much more meaningful
And that is all what we live for

Marlin Hsu

AGING

An infant am I knowing no better
how important age will be as my life pieces together

At one or two my personality starts to appear,
at three or four you'll see more and more

four and five I'm very much alive
starting to form my very own life

age eight or nine time stands still
it seems you never get close to those grownup years

at eleven or twelve you can't wait until
you hear the sounds of teenage years

at eighteen or nineteen time lingers on
twenty-one is so far away
the legal years to have fun and play

at twenty-one then to twenty-five a 1/4 of century,
has passed you by

now you hit thirty, a traumatic year for most
it seems everything is all downhill

then there's forty, they say that's the best
when life is worth living, just like the past

and now we hit fifty, a half a century gone by
it almost makes you want to cry
for what have I done with all of those years
not much you say, as it brings on the tears

June Drao

WHISPERING WINDS

Oh those whispering winds, calling out my name
calling me to younger days; but everything has changed.
It would be so much easier to close my eyes and say,
"Things aren't like they used to be; I just live day to day."

I like to think that everything works out for the best.
My memories of yesteryear just won't let me rest.
It feels like a hurricane whirling in my mind.
My true identity keeps getting harder for me to find.

Those whispering, gusting winds keep singing me a song
About my tattered, torn-up past: I thought those days were gone.
I wonder if I'm the same as I was five years ago,
The answer to this question: I'm not for sure I know.

Why can't the winds leave me alone: my past be laid to rest?
So I can live what's left of my life, doing my very best.
Oh those whispering winds; will they ever pass me by?
To let me live for the moments to come, or will they haunt me
  till I die?

Edna Jenkins

TO BE TAXED

Today I found the tree much larger than my thought,
Though ever large, could ever be.

In fact, an accurate measure, here, between
These first two branches show their tips reach
Miles apart — so far apart
Eternity could fit between their shadowed beaches.

    The day we saw the tree's first shaping —
        An August sky, distinctly blue,
        Above a stand of pines, distinctly green —
    The width we measured looked so small
    It looked like hands together,
    Linked — anonymous *(sans fils)* — within
    A common bond.

Today, these lower branches have so grown apart —
So far — you might not guess, by this far weighted
Buoyant tip, their central rooted site
Unless —
Unless you see
The same steel sap
Pervading every lengthened branch
Still tracing in the trunk the yield
And general direction,
    The accurate dimension that shapes
And bends its boughs.

E. Gray

SHATTERED GLASS

Shattered glass surrounds my everyday world
Destroying the silent dreams lost to a place unknown.
Where did they go; and why can't they be found?
I wish I knew the answer to that question.

Chaos built upon chaos, it makes my existence
  interesting and unpredictable.
That fact is evident, I receive everything
  from others
I have it made, I will always get what I want —
Shattered glass has taught me how to survive!

Rules were broken many years ago
My character was destined to be this way.
Fate: kind or unkind she was
I chose the road, right or wrong.

Different colors and shapes the pieces of glass
  are now;
Bright one moment, dull the next
I cannot recognize the colors or shapes; if
  ever I could!

The answers to the questions are still unchanged
Silent dreams will never be found.
I wish I could touch what will forever be lost
Satisfied, the victory is mine and shattered
  glass has won — forever in control; we are one.

Vicki A. Thompson

ROADSIDE SCENE

The barn door hangs wide and open,
No life is there to enter in —
The waiting stables are stark and bare —
You feel the loneliness dwelling there.

The yard wears signs the tumbled ends
Of fence and coop, for laying hens.
Fancy flowers in shoddy beds,
A footpath mends since no one treads
To back-door steps, and there it ends.

The frame door opens part-way wide,
Half-resisting what comes inside.
A tired, man shoe, lies on the floor,
With mop and pail, a woman's chore.
Now spiders spin and there abide.

The dust long kept in rest to snare,
Strangers' footprints, trespassing there.
Myopic gaze of window pane —
Watch field of weed nuzzle grain.
On tall, broad steps, we climbed the stair.
The searching sun can't chase the gloom
Of shadows lurking, in upstairs room.
Sensing, something wished us out —
We went down in haste, front door out,
In fear of this forbidding tomb.

Dorothy L. S. Strand

HEARTBREAK VALLEY

Down in yonder Heartbreak Valley
    I went back for a while yesterday,
Remember, it was our green valley
    Where we to live and pray!

You took me there when first we wed
    And I remember that you said
We'll build our little home here
    And pray for our first child, dear!

We were so happy then, my darling
    And so young were you and I
Now you both have gone from me
    And I miss you so I often cry!

The beautiful house you built for me
    Was so lonely and sad to see
Window panes broken, roof sagging too
    When once it was so pretty new!

I saw the roses we planted
    My tears were falling down
On some of the faded petals
    That had fallen on the ground!

It isn't like it was before
    Nobody lives there anymore
All are gone — my beloved — and Salley.
    Now for me it's Heartbreak Valley!

Dovie L. James

TEXAS LOVER

I'm looking for a Texas Lover,
    I need him so very much,
Someone to always thrill me
    With his ever-loving touch!

I'm looking for a Texas Lover
    And I hope He'll understand
That I'll forever love, love him
    'Cause he'll always be my man!

I'm looking for a Texas Lover
    And I can hardly wait,
He'll have a love for me
    As big as the Lone Star State!

I'm looking for a Texas Lover
    He may be in Dallas around,
Hope he's looking for me too
    'Cause I'm right here to be found!

He doesn't have to be handsome,
    Just so he's kind and true,
Did you say you're from Texas
    We'll say, it must be you!

Dovie L. James

FALL

Fall is that time each year
When angels gently toss earthward
Harvest colors of summer rainbows
Before they fade in cloudy skies.

To spread a royal robe of beauty
On the leaves of trees and bushes
In millions of breathtaking shades
Of red, yellow, orange and green.

A gift to all nature lovers
Who protect our lakes and streams
Of rot and fire and destruction
To enjoy in solitude and dreams.

George T. Higgins

A TOUCH FROM HEAVEN

Heaven, so far yet
so close.

I can feel her
touch by the soft
breeze she brings.

She brings a touch
of love no man
can give.

A love that pardons,
brings peace, joy
contentment that
answers unspoken
requests, and sends
a shining light through
our souls to conquer
all doubts and fear.

Aldena Harris

ANN

Oh, dear child of my heart,
Who never got to be.
Will someday emerge so forth
To shine in His heavenly court.

Oh, dear one, that could have been,
If only to have understood his yen.
How she cries to be free
To meet her maker, Thee.

Thou, oh my Lord, strong and with might,
Willed that it be so.
The evil one, in unceasing fight,
Will forever be foe.

So, dear child, find peace
Not in his ugly fleece,
Nor in his rotten fod,
But in your namesake, the Grace of God.

Carla Ann Bouska Lee

THE DREAM

I dreamt a dream
Of froth and lace
Elusive moths
In airborne grace;
Of breezy laughter
Swept away
With fairy dust
And moonlight rays;
Where thoughts, like castles
Touch the sky
And rainbow streams
Meander by
And Nature's tears
Are shed in dew.
I dreamt a dream:
That dream was you.

P. K. Newman

P. K. NEWMAN. Born: Indianapolis, Indiana, 11-5-54; Education: Michigan State University, B.A., Psychology; Post-graduate work in advertising/marketing; Occupation: Freelance designer; Awards: 1971-72: Publications/awards: National Poetry Press; American Poetry Press; Massport Authority Essay Award; Mass Commission on Employment of the Handicapped; Government essay/research award; Comments: *Poetry lies everywhere in the world around us; my aim is merely to espress it.*

TEARS OF LOVE

To Janie —
my ''bestest'' friend from God above.

Tears of love once filled my eyes
But for many reasons, I still might cry.
Your breath of life has slipped away
It consumed your human presence, only yesterday.

Tears of love now in my eyes
The joy you brought me was never denied.
You believed in living only for today
Why have you gone and left me, here to stay?

Tears of love never more will be
Experiences of life have been left here with me.
Did you ever once think that I would let go,
All the laughter and sorrow of your very soul?

Tears of love shall I remember forever
Passion from all you held within, what a treasure!
Of all God's gifts He has bestowed upon me
A friendship so rare and wonderful, has been seen and believed.

Vicki A. Thompson

WHERE HAVE YOU GONE?

Where have you gone?
It seems like only yesterday —
The society in which you were forced to live
Denied all true gifts you had to give.
A child so lonely, a woman confused
Why was your death so soon:
You could never reach the height and depth of
  our golden moon.
Destiny by fate: the choice was made
A child trapped inside the age of a woman,
A woman who was indeed a troubled child
Your path was full of countless, but endless lies.
From Norma Jean to Hollywood; a famous name was born.
Your beautiful yet troubled personality was left
Suffering greatly, many tears were wept.
Where have you gone?
Treasured memories you gave us!
That famous legend still fills our hearts
Marilyn, dear Marilyn: a peace within your soul
I hope you have found . . .
With all the pain, there was so much strife
Indeed ending, what on this earth — a tragedy of life.

Vicki A Thompson

FOR ITS LOVE

Love is a gift of feeling for one another,
which we share from the heart.
It's caring that makes us understand each other;
when we think about one another,
especially when we're apart.
It's lighting up her life with a kiss,
seeing her eyes sparkle when bringing her flowers or a gift.
It's settling down, to plan a life,
me to be her husband, her to be my wife.
A candlelight dinner out on the town,
sharing our thoughts with no one around.
It's the laughter and the fun,
it's being that *Team*, which means to be *One*.

John T. Savino

MY THREE DOGGIE FRIENDS

My three doggie friends, all so precious to me
Without them, what kind of life would it be?
Attracting so much attention, their actions they want you to see.
Love is so bright, it circles around the globe
Makes life wonderful, I can't let it fold,
My three doggie friends, to me you are worth more than pure gold.
Loyalty and devotion, my friends say that is what they are
Always watching out for me, they won't stray far.
All I know is my days with them will all be too few
Can't predict my future with them and am not trying to.
They are all so beautiful, they love me just the way I am
Eggs, bacon, and my toast I share with them,
covered with butter and jam.
Around our kitchen table, together we all crowd;
It is a love triangle that makes me proud.
Taking them places to show them off, I enjoy that
They will let me know when they see a loose dog or cat,
A twice-a-week brushing will keep their fur from getting a mat.
Being loved and giving love, to them this is what life is all about
My three doggie friends are the greatest, I have no doubt,
Memories are like a special light that never will burn out.

Priscilla Cohen

PRISCILLA ANN COHEN. Born: Houston, Texas, 6-23-48; Single; Education: University of Houston, B.S., Health, physical education, 8-77; Occupations: Substitute teacher; Obedience dog trainer, Basketball referee; Memberships: HPE (Delta Psi Kappa); University of Houston (Phi Kappa Phi); Park Place Chapter 731, Eastern Star Masonic Lodge; First Baptist Church, Houston; Southwest Basketball Officials Association; Poetry: 'Vision of Hope,' *Best New Poets of 1986,* 1987; 'True Love,' *Hearts on Fire, Vol IV,* 1987; 'Called Out,' 'Sweetest Story Ever Told,' 'Looking Forward,' *Words of Praise, Vol. III,* 1987; Themes: *Religious, animal, and autobiographical poems are mostly what I put together. I have written poems about the memories of some of my vacation trips and poems reflecting the love I have for my three Shetland Sheepdogs.*

IF THE BIRDS CAN SING

If the birds can sing so early in the morn,
  Then surely so can I,
    Before my day's begun.

Though neither of us know what may befall us through the
  day,
  We shall be content
    For through faith we'll find the way.

For God is the One who gives the song we sing,
  And He will give us what we need
    Like the lilies of the field.

So if you hear us singing such a bright and cheerful song,
  And if you'd like to join in
    Let God know
      He'll help you sing along.

Judith E. Reed

Part of High Fall.

SEPARATED BY TIME AND BY SPACE

Dedicated to James Dean

Well, James Dean died out on the highway one day
As he sped off the Lord stole him away
He can't tell us what was on his mind that day
That caused slow reaction — a fatal delay

James was an unusual sort of a fellow
No one dared ever say he was yellow
He was a deep thinker, he never was shallow
Don't think I'd ever describe him as mellow
He just wasn't that type

Never did a scene without something behind it
He'd dig down deep inside and he'd find it
What was he trying to say in his art
He showed his true colors, shot straight from the heart
Impulsive . . . he was that type

James had his own way of doin' his own thing
If ya called when he was busy he'd let that phone ring
Don't bother him unless he's in a good mood
Cuz he was known to be terribly rude — anger he couldn't hide

Why did you leave me? How dare you go?
When I need you, where am I to go?
A gravesite isn't my favorite place
We're still separated by time and by space
Yet you carry on strong in this world
Things happen in threes and your legend was born
Well I'm still a rebel without a cause
You're welcome to live on in me

Pam Schwetz

I TOO HAVE A DREAM

I too have a dream — That love will reign supreme
And instead of hurting one another — We will work as a team
I too have a dream — That all people will talk to one another
Without words that are like bombshells or come from the gutter
I too have a dream — Children will not be born with distortions
And that young girls will not have to seek abortions
I hope someday that teen-agers will not commit suicide
But instead — Walk this land with their heads high with pride
I too have a dream — People will not want any drug high
Whether it be a colossal city or a minute place under the sky
I too have a dream — That that white power called cocaine
Will not be snorted, smoked, or put in anyone's vein
I too have a dream — That no one will go out to rob
And for all our graduates — There will be a job
AIDS and cancer will end someday
Respect and understanding will be here to stay
Apartheid in South Africa — Will someday end
And when this happens — We shall all win
Showing love for one another is not a sin
We can treat others — Like we would a friend
These are my dreams — That I hope and pray
That they will reign supreme — For us — Someday

Bessie Frazier

GET IT TOGETHER

Message to Teen-agers

Students listen — boys and girls;
You're traveling through — your teen-age world.
You talk about this — you're into that!
You better get your business straight;
And that's a fact — or maybe you're set back;
You like to party — you like to rock.
You better watch out — that you don't get shocked.
Time keeps moving — watch that clock!
Time is going to pass — and before you know
Mother's job will be over — and you'll have to go.
Pick up that book — educate your mind,
Or you'll look for a job — and none you'll find.
Some will make it — others won't —
Because some are willing to learn
And there are those — who don't.
Ten years ago — some of today's boozers,
Pushers and frequent drug users
Had a chance — just like you.
But when they were in class — what did they do?
Some cut classes — walked the hall;
Did little or no work — they had a ball!
You know these words are true.
Who's replacing those corner people?
Don't let it be you!

Bessie Frazier

BESSIE FRAZIER. Pen Name: Munchie; Born: Brooklyn, New York, 4-9-48; Married: Edwige Jacquet, 7-22-77; Education: Fisk University, B.A., 1971; Montclair State College, M.A., 1972; New York University, Brooklyn College, post-graduate work; Occupations: Teacher, Writer; Memberships: Zeta Phi Beta, Fisk Writer's Workshop; Awards: Writing award, 1971; Other Writings: Poems, short stories and plays for Youth, Exposition Press, 1980; ''Black Creations,'' Carlton Press; ''Poetry Written by a Black Woman,'' Fisk Writer's Workshop, 1969; Comments: *Since our world is filled with so many conflicts — I would like all people to know and feel that ''a better day is coming.''*

BREATH

Life powers in man
  formed within his spiritual frame
    having the will intensified
      to inhale,
        to exhale
          a fragrant of silent wind.
            As the whispering sound of utterance
              stand to be an offering
                for life's given chance.

Geo. A. Constable

LOVING

Loving is, as loving does
Words are cheap, and free to spare
A word without an action suited
Is not fit for one who cares;
The tears inside that never fall
That well up deep inside, and drown
The "I love you's" (not love at all)
Just lost inside the heart, not found —
And when the well of tears runs dry
And love words echo freely there
And emptiness lies all around
And actions have laid love words bare —
Remember that the action suited
Does not linger with a kiss.
Loving is, as loving does
And loving does, as loving is.

P. K. Newman

THE WELL

I slipped and fell
Into a well
From which I could not rise;
The well was deep —
The walls too steep
From where the bottom lies.
Then someone spoke:
An echoed croak
From somewhere near I stood;
I gazed in eyes
Without disguise
And knew that this was good.
For through the fog
Another frog
Kept me company,
And though he might
Give some a fright,
He was a Prince to me.

P. K. Newman

FAMILY GODDESS

goddess from the sea
and me
who lured my father
to what mindless choosing
and lured me
goddess of the wave
and wind-borne spray
endlessly in motion
pulling me
goddess of the salt
and of the foam
riddling desire
and tempting me
goddess of the storm
and swirling tide
sweeping clean the beach
and wrecking me

J. Sigmund Forman

POSSESSING THE SEA

Sea past turning
slides its catch along its sucking way
the stopped shell V's the only sign
of holding back

and now a branch with seaweed laced
in place of leaves the water stole
with now a Chinese crate end wearing
poetry by its shape
but maybe only this end up
or fragile use no hooks

I claim the sea
with sandy feet
and do not shake my fist
but only cry a drowned-out plea
and raise my arms to praise
but not to beckon
and wait the tide's returning
when it will

J. Sigmund Forman

J. SIGMUND FORMAN. Born: Galveston, Texas, 5-16-30; Married: Patricia; Education: Columbia University, A.B., 1951; Occupation: Writer.

ENCOUNTER DISCO PHILODEMOS

Hello, beautiful, what's your name?
"You're not so bad yourself, what's yours?"
I want a long relationship.
"How long is long for you or me."

Let's leave this place without delay.
"Don't rush me so, cool down a bit."
My health is good and this I swear.
"My doctor can attest to me."

I'll pay my bill so finish up.
"I'm short so here's my bill with yours."
Your place or mine, my car awaits.
"Yours, and who knows how long is long."

Rann Newcomb

TO A BARBIE DOLL

Through Barbie's eyes
I've realized
there lies a world I'd love to find.
I'd live with Ken
in a world of pretend
created in a little girl's mind.
Childish notions
expressing emotions.
An unchanging smile on my face.
A life of surprise;
with love in my eyes,
living dreams, of a faraway place.
Time's but a pause.
In a house without walls,
encasing my love forever.
Life never ending.
Youth not surrendering,
yet growing old together.

Betty L. Harnly

THE PREY

I was watching the cat
playing with her prey.
Which squirmed and squeaked
trying to get away.
It started running,
looking for a place to hide.
When the long, sharp claws
struck him in the side.
Her tail twitched
as she joyed at his pain.
He tried to get away
again and again.
She batted at him
with no mercy in her touch.
She was enticed by his fear.
He died in her clutch.

Betty L. Harnly

BIRTH OF A POEM

As quick as the wind blows from nowhere
ideas breeze into my head and go to my hand.
My pen jumps across the page
as the wind would move across the sand.
Quickly, easily,
leaving ripples and signs;
words and scribbles
with rhythm and rhyme.
My consciousness cannot stop me
once my pen has hit the page.
I've felt other people's passions,
their grief and their rage.
Their fear has run through me
as the wind through the trees.
When it's all written,
what people might say,
the wind dies
and the thoughts go away.

Betty L. Harnly

IN MEMORIAM TO ABRAHAM LINCOLN

From the hills of old Kentucky, through the plains of Illinois,
Came the greatest pioneer of them all, a stalwart frontier's boy.
At night he sat alone before an old fireplace of stone,
And watched the dancing sparkling flames fly up the chimney's cone.
On bronzed bony hands he leaned, long fingers tapered fine,
This tall and somber, angular boy, plotting our history's line.
From the pattern of the flickering flames across the cabin's walls,
He watched and planned and dreamed his dreams, realized in ivy halls.
With the saber of the North drawn sharp,
  he slashed the South's rose curtains,
Ripped away the yoke that galled from slavery's pall, for certain.
Upon the canvas of his life he painted a masterpiece,
And drew a plan for all free men to live in joy and peace.
Calm and intent, so serious of mein, the woodsman's ax his tool,
His challenge the sins of all mankind, the wilderness his school.
The measure of a man, they say, is cast in the mold of what he's done.
These many years in sharp relief etch the glory of Abe Lincoln.

Lucille M. Kroner

MAGIC CARPET

There is a place where I go to be alone,
Far from the maddening world beyond.
Where adventure calls from a Matterhorn tall;
Or shimmering waters on Golden Pond.

It is a fairy-tale place, a never never land,
Where on whim I am anything I wish to be at all;
An elephant riding big game guide,
To Babe Ruth swatting in the home-run ball.

I can be a strutting Napoleon, replete with general's hat,
Standing before snowy Russia's very gates;
Or a war-bonneted Sitting Bull, crossing the Little Big Horn,
Even be President of the United States!

I am the confident, valiant hero, facing the guillotine,
In a Dickens' classic tale;
Or bronzed south seas fisherman alone in outrigger canoe,
Standing before the hurricane's howling wail.

I am soldier of fortune on China's old Macao,
Frank Baum's Oz's wicked witch mounted on a broom;
I am writer-poet and manipulator of imaginations run wild,
On this magic carpet that I call my room.

B. W. Bartholomaus

MARBLE PASSAGES

Seasons turn, years progress.
  Live a wanderer's life.
    the non-pretense of make-believe your beginning.
  Stay simple.
  Dance to the music of
    wonder, love, meaning and courageous death.
Bring no pain.
Thrive on friendship's language of meaning
    as diminished descriptions and generous emotions
    give flight to tell-tale intonations
    of unspoken loneliness.
  Give new value to each other.
  Follow each dream's direction
    as your soul's breath dwells in humble security.
I wish you long life
  long love
  'til the beautiful cheerfulness of old age
  dispels common atmospheres.

Donna Loeber

ANTIGONE

Antigone loves those most
who are stone upon the ground.

No ashes shall be made
the body will be kept for her to love.

Her ancestors were the gods
they reigned, they showed the way.

Now they have left the city
in their chariots they ride,
leaving Antigone alone to face the days of death.

She lies with cold stone dead ones.
She wishes her lust to be returned, but they are gone.

Mary Anne McCracken-Cooper

ELIZABETH

I gaze at you sleeping in my arms
and wonder at the miracle of your existence.

You let me see the world anew
through your eyes I have rediscovered life.

I never knew that love is so unconditional
and yet here I am loving you, diapers and all.

Baby daughter, how life changed when you arrived.
How is it possible that I have been so blessed?

Mary Anne McCracken-Cooper

THE COLORS OF LOVE

Yellow and brown and all the colors of sunlight was my love.
Furry and soft was his warmth, and gentle and light was his touch.
And though I tried to keep him from the world (and more),
Freedom was his nature and my sighs to tame him of no success. So —

When I'd look at him questionably and he'd turn his head,
(As often and carelessly they do) I'd scowl and say —
"What do I care!" And —
When I'd brush his fur and he'd slip away,
(Having had quite enough of this) I'd scowl and say —
"What do I care!" And —
When he'd leave for his morning stroll,
(Never leaving word of his return) I'd scowl.
And if I'd see him with another mate,
(Who seems to have more of his attention than I)
My scowl would come again. With — "What do I care!"

But, on his return for a kiss and a hello,
(As often they do) to his impatient "meow,"
I'd smile and laugh and sing, "What do I care?"
"I care."
So goes my sunlight of yellow and brown.

Rogerleen Wiggins

WINDY CITY BLUES

As you wander quietly along the shore,
I will find you.
And, like the wind that slips
the clouds above the waves,
I will caress you.
Then, having touched you with a tender chill,
I will warm you —
Like the sun when it gently
kisses your shoulders.
And, when I have presumed to be
someone your heart is fond of,
I will leave you —
Because, like the wind and the sun,
I will touch you but never hold you.

David Anthony

NEW YORK WALKER

The subways, buses, ferries, too,
disgorge their human cargo onto
dirty, filthy, littered sidewalks;
as the mass moves, nobody talks.
Light on the balls of their feet
they plunge ahead, even in sleet,
with their eyes in forward fix
trying to avoid a traumatic mix
with blankets full of many books
and junk; deflecting dirty looks.

The leisure stroller now becomes
an obstacle in the commuter's path;
as the visitor his camera lifts,
and thru the merchandise he sifts.
Strolling moms with babes in tow,
homeless people who move so slow,
don't help the walker in his plight,
divert his thought, blurs his sight;
and as he ''cops an attitude''
the walker now becomes quite rude.

P. G. Colon, Jr.

HEAR O ISRAEL

The Lord our God is only One,
and it is He who from the start
called on Abram to be set apart;
that thru this Jew He would show
His purest love, to make us glow.

In the beginning it was Elohim
calling upon His Son and Spirit
to save man as He would will it;
demonstrating His sweet salvation
which He conceived before creation.

Don't be deceived. Messiah is
who He says He is, and total man,
who took the stripes to understand
why Abba Father with such concern
did not allow the lot to burn.

Hear O Israel, once again —
Seek your heart as angels sing
a glorious chorus to Messiah King
who'll come again in all His glory
to put an end to this great story.

P. G. Colon, Jr.

QUEST IN SPACE

(1-28-86)

Ages past in Shinar's plain
a man reached to the skies;
today the quest is on again,
the Challenger's crew dies.

Orange-white in azure sky
the blast of fire confounded
as I watched the heroes die,
no hope left. Astounded!

There is One, who long ago
had set His own parameter
on how a man should come and go
without the use of an altimeter.

So if to heaven you would look,
do it with your eyes wide open.
For in the volume of the Book
it says — Knock and He will open.

P. G. Colon, Jr.

YOU ARE LOVE

You
    Give me
    Immeasurable freedom
    To spread my wings
    And try to fly,
    To attempt to find
        Who I really am.

You
    Are always there
    In the background
    Quietly supportive,
    Urging me on
    To achieve that which
        I think impossible.

You
    Make me possible
    By being here,
    Caring,
    Watching and waiting,
    Ready to catch me
        Should I fall.

You are Love.

Carol Lee Witsoe

THANK YOU FOR BEING MY FRIEND

Thank you for being my friend:
For the coffee and conversation
Through the long nights
Until the rest of the world arises,
Because I need to talk;
For the shoulder you willingly give,
Ever strong enough to bear my sorrows,
Always ready to pillow my head;
For your hand, larger and stronger,
Clasping mine when most needed
Saying, better than words, that you care;
For your smile to brighten my days;
For remembering to call,
To take the time to share
Part of your day with me;
For feeding me when I'm hungry,
Warming me when I'm cold;
For being my friend
Before you are my lover,
Thank you.

Carol Lee Witsoe

MY APRIL LOVE

Whose hair is as black as the night

Whose eyes are as blue as the heavenly sky

Whose lips are as red as a summer rose

That has the kiss of the morning dew

Whose smile is the smile of the risen sun

Whose tears are the tears of the falling rain
Of an April shower

Yes   That's my love   My April love

Raymond N. Chaput, Jr.

RAYMOND N. CHAPUT, JR. Pen Name: Captain of the World; Born: Willimantic, 11-7-41; Education: Windham Tech; Served in the Navy; Occupation: Housekeeping for the University of Connecticut; Awards: Silver Award, Golden Poet, Honorable Mention; Poetry: 'Captain of the World,' 'Just a Stranger Passing Thru the Town I Used To Know,' 'Love Me The Week Thru,' 'Pretty Little Girl,' 'Fly Butterfly Fly'; Themes: *Love, nature, travel.* Comments: *I have been writing since grammar school. 1 received awards in Orlando, Florida and Las Vegas.*

LIFE DEALT THE HAND

Once I was young and swift of feet;
    Meeting each day with great anticipation.
But lo — the passing years did take their toll,
    And yet, I am not old, but life has dealt
A hand to me — that I can't understand.

One day, I walked — with pride and head held high.
    The next, I changed — forever though it seems.
A body broken, and a mind yet strong;
    Demanding a response
My body can no longer give.

But wait! That accident was not a curse!
    For better body broken — than the mind.
Time now, to comprehend, and see and feel
    A side of life, I would have never known,
Had I not played — this hand life dealt to me.

Now I can treasure — the passing of each season:
    Noting how life awakens every Spring;
Enjoying Summer's warmth — filled with its lazy days
    'Fore Autumn marks a changing of the seasons
And Winter comes filled with nature's dormant ways.

Now boldly, I look forward to each springtime;
    Enjoying — every bit of life I see.
For I've found that my life also
    Is in part a season — a season in —
The hand life dealt to me.

Norma Russell

FADED FLOWERS

The weeds had grown, entangling the time-ravaged headstone.
Slowly, battling thorns which tore at her dress of lace,

She made her way to it, her clouded eyes seeing it
  more dimly this time.
The warm sun shone brightly upon her weathered face and,

With much difficulty, she stooped to a troubled posture,
Her gnarled hands tugging the weeds from his name.

"Hello, my dear," she said. "I'm here."
The country lane she had often walked to reach his final place

Had long since become a journey, and her frail old body
  felt the strain.
"Remember these?" she asked, smiling down
  at the tattered silk roses she held.

"From the parlor table, in that old jar?
I couldn't leave them, so, here we are."

Seated among the weeds, her head resting on his stone,
She lightly brushed his name with one hand and,

Too tired to stand, breathed a peaceful sigh,
Clutching the faded flowers in her other hand

      Forever.

Gayle Crowder

WHEN LIGHTS GO OUT

A light went out tonight — the world is darker.
  There is no way to fill its absent glow.
There are no candles to replace its brilliance,
  That we for years have loved and come to know.

Yet from this light, were other small lights kindled.
  The flame goes on — though not as bright and clear.
But each new light is filled with the potential,
  To brighter shine throughout each passing year.

Now each new light, must shine its very brightest
  And grow to kindle, new smaller lights some day.
This then, will cover darkness and its sorrow,
  Whenever lights go out — and pass away.

Norma Russell

NORMA JEAN RUSSELL. Born: Pella, Iowa, 4-7-36; Married: Carl D. Russell, 4-7-52; Education: William Penn College, Oskaloosa, Iowa; Currently studying with The Institute of Children's Literature; Memberships: Society of Children's Book Writers (SCBW); Poetry: 'Silver Love,' *Hearts on Fire*, 11-87; 'My Friend,' *American Poetry Anthology*, 1986; 'Just Yesterday,' *Impressions*, 1986; 'Only Hope,' 'Winter Birds,' *New Voices in American Poetry*, 11-87; Comments: *My poetry expresses the emotions that I feel, the beauty and humor I see, and memories. A poem I wrote, 'I Write Poems,' will be published soon. It explains why I write poems. My poetry is written in long hand on scraps of paper. I write anytime and anywhere when I'm inspired, and by request.*

SUMMER NOCTURNE

Clothed in the soft velvet of the night,
she walks tenderly among the dark petals,
knowing so well the painful burden
they must bear on her passing.
She soothes them with the warmth of her life,
and they thank her, cooling the flame
that does not burn her fragrance.

Nearby, with only the leaves breaking his meditation,
he awaits impatiently her coming, lost
in the mysteries of solitude and time.
Her steps echo above the groans that make
the trees aware of their existence.
He rises, eager to unite being and emptiness,
fearful of orange blossoms and violets.

Their mutual salutation calms the garden's stirrings.
Embraces substantiate Nature's victory over Chaos.

Charles L. Kargleder

TIM

I have a ray of sunshine,
With eyes of blue and shiny hair.
To quote a song, he is so fine,
To me, a breath of fresh air.

The clouds may darken,
I may tremble in fear,
But to love's call I will harken,
My ray of sunshine is here.

Elizabeth Waldrip

EMPTY ARMS

Empty arms
Hold your memory in a mind
Where heartache lives.
All I can see
Are dreams
Where I thought we lived;
Reality, where fantasy
Is another word for life . . .
My eyes cry
To know
You can't ever love me
And I can never love you.
And all my hopes
For a life together
Are wasted on white walls
Empty of breath
Where color is not known.
And death is as empty as life.
One becomes the other.
No line. No definition. No life.

William A. Appleby

THE TWILIGHT SLEEP

Moons of winter, I lie and watch,
Evanesce o'er boundless skies.
Snows of décembre enshroud my flesh,
and cling to wherever I lie.

A crystal surge of water, washes away,
Those snows that cloak my breast.
Immured by darkness, I sleep in twilight,
My soul is flame, my soul is dust,
one flicker burning into dusk, at twilight . . .

As shade glides along the blue water,
I embrace a reflection of the moon,
And tears stain my naked face,
like the dawn metamorphose upon the dew.

Moons of winter, sweet as silence,
With a passion of being alive.
I lay my flesh on fading flowers,
beneath an infinite sky . . .

Melody Catherine Jonet

MY FAITH IN GOD

At times the clouds had seemed dreary
And hanging over me;
I cried to God for mercy
He has surely set me free.

My burdens were very heavy
It was too much to bear,
But I was never weary
I had left them in God's care.

I was despised and forsaken
Just didn't know what to do;
I looked to God in Heaven
He has safely brought me through.

I love my dear Lord sincerely
I'll always follow him.
He healed my broken body
When life's light was growing dim.

My faith in God was the answer
To all my falling tears,
So he'll be mine forever
And throughout eternal years.

Amy Clamenta Edwards

AMY CLAMENTA EDWARDS. Born: Trinidad, West Indies; Married; Childen: Adeola Hemmingway, Ormiston Edwards; Education: Health Assistant School Certificate; Occupations: Seamstress, Nurse's assistant; Worked at a school for retarded children and at a hospital; Private duties; Awards: for 'My Doll Joan,' 'Trinidad,' 1956; Poetry: 'No Cross, No Crown,' American Poetry Association, 1986; 'A Marriage Wish,' 'Happy Anniversary,' 'My Home Beyond The Starry Sky,' 'Are You Prepared?', 'We'll Miss You Very Much'; Other Writings: "The Happiest Day of My Life," essay; I also write songs; Comments: *I have been writing poems for over thirty years. I am dedicating this poem to my children; it is based on my many heartaches and trials that I have been through in life. I have believed in God throughout my life and my trust and confidence are in Him. I encourage my children to keep on trusting in God, he never fails, I love God. I can truly say my faith in God has made a way for me. Thank God, dear reader, put your trust in God, accept him if you haven't. I thank God for this "Godgiven" talent with which I can express myself by writing poems.*

A DREAMER'S CASE
(for green and blue)

While looking at the sky today
    He said "What amazing blue
There could not be another way
    For any depth to be so true."

While gazing at the grass, said he,
    "Living green — just like the trees
Unmoved, but they're not frozen, see
    They're stretching in the breeze."

Of vegetation, any green thing grows
    Green signifies fertility
And staring at the sky, anyone knows
    That blue implies infinity.

Outstanding are these, blue and green
    They have a right to boast.
And a dreamer has now clearly seen
    Which two colors mean the most.

Yes, and that's his case for green and blue
    Colors, natural and clean,
So how highly rated now, to you
    Are these colors, blue and green?

W. Clark Davis

WHAT YOU ARE (SUSAN)

The clouds high above fight to be the one
That catches your eye through light of the sun
To let you sigh; and all the birds that sing
Hope that your ears hear the music they bring.

People you barely know depend on you
To smile and be nice, like you always do
And to strangers, you're a pleasant surprise;
While in your company, time always flies.

To the entire world, you're a precious gift
Who always finds ways to make spirits lift
The whole earth's lucky, and for the last line
I'm the luckiest; because you are mine.

W. Clark Davis

If we're bound to meet
Let's not say "good-bye"
to each other
but "take care" instead

If we're bound to meet
Let our parting
not become an end
But a beginning of hope
for our next gathering

If we're bound to meet
Then, let's wish:
Our love may grow
friendship everlasting

Marlin Hsu

THE FAN

Complacency:

The blades of the fan flap round and around.
They never get out of their place.
Swirling and swirling and moving the air
They make soft cool waves on my face.

Keeping in own Circle:

The blades of the fan whip firm and firmer.
Strong currents spark flakes in their path
Pushing and pushing and whizzing their force
They scorn all quick change with great wrath.

Fear:

The blades of the fan cut sharp and sharper.
Their mercy is naught if you're near
Slashing and slashing and slicing their foe
They cause hard knife pain in man's sphere.

Monotony:

The blades of the fan turn full and revolve.
Their movements keep up in fine style
Spinning and spinning and whirring all day
They play the same tune all the while.

Acceptance:

The blades of the fan flash swift and swifter.
Their circles cast spells on the room
Twisting and twisting and reeling the mind
They purr a mild sound as they zoom.

Dorothy M. Ainslie

DOROTHY M. AINSLIE. Pen Name: Mae Dorain; Born: Mt. Pleasant, Michigan, 5-11-14; Widow of J. Clayton Ainslie, a graduate engineer of University of Michigan, Phi Beta Kappa; Education: Michigan State Normal, B.S., 1955; Eastern Michigan University, Masters in Education, 1960, Specialist Degree in Arts, 1971; Occupation: Retired Public School Teacher, elementary education, 32 years; Memberships: M.E.A.; N.E.A.; Michigan Association of the Professions; University of Michigan Alumnae; Family: Mother of 2 daughters, Barbara Kinne and Virgina Oldt, and 2 sons, Richard Ainslie and Alton Ainslie; Poetry: 'To Share A Moment,' *Community Anthology,* Monroe County Library, 1987; 'Tragedy, Reacting To,' *Words of Praise,* 1986; 'Creativeness,' American Poetry Association; Other Writings: Social study units on geography, *Instructor Magazine;* ''AIDS, It's a Problem For Everyone,'' article, *Monroe Evening News,* 1987; Themes: *My poetic lines are snapshots focused on the world around me . . . pictures of things for real as they affect my writer person's thoughts and emotions. I receive inspiration from the lives, prayers, and works of others and am moved to share my joys and sorrows. Poetry is expression of relationships.*

Things suffer when they are not in their places:

consider the Currier and Ives dishes (A&P 1961)
how they strain
toward their first shelf
on the screened porch overlooking the white plum;
and the blue willowware tureen
leaning
toward mother's cupboard
the blue
yearning beyond its lines
the paired birds
craning above the perfect bridge;
think of the bittersweet
reaching
beyond its vase
stretching South
to the forest and the Shawnee hand —

think of things gone;
consider mother, then,
and the Shawnee
and the old white plum:

how grass pushes, always, through the ground

how words
will agonize to poems.

Jean Holmes Wilson

MEMORIAL DAY

On Memorial Day, the country remembers
  The fallen heroes who died
    That the country know
A new birth of freedom.

They gave up their rights,
  To serve in the regimented forces.
    Discipline, army rules,
Automatons, obeying a machine.

When this country remembers
  The many wars that made
    This country the great land,
We are thankful for their bravery and fortitude.

Why do men fight?
  To preserve their sacred liberty.
    America would not be free,
If heroes did not protect their country.

Every war is a capitalist war,
Fought by finance for profits.
  The war against Communism,
Is a struggle between slavery and freedom.

When the war was over,
  The Cold war began.
    Russia was trying to conquer,
U.S. always defends itself against Russia.

E. Saltz

412

I'D FLY

If I were a bird
I'd fly away from here
I'd fly to someplace far

far, far away

I'd fly forever
I'd be free

I'd be free from the hassles of people,
from the problems of life,
from the competition of friends
from anything that came my way.

If I were a bird
I'd be beautiful to everybody
My voice would not be off-tune
My feather, a gorgeous glossy color.

I'd fly over the rolling hills
The wind over the plateau would
Try and keep me back
But I'd be free.

Royale Martin

AN AUTUMN'S EVE

Early lamps, a quiet darkness
Exalted calm awaits
A white dusk of new winter.

Days of husked shadows and
Warm golden winds
Trees that shudder and sigh
Too soon unclad of finery
Forgiving summer's sad good-bye.

Lost are the echoes of summer's glee
Stilled mild schoolyard boasts
Bells that scold ring timely and old
Oh, yearn for those past lazy days.

Firelight, lamplight, hearty tasks ahead
Voices mellowed, footsteps hastened
A tart breeze in the night has left its name
Glazed in frost on the window pane.

'Tis said there's a place where winter hides
Where only sun and sand abound
To dream of such at times you do
When winter on her painterly quest has
Touched the vale with splendor.

To see the harvest fields crisp with dew
To feel the bristle and thrill, I must
For all would be missed on this,
an autumn's eve.

Betty B. Jones

THE BUTTON BOX

An odd treasure, this little button box
Here's one I see, an eagle in a pine tree
All silver and nice
Lost from a woolen vest belonging to
  Mr. Bryce.

Now this one covered in amber velvet
With lace around its edge
Graced Grandma's fine evening cape
Worn when the opera once played
In a frontier town where she long ago stayed.

This one I must study awhile
Its history is secreted with a smile
A little mustached stick-man
Is painted in a half-dollar-size round
Could it be a portrait all wise, or
Some little comical disguise?

A pearl and onyx one catches my eye
This must have belonged to the town jeweler,
Hiram Avery Dye. He in his finery left town
Owing debts, but he was mayor once
When he owned the winery.

Single buttons, lost, tossed in a faded old box
Once sewn with pride, worn in vain stride
So close the lid and put them away
Until history may fasten them on another day.

Betty B. Jones

BETTY BOELLNER JONES. Pen Names: Brittany James, Lynna Lawton; Born: Roswell, New Mexico; Married: Art Jones; Education: Attended University of Texas; Occupations: Novelist; Bestselling author of *Under Crimson Sails, Glory's Mistress;* Poets: 'A Hero He Was Called,' *American Poetry Anthology, Vol. III,* 1986; 'The Last War,' *Best New Poetry of 1986*; 'East Farm In Kansas,' 'The Movie Star I Was,' 'The Old Lady Walking Her Dog,' all *American Poetry Anthology, Vol. IV,* 1987; Comments: *People's reactions to your poetry are often very surprising: they read it, then look at you asking "Can this be the same person I know?" In the search for versatility with new themes, the creative options are endless when writing poetry. The past, the future, the present all meet on a common ground of inspiration. When asked where the themes come from, I can only reply, "They are emotions that need to be told in rhyme."*

WISHING ROMANCE

The sun shines bright
rains bring us a fresh
beginning

As day washes into night
your prosperous laugh
ignites feeling

With a life to live
our hearts touch
tension

What lost our motive?
Innocent victims of
other people's passion

April Lee Holguin

A WORLD UNDER PRESSURE

Can it be that science is wrong about gravity
an apple pulled from a tree
when the most logical thing could be
it was pushed as you and me are pushed
to the earth floor below.

When air pressure weighs us down
at night more so than in day
or density keeps us from floating away
like a balloon pushed upward out of sight.

From dawn to dust to dawn
pounds per inch weighs us down
living and dying you and me
glued forever under an atmospheric sea.

Herbert E. Wheeler, Esq.

LOVE AND LIFE

Life and Love are wonderful when they're
going right. Push the scale one way
becoming cold as night

Rain is fa-lling everywhere with
thunder just behind; watching your
creation slowly becoming dust

Started with a fire, now corrected
with a stitch. Who shall tread the
needle — ? . . . the two must make a
wwwishhhh

Create your own vibration, but nurture
every step for Life and Love are wonderful
when they're going right

Clare Sutherland

A MOCKINGBIRD LOVER

My window's the lover of a mockingbird,
Now isn't that the craziest thing, you've ever heard?
But it's as true, as true can be,
A scene so repetitious, that anyone can see!

Reading the paper in bed (as is my way),
I heard a loud *thump!* That made me say *heah!*
A bird had struck my window pane,
And left a nasty poke-berry purple stain.

His plumage was gray (as is usual for his kind),
With a beak long and pointed, and a long behind.
In no time flat, that bird was back,
And disturbed my peace, as I lay in the sack.

Over and over, he flew at my pane!
Sometimes up, then down, then back again.
He'd pause for a rest, then give me that stare,
And soon I realized, he wasn't a pair!

For two weeks now, that romantic bird,
Has assaulted my window, like a stupid nerd.
I suspect his lover is in my cat's stomach deep,
And never again will sing the slightest peep!

Each morning and evening, the mockingbird returns,
Makes love to my window (for which his heart yearns).
Then ruffled, exhausted, and satisfied at last,
He flies off again, to some other task.

Daniel Webster

DANIEL CHARLES WEBSTER. Born: Fort Wayne, Indiana, 10-30-41; Education: Anderson College, B.S., 1964; Ball State University, M.A., History, 1965; M.A., Journalism, 1975; Graduate work at Miami University of Ohio, 1974, and University of Virginia, 1974-75; Ball State University, Ed.D., 1985; Post-doctoral studies, Oxford/Christ Church, 1985, and Harvard, 1986-87 summers; Memberships: A.C.L.U., Sierra Club, P.A.G.E.; Other Writings: ''Taking the Fifth: A Contested Election in 1960,'' doctoral dissertation, 1985; ''From The Mountains To The Sea,'' Tricentennial theme song, 1969-70; ''Keeping Options Open: The 1988 Presidential Contest,'' ''Appointment With Justice,'' newspaper articles, *Harvard Summer Times,* 1986; ''Churchill, Yalta and Potsdam,'' research paper, Oxford/Christ Church, 1985; Themes: *Nature, observations in life, political and social problems, international events.*

THE TRAIN

The train is a wondrous way to travel
you really relax, hardly ever unravel.
The clickity clack of wheels on track
make going pleasant, even coming back!

It takes you to places of happiness, true
so a ride on a train is seldom blue.
It takes you to your destination —
and the scenery is a real fascination.

You pass through towns, hardly on any map,
and in between you can take a short nap.
See cows feeding in pastures green
and other things you may never have seen.

You ride over rivers, shallow and deep,
through valleys, up hills, very steep.
Some bridges and trestles give you a thrill
as you ride the train that whistles, shrill.

A water wheel here, a covered bridge there
and any time you might even see a bear!
Oh yes, a train is a wondrous thing to ride
so please keep them running, for the young to imbibe.

William H. Maclay

THOUGHTS IN AN ANIMAL SHELTER

Looking in vain for my disappeared cat
I pass the cages of woe and anxiety,
the yapping and meowing.
Then, suddenly a roomy cage of bliss and contentment,
a handsome mongrel bitch with long legs! Alone?
No, one sees a little rear-end here, a sucking mouth there,
a mutt with puppies, some five or six.
She is unaware of the terrible danger
of the approach of the repeat of the day of the week
when she was admitted; her threatening extermination.
Shall I adopt them?
What would I do with a bitch
and some five or six pups?
Let this minute isle of joy of life abide
with my hopes, my unaffirmed trust of a rescuer,
let life's flow cling to the last instant of cosmic time.
Motherdog. I failed you
and the Universe will fail me!
You are twice tricked, with the demands of man,
and those of your own mortal nature,
I await my cosmic fate.

George Mueller

WHEN DEPRESSION CALLS

When moments of depression call me,
I tend to hide away and give up on my life for awhile.
It's easy, you just forget about what's good
and let yourself feel lousy and sorry for yourself . . .
I know it well. I sleep, and I think I feel better
momentarily, which I do, but I wake knowing that
decisions must be made. How often we try to hide
from what we cannot see. How often the fear of
a moment can lead to the fear of a lifetime.
Fear lives, but it doesn't have to rule. Enough
about fear . . . we deal with it often enough anyway.

Russell R. Babington

The Light has come
   to take me home
   my time is done.
In my life
   I was happy and sad,
   Gave the best I had,
   I knew my time was here
before the ambulance had cleared;
The light's a bit brighter,
   I've got to leave now.
         But,
   we'll be together
      at the end of your rainbow
      as you seek your destiny.
Hurry now and wait for me.

Rita Lawler

A POLAROID OF YOUR FACE

the first time i met you
i was fascinated
by your face
you were so young
and so filled with life
you talked of your girlfriend
who had gone to new york
or was it l.a.?

you spoke of the two chicks
living with you now
how could one person be so loved
and others be so alone?
i needed you
couldn't you see?

you rapped about reincarnation
and read books on acupuncture and Kung Fu
you were into macrobiotics
and talked about exotic roots from Nam
you listened to the Moody Blues and
celebrated life with picnics and wine

i should have known
we never could be
we were light years apart
couldn't i see?

Virginia P. Bradbury

THE RIVER

Colorful lights shimmering on the river
Reflecting the city at night.

Moonlight shining on the water
Making a picturesque sight.

The river is beautifully crystal clear
The current is mighty and swift.

Looking at the river's beauty
Gives the innermost self a lift.

The city's reflections dancing on the river
Having a marvelous time.

The river knows all the city's secrets
And forever the two shall entwine.

Minnie R. MacDonald

THERE'S JUST SO MUCH

There's just so much one's heart
can take,
before my God, one's heart will
break.
And these wilted humans in your hands
will cry —
And cry —
Then make their plan
Some will cope, some find the strength,
to live for something worth living for.
Some will cope —
Some discover the darkness —
The darkness eliminates any further problems.

Theresa Guerra

THE OLD HOE

Half-hidden in the molded leaves,
Lay the old rusty hoe;
With many years of rest and ease
From toil of long ago.

I picked it up; it seemed to say,
"Is is already dawn?
I must have overslept today;
We'll catch up 'ere night comes."

It seemed completely unaware
Its master had long since gone —
From fields where together they shared
Their task so very long.

I laid the hoe beneath the tree,
That once was but a shrub,
I left it dreaming so peacefully,
By an old water jug.

The master hoed row after row,
From dawn 'til evening dew.
Yet left the fields so long ago,
When the rusty hoe was new.

Susan Bodenmann

U — TIME

And the Duchess was an ugly beast
and Lewis Carroll was a priest — he
wrote his story in a lonely room
with no woman to caress his . . .

and his real name was Godson and
the girl's Liedell — she was blond
and fresh and open to absorb any
story — his automat would invent —

& the Duchess was short, 2 inches
height couldn't dig her sharp little
chin unto his shoulder — "Put your head on
my . . ." no it wouldn't work — and uuu*five &
seven* took her place —

And the gardeners were laying
on their faces — scared to death
they have made an *error* — planted
a white rose in lieu of red —

Ida Fawers

TWO LOVERS

one can never know if *he* lives
alone — if his house is perfect & his Walls
Collage — if his mouse is perfect — it
needs no Walls or paper cuts — TV screen
will do.

Jacobean chairs or marble stairs
cardboard box or argyle sox and words
to tell a story — a rhyme a song —

to invent a new plot we might
speak about two lovers on a beach
and the sand humid and the sun
sets — the waves foamy — the *wind*
fresh and they are young no more
— and the lonely shore and thanks
for the privilege
            it's worse
to remain only I

Ida Fawers

RETURNING

How
as you reach out and touch the sheet and
how
you pull it over my back and
how you place your hand there then
oh how
I'm taken back to a couple we were
and can no longer be.
How
I curdle and burn and close
my eyes
afraid of yours
and how
I twist inside
tremble in my armour
            my goosebump shield
Stale beer
giggles float past the window
How
God how
I'm lost as you've found
me in your arms again
Hopelessly
lost.

Molly Shallop

RAINSONG UNSUNG

Jello emotions, wriggling.
Escape is not necessary, yet.
Notebook closed, notebook open,
Never dead, only sleeping.
I wore a sundress on a rainy day.
Funny, I felt wrong.
Even the Advil bottle in my purse clattered.
Rhythms based on the clouds.

Hester Prynne felt
Ignominy — I do, too, sometimes.
My eyes turn indigo and I try to hide
Even in my
Sundress, my flowered sundress.

Jennifer Himes

GRANDMA'S NOISY OLD TRAIN

I remember how my grandma looked fifty years ago.
Her head was always wrapped in a towel — turban style.
As I grew older, I started to know
Her anxiety, and why she would seldom smile.

''Hi! Grandma dear — how are you today?''
Then I waited for her reply.
She shouted, ''Hello! Hello! What did you say?''
As the train went rushing by.

Grandma considered her life a real hell.
The constant noise dulled her hearing and brain.
Her tenement house was againt the Third Avenue ell
Where she constantly heard the noise of the train.

Although now Grandma's gone — the Third Avenue ell
        torn down — my memories remain.
In my mind — I can still see her, and hear the rushing
        and roaring of the train.

Peggy Raduziner

TROUBLED PUSSYCAT

What do you think a pussycat thinks
When she is left in the house all alone?
I'm sure mine thinks — ''This place stinks.
I wish I could get out and roam.

''But I can't — so I go from chair to chair
Trying to get comfortable and get some fresh air.
Sitting — I look at the cracked ceiling with a frown
Any minute I bet it's going to fall down.

''Then an idea comes into my head
It might be fun to mess up this uncomfortable bed
So I jumped on the mattress — tore the stuffing out
Was sorry after I did it — she surely should shout.''

To make a long story short — Sherú was right.
I screamed when I went to bed that night.
''Come in here — you blankety-blank knuckle head''
Sadly, slowly, she slinked in joining me in
        this broken bed.

Peggy Raduziner

A NEW DAWN

I watch from afar,
As the sun begins to slowly discard,
Her coat of many colors.
She rises before me in her shining glory,
Making me feel the joy and wonder of being alive!
I know that it is my turn,
To walk away from the darkness,
Of a sorrow that should be long forgotten.
And turn at last;
With a trusting face lifted to the heavens,
So that I too, may be bathed
In the sun's healing colors.
And turn again;
To face the beginning,
Of a new dawn.

Colleen Evans

COLOR OF GLORY

My mind makes memories come to life
Thinking of things that took place years ago
When I did well and knew no strife
And the people I knew were fun to know.

Like my employer who asked me if I'm able
To have dinner with him — a special day.
I still can clearly see the long table
In the dimly lit Greenwich Village Café.

Around the table sat friends who worked with me
With their bright smiling faces and sparkling eyes
Watching to see what the reaction would be
When they raised their voices and shouted ''surprise.''

Surprised — I was — my eyes filled with tears
As they pinned a corsage of flowers on me.
For the pleasure of working 25 years.
They presented me with a watch — a beauty to see.

Then my employer rose to his feet — making a toast
Holding up a glass of red wine — a good speech about me.
But the fact that I'll cherish the most
With that moment of compliment and red wine — the color
        of glory was mine.

Peggy Raduziner

WHAT IS LOVE

Love is the glow that lights the fire of human kindness,
Opens the eyes of selfish blindness
To see values of life that are truer
And lonely hours that are fewer.
Love brings joy unspeakable, fulfillment to life.
It's mightier than riches in everyday strife.
It's elusive as shadows and softer than rain,
The most valuable blessing one ever can gain.
Its growth is tremendous when shared, we are told,
And there's never a market where it can be sold.
Like the air, it is free
For you and for me.
What is the source of true earthly love?
God himself is the answer — in Heaven above.
We take from His fountain, the loss never shows;
Love never lessens, on the contrary, it grows
When shared with a neighbor or with one another
Or given so freely to wife, child or brother.
Twice blessed is the giving when love takes a hand
In the having and sharing throughout the whole land.
Families are closer, divorces are fewer,
Lovers more faithful and marriage vows truer.
We'll have more blessings, be closer to Heaven
When love in our hearts is the softening leven.

Zula Carty

OCTOBER AFTERNOON

Time to rake the leaves
that fall on the lawn,
and wonder where, oh where,
has October gone.

Leaves fly in the air,
fall soft on the ground,
they spin and twirl,
and tease our hound.

Leaves are colorful,
though kind of brittle.
I watch them for hours
while I set and whittle.

I love the leaves
all red, gold and brown.
I'll rake them later,
when I get home from town.

Joyce Dickey

DESPITE THE AGONY

Where have all the people gone,
those who love the world,
they've gone indoors
to live alone,
their welcome mats no longer unfurled.

The willows fall prey to autumn winds,
the rivers overflow,
the heat oppresses,
the cold regresses —
and where do the people go?

I bow my head on a silent night,
praying for my friends,
the sun shines bright
after the moon does at night —
and where does a rainbow end?

Fireside chats on wintry nights,
faces once aglow,
games of chance,
a little romance —
but that was long ago.

Today we all survive,
though the world is a violent place,
but if we can utter "hello!"
to those we don't know,
then it is the *soul* we have come to embrace.

Barbara Lee Rowe

SOMEBODY CRIED

Always has been.
Always will be.
Women of great faith.
Now is our time.
God is blessing us.
No need to weep.
Once we could not.
Now we can.
Faith did it!

Ora M. Johnson

DEATH RIGHTS

The silent scream
A cry unheard.
Another one dead
Without a word.

We watch each day
But turn our back.
A crime's committed
A deadly attack.

We convince ourselves
That it's not wrong.
This world is only
For the strong.

It's murder plain
As we can see.
Why don't we
Face reality.

The time has come
We give a nod.
The life ends
And we've played God.

Stephen T. Gray

AUTUMN

Autumn is more than a stir of air;
Its colorful splendor whispers a prayer;
The rising hills are filled with gold;
There's a mystic song, soft yet bold;
Slowly the green turns to mellow wine;
Aroma fills the air with pine;
The sky so blue, the firs so green . . .
The prettiest picture I've ever seen.

Peggy Van

IN THE BEGINNING;
THEN AGAIN

Water, placid blue,
Trees green and living.
Life dipped in crystal dew,
Mother Nature giving.

Birds singing in then meadow
Animals abound in spring,
Willow trees hanging low
Meadowlarks are singing.
In the valley far below
Church bells, they are ringing.

Crystal waters
Tumble; leap,
Past tree-lined banks
To placid creek.

Life is born
And born again,
Near virgin pond
Untouched by men.

Trees and flowers, water blue;
Singing birds and morning dew,
Sunrise on the meadow grass,
Souls are mirrors of the past.

T. S. Ragan

FINAL PERFORMANCE

The old schoolhouse, we used to go
Sat back on Highway Nine.
A teacher who joined in with us
To have a merry time.
He had a way of teaching
And he didn't use the stick.
It seemed he had a thousand eyes,
He never missed a trick.
Whenever teacher left the room
Then Tom would on his desk
A feat of acrobat perform
With vigor and with zest.
'Til the day that teacher caught him
And he said, "Why, Tom that's great.
Do a hundred more just like that
And I'll take the time to wait."
Then through the air did Tom's legs fly
With vigor much diminished.
His last performance on the desk,
He'd had enough when finished!
Yes, our teacher had an insight
For he taught us all that day,
That it doesn't take a stick to teach
The mice, they shouldn't play!

M. Fauniel DeVries

IN SILENT MOMENTS

Is there sadness in the parting?
We will surely meet again
In some form or shape or manner
At a time, we know not when.

There's a memory in parting
That the years cannot erase.
Did you clasp the hand extended?
Find within your heart this grace?

Go beyond yourself a moment?
See another's point of view?
Feel compassion for a brother,
Or a wrong, did you undo?

Then, no sadness with the parting.
Nothing that you failed to say.
We will meet in silent moments
To recall the yesterday.

M. Fauniel DeVries

THE DREAM

Golden hair and eyes of deepest hue,
A baby's tiny hands I see
Within this dream — my reverie
A life begun anew.

A tremor now I feel
As held within my arms again
A something sweet untouched by sin
Would that this dream be real.

M. Fauniel DeVries

COME ON DOWN

Come on down to San Francisco,
Down where the land lies low.
After the darkness has faded into the light of new day,
View the ever-changing ocean colored red and blue and yellow,
Spreading like a magic carpet over sky and broad Pacific.
See with the eyes of wonder the mists that swirl and rise
Weaving a spell of brief enchantment
Until your heart seems lifted upward
And your day is filled with sunlight.
Or come in the cool of the evening
For rest from the cares you are leaving.
Watch the ever-moving traffic
As it comes and as it goes
On its way to unknown places.
Hurrying travelers seldom see
The dancing sunlight on the water.
They have no time to stop for views
That do no more than charm the eye;
They have no time to think, as they hurry on their way
Across the Bridge of the Golden Gate,
That the miracle of building was made by man
With his tools, his brain and his agile hand.
They have no time to ponder
Who made the man, the sea and the land.

Zula Carty

CHILDHOOD DREAMS

I look outside my window
thinking back to all my childhood dreams
all taken away by life's uncertainties

so many plans, did I have
a good life was mine to be had
a princess I'll be, or maybe a queen
everyone, everywhere, will notice me

But all I am is me

I dreamt of all the worldly places I'd see
The kings and dukes that would sit next to me

But all that would never be

I dreamt of all the riches that would be mine
diamonds and gold would surround my sides

But all this has never happened you see

plush velvets and imported silks
would entangle in my body and soul

but polyesters and cottons, is all it will hold

exquisite perfumes imported from France
would enhance my body and make the men go wild

but cheap colognes is all that I find

you see I am not a rich girl, nor a young girl anymore
and all of my childhood dreams will be gone forevermore

June Drao

GOD, THE DRIFTER AND ME

Why did you turn away that poor drifter on March 1st of 1984?
For he asked you to let him sleep that night in your jail,
 to get out of the cold.
When I heard only one of the four of you say, *Call the Salvation Army
 and see if they have a place for him to stay.* And, *I will drive
 him up to the North County line and another officer can drive
 him the rest of the way.*
When you found they were closed, God and I heard one of you say,
 Just drop him South on the county line.
One more drifter to be dropped on God's county line for that day.
God and I knew what you were thinking — *He is just a drunk and a
 drifter passing through.*
But he is a human being made in God's image like you and me.
I thought, "Why don't they call some organization or some of the
 churches, too?''
Why do we donate money to charities if not to help this man and so
 many others you drop on God's county lines for the day?
Why should you take time out to try to help him and find a place for
 him to stay? For you have nice warm homes to go to and plenty of
 food on the table waiting for you at the end of the day.
As I prayed to protect him along his way and as the tears were flowing
 down my face, I said, ''Why, God, does life have to be this way?
 Why can't they show more compassion and kindness too?''
''My child, you are not supposed to question Me. For I am the judge
 and the jury and they will answer to Me.''
So I pray the next time a drifter passes through and asks for help,
 you remember when you drop him on God's county line —
 God is judge and jury, not you.

Gloria D. Hulse

SILENT STORM PASSED

To J. B. Savage

Violent waves, outbursts that don't last,
learning to sail, not to drown,
grasping at a tenuous saving strand;
getting stronger, no longer sinking down,
a friable human form is developing now.
Calm hangs on Luna Sea as a gown;
only scanty evidence that a silent storm passed.

Hoisting the banner up the mast,
repairing the craft, stem to stern and all around,
preparing to lift anchor and return to solid land
where life remains to be lived, somehow
although there is no hero's welcome waiting to crown
this survivor of Luna Sea's piracy of man,
for no one has taken notice that a silent storm passed.

No one noticed, but one cared
to shine a guiding light and shared
the wisdom of sailors previously ensnared
by Luna Sea's ruinous silent storms past.

Inner turmoil, winds that bare
the soul to forces that fare
on ill fortune and despair;
but one more sailor has survived, the silent storm has passed.

Elizabeth S. Quintana

IMMORTAL DESTINY

Remember —
    Not with sorrow nor with tears.

Unveiled —
    At last, the mystery will be.

Recall —
    But happiness of moments shared.

My Soul
    Takes wings — Immortal Destiny.

Grieve not —
    Because the hour has come.

Death is —
    The Great Beginning not the end.

And Arms —
    Encircle now to lift.

Immortal Life —
    When Soul and Spirit blend.

M. Fauniel DeVries

GOOD-BY

Ofttimes it is left unspoken.
Sometimes said with a drop from the eye.
Whispered word that is made in parting,
'Tis the word that says good-by.

How many times in a lifetime
Are we brought this word to bear?
Why does its shadow linger
O'er cherished moments we share?

When we step from this life to the next one
And the last good-by has been said
God grant that this word is forgotten
That fond greetings be instead.

Greetings then from the many loved ones
Who have walked beyond the bend.
Fond clasp of hearts reunited
In the Land where good-bys end.

M. Fauniel DeVries

PURPLE PEOPLE

If people were purple
And turquoise and green
There would be no division
'Tween what's felt and what's seen.
There would be a revision
In how all would feel —
Blue men and green women
. . . Then children of teal.
And browns would love reds
And blacks would love blues
And Nature would teem
With teams of all hues
And views would be palettes
Of all colors seen —
If people were purple
And turquoise and green.

P. K. Newman

A SOUL BETRAYED

had You told me,
I could have Endured
the Tumultous Sea
of Emotion that inured . . .

but No;
Another broke the news;
Doubling the Woe,
Igniting a Fuse.

A Spark of Betrayal
rose in my Chest;
One did You Fail
when I learned from the Rest.

Dante's Inferno saved
the ninth, and Last
Ring for those who misbehaved
as Traitors in the past.

Joan M. Schumack

AFRAID TO LOVE

we Met, we Talked;
we talked of meeting Again.

we Will; we Won't:
we'll meet Without
a Meeting of the Minds.

we Talk so we won't
Speak our minds.
if we did, we might learn
our Talk is talk.

if I reached a Hand
Would I Reach a hand?
I keep talking.

The Comfort of Ignorance
salves the Uncertain truth.

Joan M. Schumack

A body of flesh,
Disintegrated and
Fallen into dust;

Will its deeds
Remain or its
Spirit in memory?

But after a millennium
The language is foreign,
The sense left obscure.

A spark of wit,
A span of life —
The easiest forgotten —
Has stretched a length.

W. Notta

INSPIRATION

My emotions and thoughts are awakened by
a German prince,
words from my experiences flow like the
river's current.

He caused a new sensation that makes me
feel free,
sending romantic poems to show my gratitude
seems urgent.

Inspirational fire is what he is to me,
the emotions that I speak of in prose
have never been better.

He is the inspiration of my destined
fantasies,

seeming eccentric is not a disguise,
it shows in every letter.

Rosalind Denise Hill

STRENGTH

Embarking on a desolate, sombering
new experience,
I find myself, not yet there, but
in the mist of being there, stopping
for one moment, hesitating, perhaps
the fear of not knowing what the end
of this road might bring.
Chanting to myself, reassuring myself,
that solitude can bring strength, to
one's own existence, fear then shall
not harass me, my conscience guides me
to move on.
Experience can only be a tool to wisdom,
and faith will bring me closer to the
crossroads of my life.

Susan M. Poor

I'LL BE THERE

A Special Friend

Friendship is the most beautiful thing
  that anyone can share
And it helps to know deep down inside
  that someone really cares.

There are rough times in everyone's life
  that friends can help you though
And just remember, I'll be there
  if you need a friend to talk to.

So take it slow, things will work out
  life will go on, you will see
And just remember, if you ever feel down
  the special friend in me.

Joseph M. Archie, Jr.

LITTLE FALLS.

MASTER PLAN

I possess an ageless soul,
Living through immeasurable time;
Ancient before the fossilizing coals,
In my search for life's rhyme.

I have had many forms as I passed,
Living and dying, through time.
Each more complete than the last,
In my search for the sublime.

Many spokes radiates the wheel of life,
A constant spinning, never ending;
Some enriching, some too filled with strife,
But each existence, however spent, is mending.

Tomorrow's tomorrow, I will be ready,
To accept the Master Plan achieved;
When destiny holds my spirit steady,
The Universe my perfected soul will receive.

This spiritual play, I repeat, a must,
Enacted until I have attained perfection.
In this I have placed my trust,
Awaiting, planning the final resurrection.

Kathleen Hendricks

DOORWAYS

Doorways to and from.
Into,
Out of dimensions.

Doorways wide or narrow
or arched.
Who makes them so?

Why?
Curiosity? Prying?
Change?

Through doorways.
Forward!
Never back!

Beverly A. Tadlock

TOGETHERNESS

I give to you this red rose,
To let you know my love grows,
I think of you when I'm alone,
I feel so lonely when you're gone.

When you return I'm filled with joy,
Like a child with a beautiful toy.
You make my heart skip a beat,
Every time we chance to meet.

I need your love, both day and night,
In early morning and at midnight.
As we sit before the fire,
My heart's filled with desire.

As you take me in your arms,
I feel safe from all harm.
And I slowly kiss your lips,
Then touch your face with my fingertips.

Clara L. Waller

CORINA MAE

A babe with slanted grin and button eyes,
Quiet, yet happy, but oh . . . so shy!
Hardly a problem did she ever give,
A sweeter baby never did live.

Older she became and grew into a girl,
Long flaxen hair barren of curls.
Wreaked with pain and personal strife,
She fought for happiness in her life.

Seven brothers and sisters took up my time,
While she so patiently waited in line.
Inside her I knew a war was going on,
I tried to reach her but time was gone.

Hardly naughty or so it seemed,
Even way up through her teens.
But, when she was I was severe,
I worried naught; she'd persevere.

Corina has grown into a lovely woman now,
She warms my heart and I feel so proud.
There's nothing left I can say or do,
Except these three words, "I love you."

Misty J. Ford

INDIAN BOY

Indian Boy, young yet old;
Recalling all the stories told
By Chiefs and parents, of days gone by.
Indian Boy, if you feel sad, cry.

Alone in the place you built long ago,
By the creek, in your hollow tree.
Not quite grown, yet not a child;
Grow up wild and free.

If freedom of spirit is all you have,
Then treasure it for all time.
I love you dearly, Indian Boy,
And in my heart, you're mine.

Jonni Long

I sit here wondering why we fight.
And I can't seem to think of a reason.
Could it be I'm afraid of what I feel?
Afraid of letting it show?
Afraid of waking up alone?
Afraid of hurting once again?
We've been through some tough times.
We've shared joys and sorrows.
We've been friends and lovers.
You are such a gentle, loving person.
One that I'm not afraid to love . . .
Just afraid to lose.

Ann Nestor-Hubert

STEEL

Steel once mirror shiny
Dulled red by blood
One man
One train
One siren scream

Protest now legless
cry muted in waste
Soundless
who listens
to martyrs?

wars run for profit
dream fueled by cocaine
O Jacob,
Where are
your tents?

Mortgaged for gold
power brokered in Trust
All Time
running out
On computer

And the little boy plays
in the mud building castles
And the little girl
laughs at
the splash!

Mary Ann Schacht

LIFE

I placed a precious shell to my ear
Its life not spent, echoes I hear
A roaring ocean with waves and foam
Undertows, billows on which man can roam
Over the water, through the storms
Peacefully the waters subside and you're home
Outward in life, dubious the squalls
Homeward at last, new life befalls.

I listen again to the call of the sea
In this tiny shell, as I clutch it to me
The tide took it out, the same brought it in
For the teachings in life, God has for His kin.

Christine Burkhalter Wilson

BEAUTY

There is beauty in a flower
There is hope within the seed
There is beauty in God's bosom
Which can fill our every need
There is beauty in a baby's face
In its body, feet and hands
There is beauty, honor, grace
Nourished by the land
There's beauty in trees, the birds
Build silently their nests
As trees sway, songs unheard
Come sweetly from their breast
There is beauty for all eyes behold
Thoughts of beauty, yet untold
Behold, beauty, from God the beautiful.

Christine Burkhalter Wilson

TO MY DADDY

Where were you Daddy when I needed you?
Probably in a bar getting drunk . . .
One day in December I felt a need to know you . . .
I felt it so strong that I ran away and hurt the
ones who truly love me . . .
I regret doing that now, *no* memory of you was
better than *mine* of you . . .
You see, I had this picture of you, Daddy,
so full of life and love,
and you would understand me so much better than Mom . . .
Then I learned the hard way, your life was at its end —
you might as well be dead . . .
you didn't know what love was!
To you it was just a word.
I can't imagine, love being just a word to anyone . . .
To top it all off, the only thing you understood was a bottle . . .
You weren't there for you, Daddy,
but *I'll* be there for you — because I love you . . .

Magadaline Ruth McCart

DAY'S END ON THE DESERT

Where desert hills burned brightly a short while ago
Charred shadows are now graciously cooling.
Where hot sands flamed in brilliant sun,
Brown ashes drift 'round the ground, swirling.

Yet in the sky's great copper kettle,
The sunset brightly boils beneath.
And a tired cowboy lingers to enjoy
The flood of red light seething in the silence.
Until, without a moment's warning,
Beauty spills all over flooding the west
Before it drains away in sudden darkness.

Luci A. Yeager

A BRIDE'S PROMISE

On this day I offer you myself:

I place my hand in yours,
  to walk by your side all of my life.
I place my heart with yours,
  to keep it safe from harm.
I place my dreams with yours,
  to share them, and build them, together.

On this day I give to you
  my solemn promise:
That I will treat you only
  with gentleness and understanding,
  with patience, and with love.
That I will always court you,
And consider your needs important.
And I promise that I will always be faithful,
  to you, and to our love.

  This day I ask of you:

To remind me
  of the promises I've made.
To be patient with my weaknesses,
And to forgive my failings.

  From this beginning
  May we grow together,
  And may our love be
  As the Single Rose.

JoAn A. Lee

SHADOW OF A MAN

As I wonder through days bringing to us the sun's rays
The nights, when my soul really fights
Who I am . . . I know my name
From the Lord I have come
My days, full of madness and ecstasy, the eyes pouring
through my fingers, the power to destroy
lying always within my churning heart
Who I am . . . the faces, the places
Going and walking and talking
As I wonder, the times, the joys, and the smiles.

If I could hold my entire life in the bottom of the cup
of my hand, who could I say I am
If I could walk one hundred miles a day and see
the children at play, what could I say
If I could sit by a brook and watch the tiny splashes
the little birds flitting gently among the trees
with the bees
If I could see from the highest mountain peak
christened with snow as to where I should go
If I could walk by a fawn in the forest
and sit by a summer soft daisy
then I could say
I am Me
and this is the way.

Russell R. Babington

RUSSELL ROSS BABINGTON. Born: Bristol, Pennsylvania, 4-1-61; Education: James Madison University, Physics major; George Mason University, B.A., Speech communication, 1984; Occupation: Bookseller; Memberships: Co-Ed Sports, Inc.; Poetry: 'The Life-Giver,' *American Poetry Anthology,* 1986; 'The Word Is Yours,' *Phoebe,* 1983; Comments: *I am convinced that there can never be a padlock on man's imagination. Artists should strive to let creativity spring forth and soak the soil with the richness of wonder. We should always be moving forward to open wide the doors of the unknown.*

FRIENDSHIP

I am intrigued by seers of ancient days
riddled with words/out looking for tyrants
On a long journey thrilled with — controlling fear
always unaccompanied I was deserted
hunted down by desolation
on pitiless landscapes
I'd forgotten — what is a wasted life?
Caught in suffering broken in mind
believing only what chaos chosen worshiped
I no longer pondered time and means
I learned hounded on stage —
avoid working madness in forlorn ways
hold forever your life with honest friendship

William Dudley

NIGHT WATCH

In the long and listless night
As the fry-fly takes its flight
Came a looming avalanche of thought
As tree boughs break, their battle fought
Through rain and storm though tempest tossed
Fall to the earth, their fate not lost
Back to the earth, steeped deep in the sod
As does our soul, when returned to God.

Christine Burkhalter Wilson

CHRISTINE BURKHALTER WILSON. Born: Akron, Ohio, 4-7-24; Education: North Georgia Business College, Rome, Georgia, 1945; Kree Institute of Electrolysis, New York, New York, 1971; Occupation: Retired electrologist, Companion, Aide; Memberships: Christian Business and Professional Women's Club, Past President, Gamma Eta Beta Sigma Phi; Charter Member Zi Omega, Exemplar; Comments: *I have completed a book of personal prayers and poetry, and I am currently working on a collection of music and lyrics.*

LOST AT SEA

Adolph Robinson James

My brother was lost at sea,
He loved to fish for salmon in Puget Sound,
In the bay, just past Seattle,
He would take his black dog with him,
They would go adventuring in his boat,
Then he would bear back the treasure
Of pink and silver fish galore,
And have them canned to bring
Proudly, to the other brother and I,
"Curley," they called him, and
"That blue-eyed Indian."
They found him, drowned, on the shore,
And his ring identified him —
He was my baby brother
Grown into a caring man,
I will be lonely for his laugh,
And keep the memory of his smile.

Ola Margaret James

THE ONE-THOUGHT WORK

We say we do this and that,
But we do not do as we say.
To do what we say,
Is to do the One-Thought-Work
Which builds the Human Thought-Structure,
Which is one for all, and
Which can never vary from person to person.

Doing the One-Thought-Work
Is working out a thought of one's choice
Into other thoughts,
While doing all that we do.
Doing this Work on one's own
Is not impossible to any of us
For we think that we think.

Any everyone gets this proof,
Only by doing the Work.
And when one gets it,
Doing the Work
Becomes the mission of his life,
And all the rest,
Accessories.

Ganesh Lotu Bhirud

GANESH LOTU BHIRUD. Born: India, 2-6-24; Married: Girija G. Bhirud, 4-42; Education: University of Poona, Indian, Ph.D., Education, 5-75; Occupations: Teacher, Professor, Principal of college; Awards: Paper on basic concepts in mathematics, published by the Extension Service Department, S.T.T. College, Bombay, 1965; Other Writings: "The Ideal of Education — Spirituality," article; *The Maharashtra Educational Journal*, 9-66; "Permeating The Fulcrum of Knowledge," article, *The Progress of Education*, 11-68; "Education for Life," article, *The Theosophical Light*, 1-72; "Spiritualization Is the Only Panacea for All Evils," article, *The Theosophical Review*, 4-77; Themes: *To ask mankind to do one-thought-work and gets its first-hand knowledge, which is to get the solid proof for goodness and and also the beginning of living good life.*

ONE SONG ENDS, ANOTHER BEGINS

Legends manifest, everyday
Another new song, wants to play
Open your mind, forget your fears
Let rhythm flow, into your ears

Sounds are penetrating, your desire
Burning inside, you feel the fire
Pounding out, what you've hidden away
As you begin, to hear them play

The freedom of sound, can't be ignored
Magic and motions, one accord
Imagination, takes you away
Losing you, in splendid array

Find yourself, as part of a song
Realize now, that's where you belong
Hear the music, of all origins
One song ends, another begins

Rivers of Blues, islands of Rock
Passages, only time can unlock
New Waves of emotion, keep the beat
Fields of Jazz, by every street

What one song forgets, others remind
Some play forever, in your mind
Hear the sound, of fine violins
One song ends, another begins

Paul Anthony

SHADOW DANCING

Now you see them.
Now you don't.
Our transmitters have become one
With pointillism.
Little dots and bleeps and blips
That skip
Along our neural pathways
And come together in wondrous ways.

The image of our presidency
And the Marlboro Man.
The Virgin Mary
And Marilyn Monroe.
Men can get old and wise.
Women lose their virginity and die.
Fish eggs that swim upstream
And fall into the shredder.

We can be reborn in a petrie dish
Nestled in a womb of aga-aga.
How bionic will we be
Before we launch ourselves into infinity?
Mercury has become supreme
Among the gods
As we indiscriminately and speedily
Suck up speed.

Joyce Greer

SUNDANCING

Sun dancing through me, gracefully in my heart
Gliding to the top.
Spirit of peace and joy my eyes see water blue.
Sand so deep, reaping a golden tan of delight,
In sun dancing by water blue.
Sun dancing, I love you!
Father moon and stars, forest, echo with laughter.
Yellow butterflies glisten.
Mastering the winds doth blow.
Flying with the wind aglow, turn you around.
Sun dancing! Sun dancing!
May our love open up the "skip"
Letting the angels ride, high, high by stars afar.
Radiant — on wings of a lighted dove.
Green blades of grass better than the mounds of snow.
Bright blue skip with bright sunlight.
Memories greater as we go, flowers blooming along the way —
Brighten my life more each day.
Sun dancing through me, gracefully my heart
Gliding to the top.
Spirit of peace and joy my eyes see water blue.
Sand so deep, reaping a golden tan of delight,
In sun dancing by water blue.
Sun dancing! I love you!

Bonnie Simmons Peter

BONNIE SIMMONS PETER. Born: Pontiac, Michigan, 5-22-44; Occupations: Poet, Songwriter, Author; Memberships: National Association of Unknown Players; Top Records Songwriters Association; Songwriters Club of America; Awards: Golden Poet Awards, 1985-87; 12 Awards of Merit; Poetry: 'Abraham of Love,' *Wide Open Magazine,* 1987, Other Writings: "Shoretta Love A Lovetta," song, Broadway Music Productions, 1987; "Put A Smile Upon Your Make-up," song and video, Magic Key Productions, 1987; *Blue Scarlet,* Carlton Press, Inc., 1986; "Blue Scarlet Came Aive," song, Country Creations, 1986; Themes: *"My Life," Serpents and Strife; I did not become an eternal wife. Exotic branches became lovers dances like the winds above. Lots of bonnies and bows, "I Am That I Am." A basket I covered spirit did hover into energized sparklers of the thought I became. To love and laughter I became wife in the royal journey of life.*

ALISSA AND THE TOOTH FAIRY

I wonder if her name is Ruth?
I mean, the fairy who came and took my tooth.
I kept it real close, just under my head,
Safely nestled right there between my
        pillow and bed.
Yet, while I was sleeping, somehow in the night
The tooth fairy whisked my tooth clean out of sight!
I woke up to find it gone, leaving no trace —
Instead I found a present there in its place.
Still I think I might have missed my tooth, if
        I hadn't known
That the tooth fairy is just saving it until
        I am grown.

David W. Edwards

ENTRUSTED ONE

With tear-filled eyes of joy
I watch you come into this world,
My ears embrace your cries
That speak of life to come.
In my heart I give thanks to the Giver of life
Who created you,
Entrusted one.

For the first time I touch you,
I hold you close to my breast,
I feel your soft breathing pace my heart's run.
In my heart I give thanks to our Father above
Who breathed life in you,
Entrusted one.

As I gaze in your open eyes
My heart starts to swell
With deeper feelings than any I've known.
My heart fills with love for the Giver of life
Who gave you to me,
Entrusted one.

David W. Edwards

LONELY CONCERT

Your mind revolves around a song
The lyrics, I can't fathom
You hum your tune to yourself
Not sharing your heart's melody

Can't you turn your record off
And think on your own for a moment?
You can live with the gift of the Muses
But don't sell your soul for a song

I have seen a glimpse of you
Crouching in the shadow of your music
You seemed to hold beautiful promise
Before you let your ditty become a dirge

One cannot truly live when alone
Encompassed merely by concertos of
The mind, without a partner
For life's lovely duets

All I ask is that you consider
Opening the doors of your sound stage
To admit at least one other musician
To join in your solo symphony of life

I would be more than happy to
Suggest an accompanist for your heart's songs
Even though your drummer appears to differ from mine,
Couldn't we attempt to harmonize?

Christina Ann Salisbury

THE CALLING

All alone in the station he waited that day
For the train that was coming to take him away.
Though his family and friends had all begged him to stay,
In his heart he knew he had the calling.

So he went to the city to learn how to preach,
From the scholars and elders he learned how to teach.
And then back in his home town the Lord helped him reach
His small church, for that was his calling.

Another man prayed he could know of God's will,
And he saw in a vision a crowd on a hill.
They were listening to God's Word, and eating their fill
Of bread and fish that from heaven came falling.

Now fifty thousand and more in the stands he can see,
While millions more watch 'round the world on T.V.,
And he feeds them their fill of the Truth that sets free.
To the multitudes he has the calling.

I as I listened began to receive
A Word from the Lord that has made me believe
That He has a new plan for man to perceive,
And now many will hear His voice calling,

"Go ye forth to the people, to neighbor and friend,
Let My Spirit flow through you so My Love can mend
All the soul-weary people that unto you I send."
Mighty God! May each one feel this calling!

David W. Edwards

DAVID WAYNE EDWARDS. Born: West Point, New York, 10-25-50; Education: Riverside City College; Occupation: Heavy equipment operator; Memberships: Script Coordinator for the Christian Theatre Group, Corona, California; Poetry: 3 poems, *Hearts on Fire, Vol. IV*; 3 poems, *Poetry of Life*; Comments: *All children are a heritage from God, His gift of life. Seeing through their eyes brings renewed joy to the hearts of those they touch.*

NO TOMORROW

You can laugh at yesterday
but will you laugh when there's no tomorrow?
You turn your back and close your heart
Will it kill to listen?
Aman's dying   Disease unknown
There's starvation — no communication to open minds
  And we lie here
  And breathe the little love we can find
  And now your dream's dying next to mine
My mind's just a memory
  I'm left with open wounds
How can you say the words I love you, too?
Nothing's what it seems to be to closed
minds without a trace of appreciation
  And we lie here
  And breathe the little love we can find
  And now your dream's dying next to mine

Gabrielle Vasquez

I CAN SEE

I can see the things my dad done for me. He made me strong!
Taught me it wasn't right to do wrong.
   He has long since gone, but yet it seems, even now, to me he
sends his guidance in loving star-swept beams.
   By choosing to keep his presence warm and effervescent, as my
choice.
   I imagine, the trailing whispers of his voice.
   Infrequent are those thoughts that once made me cry.
   Replaced now by happier ones; of the kite we tried so hard
to fly.
   I can see the things my dad done for me. And of myself and
he; I am still content and happy.
   Of my Dad, I was so very proud. So to harbor, sadness had
no cloud.

   I will always be happy knowing:
        You loved me Daddy.

Carolyn Baptiste

CAROLYN ANN BAPTISTE. Born: Chattanooga, Tennessee, 12-23-59; Married: Verne A. Baptiste, 6-2-79; Education: Kirkman Technical High School, 1977; Occupation: Supply clerk, aviation support; Poetry: 'Father's Golden Fields,' *American Poetry Anthology*, 1987; Themes: *Friends, family and nature inspire me to write. Writing helps me to fly outside of myself, and become the graceful bird. Special thanks to Alvin S.*

CRISIS

Suffering through so called "junk" barren years
democratic dreams come true
At long last, reached and switched funds
promised land of disaster sold short or created in panic
attractive money and mine
attractive investments spending
falling — making on grams
a money supply catalogue
supply the initial and demand — ease up
great bear and billion and on and on
absolute technology
squeeze out that positive thinking
watching the world unite in crisis
spectators are here aging psychology
living through pain and process

William Dudley

RUINS

ringed by the great souls of philosophy
my obsessionist compassion and soul
— to starve horror/gaunt and craving
I learned how to deal with ruins
spiders from the orchestra hold a towering fascination
we know where they have been
and they are only filling in time
again and again somehow somewhat I progressed from ruins
within a pocket full of hope
I found the echoes that lie — I found the echoes that live
The company of six is reduced by four
In fact these ruins echo a low king high
I'm in love with what I can't see yet
The night oddity of ruins is always dancing
dreaming in future themes of the past
I carry no ruins — I don't lie in dust
diamond stardust or scary station dogs
I'm facing myself in soft repetition
and faith clears echoes of discolored air

William Dudley

HERE ON BORROWED TIME

I have much thanks to offer Thee.
Oh my God, You have let me see
and hear the truth to set me free,
my praise for You shall forever be.

Hallowed by Thy Holy Name,
my gracious God *You* are the same
Jacob's salvation, time and again.
''Our Father . . . '' is whom Jesus proclaimed.

Ya-ha-wa-ha is what some Hebrews say,
and reverence to the name will light Your way.
It can brighten each and every day
especially when You work and play.

Thank You Father for these blessings are mine.
Long before conception, Your continuous line
had been given to me and has kept me fine.
So, I thank You again for my life's borrowed time
          Amen.

M. A. Butcher

MARC ANTHONY BUTCHER. Born: New York, 7-4-50; Education: 12th grade degree; Occupations: Creative thinker, Poet; Poetry: *Before the Divorce, Read This,* Yamoo Publishers, 1984; second printing, 1987; 'Bombs, Bombs and More B.O.M.B.S., Boosting of Military Bs,' poem about children; *American Poetry Anthology,* 1987; Comments: Before the Divorce Read This! *is my first book. I choose to publish, advertise and distribute it myself. It is poetry about relationships with a stress on positive efforts, sharing, forgiving and honesty. The first edition was 3100 softcover copies.*

YOU'RE EVERYTHING TO ME

You're everything to me.
I can go on from one day to the other,
knowing without a shadow of a doubt that we
love each other.
I can be myself and let my feelings out at any time.

Because you're mine,
I can move forward . . .
I can be independent as a modern woman but,
love you as they used to love.
Your arms around me make me one and only;
feeling special . . . as if invincible.
Looking into your eyes I gather the strength
I need for each day.
We are two individuals seeing a miracle of
total joy
together
with each other.

Lemay

ONE DREAM

I had a dream that filled my heart and soul
    With happiness,
But now, it almost feels like my dream is flying away,
    And the worst part about it is that,
        No matter how hard I try to grab it
        And keep it from leaving me,
           It seems as though it just slips
             Through my fingers . . .
                And it's gone.
As I stand there and watch my dream leave me,
    All the joy and happiness seem to drain
    From my body,
        Leaving me empty,
           Hollow and lifeless,
              Like a mannequin in a store window,
                A dummy,
                   A puppet.
It's been said
    That if you don't dream
        You'll go crazy.
If that's true,
    I'm going to go crazy . . .
        Because I have only one dream.

Douglas Beaver

TO EVERY LIFE . . . THESE COLORS

As I walked down those hallways I realized that this
was the final battle for some and a beginning for others.
It was a comforting thought of new life
but on the fifth floor I saw the eyes of death
watching me,
eating alive those people there
waiting and begging for hope long lost.

I had wanted to go alone
so scared I was to show my fears to others,
but how I needed a hand to hold, loving eyes to look into
instead of those looking at me for hope, long look.

The many signs pointing directions to various destinations
seemed to be the only guide for some,
such as me,
lost in the unemotional walls of that sanitary compound.
People walk past you there, looking right at you
but never seeing you, never knowing who you really are
and not caring to either.

How cold that must be for the dying
for those who need love and emotion, beauty and peace
are lost there on the silent walks of the doctor's room.

But with this also comes life,
the colors of pinks and blues, reds and greens,
of flourishing persons who may some day be your friends.

Tina L. Hughes

THE EXAMPLE I SET

This little body that God gave me is what I have to live in as
long as I am alive in this world. A good many things I have already
found out about this body.

I have found out if I keep this body clean it is better for me
in every way. It is better for all whom I may be in contact. If I
study to improve myself, it not only helps me but it also helps
others at the same time.

As I grew into maturity it dawned upon me
that you make disciples as you go. This can be good or bad, depending
on the examples you set.

Any person, blessed with so many of the good things of life,
has by that token a greater responsibility to be a good example.
Because of that and other good and sufficient reasons, you cannot
offer the pattern, pulling away from the mainstream of life.

When any person subverts the natural laws, that is a poor
example. When you submit to bruising your personality to prove some
point, that no longer is at issue, unwittingly maybe, but you
set a very bad example.

You are still in the land of the living.

Wake up and live.

Be a good example.

The Schuchelow Scribe

Robert L. T. Smith

BEWARE

Some conditions encountered in life dictate; Beware:

> *Beware:* Low visibility ahead;
> Bridge is out;
> Cave-in head;
> Men working ahead;
> Oversized load ahead;
> Single lane ahead;
> Deer trail ahead;
> Trucks entering;
> Ice on Bridge;
> Truck stalled on road;
> Accident ahead;

These and other warnings are written and consequently
Save many people from tragedy.
These warnings are timely.
There is an inner ear; listen.
There is an inner eye; visualize.
There is an inner voice; follow.
Beware also that you don't misuse your talents and
opportunities.
Beware that you don't misuse your fellow man.

Robert L. T. Smith

ANCHORED

Life is comparable to a trip — a voyage on waters.
It is like a vessel moving on these waters.
There are times when the waters are quiet and peaceful;
There are times when the waters are stormy, violent and
dangerous.
One cannot leave these waters and return at will.
That is why it is imperative for every vessel to have an
anchor.
The anchor is there for the sole purpose of holding the ship
in position until it is time to sail on.

The larger the vessel, the larger the anchor must be.
There must be sufficient rope to secure the anchor.
On life's journey, storms will rise and rage.
When the condition arises, let down your anchor.
Faith is the anchor, and so is love.
Preparation is the anchor and so is vision.
Courage is the anchor, and so is patience.
"Be ye steadfast, unmovable."

Robert L. T. Smith

WHY AM I SAD?

I have been a girl of a man I used to love
I was made to a woman out of my childhood ways
I learned to love and learned that I'm loved
I got everything — fame, love, and money
> *But, why am I sad?*
I was the spotlight of the town
I was an attraction of beauty
  A girl of passion
> *But, why am I sad?*
Do you want to know my story?
  My loss of dignity?
  My life full of anxiety?
All went like a dust of gold, to a dust of sand
A girl now, a woman before
> *That's what I am . . .*

Maria Loida F. Cruz

SUMMERTIME AGAIN

Eager for another drink
annoyed at Letty's awareness that
I've already had too much
Too proud to sway
and glad for the music
that will help conceal it

A bit embarrassed that
the lights have brightened
I lead the way
uneasily
bumping shoulders with college kids
and swaggering yet mellow fishermen
who seem happy
content

Expected words of gratitude
and goodnights exchange
through a haze . . .

Barely conscious I lie . . .
and wonder . . .
Happiness should be free
maybe it is
but me
I feel like I did
when my glass was empty

Marie G. Hagan

A POEM FOR STEPHEN

Imagine if the stars shined so bright
you could see inside my soul
Would you take advantage of my love
or stay and watch it grow?
Imagine if you held me tight
from the nighttime 'till the day
Would you grow tired of my love
and throw my heart away?
Imagine if we lived through death
'till the beginning of our life
hanging out on clouds,
drifting through the sky.
Imagine if I said
every word you read,
would you believe it's true?
Imagine if I told you
I'm in love with you!

Wendy Kowalsky

THE OLD HOUSE BY THE RAILROAD TRACKS

The old house looked so lonely and forlorn
On some of the windows
The curtains hung half-torn
While the other windows
Were covered with burlap sacks
At the old house
By the railroad tracks
As I passed by the house
I could see
A light shining from a small Christmas tree
The little sign, in front of it read
Happy Christmas to you and me

Rose Mary Gerlach

EXPRESSIONS OF GOD

You are the sunshine,
That shines so bright.
You are the rain,
That brings forth no blight.
You are the wisdom,
Of which you will share.
And the flame of the world,
Which burns everywhere.
You are the desire,
Of what man partakes.
You are the faith,
Of what each man will seek.
You are the freedom,
Of each man's thought.
And you are the life,
Which cannot be bought.
You are the world,
So beautiful to see.
And you are my friend,
So wonderful to me . . .

Debra Crisamore

THE POET

My expression is to paint a picture
With nothing more than words so fair
To give them meaning along with deep feeling
For they were meant for others to share

I feel the words as they flow through me
Although they were a river so deep
I give them life for you to see
And dream on while you sleep

They might contain a busy street
Or perhaps a babbling brook
The sky so blue, a baby so new
Anything seen or read from a book

They'll leave a lasting impression
On whomever that dares to read
I've planted the words in sweet succession
It has more than become my creed

A poem to me, is more than mere words
They have also become a part of me
I am the poet and their creator
Now at last, my words are free . . .

Debra Crisamore

TIMELESS

Let's try to find the point of no
solution, where there is no motion.
A timeless situation, oh Lord I've asked
for too much already. What can I do
this October when the leaves start
falling steadily. When the freeze is
just around the corner. I favor your
point of perception. Lord I feel mine
isn't working. It might not always be
the best thing to do. To stretch the
inner human and find a literary
challenge of becoming a poet in
a world that's only asking for
convenience.

Albert F. Carol III

HERO IN THE AFTERNOON

for John L.

And there you are, a hero —
The third honest man I ever knew.
Sweet mercenary lover to millions of women
   whose men forgot to care.
On-screen, off-screen, what's the difference?
At some point reality breaks through —
   no one plays a part this well.
And there you are, a hero in the afternoon.
Same station, same time
   Is it you
   I've grown to love
Or the man behind the lines?
How could you be so warm
   and not be mine — and not
pass through the camera's eye . . . please,
   stay in character
   let me sing you this love song
         just once
Until we fade
   to the real world
         again.

Suzanne Lamb-Sinkovitz

EARTH FIRE

A physical animal
   lust

Spinning nerves
   'til they
      cease to be

Good for the moment

   Binding the mind
      to void
   no thinking
      possible

Your physical
   Body
   is void
      of energy
By animal lust
      physicalé

Julia C. Gentry

LOVE

Oh to the touch of passion that burns
thy soul with its flame of lust. And I
ask thy heart, is this love?
   Oh to thy lonely soul that
dreams of love but is awakened by its
fear. And I ask thy heart, is love but a dream?
   Oh to the beauty that life for holds
that sends thy soul dancing in the spring?
And I ask thy heart, is love thy nature?
   Oh to thy soul that never questions
love and is baffled by its touch.
And I ask thy soul, is love the sensitivity
   of thy heart?

Alicha Martinez

I can still see the playful look in your eye,
Can still hear your voice, sometimes quiet and shy.
It's hard to believe you aren't here anymore.
The darkness seeps out like the plague from your door.
It cuts like a knife to the heart, to the bone,
But nothing can change it. Yesterday's gone.
The laughter that lifted me up now is still.
The warm hands now echo the tomb's constant chill.
The face full of life now is at rest.
The face that I saw at its worst, at its best.
But all of your spirit can never depart
For you left a part of it deep in my heart.
And there it will live until my life is done,
'Til forever is over, eternity gone.
I'll rejoice in the day when our souls touch again.
Until then I will miss you, my mentor, my friend.

Janet G. Fisher

CARNIVORE

Loneliness comes on midnight wings
To light upon your shoulder
And the hours grow long —
And the night, black
Illuminated only by the white faces of lost loves

The silence of the darkness
Is suddenly shattered
By the tinkling glass of your aloneness
As the distant laughter of yesterday vibrates in your silent soul

How long a night or black an hour
When the heart is only one
And the solitary spirit becomes the prey
Of the great, devouring bird of loneliness

Linda G. Collins

LIBERATED WOMAN

On an unmerry-go-round
Her belly watches moons go down
    and up —
Watches moons, softened with mist,
    emit unearthly tenderness;
    moons abrupt at dusk with quiet fire;
    moons frozen, like cold white porcelain
        in a static winter sky;
    moons that die and leave their rims
        to cradle new moons in.

Moons: young and fragile, adolescent, ripe, grown old.

With a logic, a rhythm of its own
The orb of that desert moon
    (like the makings of her empty womb)
Contracts, expands, withdraws, demands
'Til life is just the awful loony lunar up and down
    and round and round
        of many moons.

Catherine Ashley-Nelson

SLOW DANCING

Time flaked off my wings
like dandruff from an old neglected head.
Only fears were still sharp.
The things that caused tears
were tangled, drifted inside dust-balls in room corners
like pared nail moons
or flat, coarse scabs chipped off half-healed flesh.
I felt stretched, like crusted day-old gauze
over a war wound,
as glass-shattered as a mirage
hovering over a dry, desert road.
Youth's disappointments had bleached my brain like Clorox,
pulsed a sluggish fluid, eggshell colored,
through my veins.
Sins had become soft memories, simple vanities,
and stars were dulled by urban lights, by neon human needs,
while time rusted my joints
and gravity took its toll.

Oh joy! Why does it hide in the golden curl of a maple leaf,
in the folds of a hand-sized seashell?

Catherine Ashley-Nelson

FINALE

When the past lies softly against my ribs,
Its thorny edges smoothed,
When a thousand sunsets flowing through these veins
Have faded from hot vermillion to cool pale pink,
When these eyes that drank in ecstasy the crash and roar
    of all great oceans 'round the world,
        sucked by undertow through sharks' teeth
            to the ruins of Atlantis,
Now must strain, if they even cared,
    to see what floats on the placid breast of a lazy river,
When no gazelle in flight accelerates my pulse,
And no lion waking for the hunt,
When a woman's eyes captured on lonely bush roads
    beneath vases carried on the head
        can bring no pain,
When there's no other Kilimanjaro
    my legs still yearn to climb,
No tropical flower I'd fight the brush
    to whiff and frame on film,
No quivering horseflesh I long to straddle,
When the purest, cleanest blue of dawn's first light,
    even birdsong filled, can't pull me from the bed,
And when I can't remember one night's sleep inside your arms
Then I will look for the pale horse,
And I will kiss stone.

Catherine Ashley-Nelson

I have always wanted to share the happiness of love. But, time will
not allow us, and destiny has had no hand in helping us, we were but
on separate parts of the world, and only love can bring us together.

Painful days I have cried to bring us near, but I can only cry so
many tears.

The silence of being alone without him hurts me so, only a little letter
of love can hold us together.

Some days our dream of holding each other, will come true, and it will
last forever.

Sara Gonzalez

LAST SONG

Earth and wind
    fire and water
Love of life of nature
    of things animate
— waves of sound
    Bring feelings of
new life reborn,
      thru love —
By beings of space;
    Spawned yer-rans
ago — the ones
of platonic caring
   — only they would know
5996 is the year we hunt
    for food in ruins
      of brick and metal

Julia C. Gentry

JULIA CLARA GENTRY. Born: Windsor, On-
tario, ferried to Detroit, Michigan, 1-14-46; Eth-
nicity: W. Itl. O. (White Italian Oriental); Former-
ly married to Julian O. Lennon, and Raymond
Nelson; Education: Wayne State University,
Michigan, Colour design, Fashion illustration,
1963-64; Marine Tech at University of Hawaii,
1976; American Beauty Rose Modeling Etiquette
School, 1965; Occupations: Cost and proofread-
ing accountant; Memberships: I am a solitary per-
son, except for music, Patron of Music, Detroit
Symphony Orchestra; Poetry: 'Age of Julia C.';
Other Writings: "Queen Julia's Light," fiction;
Comments: *My life has been ups and downs, and
waiting. A title from my father, Francis, which I
was dared to use: "Princess of Italy," and my
mother's teaching in my youth of the Moslem and
Hasadanic faiths have always shaped my
thoughts, especially the poem 'Earth Fire.'
Though I contracted diabetes in 1983, I still take
care of myself, and of course I don't smoke or
drink. My children were scattered by my step-
sisters and my husbands. I am an octuplet!*

HI! DAD

When we're young and traveling at top speed
Who bothers a look at the clock with need;

When we are older and traveling afar
No race, no par, and slower at Del Mar,

We heed the face of the clock from afar
We are pendulus now in a chair.

    Ahh!
*What time did you say?
How far . . . You don't say!*

Nini

HARVEST MY LAST TIME

Flowers bloom the warm wind blows
it's springtime once again
time to leave my southern home
make the harvest fields one more time again.

I'll roll my clothes in a bedroll
and I'll sleep out every night
work out in the hot dusty fields
from early morning till late at night.

The hours they're long and the pay is small
and I'll go hungry half the time
wearing clothes from the goodwill store
that I can buy for nickels and dimes.

When harvest time is over
and the fields are brown and bare once again
I'll catch that southern-bound freight train
back to the warm sunny southland.

Jay Donald Foote

PURE AND SWEET AND HOLY

Lord, help us to be
more like Thee,
meek and lowly at heart.
May we live a Life
of Service with Love
To others. Yes, to others,
that even when we
are too busy in our
everyday chores, yet
may we be just like Thee,
always ready to lend
a helping hand,
To those who are
drooping in the Darkness
of Perdition and Destruction.
Yes, Lord, help us to
keep our life Pure,
and Sweet, and Holy,
That we may live
more like Thee.
For Thou wants us
to be a good example
and live the gospel
way of life,
and endure to the end.

Sister Gay G. Cabotaje

THE MASTER ARCHITECT

My life was so sin wrecked,
Until touched by the Master Architect.
He picked up every broken part,
And put in me a brand new heart.
He molded me with gentle hands,
Even in times of reprimands.
And each day He is working still,
To help me do the Father's will.
So now I can hold my head erect,
For I was touched by the Master Architect.

Patricia Lawrence

SO YOUNG AND PRETTY TO BEHOLD

*Heartily dedicated to Edna Facun,
my granddaughter*

She looks like
Sweet sixteen
Never been kissed.
Always a delight
to look at and pretty to behold,
With her sweet smiles
to everyone who comes
in contact with her.
You'll always find her to be a real friend.
Once you gain her
friendship, she will
always be a friend
to all and a lover
to the one and only.
She looks like an angel of light
from above, coming here on earth
to brighten the corner where you are.
Her sweet and smiling face
is enough to enlighten someone
in this lone and dreary world.
She is one out of a million
from among God's chosen children
whose faith and hope and love
are clothed around her
like a rainbow in the sky.

Sister Gay G. Cabotaje

GAY GABBUAT CABOTAJE. Pen Name:
Sister Gay G. Cabotaje; Born: Solano, Nueva
Vizcaya, Philippines, 10-8-08; Married: Dr. Pablo
Viloria Cabotaje, 1939 (deceased); Education:
University of Philippines, Manila, Philosophy,
Ph.B., B.A., Philosophy; Philippine Christian
University, BSE English; Occupation: Retired
high school teacher in English; Poetry: 'Take
Everything To God in Prayer,' *Best New Poets of
1986;* 'In That Beautiful Garden of Prayer,' 'So
Young and Pretty to Behold,' 'Pure and Sweet
and Holy'; 'In God I Trust,' *Poetry of Life;*
'Praises Be To God on High,' *Words of Praise;*
Comments: *I want to share the love of Christ with
everyone who comes along my way by being
loving and forgiving and keeping smiling and
trusting. My poetry conveys my trust and faith in
a loving God and my deep love for my family.
That Jesus never fails and is the same kind and
loving and forgiving being, yesterday and
forever. I always like to praise God from whom
all blessings flow like love, faith and hope — the
greatest of which is love.*

THE WORLD WITHOUT AN INTRUDER

They were born into this world with open hands,
With the hope of a brighter tomorrow to be,
Not knowing what tomorrow has for the adult,
Now, they know themselves as and called the intruders.

The intruder could be the other thing or person,
The married couples tried to prevent them,
Even all creations intentionally try to stay away from,
Their faith is always unpredictable and unbearable.

They look very attractive to all creations,
They always have those broad, smiling faces,
With such looks that would keep the original on the toes,
To always slide the intruder onto the driver's seat.

The intruder does not want to be like it is,
The making of the intruder is not by design,
The making of the intruder is just by accident,
Which nature has caused and created for you and me.

Daso Augustus Abibo

THE GREAT ARTIST

Oh such beauty my eyes behold
As I look out my window on carpets of gold
And see the dew glistening on the spider's web
And the last of the flowers where the hummingbirds fed

The fields are ready for harvest, in the valley below
That will soon be covered with blankets of snow
There is beauty and splendor everywhere to be seen
Even the glistening ice, at the edge of a stream

As I watch the squirrel and chipmunk play
I know that God in His own wonderful way
Gave us all this beauty for our hearts to enjoy
To love and cherish and not to destroy

'Tis wonderful to know, God loves us so much
He gave his only Son to keep in touch
To guide our footsteps and ease our pain
Not to seek wealth, fortune, or fame

With the passing of years my eyes have grown dim
But I still have beautiful visions of Him
Visions of a mansion built high in the sky
Where angels will carry me when I die

Melvina Jordan

TO MY MOTHER

To my sweet mother with lovely gray
A sweet smile and gentle face
She never is angry, she never is blue
She is always kind all year true!

Oh sweet mother you are always in my heart
Across the years you never have gone
Your memories are always alive
In my heart you never have depart!

Sweet mother, when I was a child you guided me by hand
When I was hungry your gave me to eat
When I was thirsty you gave me to drink
Sweet mother I love you, you never have depart!

Martha Wetzel, ASDP,
Irvington, N.J.

A TRIBUTE TO THE ONE I LOVE

I want to feel your arms around me one more time,
I want to feel your heart beat close to mine,
I want to hear you whisper, ''Darlin', I love you.''
Then I'll know that sweet heaven is in view.

I want to feel your fingers through my hair entwined,
I want to feel your lips pressed close to mine,
I want to hear the tender things you used to say,
To do the little things you did in your own way.

I want to hear you answer when I call your name,
Just to let you know, you are there to ease my pain.
I never realized the words ''Till death do us part,''
That you would go first and break my heart.

I must try to grow stronger in your strength,
And do the things that heaven meant,
And we will always remain one and the same,
And I'll try each day to grace your name.

Melvina Jordan

GRAY-HAIRED QUEEN

Cleveland, Ohio my hometown — Lake Erie runs through the
veins of this forest city, gray-haired queen.
    Sweet.
      Mean.
Thought to work-oriented, skyscrapered-size walls built
around her and her money; no fun.
A lover of Academia and art; industrious from the time she
started to run.
With her medical healing prowess in the world among the
number one.
    Ever maturing while retaining spring of a child.
    Sports-minded in nature for all seasons.
    Sense of the wild.
She can be cold hard winter.
But never forgetting to let the sun shine within her.
Rising, spreading her leaves, changing colors, falling after
breathless heated thrusts of shiny, wet, sticky summer.
    Unlikely, in her realm to go hungry, homeless, sick,
    if you can't pay.
    It's not her way.

Castella Perry

LIFE'S GARDEN

Today I try to gather my life as one would flowers.
I have nothing for a centerpiece, no beauty, no rose.
Nothing to put in place or rearrange.
My life is like a decaying rotten barren plot where
A flower garden could have been.
You take good rich soil and burn it out with hate.
You start good strong sturdy roots, and weaken
the strain with poor judgment till it bends and
is crooked and weak.
The flower starts a beautiful thing, the first years
it is a beauty, a pleasure, a garden of life.
But with time, the hardships and lack of love
the roots have nothing to draw life from. The soil
is dead. The plants die, the flowers left
are withered and dry
There is no gathering my flower garden.
My roses are dead dry thorns as the flowers
have long gone, their beauty I cannot see.
The dead weed of life has smothered
the life from me.

Vivian Sprinkles Nyberg

Sitting alone
on the water's edge
I was cold
I built a fire
I sat close to feel the warmth
I smiled as I watched the flames
dance in the cold night air
I moved closer
I could see the sparks flicker and fly away
the heat became intense
the sparks flew into my face
and burned where they hit
I moved away, crying
I hid my face in my hands
the pain went away
but so did the pleasure
I was shivering
so I moved a little closer
I began to smile again
as the familiar flames danced about
but this time I was careful
not to get too close

Sheri Sims Kaddah

The sun set upon the ocean
as if resting from a hard day's work
at first only touching the water
a little
to cool itself
then more and more
the reflection
red, yellow and orange
shone in the water
as the sun immersed itself
in the cool salt water of the ocean
and disappeared
to rest upon the ocean floor
until the morning
when it should return
in all of its glory.

Sheri Sims Kaddah

BEHIND THESE WORDS

A small child smiles sweetly,
and though frailty begets his shortened life,
his strength before the end
spurs the length of every stride
in his brother's flightful run.

A friend's long, last walk
must follow a silent path,
but sad notes echo the loneliness,
and harsh chords the bitterness
in every haunting melody.

Look behind the cloth canvas
on which an artist pretends to paint,
on tainted pages a writer strings his words.
Is passion their motivation,
or darkness their inspiration?

Robert Pignolo

BY OUR HERO'S SONGS

Sway to the cliffs
over and sometimes quite beyond
A beacon
Shines quite bright
Only so long,
As he need be supported
Run, Hide, *Fight!*
 One person's problem
Belongs to everyone.
Push the swing way over the cliff
Beware
Today the rope has grown thin

By whose light can so many sing
the
  same
    song?

Zane P. Bond

ZANE PHILLIP BOND. Pen Name: Zippy Bond; Born: New York City, 2-3-51; Married: Judy Bond, 6-8-85; Education: Alumnist of Dr. Ronald Fieve's New York City clinic for depression; Occupation: Self-employed electronics salesman; Artist; Plus anything that I can make a legal buck on; Awards: Honorary Mention in the *New York Times* for promoting a Dr. King American nickel for public circulation; Comments: *As an artist one of my constant themes is working with the desperate situations that arise in life from time to time. Cupping my hands around the tiny flames of light . . . the essence of my work tells people living horrendous times, surrender it all but defend your last splinters of hope.*

A SPECIAL LOVE

How wonderful it would be
If I could give a "forever" love
To friends constantly!
If I could learn to overlook
Surface failure.
To *discover,* the soul
Beneath . . . "mortal" cover!
If I could relate to each fear —
Understand differences;
Be sympathetic . . . to each tear!
How truly wonderful
It would be!
If I could give a "forever" love,
To friends — as God
So graciously gives to me!

Virginia E. Marx

I FOUND YOU

To Terri

Sometimes you find a friend
who's unlike any you've every known
and you stand in wonder and amazement
at the love they've shown.
They've made you laugh and
cried your tears.
How could a love so new feel
like a million years.
I think I found you
a friend so true
and on the cloudy days
I think of you
cuz you bring the sun
back into view.
Sometimes you find a friend
who's unlike any you've ever found
and when everyone else is gone
they're still around.
They've been there through good and bad
and you know in your heart they're the
best you've had.
And I know I found you
a friend so true.

Tracia Zollman

LIBERTY BELL

Bell, Bell, Liberty Bell
How many men were dead for you
But at the end of the war
All their dreams came true!

Maybe they were looking to the sky
And the clouds seemed dark not blue
But if they can see from heaven now
All their dreams came true!

If they could come back alive
They will be very happy too
Because their precious blood
Made the Liberty come true!

Bell, Bell, Liberty Bell
I am praying to the Lord
That soon you will ring again
For peace in the entire world!

Martha Wetzel, ASDP
Irving, N.J.

DEATH

Lack of light
one last breath.
Dark as night
cold hard death.
Tears of pain
people come.
Outside rain
mournful ones.
Soul has rest
no more sorrow.
Is it best
no tomorrow?

Denise Ketchum

HARVEST

Within which moon was I dwelling,
Breeding my summer silvers.
Gravid by the blue light of the quarter moon,
And reborn as its fullness pronounced?

Of which moon was I breathing out,
To turn over my fields for its seeding.
Enmeshed in the pool of its half-life,
And designed for its full term strongly.

Where did that glistened moon take me
As I ran with the threads of its weave surround me?
Charmed by the beads of its cool whispers
And rocked to the bone by the dawn . . .

Claire Burns Miller

THE SIMPLEST OF FORMS

Fingers arched in labored, piercing pulses,
Through bitter wind and winter's stinging chill,
We curl them deeply down inside our pockets,
Defying Nature's frosty charge and will.

Bravely treading on the snowy carpet,
There is no one peculiar place we seek,
I watch the execution of a snowflake
Electrified by warmth upon your cheek.

Gambling as lovers do together,
Survive we must the enervating cold,
We reminisce in fond hopes of conserving
A cherished vernal equinox grown old.

Touch my hand encircling your fingers,
Entwined as one throughout the winter storm —
Rare indeed, communication lingers,
We revel in the simplest of forms.

Rita Trapani

SNOWFLAKES IN A LANDFILL

For every message peeled and sent from someone's bleeding heart,
The pleas of ten more letters are shredded all apart.
The compositions set upon some napkin with a pen
Are shattered 'til the lull moves in and it begins again.

The poetry is burgeoning from deep inside a mind,
The memories are yearning for some corner they can find.
For every twenty dumpsters, there are thirty garbage pails
Deluged with dispatches, filled with bits of pulpy hail.

The snowflakes in a landfill, scribbled scraps with
    "love" and "please,"
The paper-weight partitions magic-marked "apologies," —
They come in every color, tissue-white and baggy brown,
Repressed, released, rejoiced, renewed, the flakes all tumble down.

Some make it to the addressees, their thoughts are freed within,
Some break or make new lifetimes, some only see the bin.
Next time, alone, you cradle lovesick remnants in a clump,
Take comfort always knowing that it's snowing — in the dump.

Rita Trapani

UNRETOUCHED

Enduring, solitary structure anchored among billowing grasses
Which pivot, green and grey, on bases as they grasp the sand.

The days are mostly overcast —
Showers sometimes delivered, sometimes threatened,
At dark it matters not —
For the galaxy is secure within partitions of decanted stone,
Like an impoverished matron cloaking her only possessions —
The tiny, helpless infants sleep in peace among the folds.

Glowing children fashioned of paper, oils, and wood —
Caught on cloth, suspended in stone — their visages
Conceived by parents who braved sharing their innermost reflections,
Realizing the possibility of tragic consequences —
Or flourishing in the warm current of approval.
No matter — still they lead them to the gallery with
    bright prospects:
Their treasured toddlers, extensions of their hearts.

Rainbows weighted with passion,
Contours molded in enchanting hues —
Blooms which know no dormant season,
Graven horses and mythical beasts champing and throbbing,
Basswood and alabaster progeny gratefully clutched
By some fearful of the slightest human touch;
Faces and longings enmeshed in textile for all time.

Tenderly placed on their pedestals, lovingly touched to the wall,
The created youngsters bubble, delighting the hearts of all —

Childless, others pace the floor, anticipating a chance to adopt.

Rita Trapani

RITA ELIZABETH TRAPANI. Born: Queens, New York, 6-8-48; Married: Girolamo J. Trapani; Education: Herbert H. Lehman College, CUNY, M.F.A. degree; Adelphi University, permanent teacher's license; Occupations: Artist, Art Instructor, Horse-drawn carriage restoration; Memberships: Long Island Poetry Collective; Guild Hall Museum, Long Island; New York State Art Teacher's Association; Long Island Art Teacher's Association; American Driving Society; Carriage Association of America; Paumanok Driving Club of Long Island; Poetry: 'Too Many X's and Not Enough Stars,' 6-87; 'Bingo,' 'The Circular Staircase,' 'For Better or Worse,' all *American Poetry Association*, 1987; 'The Huntsman,' *The Chronicle of the Horse*, 1983; Statement: *My interest in art, metaphysics, and the wonderfully creative ways people relate to each other, as well as love and friendship, provide excellent foundations for my work.*

THE BEAUTY OF THE LORD

I am looking through the window
Contemplating the trees at the fall
On this beautiful country scene.
I saw on the nature the beauty of the Lord!

Lord, as You let me see the fall
You gave me the grace of love
At the day of my departure
I want to be with You, Lord!

You gave me heavens on earth
For I have my dreaming life
I enjoy living in peace and grace
For me always is day, never is night!

There is nothing that disturbs my peace
For I found on You love and comfort
When I say my daily prayers
I feel over me the blessing of the Lord!

Martha Wetzel, ASDP
Irving, N.J.

MARTHA WETZEL. Born: Habana, Cuba; American citizen; Widow; Education: A.S.D.P., graduated 1971; Occupation: Nursing service; Membership: Essex County College Alumni Association; Poetry: 'White City of My Dreams,' 'Liberty Bell,' 'To My Mother,' 'The Beauty of the Lord'; Other Writings: In process, a book based in psychology; Statement: *My poems are clear images of my personality. The book that I intend to publish is based on psychoanalysis. My major is psychology, and I am very interested in psychoanalysis. I love the work of Dr. Sigmund Freud. I have many poems written in English and Spanish.*

ANIMALS

Animals fear.
That's why we can't
communicate.
We're not gods,
not even for them.
They are learning on their level
as we are on ours.
Trying to teach them
is easier
than trying to teach us,
but they have much farther to go.
We're all God's ideas
developing from atom
to protoplasm to fish
to dog to man to stay.

Jeff McElhone

FISH BOWL

Climb inside
Take a ride
Ride around the world

Climb out
Play a tune or two
Back in and away we go; again

Home is a bus
I'm living from a suitcase

Everybody hanging 'round my wagon
Looking for a ride
Wanting everything; giving nothing

Millions screaming, they love me
I've only a met a few

My life's for sale
Can't displease my fans

I'm looking out of the glass
Trying to live a sane life
Everyone watching me
Trapped in this fish bowl of fame

Dennis Mack

LOVE LIGHT

Love light glowing
In eyes overflowing.

Flaming so bright,
Gleaming at night.

Lips, "tasteful" like wine,
Saying, "You are mine."

Touch of your hand,
Sends love's 'demand.'

Love is forgiving,
Makes life worth living.

So — love is the reason,
When "spring" is the season.

Ronald Chatt

THE PARADOX OF THE SHINING LIGHT

It was only neon
But we thought it was saying Jesus.
(Jesus Jesus Jesus Jesus)
It was too bright to see.
We never could tell for sure
Until it burned out.
When our eyes adjusted,
We saw, and buried the thing
ceremoniously.
Come Lord . . .
(jesus jesus jesus jesus)

Beverly J. McAllister

WHITE SNAKE

Sun moon and stars
 N'oblisse obligé obilisk
  Fantasia, en physicalé
Your mind   Your body   Your soul
 Where thee meets
   me
  In astral pleasures
No boundaries
  can hold
Laser stars
  of ecstasy
Tingle along my nerves
  as your fingers
   caress my
  waiting skin
I respond
  with flowers
 of sensational light waves
Two in one
  Liaison of music
  in love
  from sphere to sphere
Electici — my love — *White Snake*

Julia C. Gentry

WISHING INTO REALITY

I want a place to live in,
I want a place to eat in,
I want a place to give in,
I want a place to sleep; and,

I want a place to love in:
'Cause I want to be with you,
And have a place just for two,
Even though two can make two more.

You know what I mean, don't you?
You know what I dream, don't you?
You know I've only one thing on my mind:
Setting up housekeeping with you.

So, go buy me a ring or two,
I'll get some pretty things,
Arrange for a proper place,
For the two of us to be "tied" as mates.

Please, get the right piece of paper,
Have a preacher there on time,
To bless our union and love sublime,
To last unto the end of time.

Va. S. Lewis

NEED FOR HOME

The need for home children on the road. Running scared and running cold having no real home.
Day after day so alone never trusting anyone. Never knowing the need for a home could feel so good until you have none.

Albert F. Carol III

DISTANT VIEW OF ST ALBANS.

BALL I.

HEN I.

BOW & ARROW & LONG POINT

PLATTSBURG FROM CUMBERLAND PT Rd

GREEN Mts FROM PLATTSBURG.

CUMBERLAND BAY.

CUMBERLAND POINT.

LAKE CHAMPLAIN, FROM PLATTSBURG TO ST. ALBANS.

THE SEARCH

Mirrors on a placid sea,
thoughts, reflecting all the past;
solitude, the cure for me,
freedom soul, free at last.

Reasons now, becoming clear,
among the misty web-spun mind;
friends and lovers, held so dear,
friends, not lovers, so hard to find.

So many people among the friends,
sharing much, but none so real;
so many beginnings, so many ends,
to share so much, but never feel.

Looking for love, prepared to hail,
the faulty promises of wedding chimes;
the dismal ache of search and fail,
the lonely reality, of endless times.

Searching and searching, fore and hind,
longing for love, among the Blue;
endless searches, never to find,
never to found . . . 'til there was You.

Glenn T. Fugitt

an old homestead
    in a tangle of cotton —
a thousand shadows

Charles B. Rodning

CHEERS

Cheers to you,
my loving friend.
Cheers to the memories,
that will never end.

Cheers to the times,
that we've shared together.
Cheers to the crisis,
that we couldn't weather.

Cheers to the lessons,
we've both learned.
Cheers to the love and respect,
we've both earned.

Cheers to the understanding,
that we still share.
Cheers to the love,
without physical fare.

Cheers to you,
my special friend.
Cheers to us both,
that we didn't end.

This is my toast,
to you I send;
a poem of gratitude,
for being . . . my Friend.

Glenn T. Fugitt

THE HULL

As the waves come crashing in,
and the fog lays light above;
the Hull, glides safe within,
the next wave's rolling shove.

Awesome, in their tremendous power,
crashing, crushing, thundering in their force;
mighty waves, with an impenetrable shower,
indomitable from their source.

Mothers of a thousand graves,
molders of a million sands;
these, the relentless waves,
infinite, in their span.

Yet the steel Hull glides,
steadfast and cold, distantly drawn;
and with each nomadic stride,
glides through . . . and Beyond.

Glenn T. Fugitt

GLENN TINO FUGITT. Born: Dreux, France, 5-18-59; Single; Education: Licensed vocational nurse, Winetaster EMT; Occupations: L.V.N., Merchant marine, Store manager, U.S. Navy hospital corpsman, 3rd Class; Poetry: 'Cheers,' *American Poetry Anthology, Vol. 7, No. II,* 1987; 'A Lover's Sleep,' *American Poetry Anthology, Vol. 7, No. III,* 1987; 'The Hull,' *American Poetry Anthology, Vol. 7 No. IV,* 1987; 'The Search,' 'Island Love,' *Poetry of Life,* 1987; Comments: *I would like to dedicate this book to my mother, Connie Ruth Fugitt. I want to thank her for all her love, trust, inspiration, and support throughout my lifetime, both as a mother and best friend. To a truly remarkable and beautiful woman who will always remain ''young at heart.'' I love you, Mom!*

OVERDONE

Am I outwitted at my task
    for pleasure.
Poems are love secret mask
    rules measure.
Be myself some thwarted fool
    time challenge.
Early sculptor attend school
    expression revenge.
Have me wisdom original
    kiss perish
Were I outcast fear is final
    none of mercy cherish.

Orien Todd

TO MAGGIE

How beautiful to observe the work of those
who love Christ, the Son, and God, the Father,
As they seek
To help the weak.

Bettye Ellis Owen

BETTYE ELLIS OWEN. Education: Baylor University, B.A., 1935; Graduate credits from SMU and TWE, 1946; Occupations: Teacher, Housekeeper; Memberships: DISD, Retired Teachers' Association; Two book review clubs, Loyal Chapter OES, AARP, Wynnewood Lioness Association; Other Writings: ''Open Windows,'' religious essay, 10-7-87.

A DEER AT DAWN

Unconscious of her matchless grace —
she nimbly bounded past my frame that
    morn —
not twenty feet from where I stood
in open-mouthed amazement —
at this flash of tan and white —
carried on four graceful legs —
across a sun-soaked land —
banked with tapered firs
where she was lost to view
before mind could fully comprehend —
or eye absorb each feature —
of God's art there on display —
in that quivering contour of a doe.

From that day forth
I never doubt —
of realms immeasurable
beyond this minute world
of rock and clay,
where an eternal Mind works even now —
in glory to create,
an Artist who is thrilled —
by every form He makes —
and lives forevermore —
to mold and to conceive anew.

William E. Mays

BEIRUT IN MY MIND

Man-made volcano erupted,
The hell went loose with loud thunder,
            and blazing fire,
Hot and humid at once the morning air!

Is there anyone who would really care
      for the fallen, sick and wailing?
Anyone who would dare to look back and slow down,
      for the little one following?
I can't say for sure . . .
Life is far too precious this morning.

The gentle folks of yesterdays
Always friendly and smiling,
Living and loving,
The proud and prosperous people
      of beautiful, beautiful Beirut,
Ah! how they keep on running and running
On this red hot morning with vacant stare
(From despair to death or death to despair!)

Is there a place called *Safe* away from all this burning
Where one can stand under the bright, blue sky
And breathe in peace a little cool air for one split second?
I am not so sure anymore . . .

Pramila Rath Chetty

I'LL HEAR THE SOUND OF YOUR VOICE

A Deaf Person's Prayer

Lord, I can't hear the words people say
And you know I'm not deaf by my choice
But I know someday when you take us away
I'll hear the sound of your voice

You gave me eyes so I can see
And hands with which I can speak
You gave me a heart and that's the best part
You strengthen me when I am weak

Thank you for knowing my heart dear Lord
You always know what I feel
Although I can't express it to everyone
My feelings are still very real

Help me O Lord to be grateful
For the gifts that you've given to me
Thank you most of all for your death on the cross
And for living so we can be free

Thank you Lord. Amen.

Joye Atkinson

ODE TO RIB 'N' RIBBON

I once had a pony named Ribbon
We both 'herd' the cows (during my youth)
'Downing' fenced 'fields'! and swimming floods 'heads up'!
They went everywhere to 'tell the truth'!
I could write a book on *Rib 'n' Me*
A-playin' like 'Robbers and Cow Sleuth'
'Til my mare shied from her 'right blind' side
And left *me 'spitting'* on *my 'buck tooth!'*

Cinderellanor

MOST IMPORTANT

The most important things in life . . .
      I hear people say . . .
Are the money they hold, and their dream of riches . . .
   So they plead!

The most important things in life . . .
      I say . . .
Are the clean air we seek to breathe, and the peace of mind . . .
   We so dearly need!

The most important things in life . . .
      Some other people say . . .
Are of their wants and needs, that leave no mountain or sea . . .
   Free, even for me!

The most important things in life . . .
      I say and plead . . .
Are a clean endless shoreline, that meets only its sea . . .
   And never to see a falling tree . . . if you please!

Tonya Ione

WE CLEANED HOUSE

The day after the giant Flea Sale
Triumph! (We) "smartly" tramped through the house
Wasn't a "scratch" left (They'd)
Hauled off "loads of junk" and "tons of louse"

We painted and polished
From ceilings to floor
How happily we worked
Didn't "itch" anymore

Everything had *sold (well)*
Fairly flew to the store
Paid for new furniture
Couldn't do that before

Our old home is beautiful
Everything's squeaky-clean
There's just one thing missing
This place wants to be seen

Folks flocked in our Open House
Laughing 'n' scratching; then to our despair
'Twas one "hopping mad" party
"Paying us back" for *flea buying nightmare!*

Cinderellanor

FLOWERS FROM HEAVEN

I see a flower in the sky coming down to the
ground. I pick this flower from the ground and
hold it in my hand.
Oh what a glorious color it has taken, and what
a beautiful shape it has. I have never seen such
a flower. I know not where it came.
I looked into the sky, and see other flowers falling
to the ground. It gave a pleasant scent, which
made my body feel at ease.
Must be angels tossing these flowers from heaven,
and how I wish someone were here to see what I see.
On the final hour these flowers fade away, and I
see no more other flowers in the sky.
My girl comes to me, and asks why I am looking
into the sky? I tell her I saw these flowers from
heaven, fall down to the ground. If only she
could believe.

Jesse Centeno

Flying cameras film good footage
Thought monitors pick up mental words
Interstellar directors feed lines
Rowdy acting is not allowed

The machine gunner producer
Doesn't want us touching
Or talking to each other
Or even remembering what we look like

We could star in a triple X movie
Or be co-messiahs
Or have a better hideout
Than Bonnie and Clyde

But our rags to riches story
Doesn't seem to be good enough
For the powers that be
Our rags are our mental illnesses
Our riches is our life together

Jeff McElhone

SURROGATE

Baby in need of gentle arms,
Tell us how you feel..
What sort of substitute
Has happened your way?
Are we who you will not speak to?
WHY do you keep us not knowing?

Pry apart your selfish arms;
The embrace holds nothing.
We'll show you interest, but
To have you we desire.
Speak in different terms to
SHOW us our control.

Self you seal as we
Mourn not fulfilling all.
We'll see you feel nothing to suffer
Only from the prophet's grasp.
Sent guilt is sorry, for
YOU will leave us for eternity.

WReNo, Mike Kirchner

I've fallen
into a cup,
Please don't drown me!
It's luscious,
They'll never get me out.
You, sitting up there,
holding on tight,
I'm glad you can't
throw me a line.
Now that I'm in,
When I look up,
I only see sky
and through coffee.
But tell me, my friend,
Since I can't see out,
How is life at the rim?

Beverly J. McAllister

FROM ME TO YOU

I give to you my love,
this heart you have
to crush.

If you should feel my pain,
these screams are yours
to hush.

You listen to my cries,

the tears you wipe
away.

No matter what is done,
you know somehow
I'll stay.

Together we shall walk,
a dream I give

to you.

Two lives we'll build as one,
our love it will
be true.

Denise Ketchum

YOUR SHADOW

One day I'll have my
child of gold.
He'll be like you so
strong and bold.
In his blue eyes will
shine your smile.
You'll love this boy, he'll
be your child.

No one shall tell him
what to do.
A will of rock he'll
live like you.
So special he will
be it seems.
We'll teach him well of
life and dreams.

We shall guide his paths
sure and straight.
Showing him roads that
he should take.
After the years of
love we'll know,
one fine day our boy
will be grown.

Denise Ketchum

WHEN YOU LOVE SOMEONE

When you love someone, please
tell them; don't wait another day,
because death just might decide to
come by and take that love away.

Rev. Robert Parker

FLYING DUTCHMAN

Sail on dear captain
Year after year
Searching for a better life
Than the one you have here
Time walks beside you
And age haunts your eyes
Still you must travel
Across countless seas
Pray for the final day
When at last you'll be free

Flying Dutchman
Ship of dreams
Sailing forever
Waiting to be set free

People have feared you
Story untold
A man who defied everything
And paid with his soul
Many have seen you
Others disbelieve
Still you must travel
Across the sea
And pray for the final day
When at last you'll be free

Flying Dutchman

Tracy D. Frost

LOVE'S HELD STRONG

Wilted flowers,
old love letters,
faded pictures.
Love's held strong
in my heart
and my hand
held out . . .
for you.
Distant dreams,
beautiful memories,
reminiscent days,
Love's held strong
in my heart
and my hand
held out . . .
for you.
Now today
waiting as always
return soon.
Love's held strong
in my heart
and my hands
held out . . .
for you.

Ondrea Jill Pehle

MY BEST FRIEND FOR LIFE

God is my best friend (for life)
He is my *hope,* my *trust,* my *strength,* and my *shield*
I saw ''Theophany'' and kneeled
He restoreth my *soul* and I became healed

God is always there (for me)
At work or play ''all through the night''
My *God, He* completely fills
My day! With *His* redeeming *light*

God knows I'm not lonely (I'm saved)
His ''sheep'' aren't left in a potter's field; When
They are safe in the arms of *Him*
He's ''The Good Life'' and the Bible fits in

My *God* is my *love (He's* caring)
Sick or well; in some dire position
He is the only one that I
''Count on,'' *He* is ''The Good Physician''

God has stuck with me (like glue)
Since *birth* . . . *He will use* Satan if He must
In ''War for Christ'' *and* stay *true*
'Til *death* and *after* ''I'm ashes or dust''

Will there be *life* after *death* (many people are *asking)?*
Yes! As the *breathlessness* of this life stills our body and sin
He promises an everlasting spiritual birth
(For *all* those who believed in Christ) to breathtakingly b-e-g-i-n!

Cinderellanor

TWO HUNDRED YEARS

We are observing the 200th anniversary of our beloved Constitution.
The document that brought about our emancipation
From rigid supervison among minorities
To a more peaceful place of worship according to God's priorities.

Thank God for men who sought His direction,
Never succumbing from the original truths and affection
For those who had fled from the stern rods of supervision,
Launching out into endless waters
    to escape from slaughters of derision.

To a place of freedom from lack of want
To a land of plenty where the stern leaders would no longer taunt.
They were to realize that they too must work hard to reach their goals
Of high esteem to obtain the wonders that they were to behold.

Such joy on their faces we were to behold
When they viewed fields of harvest that would be their goals,
Not only for their physical beings but also for
    the souls of men and women
To whom God had instructed to lead them to the fold
    and to sing, ''Amen!''

When the day's work was done
That God provided them under the sun.
What great horizons were theirs to conquer
Away from the turmoil from which they had fled for cover.

If they could but see the great accomplishments since that day,
A great metropolis with the beloved Lady beckoning them to stay
In a land blessed by the One up above
Now at long last, we thank Him for His tremendous love!

Verna Kortes Peitso

SIGHS OF A FARMER

The old farmer released a sigh of relief.
The last one of many breathed
During the harvest season, and the first
Of many more sighs yet to come.

It had been a long, wet, and cold fall this year.
Not the worst he had seen,
But surely there had been easier.

Another sigh given, but this one from
A little further down inside.
This was a sigh of satisfaction.
Of a job, though hard, had been one done
To the best of his God-given ability,
And the old farmer was satisfied.

As he walked to the house from the barn,
The evening chores completed, a snowflake
Landed on his cheek. He gave a knowing sigh
That winter was ready to begin.

Yes, the old farmer sighed many times through each year.
Sighs of knowledge, satisfaction, relief, humor, dread and sorrow.
But, as he walked into the house
His wife as she had for many years
Greeted him with a smile and a kiss.
Then the old farmer gave one more sigh.
A sigh of happy content.

Norman R. Miller

REMEMBRANCE

friends they come and friends they go
and some just remain the same
I remember you in times of true
your image still remains

times they change but the heart remains
forever lashed to the wheel
friendship's key to the door of mystery
unlock the secrets of eons feel

down exists because up allows
the comparisons room to be
one day we cried climb we tried
distant side music's mountain freedom to see

old friends through time some reappear
inside hidden layers some Autumn leaf
drifting windward through some late fall
frozen winter of life sometimes brief

I am the same yet through change remain
different at every stair
like the highway that sings destiny's song
at the crossroads someday we'll be standing there

Daniel Thomas Carr

SERENITY

A neighbor dropped in, and it
really wasn't the best time for
me. There were toys scattered on
the floor, the phone was ringing
for my daughter, and before she
left, my grandson came running down
the hall yelling, as children do.
The next day when I saw her at her
front door she invited me in. I
couldn't help notice her spotless
home. Her rugs were vacuumed, the
chrome on the furniture was polished,
and there was an air of perfect order
and serene quietness, with no
interruptions.
Upon returning to my own home, I sat
down on the couch among toys, books,
ringing telephones, children and grand-
children and thought: ''How lonely she
must be with her clean carpets.''

Garryett Fortin

FAREWELL

Faintly, I hear the cries
Of love . . . dying . . .
And the whispering
Of its pain.
Yet, I cannot go back!
Cannot hold! . . .
Or capture, its shredded
Strings again!
Sometimes I mourn
For the brightness . . .
Of its birth!
Then, I remember all
The scars given! . . .
The crashing, of its worth!
No, I heed not the cries —
Or regret its going . . .
But oh! how I long
For a . . . new way of life . . .
To come . . . a-glowing!

Virginia E. Marx

ON THE GRAIL CASTLE AND ME

A pink castle, small, but not frail,
Symbol of the Holy Grail.
The sky, when cleared, colored the cliffs,
The sands, the magical ruins,
In a pink light, a mystical glow,
A very special sacred show.

And so, as Norma's memory passed this
Vision on to me, I share it with you:
Pink soft glow, hint of inner heart, safe haven;
A legendary soul's nest, sacred place of rest.

Girded in stone, I stand alone. Mortal men
Are locked out, the weak, the un-unique,
Those who seek only overnight shelter.
A Special Sacred Warrior can hold the key
To enter into me.

Molly Ann Squire

PREYGROUND

Through the sandbox.
Up and down the see-saw. He
Climbs the slide, the ladder
Buckling under his years.
He twists as he descends.

Grey flaked with dirt,
The caked mud smells the same.
He remembers, and it fuels his frenzy.

On a swing.
Back and forth, escape the earth.
But the chains clench and constrict,
Binding tightly.

He runs up the jungle gym,
Falls through. Bars assault the landscape,
Restricting reach. He lowers,
And crawls beneath.

Around around the asphalt,
Searching for old friends.
Their footprints are below the earth.
He is caught in between.

Burdened with memories, his
Hands hold green blades
And grey strands.
The silent soil patiently waits,
He falls to it and screams.

Terry Fleming

MR. PROPELLER'S IDLE THOUGHTS

I want,
And this verifies my existence.
Continually do I pity people and
Envy them simultaneously.
Pity them for what they cannot understand,
Envy them for what they cannot understand.
Emotions adhere to my rib cage,
Close to my heart.
My manner is too rebellious,
It won't follow one feeling faithfully.
Oftentimes my mood swings are mistaken
For celebrity imitations, first some
Angry adolescent then a quick
Cyclical orbit to serene elderly.
This makes for hefty wages when
I perform (unintentionally)
On a sidewalk or roundabout.

Terry Fleming

NEW MEXICO

Look at me
stretched across
my own limitations,
like cowhide
in the sun,
I'm tanning my skin
of emotion
and bleaching white
these bones of
my own illusion.

Venetia Dawn Davison

We are indeed into
The separation time
When money moguls fall
As heroes,
And light pours down from Heaven.

Angels and judges walk
In human forms
Sun alternates with darkness,
Many have fallen.

The earth autumn spins
Its fantasy,
And many are preparing
For the cold.

Beams of light fall
From heavenly dimensions
And those who are caught
In darkness
Cannot face the light.

Virginia Weber

The lady lies alone hearing the
rain played on the piano
She dreams
staring through the glass
seeing tears falling to thunder
Visions of his eyes reflecting
back feelings of her deepest love
Hearing the fiercest wind blowing
through her, forcing her to move
to breathe life
Glistening light piercing
her eyes
She sings from the rain
and loves from hollow tears
The lady sleeps comforted by dreams
yearning for his breath
Warmth so far, so near
And candles, two
one for her heart, one for his
burning desires and hands
that touch
Sweet smelling rain
follows her visions in night
The lady lies alone
obsessed by love, possessed by him

Dianna Michelle

Sometimes i feel like a
    single feather cloud,
  lonely in the sunset sky.
    So small in comparison
        to the grey rain clouds
drifting
    behind me.
The sun colours me pink,
    and slowly
        the wind
        blows me away
        from the view
    of your gazing eyes.

Dianna Michelle

AIM

point to the star of brotherhood
in the direction of your meanest foe
this will release you from its vicious circle
feelings of pain evolve into something to know

point to the star of kindness given
to those whose lives amount to judgments fill
you reap what you sow no matter the weather
to accomplish this task you exercise your will

point to the star of the returning river
between its banks lies the ceaseless sound
of its faith and love for the mountains
of our need for each other of its need for the ground

point to the message resounds throughout your being
you are what you do in the end of all ends
desire reaps the fruit of love waiting
human seed to earth's soil growth you must send

point to the heavens if you're able to receive it
you're bound to open yourself to the rain
there is more to life than meets your eye
love is hiding its riddle right upon your pain

so design your time with plans of tenderness
to keep an even keel
for those times asunder when you go under
run over by your own wheel

Daniel Thomas Carr

FLOW

come down to the stream of consciousness
cool your weary mind
drift with the clouds that reflect in your eyes
listen to the song the river unwinds

come down to the stream of merriment
leave your reason behind to see
that it floats on moments made of magic
it's only a part of all that's meant to be

come down to the stream of enlightenment
contained in the second's glance
is the dance of knowledge with its fleeting firefly
pluck your cubic centimeter of chance

come down to the stream of brotherhood
where the intent of all men is free
the flow of kindness runs back to the ocean
will rain down as strength on our children to be

you are the world
as seen through your eyes
its as surely changeable
as your night's changing sky

and with the many faces
and your time left to abide
the ocean where the river goes
is with your love deep inside

Daniel Thomas Carr

THE POEM OF LOVE

I need to touch your dreams,
    and know that they are parallel
        with mine.

I need to run barefoot in your mind
    and catch a glimpse of myself
        and others there.

When all is spoken and finished
    I need to sit quiet
        and feel your silent wants.

Between the sun and the stars there are no differences,
    and we
        shall be closer than they.

Hours ago we fought and hurt like barbarians,
    but the cloud of peace touched our hearts
        and we are joyfully as one again.

My mind rings with impatience
    to step into this newly acquired philosophy.

When we live as one,
    but walk as two
        we darling, shall be the happiest two beings
            on the face of the earth.

            And from us,
                they will learn!

R. L. Moore

DIVA

*Dedicated to Teresa Kubiak
of the Metropolitan Opera*

Mystical, moon-drenched maiden, chanting devotion alone
Whose mighty breast is laden with armor or precious stone

Evoking a curse of ire, raging the fury of scorn
Trembling with ancient desire for vengeance of her first-born

Bride of swan-borne knight or Druid priestess spurned
Deprived of nuptial delight or joining her love to be burned

Maleficent, murderous mistress, reaching to depths unknown
Somnambulating her distress, trading her soul for a throne

Mythical goddess Norse, surrounded by magical fire
Wildly spurring her horse onto love's funeral pyre

Sensuous, sanguine dancer, writhing in treacherous grace
Uttering infamous answer, an unwilling mouth to embrace

Voluptuous, Venusburg temptress or purist of ladies divine
Pious, forgiving redemptress or demonic vixen supine

Harlot or damsel chaste, flirting or fainting for breath
Mellifluous, mad or debased, expressing all life and all death

Diva, most daring of muses, Matrix of passion in sound
All song her soul infuses, her spirit to resound

Arlene Woeckener Baldino

She is staring out her window
and falling with the rain
Breezes blow candles out
Her brandy condenses
on crystal glasses
Lovers
Her lover is so far from her
and the torn flannel shirt
can never be enough
to comfort her like his arms
She zones on the Poplars
blowing with the wind
Almost breaking
Almost dying Almost dying
She sips from crystal
Tears drop and disturb
her brandy
Candles burn out for lack of wax
Once she thought candles burned
forever
Once she dreamed
Still she stares
Her heart pounding like rain
Tears rolling Tears falling
and blowing far with the wind

Dianna Michelle

WEEPING WILLOW

I saw a weeping willow,
swaying in the wind.
I saw the tears,
fly upon a breeze,
and drop,
by the nearest tree.

Cry no more,
weeping willow.
I saw your tear,
drop upon the one you love.
I saw a shadow,
upon the tree.
The darkness,
from limb to limb.
It tells the story,
of death,
and of your love.

Wayne J. Kurpjuweit

TODAY IS MONDAY

I know today is Monday.
You know how I do tell?
My neighbors' lines are
full of clothes,
and it is raining like —

H ave I
E ver
L ied out
L oud?

Eloise Mitchell

St. Francis, the plastic statue,
hangs serenely upside-down
over an atheist bed,
thanking God
for all there is to praise.
Saint F., I've been to your city,
and you really ought to see
what they've done to you.

Beverly J. McAllister

IS LOVE A DREAM?

The Mona Lisa's lost her smile
Can't you sit and stay awhile?
Just a moment, a year or two
You know I'd move the world for you

The door slams shut on vintage thought
I clean my eyes of sandman sand
To find my sleep's been overwrought
With you and I in a far-off land

Chipping paint off playground toys
The world so full of girls and boys
With hearts that spin just like a wheel
And so much I have yet to feel

Still it's all been felt before
By others stranger than ourselves
We search to find there is no more
Than packaged love on foodstore shelves

At first a dream and now a dream
It's ended in a dream
I wake each night in cold, damp sheets
To my hollow silent scream

Patrick Sands

DEATH DOESN'T DISCIMINATE

a nursery crime

Jesse James was an outlaw
Henry VIII was king
Napoleon was a general
Caruso used to sing

Engels was a commie
Marie she lost her head
Gable was an actor
They believed what Adolf said

Gandhi was a martyr
Nicholas was the tsar
King he was a Negro
Jimi played guitar

Mao Tse was from China
Joan of Arc a saint
Einstein was a genius
Rembrandt used to paint

Patrick Sands

WHERE TRUE MORALS LIE

Walk me down from pillar to post
This broken sparrow takes to wing
The father, the son or the holy ghost
Descend with angels who softly sing

All of this a man-made dream
Placed so coyly in the mind
Our tragic flaws are made to seem
Like trifles we can leave behind

Who on earth first had the thought
That all salvation's up above
Still now bloody wars are fought
To give to Him this fallen dove

Then purify your death with life
Repent and leave without a sin
An end to all your years of strife
Now find your death where I begin

Patrick Sands

BETTER LEFT UNSAID

There are so many words
that will go unsaid
All the words in the world
could never capture the feelings

And while so much has been written
true meaning is never expressed
Words somehow fall short
of what they were to have meant

I can give you words, many words
But to say them would not be enough
Although they are given with feeling
their true depth would never be known

I use words as a tool
a well-crafted art of persuasion
believable only to those
who have searched and longed for those words

Now, I am searching, and longing
for the words that elude me
Some clever montage of words
that would melt the coldest heart

A conspiracy has taken place within me
my heart and mind toy with each other
In all their cleverness, I have learned instead
some things are better left unsaid

Susan A. Montelius

STATURE OF A PERFECT MAN

This my brothers, sisters, and friends,
This is the stature of a perfect man,
The beginning of all is faith we know.
The seeds of hope we must surely sow,
Virtue, power, goodness, and strength,
To have these fruits of the Spirit you must
go to great length.
Knowledge, wisdom, and discerning,
This we receive by teaching and learning,
Temperance, being humble, not easily provoked,
This above all we must learn the most,
Godliness with contentment is great gain,
Not seeking for wealth nor worldly fame,
Brotherly kindness, the capstone of love,
Must manifest through us like that
precious Dove.
Jesus Christ, the chief cornerstone,
Then will come soon and take his
Word Bride home.

Deborah Vaughn

WHISPER OF HOPE

I cannot be unhappy if my friend is near
He bade all my sadness depart
I cannot be lonely if gently I hear
His whisper of hope in my heart

The whisper of hope, soft whisper of hope
Gently as if a doe were wandering through a forest
I hear his soft whisper of hope
I lean to my dear friend and put my mind to rest

I cannot be weary, the days are not long
With my friend I can trust, go onward and not mope
And on this path, I pause with my heart in song
To hear the soft whisper of hope

And when, from this path my friend has taught me to tread
My footsteps forgettably lose hope
How kindly again to that path I am led
And cheered by the whisper of hope

No voice in the world is so tenderly sweet
His charm cannot let my sorrow go on for long without hope
No moments of glory, and no joy would be complete
Without my friend's soft whisper of hope

Sandra E. Carlson

THE LOWLY

We will condemn the mighty, and will condemn the strong.
    We will condemn the rich, and will condemn them all.

Who will be left then to condemn, if we don't condemn the poor?
    The cost to keep them fed, keeps mounting by the score!

Why not condemn our wrong as well, to even up the score,
    and the wrong we see in others, won't seem so wrong no more.

We'll sum up this conclusion, of how wrong are the mighty,
    how weak are the lowly, and how right are we all?

Thomas Mariano

HURT'S DEPTH

    Hurt runs deep through the mind, destroying all
the memories it touches.
    Racing and bouncing off the mind's walls, it cannot escape.
    Rendering a shock with each tremendous blow,
it is the decomposer of your mental and physical state.
    Its greedy mouth eating and eating at you till
there's nothing left.
    Of your weak and vulnerable body the infections
of hurt remain.
    Found in each wound is a sick yellow pus, which will
ooze from your wounds, unendingly.
    Crippled is your heart, living in the wildest
of fears, of ever being loved again.
    Crippled is your heart, because it could never
give itself as fully and whole as it once did.
    Crippled is your heart, destroyed by an
untrusting mind.
    Crippled is your heart, because Love will never
pass through this hollow frame again.
    And with no Love, all is lost.

R. L. Moore

DEAFNESS OF LOVE

I

Deep in my mind lies the deafness of Love.
And it will never be. Silence is its only bed.
And dreams the only comfort. It shall never be
a reality, never be lived, never be the Love I want.

II

The deafness of Love lies deathly silent in my mind.

Maybe it shall never be until death itself, for maybe it is
God's Love in its perfection I seek.

It is Love I want, pure, simple, Love. With all the affection
that presides with it. Only Love, the most powerful, meaningful
word in all.

Why do I seek then the ultimate of this, why is it not that I
am satisfied with just the small part of it?

I must have it all, or nothing, I wish nothing if I can't gain
the Love I want.

R. L. Moore

COUNTERCLOCKWISE EYES

It's not like it used to be.
Streetlights dancing off the windshield of mom's car.
She's at home.
Searching for a dark street to take you on. We're alone.
Cruisin' around town with laid back minds doing laid back
Time (time spent easier then 'cuz it was young like us and not
As many of our 'friends' had the bomb).
Looking at the world through counterclockwise eyes
We see as truth what was previously rumored. Scientist's wearing
Little white coats and matching glasses herald the perils of mind
Altering cause and effect with one hand while increasing its
Potency with the other, only to find our Jekylls becoming more
Vile and contemptible Hydes.
It's not like it used to be, or is it just that my eyes are
Seeing counterclockwise?

J. E. Lykes III

BETWEEN PAST AND PRESENT

My thoughts are wandering
somewhere between past and present
to places of long ago
where my energies were spent

My soul has become restless
with each dream that ceased to live
The will to continue has tired
of the fidelity I can no longer give

Somewhere was lost the patience
and the endurance has long since died
Somewhere the strength has weakened
and the truth is that I have lied

Somewhere between then and now
I had forgotten someone I knew
Left sleeping in the past
Its youth as fresh as dew

And now I find here and there
shades of myself aged with time
with my thoughts wandering
searching for something I may never find

Searching somewhere
between past and present
to places of long ago
where my energies were spent

Susan A. Montelius

ALWAYS SPRING

Always spring in my
heart when
I think about you.

Birds singing gay songs

A melody that softens
the heart.

Our love will always
be, no matter
how the years may
come and go.

Aldena Harris

IMPISH BOY

Impish, Tom Sawyer-like boy,
Makes my heart skip with joy,
Frog in his pocket
Snail in his hand
Love in his heart to beat the band
Cowlick in his hair
Twinkle in his eye
Waves his hand to tell me good-bye.
Pebbles in his shoes
Burrs in his socks
He'll be back with a gleeful knock.

Joy M. Parker

GRANDMOTHER'S PANTRY

The jars of jams and jellies,
stood on the pantry shelf,
my dear old Scandinavian grandmother,
made them all herself.
I smell the homemade
breads and muffins,
a tantalizing sight.
The coffee was hot
in the Scandinavian pot.
I'll always remember my grandmother,
and the delicious food she brought.

Joy M. Parker

TELEPHONE HANGOVER

Why must you scream
Your shrill song into my tortured mind?
What time is it
That you steal my liquored privacy?
Why bring me dawn
When I drank all night to find dusk?
Just hang up!
I can't force words past my tongue,
And besides,
I'm too busy to speak with you now!
God! Why today
Did I forget to use the machine?
Damn you!
I can't take any more ringing.
''Hello . . .
''No, no. I always sound like this.''

Jonathan Katzauer

MY DAD

He moves me in a silent way,
of this he doesn't know;
the strength he gives to me
and how it helps me grow.

He forces me to do the things,
I thought I'd never try;
and with comforting assurance,
I know he's by my side.

He makes me accept the challenges,
alone I'd never seek;
it's the pain he has gone through,
that makes me strong, not weak.

He teaches me how to learn,
of what life has to give;
and just living isn't enough;
first be yourself — then live.

He accepts me, just how I am,
and silently is proud,
but it's all these things he does for me,
that make his love so loud.

Denise M. Jackson

SOMETHING NEW INTO EDEN CAME

Something new into Eden came
The tempter
Though I knew not his name
Coming as from a hidden door
Now Eden, our paradise is no more

A taste, small taste
Of forbidden fruit
Sweet yet sour
Sin's first known hour

Would that I not into temptation fell
Now know of a pit
A bottomless hell

Afraid and trembling
We could not talk
Into a world of unknown
We did walk

Seeds of sin
Planted deep within
Children, I now painfully birth
Blessings with sorrow, this sowing I reap
When they as well as I
Return as dust to the earth

Something new into Eden came
The tempter
Though I knew not his name

Sharon E. Kitzler

AN ODE TO A LADY FINE SHE BE

Diane Cornelius my dear friend
a prettier lady never to be found.
Her face so noble & fine it is
her body slim yet fine indeed.

Her smile so warm
her eyes a-twinkle.
Her lips so beautiful
— and always that smile,
that kind warm & knowing smile.

She gazes at you with fire in her eyes
and releases that heat
in her laugh so pure.
A finer lady you ca'na find.

Thomas J. P. Courtney

THERE ARE THOSE

There are those who inspire me to look
There are those who inspire me to write
There are those who inspire me to dance
There are those who give me hope
There are those who hold me close
And there is you who inspires me to love
Which is all of these things
Ever-changing and free like the sea
Its waters rush in your eyes
And through your voice comes its breeze
Filling the void in between
I want you with me

Dena Beth Lesser

A CHANGE IN TIME

To Dr. Tony Berardi, a Vietnam Veteran

At times I wonder, how far can I see, with my mind and heart reaching.
  With a beginning, is there an end, or a different sense of time.

Just living what I believe, teaches me — my children, will see
farther than me.
  What they see as true, changes this — my world,
  for me and you.

Concepts of time, flexible to our senses, don't only have a beginning
or an end.
  As our young are older than us, 'cause of what we've lived,
  a rhythm folding the movement of time.

That makes our grandparents younger, than what grandchildren,
have uncovered before their eyes.
  If there is no true, beginning or end,
  then what's left is "life."

Our parents are the children of our past, our children make us,
forever young to our future.
  There's no wonder, when time has been slowed, to have a beginning
  or an end.

If we lived, past the speed of light, we'd be in the dark
of what we know.
  It's a choice — between riding the river of time in our
  hearts and mind, or walking the common ground of our lives.

To learn to live blind, trusting other senses,
till time provides the light.
  A rhythm in time, a give and take, of darkness and light.

Cathleen Chesrow

LIFE GOES ON

Twenty years from now where will you be?
Married with three kids and long forgotten about me
Your kids know mine and they get along well
It's not what we expected but only time could tell 'cause

Life goes on
Long after the pain is gone
Where the good times reigned
The memories remain
And where the damage was done
Scars heal and life goes on

The gang shares a pack
But the circle doesn't grow
It goes 'round and 'round
And with each turn someone goes

No one knows who's first (next)
'Cause it's not a game of numbers
It's just a matter of time
To see how age does wonders 'cause

Life goes on
Long after the dreams are gone
The friends you knew
Are just pictures in a book
And the logs you split together
Are just splinters of the mind as life goes on.

Joseph G. Garamella

THE HERACLITEAN FIRE

On the meandering coast of Ionia, across the Aegean Sea,
A wonder city existed once; its moira no man could see.
From its sacred fire, taken from the Athenian hearth, bright,
Unusual flare came to be. Its exceptionally effulgent light
Dissolved the mystical fog that was besetting the human mind
And with logos and metaphysical insight purveyed mankind.

As revealed by "Nature," man discerns only that which becomes,
And the world's shape from the needs of the Cosmic Fire comes.
Cosmic fire — mother of the many, mother of chronic change,
Mother of perpetual strife, mother of everything beyond range,
Mother of the ever-wrestling opposites — is what truly exists,
And what by the eternal logos and world order always persists.

Birth and death, light and night, fertility and sterility,
Concord and discord, merit and demerit, nobility and humility,
Spiritualism and materialism, grace and disgrace,
Are all pairs of antithetical forces whose never-ending race
Begets all that is "becoming" and all that is "passing away."
The ephemeral supremacy of the fittest and its giving way
To its conjugate deeply manifest the perennial "Panta rei" —
A universal mechanism in harmony with the Cosmic Fire's decree.

Great apostle of reason, enemy of belief and mysticism, wherefore
Have dogma and dismay beclouded the human mind once more?
The wheel has turned! The strife continues: night over light,
Regress over progress, pettiness over greatness. You were right!

John V. Nikas

STUMBLING STONES

I've been stumbling down this beaten road
  It seems my whole life through,
Climbing hills, choosing paths, and stumbling on stones,
  As I am often compelled to do.

The mountain road that I've been following,
  Is so steep, and very jagged.
This tedious climb up the uneven way
  Leaves me worn and ragged.

The downhill slopes are narrow and rocky,
  My steps, they jilt me to the bone,
As I stumble down the beaten track
  Towards a distant destination unknown.

The peaceful meadows are so very few,
  Great mountains spread them far apart,
And the comfort that I find in them is small
  When compared to the weariness of my heart.

Where this stoney road leads me,
  I can't begin to know,
But I am driven by an inner faith,
  It keeps me going, though progress is often slow.

You see, I know that up the road aways,
  I will no longer walk alone,
Because God will be walking with me,
  Removing all the stones.

Anne Chatterton Brown

THE OLD MAN AND THE EAGLE

The man explored as the eagle soared.
On a mountain high shared with the sky.

Thought-filled days of each other's ways.
The man pined away for the eagle's divine way.

Look down and see, don't you pity me?
The eagle in flight saw man's plight.

Sit beneath my nest, you need the rest.
The wisdom I see will be dropped on thee.

The eagle did fly, sharp eye to spy.
Many wrongs of man he did scan.

The old man recorded what he wisely sorted.
Judge you be, on what the eagle did see.

Bill Dwight Rawson

THE LEGAL(?) SYSTEM

Integrity to my dismay has faded most away.
Now we match wits from bags of tricks.

Lawyers dance and prance to a legal trance.
In joy and glee with your money they flee.

Judges preside, public trust to provide.
Truth they hide when to money allied.

Fill the pocket by the public docket.
Sway the jury in a tangled flurry.

Serve they must the dollar trust.
To laws which bend there is no end.

Pay them to say and you walk away.
Pull your last tooth if only in truth.

Foolish friend you'll find your end.
Tragic and sad, surely quite mad.

For fickle are they to truth's way.
The dollar goes first to quench their thirst!

Bill Dwight Rawson

WAS THAT A FROWN

Was that a frown
  or mistaken am I?
Furrowing the brow then down
  Followed by a sigh.
Frowns are not all bad
  Sometimes birthed in deep thought
Other times when mad
  Or when not thinking as we ought
Again love makes a frowny face
  Because you want the other to know
They set your heart arace
  and your soul aglow
Was that a frown I see?
  With a wrinkle of the nose
Was it just for me?
  I feel it love knows.

S. W. Hill

THE "OLDEST" SIAMESE TWINS

Look and see, apart they can never be.
Joined together, as two forever.

When you find one, there is the other.
Hand in hand with his poor brother.

They survive with strife, but wed for life.
You cannot say no, and let the other go.

Sure to stumble, and sure to fall.
Sore wounds they inflict upon us all.

Attached are they to names of shame.
Thru endless years of ill-gotten fame.

These blind fools none dare trust.
Name them I must, to calm this fuss.

One is called liar, and the second a thief.
Bearers are they of much of our grief.

For one must lie, if one does steal.
Look and see, apart they can never be!

Bill Dwight Rawson

"JOY" — A NEWBORN WHALE

Tell the world a whale of a tale
Tell the world a wail of a tale

Fairwinds blew on his birthday
Great strength to swim and play
Never to fall as a hunter's prey

Swam he to the ocean's song
Following fishes in many a throng

Mighty in size he grew with the thrill
Destined always to have his fill

Black was the day which found him ill
Many fishes from a toxic-spill

Deep in sorrow the whales did cry
Seep the evil, they too could die

Nowhere, nowhere a place to hide
Loss of the ages to lose this pride

Oh count the cost, count all the costs
If the wondrous whales be lost

Tell the world a whale of a tale
Tell the world to wail for the whales!

Bill Dwight Rawson

A FRAGILE BIRTH

An idea produced by man
So powerful is the idea,
Yet so delicate at birth,
A mere smirk can kill the plan.

A tremendous idea stopped
By the laugh of a fool
Who said, "Ney," to the great idea.
An idea exposed but dropped.

A good idea survives the shouts,
"That can't be done!"
The problem was, that idea had
To grow and overcome the doubts.

Non-support, our timing late,
Or no courage to start the plan.
Just think of all the ideas
That would or could have been great!

Russell E. Jones

FAIR MAIDEN

The knight in shining armour
  Has removed his metal suit;
His white horse, in the pasture,
  Has received his last salute —

For reality surpasses
  All illusions of the mind,
And the knight in shining armour
  No longer makes her blind.

She's no longer in the Castle
  Of Distress, and calling out
For the knight in shining armour
  To hear her mournful shout.

She has learned to leave the castle
  And its chains of hurtful strife,
She has broken through conditioned walls
  And learned the Art of Life.

Fair maiden, oh fair maiden,
  You are in the driver's seat,
You don't need a knight in armour
  To sweep you off your feet

And carry you away somewhere
  To make your dreams come true,
Your reality, dear maiden fair,
  Is completely up to you.

Deltalee Morgan Bilderback

SKY-DIVING

The mountain always winding ever steep to fall
I color you pure white blue
You are the sky
I see it every time I look into your eyes
My special one
Because of you I feel again

Dena Beth Lesser

446

AFTER ACTION REPORT

I see the flash, mortars.
  We get closer,
  looks like a Stone Age picnic,
  hunting for the beast
  at the end of the tunnel.

I recognize this man with his son
  and a girl handing the mortar rounds
  to her brother.

I wish I could forget tonight.

Time, 4 a.m.
  12 Jan 1970.
  3 KIA.
  1 mortar tube.
  No remaining rounds.
  Negative further.
  Charlie-2, out!

. . . Doesn't anyone want to know their names?

Robert C. Ryan

What Is Life?
Life is an ant crawling upon the ground.
Life is children laughing over an unknown
joy that suddenly makes itself known.
Life is the sunrise with its announcement
of day or the moon and stars as they shine their
way. If only one could say, *I know life,* but there
is no such way. To know life is taking another's
way. So what is life?

Life Span
Think, Think, Think, that's what they say. One
must think and do each day. Work, Work, Work, or
nothing comes your way. Time has come, Time has gone,
Did you hear the sparrow's song?

This Earth
Some say this earth will be a paradise someday.
Some say it will be destroyed by man. Some say
the earth will change within the universe. No matter
what comes, No matter what goes, the earth stands
and remains within its sphere.

Naomi Hale

THE UNKEPT SIDE OF YOU

I tend to enjoy the types of things that one does not
Routinely encounter
Circumstances or events in existence but rarely privy
The Bermuda Triangle
The dark side of the moon
The unkept side of you.

Morning sunlight reflects from the window onto the lawn
And mushrooms fade with the darkness
Grease pops on the stove while fresh bacon swims and tans
In the fryer like Sunday afternoon on the beach
The unkept side of you
The part I claim exclusive rights to
Turns to me and smiles reminiscent of sunlight
And life's mushrooms fade with the darkness.

J. E. Lykes III

THIS MAN I KNOW

This man I know
Sitting so quietly upon his soft chair.
Something to drink in one hand,
A bowl of potato chips on the little stand.
Dark as coal his wavy hair, like the sea,
Flickers as the light glows upon it in the night.
Brownish skin, showing the wisdom of his years.
But not looking a half century old.

This man I know
He only speaks when there is a need.
Helping me through the troubled times.
Stopping the hurt.
Healing the pain of the lingering sorrowful days
That come upon me now and then.

This man I know
He makes me laugh, filling my heart with warmth
As his joyful boyish spirit lifts me up.
His love for me is more than I can tell.
He's taken for granted,
But loved very dear.
Life isn't so bad, when you know, this man,
My Dad.

Barbara Ann Caton

ACROSS MY HEAVEN BLUE SKIES

High above the blue skies
Comes the roaring thunder of chariots
Streaking across my heavens blue sky.
As I rush to your side, with my angels by my side
We'll protect your inner soul that we hold.

Do not fear my children
I am not far away
Even my gates, shine brightly on your face.
My winds blow slightly across your back
Both allowing you to know, I'm by your side
Night and day, I'll never turn away.

I see with my golden light
I hear your voice that cries
I feel your cries from inside

As my tears fall upon your face
From heaven the rain will fall.
My chariot, comes roaring across the sky
With thunder and lightning, streaking across the sky.
Just to let you know, I'm here, I'm listening, I care.
Just continue watching my heaven blue skies.

Sandra Jean Keefe

AND SO GOODBYE

I wrapped her in a shroud of blue,
Just as the morning sun came through;
I buried her by a young willow tree,
My old gray cat and years of memories.
God who clothes the lilies and feeds the singing birds,
Bless your beasts and guard all small things that have no words . . .

Jeanne Louise Morgan

FRIENDS

Friends are lovers who look after thee;
Kind and humble as they can be.
When you smile, they do too . . . see:
I'm smiling broadly . . . watch me . . .

Friends bring you happiness when you are sad;
Mind you, now . . .
You will be glad;

Happiness comes when you least expect,
To crown you with many stars as you elect.

That's what friends are, as you can see:
Up there . . . that star . . . so is he.

Smile away sadness; put a twinkle in your eye;
Then you'll find friends who will never die.

My mission is complete; I bid you adieu.
Please be happy . . . don't be blue.

Rosa M. Cherry

---

*"And pain that cannot forget falls
drop by drop upon the heart."*
Æschylus

One final blow the guantlet nearly run
Dear ones reclaimed, to mark my passage none,
None but the foxes turning every bone
Nuzzling resources can never own.

But valueless I do not venture forth
My fragile trinkets here are little worth
Or even counted. There the soul gives birth
To treasures inconceivable on earth.

Oh God — to stroke again that golden head
Oh grief — unyeilding tears so lonely shed
Living at half-mast little more than dead
Ah — stroke and stroke again that golden head.

Cover my body, then be on your way
An angel waits and though my hair is grey
I shall be plain to her this golden day
And she will stroke my head — no longer grey.

Evelyn Pitel

MY KITE

My kite can sail
high and free
My kite can sway
from left to right
My kite can dip and turn
My kite can take
the hard turns
My kite can take
the soft turns
No matter how
my kite turns
It shall always fly
for it is my life
and up to me to fly it

Patricia A. Bremer

THE BIRD JUST SINGS

I wondered as I heard a bird sing
could this sound mean anything

Could the sound of a chirp and chirp
ever equate to a belch or a burp

When the bird held a whistle twice as long
was it a yell, holler, a shout, or a song

I cupped my hand around my ear
to find out what syllables I could hear

After listening intently at the little bird's sound
after over an hour of hanging around

Listening to patterns of sounds that I heard
I found none that were anything like words

I've concluded for at least a while
the bird that I heard has a beautiful style

And it's more enjoyable than many things
to hear the bird when the bird just sings

Patrick McGee

SOMETHING ABOUT YOU

There is something about you . . .

and the way you accept me
even when I cannot accept
myself.

There is something about you . . .

and your neverending
support that helps me get
through some rough obstacles
in my life, even ones you
aren't a part of.

There is something about you . . .

all the times you continue to
allow me to seek happiness
even outside our own
relationship.

There is something about you . . .

and your encouragement to
reach down deep inside myself
and be the best that I
can be.

I don't know what it is . . .

but, there's just something about you.

Tamara Kay Britain

ROLL 'n' STROLL

The way this story folds
Bewildered — no one told

Noises in my head
Movement — something is said

Talk around me
Talk for me, please
Talk with me

I don't read minds
Guessing is just a game

If you don't want to talk
Don't even start

These thoughts are here
Inside my heart

April Lee Holguin

SLEEP

O world! O life! O glory of God!
O love! O art! music! and ballad!
O fresh spring! O full summer!
Sunrise, sunset, winter hoar!
O neverending story,
I can't deny your glory!
I hate to sleep, but I have to sleep —
The road upwards is far too steep.
Sooner or later I'll fall asleep —
The road upwards is far too steep.

O Lord, O God! O Supreme Being,
O Master, save eyes for their seeing —
Preserve *me* from death's darkness
By my masterpiece, no less.
And as I reach your bosom
Make all my dreamings blossom.
I hate to sleep, but I have to sleep —
The road upwards is far too steep.
Sooner or later I'll fall asleep —
The road upwards is far too steep.

Parviz Atropat

WHITE WONDER

green mountains fade
to snowy whitecaps.
clouds gather,
crowning the peaks —
nature's own laurel.
  hot beige sands
  circle the green growth,
  protecting it from
  the harsh whitecaps
  of the ocean waves.
the earth, like a
blue iris of an eye,
surrounded by white
trapped within
inescapably together.
  White: the union
  of all color
  transfixed by light
  capturing the essence
  of the world.

Margaret Brown

CRIED A TEAR

Yesterday I smiled for you
As you held me so close to your heart
And whispered words of love so softly
Against my cheek

Today I cried a tear for you
As I tried to hold on tight
But your hand just slipped through mine
As you turned and walked away

Tomorrow you'll break my heart
As my mind drifts back to days gone by
And I'm touched by the sweet burning memories
That you left buried deep within me

Toni J. Williams

HEALTH AND HAPPINESS

Some people are happy
Some people are gay
Some are glum
Some a smile you cannot see!

Those who need assurance of who they really are,
Or what they hope to be
Are the purpose of mental health in
Our society.

Many people shun us if emotional we be;
But there are those in this world
Who believe feelings have a purpose
In making a you and a me.

So don't ignore your feelings; but
Try to do your best
To discover the real you
Is health and happiness.

Alice M. Netz

CASTLES

I live in a castle dark and cold
Narrow halls where stairs unfold –
Waters surround me protecting my life
But still all alone I dread the night.
Dungeons and cellars around every bend
Caution and wisdom never my friend.
Waiting for rescue from hills far away
Wondering if light will come with the day.
Handsome suits of armor
Shining,
Not worn
Standing and empty
Like prophecies not born.
Ladies in waiting afraid to come in
Drunken guards who brag where it is that they've been.
I'm a princess to all
That means nothing to none
Doomed to my castle
Built,
But not won.

Rossa Sharon Hahn

SELLING OUT ON A LONELY AFTERNOON

You can tell it's summer because of the flies
I watched silently as he stared out from the second
Story window into the night
Towering over me like an oak on occasion, he now
Seemed to be toppling slowly under his own weight
Falling somewhat short of the mark
Moments ago I'd watched as his seemingly distorted
Body convulsed over the john
He had said, ''A perfect society can never be obtained
From a single viewpoint. Sometimes you have to lose
To win.''
The world seems cruel when you're eleven

Now, as I pour from the bottle that sits on the shelf
And stare at my son's portrait on the wall
I raise my glass to heaven, because I know that's
Where he is, and cry
Better luck next generation.

J. E. Lykes III

COLOR THIEF

''Stop!'' I said. ''There's a broken pop bottle.''
And as I knelt down in the sand, so did she,
Sunbeams playing light-and-shadow on her face
And glistening the tangle of her hair.
As I reached for the broken glass, she cried, ''Wait!
Mama, wait. See that little sparkly place there?'' I nodded.
She looked up, eyes aglow with wonder and delight.
''Look at all the colors! There's yellow — and green there —
And pink, really really pink, and that one — I don't know
    its name —
''Violet,'' I said. ''And violet and blue and — how did they
    get there?''
''The glass has caught a bit of sunlight and taken it
    apart
And there they are.'' ''And I found them! Can we take
    them home?''
I smiled. ''No, dear.'' And I picked the shattered glass
    and threw it in the trash can.
''Oh!'' she cried, ''You threw the color all away!''
And I had. And knew that this was just the first of
    many times
When I must ''throw the color all away.''

Helen T. Widoe

I THOUGHT I SAW FLOWERS

I thought I saw flowers
But it was only what I wanted to see,
Orange and yellow bulbs of spring
In high relief against the corner of grass.
But it isn't spring; the autumn sky
Belies my false impression.
There are no flowers, only the orange and yellow
Flashing bulbs of the road barrier,
And I turn my eyes away in disappointment —
Precisely as I turned away from you.

Gianna Porter

LONG'S PEAK, FROM ESTE'S PARK.

ROBIN, PLEASE
SING ONE MORE SONG TONIGHT

All summer long you sang to me each day,
You gave the best you had to give away,
Your song was sweeter than violet's scent
As happily from bough to bough you went.

So, robin, please sing one more song tonight,
For soon the sun will sink low out of sight . . .
And nights grown cooler with each passing one —
A sign our summer trysts will soon be gone.

The flight of joy you brought, dear feathered friend,
Was one I sensed would someday, somehow, end,
For cherished mem'ries of awak'ning song
Bring happiness alas! tho' not for long.

Soon now, you will migrate to warmer clime,
To some place where the sun will longer shine,
While I, alone, shall wait through winter's frost
For spring — to greet again the friend I lost.

Walter E. Craven

THE NOSE

Listen to the tale I tell, of a nose that's big as hell.
    I'm talking about this Roman nose, I wore with pride
    now a century old.

Cyrano's was long, but not beaked, and Durante's nose I could
    beat.
One day I was taken by surprise, when a big nosed Indian was
    before my eyes.

T'was only a painting by hands of skill, from Kathy Griffin
    who had her thrill.
By painting an Indian with that same big nose.

Came Comanche Chief "Roman Nose," to look at a brother in
    similar clothes.
Took one good look and dropped his spear, looked once again
    and urged — "I go."

Now I'm sad and feeling blue, of the nose I was proud, now
    is worn by Indians too.
How many who left that distant shore, for generations tried
    to make their score.

Many have adopted the American way, but that damn big nose
    is what gives us away.

Thomas Mariano

KITCHEN BASKETBALL

All I ask is that you remember.
Remember the time when we frolicked in the kitchens of the
world, challenged by none.
Until it finally happened, the day it all fell apart.
With hoop mangled and walls shattered, we toast to the day
when it all really mattered.

Theodore M. Sievers

PRAYER #4

Days and days have filled my life, some with pain, failure
    and sorrow, and some of success, laughter and joy.

Now evening dusk, of life's approaching, and I wonder how,
    and where, I left my toll.

Life is like a treasure found, we never thank the One who
    gave it.

It does not lustre, it does not shine, it does not mean one
    rusty token.

Until that day we feel it fading, then we treasure it far
    more than gold.

The coins of life we left behind us, scattered here, and there
    untold.

Now shine so bright, but we cannot have them, they're beyond
    our reach, we are near our destined goal.

The finish line marked by our Maker, was once forgotten, because
    of gold.

How now dear friends will we cross that Goal Line? With
    loving Jesus, or into Satan's fold?

Thomas Mariano

BIG BROTHER, GONE

I followed your large footprints through the snow.
    I felt so pleased when my snowballs found their mark
on your broad back.

How I'd squeal when you tossed me high in the air.
    I was never afraid; I always knew you would catch me.

What tickling sessions! Such laughter!

On the ferris wheel, holding onto the safety bar
    as you rocked our seat way up at the top.
You'd grin while I shrieked for you to stop.

Math became easy when you explained.

Cotton candy at the circus,
    popcorn and soda-pop at the games.

It didn't seem to bother you at all
    to have me tagging along.
And, I would have gladly followed you anyplace.

    *   *   *

Now I grieve. My tears will not stop.

    *   *   *

For you are — my Big Brother, Gone.

Ann Dutcher

COMA

You lie hovering between the here and the hereafter
I touch your warm silent hand
and feel the chubby little arm I guided through babyhood
letting you share my childhood
you in your wicker carriage and I enthralled with my little
plays written to entice the others into friendship.
Little sister, come back, I need you
Now that we are both long grown and I the matriarch of the family
I need to see again your remembered face
Dancing orbs blazing with life
sometimes round with childlike wonder
Comely face contoured by warm acceptance
of yourself and your connections.
You put an exclamation point to my life
and I to yours bring understanding and a sponge to absorb
your little hurts and heartaches.
Come back, little sister
Let us enjoy our youthful dreams together
into old age.

Maliza Mildred Hoffman

THE LONELY SOLDIER

From the lonely outpost of life.
From the trench fighting his way out.
The lonely soldier sought for home.
The heaven he would fight and die for.
A proud soldier
Fighting the wars of life.
He married the runaway child.
A comrade to fight at his side.
In the trench they survived
The hostile attacks.
Fighting together.
Fighting each other.
Her fears became the enemy.
Many battles were won and lost.
The trench grew deeper and deeper.
The lonely soldier fights to live in heavenly peace.
He is tired.
He wants to go home.

A. Gregory Rosario

THOUGHTS IN CLOSING

Laughter or sadness can create a tear. Childish faith
Bonds the way for our Dreams to become Reality, but as a
Child, I live my life under the sun and moon where nothing
makes Sense and never has to. I drift through my whimsical
world, never worrying what tomorrow will bring, never worrying
about Death, for He finds us all soon enough. I merely rejoice
for the hallowed season of Autumn and marvel at the cool misty
dawns before the golden sun rises, for the earth is now buried
'neath a lake of orange and brown leaves who waltz merrily in the
chilly wind. And in my world of childhood memories I shall ride
a moonbeam o'er the blue-green ocean in search of Father Time and
Mephistopheles. Perhaps I will always reserve a place in my mind
for Dreams and Dragons, for life in the real world holds no magic
for me. Of course these are merely thoughts in closing, and I
realize I may be tottering on the edge of sanity, but I'll remain
in my world of faded memories and and hide in a blur of fantasies
where security will always be mine.

Jacqueline Smith

THE LOVING CHILD

The loving child
Sought warm, calm waters
As she held onto herself
Clinging to the side of
Her overturned boat
In the frigid, rough waters of her life.
She withstood the pounding waves from
The runaway child beating against her body.
She withstood the cold loneliness of the water.
Dreaming about her warm, loving home overlooking the calm ocean.
Her faith and love kept her above the waters.
The loving child waited for her ship to come in.
It did.
He gently rescued her from the sea and brought her home.
The home she dreamed about overlooking
The calmness of the ocean.
The calmness of her life.

A. Gregory Rosario

GREGORIO CERVANTES ROSARIO. Pen Name: A. Gregory Rosario; Born: San Francisco, California, 2-28-60; Education: B.A., Management, Columbia Pacific University; Public Relations Management Diploma, Granton Institute of Technology; Paralegal Certificate, Unilex College; Occupations: Correspondent, City News Service; Systems Administrator; Paralegal; Veteran, USMC; Memberships: Media Alliance, National Writers Club, Commonwealth Club, Silva Gradate, Fil-am Chamber of Commerce, Society of American Magicians, Center for Entrepeneurial Management; Poetry: 'Images of My Mind,' 'Wonderment,' 'Lessons in Life,' all *American Poetry Anthology,* 1987; Comments: *'Hear With, Listen With' was created by the poet through his love of his god-daughter Courtney, and their love of music. 'The Lonely Soldier' is the poet's portrait of his father, who fought in World War II and for his family. 'The Loving Child' describes his sister, Christine. Both poems describe 'The Runaway Child,' wife and mother. 'The Lonely Soldier' and 'The Loving Child' are parts of a series of the poet's "Family Portraits."*

NIGHT THOUGHTS

Sometimes I wish that I could stop
The thoughts twirling in my agile brain,
For often they whirl in endless circles of probabilities,
Problems, fears, uncertainties, hopes, despair —
Each strong, vivid, real, seemingly compulsive,
Ticking off events, scenes, people, solutions,
Invoking the past, analyzing the present,
Predicting tomorrows that never come;
I lie exhausted, energy depleted, used up,
Needlessly wasted, knowing
That thoughts are thoughts:
Fragile, elusive, volatile;
For what really matters is the now;
I rise and greet the dawn
Then gird and merge myself with the traffic of day.

Terry A. Palabrica

A LAPSE OF TIME

Oh, what a mysterious wraith Time is!
Dusty rocking chair, withered hands, lonely places,
a broken hour-glass, faded laughs, and saddened faces.
Indian summers past . . .
                    Are
                        Surplus
                            Scraps
                                Of
                                    Time . . .
Flowers that once grew a while in the meadows of my mind and
eerie images amidst the late shadows of evening.
In a child's eyes, tomorrow is too far away to grasp, so Time
is merely a sonnet of illusion, where dewy daybreaks rose and
bronze sunsets fell . . .
                    Time
                        In
                            Disguise . . .
I have often heard Grandpa say Time is lost, but Time is never
lost, nevertheless I would toss rose petals into the cool winds
of Time and envy them as they seemed to be scattered to the far
corners of the earth, for I too wanted to be like the petals . . .
drifting through life carefree with nothing but Time on my hands.

Jacqueline Smith

PLATEAU

Trembling hands pick, search, and choose
Making painful mistakes ending in skinned knees.
Powdered face chalked with the climb
Peers over a protruding obstacle of stone.

Reaching, sometimes finding crevices
Powerless arms fatigue, but I continue.
Afraid of the height, even more afraid of the fall,
I struggle with the thought of continuing on.

No guidelines or ropes stretch in front of me
No maps lead the way to provide me comfort —
Hindsight fails in showing me where I'm going.
I climb and dream, climb and dream.

I stop, rest, secure on the flat rock
Look around, observe, cherish, remember,
Adding new scenes to an already picturesque
Collection in my soul-searching mind.

Making preparations to further my climb,
I have rested; but rested enough?
I struggle inside and my decision,
Whether right or wrong, never knowing,
Is to push hard and climb, again, still.

Mark A. Evans

WORDS UNSPOKEN

Some words don't have to be spoken
When you look into my eyes,
We both feel the love that is reflected off each other's heart
The words unspoken
The meanings are all the same
They wrap us around each other like a warm blanket thrown across
Each other's body
The fragrance of love fills the air around the room
Soft candles burning
A smile to each other's eyes
The words are still unspoken.

Peggy Leyva

MISTRAL

And now that wind comes again
    Blowing from the mountains,
    Wailing through the valleys,
    And ripping across the desert.

It is a hot, wicked, and uncaring wind
    Charged with electricity and life,
    A malevolent gale whose reckless gusting
    Is bearer of its own foreboding.

There are evils yet to come, and passions yet to feel,
    Loves to be made, and madness still awaiting to happen
    Before this tumultuous tempest will cease its blowing
    And pull back its banshees from feasting on our souls.

Oh, wickedest of winds,
    You that darken our hearts and bring madness upon us,
    We are human,
    We need you.

Justin Farlow

ALL HALLOW'S EVE

The Macabre —
Its stench burns thick
In our nostrils,
On this,
The night of All Hallow's Eve.

The evil foreboding
Of this deadly Samhaine,
The spirits of Druids,
O, those wicked Celts,
They so much want to possess us
On this,
The night of All Hallow's Eve.

Our spirits turn black
With the darkness inside us,
That which we name goblins and ghosts,
Witches, devils, monsters and such
Are our own evil apparitions,
On this,
The night of All Hallow's Eve.

Darkness — How it lingers in the flavors of candy fed
To our own little Children
Who unknowingly celebrate
This, the night of the dead,
Which we all call Halloween.

Justin Farlow

SONNET

Compare you? What to? Neither amethysts
Nor diamonds evoke a love immortal,
Faithful, honoured, untinged by betrayal,
Unhindered and unhindering; my wrists
Glittered with these stones, ago — we'd not kissed
Then: I was yet a child. My girlhood hails
Diamonds — dozens of them — in sedimented pails;
By elfin hands pitched in, they clicked and hissed.
No. — Endow me yourself, and I'll compare
You to many other selves I behold;
Yourself, in love; yourself ecstatic, far;
Yourself right-seeming, true-speaking, and bold;
Yourself in thought or overwrought. — You choose
The self, and I, the one on which I muse.

Y. A. Reid

IF I WERE A PRINCE

There will be a great deal of happiness in my life,
Leaving my estate, with chauffeur-driven Rolls-Royce
With this fulfillment, love, money, also a good wife,

If I were a prince, If I were a prince,
There will be no more hungry-poor-poverty-people for good,
For emotionally, physically, reflection,
I personal, help, you, me, and all if I could.

If I were a prince, If I were a prince,
My mother, father, sister, and brothers,
With respect, I love to help them all
Confidence, seriousness, rendezvous, with my heart.

If I were a prince, If I were a prince,
With compatibility and understanding, from one to the other,
Perhaps all this will not be unnoticed and by public,
Making engagements, here and there is uncover,

If I were a prince, If I were a prince,
A home, red corvette, a little boy at times
Idealistic, and optimistic sense of life,
Wishful thinking, dreaming, health, come to mind.

If I were a prince, If I were a prince.

Calvin Rogers

TO GRANDMOTHER'S HOUSE

Going across soft green fields to my grandmother's
Was an exciting adventure of my childhood.
With me were a little sister and two brothers
Skipping quickly along the path close to the wood.

Dear Grandmother was at the front door to greet us.
Young uncles, aunts, cousins, too were ready to play.
Grandfather was much too busy to make a fuss.
In store for all of us, we knew was a great day.

From home to grandmother's house, the miles were just two.
But in the later years, life's miles became too many.
Grandmother and grandfather have both said adieu.
Uncles and aunts, also gone — there aren't any.

Cross the fields to grandmother's in memory, I go.
The dear old house in its ancient beauty, still stands.
But it will never be the same again, I know.
Because the door will be opened by a stranger's hand.

Marie Talbert

THE AMAZON LILY

For two sunsets, the crimson Amazon
Lily holds beetles the size of women's
Nails in its sticky center, as jejune,
Girlish stilt-birds patinate on green
Five-foot leaves. A phosphorescent, bright-wan
Afterglow hallows these livings, 'til dawn,
When the cycle duplicates. Exaggeration,
Starkness, is this land's trademark. Elsewhere life wanes
In blandness. So is my love an ample
Lily; immense, it shall endure for two
Millennia, curve 'round your bloom-hands that pull
You to me. Our spirits shall not re-hew
Nature's stark commandments. Rather, love will
Propagate itself the length of God's while.

Y. A. Reid

THE MOUNTAIN LEAVES

The mountain leaves, a story they tell,
a song they sing, as life begins, early in spring.
The leaves come forth, early in spring, coming
forth, in shades of green; Waving in the winds,
waving a friendly hell-o, to those below,
below their shade, the shades of green.

Then comes summer, a warm song they sing,
still shading in shades of green and wave in the wind,
as laughing and waiting as they sing, sing
their songs, in summer's winds, their warming sing!
Shading creatures and creeping things, flowers of
the wilds and people too; for some like hiking
and picnicking too, a friendly scene they do make,
a scene for fishing in waters cool and blue.

Then comes fall, the leaves change colors, as
that of fire, as they coat the hills like the coat of
many colors. Then by winter they all fall, till spring!

David I. Nitz

LIFE

Paraphrased

In the beginning there was no life until the word of life
Became life, Nothing before,
Then God spoke!
And life within itself came into being a life,
A life within itself.

And any life before it comes into existence is not existent
Until life is manifested within itself,
There was life before the blood
And spirit before the soul of life
And that soul contained the life which is in the blood.

There is no life without life except the life that lives within
Wherein is life itself,
So when life within comes outwith
That without is within,
Not being in the flesh but being in the innermost part
Of the inner man;
The spirit of God? Is the life of man.

Roslyn Pasley

THE WHIPPOORWILL

We walked alone down a green country lane,
While the night whispered down like soft falling rain.
When out of the darkness, from a far away hill,
Came one lonely cry from a sad Whippoorwill.
My Darling voiced an answer into the dim sky,
Then said, "That's my lover calling goodbye."

The years went away, and while sitting one eve,
Beside a great river, I felt its slow heave.
When from out of the darkness, on a far away hill,
Came one lonely call from a sad Whippoorwill.

My soul shrank within me, tears slurred my sight,
And my heart burst asunder in the darkness that night.
But from the ruins rose an answer to that faint, fading cry,
To you too my Darling, this final goodbye.

Lois Harrison Gilbert

OH BEAST OF TIME

The beast claws at my complexion,
Filling me with sadness.
What is this animal taunting me?
How can I eliminate its aggression?

Oh the beast . . . the evil wrinkling beast!
How will I learn to live with it?
Over and over, I search for the answer,
Never found . . . never gained.

'Tis a joke played on us all, I tell myself.
From youth to our prime it comes;
Slowly, but fiercely creeping in,
Grabbing hold, to leave only its . . .
Haggard and emaciated look . . .
Taking with it . . . freedom of mind . . . of beauty . . .
Of agility.

Oh beast of time, I give myself up,
For fighting is to no avail . . .
But there is one part of me,
You will never hold in your possession,
    You can't have my soul!

Georgi Clark

RICK'S ROSE GARDEN

The heart grows within time,
It prospers like the seed that is planted in a rose garden
By the means in life it can be carried into full blossom,
Springing into two people's heart
Growing together with time,
We find we are like the instruments in music all repeating the
same sounds to one another,
It is our rose garden filled with love and understanding
We make a toast to the sun for today.
In hopes of a brighter tomorrow which blossoms into a full rose.

Peggy Leyva

PEGGY ANN LEYVA. Born: Hollister, California, 7-13-62; Education: San Benito Joint Union High School, 1981; Art Merit Scholarship, Tying Award, Cabrillo College, Business courses; Occupation: Document controller, Secretary, Artist, Writer; Memberships: Artist Society International, San Benito Artist, American Poetry Association; Awards: Many San Benito artist awards, ribbons, sold several paintings, show art work in shows & restaurants; Writing "Life's Depths," poetry manuscript, Appreciation of Artist, 1987; Poetry: 'Mother,' 'Season of Time,' 'Warmth Within,' 'Dance Me Away,' 'Soft Touch,' all *American Poetry Anthology,* 1987; Comments: *I find expression in creating a tool of a person's mind and heart, it is the dancers' and pipers' songs of today for who we are and who we become. Art is the center of a person's soul, words are treasures of our heart. My writing is based on human emotions, experiences, love, spirituals, feelings, places and art. I enjoy piano playing, writing song-lyrics, tennis, snow skiing, and the beach.*

UNTO YOU

I nursed him from the day he was born.
I washed his cuts, kissed his bruises.
I held him when he was sick.
I comforted him when he was sad.
I laughed with him when he was happy.
I shared his joy and his sadness.
I gave him encouragement and understanding.
I was an island for him to retreat to when life became overwhelming.
I have nurtured him through all his life —
Until this day.
This day I cede my place in his life to you.
From this day on, he will share his life with you.
Please share in his joys, sorrows, triumphs, and defeats as I have.
Please be an oasis he can come to for solace, peace, and love.
Please promise me this, because he is my son,
And he will always be a part of me.

K. Lynn Mogle

I AM AN OCEAN WAVE

I AM AN OCEAN WAVE
SIPHONED UP FROM THE GUTS OF THE SEA
ONE AMONG MILLIONS
YET THE MILLIONS ARE ME
ASCEND FALL CRASH
ACKNOWLEDGING AN ANCIENT SCRIPT
ARTEMIS HAS SPELLED FOR ME
LONELY — MAGNETIC — AND LUNATIC
THE MOON HER MIRROR
EVER PUSHING PULLING
WITH INVISIBLE LIGHT LAUGHING AT
THIS MY SILVER-SCORNED DESTINY
TO ASCEND
        FALL
            CRASH
ONLY THE FALLEN STARS IN MY SOUTHERN SKY
BRING BRIEF FIRE TO THEIR WICKS TO
MOURN FOR ME
AS I DENOUNCE THIS CRUEL FATE
ASCEND NO MORE
I SCREAM
AND THE SHAMELESS SALT OF MY TEARS
SCOURGES THE SANDS
OF AN UNDECREED SHORE

Cynthia Clark Withers

REFLECTION

Some light glitters and I know not where.
Sunglint smiles there on some windblown hair.
Somewhere river flowing mirrors face
Somehow caught away in life's long race.
Sunlight glints on ripples as white danc-
Ing horse green liquid field may prance.
Over driftwood, over thousand leaves
Sparrow flutters south from autumn eaves.
I am driftwood, I am sparrow, leaf,
Horse prancing, sunlit river — thief,
Capturing moments while the hours chime,
Hoarding the sense of timelessness in time!

Shirley Mohr

WHITE WINGS OF EVENING

To my most beloved, Peter Andolino

The moods of escape this bewailing day,
are beckoning me to hurry away.
The measures of time and life,
send portal's solace from trialing strife.

Make my flight to the regions never deceiving,
to peaceful Haven's Wings of Evening.
A presence unfettered, a passage to hide,
Bounteous skies bursting azure-reaching planets wide.

Needle instruments convey abstruse questions within,
human mankind, benevolence shall win.
Perchance the strings of bead shall yield blossoms there,
once again the sugared sun shall awaken silver hair.

Death is not, the not is final death,
a devotion flaunts enduring perseverance wealth.
My soul is receptively bare to your sensitive strength,
White Wings of Evening shall bridge the broken length.

Attention my listening post with new depth and really hear,
the intrinsic nature of your voice which produces no fear.
Magnetic effects germinate into beauty breathtaking,
White Wings of Evening, O what an awaking!

Elayne Gocek Walden

BELIEVE IN YOUR DREAMS

To my friend, James

They say "Believe in your Dreams."
And you, my friend, have special dreams, like myself.
Dreams of happiness.
Dreams of success.

Like myself, friend,
You have to follow your Dreams.
But remember, my friend, it is not easy to achieve our dreams.
The path we choose can be hard, weary, and sometimes lonely.

When those lonely times come,
Remember those you hold dear.
If you need a friend,
On me you can depend.

Don't stop believing in your dreams.
Don't forget those who shared your dreams.
Our dreams are different and yet so similar.
Remember that someday our dreams will become, Reality.

My friend, it is time to say good-bye.
But good-bye sounds so final.
So I will say — "See you soon, my friend,
Best wishes to us as we pursue our dreams."

Edward H. Kwantes

IMAGES

In the sweet pre-sleep of night
Even as the mind begins to draw its curtain,
A thin transparent veil at first, but fast opaquing,
Shading conscience form consciousness.
Even then I gaze through incessantly,
Straining to see your sensuous body
Dancing across the room on winged feet,
Teasingly, just beyond my foolish grasp,
Yet close enough to keep me ever reaching.
Gliding, weightless upon the midnight air
As though mass and gravity were not there,
And beauty were all defiance needed
To rule supreme in that twilight realm.
Sublime, holographic wonder of the mind!
Fading swiftly now into the darkening deep
To the point of total transition:
When all the mind's light drowns,
And the world is suddenly submerged
Into an ocean of darkness.
Then, like the fiery sun rousing half the earth
While yet lulling the other half to sleep,
Your lovely face returns to me
Crowning the crest of a wave of dreams.

Hemson J. Zenon

YOU DID IT

I was like barking at the moon, due to my many emotions
I asked God why He had to get, my husband and my sons too soon
You gave to me consolations, showed much concern and compassions
Your very nice explanations, did suddenly change my notions
You emphasized to me often, that over spilled milk I must cry no more.

My life was dreary and hopeless, then you brought sunshine into it
You changed my sobs into laughters, relieved partially all my griefs
I was in despair and hopeless, encouragement to me you gave
You changed my frowns into smiles,
  by the jokes and wisecracks you made
You helped me to forget my griefs, and I know that you did your best.

Endearing words of compassions, helped me lessen my emotions
You said, Jesus suffered for us, and so I have to carry on
You pushed me to attain my goal, you admired and enjoyed my poems
I found out it is wonderful, my busy mind kept me cheerful
I was so very much inspired, because of your appreciations.

A divine help came unto me, I did not spend time uselessly
I compiled poems to be busy, it kept me from being lonely
Were it not for you, my dear friends, I would now be a total wretch
The death of my husband and sons, was to me so very tragic
And because of your advices, you changed my life and *you did it*.

Marcela Monterey Vda de las Balagtas

BLUES

I think not "blues" in my lament tonight,
In fact, no color flows through eyes closed tight.
Then why make plural a color of such hue
That could only mean joy when it comes into view?

The royal tint of heaven seems peace to reach,
A blending of liquid lines that edge each beach;
Blues of sky and water have but one accord,
To beautify the wonders made by God, our Lord.

I think not of "blues" in this night filled with prayer,
But of faith, strength and thanks that any shade of care
Can artfully blend, on a canvas of life,
Into a regal horizon, a mosaic without strife.

In rapid succession, I opened and closed,
My eyes — at rest, they reposed.
At one stroke of the brush, "blues" changed to blue
And pure beauty filled my spirit in a minute or two.

Jeanne Ackiss Davis

SONNET TO THE NIGHT

When I awake to the bright morning light,
Freeing myself from the dark, eerie phantoms
That fill my sleep with haunting, reckless flight.
I think to myself, how like chrysanthemums,
These shadowy, mop-headed demons are;
How wildly do they jump and dance,
Where do they come from, how near, how far?
Even now, my mind's eye views them askance.

Then, can I release my pent-up fear,
Of incubus waiting to entrap me
In a night, rigged with his cunning lair,
And cries, much like, the Highland's banshee.
When I go to sleep in the still of the night,
Will I awake, with the morning light?

Andrea McDonald-Black

HARPER'S FERRY

My heart feels the magic that my eyes, here behold.
On this splendorous mountain, from which history unfolds.
This place where two rivers dare to run free,
And, John Brown long ago, gave his life just for me.
Like Jesus before him, he saw something wrong,
He dared to be different, he dared to be strong.
He saw men in bondage, he saw men in chains,
Their sorrows were such that tears seeped through their veins.
Here in the ferry John Brown saw their plight,
And with God as his leader, he aided them in their flight.
He was hung for his trouble up there on that hill,
But the memory of his kindness remains with us still.
I stand here by the rivers looking around and above,
Surrounded by his glory and wrapped in his love.
How could I thank him for all he has done,
He led us through darkness and gave us the sun.

Andrea McDonald-Black

ILLUSIONS OF MY PRISON'S REALITY

my love eludes me at night
    like the sleep
that has eluded me for weeks
    like the freedom
    of my future
trapped in a time
surrounded by illusions of mankind
questioning my own sanity
in a place like a skinner box
trying to find my way
like a trapped animal
to the goal of freedom
    which eludes me
like my manhood being in question
    since i cannot express
what i feel as a sensitive human being
    to those i love
where interpersonal relationships
    have no meaning and
you look upon yourself
    as an individual
yet you are as trapped
    as the next man
    differing only
    in consciousness

Ronald James Dessus

RONALD JAMES DESSUS. Pen Name: Rafeek Naeem Aleem; Born: St. Luke's Children's Hospital, Philadelphia, Pennsylvania, 8-22-45; Single; Education: Allegheny Community College, A.A., Social studies, 1972; University of Pittsburg, B.A., magna cum laude with departmental honors from the Department of Black Studies, 1974; Northampton Area Community College, A.A., General education, Para-professional Teacher's Certificate, 1978; International Correspondence Schools Center for Degree Study, Associate in Specialized Business Management Degree; Now enrolled at The Institute of Children's Literature; Occupations: Machine operator, Welder, Teacher of history, math, science; Memberships: Sustaining member, Republican National Committee, Astara; Awards: Golden Poet Award, 1987; Poetry: 'I Dream Like You, Anne Sexton & Sonia Sanchez,' *Prison Writing Review,* 1980; 'Geronimo,' *The Light From Another Country,* 1984; 'Surrounded by Walls A I Ta Wa Nee,' *Poetry from American Prisons,* 1984; 'The Shuttle Launch Challenger,' *American Poetry Anthology,* 1986; Comments: *I have been incarcerated for over twenty-one years. I do not consider myself a prison poet, despite the fact that many of my poems reflect incarceration. I realize, as Jean Paul Sartre said, "Suffering breeds consciousness"; this consciousness has given birth to the reason for my being in prison. It is said that the power of choice, the will, is given to us by God; freedom of the will is one of the basic principles explained in the bible. I made the wrong choice many years ago, but I do have the freedom of a new beginning as difficult as it may seem. I am now enrolled at the Institute of Children's Literature. I hope my writings will help some child, teen or maybe an adult continue to make the right choice and know that God is real and alive in each of us despite our circumstances. We have the choice to make what we will of our lives.*

SIMPLY BEING WITH THE CREATOR

Isaiah . . . 40 . . . Verse . . . 22
*"It is God who sits above the circle of the earth.
(The people below must seem to him like grasshoppers.)
He is the one who stretches out the heavens like
a curtain and makes a tent from them."*

I sensed a need to bare my soul.
The swinging frame of enclosure gave admission.
Passageway's wisdom arose to the Gatekeeper,
and great fathom plains in Heaven did roll.
I met with the Creator, simply to rest.
The Force attraction dispelled locked gray matter.

I reveled dancing until the day-spring.
The power storehouse became as the loftiest eagle's-eye nest.
Pasture's Throne roses which never wither nor fade,
and praise prophecies, rare beauty to sing.
I lay at the feet of the Creator, the Best.
The Grace binding blood together, my sins paid.

Elayne Gocek Walden

ELAYNE GOCEK WALDEN. Born: Archer, Florida, 9-24-27; Divorced; Education: Archer High School, 1947; One year at Louisville School of Art, Some college courses in the arts; Occupation: Floral designer, Fashion designer, Crafts artist (with the tradesname Elayne the Fair), Gardener (bonsai); Poetry: 'Someday Forever,' 'Yesterday's Roses,' songs, New Nashville Music, Gold Edition, Coltrain Records, 1-87; 'Now is the Time,' *American Poetry Anthology,* 1986; 'Sweet Stolen Moment,' *Hearts on Fire: A Treasury of Poems on Love, Vol. IV,* 11-87; Comments: *I am writing four books in the form of poems and songs. Basically the story of my life, I have lived every piece of work. Each book is a sequel to the other. First book,* God's Grace and Memories; *second,* Being With God in Every Thought; *third,* Without a Song There Would be No You; *fourth,* Wings in Flight. *They are nearing completion. My poems and songs are inspired from God. Many come from dreams and visions. They are also created from people who have touched my life in a special way, from nature in every respect, and my pets. Up until about eleven years ago I never dreamed I would become a poet, but God called me in a dream: To this you have been ordained. He has been my soul teacher.*

PLAYING SNOOP AND POOP

The hunter, red hat tossed jauntily back on head
Dressed in blue jeans and a shirt of bright plaid
Started thru the woods — gun shoulder high
Behind him, unbeknown to the man
Followed a young deer in its coat of tan
When the hunter would pause — the deer dashed to a tree
Peeked around as if to say "You can't see me"
The hunter became wise and entered the game
Playing snoop and poop with the deer, almost tame
They snooped for hours, then becoming tired of their play
The hunter lay 'neath a tree — the deer went away.

Doris Brubaker Walter

MUSIC BOX

Locked up in your tower,
love can't escape your life.
Wanting someone so badly,
someone to share your dreams with,
someone to hold you close at night.

Trying to break ties that were on you,
just trying to understand your own thoughts.
Alone and lost in your ivory tower,
love can't escape your thoughts.

Happiness will bring you memories of your lover,
memories that passed you last night.
Stardust comes in through the windows,
letting love back into your life.
Happiness will bring you memories of your lover
that was with you last night.

Larry Shuffle

LARRY SHUFFLE. Born: Sanquankind Valley; Married: Linda; Son: Larry Lee; Occupation: Professional karate instructor, Musician, Poet, Songwriter; Poetry: 'Making Love,' 'Ballet of a Twilight Princess,' *American Poetry Anthology,* 1987; Comments: *If you have an imagination you don't have to think because you can wander into a world of dreams.*

THE DREAMER

If I were an artist, and could paint anything
I'd paint all the loveliest wonders of spring . . .
Green trees and flowers and birds on the wing,
Then I'd paint a mockingbird and dream it could sing.
Its throat I'd paint golden, its voice to make sweet,
Then add a bit of silver, my painting to complete.
I'd listen for its golden song all the long day through,
And when sweet melodies I hear, I'd know that dreams come true.

If I were an artist, and were asked to paint
The most enchanting thing of which I could think,
I'd paint spirited dancers in costumes bright
With motions and rhythms to bring viewers delight.
And when my work on "The Dance" was done,
I'd share my painting with everyone
That all may know there's art in the dance
And its artistic beauty your life may enhance.

If I were an artist and I could create,
This talent to my people I'd dedicate.
My brush, I'd drip in the nectar of flowers,
Adding a ray of sunshine from life's brightest hours.
I'd capture the sparkle of the nocturnal sky;
From the rainbow its multiple colors I'd pry.
On life's canvas, I'd add all the love I could find
And bring the magnificence of color to all humankind.

LaVerne Byrd-Smith

FORCE HIM TO THE LEFT

Force Him to the left
He'll always turn over the ball.
Force Him to the left.
He'll fall on His face in front of all.

He never listened to the coach.
You can't go the same ole way.
Like the run you get in with sin,
You got to practice and work every skill.
And start today.

Today is a new beginning,
As He worked hard to be his best,
Just in time for game day.
'Cause He knows they'll force to the left.

The coach is with his player,
As he helped him to be his best.
This time he didn't fall on his face,
As you heard *swish!*
When they forced him to his left.

Larry Grogan

LARRY EUGENE GROGAN. Born: Chanute, Kansas, 7-27-61; Poetry: 'There is a Man,' *American Poetry Anthology*, 1982; 'God Is,' *Best New Poets of 1986*; Comments: *I write about things that mean a lot to me like a special friend and God, because without Him nothing is possible; so the glory should go to Him.*

MEMORIES OF NEW ENGLAND

Yes, I grew up along your craggy coast
Learned of life and lobster pots
Upon your frigid shores.
Built snow forts in your
Crisp, bright winter
And sand castles
In your surly summer.

Explored your soft pine thickets
In fingerpainted autumn.
Devoured sandy clams and codfish cakes
In your strident springtime.

    Now that I have grown
    and left your womb,
    your jagged shores
    are calling me back home.

    Someday, I vow
    I'll make it back to you,
    My ashes dancing
    On your seething seas.

Lorraine Standish

I used to want to die,
so one day I pretended.
You vultures picked my brain.
The scars are hidden
by a full set of hair.
Just recently I've
learned to love life,
and now I have cancer.
I know it won't kill me,
and I am certain
that when I lose my hair
the scars won't show.

James Deisch

LIFE'S SIEVE!

The 'Sands of Time,' so sages say:
  Are sifted daily, come what may!
  This sifting process — as they say,
Extends through life: Day unto day!
  Small grains pass through —
    The chunks remain! —
  Large flakes alone
    What we retain!
Questioning ever: Loss or gain?
  The puzzle's answered,
    As we live,
Not what we get, but what we give
  Does *not* sift out
    Of our life's sieve!
Love gives the most —
    We found this so.
Love is the power — and this we know!
  So let us love,
    And all forgive —
Then —
  Life will have *no* empty sieve!

Alice Cummings

TATTING

She folds the afternoon around her
Like unbleached muslin.
Fire in the sky comes down
To play with the goldfish
In a bowl beside the loveseat —
Hard to catch a sun that sets
Like honeydew melon
Over window-box begonias.
"It's hot," she murmurs, "much too hot,"
As rays of material in the torn skirt settle.
She waits alone in a stiff-backed chair
Her father brought from Boston.
His picture pouts on the piano —
A big-mouthed, wounded bass
Holding a booty of speckled trout.
Condensation drips from the iced tea
In an old canning jar,
Baptizing the skirt.
Tomorrow she'll mend the moth hole
In the lace curtains.

Jill Hatfield-Bland

Life is a test,
    only God knows whether we pass!

Timothy J. Cooper

VIKING SUN

Born again, reincarnated
  it seems we've traveled
Together before
  our souls feel as one
Two hearts aflame
  to right, to be wrong

An embrace left lone through
  eternities
For a moment together
  past times reunited
Flesh to flesh, free

Expressions, conversation
  the salt of your breast's
Memories locked in the subconscience
  spiritual mysteries unknown

Those minutes
  now again too soon washed away
And to when you will return
  if ever, I do not know
But somehow I know my love
  We have walked this way, before

Stephen D. Green

WINDOWS OF THE MIND

Windows of the mind
  what do they mean to you
Can you begin to count them
  or are they just too few

From the moment of our birth
  to the minute of life's end
There are so many things
  that we can't comprehend

The windows of a house
  are just like in the mind
We can see right through them
  yet sometimes we are blind

We can look through windows
  the world is all around
Are we looking at ourselves
  can reality ever be found

Do we really have a mind
  is it worth its weight in gold
Can we make decisions
  or are we just controlled

The windows of the mind
  are not like any tokens
Like the windows of a house
  they are easily broken

J. E. Zawacki, Jr.

THE JOURNEY OF THE FRUIT TREES

Living in her car
dreamin' from afar

holding one baby
with another on the way

lay the children down
on a dusty car seat
ragged, faded towel draped across
the cracked window
forms a ray of shade on the baby

working hard and working long
working all day long
from sunrise
until the mid-day heat
drives them away from the fields
seeking any shade they can find

to rest their tired, aching bodies
and their tired, aching feet

ankle-length, billowing dress
hand-stitched together
from the remains of two, once very formal, gowns
castaway, rescued
from garbage cans passed along the journey
of the fruit trees

weary, weather-lined faces
and, gentle almond eyes.

Sally Rhodes

RUNNING AT MORNING

Run in the cool shadows of the road
At daybreak under broad-leafed oaks
With long aching branches, when sun's
Red eye is still hazy with brown sleep
And let the mind be at peace.

Let lostness wander into dark ploughed down
Fields sheared up to receive scorching light of sun
Wafting into sweet sense of sodden prairie grass
Cut and laid in neat rows for baling
Where insects chirr the night away.

By the road watch young cottonwood shiver
Or cold curious muzzle of nervous coyote
Jabbing thickets of brush ahead.

Listen to rows of sunburnt cornstalks rotted
Before harvest time rustle from their dead sleep.
"Old Jim will go under this year. Everything must go:
John Deere, the house, the farm."

Now peace lopes in the heart
Like a faithful dog come to trot at the heels
Of a man and poisoned thoughts of yesterday's
Ruin and destruction drip away
From the mind like sweat in the sonorous wind

Run . . . and intense Love's wet ashes
Plop down to the jutty road underfoot in dirt red.
Pounded solid by muscle, instincts back into the primitive.

George D. Scott

CYCLICAL

A Dedication to Marie

I look with wonder as early morning's faint blush
Spread o'er sleeping scapes of land and city in array,
Which lie like sparkling jewels at the end of each yesterday,
Fresh from dusk's cooling shower after sunset's fiery flush.

My heart stands still as slowly you open your dark brown eyes,
Which like bright stars twinkle merrily with your enchanting smile;
A bundle of heavenly joy you are, a gift from the laughing skies
To brighten up my twilight days as I linger here a little while.

Lovingly and very softly I kiss your tiny hand and touch a finger,
That grasps and captures my heart with a love innocent and tender;
In a moment I see yesterday's varied scenes flashing back swiftly
Stormy but spicy that you, too, in the future shall taste heartily.

With laughters we walk the rainbow-colored path of your childhood,
Fairies, dwarfs, castles, and witches you gobble as you do fast food;
Then endless questions of what's, why's and how's you now ask,
Answering them was pleasant, it was such an easy and funny task.

Rosy dawn and golden sunset shall blend into a pattern of harmony,
As my life and yours merge serenely into a delightful continuity;
The cycle goes on and with a child's smile shall always glow,
A grandparent's memories in one wonderful kaleidoscopic show.

Connie V. Espeleta

CONNIE VILLAMOR ESPELETA. Born: Agusan, Philippines, 12-12-20; Married: Ramon Espeleta, 12-12-45; Education: Osmena Colleges, B.S.E., 1965, Centro Escolar University, Manila, Philippines, M.A., 1973; Occupations: Retired educator; Homemaker, Writer; Memberships: Philippine Public Schools Teachers' Association; Centro Escolar Faculty Association; Awards: Antonino Bronze Plaque for writing pageants and poetry (R.P.), 1972; used by fellow educators (Masbete); Poetry: 'Tribute to the Power of Poetry,' *American Poetry Anthology, Vol. II*, 1983; 'Love and Perfidy,' *Hearts on Fire, Vol. II*, 1985; 'Praises and Prayers,' *Best New Poets of 1986;* 'Praise the LORD for His Eternal Goodness,' *Words of Praise*, 1987; 'Let Your Joyous Sounds Fill the Chilly Air,' *American Poetry Anthology, Vol. VII*, 1987; Comments: *Life is ephemeral, but beautiful thoughts expressed in poetry are eternal. Thus, I bequeath to posterity in particular and to the world in general my writings about God's beautiful masterpieces and His boundless love to mankind, and also about friendship, understanding, and peace among nations.*

SALUTE TO THE BIRTH OF BABY DREW, THE DAY THE EARTH TREMBLED

Dean, Meg, and son, Patrick, were having
  Their dreams at three o'clock in the morning,
Meg woke with a shake,
  The earth gave a quake,
    And to the hospital they went flying,
In the early morning dawn,
  Drew came along
    With a cry and a song!

Pamela Delis

MY VALLEY

I walked in a valley that you wouldn't believe,
With tall green grass and a beautiful breeze.
With lusty fields and clean fresh air,
And once or twice, even a bear.
I looked and saw the light blue sky,
And then I saw the mountains so high.
I drank from blue rivers and tremendous falls,
Believe it or not, there was no smog.
There were no buses, not even a car,
No tall buildings, just a few small farms.
I watched the most beautiful flowers in bloom,
At night I looked upon a shiny full moon.
I looked at all the wonders I'd seen,
And then I awoke, it was only a dream.

Edward W. Green

IF . . .

If I could be
Tall as a tree
Birds would come
And sing to me

If I could run
Swift as a brook
Fish would come
To take a look

If I could fly
As eagles do
the sky would show
A different view

If I could be
The man in the moon
I'd let the sun
Sleep 'til noon

If I could be
An angel fair
The world would live
Without a care

Kathleen S. Peterson

A SILENT TIME

Quiet night, a halo moon,
A luminous, hazy moon,
On a summer's night.
The Ancient Mariner's call,
To the heavens for all.
While mermaids keep watch,
On souls of many who sail,
As they sing by the shores,
Of the Seven Seas.
Stars with twinkling eyes,
Looking down without a sound;
As the summer breeze,
Comes blowing in with ease.
Northern lights light the way,
Across the Southern Bay,
To make an enchanting night,
In seasons all around;
Coming up to meet the dawn,
A silent time without a chime,
Ringing without a Rhyme.

Debra L. Wilcox

REPETITION

History repeats itself
you think they'd learn by now
the powers of the men in charge
have been misused somehow

With weapons they try to control us
apartheid, famine, war games
enough to ten times over destroy us
what do they think they'd gain?

If they annihilate the people
there'll be no one to live by their rules
we'd be the ones in heaven
so they must be the fools

It's not too late to change it
but it's gonna take us all,
if we don't learn that Peace is Best,
the world is going to fall

So stand up and tell them,
any way you can, have your say
'cause our children have to live here,
even if they blow us away.

Teeka Lynne Stevenson

FRUIT OF LIFE

The moon was full and O so bright,
When I awakened and peered outside,
Taking my time to truly think,
About this dream of "The Tree of Life!"

O this tree would take your eyes,
Being so big and being so green,
With all fruits of fancy colors,
Hanging from the limbs full of grace!

Yes, only let me pick just one,
Was my thought as I reached high,
To pick one from this special tree,
When a voice said to me!

"So you would like to pick my fruit,
The fruit of life I took from man,
Because of sin all must die,
Because of Christ all can live!"

Yes, my God, Your word is truth,
I do desire to pick Your fruit,
And have a sip from Your fountain,
So thank You God for eternal life!

Doris Burleigh

TOO EASY

If things came too easy
there must be something wrong!
If things came too easy
there would be nothing
to make us strong!
In opposition comes strength
in body, mind and soul.
So the stumbling blocks
that often get in our way
sharpen our wits and
make us strong as a whole.
God's Celestial Cunning
is part of a unique plan
to mold and temper *matter*
into needed Superman!
It takes strength
to do the impossible,
which is possible
when you know how!
So don't curse this cunning
because you know what it is now.

Clodah G. Summer

CLODAH GERALDINE SUMMER. Born: Hudson, Ohio, 1-23-18; Education: Dr. of Concept-Therapy, San Antonio, Texas, 1955 (being self-taught in my early years has shown me that observing life itself was my real teacher); Art, Incarnate Word College, 1961; Art, Music, and Photography, San Antonio College, 1962-67; Occupations: Writing, Poetry; Memberships: A beamer in the International On The Beam Club; Bulverde Area Humane Society; Awards: Golden Poet Awards, 1986-87, for 'Easter Time' and 'A Revolutionary Revelation,' plus 11 honorable mentions; Poetry: 'Cackling Hen,' humor and facts poem, *Prickly Pears,* 1985; 'The 4th of July,' humor and facts animal poem, *Great Poems of Today,* 1976; 'Santa Speaks Intelligence,' symbolic poem, *World Poetry Anthology,* 1981; 'Life Speaks in Haikus,' a laws of life poem, *Many Voices, Many Lands,* 1986; 'Too Easy,' an "Obstickles" explanation poem, *Best New Poets of 1987;* Comments: *To entertain and make people laugh, I try to put the humor I see in life in poetry. To help people learn facts about life they do not have time to think of by themselves, I put scientific facts in with humor or very serious lessons in life. Metaphysical ideas show up from my 37 years in Concept-Therapy. To me it is more important to teach than to be a good poet, as I hear good poetry is not like a lesson in a science class.*

A SHIZOPHRENIC EPISODE

Day after day she sits and stares,
She paces around, twists her hair;
And laughs at visions only she can see,
Talking to no one else but Life and Xee.

She draws away from others' touch,
And thinks they're there to catch and scratch;
She says they're there to see her withering
And fears their whispers and their gathering.

The word she hears would race around
Her head, with objects, lights, and sounds;
Her actions are regressingly bizarre,
She claims she is the "Queen of Martian Stars"!

She turns away from what is here
That then she may her burden bear;
These flights assist her ease the psychic pain
Anxiety leaves upon her burning brain.

She knows she's sick, "Schiz" of some sort.
As her perception still distorts
People as cardboards, and the world as tin,
She takes her adjunct therapies with grin.

And while for others it may seem
Her mental health she can't redeem,
With chemotherapy, milieu and care,
And kind support, some normal life will share.

Inday Nabor Lombardi

MILDRED NABOR LOMBARDI. Pen Names: Inday Lombardi; Born: Libacao, Aklan, Philippines; Married: L. M. Lombardi; Education: ONPH School of Nursing, Diploma in nursing; La Consolacion College, Philippines, B.A., History, cum laude; Central Michigan University, M.A., Personnel management and supervision, 1980; Occupation: Nursing instructor; Memberships: American Nurses' Association, Delaware Nurses' Association, Philipino-American Association of Delaware; Sigma Iota Epsilon; Awards: 'Wishes,' first prize, *The Ripples,* Philippines, 1960; Poetry: 'My Song,' *The Lamp,* 1958; 'Communism,' *The Elite,* 1962; 'Beauty,' *Poems for Little Angels,* 1986; 'Philippines — Queen of Asian Lands,' *New Voices in American Poetry,* 1986; 'The Homeless One,' 1987; Comments: *I love to write poems with historical, philosophical, religious, psychiatric, analytical and romantic themes. Poems for Little Angels is my first attempt at children's poetry and is composed of 23 poems that emphasize values, all with illustrations by former Fulbright-Hays and International Rotary scholar and painter, Jose Dureza. Currently, I am working on an epic poem on ancient Philippines, "Starlight of Long Ago."*

THE BALLAD OF THE ICICLES

The debate is hot and your case isn't clear
Everyone turns against you
The moment crowns the line and leaves a residue of fear
Intentions provoke misunderstandings
Words are misconstrued
Unfriendly feelings revealed by chance words
Clouds cover the sunshine and weary rain seems endless
Days start hesitant and unsure, echoing yesterday's
    bleakness.
You stand in deepest shadow caused by latest grief
Discovery of a pain thought long ago eased.
Guilt because you know you received your just due.
Bad taste in your mouth because you wasted the
    trust you needed so badly.
Icicles have taxed your strength, health and faculties.
You are finally allowed to lick your wounds.
You pray. You ask forgiveness
The breakaway has now begun.
Icicles slowly melt as the first ray of the
    Son of God shines on them.

Katherine M. Brady

WHEN LIFE'S STORMS COME

The lonely ancient house sighing, creaking, and shaking shamelessly,
As gusty winds howled and deafening thunder rolled unrelentlessly,
Conspired with the night and spewed out sounds and forms quite eerie;
Iron chains dragging, people moaning and wailing intermittently,
Made the child in me tremble, whimper, and cower in fear.

Blinding lightning streaked down and ignited some pines nearby,
Turning them to an inferno licking the house and curling up high;
Pandemonium and burning fire caused reason from out of my mind fly,
Petrified with fear my frail heart froze, I thought I'd soon die.

But the will to live, to stay alive, sparked the instinct to survive.
Rushing from the smoke-filled house, I shouted loud to heaven above,
Called His name again and again, asked help for the sake of His love;
The wild elements still around became tame at the sound of His name,
And the sweet pouring rain came quenching every greedy hungry flame.

I raise my eyes to the skies and stared at a mystic silvery light
Descending to my garden and changing it to an ethereal sight —
    swaying plants with flow'rs and leaves glistening
    became dancers with bejewelled tresses glittering;
    bending and tiptoeing gracefully to the tempo
    of drums, cymbals, and flutes played fortissimo.
In those brief seconds of heavenly relief and ecstatic delight,
I felt His holy presence, comforting me all through the night;
Whene'er life's storms come, let's raise our voices in pray'rs,
In His own mysterious ways He shall send help because He cares.

Connie V. Espeleta

LOVE

As days grow longer,
And birds fly higher in song —
Dogwoods blossom pink and white,
And our love grows strong.

Like a falling star,
Love may seem to disappear,
But ours is steadfast love and
Always will be near.

It touches our hearts
Like a misty summer rain —
Refreshingly light and warm —
Healing any pain.

Tho' skies may darken
Tho' the air be cold and dry
Love will warm us always and
Ever, you and I.

Debra J. Barba

HERALD OF SPRING

Crocus

Like an effervescent bubble
On lawns, in gardens, mayhap in stubble,
All heedless of the weather
Scattered widely, sometimes close together.

Exquisitely beautiful petals unfold
Awakening emotions in young and old.
Gorgeous, colorful herald of spring
And the fragrance it will bring.

Gold, and purple throats
Cupped in petals, white as the cloud that floats,
Windblown across the blue
Colors that rival the rainbow's hue.

The rainbow is a token
Of a promise that can't be broken.
And the crocus seems to sing,
"Every year shall have a spring."

Agnes Angel Stiles

SPELLCASTING

Hide yourself in the moonlit dark,
Set free the love-torn lark,
Spin the spell to be reborn,
Cast off the cloak of love bitterly
worn.
Throw his ashes into the wind,
Dance with the spirit . . . now begin,
Turn the wheel once more,
Reap the fruits of beloved Kore.
Heal the dove's wing,
Listen to the caged bird sing,
Unburden your weary heart,
Forget the one who tore it apart.
Watch the dove fly,
Gone is the past from your eye,
See the new day dawn . . .
To you, a new soul is born.

Geri Nostrand

MR. SUNDAE

I wet my finger and
put it to your lips –
just to see if you are real.
Gently, you bite it, and I know you are.

Wrinkling my nose at the flash of
white teeth, I lick your fingers slowly –

just to see if you respond.
Eyeing you sideways, I
see that you do.

You say, "I have weak moments,"
times you need me, places you want me.
I say, "I'm glad," 'cause to me
you're like an old ice cream sundae
going someplace just to taste good.

I lick you all over, Mr. Sundae,
your tongue, lips, cheek, chin,
but you don't melt away.
You just get warmer and sweeter,
rising to meet my appetite.

I wet my lips and go wandering,
in search of dessert, glad
that you have weak moments.
You smile, and you are real.

Barbara Whetstone

I AM OF AN OYSTER NOT!

I am of an oyster not!
    No pearl will grow on any spot!
    Of my anatomy!

No matter how antagonized!
    Ragèd mores lashed unwise!
    Upon a nuded me!

Gretchen Weiner

SOMETHING MORE LIES BEYOND

Streams of sunlight rays,
Glistening through white clouds,
Reaching to touch the earth below,
Like an elegant, golden shroud.

While pondering this wondrous beauty,
Which moves without a sound,
I behold the clouds and golden rays,
Knowing something more lies beyond.

This heavenly paradise land,
Is part of an infinite plan,
From the first tiny droplet of water,
To the last minute grain of sand.

My existence on earth is enraptured,
By life forms which suddenly appear,
Each moment is very precious,
To be lived fully while I am here.

My passion for life is aroused,
Consuming all that exists around,
Though someday I'll break my earthly bond,
Knowing something more lies beyond.

Marjorie Daly

PEOPLE PROFILE IN THE SCHEME OF THINGS

Does destiny
  define, or limit
  man's accomplishments?
Are people's feats ordained
  to be large, or small?
Ponder man's aspirations,
  and known
  achievements;
Did an all-wise creator
  design, and foresee all?

Warring nations,
  expound differing views
  on religion;
As to a God to worship,
  men disagree.
Consider the magnitude
  and functioning
  of the Universe;
Can man deny, there's
  a "Universal Diety?"

Lucille S. Weaver

LUCILLE SMITH WEAVER. Born: Putneyville, Pennsylvania, 3-26-13; Education: University of Iowa, Psychology and business administration, 1949; Occupation: Personnel and wage administration specialist with federal government; Poetry: 'Critical Judgments,' 1986; 'Seaside Therapy,' 1986; 'The Mystery of Religion,' 'Tomorrow the Sun,' 'The Nature of God,' all *Words of Praise,* 1987; Comments: *The primary focus of my poetry is on nature and people. Giving expression to people's thoughts, feelings, expressions and experience and my own reaction to nature and the thoughts called to mind. The first poems done on religion were done in response to a specific request.*

RENDEZVOUS

The wild flowers adorn the lush vegetation,
  down by the ocean
White sand stretched beyond the beach,
  she sat right by my side.

The frothy waves danced upon the shore,
  the brilliant coral shown,
She sat there till purple dusk,
  like a queen upon a throne.

Warm breezes teased her flowing hair,
  the glossy seals did share,
This lovely secret rendezvous,
  etched in my heart with care.

Joy M. Parker

SYLVIA

What such sweet melodies in her name
To match the fine fluidity of her frame;
She has the face with the pulchritude to mellow
The fast, furious hearts of many a fellow.

She is living proof flowers grow in the desert
And she's an oasis to a heart bereft of pleasure;
Her laughter is such music that I hear
Until no other silly sound could ever compare.

When I drink to her beauty I make toast
And in my feeble lines I try and boast;
Yet I haven't the ability with words to do her justice
My meager words sound to my learned ear as just ice.

She always inspires my heart to uplift and sing
All I but need to do is call out her sweet name;
Then I hear all notes and chords in full harmony
Because she like her name possesses all melody.

Charles Henry Powell

TREASURE AT THE END OF THE RAINBOW

I searched and searched to find a bit of happiness;
I tried in different ways to be content.
Then I heard about following the rainbow;
And the treasure that was at the other end.
Well, Honey, I have chased a lot of rainbows,
Searching for the treasure there to find.
But I never found the end of the rainbow,
Until the day that you asked me to be your wife.
You're the treasure at the end of the rainbow,
You're the pot of gold most people hope to find.
You're the treasure at the end of the rainbow,
And, Honey, I'm so glad that you're mine.
After searching for so long, I nearly gave up;
I thought there was no treasure to be found.
But your love was all I needed to convince me;
There's Treasure if you only look around.
Now I'm no longer chasing after rainbows,
Searching for that elusive pot of gold;
For I've got all the gold I ever needed,
On my finger and in all the love you show.
'Cause you're the treasure at the end of the rainbow;
You're the pot of gold most people hope to find.
You're the treasure at the end of the rainbow,
And Honey, I'm so glad that you're mine.

J. R. Moses

ICE CAPADES

*Dedicated to Shirley Penkivich for editing my poems,
and to my mother and father, Ray and Lee Qualls.*

The scraping under my feet from the blade on
my skates on the ice, The pounding in my body of
excitement of performance, The crowd applause
thrilled with the brilliance of style. I glide
like a swan with grace, beauty, and eloquence.
I'm lifted higher and higher, my arms lift me,
twirl me. I reach out like a ballerina with toes
to the ice, I perform like a champion. Performing
with great enthusiasm and style, with aerobatic
skills of brilliance that are breathtaking. With
great competition, skill and speed. My heart races,
my soul soars, exploding with sheer happiness to
its peak.

Juanita Cossey

CHOICES

Choices are the most important function of mankind!
By your choices you rise or fall,
By your choises you win or lose,
By your choices you rule your destiny.

You can choose good or evil,
You can choose right or wrong,
You can choose work or indigence,
You can choose independence or dependence.

Every choice you make day by day,
Makes the next choice easier or harder,
Choices of wrongdoing lead to more wrongdoing,
Choices of good lead to more good.

Consider all things before you make your choice.
Will your choice help or hinder you?
Will your choice strenghten or weaken you?
Will your choice lift you up or drag you down?

Wrong choices can be reversed,
But often with great pain and sorrow,
The choice is yours, *choose wisely!*
Do not let anyone make the choice for you!

*Faith or unbelief will decide your eternal destiny!
God or Mammon — Paradise or Hell!
It's your choice! You choose! The choice is forever!
God gives you your own free choice! What will it be?*

Eliza Tyler Taylor

MY DEAREST FRIEND

At the age of twelve
I met my dearest friend,
And from that time on
He became my constant companion.

No matter what the crisis or trouble,
No matter what the joy or pain,
In all my troubles and excitements,
Wherever I would go, my dearest friend was always there.

Always loving, protecting, caring for me,
Helping me make right decisions
Concerning home, family, jobs, everything,
A faithful, loving, caring companion.

As time passed and life became more full
Of everyday living and pressure from others,
I sometimes neglected my dearest friend,
And would go without visiting, for a time.

But — always, always, always,
He was there waiting for me
To get in touch with him.
No matter what the reason, *He was there!*

*My dearest friend is Jesus Christ!
My Savior, the Lord and King of Glory!
And I will live with Him forever,
In Paradise!*

Eliza Tyler Taylor

King's Bridge.

GOD IS NOT DEAD

How do I know?

Because I talk to *Him* every day,
And *He* answers in truth, love, comfort and peace.
He is always the same, yesterday, today and forever.
He is without beginning and without end,
From everlasting to everlasting.

He is God! He rules!

The sun in its rising and setting,
On split-second timing since its creation,
Burning with inestimable heat but never consumed.
The moon, planets and stars, moving in their appointed places,
The earth, man's temporary abode, moving in its assigned orbit.

Through the millenniums since earth's creation,
He controls its seedtime and harvest,
Ebb and flow of its mighty waters,
Thunders and lightnings, rain and snow, fog and mist,
He causes the earth to tremble at *His Word*,
But remain in its place in the heavens.

If God is dead, who is in control of the universe?

Not mankind, who says, God is dead!
God's laws are immutable, infallible, unchangeable,
Until He, not man, changes them.

Thank You God! You are alive and in control, forevermore!

Don't tell me God is dead! I know better!

Eliza Tyler Taylor

ELIZA TYLER TAYLOR. Born: Benson, North Carolina; Lived in Goldston, North Carolina until 1946; Has lived in Redondo Beach since then; Married: Myron Taylor, deceased; Three children: Myra Taylor Dunn, Jean Taylor Johnson, William J. Taylor; Education: Two years of college; additional college and university courses and seminars; Occupation: Manufacturing engineering planning, senior, retired; Writer; Poet; Poetry: *Impressions and Reflections*, a collection of poems; Themes: *Spiritual truths and insights concerning the Almighty Godhead and the Kingdom of God. Also living life at its fullest and best.*

THE SPARKLING BROOK

Did you ever look at a brook?
When it goes sparkling down a hill?
There are many hidden pools among the rocks.
Fish darting here and there and even bugs.
Fisherman trying for a strike
Along the brook, one can find pebbles, stones, small and large.
People have been wading
One can find quiet and peace.
Well the sparkling brook goes on its way
Life seems much the same to me as the brook.

Hazel A. Gould

A TIME FOR EVERY PURPOSE

In the eve of my life I see
  all those above
  and beyond me.
But as I think of the noontide
  sweet memories flood my soul
  and I am happy.
And as a babe (in the dewy dusk)
  I may see all that lies ahead
  — all I've seen —
    and my heart swells with the joy of confrontation.
But now, after the battle's won,
  and I retreat to lick my wounds,
    I live only to count the stars of my
    daydreams.
      For soon 'twill be midnight.

Scott Rawlinson

MEN WORKING?

When I am driving down the street,
Why, there's a sign that my eyes do meet.
It'll say some words like "Caution, Men Working,"
But as I observe them, there's cause for some smirking.
There's a hole I notice that seems to need fillin'
And there's a machine for the job of a-drillin'.
There's a great big truck and some goop that is black,
And a roller to smooth it and pack it real flat.
But where are the men who we're told are a-workin'?
They're under the shade tree drinkin' coffee that's been perkin'.
They're laughing at some joke they shouldn't be tellin'
And they're tellin' each other how their wives been a-yellin'.
There's only one man with any reason to brag.
It's the man who so proudly does wave that red flag.
Even then I wonder if he really is needed,
Since my car's the only one in sight to be heeded.
As I sit and wait for the flag to wave me through,
I ponder, I wonder, as I look at that crew,
Why has a sign ne'er been seen far and wide
That says "Women Working" when we're working outside?
I guess 'cuz it's obvious what we are a-doin'.
We don't need a sign to be givin' a clue'n.
So you men, with your signs that say "Caution, Men Working,"
To be truthful, your signs should say "Caution, Men Shirking"!

Rosemary Beecner

ON BEING: A HUMANISTIC CONJUGATION

I *am* . . . but you *Are* . . . and he, she, or it *is*
That's the nature of being, I'm told.
When I *was,* you *were,* and he, she, or it *was*
But that conjugation didn't hold.

"If you *can be, I can be;* he, she, or it *can be* too!"
The Am(s) and Is(es) and Was(es) did declare.
"If you *should be,* we *should be,* and they too, *should be.*
This just seems 'subjunctively' fair."

For if *we are,* and *you are,* and *they* also *are,*
The future for all can be bright.
If you *will be,* we *shall be,* and they *shall be* too.
Then *being* will come out just right.

Consider "being" from an ethnic perspective,
from an economic, or world point of view,
Or in relationships with family and friends,
Where in this conjugation are *You?*

LaVerne Byrd-Smith

FOR A YOUNG WOMAN ON THE STREETS

Riding safe bus to safe job
I saw you and cannot forget

Lying on the sidewalk
Your morning stirs so heavily
Dark tangles fill your face
Sway raising shoulders from the ground
And roll, leaning on one arm, to your side

Shoulder waist hip slim leg
silhouette against a chasm
I see no bridge, no wall
to stop your falling and I fear
I fear for you

There is no parapet
no tender ear to hear your craziness
No one to cry with at your rapes
or keep you from destruction

I look down and toward another morning

Cheryl Tupper

SOLAR WINDS

Quiescence of life fills the
  encompassing wind

The sand dunes enjoin its visitations

Trees reach out to absorb life force
  rich with photons

Soil and water listen to airy recitations

Are there angels dancing in the storms
  and thunder clouds?

The solar spoon stirs a thickening soup

Swirling condensations and evaporations
  toss the atmospheric dress

Earth reclines in the star gaze loop

Cora Mendeola

A PART OF ME

You've been a part of my eyes,
  you help me see the things
  I should.

You've been a part of my ears,
  to help me listen to your
  wisdom and counsel.

You've been a part of some of
  my big decisions, so that
  I make the right ones.

You've been a part of my life,
  that's strong, loving and
  special . . . my dad.

Thanks for being a part of me!

Tamara Kay Britain

REMEMBER

Remember when it was you
Remember when it was me
Remember how we would miss each other
the long lonely nights
the sad phone calls
Remember those special weekends
the times you arrived
the times you left
Remember when it was us against the sea
the nights on the beach
the days in the park
Remember when I cried
the time you cried
Remember when it was us
Remember me the one you love
Remember you the one I love

Patricia A. Bremer

PATRICIA ANN BREMER. Pen Name: Honey West; Born: San Jose, California; Married: Howard West; Education: High school graduate; Occupations: Teacher's aide, Yard duty teacher; Poetry: 'You and I,' 4-87; 'My Kite,' 5-87; 'Remember,' 9-87; all American Poetry Association; Comments: *'You and I' is dedicated to Howard West for his faith in my work. 'My Kite' is dedicated to my family for all of their support.*

DA VINCI, A GIFTED MIRACLE

A Florentine genius this
      Renaissance man,
Unequaled comparison,
      a rarity indeed,
Quality surpassed a mortal with a
      thought to
Transpire everyday activity into a
      phenomenon.
In an era of timeless endeavors and
      unlimited adventure.
Captured the mind of a king,
      artistic ability
Of lifelike ingenuity,
      Leonardo's respect
For life enabled his aesthetic
      aura to
Uphold hierarchy of aristocratic
      nobility.

Rita Marie Knecht

MY MOTHER, MY FRIEND

When I was a little girl,
  I pretended to be
  this young pretty lady
  that I loved so very much.

Then after I reached my
  teenage years, I
  desired to model my
  character like that
  same beautiful woman
  I admired as a child.

Now that I am older,
  I often seek counsel
  and receive comfort
  from her after all
  these years.

I say these things because
  I was her little girl.
  The daughter I am
  proud she raised into
  a young woman.

She is still an intelligent
  and beautiful woman
  whom I adore and love
  with all my heart.

My mother, my friend.

Tamara Kay Britain

I AM A POET

I am a poet . . . a painter of the soul.
  I need no brush, no canvas,
  no dye to mix or control.
I can create a world of beauty,
  wring the sorrow from swollen eyes,
Or type out a tune so sad
  it will make the most cold-hearted cry.

I am a poet . . . the rhyme is the heart of me.
  I can take a creature of sadness
  make you believe it is his destiny.
I can write of the love that warms me,
  that stirs me through and through,
And from my lyrics you will sing
  of the love that stirs you too.

I am a poet . . . my life is to entertain,
  to leave behind when I am gone
  a song from my soul, a bittersweet refrain.
I will take the things that haunt me
  that make me laugh or sing,
And from my poet's eye I'll change them
  to colors that pull at your heart's string.

I am a poet . . . I deal in verse, in rhyme,
  a mirror for the eclectic soul
  of the poet I'm coloring in my lifetime.

Mary Ann Taylor

467

FRIENDS

'Twas said one day, in the cool quiet dawn,
Look, look over yonder,
And lo, who did we see coming,
But, Nell and Danny Ponder.

Loaded with gifts they came our way,
And as they came closer we heard them say,
"Come friends, come share God's gifts today."

Freely he gives, and freely we receive,
All that he asks is that we believe.
So come and take freely of the gifts he has sent,
And we gave thanks to our God, as on our knees we went.

So truly today, our hearts sing with joy,
As we share God's love with these he has sent.
So Danny and Nell, God's blessings on you we pray,
As you turn to go on your merry way.

Knowing you answered God's call to you,
It's to feed my sheep, and you did too.
For God to bless and keep safe all that is yours,
This is our prayer for you today,
As we turn now and go on our merry way.

Jean Reed

PASSÉ

It seemed casual enough Our meeting on an Army installation
I heard your greeting A simple "hi" You walked by
That's all there was.

I didn't return the "hi" — Involved in a conversation with a girl
From the home town Discussing a scene at the station preceding
Entrance into the Army.

Basic was rough — Fun 'tho — Weekends came fast. Off we'd go
Neighboring towns Did lots of running around I think I loved you then.

We split, far and wide after sixteen weeks — Again — Side by side;
Stationed together — For good?

Get along? Not always arguments? Not always. Days were good
    Some were bad
I could appreciate them now (wish I had!).

Plans drawn. A home of our own Greenwich Village You and I happy,
    together
All kinds of weather.

Orders. Don't hold your breath. We're sure to be separated. Anyhow,
You're unhappy I'm temperamental. You've tried to understand —
    But you can't.

Comparison, weather with a love affair — One day's dark
    Another fair
Hot, cold, Sunshine sometimes bright as the old. It comes back tho'
    Doesn't it?
The sunshine that is — Do you see any traces Of the rain on
    the places It's rained on?

Sometimes. You're gone. Not by miles Mostly I miss your smile.
    I was wrong
You were right. These thoughts reach me Far in the night.

You came, you saw, you conquered My love my life. Beaten into
    submission
I throw myself at you Empty blue needing you, as always.

E. M. Albritton

THE SEA

It wants to take me with it! Very much against my will,
The feeling that passes over Leaves me bewildered, upset, ill.

"Come to me" it says "Put your trip aside.
Throw your cares to the winds. Away we can ride."

Close your eyes   Don't be afraid
Everything went haywire. All the plans you had made.

You're blue, lost, forsaken   There's nothing more
Nothing behind you — Nothing before.

Stop your procrastination   Don't try to remember
Forget your destination   You were due in November?

So what! You're late for your trip.
It roars on beneath   I feel my insides rip —

Apart — My insides — or you and I?
I can't seem to remember   Oh do or die?

How fascinating   This calm yet wild sea
What pathetic messages   It delivers to me.

The ship lurches. I wake with a start
This numb aching reeling   Encases my heart.

I hate myself   For allowing the sea
To disturb my whole being   To disturb you and me.

E. M. Albritton

THE DANDELION PRINCESS

A chubby little girl

I saw you laughing with your friends, and I wondered if I should
    let you be —
I wanted to join in the fun, but you turned your back on me —
I saw all the children playing, and I wished that I could stay,
but, everyone turned, looked at me, they said, "No! Go . . . get away!"

The park is before me, its nature called me there,
in it I am at home, I am a child so fair —
I walk barefoot through the grass, the flowers: yellow, white and blue,
I am surrounded by my friends: elves, animals, plants, and friends,
    the fairies too —
To them I look no different, my real beauty they can see,
They look with their heart, they don't make fun of me —
I sat amongst nature's children, yellow dandelions make my bed,
with loving thoughts I tie them, and their crown I place upon
    my head —
"Oh, I am a pretty princess, just as I always wanted to be,
Oh, I am a pretty princess, the beauty out is inside me — "

Oh, why do you only see the shell, the thing you think is me?
Oh, why are you so unkind, why can't your "blindness" you let be?
Why can't you open up your heart, and let the real you see?
And then you'll see the real, true beauty:

    ". . . I am you, and . . . you are me . . ."

Ruby M. Lowery-Obermeyer

FLAVORING

You leave my heart warm.
Tongues speak poorly,
      incompletely
           in this.
You are special people to me.

Memories are nice
      dreams
           lived and
           turned inside out
  but
Memories
Need a taste of reality
As spicing . . .

You have flavored my life
      with your realities.

M. D. LeDoux

THE LADDER OF LOVE

Some days are dark and dreary
others are sunny and sweet,
but what are all but a ladder of
    love
Leading to God's dear feet?
No matter how deep the shadow,
or how friendless we may stand
we know our feet will ever be firm
if we put our trust in God's sure hand.

And yet on that upward journey
there are dangers hidden from all,
and even from the loftiest height
the unwary feet may fall;
But if faith and love, twin beacon
    light,
shine on us from above,
we shall reach our Father's home at
    last
On Life's great Ladder of Love.

Claudine L. Evans

JOEY

Tell me, my love,
my sweet young boy.
What is it I can do
to open you like
the flower that
you are?

I open your hand,
and slowly, softly,
kiss the tender
hollow of your palm.

If only you
could be opened like
a hand, or a flower,
would you tell me?
Could you whisper
it . . . gently?

(i know better than to ask)

Barbara Whetstone

INCARNATE JEWEL

A dawn radiates, from your deep
  Piercing blue eyes;
Whispers of things – nearly forgotten,
  ''Man's ultimate prize.''

How can the eyes of an infant
  Baby girl; communicate so *profoundly*
With a – grown man's soul?

You illumine my world
  Like the *flower* of crimson –
And deep forest green;
  The *monarch* of Beauty – Love, and a
Mysterious *beam*.

Its tender petals unfolding with *grace*
  Majestically – bestow their
Enchanting bouquet; as a *rose,*
  You christen the Earth – by existing,
Your daddy's heart – in every way.

A love that sings – and freely soars,
  For *you* pours forth, from the deepest
Part of me; perennial – effervescent,
  As gulls and foam – of the
Crystal Sea –

Peter Moser

I

Oh, yes! Judgment ran rampant that day!
The day I lived as a child I was urged to
  ''Act maturely!'' The
  Day I lived as a tee
  Nager the testimony
  Was that I ''Acted li
  Ke a child!'' And, l
  Ater, ''Act your age!''
  Still, later, ''Why w
  Ould anyone your age
  Do this?'' And, even,
  Still later, ''What i
  N the world moves yo
  U to do that, and t
  His And this?'' Ah,
  Judgment ran rampan
  T that day! But, ye
  T, today, I say, ''I
  Will be me! You ha
  Ve had your day! L
  Et me have mine, and
Be and be nothing any different to see!''
And, yet, judgment runs rampant today!

DENTITY

Raymond Befus

HOURGLASS

Fanciful spree
 fanciful touch
  why count?
   the midgets
    ferried by the streams
    why retrace?
     your footfalls
     in the shade
     why dig?
      twigs and eavesdrops
      sticks of ages
       long been gone
       why turn?
        rusty keys
        spinet, doorknob –
         spilled wine
         never will again
         refill
        this empty bottle.

Concordia B. Braña

CONCORDIA BARRAMEDA BRAÑA. Born: Phillipines, 9-5-39, U.S. citizen; Married: Dr. Lejo C. Braña, 2-22-64; Education: Phillipine Women's University, 1962, B.S. in Health Education, major Nutrition; La Salle University, Chicago, Interior Decoration, 1972; Occupations: Avon dealer, Interior decorator; Memberships: National Association of Female Executives, 700 Club; Awards: Write-up in *Phillipine Journal of Health Education,* 1962; Poetry: 'Hourglass,' *American Poetry Anthology,* 1985; Comments: *I want to praise and honor the Lord with great reverence because without Him my depth of words would not be realized.*

Dedicated to E. E. Cummings

    As all Sound
is not definite

    Value Being

 in the not Yet having taken place
thus I condition without being Conditional
   Consider as if you were to con si der
   connaitre in order to dis co ver
    reconnaitre A Vers

Harry Fulson

HIDDEN LOVE

Deep within my soul there is a struggle
Of thoughts and intents and constant meditation
Believing that beyond my very existence
Are the solutions of a love with eternal implication.

Reclining under a canopy of wide oak tree
I cannot help but reflect on several scenes
Memories of fond times and pleasant places
Where we have been together, yes, even in my dreams.

For the moment this seems so very impossible
That the love I foster and hold so dear
Like the squirrel hides his food supply in secret
May one day in spring be real, and suddenly appear.

Such a fool I dare not choose to play
And carry on in delirious delight of one's reflection
But faithfully hold on to a bright, bright hope
That one day our hidden love will shine as the noonday.

Yes, I believe that this love is now just a seed
Held by the hand of God Himself, far, far above
And, soon will be released on all the four winds
And planted into us, once hidden, but then a blossoming love.

Ronald A. Aldrin

PARADE COUNTRY STYLE

Take a small country town.
Add sunshine and warm breezes.
Mix in people, large and small,
Old and young, all tanned and brown.
Throw in some hot dogs, cotton candy,
Balloons, fireworks, and Sam the Clown.
And everyone is ready for one thing:
The annual hollerin', squealin',
Bright and colorful best parade around.
No greater thrill to a child's eyes
Or grander tug on anyone's heart
Than to see a parade — country style.

There's ol' Uncle Pete on Fire Engine #1,
And cousin Susan and all her friends
From Pierce Junior High's Eagle Band.
Of course, there's Henry and Alice in their Model T,
And all the vendors along the way.
But, best of all are the dressed-up smiles
On all the faces of those who line
The sidewalks of Countrytown, U.S.A.
"Picture perfect" many would say.
A day of cheer, of hope, and love.
A day of tradition, yes, but a day set aside
With all fear, worry, and doubt left outside of town.

Ronald A. Aldrin

B is for breathing, a vital sign of life
E is for Eden, garden of earthly delights
A is for amnesty, for those who fled from war
U is for understanding in welcoming them back to our shores
T is for touchdown, and the smile it projects
I is for intercourse and the niceties of sex
F is for forgiveness and washing of sins
U is for unity and mixing of skins
L is for love and that one special girl.
  Such beautiful things for an ugly world.

George W. Poitras

THE GOD KIND OF LOVE

You are a special, sparkling jewel in my heart
Wherever we may travel, either together or apart
That we not forget our God Kind of Love
Forged and fashioned from God Who dwells above

I'll remember your bright, smiling face
You know, the turning part — so soft and new
Saying with your mouth, the speaking part, how
God reached out with love and healed you

Those eyes, like a fountain in the center of a landscape
Shine as the noonday because of His perfect love
And your hands, willing to greet someone who
Is lonely and depressed, needing His love from above

God's Kind of Love flows through you
Like sweet, sweet syrup of a stately maple tree
And, like fresh anointing in morning of mountain dew
Yes, He healed you — a testimony of His love for all eternity

May Jesus continue to touch your life with healing virtue
Constant joy, and precious promises all the days of your life
And in that eternal splendor we can walk and talk, both me and you
Saying how God really did love us, and the whole world *all the time!*

Ronald A. Aldrin

RON ALDRIN. Pen Name: KAS (Kenneth Alfred Selvin), my natural father's last name; Born: Brooklyn, New York, 7-19-32; Married: Dody Aldrin, 8-9-58; Education: North Park College, Chicago, 1951-53; Word of Faith Bible School, Dallas, 1984; Occupation: Freelance writer; Poetry: 'Faith Over Worry,' 'I Still Love You,' 'Recreated Citizen,' *Words of Praise, Vol. III* 1987; 'Hidden Love,' *KAS' Komments,* 1987; Other Writings: "Names You Can Depend On," Biblical teaching on Hebrew names of God, 1984; Themes: *Most of what I write is poetry or prose in illustration format. Some are Biblical teaching in pocket-size handbooks ("Names You Can Depend On"). I am working on some novels,* Desperate Minutes, Survival During Atomic Attack, *and,* Slaymaker — Hitman on the Run. *Most of all I do is personal reflections and incidents in my own life and healing by God of my mind and body. Other poems reflect human behavior and responses to life.*

DILEMMA

My grandchildren perceive me to be omnipotent
Although the word surely is not in their vocabulary.
I'm bracing myself against the day
When realization reveals to them I'm only ordinary.
The warmly exhilirating initial taking of a little hand
Offered so willingly in confident expectation
Of a safe convoy across the as yet untried course
Of life's broad strand
Gives me determination to give this awesome undertaking
My level-best effort hoping to accomplish some part of it
Before these precious ones learn that I have come to know
As much or more from this God-given opportunity
Than they have ever learned from me.
Lord, help me to stand up under their disillusionment
In discovering their idol has feet of clay!

Robert L. Campbell, Jr.

WHAT IS A MOTHER

To the best mother in the world

A mother is someone who
is always there for you when
you need her.
    A mother is someone who
takes care of you from
the day you're born.
    A mother is someone you
can talk to when you're
having problems.
    A mother is someone who is
there for you if you need
a shoulder to cry on.
    A mother is the most important
person in a girl's life.

    That's why I'm so lucky
to have a mother like mine.
    I love her more and
more each and every day.

Lori Nichols

THE CUP

With weak resolve
I kneel in prayer
confessing my slowness
to drink from His cup.

Dear Father, change my will
to Your will. Then,
strong I rise –
completely dependent on You.

Luke 22:41-42
    And he knelt down and prayed this prayer:
Father if you are willing please take away
this cup from me, yet not my will,
but yours be done.

II Corinthians 12:10
    For when I am weak, then I am strong,
the less I have the more I depend on him.

Sharon J. Daley

Dedicated to Robert Bly

            As We Sense We See
As we see We recognize Ourselves
        there should be a break
As in weather
        the Sun shines through
    there should be a way for you to have
whom you become
            You only have to Affirm
Your Presence
        In the field of Form

Harry Fulson

FRUIT TREE

Apple blossoms dress the tree
in my back yard in May.
A radiant bride
in a dainty gown of white.

From gentle breezes
delicate petals float,
lacy patterns
forming her train.

Blessed by bees and sunshine,
with intervals of rain
she brings forth
luscious fruit.

God's design in nature
can be plainly seen.
Life is not just taking.
Its glory is in giving.

Galatians 5:22
    But the fruit of the Spirit is love, joy,
peace, patience, kindness, goodness,
faithfulness, gentleness and self-control.

Sharon J. Daley

SHARON JEAN MILLER DALEY. *I was
raised in upstate New York in the foothills of the
Adirondacks. There I've had an excellent oppor-
tunity to experience God in nature. As an
American wife and mother, I feel a compelling
responsibility to give something beneficial to my
community, church, family, and society in
general: through my daily activities as
homemaker, piano teacher, church organist, and
avid student of the Bible, I seek to express in a
quiet and loving way the values of the Christian
faith, upon which I have centered my life.
Through the art of poetry and the art of music
I've sought to reveal basic scriptural values and
to elicit guidance for positive living.*

IMAGINE

    Imagine, if you will,
another world outside your window-sill.
A world of creatures, fat and small,
a world of creatures, thin and tall.

    Different sizes, shapes and colors,
one of them is never like the others.
With little bodies and lots of love,
all the creatures live as one.

Donna Wise

STIFF UPPER LIP

For years I have glazed over
All the hurt inside me,
Letting others witness
Only my success.
Now I am trapped forever,
Like a fly in amber,
In the tinted clarity
Of my own brittle deceit.

Shirley Mohr

EVENING BY THE RIVER

Motor boats purr
skimming down the river,
    waves widen ripples
to the edge of the bank.

    Backwash slaps against the hulls
boats rock gently,
    Sunshine on placid waters
        shimmers and gleams.

    There is a cool breeze
drifting across the shores,
    skiers whizz by
    leaving a wake behind.

    Far down the stream
fisherman sits on the bank,
    happily casting his reel
    waiting for the big bite.
    He'll sit and wait
        if it takes all night.

Children splash and squeal
        clinging to the inner tube,
        holding nose, hands in air
jump daringly into the depths.

Marilyn Vanistendael

THE HARBOR

A vantage point –
I have stumbled upon this spot
    To view the bay
    For part of the day,
With Staten Island
    Slightly rising
    To the right with trees,
    Nature furnishes a small breeze
    To ripple waves
A giant freighter
    Deck stacked with huge containers
Laboriously creeps upon the bridge
Slowly slides under at the Staten Island edge,
Mysteriously the stack
    Rides past the
    Fuel tanks in
        Bayonne.

Soon the ship will be gone
Smaller tugs plow back and
    Forth past green
    Shooters Island.
Diving gulls dive for fun
    Waves ripple
    The ship is gone.

James T. Mackey

SCREAMING

I'm screaming.
I can feel myself screaming.
I'm screaming so loud that my body is shaking.
I'm screaming so I don't have to listen.
So I can close my eyes and concentrate on screaming.

But no one can hear me.
I guess they can't hear me
Because no one is coming.
I don't feel arms around me.
I don't hear voices.
I don't see anyone coming.
So I stop screaming.

I'm dying.
I can feel myself dying . . .

Lori Simonton

IN GOD WE TRUST

When we are weak and react to fear,
We need remember the holy spirit is near.
A reminder to you and me,
Is inscribed on every penny.

The wisdom of our forefathers made sure we all know,
We should trust in God as through life we go.
Instilling in the hearts of young and old,
The message God's word does hold.

''In God We Trust,'' should a reminder be,
It is right out front for all the world to see,
A silent witness to many every day,
May it be the inspiration for them to pray.

Gladys Ritenour

AN APPEAL TO THE U.S.

On behalf of Ethiopia's hungry.

Tears are gently rolling down my face,
Enveloping the pain I can't erase,
When I see Ethiopia's hungry, and unending drought,
I feel compelled to do something to help these people out,
Faces of starvation, the stench of death in the air,
As a nation, sending resources can show them that we care.

Most of us have food and nice places in which to live,
Let's forget our own problems, and, for once, try to give,
To Ethiopia's hungry, homeless and poor,
This is not a political fight or a Marxist war,
These people are struggling, solely to survive,
So, let's help them in their efforts to keep themselves alive.

Send food and money; there's no alternative route,
These people will be grateful, beyond the shadow of a doubt,
Tho' they cannot express it in our native tongue,
Their survival will convince us that God's will is being done,
That these people are dying seems so unfair, somehow,
Let's not delay in our commitment to help these people now.

L. Joy Hunter

FEEL ME, TOUCH ME, KNOW ME . . .

Innermost portrait of one woman

For I am the wind that blows o'er the trees,
And shadows the clouds in the heavens,
Feel Me, Touch Me, Know Me.

For I am the ocean that wipes all impurities away,
With the ripples of my waves,
Feel Me, Touch Me, Know Me.

For I am the moon that enfolds the night
And its glistening stars, with my eclipse.
Feel Me, Touch Me, Know Me.

For I am the sun; feel the heat of my rays,
As they scorch the earth in fury,
Feel Me, Touch Me, Know Me.

For I am a nightingale, singing a song,
Blending rhythmic sounds, with melodic tones,
Feel Me, Touch Me, Know Me.

For I am an unending poem, a collection of words,
That communicate my secrets . . . innermost portrait of
one woman . . . Feel Me, Touch Me, Know Me.

For I am your Alpha and your Omega,
The beginning and the end of time,
The on-going reason for the existence of your life,
Feel Me, Touch Me, Know Me.

L. Joy Hunter

WITH LOVE

Through love the Son of God was born,
Not in a castle, heir to a sceptre
        and throne;
In a stable, His destiny,
    A shepherd's staff, a flock of sheep . . .
A flock He tended and healed with love.

In mockery, a scarlet robe, a coronet of thorns,
        a reed
By Roman soldiers to Him given,
With scorn called, ''King of the Jews.''
Upon a cross He died a King . . . The King of Kings,
        With Love.

Through Love He conquered death,
Ascended into His Kingdom in the heavens above.
Still tends and guides His flock,
        With Love,
Hoping soon, no matter color or creed,
Joining hands His call to peace they will heed,
        With Love.

Then there shall be,
        One flock,
            One Shepherd,
                Through Love.

Elia Vann Colmenero

RANDOM THOUGHTS

Random thoughts invade my mind . . .
　　Such discipline required:
　For the good ones must be filed,
　　The others turned away;
　But they refuse rejection . . .
　　Persistence is their bag.

Although kept in the lowest drawer,
One day, emotion or some casual act,
　　Will ring a wild alarm.
Up they spring, to go rampaging
　　On some sea of discontent,
　Like old and cunning cats
　Escaping from great bags of care.
　Who knows where they reside
　　When not contained?

Is there some well – some cesspool
Of decay – where thoughts are reared
Like cultures on some mental mold?
　　Perhaps, but if there is,
　There must be yet another well
　Where crystal may be tapped.
　Is that one lined with gold?

Barry Green

PUZZLE

Every place she leaves improves!
　　Speak out and please be fair.
Is the cause that now she's gone,
　　Or that she once was there?

Virginia F. Brown

A REMEMBERED LOVE

I've been there.

　You brought me.

　　I've done this.

　　　You taught me.

Our thoughts are these,
　Bold and real.

Your sounds fill me,
　And I close my eyes,
　　Carried to embrace you.

Your warm, ample breast,
Secure.
　　Abating fears of all.

You leave me,
　In the morning spent.

　　Yesterday brings a smile.

You were there,

　As I.

You've done this,

　I learned.

J. Scot Sequin

A BEAUTIFUL STORY

There is a wonderful, beautiful story
It has been told many time before
Of a beautiful land just over the river
Just over the far eastern shore.

For there is that beautiful city
Its storehouses not found here below
Treasuring the prayers of the martyrs
This beautiful truth God wants us to know.

The prayers of the martyrs, God will answer
God receives them, they are His own
For His cause they bled here and suffered
And now up to heaven have flown.

So rejoice when trouble comes upon you
Rejoice if in His name, you suffer loss
Know that you partake of His glory
Of the suffering Jesus knew on the cross.

Now that our saviour has suffered
Know that His own will suffer here too
When they are found worthy to be like Him
Doing the works that He gave them to do.

Sing, for we cannot keep silent
We can shout, for our cup runneth o'er
Praise the Lord for His blessed Holy Spirit
Fills us from our heads to the floor.

Calvin R. Skeen

GIVING IS LIVING

When it seems that you have given all
And you have nothing left to give
Reach down deep within your heart
And learn how to really live.

For way down deep within your heart
Like a sponge its treasures keep
And when you give from way down deep
Bounteous joy you will reap.

For selfish love takes all it can
And grabs for even more
No matter how much it has
It never fills its stores.

The more it gets the more it wants
It thrives on hate and greed
But it is sure it never lives
For into death it leads.

The one who gives has learned to live
And a full life he can lead
For he has heard his master call
And his call he did heed.

Calvin R. Skeen

Dedicated to Delmore Schwartz

　　　　As
caricature perpetuates that which is not
　　character shows through
　　As sure as certainty
comes after
　　　　Qualify
　　　And if Quantity
overshadows substance
　　　Look for the I
to weigh in the Balance
　　　　there
　　　　　　and if she is
undefined
　　in the way she asks of you
　　Answer to her
　　　Say

Harry Fulson

ANGELUS DUBIOSUS

For Geoffrey Hartman

We touched upon the Prelude
Like Paolo preying on a book
Omphalic intimations of the text
To build on hell the intercourse of sense

The wind was very gentle and yet urgent
To plant a voice among the vine

That day they did read on and on
The wings of the averted angel
Named and caught and
Laid to rest
In language and in time
The dark child:

Terrified.

Mechthild Cranston

SUMMER FEELINGS

Sunlight cascades
　　　mirrored images
dancing in the early dawn hours
In the distance
　　a train whistle
disrupts the stillness
　　of this warm summer morning
As i touch
　　your slumbering body
I wonder how i feel to you
As i gaze
　　into your waking eyes
I wonder how they see me
As i search
　　your wandering mind
I wonder what your thoughts of me
　are about

Billy Mac

AN ODE TO MISTRUST

I've gazed at the once friendly tide,
and its waters nearing drought,
felt the foot of injustice as it kicks us about.
Witnessed faces taut with anger, lined by stress,
stumbling lifeless through the sordid mess,
stripped of dignity to the very limb
fallen victims of some unseen whim.
Your strength is dwindling and so is mine
but where must we finally draw the line?

This world and its dreadful sobriety
say a thing or two about our so-called "society,"
commentary on such a place could never expose
the stifling effect running rampant its throes.
What in this world could we possibly obtain,
what things are really of merit in our realm humane?
All I see is a lack of sincerity
and when I do it is indeed a rarity,
so from this day forward my space do not endanger
only an arm's length allowance for you unfair stranger.
Today I become as faceless as all humanity
I trust you sense my upright sanity,
and just as the lights fight the shadows at night
another soul disappears fading till it's forever out of sight.

Mark Brookshire

DOWN ON HER LUCK

When he left and said "Good-bye Honey"
She and her children were left with no money

She tried hard to work and do socially right
With typing, pouring coffee, slinging hash at night

Low pay and no benefits do not go far
Sitters to pay, clothes to buy, parts for the car

Years passed by, but with no avail
Juggling jobs, children, no money, no food, a living hell

She pondered long and hard hating this rock bottom she had hit
Pressures, problems, alone and at her wits

With much remorse she knew what she must do
Welfare? "Oh no!" she cried, "Not that too!"

Head held high into the office she asked for help and care
Humble she said, "My children are hungry, they need clothes to wear."

She sat through much paperwork, burning inside
She thought, "This can't be happening to me, I want to run and hide."

She left with approval that money and food stamps would arrive
  in the mail
She felt beaten, lost, helpless; so young to look so frail

She is a humble mother with much pride and grace
In public it's difficult for her to take what she must face

She wants the good life and prays each night
That classes at college will help end her fight

So checkers at groceries show her kindness and a smile
She is not trash or too lazy to work, she's just down on her
  luck for a while

Patty Linville

EMPTINESS WITHIN

The world you know is not the same,
  The innocence is gone.
    You realize what you now face
      And try to right the wrong.
So many things you face alone;
  There's anger and despair.
    But brave the fight, with strength unite
      And lose the will to care.
Within you grows the emptiness
  To armor all you feel.
    You're cold as ice, but safe from harm,
      And nothing more seems real.
The battle scars purge deep within,
  The rage within you grows.
    That even you are shocked to see
      The anger you now show.
Is this what's left, a world of hate,
  With cold, unfeeling droids?
    The child in me appeals for more,
      Some warmth to fill this void.
Afraid to break, the shields protect,
  Then nothing can begin.
    My heart cries out for love to melt
      The emptiness within.

Lisa Eileen Baumgartner

THE MASTER ARTIST

God's art gallery is open night and day.
There is no admission to pay.
Perfect colors varied and abundant
abound in the sky, water and Earth —
Showing endless radiant lights, elegant shades and soft hues
equally beautiful in every season —
Spring blossoms, Winter snow,
Summer green and Autumn harvest placed within everyone's view;
Abstract to action
endless living art
with love from omnipotent God, the master artist.

Sophia L. Eaton

MENSA

Only 2% of the population can lay claim
To equal your intelligence.
So I'm somewhat hesitant to tell you this,
But the price you paid for your achievements
Does not equal
Our Fault.
Except for certain tragedies and sudden death
  (over which we have limited control),
The quality of life in these United States
Is mostly dependent upon
Our choices.
It's the democratic way.
And you don't even vote.
Percentage-wise,
  your misfortunes should have been a wash.
If you'll study your spreadsheet,
You might discover your assets
Omit those who once admired your courage.
But, the IRS would likely agree that the omission
  wasn't a qualified gain anyway.
Perhaps the only mistake, then,
Is that you underestimate
  98% of the population
Who cannot lay claim to equal your intelligence.

Susan Williams

HE WAS NAILED TO A DOGWOOD TREE

From a hill far away I heard one day
  Of a man who was crucified.
He was nailed to a tree a dogwood tree
  It was for me my Saviour died.

On the cruel cross of Calvary
  He died for you and me
Alone upon the cross in shame
  To save and pardon me

On the cross the tree of agony
  There His blood was shed for you and me
He was born to die, but He lives again
  He has cleansed us from all sins

Up the hill of stones and thorns
  Beneath His cross He bore
He did this all for you and me
  Never to live in sin no more

The thorns that pierce His raven head
  As He looked up to the skies
It is finished He in anguish said
  Then He bowed His head and died

O lamb of God thou son is He
  Forevermore He will be free
For He has gone to His heavenly home
  To prepare a place for me.

Myra M. Williams

I can feel it
  when I'm near you
    your heart is there
      then you act like
        you don't care
          leaving me standing
          hopelessly handing
            you my heart
I just can't accept it
  the way I'm supposed to
    you have to want
      but you turn away
        to tease and taunt
          leaving me dwelling
          pointlessly telling
            you my dreams
I guess I could forget you
  leave what I want
    I just can't refrain
      when I feel you
        touch and detain
          leaving me trying
          resentfully lying
            to my soul

Shawna Lee Benson

HAUNTED

Who is this mysterious guy
To make my heart beat wild?

Is he from out of my dreams –
Or am I just chasing moonbeams?

Could he be a fantasy of mine –
To meet somewhere in time?

Right from the very start
He had captured my heart.

I am mesmerized by his sound,
And there is music all around.

What I feel I dare not say
For fear he might go away.

I find comfort in his tenderness
And seek to give him happiness.

His voice is intoxicatingly sublime.
It warms me like a glass of wine.

My spirit is set free,
As if he were calling me.

His soul haunts me
Like a romantic melody.

Merla Cumbow

CREATION STILL WORKS AND ALL IS WELL

The rooster crows
With joy to tell
Of the coming day,
And all is well.

The sun comes up
Or rain clouds pour,
But a new day dawns
As it has before.

The Creator, who with infinite wisdom,
Put each little star in place,
Still loves and cares about us all,
And knows us, by name and face.

The oceans roll
Their tides still swell
With the changing moon,
And all is well.

Faye Teague

IF I BUT KNEW THEE

If I but knew thee
before it all began.
Before the wind did blow,
before the sun did shine,
before the rain did fall,
or the waters ran.
What would you have been
if I knew thee then –
What paths would we have walked
or valleys seen,
or oceans swam,
or meadows gleaned?
Would you have been
a part of me as you are now –
Would our souls intertwine,
and fingers touch
or lips brush each other
in the first faint flush of love?

What would we have been then,
if I but knew thee,
before it all began?

Dee Michel

YOU'RE AN EXCEPTION

You're there when the light in my eyes
begins to fade.
You're there when a link loosens upon the
chains surrounding my heart,
that has been filled with our love.
You're always ready to help when my smile
begins to weaken,
and you're the only exception in my life.
You're strong for me when my shoulders
can't lift another thought.
You're always close enough to touch when
my body begins to slide down the
slope of life,
and when I listen to the sound of your
voice, my loneliness and past
ventures vanish.
You're the only man, and forever the only
exception in my life.

Sherie L. Mullen

DARKNESS

The warm red fire has ceased
all I see is darkness

Your golden words of wisdom
echo in my empty heart

The fresh life of spring
is no longer green

I feel the heavy drops
the tears from my sorrow

No light
    No reflections
        No peace

Just darkness

Maria-Isabel Campos

YOU HAVE FOUND A PLACE

We know life is rough
We know life can be tough
We must if you can trust
Trust yourself not standing still
With these thoughts you will make it up hill

Did you drink from the cup of courage
Did you face your face with love
Did you open your heart with pride
Did you open your mind with kindness
Did you walk the roads of respect
Did you fill your eyes with wisdom
Did you shake hands with faith
Did you tell death no
Did you smile when you awakened and the sun shined
When you slept did you leave your troubles far behind

If you try doing one or more of these things
You might have found your place in the humanitarian race

Melvin Sykes

RISE UP MY LOVE

Who is this that looketh forth as the morning —
   fair as the moon, clear as the sun — terrible as
an army with banners — it's the bride of God's Holy Son!

Rise up my love and come away — the winter is over
   and gone — flowers appear on the earth — and the
singing of the bird is come — the voice of the turtle
   is heard in the land — and the little green
figs do appear — the grape of the vine hath a
   goodly smell — our beloved will soon be here!

Libby Morris Williams

THE PLEASURES OF YOU

Whenever I reach to touch you and I find you
   warm and waiting at my side,
I can feel my loneliness slip away, lost
   within the pleasures of you —

The tingle of your touch on my skin,
   The taste of you sweet upon my lips
     And, most of all, the perfume of the passion
      I always seem somehow to find in you.

As the love we feel becomes the love we make,
   I find myself falling into the deep and the velvet
     until all that I know is the sweet abandon that
      I feel whenever you take me to you.

The dance becomes the music and the darkness
   explodes into brilliant, white-hot light —
     in the tender chill that follows, all that I want
      to be comes true in the dream that is me and you

When I finally lay spent in your arms, your
   breathing warm upon my neck, sleep comes to
     steal me, promising me dreams that are
      mine awake because I am with you.

Then, reaching to touch you again, I drink in the
   warmth and ease of loving you.
So much of what I am about, so many of the things
   I want and I need, I find
     within the pleasure of you.

David Anthony

I'M CAPTAIN OF THE WORLD

I'm captain of the world
Up over the mountains, down thru the valleys, I've wandered
And roamed
I've sailed far and wide across the deep blue sea
North, East, South and West
I've been all over this land
The seven wonders of the world I've seen
I'm captain of the world

My life is like the lapping of the oceans' tides, endlessly
Searching for the pleasures of the world
Stopping at many distant ports along the way, meeting and
Making new friends
Many arms have held me, many lips I've kissed
Then I've sailed off again thru life's many stormy seas,
Till again I find a calm in a friendly port
I'm captain of the world

Always knowing in my heart that through life's storm there
Is a place where the water's calm and a friendly port is
Near in which to anchor
I'm captain of the world

Raymond N. Chaput, Jr.

ONE LITTLE KISS

One little kiss
Yes, just one little kiss will do for now
For the old year is almost over and the new year here
So let's start it right with just one little kiss
Who can tell what one little kiss will do, it
   Could start a whole new love affair
Yes, just one little kiss will do for now

I'm not asking for two, three or four
No, just one little kiss will do for now
So let me put my arms around you, and put your
   Lips close to mine
Yes, just one little kiss will do for now
Yes, just one little kiss will do for now

Raymond N. Chaput, Jr.

MY MOTHER WENT SHOPPING

Mother's gone shopping — trusted home alone
left with promises

Shadows' interminable presence — day becomes night
falls with vengeance

Window pressed face — frost visible breath
quickens with fears

Eyes blinkless glare — vexation clouds perception
moist with tears

Mind knows consequence — heart feels abandon
isolated without Mother

Child's desolate existence — place called home
when Mother was there.

Karen S. Wolff

MAID POETRY

To make faint heart wildly beat
  My soul must need to write.
Like carillon's ringing peal so sweet,
  Maid poetry is my delight.

Love's passion dwells within me
  Like a mighty raging fever.
Poetry is my love my might,
  Never could I deceive her.

She has me write of you and me
  And what has never been.
Heart laid bare for all to see,
  Life's painting, with my pen.

Love's light and airy beauty
  Is not all she has me write,
Like compelling prisoning duty,
  I list your fears and fright.

She belongs to no one being.
  It's really all that's fair.
May my hand and eye keep seeing,
  Maid poetry's lines and rhymes –
          So rare.

Harold D. Gascoigne

WILD BIRD

Love is wild and sweet as music
  The wind sings.
If you fasten love with threads as
  Light as moon beams,
He will shatter, with silken wings,
  Your fragile dreams.
If you imprison love in a pretty cage,
  Love will age.
His silver plumes will fade,
  And his voice will vanish into the realm
    Of the shade.
If you hold love close in your hand,
  Love smothers and dies.
If you stretch out your hand
  Love will come and stay –
To charm you with songs of
  Purple night,
Lyrics of rosy day,
And melodies of silver rain
Written in the minor key of
  Dark delight
And golden pain.

Nell Rawlinson

SEPTEMBER

Come walk with me through the Valley,
Where lovely wildflowers grow.
For soon the flowers will fade away,
And winter will bring the snow.
And when winter has dropped her blanket,
And we dream by the fireside's glow,
We'll have these days to remember,
Of the Valley where wildflowers grow.

Frances Beasley

DID YOU KNOW

Did you know
  I wonder, how much I loved you
  That night you walked away
  Not knowing it was forever.
  Or how your quiet smile brought
  Bright sunshine into my heart.

Did you know
  That when you took my hand
  In yours to walk
  Our nightly walk, that the
  World was mine, because
  It held you?

Did you?
  I pray you did, for this
  Life without you in it,
  Is like a deadly silence.
  Nothing is the same, my love,
  I wonder every day, why I am
  Here when you are gone,
  My husband, my love,
Did you know?

Petal A. Beebe

AUTUMN

The sun turns a blazing orange,
  as it falls into the earth.
The leaves are turning,
  a crimson gold, and parchment.
The clouds are chilled,
  the air finds an autumn.
The sea reaches out,
  but the sky only meets it halfway.
The birds are gathering,
  to take their flight southward.
The days grow shorter,
  as the darkness devours the light.
The morning fog thickens,
  obstructing our view of reality.
The earthly array of colors,
  will soon dissolve into few.
The fragrance of summer,
  shortly will take its total absence.
It's all a kind of sadness,
  in a beautiful mode.

Jean Ponting

GONE AWAY

So near yet so far,
  So close and yet,
    I cannot touch.
So happy yet so sad,
  So glad and yet,
    There are tears.
I felt your tender kiss,
  Whisper-soft and warm.
I saw your sunny smile,
  Looked into your fiery eyes,
    And then it was gone —
Your eyes, and smile,
  Your gentle kiss,
— gone . . .

Donna Wise

RISE UP

We want a new world
We want to live alright
We want world peace
We want to see the light.

There is a new place
They are singing new songs
They've got the power
Their spirit times have come.

Come share the new world
Come sit here by me
Share my freedom
'Cause we've got that peace . . .

Rise Up, Rise Up
Up Rise, Up Rise

Carmen Billops

CARMEN LORRAINE BILLOPS. Pen Name: Sareal Magellen DeBernard; Born: Detroit, Michigan, 1-4-74; Education: Currently attending Robinson Junior High School, eighth grade; Occupation: Student; Memberships: National Junior Honor Society, serving as the president of the organization at Robinson School; Awards: Martin Luther King Junior Oratorical Contest, Young Writers' Hall of Potential Fame Award; Poetry: 'Lost,' *Seventeen*, 9-8-84; Other Writings: "I'm Sorry," essay, *Top British*, 10-5-86; "Nine Through Fourteen," short story, *Star (Tiger Beat)*, 11-3-85; "The One That Was," short story, *Top British*, 12-6-85; Comments: *Life is a place that keeps us alone, because only we own our lives. Love is all and all good is of God who is my love and good life forever.*

CAN YOU HEAR THE MUSIC?

Can you hear the music
  as it drifts upward in the air?
Can you feel the rhythm of child feet
  pounding with the beat of the sound?
Dancing in the air, are the spirits
  to the free notes of beautiful sound.
Light sound and then heavy, faster.
  Beats of purple music,
    the music that escapes
      from the strings of
        his guitar.

Donna Wise

EACH TIME I BLINK (STACY)

The best personality that's ever been shown
In any female that I've ever known
Is in a teardrop six years behind
And eight hours away from me at this time.

My corkboard is graced, for she is there
In the latest picture, with touseled hair
She's growing sexier ev'ry day, I see
This, while touching the very heart of me.

She seems to look better each time I blink
And I love her, but not like one might think
For physical thoughts are fairly far
From where my brotherly duties are.

And I'm going to help her keep learning, with style
To stun the world; make it stare and smile
I'll share in her growth, as she will in mine
And, between us, both of us ought to do fine.

Written feelings don't show as much as they should
But I'd hug her twice a day if I could
It's hard from afar, but we do try like hell
To stay close in touch, and we do pretty well.

W. Clark Davis

HOPE FOR A BETTER DAY

Trouble and worry on every hand! Panic grips our land!
Peace is nowhere to be found! Even the word has an empty sound!

The cost of living is constantly rising,
  With inflation there is no compromising.
    A dollar isn't worth much anymore,
      Our money seems to buy less than ever before.

People are grasping for security,
  Striving hard for prosperity!
    Making money any way they can,
      Constantly hurting their fellow man.

Yes times are hard, the future bleak! Whom can you trust,
  Whom do you seek?
Worldly possessions will all pass away — is there hope
  for a better day?

These words of Jesus hold the key,
  "I've come that you might have life more abundantly!"
    His own life He gave as a token
      Of a promise that will never be broken.

He gave His life that we might live;
  The eternal sacrifice He freely did give.
    Grace and forgiveness are in His name —
      Accept Him — your life will never be the same!

In Him is found peace, rest and happiness!
  Freedom from panic and from stress,
    In Him is life eternal, abundant and free,
      Not someday but *now* for you and me!

Susan Elaine Neill

YOU'LL TAKE ME ONCE MORE

You'll take me to the seas once more
watch with me waves, icebergs, unhindered tides.
You'll take me to the seas once more on ships
know of undiscovered ports, visit foreign shores.
You'll take me to the seas once more to sail in the sunset
recaptured memorable dreams of long ago.
You'll take me on ship decks; feel the salty sprays on my face,
as an unwielded knife the winds rippled my inner soul.
You'll take me to the seas once more, to walk along the sea shore,
long searching glances toward the seas I search for silent tributes
of recent ventures.
You'll take me to the seas once more, to watch the migration flight
of wild birds gliding through the evening hues.
You'll take me to the seas once more.

Eliza Ann McNair

ELIZA ANN McNAIR. Pen Name: Ana Elisa Little; Born: Anson County, North Carolina, 1-8-53; Education: Chesterfield-Marlboro Technical College, 3-76 to 2-80, A.A., Associates of Business; Occupations: Business administration, Poet, Screenplay writer; Awards: Honorable Mention, Golden Poet Award, 1987, for 'Pearl Harbor, Again!'; Poetry: 'The Youths of No Return,' 1977; Other Writings: "The Children Who Came to Dinner," "Her Royal Highness Kinsfolk," 1985; "It's Grandpa's Turn, Now," 1986, screenplays; Themes: *Modern, realistic, serious, and people; I want to stir readers' emotions, make them more aware of modern civilization's problems.*

ABOUT THAT WAYWARD TOWN

It was the morning of a day when
Lucy James ran away
Those who knew her at all well
Found nothing busy that they could tell
The talk was such, Lucy had simply run away
That's all, and no one seemed to care very much.

The years between were sore and mean
For that wayward town
Mr. Skeen, the pharmacist at Owl Drug Store
Said the town would die, wouldn't last much more
But he was old and cross
And what he said, had all been said before.

The old Santa Fe train that used to puff into town
Brought Lucy James home one day
Few recognized her, or thought she meant to stay.
She walked down Main Street looking in store windows
Her with a worldly air, like she'd never in her life
Before been there.

"Are you Lucy James?" someone had to ask.
But she never would admit to anyone a word
About her past. Arguments played, rumors strayed,
Gossip was, it was Lucy
Home to mend her wayward ways.

Betty B. Jones

UNKNOWN

Our body, pulsating, transparent,
  cushions compassionately our falls
    from birth
    from our ideals
    from sudden death and . . .
      all the silent tears.

Worn out from its ordeal,
  it disconnects from Life
    one strand at a time, releasing
      a vessel,
        then its heart,
      a muscle,
        then its brain,
          the Captain of its form.

No tears are shed for it
  no celebration given for its labor
  no gratitude bestowed.

  We are incensed
  that it will work no more.
  How dare this Body cause us
  such inconvenience!

With still no gratitude,
  quietly, Unknown, it slips away
  into another form.

Clo Wilson

WINGS OF PEACE

On the wings of a butterfly
    I rise.

An ethereal emissary from heaven
    it flies;

As with grace if floats and soars
    and ties,

My soul far beyond earth to
    the skies.

On its quiescent beauty I rest
    my eyes.

A healing warmth flows in,
    tension dies.

In peace and contentment my heart
    sighs,

A thanks to God for his
    butterflies.

Joyce Gehman Rich

REMEMBER

Remember when?
Yes, I remember.
Nights cold, blankets by the fire.
We laughed till we cried.
Shaking yet knowing.
We loved so deeply.
Do you remember?
Yes, I remember.

Mikki Lynn Neuwerth Garding

WHY

Oh, another moment
Of nonexistence.

The story of living
For a bleak unknown

    Seated in the darkness,
  Dying —

Am I a person
With meaning

Sucking in cloves for the blood
Coughed into a toilet,

Draining a glass of rum
For distortion.

    A method of placing
    A moment onto

    A grain of sand
    That falls through space

    Crashing hard upon the matter
    Filling the hourglass

    That God lightly tossed
    Into a toy box

      Of his youth.

Mark Oliver

NO MORE ROOM

I don't love you. Me got no more room
  the little boy said
  perched on his haunches.
Heart full of building blocks
  teddy bears
  tricycles
  pizza
  spacemen
  Mommy
    and
      honesty.

  So much to fill
  his eager mind
  thought Grandma
  half-teared eyes
  wide with amazement.

Oh, sure you do.
Scoot over those stuffed bears
and make room for
the biggest teddy of all.

Donna Loeber

I AM

I am I cry . . .
Take me I cry . . .
With fears and cares,
I want you to know.

This is me . . .
I'd like you to stay.
But if you can't now .

        .

          . Perhaps,
someday you will.
And I'll be here,
Just as me (whatever that is)
    as I can be.

Lemay

GBLORMEHN GENEVA STANLEY. Pen Name: Lemay; Born: San Francisco, 5-31-64; Married: Patrick C. Stanley, 10-24-84; Education: University of LaVerne, B.S., Criminology 1986; Occupation: Criminologist; Poetry: 'A Cloud,' *American Poetry Anthology*, 4-87; *I Am*, compilation of short stories and poetry, 12-86; Comments: *I believe in love and life and happiness. I believe in honesty and truth. I hope for a world where my daughter and other children can grow up smiling and having that greater strength that comes from within. Let's all believe in ourselves and be who we are.*

PLAY, OH PLAY, MY GUITAR

Under stars gleaming brightly
Under magical moonlight
Everything so aglow
My love for you I know
Will never, never die.
'Neath the star-studded sky
To you I declare
This love song of romance
All beauty will enhance
And love will never die.

Play, oh play, my guitar
Tell my loved one I am dreaming
In this night of starlight gleaming
All my dreams I shall share
Tell, oh tell him, I am yearning
For the day he'll be returning
'Neath the lovely silver stars
Play, oh play, my guitar.

Grace P. Quattrone

View from Red Hill, back of Georgetown.

As I listen to their sounds,
 from a playful scream
 to singing a song
 that hasn't been written,

I try to lock them in my heart
 for safekeeping.

I know full well
 of my guilt.

I will always carry with me
 the memories
 of dying children.

First, last, and always,
 Vietnam.

Robert C. Ryan

THE BOOK

 Great, is the mystery, of love, for a Book.
Moving, is its written word —
Passion, tears, and desire,
Does the written word inspire.
Sad — with anguish, was its beginning,
Sorrow, and heartache its meine,
Joy and gladness, its hidden meaning.
 For—
Great, is the mystery, in its silence,
And profound, when it is expounded.
Oh, Written Word, whence cometh thou?
From the ages, from the ages,
Words, poured forth, from its pages,
Spirit, and soul, of man uplifted,
By the beautiful words, there in it.

Annette N. Ashbough

ANDHI

Andhi is *Enchanting*
         Affectionate
           Magnetic
             Exhilarating
               Peaceful
                 Kind

         Intelligent
           Sensitive
             Mindful
               Loyal
                 Just

         Melodramatic
           Imaginative
             Giddy
               Lighthearted

Andhi is *The Flower of My Life*
God's most precious gift to me.

A. Mozelle Michaux

LOVE FOREVER

Dedicated to my precious mom

Day and nite she cares about me
No matter where I am, far or near
Her heartstrings are tied to me
For her motherly love never dies
Her million sacrifices show me
How much she loves her child.

Though now she is gone from earth
Her unending love lives on
                    eternally
From the heavens she watches
Over all of her children daily
The Shining Star I see at nite
Tells me her love is there forever!

Sun Sato

RETURN TO NEW YORK

The city beckons at horizon's line,
Its hustling bustle of Times Square glamour
Flashing etched on the mind; the vive d'amour
That Broadway shows, wrought in fantasy's mine.

Babel's towers shimmer with lives of wealth
As brokers curse Manhattan's merry bourse;
And doctors challenge nature to its course,
Straining to cure the city's indexed health.

Trains wind serpentine through crowded litter,
Screeching in protest to wild hordes pushing
With dollar-crazed fury. Above, strutting

Hookers at corners smile, cracked and bitter.
As old unbroken children rape, kill, fight,
Demonic sirens scream to deified night.

Jonathan Katzauer

WHEN THE PAST IS PRESENT

When the past is present,
    Nothing goes as planned.
The heart is heavy with languishment.
    How I wish I could understand!

When the past is present,
    Its memory haunts my soul.
The life is full of enticement.
    How I wish I could let go!

When the past is present,
    Its darkness hides the day.
The mind is swelled with wonderment.
    How I wish I could get away!

When the past is present,
    Nothing wants to give.
The soul is supplied with presentiment.
    How I wish in the present I could live!

Johnny E. Parker

THE TRUTH SEEKER

She was a person seeking truth,
    The highest she could gain,
    She said "Illusion just brings pain
    And adds to an energy drain."

She met a Yogi on the Path,
    He said, "Why did you call?"
    She answered, "I don't want to fall
    By Illusion's wayside, or wall

Myself into limitations;
    So mentally I called for you
    Because as master you know true
    What I really need to do."

He smiled in understanding; joy,
    And said, "With you I'll gladly share
    The wisdom I have learned. Prepare
    To learn Life's lessons. How you fare

Depends on how you want to work,
    Center in serenity;
    Learn joy in living — you will see
    With eye of perception what needs to be.

Truth Seeker, open to the truth,
    I can wisely just advise
    When situations do arise
    And you need guidance that applies;
    Be aware of where illusion lies.

Deltalee Morgan Bilderback

A LONG NIGHT THINKING OF YOU

When the moon shines through my window
and the light beats on my face
I let my mind go

It's all cluttered with thoughts,
thoughts of you
You're something new,
something I've never had
something I've always wanted
and always needed

I think about seeing you the next day
but it's sad
because you don't realize
what you mean to me
You're my gift from Heaven
I've been praying for all my life

I've met many girls
None had a hold on me as you do
but I won't let myself go
'til you realize . . .
            I Love You!

Joseph G. Garamella

LET THAT LAST DAY BE WRAPPED . . .

Let that last day be wrapped in the
cocooning sense of safety with which
I wrap me up tonight. Goodnight
good night. Will the bedbugs bite?

Will all the old sassy mates be there,
pain, love and hate and ecstasy,
to wander with me in that Keep,
or does the Randy Reaper unsplice
you whole and free forever from
those antique partners of your blood?

Enlightened at last?

Older Towers of Trite have said
it so, and newer ones tack it
to their Tents of Tinker and Toy.

Should death reveal the answer to us, and
we see the why of this saddle-fart stew, could peace
be found in some well-lit room, therein,
say you,

For the fifteen million years of murder, rape and greed,
Which have seized us like a saw?

Could bliss be caressed underneath death's roof, in bed
with the razor rage and grief of billions
tortured, trashed, atomized with lies,

In fifteen million years of murder, rape and greed,
which have seized us like a saw?

R. A. Calvert

SONG OF PREY

Do you see, song of prey, distant moments calling for you?
Questions, hold the answers.

Past still believe, but was it real?
Reflections, tell the story.

Time, erasing memories, trying to hold.
Exposing every challenge, you try.

Song, can't help but sing, don't want to know secrets from you.
Share a passing smile.

Balance the high wire, skies of love, pools of tears below.
Can you risk any higher?

Wonders spoken, echo, never seem to fade away.
Exposing every reason, you try.

Look through your veil, worn for the distance of man.
Do you hide behind it?

Won't interfere, with what's held dear.
Honest, to be trusted.

Spirits of laughter, inspire emotion.
Exposing every new dream, you try.

Paul Anthony

JUSTICE

"As thou hast sown, so also shalt thou reap!"
How will you plead, O proud America, should you be called before
     the judgment bar?
How answer your accusers in the court? The Africans
Torn from their homes, their families, their way of life
To die in fetid holds of ships at sea or in slavery's chains?
How of the Red Man, fighting to the death for life, for loved ones,
     for his native land?
And now what infamy is spread abroad — rape, murder, drunkenness
     and drugs,
Our youth destroyed in body and in mind for gain!
Your wealth expended for new ways to kill while millions rot
     in hopeless poverty!
Can you believe that One Who died on Calvary, your mouthings of
     vague rituals by church approved
And waters of baptismal fonts can make you pure while you still
     violate the rules He gave?
If God is just, this thing can never be! For it was truly said
" 'Tis by their works they shall be known! Do thorns bear grapes
     or figs on thistles grow?"
Self-righteousness, bigotry, greed, sensual lust, jealousy and hate,
Their rottenness pollutes the air of earth! Cleanse it before we
     suffocate!
Let in the pure, clean air of Truth and Love and caring for our
     fellow men!
So shall we usher in the New Jerusalem!

George N. Heflick

THE RESURRECTION MACHINE

Give me a voice once again, dear Donna, I need
Your teasing and your needling to be heard.
Spin me again as we spun in the shadows of
The moonlight prom, when your golden hair
Mirrored the lantern light to halo an angel's
Face, and our love was as fresh and tender as
The petals on your corsage, petals that suddenly
Turned cold and fell like lovers' teardrops to
Wither in the snow. Don't let those cruel winter
Winds blow away all that we shared, turn me on
Again and let's groove once more for an eternity.
Let me serenade you till the music fades and the
Lanterns have dimmed. You know that I left you
For just a short time. Give me a lifetime with
You again.

Richard W. Simenson

REPOSSESSION

Why do you give us things; people?
Only to take them away,
at no specific time,
no specific moment,
at your leisure,
and at ours,
when everything is going right,
and is picture perfect.
Only to leave us in a dejected, downtrodden, and
maudlin state.
Why do you give us things?
People whom we have grown to love,
and cherish, and adore.
Why do you give and take away,
all that we have in the most abrupt way?

Darryl Lance Lockett

THANKSGIVING

For Norman J. Greene, Sr.
(1898-1985)
Past Governor General,
Gen'l. Society of Mayflower Descendants

For love of God and liberty the Plymouth Pilgrims came,
And from that fearful time to this our land's not been the same.

Where once each tribe shunned all the rest,
  And fear and hatred reigned,
Cooperation came to dwell,
  And freedom rose unchained.

When faced with famine and disease,
  They shared their dwindling fare;
Though half a hundred Pilgrims died,
  Their faith lived on in prayer.

Then Samoset and Squanto came
  In answer to their need,
And told them where to hunt and fish,
  And when to plant their seed.

At harvest time they held a feast
  To celebrate the yield
Of fish and turkey, beans and corn
  From river, wood, and field.

Inviting the Wampanoags
  To share the season's cheer,
They gave their thanks to God and man
  For the bounty of the year.

We too, as pilgrims, should give thanks for blessings we've received,
Since all our gifts from God and man presaged what we've achieved.

David Cole

YEARS

Years pass and bring no anodyne.
And in the intervening time
A hundred faces have looked into mine
With hope we intertwine.

Yet, quaking aspen marked with ILY copious,
Smooth stone covered with wet green moss,
Mountain meadow with bright colors embossed,
Hold greater promise.

In solitude I improve my mind, my rationality,
In evenings occupied at community library:
Week's news, medical journals, elementary logic.
Ever heartsick.

With people in public I fear interaction,
Being Universal Reactor is chief causation:
Perfume, cologne, cigarette smoke, multiplicity
Affect brain chemistry.

Memory difficulties, mental confusion,
Intellectual degradation, personality disintegration,
Present obstacle to finding a mate.
So I wait.

Rare the individual who might want to combine
With arms wound 'round mine,
Take away gnawing, and understand brain
Inextricably linked to mind.

Dan M. H. Wilcox

WONDER

When I was little, I used to wonder,
Oh, wondered what little minds wonder,
What is? How come? Why?

In Sunday School, we always sang
"Jesus Loves the Little Children"
And when we got to the part
"Red and yellow, black and white" I wondered,
What is red? How come they're red? Why?

And I would go home after church
And think about all the red and yellow, black and whites,
In Africa, China, all over, and wonder,
What would they be doing
After church on Sunday afternoon?

The one Sunday afternoon, I fell off my bike,
And I cried. Then I wondered,
Do all the other kids, in Africa, China, all over,
Do they cry when they're sad,
Or laugh when they're happy?

Today, I'm a little older. I went to college. I developed
A taste for beer. And I left home to travel.
And I heard a child laugh
As he chased the pigeons,
And I heard a child cry
When he dropped his ice cream cone.

And I didn't have to wonder anymore.

Andrew J. Kromminga

HOPE

In a gloomy depressed, unenthusiastic mind,
A streak of light of hope
Bursts into the showers of
Delightful flowers
Revealing
Life has conquered death.

Dr. Ram R. Sharma

A NEW SONG

It's hard to imagine our world before you came along . . .
And brought to our lives such a sweet, happy song!

It's a song filled with wonder at each new day —
And those strange little sounds you sometimes say!

It's a song full of toys all over the place —
And those interesting expressions we see on your face!

It's a song filled with smiles and a laugh all your own —
That brings such joy to us that we've never known!

It's a song full of splashes, wiggles and crawls . . .
As well as a few bumps, bruises and falls!

It's a song with a verse repeated o'er and o'er —
That says, "I'm hungry again, feed me some more!"

It's a song that fills us with pride as we watch you grow —
And learn all the things you need to know.

It's a song that sings of God's love and His miracles too . . .
Because that's just what happened when God gave us you!

Marsha Goff

Time, where is it going to
where has it been?
I reflect to yesterday and it is no more than a dream.
I look for tomorrow yet I cannot see past the clouds.
I would look at today, but by the time I do it's gone.

C. Pikula Gallagher

DEPTH

To some, depth is a pit, a hole,
                              a hollow, a well
Or a lonely trip down into Hell
For those they might perceive have sinned.

To others, depth lies inside the soul
An empty recess filled with light
To see without; as well, within.

P. K. Newman

P. K. NEWMAN. Born: Indianapolis, Indiana, 11-5-54; Education: Michigan State University, B.A., Psychology; Post-graduate work in advertising/marketing; Occupation: Freelance designer; Awards: 1971-72 Publications/awards: National Poetry Press; American Poetry Press; Massport Authority Essay Award; Mass Commission on Employment of the Handicapped, Government essay/research award; Poetry: 'The Well,' 'Loving,' 'The Dream,' *American Poetry Anthology,* 1987; 'Affairs,' 'The Inner Voice,' *The Poetry of Life: A Treasury of Moments,* 1988.

MOVING

I left my country to go learn about the world.
Despite colorful travels and eye-opening experiences,
The ease of home-life, like a magnet, pulled me back.
Now I sit restlessly while reading at home, passing time,
   daydreaming of Roming to roam,
   awaiting the next flight abroad . . .
   vingt jours, neunzehn Tage, dix-huit jours . . .
This time I leave with a new piece of wisdom —
   That coming home to old friends, now infrequent pen-pals,
   dry brown plants, and dusty stuffed animals,
   moving time stands still, inanimate.
I've returned to an illusion of my childhood
Expectant that friends would gather 'round the kitchen table
   to hear of my adventures, but instead
   I find their phones are disconnected —
   They've moved to make money or babies.
This time I leave with the hope
That I can make the happi-nesst mobile
Starting today in the You.S.A. . . Won't U join me?

Lorraine Clayton Kandor

ISLAND RAINBOW

Island covetness hovered by a rainbow of captivating colors:
Sheiled tropical palms shelter an oasis from worldly turmoil;
Soothing breezes and rays of warmth calm attitudes, tranquil
sunsets follow moonbeams of tantalizing attractions and
starlit passions;
Hovered rainbows harbour color of extended youth where
treasure of unstressed expression and Island covetness
cherished . . .

Rosemarie Scorza

ROSEMARIE A. SCORZA. Born: Glens Falls, New York; Occupations: Hairstylist, Body builder, Real estate; Comments: *From people I meet and places, my writing helps me analyze all situations.*

SUCH LIES

I look down at your baby soft face
you lay on blankets of ribbon and lace

I look at the purity in your eyes
how do people learn such lies

What happens to the innocence of childhood
where do we learn the difference between bad and good

Where do we learn to hate
is it all a part of fate

What happens to the smile of simplicity
where is the feeling of tranquility

Behind the locked door we hide
fearing who might be on the other side

People are feared by us all
where did the human race fall

How can a baby grown to adulthood
turn out to be ''no good''

To shoot a man to the ground
and knock an elderly woman down

I look down at your baby soft face
you lay on blankets of ribbon and lace

I look at the purity in your eyes
how do people learn such lies?

Linda A. Vanderbilt

BLESSED ASSURANCE

Sometimes we let ourselves get so distraught
that we forget the lessons that our Lord has taught.
We get so frustrated that we run and hide
not to think that for us, does His Love abide.
We put our minds on what others think our lives
should mean.
But God is our rock, upon whom we should lean.
We try so hard, though they put us down,
so we need to keep our eyes on Jesus, to wear His
blessed crown.
To live for Him can mean pain, you see,
though such a small price, for His love, eternally.

Bryan Humphrey

EXPECTED TO FAIL

In my lifetime I've seen a falling star
And, through a sadness that has been know by many
   I've seen a few men cry.
But, to feel as I do now none of the above could be as unusual as this
For our love that was expected to fail grew stronger and more
   beautiful even with the twenty years in age difference as a risk
Your not being able to do all the many things that you once did
   yet can't be expected to do
You still do far more for me than I could ever do for you.
Your love and your happiness mean everything in this world to me
You are my falling star, my silvery ocean view and tropical evenings
   by the sea
You are the most thoughtful and considerate man just the way you are
You are the very dearest person that I have ever known by far.
I just pray that I shall always be able
   to keep you contented with my love
For, I know that this marriage, this love, is truly
   one of the many treasures from above.
So in our lifetime we'll share the excitement of many falling stars
But, may I always make you so very happy and content
   there will never be a reason for sadness and no reason to cry.

Rachael Johnson

LONELINESS

Loneliness can take you and grasp you into its hold
Loneliness can creep upon you without your being told
Loneliness comes from thinking only of yourself
Not wanting to do for others or offering any help
Loneliness comes from selfishness, too
Not caring to share with those around you
Loneliness can defeat and destroy the very best
And loneliness can separate you from those that you once
   knew and all the rest
Never let loneliness creep into your life even for a day
Find something to do to help others with their burden along the way
Doing for others, just the smallest and most simple things
Let your heart guide you and help you to bring
More love and joy into these persons' lives and yours, too
Then you'll have forgotten loneliness
   and you'll no longer feel "blue."
You will no longer feel that loneliness is the only way
It will soon become a habit doing for others and saying
   pleasing things throughout the day.

Rachael Johnson

LIFE'S ROAD

Life's road can be long and it can be rough
But the way you live it can make it easier for you or tough
Choosing the right path and choosing the right friends
All of that matters greatly when we reach the bitter end
So, think things out clearly — never be in too big a rush
And, if you need someone to talk with — talk with someone
   you can trust
Make your plans carefully — plan each step of the way
Changes may come up — those can be allowed for and can be altered
   until another day
But remembering the rules — that right rules over wrong
One must never take shortcuts, falter along the way —
   one must remain strong
Do what you truly believe in — what you sincerely believe
   is for the good
Never trying to take advantage of anyone, be fair,
   and do what you should
That just about completes the pattern for making a good life
But, you're always going to have to figure on a certain amount of
   stress and strife
But if one is lucky and can find a wonderful and loving mate
That can surely renew one's hopes and prayers in the power of Faith.
Yes, that loving and thoughtful and kind and true lover and friend
Can make every day of hard labor a day of pride and pleasure right
   up to the end.

Rachael Johnson

LONELINESS

Loneliness is like paper without words,
it's like a painting without the paint.
It's also been referred to as candy without sugar.
It has also been called me without you!

It hits you without warning,
it comes like something right out of the blue.
Your mind refuses to focus,
your eyes fail to see,
your heart stops working logically;
you fail to start forgetting.

The basic life force inside of you tries to go on,
but the hurt inside of you attempts to stop.
The pain welled up inside of you surmounts to a never ending high.
The hurts start multiplying to an exaggerated amount.

Steve Whitenburg

SADNESS

Like the mist of the dark night,
   Sadness clouded over the burning delight.
Without any sound or warning,
   It took away my sun and morning.
Months and years and nights and day,
   It drifted on in a dreary way.

Who took away the sweet, innocent dreams?
   Who stopped the laughter's joyful streams?
      Who ended the spiritual, shining strife?
         Who stole away the golden rain of nature's life?

To the deep green ocean and the lonely sky,
   I asked these questions and the reason *why*.
And by the wind's songs, the bitter air, and the rushing tide,
   I found sadness with a painful trembling sigh.

Nancy Chang

WHEN I LOOK INTO YOUR EYES

When I look into your eyes, I just get this urge
  to hold you in my arms so tight
To have the chance, to have you hold me too
  this thought just seems so right

When I look into your eyes, I just get this urge
  to show you the thoughts and feelings of me
And my future thoughts would be nothing more
  than to share my life, that's the way it should be

When I look into your eyes, I just get this urge
  to kiss your lips so sweet
And I'll patiently wait, for the chance once again
  for the next time our eyes should meet.

Joseph M. Archie, Jr.

JOSEPH M. ARCHIE, JR. Born: Philadelphia, 11-23-60; Single; Education: Monco, no degree; Occupation: Regional Coordinator, El Torito Restaurants, Inc.; Poetry: 'Resume to Love,' 'People,' 'Every Day,' 'A Special Wish,' 'Naturally,' *Thoughts and Feelings From the Heart,* 1987; Comments: *Sometimes I can't always say how I feel, so I write these thoughts and feelings down. I try to write about the beauty in the world, people, places, etc., because I know there are a lot of people who feel this way. I hear all the bad in this world and yet I still see the beauty.*

YOU'RE THE POTTER, I'M THE CLAY

Oh Father,
  When I think of how You've made me
  in such a unique miraculous way,
  My soul bows in Praise to You
  For You're the Potter, I'm the clay.

  How can I help but worship you
  How can I be anything but happy and gay,
  It was You who knitted me inside my mother's womb,
  Yes, You're the Potter, I'm the clay.

  You had a purpose for my life
  For my being alive this very day
  And I know You're guiding each step I take
  You're the Potter, I'm the clay.

Oh Father,
  My heart is so lifted
  When I think of Jesus and the price
  He had to pay —
  to redeem me from the clutches of the devil
  You're the Potter, I'm the clay.

  Now mold me and shape me
  even if it hurts me; don't let me go astray.
  I want nothing but to stay close to You, my Master
  You're the Potter, I'm the clay.

Quincia Clay

THANKSGIVING PRAYER

As Thanksgiving Day approaches and my heart is feeling glad
I bow my head in ''Prayerful Thanks,''
  for the many Blessings I have had.
I ''Thank God'' for my ''Loving Friends,''
  told Him what they mean to me.
Gave ''Thanks'' for *Health, My Work* . . . AND, for my
  ''Precious Family.''

I told Him of my Broken Heart, when ''Death's Sadness'' . . .
  came my way,
Ask if somehow . . . He'd make *Reasons* clear . . .
  so I'll understand some day?
I ask Him, if He'd tell each ''Loved-one'' . . .
  in a way they'd understand,
How I've been so grateful for them . . . and each kindly helping hand.

I Willed . . . to make *each day* ''Thanksgiving,''
  each in some ''Special-way''
To make me ever realize ''My Blessings'' . . .
  and take time each day, to pray.
I prayed for *''Blessings of this Season,''*
  to reach throughout the World,
And Bless each *Living Person* . . .
  'til *All ''Peace Banners''* are unfurled.

Lucille Kerr Rawling

SIGNS OF FALL

Green Summer Lawns . . . adorned with carpets of Gold,
                as falling leaves scatter about.
Smells of Autumn, can be perceived everywhere
                a chill can be felt when you're out.
Fragrance of Burning Leaves . . . permeates the Air
                carrying pungent reminders, Winter soon will be there.

The Honking of Geese . . . as they migrate South,
                a Tree of Red Apple, that survived the Summer's drought.
Huge piles of wood . . . for fireplaces abound
                Squirrels hiding nuts, in the ground all-around.
Flocking Birds stop-over, to rest and feed, on their flight
                to a warm Winter Clime,
Butterflies too, are wending their way, with fluttering ease
                and grace so sublime.

Fall colors leave us breathless . . .
                this fact, we cannot deny,
But there is a sort of sadness we feel,
                as we watch the Summer die.
God planned the Fall, giving His Creatures time
                to gather supplies and prepare,
For the long months ahead, with Winter's cold . . . that all too soon
                would be there.

Lucille Kerr Rawling

GIVE ME A FRIEND

Give me a friend, who is loving and true
One I can open my heart and really talk to.
A friend who can overlook a human mistake
Never giving the impression, her feelings are fake.

Give me a friend, who will laugh with me
One to share my sad times, let me feel free
To respond in my heart-felt, God-given way,
As our lives unfold . . . each mysterious day.

Give us a fireside where we can chat
Talk over old times and things such as that.
With a faithful dog, laying at our feet,
Knowing a loving friendship, is a "God-given Treat."

Let me forever treasure, the gift of this friend
With never a need any quarrels, to mend.
No matter if we're near . . . or far apart
Always remaining . . . true friends in our heart.

Truly knowing there's someone . . . on whom I can depend,
Who will ever be ready, a broken heart to help mend —
Or to just stand by, with support if need be,
To help me through . . . any life Tragedy.

Give me a friend, who will bring out "My Best,"
With a Friendship like this, I will surely be Blest
And "Thank God" for the gift . . . always striving to be
As good a friend in return, as this friend is to me.

Lucille Kerr Rawling

LUCILLE KERR RAWLING. Born: Morrisonville, Illinois, 9-3-13; Married: Walter J. Rawling, 12-2-33, Deceased, 7-8-87; Education: High school and some college correspondence courses; Occupations: Semi-retired, Cashier, Secretary; Awards: 4th Place, 'Happiness Creed'; Golden Poet Awards, 1986-87, 'Face Up To Your Woes,' 'Be Kind and Loving to All'; Several Merit Awards.

IN YOUR EYES LOVE LIGHTS A DISTANT FIRE WE KNEW

In your eyes love lights a distant fire we knew
somehow together, somewhere, something we were
or shared back through the endless ribbons of time.

Scattered fragments of a lost and ancient unity
meld us still, at moments, when our eyes
meet and hold in that releasing, hot
white flame, encircled by a spacial blue
unfolding infinitely to you.

Love is a joining with the past which we know
and know not, feel and forget and oh that we
could light that past again, reach through this soiled
and seamy sock of being to that fingering fire
and rise flesh in flesh to a higher home of self
where that fire, prickly pure, reseeds the soul
with joy forever.

R. A. Calvert

WHAT MAKES LIFE WORTH LIVING

Isn't it the small everyday occasions
  that make life worth living?
A telephone call, a pleasant hello
A baby's first toothless smile
A friend who walked in your shoes an extra mile
A small boy with a dirty face
Your heart beats at a faster pace
A little girl dresses up like mom
Wishing it were possible to keep her always young
A hug from a son who is taller than you
A daughter who will go with you anywhere
A loving husband, a broad grin on his face
A lovely bouquet in his hand, showing he understands
Sharing a day with shut-in friends
A good cup of coffee, an excellent book
Sitting in church singing praises and hymns
  to our Heavenly Father
His love is sufficient, His peace overflows
That's what makes life worth living.

Louise Minnick

GOLDEN THREAD

Like a flicker of a candle I leave behind
The sordid displeasures that come to mind.
Like a flash of light I do glide away
An earthly body gone . . . yet stays.

A phantom body seeking knowledge below
Into a disembodied plane I must surely go.
O'er craggy mountains and moons I expand
Past planets and suns more ancient than man.

Still there is more as the cosmos bursts near
Awesome, stupendous I find knowledge so clear.
Unhindered no more by this bound plane
This golden thread stretches where no man reigns.

By my slender gold thread I suddenly descend
With knowledge that surpasses that of most men.
Intelligence is continuous so I've now found
The shadow of death no more holds me bound.

Misty J. Ford

THE TURNING POINT

Shall I remain as a little child
Gazing up at the sky, watching the clouds
That float by or running through a field
Trying to catch a butterfly
Happy and not knowing the fears that
Growing up can bring,
Only aware of the beauty around me
And the glorious songs that the birds sing?

Shall I remain as a little child,
Free of pain and anxious ways
Only caring what the moment brings,
Never concerned with grown-up things
Or shall I venture to grow up
To endure the pain and fears that will
Surely come my way, wondering what tomorrow
Will bring or if I'll have time to
Hear the birds sing or catch a glimpse
Of the clouds that pass by or see a rainbow
High in the sky?

Shall I remain as a little child?

Edith Driscoll

MELISSA

For Dave and Michelle; Dedicated to the memory of
Melissa Carr (1974-1987),
Melissa Danielle (1976-1977),
and Melissa Stockton (1957-1964).

There's a little girl on the cross road
When the afternoon sun signals the end of school
And she takes the hands of the children, laughing
They don't know she's there.
But she holds them back with a whisper . . . as the cars
pass with a roar. And she remains until the last child
runs out the schoolhouse door.

Melissa, Melissa . . . Melissa, you didn't die in vain
Hold the hands of the children; lead them in the rain.

There's a baby in the shadows of the hallways of my
mind. And she plays with her brothers, and her face looks like
mine. A little life, suspended in time.

Melissa, Melissa . . . Melissa, you didn't die in vain
The love you missed lives on in all the lives you saved.

There's a young, pretty girl on the train tracks
When the afternoon sun signals the end of school
And she takes the hands of the children, laughing, on the hill.
As the wheels thunder past, she leads them down to a picture
in the grass — a name etched in stone;
and when the whistle blows . . .
She points them home.

Melissa, Melissa . . . Melissa, you didn't die in vain
Whisper to the children,
    "Don't take that train."

Suzanne Lamb-Sinkovitz

MY DREAM: A REVELATION

I had a dream that seemed so real to me,
My thoughts came alive and demanded to be set free.
My hunches raged as a live creature in me,
Tearing at my spirit, begging to be set free.

I sought the Lord, and he had a mission for me.
There was one down here in distress — struggling in poverty.
Sin had made its mark, threatening the right to liberty.
I yielded my vessel, and Jesus responded faithfully through me.

I became his friend, and he sought Jesus through me.
He became my friend, and the spirit of God set us both free.
I now have a new friend and Jesus is pleased with me.
Happy is he who has friends and the assurance of liberty.

Mercedes Barnes Thompson

LONG THOUGHTS

Sometimes I think the world is bright — sometimes I think it gay.
I sometimes think there is no light, and sometimes think it's gray.
Yet one thing now I seem to know, I've found it out you see,
That whether sunshine, rain or snow, it all depends on me.
Sometimes I try to do my best — sometimes I do not care,
But when I try with greatest zest, 'tis then the world is fair.
Now listen when I say to you before it is too late —
When to himself, each one is true — the storms will soon abate.
Each one must have his "sometime," each one must learn to know.
That though the seeds be very small, they take some time to grow.

Olive Ruark

RAGING AMBITION

I'm reaching for the top, but it's too far down to climb.
I'm never gonna stop, how else can I spend my time.
I'm gonna throw it all away, gonna start all over again.
I'm gonna prove once more that nothing makes sense.
It doesn't now, and it didn't then.

I hear it's lonely at the top, but it's hectic at the bottom.
So how can you ever win.
If you never start, then you'll never have to stop.
When you stop, you only begin.

Oh yes I know it's crazy.
It's the same now, just as it was then.
To be reaching so far, for something so close.
My mind crazed with raging ambition!

James Garland Brosamle

TIME GAME

Such simple aspirations are becoming complex complications,
Once distant revelations, have turned to history's observations,
Moving memories ahead, we push the future back,
Letting loose all the chains that had once held me back . . .
    "I'll take the chance."

If history can repeat itself I'll take the chance . . .
Somewhere in the afterglow the music makes me dance.
Now intentions close at hand leave only footprints in the sand . . .
While dreams from which I awake, "Only tend to make me late."

From a boy to a man,
    "All those dreams of future goals lay across empty land."
Still I dance my way along, a dance from boy to man,
Such simple aspirations less than a dream from mind to hand . . .

But they've got me crying out for help, even looking under rocks,
For the guarantees I need, "When will it ever stop?"
I'm wishing upon dreams, until my mind begins to scream . . .
Still searching for someone to make me smile again . . .

Listening as the seconds pass away, watching the clock's
    pendulum sway . . .
Dreaming of yet-to-be times, no longer speaking overheard lines . . .
Solving riddles now with rhymes, I solve rhymes now with riddles . . .
Looking back the memories taunt me . . .
I've been playing with time, "When time is so little."

James Garland Brosamle

THE WONDER OF SURVIVAL

Wandering through the forests by the mountains
Our eyes were wide with creation's wonder
But darkness came like a thief to surprise us
And we were lost in the lofty woods.
Our wonder turned to fear as we heard a bear
Like Faulkner's, a giant anachronism,
Lumbering near us and growling fiercely.
By God's grace, he smelled something more tempting
And we stood safe but shivering.
Cuddling together with only our clothes,
We survived the long night of wildness
And when the golden glare of sun awakened us
We felt the glory of life pulsing in our veins
And knew the wonder of survival.

Norman J. Hansen

SAY GOODBYE

Dedicated to Kimberley Ann Shepherd

I guess it's time for me to leave, I guess it's time to go,
I guess I didn't give enough, I guess I didn't know . . .
Tell me, tell me why . . . Tell me, tell me how . . .
Show me, show me please . . . Show me, show me now.

My heart said, "No room for another chance!"
Don't wanna cry again . . .
But if we met several years from now, would we try again . . . ?
I thought that if we parted, I could make it through . . .
Yet now that it's all over, "I don't know what to do."

Tell me, tell me why . . . Tell me, tell me how,
All I, all I have . . . Is memories of you now.

I guess it's time for me to leave, I guess it's time to go,
I wish I knew where all the time went, I guess I'll never know . . .
I wished it was a fairy tale, I wished it was a show,
I wish it didn't end this way, I've been wanting to let you know.

I wasn't ready for this, your feelings didn't show . . .
It was the last thing I expected, I guess it's time to go.
Remember all the good times, don't let them slip away,
The memories that we have, in our minds will always stay.

I really, sincerely wish, "I didn't have to go" . . .
    Just had to say a few things,
I thought you'd like to know . . . "Say good-bye."

James Garland Brosamle

IN THE BEAUTIFUL GARDEN OF PRAYER

When in far field you may then be,
And no more you shall see of me,
Just remember our first meeting
In that Beautiful Garden of Prayer.
Yes, it was there where we met each other
together with our Lord and Saviour, Jesus the Christ.
He was patiently waiting for us to come
to Him in His Beautiful Garden of Prayer.
That will always be long remembered by us
through time and eternity.
For it is said, that prayer is the language
of the soul, and prayer changes things;
And there is no distance in prayer
For whatsoever we ask the Father in
the name of His Beloved Son,
will always be given to us provided it is good;
and in faith believing it will be answered.
So let us then be joining our heart and soul
together in prayer by putting our faith and trust
in Him that in the due time of the Lord Jesus Christ,
our prayers will be answered. That each day and
each hour will bring us closer to our Father
in heaven as well as to each other.
In faith believing we praise God
for answered prayer.

Sister Gay G. Cabotaje

Born on a day just like any other
you brought both joy and sorrow to your mother.

For now she had another son to give in battle
you learned to hold a gun when you learned to hold a rattle.

Childhood passed too quickly inside the refugee camp
houses half-destroyed, often cold and damp.

Then sent out to fight for a land you've never seen
you were told of the cause, but what does it mean?

Wide-eyed, enthusiastic, you headed for the fight
to protect your people and do what you think is right.

Soon the glamour's gone and the many become few
of all the friends you left with, now there's only you.

Fighting side by side you said you'd conquer them together
now their lives are gone, but the pain goes on forever.

So you stand alone, feel the loneliness of one
armed with your sorrow and a freedom fighter's gun.

Sheri Sims Kaddah

HOME

To all my loved ones in Ohio

I've been away for such a long time
from the place I call home in heart and mind.
The essence that's me aches for that place
where life was lived slow, and easy the pace.

I long for that place where friends were dear
my arms so empty for want of holding them near.
I miss the wild roses that grow by the lane
and walking down the street that they call Main.

It was a small town, not too many people
a few stores, a church with a tall steeple.
If driving through, don't go too fast
'cause if you blink, the town you'll pass.

Now I'm here and many are the miles
away from friends, their warm, loving smiles.
Each day that passes brings an ache in my heart,
I think I'll return and make a new start!

Rachel A. Anthony

TO TUX

We were once owned by a cat
  Now what do you think of that?
We called him Tux because of his beautiful black fur coat,
  white vest and black tie.

If you bet Tux was a boozer,
  You'd never be a loser.
Tux would stagger drunkenly from one
  beer mug to the jug.

Tux became famous. He was a poster cat,
He sat drunkenly against a wall under a
  banner reading "I'm not as think as you drunk I am."

Bettye Ellis Owen

A FRIEND IN NEED

To Eva Taylor

There's a woman that I know
Old and frail, hair white as snow
Walks gingerly on legs not so spry
Never gives up, always has to try
Though her speedometer is set on slow.

Her husband died and she's been alone
From the nest her children have flown
  to stretch their own wings
  and do their own things
While she sits waiting by the phone.

Will someone come today to take her for a ride,
Out for some fresh air, to see the countryside?
Will she hear footsteps and a rap at the door?
Even if it's someone who's a total bore,
To just have a visitor, anything she'd abide.

All she needs is a person to call "friend"
Someone on which she can now and then depend
To visit, or phone, if only for a short while
A shoulder to lean on and a great big smile
A friend who could lend a hand to help an old lonely heart mend.

Rachel A. Anthony

A GYPSY YAM

Glowing with a marshmallow softest all over,
This very unite beauty of sheer smoothest,
Has the keys of a banjo leading her daring eyes.

Barefooting all around,
Showing a cranberry color rose,
Touching her beautifully shaped breast
And yet there are petals of glorious flowers,
Like bees crawling all around her feet,
Displaying its wonders and giving mounts of honey.

Let not the beast roar through her beauty,
She is calmly exhibiting her utmost gentle gloves of flexibility,
Hypnotizing not your fortunes only crystal gazing at the architect.

For this classic *Gypsy* woman is indeed a golden yam,
With a bondage of compassion appalling,
How wonderfully and brilliant the boost,
When releasing one's exciting supplies
And recognizing the thunder it can give,
Whereby the stardust can sprinkle,
The wishes of one's dazzling thoughts all around.

As she is captivating the minds as being the best,
In whatsoever one's bones lead you
And clearly checking always to handle herself superbly well,
With her delicious tropical feelings that can spread like a heat wave
Bringing the grass roots of survival to your touch while adding,
The fruits of foundation and companionship together very softly.

Constance Edwards

OLLIE AND HIS FOLLIES

We hear and read a lot about Ollie and his "follies."
On stage, his charisma won over many of us "dollies."
Looking at him, though, you doubt that he was ever a dancer.
Yet, in his mind a dance was going on all or any old time,
To tunes he dreamed up to fit each occassion so they rhymed;
Was even proud his steps turned out brand-new and so fine — that,
Perfectly executed, removed all the popular good old "standards."
  Does that include, perhaps, any and all conduct too!
 He chose his steps very well to cover the territory he held, for his:

Charleston turned into the "Contras" transacted secret affairs.
Fox trot, many intricate moves on the make to be there "first."
Jitterbug, nervous about the money that ended up God knows where.
Fire dance, leading his superiors astray: or, was it the other way?
Ballet, rising to his height to proclaim his "truth" — nothing more.
Tango, having a time a-plenty to "tan," yet always be on the "go."
Indian-war-dance, going primitive — and that worked for him too.
Turkey trot, private code for "fast" planes, "fast" lanes, "fast!"
Waltz, perfect military pace to arrive anyplace and on time.
Sorry, he never sways at "polka-er" — says at that he never plays.
Put all these great dance steps together, and what have you got?

Rhymes and rhythms that blend a lot, yet "Ollie" ends up on the spot,
Sorting covert operations, diversions, missile wheeling and dealing.
Facts, words, truths, you bet: Lies! Will much end up just that?

Can the real Ollie North "two-step" ever be untangled or understood?
Or, could it be that this is what "folklore" heroes are made of!

Va. S. Lewis

THE LAST INDIAN

He drifts through time as he soars with the wind,
On his faithful horse Stormcloud.
His only companion and last living friend,
He rides so tall and proud.

He's the last of his generation
And from birth all he could see,
Was a lonely barren reservation,
A world of misery.

He rides upon the moonlit shore,
And he looks across the misty sea.
The wilderness gone forevermore,
City lights reflect lost identity.

He rides to the crowded city at night,
The people laugh and stare.
Blinded by the neon lights,
He can't run anywhere.

He looks up to the clouded skies,
And he clenches his calloused hand.
As a tear streams from his eye,
A lost and broken man.

He continues on from dusk to dawn,
A man of dignity.
Though his world is forever gone,
He searches desperately.

Mary Morley

THE RACE WITH TIME

A sapling stood upon a hill.
The sun rose in a virgin sky.
Everything fresh and green had filled,
A mass of clay once so dry.
God took this clay, and with His hands,
Molded the earth, and created man.
With earth's awakening the pace had now begun,
For this planet of life to revolve the sun . . .

An old tree stood upon a hill,
The sun sank in a neon sky.
Most living things had lost their will.
The dove had forgotten how to fly . . .

In the desolate ruin of factories,
Standing alone upon a hill,
Is the decaying stump of an old oak tree,
Was there anything left man could kill?

Something is seen in the heavens afar,
Floating in the massive galaxies.
It looks like a cinder among the stars.
The bitter ruin of man's destiny.

The race had now ended, with the dying sun,
For this lifeless cinder, can you tell me who won?

Mary Morley

MARY CATHERINE MORLEY. Born: Meriden, Connecticut; Single; Education: Associates degree in human services; Occupation: Vocational instructor, Homebound instructor; Memberships: Member of the Meriden Wallingford Society of Handicapped (MWSH) New Horizons; Poetry: 'Traveler in Time,' epic style poem; 'Exist,' 'Who Knows,' 'Memories,' *American Poetry Anthology*, 10-20-87; 10-25-87; Comments: *Poetry is the constant expression that begins in depths of quiet emotion — and surfaces into sparkling words of personal experience; yet often relates to the universal experience, eternal.*

PAPA WAS A WATERMAN

Sailing gently on the waters, a great ship wends her way.
Yes, it is the good ship Olive, for she's due in port today.

Rapidly on her way she rolls with her cargo of fish and men.
With her lovely flag flying in the breeze,
  she is far more beautiful then.

On the high white deck the captain stands,
  as he turns the wheel o'er and o'er,
Safely through the waves she rolls, as she oft has done before.

God keeps his eye on the work boats as they toil from shore to shore.
He knows their ways and their havens — He has seen it all before.

Now, slowly up the creek she goes to put her freight ashore
God blesses the good ship Olive, bring her safely home once more!

Olive Ruark

THE VISION

Within are lights, and music, without is dark and cold
Yet as I now sit dreaming, a vision does unfold.
This room is filled with sunshine, the night fades into day.
Yes, I am in the meadow fair where once I used to play.
I pick the snow-white blossoms there, my joy I do not know.
The vision fades and here am I with hopes and joys and fears
O, could I live in days gone by, those happy days and years!
We wish in vain for yesterday, and now it cannot be,
Let's do the very best we can, then happy I will be!

Olive Ruark

OLIVE RUARK. Born: Cambridge, Maryland; Single; Education: Cambridge High School, 1915; Mid-State Normal School, Towson; Two-year course, Lifetime Teacher Certificate in State of Maryland, 1915-17; Occupations: Bookkeeper, Credit manager, Office manager, Administrative assistant; Awards: Woodward and Lothrop, Washington, D.C., "Best Jingle," stating the advantage of evening shopping hours, 1935; Employer invited ideas for improvements, my idea was accepted and used for many years, 1926; Gold Medal Award from Dartnell Corporation for excellence in business letter writing, 1958; Gold Medal Award from Dartnell Corporation for a letter which welcomed new customers; Memberships: Credit Women's Breakfast Club, Retail Credit Association; Comments: *I'm partial to stories of oceans, seas, lakes, rivers, as my father and ancestors "followed the water" for years, centuries. Many other verses are special for special people. The last one in 1960, when I retired, was named 'Swan Song.' It was for my associates at the company. It was highly prized and I felt rich, indeed!*

GAMES LOVERS PLAY

Only strangers lost and lonely
passing through the night;
coming face-to-face
feeling insecure — yet reaching out for love.
Embracing,
as the feeling of security mounts within them.
The tenderness of an innocent kiss
the excitement of a gentle touch
the emotions struggling to comprehend
as they are driven with passion and lust
giving in — making love
never feeling the same afterward.
Forsaking each other and using others
as the wave of jealousy burns within them
being torn inside with feelings of guilt
as those sturdy ties that held them together
slowly drift apart.
Once strangers — now once lovers,
never retaining what they shared together.
They try to keep hanging on
each too tight, but both, loose enough to get away.

Cheryl Kramer

A MOTHER'S NESTING INSTINCTS

As a busy day's work slows to a standstill,
the sun pulls the earth up around its blazing girth.

As day sounds die and
     night chirps fill the sky,
as the blinds are drawn over the dark windows
my heart calls the roll of all the absent children and
 I wish to tuck each one under my wing in order to sleep until
  morning knowing my brood is safe and secure.
   Otherwise the long night is hard to endure.

Bettye Ellis Owen

ETERNAL THANKS

Whatever lies beyond these shades of dark and light —
encompassed by the vastness of eternity,
be thankful for two eyes beholding beauty every passing hour —
a voice that can express a heartfelt wish —
and soul that doth wake up — with songs to sing.
No matter how remote that fondest wish —
how toilsome or how long a day may be —
to have horizons far that beckon on —
is ever to possess a peace — that God alone can bring.

He brought it to those shepherds long ago —
and to those Wise Men three who journeyed far.
And e'en to you and me He giveth light and life —
if we will but look up — behold the Star —
that shineth even now —
for eyes that see —
for voices swelled in song —
of souls made new —
by faith in Him who lay within a manger bed —
and on a Cross pierced darkest doubt —
man's hopes forever to renew.

William E. Mays

GRANDPOP'S LOVE

Father was never around when needed
 Never was too dear to me
 Too far to be near to me
Mother's life was a fight to survive
 I'll always love her 'cause she always tried
But there's none I place above
 Over the potency of Grandpop's love.
If the world was his he'd give it to me
 Didn't just show his love through gifts and money
He gave of his heart and of his soul
 Just wanting to be loved was his goal
Always there when needed
 He never lied, he never cheated
If there was a saint on this earth
 His name was Ebenezer at birth
Worthy of his love, I have to ask
 Giving so much, wanting nothing back
I say whatever would I do.
 Because of all the heroes in my mind
He is number one time and time
 He is the gift of life unbounded
Never challenge never sounded.
 Grandpop, you are eternally etched in my heart.

Toure Fernandez

THE GIRL OF MY DREAMS

Where have you been all my life?
You're the best I've ever seen.
You must be the answer to all my prayers,
Truly the girl of my dreams.
Although we just met, I think I've known you all my life,
You're the best thing that ever happened to me.
I thought you were a figment of my imagination,
But you're better than I thought you could be.
Since you walked out of my dreams, and into my heart,
I don't think I can stand it when we're apart.
I'll love you forever, but there are a few things I'd like to know.
Like how did I get so lucky as to meet you.
And what happened to your wings and halo.

Grant Wilson

SCARLETT O'HARA
THE ONE   THE ONLY

Scarlett and her "Rhett": Everyone knows of their rosy love story.
Back in 1936 it appeared in its first print — and away it went.
It's one-of-a-kind to end all great loves, with the usual worry.
Now, a group in 1987 wants to re-create and carry it along.
Would a "concocted" script for a brand-new film be right or wrong?
Scarlett and Rhett are no more: shouldn't be seen on any type screen.
Their curtain came down, as well it should — both pulled its rope.

When love leaves one or both, that's it; it's over — there's no hope.
They can't resurrect these two from the rubble the North left behind.
So: let their affair end as it did in that great book and be kind.
Its memories are sweet; full of defeat; in spite of the rebel yell.
They lost each other: the South lost its cause: what's more to tell?
Besides, what fun to make up different endings that end up just swell.

Please let the beauty and glory of their love last in memory,
Like those "blue and gray" soldiers who rest in the cold, old ground,
For fighting to save "then," for us "now," everybody's "old glory."
So, right hand to your head to salute our flag — 'cause of the story.
There is only one Scarlett: therefore, only one Rhett Butler, you bet.
They both went away, back then, to where the wind blow - s - s, yet.

Leave their names, please, with all the others, in perpetual repose.
   For that wind now blows in peace.

Va. S. Lewis

A MOMENT OF SADNESS IS A THOUGHT OF LOVE

Think of love when laughter is near
Understanding is to be sufficient
Believe is living
A thought of love makes sadness disappear

Today's dreams of yesterday's sorrows
Fading away in the distance of a grain of sand
Tomorrow's sunset relates yesterday's dreams

Think not what you say what you do
Do what you say think not what you do
Do what you think say not what you do

Be wise is forgiveness
A Thought for tomorrow's dreams
Tomorrow's dreams become today's dreams
Today's insight becomes tomorrow's true
The true of the past becomes tomorrow's courage
A lesson learned becomes well deserved

Melvin Sykes

MYSTIC REVELATIONS

In mystic revelations we create the time spot
Marking sounds that tumble, twist, and turn
        for
the natural forces to elaborate for the time being
      Nesting images
Noting mechanisms to spin only notions of your
       reality
        not anyone else's
Therefore, we may hear the same thing
But — the times tingle differently
Saying something worthwhile
      to you,
       to me,
        to anyone,
         with a revelation

Lori Richardson

BEING EQUAL

Remember to treat your children always as your equal
Never look down on them, remember they're your sequel.
You started their lives and they've just begun
Conquering the world through work and fun.

Remember it was we who brought them here
Just you and me, our love is clear.
They will think back from day to day
Remembering how we would always say
'I love you, Dear' and 'I love you, Honey.'
But, to them right now, this sounds funny.

They'll always remember the chances you took for them
So, they could grow to become better women and gentlemen.
Thinking of their lives from the start
Will forever bring happiness to their hearts.

Linda Babcock

GROWING UP IN THE SIXTIES

I grew up in the sixties
People referred to us as hippies.
We had long hair, both girls and boys
We did anything to make noise.

Then flower children we were called one day
Where people got this one, it's hard to say.
Could have been the flower we wore in our hair
When they'd walk by, they would laugh and stare.
But, if it looked nice, we didn't care.

They scorned us, they blamed us
And made such a fuss.
But, I grew up and I could see
Why the blame was put on me.

Our minds are shallow, our brain sometimes lame
A generation to follow with a new name.

Let them grow, let their minds expand
Let them conquer their own horizons.
If they should just happen to ask?
Lend them a hand, and enjoy the task.

Linda Babcock

THE BOOGIE MAN

The boogie man always comes at night
Scaring children and causing fright.
There's no such thing as a boogie man, kids
Put a smile on your face, and close your lids.

Your parents have told you, many times
Over and over, you've heard the same lines.
''Don't be afraid, 'cause we're right here . . .''
As they wipe from your eyes, your very last tear.

They've left the door opened and turned on the light
The boogie man's gone, somewhere else, tonight.
Dad and Mom are close, so I'll give a wave
To the boogie man, tonight, 'cause I know I'm saved.

It's nothing real, only a thought in my head
But, before I go to sleep, I'll check under the bed.

Linda Babcock

THE LAST ENCOUNTER

Existence so bold so cold
with pressure of two extremes
a world of heat and cold
pushing pulling a wonder to behold.

Cold come from the six corners of space
where existence leaves not a trace.
     However,
we live in this section of space
plants animals and the human race
here where heat exists for sure
without it we would be nevermore.

The war of all wars shall not be fought by man
but by two forces no other force can withstand.
A war which the outcome will never be known by man
rather there will be forever fire and forever cold.

Cold appears to be the winner here
since all things cool at a point in time
and sleep with the everlasting power
almighty God in cold and darkness.

Herbert E. Wheeler, Esq.

PLAN OF SALVATION

Repent ye, for the kingdom of heaven is at hand
Believe in Jesus and the Promised Land
Confess and turn away from your sins with a godly sorrow
Do it right now, for you may not be here tomorrow

Today, when you hear Christ speaking to your hearts
Harken unto Him, and I promise you, it won't be
  for naught

Invite Him into your heart today
Trust in Him, 'cause He is the way

Draw nigh to God and He'll draw nigh to thee
For salvation is a free gift from God
That Jesus has already paid for on Calvary.

Jheri Rivers

SNOWFLAKES II

Blanketed was the whole earth
With a beautiful fleece of white
Slanted from underneath by the frozen
Stubble of mown grasses,
And early springtime crocuses that had
Just begun to peck,
Felt from a single crack of ground
With one green sprout each.

Through windows, water-streaked by
Steam that warmed the passenger car,
Projected countless, tiny travelers from outer space
Swirling and turning, the various geometric crafts,
Each gyroed into view on some mysterious flight
Then lighted gently and rested there.

Pine needles, their frigid faces upturned
To greet the snowflakes from their treetop perch,
Had slender branches laced with white frosting
Held steady by strong earth-thronged roots.
Dried and still the oak tree
Dwarfed by tall timber on a wooded hill,
Held an ice-capped head that bowed in the drift.

And one deserted child of the oak, a tiny acorn,
Made a visible black dot in a spot
Slightly bare,
That punctuated the starless night.

Barbara J. Lewis Everette

VISIONS OF CHRISTMAS

The Christmas gala that awakes all dreams
And most definitely takes the place of all wishes,
With the bulbs from the tree lighting up all the points of love,
Giving a bodily toast that scores very high,
For the ingredients have a mixture of desires,
Which can be sweeter than tons of fine sugar
And more tangy than the bees' honey.

The winter whites with its snowflakes of innocence spreading,
Gladness to all while making a scenery of another place appear,
As its tinkles being to make inches,
Bringing precious fun upon which to play in again
And giving its pure softness to the tree's branches.

Sleighbells ringing yet underneath those mistletoes are dating kisses,
With Old St. Nicholas creeping around with magical gifts for everyone
And those greatly adoring angels bring all their blessings for us.

As your red and white stockings are hanging next to the fireplace,
Ornaments and decorations of all sizes are displaying a sheer beauty,
Presents are wrapped in pure sincerity all around the Christmas tree.

The harmony of love made those musical carols sound so beautiful
And brought together voices gathering laughter,
As it made rapid feet and busy hands move together.

Viewing maybe a cute vision of Frosty the Snowman as he is smiling
Or Rudolph's red nose re-lighting the sky with his merry feelings.

The splendor of joyness and prosperity will echo and spread exquisitely
As prayers are circling the globe in honoring our Savior's birth.

Constance Edwards

GIVING FEAST

A feast of giving may bring humans out for dinner,
While sharing with acqaintance,
The great and wonderful gravies of Thanksgiving,
With its many different styles of dressing to delight all.

The shy, selfish and the slick,
For they talk good of the feast
But never of the love and giving,
For being narrow-minded brings a bias form around,
With fields of limit and lacking decisions,
That will gather an unforgettable oath on any opinions and reasons.

Let not the old tradition be distorted,
Which are of the utmost vital importance,
For those troubled and worried throbbing cells,
Can lead directly to the line of one's brain
And then may splash quickly its vibrations into the vessels.

For those vibrations can flow a closeness,
That has never been felt before,
While its beauty of joy is roaring,
A strange fear of gladness together.

As it's now displaying a pearly figure
  of spring enrichment all around us
And now awaiting the wishbone with its delightful dramas,
For this magnificent feast has a brilliant grace to give,
To love and being loved with a deep embedded spirits
  of continuous crystals.

Constance Edwards

CONSTANCE EDWARDS. Born: Chicago, Illinois, 4-9-47; Education: George Washington Carver High School, 6-24-65; Occupation: Clerical; Honors: Authored short story and poem to recite at the DuSable Museum in honor of Dr. Martin Luther King, Jr., at his birthday celebration, January, 1983, in Chicago, Illinois; Comments: *The basic essentials I used in creating my ideas are indeed all around us in this world such as love, joy, happiness, sorrow, fear, hurt and pain. Whereby, when I expound upon these emotions it enables me the ability to combine a combination of words or phrases together to hopefully capture and reach an individual imagination. I enjoy tremendously creating the many dreams of life itself into sentences.*

LITTLE GIRLS

Little girls in ruffles and lace,
Look so sweet with a smile on their face.
Ribbons and dimples and dainty feet,
Pitter and patter as they walk down the street.
Gold in their hair and stars in their eyes,
Catches a butterfly as it goes by.
Little girls as you can see
Are ever so dear to you and me.

Joy M. Parker

FADE TO BLACK

What happened to those 'yesterdays,' when man and woman met?
  And fell in love then married. Had kids, and that was it?
She was there for only *him,* and he was there for her,
  And the thought to seek another mate, back then, did not occur.

As long as I remember, we've prayed for Unity —
  For this world to stand 'as one' in peace, from sea to shining sea.
Well, there's unity among us now, but nowhere is there cheer.
  For in every corner of the world, we stand 'as one' in fear.

In fear of a deadly virus, that's better known as AIDS —
  And we watch it spread across this land, as our population fades.
No one ever knowing, the next time it may strike
  And make another victim of both young and old alike.

Yes every human life's affected by it, that's for sure.
  There is no prejudice with AIDS; just like there is no cure.
Will our children reach maturity? Are they guaranteed their place?
  Or will they be the victims of a fading Human Race?

When wedding vows are spoken, ''Until death do us part,''
  Do they have a strike against them, before they even start?
Do couples ever wonder, if the wedding night they spend
  Is really the beginning. Or could it be the end?

Garryett Fortin

HEART AND SOUL

Lonely tears that hide the child's laughter in my heart.
  And pain that's driven into the depths of my soul.
Stars shine brightly in the sky, but oh not for me.
While the willow weeps its tears for my heart and soul.
  Run! Run! I ask my soul, and do not look back
for Pain grows strong when it is felt.
  Laugh! Laugh! I ask my heart, for my tears will
fall as long as you shall frown.
  Oh rivers that flow gently down the stream, you
always seem to pass me by.
  Move on! Move on! I ask my heart and soul, for you
will never heal my pain and tears if you don't move on.

Alicha Martinez

MY LITTLE BLACK BOOK

My black book is sort of badly worn
  It's been paged and paged and even torn
Some are new, some are not and some are blue
  Others are white, some are changed, and may not be true.

Some print is small and hard to even read
  For some or even me, would glasses be my need
Could be we change and need a repair and lift
  But my little black book reads the same and tells of a gift.

God gives to all who will receive free from Him
  Some it is not true. Because they cannot see Him anywhere
Yet who can see the wind — or feel the stars so dim
  But oh the power of wind that even raises buildings into the air.

So when I read and trust in prayer and its power
  And through Him who lifts a man or a woman or youth
    from the gutter
Make a winner from a loser, and a standing tower
  Sort of explains why my little black book is like a shelter and a shutter.

Alma A. Carlson

HOW COME MAGELLAN SAILED AROUND THE GLOBE AND I CAN'T CIRCUMNAVIGATE ONE TEEN-AGE LOBE?

His billowy sky's stuck 'tween Mother Earth and the vast unknown —
My son's suspense, his heir space, his crumpled, rent-free battle zone.

He bulks up that sky with ripe castoffs, slushpiled from teen events.
They're oxidizing, those stockpiled socks, piquing indignant tense.

And, geez, his snoz, it's like New York
  with stoplights stuck on bright-red.
I'm supposed to love this geek and his putty-thick 'Clearasil' head?

Bellowing decibels substantiate — 'Hey Ma, lemme be.'
Filial affection mauls feelings with each shrug at me.

I'm not your bailiff, Son. Shut your door. Whaddah ya trynnah do?
Hold up the universe with noise and fill up the sky with rue?

I know in his wallet Miss June unfolds, see the way he gawks.
His tongue hangs way out, his nostrils flare, how awkwardly he walks.

Yetch, clam up. What's to talk about?
  That hickey on his neck? 'Son . . .'
Discussion? R-I-G-H-T. That's teen taboo,
  any subject that's begun.

I can't navigate this new stage. It's uncharted, I can't plot.
Fourteen years, now this blockade . . .
  our relationship, it's just shot.

Oh grief, oh stress, oh mother load, swear by sexton, skies and earth.
The hardest stage is teenager time; the least hard, giving birth.

Susan L. Maguire

COMPLEXITIES

Life is complex and full of unwanted certainties.

  People searching for higher levels of spiritual and emotional
  ties. It seems most often to become an insurmountable task.

Will we be able to forge ahead without the constant mental games
  and fears of entrapment? Or just perhaps, when we find that
  other person, our fears and defensiveness can be subdued to
  the point of enjoyment.

Yes, life is complex! But we can't give up the hope of finding
  that special person.

Bernard Ginsberg

LIFE'S PRICE

If you didn't struggle, you never earned it.
If you didn't fall, you didn't learn it.
If you've never been hurt, you've never been loved.
If you've never cried tears, you've never been happy.
For in life there's always a price.

Alicha Martinez

THE UNKNOWN

We met by chance.
  An evening of dance, quiet conversation, and more dancing.
  Oh, my feet ached all night from dancing!

It was a splendid encounter. Meeting a woman full of energy and
  great magnetism.
    We now know each other what others would consider many months,
      but, reality says less than two.

It was fortuitous that we met.
  A stumbling act by two, while many others trying for the same.
    Hoping, just hoping, that their evening would end on a
      high note by meeting just that one!

During this time I have allowed myself the luxury of tearing away
  many of my walls. Only for her, did I show my vulnerability.
    But, what good is it? It becomes too painful when the
      Achilles heel becomes touched!

We're together, but, are we there as one?
  Or, are we two strangers, never to be united as a single entity?
    Similarly, as two ships approaching, then passing alone in
      the dark. Excited for that fleeting moment of time.

Why do I feel uncertainty and unknowingness?
  Which creates a void sensation.
    The time now indicates to reach out as one, or, sever all ties.

Bernard Ginsberg

HUMILITY

Of a humble, modest and contrite heart
Do ye surrender all to thee
Omnipotent Lord, please set me free
Free from my own will and selfish plight
Yielding and submitting all to You, Master,
  for this is right

Giving all of yourself in an unselfish manner
Taking the blame and forgiving when you'd rather
  fly the pride banner
Humility is repenting and seeing how low you can go
To climb the mountain to reach Heaven's door.

Jheri Rivers

FAITH

Trusting in His unseen power and grace
Though you have not seen Him face to face
Listening to your inner heart for conscience sake
Being pure in your heart and not a fake

Faith is reaching for something that's not there
Holding on to hope when no one cares
Rejoicing in times of suffering, tribulation and strife
Leaning and trusting on Jesus, knowing He'll make it right

Faith is repenting and believing that Jesus is the Son
  of God, truly the Christ
The Everlasting hope of peace in your heart, the promise
  of eternal life.

Jheri Rivers

WOODLAND REVISITED

Penetrating the taciturn air,
  Cicadas' shrills pierce
    solemn silence.
Staccato-warbling of birds
  melodically trail the woodland sounds, as
Cascading leaves from trees find response
  in the soothing soil
Weary, from daily toil.

Placidly, the sky envelops verdure
  embracing it with a mother's enduring love, while
Sun-drenched rays flood paths and patches,
  reflecting patterns of light, interlacing
  branches, hills and mounds,
  forever bound.

Voice-less humanity rests, while cicadas sing
  their best
Intensity of sounds re-bound,
  from infinitesimal insects whose momentary shrills
  mirror the brevity of happiness
It's mercurial fleeting visits in man's path,
  to meet death's veil where, perhaps
  love hides away from wrath.

Angela Puglisi, Ph.D.

CHRISTMAS HOLIDAY MEMORIES

In Memory of my mother!

Christmas means many things to me!
Happy days that used to be —
Recalling all the time that was spent,
In preparing for the happy event —
Seemed — being kids, we didn't appreciate,
The many nights you stayed up late —
Making cookies and presents for that date,
Always working for our happiness —
Surely, you made our Christmas always blessed!

How you dressed us up for church plays —
Oh! you made us angels — singing God's praise.
Love was present in every room —
It filled our hearts and chased away gloom,
Dear to our hearts you will always be —
A blessing from God to our family,
Yes, you made Christmas pass so pleasantly!

Many children never did possess —
Even a small amount of our happiness,
More was given by you each year —
Only love was present — never fear,
Remembering all those pleasant days —
I'll never stop singing of your praise,
Etched in my soul — is a deep wealth —
So, I wish you luck, happiness, love and good health!

Thelma G. Mark

THE TEST

The test of a true friend is the challenge in accepting one's
  faults, frailties, and fears. The outcome shall bear full
  fruits which will be an everlasting bond between the two.

Bernard Ginsberg

WATCH THE SPIDER WEB

As I watch the tiny spider web
  The sun is shining so bright
But this little guy is hard at work
  Not in the sun, but a darker corner.

He is up and down, over and around
  I cannot see his thread or machine
But down and up and just all over
  And then the sun moves, and shines on his glitter.

I watch him, and away he is gone, down his web
  Just how did he make the pretty design
His body so tiny — with time so short
  And yet so strong, as he strings up or down to the floor.

Or stops halfway, or up again to the top
  I sweep him down, yet he is back the same way
Up and over, down and around, in all my anger I have
  to say he makes a most interesting pattern and not a stop.

Then I watch a fly passing by, and at once he
  the tiny spider captures the fly and folds it gently
and neatly into his web. It looks so neat and shiny
  I ask just how can it be 'so' as I watch, the spider web.

Alma A. Carlson

GOD'S LITTLE CREATION

This morning I was blue, it seemed so empty and alone
  The wind blew the branches and leaves all around
One robin hopped to and fro, but sat another as on a throne
  Still another came, she seemed to search the ground.

As I watched she pulled and pulled, she had a nice worm
  Soon other birds came, some flew far out of my sight
Back came the mother, how did I know? I saw the tree and
  babies squirm
  The wind blew, yet her nest hung so perfectly neat and tight.

Then came a rabbit, a hop and a hop and then a stop
  What do I see, out by my flower bush sat another rabbit
Down from a tree came a red squirrel and up again to the top
  Cheerful and full of pep, this is fun to watch, I'll
    make it a habit.

So when my hours seem empty, I just watch them and think of God
  How He created and how He cares and feeds them all
How He gave them keen eyes to see a worm as a farmer turns the sod
  The squirrel who hides his food for winter, the feathered birds leave in
  the fall
My lonely self turned to joy by God's little creation.

Alma A. Carlson

I FOUND MINE

All girls are lovely
Some are more sugar while others lean toward spice
And every so often you may find one
Who has the proper portion of both

When they have grown up
A woman some will become while others a lady by choice
And every so often you may find one
Who knows when, where and how to be —
All three at the very same time

E. Arnold Musgrove

GOD'S PRESENCE

*For Dr. Eugene Chesrow who said, ''Get the children out
of the cities to grow in the freedom of life.''*

What's the cost of our lives when our cities' children don't even
have the right.
  To stand at wonder and see the stars at night or the breath
  of trees at daylight.

A pecan tree spreads its leaves and drops beneath food for free,
  A magnolia bursts with fragrance, a scent song, floating on a
  Soft gentle southern summer's breeze.

The honeysuckle trumpets its nectar, to a child taught the finesse
to collect its sweetness.
  Taught the effort to pull the stem and wonder at the world
  constructed with exquisite completeness.

To see the power and the glory, the pain and the stories, told by
storm-washed fields.
  Seeing the freshness amidst the wreckage left by the cresting
  of pure energies.

Hearing the voices piping and hoarseness from crickets to frogs,
bulls, or hogs.
  Hearing the grate of the bark from trees needed to bend with the
  breezes they helped conceive.

Harmony pleases, chromosomes weaving in time, seeking the music;
creating life.
  Whether it be a leaf in fall its colors changing, or the children
  learning the sayings of different songs of life.

Cathleen Chesrow

DAD

To Dr. Tony Berardi, a Vietnam veteran

Mr. Davie, if divorce court were the Navy, you'd have a lady in every
port.
  So I set out to be just your girl, the daughter you felt you
  could help by just being yourself.

It was fun to see the surprise as your world-weary eyes had to learn
to resist.
  It was love you perceived as I sat on your knee and gave you
  a hug so quick.

That pipe smoke encircling your head, when you wanted to consider
why our roles were reversed — quixotic at first.
  Christmastime all the time and you didn't have to be the giver,
  saying, ''I can't figure — why you always look so fresh.''

When the court case was finished — you as the winner — saying,
''They can't take what we had.''
  I knew as I'd sit down to dinner — evening prayers said,
  ''That there was never — a winner — a friend when you
  became one of the ones who have stood in as my dad.''

Oh now there will be husbands and friends, brothers and kin, and if
they have taken the time to see
  It's that toughness, an Irish loving roughness, they love; I saw in you
  and choose to become a part of me.

Cathleen Chesrow

HIS LIVING SPIRIT

He had a dream,
    and we dreamed
Through his eyes, we as a people
could see what time had dared us not to see

He believed,
    and we believed
in a life others dared us not to live
but only through believing could we hope to achieve
      it

He had courage,
    and through his courage
we faced a lifetime of unknowns
that too soon ended dreams and beliefs

and challenged our courage to exist
The years have not changed our dreams
nor dampened our beliefs, but because of
one courageous man, we as a people

are united; we can believe in
ourselves, our goals, and face
our unknowns with a courage that he,
Dr. Martin Luther King, instilled in us

He had a dream; and we dreamed
he believed, and we believed
He dared to exist; and today
his spirit continues to exist within us all

Susan A. Montelius

TO GIVE UNENDING

Sometimes the ways of life make one wonder,
How to go above or get out from under.

Into the maze of burdens one must go,
Reality so strong a force does show.

Left alone my children can you bear the force,
Each day of crashing waves does block your course.

Yet standing as a barrier reef so strong,
Behold! Two pillars so straight and long.

Each takes its place and backs its voice,
No mention of any alternative choice.

Just to give unending with heart and soul,
And never a thought for the personal toll.

Can one ever repay such endless support?
Has eternity the means for sustaining the thought?

To offer some praise, a prayer and a yell,
Each person here mentioned through poetry can tell.

Reflect and consider the light you have shown,
How words best describe what forever will be known.

Joel Greenman

Sometimes when I look at the bright blue sky without a cloud in sight
I feel that I want to jump right up — just   take off in flight.
Picture it and just imagine how happy I will be
saying that I declare I am nothing else but me.
The wind blowing in my hair, on my face a smile
all the things I had to do will wait a short-long while.
Flying fast and high and free I see the whole world too
with it realizing just how much I can learn and do.
Suddenly there is no time — no time at all to waste
for with the short life that I have I should rush but without haste.
My life I will live hard and put to a test
for how can I leave the world alone until I do my best?
I want as much as possible to do what is to be done
to make this world a better place to live — for everyone.
All that I accomplish I will use to dream, to fly and call:
Unless I take every man along, I am not me at all!

Shira Verbit

THE LAST ROSE OF SUMMER

The chill of November quickens my pace
As I walk along a leafy path
Where trees seem reluctant to face
The inescapable winter's wrath.

The season's first snow, just beginning,
Obscured my view where the pathway led,
But through the pure and white descending
I caught a glimpse of something red.

I strayed from my path where the creek gently flows
To behold what had survived the deepening snow.
On a leafless bush clung a single red rose,
Fighting against Fate for one more tomorrow.

As I continued my walk along the rill,
I kept on wondering, trying to determine
What gave that rose a stronger will
To cling with such hope when death was so certain.

Then turning again to bid a farewell,
I suddenly knew the message it sent.
Like the last rose of summer, as the last petal fell,
I would cling to life till the last precious moment.

Elizabeth Ann Jones

RETURN TO NEW YORK

The city beckons at horizon's line,
Its hustling bustle of Times Square glamour
Flashing etched on the mind; the vive d'amour
That Broadway shows, wrought in fantasy's mine.

Babel's towers shimmer with lives of wealth
As brokers curse Manhattan's merry bourse;
And doctors challenge nature to its course,
Straining to cure the city's indexed health.

Trains wind serpentine through crowded litter,
Screeching in protest to wild hordes pushing
With dollar-crazed fury. Above, strutting

Hookers at corners smile, cracked and bitter.
As old unbroken children rape, kill, fight,
Demonic sirens scream to deified night.

Jonathan Katzauer

NUCLEAR WINTER

I once owned an orchard blossoming trees
That promised great harvest from newborn Springs,
When conceptual fruit flew on wings
Of sunlit breezes, floating golden bees.
The Summer brought its youthful innocence, gazing
In wonder at life growing, myriad forms
Living on light and hope and warmth and storms,
Looking to endless time of timeless dancing.
In Autumn's golden fall my apples ripened
To the rustling of a maturing world,
Where sheep grew shining fleece in rustic wolds
And farmers planned to years not yet wakened.
    But Winter blew early with deadly snows,
    And killed my trees when their orchard froze.

Jonathan Katzauer

AT WHAT LONELY TIME?

When does the Boy cease to watch for and to search out the
    wonders of his commonplace world?
And where does an ice cream cone lose its delicate vanilla
    perfume to become something cold, sweet and fattening?
And at what moment, in the swift flight of time, does he
    forget his fear of Goblins, or of houses turned old
    and sinister at night;
Or his delight in lying on heaps of acrid-smelling leaves on
    nippy autumn afternoons,
Looking off into a cloud-infested sky or at nothing at all?
When does the Boy forget his games and how to play?
When does the Man, walking along a quiet street, discover some
    half-remembered scene out of joint with time;
To hear faintly the cry of the long-deposed peddler, loudly
    sing-songing praises of his simple wares?
And when does the Man forget his joy of climbing into tall trees,
    to see and to be the silent master of the vibrant, pulsing
    world below . . .
At what time and place did the Boy and the Man meet in quiet
    embrace — and then forever part?

James Taylor Forrest

THREE FRIENDS

The day began early so I decided to stop and relax
for a while — on a cliff so high above the ocean's roar
Its waves were as whispers when they kissed the shore

As I looked up the sky began to fill with millions of
stars for me to pluck
With a big yellow moon on the rise — over the crest
of a hill just off to the side

Then as I lowered my eyes to my utter surprise —
A stag I spied near enough to all but reach out
and touch
And within the speed of a blinking lash —
There were now two standing side by side
To bid me welcome on this beautiful night

Then I thought to myself wouldn't it be grand
if the rest of the world could join in to find peace
with each other and with their self

As had the new-found friends — the stags and I

E. Arnold Musgrove

MITTENS

My Kitty Kat had five little kittens
    Alberta got one and named her "Mittens."
She herself was grey but her feet were white,
    and by all the neighbors she was so much liked.
When they were big enough they were given away,
    and poor Mittens thought they with her should stay.

And not many days, quite soon after that
    again she became my own little cat.
When she crawled through the bushes under my fence,
    and no one but me ever knew where she went.
Her secret was mine and I let her stay,
    I knew she was pregnant, and then one day,
She had five kittens by some boards in the hall,
    but I told not a soul, nobody at all.
I fixed them a place on the porch to stay,
    where they had lots of room to romp and play.
And there they stayed 'til they were grown
    big enough, till I found them another good home.

Agnes Westmoreland

BEEKEEPER

I was a beekeeper for more than thirty years,
And through all my experiences I had no fears,
I learned it from my son who first found a hive,
Way up in the mountains, not a bee was alive,
The bears had gotten to them, and the hives were knocked about,
They had eaten all the honey, and all the bees were out.
He nailed things together for another swarm of bees,
Might find one on a fencepost, or nesting on a tree.

Another name for colony is also called a swarm,
When they get overcrowded, they are then less calm.
Then the queen gathers followers, she's the leader of the swarm,
No one should molest them or do them any harm.
They fill themselves with honey just before they travel on,
In just a little while they will all be gone.
They have made a new queen to take the old one's place,
For one queen would be killed if they met face to face.
They'll rest a little while in a place, then send a scout
To find a new home for them a way out.
This usually happens when the moon is very light,
Did you ever know an insect that could be so bright?

Agnes Westmoreland

UNTITLED

Last night I put my hands together and I hoped He'd hear my call
to put a wall around my brother deep within South Africa.
He dropped a match in a dead forest and a fire's about to start.
Let the flame blaze across the world and singe the fists of
blackened hearts.

Please keep Him in mind — Please keep Him in mind. The world is
baking now — soon it's going to burn. For none of us — none of us
get in except by the Grace of God.

A child reached from my TV set and then he clutched my eyes —
instead of baby fat he had tired bones in place of thighs.
Nothing filled his stomach but a dream to stay alive — So far
his screams for a hope seem to be whispers that die.

Howard Dantzler

CHRISTMAS PAST

I would change Christmas, to simple old days
When we were just children, with few toys to play.
We talked of the shepherds, on hillsides so far,
While guarding their flocks, they saw a great star.

We lived in a house that was not very old,
On a farm in Montana, where winters were cold,
Jack Frost painted windows, you could hardly see through,
All the scenery outside was hidden from view.

We'd go to the mountains, to chop down a tree,
We'd pick the best one that Papa could see.
A fir tree so fragrant, some branches had cones,
We'd hang extras of them, over doorways at home.
A candle holder, on each branch we clipped,
To each hold a candle, we eventually lit.
These bright-burning candles, we watched every one,
Lest one would catch fire and burn up our home!

Soon Mama told us "It's time for your bed!
Put on your nighties, nightcaps on your heads."
And soon my dear Mother and Father, we knew,
Would blow out the lamp and go to bed, too.

Agnes Westmoreland

AGNES M. WESTMORELAND. Born: Montana, 4-12-04; WWII Navy widow; Education: State University of Missoula, Montana, B.A., 1928; Occupations: High school teacher; Recreation leader; Drama director and entertainer, 2-1/2 years; Short story writer; Poet; Government worker during WWII: Machine operator, Electrician's helper, Seamstress; Secretary, 15 years; Hobbies: Writing, Sewing, Beekeeping, Humanitarian projects; Poetry: 'Wilderness'; 'Threshing'; 'Lament of a Kitten,' *Anthology,* 1986; Other Writings: Beekeeping stories; ''Our Special Hen,'' story; Themes: *The poems and stories I write are largely about my life on a farm where I lived and worked for many years. I also enjoy writing about my many experiences as a beekeeper.*

ON HAVING A CHILD

Crystals of fine joy cover me
when I think of my child
a warm frontal flush
sweet ache in my middle to enclose him, tenderly
Wistfulness (and some relief)
when I think of his outgrowing me

I have never loved another so unconditionally
Nor played servant nor master so well
Nor had such a good reason
to be good, not so reckless
and expand my idea of myself

I am thankful
my dear beautiful baby
thankful that you are

Cheryl Tupper

TO SPIDER, 16 YEARS OLD IN A ONE-ROOM APT.

If you were a moth, you'd be a night-life butterfly
But you
Are a spider.

The webs you spin are in your head, not in any bottle;
Skeins of tight dreams, unwoven, unwinding —
Nor vial of silk
Whose threads cocoon your daily loaf, your loaf-mind,
As in a spool —
But you
Must believe it.

From your fingertips and feet come spun gold
Which you design across the corner of a wall;
Threads are for sewing wounds shut, curtains, patches.

Why couldn't I give you any more than a simple wish
For a good night's sleep:
The cool sheet flying out over you
Like a wing of light through web patterns.

For your home you need
Spider-magnets for a mini-fridge
Or a two-dollar, styrofoam cooler.
Filled with juice and fruit.

Vickie Graeff

LOVE #1 'CAUSE IT MAKES LIFE MORE FUN

Love is something that I understand
You've got to know how to get it, and how to demand
You've got to know what you want, put all games to the side
Love at every minute so you both can abide
By the rules — of the loveliest game — don't be fools
Where love is the name.
Take the time to show it, because without it you blow it
What you once had, now someone feeling bad
You or the other lost and lonely lover and oh so sad.
  Love #1 b-cuz it makes life more fun.
This is how you do it, so put your mind to it
And take over her heart, she loved you right from the start
Every drop, please don't stop, nothing will tear you apart
Hug and squeeze, play and tease, show your love with
the ease. Hands and toes, rub your nose with the touch
Very much because it shows where it goes like a finagle of
such. Love, under the sheets — in the streets — another love
It defeats; can put you where you belong it's so strong . . .
And starve a person that eats. If I didn't know love
I'd wonder what's going, but it comes from within and if
Misused then it's gone.
  Love #1 'cause it makes life more fun.

James Kyser

LOVE

There is no other love other than the love that parents bring,
the love they share is genuine love.

No other male or female can give the same love that parents,
give it is a true and everlasting love.

So be advised and give respect where respect is due, because no
one will ever love you like your parents do.

Selene L. Christian

EMPTINESS

Oh, what does it mean in your emptiness to sit?
Rather, the question is:
Are you able so to do on your own?
And is there a God as we when children are taught?

The question last propounded is one to so hurt
that we all unable alone to ponder —
let alone answer — are

But who is it that is there —
shall we say "what" for those poor few
who don't believe in a personal God, Who —
crazy it is — is revealed in those same old yet even new
words in the Bible they are

Now what is it I've said —
And am I advancing a religion new?
Not at all say I, only saying am I,
What is so wrong with reexamining the old,
for truths there are aplenty for those who apply
the old yet ever new
"let go and let God"

Thomas J. P. Courtney

THIRTY YEARS

Thirty years unable to speak suffered I
a pain unspeakable such as to bear
as I fought and fought against what I knew not
As I tried and tried to free do break.

And never did I give the slightest of thought
to the pain to others I caused —
though heavy for me, it was so to bear.
For no counting for what was never uncountable . . .

Friendships unborn and people unknown —
and all because uncommunicative was I.
Whose fault, whose fault, this you may wonder
And maybe a lot my iron will it bears . . .

But my iron will my savior has been,
for, after all is said, a balance is needed,
between "community" and individualism, that is.
And while the will it is neither, its force it is needed . . .

To balance between the aforesaid two
is an easy task never at all.
And here it is that an iron will it does become,
the fulcrum, the balance, the chasm between.

Thomas J. P. Courtney

THOMAS J. P. COURTNEY. Born: 12-9-48; Married: Maribeth, 6-26-71; Education: Fordham College, B.A., 1971; Fordham Law, J.D., 1974; Occupation: Attorney at Law; Writings: As a lawyer, I write incessantly.

GET WELL FATHER

My father is not a lawyer, doctor, or millionaire, but a hard-working, Polish-American, foundry worker, of whom I am proud, no matter, rich or poor, sick or in health. When I was a little girl, my father was always there for me, when I needed him. He would work very hard, every day, to keep food in our stomachs, and a roof over our heads. Even though we were very poor, my father made sure we had clothes, and lots of presents every Christmas. My father would always be ready to read to me, even after a hard day's work. I remember, he used to bring me home books on dinosaurs, Sherlock Holmes, Poe, and more. My father had this story he used to tell us kids, every day he came home from work, about his talk with Peter Rabbit and his family about our family. He was strict, but as I got older, I realized he was, because he loved us and wanted us to become good adults. Most of all, my father is the very best father anybody could ask for, in the whole world, because he never gives up. Dad, I love you. Please don't give up. We need you, and mostly, so do I.

I love you
Your daughter

Marci Bilyue

THE "LAW" OF LAWS!

To the making of laws there is no end.
No tree so great that would not bend.

Adorned with all the rules, hung there by fools.
Thru each city and town endless laws abound.

The elected compose, as this sea of vain-ness grows.
Each, casts a stone, from his shiny little throne.

Contained it seems, as these dreamers dream.
Go search the ages, waves of meaningless pages.

Have never calmed troubled seas from rages.
Countless rules are fearful tools of shallow fools.

The answer can be found, with a heavenly sound.
The laws which "free men" will always be the *Eternal-Ten*.

With freedom ever so dear, pray we seldom hear.
There ought to be a law. *There ought to be a law!*

To end the burdens men place upon free men.

Bill Dwight Rawson

BILL DWIGHT RAWSON. Born: Colby, Kansas, 2-26-37; Education: High school, 2 years college, Several business seminars; Occupation: Owner, Market Maintenance and Construction, Inc.; Memberships: Business clubs; Themes: *My viewpoint on some of today's problems. I like to use poetry to express my ideas and feelings to awaken my fellow man to a realization of truth and integrity.*

A BOOK I NEVER FOUND

In the late thirties, Anaheim High
Was my Alma Mater. Memories fly
    Back to the teacher who worked with me —
    I was class poet — I wrote poetry
For the teacher who watched both meter and rhyme
In historical poems of Discoverers' time.

A boy artist, in a seat just behind,
Illustrated my poems. I see in my mind
    A boy, very tall, with dark eyes and hair,
    We worked on the book for Pomona State Fair.
My folks, then, sold their Main Street Cafe,
So I never saw that Pomona State day.

I never saw the poems and the art
Of the book of which I was so much a part,
    But I saw a shy. I was a shy,
    Shy teenager, using poetry to fly
From emotional pain. Oh, the tears
That flowed when I left those years

Spent in that small California town,
And now it has grown into world renown
    With Disneyland. Before this fame
    Beautified and expanded Anaheim's name,
I was there, with orange groves all around,
Writing a book that I never found.

Deltalee Morgan Bilderback

CANDY CANE GATES

In the land of make-believe, I saw
flowers that smiled, and popcorn that talked!

And while strolling along chocolate block, I saw
lollipops dance, and gumdrops on roller skates!

There were cookies that ran past me, oh! so very
fast, and fudge sundaes that wore cowboy hats!

I love this land of make-believe, where time
is but a cupcake, and the world a cherry pie

The streets are made of lemon drops, the buildings
of gingerbread, and every tree I see, is made of
non-other, than taffy!

Cotton candy clouds float across the licorice sky,
and soda pop raindrops seem to always fall, in
spite of the bubble gum sun, that always shines.

I think I shall never leave this place, I'll
become a sno-cone that never melts, and I'll
never be like all the people who go thru their lives
unnoticed, who fade away and die, outside of
these candy cane gates.

Theresa John

ODE TO A TEACHER

Terrific in helping us learn new,
Eager to show us the right thing to do,
Adored and beloved by all of the students,
Cordial and cheerful with kindness and prudence,
Helping us gain the knowledge desired,
Enchanting in spirit, esteemed and admired,
Resplendently keeping us deeply inspired.

Ruth J. Colella

CHILDREN OF THE STARS

They carry the blood of their parents, but ancient memories
dance in their heads. They have a consuming hunger that cannot be
sated. The secret of the first flame, creation of the wheel, gravity's
pull, why the winds blow, and calendars of amazing accuracy . . .
just a few marks of their talent!

The waves reflect the pounding of their pulse, the seasons pace
their growth and nadir. Left behind by explorers of the past?
    Forgotten
by forebearers of long ago? Scattered, multi-colored remnants of a
cosmic sailing breed, floated on reed rafts, rowed with the
    Phoenicians and
Vikings, created form and beauty in Greece, raised megoliths and
    pyramids,
and awed millions with the Renaissance . . . still they are restless.

They do not despise the gift of Earth or mortal kin, but they have
    lit a candle in the
darkness, and still it is too dark . . . Raged at the darkness . . .
    Struck sparks for more light, and suffered impotence.

Their spirits strain against time, they are inpatient with life,
they are painfully aware of their flaw of mortality, with lifespan
clocks a-tickin', and more to do and learn than Earthlings should
ever dare to dream! They race ahead because they instinctively know
that a century, even a millennium, is inadequate to reach their
    destination,
their timeless place of origin.

Others do not understand these throwbacks of a race long gone.
They are lonely . . . craving a reunion with their progenitors. They
seek the satisfaction of a world, nay, a universe complete. In their
moth-like flutterings, they struggle to reach the ancestors they
never knew. Though they may not achieve relief of their yearnings . . .
    may forever tread
the wheel of fate . . . they will lift mankind just a little higher,
    a little nearer to the stars.

Daniel Webster

RELATIVES

For a man to have a relative
can be sometimes an irritative . . .
though he might often be glad
to have one when he is sad,
to share sorrow, or mishap,
or rescue him from life's trap.
But never forget this truth:
your brother and sister both,
as relatives, may bring troubles to you,
even the worst misfortune, that is the issue.
Your dilemma won't be merely strife,
through them you may lose your living, even your life.

Always remember that glass
belongs to a family, a class.
Diamond, rock and stone are all
of the glass family: small, big, short, or tall.
They share origin, nature, entity, alas!
A diamond scratch on the face of glass
makes the glass ready to crash.
A stone that hits glass produces a smash.

Parviz Atropat

CEMETERY

There is an ancient land far, far away.
It was called Persia, and it stands by the sea.
There are no birds, laughter, music; all is dismay.
Day after day more wickedness and misery.
In this land millions of moving dead, young and old,
are dressed in mourning — deepest black —
for what they have buried because they were blindfold:
they have buried and lost their all under evil's attack.
This was a land of ancient culture and rich history;
but no more. Now it is controlled by the devil's squad.
Now it is merely the graveyard of a great story.
All good has been buried: freedom, honesty, humanity, even God!

Parviz Atropat

A MIRROR IN THE SAND

After I lose the world and all that I've got there's sleep
Crystal vibrant airiness sockets of sound which they can't hear
But I can see how dear you are to me
So close that I mayn't breathe
Breath exhales itself nothing is possessed because foreverness
When all of time's a day where I want to be with you unleashed
Not behind this hedge but inside everything just listening to see
A mirror in the sand tells me who I am someone not alone
I see you in my sight of mind I hear you in my heart of thought
I feel you like the wind
Dispersed into emptiness together alone no body only space
If I touch your hand you are gone but if I hold my breath we are
    at rest
I want to know the spirit of you and nothing else
The mindless naked breast the childless very self crying until
    needlessness
When only wonder cares at all and we want nothing more
Regret is not a word living has no meaning
We are faceless when we bear no fruit
It is because I am you and you are me

Dena Beth Lesser

DENA BETH LESSER. Pen Names: Dena, Dena Amour; Born: Los Angeles, California, 10-30-54; Single; Education: University of California, Los Angeles, and Antioch College, undergraduate, 1972-75; Occupations: Actress, Dancer, Poetess, Make-up artist, Screenwriter, Astrologer; Memberships: Screen Actors Guild, Federation of Television and Radio Artists, Actors Equity Association; Poetry: 'Child of Faith,' *Words of Praise: A Treasury of Religious and Inspirational Poetry, Vol. III,* 1987; 'Identity,' *American Poetry Anthology, Vol. VII, No. 2,* 1987; 'Romance,' *Hearts on Fire: A Treasury of Poems on Love, Vol. IV,* 1987; Other Writings: "Children's Leukemia," medical research article, nurses files, City of Hope Cancer Institute's Children's Hospital, 1966; "The Camel Pusher," screenplay, registered: Writer's Guild of America (West), 1979; Statement: *Is there any difference between peace and power? It seems to me that religions and nations believe force yields power while preaching peace and freedom for all mankind. Whereas individuals seek personal control of each situation in order to feel superior or at the very least a sense of security. But why fight, when ultimately there is no greater power on earth or in the heavens than love. It is for peace I write.*

I MOVE AMERICA

The coal and water are gone.
Where? I don't know. Advancement in
technology? Things will not be the same.
I am large and powerful and blue. That
is my color; not my mood. The 3/4 circles
and lines on my side are a symbol of pride
and loyalty; not ownership. When my
whistle blows, don't say I dry up your cows,
cause your chickens to stop laying and scare
children. When you hear me and see my red
flashing lights, pay heed. Don't try to
beat me across my path. You may lose.
That saddens me and causes my crew unnecessary
stress. I am on the job day and night while
you work, play, and sleep.
I move the cars you drive.
I move the coal for your electricity.
I move the grains for your breads.
At times I move you.
I am a Sea Dust engine working always for Conrail.
Respect me and help me to keep on moving America!

James R. Clark

A DAY IN THE COURT OF LOVE

In Kangaroo Court the verdict is read to the
accused. GUILTY! Guilty of loving someone who doesn't
wish to return it. The sentencing follows.
LIFE! A life term of waking up cold and lonely.
Without a fair trial of the relationship proposed,
I stand before the one-woman judge and jury.
She decrees without cross-examination that nothing
beyond a friendship can be or exist. The bridge
goes up in flames as the heart breaks. Appeals will
not be entertained. She leaves with a smile on her
face to advertise to the world the grandeur of her
new lover. I depart to the prison of sadness to
repair the damage as I have done in the past —
alone.

James R. Clark

THE CHRISTMAS BAZAAR

The little old woman hobbled 'round with her cane
Laughing and calling to all a "Hello!"
Happiness showed on her wrinkle-lined face
As she tapped hand-block patterns of quilts in each row.

"Hi! How be you, Viny?" greeted this one and that
Roaming and buying sale goods at bazaar.
Homemade pies sat on cloth-covered wood shelves
As she whiffed the spice odors of sweets from afar.

The woven plaid holders recalled life in the past
Cooking and baking in an old home kitchen
Heavy pans placed on black iron woodstove,
Hot pads jogged memories of Gran-pap's loud bitchin'.

"Ah —" Crochet-edge towels pattern stitches on top
Cutting and sewing fine cloth with finesse —
Baby bibs piled in neat labeled high stacks
Made her feel once again her own infant's caress.

"Yes!" Rampant remembrance filled the air with good cheer
Caring and serving kin folk 'long the way
Enjoyment showered her friendship-strewn path
As she paid heartfelt "thank-yous" with smiles on this day.

Dorothy M. Ainslie

CAUGHT IN THE STORM

Downpour: The rain pounds on my car.
I sit and hear the bang of blasting water.
I see bouncing bubbles on my hood.
The sky is dark and grey.
Lightning zig-zags streaking fire through the air.
Big drops fall in bunches on the road. Thunder roars.

Submission: I sit and wait for time . . .
      Time to let the raging storm work out.
      Time to see the fury — feel the wet.
      I sit and feel remorse.

Recovery: The rain slides off my car.
I sit and hear the spills of sprinkling water.
I see smoothing splatters on my hood.
The sky turns white and bright.
Lightning zip-zaps cruising blinkers through the air.
Big drops rest in puddles on the road. Thunder quits.

Rejuvenation: I rise and know it's time. . .
      Time to let the killing storm be done.
      Time to see the beauty — feel the calm.
      I rise and feel relief.

Dorothy M. Ainslie

CHRISTINE

Bundle of curls, big saucer eyes behind my friend's skirt;
A sweet laughing child (sometimes too wild — sweet
    goes out the window: it's a stage).
My charge when the band played; an excuse for
    some cozy cheap high school dates.
Charming my lover, when he was the charmer —
A whole bag of candy, and then off to sleep . . .
A tiny package of pink in his halfback arms.
One day I looked and your hair was in pigtails
The next it was even more grown-up than mine
    And you babysat others/with lovers
        of your own.
So: you fit in my clothes, make jokes like a human —
And suddenly your opinion matters.
Still sometimes a child steps out, in back
    of the badge of a lady in blue
And I pull her close, my
    sweet, surrogate daughter —
        Grown to love: that's
        You.

Suzanne Lamb-Sinkovitz

TKO

Who is the winner
and who is lost;
Or is this a draw
where both lose and end up
as we started:
Alone,
Unsure,
With each other to blame
when it's within each of us
that the fault lies.
You wanted a fight, so
I gave you one.
Now both of us are bloodied.

Gregory J. Borden

FULL CIRCLE LOVE

Given to Ruth, 3-29-75

How much do I love you?
  How much do I care?
I'll tell you, my darling,
  No words will I spare.

I love you as green things
  Love sunshine and rain;
I love you in pleasure,
  I love you in pain.

I love you as roses
  Love moonlight and dew;
I love you in springtime
  And all the year through.

How much do I love you?
  How much do I care?
I love you completely,
  Beyond all compare.

When you're among others,
  It's all very plain:
I love you full circle,
  And then back again.

I love you full circle,
  And then back again.

John C. Slemp

JOHN CALVIN SLEMP. Born: Butler, Tennessee, 3-29-02; Died: 8-23-81 Married: Ruth Weaver, 6-17-25; Education: Carson-Newman College, B.A. magna cum laude, 1924; D.D., 1935; Southern Theological Seminary, Th.M, 1929, Highest in all classes in history of seminary; University of Tennessee, Graduate work, summers, 1935-37; Occupations: Professor of English literature, Carson-Newman College; Assistant editor; Editor, Southern Baptist Convention; Memberships: American Baptist Churches; International Bible Lessons Committee; Curriculum Committee, American Baptist Convention; American Baptist Historical Society; Awards: Award of Merit for Christian journalism, editorials in *Missions;* inclusion in *Who's Who in the Clergy,* 1936; *Who's Who in the East,* 1955; Poetry: 'Breathe O'er Our Waiting Spirits, Lord,' *Broadman Hymnal,* 1936; 'I Sought the Living God,' *Christ in Poetry,* 1952; 'Worship,' *The Christian Century,* 1940, *Words of Praise,* 1985; 'Creativity,' *International Journal of Religious Education;* Comments: *I cannot remember a time when poetry was not a part of my life and thought. At an early age I was fascinated by words that rhyme and by rhymes that make poems. I read all the poems that came to my attention in school, memorized many of them, and wrote my very own, now long since lost to posterity. However, it was not until several years later that I began to write the poems that appear in books of poetry. For the most part, I wrote about ideas that appealed to me and events that challenged me. Always my purpose was to say something about life as I saw it and events as I interpreted them.*

DISCERNMENT

I sit here wondering about my life's current situation
  All of which I have complete control if *I am true* to
    My God and *my* life's *destiny* . . .

There are times when I feel despondent that it seems as though
  My happiness in this *life* is just a *mirror of illusions*
    ''An erroneous perception of reality'' . . .

  It's during these times that the *gentleness* of my being
    Languishes into *non-existence* . . .

It's funny how *we* as *physical beings* let so many *outside forces*
Assume control of *our lives* to the point where *we* become *encumbered*
And *filled* with much *pain* and *mental anguish* . . .

It's during these times that *we shrink* into the *nothingness* of
Our true *purpose* and *existence* in this *life* — thus eliminating *God's*
Simple gift of gentle pleasures, ''*love, friendship, and happiness*''

I am at a point where I must *break through the barrier of illusions*
  And *regain* the true reality of *my existence* in *this life* . . .

If *I am to attain and fulfill my Lord's will* — I must *first* put my
  Faith and *trust* in *Him* who gave me *life* — and come to the
    Realization that we are living in ''*a time of atrocity*'' . . .

. . . To fail, is to become *devoid* of *warmth, comfort,* and *all hope* . . .

    A. Mozelle Michaux

GIFT OF LOVE

Let the spirit of love charge my soul
until it is one

This ''Gift of Love'' radiates from the very core
of my soul — nothing has ever held this heart
of mine in captivity before

This ''Gift of Love''
God's supreme blessing has illuminated my life
for I am not longer the footstool of man's wretchedness
but the sure and pure existence of God's
true promise and glory to all who seeks Him

This ''Gift of Love''
has beautified my surroundings
uplifted my thoughts
purified my soul
simplified and endowed my life
entrusted me with enchanted friends
an honorable son
an honorable mate
and family

What greater joy is there for one who seeks happiness
but the word and love of God
''The true meaning of life''
The crystallization of grace and grandeur

    A. Mozelle Michaux

PARIS

Ah, the ambiance: Montmartre, the Rue de la Paix,
  the Arc de Triomphe, Sacré Coeur,
  Place de la Concorde, and Champs-Elysées.

The placid, shimmering Seine, winding between
  Left Bank and Right with unhurried grace,
Under bridges ornate in loveliness glides
  Like a ribbon through eyelets of lace.

A filigreed spire, a pyramid touching the sky,
  Towers the Eiffel in slim silhouette —
A beacon to herald each morning the sun,
  The moon and the stars when the sun has set.

Notre Dame, the cathedral, in beauty abounds:
  Gothic the portals where the saintly have trod;
The windows: medallions in rose-tinted hues;
  The towers: like arms uplifted to God.

The fabulous Louvre, museum beloved and renowned,
  Resplendent and proud, with antiquity teems;
Palatial the walls that gently enfold
  A myriad mementoes, a myriad dreams.

    Lenore Llewellyn

VIETNAM '69

Killing hot,
  the heat of the writhing bodies
  still sweating and you wait
  for that last reach for life.

You don't want anyone to touch you, talk to you,
  interrupt your rapport with the dying.

It is a very private moment,
  as though you are awaiting a transformation,
  a rebirth before your eyes.

But it usually ends with a wimper
  and it's very, very close.

And then you pray.

    Robert C. Ryan

ROBERT C. RYAN. Pen Name: Charlie-2; Born: Cambridge, Massachusetts; Married: Maureen Olivia Ryan, 11-1-80; Education: University of Massachusetts at Amherst; Occupation: 100% disabled veteran, Vietnam; Memberships: Disabled American Veterans, Vietnam Veterans of America, Military Order of the Purple Heart, Society of the the First Division; Awards: Runner-up, Daily Life category, *American Poetry Anthology, Vol. VII, No. 4;* Comments: *My poetry is my only means of outside communication because of Post-traumatic Stress Disorder, 100% from Vietnam, which renders me totally lost at times. I have a severe short-term memory deficit because I live in Vietnam every day. My poetry is fact, not fiction. I write it, line by line.*

THE HALLS OF THE WHISPERING NIGHT

Were you there when that first faint whisper
Stirred in the muted halls?
Did the fragrant breezes hold you
Where voices caressed the walls?

Will you still be there in the darkness
When I return once more,
Or be gone on the breath of the morning
To some lonely, misty shore?

Will you race to the portal to meet me,
And greet me with tears in your eyes?
Or will there be nought but the twilight,
In a room that is heavy with sighs?

Whenever you come you will find me,
Though eons may sing in their flight;
By the walls where the voices are muted,
In the halls of the whispering night.

Barry Green

HAROLD SANDERS GREEN. Born: Oxford County, England, 2-11-14; Married: Catherine Sanders, 4-15-39; Education: St. Andrew's, B.A.; other degrees and diplomas; Occupations: Educator, Entertainer, Director, Philosopher, Poet; Memberships: formerly Musicians, Variety Artists, Actors; Poetry: 'Kosmosava,' light verse, 1966; Themes: *My work covers a very wide spectrum, from religious, philosophical, humorous, and many song lyrics. I also wrote articles concerning international affairs, and Naturopathic health, for two English magazines:* Health for All, *and* New Vision.

FEEL THE COLOR OF WAR

Taste of a distant memory, a time when the world seemed young.
Broken archives of a dream, still running to catch the sun.
Feel a candle whisper, then fade to an echoing dun.

And in

    a corner of night

        two lovers

            are making love.

Odor of chrysanthemums, flavors of frankincense.
Feel the color of war, you can taste it in the wind.
My naked body exploding, as sweat drips off my skin.

And in

    a corner of night

        I hear the whisper

            of a dove.

Donald M. Cline

DIDO'S PRAYER

The quiet is without, but the silence is within;
and menacing is the hunger that couples with this dark.

And the abstract is born of the impact.

And Dido, poor Dido,
vainly seeks to embrace the infinite.

Better she were never born.

The river is wide before her,
yet she chooses to cross it anyway;
and may the gods forgive her for the passions of her heart.

And she would come to pray:
  As Juno is my guide,
  to the moon I pray this night.
  He lies here, tonight,
  in the chambers of my house.

  By Carthage I solemnly swear —
  and the gods —
  and Sychaeus —
  he lies here, tonight,
  in the chambers of my heart.

  For want I'd be his wife.
  For love I'd bear his child.
  And I pray, Heaven, that I,
  am in his dreams, tonight.

  I — Dido.

And then, Dido sleeps.

Donald M. Cline

THE FALL-OUT FACTOR

The fall-out from your alluring laughing eyes
rushes o'er me like a bubbling fountain
and bathes my captive mind with its magic art;
it gently overwhelms me with a secret happiness
that flows slowly over the emotional borderline
and suddenly . . . desire is born in my heart.

The overflow runs through the halls of my mind
and carries my spirit into a white fog that cradles
me high above reality's cold grasping fingers,
and though 'Old Man Sorrow' knocks and kicks;
screaming a warning at the tattered back door
of my heart . . . the closeness of you lingers.

The feeling sweeps slowly over me and tenderly
awakens my sleeping heart to sing again;
a loving song, that releases the sunshine of dawn
and drifts on, echoing your special melody into
my trembling body and fills me with the sweetness
of your nearness . . . even after you have gone.

Alice M. Miller

BREAKING FREE

Sometimes I feel as though I am a butterfly floating
  through this pathway called life;

Along the path I fall upon the prison of a web;

To escape the confinement of the web I learn its
  structure, its strength, its weakness, thus its origin;

Once I achieve understanding, I break free to float on
  ahead to find myself caught in another web of life
  and ahead of that yet another;

Each time I learn more about life's webs;

But each time I encounter these prisons I lose a little
  of that precious powder that keeps my wings moist to
  fly, and I grow tired;

But become lighter.

William Arthur Shoemaker

CHRISTMAS EVE NIGHT

Little children with your eyes shut so tight,
What are you dreaming on this Christmas Eve night?
Are you dreaming of nuts and candy canes,
Or of Santa holding the reins?
Are you dreaming of toys you're going to get,
Or if you don't are you going to fret?
Are you dreaming of delicious foods and fruit,
Or a train with a horn that goes *toot! toot! toot!*
Are you dreaming of a doll, with eyes so big and brown,
Or of candies, that you could eat by the pound?
Are you dreaming of the Christ child, with his mercy mild,
Or the snow that comes, at times so wild?
You with your eyes shut so tight, what are you dreaming
Tonight?

Etta Person

ETTA JANE PERSON. Pen Name: Ben. Jr.; Born: Sapulpa, Rural Creek County, Oklahoma; Married: Benjamin Franklin Person; Education: Grossmont Adult Night School, El Cajon, California, 5-68; 2 years, Grossmont Junior College, San Diego, California, 5-70, 4.0 G.P.A.; Occupations: Laundry worker, Housekeeper, United States Navy; Mother of 6; Memberships: Ordained minister; American Legion Auxiliary, 15 years (one year as district historian); D.A.V., auxiliary member, 7 years; Founder, Over-25ers Club, 2 years and lots of fun; Awards: ''A+'' for thesis in college English, 1970; Honorable mention, 1935; ''A'' grade, Grit Junior Writers, 1942; Other Writings: ''I Think,'' shory story, *Mrs. Nurse's Blackboard*, 1929; ''Who Am I,'' college theme paper, 1970; ''This Too Shall Pass,'' reports to club on campus college paper; Items for Over-25ers newsletter; Themes: *Nature, life in general, Christian life, knowing myself, letters to friends in politics, governors, senators, congressmen, state representatives. Vital issues concerning you and me. Today, yesterday, and forever. For all time, Dwight, I will always be your grandmother! The three-year-old child. What a mother is.*

A SOUL'S RHAPSODY

I have the moon in a big gold spoon
And the stars are a halo for my head,
The clouds at night are silver and white
And I have their softness for my bed.

Butterflies and I are free as the wind
We can soar where eagles fly,
O'er white-topped mountains and blue-green rivers
Past sweet smelling pines half-way to the sky.

My spirit wings and my soul sings
As I listen to a soft lullaby,
Or hear a choir sing praises to Him
Or watch a baby fall asleep with a sigh.

My heart pounds when I hear the sounds
Of a military marching band,
See Old Glory wave o'er land of our brave
Watch the torch light up in Liberty's hand.

Vonda Blum Wyatt

MY SON

I remember the night God sent a child to me,
a precious boy my eyes to see.
A tiny boy to grow big and strong,
mine to teach right from wrong.
I picked him up when he fell down,
turned into smiles all of his frowns.
I walked him to school that very first day,
watched him mold tiny people from a hunk of clay.
I helped him ride his trike and bikes of red,
listened to his prayers at night before bed.
From every birthday cake a candle I secretly saved,
never forgot to thank God the wonderful years he gave.
I worked very hard to make his college years right,
watched him cram for exams late into the night.
Then graduation day quickly came and went,
I knew my money had been wisely spent.
I knew I'd explained well all the facts of life,
when the minister pronounced them man and wife.
It was late last night I heard the telephone ring,
my son told of the child God would soon bring.
I know my son will feel the same as I,
as through the years memories fly by.
It all began the night God sent a child to me,
a precious boy my eyes to see.

Carolynn Ward

WHAT'S LIFE?

Ocean waves racing to shore
Sweet rain falling upon the ground
Soft wind blowing
Mountain peaks covered with first winter's snow
Beauty and fragrance of first season's rose
Warm sun shining through clear blue skies
 A newborn baby's first cry

 What's Life?

Ocean waves stealing sand from shore
Sweet rain and wind turned to thunder and storm
Snow peak mountains melted forming rivers below
Full bloom rose withers and falls to the ground
Warm clear skies turned cold and grey
 Newborn baby, seems like yesterday
 Grown old, died today.

 That's Life

 Christina Grisco

OUR GRANDKIDS

Reflections in a looking glass, first born, first son,
Inside the struggle for life begins, we're not the only one;
Come ride the carousel with me on beautifully painted
Horses, come play in a garden of flowers and pumpkins
And ponder the water courses; chickens gather
Round the squash to search for those tasty seeds, while
Dragonflies float lazily on a summer's breeze;

A sensitive mind at three, walking with the tin man and me,
Next day a winding path of golden bricks leads to a new
Dawn, a world without war or a wicked witch, that is free;

Along this road of fall-colored leaves we travel, to be
Near the sounds of football and the cheerleaders' razzle
Dazzle; the smell of fireplace smoke, wafting from
Red-tile chimneys and just around the bend, a park with
Easy swings and harder slides and bounding springs
With elephants, turtles, porpoises and wild rides;

My dreams are with these kids and Bev as we sit
On the fence and feed the llamas, Mark and Lori are
Raising two fine boys, a model for all papas and mamas;
In time, Rich and Andy will reach for that shiny brass ring, the
Next carousel ride will offer a different tune to sing.

 John B. Passerello

SNOW IS POETRY

Oh snow so pure and white,
you glorify the black of night.
You glisten in the light of day,
like a million diamonds on display.
Silent snowflakes shimmering down,
gently coating the pine trees all around.
Your majestic blanket of white
embraces everything in sight.
Traveling over hill and dale,
you cover the land in a white bridal veil.
What a lovely sight to see.
Snow is poetry!

 Marie Belfiore

BEV

Meet me in Mendocino where crashing waves create rainbows
 in the mist, where sea gulls slice a piece of
Yellow sun and Summer's Harmony is a place where dolphins
 kissed;

We walk along MacKerricher's beach in that space where
 sandpipers play, where kelp appears
In many forms and hides the spot where sand dollars lay;
 pelicans fly in
Formation just above the ocean swells, searching for fish at
Eventide and matching the motion of dune grass as the sun
 marks eight bells; you will always

Be with me as we sit on the dock in Noyo Harbor, where the
 seals frolic like our otter friends and where
Every brightly painted boat is filled with anticipation,
 waiting for the salmon and urchin to fill their larder;
Volunteering for love, rose-colored glasses and a yellow
 brick road that leads to the land of Oz and
Eternity, you are all the dreams I have ever had and create a
 future with serenity; as Neil sings come play with me and
Rhymes along the coastal highway, we head for a place
 where twilight dwells, where moonlight
Leaves a silver track upon the waters of the bay; and
 when the stars appear and
Your warmth melts my heart, remember that calico ocean
 cat and the scenes we treasure as art.

 John B. Passerello

HUMAN FEELINGS

Loneliness is the broken bridge
With water flowing by.
There is no way to get across
No matter what you try.

Loneliness is the lost soul
Wandering the long and lonesome road.
No bright faces, no smiling friend
To lighten the heavy load.

Loneliness is missing loved ones' laughter
And knowing no one's there to care.
Searching with a broken heart, crying out
For feelings only two can share.

Jealousy is the ugly gray-black film
Covering joys and delights,
Suffocating love, breaking marriage vows,
Turning bright days into darkest nights.

Happiness is the pair of doves sharing life,
Caring for each other, close or far apart,
Happiness is the springtime thaw, melting snow,
Bringing sunny summer warmth to the cold, cold heart.

 Ginger Chapman

LANTERNS

Yellow plastic roses
Pink plastic roses radiated
between 2 beer cans
that hung on both sides
of her pushcart
filled with old and yellowing newspapers
   and garments colored green, overlapping
   red-colored ones overlapping striped ones.

A woman beside the cart
plump, overdressed for summer
   and eating Chinese food
from a small carton.

I said overdressed, the truth is
A sweater
A couple of coats, a dress.
I didn't see her feet.
What impressed me?
 Her sense of perfection
   anyhow.

I gave the credit
 to the Lanterns
  Made with beer cans.

    Rhonda Desilus

GOD SAVE ME & THEE
& SET MY COUNTRY FREE

Dedicated to L. A. Wertz

We pray with love to the holy one that before He's done,
He'll save us from this *capital* mob that's trying so hard
to do God's job.

Pray to our God above that in His love, He'll save both
thee and me and set our country free, oh please God save
us all from the sin of these shanty boat Irishmen.

As for them, save your breath, nothing can save these
ministers of death, of those who deal in the gun, ask
yourself, What have they really won?

We do it for freedom there cry, but they don't have to
face those who must die, it's easy to be brave when
you're not the one who goes to the grave!

There's these things more, if it were those who make, and
those who make money from, who died, instead of the
innocent and the poor, there would be no more *war!*

They shouldn't have so much pride, the truth will out and
there's no place to hide, they want to save face even if
it wipes out a human race, Alas this too shall pass, pray
and work hard to make sure their shoes aren't filled by
another without *class!*

    Leland D. Wertz

TO MICHAEL

One day I turned to face the sun, a moment to remember
And from the endless skies a silver light came pouring down
And you were there. You, who made the sunlight real
Dear Prince with auburn hair and golden eyes
That mirror the sweet harmony of the universe
Although our hands did not touch
My soul was meshed to yours forever
In your sad eyes I saw the dream of honor
The vastness and splendor of truth
Your music rises like great opalescent fountains
Weaving wondrous patterns on the sky
You are love, noble and kind
Like the forlorn call of a nightingale
That echoes across the earth
You are the one whose footsteps fill my dreams
While enchanting earth-songs sound through silent halls
A kaleidoscope of beauty lights my way
The purity of starlight on the sea
The trees, emerald mansions that inspire the dawn
The gentle sway of lilac's sapphire light against the morning sky
The rhapsody of autumn's song and twilight waterfalls
The swallows' melancholy tribute to the sun
The winter earth, swept with silent, glistening snow
And all the beauty holds, and life profound and cherished hopes
are you

    Geraldine Nathan

THE ETERNAL VIGIL

Sometimes as I gaze at the vast starry sky,
  the eternal question arises — Why Lord, O Why.
    Where did I come from and to where do I go —
      And why was I put here — when and how shall I know.

Yes we seek out a life free from troubles and cares,
  and we pray for our needs, and for someone to share.
    The world and its treasures may be ours to command,
      but without someone to share them —
        they meet neither our needs or demands.

So if self-centered we be, as our natural way,
  then alone in a crowd, we will be doomed to stay
    That "No Man Is An Island" — is a very true quote
      And we require this mate to help keep us afloat.

    Barney Reilly

THE QUILT

ever work on a quilt?
i've made many of them
each one is different
even if i use the same basic pattern
i think that's kinda the way
God's made mankind (person kind?)
we are all different
but each has a place
in a master plan
red, black, brown
beige, white, yellow
from above
it's beautiful to the creator

    Grandma Rice

COUNTRY BOY

This is for Billy Paysinger in Missouri . . .
One guy I'll never forget!

Things weren't supposed to happen the way that they did
I wasn't supposed to fall in love with this silly country kid
I should never have believed all the crazy things he said
But I did everything he told me and I followed where he led
We'd met only a few days ago and now it was time to part
But no matter how far I go he'll always have a little piece of my heart
We held each other closely with tears in our eyes
Neither one wanted the time to come that we'd have to say good-bye
With a gentle kiss and a whispered "I love you" in the darkness
I got up and walked to the door
I knew it was over, even though we wanted so much more
He was looking at me with those hound-dog eyes
And then he grinned that country-boy grin
He said, "Hey don't worry, I'll find you someday
And we'll be together again."
"I love you. Please don't forget me. It's so hard to tell you good-bye,
But I know I have to do it and I guess that now is the time."
It was hard to leave but impossible to stay
And because of this he could never be mine
It would have been so much easier if we'd have never met
Now it's going to be impossible to forget
That he loved me for a little while
And I loved him.

Jody Blaney

LOVING YOU

Seeing you for the first time was like seeing the sun peek out
from behind a tall mountain and fill the world with its radiance
and warmth.

Seeing you for the first time was like sitting in quiet solitude
watching a peaceful ocean sway back and forth in perfect harmony
with nature.

Loving you for the first time was like a rush of wind felt before
a spring rain.

Loving you is like dew kissing nature and renewing the earth
each day.

Loving you is the peace felt after love's fulfillment as you cradle
me in your arms and rock me gently to sleep.

Loving you is a refreshing drink of spring water nurturing my mind,
feeding my body, and quenching my soul.

Loving you is the promise of infinite life, infinite love, and eternal
serenity.

Shirley Delores Bolden

THE CLOSING OF PARADISE

There was a time when things were natural and good,
there was a time when some things weren't to be understood —
But curiosity could have been the cause,
that made them act without a pause —
They must have decided, it was time to move on,
they were ready for the close of the "Golden Dawn" —
They took that step that closed the first chapter,
and moved to the next stage to learn disaster —
They closed that door to paradise,
to experience more through their pair of eyes —

. . . So closed the first chapter,
and the second begun,
of the life of God's first daughter,
and God's first son . . .

Ruby M. Lowery-Obermeyer

THE SOUNDS OF ROME

Beyond the sea and its billowing foam,
Listen to the heartbeat of immortal Rome.

The stranger in Rome might seem to hear
The measured tread of warriors marching by,
The wail of babes, the wolf of fabled lore,
A martyr's prayer, a gladiator's cry.

— Or he may hear at morn cathedral bells,
A warbling bird, the breeze among the pines,
The ancient Tiber's low and languid song,
And buzzing bees in nectar-scented vines.

— At close of day, in quest of solitude,
The weary one may sense, along the trail,
A mood sublime, as evening shades enfold
The wooded glen where sings a nightingale.

All through the city, the hills, and the dells,
Tinkle softly the fountains like faraway bells.

Lenore Llewellyn

ELEVEN FORTY ONE

I am writing this for those
Of us
Who have failed
For the paltry few
Of us
Who have crawled
To the end
Pulling ourselves up
By sheer will,
And will alone
Lest we give up
I am dedicating this
Small prize
To us.

Sharon Avant Shiree

POINT NOIR, TRINITY ROCK, AND CAPE ETERNITY, SAGUENAY RIVER.

GRANT RECIPIENTS

$1,000
PASSENGER

I am in the body of an immense silver bird streaming
through wind and sky.

It is the night's time.
All the other passengers
are asleep, but I am awake somewhere over the Atlantic —
looking through a window into darkness.
It seems poets are always looking through windows
trying to bring a poem to light.

In these speeding moments,
I think of how I am so often a passenger
wondering where I am going — yet remembering,
my mother's strong smile, and the fading blue images
of the friends I leave behind.
How I love them. How I carry with me the memory of their dreams,
and even now, we are all moving and streaming through the
starlit darkness.

Once, an immense silver horse came running to me out of a fog
over the hill across the pasture.

Now the sun comes rising
over the wings of birds and Ireland,
and I have crossed the ocean again.

Cecily Markham

CECILY KINSEY MARKHAM. Born: Harrisburg, Pennsylvania, 4-17-
56; Married: Patrick Markham, 6-14-80; Education: University of Vir-
ginia, B.S., 1979; Poetry: 'This Moment We Have,' 'The Everlasting
Life,' *Words of Praise, Vol. III, 1987; Deer Fields Near the Sea,* collection
of poetry, 1985; *Father of the Free,* collection of poetry, in progress.

$500

sunlight turning
    mill stone shadows —
falling water

Charles B. Rodning

$300
HE CALLS

He calls us
By the name we know
To give us the name he wrote
Upon our hearts
When they were just a thought
Who am I to say He doesn't
Know me
And remind him of my given name
He who named himself
And all from me to him
Not for poetic rhythm
But for purpose
Knowing my heart would answer
In a quiet moment
As if I'd known no other

Carolyn Coffee

$200
TEARS

Silver cascades of water fall down barbed rocks,
curiously soft and absorbing. Wet mist reaches us here,
slowly penetrating our porous bodies. Suddenly,
we become pregnant with moisture, like water-driven logs.

My wife stands beside me. Our hands touch lightly.
She wears my face. I wear hers. Tears have carved
our cheeks. Against our will, we have become
a part of the landscape, like furrows in the soil.

Tadeusz Rybowski

$100 (In alphabetical order)

BOBBY — EVENTUALLY

This year, I met my half-sister — Jan
She's thirty-one and I'm twenty-three
She has a nice husband — Gary,
A five-year-old son — Jeremy,
And a three-year-old daughter — Janae.
Now, they live in Bruchmülbach, West Germany
And I, by coincidence, Lorraine in France.
We're not far by train — about three hours.

Ten years ago, I met my father in a Pennsylvania courthouse
When my mother and step-father decided to change my name.
When I was fifteen, for the summer, my mother sent me
To live with her sister near Miami.
One weekend I snuck away to see my father in Jacksonville.
I haven't seen him since.

I have another half-sister — Diane, in Hawaii,
And one half-brother — Tommy, in Florida,
And another half-brother — Bobby, in Heaven, I hope.

The whole "family" will end up with Bobby — eventually
Until then, I'm tormented with resentment about the break-up
Yet at age eighteen, when I last saw my mother and step-father,
I decided that the three of us would be better off apart.

Since then, a widowed sister-in-law of my step-father
Has welcomed me as her third child — blood may be
Thicker than water, but kind hearts which dry tears
Conglomerate substantial grace.

L. E. Clayton Kandor

DAYDREAMING

Daydreaming is no longer undesirable,
no longer an indication of laziness.
Fantasizing is considered a sign of good health.

Now your dreams of power,
hopes of achievement are welcome —
not just reveries of new homes
when shopping for real estate and how
you would decorate and furnish them,
but unrealized plans for study fields
and work developments and achievements.
Would they ever become reality?
Fantasizing about how to accomplish
these goals and what life would be like then
may be a part of your life.

It is a release for a person's self-esteem
to be allowed to dream and fantasize.

The wistful fields of personal relationships
can be expanded to the limits of galaxies
and you realize that it is only wishful thinking.

Florence K. McCarthy

CRAZY HEART

My mind is so neat, ev'ry thought is filed,
But my Crazy Heart is so wild — so wild!
My life ruled by my mind would be so mild,
But my heart by ev'ry charm is beguiled!

My mind knows ev'rything from A to Z;
My heart is stupid to the Nth degree!
My mind knows just what is the best for me,
But my wild heart wants to go on a spree!

My mind went to school, is educated;
My foolish heart for folly is fated!
My mind would wait 'til passion abated,
But my untaught heart wants to be mated!

Carol Boyer Mitchell

CAROL BOYER MITCHELL. My childhood was spent in a beautiful Montana wilderness, where my parents were homesteaders. There we saw a lot of bear and elk, the ever present coyotes (who always howled at night), and jackrabbits (which we caught and ate), as well as rattlesnakes. Also we saw many Crow and Blackfoot Indians, with whom we became good friends. Poetry: 'Another Day,' 'April,' 'A Challenge,' 'Christmas,' 'Picture Memories'; Comments: *Poetry has a lilting sound. When I recite my poetry, I feel like singing.*

PERSPECTIVE

Where I used to live there are no elevators nor escalators
to take one up or down to grocery stores,
plush restaurants, theaters, or haberdashery,
where he makes his pick of what money can buy,
or if he chooses, to whisk him to the top of skyscrapers
where he can watch toy-like cars whizzing by
and hail airplanes and helicopters whirring;
To see the world around I'd shin up tall trees,
skinning hands and legs, and slowly parting
the heavy dark foliage, peer out,
but often rooftops blocked the view;
Or better, I'd climb the highest hill to the summit
(panting with each labored breath wheezing
through oxygen-hungry lungs, knees and chin rubbing)
for an unobstructed sight of towering emerald mountains
like gigantic jagged teeth against the clear blue sky
and, at their feet, rice fields like Bermuda grass patches
where turbaned brown women wade knee-deep in mud
to pull the weeds choking the plants;
Through upward winding trails, bare-backed brown men like ants
bear on their stooped shoulders white sack of rice;
They do not ask for much: sufficient for them
a bowl of rice, a corner to sleep in, the leaky roof
over their head, and hopes for a good harvest.

Terry A. Palabrica

an old barn
    jammed with hay —
nesting swallows

Charles B. Rodning

Strange though it may seem, we can easily become
prisoners of ourselves;
barred from the outside world by an ailing body.
All those headaches, toothaches, backaches
suddenly gain significance,
make us self-conscious, self-centered, vulnerable.

And only with insomnia it is different;
one can see the world so clearly
after a sleepless night.

One changes beyond recognition with the passing years,
and everything starts with one's hands.

And only the sunlight remains. We sit in the park,
withered like autumn leaves, thin and dried.
One feels so secure with one's eyes closed.
Nothing can happen to us when the danger is unseen.

Tadeusz Rybowski

$50 (In alphabetical order)

THE FALL OF BIG BEN

Well, I didn't mean to see your wife again.
She's the one who called me, honestly.
You know I would never go against you, Big Ben.
Let's just call it fate and let it be.

You broke old Leonard's back because he danced with her.
Ben, he really didn't get that far.
You threw him off Brewer's bridge last Thursday eve.
You caught him as he walked out of the bar.

Don't expect for you to show no mercy.
She told me not to expect that from you.
I won't even waste time begging your forgiveness, no.
Go ahead and do what you want to do.

Just one thing you should know before we start.
She left on the old eight thirty-five.
She said she don't want to be beat no more.
She said she is lucky to get out alive.

Raise up your hands, cave in my head, Ben.
I'll take your best and smile through it all.
Because I paid ten thousand dollars today to a strange man,
Who said if I did it that later tonight, you would take a long fall.

Anthony John Ciccariello III

ANTHONY JOHN CICCARIELLO III. Pen Names: Thomas Coran, Chick Jackson, Wkyie; Born: Staten Island, New York, raised and reside in Jackson, New Jersey; Education: St. Josephs High School, Ocean County College, the world; all my wanderings through America and my travels through the Far East; Occupations: Fast food chef, Bum, Sailor, Cashier, Singer and Guitarist in Band, Composer; Memberships: Golden Shellback, Amvets, Order of the Golden Dragon; Poetry: 'Peaceful Dreams,' *American Poetry Anthology,* 1986; Comments: *My works are primarily the lyrics of my songs, I've been writing since 1978. My first works were sparked by the Ocean County area of New Jersey. The beauty of the woods and my vast inexperience. The once I began to travel across America and get a little worldly my works changed, and once I traveled the Far East my works became the stories of people and places I had seen; it's about life.*

NOT AN ATHEIST

I believe in spinach.
It's green, it's large, it's god.
If you don't plant it early,
It will go to seed.
If you don't cook it right,
It will shrivel;
Arrogant, impossible, voluptuous miracle.
To eat and to grow.
To stand in rows, flamboyant,
To stretch paddle-limbs upward,
Yet to curl enough to protect the new growth,
The yellow pale heart.
I believe in spinach.

Vickie Graeff

UNTITLED

I dreamed you: sailors dream seas
nights before they sail.
At sea, they dream of sleep on land.
You dreamed me: sleeping one last
night at home before you
gave up, and let me dream you.
Some sleep is dreamless: take it as a gift,
wrap it all around yourself
keep yourself so safe that you
rest, hide, wait
for the dream
that lets us
vanish
through secrets
into seadreams.

Larry Johnson

ADOPTED

I never felt adopted until today.
When you married someone else;
Someone other than my mother.

I was never unsure of your love,
Never scared someone could take you away
Until today.

If it were your blood
Coursing through my veins,
I would always have a claim on you.

Ties made up only of love and commitment
Seem so fragile today.
Suddenly, I feel so easy to replace.

You love me. I know you'll never stop.
I just never felt adopted
Until today.

Deedria L. Martin

THE CORNER COFFEE SHOP

At the corner coffee shop there are two
obvious groupings — the morning cup of coffee
crowd and the evening cup of coffee crowd.

In the morning there are some spaces at the counter.
There are early-to-work people, just a cup of coffee,
maybe with a cigarette, in a comparative rush.
And there are not so early-to-work people, some eating
large breakfasts — potatoes, eggs, toast with jelly as well
as butter; others danish and coffee.
The talk is of the news on the radio, the possibilities
for the day's horse races, the employment angles.
Some taciturn souls just read a newspaper.
The persons who work in the shop are cheerful,
efficient, and amiable to all comers.

In the evening there are some spaces at the counter.
From mid-afternoon on there are the people who started
work early or leave a shift early; a bit later the office
workers and people staying in town for the evening.
The talk is of management changes, relatives, and a girl
up the counter explaining every key on her keyring is
the key to a different man's apartment.

The people who worked in the shop from early morning
are still wearing spruce uniforms, but are a little tired.
The radio is playing music rather than news.

Florence K. McCarthy

MATTERS OF LIFE AND DEATH

The corridor is empty.
Until yesterday, patients were in the rooms
And nurses were at the station,
But now, they have cleared out because of remodeling.

The corridor is empty, except for my sister and me.
We sit outside the Intensive Care Unit
And listen to the rhythmic breathing sound of the respirator,
On which our mother lies.

Until yesterday, she was a patient in one of those rooms,
  and then, Code Blue.
She, who always protected me, now looks so helpless.
I try to think, ''Well, she is eighty-six and has Alzheimer's.''
But that does not help. Oh, how she loved me!

I look down the hallway through many open doorways,
And I think of the future before me. At fifty, I am at a turning point.
The next twenty years will tell the story.
What may I yet become?

The sound of the respirator brings me back to the moment.
I think of the one lying there.

Again, I look down the hallway and think of my own possible demise.
Yet, I see my life beckoning to me. There is so much remaining!

I know I must go on: to think, to do, to act.
She, who gave me my life, would want it that way.
But now, in this brief moment, it seems as if
The corridor is empty.

Janice R. Meyer

DAYS OF DARKNESS: MARTIAL LAW

I was mute: numbed by the shock of seeing
innocent men and women led to prison,
of hearing the cries of hungry mothers and children
vainly awaiting fathers, brothers, sisters, or kin
languishing in filthy and lawless stockades
guarded by insensitive stolid soldiers
sworn to servile loyalty to a cruel wealth-crazed despot;

My heart and mind rebelled,
but my tongue was silenced by fear gripping me:
friends turning traitor for favors desired,
kin against one another, divided not by race,
but by greed, ambition, creed . . .
the lust for power all too compelling, irresistible, insatiable;

I marched along with millions — living cowards like me —
shouting *mubuhays,* terror urging us to shout the loudest,
lest someone near would say, ''You are undesirable,
undeserving, of office, job, or even life.''

In the middle of the night I cowered
trembling, crying, enraged at my utter helplessness,
afraid to say outright my thoughts lest loved ones suffer;
Desperate, I longed for the bright morning,
Yet dreading it, knowing that the tentacles of power
could reach out and blot the brightness from our lives.

Terry A. Palabrica

GRIEF

Trouble rising from my mourning
to leave what was our dream-filled bed
Put on my clothes, my face, and go

And for some hours escape you

But I still dwell in our old places
Entering, my heart beats fast
With a feeling from before
I'll see the curve of your back
Your head inclined to reading
and you'll raise a smile to me

But no, beloved, no more

Late at night I am alone
with your absence, legacy, decay
All is the same
And centered in my longing for you

Cheryl Tupper

A SIMPLE POEM

Mona Rose cooks patiently
from herbs and scratches of large green leaves
a salad for our dinner. She heats the house
with the water boiling spices through the air.
Back on earth, we sit poised at the table
praying in silence. Mona Rose sparks the candles
and they leap up like torches in the shape of thin hearts.
With hungry eyes I've watched for dinner,
have waited home half the day to see Mona Rose
create my life. I am a strange party to love
as perfect as a deadly avalanche, or a lily
against the sky. I have not seen many fields of grain
directing the wind, I have not seen myself dancing
with the bread of life in hand. Now I see myself
— my spirit, my heart, my body —
breathing like a man the breath of another.
I am the lover of Mona Rose, and eat
so much so fast I am liable to explode
and die in my sleep.

Joseph Walker

SUNDAY

We ironed our hair ribbons
On a lightbulb
Church bells
Brightening the sun

And mother
Took the jelly
Out of the tumbler
All in one piece
But only if
The minister were coming
And upended olives
On carnival glass

Dust motes
Lazed in the light

Grandmother
Fingers fat as sausages
Played the piano
Her bottom hung
Over the stool
And mother
Who once shook hands
With Valentino
Sang
And father and I danced to
"Can't you see my new shoes."

Jean Holmes Wilson

$25 (In alphabetical order)

THE SHIFT OF LIGHT FROM THE WINDOW ON ST. PATRICK'S DAY

The sun is all the way back now
To the last building, to the front —
The New York sun is especially bright, as it goes
On the brown-red brick, tiny windows, lined up in a row.

The windows go up to the balconies, and then
Into the spires, at the top, to the sky
Which is very blue; with large white fleece
Shading the clouds as this rear-view
Window, lets the sun escape.

It transfers itself from the first
Building window, to glare on the
White-wash painted years ago, left abandoned as
Offices of yesterday's affluence, now empty
Warehouses cluttered inside with filth and
Remorse for their mistakes financially.

As I type my secretary's work on St. Patrick's Day, '87
The stare of the sun fresh in the face
Tells what is left of what happened before.

Geneve Baley

SATURDAY MORNING

We sleep late and wake up
Together in the same bed
Smiling good morning at each other,
You with an extra smile
At your nightshirt on me.

We can spend all morning in bed
If we want to!
Making Friday night last
With the closing of the shades.

No appointments
No demands
Breakfast in bed for two.

We revel in bed for hours
Watching television, sometimes not
Touching, talking, caressing, caring
Into the afternoon.

Peaceful, restful, full-of-fun hours together.
Saturday mornings with you are my very favorite times.

Rosemarie Bem

REFLECTIONS OVER KITTY LITTER

Oh! To be a Hemingway,
    Whose literary ease
Has claimed a paying public
    At home and over seas.

Oh! To have an island farm,
    An isolated place,
Where cats and kittens caper
    Unlimited in space.

Oh! To have a haven far
    From human kind's complaint,
Where creatures freely frolic
    In caves and castles quaint.

Oh! To be a Hemingway,
    Whose staff of servants could
Feed the felines fully,
    Then chase them to the wood.

Virginia F. Brown

WONDERLAND

The mad hatter
Is not as mad
As he appears to be.

Animals age
A multiple of years
To our one.

That gives them
A lot of unbirthdays
We forget to celebrate.

Henry W. Butler

PLENTY

My father was fat since I first remember.
My mother had a knack for picking things up —
    whatever came in reach, useful knick-knacks,
    conversations, and the invisible dread
she grabbed onto, dug her home into that heap.

She bore and raised me there.

I'm short
    and now I'm old and done.
I've scraped off some of Daddy's weight,
looked him in the face, I did, before he died,
and I thought I'd left my mother's junk behind.

But I'm small
    and now I'm old
and at night I often stay awake alone

unable to select amongst the loot what should be mine.

Jean Esteve

NIGHT FISHING

and caught the night
with nets and hooks and lines
for dreams that dive
and rise again
and dive

and caught the night
with sleeping upturned ear
for water wounds that sift
through crack
and crevice

and caught the night
with molds and jars and baskets
to carry darkened
visions
to the light

J. Sigmund Forman

OH — TO BE SEEN BY AN ISLAND

for Jonathan

Still, in the old canoe we are
whitely watched by egrets perched
in salt dry trees at the river's edge.
You feather your stroke to press
the upturned bow toward shore.
Held by the current you do not let
the sandy ledge scrape-catch
the varnished spine.

Across my lap I lay my oar
and point slowly to an osprey
settled on an inland birch.
They have returned.
I feel your eyes rest on me,
not where my fingers lead.
I would not look, but bow my head
and let my fingers turn
their wake in the brackish water.

Melinda Underwood Griggs

FIRST CHRISTMAS REMEMBERED '63

The snow, blanketing the Jersey hills and pine trees,
seemed to cover up the world as I knew it then
I felt the snow came up to my thin four-year-old neck
Bells and colored lights dotted the wooden houses in the village
where I lived, all with black roofs — now all also turned white
under the domination of the fanciful white flakes
fallen from the normally blue and clear skies
where my mother said God sat in Judgment and Forgiveness of us

Inside our house, the odors were sweet and clean
the potato pies doused with shredded coconuts baking in the oven
the house spotless, smelling of pine

On the TV set there were pictures of black boxes for a fortnight
The man on the TV called them ''coffins''
The coffins were draped in a red, white and blue curtain
with stars that seemed to have fallen from the clear darkened sky
when the sun fell from it
The TV man said it was as though ''King Arthur had been taken from us,
like Jesus' Crucifixion . . . As though Christmas wouldn't come
to the great Land this year.''

Mama had said Christmas was a happy time — not sad like this
She said there'd be gifts and good things to eat
and love abounding throughout ''God's good earth''
And now the TV man said it wasn't coming this year
Why had an evil person killed the great King President
and taken Christmas from me?

John L. Howard

ONE SMILE

Letting go is the one thing I never wanted to do.
I let go one time before, before I loved you. Even then,
in the shallows of our beginning, I knew it was just
that, our beginning. You had tomorrow written all over
your face. You drove a truck and so did I. We shared
white line fever on separate hiways, sharing the same
base with so many crowded faces. Always searching
for that one smile, that came only with one face.
That smile came straight from your toes, a smile
stranger to mortal man. Nine long months and I've
only known your touch seven times. I'm a trucker at
heart, but my heart's having a hard time loving
another trucker. There's no doubt I'll always drive a truck
and so will you, our first love has eighteen wheels. My love rolls
eastbound, and yours westbound, as we share a whole lot of lonely.
We've never shared a day off, only two trucks seldom meeting at
the truckstops only to hear you say ''I have to be in Dallas by
morning,'' and I reply, ''And I have to be in Green Bay by morning.''
We share no dreams, no goals, only trucker stories. We never planned
yesterday nor does tomorrow seem to be troubled with any plans. But
the trouble seems to be, I look at you and I can see the future,
I look away and I see we have no direction in our lives what little
we share. The only direction we know comes from each new load. We count
days by miles, weeks by an average and months by loneliness.

Rose A. Pope

AT THE FAIRGROUNDS

A girl from Elizabeth Colo got her face blown off
today
by a steel lid flying from
an exploded barrel of propane
that was ignited
by someone's fallen cigarette
ash. Her face was
turned
slightly to the side, away
from the explosion.
A man watching
saw her blue eyes
staring
with that calm shock before
the pain
and the bleeding
begin.

Michael Strickland

CUMBERLAND GAP, FROM THE EAST.

Index